THE AMERICAN CHALLENGE:
A New History of the United States, Vol II
Sixth Edition

THE AMERICAN CHALLENGE:
A New History of the United States, Vol II
Sixth Edition

Keith J. Volanto
Collin College
Plano, Texas

Michael Phillips
Clements Center/SMU
University Park, Texas

M. Scott Sosebee
Stephen F. Austin State University
Nacogdoches, Texas

Edited by
Keith J. Volanto
Michael Phillips

Abigail Press   Wheaton, IL 60189

Design and Production: Abigail Press
Typesetting: Abigail Press
Typeface: AGaramond
Cover Art: Sam Tolia

THE AMERICAN CHALLENGE:
A New History of the United States, Vol. II

Sixth Edition, 2023
Printed in the United States of America
Translation rights reserved by the authors
ISBN 979-8-9857619-1-7

Contents in Brief

Contents

MAPS

Preface

Every nation encounters challenges during its existence. Some are common to all countries, some are quite unique. How a people rise to overcome these challenges, or fail in their attempts to address them adequately, engenders much of that country's history. Americans experienced a series of internal and external challenges over the past 500 years even before the creation of the United States: exploration of unknown lands, intense military conflicts, demanding technological problems, divisive political battles, and epic social upheavals, just to name a few. This textbook is an attempt to relay how Americans have risen to their own set of challenges and either prevailed over them or continue to deal with those not yet overcome.

The work's subtitle—"A New History of the United States"—refers to the effort by the authors to synthesize the latest historical scholarship (and borrow, when pertinent, from other disciplines) to provide a fresh account of this country's national story. Unlike many older textbooks originally produced during the Cold War era and simply updated with token changes, the authors of *The American Challenge* have written their chapters entirely from the perspective of the early twenty-first century. At the conclusion of each chapter, the authors have included a list of suggested readings consisting of a few classic works and numerous recent publications that influenced their interpretation of a particular period. These books can also provide an important starting point for students interested in delving deeper into the introduced topics.

Every textbook contains a tremendous amount of information. To guide the retention of material, the authors of *The American Challenge* have emboldened key terms to aid readers in distinguishing the most important persons, events, and concepts appearing in each chapter. A glossary at the end of the book serves as a compilation of all bold terms, providing informative descriptions. To further help digest the information, each chapter also contains a chronology to act as a quick-guide for those wishing to keep track of key events over time, and a set of five summary review questions that students should feel comfortable answering before moving on to the next chapter. To enhance the overall learning experience, all chapters include helpful maps, interesting photographs of noteworthy people and everyday scenes, and other enlightening illustrations relevant to a particular period. A supplemental reader for *The American Challenge*, containing primary source documents and an assortment of vignettes, is also available from Abigail Press.

I am very proud to be associated with the fine group of scholars who authored *The American Challenge*. Each professor channeled their broad experiences as academics and classroom educators to produce a book that not only reflects the latest historical scholarship, but also written in a compelling manner which will resonate with today's college students. Michael Phillips, earned his Ph.D. in History from the University of Texas at Austin. His teaching and scholarship on race in Dallas and Texas House Speakers demonstrate his strong interest and expertise in American government as well as race, class, and gender issues. He is currently a Senior Research Fellow at Southern Methodist University's Clements Center for Southwest Studies. Doug Cantrell holds the rank of Professor of History and chairs the History Department at the Elizabethtown Community and Technical College where he has taught for the past 30 years. Professor Cantrell studied at the University of Kentucky and has authored numerous articles and book reviews in academic journals and encyclopedias in the field of immigration and ethnic history. Andrew Lannen is an expert on colonial and revolutionary America who received his Ph.D. from Louisiana State University. His publications have focused on the Native American experience and colonial warfare. He has taught American history for over 20 years and is currently an assistant professor of history at Stephen F. Austin University. Andrew's colleague at Stephen F. Austin, Scott Sosebee, received his Ph.D. from Texas Tech University. In addition to his position as Associate Professor of History, he currently serves as the Executive Director of the East Texas Historical Association. Dr. Sosebee's published works and research interests focus on twentieth-century economic and political history, centered on Texas and the American South. Roger Ward completed his Ph.D. coursework at the University of Kentucky before becoming Professor of History at Collin College where he has taught for over 15 years. A specialist of the early American Republic, his research focus is on nineteenth century race and class, as well as rural history, especially with regard to Appalachia. Finally, I received my Ph.D. in American history from Texas A&M University and currently serve as Professor of History at Collin College. I have taught American and Texas history for the past 25 years and published a book as well as a dozen articles reflecting my interests in twentieth-century American politics and race relations. The authors hope you enjoy this effort and welcome feedback from our readers. We wish to acknowledge the assistance of James Page, North Central Texas College, faculty members from Collin College, and our students for all of their feedback. Also, we appreciate the love, support, and patience of our family members during the long publication process.

Keith J. Volanto

Chapter Sixteen

A BROKEN PROMISE OF FREEDOM: Reconstruction, 1863-1877

On April 9, 1865, Confederate General Robert E. Lee, the commander of the Confederate Army's largest and most resilient fighting force, surrendered to Union General Ulysses S. Grant, ending the Civil War. With the war concluded, the nation awaited Abraham Lincoln's ideas on how to piece the country back together again. The president gave a hint two days later, delivering a fateful speech in which, for the first time, he called publicly for granting full citizenship and the right to vote to at least some African Americans—"the very intelligent, and . . . those who serve our cause as soldiers." In the audience, an embittered, Confederate sympathizer named John Wilkes Booth grimly vowed, "That's the last speech he will ever make."

Just 27 years old, Booth had been plotting against Lincoln for months. Born in Maryland, Booth supported the South throughout the Civil War, but his enthusiasm never moved him to enlist in the Confederate Army. A heavy drinker, Booth acted for a living but never quite measured up to the talent or fame of his older brother Edwin Booth, the most admired Shakespearean performer of his generation. Booth despaired as it became clear the South would lose the war and resolved as early as August 1864 to rid the country of its "false president."

Booth hoped he might snatch southern victory from the jaws of defeat by kidnapping Lincoln and holding him hostage until the North agreed to recognize Confederate independence. After stalking the chief executive in early 1865, he decided that kidnapping the tall, strong, and always guarded president would be too difficult. Frustrated, he resolved instead to kill Lincoln after hearing the president's April 11 call for what Booth termed "nigger citizenship." He had already gathered around him a gang of conspirators, which met at a Maryland tavern owned by Mary Surratt. The clique now planned to murder Lincoln and other top administration figures.

The conspirators included Mary's son John Surratt, a Confederate spy; another Confederate agent, George Atzerodt; David Herold, a pharmacist in Washington, D.C.; and Lewis Powell, a veteran of the Confederate Army. Powell was assigned the task of killing Secretary of State William Seward while Atzerodt was to kill Vice President Andrew Johnson. Always seeking the center stage, Booth assigned himself to kill Lincoln.

April 14 was Good Friday, a day when Christians commemorate the crucifixion and death of Jesus. For much of his presidency, Lincoln had trouble sleeping and often seemed depressed. Yet, the awareness that the Civil War was winding down lifted the president's spirits. "His whole appearance, poise, and bearing had marvelously changed," his friend, Illinois Senator James Harlan later remarked. The First Couple planned to spend the evening forgetting about their troubles, attending a lighthearted comedy—***Our American***

Cousin—*at Ford's Theater. The Lincolns convinced a friend, Major Henry Rathbone and his fiancée to accompany them. They took a carriage ride that afternoon and after Mary commented on his happy mood, Lincoln remarked, "I consider this day the war has come to a close."*

That night, the Lincolns received a standing ovation to the tune of "Hail to the Chief" when they entered the colorful presidential box decked in red, white, and blue bunting and a big portrait of George Washington. The Lincolns and their friends laughed at the misadventures on stage when Booth, who often performed at the theater, arrived and worked his way upstairs to where the honored guests sat. Lincoln's lone bodyguard, an incompetent police officer named John Parker who had been repeatedly disciplined, had abandoned his post at intermission to grab some drinks at the nearby Star Saloon.

Unimpeded, Booth entered the box and shot the president in the back of the head at close range at a pre-planned moment when as the audience loudly laughed during a particularly funny scene. Lincoln fell forward, already unconscious. Mary Lincoln screamed as Booth stabbed Rathbone on the arm and pushed him aside before leaping from the box. A spur on one of Booth's boots got caught on a flag decorating the box. The assassin broke a leg as he landed on the stage. He still managed to yell at the confused audience, "Sic Semper Tyrannis!" (the state motto of Virginia, which translates as "Thus Always to Tyrants!") before limping to the exit and leaping on a horse he had intentionally left outside the theater.

The other conspirators were unsuccessful in carrying out their assigned tasks. Lewis Powell came the closest to achieving his goal of killing William Seward. After arriving at the Secretary of State's home, Powell pretended that he was delivering medicine and forced his way to the Seward's upstairs bedroom. The Secretary was convalescing from a broken jaw and shattered arm he suffered after being thrown from a carriage. Powell stabbed Seward repeatedly and then escaped, only to be captured later. George Atzerodt lost his nerve and got drunk instead of attacking Andrew Johnson at the vice president's hotel room. Meanwhile, Lincoln was carried to the home of William Petersen, a German tailor, located across the street from Ford's Theater, and placed in a bed not long enough to fully accommodate his tall frame. He died the next morning. Looking upon the president's body, Secretary of War Edwin Stanton said either, "Now he belongs to the angels" or "Now he belongs to the ages."

Booth evaded capture and Union troops did not corner him until April 26, when they discovered the assassin in a barn on a northern Virginia tobacco farm. Booth refused to surrender. Soldiers set fire to the barn, but a soldier shot Booth, who was carried out of the building still alive. Staring at his hands, he reportedly muttered, "Useless . . . useless" before he died. After a brief trial, the federal government executed Powell, Herold, Atzerodt, and Mary Surratt

John Wilkes Booth

on July 7. John Surratt escaped to Canada and then to England before he was arrested. In 1867, a jury failed to convict him of conspiracy to murder the president and the conspirator lived to the age of 72. Lincoln became the first of four U. S. presidents to die through gun violence. His death caused shock and profound grief across the North. The assassination added to the fears and uncertainty that many Southerners felt as they wondered what postwar life had in store for them.

When Abraham Lincoln delivered his Gettysburg Address on November 19, 1863, he expressed his hope that from the horrors of the Civil War the nation would experience a "new birth of freedom." The war indeed ended slavery. Though the Thirteenth Amendment was not ratified until December 1865, the year of the war's end, under terms of Lincoln's Emancipation Proclamation, the vast majority of the country's slaves were legally freed beginning January 1, 1863. African Americans soon hoped to start the long, hard struggle to move from being slaves to exercising their rights as citizens.

During the postwar period, while African Americans felt joy at their liberation, many southern whites would repeatedly conspire to claw back much of former slaves' newly won freedom. As African Americans experienced this difficult transition, the nation as a whole, and the defeated South in particular, faced a major rebuilding of many of its political, social, and economic institutions—what came to be known as "Reconstruction"—a daunting task for which neither section was prepared.

As the war concluded, the federal government endeavored to reconstruct the South while reviving a shared sense of American identity between the regions. Daunting obstacles loomed as leaders sought to create a "New South." About 750,000 Americans died in the war, the highest death count for any military conflict in the nation's history. About 290,000 out of a population of 5.5 million southern whites in the eleven Confederate states died in the war. Virtually everyone south of the Mason-Dixon Line separating the regions knew someone killed in the conflict. These soldiers died for a failed cause, leaving a mourning population angered and resentful toward the federal government. As the Union troops gained control over southern territory, many local whites saw them not as fellow citizens but as conquerors.

The white South had lost the labor of not just the war dead and the severely injured, but also the approximately 4 million slaves freed by Lincoln's proclamation. White Southerners had defined those black humans as property. The financial investment in those flesh-and-blood assets had, by the time of Lee's surrender, reached more than $10 trillion in today's money, wealth lost forever to the former masters. At the same time, on top of the destruction normally expected by mass, mechanized warfare, northern troops had torched some southern cities and towns, as well as plantations and farms, to deny supplies to the enemy and break the Confederate will to fight. To impede the ability of the Confederate Army to move troops, weapons, and supplies, Union forces also wrecked the South's relatively small network of railroads—vital infrastructure that the South would need to bounce back from the war. The damage impoverished the region. Overall, some economists estimate that the value of southern property dropped 75 percent from 1861, the year the war began. If rich Southerners took a massive fiscal hit from the war, poor Southerners faced hunger, with many of their hardscrabble farms looted or destroyed while others decayed from neglect as the male owners served in the Confederate military

Upon emancipation, most African Americans in the South dreamed of becoming landowners and independent farmers, but they began life as freedmen with no land and, except in rare cases, no money. With the tiny southern industrial base shattered from the war, the primary jobs remaining for most African Americans involved working on land owned by their old masters, although the details of that relationship, post-emancipation—including wages—remained unclear. Before and during the Civil War, ten of the southern states had legally prohibited teaching African Americans how to read and write, arithmetic, and other basic skills that would have greatly aided their quest for financial independence. After the

war, southern white landowners wanted to keep African Americans working at low wages, or even no wages, and stood in the way of blacks seeking education as a pathway to a better future. Additionally, the South suffered from the highest rates of white illiteracy in the country. Before the war, southern elites had shown little interest in spending tax money on educating their hard-luck white neighbors. Rebuilding the southern economy on the basis of freed laborers proved devilishly difficult with such a poorly educated workforce in an atmosphere of mass poverty and with an elite contemptuous of universal public education.

As poisonous as race relations had been before the war, racism in many ways actually intensified when the war ended. Whites believed their loved ones had died in a war over slavery and blamed African Americans for their losses. They saw black liberation, and the citizenship and voting rights soon won by the black community, as coming at their expense. As violent as slavery had been, slave owners often restrained themselves from killing or permanently disabling their expensive property. Now that African Americans represented replaceable free workers, that restraint disappeared, and white violence against blacks escalated.

During the Reconstruction Era, from 1863 until the northern political leadership essentially gave up on reforming the South in 1877, the federal government would be asked to involve itself in aspects of southern life where it had never ventured, finding itself, for the first time, operating schools, providing aid and legal services to the poor, and defending voting rights for the previously disenfranchised. For African Americans, the era opened with great hope, but in less than 15 years it came crashing down in a reign of terrorism and dashed dreams.

ABRAHAM LINCOLN AND RECONSTRUCTION

The Hesitant Emancipator

From the time that the first shot of the Civil War was fired at Fort Sumter, African Americans knew that the outcome of the conflict would seal the fate of the "peculiar institution." African Americans supported the cause of the Union in myriad ways, understanding that a northern victory would lead to the abolition of human bondage. In his classic work *Black Reconstruction in America, 1860-1880*, the scholar W.E.B. Du Bois notes that as many as a half-million slaves escaped their southern masters during the Civil War, a movement he called "The General Strike." This loss of labor gradually undermined the southern wartime economy. Slaves who remained often served as spies for northern troops and saboteurs wrecking Confederate farm production and military equipment. Abolitionist leader Frederick Douglass, an escaped slave, repeatedly urged the U.S. military to recruit African-American soldiers and to assign them to combat duty. No group in America, he argued, held a more passionate interest in defeating the southern slave owners. "Let the slaves and the free colored people be called into service, and formed into a liberating army, to march into the South and raise the banner of emancipation among its slaves," Douglass declared. President Lincoln, however, initially resisted this message and, to Douglass's great exasperation, delayed making the end of slavery in the Confederacy a war aim until almost two years into the conflict.

Abraham Lincoln was in many ways a product of his time. Born in Kentucky, a slave state, he lived most of his adult life in Illinois (a northern state heavily settled by southern whites), and married the daughter of a slave owner. He absorbed many of the racist ideas common among most white people in the first half of the nineteenth century (although some abolitionists in Lincoln's time did believe in racial equality). Lincoln publicly expressed a belief in black inferiority, though his words have to be placed not only in the context of his times, but also in consideration that he was a politician seeking to win the votes of whites hostile to the idea that African Americans shared full humanity with whites. Throughout his political career, he had opposed the spread of slavery to new U.S. states and territories. He condemned slavery, which he called a "monstrous injustice," as physically cruel and as a type of theft, which stole the fruits of labor from its victims. Lincoln further predicted in 1858 that the Union could not forever remain "half slave" and "half free."

Yet, until his presidency he always stopped short of calling for abolition in all the states. He angered Frederick Douglass and other anti-slavery crusaders when he proclaimed in his First Inaugural Address: "I have no purpose, directly or indirectly, to interfere with the institution of slavery in the States where it exists." These comments led Frederick Douglass to dismiss the new president as an "excellent slave hound," referring to the dogs used to track down escaped slaves. As late as an August 22, 1862 letter to the abolitionist Horace Greeley, less than four months before he issued his Emancipation Proclamation, Lincoln wrote, "My paramount object in this struggle is to save the Union, and is not either to save or to destroy slavery. If I could save the Union without freeing any slave I would do it, and if I could save it by freeing all the slaves I would do it; and if I could save it by freeing some and leaving others alone I would also do that."

Abraham Lincoln

Lincoln also sent mixed signals regarding his racial views and what rights African Americans should enjoy if they were free. In one of his speeches delivered during the Lincoln-Douglas Debates taking place during his 1858 campaign against Democrat Stephen Douglas for his Senate seat, Lincoln stated: "I will say then that I am not, nor ever have been, in favor of bringing about in any way the social and political equality of the black and white races—that I am not nor ever have been in favor of making voters or jurors of negroes, nor of qualifying them to hold office, nor to intermarry with white people; and I will say in addition to this that there is a physical difference between the white and black races which I believe will forever forbid the two races living together on terms of social and political equality." Still, during the same campaign he told a different audience, "Let us discard all this quibbling about this man and the other man—this race and that race and the other race being inferior, and therefore they must be placed in an inferior position . . . Let us discard these things and unite as one people . . . declaring that all men are created equal."

Lincoln's contradictions stem from his attempts to appeal to a Republican Party united in opposing the spread of slavery but divided on abolitionism and uncertain on what to do with African Americans should they be emancipated. For most of his political career, he expected that slavery would eventually vanish, though he was unsure how, and—believing that African Americans lacked the intellect to compete and thrive in a white-majority country—he favored "colonization," a scheme in which freedmen would be sent to their African ancestral homeland. Most African Americans rejected this plan as unfair and cruel. As far back as the early 1600s, many black families arrived in the British colonies that became the United States. Many black families had lived in North America longer than many white families. Most black Americans had never seen their ancestral homeland. "We live here—have lived here—have a right to live here, and mean to live here," as Douglass wrote in an 1849 editorial for his abolitionist newspaper *The North Star*.

Lincoln also proposed in 1862 a gradual emancipation scheme that would have taken 31 years to fully implement and would have provided financial compensation for slave owners for their freed human property but offered nothing to the freedmen for their unpaid work. Rather than a "slave hound," however, Lincoln represented a work in progress regarding human bondage and the status of free blacks in America. African Americans lobbied, pressured, and by their valor in the Civil War, pushed Lincoln towards an increasingly more just position on ending slavery and, eventually, African-American citizenship.

The Start of Reconstruction: The Emancipation Proclamation

The performance of African-American troops in the Union Army greatly influenced Lincoln's views on race. Four slave states—Missouri, Kentucky, Delaware, and Maryland—remained in the Union, but most of their residents had no desire in 1861 to abolish slavery. Lincoln feared the pro-Union slave owners would interpret the arming of black men as a prelude to emancipation. These fears became less important as the war turned out to be much harder than most Northerners expected, the casualties escalated, and the number of white volunteers sagged. Lincoln knew he could not spare potential military manpower. As military frustrations piled up, he also realized that he had to quickly change the tone of the war and boost morale. The stubbornness of southern resistance in the war had dramatically enhanced support for abolition in the North. Lincoln sensed a political advantage in transforming the war into not just a struggle to preserve the union but a crusade for human liberty. The thousands of slaves who began flocking to the Union lines in hope of freedom and who indicated a willingness to serve pushed Lincoln in a new direction. The president was also heartened by Union military's ability to secure control over large portions of the pro-Union slave states. In April 1862, he signed a law that immediately freed the 3,000 slaves within Washington, D.C., but a more dramatic step lay in the future.

Lincoln waited until a military victory so it would not appear he made the decision for emancipation out of desperation. The Union victory at the Battle of Antietam opened that door. On September 22, 1862, he announced the Emancipation Proclamation, which declared, as of January 1, 1863, "all persons held as slaves within any State or designated part of a State, the people whereof shall then be in rebellion against the United States, shall be then, thenceforward, and forever free." The proclamation also specified that emancipated slaves "will be received into the armed service of the United States to garrison forts, positions, stations, and other places, and to man vessels of all sorts in said service."

The proclamation was far from universally popular. Major Charles J. Whiting, a Union Army cavalry officer from Maine, complained bitterly about fighting in a "damned abolition nigger war." Yet, the proclamation changed the politics of slavery in the North; and the border states of Delaware, Maryland, Kentucky, and Missouri soon acted to end chattel servitude on their own before the Civil War ended. The proclamation furthermore marked the beginning of Reconstruction, and the war became a rolling revolution that destroyed the old southern economy and the relationship between the races there, battle by battle. The first phase of this key turning point in American history—"Wartime Reconstruction" or "Military Reconstruction"—began as a moral crusade. African Americans flocked to Union Army and Navy recruitment centers to serve. Nearly 200,000 African Americans enlisted in the Union military during the Civil War, and they made up about 10 percent of the northern Army. They performed with valor.

African American combat performance eroded racism among white soldiers. As one white solider put it, "I've been one of those men who never had much confidence in colored troops, but these doubts are now all removed, for they fought as bravely as any." The service of black soldiers convinced one Illinois man that it was "safer to trust 4,000,000 loyal negroes" than "8,000,000 disloyal whites" and that, therefore, "the faithful and patriotic negro soldiers have richly earned . . . suffrage." Lincoln became another convert, abruptly ending his talk about colonization.

Radical Republican Opposition to Lincoln

Even as Lincoln and other northern political leaders struggled with how to define the political status of black freedmen in the post-war world, they wrestled as well with the future status of states that had seceded and had been brought back by the Union Army. Lincoln's Republican Party not only controlled the White House, but also controlled both chambers of Congress. The Republican majority emerged in 1861 because, as the eleven states that formed the Confederacy left the Union, their Democratic-dominated congressional delegations resigned. At first, no consensus formed among Republicans on the requirements for reunion (if any) that should be imposed on the states retaken by northern troops. Conservative Republicans in the Congress advocated minimal change. Southern states should be readmitted, the conservatives argued, minus slavery but still firmly in the hands of the wealthy planters, politicians, and businessmen who had dominated the region before the war. Conservatives saw blacks as morally and intellectually unfit for citizenship and could see little role for them in the postbellum South other than providing physical labor. They viewed wealthy Southerners as the natural leaders of the region. To the conservatives, national reunification trumped all other issues, even if that unity came at the expense of the freedmen.

So-called **Radical Republicans** (those adamantly in favor of abolition and securing civil rights for freed slaves) recoiled at this thought. Led by Senators Benjamin Wade of Ohio and Charles Sumner of Massachusetts and Representative **Thaddeus Stevens** of Pennsylvania, the Radicals believed that the Conservative Republican approach would return men they saw as traitors to power in the South. Radicals also feared that should the former Confederate states re-enter the Union too quickly, the Republicans might lose their congressional majority and even the White House to the Democrats in the upcoming 1868 elections.

The Republican Party, which had formed only in the mid-1850s, did not exist in the South prior to the Civil War, therefore, Radicals wanted time to build the party in the southern states before allowing them back in the Union. Radicals believed they could recruit pro-Union white Southerners into the party, but to have any chance of success, they needed freed slaves to join as well. Freedmen had an obvious reason to back the Republican Party, the party of Lincoln and the Emancipation Proclamation. However, for the freedmen to be active parts of a new southern Republican Party, the Radicals would have to change state and federal laws to grant citizenship to African Americans and to give black men the right to vote. Such dramatic reforms would take time. Political calculations aside, men like Stevens and Sumner saw black voting rights (suffrage) as a matter of justice.

Radical Republicans also knew that African Americans could not defend their political rights without economic independence. If blacks were left as landless workers dependent on their former masters for their livelihoods, the white landowners could pressure African Americans to not vote or to vote as the landowner wished. Many Radical Republicans, therefore, also pushed for redistributing land in the South, seizing land from wealthy families that had supported the rebellion and giving it to freedmen who could then become independent farmers. Radicals also wanted to secure loyalty oaths from former Confederates before allowing them to vote or run for office. Stevens declared that true reconstruction must "revolutionize southern institutions, habits, and manners. . . . The foundation of their institutions . . . must be broken up and relaid, or all our blood and treasure have been spent in vain."

As with emancipation, Lincoln positioned himself as a moderate. Like the Radicals, he wanted to provide African Americans education and believed in at least limited black suffrage. However, he did not want to break up the large plantations for the benefit of freedmen. Agreeing with the Conservatives, Lincoln placed a premium on reconciliation between the white North and South. He wanted to reassure white Southerners that they would not be punished for secession and the war and that they were welcomed back in the Union. Once true unity had been achieved, he hoped, maybe then other reforms could be pursued. With this mindset, Lincoln formulated plans he hoped would be consistent with his pledge in his Second Inaugural Address delivered in March 1865, to guide Reconstruction with "malice toward none, with charity for all."

On December 8, 1863, Lincoln shared his vision for the postwar order with the issuance of his Proclamation of Amnesty and Reconstruction, in which he provided pardons for those who had fought for or otherwise supported the Confederacy (with the exception of top Confederate political and military officials). The president's proclamation established a process for how states that left the Union could rejoin, stipulating that when the number of voters in a state applying for readmission who swore loyalty to the Union and its laws (including the Emancipation Proclamation) equaled 10 percent of the number of people from that state who voted in the 1860 presidential election, then the people there could hold statewide and local elections and revise their state's constitution to abolish slavery. That state could then apply for readmission and hold congressional elections.

Lincoln's plan generally met with enthusiastic approval in the North. The war was not yet over, but the public was tiring of conflict, and the proposal—which came to be known as "the **Ten Percent Plan**"—seemed to offer a rapid path to reunification once the shooting stopped. Radical Republicans, on the other hand, saw the Ten Percent Plan as a betrayal, as did African American leaders like Frederick Douglass. The plan made no mention of African-American political rights. No requirements that southern blacks be recognized as citizens, have the right to vote, or any other freedom other than the right not to be bought and sold were included. Abolitionist leader Wendell Phillips argued that the amnesty program "makes the negro's freedom a mere sham." Douglass said that the plan would "hand the Negro back to the political power of his master, without a single element of strength to shield himself from the vindictive spirit sure to be roused against the whole colored race."

Lincoln's Ten Percent Plan hit a roadblock erected by members of his own party. Henry Davis, a Maryland representative, and Senator Benjamin Wade collaborated on a Reconstruction bill that set a much higher bar for southern states seeking readmission. The **Wade-Davis Bill**, passed July 2, 1864, would have required a majority of the state's white citizens to swear loyalty to the Union before it could be considered for re-entry. Only when that happened, could a state hold a constitutional convention to write a new state constitution that prohibited slavery and barred Confederate officeholders and military veterans from serving in elective office. Under the bill's provisions, a resident of a former Confederate state would not be allowed to vote until they took a so-called "ironclad oath" that they had never willingly aided the Confederate cause.

Lincoln pocket vetoed the measure. Under the Constitution, while the Congress is in session, a president has ten days (excluding Sundays) to decide whether to sign a bill or veto it. If he or she declines to sign it without issuing a veto, the bill becomes law. If the Congress is in recess, as it was after passage of the Wade-Davis legislation, the bill fails if the president does not sign it. Lincoln believed the law would have undermined the Union-friendly governments established in the states already under federal control—Tennessee, Louisiana, and Arkansas. Radical Republicans fiercely criticized the president. Wade and Davis issued a "Manifesto" in which they accused Lincoln of unconstitutionally usurping Congress's power, but Lincoln's sound victory over his Democratic Party opponent in the November 1864 election, Union General George McClellan, limited any political damage caused by this conflict within the Republican ranks.

The Thirteenth Amendment

Despite divisions within the Republican Party, Lincoln and the Congress made an epic break with the American past. Lincoln spent much of the final months of his life not only leading the war effort, but also ending slavery once and for all across the union. Lincoln had finally become an abolitionist. He worried that the conservative

Supreme Court might overturn the Emancipation Proclamation on the ground that the president had exceeded his Constitutional powers with this act. Such a court reversal would re-legalize slavery in the southern states then under Union control.

Lincoln and his allies in the Congress, including Senator John B. Henderson of Missouri, pushed for a Constitutional amendment abolishing slavery permanently in all U.S. states and territories. An early version of the amendment died in the House in the summer of 1864, falling short of the required two-thirds majority. After winning re-election in November 1864, Lincoln lobbied intensely for passage of the **Thirteenth Amendment**, one of the shortest and simplest in the Constitution, and which in its final form said in its first section, "Neither slavery nor involuntary servitude, except as a punishment for crime whereof the party shall have been duly convicted, shall exist within the United States, or any place subject to their jurisdiction." The Congress passed the amendment on January 31, 1865 and the necessary three-fourths of the states ratified it as of December 6, 1865, almost eight months after Lincoln's death.

The Thirteenth Amendment forever changed the lives of African Americans, but it contained one unforeseen loophole. The amendment, which marked the first time that "slavery" was ever explicitly mentioned in the Constitution, allowed involuntary servitude as a punishment for a crime. Southern states would later exploit that clause. Local law enforcement would soon arrest African Americans on dubious grounds and the courts would sentence these defendants to toil without pay for wealthy landowners or to perform uncompensated work on public projects, thus allowing a continuation of slavery under a thin disguise.

A NEW LIFE FOR AFRICAN AMERICANS

General Sherman Promises "40 Acres and a Mule" to Former Slaves

With the ruling Republican Party at odds with itself, the Congress and the White House could not agree on what to do with the slaves who had escaped from behind Confederate lines or had been liberated by the Union Army. Such freedmen posed a dilemma for military commanders. The freedmen needed food and protection from possibly vengeful southern whites, and desired a chance to earn an independent living. Still facing the Confederate enemy, the Army was reluctant to devote resources to serve as a social agency helping one-time slaves adjust to their new lives. With no clear directions from Washington, D.C., Union generals concocted policies under the pressure of war regarding the employment of freedmen, with different generals experimenting with wildly different solutions.

In New Orleans in 1862, prior to the Emancipation Proclamation taking effect, the army initially felt overwhelmed by the slaves who flocked to their camps and ordered the escaped slaves to go back to their masters. Slaves, however, resisted this, and General Nathaniel Banks improvised a new plan where the black work force, though not yet free, received wages from the military for the work they did on their masters' properties. The masters, now more like employers, were obligated to provide meals and shelter. The slaves had to sign one-year contracts with their "employers" and could only change who they worked for after completing that term.

General William Tecumseh Sherman took a far more revolutionary approach. After leading a force of 60,000 troops that punched through the heart of the Georgia Plantation Belt, and Sherman had, by September 1864, seized the city of Atlanta. Whenever his force arrived in a given area, slaves ran towards the men in blue and sought protection. "They flock to me, old and young, they pray, they shout, and mix up my name with Moses . . . as well as Abraham Lincoln," Sherman wrote from the field. Secretary of War Stanton traveled to Georgia to confer with the general and urged him to meet with a group of freedmen in Savannah. The gathering, attended by about 20 men mostly from the clergy, convened on January 12, 1865. The ministers were asked what slavery had meant to them. One of the ministers, 67-year-old Garrison Frazier told Sherman that life in bondage meant masters "receiving . . . the work of another man, and not by his consent" and he said he dreamed of a day when his people would "reap the fruit of our own labor."

While possibly moved by the minister's words, Sherman was primarily motivated by the practical necessities of running the Union's western forces when on January 16, the general announced Special Order No. 15, in which the military seized the Georgia Sea Islands, the South Carolina low country, and part of northern Florida's Atlantic Coast, that had been abandoned by Confederate owners. Sherman set aside this rice-producing land for black settlement. Freedmen families could apply for use of 40 acres. Upon request, the military also loaned each family an army mule. Sherman may have only intended what came to be known to some as "Sherman land" as a temporary expedient to get freedmen back to work and producing crops, but African Americans jumped at the opportunity to become landowners.

By June 1865, 40,000 freedmen had taken up Sherman's offers and, using their farming expertise, soon were successfully cultivating about 400,000 acres. About 1,000 freedmen occupied Skidaway Island, off the Georgia Coast, and declared Ulysses L. Houston, who had participated in the meeting with Sherman in Savannah, the "black governor." Freedmen would get little opportunity to celebrate their achievements. By the fall of 1865, Lincoln had died, and Andrew Johnson, a one-time slave owner possessing no sympathy for African American aspirations, reversed Special Order No. 15 and ordered the Sherman Land returned to the previous white owners. Sadly, Special Order No. 15 would be one of the few substantial attempts to address black poverty. Sherman's directive became the first of many broken promises made to African Americans in the Reconstruction Era.

The Freedmen's Bureau

At the Civil War's end, African Americans in the old Confederacy remained in limbo. They were no longer property but they held little or no property themselves. They possessed meager resources with which to start their lives as freedmen and their white neighbors had little interest in aiding them. Any assistance would have to come from Washington, D.C., which posed a further problem. Prior to 1865, the federal government had never provided direct aid to the poor, even during the brutal depression that occurred from 1837 to 1843. The U.S. government had spent no money on public schools and no tradition yet existed of the federal government tackling poverty, illiteracy, or workers' rights. Yet, these were precisely the type of social services freedmen would need to get a firm start on their new lives.

In their last major collaboration, President Lincoln and Congress engaged in a bold, unprecedented experiment. Congress provided direct aid to the former slaves with the March 3, 1865 passage of a bill creating the Bureau of Refugees, Freedmen, and Abandoned Lands, better known as the **Freedmen's Bureau**. The War Department operated the Bureau, which would be staffed by U.S. Army personnel. At first, the Bureau provided relief not just for freedmen but also whites left destitute and homeless by the war. The Bureau tended to basic needs for its clients such as food and clothing. Congress also gave the Bureau authority over land owned by individuals who could not be traced, either because they were missing in action from the war, or they were Confederates who fled before the advance of Union armies. The Bureau could then lease 40 acres of abandoned land to former slave families for three years at a rate of 6 percent of the value of the land per year. After the three years, the freedmen enjoyed the option of purchasing the tract at its full value.

The most important part of the bill gave the agency responsibility for "all subjects relating to refugees and freedmen." This broad mandate allowed the Freedmen's Bureau to educate African Americans by establishing schools across the South, which, in turn, led to dramatic increases in African-American literacy rates. The Bureau also became a legal aid agency. As former slaves became free workers, landowners offered them contracts with confusing wording that deliberately locked them into years of service in return for miserably low wages. Most freedmen still lacked the education to understand what they were being asked to sign. Army lawyers began to review the contracts and help freedmen renegotiate the terms. Finally, the soldiers assigned to the Bureau became the blue shield protecting African Americans from white vigilante violence. Crimes against blacks, including rape, assault, robbery, and murder escalated during Reconstruction. Law enforcement would only rarely arrest any white person for these crimes even when the identity of the suspect was widely known. Grand juries routinely failed to indict whites for crimes against freedmen and, if a trial were ever held, white defendants would not be found guilty. Law enforcement officials themselves often participated in the crimes. As the violence mounted, the Bureau began to hold such assailants accountable, presiding over military trials for such suspects.

All of these federal interventions on behalf of the freedmen outraged southern whites, but the Bureau's schools may have been the most subversive example of Reconstruction Era social engineering. Most southern whites convinced themselves that black men and women could not learn beyond a basic level and insisted that formal schooling would only inspire black discontent with their economic and social plight. African Americans enthusiastically embraced education. "The free people are aroused to the possibility of educating their children," observed William H. Horton, the Sub-Assistant Commissioner for the Freedmen's Bureau in Dallas, Texas, two years after the Emancipation Proclamation.

Black schools received funding from federal allocations to the Bureau, and from northern charitable societies. When Republicans began winning control of state governments in 1868, they also provided money for black education. Within a month of the arrival of Union troops, more than 1,000 black boys and girls sat at school desks in Richmond, Virginia, the schooling provided by white and black churches. Learning became contagious, with children returning home and teaching their parents the alphabet.

Teachers—white and black, male and female, often inspired by religious faith—trekked South to teach under the most difficult, and sometimes physically dangerous, circumstances. Even with these hardships, by 1870 the impoverished African-American community in the Old Confederacy pooled their meager resources and expended more than $1 million to build schools, buy classroom supplies, and pay teachers. These schools helped train a generation of post-slavery African-American political, cultural, and spiritual leaders.

Sharecropping

Much of the drama during Reconstruction occurred in places other than Washington, D.C. In this era, the

The Freedmen's Bureau by A.R. Waud. An army officer representing the Freedmen's Bureau stands between armed groups of white Americans and African Americans. 1868.

southern economy dramatically evolved. Lacking money and without land, freedmen fought to become independent farmers. "They appear to be willing to work, but are decisive in their expressions, to work for no one but themselves," an officer with the South Carolina Freedmen's Bureau reported in 1866. With the experiment in Sherman Land aborted early in Reconstruction, most freedmen were forced to labor for their former masters. Two systems of farm labor arose in the South to replace slavery: farm tenancy and sharecropping.

In spite of their continued poverty, many African Americans at first greeted their new circumstances with hope. Landowners improvised new systems of labor because they had lost their workforce, but they would rig the system to ensure maximum benefit for themselves while maintaining tight control over their workers. Under tenancy, the landowner divided his property into lots rented by the freedmen who owned the crops that they grew. The tenant farmers were not limited to growing only cash crops like tobacco and cotton, and could devote some land to growing food for the family. At the end of the growing season, the freedmen sold the crops and used the proceeds to pay off the rent, which was often one quarter of the crop. Such farmers believed they had taken a mighty step from slavery. They were no longer subject to the lash. They controlled, to a larger degree, their own work schedule. The husbands and fathers in freedmen families were thrilled if their wives could tend to the children rather than working in the fields and if their children could attend Freedmen Bureau schools rather than toil.

Under sharecropping, the freedmen owned virtually nothing, but instead signed contracts to obtain everything not necessary to grow the crop on credit from the landowner. Whereas the planter usually provided seeds, planting equipment, and work animals such as mules, the growers borrowed to purchase food, clothing, medicine, and others life essentials. At harvest time, sharecroppers typically were contracted to receive one half of the proceeds from the crops they had grown that year. The problem with both tenant farming and sharecropping was that landowners and sometimes owners of nearby country stores (often the same individuals) held local monopolies on providing credit and thus charged exorbitant interest, sometimes 50 or 60 percent, on all the items the freedmen borrowed since the beginning of the year. When these costs were subtracted from the share of the crop, and when unscrupulous landowners lied about the profits received from crop sales or the amount borrowed, the freedmen usually ended up in debt. Their contract required sharecroppers to work off the last year's debt and then the freedmen had to borrow again for all their necessities for the coming year. Essentially, sharecroppers never got paid for their labor, a situation heartbreakingly close to life under slavery.

Sharecropping became a cancer that ate at the southern economy. Greedy landowners, thinking only in the short term, insisted that the sharecroppers devote more acres to cash crops and less to food production. This aggravated a worldwide glut of cotton, which caused prices of that commodity to tumble. As their incomes fell, poor and struggling white farmers who owned their land eventually could not pay their mortgages and were sucked into tenancy and sharecropping as well. This meant the South could not produce a consumer base that might have sparked industrial development, leading much of the region to languish in poverty.

Celebrating Freedom

African Americans celebrated their liberation in myriad ways, public and private, in manners great and small. As the historian Leon Litwack observed, upon realizing the day of emancipation had arrived, African Americans in Athens, Georgia, erected a liberty pole and danced and sang around it, while more than 4,000 black men and women marched through the streets of Charleston, South Carolina, wildly cheered by about 10,000 mostly African-American spectators. The parade featured a mule-drawn cart with a coffin draped with the message, "Slavery is Dead." Resentful whites made such open celebrations of black freedom dangerous. When freedmen celebrated emancipation in the streets of Huntsville, Texas, an angry white man on horseback rode up to the crowd and swung a sword at an African-American woman, slicing her in half. Annie Row, a former slave interviewed in the 1930s, remembered her childhood at a Rusk County, Texas, plantation. "Marster Charley," she said, received a letter informing him of his son John's death in the Civil War. The loss of his child and the imminent disappearance of the fortune he had invested in slaves proved too much for him to bear. He "started cursing the war, and he picked up the hot poker and said, 'Free the niggers, will they, I'll free them.' Then he hit my mammy on the neck, and she started moaning and crying and dropped to the floor . . . He took the gun off the rack and started for the field where the niggers were working. . . . But the good Lord took a hand in that mess, and the master hadn't gone far in the field when he dropped all of a sudden . . . He couldn't talk or move, and they toted him in the house. The doctor came, and the next day marster died."

Some white landowners living in remote rural communities kept news of the emancipation from their African-American workforce, which kept them toiling as slaves for years. In some cities, Union troops arrived and announced to the freedmen that their chains had fallen, but when they moved on to the next front, local whites placed them back in bondage. Slavery thus died a slow death in the South.

When it came, African Americans acted upon their freedom. African Americans sought autonomy in their political and spiritual lives. After slavery, African Americans formed their own religious establishments across the South, including new African Methodist Episcopal (AME), Baptist, and Methodist churches—black churches led by black preachers supporting the dreams of black congregations. These churches became hotbeds of political activism, as ministers urged their flock to fight for full citizenship, including the vote, the right to serve on juries, and the right to run for office. When African Americans won citizenship and the right to vote, black preachers recruited candidates and urged church members to register to vote and to show up on Election Day.

Hence, for the next 100 years, whites targeted black churches for terrorism because of their role in resisting white supremacy. From the 1860s through the June 17, 2015 mass shooting at Emanuel AME Church in Charleston, South Carolina (which once claimed famous slave rebel Denmark Vesey as a member), black churches suffered arson and bombings while white assassins slew ministers and congregants. The black church also became the launching pad for many of the twentieth century's most important African American political figures, including civil rights leaders Martin Luther King, Jr., Ralph Abernathy, and Jesse Jackson.

The African-American Family during Reconstruction

Slavery had represented not only an act of kidnapping and the theft of black bodies and black wages, but also an assault on the black family. Out of self-interest, slave owners had tried to keep together slave couples that fell in love and sought to not split slave parents from their children. Slave "marriages" had no legal standing because recognizing such unions would interfere with what southern states assumed was the absolute authority slave owners held over their flesh-and-blood possessions. Yet, slave couples built lives together and informally married, improvising ceremonies such as "jumping the broom" to mark the occasion. Nevertheless, because of debt, the loss of a lawsuit, the need for cash, or to display their power, owners sometimes split up slave families, selling children, spouses and other relatives away from their loved ones.

Whites who broke up slave families assured themselves that black human beings quickly forgot such attachments and pain. Even after emancipation, southern whites refused to acknowledge that African-American couples could fall in love and desire a lifetime relationship with each other. "Now what does the Negro know about the obligations of the marriage relation?" wrote former U.S. senator and ardent secessionist Robert Toombs in the *Atlanta Constitution* in 1871. "No more, sir, than a parish bull or village heifer."

Such whites were in for a shock when African Americans rebuilt their families after emancipation. "It was commonly thought that the negroes, when freed, would care very little for their children, and would let them die for want of attention, but experience has proven this surmise unfounded," one white observer from a former plantation-owning family, David G. Barrow, wrote in 1881. Freedmen proved their devotion in several ways. They sacrificed all they could to see that their children got an education and provided for them as best they could even though they were denied decent wages. In large numbers, they flocked to authorities to have their marriages sanctified and legally recognized. Freedmen raced to Union Army chaplains wanting the legal protections for their relationships that marriage provided. Army chaplains later reported that they could have performed freedmen marriages around the clock in the final days of the war. In 1864, the War Department authorized Freedmen Bureau agents to preside over freedmen marriages as well.

One of the more poignant tasks faced by too many freedmen was piecing together families broken under slavery. Freedmen started newspapers and these publications filled with advertisements bought by money-starved husbands, wives, and parents seeking kin who had been sold away, sometimes decades earlier. A northern reporter touring the postwar South later wrote of meeting an exhausted middle-aged African American in North Carolina. The freedman's feet ached and his heart did as well. He had walked about 600 miles believing his wife and children had been sold there four years earlier but he had not yet finished his quest. Freedmen made these epic journeys and sometimes never reunited with their loved ones. In other cases, they discovered with heartbreak that partners they had considered husbands or wives had started new romantic relationships at their next master's property.

PRESIDENTIAL RECONSTRUCTION UNDER ANDREW JOHNSON

Lincoln's Unfortunate Successor: Andrew Johnson

A dramatic decline in the quality of leadership befell the country when Lincoln died and Vice President **Andrew**

Johnson took power. If diplomacy defined Lincoln's approach to leadership, divisiveness defined Johnson's. If Lincoln worked well with rivals and sometimes won them to his side, Johnson needlessly made enemies. If Lincoln could handle brutal criticism and stay focused, Johnson was thin-skinned and easy to anger. If Lincoln grew in his worldview and became more tolerant and supportive of black rights as he aged, Johnson remained a white supremacist who could see no place for former slaves than as the tightly-controlled servants of their supposed white superiors. With a reputation as a heavy drinker and a combative personality, Johnson provoked Republicans in Congress, and he became the first president to be impeached. At a time when regional and racial relationships were at their most delicate point, he was remarkably ill suited to occupy the White House.

Johnson grew up in poverty in Raleigh, North Carolina. Strapped for cash, his widowed mother Polly apprenticed Andrew to a tailor so he could learn a profession. At age 15, he ran away, eventually settling in Tennessee where he perfected his tailoring skills and became a successful businessman. Johnson's new home shaped his political destiny. Greeneville sat in Eastern Tennessee, in the foothills of the Appalachian Mountains, a terrain not suited for the establishment of large plantations run by wealthy landowners and worked by armies of slaves. Whites in eastern Tennessee in general were poorer and far less likely to own slaves than their western neighbors. This region would oppose secession, and many there would fight for the Union during the Civil War.

Johnson married and ran a successful tailor shop, investing his profits in real estate, and owned up to nine slaves. Now a prosperous man, and one who seemed to relish an argument, Johnson plunged into politics and climbed up the state's political ladder, along the way winning races for the U.S. Congress, for governor, and in 1857, the United States Senate. Johnson always positioned himself as the voice of the common folk speaking out against the recklessness and greed of the wealthy.

Throughout his political career, Johnson vigorously defended slavery, insisting that the Constitution guaranteed property rights, including slaves. He denied that the federal government or even states had the right to abolish slavery. He frequently expressed the deep-seated racism that would shape his policies towards freedmen during his presidency, including his lack of support for anything but token voting rights for African Americans. While serving in Congress, Johnson argued, "the black races of Africa were inferior to the white man in point of intellect—better calculated in physical structure to undergo drudgery and hardship—standing as they do, many degrees lower in the scale of gradation . . . than the white man."

Andrew Johnson, 1866.

Johnson infuriated most white Southerners by his actions after Abraham Lincoln won the 1860 presidential election. When most of the slaveholding states, including Tennessee, seceded from the Union, Johnson became the only U.S. senator from a Confederate state to remain loyal to the Union and remain in office. For Johnson, the regional conflict was about the survival of the Union, one he hoped would still preserve and protect slavery. "Damn the negroes," he once said. "I am fighting these traitorous aristocrats, their masters."

Johnson's loyalty to the Union caught Lincoln's attention. At the end of Johnson's Senate term, the president appointed him to serve as the military governor of Tennessee, where much of the state including the eastern section had returned to Union control. Johnson played a surprising role in promoting black enlistment in the Union Army, with 20,000 African-American soldiers enlisting from Tennessee, but his relationship with African Americans would only go downhill from there. Because Lincoln faced a tough re-election bid in 1864, Republican leaders wanted to add a pro-Union Democrat to balance the ticket. Lincoln convinced Johnson to join him as running mate under a temporary "National Union Party" label. The ticket prevailed, and this placed Johnson next in line to the presidency.

Johnson's Reconstruction Plan

When Johnson became president after John Wilkes Booth's murder of Lincoln, he stepped into a power vacuum. Congress would be in recess for most of the time between April 1865 and the next session in December. Lincoln and the legislative branch had been unable to reach a consensus on Reconstruction policy, so there was no official plan on the table. Johnson saw an opportunity, and he asserted his authority as chief executive to implement his own road map to national reconciliation. His approach would be a disaster.

In spite of Johnson's condemnations of wealthy slave owners as greedy traitors, the new president decided he needed the southern elites to restore order and to keep what he feared were potentially lawless African Americans in their place, under white control where they could not start a race war. Johnson generously handed out pardons to top Confederates. African-American leaders including Frederick Douglass met with the new president, hoping to win his support for black voting rights. Johnson could not take seriously the African-American aspirations for fair treatment, equal opportunity, and especially, voting rights, insisting that poor southern whites had lost more in the war than any other group while African Americans had gained the most. To grant black voting rights would only provoke deeper racial tensions. Johnson also believed that supposedly childlike former slaves would meekly vote as their one-time masters instructed them, which would only strengthen the dominance of the old planter class that had caused the Civil War. Douglass scoffed at the notion, pointing out that African Americans had been deeply loyal to the Union and had suffered at the hands of those planters. Blacks would be the most likely political counterbalance to pre-war white elites. Johnson did not budge from his opposition to a constitutional amendment enfranchising African Americans, arguing that voting rights were a state matter. The president did not take kindly to being challenged by a black man. After the conference, Johnson ranted about Douglass and his compatriots. "Those damned sons of bitches thought they had me in a trap. I knew that damned Douglass; he's just like any nigger and he would sooner cut a white man's throat than not."

Johnson's Reconstruction plan—what came to be known as "Presidential Reconstruction"—prioritized readmission of the southern states into the Union over even a minimal nod to African-American rights. Johnson set a low bar for readmission. He viewed emancipation as a mistake but felt it was too late to reverse course on that issue, so his plan required states seeking readmission to ratify the Thirteenth Amendment. Under Johnson's scheme, the interim governors that the president had appointed would have to convene state constitutional conventions. These conventions had to officially renounce their state's right to secede. Because Johnson wanted to

punish those who had bankrolled the rebel war against the Union and discourage those who might fund future treason, returning states also had to renounce their war debt. Johnson did not make black suffrage a requirement. He did, however, support extending token voting rights for freedmen, first granted to those who served in the Union Army, then to literate African Americans holding personal property between $200-$250 (about $3,300 to $4,100 in today's dollars). Such policies would leave most African Americans disenfranchised. Once states met these requirements, they could hold congressional elections and resume their old status in the Union. The region would remain a land of, by, and for white men alone. He still required those Confederate supporters who owned $20,000 or more in property (about $313,000 today) to personally apply to Johnson for a pardon. Those pardons, and full restoration of property minus slaves, flowed easily from President Johnson's pen.

Rather than being relieved at Johnson's lenient terms, southern leaders saw the plan as a sign of Johnson's weakness and sought to restore the South as close to its pre-war condition, and African Americans in as close a condition to slavery, as legally possible. Johnson, in turn, responded to this continued southern resistance passively, which would provoke a backlash from even moderate Republicans.

The Black Codes

Seeing Johnson's leniency as a sign of weakness, delegates to the state constitutional conventions in mid-1865 clearly expected they would face no consequences if they ignored Johnson's requirements for re-admission. Mississippi declined not only to repudiate its Confederate war debt, but also even to ratify the Thirteenth Amendment abolishing slavery. (Although the amendment went into effect across the United States when ratified by three-quarters of the states in December 1865, Mississippi would not get around to approving it until 2013.) Other states also refused to repudiate their debts. Regardless of this intransigence, Johnson not only appeared ready to accept the old Confederacy back in the Union, he continued to defend their interests, for instance vetoing a bill in 1866 admitting Colorado as a state, insisting that no such move should be made until the South was completely represented in the Congress.

As new and still unreconstructed governments took power in southern states Johnson remained indifferent as they implemented a series of cruel limits on African-American freedoms that came to be known as "**Black Codes**." Each former Confederate state passed a different set of laws that applied only to black people, but most of these codes included provisions that harshly punished "vagrancy," or lacking what the local authorities decided was adequate employment. Under the Black Codes, African Americans had to carry documents written by whites certifying that they had jobs, which echoed the written passes slaves had to carry when they traveled.

Black Codes in some states required African Americans to work from sunrise to sundown. Upon freedom, many African-American families celebrated the freedom to allow women, who as slaves had been forced to leave offspring each day with grandparents or other relatives too old to labor, to stay with and care for their own children. In Texas and Louisiana, the Black Codes mandated that all members of a freedman family, including young children, were required to work.

The Black Codes in many cases prevented African Americans from developing job skills and business experience that would take them off the farm. Even though African Americans had acquired many skills under slavery, working for instance as blacksmiths, saddle makers, animal trainers, leather craft workers, or even distillers, some states now banned African Americans from having any job other than working in the fields. Mississippi even outlawed African Americans from owning or renting farmland, thus requiring them to be field hands toiling for white people. In South Carolina, the state forced African Americans to pay annual taxes between $10 and $100 (between $163 and $1,634 in today's dollars) if they worked at any occupation other than servant or farm laborer.

In Florida, courts could order a freedman who violated a labor contract to be whipped and sentenced to one year of uncompensated labor. Black Codes prohibited African Americans from serving on juries and all-white juries without fail found African Americans charged with vagrancy guilty and sentenced them to work without wages for white planters or the local government. African Americans could also be forced to perform unpaid work if they failed to show proper respect to a white person, for instance looking them straight in the eye or not bowing or failing to bow quickly enough.

At a time of intense white violence against African Americans, many freedmen were denied a right to self-defense and were banned from owning firearms. At the same time, states across the South also did not allow African Americans to testify against whites in court. Since African Americans were often the only witnesses to crimes whites committed against the black community, such laws meant that these crimes went unpunished. The most mean-spirited of these Black Codes, in states like North Carolina, allowed courts to take stewardship of black orphans or of children whose parents supposedly could not adequately care for them and hand them over to white "guardians," who then exploited them as servants. Under this form of legal kidnapping the guardians were allowed to whip or use other physical punishments against black minors. African Americans who worked so hard to put families back together after slavery now saw white authorities seizing control of their loved ones again by the thousands.

Many whites embraced terrorism to beat their former servants back into a position of subservience. According to research by historian Barry Crouch, former Confederates murdered about 1 percent of all African-American men from ages 15 to 49 in Texas from the years from 1865 to 1868. Another scholar, Eric Foner, noted that age or gender did not shield African Americans from beatings, torture, or murder. Whites in Bosque County, Texas, during the first years of Reconstruction raped a black girl, castrated a black boy, and whipped another child to death without legal consequences. In Limestone County, Texas thugs seized Jo Brooks and hacked off her arms for no reason other than her black skin. "Damn their black souls, they're the things that caused the best blood of our sons to flow," one white man exclaimed in Mississippi.

The Black Suffrage Issue in the North

Racism still warped northern society, but many whites there had embraced black emancipation as a sacred cause for which their fathers, husbands, sons, and other loved ones had given their lives. Northern whites watched in horror as the Black Codes robbed African Americans of the freedom they had just won at so high a cost.

Yet, southern leaders refused to accept the consequences of wartime defeat. They believed that their continued resistance would incur no consequences from the Johnson administration. Even though some of the states applying for readmission had failed to meet Johnson's minimal requirements, the former Confederate states held Congressional elections in the fall of 1865 and sent to Washington, D.C. a delegation dominated by leaders of the failed rebellion including 15 former officers in the Confederate military and 25 officeholders from the Confederacy, prominent among them the former Confederate Vice President Alexander Stephens. African Americans had not been allowed to vote or run for office in those elections.

Northern voters were furious at the prospect of men they saw as traitors returning to power. Even moderate Republicans worried that returning southern states controlled by the Democratic Party to the Union too quickly threatened Republican Congressional majority. When the Congress convened in December 1865, a majority voted not to accept the credentials of the 80-member southern delegation and sent them back home.

CONGRESSIONAL RECONSTRUCTION

Moderate and Radical Republicans in the Congress temporarily bridged their differences during Andrew Johnson's presidency. Both factions blamed Johnson for continued southern intransigence. Rather than reconciling the regions, the president had deliberately or through incompetence reinforced regional grievances. The alliance between moderate Republicans and their Radical peers began with the refusal to seat the southern delegation and deepened in 1866 as Johnson vetoed two bills enjoying broad support.

The law creating the Freedmen's Bureau in March 1865, specified that the agency would cease operations one year after the Civil War ended. That deadline loomed in the spring of 1866, but it became clear that the Bureau had become a critical lifeline for African Americans in the South and that much work remained undone. Majorities in both houses of Congress passed a bill extending the life of the agency, but Johnson vetoed it, arguing that the federal government had no constitutional mandate to provide education or financial assistance to the poor and that Congress should pass no major legislation as long as the old Confederate states were unrepresented. An attempt to override Johnson's veto by the required two-thirds majority barely failed.

Johnson's relationship with Congress had already soured, and he did not improve matters when, speaking to White House visitors on George Washington's birthday, he improvised a speech in which he compared Radical Republican leaders like Representative Thaddeus Stevens of Pennsylvania and Charles Sumner of Massachusetts to Confederate leaders, accusing them of dividing the Union. Johnson made a split with Congress inevitable when he vetoed the 1866 Civil Rights Act, the nation's first civil rights bill, which aimed to undo the Black Codes widely despised by the Republican majority in Congress. The bill defined all born in the United States, except for Native Americans not taxed, as citizens due "the full and equal benefit of all laws . . . as is enjoyed by white citizens." The proposed legislation specified that African Americans had the right to sue, to testify in court, and to enter into contracts, and that states could not give unequal punishments for violating the law based on race. Johnson again wielded his veto pen, claiming that state citizenship was not a federal matter.

Given the clear human rights abuses unfolding in the South, Johnson's March 27 veto shocked even the moderates in Congress, who had become partners with the Radicals. The Congress overrode the veto in April. In July 1866, Congress again passed another bill extending the life of the Freedmen's Bureau, prompting yet another Johnson veto which the House and Senate promptly overrode. Power clearly passed from the White House to the House and Senate, thus beginning the third and most significant phase of Reconstruction, Congressional or Radical Reconstruction.

The Fourteenth Amendment

Fearing that the Supreme Court might overturn its 1866 civil rights legislation, congressional Republicans fought to permanently enshrine the legislation's principles. In April 1866, moderate Republicans proposed the **Fourteenth Amendment**, destined to become one of the most important and complicated additions to the U.S. Constitution. The amendment for the first time specified that all born in the United States, and naturalized immigrants, were not only citizens of the United States but also of the state in which they lived. This clause undid the Supreme Court's infamous *Dred Scott* decision, which held that the writers of the Constitution never intended African Americans to be citizens and viewed them as "beings of an inferior order . . . altogether unfit to associate with the white race . . . and so far inferior, that they had no rights which the white man was bound to respect."

The Fourteenth Amendment not only guaranteed African-Americans rights but also specified that as citizens they enjoyed the same "privileges and immunities" as white citizens, and could not be denied "life, liberty, or property without due process of law." All citizens, it said, were due "equal protection under the law." No longer could a state legally target African Americans, requiring only blacks to carry proof of employment, for instance, or prohibiting only them from testifying in court. In response to the elections that took place in the former Confederate states in the fall of 1865, the Fourteenth Amendment prohibited anyone who violated a military or civil oath by participating in the rebellion from holding elective or military office in the future unless specifically allowed by a two-thirds vote of Congress. States were also prohibited from repaying their Confederate war debt.

Finally, although the amendment did not specifically grant voting rights for African Americans, it did allow Congress to reduce a state's representation in the federal legislature by the proportion of African-American men 21 years and older represented in that state's total population if that state disenfranchised black men. Cynicism lay behind the wording of this section. Many white northern voters still adamantly opposed black suffrage, and some states outside of the South still denied African Americans the franchise. The black population, however, still overwhelmingly resided in the old Confederacy. In states like Vermont and Maine, the black population amounted to less than 1 percent while in several southern states the African-American population exceeded 40 percent. African Americans were a majority in Mississippi and South Carolina. After ratification of the Fourteenth Amendment, southern states rejoining the Union would suffer a major penalty in terms of political power if they denied black voting rights while the impact on a northern state blocking black suffrage would be minimal. Republicans supporting the amendment, meanwhile, knew they would gain politically by promoting black voting in the South. Congress passed the Fourteenth Amendment by the required two-thirds vote on June 13, 1866, and three-fourths of the states ratified it less than two years later.

Johnson's Failed "Swing Around the Circle"

Tennessee ratified the Fourteenth Amendment on July 19, 1866, and became the first southern state to satisfy Congress's expectations for readmission. Ten former Confederate states remained unreconstructed. As black rights advanced, the mood got uglier in the South, and President Johnson added kindling to the fire by touring the country that summer in a large circular route. On this grand "swing around the circle," he denounced Radical Republicans and the Fourteenth Amendment while promoting the congressional candidacies of fellow conservatives. Johnson wanted to win a presidential term in his own right in 1868, but he realized that he was in deep political trouble since Democrats regarded him as a traitor and Republicans saw him as an obstacle to their Reconstruction program. Johnson hoped that if he elected allies to the next Congress, he might use that foundation to build a third political party that would nominate him for president. Like many Johnson initiatives, this effort proved a disaster.

Race riots stained the summer of 1866. Violence wracked Charleston, Richmond, and Atlanta, with particularly appalling bloodshed as well in New Orleans and Memphis. In Memphis, African American Union soldiers and freedmen forced the release of a black man arrested on dubious grounds, sparking white fury and a riot that claimed the lives of 46 African Americans (including two children) as well as a white policeman and a firefighter. Rampaging whites burned down much of the African American part of town, torching schools, churches and homes. In New Orleans, chaos reigned when black workers paraded, demanding voting rights during a state constitutional convention, sparking an upheaval that slew 48 and wounded 166 in an incident a congressional investigation later labeled a massacre of African-American civilians.

Rather than using his high office to unite the country, Johnson exploited the tragedies, attempting to blame his radical political enemies for the melees even as he showed complete indifference to the loss of African-American lives. In speeches delivered in August and September, he compared Radical Republican leaders like Thaddeus Stevens and Wendell Phillips to Satan, to Judas Iscariot (the Biblical betrayer of Jesus) and to the Confederate rebels. As a result of his angry outbursts, Johnson probably lost more votes for his allies than he won. Republicans, now solidly anti-Johnson, gained more than a two-thirds majority in both the House and the Senate, meaning they could (if they maintained unity) override any Johnson veto of congressional legislation. The election threatened to make President Johnson a bit player in the ongoing drama of Reconstruction.

The Reconstruction Acts of 1867

By March 1867, moderates and Radical Republicans largely agreed that Johnson's policies were a failure, and they decided to hit the reset button and to begin the process all over again. They passed the **Reconstruction Acts of 1867**, four laws under which the southern state and local governments created under Johnson in an atmosphere of terror and without black participation would be replaced. The legislation placed the ten unreconstructed states under direct military rule and were divided into five military districts, each under the authority of an Army general whose first task was to impose law and order.

Once violence ended in a military district, the army would initiate voter registration. The law required each state to hold new constitutional conventions, with the delegates to be elected by male citizens age 21 and older registered to vote. The law required that African Americans must be allowed to register, cast ballots, and run for the delegate slots. Men who had been major military or political officials in the Confederacy would not be allowed to participate in the constitutional convention delegate elections. The law also set requirements for these conventions. Each of the ten states was required to grant voting rights for all adult male citizens 21 years of age and older regardless of race, and to ratify the Fourteenth Amendment. Once all these requirements were met and the voters approved the new state constitution, that state could then hold elections and apply for readmission to the Union.

Unlike Lincoln's 10 Percent Plan and Johnson's program for Reconstruction, the Reconstruction Acts dealt directly with the political status of African Americans post-emancipation. Blacks would have the legal right to vote, and for a time the Union Army would ensure that those rights were respected. However, like its predecessors, the congressional plan did not address the freedmen's poverty and landlessness. African Americans would continue to be economically vulnerable and subject to financial pressure to not assert their political rights. Reaching his desk only 10 days before the end of the 1867 regular Congressional session, Johnson had the opportunity to pocket-veto the first Reconstruction Act but instead decided to grandstand, issuing a veto with an angry denunciation, only to see the Congress override the veto that same day. Johnson had been sidelined, and by this time many Radicals sought to eliminate him from the political process in Washington completely.

The Impeachment of Andrew Johnson

The authors of the Constitution deliberately made it difficult for the Congress to remove high-ranking federal officials, such as a president, vice president, cabinet member, or federal judge. Under Article II, Section 4 of the Constitution, the House of Representatives is given the power to impeach such officials for "Treason, Bribery, or other High Crimes and Misdemeanors." The role of the House in such cases is similar to that of a grand jury in a criminal case. The House determines if sufficient evidence has been presented to justify **impeachment**, and it takes a simple majority in the lower chamber to move the case forward. An impeachment is, therefore, similar to a grand jury indicting a defendant. Guilt has

not been determined and an impeached official does not yet have to leave office. The Senate must then hold an impeachment trial. The accused official can present a defense through lawyers, while the "prosecution" is handled by House managers, members of the lower chamber who act as prosecutors. The Senate acts as the jury, with the Chief Justice of the Supreme Court presiding over the trial to rule on legal issues. The Senate must vote by at least a two-thirds majority to remove a president or other officials from office.

Johnson still worried congressional Radicals. Even if the large Republican congressional majority severely limited his ability to block Republican Reconstruction plans, Johnson remained commander-in-chief. This gave him authority over the Freedmen's Bureau, an agency that the U.S. Army administered and Johnson had wanted to destroy. The president had authority over Secretary of War Edwin Stanton with whom he had battled over policy. Stanton frequently allied with the Radicals on Reconstruction matters. Radical and moderate Republicans both trusted Stanton and feared Johnson would fire him and replace him with someone sympathetic to the former slave owners.

With this conflict between Johnson and Stanton in mind, Congress passed the **Tenure of Office Act** over the president's veto in March 1867. The law prevented the president from firing any officeholder in the Executive Branch who had been approved by the Senate until that body approved a replacement. Johnson would not be deterred in his attempt to dump Stanton and made two legal arguments against the act. First, Lincoln had appointed Stanton and not Johnson. Based on the precise

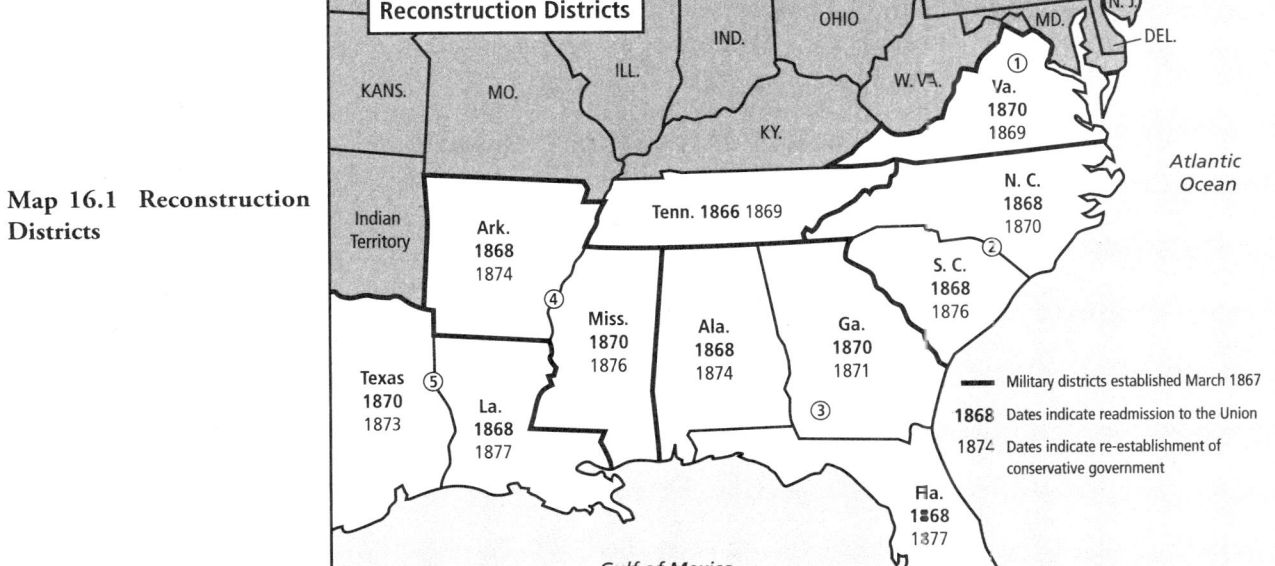

Map 16.1 Reconstruction Districts

Reconstruction Districts

KANS. — MO. — ILL. — IND. — OHIO — PA. — N. J. — MD. — DEL. — W. VA. — KY.

Va. 1870 1869 — ①

N. C. 1868 1870 — ②

Atlantic Ocean

Indian Territory — Ark. 1868 1874

Tenn. 1866 1869

S. C. 1868 1876

Texas 1870 1873 — ⑤ — ④ — Miss. 1870 1876 — Ala. 1868 1874 — Ga. 1870 1871

La. 1868 1877 — ③

Fla. 1868 1877

Gulf of Mexico

Military districts established March 1867
1868 Dates indicate readmission to the Union
1874 Dates indicate re-establishment of conservative government

STEPHEN SWAILS:
A VOICE FOR BLACK RECONSTRUCTION

Perhaps no man more completely embodied the fears of southern whites during the Reconstruction Era than Stephen Atkins Swails. Of mixed-race heritage (with a black father and a white mother), Swails was a war hero who became one of the first African-American officers in the U.S. Army. Though derided by ex-Confederates as a so-called "carpetbagger" (a Northerner who moved to the South after the Civil War), he could not be intimidated by white threats and violence. Swails worked for the Bureau of Refugees, Freedmen and Abandoned Lands, commonly known as the "Freedman's Bureau"—an agency run under the supervision of the U.S. Army that provided education, legal aid, and other services to the former slaves to aid them in their transition from slavery to freedom. The Freedman's Bureau became a focus of hatred for bitter, unrepentant Confederates. During Reconstruction, Swails enjoyed a remarkably successful political career. Terrorist groups such as the Ku Klux Klan, horrified by the "race mixing" that the Swails family represented, arose during the period to silence the voice of politically empowered black men such as this northern transplant.

Born in 1832, Swails spent his first two years in Columbia, Pennsylvania, a town with an unusually large African-American population (about 32 percent) where black men experienced an unusual degree of prosperity in business. The size and success of the town's black community, however, sparked increasing resentment among whites. In 1834, a year that witnessed race riots erupting across the North, violence shattered the town, with a white mob destroying a lumber business owned by Stephen Smith, Columbia's most prominent African-American entrepreneur. White violence prompted a black exodus that included the Swails family, which moved to nearby Manheim. Receiving a modest education, Stephen Swails worked for a time as a waiter in Cooperstown, New York and got married. However, he felt restless, so when the Civil War started in 1861, he wanted to join the crusade to end slavery. Swails eventually signed up with the Massachusetts 54th Regiment, with all-black enlisted men led by a white abolitionist colonel, Robert Gould Shaw.

Although initially turned down for a promotion because of his black heritage, he earned the rank of First Sergeant. The 54th achieved fame for bravely spearheading an ultimately ill-fated assault on Fort Wagner near South Carolina on July 18, 1863. Due to Swails's bravery under fire and the huge losses suffered by the regiment, the unit's new commander, Colonel Edward N. Hallowell, named him acting Sergeant Major. In February 1864, Swails fought bravely at the Battle of Olustee, where he received a head wound. After the fight, Colonel Hallowell recommended to Massachusetts Governor John Andrew that Swails be promoted to Second Lieutenant. The governor approved the request, but the U.S. Army initially refused to recognize Swails's new rank because of his race. Under pressure from Andrews and Hallowell, however, the Army finally relented, making Swails one of the first black officers in United States Army history.

*After the war, Swails remained in South Carolina, serving as an agent for the Freedmen's Bureau in Charleston. Even though many former Union soldiers decided to settle in the South after the Civil War, Swails was one of the few African-American soldiers to do so. To meet congressional requirements for readmission to the Union, South Carolina held a state constitutional convention in 1868, and African Americans were allowed to participate. Williamsburg County picked Swails as its delegate. The convention gave African Americans the right to vote. The large black population in the state briefly made African Americans a powerful constituency, giving Swails a chance to lead. He had moved to Kingstree, South Carolina, in 1868 and won election as mayor, an office he held for the next eleven years. Swails also edited a newspaper, **The Williamsburg Republican**. He represented his district in the South Carolina State Senate until 1878, serving three terms as Senate Pro Tempore. Along the way, he became a delegate to the Republican National Convention three times and served as a presidential elector in the Electoral College. No black man had ever achieved such political stature in the Palmetto State.*

South Carolina, however, descended into a nightmare of violence as the curtain fell on the Reconstruction Era. White Democrats essentially staged an insurrection to end Republican rule of their state and to return African Americans to a condition of political and economic powerlessness. Hundreds of Republicans, mostly African Americans, died or were injured in an orgy of racial violence between 1876-1877. A white mob tried to murder Swails, who decided to resign from the state senate rather than leave his four children fatherless.

Through his Republican Party connections, Swails managed to secure positions with the United States Postal Service and the Treasury Department in Washington, D.C. After a lengthy absence, he returned to Kingstree where he died in 1900, as a largely forgotten man, buried in an unmarked grave in Charleston. In 2006, after research by a local history buff uncovered his remarkable career, activists erected a five-foot-high granite monument to the memory of this overlooked hero of one of the country's most troubled epochs.

wording of the law, Johnson believed the law did not apply to him in this particular case. Second, the law violated the Constitution's "separation of powers" doctrine. If the law stood, the president would not be able to fill the executive branch with individuals he trusted for advice and to implement policy. Congress would be interfering with the functioning of the Executive Branch, which was designed to be equal with the federal legislature. Johnson wanted to challenge the constitutionality of the law. He suspended Stanton from his position on August 12, 1867, while the Senate was in one of its lengthy recesses. Johnson named General Grant as Stanton's interim replacement, hoping to tap into the former Union commander's popularity.

Radical leaders believed that they held the upper hand and, when Congress reconvened, they declared Stanton's firing violated the Tenure of Office Act and voted to reapprove Stanton as Secretary of War. Grant desired the presidency in 1868, and he had no motive for helping out the politically unpopular Johnson, so he resigned as Stanton's temporary replacement. Johnson refused to give ground, firing Stanton on February 21, 1868. To prevent being physically removed, Stanton barricaded himself in his office for the next three months, only occasionally sneaking off to visit his home. The House of Representatives, out of patience with Johnson, approved eleven charges of impeachment against him, including firing Stanton, not enforcing Reconstruction laws passed by Congress, libeling members of Congress by denouncing them as traitors, and bringing into "disgrace, ridicule, hatred, contempt, and reproach the Congress of the United States." The House overwhelmingly voted for impeachment March 24, 1868, by a margin of 126-47, a coalition that included many moderates.

The president's fate now rested with the Senate, where many Senate moderates there doubted that Johnson's actions rose to the level of "high crimes and misdemeanors." Several senators believed that Johnson was on trial not because of a serious breach of law but because he disagreed with the Congress on Reconstruction. To force a president from office under such circumstances, they worried, would weaken the presidency to the point that future chief executives fearing impeachment and removal would hesitate to challenge the Congress on policy matters, even if a president viewed acts of Congress as unconstitutional. Furthermore, by the time his trial began March 4, Johnson had slightly less than a year left in his term. Some questioned the value of taking so drastic a step when the president had so little time left in office.

In addition to their concerns over what precedent the impeachment might set, moderates who did not care much for Johnson, strongly disliked his potential replacement even more. At the time of Lincoln's assassination, there was no process for replacing a vice president who rose to the White House. The country had to wait until someone was elected vice president the next election. With no vice president in place, and by a law earlier passed by the Congress, the person next in line was Senate President Pro Tempore Benjamin Wade, a Radical whose support for African American and women's rights, placed him at cross-purposes with more conservative Republicans. "There are Republican [news]papers that believe the president guilty of crime and favor impeachment, but they hate the idea of Mr. Wade becoming Acting president," a writer for the *Cincinnati Gazette* noted. The Senate reached its verdict May 16, with 35 voting for conviction and 19 for acquittal, exactly one vote short of the two-thirds majority required for Johnson's removal from office. Johnson would stay president, but his influence over events had completely evaporated. Stanton, meanwhile, resigned as Secretary of War that same month.

The Fifteenth Amendment

During congressional Reconstruction, Republicans wanted to permanently secure an African-American voting base in the South. Widespread poverty, however, would play a role in hindering black political rights. If the Fourteenth Amendment represents one of the most complicated additions to the U.S. Constitution, the **Fifteenth Amendment** proved to be one of the briefest yet most poorly worded. On the surface, the amendment seemed to guarantee African-American suffrage, but the amendment's authors unintentionally opened the door to poll taxes and literacy tests.

The Fourteenth Amendment pressured only states with large African-American populations—specifically those that had formed the former Confederacy—to adopt black suffrage. The Fifteenth Amendment eliminated this inconsistency, as it would apply equally to all the states. The brief first section declared: "The right of citizens of the United States to vote shall not be denied or abridged by the United States or by any state on account of race, color, or previous condition of servitude." The amendment passed the House and the Senate February 25-26, 1869. A handful of Radical Republicans, most notably Charles Sumner, voted against it because they believed the amendment did not go far enough to safeguard black voting rights. These concerns turned out to be prophetic. By February 3, 1870, three-fourths of the states had ratified the amendment.

Unfortunately, the amendment did not guarantee the right to vote to all U.S. men age 21 and older. It only prohibited states from barring a citizen from voting for three specific reasons, leaving the door open for states to later contrive any other reason for denying suffrage. Georgia pioneered one such method by passing the first poll tax in 1877. Poll taxes were not large by today's standards, upwards of $2 (about $38 in 2016 dollars). But they were unreachable particularly for sharecroppers who rarely received cash payments for their work. Polls taxes spread throughout the South from the late 1870s until Texas finally implemented one in 1902. By themselves, poll taxes cut black voting by half in the South. Because such laws could not directly refer to race, they applied to whites as well. White political participation in the South dropped to a third between the 1880s and the 1930s. Other states required literacy tests, designed to be difficult or impossible to pass, beginning in the 1890s. This requirement disproportionately affected African Americans, since, even more than two decades after slavery, African Americans had been denied equitable access to education and upwards of 60 percent still could not read or write.

The passage of the Fifteenth Amendment caused an unfortunate rift between movements for the African American rights and women's rights. Women such as Lucretia Mott, Elizabeth Cady Stanton, and Sojourner Truth had heroically fought against slavery for decades and saw the spirit of radical reform in Reconstruction as opening the door to women's suffrage. Mott, Stanton, and Truth fought to include women's voting rights in the Fifteenth Amendment. They could not prevail against men like Frederick Douglass and women like longtime abolitionist Lucy Stone who argued that asking to enfranchise both African Americans and women at the same time was too much and could end up politically dooming both efforts. In particular, southern white women fighting for voting rights argued that it was an injustice that they were denied the franchise while it was held, technically at least, by African-American men.

Republican State Governments

For a brief time, black voting dramatically changed southern politics. With some whites still disenfranchised because they had not met the loyalty requirements of the Fourteenth Amendment, and others boycotting elections that included black voters, Republicans took control of the governments in all the former Confederate states, ushering in (for a short while) one of the most progressive, modernizing, and democratizing periods in the region's history. African Americans flocked to the Party of Lincoln, and comprised eight of ten Republicans in the South, but the party had two other important constituencies.

Northerners who moved South at the end of the war, migrating from a region already dominated by the Republicans, carried their party loyalties with them. Southern Democrats later villainized this group, the smallest within the Republican Party, as "**carpetbaggers**." Such migrants were stereotyped as lowlife con artists who, living on the margins in their home states, stuffed their few possessions in a cheap carpetbag, and headed South, where they hoped to con their way to riches and political office. In fact, carpetbaggers were mostly teachers and missionaries associated with the Freedman's Bureau, Union veterans, and respectable businessmen who felt a humanitarian urge to teach freedmen and poor whites, to spread the Gospel, or who saw the South as a place ripe for economic development. A large number remained committed to the South and lived there past the end of Reconstruction. Even though they were the smallest Republican faction, Northerners took the initiative in forming local Republican Party organizations. Their leadership, however, soon passed to a much larger Republican Party demographic that Democrats derided as "**scalawags**."

The origins of the term "scalawag" are controversial but evidence suggests that the word came into use in the early 1800s and referred to worthless livestock. The term transformed into an insult directed at supposedly worthless people, a description southern Democrats thought applied to southern Republicans. Democrats smeared scalawags as ignorant, uneducated, and prone to crime, reflective of the party elite's disdain for the poor. While scalawags included many poor whites, non-slaveowners or owners of few slaves, who struggled to raise crops on hilly, hard-to-farm land, a large number came from the economic middle and some were elites. About 40 percent of them held public office at some level before the war. Many had been Whigs or pro-Union Democrats before the first shots were fired at Fort Sumter. They supported government investment in internal improvements such as building bridges and roads and bringing back a centralized banking system. Frequently, scalawags simply resented the power and the arrogance of the old slave owner class.

These three groups catapulted the Republicans to dominance in elections selecting delegates to the state constitutional conventions. Republicans made up 75 percent of the delegates at these conventions. Later southern-sympathizing historians like William A. Dunning, who taught at Columbia University in the late 1800s and early 1900s, promoted a racist myth still prevalent among many today that this period marked when the South temporarily came under "negro rule," the government falling under the control of corrupt and unqualified officials placed into power by ignorant, enfeebled freedmen. This interpretation not only insultingly misrepresented African Americans, it was also inaccurate in terms of numbers. Only 258 African Americans served as delegates in the southern constitutional conventions out of 1,027 overall. The so-called scalawags comprised six out of ten convention delegates. In the Reconstruction era, only two African Americans reached the United States Senate—Hiram Revels and Blanche Bruce—and only sixteen served in the U.S. House, with almost half of that number from South Carolina, a state with a large African American population. Only in South Carolina, did African Americans win a majority in a chamber of a state legislature, the state's House of Representatives. Although African Americans played a significant part in shaping subsequent reforms, this era reflected not African American but a different type of southern white rule.

Rather than ushering in an era of unprecedented waste, fraud, and abuse born of African-American immorality and incompetence, African Americans helped turn the Reconstruction Era into one of the most-forwarding looking in southern history. The constitutional conventions dropped property qualifications for voting or holding office, and shielded homes from seizure in bankruptcy proceedings. In nine former Confederate states, laws were passed that protected married women's property rights for the first time. The number of elective statewide offices expanded, changes that increased the voice of poor whites in their government. In state after state, the southern Republicans made a priority of creating the first viable, widely attended public school systems. Although segregated, these provided education for African Americans. South Carolina implemented its first-ever compulsory school attendance law.

The most important innovations involved the public schools. Southern-born whites, even in the Republican Party, would not countenance black and white children sitting together in classrooms. So except in a small district in New Orleans, these schools were racially segregated. All ten states covered in the Military Reconstruction Acts provided public schools for blacks and whites between the ages of five and twenty-one. By the 1870s, around half of children received regular education in South Carolina and Mississippi, with numbers ranging from 30 percent to 40 percent in Georgia and Alabama.

Finally, Republican state legislatures tried to modernize and stimulate the southern economy as well, subsidizing railroad construction. This move proved controversial because of the taxes required to fund the subsidies, especially when an economic depression in the 1870s left many of these railroad lines unfinished. Taxes and spending did dramatically increase when Republicans controlled the southern state governments, as they tried to address the many issues that the antebellum slave-owning planter class had ignored, such as education, public health, and developing industry and infrastructure. Reconstruction Republicans tried to accomplish all this with what was still largely a one-crop economy devastated by war, a planter class set on obstruction, and a profoundly undereducated population. It was remarkable that the Republican Reconstruction governments accomplished as much as they did with so few resources in such a short time (roughly from 1868 to 1874).

The Acquisition of Alaska

Even as it struggled to exercise its full authority over the unreconstructed states, the federal government expanded the American borders and took tentative steps towards the imperialist empire building that would commence full-throttle at the end of the nineteenth century. The purchase of Russian America, soon to be designated by Secretary of State William H. Seward as the **Alaska Territory**, provides one of President Johnson's few clearcut achievements. The company contracted to run the colony for Moscow was rapidly losing money even while the Russian government feared a military conflict with the ever-expansive British Empire. The Russians did not know if it could adequately defend their North American possession against their European rival even as they encountered resistance from indigenous people. Seward concluded a treaty with the Russian envoy on March 19, 1867, to buy Alaska, about 500,000 square acres of real estate, for $7.2 million (just over $123 million today). The president presented the agreement to the U.S. Senate for ratification the following day. One newspaper ridiculed the Alaska purchase as "Johnson's Polar Bear Garden" and for years it was famous as "Seward's Folly." Because of its vast oil and gas resources and the military value of its geographic position in the North Pacific, the purchase, then at two cents an acre, has since generally been seen as a lucky gamble.

THE PRESIDENCY OF ULYSSES S. GRANT

Grant Administration Scandals

After Lincoln's death, **Ulysses S. Grant** stood as the Union hero of the Civil War, and there was little chance he would not be elected the next president of the United States. On May 20, 1868, just four days after the Senate acquitted Johnson of impeachable offenses, the Republican National Convention opened and quickly handed Grant the party's nod. The badly divided Democrats, tarnished by the Civil War and the continued resistance to Reconstruction in the South, took twenty-one ballots to nominate a bland former New York governor, Horatio Seymour. That November, Grant won twenty-six of the thirty-four states and crushed Seymour by a 214-80 margin in the Electoral College.

Grant was well meaning but politically inexperienced and completely unqualified for the presidency, relying on men he trusted but who often took advantage of him or otherwise let him down. His presidency unfolded during a period of record fortunes made by reckless and unscrupulous men while governmental ethics were rarely policed. One irony of the corruption charges made against Reconstruction Era governments in the South is how clean most were compared to what unfolded across the North and the West at the same time. Grant's administration reflected the period's relaxed ethics. Though never directly blamed for the numerous scandals that unfolded during his eight years in the White House, the former military commander made astonishingly bad choices for his cabinet and Grant suffered from guilt by association. At the Treasury Department, officials accepted bribes from distillers to falsify records on how much liquor they manufactured and distributed, in order to avoid paying federal taxes. One 1874 estimate placed the federal revenues lost to the so-called "Whiskey Ring" at $15 million in taxes (about $318 million today.) As negative as the reactions were to these incidents, the **Crédit Mobilier Scandal** of 1872 stands as the biggest and most complicated scandal to rock the Grant White House. The Lincoln Administration in 1864 had chartered the Union Pacific Railroad to build a transcontinental line, providing $100 million for the project and $60 million in low-interest loans (an astronomical $3 billion today when accounting for inflation.) Much of this money was not spent on

railroad building. The Union Pacific Company Directors set up a shell company they called Crédit Mobilier, supposedly the subcontractor that would actually build the railroad. Receiving payments from Union Pacific, Crédit Mobilier used the cash to buy stock in Union Pacific at below-market value and then sold the shares publicly at greatly inflated values. The Union Pacific directors split the proceeds among themselves. This financial shell game may have eventually generated more than $877 million at 2016 values. Beginning in 1867, before Grant became a candidate for president, the railroad company sought to prevent this theft from becoming public and to sway Congress to pass more legislation favorable to Union Pacific. They sold shares of Crédit Mobilier stock to House and Senate members at discount rates. An 1872 report made these bribes public, prompting a Congressional investigation of 13 of its members for involvement in the scandal. Grant had no personal involvement, and since both parties were implicated, he did not have any baggage from this particular scandal to carry when he ran for another term in 1872. These tawdry affairs eroded Grant's influence within his own party.

The Ku Klux Klan

Even with the swirl of controversy over scandals and foreign affairs, Grant could never direct his attention far away from the South. There, an organization soon channeled unfocused white cruelty and rage at freedmen into a more precisely defined political and economic agenda aimed at crushing the Republican Party in the South,

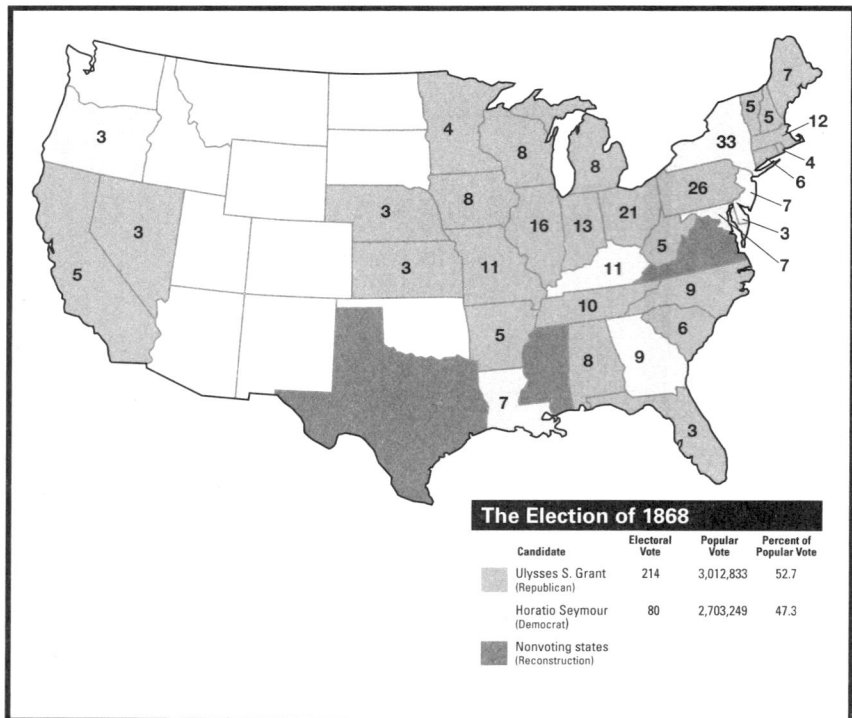

Map 16.2 The Election of 1868

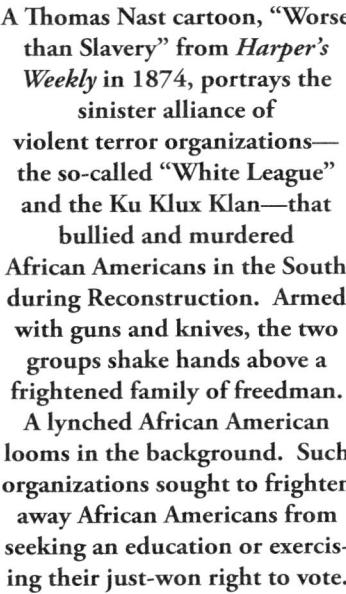

A Thomas Nast cartoon, "Worse than Slavery" from *Harper's Weekly* in 1874, portrays the sinister alliance of violent terror organizations— the so-called "White League" and the Ku Klux Klan—that bullied and murdered African Americans in the South during Reconstruction. Armed with guns and knives, the two groups shake hands above a frightened family of freedman. A lynched African American looms in the background. Such organizations sought to frighten away African Americans from seeking an education or exercising their just-won right to vote.

ending all northern occupation of the region and putting black people "back in their place" as tightly controlled and powerless farm and manual labor.

In December 1865, six bored young men, mostly college educated and former Confederate officers, gathered in Pulaski, Tennessee, a place filled with old slave plantations on the state's mid-southern border. They decided to kill time by forming a fraternity devoted for a brief time to pulling pranks and drinking. The group soon dubbed itself the **Ku Klux Klan**, derived from the Greek word *kuklos* (meaning circle) and "clan" (spelled with a "k" for alliterative effect). As the Klan expanded beyond its original membership, it developed secret rituals, initiation rites, and code words to be used in greetings. Some started wearing sheets or similarly ghostly outfits because Klansmen thought this clothing would frighten allegedly superstitious freedmen. As they turned political, seeking to roll back black freedoms, the Klan grew the largest in counties without large African-American populations, and before long the "Invisible Empire" penetrated almost every southern state. Former Confederate General Nathan Bedford Forrest of Tennessee emerged as the Klan's original Grand Wizard.

The Klan, the Knights of the White Camellia, and similar groups served as goons for big planters to enforce sharecropping contracts. They beat and whipped African Americans who dared speak up to white growers. The

Klan sought to suppress any incipient black revolt by assaulting and even murdering "uppity" freedmen who expressed pride and independence. The Klan waged war on all three major factions of the southern Republican Party, not just freedmen but also carpetbaggers and scalawags. Among so-called carpetbaggers, black and white teachers, seen as dangerous outside agitators, drew the most intense Klan fury. Even if instructors stuck to the ABCs in the classroom, teaching black children in the 1860s and 1870s was an act of political dissent. The planter class whites and their Klan enforcers knew teachers reinforced the black demand for economic justice. They responded by disrupting classes and intimidating students, torching schoolhouses, threatening teachers that they would be burned alive if they did not leave town immediately, and by raping and hanging teachers who stayed.

Republican politicians and activists (including Freedman's Bureau agents) who registered African Americans to vote became the most numerous Klan victims. The list of Republican public officials assassinated by the Klan included state representative Richard Burke of Alabama, Republican state judge George Ashburn of Georgia, and state representative James Martin and state Senator B.F. Randolph of South Carolina. A political dispute instigated a Klan massacre of Republicans in Colfax, Louisiana, April 13, 1873. The killings took place after a racially charged gubernatorial race the previous year. Democrats in Colfax Parish formed a militia to do battle with the mostly African-American state militia and overthrow the local government. On Easter Sunday, the white militia, the Klan, and members of the Knights of the White Camellia amassed in a 300-man force and attacked the courthouse. After gaining control of the building, whites hunted black members of the state militia and African-American residents. Eventually, 150 African Americans and three whites died in the battle. The Klan literally got away with murder because the general white community protected them, or feared them too much to speak out.

The level of violence forced the Grant Administration to act. In 1870-1871, at Grant's behest, Congress passed a series of three laws known as the "Ku Klux Klan" or "Enforcement" Acts. The laws enforced the Fourteenth and the Fifteenth Amendments by making, for the first time in the republic's history, interfering with voting a federal crime and gave the federal government the power to prosecute such violations. Under the law, the president could declare a county to be in a state of insurrection, impose martial law, and suspend the writ of *habeas corpus* in those places. (Under *habeas corpus*, authorities cannot detain suspects indefinitely without presenting legal justifications in court.) The three laws went into full effect in nine upcountry South Carolina counties, prompting 800 Klan members to flee the state. Under these statutes, the U.S. Army arrested thousands of Klansmen. Courts convicted hundreds and sent sixty-five Klansmen to prison. Klan membership dwindled.

By the mid-1870s, the Klan's usefulness had passed because they had largely achieved their goals. Federal troops began to withdraw from the South, removing the force protecting African-American civil rights. The Democratic Party began taking control of the former Confederate states. Most freedmen had been reduced to sharecropping. The Klan itself disappeared by the end of Reconstruction in 1877, to be replaced by smaller, local terrorist cells that operated under names like the White League or designated themselves as "rifle clubs." The Klan would return in much bigger form as not just an anti-black group, but also an anti-immigrant, anti-Catholic, anti-Jewish, anti-alcohol, and anti-women's rights organization in 1915.

The Santo Domingo Affair

The acquisition of Alaska during Andrew Johnson's presidency also provided a jumping-off point for further American imperialist adventures. European empires began to see China and the rest of the Pacific Rim as a treasure trove of easily exploited labor and natural resources. As early as 1861, thirty-seven years before the Spanish-American War, William Seward advocated starting a war with Spain to gain control of Cuba as a way to heal North-South conflict with the tonic of shared militarism. Seward also spoke of buying Hawaii, Samoa, or the Fiji Islands. **Santo Domingo**, now known as the Dominican Republic, also sat high on Seward's expansionist wish list, and he lobbied for its annexation. He encountered strong resistance, however, from whites who might have loved to seize foreign lands and their riches but, echoing anxieties in the 1830s and 1840s about conquering Mexican territories, many politicians and opinion makers did not want to add the dark-skinned, non-English-speaking in Cuba and the other lands to the American population. *Harper's Weekly* insisted that it would be impossible to make citizens of "a people wholly alien from us in principles, language, and traditions, a third of whom are barbarously ignorant."

Administrations changed but ambitions to take over Santo Domingo did not. That nation's president, Buenaventura Báez, had hoped to personally profit from selling his nation to the highest bidder, regardless of the consequences to his people. Santo Domingo already produced much of the coffee and sugar Americans consumed and, if the nation were conquered by one means or another, the cost for those products would drop for American consumers. Santo Domingo annexation would provide the United States a plantation for tobacco, chocolate, and tropical fruits, all grown by pitifully low-wage labor. Again, racism trumped greed as opponents of a Santo Domingo expansion warned about the dangers posed by its largely African-descended and Catholic natives.

Grant was undeterred and dispatched his secretary Orville Babcock and General Rufus Ingalls to negotiate an annexation agreement with President Báez. A proposed annexation treaty offered $2 million (about $38 million today) for Samaná Bay (also on the island of Hispaniola). In an unwise move politically, the agreement also included a provision that would allow Santo Domingo to apply for U.S. statehood. Grant sent the treaty to the Senate on January 10, 1870. When Babcock spoke on behalf of the treaty to the Senate in March 1870, it provoked fury. The Senate had not been consulted about the negotiations in advance. Babcock treated the Senate with arrogance and, when some objected to the treaty, became threatening. Treaties must receive a two-thirds majority from the Senate to be approved, and the Santo Domingo pact failed in a 28-28 tie on June 30.

The 1872 Presidential Election

Grant's actions in the Santo Domingo Affair opened a rift within the Republican Party by the end of his first term. Carl Schurz, a Senator from Missouri, led a revolt against Grant in 1870. By the time of the 1872 election,

Charles Sumner of Massachusetts, who had opposed Grant on Santo Domingo annexation, joined him. Aware they could not block Grant from winning re-nomination at the Republican Party Convention, they formed the Liberal Republican Party, which held a convention in Cincinnati, Ohio in May 1872. Prominent Republican newspaper editors like Horace White of the *Chicago Tribune* and Horace Greeley of *The New York Tribune* joined the splinter group. The **Liberal Republicans** professed disgust at the myriad Grant administration scandals. They also deemed many of the Reconstruction policies pursued since Lincoln as failures. Liberal Republicans were unimpressed with the results of black voting in the South, which they believed had placed unqualified men in office and had worsened racial tensions. The splinter party nominated Greeley for president.

Democrats, still crippled by their association with the southern rebellion, decided to merge with the Liberal Republicans and nominate Greeley and his running mate, Governor Benjamin Brown of Missouri, for president and vice president as well. The effort was doomed to fail, with Grant winning by a landslide. He carried the popular vote by a nearly 56 percent to 44 percent margin. The Electoral College gap was wider, 286-66, though Greeley died only 24 days after the election and his freed electors were scattered among various third party candidates.

Strangeness aside, this election marked an intensification of the women's suffrage movement as Victoria Woodhull and her allies formed the Equal Rights Party, which nominated the feminist Woodhull for president as a protest against female disenfranchisement. The Equal Rights Party nominated Frederick Douglass, a strong backer of women's suffrage, for vice president. Douglass ignored the symbolic gesture because of his urgent hope that Grant would earn another presidential term. The party advocated the right of women to file for divorce. Woodhull campaigned although she was barred from serving as president because of her gender and because she had not yet reached the constitutionally mandated age of 35. Her campaign consisted of a series of protests aimed at heightening consciousness about the women's suffrage cause, which would not reach fruition until 1920.

The Panic of 1873

Jeopardizing both Republican dominance of the political landscape and the continuation of Reconstruction in the South, a sharp economic downtown in 1873 enveloped the United States and soon the world. This depression, which lasted five years, had multiple causes. What became known as "**The Panic of 1873**" began on September 18, 1873, when Jay Cooke & Company announced it could not pay off railroad bonds after its Northern Pacific Railroad project fell apart. Investors began to dump railroad portfolios. In days, 5,000 investment firms went bankrupt and stock prices plummeted. On September 20, the New York Stock exchange suspended trade for the first time ever as top stocks tumbled. The Grant administration tried to calm nerves by buying $13 million in railroad bonds to revive confidence in what seemed like a collapsing industry, but the move failed. The post-Civil War economy seemed to be unraveling.

Reckless real estate speculation resulting in artificially inflated land prices triggered a collapse of property values. When land speculators could not pay loans, banks failed, leading panicked Wall Street investors to dump stock. Across the country, retail stores, laundries, and restaurants closed. Manufacturing output markedly declined. Flour, cotton, and iron mills shut their doors. The unemployment rate hit 25 percent in New York City. Civil War veterans and others formed armies of the unemployed who tramped across the country in desperate search of work.

Strikes broke out across the country. Rejecting charity as an undesired alternative, workers and the unemployed formed the Committee for Safety in New York City in December 1873, demanding that the city create public jobs to provide relief. They planned a massive rally drawing thousands in Tompkins Square Park leading to a march on city hall where they would present demands and called for the city to spend $100,000 on a Labor Relief Bureau to offer public works jobs. Conservative newspapers spread the rumor that jewel-stealing radicals in Paris bent on destroying capitalism had funded the committee. The committee decided to not march on city hall but simply stage a January 13, 1874, demonstration at the park. The city revoked a permit for the rally, but 7,000 showed up anyway. Armed with clubs, police charged into the peaceful crowd, beating demonstrators and even patrolling nearby streets on horseback where they assaulted pedestrians unlucky enough to be nearby.

In 1874, Congress finally responded with a bill to increase the money supply as a means of stimulating the economy, but Grant vetoed it. Congress tried a much more conservative approach in early 1875 with passage of the Specie Resumption Act, under which the government bought back currency with gold, further tightening the money supply, but boosting its value. The move benefitted the wealthy and stabilized the investment climate but still left millions unemployed or struggling.

Retreat from Reconstruction

The economic spiral had immediate political consequences. The Republicans held the White House, the Congress, and most of the nation's statehouses. The public blamed them for the depression. In 1874, for the first time since before the Civil War, Democrats won a majority in the House of Representatives. Republicans held onto the Senate, but a conservative Democratic majority in the lower chamber spelled doom for any more dramatic efforts to reconstruct the South.

Reconstruction by this time had languished. Due to recent appointments, the Supreme Court by 1873 had shifted in a conservative direction. The justices strictly narrowed the application of the Fourteenth Amendment in a set of 1873 decisions called the Slaughterhouse Cases. The Court ruled that Fourteenth Amendment only barred states from denying the equal protection of the law to all citizens but did not pertain to individual acts of discrimination. In a subsequent case, *Minor v. Happersett* (1875), Virginia Minor sued after she was denied voter registration in Missouri because of a state law that limited the franchise to men. The Court ruled that voting rights were not one of the privileges of citizenship protected by the Fourteenth Amendment and that states could regulate who qualified to vote, a decision reinforced by the 1876 *United States vs. Reese* decision, which held that the Fifteenth Amendment did not guarantee an absolute right to vote, but only set limits on the grounds on which the states could limit suffrage.

Meanwhile, Grant began to privately say that the Fifteenth Amendment had been a mistake. "It had done the Negro no good, and has been a hindrance to the South, and by no means a political advantage to the North," he told his cabinet. In this atmosphere of retreat, it was not surprising that the Republican control of southern states slipped. In the old Confederacy, so-called "**Redeemer**" Democrats accused Republicans of spending too much, raising taxes too high, and of having handed the region over to corrupt and incompetent "negro rule." By 1870, all eleven former Confederate states had reentered the Union, and the Redeemers had gained control of the state governments in Tennessee, Virginia, North Carolina, and Georgia. The Redeemer rollback of reform picked up pace after the 1873-1878 depression started, as Republican control ended in Texas, Alabama, and Arkansas between 1873-1874.

Democrats gained control of the Texas legislature in 1873 and stripped Republican Governor Edmund J. Davis of many of his powers. Beginning in 1875, "the Mississippi Plan"—the label given to describe the use of armed gangs, strategic murders, threats, and bribes to prevent African Americans from voting, brought Redeemers to power in that state. In an 1875 election in one black majority county there, not a single African American voted. A massacre of blacks in Vicksburg may have claimed as many as 80 lives. Whites followed similar tactics in South Carolina, where as many as 150 African-American politicians and voters fell to white assassins. The Grant administration lost the will to intervene on behalf of its southern black constituents. Mississippi fell completely in the hands of the Redeemers by the fall of 1876. Going into November of that year, Republicans only held the governorships in Florida, Louisiana, and South Carolina.

The 1876 Presidential Election

It is perhaps fitting that so violent and scandal-ridden an era as Reconstruction should end in one of the most corrupt and controversial presidential elections in United States history. The ballots closed on November 7, 1876, but the disputed final results were not determined until March 2 of the following year, the announcement coming only two days before the new president was to be sworn in. During the five-month interim, the two major parties accused each other of attempting to steal the election. Some Southerners threatened another civil war if the Democratic candidate was not declared the winner, and terror gripped African Americans that they would be re-enslaved if Republicans lost.

Grant's influence within his party had waned and, even though he likely could have secured a third nomination, Grant's association with scandals and the ongoing economic depression worried Republicans that he would lose to the Democrats in the fall. Instead, Republicans settled on a compromise candidate, Ohio Governor Rutherford B. Hayes, an ally with the 1872 Liberal Republican faction whose nomination seemed a rebuke to the corruption of the sitting administration. Hayes told southern friends that he was skeptical of the president's Reconstruction policies. The Democrats also nominated a reform-minded governor, Samuel J. Tilden of New York, who also was a critic of Grant's actions in the South.

Operatives from both parties stuffed ballot boxes, and, in the South, Democrats sometimes placed armed gangs near courthouses to keep Republicans from voting. Tilden clearly won the popular vote, 4,288,546 to 4,034,311, but both parties claimed that they had won the electoral votes in four states: in Oregon where one elector had been replaced when his credentials were challenged, and the three southern states that still had Republican governors and where Union troops still protected black voters. Minus the tally from those states, Tilden had won 184 Electoral College votes, one short of victory. Hayes would have to win all 20 unresolved votes to win the White House. The Constitution states that Congress receives and tallies Electoral College votes before it certifies the results, but it had recently adopted rules that granted

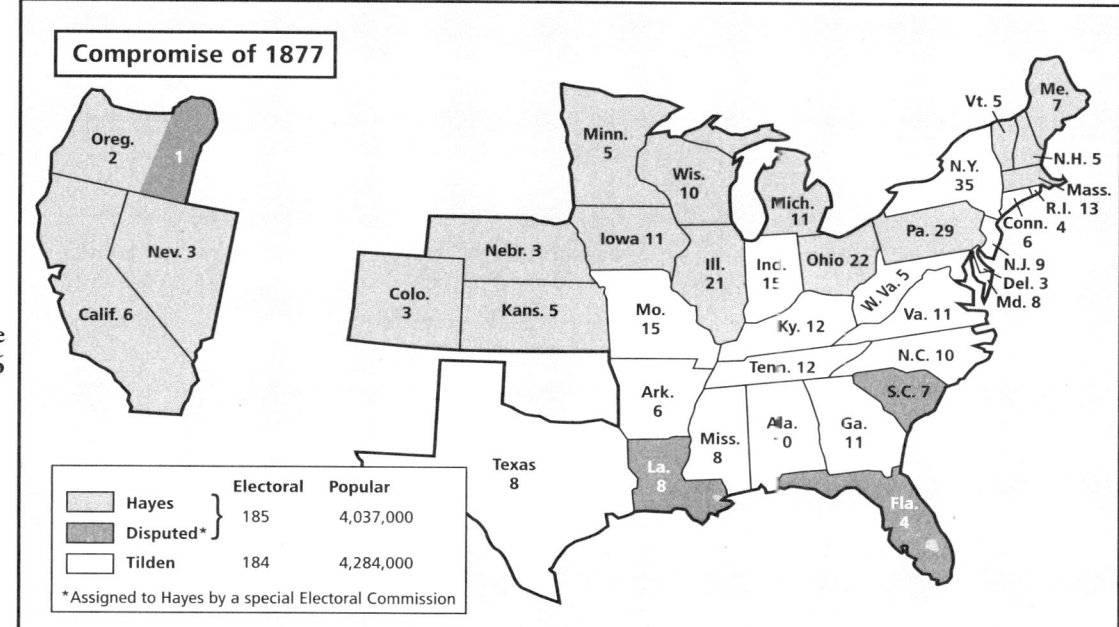

Map 16.3 The Election of 1876

	Electoral	Popular
Hayes }	185	4,037,000
Disputed* }		
Tilden	184	4,284,000

*Assigned to Hayes by a special Electoral Commission

members of the House or Senate the power to challenge any Electoral College votes. The House, controlled by Democrats, could block Hayes from winning, and the Senate, controlled by Republicans, could deny Tilden the one remaining vote he needed for victory.

To resolve this logjam, the Congress voted to create a special Electoral Commission, designed to be as balanced as possible in such a hyper-partisan environment. The commission featured five Republicans and five Democrats from the Congress and five justices from the Supreme Court. Congress picked four justices, two Democratic and two Republican appointees and left it to the Court to pick a fifth member to round out the 15-member commission. Both parties expected Justice David Davis of Illinois, a genuine independent, to become the last member of the commission, but the night before the Congress approved the commission's creation, the Illinois Legislature named Davis to the United States Senate. (Voters did not directly elect senators until the Seventeenth Amendment, ratified in 1913). Congress established the commission anyway. Instead of Davis, a Republican, Joseph Bradley, filled the last seat, leaving the commission with eight Republicans and seven Democrats. Predictably, the commission voted 8-7 along strictly party lines to award all twenty disputed electoral votes to Hayes, and thus Hayes edged Tilden by a 185-184 count in the Electoral College.

Throughout this crisis, southern newspapers ran headlines like "Tilden or War!" Yet, the reaction to the commission's decision turned out to be mild. Some historians believe that the waters had been calmed behind the scenes through the so-called "**Compromise of 1877**" in which, in return for Democrats agreeing to accept Hayes

as president, Hayes would withdraw troops protecting the Republican state governments in Louisiana, South Carolina, and Florida. After the election, the Union troops were withdrawn, bringing a final, fitful end to Reconstruction. As one Louisiana freedman put it, "The whole South—every state in the South—has got into the hands of the very men that held us as slaves."

RECONSTRUCTION: THE TURNING POINT THAT NEVER TURNED

The Compromise of 1877 brought black dreams in the South to a crashing halt. After Reconstruction, sharecropping, which left black farmers in an endless cycle of debt and poverty, became their typical destiny. As Redeemers assumed control of southern states, they rolled back state spending and many reforms Republicans had enacted. Black schools vanished in many places, and the remaining schools struggled with meager funds. Meanwhile, segregation in the following years would become a new means of enforcing white supremacy. What came to be known as "Jim Crow" aimed at preventing poor blacks and whites from making common political cause.

When Union troops withdrew, enforcement of the Fourteenth and Fifteenth Amendments vanished, making citizenship for African Americans largely symbolic and voting rights almost entirely fictitious. Northern whites disillusioned about progress in the South looked the other way. The states north of the Mason-Dixon line and on the West Coast would, from the 1880s until World War I, experience an unprecedented wave of immigration primarily from Northern and Southern Europe, and from China and Japan. Americans of Northern and Western European descent in the North and West saw these newcomers as racial aliens, as inferiors. Anti-black racism had never disappeared in the North. Now it spiked again along with anti-immigrant prejudice, and northern whites empathized to a greater degree with the bigotry of their southern neighbors. Northern whites largely responded with apathy as southern lynchings of mostly black men, women, and even children became a weekly spectacle of violence that sometimes drew an audience of thousands.

The South, meanwhile, became a nation within a nation. It remained deeply rural as the North became more industrial. Its society was defined by the divide between black and white, while the North and the West became ever more diverse. The South remained poorly educated as public schools advanced on the other side of the Mason-Dixon line. As voting rights and democratic participation expanded in the North and West, the South increasingly blocked voting and the Democrats suffocated dissent in the South until one-party rule began to collapse in the 1960s. Technically, the United States became a single nation again between 1863-1877. In reality, the South in many ways increasingly became a land unto itself, cut off from the dramatic changes enveloping the other states in the emerging industrial age.

Table 16.1

Important African American Officeholders During Reconstruction

Officeholder	Offices Held and Term	Significance
Blanche Bruce (1841-1898)	U.S. Senator from Mississippi, 1875-1881	First African American Senator to serve a full term. Supported railroad construction and advocated civil rights for African Americans, Native Americans, and Chinese immigrants.
Richard Cain (1825-1887)	U.S. House Representative from South Carolina, 1873-1879	Advocate of the Civil Rights Act of 1875 and of integrated public schools
Robert Brown Elliott (1842-1884)	U.S. House Representative from South Carolina, 1871-1875	Strong supporter of the third "Ku Klux Klan Bill," which authorized the president to intervene, to the point of using military force, in any state where the 14th Amendment rights of citizens were being violated.
Joseph Rainey (1832-1887)	U.S. House Representative from South Carolina, 1869-1879	The first African American to serve in the U.S. House, and for the longest tenure, he supported the three anti-KKK bills and the 1875 civil rights law, and denounced rampant racial terrorism in his home state.
Hiram Revels (1827-1901)	U.S. Senator from Mississippi, 1869-1871	Led resistance to attempt by Georgia state legislature to unseat African American legislators and fought attempt to segregate Washington, D.C. schools.
Robert Smalls (1839-1915)	U.S. Representative from South Carolina, 1875-1887	A Civil War hero who seized control of the Confederate ammunitions transport vessel and delivered it to the Union Navy, Smalls increased appropriations for Port Royal Harbor and fought to integrate the U.S. military.
Josiah Walls (1842-1905)	U.S. Representative from Florida, 1871-1877	The only African American to hold a seat in the United States House representing Florida until the 1990s, Walls fought for national funding for public schools.

Revisionist History:
Creating the "Lost Cause" Mythology

Before President Rutherford B. Hayes withdrew the last of the Union troops from the South in 1877, white Southerners who had supported the Confederacy during the war began concocting legends about the Civil War and Reconstruction that came to be known as the "Myth of the Lost Cause." The Lost Cause mythology portrayed the leaders and soldiers of the Confederacy as virtuous people in a sinful world and closer to God than their materialistic "Yankee" combatants.

After the Civil War, Lost Cause mythologists insisted that southern slaves had been treated lovingly like family members by their masters. Confederate defeat, the mythology insisted, emanated from the wiles of Satan or was God's test of faith, similar to the travails endured by the Hebrews during their forty years in the desert after leaving Egypt. Pastors like Episcopalian cleric Randolph McKim compared the suffering of Confederate leaders like General Robert E. Lee to that of Jesus on the cross. In any case, the legends insisted, the Confederate soldiers had been braver and smarter and had lost only because the northern states were richer, more populous, better-armed, and more ruthless. Promoters of the Lost Cause portrayed men who waged war on their country not as traitors but as patriots and heroes.

By the end of Reconstruction, white Southerners observed annual memorial days for fallen Confederates. Meanwhile, groups such as the Sons of Confederate Veterans, established in 1889, and the United Daughters of the Confederacy (UDC), organized in 1894, dedicated themselves to spreading the Lost Cause Gospel nationwide.

The UDC raised money to build and maintain at least 700 Confederate monuments honoring the Lost Cause across the United States. Most rose on the national landscape during the peak of segregation, voting restriction laws like the poll tax, and lynching between the 1890s and the 1930s, and during the struggles over desegregation in the 1950s and the 1960s.

Mildred Lewis Rutherford, the historian general of the UDC from 1911-1916, declared in one speech "The Negroes under the institution of slavery were well-fed, well-clothed, and well-housed. How hard it was for us to make the North understand this!" In another speech, she asked whether African Americans had benefitted from freedom since the war. "As a race," she said, "unhesitatingly no!"

The UDC also tried to erase the memory of the many white Southerners who, along with slaves, resisted the Confederate government. In 1911, a monument went up at the Cooke County Courthouse in Gainesville, Texas, the scene of a mass hanging of 42 suspected Union supporters by backers of the Confederacy in 1862. The inscription at the bottom of the Gainesville monument reads, "No nation rose so white and fair/None fell so free of crime." Monuments also went up in southern states that stayed in the Union, such as Kentucky, Missouri, and West Virginia, the latter of which broke off from Virginia to stay in the Union.

Even historians like William Dunning at Columbia University in New York took up the Lost Cause. Many of Dunning's graduate students wrote public school textbooks that were used across the United States. These books portrayed pre-Civil War abolitionists as deranged fanatics unconcerned about tearing the country apart. These historians described freemen as ignorant, unintelligent, and childlike, and completely unprepared to become citizens. The "Dunning School" also falsely claimed that terrorist groups like the Klan had saved the South from "Negro rule," an era of supposed black domination marked by political corruption and incompetence.

These scholars gave credibility to the UDC, which held annual history essay contests. A Seattle student won a UDC "loving cup" for her pro-KKK essay. The scholars also influenced American popular culture and inspired the hit 1915 silent film **The Birth of a Nation***, which depicted black Union soldiers as rapists and the Klan as southern saviors; and the novel* **Gone with the Wind***. In Margaret Mitchell's novel, she describes the freedmen as "creatures of small intelligence" who handled their right to vote "like monkeys or small children . . . they ran wild." As the historians Warren Beck and Myles Clowers noted, "More Americans have learned the story of the South during the Civil War and Reconstruction from Margaret Mitchell's* **Gone with the Wind** *than from all of the learned volumes on this period."*

Gone with the Wind *was adapted into a highly popular movie in 1939. Confederate monuments became a political controversy in recent years. Neo-Nazis rallied in Charlottesville, Va., on August 11-12, 2017, to protest the proposed removal of a Robert E. Lee statue. An anti-monument protestor, Heather Heyer, was murdered by one of the white nationalists. In the last two years, statutes of Lee and other Confederate heroes have come down in Austin, Baltimore, Dallas, New Orleans, and other cities.*

Chronology

1863 The Emancipation Proclamation goes into effect and Lincoln issues his Proclamation of Amnesty and Reconstruction.

1864 Lincoln pocket vetoes Wade-Davis Bill.

1865 The Freedmen's Bureau is established.
The Civil War ends.
Lincoln is assassinated.
General Sherman issues Special Order No. 15.
Black Codes enacted by southern legislatures.
Thirteenth Amendment is ratified.

1866 Congress passes Civil Rights Act and extends the life of the Freedmen's Bureau.
The Ku Klux Klan founded.

1867 Congressional Reconstruction Act.
U. S. purchases Alaska from Russia.
Congress passes Military Reconstruction Acts, Tenure of Office Act.

1868 President Johnson is impeached but acquitted.
Fourteenth Amendment ratified.
Ulysses S. Grant elected president.

1870 Ratification of the Fifteenth Amendment.
Last four southern states admitted to the Union.
Enforcement Act.

1871 Ku Klux Klan Act.

1872 Grant re-elected president.

1873 Financial panic leads to five-year depression.

1875 Whiskey Ring scandal further discredits Grant administration.
Civil Rights Act.

1876 Disputed presidential election of Hayes vs. Tilden.

1877 Electoral commission awards presidency to Rutherford B. Hayes.

SUGGESTED READINGS

Paul H. Bergeron, *Andrew Johnson's Civil War and Reconstruction* (2011).

Josiah Bunting, *Ulysses S. Grant* (2004)

Richard Carwardine, *Lincoln: A Life of Purpose and Power* (2006).

David M. Chalmers, *Hooded Americanism: The History of the Ku Klux Klan* (1987)

Richard Nelson Current, *Those Terrible Carpetbaggers: A Reinterpretation* (1988)

David Herbert Donald, *Lincoln* (1995).

W.E.B. Du Bois, *Black Reconstruction in America, 1860-1880* (1935).

Laura F. Edwards, *A Legal History of the Civil War and Reconstruction: A Nation of Rights* (2015).

Douglass R. Eggerton, *The Wars of Reconstruction: The Brief, Violent History of America's Most Progressive Era* (2014).

Eric Foner, *Reconstruction: America's Unfinished Revolution, 1863-1877* (1988).

___, *The Second Founding: How the Civil War and Reconstruction Remade the Constitution.* (2019).

James K. Hogue, *Uncivil War: Five New Orleans Street Battles, and the Rise and Fall of Radical Reconstruction* (2006).

Richard L. Hume and Jerry B. Gough, *Blacks, Carpetbagger, and Scalawags: The Constitutional Conventions of Radical Reconstruction* (2008).

Jacqueline Jones, *Labor of Love, Labor of Sorrow: Black Women, Work, and the Family, from Slavery to the Present (2010).*

Stephen Kantrowitz, *More Than Freedom: Fighting for Black Citizenship in a White Republic, 1829–1889 (2012).*

Leon F. Litwack, *Been in the Storm So Long: The Aftermath of Slavery* (1980).

Louis P. Masur, *Lincoln's Hundred Days: The Emancipation Proclamation and the War for the Union* (2012).

Eric L. McKitrick, *Andrew Johnson and Reconstruction* (1960).

Elaine Frantz Parsons. *Ku-Klux: The Birth of the Klan During Reconstruction* (2015).

Hannah Rosen, *Terror in the Heart of Freedom: Citizenship, Sexual Violence, and the Meaning of Race in the Postemancipation South* (2009).

Jean Edward Smith, *Grant* (2001).

Mark Wahlgren Sumners, *A Dangerous Stir: Fear, Paranoia, and the Making of Reconstruction* (2009).

___.*The Ordeal of the Reunion: A New History of Reconstruction* (2014).

Review Questions

1. What was the Emancipation Proclamation and why did Lincoln word the document the way he did?

2. How did freedmen respond to news of their emancipation?

3. Describe the three major phases of Reconstruction—Wartime (under Lincoln), Presidential (under Johnson), and Congressional. What were the goals for each phase? How successful were they? How and why did each phase end?

4. Explain how sharecropping worked. How was it that sharecroppers were never able to escape debt?

5. Describe the Southern backlash to black political gains, including the rise of the Ku Klux Klan.

Glossary of Important People and Concepts

Alaska purchase
Black Codes
"Carpetbaggers"
Compromise of 1877
Crédit Mobilier Affair
Fifteenth Amendment
Fourteenth Amendment
Freedmen's Bureau
Ulysses S. Grant
Impeachment
Andrew Johnson
Ku Klux Klan
Liberal Republicans
Abraham Lincoln
Panic of 1873
Radical Republicans
Reconstruction Acts of 1867
Redeemers
Santo Domingo Affair
"Scalawags"
Thaddeus Stevens
Ten Percent Plan
Tenure of Office Act of 1867
Thirteenth Amendment
Wade-Davis Bill

Joseph, Chief of Nez Percé

Chapter Seventeen

INDIAN EXPULSION AND WHITE SETTLEMENT IN THE TRANS-MISSOURI WEST

By the 1880s, starvation, disease, warfare with the United States Army, and the mass slaughter of buffalo and other big game had devastated the Native American population. Less than 300,000 Indians remained in North America, compared tao a Native population of approximately eight million at the time of Christopher Columbus. Many Plains Indians sought relief from suffering and fear through religion. In 1870, Tavibo, a Paiute shaman in Western Nevada, proclaimed that while meditating he received a vision from "The Great Holy Force Above" that promised Native Americans salvation from hunger, want, and the persecution of whites. A worldwide earthquake would soon swallow American soldiers, missionaries, railroad builders, ranchers, and unbelieving Indians, Tavibo prophesized, the whites enduring eternal punishment in the afterlife. Native Americans alone would survive, and their old way of life would return.

Initially met with scorn from other Native Americans, Tavibo began to preach that the Great Holy Force Above allowed Native Americans to suffer and die because they had abandoned their religious traditions, lost virtue, and imitated the ways of the white man. He gained followers among not just the Paiutes but also the Shoshone, Ute, and Bannock peoples. When Tavibo suddenly died, the prophetic mantle fell upon his son Wovoka, who received his own revelations beginning in 1889. Wovoka, called "Jack Wilson" by whites, told his audience that he had suffered a fever as a solar eclipse unfolded in the heavens. Spirits revealed to him a coming paradise in which Indian warriors slain in battle and their women would return to life, grass would spring abundantly from the plains, and buffalo would once again roam the land unimpeded.

Wovoka said that God had turned against white men because they had killed Him when He came to Earth as Jesus Christ. Wovoka told his audiences that he was the Second Coming of Jesus and that he would lead the Native people to salvation. Wovoka's followers began meditating, praying, chanting, and performing "Ghost Dances" in rituals lasting five consecutive days. Dances varied by tribe and by location, but all involved moved in a circle, often falling into a hypnotic trance. Some dropped from sheer exhaustion.

The Ghost Dance religion, with its promise of future redemption, lifted Indians out of despair. Nations as diverse as the Arapaho, Cheyenne, and Pawnee danced in Idaho, Montana, Utah, Wyoming, Colorado, Nebraska, Kansas, the Dakotas and the Oklahoma Territory. It represented a non-violent movement, with the faithful waiting for the intervention of the Great Spirit to end white oppression. Among the Sioux, however, especially the Oglala, Blackfeet, and Hunkpapa, the dances had a more militant tone. Sioux Ghost Dance leaders taught adherents that wearing white ghost shirts would make Indians immune to the bullets of white soldiers.

One Sioux, Tatanka Yotanka (called "Sitting Bull" by whites), emerged as a political leader among the Plains Indians as the Ghost Dance swept the Plains. Nearing his sixties, the charismatic Sitting Bull helped destroy General George Custer's forces at the famous Battle of the Little Bighorn in 1876. Held prisoner by the United States Army for two years, he was a featured attraction for a brief time in

Sioux performing the Ghost Dance, 1891.

Buffalo Bill Cody's circus-like "Wild West" show as it toured the eastern United States. Cody dressed his Native American performers in brightly colored war bonnets and face paint, with men like Sitting Bull mounted on horses and acting out frontier battles. Feeling humiliated by the experience, Sitting Bull became a bitter critic of white society. "The love of possessions is a disease with them," he bitterly observed. "They take tithes from the poor and weak to support the rich who rule. They claim this mother of ours, the earth, for their own and fence their neighbors away."

As the Ghost Dances spread, terror gripped whites living in the Plains. James McLaughlin, an Indian agent, refused to acknowledge how much the new Native faith derived from Christianity. "A more pernicious system of religion could not have been offered to a people who stood on the threshold of civilization," McLaughlin fearfully said. "Our religion seems foolish to you, but so does yours to me," Sitting Bull retorted.

Army personnel became alarmed that the movement might lead to an uprising and that the Ghost Dance rituals whipped the Indians into a bloodthirsty frenzy. "Indians are dancing in the snow and are wild and crazy," a Bureau of Indian Affairs agent at the Pine Ridge Reservation in South Dakota wrote frantically to President Benjamin Harrison in 1889. Several thousand federal troops were dispatched to the Sioux reservations to crush any rebellion.

In December 1890, when Sitting Bull asked permission to meet with Wovoka at the Pine Ridge Reservation, the local Indian agent sprang a trap. Soldiers ambushed Sitting Bull, fatally shooting the Sioux leader. Sitting Bull's entourage fled the scene, only to be apprehended near **Wounded Knee Creek**, South Dakota, by the Seventh Cavalry, Custer's old regiment. The Indians surrendered December 29, 1890. A rifle accidentally discharged, however, and nervous soldiers opened fire. In the following battle, Native warriors killed 30 soldiers, but they were badly outgunned. The army's new Hotchkiss machine guns mowed down scores of indigenous men, women and children in minutes. More than 200 Sioux lay dead or dying in the snow. Even nursing babies numbered among the victims.

Jules Sandoz, a settler, inspected the scene the day after the massacre. "Here in ten minutes an entire community was as the buffalo that bleached on the plains," he later wrote. "There was something loose that hated joy and happiness as it hated brightness and color, reducing everything to drab agony and gray." Some of the wounded Indians were carried to a church at nearby Pine Ridge. Borne on stretchers, they passed beneath a Christmas banner that read, "PEACE ON EARTH. GOOD WILL TOWARDS MEN."

Before European colonists reached the Western Hemisphere, the native peoples of the Great Plains, the Southwest, and the far West had occupied the land for more than 20,000 years. Hundreds of Indian nations cultivated corn, foraged for wild plants, hunted and fished, and built cities of several thousand inhabitants. The invasion of their territories by Spanish and other European intruders brought disease, missionaries and new trading patterns, but relative geographic isolation gave the Western tribes a margin of survival unknown in the East.

Prior to European contact, Indians in the North American West combined hunting and gathering with settled agriculture and the raising of domestic animals. Some peoples, such as the Anasazi in the modern Four Corners region of Arizona, New Mexico, Utah and Colorado, built elaborate cities of terraced cliff dwellings. Although wide diversity existed among the different Native cultures, in general Indian societies rested upon extended kinship networks and valued cooperation and mutual responsibility as opposed to the extreme individualism and competition that came to dominate white culture. Different Indian societies designated certain hunting grounds or lakes or rivers as especially sacred to the group, but typically land was seen as a shared resource, whereas Anglos viewed land as a commodity to be bought, traded and fenced in.

The arrival of the Europeans and their American successors, however, forever altered the Indian civilizations in the West even before the mass white invasion of the Trans-Missouri region in the late 1800s. Spanish conquerors realized the huge advantage they enjoyed due to their monopoly on horses and tried to keep their herds out of Native hands. However, Spanish military raids and their kidnapping of indigenous people for slavery provoked a violent and acquisitive Indian response. Nomadic bands like the Apaches began punitive raids on Spanish settlements. Obtaining horses for transportation, hunting, and warfare became a major goal of these expeditions.

Acquiring not just horses but also firearms, western Indians developed a new equestrian culture. Transformed into highly mobile hunters who followed buffalo herds with greater efficiency than before, Plains Indians enjoyed vastly expanded hunting grounds. For all their mobility, however, these Native Americans could not avoid a fatal collision with white America.

NATIVE AMERICANS AND THE CIVIL WAR

Choosing Sides

During the Civil War, American Indians faced a dangerous choice in deciding whether the United States Army or the Confederate forces presented the greater danger. Whites did not allow Native Americans living near the borders of the Union and the Confederacy the option of neutrality. The Confederate government expected that, as owners of African-American slaves, the so-called Five Civilized Tribes (the Cherokee, Chickasaw, Choctaw, Creek, and Seminole peoples) would side with the South. Living in the Indian Territory (modern-day Oklahoma), the tribes shared a border with the Confederacy and felt great pressure from their southern neighbors. John Ross, an elderly Cherokee and a survivor of Andrew Jackson's Indian "removal" policies in the 1830s, begged the Confederate government to leave Native Americans alone. "[W]e do not wish to be brought into the feuds between yourselves and your Northern Brethren," Ross

wrote to one supporter of the Rebel cause. "Our wish is for peace. Peace at home and Peace among you."

Caught in the crossfire, and facing pressure from both North and South to choose sides, many Native peoples reflected on their long-term victimization by the federal government in Washington, D.C., and placed their bets on the Confederacy. The Wichita, Caddo, Osage, Shawnee, Delaware, and Quapaw nations, in and near the Indian Territory, allied with the South and fought northern troops as warriors or served as scouts and spies. The Comanche and Kiowa Indians in particular provided military aid to the Confederate cause, conducting raids in Union territory in Kansas. Comanche and the Kiowa raiders regularly attacked mule-driven caravans carrying provisions, ammunition, and other equipment from Fort Leavenworth in Kansas to Union troops in New Mexico.

Some Indian nations, such as the Cherokee, mirrored the larger conflict. The Cherokee split into supporters of the federal government and backers of Dixie. The war gave Union commanders an excuse to encroach on the Indian Territory as pro-Confederate Cherokee battled Union troops. By the end of the Civil War, the Cherokee lost land, political unity, and a quarter of their population.

Although Abraham Lincoln never committed northern society to total war, the Civil War thoroughly militarized northern society, with devastating effect on Native Americans. Volunteer American army regiments were raised in every western state. When the Confederate threat passed, these western volunteers turned their guns on the Indians. Moreover, the development of mines, the expansion of the railroads, and federal legislation in Washington drew thousands of Anglos to seize Indian land west of the Mississippi. Mining exploration expanded in Colorado, New Mexico and Arizona, precipitating wars between Indians and whites that led Washington to seek a final solution to the Indian problem.

Wartime Massacres and Detention

Whites often responded to Indian defense of their land with extreme violence. One of the most heartbreaking white-Indian incidents in the West broke out in Colorado. There, in 1861, Cheyenne and Arapaho had been forced onto a reservation in the southeastern part of Colorado, a "dry and desolate" region called the Sand Creek Reserve. Mines, white settlements, and the fencing of white-owned farmlands had disrupted buffalo migratory routes. Food became scarce. The Cheyenne and Arapaho began staging raids along the Platte River, attacking trains in search of food and other supplies.

The territorial governor, John Evans, warned the Cheyenne and Arapaho that unless they remained confined to the reservation they would "suffer the consequences." With Evans's encouragement, the civilian Colorado Volunteers launched attacks on Cheyenne campgrounds. Chief Black Kettle sought protection for 800 Cheyenne and returned his entourage to Sand Creek, after getting reassurances about his people's safety. Black Kettle sent his men out to hunt while the elderly, women and children stayed at the camp. Spotting a vulnerable target, the Colorado Volunteers attacked on the morning of November 29, 1864. Desperately hoping that the whites would stop their assault on an unarmed Indian community, Black Kettle flew an American flag and a white truce banner, but to no avail. Many of the 700 Anglo men were drunk as the assault began. They massacred 200 Cheyenne men, women and children, desecrating the corpses and collecting scalps for trophies. One eyewitness, a Cheyenne woman named Iron Teeth, later testified about seeing a woman "crawling on the ground, shot, scalped, crazy, but not yet dead." Over the next several months, the **Sand Creek Massacre** (also known as the Chivington Massacre) provoked retaliations from Cheyenne, Sioux and Arapaho who attacked civilian outposts and killed entire families.

Some of the most brutal fighting between whites and Indians during the Civil War took place in the New Mexico and Arizona territories. A Confederate expeditionary force sought to occupy these territories and repeatedly attacked the Apaches and Navajos in the region. The Navajos and Apaches responded with numerous raids on white settlements. All-out war broke out between Texas troops and Apaches, with the Texans faring poorly. In a single month, August 1862, Mescalero Apache forces killed 46 whites, seized large herds of horses, cattle and other valuable livestock, and kidnapped dozens of white children. Union General James H. Carleton, commander of the First California Regiment, ordered an offensive against the Mescalero. Desiring to teach the Natives a "wholesome lesson," Carleton issued harsh orders to his men, insisting that there would be no negotiations with the enemy. "The men are to be slain whenever and wherever they are found," Carleton said. "Their women and children may be taken prisoner."

By the winter of 1862-63 constant military pressure forced the Mescalero to abandon their traditional lands. General Carleton directed that a forty-square-mile area along the Pecos River be set aside as a military reservation, Fort Sumner, and ordered construction of an internment camp for Indian prisoners. With the Mescalero placed in a concentration camp, Carleton turned his attention to Navajo warriors, who had battled with gold and silver miners in eastern Arizona and western New Mexico. Carleton then defeated the Navajo and forcibly relocated them to the Fort Sumner reservation by 1864. By this time, the camp was home to 10,000 Indian prisoners.

The Natives were expected to support themselves by raising their food from garden plots and fields, but the hot sun and repeated droughts withered the corn and other food crops. The prisoners suffered from the heat, malnutrition, and disease. They faced starvation but were delivered from the brink by occasional government rations of low-grade flour, corn, salt, pork and beef. Stagnant water standing in the riverbed provided a perfect breeding environment for mosquitoes, resulting in an outbreak of malaria. The unclean water also promoted the spread of dysentery. Troops at Fort Sumner infected many of the indigenous women with syphilis and gonorrhea, which spread throughout the Indian community. About 25 percent of the Indians at Fort Sumner had died by 1868 when the survivors were finally freed to return to their traditional homelands.

AMERICAN WESTWARD EXPANSION DURING THE CIVIL WAR

Conquest by the Railroad

The Mescalero War replayed with deadly regularity in the next three decades, with increasing numbers of white settlers drawn into Native territory with the promise of gold, silver, or Indian land that whites regarded as free and theirs by racial right. The indigenous people responded with armed resistance, provoking a massive military response from the U.S. government. This led to the slaughter of Native Americans and their expulsion to ever-smaller reservations.

The railroad served as a harbinger of Indian doom. In the last 35 years of the nineteenth century, the white population west of the 95th meridian (a line from Galveston to Kansas City to Minnesota) climbed 400 percent, increasing to more than 8,628,000. This population increase exceeded the rate in the remainder of the United States by a factor of five. Much of this white migration west resulted from Republican Party legislation passed during the Civil War and Reconstruction.

Abraham Lincoln won election as president in 1860 on a Republican platform that included a call for constructing a railroad to the Pacific coast. With the Democratic opposition greatly reduced in the Congress from 1861 to 1874, the Republicans passed much of their pro-business economic agenda. Protective tariffs (taxes on foreign-produced goods) raised needed revenues for the army but also gave a competitive edge to northern manufacturers who were now able to sell goods at a lower price than their European competitors.

One of the chief beneficiaries of Republican political dominance proved to be the railroad industry. Before the Civil War, congressional Democrats fiercely opposed spending federal money on infrastructure such as railroads and canals. By the 1850s congressional Democrats finally agreed on the desirability of a transcontinental railroad line that would link the country from the Atlantic to the Pacific, but those dreams would be deferred until the Civil War.

Once the war started, however, money flowed to the railroads not just from stock speculators, but also from generous state legislatures and the federal government, which granted huge direct subsidies, land grants, and tax breaks to railroad companies. The railroads received public land from the federal government not just for the tracks themselves but alternating sides of the track, the "right-of-way," to dispose of as they pleased. Most often, railroads sold this land to settlers who followed the tracks west. Over the years, the federal government distributed to already wealthy railroad company executives over 180 million acres, an area larger than Texas. Towns realized the economic benefits of becoming a stop on the railroad line and offered rich cash incentives to persuade rail executives to route railroads through their boundaries.

Technological improvements in the manufacture of steel contributed to an exponential spread of the American railway network. In turn, the construction of more than 72,000 miles of railroad track beyond the Mississippi River spurred the rise of western cities like Reno, Cheyenne, Kansas City, and Omaha, which in turn encouraged more white immigration to the West.

Engineering innovations rapidly improved travel speed, safety, and comfort for customers travelling across what once had been known as the Great American Desert. Technicians invented the swiveling truck, which allowed trains to negotiate the sharpest curves. Other innovations kept trains on the track over the roughest patches of land and allowed them to climb ever-steeper angles through mountain passages. Thousands of African American, Mexican and Mexican American, Chinese, Irish, German, English, African and South American workers served in crews that toiled through Indian attacks, high altitudes, bad food, lack of water, scorching heat, blizzards, and disease epidemics. Workers transported dirt dug from construction sites with carts, used drills and sledgehammers to start tunnels, blasted through mountain passages with dynamite, laid the rail ties, and drove in the spikes that held the rails in place.

The Homestead Act

The West became a multi-racial region, but an Anglo majority ruled it. Besides bills directly supporting the railroad companies, other Republican legislation encouraged white immigration and contributed to the Anglo conquest of the West. In 1862, Congress passed the **Homestead Act**. Fearing that it would lead to the admission of more free states to the Union, southern lawmakers blocked passage of this legislation before the Civil War. After the southern states seceded, the new law sailed through Congress. It allowed farmers to obtain 160 acres out of the public domain for free, provided they cultivated it for five years. Farmers also could buy the land for $1.25 an acre if they cultivated it for six months. Meant to provide financial independence for families of middling and humble means, the bill actually allowed northeastern land speculators to hire proxies to purchase much of the land, who then sold on the market at greatly inflated prices.

Along with the Morrill Act (a law also passed in 1862 that gave states land that was then sold to endow the construction of "agricultural and mechanical colleges"), these Republican-sponsored laws fueled a mass movement of white farmers who rode the rapidly expanding railway networks west to claim their homesteads. In the last three decades of the nineteenth century, the number of American farms more than doubled, from 2.5 million to 6 million, and the production of corn, wheat and oats nearly tripled. Farmers poured into Texas, Kansas, Nebraska, and the Dakota Territory. Mass immigration resulted in the admission of nine new states into the Union between 1867 and 1896.

THE WESTERN ECONOMY

The Great Western Cattle Trails

Cattle ranching became an engine of the western economy. Before the 1860s, profit margins from cattle suffered due to poor rail connections. Ranchers had few customers in the low-population West and could not deliver meat to the vast eastern market. The Civil War changed that. The federal government became the largest customer for beef needed to feed Union troops. Prices climbed to a record $40 a head. The railroads built during and after the war closed the distance to eastern and California markets, boosting the profitability of cattle ranching. Some rail lines existed in Texas but crossed such great distances that their use greatly reduced profit margins. As a result, as early as 1866, the year after the Civil War ended, cowboys led the first great cattle drives from Texas to Missouri, where the livestock were put on trains bound for the eastern markets. Cattle drives became the industry norm by the following year, aided in large part by the construction of the Kansas-Pacific line to a new railhead in Abilene, Kansas. Previously forced to march cattle across Missouri to the nearest depot, cowboys could now simply cross the Indian Territory along the Chisholm Trail to the new railway station, which was 150 miles closer to Texas. Later, as the westward expansion of settlers increasingly closed off the corridor to Abilene, the **Dodge City** (or **Western**) **Trail** to western Kansas became an even more popular route with over 5 million head of cattle being driven from 1875 to 1885. The invention of the refrigerated railcar in the 1870s turned Chicago into the famed cattle and "hog butcher of the world," as the poet Carl Sandburg put it, allowing trains to pick up beef and pork processed in the Windy City and ship the goods to the four corners of the country.

High profits in ranching, however, carried a heavy price. "The introduction of cattle, sheep, and goats was, in many regions, a shock to the ecological system from which it never quite recovered," observed historian Patricia Nelson Limerick. Overgrazing and the repeated planting of the same grasses to feed livestock led to depletion of nutrients in western soils, the erosion of topsoil, the removal of trees needed to anchor the soil, and other factors that would create the devastating Dust Bowl in the Plains states in the 1930s.

Large ranchers would soon graze their cattle on millions of acres of free, unfenced public land, cutting into the grazing land left for the buffalo that the Plains Indians depended on for food and clothing. These moves increased Indian poverty and hunger. Meanwhile, needing wide-open spaces to feed their growing herds, cattle ranchers also fought "range wars" with farmers and sheep ranchers. In the 1890s an oversupply of beef caused prices to spiral downward. Ranchers abandoned the cattle trails, cut the size of their herds, and started buying or renting land, using barbed wire to fence in their livestock and feeding them hay or other feed stored for the winter. These barbed-wired ranches further disrupted buffalo migratory patterns, contributing to their disappearance from the Plains. Ranchers also began breeding Angus and Hereford cattle that were significantly meatier than the leaner longhorns the cowboys had driven in the cattle drives. The increased volume of meat produced more than made up for the increased shipping costs ranchers encountered after the abandonment of cattle drives. The brief age of the cowboy disappeared as rapidly as it had arisen.

Western Mining

Before the Civil War, mining served as a major engine of the West's economic growth. The 1858 discovery of gold in the Pikes Peak region of Colorado, and subsequent finds near modern-day Denver and Boulder, drew 100,000 prospectors into the area. Residents declared the birth of the state of Jefferson and applied to Congress for admission to the Union, but the Civil War delayed action, with Colorado not made a territory until 1861. It became a state in 1876. At the same time as the Colorado strikes,

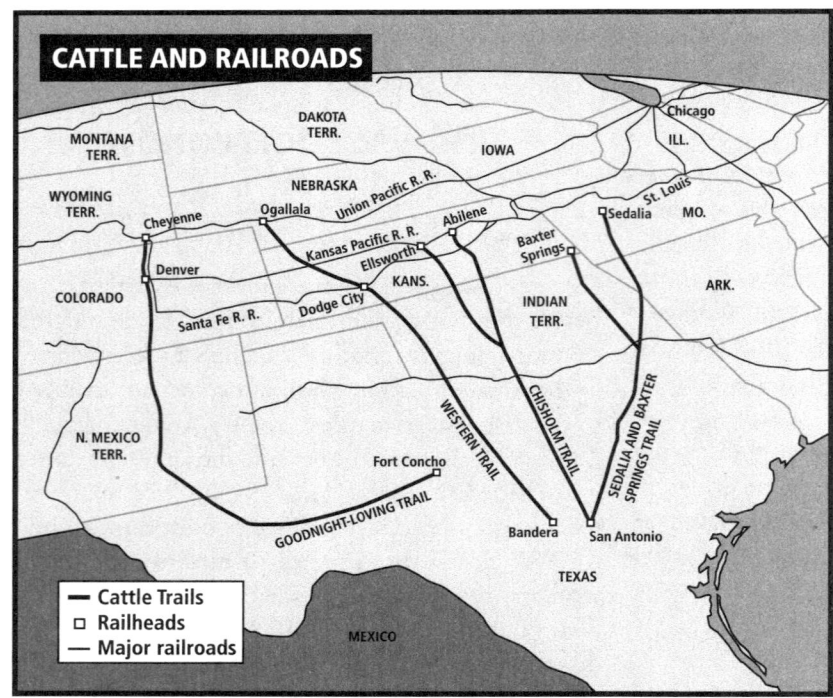

Map 17.1 Major Texas Cattle Trails and Western Railroads

gold discoveries in Nevada sparked rapid population growth in that area as well, so that by 1864, just six years after the mines opened in Carson City and Virginia City, Nevada became the newest state.

Scientific discoveries in the northeast also added impetus to western migration. Profitable copper mines opened in Montana and Arizona partly as a result of several late nineteenth century inventions including Alexander Graham Bell's telephone in 1876 and Thomas Edison's light bulb in 1879. These inventions created a demand for thousands of tons of copper wire. Mining towns sprang up across the western frontier.

Western bloodshed joined with violence against nature. Mining camps drew diverse populations, with Anglos from across the country joining Civil War draft dodgers and deserters from the North, migrant Mexican workers from the New Mexico territory, eastern and southern European immigrants, and imported Chinese labor. Mining towns often became anarchic centers of violence. The discovery of precious metals and ores often spurred both rapid economic development and lawlessness. The hydraulic mining used at the **Comstock Lode**, a rich source of silver found in western Nevada in 1859, poisoned salmon streams and filled the soil with toxic metals. To fuel metal smelting, loggers stripped forests near Virginia City, Nevada. Mercury mining poisoned San Francisco Bay. Elsewhere, hydraulic mining of copper created huge heaps of tailings, poisoning the soil and leaving an often barren, strip-mined landscape, with mountains reduced to ugly streams of muddy ooze.

The discovery of nearby silver in 1878 led to the breathtaking industrialization of Tombstone, Arizona, which lay fifty miles south of the Southern Pacific Railroad line. In spite of its distance from a main travel artery, prospectors swamped the region even as quartz mills dotted the surrounding landscape. From 1881 to 1882, Tombstone's population exploded from just below 1,000 to perhaps as many as 14,000.

Tombstone's unexpected economic boom turned quickly to bust, and the aftermath left ugly ruins. Searching for ever-deeper veins of silver, miners in 1881 hit an underground river, forcing companies to purchase expensive pumps in order to keep the pits from flooding. By the end of the 1880s, a glut in the silver market drove prices for the precious metal rapidly downward, and the busy buzz of Tombstone's boomtown days gave way to an eerie quiet. Mining companies left behind burned-out mills, waterlogged mines and abandoned homes, the townspeople migrating in search of the next rich strike.

As housing, saloons, and the other infrastructure of frontier towns rapidly rose in the desert landscape, new residents denuded the surrounding countryside in search of lumber for buildings and cordwood for cooking and warming hearths. Population growth attracted livestock ranchers, and a one-time isolated blip on the arid landscape gave birth to a vibrant livestock industry, which further stressed the local environment.

CRIME AND PUNISHMENT IN THE OLD WEST

The presence of silver and livestock attracted bands of robbers and cattle thieves organized into criminal gangs, such as the Clanton family and the McLaury brothers, that often preyed on the local Mexican population. These gangs crisscrossed the Arizona-Mexico border, stealing cattle in Sonora in northern Mexico and selling it in the United States, or vice-versa. These raids often resulted in murder, such as the mass killing of eight Mexicans in Skeleton Canyon in July 1881.

Mining regions often improvised a legal system, well ahead of establishing a territorial or state government. In Jacksonville, Wyoming, for instance, miners elected a magistrate and a sheriff. The prospectors and miners served on improvised juries in criminal and civil cases. Any murderer, horse or mule thief, and anyone who stole gold dust from a miner's tent, or any items valued at more than $100 (around $2,379 today) faced a possible hanging. Thieves taking less than $100 faced having their heads and eyebrows shaved and expulsion from the mining camp.

Vigilante justice remained part of western life even after formal courts and government institutions had been established. According to western historian Michael J. Pfeifer, twenty-three lynch mobs killed thirty-six persons in Wyoming between 1878 and 1918. Whites accounted for most of the victims, twenty-five, while mobs murdered four blacks, four Indians, and one Hispanic victim. In California from 1875 and 1947, forty-two lynch mobs murdered thirty-four whites, fourteen Hispanics, eight Indians, three Chinese immigrants, and two African Americans. Accusations of interracial sex and job competition between racial and ethnic groups often preceded such mob actions.

Outside of mining and logging camps, robberies and vengeance killings became part of the West's daily routine. One murder per night is estimated to have taken place at Gibson Station in the Indian Territory. The Indian Territory became known as the "Robber's Roost" and a local proverb proclaimed, "There is no Sunday west of St. Louis—no God west of Fort Smith."

Outlaw Chic

In the social chaos of the late nineteenth-century West, gun-slinging lawbreakers and lawmen achieved celebrity status and won admiring fans. Jesse James became such a media-savvy robber of banks and trains that once, after he and other members of the James-Younger criminal gang robbed $22,000 in gold and currency (more than $446,856 in today's dollars) from a train in Gadshill, Missouri in January 1874, he startled the engineer by throwing him a stick that was wrapped with a press release James had written. Headlined, "THE MOST DARING TRAIN ROBBERY ON RECORD," the blurb read in part, "The robbers were all large men, all being slightly under six feet. After robbing the train they started in a southerly direction. They were all mounted on handsome horses. P.S. They are a hell of an excitement in this part of the country."

The brutal career of James reveals why such outlaws attracted so much attention and even admiration among contemporaries and figured so largely in later "Wild West" mythology. During the Civil War, Missouri natives Jesse and Frank James rode with the murderous William Clarke Quantrill and his band of Confederate guerillas. "Quantrill's Raiders" in 1864 looted and burned Centralia, Kansas, before coldly executing seventy-five Union prisoners of war. After the bloody excitement of the war, the James Boys found farm life too boring and sought the thrills of bank robbing. The James Brothers, joining the four Younger brothers (Cole, Jim, John, and Bob), and other hoodlums in a series of holdups. They gave voice to the regional and class resentments of the era, blaming northern bankers and railroad executives for their financial troubles, sentiments widely shared by the general public that elevated these violent criminals to heroic status.

No matter how ruthless the tactics of the **James-Younger Gang**, their perceived resistance to Yankee invaders and the unprincipled actions of law enforcement continued to win the gang admiration and sympathy. The gang's end came the next year with a daring but unsuccessful robbery in Northfield, Minnesota, which resulted in the deaths of some members of the gang, the surrender and imprisonment of the Youngers, and a change in the public image of the James Brothers. Having killed a cashier and others in the misadventure, the James Brothers were now seen by many as mere murderers. They now drew hundreds of pursuers who searched for the outlaws in vain across the Midwest. The formerly tight-knit group included several new, less reliable members and Jesse began murdering associates he suspected of wanting to turn him and his brother Frank in for a $10,000 reward

Jesse James

(worth more than $238,000 today). In return for the reward, on April 3, 1882, gang member Robert Ford shot Jesse James in the head as the notorious gunman stood on a chair to straighten a picture at his home.

The public generally saw Robert Ford as a traitor and a coward. Ford used his reward money to open several saloons but ended up drifting from town to town before being murdered himself at the age of 30 in Creede, Colorado, June 8, 1892. By then, the public again transfigured Jesse James into a folk hero, a Robin Hood who resisted unjust authority, robbing from the rich and helping the poor.

Romanticized in dime novels, plays, and "true detective" magazines, the western outlaw provided nineteenth-century urban readers with fantasies of adventure in the wide-open spaces and vengeance against the wealthy and powerful. In the end, many Americans saw Billy the Kid, Jesse James, and other gunslingers as less lawless, sinister and greedy than "robber baron" business titans like the Rockefellers and the rest of the callous rich whose gaudy wealth stood in shocking contrast to the appalling poverty seen in America's spreading urban landscape.

WOMEN IN THE WEST

The outlaw culture of the West crossed gender boundaries. Myra Maybelle Shirley, who later assumed the alias "**Belle Starr**," won fame as a stagecoach robber, cattle rustler, and horse thief in the 1870s and 1880s. In addition to those criminal activities, she fenced stolen goods and became known for successfully harboring wanted criminals. Working as a card dealer at a Dallas, Texas, saloon in the late 1860s, she gave birth to a daughter fathered by one legendary gunman (Jesse James' crime partner Cole

Younger) and married outlaw Jim Reed, the couple fleeing to California after a warrant was issued for their arrest.

The couple returned to Texas, and Shirley again dealt cards and worked as a prostitute until Reed was killed in 1874. Shirley entered into a series of volatile relationships with six common-law husbands, all of them criminals. Living in the Indian Territory, she died mysteriously from several shotgun blasts in 1889, shortly before her 41st birthday. Though no one was ever arrested for her murder, two of her sons were prominent suspects.

Martha Jane Burke, a sometimes prostitute who became famous as "**Calamity Jane**," earned fame by dressing as a man at age 23 and joining an otherwise all-male geological exploration of the Black Hills in South Dakota. Then, in 1876, again in disguise, she volunteered for service with a 1,300-man force commanded by General George Crook in a war expedition against the Sioux and Northern Cheyenne peoples. She rapidly traveled 90 miles, including a swim across the Platte River , to transmit secret military dispatches. Burke later made dubious claims that she had married and borne a child with another Wild West celebrity, gunman James Butler "Wild Bill" Hickok and that she also was a friend of General George Armstrong Custer, famous then for his defeat and death at the Battle of the Little Bighorn. In 1893, Burke performed in the popular "Wild West Show" of **William "Buffalo Bill" Cody**, entertaining crowds as an expert horse rider and trick gun shooter. Sadly, alcoholism destroyed her entertainment career and hastened an early death at age 51 from pneumonia.

The West, however, offered much less excitement and drama for many women, some of whom endured lives of isolation. Elite women, in particular, chafed against the lack of culture and community. A doctor's wife, A.K. Clappe, complained bitterly in letters of life near the California gold mines, sharing with her sisters the emptiness of subsisting with "no newspapers, no churches, no lectures, concerts or theaters; no fresh books, no shopping, calling nor gossiping little tea-drinkings; no parties, no balls, no picnics, no tableaus, no charades, no latest fashions, no daily mail . . . no promenades, no rides or drives; no vegetables but potatoes and onions, no milk, no eggs, no nothing."

Such cultural niceties did not concern working-class women who faced exhausting work but also missed the extended family networks that they left behind in the East. Women constituted only about 20 percent of the adults in western mining communities. As one Denver prospector's wife put it in her diary in an 1863 passage, "I never was so lonely and homesick in all my life. My sweet sweet home! Why did I ever leave you in the stranger's land to dwell?"

Men and women struggled side-by-side to survive in the West, whether they lived in one of the new frontier cities, in mining camps, in the desert, or in farming communities. The family farm depended on hard work from both the men and the women, with women assigned not only the endless chores of feeding the chickens and other poultry, planting seeds, watering the crops, and helping with the harvest, but also cooking, caring for the young, doing the laundry, hauling water to the house from the well, making and repairing clothes, and acting as a physician when someone in the household fell ill. Women milked cows, churned butter, and gave birth to large families.

In mining towns, women often earned incomes as domestic servants. Some women contributed to the family income by taking in renters, and cooking or doing laundry for other families. In many cases, family structures were informal. In several Central Arizona mining communities in the 1860s and 1870s, almost half the adult women were not married to the men with whom they lived. These couples often defied the racial mores of the time. White men often cohabitated with Hispanic women, though Mexican men could pursue relations with Anglo women only at great risk. Such women dealt with a sexual double standard in which the community looked the other way when men had sex outside of marriage but defined a woman as being immoral for engaging in the same behavior.

In spite of the more loosely structured gender roles in the West, however, in mining camps, more than 90 percent of women "kept house," according to late nineteenth-century censuses. Marriage became more common as frontier towns became more settled. Recent studies suggest that spousal abuse, marital rape, and violence against children were commonplace in the region in the late-nineteenth century.

Mining camps in particular posed hazards for mothers raising young children. Foul water, streets strewn with garbage, and crowded living conditions helped spread diseases such as cholera, diphtheria, influenza, and measles. Childhood mortality became a cruel commonplace for these mothers, including one who lost three children in four days in Caribou, Colorado, in 1879. The landscape posed another lethal hazard. Young ones were liable to accidentally tumble into mine shafts, be exposed to lethal amounts of mercury, swallow lye or wander into the paths of fast-charging horses or heavy wagons. "This is an awful place for children and nervous mothers would 'die daily,'" as one woman wrote in Rich Bar, California.

Women lived public as well as private lives. Women married to or living with miners on strike brought food to their husbands on the picket line and threw projectiles at

Graceful as a Cat: The Life of Billy the Kid

In western communities that lacked deeply established social institutions, outlaws often became admired anti-heroes. In Lincoln County, in the New Mexico Territory, a teenager named Henry Antrim (who already went by the alias Billy Bonney) was well on his way to becoming both famous and infamous as Billy the Kid. A drifter and horse thief, Billy became a "soldier" in the so-called Lincoln County War, a bloody battle between two rival criminal rings that sought monopoly control of trade and political dominance in South Central New Mexico.

Racist tensions simmered between Anglos and the local Mexican population and pitted white residents against "nigger soldiers" stationed at the Fort Stanton army base, even as all these groups feared and hated the native population at the nearby Apache reservation. With local law enforcement sporadic and weak, alcohol-fueled murders and disfiguring assaults became part of the county's weekly routine.

Bonney first reached prominence in a gang war with "The House," a criminal outfit that dominated local business, holding a lucrative contract providing beef for the United States Army obtained when enforcers for the gang, called "The Boys," terrorized opponents and stole local livestock. A wealthy Englishman, John Henry Tunstall, challenged the power of The House, and won backing by the powerful cattle baron John Simpson Chisum, who had tired of the gang's cattle rustling.

Tunstall opened a bank and a store to compete with The House's businesses and won a monopoly of his own on all livestock feed grown in Lincoln County and near-total control of local water rights. At the instigation of The House, a sheriff's posse shot Tunstall to death on February 18, 1878. One of Tunstall's henchmen, Alexander McSween, gathered an army of local outlaws to retaliate, a force called "the Regulators," that would include the 18-year-old Billy the Kid. The Regulators hunted down men they blamed for the Tunstall killing, eventually assassinating Sheriff William Brady, a puppet of The House.

Billy Bonney would be implicated not only in Brady's death, but also the killings of two deputies. Eventually Bonney would be blamed for more than twenty murders, though he likely killed no more than four men. Just a teenager, Bonney already displayed a charismatic personality and physical courage that impressed his partners in crime. "The Kid was as active and graceful as a cat," one sidekick remarked. ". . . He was very proud of his ability to pick up a handkerchief or other object from the ground while riding at a run."

In mid-July, a sheriff's posse eventually trapped several of The Regulators, starting a siege known as the Five Day Battle that ended on July 19. Billy and other members of the gang successfully slipped away. McSween died in the battle and the Lincoln County War basically ended. Newly appointed Territorial Governor Lew Wallace proclaimed a general amnesty for anyone involved in the Lincoln County War not already under indictment.

Bonney fled to Texas. Charged with murder, he requested amnesty from Gov. Wallace in return for his testimony on the Lincoln County War. When the two met, Bonney greeted the governor holding a rifle in one hand and a revolver in the other. As part of the amnesty deal, Bonney was supposed to be jailed for a short time and released, but District Attorney John Dolan (affiliated with The House) reneged, forcing Bonney to escape.

Pat Garrett won election as Lincoln County sheriff in November 1880, running on a law-and-order platform. His posse captured Bonney in December. Found guilty of murder on April 9, 1881, the 21-year-old faced death by hanging on May 13. Bonney escaped again with help from local friends. The daring getaway captured headlines nationwide and added to The Kid's mystique. Garrett and two deputies were interrogating a local resident, Pedro Maxwell, about the Kid's whereabouts when Bonney unexpectedly showed up at the residence. Accounts on what happened next widely differ, but Garrett shot Bonney just above the heart, killing the outlaw.

Five wildly inaccurate and florid biographies of Billy the Kid reached readers within a year of his death, but the legend of this outlaw received its biggest boost with the publication of Pat Garrett's book (co-written with M.A. "Ash" Upson), The Authentic Life of Billy the Kid, in 1882. Garrett portrayed Bonney as a divided soul, an outgoing and charismatic youth who could suddenly turn into a cold-blooded killer. During another period of flamboyant gangsters, the 1920s, newspaperman Walter Noble Burns' bestseller, The Saga of Billy the Kid, depicted the robber as a latter-day Robin Hood, a good-hearted thief motivated to commit his crimes by his frontier sense of fair play. In a society in which corrupt politicians and greedy business tycoons robbed the public with impunity, such working-class outlaws hardly stood out as villains. Instead, they seemed glamorously rebellious and comparatively honest not just to nineteenth-century reading audiences but to twentieth-century book buyers and fans of radio, television and movie Westerns.

soldiers and Pinkerton Guards sent to quash the uprising. Women campaigned publicly for the right to vote and sometimes lobbied influential husbands to back suffrage. The Patrons of Husbandry, also known as the Grange, and other farmers' organizations allowed women not only to join but also to hold offices within the organization, and women took the leadership role in the campaign for the federal and state prohibition of alcohol.

Women won the right to vote in the West before any other region. In the 1876 Colorado state constitution, women won the franchise in school elections and to hold seats on local school boards. By the 1890s, Wyoming, Utah, Colorado, and Idaho had approved women's suffrage. By 1914, they were joined by California, Washington, Oregon, Arizona, Kansas, Nebraska, and Montana. Many historians have argued that the central role women played in the family economy in the West persuaded men to accept full citizenship rights for women. Such men also sought greater female migration to the West to up congressional representation for the region and thus expand the region's political clout.

Prohibition emerged as a feminist cause for many reasons. Women argued that alcohol led to spousal and child abuse, that it was a factor in workplace injuries suffered by wage-earning husbands, that money spent on spirits could be better invested in the home economy, and that much alcohol consumption took place in male-intense environments like saloons where men solicited services from prostitutes, often contracted social diseases, and later infected their wives.

Women also formed church groups, literary clubs, and organizations that sought to improve city sanitation, hospitals, and schools. These groups often attacked issues considered part of the "domestic sphere," for instance addressing the needs of children and preserving the safety and sanctity of the family. Nevertheless, woman gained vital political experience in these groups.

Abortion Restriction in the West

In one realm of their lives, western women steadily lost autonomy as the nineteenth century progressed: reproduction. As in the East, fear of the nation's changing racial and ethnic demographics and increased male domination over women's medical care led to the outlawing of abortion in several states. The criminalization of abortion did not begin until the second third of the nineteenth century. Early on, **abortion laws** did not focus on the morality of the issue but instead were aimed at outlawing specific abortion methods said to threaten a mother's health. Several early laws, for instance, prohibited the use of poisons to perform

abortions. By 1840, only eight states had enacted laws restricting abortion.

The struggle of the American Medical Association (AMA), founded in 1847, to ban abortions overlapped with the campaign by male doctors to "professionalize" the medical field and eliminate competition from female midwives who provided most health care to women. Before the mid-nineteenth century, most women, if they sought help in childbirth outside of friends and family, consulted midwives, who also provided information on natural methods of birth control, abortion, and women's health and nutrition. To many male doctors, midwives represented a loss of income.

The AMA successfully lobbied states across the Union to require medical licenses for practitioners. Since medical schools of the era did not admit women, this legislation effectively eliminated women as health-care providers. Deaths and injuries occurring at the hands of midwives and other female medical providers during abortions provided major sensational evidence for male doctors in their arguments for excluding women from the profession and for outlawing abortion. Abortions at the time had a 30 percent mortality rate for women, as opposed to 3 percent mortality in live births.

Rivalry between male and female medical providers and concern about women's safety did not alone account for the new interest in abortion. Between 1800 and 1900, the rate of fertility—the average number of children born to each woman—dropped for white women by almost 50 percent, from seven children per woman to 3.56. Anglos expressed a fear of "**race suicide**" instigated by the failure of white Protestants to have enough children to keep up with the birth rates of Catholic, Jewish and East Asian immigrants and African Americans. An 1865 tract by anti-abortion physician Horatio Storer, for example, warned that abortion was "infinitely more frequent among Protestant women than Catholic."

The West, with its proximity to Mexico, its importation of Chinese railroad workers, and its still large Native American population, helped lead the national trend toward abortion abolition. Politicians in five western territories in the West drew up anti-abortion clauses in the region's new legal codes. Performing an abortion "on a woman then being with child" became a criminal offense in the Colorado and Nevada Territory in 1861, and in the Arizona, Idaho, and Montana territories by 1864. Farther west, legislators moved from restrictions on procedures that physically harmed women to outright bans on abortion itself. In 1864 in Oregon, the state legislature eliminated allowances of abortion before the "quickening," when the fetus begins moving in the uterus, and defined the aborting of any "child" in utero as manslaughter, whether or not the mother suffered injury from the procedure. By 1869 in Nevada, the legislature outlawed even the dissemination of information on abortifacient drugs and abortion procedures. By the 1880s, states had passed 40 different anti-abortion statutes, laws that generally provided an exception only when abortion was necessary to save the life of a mother. Men saw women as a reproductive weapon in the conquest of the West and had enacted laws to make sure Anglos remained a demographic majority in the region.

CHINESE WORKERS

Perhaps no group inspired greater nativist panic within the Anglo community in the West than Chinese immigrants. Dangerous railroad construction depended heavily on low-wage Chinese workers, buffeted on one side by the resentment of Anglo workers and on the other side by the exploitation of bosses who kept their wages low with the threat of deportation. The West Coast in particular experienced an explosion in immigration from Asia that, though small in numbers in comparison to the total United States population, made a major impact on the California economy. In the years between 1850 and 1880, the number of immigrants from China in the United States skyrocketed from 7,520 to 105,465, with such newcomers comprising almost 9 percent of California's total population and about 25 percent of the state's total workforce.

Only 5 percent of these immigrants were women. Railroad companies at times purchased women from China who were used as prostitutes servicing the male workers. Chinese workers built the particularly difficult Sierra Nevada portion of the first transcontinental line, a project that resulted in thousands of workers' deaths. Toward the end of the nineteenth century, immigrants worked not only in railroad construction but also as domestic servants and in textile, shoe and cigar manufacturing.

Western companies happily played a game of divide and conquer with Anglo workers and their Asian peers. The press published stories accusing Chinese men of forcing white women into prostitution and Asian businessmen cheating white customers. Workers simmered with anger at the use of immigrants as replacement workers, which allowed employers to stymie white-run unions' demands for higher wages. Adding fuel to the fire, popular magazines and newspapers printed stories accusing Chinese men of being sexual predators. "No matter how good a Chinaman may be, ladies never leave your children with them, especially little girls," *Scribner's Monthly* warned. Not surprisingly in this atmosphere, violence against the Chinese reached pandemic levels in California and other western states.

In 1871, in Los Angeles, Anglo mobs murdered twenty-one immigrants, while in 1885, whites in Rock Springs, Wyoming, killed twenty-eight and wounded fifteen in a Chinese neighborhood. White workers battled to end Asian immigration to the United States. Cigars made by whites in California bore a "union label" signifying that no Chinese worker had been involved in the manufacture of the product. In San Francisco, the home of the nation's largest Chinese population, an Irish immigrant named Denis Kearney formed the Workingman's Party in 1878, its platform proclaiming, "Treason is better than to labor beside a Chinese slave." Such sentiments fostered political pressure that led to the passage of the **Chinese Exclusion Act** in 1882, which forbade further immigration of Chinese laborers into the United States. In spite of Anglo worker unrest, Chinese work crews contributed to the completion of five transcontinental rail lines between 1869 and 1893.

MEXICAN LABOR

An emerging source of labor came with Mexicans and Mexican Americans, who drew Anglo hostility that often matched that shown the Chinese. Protestant whites saw Mexicans as descended from three inferior racial groups: Indians, blacks, and the Spanish and also disdained the Catholicism of their neighbors from south of the United States border.

Most Latinos within the United States were poor, working their own small farms or serving as migratory agricultural labor. Before the Mexican American War, wealthy *Mexicanos* in California owned about 15 million acres of land. Anglo judges repeatedly invalidated these land claims. Whites often supplemented lawsuits with petty harassment or even violence. White merchants, bankers, and lawyers in New Mexico conspired to raise property taxes to force Mexican landowners to sell. By 1854, Anglos had seized all but one Mexican land grant in Texas. The **Texas Rangers**, a state law enforcement agency, along with white mobs and individuals, initiated a campaign of terror against Mexicans and Mexican Americans within the state, murdering as many as 5,000 in the nineteenth century. The seized land would then be distributed to whites, who subsequently made fortunes as ranchers and farmers.

Formerly rich Hispanics declined into poverty and worked as migrant farm labor or as low-wage workers in urban barrios (ghettoes). The spreading railroads expanded the marketplace for western farmers, who employed the wave of Mexican immigrants pouring into the United States in wake of the bloody Mexican Revolution of 1910-1920.

Mexicans faced particularly harsh discrimination in many parts of Texas. No state law mandated segregation of Latino students in any Texas school system, but administrators assigned Anglo and Hispanic children to different schools as a matter of custom. Where there were few Mexican children, no segregation occurred. In farm communities, however, separate quarters for Mexicans and Anglos were established early on. In 1902, Seguin, in South Texas, became the first school system to segregate Hispanic children but the practice spread until, by 1930, 90 percent of South Texas schools provided separate facilities for Anglo and Mexican and Mexican American children. Restaurants in Texas and other Southwestern states often would not serve Mexican customers or would require them to wait outside for food. Park and public pool managers frequently excluded Hispanics.

AFRICAN AMERICANS IN THE OLD WEST

Buffalo Soldiers

Partly in grudging acknowledgment of the brave service provided by 200,000 black soldiers in the Union Army during the Civil War, in 1866 the federal government created the first all-black infantry and cavalry regiments to serve in the western United States. Even "Radical" Republicans were not fully immune from the white supremacist ideas of the era, however, so the law establishing these segregated units required them to be led by white officers. These black units primarily served in the American West where they provided security for stagecoaches, wagon trains, and railroad cars. They battled outlaws and sometimes built roads and strung telegraph wire as the line of American settlement moved further westward. While African Americans in the South and the East suffered confinement to the lowest rung in the nation's racial hierarchy, in the West they formed part of a conquering army that suppressed Native American resistance and paved the way for white and black seizure of Indian lands.

With African Americans composing 10 percent of soldiers serving from the end of the Civil War to the Spanish American War in 1898, black fighters played a highly visible role in the "Indian Wars." Native Americans reportedly dubbed these men "**Buffalo Soldiers**," either because Indians thought the hair and skin color of African Americans resembled that of buffalo, the soldiers wore buffalo skin robes in the winter time, or because of their reverence for both the buffalo and their respect for African

Americans as fighters. Most black soldiers served in Texas, Kansas, Oklahoma, Arizona and New Mexico territories. The African American Ninth Cavalry played a key role in defeating the forces of Chief Victorio, a Warm Springs, New Mexico, Apache leader, in a war that lasted from 1876 to 1880.

African-American troops often suffered as the U.S. Army placed them in the uncomfortable role of restraining white settlers intent on illegally taking Indian lands. Others served as strikebreakers. After the victory over Apache leaders Victorio and Nana in New Mexico, commanders dispatched the Ninth Cavalry to restrain white "boomers" from crossing the Kansas border and taking land illegally in Oklahoma, action that often resulted in violence between black soldiers and would-be settlers. In more than fifty cases, beginning in the late 1870s and continuing until the start of the twentieth century, railroad and mine owners and other powerful western business owners exploited black soldiers to replace striking white workers.

Sadly for the black servicemen in the West, an anti-military mood gripped the country after the Civil War and soldiers in the late nineteenth century did not enjoy the respect accorded their wartime predecessors, a problem intensified by racism. African Americans frequently endured hostility from the whites they encountered. When whites murdered black soldiers, as often as not, authorities looked the other way. Meanwhile, local law enforcement often harassed black soldiers, arresting them on trumped-up charges, beating and killing them, or sentencing them to lengthy sentences for the most minimum of offenses.

Meanwhile, the Army discriminated against black men. In spite of their often-acknowledged bravery, black soldiers received only 4 percent of the Medals of Honor awarded in the period between the end of the Civil War and the Spanish American War. The Army promoted no African American enlisted man to the rank of officer in that time period, though no military rules prohibited such an action. Only 22 African Americans received appointments to the West Point military academy in the late nineteenth century, and only three could overcome the racism at that institution and graduate. Military records also note repeated instances of black soldiers denigrated by their officers with racial slurs.

African Americans and the Western Labor Movement

Black soldiers were not alone in being used as strikebreakers by ruthless businessmen west of the Missouri River. In 1891 in Washington State, African-American civilians, excluded from unions and needing decent-paying jobs, arrived under the protection of Pinkerton guards in Newcastle, near Seattle, to serve as replacement workers at coalmines owned by the Oregon Improvement Company (OIC). White workers had gone on strike against the OIC, which subjected its employees to long hours in unsafe conditions and housed them in "company towns" where the OIC served as landlord. Miners received wages not in cash but in company "scrip" redeemable only in OIC-owned stores. White workers attempted to affiliate with the Knights of Labor, an effort that led the company to bring in African-American replacement workers from Iowa, Illinois, Indiana, and Missouri.

One group of white workers assembled in Pierce County near Seattle and resolved that "we will no longer submit to the introduction of the negro race among us, and that we cannot and will not recognize the negro as worthy of association with us; neither will we submit to any association with them in any manner whatsoever." Some white labor leaders believed that black workers were naïve dupes of the mining company and expressed the hope that once they realized how bad conditions were at the OIC mines they would leave. In fact, leaving was almost impossible for most of the imported miners who were too poor to return home and who, in any case, were closely monitored by OIC guards told to prevent their escape.

Regardless, most black replacement workers had rational reasons for staying. They needed the wages, as paltry as they were, and to escape the low prestige that came with work as farm labor. If white workers demanded class solidarity from their marginalized black peers, they proved incapable of maintaining it themselves. White miners started returning to their jobs by late June. In any case, the strikers' virulent racism had fatally undermined their cause and allowed the OIC to split the work force along racial lines.

Black Colonies in Kansas and Oklahoma

Some African Americans migrated west after Reconstruction out of fear. With the final withdrawal of Union troops from the South as part of the Compromise of 1877, many freedmen panicked that slavery would be re-imposed and that northern politicians, sick of being involved in the racial turmoil in the former Confederacy, would do nothing to defend them. Ku Klux Klan violence also led to a migration of approximately 40,000 African Americans, known as "**Exodusters**," from the south to Kansas, Oklahoma, and Colorado. As sharecropping increasingly became the fate of blacks who remained in the old South, many African Americans

hoped to take advantage of the Homestead Act and became landowners.

Kansas became a popular destination for migrating African Americans for practical reasons, such as its nearness to southern states. Also, many African Americans associated Kansas with pre-war radical abolitionists like John Brown. The black migration began in 1874 in Tennessee when Benjamin "Pap" Singleton proposed the creation of black-governed towns in Kansas. A "colored person's convention" created a committee to promote the African-American exodus. The migration hit full throttle in 1879 when 6,000 Exodusters left Texas, Louisiana and Mississippi for what they hoped would be freer and happier lives. Southern whites became alarmed at the departure of cheap labor and demanded a congressional investigation into the movement. White terrorists beat and threatened African Americans, and arrested them on trumped-up charges to stop the departures, but the human tide continued.

Exodusters generally passed through St. Louis on the way to Kansas. There, a white witness reported, the banks on both sides of the Mississippi River were "literally covered with colored people and their little store of worldly goods [and] every road leading to the river is filled with wagons loaded with plunder and families who seem to think that anywhere is better than here." Some ran out of food and money before they reached their destination and received some help from local churches, although many whites resented and feared the black influx. Whites blamed an outbreak of yellow fever on the migrants and imposed a quarantine on them. Nevertheless, the African-American population in Kansas shot up from just over 16,000 in 1870 to more than 43,000 a decade later. The newcomers would still experience white racism, but many felt they had achieved real liberty for the first time in their lives. "When I landed on the soil [of Kansas] I looked on the ground and I says 'This is free ground,'" remembered one Exoduster, John Solomon Lewis. "Then I looked on the heavens and I says them is free and beautiful heavens. Then I looked within my heart and I says to myself, 'I wonder why I was never free before?'"

In 1889, when the United States government opened up much of the Indian Territory in present-day Oklahoma to non-Native American settlers, thousands of African Americans participated in the land rush. For a time the federal government split the future state into separate Oklahoma and Indian territories, and a land rush commenced in both sections. These colonists joined blacks who had once been or were descended from slaves brought to the territory by the "Five Civilized Tribes"— slave-owning Indians forced to migrate west from Georgia and nearby states in the 1830s. African Americans frequently merged their land claims and created all-black towns. Nearly 40,000 African Americans lived in the Indian Territory by 1900. Once there, African Americans built churches, school systems, businesses, and local governments.

African-American "boosters" promoted many of these colonies. **E.P. McCabe**, an African-American Republican politician from Kansas, founded the town of Langston and used his newspaper, the *Langston Herald*, to promote black migration from the former Confederacy to the Indian Territory, which he portrayed as a black promised land. "What will you be if you stay in the South?" he asked in one editorial. "Slaves liable to be killed at any time and never treated right; but if you come to Oklahoma you have equal chances with the white man, free and independent. Why do southern whites always run down Oklahoma and try to keep the Negroes from coming here? Because they want to keep them there and live off their labor. White people are coming here every day."

Rumors spread that McCabe planned on creating an all-black territory and African Americans hoped he would be appointed its governor. McCabe also supposedly planned for Oklahoma to become the first all-black state. Panicked whites and Native Americans warned of the dangers that would be posed by such "Negro supremacy." Ultimately, President Benjamin Harrison decided not to appoint McCabe territorial governor. Black immigration to the territory slowed dramatically because the financial hardships of relocation proved too steep for most African-American families. McCabe focused then on the economic development of the twin territories' all-black towns.

Gary O. Carney, a chronicler of these communities, said various motives spurred immigrants to settle in the all-black towns. "Some blacks wanted to live with people of their own race, which gave them a sense of security in a new homeland," he wrote. "Others saw the black towns as an opportunity to control their own destiny, politically and economically, without interference from whites. Many viewed the towns as a safe haven from groups such as the Ku Klux Klan." These communities quickly declined after Oklahoma statehood in 1907. McCabe departed Oklahoma the following year and resettled in Chicago, fading into obscurity as the years passed. As of the 1990 census, thirteen of these towns still existed.

THE RESERVATION ERA

As white, Chinese, Mexican, and African-American men and women followed the railroads and staked a new life in the West, those trains brought death and destruction to the Native Americans living along the path. In response,

Sioux and Cheyenne warriors attacked rail line workers and tore up track laid by the Union Pacific line in the late 1860s. Yet, Indians were still expelled from their remaining homelands and herded onto reservations.

Many whites doubted if Indians could ever be incorporated into white society and concluded that they represented an obstacle to Anglo wealth and progress. Some white newspapers and politicians openly called for Indian extermination. Civil War General Philip Sheridan famously declared that the "only good Indian was a dead Indian." Sheridan was hardly alone in his sentiments. The *New York Herald* declared that for the Indian the drawing of blood was "as much of a passion as it is to the tiger, or the shark, who has no possibilities of civilization, and whose fate must be extermination . . ." Even as the *Herald* declared the Indian doomed, however, the newspaper preferred the more passive approach of penning Native Americans in overcrowded, disease-ravaged reservations, hoping that nature would eliminate the troublesome Natives.

Toward this end, the **Medicine Lodge Treaty of 1867** assigned reservations in the Dakota Territory to Arapaho, Cheyenne, Comanche, Apache, and Kiowa, squeezing these peoples together with already imprisoned Bannocks, Navajo, Shoshone, and Sioux. Eventually more than 100,000 people scrabbled for existence on bleak, shrinking lands. These different Indian nations battled over dwindling resources. At the same time, corrupt **Bureau of Indian Affairs** officials routinely stole government aid meant for the Indians. This embezzlement reduced Indian food supplies, thus promoting malnutrition, disease, and widespread depression on the reservations.

The so-called "reservation period" of Anglo-Indian relations lasted roughly from 1867 to 1887. Well-meaning liberals, ignoring the diversity and complexity of Native American culture, hoped that the reservations would provide an atmosphere in which "primitive" migratory Indians could be converted into stationary, law-abiding wards of a white republic. **Helen Hunt Jackson** wrote a shocking 1831 bestseller, *A Century of Dishonor*, that detailed white brutality toward the Native population, and inspired many readers to call for reform in Indian policy. Reformers hoped that Indians would win acceptance by whites and would rise from poverty if they could be induced to surrender their language, culture, religion, and traditions and accept white cultural norms. Reformers saw reservations as training grounds for Indian citizenship.

Tragically, for many indigenous people, the reservations more closely resembled a concentration camp. The Indian population had dropped to about 250,000 by 1890, and continued to shrink, a situation attributable to the food shortages and poor sanitation that prevailed in overcrowded reservations. Indians entered the reservations with their minds reeling from the loss of their homes, the pain of battling for a lost cause, the pressure of white reformers who wanted to strip away their traditions and faith, and the fear of being under constant surveillance of corrupt and abusive federal agents.

The Buffalo Slaughter

The Lakota, or Sioux, in particular resisted the white invasion of the West. With the arrival of the horse, the Lakota adopted an itinerant culture of following and hunting buffalo herds. In the late nineteenth century, however, whites launched a mass slaughter of buffalo, threatening the survival of the Lakota people.

In the early nineteenth century, eyewitnesses reported that the ground literally shook when massive buffalo herds charged across the landscape. Between 30 million and 60 million buffalo roamed the land from Canada in the north to the Mexican border in the south, and east to west from Pennsylvania to California. Buffalo rapidly vanished, however, when railroad companies paid hunters armed with rifles to kill buffalo to provide meat for rail construction crews. Others sought the buffalo for their hides. After skinning the animals, they would leave the rest of the carcasses to rot in the sun. Railroad executives and mining camp managers viewed the buffalo as a nuisance, since herds sometimes charged across the tracks in front of incoming trains, knocked over telegraph poles, or wrecked storage buildings or other structures.

Railroad companies provided rifles for passengers, encouraging them to fire at the herds purely for sport, leaving the dead animals behind as the train chugged on. The newest rifles, such as the .50 caliber sharpshooters, were accurate within a range of 600 feet. Thus armed, sportsmen devastated buffalo herds. Western showman William "Buffalo Bill" Cody bragged that he had killed 4,000 buffalo in 18 months. One hunter said, "I saw buffaloes lying dead on the prairies so thick that one could hardly see the ground. A man could have walked for twenty miles upon their carcasses."

The United States Army saw the **buffalo slaughter** as a tactic in the war against Native Americans. The army referred to the animals as the "Indian commissary." Indians ate buffalo meat, clothed themselves in buffalo hides, made their tents from buffalo skin, and used buffalo fat to make candles. Military commanders reasoned that the extermination of the buffalo would force Plains Indians to abandon their nomadic ways and accept confinement on reservations. If Indians starved to death along the way, many Army officers thought that was all

for the better. "Kill every buffalo you can," one officer said. "Every buffalo dead is an Indian gone."

The Lakota and other hunting nomads began to experience hunger and had to travel over broader swaths of land in search of prey. In the 1870s, Anglo hunters killed as many as 200,000 buffalo a year. An 1883 scientific expedition found only 200 buffalo in the Western United States. Their access to their chief food source gone, Lakota, Oglala, and other Plains Indians concluded the only options left to them were waging war against whites or accepting their own extinction.

Little Bighorn

One of the fiercest Indian wars pitted the United States Army against the Oglala Sioux. In 1851, the Oglala surrendered vast lands to the United States government. Oglala leaders underestimated the number of white miners who would swamp their territory. They also did not anticipate that the U.S. Army would construct a chain of forts in the middle of their most important buffalo range along the Bozeman Trail in Wyoming. Oglala Chief Red Cloud temporarily halted the white advance, battling to an impasse with the U.S. Army in the Great Sioux War of 1865-1867. Unable to suppress Oglala resistance, the government abandoned Fort Reno, Fort Phil Kearny and Fort C.F. Smith. The Oglala burned these forts to the ground.

Under the 1868 Treaty of Fort Laramie, the federal government created the Great Sioux Reservation, located within the present state of South Dakota west of the Missouri River, but territorial disputes remained unsettled. The northern tribes pledged to allow the peaceful passage of railroads near the territory. Unfortunately, construction in the area, and the railway companies' policy of buffalo eradication, disturbed the buffalo herds that ranged farther away from the Oglala settlements. This forced the Oglala to hunt over larger territories, which brought them into conflict not just with whites but with other Indian groups as well. Numerous small battles broke out between the Sioux and Cheyenne warriors and the Army between 1868 and 1876.

The Treaty of Fort Laramie guaranteed the Sioux the right to live and hunt within the Black Hills for "as long as the grass shall grow." That promise became unimportant to the U.S. government and white prospectors when they realized that the Black Hills contained rich gold deposits. Prospectors intruded on Sioux land, and Colonel George Armstrong Custer directed his troops to conduct a surveying mission during the summer of 1874. Custer reported to Congress that the Black Hills contained abundant veins of ore and recommended that the U.S.

"Kill the Indian, Save the Man": Indigenous Culture and White Boarding Schools

To the Bureau of Indian Affairs, education for indigenous children was as much about unlearning as it was learning. From 1870 to 1900, the federal government boosted the budget for Indian education from $140,000 to about $2 million. By 1879, the BIA contracted churches and businesses to run 27 boarding schools for Native Americans across the country.

Attendance at these special schools was not voluntary. BIA agents, police, or even the U.S. Army regularly seized native children from their parents to ensure that each school taught its quota of students. Indian parents who refused to hand over children faced jail time.

Arrell Morgan Gibson, a scholar of Native American history, noted that the roundup of Indian children at the beginning of each school term often inspired terror. Taylavesa, a Hopi in what is now the state of Arizona, recalled in his biography the experience of being herded by school agents. As the police grabbed the children, he wrote, "The people were excited, the children and the mothers were crying and the men wanted to fight."

Students lived at these remote schools for up to four years, isolated not just from their families but from their nations, sometimes not allowed to return home even during holidays. At places like the Carlisle Indian Industrial School in Pennsylvania, white educators pushed children to adopt "white" names, convert to Christianity, and stop use of their birth language in favor of English. School officials burned the students' indigenous clothes and forced them to wear "white" clothes and chopped their hair to match shorter, white fashion.

By the 20th century, even the limited entertainment at Indian schools had the purpose of making the students ashamed of their identity. "Saturday night we had a movie," recalled Lucy Toledo, a Navajo woman who attended the Sherman Institute in Riverside, California in the 1950s. "Do you know what the movie was about? Cowboys and Indians. Cowboys and Indians. Here we're getting all our people killed, and that's the kind of stuff they showed us."

Students who used their native languages, even one Indian word, were hit to the point of bleeding. Teachers sometime denied children meals for other rule infractions. Students received little education in math or writing, and subjects like science were ignored. Students spent about half of each school day in labor or receiving vocational training such as carpentry skills. After receiving their training, the children spent up to three years apprenticed to nearby rural white families where they were used as labor.

White educators of Indian children made cultural genocide an explicit goal. "A great general has said that the only good Indian is a dead one, and that high sanction of his destruction has been an enormous factor in promoting Indian massacres," the founder of the Carlisle School, Richard Henry Pratt, said in an 1892 speech. "In a sense, I agree with the sentiment, but only in this: that all the Indian there is in the race should be dead. Kill the Indian in him, and save the man."

Only by mimicking whites, Pratt believed, could Indian children thrive in the modern world. By the 1920s, however, even the federal government conceded the schools had failed and were in terrible shape, with students overworked and undereducated. "The boarding schools are crowded materially beyond their capacities," noted a report, "The Problem of Indian Administration," written by Lewis Meriam and released in 1928. "The toilet facilities have in many cases not been increased proportionately to the increase in pupils, and they are fairly frequently not properly maintained or conveniently located. The supply of soap and towels has been inadequate."

In spite of years of pressure to abandon their identities, many indigenous children faced ridicule for acting white when they returned to their reservations and their traditions. Others suffered a lifetime of nightmares inspired by the beatings and the separation from loved ones they suffered as part of their supposed education.

expel the Sioux living there. Suspicious of white activities in the area, Oglala Sioux, Cheyenne, and Arapaho formed an alliance and prepared for battle.

Federal agents commanded the Indians to return to their reservations by February 1, 1876, or face an army assault. By this point Red Cloud had stepped down as the Oglala military leader because he believed resistance was futile. Crazy Horse now led the Oglala, who fought alongside Hunkpapa Sioux under the command of Sitting Bull. Four columns of American troops arrived, and the soldiers engaged in several skirmishes with local Indians and destroyed 100 Indian lodges. Army scouts detected a major Sioux encampment in a valley at a site known to the Oglala as Greasy Grass.

Custer decided to divide his forces into four groups and positioned three of them to prevent Indians from

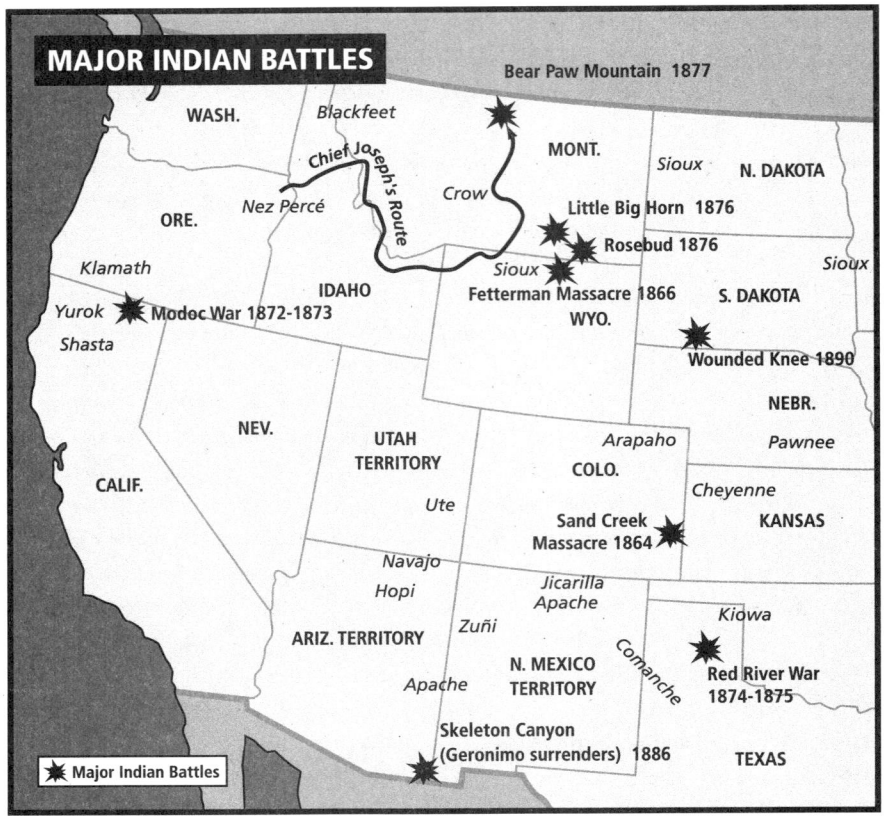

Map 17.2 Major Indian Battles

retreating from their settlement. He then led 225 men in a charge along the Little Bighorn River into the valley on June 25, 1876. Between 2,000 and 4,000 Cheyenne and Sioux warriors closed in on the American forces and slaughtered Custer and all his men. In militarily defeating Custer at the **Battle of the Little Bighorn**, the Oglala and their allies unintentionally handed the American government a propaganda tool that whipped up anti-Indian frenzy in white society. Reportedly upon hearing of Custer's death, Chief **Sitting Bull** remarked, "Now they will never let us rest." Custer's "Last Stand" became the battle most frequently depicted in American paintings, art prints, and newspapers illustrations. These works depicted the cavalrymen bravely fighting off an overwhelming force of near-naked savages. Custer's defeat became a public symbol of the American resolve to fight on for a just cause to the last drop of blood. The *New York Herald* quoted the commissioner of Indian Affairs as responding to the massacre with the remark, "A white man's life is worth more than an Indian's" and that, "It is not too much to say that the prevailing feeling among the public favors the policy of extermination." The U.S. Army pursued warring Indian nations until, by 1877, the Sioux leadership of Indian resistance in the Plains ended.

Geronimo and the Twilight of Indian Resistance

The western Apaches would be the last Indian peoples to surrender. Federal authorities attempted to pin Apaches down on one reservation in New Mexico and three in Arizona. In the 1870s and 1880s, Apache warrior bands rejected confinement, gained control over previously white-ruled territory, and raided ranches for cattle and other livestock. Meanwhile, a loose confederation of Cheyenne, Kiowa, Kataka and Comanche warriors joined the Arapaho in one of the bloodiest conflicts in the West, facing off against troops led by General William T. Sherman in the Red River War of 1874-1875.

Years of pursuit by the American Army in the difficult desert climate added to high casualties and eventually depleted Native American morale. Nevertheless, a decade-long series of small battles followed, with **Geronimo** leading Apache attacks on small white settlements across the hot and dry Arizona terrain. Geronimo resisted until only thirty of his once powerful warrior band survived. In September 1886, Geronimo finally capitulated, thus concluding two decades of intense warfare in the American Southwest.

Humiliation awaited Geronimo in his final years. Stripped of his right to hunt freely and needing to make a living, he became a chief attraction at the St. Louis

Table 17.1

Important Late 19th-Century Native American Leaders

Leader	Indigenous Nation	Significance
Black Kettle or Mo'ohtavetoo'o (1803?-1868)	Cheyenne	Tried to return 800 of his people to the Sand Creek Reserve in Colorado after an expedition for food but they were massacred by the white "Colorado Volunteers" on November 29, 1864
Cochise or Shi-ka-She (1805?-1874)	Apache	Led indigenous resistance in 1861 to white incursions into modern-day Arizona before a heavily-armed California militia overwhelmed his forces in 1862. He evaded capture for a decade.
Spotted Elk or Uŋpȟáŋ Gleška (1820?-1890)	Minŋecoŋjou Lakota Sioux	The half-brother of Sitting Bull, he led his people at the Cheyenne River Indian Reservation, and encouraged assimilation to white norms, until widespread hunger at the site led him to join the Ghost Dance Movement. He was murdered during the Wounded Knee Massacre.
Red Cloud or Maȟpíya Lúta (1822-1909)	Oglala Lakota	Won numerous victories over the U.S. Army in the area near Fort Laramie, Wyoming and forced the American government to abandon land claims in a peace treaty in 1868.
Geronimo or Goyathlay (1829-1909)	Apache	Led a diverse band of indigenous people battling white encroachment in modern-day New Mexico and Arizona, evading capture until 1886. In poverty, he was exploited as an exhibition at the 1904 St. Louis Exposition and other events.
Sitting Bull or Tatanka Iyotake, (1831?-1890)	Hunkpapa Lakota	A military leader during the Great Sioux or Black Hills War of 1876 in which he defeated U.S. Gen. George Armstrong Custer in the Battle of Little Big Horn.
Crazy Horse or Tȟašúŋke Witkó (1840?- 1877)	Oglala Lakota	Forced the U.S. Army under Gen. William Tecumseh Sherman to abandon forts and give indigenous people control of the Black Hills in South Dakota and Wyoming, defeated white forces in the Battle of Rosebud in Montana, and played a role in the Battle of Little Big Horn before being captured by the U.S. Army and fatally shot in 1877.
Chief Joseph or Hin-mah-too-yah-lat-kekt (1840-1904)	Nez Perce	Attempted to negotiate peace with white colonizers in modern-day Oregon, efforts that failed when gold was discovered in the area. After a Nez Perce warrior killed whites in a violent exchange, Chief Joseph led his people on a 1,400-march to find a new home in Canada and came within 40 miles of that country, but all but 87 died on the journey.

Geronimo, the great Apache chieftain, stands still erect and proud at the age of 70, at the St. Louis World's Fair, 1904.

land. The already small amount of land controlled by Indians shrank even further. In 1881, Indians controlled about 155 million acres. Just nineteen years later, in 1900, the land under Indian control had shrunk to 78 million acres.

By 1890, the Indian struggle for survival limped to an end in the Wounded Knee Massacre. Resulting from a white misunderstanding of a native religious movement with no apparent warlike intentions, the killings summed up four centuries of dishonor that began when Columbus encountered Native Americans for the first time in the Caribbean in 1492. The Indian population hit an all-time low by 1900, dropping to 237,000, but eventually recovered. About 1.9 million Indians were counted in the 1990 census. The Indian way of life, however, had been destroyed. Reservations would become pockets of poverty, bad health, and inadequate education throughout the twentieth century and serve as symbols of infinite broken promises made by the United States government to the original inhabitants of North America.

THE REAL AND MYTHIC WEST

Even before a more realistic view of the West faded from public discussion, a mythical West filled the American imagination. Memories of the violent business of forcing Native Americans into reservations, the environmental disaster of Western mining, and the corruption and greed that spurred the development of the railroads gave way to more inspiring legends. The West that captured first American and then worldwide audiences starred lonely cowboys wistfully following cattle trails, brave cavalrymen battling villainous Indians, sheriffs in white hats hunting down bad men wearing black, and gunslingers with hearts of gold putting the greedy and politically corrupt rich in their place. Such stories became a mainstay of the dime novel, the forerunner of the twentieth century's mass-market paperback. These widely read books turned colorful figures such as Billy the Kid, Wild Bill Hickok, Butch Cassidy and the Sundance Kid, and Calamity Jane into household names and fed urban children and adults with dreams of life in the wide-open spaces.

Immortalized as well in the paintings of Frederic Remington, the mythic West became flesh and blood in the late nineteenth century with Buffalo Bill Cody's "Wild West" shows. Cody first starred in the dime novels written by Edward Judson (under the pen name of "Ned Buntline") in which Buffalo Bill saved damsels in distress, and beat bad men and Indians with his quick draw and flawless aim. Cody's shows starred famous Native Americans like Sitting Bull, rope twirlers and

Exposition in 1904 where he sold pictures of himself for 25 cents apiece. He also accepted an invitation to ride in President Theodore Roosevelt's 1905 inaugural parade. Depressed, Geronimo said in a newspaper interview that, "I want to go back to my old home before I die . . . Want to go back to the mountains again. I asked the Great White Father to allow me to go back, but he said no." The federal government had banned Apaches from returning to their traditional lands in Arizona. Instead, when Geronimo died in 1909, his remains were interred in Oklahoma.

The Dawes Severalty Act

Having stripped Indians of their land, the federal government now sought to shatter their cultures. In 1887 Congress passed the **Dawes Severalty Act**, which authorized the president to distribute land to individual Indians provided they broke all ties to their tribes. The stated intent of the law was to turn hunting, nomadic Indians into small farmers and to bring them into the American economic mainstream. Nevertheless, greed played a big part in the drafting of the legislation. Knowing that Plains Indians were unfamiliar with farming, white currency, and Anglo courts, and that the land they were given was poorly irrigated, sponsors of the bill realized that many of the Indian "farmers" would soon be forced to sell to speculators what had once been tribal trick shooters such as Annie Oakley (Phoebe Butler), who could shoot a small coin out of her husband's hand at a distance. Cody's show crisscrossed America and Europe for three decades, bringing the thrill of the imaginary West to generations.

The invention of the motion picture camera came in the 1890s just as the western frontier was declared closed by the federal government. "Westerns," set in the late nineteenth century, were the most popular American movie genre from the first decade of the twentieth century until the 1950s, beginning with *The Great Train Robbery,* produced by Edwin S. Porter in 1903.

In the coming decades, cowboy serials starring actors like Tom Mix, and musicals featuring singing cowboys like Roy Rogers, filled theaters. Westerns became the most popular radio and TV dramas of the 1950s and 1960s, including *Bonanza*, and encompassed one of the longest-running television programs in history, *Gunsmoke.* The imaginary West depicted in popular books, movies, and radio and TV dramas did not include African Americans, Mexicans, or Chinese workers. Women were passive audiences as courageous men stood off evil, challenging villains to gun duels. A handful of Indian characters, like Tonto in the popular *Lone Ranger* radio and TV programs, were portrayed positively, though in a subservient, patronizing light, but Native Americans usually served as the enemies of white progress in these cowboy melodramas. The so-called "frontier" West became a racist fantasy, a metaphor for American invincibility and of white modernity overcoming dark savagery.

Chronology

1862	Homestead Act
	Sioux War erupts in Minnesota
1864	Sand Creek Massacre of Cheyenne
1867	Joseph McCoy organizes cattle drives to Abilene along the Chisholm Trail
	Treaty of Medicine Lodge
1869	First transcontinental railroad completed
1872	Yellowstone National Park established
1873	Giant silver strike discovered at Nevada's Comstock Lode
1874	Gold found in Black Hills of South Dakota
	Barbed wire invented
1876	Custer and his troops annihilated at Battle of the Little Bighorn
1877	Chief Joseph surrenders
1880s	Buffalo herds decimated
1882	Chinese Exclusion Act passed
1883	Buffalo Bill Cody introduces his Wild West show
1886	Droughts and blizzards on the Plains devastate cattle ranching and wheat farming
1886	Geronimo surrenders
1887	Dawes Act passed
1889	Indian Territory in Oklahoma opened to settlement
	Rise of Ghost Dance religion
1890	Massacre of Sioux at Wounded Knee, South Dakota
	Sitting Bull killed

SUGGESTED READINGS

Najia Aarim. *Chinese Immigrants, African Americans, and Racial Anxiety in the United States, 1848–1882.* (2006).

Stephen Ambrose, *Nothing Like it in the World: The Men Who Built the Transcontinental Railroad* (2000).

Susan Armitage and Elizabeth Jameson, eds., *The Woman's West* (1987).

Monroe Lee Billington and Roger D. Hardaway, *African Americans on the Western Frontier* (1998).

Dee Brown, *Bury My Heart At Wounded Knee: An Indian History of the American West* (1970).

Arrell Morgan Gibson, *The American Indian: Prehistory to the Present* (1980).

Pekka Hämäläinen, *The Comanche Empire* (2008).

Robert V. Hine. *The American West: A New Interpretive History* (2000).

Shari M. Huhndorf, *Going Native: Indians in the American Cultural Imagination.* (2001).

William Cronon, et. al., eds., *Under the Open Sky: Rethinking America's Western Past* (1992).

Reginald Horsman, *Race and Manifest Destiny: The Origins of American Racial Anglo-Saxonism* (1981).

Andrew C. Isenberg, *The Destruction of the Bison: An Environmental History, 1750-1920* (2000).

Ari Kelman, *A Misplaced Massacre: Struggling over the Memory of Sand Creek* (2013).

James C. Mohr, *Abortion in America: The Origins and Evolution of National Policy, 1800-1900* (1978).

David Montejano, *Anglos and Mexicans in the Making of Texas, 1836-1986* (1987).

Joane Nagel, *American Indian Ethnic Renewal: Red Power and the Resurgence of Identity and Culture* (1997).

Nyan Shah, *Stranger Intimacy: Contesting Race, Sexuality, and the Law in the North American West* (2011).

Richard Slotkin, *The Fatal Environment: The Myth of the Frontier in the Age of Industrialization, 1800-1890* (1985).

Ronald Takaki, *The Indispensable Enemy: Labor and the Anti-Chinese Movement in California* (1971).

Samuel Truett, *Fugitive Landscapes: The Forgotten History of the U.S.-Mexican Borderlands* (2006).

Robert M. Utley, *Billy the Kid: A Short and Violent Life* (1989).

James Wilson, *The Earth Shall Weep: A History of Native America* (1998).

Ronald Wright, *Stolen Continents: 500 Years of Conquest and Resistance in the Americas* (1992).

Review Questions

1. How did the Civil War affect Native Americans?

2. What were the ecological consequences of economic development in the West?

3. What economic role did women and immigrants play in the West?

4. How do the details of Jesse James's real life compare to his legend?

5. What impact did federal government policies such as the Dawes Severalty Act, the creation of Indian reservations, and the vast buffalo slaughter have on Native Americans?

Glossary of Important People and Concepts

Abortion laws
Antrim, Henry, also known as "Billy the Kid"
Battle of the Little Bighorn
Buffalo slaughter
Buffalo Soldiers
Bureau of Indian Affairs
Burke, Martha Jane, also known as "Calamity Jane"
Chinese Exclusion Act
William "Buffalo Bill" Cody
Comstock Lode
Dawes Severalty Act
Dodge City (Western) Trail
Exodusters
Geronimo
Homestead Act
Helen Hunt Jackson
James-Younger Gang
E.P. McCabe
Medicine Lodge Treaty of 1867
"Race Suicide"
Sand Creek Massacre
Sitting Bull
Belle Starr
Texas Rangers
Wounded Knee Creek Massacre

ELLIS ISLAND

Chapter Eighteen

WEALTH, POVERTY, AND THE GILDED AGE, 1870-1900

Sadie Frowne always remembered the first time she saw the Statue of Liberty. "It took us twelve days to cross the sea," she said to a reporter in 1902, "and we thought we should die, but at last the voyage was over, and we came up and saw the beautiful bay and the big woman with the spikes on her head and the lamp that is lighted at night in her hand." A Jewish girl from Poland, Sadie had fled her homeland at age thirteen with her mother. In her short life, Sadie had lost a parent, seen a family business fail, and now she had crossed an ocean to begin a new life in a strange land. Back in Poland, then a Russian province, Sadie's father died when she was ten, and for three years her mother ran a grocery where they lived in one room. Her mother displayed many talents as she struggled to support her child without her husband. "She was well educated," Sadie said, "being able to talk in Russian, German, Polish and French, and even to read English print, [though], of course, she did not know what it meant . . . [M]other had charge of a gate between [Russia and Poland] . . so that everybody who came through the gate had to show her a pass. She was much looked up to by the people, who used to come and ask her for advice. Her word was like law among them."

The grocery store did not earn enough money for the Frownes to afford the rent on the building. Sadie's Aunt Fanny already lived in New York City. Fanny encouraged Sadie and her mother to move to America. They raised money among relatives to pay for the trip. The voyage across the ocean on an overloaded steamship was miserable. They slept in bunks in steerage, the crowded lower deck of a ship sometimes used to haul cargo. "There were hundreds of other people packed in with us," Sadie later recalled. "Men, women and children, and almost all of them were sick." Upon ar-

rival in New York, family members welcomed the Frownes, but they had not left hardship behind. While her mother labored at a factory making underclothing, Sadie became a domestic servant earning about $9 a week ($259 in today's dollars). The Frownes struggled but managed to make it from month to month. Tragedy, however, soon struck the family again. "[Mother] caught a bad cold and coughed and coughed." Sadie said in an interview. "She really had hasty consumption, but she didn't know it, and I didn't know it, and she tried to keep on working, but it was no use. She had not the strength." Two doctors tended to her, but they could not save her life. ". . . At last she died, and I was left alone . . . [N]ow I had to begin all over again."

The still-teenaged Sadie sewed clothes at a sweatshop on Allen Street in Manhattan where she faced constant scolding from her foreman and sexual harassment from male employees. Her boss derided her as a "stupid animal" whenever she made mistakes. Typically, she awakened at 5:30 each morning, gulped back a cup of coffee, had some bread and fruit for breakfast, and got to work, where her shift lasted from 7 a.m. until 6 p.m. If she fell behind on her production quota, she would have to keep working until she caught up. She said that when she ended each 11-hour workday, she felt like doing nothing except lying down.

Sadie did not have much time for fun, but when she did, she loved to dance. By 1902, a steady boyfriend, Henry, began talking to her about marriage. Ever responsible, Sadie attended some night classes in spite of her exhausting work schedule, hoping to get a better job. Her hardship and determination in spite of exploitation and personal tragedies made Sadie's story a common one among immigrants in the Gilded Age.

Reconstruction had not yet ended when the United States entered into what the historian Howard Zinn called America's "other civil war." Set against the rise of industrialization, urbanization, and mass immigration from the 1870s until the early 1900s, workers and the upper class organized into informal armies and at times engaged in violent clashes causing injuries and deaths over basic issues such as fair pay, reasonable working hours, safe working conditions, and the right of laborers to organize into unions.

This conflict unfolded against the backdrop of a rapidly growing population in the last decades of the nineteenth century. The national population almost doubled in 30 years, growing from about 39 million in 1870 to more than 76 million in 1900. Much of this demographic growth came from overseas. Newcomers arrived mostly from eastern and southern Europe, but also from eastern Asia and, after a revolution south of the border in 1910, from Mexico. The number of Americans born outside the United States increased from almost 5.6 million in 1870 to 13.5 million in 1910, and most of those immigrants settled in the country's growing urban centers. In 1920, when slightly over 50 percent of all Americans lived in towns and cities, about 75 percent of immigrants were urban residents. By 1910, approximately 500,000 Jewish immigrants and their children lived in just 1.5 square miles of the Lower East Side of Manhattan in New York City. Those immigrants added demographic complexity to a nation that now included millions of Jews and Catholics who spoke languages other than English.

Migrations also occurred within the United States. Americans moved from the South to the North, from the East to the West, and from rural communities to the rapidly expanding cities. African Americans began to trickle out of the South hoping for freer lives in the North. Farmers tired of struggling with debt and unpredictable weather moved to the cities. Between 1870 and 1900, the percentage of Americans living in towns or cities with 2,500 or more people grew from 25 percent of the population to just below 40 percent. Sometime between 1910 and 1920, for the first time in American history, a majority lived in towns or cities. Many of those cities became modern metropolises. By 1900, New York City, the largest, boasted a population of almost 3.5 million. Chicago, with 1.7 million, and Philadelphia with about 1.3 million, followed, while two other cities, Boston and Baltimore, could claim more than a half million residents each.

The passage of the Homestead Act of 1862 (see Chapter 18) and a binge of railroad construction nationwide enabled this internal mobility. Crews laid down about 40,000 miles of railroad track between 1870 and 1880, and more than 70,000 miles between 1880 and 1890. Ten years later, the United States boasted the world's largest railroad network. The rapid spread of railroads fed the growth of another major American industry, steel. The railroads also turned the North American continent into a more tightly bound marketplace. All the while, money concentrated into fewer hands. Grotesque wealth often stood side-by-side with grinding poverty. The novelist Mark Twain called the era "The Gilded Age." A gilded object has a gold veneer but can have a rotten interior. As the saying goes, "not all that glitters is gold." Twain urged the readers of *The Gilded Age: A Tale of Today* (1873), a book he co-wrote with Charles Dudley Warner, to look past the shiny fortunes produced by the business titans of his time. The Gilded Age, he wrote, represented a time "when one's spirit is subdued and sad," when "life is a vanity and a burden," and when the average person wandered with "vague longings" and dreamed of "flight to peaceful islands in the remote solitudes of seas." Rampant economic exploitation, however, provoked millions not to the passive fantasies that Twain described, but to battle for a better life in the caldron of the real world.

THE INDUSTRIAL REVOLUTION

The industrial revolution that followed the Civil War transformed the everyday lives of American citizens. Every facet of life was demonstrably different for most people than just a few decades before—how people worked, how they moved around, how they lived in their homes, what foods they ate, what clothes they wore. All had changed due to industrialization. Many factors combined to make industrialism possible: an abundance of natural resources, unskilled labor, and investment capital; expanding markets provided by interstate railroads and foreign trade; and a copious amount of local, state, and federal government aid. Perhaps most important of all the stimuli to the industrial revolution was the explosion in technological advances that took place during a relatively short period of time, enabling the country in a single generation to emerge as one of the world's foremost economic powers.

The Transformative Power of Technology

A slew of scientific breakthroughs applicable to industrial processes enabled inventors and entrepreneurs to improve the manufacturing of standard goods while also creating a host of entirely new products mass-produced for the marketplace. The development of the refrigerated railroad car in the late 1870s and the spread of household "ice boxes" in the 1880s and 1890s, greatly enhanced the ability to transport and store food, which in turn improved

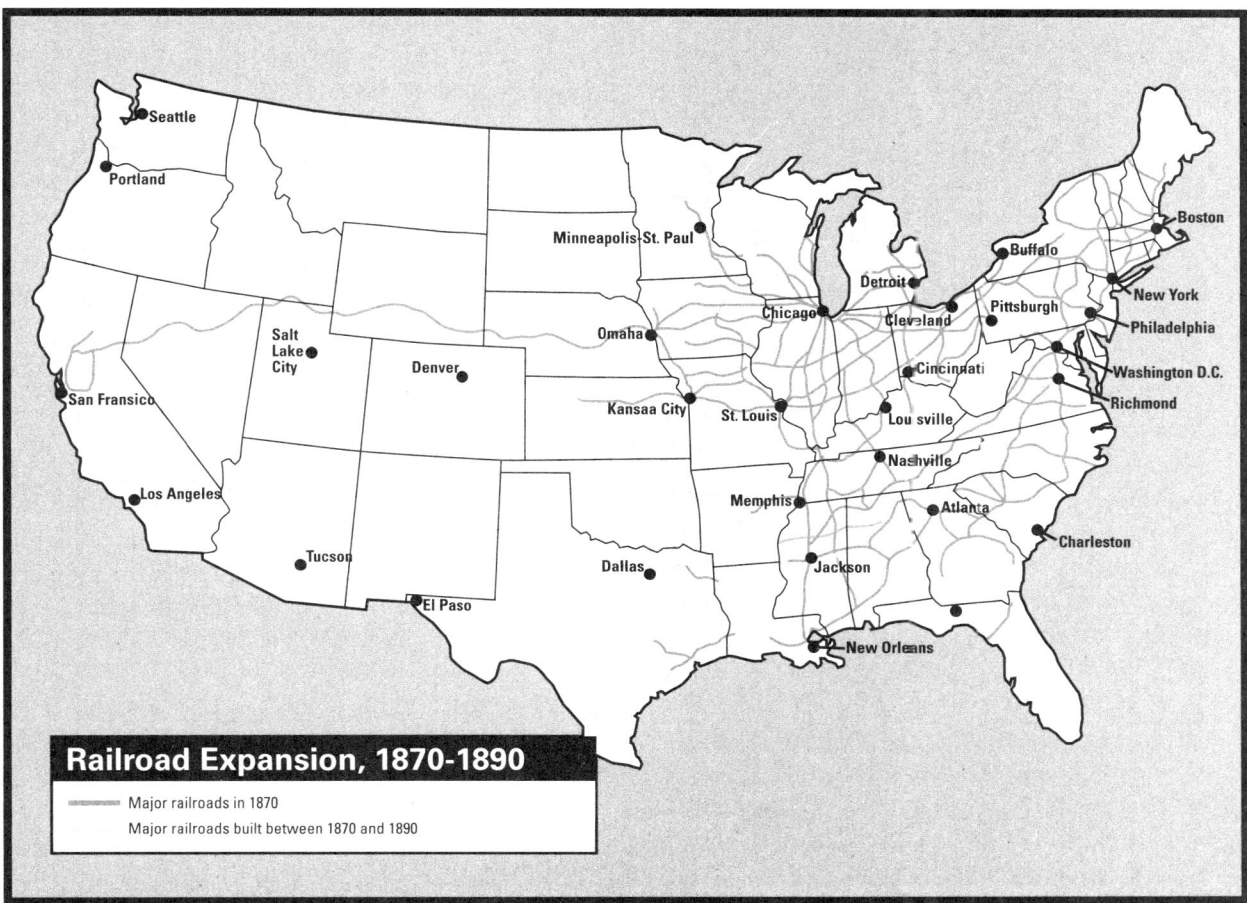

Map 18.1 Railroad Expansion, 1870-1890.

the quality of the American diet. British engineer Henry Bessemer's invention of the converter allowed for the first time for large batches of iron ore to be transformed into molten steel at lower costs than ever before. Chemists during these years determined the means to refine petroleum into kerosene and gasoline. Jan Matzeliger's invention of a mechanical lasting machine opened the door for the mass production of shoes.

Among the most important breakthroughs enabled the widespread use of electrical power. The expansion of telegraph lines in the second half of the 1800s and the invention of the telephone in 1876 by **Alexander Graham Bell** shrank distance for those separated by hundreds of miles from loved ones and greatly increased the speed by which news spread and diplomacy and government administration could be conducted. The invention of the light bulb by **Thomas Edison**'s workshop of technicians in Menlo Park, New Jersey in 1877, and silent movie cameras and projectors in the 1880s and the 1890s revolutionized entertainment for the masses and the preservation of historical memories. Edison's invention of a practical light bulb in 1879, of course, became his signature achievement, allowing homes and businesses to no longer depend upon the cumbersome use of candles or dangerous oil and gas lamps for indoor lighting.

Edison was also a pioneer in the effort for long-distance electrical distribution over power lines. He worked diligently to build power stations and provide electric current, but his system had one serious drawback: it relied on direct current (DC), which for technical reasons limited its effective power distribution to only two miles from a generating power plant. George Westinghouse, already known for inventing the compressed air brake for trains, solved the problem by developing a workable alternating current (AC) system by which electricity could be transmitted over long distances with minimal losses compared to DC. Westinghouse saw the potential for great profits and created his own company to compete with Edison's General Electric Company. He eventually won this "War of the Currents," and his superior alternating current system became the accepted standard for electric power distribution. Contributing greatly to this victory was Croatian immigrant scientist Nikola Tesla's successful development of the first AC motor, which converted the transmitted AC electricity to a wide range of mechanical uses. By 1900, electricity had become, like the telephone, a major part of American urban life. Electricity powered trolley cars, subways, and factory

Alexander Graham Bell, 1904.

machinery (which now could be located anywhere, not just near falling water to drive turbines as was the case previously). It lighted homes, apartments, factories, and office buildings. As late as the 1930s, however, only 10 percent of rural American homes enjoyed or had access to this most important product. As was the case with the telephone, those who controlled the electrical power busi-

Thomas Alva Edison, standing in his laboratory. East Orange, New Jersey, c. 1901.

ness, like Westinghouse and others, hoped to personally profit and thus only provided to markets where money could be made—the cities.

THE RISE OF THE MODERN METROPOLIS

The impact of industrialization on American life was most directly felt in the nation's urban areas, especially those in the Northwest and Midwest, which grew massively in size and in a haphazard manner due to the swarm of factories and workers that descended in torrents upon the landscape. Whereas among American cities only New York had as many as a half million people in 1850, six cities topped that level just fifty years later. In addition, the top three cities (New York, Chicago, and Philadelphia) all had populations over one million, with over three-quarters of their residents consisting of foreign immigrants and their children.

Urban Growth, Outward and Upward

Before the Civil War, emerging American metropolises were "walking cities." Most urbanites could navigate their way across town by foot since these cities measured only a few feet across at their widest points. Advances in electric-powered transportation would help spur the expansive growth of the modern city outward. By the 1890s, many cities built electric streetcars to move around town the people who could afford the fares. Some cities overwhelmed by street traffic, such as Chicago, built electric-powered elevated train systems, which operated on platforms constructed of sturdy steel frames in order to allow people, wagons, and soon automobiles to move beneath them. Many more cities endeavored to build subway systems below ground to facilitate the movement of people and alleviate surface congestion. New construction techniques and the advent of steel materials also allowed for the construction of bridges over large rivers and bays thus ending another barrier to urban growth. In addition to aiding the movement of people around the ever-widening city limits, streetcars stimulated the beginning of the nation's first suburbs—middle- and upper-class residential areas located a considerable distance away from town centers where its inhabitants frequently worked, shopped, and entertained themselves.

Technological breakthroughs allowed for the construction of the nation's first skyscrapers, which dramatically changed the look of modern cities when compared to their antebellum counterparts. Before the Civil War, the largest city buildings, usually made of brick, rarely topped three stories as it would be difficult for the structures to support their own weight. Chicago-based Louis Sullivan and other innovative architects in the 1880s, however, began to apply new construction techniques using a variety of new materials such as steel beams, girders, and tempered glass, as well as new inventions such as the electric-powered elevator and escalator to create residential buildings, commercial buildings, and factories of unprecedented height and overall size. These new creations allowed residents to maximize space in order to try to cope with the immense crush of people existing in the new metropolises.

Department Stores and Mail Order Houses

The streetcar lines facilitated the appearance of a new commercial institution on the urban landscape catering mainly to female customers—the modern department store. Located in central business districts, middle- and upper-class shoppers began to flock to the new stores via streetcars from the outer areas of cities and the suburbs, attracted by the large variety of new manufactured household items on display—furnishings, appliances, and especially clothing.

As important as the department stores were to the distribution of the large array of goods produced in the nation's factories, their impact would pale in comparison to the degree of business undertaken by another new urban commercial institution: mail order houses. Montgomery Ward in the early 1870s and Sears, Roebuck Company in the mid-1880s, both were headquartered in Chicago, pioneered the mail order business, employing large numbers of workers overseeing inventories in vast warehouses. The mail order houses greatly aided the distribution of manufactured goods by catering to rural customers through the U.S. Postal system via the emerging national network of railroads. Ward and Sears used immense economies of scale to purchase large quantities of products from wholesalers allowing the companies to offer dramatically cheaper prices to rural customers across the country than what the country stores charged.

In the most remote locations, women could now buy knock-offs of the latest Paris, London, and New York fashions. Before the rise of retail, most women made their own clothes. That clothing was custom-fit. Mass-produced clothing shipped from department stores in New York and Chicago could not accommodate the unique shape of each woman, so the clothing delivered by train to distant outposts came in mass-produced standard sizes. Women had to accommodate their bodies to their clothing. This produced a shift in the cultural standards of beauty. Women hailed as appealing in the nineteenth century would be considered "plus sized" today. With the advent of standardized clothing sizes, women were increasingly encouraged to view themselves as overweight.

Mass Marketing and Advertising

Advertisers increasingly shaped how the public saw reality due to technological improvements in printing technology and the rising importance of newspapers. The first professional advertising agents appeared in the 1850s and 1860s, and this new industry was male-dominated in cities such as Boston, Chicago, and especially in lower Manhattan near the headquarters of some of the nation's largest and most influential newspapers. Advertisements with wildly exaggerated claims of so-called "patent" medicines filled newspapers after the Civil War.

Gilded Age advertising aimed to create a sense of need where none existed by making men and women feel unattractive, unhealthy, and out-of-fashion. As awareness of the importance of hygiene in health increased, advertising played on a fear of filth. This age saw the birth of the advertising slogan. The makers of Ivory Soap declared, without explaining how they derived their measurement, that their product was "99 and 44/100s percent pure." Royal Baking Powder, meanwhile, was "Absolutely Pure." As the industrial age rendered job competition more fierce and career anxiety became more intense, readers of newspaper and magazine ads were warned to worry about maladies, such as constipation, that might make them less competitive and more vulnerable to being fired. Other advertisements celebrated the joy and wonder of life-simplifying technology, such as when the Eastman Dry Plate and Film Company told customers that they could make quality photographs with their new Kodak camera with ease. "You press the button," ads said. "We do the rest." More sophisticated advertising created "brand loyalty" for products such as sodas, pancake mixes, and cereals. Gilded Age awareness of popular brands became so deeply woven into the American culture that intelligence tests in the early twentieth century asked respondents to identify advertising characters associated with particular products.

Entertainment for the Masses

Electric lighting and the streetcar encouraged a vibrant nightlife in the modern metropolis. While many continued to attend operas, dance halls, and theaters as urban residents had done before the Civil War, the most popular form of indoor entertainment in Gilded Age cities was the vaudeville show. Providing a wide range of comedic acts, musical numbers, acrobatic displays, and

An advertisement of a pioneer washing with Ivory soap at his campsite. Procter & Gamble, c. 1898.

farcical melodramas, these variety shows catered to men, women, and children of all classes and backgrounds in order to promote city unity while maximizing profits.

The most popular stopping place for urban male workers proved to be the local saloon. Financed by the nation's leading brewers, the saloons were usually owned and operated by immigrants who served the breweries' brands while providing an escape from work in the factories and home life in the tenements. More than just a place to eat and drink, saloons offered their customers the benefits of a social club without a membership fee—an urban enclave where patrons could play games, argue politics, and discuss local affairs. Prohibitionists, however, concentrated their fire on the vast consumption of alcohol that occurred within saloon doors and resolved not to rest until the establishments were closed forever.

Sports stadiums and amusement parks provided the urban venues with the largest group attendance. While boxing matches, horse races, and collegiate football clashes drew sizeable crowds, professional baseball was the most popular of the spectator sports fast becoming a national cultural phenomenon. Beginning with Coney Island in Brooklyn, New York, amusement parks entertained millions of urban residents by maintaining a perennial state fair atmosphere of loud music, fast rides, games of chance, and copious amounts of food.

THE "ROBBER BARONS"

Technology and changes in American law paved the way for a new type of businessman. Called "**Robber Barons**," (a term derived from an 1859 column written by *New York Times* editor Henry J. Raymond), an emerging financial royalty built their fortunes running monopolies that restrained trade and bought political influence. Most Robber Barons inherited their wealth. (Andrew Carnegie was the major exception.) An estimated 90 percent of top executives in the major American manufacturing industries came from affluent family backgrounds. They were rich because they usually started rich, with all the advantages of education, social and political connections, and business networking that their family backgrounds provided. John D. Rockefeller, later an oil titan, got a head start in life from his father, William Avery Rockefeller, a con artist who built a fortune selling "patent medicines"—phony elixirs that supposedly cured maladies ranging from baldness to stomachaches to cancer. Such medicines, completely unregulated by the government in the nineteenth century, often contained heavy doses of alcohol and even narcotics such as morphine and heroin. Other patent medicines contained morphine and heroin. William Rockefeller falsely presented himself as a doctor, specializing in selling fake cancer cures at camp meetings. He accumulated a small fortune from his sick patients and later frequently made loans to his eldest son John to give him a start in business (though the elder Rockefeller always charged his offspring high interest rates).

Industrialization created both fabulous riches and devastating poverty, and in big cities both realities sat side-by-side. The Robber Baron class enjoyed access to riches rarely seen in the United States and embraced conspicuous consumption, flaunting wealth to enhance one's social standing. They lived opulently in places like San Francisco's "Nob Hill," the name derived from the word "nabob," a term referring to a person of high status. San Francisco residents liked to sneer at the rich neighborhood as "Snob Hill." There, railroad executive Mark Hopkins ordered construction of a 40-room Gothic mansion that took three years to build starting in 1875, cost $1.5 million to construct, and remained unfinished before he died in 1876. The mansion featured medieval-style columns, a turret, and towers that one local writer compared to a garish candy castle on an elaborate cake.

Charles Schwab, president of U.S. Steel, resided in a 50,000-square-foot, 75-room mansion on Riverside Drive

Movies as the American Dream Machine

As was true of most of the inventors who toiled in Thomas Edison's laboratory in Menlo Park, New Jersey, William Kennedy Laurie Dickson worked underpaid, underappreciated, and in the knowledge that his boss would get much of the credit for whatever the Scottish immigrant created. In 1891-1892, Dickson completed a prototype of the world's first motion picture projector, a device that gave still pictures the illusion of motion by running perforated film in front of a light source and projecting the images onto a screen.

Back in 1888, Edison had called for a device that would do "for the Eye what the phonograph does for the Ear" and Dickson and his team had made this device a full reality. Shortly, so-called "moving pictures" would be on display at penny arcades, storerooms often set up at boardwalks and fairs that featured coin-operated machines. Viewers inserted coins into machines called "kinetoscopes" and through viewers enjoyed primitive films that were sometimes just a few seconds of footage shot at landmarks like the Eifel Tower, street traffic in downtown Manhattan, snippets of horse races, women and men dancing, or even short, pornographic images featuring female nudity.

The novelty of slice-of-life shorts began to wear off and early movie directors, like Georges Méliès in France, used crude early special effects to make films that told stories like **Cinderella** and **A Trip to the Moon**. Edwin Porter at Edison's studio made a landmark western, **The Great Train Robbery**, in 1903. Audiences, who found these early examples of cinema sometimes disturbingly lifelike, reportedly jumped and ducked behind their seats at the end of Porter's film when an actor pointed a gun directly at the camera and pulled the trigger.

These films, displayed at the first "movie houses," were short, often less than ten minutes, silent, and in black and white (although sometimes artists hand-painted films frame-by-frame to give at least some scenes color). The musical score was often played live on piano, and the movies were often sandwiched between live comedic and musical productions on stage.

In the earliest dramatic and comedic films, directors often kept the camera still from a distance, like a modern parent holding a cell phone while recording a child's play. D.W. Griffith, the son of a one-time Confederate Army officer, revolutionized filmmaking when he began his directing career in 1908. He made the camera mobile, zooming in for emotionally intense close-ups, then backing up and widening the lens to reveal to the audience sweeping vistas. Griffith also pioneered techniques like cutting back and forth between scenes to suggest simultaneous action.

Griffith and other major filmmakers began moving their operations from New York, where production was expensive, to a rural backwoods of orange groves near Los Angeles that became known as Hollywood. Griffith essentially created the modern grammar of moviemaking, innovations he put to full and devastating effect in his 1915 pro-Ku Klux Klan film **The Birth of a Nation**. **Birth** became the first Hollywood epic, screened at the White House and earning a stamp of approval from President Woodrow Wilson. Unlike its early predecessors, **Birth** ran for more than three hours and, in an era in which movie tickets often cost a dime or less, audiences were willing to shell out as much as three bucks to watch the controversial and racist depiction of Reconstruction-era South Carolina.

Movies provided a home for immigrant Jews who found themselves locked out of advancement in most industries in the United States. Jewish men like Louis B. Meyer, Adolph Zukor, and Jack Warner created the biggest movie studios and made films that gave an increasingly immigrant audience a fantasy escape from the poverty and other hardships of industrial America. The early movies often brimmed with patriotism and conveyed American dialect and culture—as well as highly distorted versions of American history—to the millions of newcomers who came to call this country their home.

in Manhattan that sported a great view of the Hudson River, a gymnasium, a bowling alley, a pool, and three elevators. Mrs. Stuyvesant Fish spent part of her riches to throw a dinner party for her dog. At a time when the average worker made $500 a year (a little more than $13,000 in today's dollars), Fish bedecked her pet with a $15,000 diamond collar.

Though many Americans experienced an increase in their personal wealth during the latter half of the nineteenth century, the fortunes created by the Robber Barons generally did not trickle down to the masses as the tycoons accumulated many of the largest fortunes in American history. According to one estimate, five men who rose to power and prominence in the Gilded Age stand among the 13 richest Americans of all time: department store magnate Marshall Field (ranked eleventh with a fortune at his death of more than $66 billion in modern dollars); Jay Gould (ninth with $71 billion); lumber king Frederick Weyerhauser (eighth at $79.9 billion); and the two richest Americans of all time,

Andrew Carnegie

Andrew Carnegie (at $309 billion) and Rockefeller (at $336 billion). The economic top 1 percent in the United States held 29 percent of the wealth in 1860. Three decades later, the top 1 percent possessed 50 percent of the nation's wealth. (By contrast comparison, today it is estimated that the top 1 percent control 40 percent of national wealth.) Greater income inequality existed in the United States in the 1880s than in England, another rapidly industrializing world economic powerhouse. The economist Thomas G. Sherman noted that in England, 1/70th of the population possessed 67 percent of that nation's riches in the 1880s, while the American top 1/70th held about 80 percent. The Robber Barons won some admiration for their vision and their success but earned even more public hatred for their greed and indifference to the suffering of their workers.

Jay Gould

As he solidified control of his vast railroad network, **Jay Gould** emerged as one of the nation's first Robber Barons. Like Leland Stanford and other successful railroad executives, Gould used not just profits, but also generous public subsidies to build his empire. Buying up the Manhattan Elevated Railroad, as well as the Western Union Telegraph Company, Gould gained control of the Erie Railroad in New York in collaboration with stock market speculator Jim Fisk. In 1869, the two men worked together again on an effort to corner the gold market. When the attempt failed, the value of gold tumbled, and the stock market fell 20 percent on September 24, 1869, a day

that came to be known as "**Black Friday**." The crash left thousands of investors insolvent, and drove one stockbroker to suicide. Corn and wheat farmers suffered massive losses, with the value of their crops dropping by half.

After Black Friday, Gould became known as the "Mephistopheles of Wall Street." Such shady wheeling and dealing led contemporaries to view him as a vampire, a hustler and, in the words of one early twentieth-century biographer, a "human carnivore" feeding on the helpless. Yet Gould, through his uncanny knack for timely stock buying and selling, gobbled up a string of financially failing rail lines and merged them, thus stitching together much of the American railroad network from the Atlantic to the Pacific. Gould bounced back from Black Friday and gained control of the Union Pacific Railroad in the early days of the 1873-1878 depression. He embodied the attitude of an industry that squeezed long hours from workers in return for low pay. During a wave of strikes against his railroads in 1886, Gould reportedly said, "I can hire one half of the working class to kill the other half." His cost cutting at the expense of his employees, however, came at a price and provoked a series of major strikes throughout the Gilded Age.

Andrew Carnegie

Andrew Carnegie came to control most steel production in the United States in spite of a humble background as a Scottish immigrant. Clever and determined, Carnegie worked in a Pittsburgh textile mill at age 12 as a bobbin boy before starting his climb up the corporate ladder when he got a job as a telegraph clerk and delivery boy for the Ohio Telegraph Company. His new job enabled him to establish contact with powerful local businessmen, including Tom Scott, the head of the Pennsylvania Railroad. Scott took a liking to Carnegie and gave him a series of jobs, eventually promoting him to the level superintendent. Scott also loaned Carnegie money to invest in companies that dealt profitably with the railroad—an obvious conflict of interest, but an arrangement that allowed railroad executives like Scott and Carnegie to accrue more money than they received from their corporate salaries. Armed with this windfall, Carnegie quickly became a master of insider trading, using information not available to the general investing public to buy and sell right before a company made an important move or when positive or negative news about its earnings were about to become public. He achieved his status as a millionaire Wall Street broker peddling the railroad bonds that became a mania for investors in the late nineteenth century before he turned his attention first to iron production, and then to steel.

When the United States imposed a $28 per ton tariff (import tax) on foreign produced steel in 1870, Carnegie saw an opportunity to undersell British manufacturers and build an American business empire. First purchasing a Braddock, Pennsylvania mill near Pittsburgh, he used profits to buy failing competitors during the 1873-1878 depression. Carnegie's approach to monopoly building came to be known as "**vertical integration**." To avoid paying outside contractors, he sought to control every aspect of steel production: prospecting for iron and other raw materials, mining it, processing it, and selling it. Carnegie also absorbed competitors, sometimes honestly and sometimes through questionable means, such as when he slandered the products of the rival Duquesne Steel Company, which had developed a means of making quality railroad rails at a cheaper price than Carnegie Steel. The end result of his successful smear campaign was the sale of the Duquesne Company to Carnegie Steel, with the more efficient Duquesne method of rail manufacturing soon becoming the new Carnegie method.

By the 1890s, Carnegie controlled more than 60 percent of the industry. He fattened his profit margins by pressuring foundry managers to ruthlessly cut costs, which they achieved by forcing workers to churn out steel in 12-hour shifts, six days a week, at low wages, with few breaks. In the interest of saving money, Carnegie invested next to nothing on safety at his plants. Working in an inferno where explosions could occur and workers could be, and sometimes were, burned to death, Carnegie's employees wore only two layers of long-johns as "protective gear," which proved an inadequate shield against molten metal. Families of steel workers near Carnegie's plants feared the sound of factory whistles blowing unexpectedly, knowing that the alarm meant that production had been halted because someone inside had been hurt or killed.

In spite of his hard-hearted management style, Carnegie endeavored to create a benevolent public image in the press by investing a large share of his profits in philanthropy. Showing a charity that he never extended to his workers, Carnegie funded the construction of 2,800 libraries across the country. By the time he died in 1919, he gave an estimated $350 million to charity, including establishing the Carnegie-Mellon Institute (now Carnegie-Mellon University), the world-renowned music venue in Manhattan that came to be known as Carnegie Hall, and the Carnegie Foundation that funded scientific research for good and ill. The tycoon realized that a positive public image formed an important part of running a successful business. Carnegie's charitable reputation bought him good will with state legislatures and the Congress, which could do him favors in the form of tax breaks, resistance to efforts to regulate workers' wages, and tariffs on foreign steel.

John D. Rockefeller and the Birth of Big Oil

The only individual American during the Gilded Age to acquire more wealth than Carnegie was **John D. Rockefeller**, who eventually controlled petroleum refining more completely than Carnegie dominated the steel market. By 1913, Rockefeller's total personal assets equaled 2 percent of the American gross national product.

With a talent for mathematics, Rockefeller started his career as a bookkeeper. As a clerk at age 18, he handled the complex logistics of organizing shipments of freight transported by boats, wagons, and railroads. He also sold various commodities by the outbreak of the Civil War. During the war, a new industry attracted Rockefeller's attention. The American oil industry, based on oils from animal fat, had existed for decades. American ships sailed the seas to hunt whales for the blubber to be used to make soap, kerosene, and fuel for oil lamps—an industry immortalized in Herman Melville's 1851 novel *Moby Dick*. The industry changed forever on August 27, 1859, when Edwin Drake discovered major petroleum deposits near Titusville, Pennsylvania. Fossil fuel-based oil soon provided much indoor lighting before the dominance of electricity, as well as heating, and lubrication for

John D. Rockefeller

factory machinery. When German and French inventors developed the first gasoline-powered automobiles in the 1880s and 1890s, a major additional market for oil opened.

With partners, Rockefeller bought his first oil refinery in Cleveland, Ohio in 1862. After avoiding service in the Civil War by paying a substitute, he used the refinery's profits to buy out his partners and become sole owner three years later. In 1870, he formed a partnership with his brother William and other local businessmen, and the newly named Standard Oil Company of Ohio quickly gained control of almost all refineries in Cleveland. Soon, Standard Oil would branch out to other states.

By 1878, Rockefeller's company controlled enough of the refining industry that it could demand that railroads pay it a rebate of 20-35 cents ($5-$9 adjusted for inflation) per barrel of crude oil shipped by any of Standard Oil's competitors. This move hiked the price of oil sold by Rockefeller's competitors, which hurt sales, making these companies vulnerable for takeover by Standard Oil. By 1879, Standard Oil controlled 90 percent of the oil refining in the United States. Instead of Carnegie's vertical approach, Rockefeller ruled over oil through **horizontal integration**—dominating the most critical part of production. For oil, that meant refining, which made the crude petroleum pumped from the ground usable for consumers.

Rockefeller not only refined oil, but also created a new form of business organization called the "trust." In a trust, members of the board of directors of a company buy up stock shares of competitors and suppliers, which they hold as individuals in "trust" for the company. This served as a dodge to mask the creation of a near monopoly at a time when large corporations became increasingly unpopular politically. Through such maneuvers, Rockefeller was on his way to becoming one of the wealthiest men in the history of the world by the time he celebrated his 40th birthday.

Social Darwinism

In spite of largely building their fortunes upon a foundation of low wages, long hours, unsafe working conditions, child labor, bullying competitors, and overcharging customers, many Robber Barons believed that recent science provided a justification for their behavior. In 1859, British naturalist Charles Darwin shook the scientific world with publication of his groundbreaking *On the Origin of Species*. His work explained how species evolve over time as the environment changes, and how some biological modifications are useful in allowing a species to thrive, while other traits become a hindrance under changing conditions. As certain traits become more suitable for an environment, helpful adaptations are reinforced through sexual reproduction and unsuitable biological traits disappear. Over the long run this leads to the physical modification of species and the rise of new ones. Darwin called this process "natural selection."

Darwin's book focused on the animal world, but some British and American thinkers quickly saw in Darwin's work an explanation for why some individuals rise to wealth and power in human society while others fall into poverty and crime. British philosopher Herbert Spencer (who coined the term "survival of the fittest" to describe how evolution worked) and Yale University sociologist William Graham Sumner believed that Darwin revealed a truth about human society as well. According to Spencer, Sumner, and others who came to be known as "Social Darwinists," the human world is not too dissimilar from the natural one. Individuals of all abilities compete not just for food, shelter, and water with other humans, but also for wealth, power, and status. The fittest—the smartest, the bravest, the most innovative, and the most determined—prevail, while the "unfit"—the least intelligent, the laziest, and the fearful—fall to the bottom. Wealthy individuals like Andrew Carnegie, John D. Rockefeller, and Jay Gould were able to build their fortunes, the Social Darwinists argued, because they were the most biologically capable, while the poor were unfit. Social Darwinists ignored that their own wealth was not necessarily a measure of their hard work and fitness, but of their good luck in having wealthy parents (or a wealthy benefactor, in the case of Carnegie). Social Darwinists also ignored the degree to which ruthlessness, corruption, and inherited social networks allowed the children of the wealthy to climb to the top while blocking the poor from rising.

In his 1883 book, *What the Social Classes Owe Each Other*, Sumner argued that society should do nothing to help the poor and the struggling. Social Darwinists worried that advances in medicine had made it possible for unfit humans to survive and reproduce and that the unfit, because they were supposedly less disciplined, would have far more children than the fit. The future of the human race would thereby be imperiled. Sumner argued that charity would only make the situation worse. Social Darwinists also opposed any legislation that would improve workers' wages, reduce working hours, or in any way improve the lot of the lower classes. They suggested that hardship weeded out the biologically dangerous and that if capable children by some unpredictable set of circumstances found themselves in poverty, these challenges would sharpen their intellects and their instincts, leading them to inevitably rise to the top.

Social Darwinism reinforced the elite commitment to *laissez-faire*, the idea that the federal and state governments should not interfere in the workings of the economy in terms of regulating wages, working conditions, consumer prices, or forbidding trusts. Carnegie offered an alternative to pure *laissez-faire* and Social Darwinism in an article that he authored in June 1889, "Wealth," published in the *North American Review*, an essay that later became known as "The Gospel of Wealth." Carnegie chided others of his class for conspicuous consumption, warning that the lavish lifestyles of the superrich yielded resentment and even radicalism among the poor. He disdained the recipients of inherited wealth and advocated high taxes on inheritances to force heirs to work their way up as he did. Carnegie advocated that excess wealth be used to underwrite a trust fund to create opportunities for the less advantaged to climb the economic ladder, but he also rejected traditional forms of charity providing direct financial aid to the poor. His admonitions won few converts among other Robber Barons. In any case, the tycoon's behavior as a business manager did not align with his printed words.

THE IMPACT OF IMMIGRATION

"Old" vs. "New" Immigration

Industrialization led to a massive influx of workers to the Western Hemisphere. Although large numbers of laborers traveled to Argentina and Brazil in South America, and Canada also received a fair share of industrial workers, over 17 million people immigrated to the United States between 1880 and 1919—the largest stream of immigrants in American history. Not only did the volume of immigration to the United States notably increase during this period, but the primary source of immigration changed dramatically as well. Demographers, social scientists who study patterns of immigration, divide nineteenth-century immigration into two periods: the era of so-called "old immigration" followed by the emergence of a "**new immigration**" pattern.

Before 1880, most immigrants to the United States arrived from northern and western Europe (primarily England, Scotland, Wales, Ireland, and Germany, with smaller numbers from France, Belgium, and the Netherlands, as well as the Scandinavian nations of Denmark, Norway and Sweden). These old immigrants were drawn to the United States because of the availability of inexpensive land and to seek new job opportunities. In addition to these "pull" factors, these immigrants felt "pushed" to relocate because of chaos in their homelands. A wave of revolutions broke out in Europe in 1830 and 1848, creating political and economic chaos. In Ireland, the potato famine drove about 500,000 to cross the Atlantic and resettle in the United States.

Much had changed in northern and western Europe by the 1880s, as these regions entered an unusual period of political stability. After Germany unified in the 1870s, it quickly became an industrial power rivaling Great Britain and the United States. Wages rose and the German state created the world's first social security system. European labor unions won some victories, and France saw improvements in living standards. Immigration from northern and western European countries subsequently began to stabilize, though many immigrants from these regions continued to arrive.

Immigrants from eastern Europe on the deck of the *S.S. Amsterdam*. 1899.

"THE MOST DANGEROUS WOMAN IN AMERICA":
EMMA GOLDMAN

During one of the worst depressions in American history, a time when families feared starvation and men and women begged for work, a Jewish immigrant named Emma Goldman stood up on a soap box in Union Square in New York and, pointing her finger at the regal Robber Baron mansions that lined 5th Avenue, urged an audience that had grown to 3,000 to take direct action. Demand jobs, she said. "If they don't give you work," she said, "ask them for bread. If they deny you bread, take it." The crowd exploded in cheers. The police monitoring the rally had a different reaction. Seeing her words as a provocation to revolution, they arrested her for "inciting a riot" and sentenced her to two years in prison. This didn't faze Goldman, who saw jail time as a price paid in the struggle for social justice.

Born in 1869 to shopkeepers in 1869 in Lithuania, Goldman suffered severe abuse as a child at the hands of her father, who found her unruly and used a whip to discipline her. This only reinforced her rebellious nature. She supported revolution against the Russian czar as a teenager. She fled her father's brutality, immigrating to the United States in 1885. Settling in Rochester, New York, she almost immediately plunged herself into the world of radical American politics. The execution of labor leaders blamed for the November 1886 Haymarket Square bombing shocked her. She embraced anarchism, the belief that any level of formal government serves only the rich and oppresses the masses.

In 1889, she moved to New York City. There, she met and fell in love with another anarchist, Alexander Berkman, who encouraged her to make her first public speeches advocating revolution. In 1892, Berkman would be convicted of attempted murder when he shot and stabbed Henry Clay Frick, the man who crushed a strike by workers at a steel mill owned by Andrew Carnegie in Homestead, Pennsylvania. Goldman had offered to work as a prostitute to finance the purchase of explosives Berkman wanted to use in the attack

Separated from her lover as he served 14 years in prison, Goldman became a social worker. Her life intersected with another moment of political violence in 1901 when a fellow anarchist named Leon Czolgosz assassinated President William McKinley and later claimed he had been inspired in part by a speech Goldman had given. Receiving hostile press attention after the murder, Goldman refused to back down. "As an anarchist, I am opposed to violence," she said. "But if the people want to do away with assassins, they must do away with the conditions which produce murderers."

She became a sought-after public speaker who never shied from embracing unpopular ideas. The Spanish-American War inspired an intense wave of flag-waving patriotism, but Goldman did not hesitate to condemn it as a grab for money and poor people's resources. "...[T]he cause of the Spanish-American War was the price of sugar... the lives and money of the American people were used to protect the interests of the American capitalists." An open atheist, Goldman asserted women's right to sexual freedom outside of marriage, advocated abortion and birth control at a time distributing information on contraception could be criminally prosecuted, and called for women to be paid equally with men for their labor. She called granting the women the right to vote symbolic absent those other freedoms. Speaking of women in early twentieth century America, she said, "Her development, her freedom, her independence, must come from and through herself. First, by asserting herself as a personality. Second, by refusing the right to anyone over her body, by refusing to bear children, unless she wants them; by refusing to be a servant to God, the State, society, the husband . . . Only that, and not the ballot, will set women free . . ."

Goldman would be sentenced to two years' imprisonment at the Missouri State Prison in Jefferson City for opposing the draft in World War I. Berkman, who had been released for his attack on Frick, also went to prison for his anti-draft activities. On December 21, 1919, amid a national panic about radicalism called The Red Scare, the Justice Department gathered up Goldman, Berkman, and 247 other anarchists, communists, and socialists without citizenship and deported them to the Soviet Union. J. Edgar Hoover of the Bureau of Investigation (who would later, for decades, head the renamed Federal Bureau of Investigation) had already dubbed her "the most dangerous woman in America." Like many leftists, she had hopes for the revolutionary regime in Moscow, but the pair left the Soviet Union after two years, condemning it for its corruption and suppression of free thought. She was allowed to tour the United States in 1934 on the condition that she only promote her autobiography and not talk about current events. Due to health problems, Berkman shot himself in 1936. Goldman died in Toronto in 1940 after suffering a stroke. The United States government allowed her to be buried next to the men executed for the Haymarket Square bombings. Goldman spent her life as a dissident, always on the political fringe, but she never lost hope that her dreams would be a future reality. "Every daring attempt to make a great change in existing conditions, every lofty vision of new possibilities for the human race, has been labeled Utopian," she said.

Radically different conditions prevailed in southern and eastern Europe after 1880, prompting a sharp increase in what came to be known as "new immigrants" from Russia, Poland, the Balkans, Hungary, Romania, Bulgaria, Italy and Greece. The Russian Czar (Emperor) Alexander II emancipated the serfs—peasants owned along with the land by large estate holders in the empire's vast countryside. His reform unintentionally left the rich even wealthier and pushed many of the Russian rural poor into an even more desperate state, not just penniless but now often landless. This bungled transition from serfdom followed by Alexander's assassination by a socialist revolutionary in 1881, led to a violent crackdown on radicalism by the Russian government. The chief victims of this oppression were Jews, a favorite target of the Romanov royal family when they desired to distract the public from their military and political failings. Encouraged by the government, mobs murdered at least 40 Jews between April and October 1881. Jews were beaten, shot, stabbed, and their homes and businesses were burned to the ground. This persecution prompted two million Jews to leave the empire between 1880 and 1920, most ending up in the United States. About 800,000 people left Poland (controlled by Russia) and arrived in the United States between 1880 and the start of World War I in 1914. Almost concurrently, more than four million Italians (fleeing economic hard times) resettled in the United States between 1870 and 1920.

New Immigrants and "Whiteness"

Protestant Americans of northern and western European descent typically viewed the new immigrants as non-whites and, therefore, as inferiors. Racial categories have no scientific basis. No definition of racial categories is logically, culturally, or historically consistent. As a result,

the number of artificial racial categories that society creates, and who belongs to those categories, changes at random over time. By the late nineteenth century, Americans of northern and western European descent, particularly the wealthy and the growing middle class, defined themselves as "white," and regarded whites as the master race. A majority of citizens in the early 1800s accepted the "Old Immigrants" as whites who would easily assimilate into American society. Irish immigrants became one notable exception. When they conquered Ireland and stole land from the inhabitants, the English justified their conquest on the grounds that the Irish represented animal-like savages. The English-descended elites who ruled the United States carried the same prejudice and, in political speeches, cartoons, and theatrical presentations depicted the Irish as drunkards and near-animals fit for only the lowest-paid labor. The Catholicism of most Irish did not sit well in nineteenth-century Protestant-dominated America. Anglos did not generally see the Irish as white but as an inferior race. The press routinely used phrases like "simian [ape-like]" or "low-browed" to describe the Irish. However, as the Irish increased in number, came to control law enforcement agencies in cities like Boston, and began to achieve political power, this earlier prejudice began to slowly ebb. The Irish gradually "became" white.

The "New Immigrants" faced a hard road similar to the Irish. Japanese and Chinese immigrants immediately saw themselves cast as racial outsiders. As the nineteenth century progressed, American elites limited the definition of "white" to those of northern and western European heritage. Jews, Poles, Russians, Italians, Greeks, and other New Immigrants routinely found themselves categorized, as Massachusetts congressman and future U.S. Senator Henry Cabot Lodge put it in 1891, as "races most alien to the body of the American people." Journalist and political philosopher Henry George characterized the

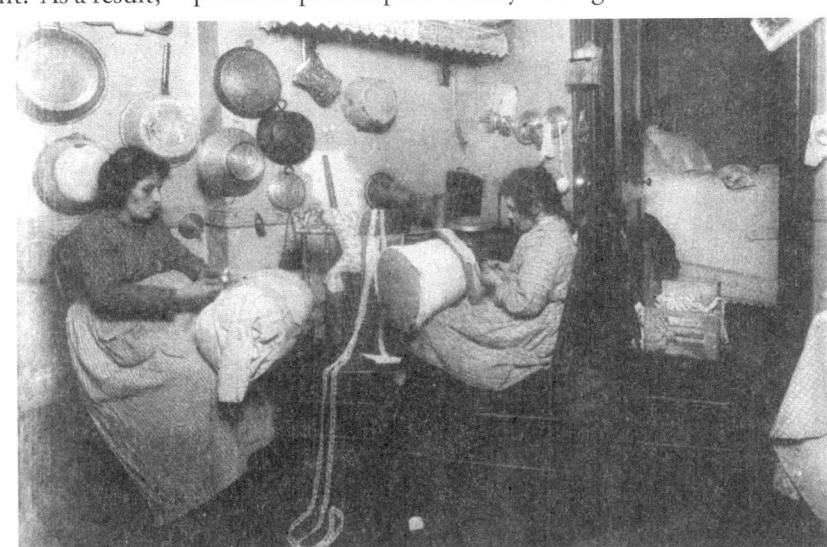

An immigrant mother and her daughter working on fancy lace, perhaps for a pillow, in the kitchen of their tenement house. Women and children often earned additional income at home by doing such piece work. December 1911.

new immigrants as "human garbage." Anglos stereotyped eastern and southern Europeans as violent, self-indulgent, and prone to dangerous revolutionary ideologies like socialism, communism, and anarchy.

The Anti-Immigrant Backlash

As the nineteenth century wound to a close, anti-immigrant forces gained momentum. Several states had already passed laws against the use of foreign labor. The ugliness of the anti-immigrant rhetoric by nativists intensified during and after the depressions of 1882-1885 and 1893-1897. *Public Opinion*, a national journal, described New Immigrants as "long-haired, wild-eyed, bad-smelling, atheistic, reckless foreign wretches, who never did an honest day's work in their lives."

Sicilian workers in particular became targets of violence, particularly in the South, where they were often compared to African Americans. Employers frequently exploited underemployed and underpaid Italians as replacement workers during strikes, which made them convenient targets for retaliatory violence. Mobs lynched Italians in Mississippi and Virginia for allegedly participating in crimes or for socializing with African Americans. The worst incident of anti-Italian violence occurred in New Orleans in 1890, when a group of men shot the city's Police Superintendent, David C. Hennessy. Conscious until the next morning, he told those attending him before he died that he had been attacked by "Dagoes" (an anti-Italian slur). Hennessy had conducted a war against the local Mafia, an organized crime syndicate that traces its origins to 1860s Sicily. The Mafia had become active in the New Orleans area and may have been responsible for as many as 100 unsolved murders in the 26 years following the Civil War. Local authorities eventually indicted 19 defendants for Hennessy's murder. The New Orleans press whipped up fury at the defendants, and elites were convinced of their guilt. Shock reverberated through New Orleans when a jury found six defendants not guilty and declared a mistrial for three others. Since nine defendants faced further charges, authorities kept them under lock and key.

That night, a lynch mob of about 6,000 gathered on Canal Street. They forced their way into the parish prison where the jailers handed over the defendants. Five of the prisoners ran, but the mob chased them down and shot them. The vigilantes hanged two others. In all, locals murdered eleven Sicilians, provoking a protest from the Italian government, which for a time openly spoke of war with the United States. The federal government eventually paid reparations to the families of the lynching victims who had obtained American citizenship.

Chinese immigrants to the West Coast also experienced tremendous prejudice and occasionally violence from members of the dominant white community who resented the large numbers of Asians in their midst. By 1880, some 75,000 Chinese made up a little over 10 percent of California's population. Chinese laborers initially came before the Civil War during the Gold Rush, then later to help construct the transcontinental railroad. In response to voter complaints, Congress passed the Chinese Exclusion Act in 1882 over President Chester Arthur's veto, barring most Chinese from entering the country—the first U.S. law ever to exclude an entire group from entry based on their ethnicity.

The nativist response to mass immigration led to the creation of the American Protective League, which dedicated its efforts to limiting foreign entry into the United States. Pressure on Congress ultimately led to the creation of the Bureau of Immigration in 1890 and the construction of new immigrant processing centers, the most famous being the most used processing facility of them all—New York's Ellis Island. Located in New York Harbor, the Ellis Island facility opened its doors in 1892 and for the next 60 years processed more than 12 million immigrants. In 1907, its busiest year, over a million immigrants arrived (an average of 5,000 per day). Though part of the bureau's job was to screen the arrivals looking for those who fit such exclusionary categories as unaccompanied minors, carriers of contagious illnesses, signs of "imbecility," and known criminals and political radicals, over 98 percent were allowed entry into the United States after basic information was obtained on the immigrants including their names, places of origin, amount of money they possessed, known contacts in the country, and their employment expectations.

LIVING AND WORKING CONDITIONS OF INDUSTRIAL LABORERS

Life in the Tenements

Industrial workers of all backgrounds dwelled in working-class slums located near the factories where they toiled. Not far from the Robber Baron mansions, tenements (low-rise apartments as tall as seven stories) spread across the urban landscape. At one point, more than 2 million people (two-thirds of the New York City population) lived in cramped, foul smelling, and poorly ventilated tenements that often lacked indoor plumbing. Immigrants formed the bulk of tenement residents. Families struggled to pay rent in these tiny apartments, concentrated in Manhattan's Lower East Side where it was not unusual for six to eight people to share a single room just 13 feet across.

Such overcrowding facilitated the rapid spread of disease. Cities provided only scant police protection in poor neighborhoods, turning them into crime centers. At the same time, merchants running stores in or near ghettos, aware of the vulnerability of their customers, routinely overcharged them. Meanwhile, animal and human waste often piled up on the streets along with garbage. Rats thrived in these neighborhoods. Infant mortality in poor and working-class neighborhoods reached a level three times higher than in middle-class ones, particularly during hot summers when filthy streets became breeding grounds for disease-bearing pests. (Nationwide during the Gilded Age, 215 children out of every 1,000 did not live to see a first birthday). Children died from gastroenteritis and diarrhea, outbreaks of flu and measles, and sometimes from complications from malnutrition.

During these years, European scientists confirmed the germ theory, the idea that microorganisms cause illnesses. The concept slowly took hold in the United States in the last third of the nineteenth century, although doctors continued to use blood-splattered gloves and other equipment in hospitals and operating rooms until the 1880s and still did not cover their faces or hair while performing surgery until the start of the twentieth century. Nevertheless, there was a greater emphasis on sanitation, with doctors and other medical care workers washing their hands more frequently and replacing bloody equipment, moves that reduced post-operative morbidity. As cities made greater efforts towards public sanitation—garbage collection and cleaning streets of human and animal waste—infant mortality dropped. Life spans gradually climbed upward. A girl born in 1870 could expect to live on average about 43 years, while a boy could expect to reach age 39. For children born in 1900, girls lived on average 58 years, while boys could expect on average to reach age 51. Life spans would reach the 60s by the 1920s. Unfortunately, public sanitation in poor neighborhoods remained woeful, and members of working-class families died prematurely and unnecessarily.

Reformer Jacob Riis shocked the American reading public by documenting life in New York City's slums with the 1890 publication of *How the Other Half Lives*. Riis's photographs of tenement conditions supplemented the author's heartbreaking words. He described the death of a child in a tenement on Mott Street. Arriving in the rooms a poor family rented, Riis saw "a child dying from some unknown disease . . . the patient . . . stretched upon two chairs in a dreadfully stifling room." The girl was "gasping in the agony of peritonitis that had already written its death-sentence on her wan and pinched face." A doctor diagnosed the cause of her impending death "improper nourishment." Riis went on to describe how the rest of the family had been victimized by Robber Baron era corporate greed. The girl's father had hands "crippled from lead poisoning." Contagious eye diseases left the mother and a little boy nearly blind. "The children cried with hunger," Riis wrote. ". . . For months the family had subsisted on two dollars a week from the priest, and a few loaves and a piece of corned beef which the sisters sent them on Saturday." Riis's book prompted reforms regulating housing quality in New York, including requirements

Miners at the main entrance to the Gary, West Virginia Mine preparing for a ten-hour shift. September 1908.

for ventilation, availability of light in living quarters, increased living space per occupant, and stricter fire safety rules, but none of these laws addressed the underlying cause of the child's death that Riis documented: the miserably low wages paid to immigrants in New York City.

To make ends meet, the poor, including immigrants, sometimes broke the law. Red-light districts offering saloons, drugs, and prostitution grew in cities across the United States. At one point, 200 brothels operated in Chicago and 2,000 prostitutes labored there. Red Light Districts like "Guy Town" in Austin, Texas, "Frogtown" in Dallas, "Hell's Half Acre" in Fort Worth, "Storyville" in New Orleans, and the "Barbary Coast" in San Francisco became popular tourist attractions. Prostitutes received higher wages than they would as factory workers, but endless hardship marked their lives. Some prostitutes began their careers as young as thirteen. Such girls and women faced harassment from police who demanded "protection money" in return for the promise they would not be arrested. In one precinct in New York, police were one-third of the customers. Called "Johns," customers often beat and raped sex workers, who endured abortions, sexually transmitted diseases, and drug and alcohol dependency. Almost 10 percent of sex workers in the era committed suicide.

Company Towns

Gilded Age industrialists sought every way they could to tightly control their workers. During the late nineteenth century, employees at iron and steel foundries, textile mills, and mines often lived in "company towns," where employers built housing, stores, saloons, churches, schools, and other amenities. They hired the teachers who taught the workers' children daily lessons that heaped praise on capitalists and condemned labor unions. Companies hired ministers who preached a similar message. Corporations also employed spies who lived in the town and posed as fellow workers, bartenders, and so on, and reported to management any complaints about supervisors, working conditions, and any desire by workers to unionize. Indeed, the purpose of the company towns was not to facilitate expansion of their operations beyond the confines of the central city as much as the desire to remove their employees from outside influences such as labor unions and socialists.

Employees living in company towns such as Steinway Village in New York (where workers manufactured Steinway pianos), Pullman, Illinois (where employees made railroad and subway cars), Hershey, Pennsylvania (a chocolate manufacturing center) and the mining town owned by John D. Rockefeller in Ludlow, Colorado, lived under constant surveillance. That made resisting exploitation difficult, but the way company towns paid workers gave management even more control. Company towns paid workers in "scrip"—paper slips printed as a substitute for legal tender. This private money could be spent only to pay rent for company-owned housing, or to buy items at company-owned stores. Scrip held no worth outside the company town. This arrangement allowed companies to overcharge for all items sold within the town. Workers fired by employers in company towns faced multiple hardships. They became homeless after they were kicked out of company-owned housing. Company stores no longer sold items to them and the scrip they carried became useless, leaving them penniless. Companies placed such workers on "blacklists," a list of alleged troublemakers distributed to similar companies. Workers on these lists had trouble getting new jobs. Such a system of near total control made fighting for better working conditions an even harder challenge.

Industrial Working Conditions

The low wages, long hours, brutal pace demanded by supervisors, and the dangerous working conditions at "respectable" jobs at factories and mills explain why prostitution and other criminal activity might have seemed a viable alternative. Management routinely engaged in "wage theft," or financially shortchanging their employees. Workers at cloth mills received pay by how much they produced and supervisors routinely under-measured their output. In mines, supervisors intentionally under-weighed the coal and other raw materials miners produced in order to claim a quota had not been met and to keep the miners working even after they had met the requirement for a shift. Seamstresses and other workers in the clothing industry were denied the use of chairs during shifts that could last 12 or more hours and faced steep fines for minor infractions, such as a quarter (the equivalent of $6.65, or two days' wages) for being five minutes late for a shift and similar penalties for eating at their work stations, or taking time off to drink a glass of water.

Mechanical clocks began appearing in American mills in the 1830s, which allowed supervisors to more tightly police the working hours of their employees. As indoor electricity spread across the United States in the 1880s and 1890s, factories increasingly operated around the clock and supervisors told workers to speed up production or get fired. Some factories hid clocks from workers in order to trick employees to toil past their shift.

If not a high concern for management, safety on the job was a perennial concern for workers. American factories had the highest accident rate of all the industrializing nations yet, unlike other countries, had no workmen's compensation system. In 1913, over 25,000 worker fatalities took place in the U.S. while 700,000 experienced serious workplace-related injuries. At one Butler, Pennsylvania steel mill, four men died after the molten steel poured on them and 30 suffered serious burns when a pot of molten metal accidentally spilled on wet sand, sparking an explosion. A coffin factory became a deathtrap when a boy got caught on a shaft rapidly spinning at 300 revolutions per minute. The machinery decapitated him and yanked off both of his arms and legs. A machine at a caramel factory in Philadelphia tore another worker, Martin Stoffel, limb from limb in front of about 100 coworkers when he got caught in the gears. "Before the machinery could be stopped, Stoffel had been literally chopped to pieces," a report read.

Women and Child Labor in Industrial America

Women made up 20 percent of the paid workforce in the United States by 1900. Both economics and technology drove the trend towards more women in the workplace. Factory machines erased differences in average upper-body strength between men and women, expanding the number of jobs that even teenaged girls could perform in a factory setting. Women proved to be tough, productive and reliable workers. Due to sexism, employers paid them substantially less than men for the same work. Therefore, women in eastern seaboard cities came to dominate clothes manufacturing, cigar making, and other fields due to wage discrimination.

At the sweatshops that manufactured clothing, the owners paid women per piece of clothing completed. Companies required women to pay for the sewing machines and the thread they used to make clothes and in the mid-1880s in New York women only earned $1.50 for making a dozen trousers, 15 cents for vests and 90 cents for completing a dozen gloves (approximately $40, $4, and $24 in 2016 dollars). Yearly wages worked out to about $12,000 a year or less, adjusted for inflation. Sweatshop labor led to chronic backaches, repetitive motion stress disorder, and respiratory problems from breathing in fibers. Bosses also often sexually exploited female workers. The buildings themselves were life-endangering firetraps.

Women participated in the American Federation of Labor, but by the 1890s that labor organization offered only tepid support for women fighting against hiring, promotion, and wage barriers. Women responded by forming their own unions, such as the Collar Laundry Union in 1863 in Troy, New York; the Women's

Typographical Union No. 1 in 1869; the International Ladies Garment Workers Union in 1900; and the Women's Trade Union League in 1903. Teenaged girls often did the important work for local unions, recruiting new members, forming strategy, and carrying the signs on the picket lines during strikes.

In the northern industrial states, and (not long after emancipation) in the South, financial pressures forced African-American women to work outside of the home as field hands, domestics, or other low-wage jobs. Employers discriminated against black men in terms of employment opportunities and wages, which meant that African-American men struggled to support their families with their wages alone. In 1900, 43.5 percent of non-white women ages 16 and older worked outside the home as opposed to just under 18 percent of white women.

The exploitation of one particularly vulnerable group of workers, children, would provoke the most intense outrage of reformers in the late nineteenth century and early twentieth century. As slaves, and then as sharecroppers, African-American children had spent their days picking crops or performing other grueling labor almost as soon as they could walk and understand instructions. The use of white children as workers, paid and unpaid, extended back to the beginning of the colonial era, when girls in particular essentially became domestic servants once they grew past the toddler stage. During the Gilded Age, many parents, either out of desperation to supplement their family's income or because they simply did not think that there was anything wrong with putting their young children to work, sent their kids out to find gainful employment. Children were the lowest paid of all workers in urban-industrial America. In addition to working as delivery boys, food vendors, and shoe shiners on the city streets, many worked in factories, especially in the South, where many worked in textile mills. By 1900, children made up almost 20 percent of the paid American workforce.

In many industries, such as mining, children often performed dangerous tasks. In the nine coal counties in Pennsylvania, workers suffered 513 fatalities in 1901 out of 148,000 employees. Coal mines employed boys between the ages of 8 and 12 to break coal into nearly standard-sized pieces, removing clay, soil, rock, and other impurities in the process. "Breaker boys" worked in the anthracite (hard) coalmines of northeastern Pennsylvania. As they broke chunks of coal, dust covered their bodies and entered their lungs. This exposure commonly led to black lung disease, severe bronchitis and chronic obstructive pulmonary disease, conditions pandemic among coal miners. Boys sometimes wore gloves to protect their hands from getting cut by hard rocks, but

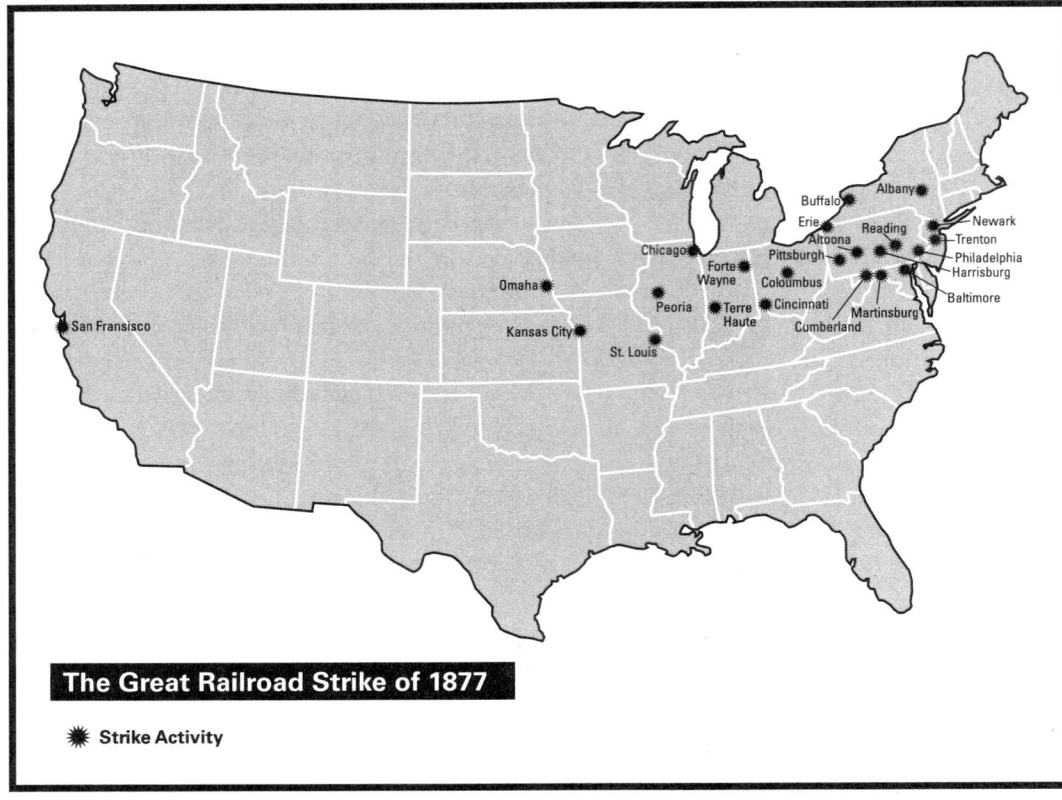

Map 18.2 The Great Railroad Strike of 1877 that brought rail traffic in much of the country to a standstill.

bosses noticing this beat them. Children working near coal crushing machines often went deaf. They pulled 11- or 12-hour shifts, with only one day a week off. They rarely saw sunshine, had no time for the schooling that might give them a better life, and no opportunity to play.

THE RISE OF ORGANIZED LABOR

While a few dedicated reformers endeavored to create national labor unions during the antebellum years, the movement began in earnest after the Civil War in response to the new industrial conditions. Some of these efforts were limited to organizing skilled craftsmen in a given industry, but many others sought to unite a wide range of skilled and unskilled workers involved in each sector of the economy. Though a few dedicated labor activists desired upending the capitalist order and promote social revolution, most desired to achieve what they viewed as basic economic justice in the form of better pay, reasonable work hours, and safer working conditions.

The Great Railroad Strike of 1877

Reconstruction had barely ended when the **Great Railroad Strike of 1877**, one of the largest collective labor actions of the nineteenth century, began on July 16, 1877. Railway workers, unable to absorb a deep pay cut after multiple previous wage reductions, walked off the job after the Baltimore & Ohio Railroad announced it would slash pay 10 percent. Gould and other railroad executives implemented the same wage reduction nationwide, inspiring strikes across the nation. Workers' uprisings unfolded in Baltimore, Buffalo, Chicago, and San Francisco. Only New England and the Deep South remained untouched by the labor unrest. Workers held sympathy strikes in other industries. Evolving into a national movement, the strike turned violent in Pittsburgh when workers seized control of railway switches, preventing the lines from operating, leading the company to dispatch armed guards to regain control. The private army fired on the strikers, killing 20, which provoked workers to set fire to more than 2,000 railroad cars.

Strikers in Chicago and other major cities called for the federal government to seize the railroads and for the industry to be turned into a public utility. Workers demanded a national law setting the workday at eight hours, and the abolition of child labor. By 1876, unemployment due to the depression reached a peak of 14 percent. Numerous towns and cities passed "tramp ordinances," which allowed police to arrest the unemployed caught begging for work or food. Strikers demanded an end to these laws. The movement broke the color line, with whites and African Americans marching side-by-side in Galveston, Texas, where dockworkers and employees of the Texas & Pacific Railroad manned the picket lines side-by-side. In an ominous foreshadowing of future tactics, employers played a game of racial divide-and-conquer by bringing in underemployed African Americans as replacement workers.

Mayors and governors sent desperate messages to President Rutherford B. Hayes to bring the strike to an end. Hayes was in the process of ending Reconstruction by withdrawing troops from Louisiana, Florida, and South Carolina, and dispatched some of these men to break the strike. Soldiers captured control of railway lines, protected replacement workers, and broke up union meetings. In all, police and local militias killed more than 100 workers nationwide. By August, the strike was basically over, although a few pockets of resistance remained. Workers' demands remained unmet, but repeated major strikes would mark the next four decades.

The Emergence of National Labor Unions

Several notable northern labor leaders who had fought in the Union Army during the Civil War and had been proud of their role in ending slavery began after the war to call for the eight-hour workday as another struggle against bondage. Twelve-hour shifts made education and recreational opportunities almost impossible. Union leaders argued that recreation was part of the life of any truly free person, but the industrial age denied workers the right to pleasure by entombing them almost every waking hour in factories and mills. Unions called for eight hours for work, eight hours for rest, and eight hours for everything else. Congress implemented an eight-hour workday for federal workers on June 25, 1868, but the

fight for the 48-hour workweek in the private sector proceeded at a snail's pace. The Illinois state legislature, for instance, passed an eight-hour workday law in 1867, but major employers in the state largely ignored it, prompting a pushback from labor unions.

Almost three-quarters of a million workers joined the **Knights of Labor** by the mid-1880s. The group's constitution adopted in 1878 called for a prohibition of child labor and convict labor (the use of prisoners as unpaid workers), a graduated income tax on the wealthy, and the creation of a labor arbitration system to make strikes a thing of the past. Many Knights were socialists who advocated government ownership of the railroads, which were widely despised for their high rates and poor service. Dreaming of creating "one big union" that encompassed all workers, the Knights of the 1870s and 1880s advanced a degree of tolerance unusual for the late nineteenth century, welcoming African Americans and supporting equal wages for women, who represented one-fifth of the group's membership.

A more conservative union arose to challenge the Knights. The Federation of Organized Trades and Labor Unions, established in 1881, changed its name to the **American Federation of Labor** (AFL) in 1886. Led by Samuel Gompers, a British-born son of a cigar maker who participated in his first strike at age 18, emphasized organizing highly skilled workers not easily displaced by technology. Gompers and the AFL did not promote socialism or call for revolution. Instead, Gompers focused on what he saw as pragmatic, attainable goals, such as the eight-hour workday and higher wages. Though there was no formal ban on their membership, few women and even fewer African Americans joined the AFL. The Knights of

The Haymarket Square bombing in Chicago.

A bomb exploded during a mass labor rally in 1886 calling for the eight-hour work day and protesting police violence against striking workers at the nearby McCormick plant.

Labor overshadowed the AFL in terms of membership in the mid-1880s and sought more radical action.

The Great Southwest Strike

Although it played no major role in the 1877 railroad strike, the Knights of Labor became one of the chief beneficiaries of that action, and the group saw a major boost in membership afterwards. Beginning in 1883, the Knights began a campaign against Jay Gould's railroad empire in the Great Southwest Strike of 1886. The Knights led a successful strike in 1885 against the Wabash Railroad, owned by Gould, after he fired some members of the union. The Knights completely shut down the Wabash line in the southwestern United States. Gould ultimately promised not to target Knights members for termination in return for the Knights' leader, Terrence Powderly, agreeing not to stage any future strikes without first holding negotiations with Gould.

The next year, Gould broke his promise when his Texas and Pacific Railway fired a foreman in Marshall, Texas. This action led to a strike that spread throughout the Southwest. Workers snarled up rail traffic by uncoupling cars and gaining control of key junctures. Gould refused to negotiate and then persuaded Texas Governor John Ireland to use Pinkerton detectives, the Texas Rangers, and local militias to protect strikebreakers. This combined armed force regained control of the lines. Powderly conceded the futility of the strike, and the Knights surrendered, beginning its long decline, with the group's more utopian vision giving way to the AFL's more piecemeal approach. The struggle to create "one big union" uniting all industrial workers to end the dominance of capitalism morphed into a more immediate struggle to win the eight-hour workday.

A Bombing in Haymarket Square

A combination of worker anger, elite fears of immigrants, a violent, renegade police force, and a hyperbolic, conservative press fanning panic over political radicals provided the combustible elements leading to a terrorist bombing at **Haymarket Square** in Chicago in 1886. Throughout the 1880s, the pages of the *Chicago Tribune* newspaper were filled with alarming stories of Irish nationalists seeking liberation of their island from Great Britain, as well as tales of anarchists setting off bombs and assassinating political leaders in Europe. The Chicago press also expressed alarm at the immigrants pouring into the city and the allegedly high number of anarchists, socialists, and communists who lurked among them.

Labor discontent boiled over the years as the McCormick Reaper Works increasingly replaced workers with machines and hired guards from the Pinkerton Detective Agency, which stood ready to use violence to crack down on any potential strikers. Workers increasingly spoke of the need for self-defense while a German anarchist who had resettled in Ohio, Johann Most, published a book on how to make explosives from nitroglycerine and how to use dynamite.

All this anger, paranoia, and xenophobia came to a head in the spring of 1886. Years earlier, union leaders set May 1, 1886, as the target day by which they hoped that the eight-hour workday would become standard nationwide. When that date arrived, workers across the nation held demonstrations. In Chicago, where workers called May 1 "Emancipation Day," 30,000 did not report to work in support of the eight-hour movement. Many others who did work walked off the job after clocking their eighth hour. Mill, steel, and slaughterhouse workers marched in the city waving red flags, a symbol of the socialist movement,

At a 3 p.m. rally on May 3 outside of the McCormick plant, where experienced skilled workers had recently been fired and replaced with lower-wage, younger workers, a fiery socialist newspaper editor, German immigrant August Spies, delivered a speech to workers who had been locked out by the plant managers. McCormick had hired replacement workers called "scabs" by union members. The replacement workers received protection from heavily armed police. Spies urged the strikers to stand united regardless of the pressure they might face. As Spies spoke, shifts changed, and the replacement workers filed out, walking past the angry strikers. Spies called on all to stay calm. A fight still broke out between the two groups. The police, 200 strong, waded into the crowd hitting strikers with nightsticks, and fired their guns, killing two strikers.

Workers held another rally the next night at Haymarket Square. Speakers continued their demand for the eight-hour day, and also condemned the recent police violence. The group of orators included Spies and Albert Parsons, a Texan who (though he had served in the Confederate Army during the Civil War) supported black voting rights in his home state during Reconstruction and had married a mixed race woman before moving to Chicago where he edited a radical newspaper called *The Alarm*. Mayor Carter Harrison had been watching the rally, which at its peak drew 1,500 people. Concluding it was peaceful, he instructed the police to go home. Police ignored Harrison. As the rally wound down and the crowd dwindled to 600 people, Police Inspector John Bonfield loudly announced, "I command you in the name of the law to desist and . . . disperse." At this signal, 176 officers started beating the protestors. This time, however, a bomb went off. After hearing the explosion, police fired wildly into the panicked crowd. Seven officers died that night, with two dying later from wounds, many of them accidentally shot by their fellow officers.

The next morning, the Chicago press, including the *Chicago Tribune*, declared the rally organizers had conspired to murder police officers and plotted the bombing as the first stage of a revolution. For the next two months, police raided the homes of hundreds of working class men and women, often in the middle of the night, ransacking their residences, and beating witnesses. Police attempted to coerce confessions from suspects by locking them in "sweatboxes," cramped enclosed spaces deliberately kept uncomfortably hot. Meanwhile, newspapers suggested that lynching the suspects, including Spies and Parsons, might be appropriate. The movement for the eight-hour day lost steam. Even as the strikes ended, some Chicago employers who had agreed to pay their workers ten hours' pay for an eight-hour shift reneged on their promise.

A grand jury indicted ten men for murder, and eventually put eight on trial. The suspects were mostly targeted for being immigrants or anarchists rather than on the basis of evidence. Police found explosives in the residence of only one suspect, Louis Lingg. One suspect was charged with murder largely because he possessed copies of one of the local radical newspapers. Only two defendants were actually in Haymarket Square when the bomb exploded. As the trial began June 21, 1886, prosecutors paid witnesses for their incriminating testimony. The jury announced its verdict on August 20, sentencing seven defendants to be hanged and one to serve 15 years of hard labor.

On November 10, Illinois Governor Richard J. Oglesby commuted two death sentences while another defendant, Lingg, committed suicide by chewing a blasting cap that had been smuggled into his jail cell. Jailors marched the four condemned men, including Parsons and Spies, to the gallows the next morning, on November 11. Alarmed by the dubious evidence and the biases of the judge and jury at their trials, Illinois Governor John Altgeld pardoned the three surviving men in 1893. Chicago Mayor John Roche later fired John Bonfield, the police inspector, who directed the police violence at the McCormick plant and the next day at Haymarket Square, when it was revealed that he had taken bribes from saloonkeepers and prostitution rings and sold personal property stolen from suspects. The bombing damaged the movement for the eight-hour workday for years and was exploited by the media as a warning of the dangers supposedly posed by unions. Meanwhile, the executed men became labor movement martyrs, and May 1 became International Workers Day, a major commemoration celebrated globally in honor of the Haymarket Square incident.

The Battle of Homestead Mills

Much to the consternation of his fellow industrialists, Carnegie went out of his way to publicly praise unions and the right of workers to organize. More than any other Robber Baron, Carnegie cared about his public image perhaps not just for politically strategic reasons but also for emotional ones as well. Criticism apparently deeply hurt the steel magnate, and he celebrated when one union named a meeting hall after him. Seemingly desperate for approval, he would visit steel mills and joke with the workers. Witnessing the labor unrest in the country, he wanted to make sure the public saw him as a peacemaker. In an 1886 article for the magazine *Forum*, Carnegie hailed the "triumphal march of labor" in the previous 300 years, and proclaimed that in his view workers enjoyed equal status with employers and he insisted that the right to form unions was "sacred." The attitude that Carnegie presented towards the workers at his steel mills could not have been in starker contrast to his published words. By the dawn of the twentieth century, Carnegie Steel out-produced Britain, France, and Germany combined. American steel companies had grown rich from railroad construction, but now it provided an extensive network of pipes for the oil industry, beams and girders for skyscraper construction, factory machines, and armaments for the world's militaries. In 1890, Carnegie's company made $5 million in profit in one year ($133 million today, adjusted for inflation) In spite of his kind words about workers, a significant part of that profit margin came from reducing costs by overworking his employees and keeping their wages as low as possible.

Carnegie sought to not waste a penny at his mills. He required detailed records from his employees, with logs tracking the productivity of each worker and their supervisors. Managers were rewarded with promotions and bonuses for cutting costs or were fired if they failed to keep up with their peers. "If he can win the race, he is our racehorse," Carnegie once said of his managers. "If not, he goes in the cart." The savings from this exploitation allowed him to undersell his competition, acquire more mills, and dominate even more of the industry.

Carnegie made a fateful decision in 1886 when he hired Henry Clay Frick as chair of his steel company. The Pennsylvania businessman had founded the H.C. Frick Coke Company, which provided a fuel used in steel production, and he had been a major supplier for Carnegie's steel plant. Carnegie admired Frick's aggressiveness, confidence, and willingness to take risks. A man who took no holidays, and who showed up at work by sunrise and stayed at his desk well past sunset, he meticulously learned every detail of the steel business. In three years, he rose to the position of company chairman and had increased company profits by a third.

Unlike Carnegie, Frick made no pretense about supporting unions. In 1886, workers formed the Amalgamated Association of Iron and Steel Workers (AAISW) and staged several walkouts at Carnegie mills when the company sought to re-impose 12-hour shifts where employees had won the eight-hour battle. After the company tried to reduce wages in 1889, union members argued that higher wages were justified because of the dangers and high death rates at Carnegie mills and walked off the job. Carnegie Steel took out ads for replacement workers. When the replacements showed up at the Homestead Mills plant, east of Pittsburgh along the banks of the Monongahela River, 2,000 strikers blocked the gates. Workers at another Carnegie mill threatened a sympathy strike. The company avoided a crisis by agreeing to recognize the AAISW, meaning that the union won the right to negotiate contracts on behalf of all workers and to approve or reject any new hires. Both parties singed a new contract set to expire on July 6, 1892.

About 1,000 of the 4,000 workers at Homestead Mills belonged to the AAISW. Frick made a priority of breaking the union. As the deadline for a new contract approached, he insisted that steel workers get paid per ton based on the price of steel. Overproduction meant that steel prices were dropping, and Frick's proposal meant a significant pay cut. The union rejected this proposal, and Frick hired 300 Pinkerton guards to use as security and as replacement workers. The Carnegie Steel chair prepared for war. In May 189s2, Frick ordered a solid wood fence topped with barbed wire, spotlights, and sniper nests built around the mill's three-mile perimeter. Workers jokingly referred to the foundry as "Fort Frick." AAISW members seized control of a railroad loading platform that they feared would be used to bring in replacement workers. By June 29, the plant had shut down. Meanwhile, Frick outfitted barges to transport Pinkertons to seize control of the foundry.

On July 5, at 3 a.m., three barges bearing Pinkertons armed with pistols and Winchester rifles sailed down the Monongahela. A giant alarm whistle alerted union members of the approaching force. By 4 a.m. thousands of workers, their relatives, and sympathetic citizens gathered on the river's banks to prevent the guards from establishing a beachhead. One of the barges reached the dock in front of the mill and another stayed nearby. (The third barge eventually left). Thousands of strikers gathered on the shore in front of the barge. A Pinkerton captain ordered the crowd to disperse. The guards started coming ashore, swinging clubs. Two shots rang out and soon a guard and a union member fell to the ground, hit by bullets. The gun battle lasted 10 minutes, with 27 union members and Pinkertons wounded. A second round of gunfire erupted at 8 p.m. when a group of Pinkertons tried to get ashore, and four union members died. The battle went on for 15 hours, when a white flag went up on one barge and the Pinkertons surrendered. Exhaustion and rage boiled over, and the strikers forced the surrendered Pinkertons to run a gauntlet. The crowd kicked and beat them with fists, clubs, and the butt ends of rifles. In all, six workers died that day, with 17 suffering wounds. One Pinkerton guard committed suicide rather than surrender to the strikers while two others died in the exchange of volleys, but more than 200 had been wounded.

The public initially backed the workers during the **Homestead Lockout** even as Frick and Carnegie resolved that no union member would ever work at the plant again. To prevent another siege, Pennsylvania Governor Robert E. Pattison dispatched the National Guard to seize the plant on July 12. Police arrested union leaders for murder and treason, though they were acquitted. Later, some Pinkerton guards would be arrested for homicide as well.

The Homestead uprising had already shifted in favor of Carnegie, but the strikers' efforts died on July 23, 1892, when Alexander Berkman, a Russian-born anarchist, made a failed assassination attempt against Frick at Carnegie Steel headquarters. Although there was no connection between Berkman and the AAISW, the union got blamed by the public for the murder attempt, which played into every anxiety that middle class Americans had about immigrants, unions, and violence. The public turned against the strike. A court sentenced Berkman to 21 years in prison for the attempted murder. He served until 1907.

The strike continued, but in November most of the workers gave up and returned to work. The AAISW collapsed. Wages for workers fell to half the pre-strike levels even though Frick re-imposed the 12-hour day. The chief effect of the harsh struggle had been to kill unionism within the steel industry for many decades. The last steelworkers' union folded in 1903. Organized labor would not organize steel workers again until 1937. Meanwhile, Carnegie Steel's profits multiplied tenfold between the year before the strike to 1900. In 1901, Carnegie sold his steel company to a pool of investors organized by financier J.P. Morgan for $480 million (about $1.4 billion today).

INDUSTRIALISM AND THE "NEW SOUTH"

Henry Grady, the editor of the *Atlanta Constitution*, witnessed the explosive growth of industry in the North, the emerging northern middle class, and the giant fortunes accumulated by men like Rockefeller and Carnegie, and feared that time had passed by the South, which seemed mired in a backwards, agricultural past. His worries deepened as cotton prices dropped in the last third of the nineteenth century and the region's widespread poverty only deepened.

Across the South, a cult of the "Lost Cause" arose. Almost every town and city in the region erected statues of Confederate heroes and commemorated the war's fallen combatants on Confederate Memorial Day and the failed noble crusade they had supposedly died for. Southern preachers taught that the "Old South" before the Civil War had been a land of virtue, and that the commander of the Army of Northern Virginia, Robert E. Lee, had been a secular saint. God was supposedly testing the faith of white Southerners, like the ancient Hebrews in the Christian Old Testament, by subjecting them to post-war hardship.

Grady tried to convince his fellow Southerners to move this past antebellum nostalgia. Northern industrialists had much to teach Dixie, the editor said, suggesting that defeat in the Civil War had been a hidden blessing. "The Old South rested everything on slavery and agriculture, unconscious that these could neither give nor maintain healthy growth," he said in a speech to the Bay State Club in Boston in 1899. "The New South," he declared, "understands that her emancipation came because through the inscrutable wisdom of God her honest purpose was crossed, and her brave armies were beaten." Grady cajoled Northerners to locate textile mills and other manufacturing concerns to the former Confederacy and help create that "New South." He promised his fellow Southerners a happier era with an economy not dependent on something so unpredictable and hard to control as cotton prices.

Grady's New South turned out to be less than the Millennium. Unwilling to pay decent wages to northern workers or negotiate with unions, textile mill owners shut down in New England and reopened in Alabama, Georgia, and the Carolinas, where the labor force received even lower wages than their Yankee peers. Mining increased, with Alabama ranking second among the states in iron ore production by 1889. Coal mines, steel plants, bottling works, and brickyards began to dot the southern landscape. Sheriffs cracked down ruthlessly on union organizers to the point of murder, and employers could count on a racially divided pool of employees. However, the economic impact was less than expected and most in the New South remained as poor as their predecessors in the Old South.

The New South rested upon white supremacy. As Grady himself said, "the supremacy of the white race of the South must be maintained forever, and the domination of the negro race resisted at all points and at all hazards, because the white race is the superior race . . ." Grady believed that he had to reassure poor and struggling whites, who felt mired at the social bottom, that they formed part of a racial ruling caste. In the slavery era, poor whites knew that, as powerless as they were economically and politically, they could never occupy the lowest social rung. Since the Civil War, African Americans had risen from slavery and gained voting rights and legally stood equal with their white neighbors. Too many southern whites saw this as coming at their expense. To ensure the loyalty of poor whites who had so little to gain from the status quo, to restore their sense of privilege as part of a "master race," and to create physical and psychological distance between blacks and whites so they would not make common political common cause against the era's leadership, southern states began to implement **segregation** laws mandating physical separation along color lines.

These statutes came to be known as "Jim Crow" laws, named after a stock character in minstrel shows, live variety shows performed on stage in which white actors wore black makeup as they comically impersonated African Americans and imitated their music styles. Even Republicans required segregated schools during Reconstruction. The concept spread in the 1880s and 1890s, especially with the spread of southern railroad networks. The railroads set aside cars for "whites only" and "blacks only." Usually, a train had only one black car and these crowded accommodations were kept intentionally shabby. The railroad companies required black and white customers to use separate waiting rooms as well. Soon, segregation laws mandated separate seating in theaters, with African Americans confined to balcony seats if they were allowed to enter at all. Restrooms were set aside for men, women and "colored" and many buildings provided no bathroom facilities for African Americans. Blacks found themselves barred from white-owned barbershops, hotels, restaurants, saloons, and dance halls. Eventually, blacks were not allowed on "white" ambulances and had to form their own ambulance companies; hospitals even racially separated blood supplies. Ironically, Jim Crow opened the door for the rise of an African American business community that provided services whites denied black customers.

The Fourteenth Amendment provided for "equal protection under the law" for all citizens regardless of color, but the United States Supreme Court refused to acknowledge that segregation laws violated both the spirit and the letter of this clause. In 1896, the Court with its ***Plessy vs Ferguson*** decision upheld the constitutionality of segregation laws. Homer Plessy, a Louisiana resident, sued when he was denied seating in a "white-only" section of a train. By a 7-1 vote, the Court ruled that separate facilities did not stamp "the colored race with a badge of inferiority." As long as accommodations provided to African Americans were equal, they could be separate and still be consistent with the Fourteenth Amendment. The notion that poorly-funded Jim Crow schools and hospitals, intensely-crowded blacks-only neighborhoods, or the inadequate space given black customers on trains could be considered remotely equal was absurd on its face. Southern school systems in the first two decades of the twentieth century spent more than three times on white students than they spent on black students. But the Supreme Court stuck by its "separate but equal" fiction until its 1954 *Brown v. Board of Education* ruling that banned segregation in public schools.

Southern voting restrictions imposed in the 1880s and 1890s rendered African Americans politically powerless to stop the Jim Crow onslaught. The former Confederate states required citizens pay poll taxes in order to be able to vote, a levy that most African Americans could not afford. Some southern states also required citizens to pass literacy tests, exams designed to be almost impossible to pass in order to be eligible to vote. The tests were particularly difficult for an African-American population that had been systematically denied an adequate education. Since the laws imposing these requirements did not mention race, color, or previous condition of servitude, the courts for years ruled that these laws did not violate the Fifteenth Amendment, even if the intent of these laws was to disenfranchise African Americans. Unintentionally, many poor, illiterate whites could not vote because of the new barriers to the ballot. The racial intent of poll taxes and literacy tests became clear when states responded by adding "grandfather clauses" to election laws. Louisiana became the first to pass such a statute in 1898. The law said that if an individual was eligible to vote before 1867, or had a parent or grandparent who could vote before that date, that citizen could vote without having to take the literacy test or pay the poll tax. Since African Americans could not vote before 1867, they still had to meet those requirements. North Carolina, Alabama, Georgia, Maryland and Oklahoma soon passed similar laws. The Supreme Court ruled that grandfather clauses violated the constitution in 1915 in *Guinn v. United States*, but states

with such laws found new ways to deny African Americans the ballot. Like the Old South, the New South remained an unwelcoming place for people of color.

GILDED AGE POLITICS

Corrupt politicians in the palm of big business enabled the rise of the Robber Barons. Much of the idealism that fueled the Republican Party in the lead-up to the Civil War and during Radical Reconstruction drained after the war, with the intense reformers in the party nudged aside by party hacks who placed in the White House a series of ineffective, mostly forgettable presidents. Marked largely by mediocrity in leadership, the Gilded Age nevertheless remained a time of intense political passion. As the historian Mark Wahlgren Summers points out, the nation's strong interest in politics led to a golden age for newspapers, a time when cities like Chicago could support 18 dailies, Detroit published eight, and most towns at least a pair of competing papers. During the 1880s, an estimated 80 percent or more of all eligible voters cast ballots on election days, while in some heated races, the turnout of registered voters reached as high as 95 percent. Political cartoonists like Thomas Nast of *Harper's Weekly*—responsible for such images as the elephant and donkey that came to symbolize the Republican and Democratic parties, respectively—became celebrities as they lampooned shady officeholders. Meanwhile, two magazines devoted to political humor—*Puck* and *Judge*—enjoyed big readerships and political rallies and speeches served as a major form of entertainment. All this political obsession, passion, and derision, however, did not lead to any significant effort to cope with such important issues of the day as income inequality, the disenfranchisement of women, or the ongoing oppression of African Americans in the South.

American Law and the Rise of Big Business

The court system nurtured the growth of American big business and its Robber Barons in the post-Civil War era, often at the expense of consumers, small business, and workers. Cities, counties, and states increasingly employed eminent domain—exercising government power to seize private property so it can ostensibly be utilized for the public good. Government entitites condemned farms, small homes, etc., so the land could be used by railroads, factories and other big businesses, even as judges increasingly shielded major corporations from government regulation. The late nineteenth century saw the rise of the concept of "corporate personhood."

William Marcy "Boss" Tweed

Courts began to treat corporations, in terms of law, as being "persons" enjoying all constitutional rights that flesh-and-blood humans enjoyed.

This legal status provided corporations a shield from government regulation after the adoption in 1868 of the Fourteenth Amendment, which said that no state shall "deprive any person of life, liberty or property without due process of law . . ." When the Fourteenth Amendment was ratified, the amendment was understood to apply to freedmen and to protect African American civil rights. The rights of corporations never came up in the ratification debates. Yet, even as state and federal courts ignored repeated violations of African American civil liberties, they used the Fourteenth Amendment to shield businesses from regulatory laws, ruling that such statutes violated these companies' right to due process. For example, in the 1905 *Lochner vs. New York* decision, the Supreme Court overturned a law that prohibited bakeries from requiring employees to work more than 60 hours a week, claiming that the law represented a denial of property (the money a bakery would have to spend to hire additional bakers because of limits on the work week) without granting bakeries due process (the right to resolve conflicts over pay and the length of the work week in a civil court before a jury).

Urban Political Machines

The moral rot that lay at the heart of American politics stood in full view in almost every major American city: New York, Chicago, Philadelphia, Boston, Baltimore,

Cleveland, St. Louis, and Kansas City. Sometimes the "boss" controlling a **political machine** held a high elective office, such as mayor, but often they operated entirely in the shadows like an organized crime chieftain. In corrupt municipalities like New York, political machines expanded the number of public offices in order to create jobs for political supporters. Such employees often paid back a portion of their salaries to the machine to keep their positions. Jobs were given with no regard to qualification. City employees such as police officers, fire fighters, building inspectors, and health officials used their new positions of authority to collect graft, which they shared with the machine. Police officers often demanded a percentage of the profits from illegal gambling, prostitution, or rigged sporting events like boxing matches, in return for not arresting the participants in these crimes. Owners of saloons and other businesses paid bribes to keep from having their operations shut down and any licenses revoked because of alleged safety or health code violations. Builders and other contractors had to pay bribes if they wanted to do business with the city. These contractors ended up paying back as much as two-thirds of what they got from the city, but made that up by grossly overcharging for their frequently shoddy work.

Tammany Hall, run by New York City's Democratic Party leader William "Boss" Tweed, became the most infamous political machine in the United States. As a young man, Tweed won an election as a New York City alderman and then captured a seat in the United States House of Representatives. Essentially running the city, he held no law license but still demanded fees from local corporations for "legal services" and used these bribes to buy up valuable real estate. Winning a race for the New York State Senate in 1870, he still ran New York City's municipal government, particularly its treasury department. He embezzled a fortune through a number of swindles. Tweed's ring stole as much as $200 million in public money in 2016 dollars.

A fiscal crisis developed as a result of this corruption. Investigations by *The New York Times* and a slew of hostile cartoons by Thomas Nast outraged the public, leading to Tweed's conviction on larceny and forgery in 1873. Released two years later, he was taken into custody again in 1875. Tweed escaped and made it to Cuba, and then to Spain, but was arrested when someone recognized him because of Nast's cartoons. He died of pneumonia in a New York City jail in 1878 at the age of 55.

Political machines could not have maintained power for as long as they did if they did nothing for their constituents. Political bosses operated in a generally corrupt political environment in which supposedly clean campaign donations from oil, steel, railroad, and other major business interests bought favorable legislation. Establishment politicians, in return, ignored poverty, workplace injuries, and other hardships suffered by the working class. Many workers backed the political bosses and sometimes embraced them enthusiastically. One Tammany Hall operative, William "Big Bill" Devery, the superintendent of New York City Police (later a co-owner of the New York Yankees professional baseball franchise), became a master of graft, building a million-dollar fortune under the table while earning a mere $6,000 a year salary at his government job. Devery, however, cleverly plowed back some of his ill-gotten gains into his constituents' neighborhoods. He dispatched an army of women called "Devery's Deaconesses," who searched for financially struggling families. After reporting back to their boss, he arranged for these families to receive medical care, food, milk, and clothing. Devery's network treated children in the city to a "Himalaya of ice cream," and the superintendent arranged for bands and theater troupes to entertain striking coal miners. Such machine politicians could buy a lot of love simply by occasionally acknowledging the needs of constituents ignored by supposedly more ethical public figures. Such love, however, was always conditional. At election time, these recipients were expected to vote for Tammany candidates if they wished for such help to continue.

The "Spoils System" and Civil Service Reform

The longstanding "spoils system" whereby jobs were dispensed by incoming presidential administrations as rewards for political loyalty and in return for favors, had long been an engine for corruption, a problem that only worsened as the federal government expanded in size during the Gilded Age. Federal departments minus the military employed 53,000 people in 1865, the year that the Civil War ended. Two decades later, that number had risen to almost 130,000. As with the urban political machines, federal departments routinely gave contracts to the supporters of the current administration. Local postmasters subsidized newspapers that backed the party they supported and refused to deliver newspapers endorsing the opposition.

Scandal may have defined the Grant administration, but Rutherford B. Hayes of Ohio, perceived as having been awarded the White House due to a backroom deal (the Compromise of 1877) in spite of losing the election, entered his presidency under an ethical cloud. He surprised his peers, however, when three months into his administration, he issued an executive order that barred federal employees from participating in politics. Hayes urged Congress to pass **civil service reform** legislation that would require those applying for some jobs in the federal bureaucracy to pass an objectively graded exam before they could be appointed, but Congress refused to move. Hayes then picked a fight with New York's famously corrupt Senator Roscoe Conkling, a so-called "Stalwart Republican" who hoped that Ulysses Grant could come out of retirement, win the 1880 election, and serve a third term as president. Conkling's feud with Hayes began when the president tried to dump the senator's three cronies who had been running the New York Customs House. Hayes wanted to appoint more reputable men, but this led to a split in the Republican Party leading up to the 1880 presidential election.

President Hayes had promised that he would serve only one term when he ran in 1876. The Stalwarts at first lined up behind Ulysses S. Grant, but the former president was unable to shake memories of his tarnished tenure in the White House. Grant also lost the support of powerful Republicans such as Senator James G. Blaine of Maine, who decided to seek the presidency himself. Blaine, committed to civil service reform, enjoyed widespread approval from like-minded Republicans, insultingly labeled "Half-Breeds" by the Stalwarts because they were supposedly not pure party loyalists. Neither Grant nor Blaine could win a majority of the delegates at the 1880 Republican National Convention. The Half-Breeds switched their support to Representative James Garfield, a bright congressional leader from Ohio who had survived revelations that he had received discounted stocks from the Crédit Mobilier Company, which sold the shares in return for friendly legislation. For party unity, Garfield named a Stalwart, Chester A. Arthur of New York, as his running mate.

Garfield's commitment to cleaning up corruption was weak at best. Conkling refused to help his campaign until Garfield met with Conkling's associates and promised to consult the New York senator before he made any appointments related to the Empire State. To win Wall Street support, Garfield campaigned for raising the tariff on foreign-made goods and told the old railroad executives that he would give them final say on any prospective Supreme Court nominations. The Democrats nominated Winfield Scott Hancock, a Union general during the Civil War. Hancock opposed a higher tariff and drew opposition from labor because of his role in cracking down on the Great Railroad Strike of 1877. The popular vote in the election that fall was close, with Garfield winning 48.3 percent to Hancock's 48.2 percent. Garfield won the Electoral College by a wider margin, 214-155. His coattails did not extend far, however, as the Republicans maintained only a 12-seat majority in the House of

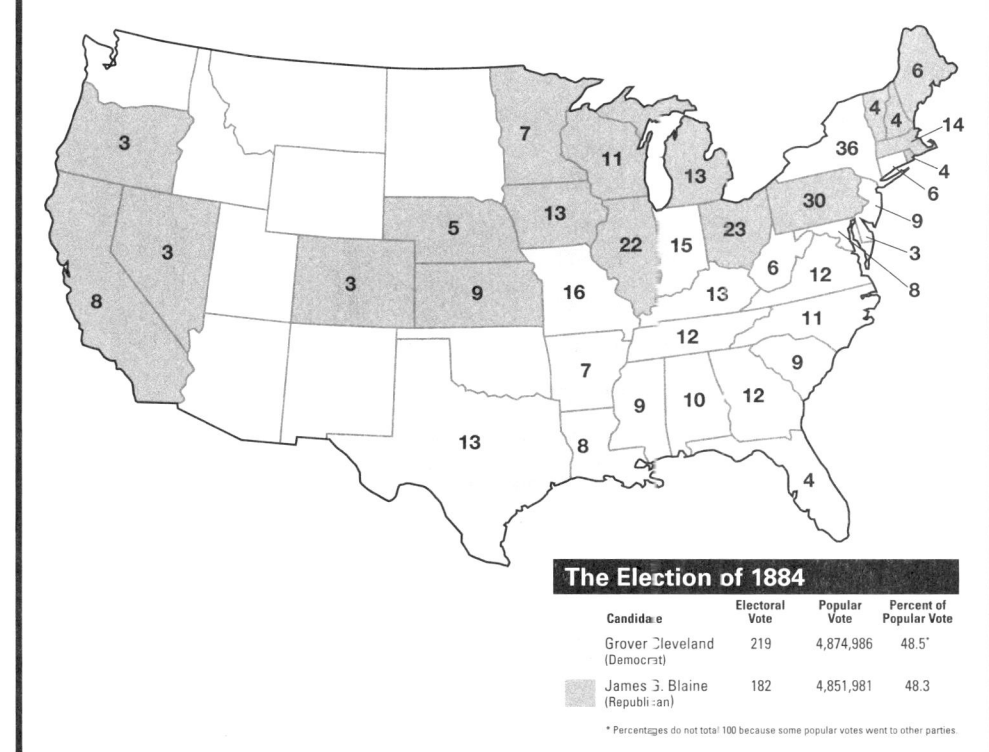

Map 18.3 The Election of 1884

The Election of 1884

Candidate	Electoral Vote	Popular Vote	Percent of Popular Vote
Grover Cleveland (Democrat)	219	4,874,986	48.5*
James G. Blaine (Republican)	182	4,851,981	48.3

*Percentages do not total 100 because some popular votes went to other parties.

Representatives while the Senate evenly split between the two parties.

Garfield's presidency lasted only four months before he was killed by a crazed assassin. Office seekers had been swamping the White House after Garfield's election, and the new president had a hard time turning away party members wishing appointments. One of those office seekers was Charles J. Guiteau, a mentally ill man who had failed earlier in life as a lawyer and a preacher. He convinced himself that he stood next in line for the throne of Great Britain and that he had played a major role in electing Garfield president. Guiteau expected to be appointed ambassador to France as a reward, and he stalked the new president for weeks. Incensed at being ignored, on July 2, 1881, Guiteau followed Garfield to the Baltimore & Potomac Railway Station in Washington, D.C. and shot him twice in the back. Garfield survived until September 19, but probably died from infections caused when doctors inspected his gunshot wounds with unsanitary instruments and unwashed hands rather than from his initial injuries. Guiteau insisted on representing himself at his trial. Found guilty, he died at the gallows in Washington, D.C., June 30, 1882.

Garfield's premature death made civil service reform inevitable, with Guiteau symbolizing the madness of the spoils system. Few had high expectations of the new president, Chester Arthur, a creature of the national capital's pay-to-play culture. Nevertheless, two years into

his term, Arthur signed the **Pendleton Act**, sponsored by Senator George H. Pendleton, an Ohio Democrat. The legislation required applicants for jobs classified as civil service positions to take open, competitive exams, made it illegal for officeholders to demand political contributions from federal employees, and imposed limits on nepotism (appointing relatives to office). Under the flawed law, government departments and not the newly created Civil Service Commission administered the exams and the fairness of the results were often suspect. Major departments like the Post Office and the Internal Revenue Service also remained under the spoils system.

The law, nevertheless, provoked controversy within the Republican ranks. Arthur's sudden commitment to reform alienated his Stalwart base and doomed his chance to be nominated for a term in his own right in 1884. Stalwart Republicans instead pushed through the nomination of Blaine, the former Maine senator and Garfield's former Secretary of State. Blaine could not win the support of reformers, who saw him as corrupt because of his involvement in the Crédit Mobilier imbroglio. When Blaine secured the nomination, yet another dissident faction of Republicans called the "**Mugwumps**" split from the party and campaigned for the Democratic nominee, New York Governor Grover Cleveland, who enjoyed a reputation as a clean politician. (Republican loyalists coined the sarcastic Mugwump label, which derived from the Algonquian word "bigwig." Party regulars viewed them as self-righteous purists.)

The 1884 presidential race soon sank into character attacks, with Democrats calling Blaine a crook, and the Republicans revealing that Cleveland had fathered an illegitimate child while a bachelor. Republicans chanted at rallies, "Ma, Ma, Where's my Pa? Gone to the White House, Hah! Hah! Hah!" Mugwump defections probably cost Blaine the election, causing him to lose New York's 36 Electoral College votes. Only 57,577 votes out of almost 1.2 million cast separated the two candidates in the popular vote, which Cleveland won, but in the Electoral College Cleveland triumphed by a 219-182 margin to become the first Democrat to win the White House since James Buchanan captured the presidency in 1856.

The Impact of the "Long Depression"

Neither the Republicans nor the Democrats had any imaginative solutions to cope with what economic historians have called "The Long Depression"—a series of sharp economic downtowns that plagued the nation from 1873 to 1878, 1882 to 1885, and 1893 to 1897. In fact, the ideology of both parties made the country's economic situation worse. For elites, the period from the 1870s to the turn of the twentieth century represented boom times. For farmers and industrial workers, disappointment, hardship, and despair marked the period. The government withdrew "**greenbacks,**" paper currency not backed by gold that had financed the Civil War and boosted wages and increased profits for manufacturers supplying the Army and Navy. Farmers received top dollar from Washington, D.C. for feeding soldiers, sailors and marines, and the horses, oxen and other animals the military needed for transportation. Employment increased, and flush farmers invested heavily in new land, building barns, fences, and other infrastructure, and purchasing farming equipment.

The conventional economic wisdom of the nineteenth century held that "fiat currency" (paper money not backed by precious metals of "intrinsic worth") was unstable in value and likely to spark out-of-control inflation. Government officials listened to this view and returned to a policy of "hard" currency. As greenbacks were taken out of circulation, the money supply shrank even as the postwar population expanded. Farmers earned less money for what they produced, industrial workers earned lower wages, and products sold for lower prices, thus triggering rapid deflation. The shrinking money supply particularly injured heavily mortgaged farmers who often defaulted on loans, lost their land, and fell into tenancy or sharecropping. Meanwhile, the factories and mills

of the nineteenth century overproduced almost every product, which further depressed prices. The low wages paid to workers gave them little spending money, which cut business profits. As a result, recurring bouts of high unemployment stalked the U.S. economy from 1870 to 1900.

Organized Farmer Protests

Industrial workers did not suffer alone as the Gilded Age unfolded. The misery in urban tenements found its match in the vast American farm belt. While workers fought to gain a voice through labor unions, farmers over three decades formed one of the most significant radical political movements in the United States. Active in what came to be known as the "Populist Movement," from the 1870s, growers threatened to overturn longstanding economic policies, democratize the political process, and even to revolutionize race relations in the South. This effort inspired a furious backlash from the Democratic and Republican establishments, leading to the birth of a third political party, **The People's Party**, which became more commonly known as "The Populist Party."

With the end of the Indian Wars, more white-owned farms sprang up on the Great Plains and the western states. Droughts, freezes, hail storms, and waves of locusts, however, battered the newcomers. Nevertheless, American farm production increased 135 percent between 1870 and 1900. Still, these bountiful harvests, coupled with increasing foreign production, contributed to falling crop prices that slashed farmers' incomes. Wheat and cotton prices dropped about 60 percent between the 1870s and 1890s.

Government policies tightening the money supply made the farm crisis worse by ending the printing of greenbacks and halting the minting of silver. Financially battered and losing their land to foreclosure, Western farmers banded together to establish the National Grange of the Order of the Patrons of Husbandry, better known as the Grange, in 1867. The group grew exponentially, eventually claiming 1.5 million members concentrated in the Plains States and the South. The Grangers took a two-pronged approach to alleviating farmers' plight. They lobbied state legislatures in Wisconsin and Illinois to pass laws regulating the rates that railroads could charge farmers and prohibited price-fixing conspiracies in which companies agreed to suspend competition and charge customers similar prices at high levels. The Supreme Court, however, overturned these "Granger Laws." The Grange also sought to address the overcharges that they suffered at the hands of merchants who sold farm equipment and supplies like seeds, and warehouses and silos that stored grains. They established their own country stores, warehouses, and grain elevators. Through these cooperative businesses, the organization hoped to provide low-interest credit and discount prices to farmers. Unfortunately, financial institutions had little interest in helping potential competitors get off the ground, so the Granger co-ops had a hard time obtaining credit. Additionally, the depression of 1873-1878 swamped the Granger-operated businesses. The group's political and business failures led to a sharp decline in Grange membership by 1880. Nevertheless, the Grangers established a precedent for farmer activism during the 1880s and 1890s.

Farmers not only battled with overcharging creditors and railroads, they also rebelled against the two-party system. A policy of "hard currency" backed by gold enjoyed bipartisan support. Frustrated by this consensus, farmers established the National Greenback Party in time for the 1876 presidential election but only gained 80,000 votes. Discontent caused by the depression, however, and an effort to expand its appeal to urban workers helped the party grow. The renamed Greenback-Labor Party won more than 1 million votes in the 1878 off-year elections and elected 14 members to the Congress. The 1880 party platform, far more progressive than those of Democrats and Republicans, called for an expansion of the money supply, women's suffrage, an eight-hour workday, a graduated income tax, and federal regulation of interstate commerce. The depression ended two years earlier, however, which took the urgency out of the money issue. Former Union General James B. Weaver waged a spirited, eloquent campaign for president in 1880. Nevertheless, Weaver received only 308,578 votes (3.32 percent of the total). The party competed in one more presidential race, in 1884, but its support dropped almost by half and most members drifted back into the Democratic or Republican Parties.

The Farmers' Alliances

The struggle against tight money and overcharging by so-called "middlemen" did not end as the Grangers went into decline. During the 1880s, tens of thousands of farmers formed "alliances," to provide mutual aid and lobby for political reform. As the movement grew, the farmers consolidated into two regional alliances, the Northwestern Farmers Alliance, which included the old Grange states of the Midwest and the Plains and the far more radical Southern Farmers Alliance, which began in Texas but spread as far east as the Carolinas. By 1890, the federation claimed more than 3 million members. The Southern Alliance reached across the color line and recruited black farmers, although on a segregated basis,

by encouraging a separate National Colored Alliance that enrolled another quarter of a million members.

Borrowing an idea from the Grange, the Alliance established farmers' cooperatives. Farmers sold commodities as a group instead of competing with each other in the hope that they could command higher prices. The Alliance also established country stores, which became sources of low-interest credit for its members. Alliance stores and other businesses ran into the same problem that the Grangers had in obtaining credit, and these cooperatives closed. After this failure, farmers concluded that reform could succeed only through political reform.

Alliance members met in Cleburne, Texas in 1886 to draft a set of demands that called for state legislatures and the Congress to regulate railroads, outlaw land speculation, ease access to credit for farmers, and issue paper and silver currency to expand the money supply. These reforms languished, however, stymied by Democratic and Republican politicians dependent on the campaign contributions provided by big businesses.

Democrats, Republicans, and "Hard Money"

Alliance leaders began to consider formation of a third political party as the only means to get their demands met. The Democrats had dominated the South since the 1830s, with the exception of Reconstruction. Grover Cleveland, a former sheriff, mayor of Buffalo, and governor of New York, assumed leadership of the party in 1884, when he became the first Democrat to win the White House in 28 years. In an age of corruption, he enjoyed a reputation as the rare "clean politician." He also turned out to be a hard-core economic conservative, vetoing popular spending measures, including a pension bill for Union Army veterans. In 1887, he did sign the Interstate Commerce Act, based in part on ideas proposed by the Greenback Party the previous decade. The law created the Interstate Commerce Commission, the first-ever federal regulatory agency. The statute gave the ICC the power to ensure that railroad rates were "reasonable and just" and banned the rebates railroad companies had given giant corporations like Standard Oil and Carnegie Steel to the disadvantage of smaller competitors. Cleveland, however, would not budge on printing greenbacks or resuming the coining of silver. This "gold bug" stance played a role in a depression lasting from 1882-1885.

That downturn had ended before Cleveland mounted his reelection campaign in 1888 against Indiana Senator Benjamin Harrison. After a dull, passionless campaign in which Cleveland made only one public appearance and the main debate centered on the incumbent's support for a lower tariff and Harrison's backing of a high one to prop

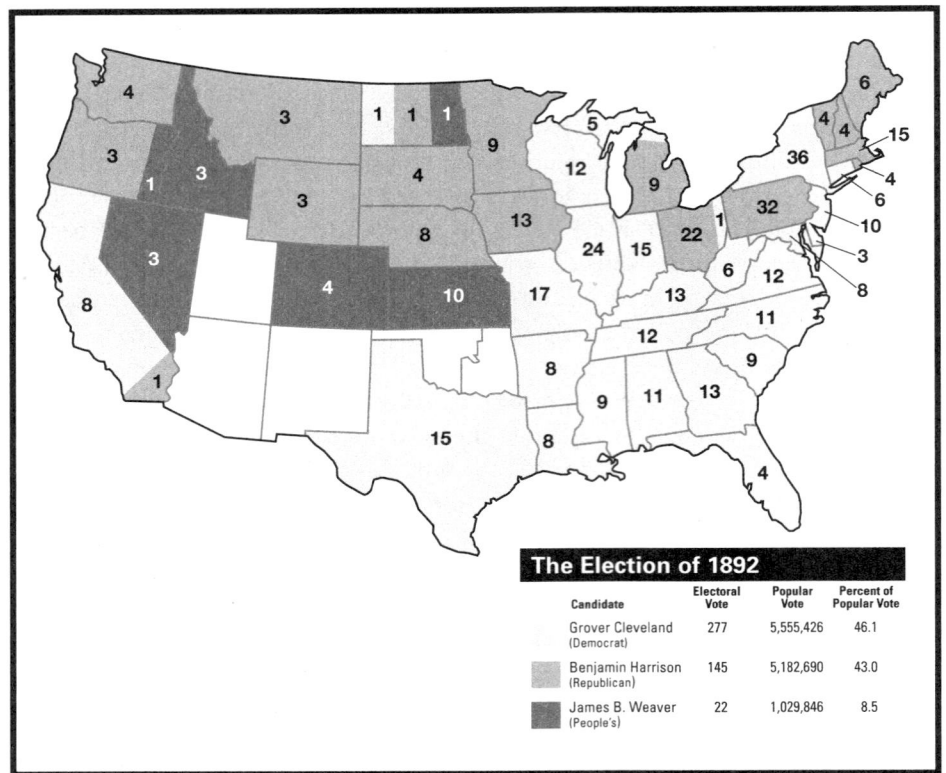

Map 18.4   The Election of 1892

The Election of 1892

Candidate	Electoral Vote	Popular Vote	Percent of Popular Vote
Grover Cleveland (Democrat)	277	5,555,426	46.1
Benjamin Harrison (Republican)	145	5,182,690	43.0
James B. Weaver (People's)	22	1,029,846	8.5

up American manufacturing, Cleveland won the popular vote by over 100,000 votes, but lost the Electoral College in large part because he could not carry his home state of New York. There, the Tammany Ring in New York City had bitterly opposed his campaign against corruption in the state government. Seeking revenge, they undermined Cleveland's re-election bid.

Harrison continued his predecessor's hard-money policies. He did, however, sign the Sherman Silver Purchase Act, aimed at helping Western mining interests that were hurt when the government stopped minting silver coins. The bill required the United States Treasury to buy 4.5 million ounces of silver a month at full market price, nearly the entire output of Western mines. In response to the widespread public dislike of business oligarchs like Rockefeller, Harrison also signed into law the 1890 Sherman Anti-Trust Act. The bill outlawed "every contract, combination in the form of a trust or otherwise, a conspiracy in restraint of trade." Unfortunately, the law vaguely defined "trusts" and the United States Supreme Court, in its 1895 *U.S. vs. E.C. Knight* decision ruled that the law only applied to commerce—sales—and not manufacturing, thus placing the competition-stifling actions of Carnegie and Rockefeller at least momentarily out of reach. Presidents made little use of the law to curb monopolistic business practices for more than a decade until Theodore Roosevelt became president in 1901. Yet, even though the law never mentioned labor unions, the courts used the legislation to break up strikes, holding that when unions led job walkoffs, they were acting in restraint of trade and therefore constituted a "trust" of workers.

The Populist Challenge

With conservatives dominating both major parties, Alliance movement farmers decided to break with their old political loyalties. Forming the People's Party in February 1892, candidates under this banner called for creation of the so-called subtreasury system, which would act as a combination of government warehouse and lender. Farmers could store nonperishable crops in government facilities until commodity prices allowed them to sell at a reasonable profit. In the meantime, farmers would receive credits from the federal government based on the amount of crops they stored, which would allow them to maximize their earnings and "get by" until the next growing season.

Populists also called for excessive land bought for speculative purposes by foreign investors and railroad companies to be seized by the government and redistributed to poor farmers. Other demands called for government ownership of the railroads and telegraph lines as a way to end overcharging. Addressing the tight money supply, the Populists called for the coining of silver and the printing of greenbacks. Wishing to expand their appeal beyond the farm belt, they also supported the eight-hour workday and the abolition of convict labor. Finally, pushing for reforms to further democratize the political process, the party platform advocated laws requiring the secret ballot, the direct election of senators, and the right of referendum and recall of elected officials.

Harrison won re-nomination on the Republican ticket, while Cleveland won the Democratic nomination, thereby earning a chance for a rematch of the 1888 race. Supporters of Harrison and Cleveland spent the fall arguing about the 1890 McKinley Tariff, which raised the tax on foreign-made goods by a stunning average of 48 percent. Farmers especially hated the tariff, which came on top of a financial panic that year. This one-two punch devastated Republicans in the 1890 congressional elections, with Democrats becoming the majority in the House after gaining 86 seats. The Populists won eight seats. Republicans stilled controlled the Senate. Two Populists—William Peffer of Kansas and James Kyle of South Dakota—won seats in the upper chamber. Republican candidates still bore the burden of their unpopular policies in the 1892 elections, with Cleveland becoming the first and to date the only president to win non-consecutive terms; he captured both the popular vote, 46 percent to 43 percent, and the Electoral College by a comfortable margin. The People's Party did well for a third party, capturing more than a million votes in the 1892 presidential election, about 8.5 percent, and twenty-two electoral votes. The Populists won three more seats in the U.S. House and captured a third seat in the Senate.

A tragedy prevented the Populists from gaining even better results. The most acclaimed leader of the Populists, Leonidas Polk of the Southern Alliance, was a sure bet to win the party's presidential nomination but died from a hemorrhaging bladder before he could be nominated. A veteran of the Confederate Army, Polk had worked extensively to build the Northwestern Alliance and was well liked across regional lines. His replacement, James B. Weaver of Iowa, carried the baggage of being a former Union commander, which hurt him in the South. Southern Democrats also claimed that Populists would split the white vote and, if they succeeded, the supposed "negro rule" of Reconstruction would return. Populists stood accused of being race traitors and of insulting the memory of the Confederate dead by supporting a northern officer for president. In the North, Republicans also played on regional passions, bashing Populists for voting side-by-side with former Confederates. This political exploitation of unresolved bitterness from the Civil War came to be known as "waving the bloody shirt." The tactic proved effective in many communities.

Southern Democrats feared the willingness of Populists to form alliances with black farmers. Tom Watson, a disillusioned Democrat who joined the Populist Party and represented it in the United States House from 1891 to 1893, argued that Democrats manufactured conflict between blacks and whites in order to keep both groups distracted from the theft committed against both groups by wealthy whites. "You are kept apart that you may be separately fleeced of your earnings," Watson said. He promised that the Populists would erase this racial division.

Republicans and Democrats alike brutally oppressed the movement. In the North, Republicans turned to vote fraud, bribery, and intimidation. In the South, these methods were supplemented with violence, up to and including the murder of Populist leaders and supporters. Nevertheless, Populism grew even stronger as a result of a national depression that began in 1893. Both farmers and factory workers were devastated by this downturn, which lasted for four years. At one point, three million people, or 20 percent of the country's workforce, could not find jobs. Hunger and suicide became rampant as hard times dragged on.

In 1880, George Pullman, manufacturer of elegant dining, parlor, and sleeping cars for the nation's railroads, constructed a factory town named after him located ten miles south of Chicago. The planned community provided homes for workers, parks and playgrounds, and even its own sewage-treatment plant. In 1894, the Pullman Palace Car Company laid off hundreds of workers and slashed wages by 33 percent without reducing rents. In response, thousands of workers joined the newly formed American Railway Union (ARU), led by Eugene V. Debs. The Pullman workers joined an ARU-staged strike. Union members working for the nation's largest railroads refused to switch Pullman cars, paralyzing rail traffic in and out of Chicago, one of the nation's most important rail hubs. The strike spread nationwide, with railroad workers refusing to handle trains carrying Pullman Cars. The company would not budge, and workers in some cases set fires to Pullman cars. Workers not belonging to the ARU also joined the struggle.

In response, the General Manager's Association, an organization of top railroad executives, decided to break the union. The managers imported jobless scabs from the East Coast and asked U.S. Attorney General Richard Olney, a former railroad attorney, for a federal injunction (court order) against the strikers for allegedly refusing to move railroad cars carrying U.S. mail. Bolstered by President Grover Cleveland and citing the Sherman Antitrust Act, Olney secured an injunction against the union's leaders for restraint of commerce. As a federal court issued an injunction calling on strikers to return to work, Cleveland dispatched 12,000 troops to crush the uprising and reopen rail lines. Federal marshals killed

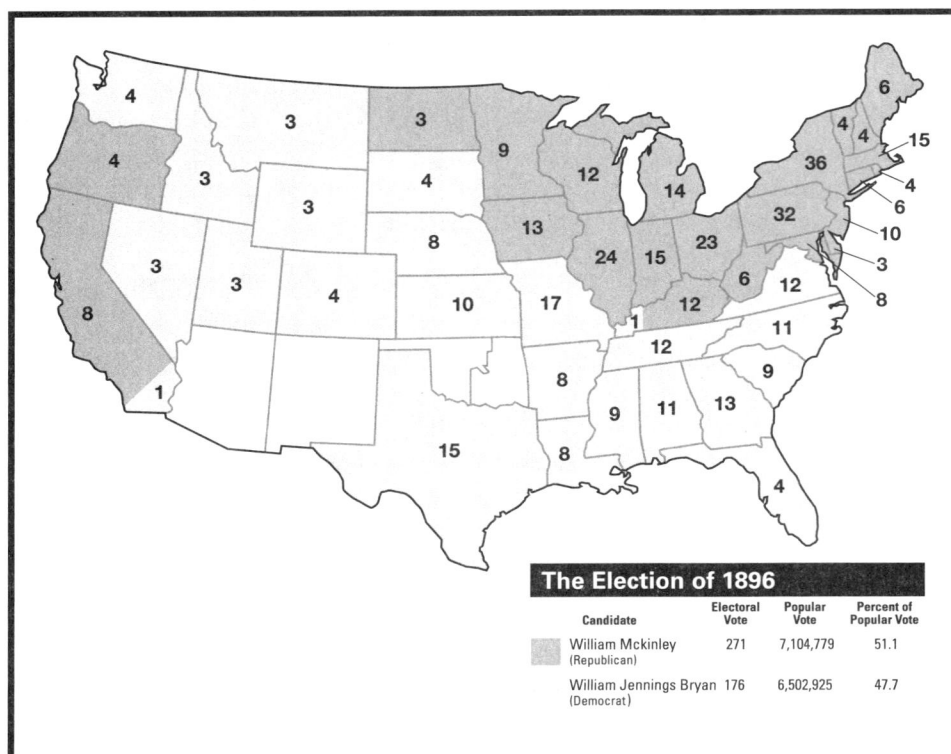

Map 18.5 The Election of 1896

The Election of 1896			
Candidate	Electoral Vote	Popular Vote	Percent of Popular Vote
William Mckinley (Republican)	271	7,104,779	51.1
William Jennings Bryan (Democrat)	176	6,502,925	47.7

two strikers in Kensington, Illinois, not far from Chicago, while authorities arrested Debs and put him in prison for defying the court order by continuing the strike. When the Supreme Court in the 1895 case, *In re Debs*, upheld Debs's prison sentence and legalized the use of injunctions against labor unions, the judicial system made its support of big business clear. To ease the workers' anger, the House and Senate unanimously passed a bill creating Labor Day, which Cleveland signed within days of destroying the ARU. The new holiday, however, did nothing to defuse the spirit of rebellion energizing the Populist movement,

The 1896 Presidential Election and the Collapse of Populism

With discontent turning to despair, voters seemed eager for an alternative to the Republican and Democratic Parties, and the Populists looked like a serious threat in the 1896 presidential race. The coinage of silver became a particularly popular political stand in Western states where silver mines operated. Populists pinned their hopes of victory on being the only political party advocating the coinage of silver. These hopes grew when the Republicans ignored public discontent with the status quo, nominating a conservative, Ohio Senator William McKinley, for president in 1896. Throughout the campaign, McKinley remained a solid supporter of the gold standard.

Southern and western Democrats rebelled against the incumbent Democrat, Cleveland, whose economic policies were indistinguishable from McKinley's positions. Instead, the party nominated former Nebraska Congressman William Jennings Bryan, who attracted a national following by focusing on the miseries of the farm belt and by blasting the greed of bankers and big business. In a speech at the 1896 Democratic National Convention, Bryan loudly declared his support for coining silver, telling a rapturous audience, "Having behind us the producing masses of this nation and the world . . . we will answer [the financial interests'] demand for a gold standard by saying to them: 'You shall not press down upon the brow of labor this crown of thorns, you shall not crucify mankind upon a cross of gold.'" Bryan aimed his speech not just at the Democrats at the Chicago convention, but at the millions of Populists he hoped would join a common front with the Democrats against a still solidly pro-business Republican Party.

The Populist leadership grew impatient with the third-party strategy and concluded that they should back Bryan's campaign. As a result, the People's Party also nominated Bryan for president, although they replaced Bryan's Democratic running mate, economic conservative Arthur Sewell, with former Congressman Tom Watson, as the vice presidential candidate. Ultimately, the nomination of Bryan undermined Populism. Bryan's policies represented pseudo-Populism at best. He embraced only the least significant part of the Populist program, the coining of silver. More substantial reforms called for by the Populists, such as providing access to government credit for farmers, the establishment of cooperative warehouses, and government ownership of the railroads and telegraph lines, were ignored by the Democratic nominee.

Many southern Populists could not swallow supporting the Democratic presidential nominee when so many had been the target of Democratic fraud and violence in the 1892 and 1894 elections. Support for the Populist Party dropped in the South. Nevertheless, even though McKinley raised an unprecedented $16 million in campaign contributions from corporate interests (about $460 million today), the election proved to be surprisingly close. For his part, Bryan had only his eloquence and his tirelessness as he toured the country, delivering hundreds of speeches that reached 5 million voters in the three months after the convention. The heavily populated Northeast backed McKinley, while Bryan carried most of the Plains States, the Rocky Mountain West and the Old Confederacy. Several factors hampered Bryan. An improvement in the economy just before the election made many voters reluctant to back a candidate widely perceived as radical and, as in past elections, Republicans north of the Mason-Dixon Line padded their vote total through deceit. Southern voters supportive of the Democrats also suffered confusion since Bryan's name appeared on the ballot twice, once as a Democrat and once as a Populist, and he was paired with two different running mates. In the end, McKinley carried twenty-three states to Bryan's twenty-two, even though the Electoral College gave the Republican a comfortable 271-176 margin.

"Fusion"—joining forces with the Democrats -- proved a disaster for the People's Party. In their clamor to support the Democrat Bryan, Populists had lost their separate identity. With an improved economy, southern whites returned to the party of their fathers, the Democrats. The People's Party straggled on for years, a shell of its former self. The party withered, and with it, the agrarian revolt that had emerged during the 1880s and 1890s. The Democrats would gain a near monopoly on political power in the South that they would hold until the 1960s and 1970s. In Populism's aftermath, the Southern Democratic Party incited lynch mobs to kill thousands of African Americans. State constitutions were rewritten to take the vote away from not only blacks but also poor whites who might become African-Americans' political allies.

FARMERS AND LABOR VS. CAPITAL: A ONE-SIDED WAR

If, as Howard Zinn wrote, the late nineteenth and early twentieth centuries marked "America's Other Civil War,"

this conflict turned out to be a one-sided affair. Workers and farmers badly outnumbered the wealthy, and this numerical advantage provided a weapon. If they stood united, they could shut down factories, entire industries (as in the case of the 1877 railroad strikes), or cities (as the case with much of Chicago during the Haymarket Affair). Industrial workers occasionally won battles over the eight-hour day or wages, and farmers, through the pressures of third parties, won passage of piecemeal reforms like the Interstate Commerce Act, but these victories were often short-lived or purely symbolic.

Most of the weapons in the war between labor and capital rested in the hands of economic elites. Wealth was an inherent, built-in advantage. Rich corporations could starve out unions during long strikes. But money was also important for what it could buy. Corporate elites used money to fund the campaigns of politicians who passed legislation favorable to the financially favored, such as tariffs that made foreign-made products more expensive. Corporate-funded politicians resisted regulations that mandated decent wages, workplace safety, clean food and water, banned child labor, provided medical care and compensation for workers injured while on the job, and a graduated income tax in which the wealthier would pay more in order to fund quality education for the common person. The corporate-financed politicians who ran city halls across America hired police departments that were used to spy on, harass, intimidate, and in some cases assassinate union leaders. Corporate-supported governors and presidents appointed judges who used the Fourteenth Amendment not to protect African American civil rights, and the Sherman Anti-Trust Act not to curb the monopolistic practices of large corporations, but to shield big business from regulation, and to halt strikes. The wealthy owned the largest newspapers in the country, which usually depicted unions as overrun with murderous revolutionaries who would sow bloodshed and chaos if they prevailed.

Among their many advantages in the "Other Civil War," the fact that the wealthy overwhelmingly came from a similar background (as mostly English-speaking, white Anglo-Saxon Protestant males) ranks as one of the most important. Except regarding immigration laws, generally American economic elites, even if they remained business competitors, saw the world the same way, knew how to translate their desires into public policy, and had the financial means and the influence to achieve their political goals.

The one great advantage the working class had, their sheer numbers, was also their greatest weakness. The working class divided along cleavages of race, ethnicity, gender, language, and religion. Thus, African Americans, generally shunned both by employers and by unions who saw them as lower-wage competitors, served as strike breakers alongside Italian immigrants desperate for work under almost any conditions. The wealthy manipulated tensions within the working class, and the labor unions thus often failed to effectively enlist women, African Americans, Chinese immigrants, and other marginalized groups to their cause.

Given these disadvantages, the labor movement displayed remarkable persistence. Through strikes, political activism, and lobbying, unions would begin to see some victories in the twentieth century: minimum wages laws; the eight-hour work day and the five-day work week realized; legislation providing for workman's compensation and overtime pay passed; statutes required protection of workers from toxic chemicals enacted; and child labor was banned. The government provided lax enforcement of these laws, but by the mid-twentieth century a measurable improvement of working people's lives had been achieved, a triumph paid for by bloodshed in the country's unacknowledged civil war.

Table 18.1

Immigrants to the United States
1820s to the 1920s

Immigrant Group	Approximate Numbers and Peak Years of Immigration	Reasons for Leaving ("Push Factors")	Reasons for Coming ("Pull Factors")
Irish	4.5 million between 1820 and 1930.	Oppressive British occupation of Ireland, the Potato Famine (1845-1852), and escaping poverty.	Job opportunities and the chance to reunite with family members already in the United States
Chinese	More than 300,000 immigrated to the U.S. and more than 105,000 stayed from 1850 to passage of the 1882 Chinese Exclusion Act.	Poverty and the political decline of the Chinese Empire.	Sending wages home as they were hired as low-wage miners, agricultural and factory workers, domestic servants, and railroad workers
Czech and Slovak	Between the 1850s to the start of World Wa I in 1914, about 1 million Czechs and Slovaks arrived in the United States from Central Europe.	Finding refuge from the political chaos and oppression that followed failed revolutions across Europe in 1848, high unemployment, and the scarcity of farm land because of overpopulation.	Seeking the expanding number of jobs provided by the American industrial revolution, supporting families back home, and dreaming of upward mobility.
Japanese	From 1880 to 1920, more than 400,000 immigrated to the United States and its territories and 100,000 stayed by 1920.	Leaving the economic and political instability caused by industrialization, job losses caused by increasing imports, and the decline of agriculture in Japan.	Earning money for families in Japan as agricultural workers, as loggers, as miners, as fishers, and as railroad workers
Italian	Between 1880 and 1924, 4 million Italians immigrated to the United States.	To escape grinding poverty and violence and disease that broke out in the aftermath of the struggle for Italian reunification. Sicilians escaped discrimination.	To send back money to struggling families, to reunify with relatives already in the United States, and to improve their economic standing.
Jewish	Between 1881 and 1910, more than 1.5 million Jewish immigrants arrived in the United States, mostly from the Russian Empire.	To flee the violent anti-Semitic persecution and harsh anti-Jewish laws that followed the assassination of Czar Alexander II by an anarchist in 1881.	To find jobs, greater tolerance, less discrimination and violence, and to connect with the growing Jewish communities in American cities.
Greek	In the first two decades of the 20th century (1900-1920), more than 350,000 Greeks arrived in the United States.	Because of widespread debt, bankruptcy, and poverty among farmers.	Encouragement by the Greek government and the hope for jobs and decent wages.
Mexican	The number of Mexicans living in the United States tripled from 200,000 to 600,000 from 1910 to 1920, and as many as a million crossed the border, sometimes multiple times during the Mexican Revolution.	Seeking shelter from the violence, social and political chaos, and poverty during the revolutionary period.	The hope for safety, decent wages, and a way to lift their families back home from impoverishment.

Chronology

1868   The eight-hour workday is established for federal workers

1869   Completion of first transcontinental railroad. Knights of Labor founded.

1870   Standard Oil incorporated.

1871   Chicago department store Montgomery Ward begins mail-order delivery

1873   Panic of 1873 causes worldwide depression. Congress demonetizes silver, tightening the money supply
Mark Twain and Charles Dudley Warner's *The Gilded Age* published.

1876   Alexander Graham Bell demonstrates the telephone.

1877   Workers stage The Great Railroad Strike. Thomas Edison's workshop invents the phonograph.

1879   Thomas Alva Edison invents the first light bulb.

1882   New York City establishes a Labor Day holiday.

1883   The Pendleton Civil Service Act passed. William Graham Sumner's *What the Social Classes Owe Each Other* published.

1886   The American Federation of Labor established. The Haymarket Riots unfold in Chicago. Supreme Court's *Wabash v. Illinois decision*.

1887   Interstate Commerce Act becomes law.

1888   Benjamin Harrison elected president.

1890   Jacob Riis *How the Other Half Lives* published.

1892   Steel workers strike at Carnegie's Homestead Mills Plant in Pennsylvania. The People's, or Populist Party, competes in the presidential election.

1896   William McKinley defeats William Jennings Bryan, the Democratic/Populist fusion ticket

SUGGESTED READINGS

Robert C. Bannister, *Social Darwinism: Science and Myth in Anglo-American Social Thought* (1979).

Gregg Cantrell, *The People's Revolt: Texas Populists and the Roots of American Liberalism* (2020)

Roger, Daniels, *Coming to America: A History of Immigration and Ethnicity in American Life* (1991).

Rebecca Edwards, *New Spirits: Americans in the Gilded Age, 1865–1905* (2005).

Rosemarie Feurer and Chad Pearson, eds., *Against Labor: How U.S. Employers Organized to Defeat Union Activism* (2017).

Leon Fink, *The Long Gilded Age: American Capitalism and the Lessons of a New World Order* (2015).

James Green, *Death in the Haymarket: A Story of Chicago, the First Labor Movement, and the Bombing that Divided Gilded Age America* (2006).

Matthew Frye Jacobson, *Whiteness of a Different Color: European Immigrants and the Alchemy of Race* (1998).

Jacqueline Jones, *Goddess of Anarchy: The Life and Times of Lucy Parsons, American Radical* (2017).

Jackson Lears, *Rebirth of a Nation: The Making of Modern America, 1877-1920* (2009).

Rachel Maines, *The Technology of Orgasm: "Hysteria," the Vibrator, and Women's Sexual Satisfaction* (2001).

Michael O'Malley, *Keeping Watch: A History of American Time* (1990).

Chad Pearson, *Reform or Repression: Organizing America's Anti-Union Movement* (2016)

Kathy Peiss. *Hope in a Jar: The Making of America's Beauty Culture* (1999).

Kevin Phillips, *Wealth and Democracy: A Political History of the American Rich* (2002).

Edward J. Jr., Renehan, *Dark Genius of Wall Street: The Misunderstood Life of Jay Gould, King of the Robber Barons* (2005).

Les Standiford, *Meet You in Hell: Andrew Carnegie, Henry Clay Frick, and the Bitter Partnership that Transformed America* (2005).

Peter N Steams, *Fat History: Bodies and Beauty in the Modern West* (2002).

Alan Trachtenberg, *The Incorporation of America: Culture and Society in the Gilded Age.* (2007).

Kyle Wilkison, *Yeomen, Sharecropper, and Socialist: Plain Folk Protest in Texas, 1870-1914.* (2008).

C. Vann Woodward, *Origins of the New South, 1877-1913* (1951).

Review Questions

1. What are some major technological and scientific innovations from 1870-1900 and how did these inventions influence American life and culture?

2. What are "trusts" and "vertical" and "horizontal" integration, what industries are associated with these forms of business organization, and what "Robber Barons" are associated with each?

3. Detail developments in American law in the late nineteenth and early twentieth centuries such as: new attitudes towards corporations; the concept of eminent domain; the definition of corporations as legal "persons"; and the use of the Fourteenth Amendment to overturn regulatory statutes and analyze how these developments aided the rise of corporations in the late nineteenth century.

4. Describe the trends in immigration to America from 1870-1900, including the shift from "old" to "new immigrants," the reason for this shift, and the attitude of English-descended Americans to the new immigrants.

5. What were some of the major acts of labor resistance in the late nineteenth century and what obstacles did workers face in forming unions and improving wages, worker safety, and making the eight-hour work day the American standard?

Glossary of Important People and Concepts

American Federation of Labor
Alexander Graham Bell
Black Friday
Andrew Carnegie
Civil Service Reform
Thomas Edison
Jay Gould
Great Railroad Strike of 1877
Greenbacks
Haymarket Square
Homestead Lockout
Horizontal Integration
Knights of Labor
Laissez Faire
"New immigrants"
New South
Pendleton Act
People's (Populist) Party
Plessy v. Ferguson
Political Machines
Robber Barons
John D. Rockefeller
Segregation
Social Darwinism
Vertical Integration

THEODORE ROOSEVELT

Chapter Nineteen

THE IMPERIAL REPUBLIC

After the terrorist attacks of September 11, 2001, the United States engaged in a series of conflicts abroad including military incursions into Afghanistan (where the government gave safe haven to 9/11 mastermind Osama bin Laden) and Iraq (where officials in the administration of President George W. Bush believed, falsely it turned out, that dictator Saddam Hussein was developing weapons of mass destruction to be used by future terrorists). During the course of this "war on terror," U.S. soldiers and their allies began capturing high-value prisoners. Some of these captives, the American public began to find out through the media, were subjected to brutal interrogations by operatives of the Central Intelligence Agency (CIA) in order to extract information. Among the most notable techniques employed was waterboarding, in which a prisoner is held down while water is forcibly poured down the person's nose and throat until they almost drown. President Bush, Vice President Dick Cheney, and other administration officials played a game of semantics, refusing to admit that their tactics were akin to torture, preferring instead the more ambiguous label "enhanced interrogation techniques." The furor over revelations of the CIA's methods paralleled a similar controversy over the mistreatment of prisoners that occurred almost exactly 100 years earlier during the American fight against Filipino insurgents then resisting American annexation of their homeland after the Spanish-American War.

The four-year-long conflict in the Philippines was a brutal affair between U.S. occupation forces and Filipino allies in league against Filipino rebels under Emilio Aguinaldo and other leaders who had originally fought against their Spanish colonial rulers and were now determined to dislodge the Americans. Guerilla-style attacks were employed against the occupiers—ambushes, snipers, hit-and-run assaults, and

bombings—while assassinations and atrocities against Filipinos sympathizing with the Americans terrorized the populace. U.S. army troopers often responded with impunity, shooting civilians suspected of aiding rebels, burning entire villages, forcibly relocating peasants, and mutilating the bodies of dead enemy combatants—basically the same acts that writers and editors in American newspapers condemned the Spanish for performing in Cuba before the Spanish-American War.

In addition to controversies surrounding these aspects of the Philippine War, the American public also became aware that U.S. soldiers and their Filipino allies frequently used a technique similar to waterboarding known as "the water cure" to force prisoners to cooperate and provide useful information. Word first began to appear in American newspapers after letters sent home by soldiers detailing the treatment of prisoners began to be disseminated by anti-imperialist activists and eventually caught the attention of like-minded senators serving on the U.S. Senate's Committee on the Philippines, established in December 1899, to examine various aspects of the American occupation, including the conflict against the rebels. The committee held hearings on the conduct of the war from January to June 1902, in response to a furor over comments made by an American general stationed in the Philippines who stated to a Manila newspaper that he wished to set an entire island ablaze in order to root out rebel resistance there. Chaired by Republican Henry Cabot Lodge of Massachusetts who supported the nation's imperialist ambitions in Asia, the committee began its hearings with the testimony of Governor (and future U.S. president) William Howard Taft who conceded that the water cure had been used "on some occasions" to extract information. He was followed by a parade of pro-imperialist witnesses who cited atrocities perpetrated by the rebels and attempted to justify the razing *of villages and the forced relocation of civilians as militarily necessary. When one senator asked a general whether such actions were within the ordinary rules of civilized warfare, the general famously responded: "These people are not civilized."*

Though Senator Lodge proved skillful in controlling much of the agenda of his committee, he could not completely prevent shocking disclosure from being entered into the public record. Among the most shocking revelations was provided by Charles S. Riley, a former volunteer sergeant who testified before the committee to witnessing the use of the water cure upon Tobeniano Ealdama—a local town official accused of aiding the insurgency. Riley described in detail how an Army captain, Edwin F. Glenn, ordered his men to tie up Ealdama, place a large stick across his mouth to prevent it from closing, then poured a large amount of water down his throat which entered his stomach and lungs until forced out by stepping on his torso. After repeating the process a second time, Ealdama "confessed" to aiding the rebels and took them into the countryside looking for an enemy stronghold that did not exist. Upon their return to Ealdama's town, Glenn ordered his men to burn all of its 500 houses to the ground. Riley's testimony was confirmed by another member of his unit, as well as by Ealdama himself who told the senators that he only stated that he supported the insurrection because of the intense pain he experienced, his inability to breathe, and great fear at that moment that he was going to die. (After his testimony, he was returned back to his prison in the Philippines where he was serving ten years of hard labor based on the statements he gave after receiving the water cure.) Captain Glenn was eventually found guilty of minor offenses, docked a month's pay, and fined fifty dollars. He retired from the Army after World War I with the rank of brigadier general, so the affair obviously did not significantly impact his military career.

For his part, President Theodore Roosevelt characteristically tried to stay above the fray while condemning agitators on all sides. While condemning all acts of barbarity perpetrated by U.S. troops, stating at one point that "torture is not a thing that we can tolerate," he also believed that the water cure was "a mild torture" that, in his estimation, did not cause permanent damage to its victims. Roosevelt thought the enemy to be especially treacherous and lambasted American anti-imperialist critics who only brought up negative aspects of the war committed by Americans instead of focusing on the peace, order, and freedom for the Filipino people for which the U.S. forces were supposedly fighting.

Though the Committee on the Philippines continued until 1921, the hearings on the conduct of the war ended upon President Roosevelt's declaration of victory in July 1902. Despite efforts by activists demanding further inquiries, Senator Lodge's Republican-controlled committee soon voted to end all investigations of torture allegations and moved on to other matters, as did most of the American public.

AMERICA'S QUEST FOR EMPIRE 1880-1900

The United States expanded beyond its previous continental limits during the second half of the nineteenth century, primarily by gathering new possessions in the Pacific Ocean. Some of these acquisitions were by design while others resulted from wartime opportunism. Unlike the powers of Europe (and Japan in Asia) who expanded their global empires during these years largely to gain access to raw material resources not available at home, the U.S. secured control of new territories in the Pacific mainly to facilitate and protect trade with the emerging markets of Asia. With American industrial and agricultural output reaching record levels, business and government leaders were very much interested in expanding exports to relieve potentially burdening surpluses of manufactured goods and crops, a view only strengthened during the national economic crisis of the mid-1890s. Some Americans also wished to expand in order for their country to be acknowledged by the global community as one of the world's great powers. After the nascent empire was obtained, foreign policy concerns centered on how best to maintain this new domain—an unknown concept for Americans whose expansionist mindset throughout the 1800s had been limited to the vast expanse of North America.

The Imperialist Impulse

Eager to assist the expansion-minded capitalists who believed that the acquisition of overseas markets would be the panacea for the nation's economic instability, many politicians, intellectuals, and military strategists emerged who viewed acquisition of overseas territory as essential for the United States to assume great power status alongside Great Britain, France, Germany, and Russia. Enviously watching European nations extend their control over various regions of the world, American imperialists began to agitate to join this scramble for empire, often resurrecting the rhetoric of Manifest Destiny that propelled westward expansion before the Civil War.

Just as some capitalists had used Social Darwinism to rationalize income inequality and unsafe workplace conditions, many imperialists distorted Charles Darwin's theory of evolution to explain American overseas expansion. Others, such as the evangelical Protestant clergyman, **Josiah Strong**, used their belief in Christian uplift to justify expansion in the name of progress. At home, Reverend Strong was a leader in the Social Gospel movement that called for the application of Christian ideals, such as basic social justice, to combat the vast array of social problems caused by industrialization and urbanization such as income inequality, poverty, child labor, and the development of slums. When looking outward, Strong's religious zeal promoted missionary work with a racist bent. In his 1885 best-selling book, *Our Country,* Strong praised the nation's economic progress, supposedly due to the Anglo-Saxon blood of its majority population, and asserted his hope that the United States and other Anglo-Saxon nations would expand across the globe and exert their dominance for the uplift of the "savage peoples" by Christianizing and civilizing them.

Even more influential was a cadre of imperialists serving in the military and the federal government who promoted a naval buildup and overseas expansion as essential for the nation's strategic and economic prosperity. These leaders pointed out the sorry state of the U.S. Navy after the Civil War, mostly consisting of outdated vessels poorly maintained in an effort to save money. From his position as president of the Naval War College, **Alfred Thayer Mahan** sought to change the prevailing mindset of the navy as little more than a glorified coast guard. He promoted a more visionary outlook for the importance of a modern navy through correspondence, speeches, and a series of published works. In his most important work, *The Influence of Sea Power on History, 1660-1783* (1890), Mahan argued that sea power was the dominant factor in the European conflicts of the period from the mid-seventeenth century to the end of the eighteenth century. He asserted that the lessons learned from that period could and should be applied to the present—that the nation needed a vibrant merchant marine and a modern navy of battleships and heavy cruisers strong enough to make its presence felt across the globe in order to promote and protect its growing world trade of surplus industrial and agricultural goods. To accommodate this new fleet of steam-powered military and trading vessels, the U.S. also needed to acquire an array of island bases in the oceans of the world. These ports would serve as vital stations for the ships to take on needed coal and water, serve as repair facilities, and provide safe harbors from foreign foes and inclement weather. Also imperative in Mahan's vision was the construction and control of an isthmian canal in Central America to allow for the rapid movement of American vessels between the Atlantic and Pacific Oceans. Mahan's ideas had a strong influence upon government officials, business leaders, and the general public, laying the groundwork not only for the nation's first significant peacetime military buildup in its history, but also for the acquisition of new overseas territories.

Samoa and Hawaii

The **Samoan Islands** of the southwest Pacific Ocean, strategically situated along the route between the United States and Australia/New Zealand, had been occupied by Polynesians for over 3,000 years before Europeans and Americans began arriving to establish trade relations in the mid-1800s. While German companies established rubber, coconut, and cocoa bean plantations on its western islands, American naval officials salivated over the beautiful natural harbor of Pago Pago on one of the chain's eastern islands, leading to a treaty between the U.S. and local Samoan leaders for exclusive American rights to its port facilities. The English also sought a commercial and strategic foothold in the islands and allied with some native groups there. Internal tribal tensions, exacerbated by the differing allegiances with the outside powers, led to the outbreak of a prolonged civil war in Samoa with Germany, Great Britain and the United States aiding the various rival factions. In 1889, just as the fleets of those powers arrived and looked to directly intervene, possibly engaging in combat against each other, a great typhoon enveloped and destroyed most of the ships. In response, the three nations agreed to a joint protectorate over the islands in an effort to maintain peace. Ten years later, when the civil war resumed, Germany and the U.S. formally partitioned the islands, with the United States assuming control over Pago Pago and the eastern islands (now the U.S. territory of American Samoa).

As with Samoa, many global powers eyed the Hawaiian island chain because of its strategic location (in the middle of the Pacific Ocean) and economic potential as a producer of raw materials and consumer of manufactured goods. A unified kingdom since 1795 when Kamehameha I conquered most of the islands, Hawaii began to receive a growing number of traders and missionaries by the mid-1800s. American missionaries had tried to convert the islanders to Christianity since the 1820s. Their children increasingly became engaged in commerce and landholding, buying up huge parcels of real estate and establishing tropical fruit and sugar plantations. By 1875, King David Kalakaua signed a reciprocal trade agreement with the United States allowing for the tax-free flow of American commercial goods into Hawaiian markets in exchange for tariff-free entry of Hawaiian sugar into the United States. The American sugar planters took advantage of the deal by expanding their holdings and importing thousands of Chinese and Japanese agricultural workers to turn the islands into one vast sugar-producing economy under their control. Over time, the introduction of smallpox and other foreign diseases would ravage the Hawaiian population and leave the natives a minority in their own land. In 1887, the king signed a new treaty with the United States, renewing the reciprocal trade deal and allowing the Americans to build a naval base at Pearl Harbor near Honolulu on the island of Oahu. In granting the United States sole use of the port facilities, the monarch believed that he would protect the islands from seizure by a foreign power as the U.S. would defend its hold on Pearl Harbor at all costs. Together with Pago Pago, the United States now had two major Pacific fueling stations for its growing naval fleet.

The same year that the king agreed to the Pearl Harbor arrangement, the American sugar planters moved to gain political control of the islands. Believing David Kalakaua to be a weak ruler who spent too much government money and had unrealistic ambitions (such as his desire to create a Polynesian confederation with far-away Samoa), the planters forced the king, literally at gunpoint, to sign a constitution that denied voting rights for a majority of native Hawaiians, stripped the monarchy of numerous executive powers, and greatly increased the influence of the planter-dominated Hawaiian legislative assembly. After Kalakaua's death in 1891, his strong-willed sister, **Liliuokalani**, assumed the throne. Determined not to be a puppet of the sugar planters, Queen "Lili" tried to assert her independence by drafting a new constitution that would give the monarchy veto power over the legislature and restore voting rights to disenfranchised native Hawaiians.

Wishing to maintain their dominance over the islands, and upset with a new U.S. tariff law that allowed tax-free entry of all foreign sugar into the United States and granted a government subsidy to all American sugar producers, the planters overthrew the queen in 1893 with the help of 150 U.S. marines provided by the American naval commander at Pearl Harbor in league with John L. Stevens, the U.S. ambassador to Hawaii. Led by Sanford B. Dole, the planters established a provisional government before formally asking the U.S. government to annex the islands. Queen Lili, who asked her guard to stand down and end resistance to avoid further bloodshed after the U.S. marines became involved, petitioned American government officials to help place her back in power.

In the United States, Republican congressional leaders and President Benjamin Harrison both supported annexation, but Harrison had recently been defeated in his reelection bid by Democrat Grover Cleveland and the Republicans lost control of the Senate and House of Representatives. Before assuming office, President-elect Cleveland successfully convinced Senate Democrats during the lame-duck session to stall on a proposed annexation treaty before they formally took over control of Congress in the next session. After an investigation revealed the role of the American troops in the insurrection and that most native Hawaiians preferred the return of Queen Lili, Cleveland refused to pursue annexation any further, telling the planters to restore the queen to her throne. The planters balked at the notion, declaring the independence of the "Republic of Hawaii" under the presidency of Sanford B. Dole. In 1898, however, after the conclusion of the Spanish-American War, the United States annexed Hawaii by joint resolution of Congress. Two years later, Congress granted the islands U.S. territorial status.

THE SPANISH-AMERICAN WAR

Crisis in Cuba

By the 1890s, Cuba and Puerto Rico were the last remaining Spanish possessions in the Western Hemisphere. Since the late 1860s, Cuba had seen a series of revolts erupt against Spanish rule. Though suppressing these earlier uprisings, by the late 1890s, the Spanish found these rebellions increasingly difficult to subdue. A revised tariff passed by the U.S. Congress in 1894 helped to ignite a new insurrection in Cuba as the island's main export, sugar, became too expensive for the American market. The tariff caused an economic contraction, which intensified Cubans' resentment toward their Spanish rulers, even though they had not caused the depression. Fighting between Spanish soldiers and Cuban guerillas became brutal, as both sides often committed unspeakable atrocities. The rebels made many areas of the island uninhabitable as they destroyed tobacco and sugar crops while razing large swaths of the countryside. In an effort to better protect his troops in the rural areas from sporadic ambushes, the Spanish commander in Cuba, General **Valeriano Weyler**, controversially ordered the rounding up of thousands of Cuban civilians to be relocated into designated "reconcentration zones" (usually armed camps and villages) where they suffered from low food supplies, poor sanitation, and general abuse leading to tens of thousands of rural Cubans dying of starvation and disease.

News of the outlandish policy spread to the United States and greatly upset many Americans who read the accounts often depicted as examples of "Spanish barbarism" by the major competing newspaper chains owned by William Randolph Hearst and Joseph Pulitzer, who together owned the majority of the nation's largest dailies. Hearst and Pulitzer were revolutionizing American journalism in the late nineteenth century by creating a new kind of newspaper that catered openly to citizens from low socioeconomic backgrounds rather than those who read the more traditional press. Berated by the members of the mainstream press as unprofessional, the practitioners of the so-called "**yellow journalism**" specialized in sensationalized news to increase their readership. When instances of actual news slowed down, editors were not above making up stories to fill their pages. By the 1890s, both publishers were engaged in a ruthless circulation war and saw the struggle in Cuba as a great opportunity, sending scores of reporters to the island with orders to provide accounts of Spanish atrocities committed on innocent Cubans. As they did in the United States, the correspondents frequently exaggerated or distorted what took place in Cuba, if not blatantly fabricating stories, to please their bosses.

Helping the jingoists agitate the American public were the thousands of Cuban émigrés in the United States living primarily in Miami, Philadelphia, and New York City who gave extensive support to the Cuban Revolutionary Party. Headquartered in New York, they helped to make their slain leader, José Martí, a "freedom-fighting" hero and martyr in the eyes of many sympathetic Americans. With the financial backing of prominent American capitalists, Cuban Americans formed other associations to support the cause of *Cuba Libre*.

The increasing public outcry against alleged Spanish brutality and agitation for U.S. intervention in Cuba failed to move President Grover Cleveland to action. He proclaimed American neutrality and urged New York City officials to muzzle Cuban émigrés trying to rally New Yorkers to the cause of Cuban independence. Cleveland's Republican successor, **William McKinley**, elected in 1896, appeared more amenable to the increasing calls for intervention. Soon after taking office, McKinley formally protested Spain's actions in Cuba. After a new government took over in Spain, the prime minister announced that he was recalling General Weyler, modifying the reconcentration policy, and offering limited autonomy (self-rule on an assortment of domestic matters) to the Cubans if they would lay down their arms. While militant critics believed that it was their "saber rattling" that had caused Spain to modify their Cuban policy, the Spanish government was merely attempting to placate American public opinion. (The reconcentration policy continued under the new commander and autonomy was only offered because the new prime minister knew anything short of independence would be rejected by the rebels.) Upon hearing that General Weyler had been removed by authorities seeking to appease critics of the military's reconcentration policy, troops loyal to the commander undertook a rampage that killed and injured many Cubans, destroyed Cuban property, and threatened many Americans living in the city. In response, President McKinley ordered a new battleship, the **U.S.S. Maine**, to dock in Havana Harbor in order to evacuate Americans wishing to leave and also to send a message to the Spanish that the U.S. government was continuing to monitor events in Cuba.

America and Spain Go to War

Ultimately, the events of early February 1898 mitigated any chance for a peaceful settlement. The first crisis occurred with the publication in American papers of what would become known as the **de Lôme Letter**, a diplomatic communiqué written by the Spanish ambassador in Washington, Enrique Dupuy de Lôme, which had been stolen by a Cuban agent in Havana and found its way into William Randolph Hearst's *New York Journal* under the headline "Worst Insult to the United States in Its History." In this correspondence, de Lôme described McKinley as a weak man and "a bidder for the admiration of the crowd." Many Americans thought the same way about the president, including Assistant Secretary of the Navy Theodore Roosevelt, who privately declared that McKinley had "no more backbone than a chocolate éclair." Still, though Americans accepted the right of citizens to openly criticize their president as part of partisan politics, no foreigner in their opinion should be accorded that privilege. The resulting media firestorm led to de Lôme's prompt resignation.

Just as anger over the de Lôme Letter was beginning to abate, the *Maine* suddenly exploded under mysterious circumstances in Havana Harbor, causing the deaths of 260 sailors. No sooner did the disaster take place than the imperialists screamed for revenge, certain that the Spanish soldiers (either upon direct orders from their superiors or under the initiative of rogue elements within the army) had sunk the warship. Helping their view, a rushed U.S. Navy inquiry board declared that an external explosion, possibly caused by a mine, had caused the disaster. Subsequent investigations performed decades later have demonstrated that the incident most likely occurred as a result of an accidental explosion in the gunpowder

The battleship *Maine* in Havana Harbor, February 1898.

magazine, probably triggered by an undetected fire in a nearby coalbunker. By poor ship design, the bunker was situated too closely to the magazine, only separated by a bulkhead that did not prevent enough heat from transferring to the magazine and igniting the gunpowder. With the true cause unknown at the time, sufficient numbers of Americans were convinced that the blast was an act caused by the Spanish. Soon, war hysteria swept the country. Congress responded to the public clamor for retaliation by unanimously appropriating $50 million for military preparations as "Remember the *Maine*" became the mantra for revenge against the Spanish.

A Civil War veteran who had experienced combat firsthand, McKinley still hoped to avoid a conflict while others in his administration, including Theodore Roosevelt, clamored for a fight. In late March, the president notified the Spanish government of his conditions for avoiding war: Spain would have to pay an indemnity for the *Maine,* abandon its reconcentration policy, end the fighting with the rebels, and commit to Cuban independence. On April 9, Spain agreed to all but one of the demands—Cuban independence. Though McKinley was inclined to accept Spain's bid for peace, the imperialist pressures from within his own administration, as well as from the general public, proved too great to withstand. Propaganda had been successful in whipping the American public into a war frenzy. The nation's new war machines, especially the navy, had been modernized at great expense,

and now the opportunity presented itself to see whether it was sufficient to earn the respect that the United States deserved as a great power. The imperialists believed it was imperative for the country to go to war. If Spain simply acquiesced to American demands, then the U.S. would not have the opportunity to demonstrate its awesome military power. Thus, on April 11, 1898, McKinley asked Congress for authority to go to war. Nine days later, he signed a joint congressional resolution granting his request and calling on Spain to vacate its hold of Cuba. The resolution included a declaration known as the **Teller Amendment**, which declared the U.S. had no intention of acquiring Cuba. Spain promptly broke off diplomatic relations with the United States. The president soon ordered a blockade of the Cuban coast and issued a call for 125,000 volunteers to join the U.S. Army. In response to these perceived affronts to national honor and strong public pressure at home, the Spanish government declared war on the United States on April 23. Two days later, Congress voted a formal declaration of war against Spain, retroactive to April 21, the day that the Cuban blockade began.

"A Splendid Little War"

Secretary of State John Hay famously labeled the Spanish-American conflict "a splendid little war," because of its short duration (four months), relatively light number of combat casualties (460 deaths), and the large amount of territory taken from Spain at the war's conclusion. Such a view ignored the large number of American military personnel who died as a result of diseases and food poisoning in Cuba (over 5,200), let alone the effort to subdue the Philippines after the war, but the gains for the country in such a short time were indeed profound.

U.S. naval superiority soon became a major factor in the American victory. In the war's first major engagement, the **Battle of Manila Bay**, fought in the Spanish-held Philippines on May 1, 1898, an American flotilla commanded by Commodore George Dewey destroyed the entire Spanish Pacific fleet while losing only one sailor who succumbed to heatstroke. Unprepared for such a resounding victory, Dewey soon left and did not return occupation forces until mid-August.

In Cuba, the story would not be as simple. Though no longer a great power, Spain was determined to hold onto its remaining empire and had 80,000 troops in place on Cuba to defend the island. When the war began, the United States had a weak standing army of only 26,000 troops, mostly used to man western frontier outposts and whose only combat experience had been skirmishing with Native Americans or chasing local bandits. Congress

Map 19.1 Spanish-American War in the Philippines

The Teller Amendment

On April 11, 1898, President William McKinley asked Congress to "to authorize and empower the President to take measures to secure a full and final termination of hostilities between the government of Spain and the people of Cuba, and to ensure in the island the establishment of a stable government, capable of maintaining order and observing its international obligations, ensuring peace and tranquility and the security of its citizens as well as our own, and to use the military and naval forces of the United States as may be necessary for these purposes." For the better part of a week, congressmen in both houses debated the terms and conditions of the president's request. Senator Henry M. Teller, a Republican from Colorado, joined the chorus by proposing an addition to the joint resolution stating that United States had no intention of establishing permanent control over Cuba. The so-called "Teller Amendment" asserted that the United States "hereby disclaims any disposition of intention to exercise sovereignty, jurisdiction, or control over said island except for pacification thereof, and asserts its determination, when that is accomplished, to leave the government and control of the island to its people." On April 19, the Senate passed the amendment with a 42 to 35 vote, with the House concurring soon thereafter by a 311 to 6 margin. President McKinley signed the joint resolution the next day.

While the inclusion of the Teller Amendment allowed the United States to gain some moral high ground in the approaching conflict by publicly disallowing any desire to annex Cuba, many inside and outside the halls of Congress had diverse primary reasons for supporting the amendment. In addition to those genuinely idealistically supportive of Cuban independence, the coalition also included large numbers of those opposed to annexing territory containing large numbers of blacks and Catholics (over fears of their possible migration to the U.S. mainland) as well as those supportive of domestic sugar interests, such as Senator Teller who represented a state with a sugar beet industry that did not welcome the possibility of competition from Cuban sugar producers who no longer hindered by American sugar tariffs if Cuba became part of the United States.

Ultimately, Cuba achieved its nominal independence after the Spanish-American War, but the young nation would remain strongly within the orbit of the United States, both economically and politically, well after U.S. troops left the island (with the notable exception of the Guantanamo Bay naval base) in 1902. The Cuban economy depended heavily on trade with the United States and American investment capital. U.S. forces intervened in Cuban affairs on multiple occasions and supported the government of pro-U.S. dictator Fulgencio Batista after he assumed power in a military coup in 1952. American corporate influence over the Cuban economy swelled during the Batista era, which lasted until 1959 when rebels under Fidel Castro succeeded in overthrowing the dictator's regime, beginning a new antagonistic phase in U.S.-Cuba relations that continues to the present day.

increased the size of the regular army by another 50,000 men, and the government soon issued a call for over 100,000 temporary volunteers who would somehow have to be equipped, trained, and shipped to Cuba.

Theodore Roosevelt, McKinley's former Assistant Secretary of the Navy helped to lead a volunteer cavalry unit comprised of his Harvard classmates and a host of recruits assembled at the Menger Hotel next to the Alamo and trained in the San Antonio, Texas area. Nicknamed the "**Rough Riders**," they gained fame (with the help of Roosevelt's journalist friends imbedded within the unit) attacking the heights overlooking the city of Santiago de Cuba, which proved to be the main theater of action on the island because the port on the southeastern coast of Cuba served as the base for the blockaded Spanish Atlantic fleet. Most famously, the Rough Riders successfully charged San Juan Hill on July 1 to complete the American conquest of the high ground. Overlooked in contemporary accounts of the Rough Riders' bravery and ultimate success were the contributions of the regular army

units, including black regiments or "Buffalo Soldiers," who engaged in heavy fighting leading to the capture of nearby Kettle Hill, which cleared the way for the final assault on San Juan Hill in which they also participated.

By mid-July 1898, American forces were feeling the effects of the environment, increasingly succumbing to a host of tropical diseases, but their enemy bottled up in Santiago had few tangible options. Before long, American artillery placed on San Juan Heights would decimate the Spanish Atlantic fleet. Rather than suffer the humiliation of a surrender, the Spanish commander ordered his ships to make a run for the open sea. The blockading U.S. Navy quickly pounced, destroying every Spanish vessel as it emerged from the narrow harbor entrance, killing almost 500 Spanish sailors. The Spanish army in Santiago capitulated on July 16. Two days later, the Spanish government sued for peace. While Spanish and American officials negotiated the details of an armistice, U.S. military forces captured the Caribbean island of Puerto Rico and Manila Bay in the Philippines. In the

Map 19.2 Major Battles in Cuba

ensuing formal peace settlement, finalized in the **Treaty of Paris** in December 1898 and ratified by the U.S. Senate two months later, Spain recognized Cuban independence, ceded Puerto Rico and the Pacific island of Guam to the United States, and reluctantly sold the Philippines to the U.S. for $20 million.

A NEW WORLD POWER EMERGES

The Philippines, Guam, and Puerto Rico were not involved in the events leading to the Spanish-American War, but each was gobbled up by the United States as a result of the Treaty of Paris, much to the delight of American imperialists, as the legitimate "spoils of war." President McKinley soon asked Congress to annex Hawaii, giving the U.S. permanent control of the deep-water port at Pearl Harbor, then, set his sights on establishing a naval base in the Philippines at Manila. Never before had the United States pursued such a large military presence outside the Western Hemisphere.

Of even greater significance, the McKinley administration announced that the newly acquired territories would be governed as colonies. Among the new possessions, only Hawaii (largely due to the presence of its powerful American sugar planters) would follow the normal procedures for U.S. territories to apply for statehood. In 1900, Congress extended citizenship to all Hawaiian residents and placed the islands on the road to statehood (though this was not achieved until 1959).

Guerrilla War in the Philippines, 1898-1902

Unlike the Hawaiian Islands, the acquisitions from Spain were saddled with a host of special conditions attached to their territorial status. Few Americans had interest in the Philippines beyond controlling Manila Harbor. The

decision to convert the entire archipelago into a U.S. colony was based on the desire to prevent other powers, such as Japan and Germany, from gaining a foothold there. The McKinley administration might have taken a different approach toward the Philippines had it not been for the racism that dominated imperialist attitudes at this time. Helping American forces to defeat the Spanish in the Philippines was a broad-based indigenous rebel movement led by **Emilio Aguinaldo** who, like his Cuban counterparts, looked to the United States as the liberator of his country. Much to Aguinaldo's eventual disappointment, the U.S. never had any intention of granting the islands their independence, which they could have done in exchange for a naval base at Manila. An American fleet stationed there would have protected the islands from aggressive nations and served the larger interests of both the U.S. and the Filipinos. Outright annexation was also an alternative, granting the Filipinos the same status as the Hawaiians and putting them on the road toward statehood. McKinley chose none of these possibilities, believing that the Filipinos were an inferior people incapable of self-government. The president thought that American rule would enormously benefit the Filipinos, who he called "our little brown brothers." A devout Methodist, he explained that America's mission was "to educate the Filipinos and to uplift and Christianize them, and by God's grace do the very best we could by them." The majority of Filipinos were already Christianized, Catholic in fact, a legacy of centuries of Spanish rule. A substantial percentage of the islanders not only had assumed Spanish names but were bilingual as well, able to speak both Spanish and their native tongue. They were hardly a people bereft of civilization. Nonetheless, until U.S. officials deemed them ready for independence, the islands would be ruled by American governors appointed by the president.

When Aguinaldo and other Filipinos resisted the imposition of American rule, a bloody struggle lasting nearly five years ensued costing the lives of over 4,000 American soldiers, at least 20,000 Filipino resistance fighters, and an estimated 200,000 civilians from war-related violence, famine, and disease. The war brought Americans face-to-face with a disturbing reality: U.S. military actions on the islands were often no different than those perpetrated by the Spanish in Cuba. Residents of hamlets suspected of aiding rebels were imprisoned and their villages razed. Captured enemy fighters and sympathizers were often tortured, frequently enduring the "water cure"—a version of waterboarding—in order to induce them to provide information.

American forces began to prevail after General Arthur MacArthur (the father of World War II General Douglas MacArthur) assumed command in 1900. Realizing that victory required a combination of military might tempered with diplomacy, the general initiated an amnesty program for all Filipino rebels who laid down their arms. He also cultivated close relations with the island's wealthy elites. His efforts were aided by the arrival of the new governor, future U.S. president William Howard Taft, to establish a civilian government. In 1901, Taft became the colony's first governor-general. Taking a page from British imperialism, Taft and subsequent American governor-generals created the façade that the colonists were governing themselves, ruled through allied local elites. Many governmental functions were transferred to Filipino control, and Taft initiated a vigorous program of public works (roads, bridges, schools) that provided the Philippines with the infrastructure necessary for future economic development and political independence. By 1902, the combination of ruthless suppression, the capture of Aguinaldo and other rebel leaders, and some granted concessions ended the revolt. Though sporadic fighting continued until 1913, American control of the Philippines was secured. Filipino independence did not occur until 1946, a year after the end of World War II and nearly half a century after Admiral Dewey's guns had boomed in Manila Bay.

Special Provisions for Cuba and Puerto Rico

Though the U.S. government renounced acquiring Cuba in the Teller Amendment American government officials after the war's conclusion began to assert control over the island while undertaking the process of granting the islanders their official independence. With President McKinley's blessing, Congress attached the **Platt Amend-**

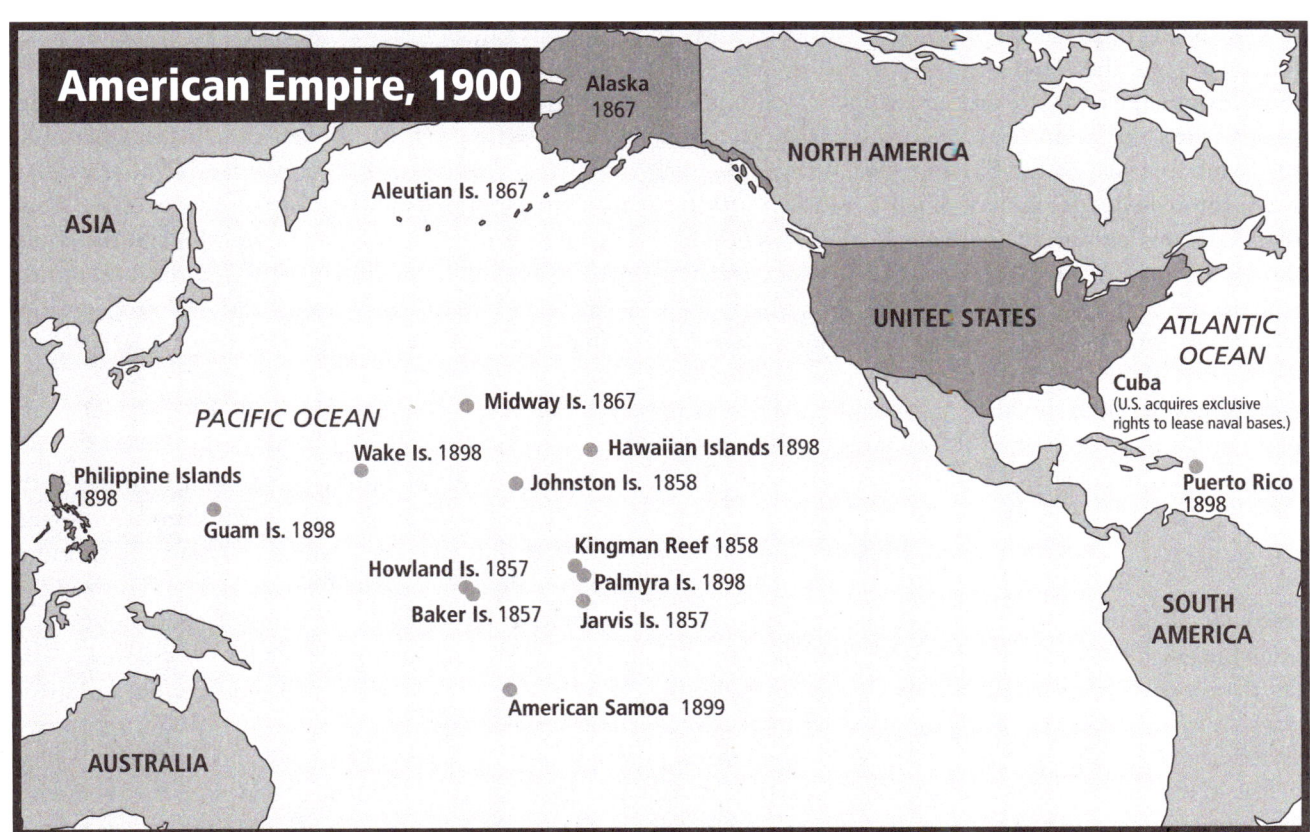

Map 19.3 American Empire, 1900.

ment to a 1901 army appropriations bill, laying a host of conditions that Cuba was expected to accept in return for the removal of American soldiers. The amendment's terms (which were added to Cuba's constitution in 1903) ensured Cuba's dependence on the United States by stipulating that the island country could not make treaties with other foreign nations, would accept the right of the U.S. to intervene in Cuban political affairs (ensuring no one would rule Cuba without the acceptance of the United States government), and Cuba would sell or lease land to the United States for naval stations such as Guantanamo Bay on the eastern tip of the island (still held by the U.S. today).

The Cuban economy came to depend on American trade and investment. The United States intervened in the island's political affairs by sending in military forces five times between 1906 and 1921. As in the Philippines, the United States ruled in Cuba through pro-American local business elites who remained in power until 1959 when rebels led by Fidel Castro overthrew the last of such puppet regimes. Until then, the Cubans endured a half-century of exploitation. The economic, military, and political control that the United States imposed on Cuba would fuel anti-American sentiment for years to come and helped prepare the way for the success of Castro's revolution.

With regard to Puerto Rico, the U.S. government refused to grant the island its independence, even though its residents enjoyed a large measure of political autonomy under Spanish rule. Instead, the United States annexed the island in 1900 via the **Foraker Act**. This legislation was unprecedented for its lack of a provision for making its inhabitants citizens of the United States. Eventually, Puerto Ricans received better treatment when granted American citizenship in 1917 and the ability to choose its own territorial legislature, followed thirty years later by the election of their own governors. Nevertheless, Puerto Ricans had a skewed distribution of wealth and the lack of an industrial base leaving the majority of the island's residents in dire poverty.

The Open Door Policy

The U.S. relationship with China became a prime interest and concern for American foreign policy makers in the last decade of the nineteenth century. As for other global powers, China represented a vast potential market for American capitalists, but after suffering a demoralizing defeat in the first Sino-Japanese War of 1894-1895, the weakened Chinese government could not prevent efforts by the Russians, Japanese, British, French, and Germans to partition much of China into separate spheres of economic influence. In these occupied zones, the foreigners began exacting trading and investment privileges and other concessions in efforts to close off all outside commerce with other countries. Much to the dismay of American capitalists and their imperialist allies, the United States faced being shut out of the lucrative China market.

McKinley's Secretary of State and noted imperialist, John Hay, led the effort to convince the other powers to open up their spheres of influence in China to outside trade. To prevent the possible division of China into foreign-dominated colonies while accepting the concept of free trade in order to maintain American trade with China, Hay sent a statement of principles known as the "**Open Door**" notes to representatives of the major powers, asking each of the powers to keep their respective spheres of influence open to outside trade. He also asked the powers to respect Chinese sovereignty by affirming the right of the Chinese to collect tariff duties on an equal basis.

Hay's overture engendered little enthusiasm among the other nations, who had nothing to gain by supporting his effort. However, not wishing to insult the United States, an emerging world power who might side with one of their rivals in future dispute, they all refused to formally reject his proposals. Not wanting the United States to appear weak by being unable to convince others to heed its requests, Hay simply declared to the American public that the powers occupying China had agreed to observe his Open Door principles and that he regarded their "assent" as a "final and definitive" acceptance of his initiative. Flushed with nationalist pride after displaying their supposed military superiority over a corrupt European nation (Spain), most simply bought the notion that Hay's diplomacy convinced the Europeans and the Japanese of the righteousness of the American position with respect to China.

The Boxer Rebellion

China's defeat in the Sino-Japanese War (leading to the loss of Korea and Taiwan), the establishment of foreign spheres of influence on Chinese soil, and the spread of western culture in China by missionaries bred strong resentment within many young Chinese nationals who were members of a radical group known by Westerners as the "Boxers," because of their clenched fist symbol and strong devotion to the martial arts. In May 1900, the Boxers rose in armed rebellion in order to "cleanse" China of all "foreign devils" and influences. Considering themselves the protectors of traditional Chinese culture, and claiming that European occupation had destroyed centuries of security, the Boxers killed hundreds of American and

European missionaries, as well as many Chinese men and women who had converted to Christianity.

The **Boxer Rebellion** caught the foreign community by surprise. At the beginning of the insurrection, the Boxers appeared to be winning. For 55 days, they laid siege to the foreign legations in Beijing, cutting off communication between the city and the outside world. In order to raise the siege, the foreign powers momentarily put aside their own rivalries and formed a multinational expeditionary force to rescue the diplomats and punish the rebels. At this juncture, the U.S. government officials found themselves in a dilemma: although sympathetic to the Chinese nationalist movement, which if successful could economically benefit the United States, not joining the international coalition would alienate the very powers they were attempting to woo into accepting the Open Door initiative. Eventually, the McKinley administration opted to side with the other imperialist powers and ordered 5,000 American troops to be rushed from the Philippines to help break the Beijing siege and crush the Boxer insurrection, which was accomplished by October 1900. Approximately 100,000 people, mostly civilians including thousands of Chinese Christians and over 200 European missionaries, died as a result of the violence.

Hay feared that the Boxer Rebellion might permanently shut the Open Door by leading the other major powers to seek even greater control over China. He sent another round of notices, reiterating his original policy. Impressed by America's show of military prowess in helping to suppress the Boxers, and worried that the Chinese rebels might strike again, the main imperialist rivals in China—Great Britain, France, and Germany—publicly endorsed the Open Door Policy, enabling Hay to check the designs on Chinese territory by the Russians and Japanese, who eventually capitulated to the Open Door once they saw the forces arrayed against them. Hay was also able to convince the Chinese government to pay (and the foreign powers to accept) cash reparations for damages to life and property inflicted by the Boxers in lieu of territorial compensation. What remained of China was kept intact, and for the time being, open to free trade. The United States had achieved, largely by Hay's persistent diplomacy, a major foreign policy victory.

THE FOREIGN POLICY OF THEODORE ROOSEVELT

Rarely in the history of the United States has one individual left as indelible a mark on both domestic and foreign policy as Theodore Roosevelt. Mostly because of his personal initiatives as president, the United States became the respected (and often feared) world power that Roosevelt and other imperialists envisioned. He emerged during the 1890s as one of the most outspoken champions of utilizing the nation's industrial might to transform the United States into one of the world's great powers. Roosevelt and his cohorts had worked assiduously, both publicly and privately, to convince their fellow Americans to embrace their vision for the nation. For Teddy Roosevelt, the United States must also exercise its power for the preservation of world peace, displaying what he believed were the true virtues of a democratic republican government. He captured this fundamental premise with his quip, "**Speak softly but carry a big stick.**" In effect, he wanted to project to the world an image of the United States as a nation dedicated to world peace, stability and freedom, yet not afraid to unleash its awesome military upon an adversary if provoked.

For all his public bluster, Roosevelt was not a saber-rattling warmonger. He understood the complexities and imperatives of international relations and power politics. Rather than seeking American domination over the globe, he pursued a policy of promoting a balance of power among the great industrial nations through negotiation in different regions of the world. In this manner, he believed, they would all peacefully resolve tensions among themselves while pursuing agendas that preserved their dominance and ensured their prosperity. By safeguarding their interests, the powers would maintain world peace. Of course, this thinking left out the perspective of the world's least powerful nations. Reflecting not only his own inherent racism but also that of the leaders of the other great powers, Roosevelt turned a deaf ear to the cries of sovereignty and human rights coming from small countries, whose people he believed weak, inferior, and incapable of self-government.

The Roosevelt Corollary

Perhaps no initiative better reflected the president's desire to establish American hegemony in a vital region of the world than his 1904 "**Roosevelt Corollary**" to the Monroe Doctrine. The original 1823 Doctrine's purpose had been to promote a degree of hemispheric solidarity against any further European intrusions in New World affairs. Most important, the United States declared itself the hemisphere's guardian by asserting its right to use force if necessary to keep the European powers from meddling in the hemisphere's business, especially in matters relating to Latin America. However, at the time, the United States lacked the military might to prevent European intervention, and thus, throughout most of the nineteenth century, the powers of Europe often violated

Political Cartoons and American Imperialism

One of the most revealing, poignant, and entertaining ways of recovering past attitudes and values is through political cartoons. Ralph Waldo Emerson once said, "Caricatures are often the truest history of the times." A deft drawing of a popular or unpopular politician can freeze ideas and events in time, conveying more effectively than columns of words the central issues of the day and creating an immediate viewer response. This freshness makes caricatures such a valuable source when attempting to understand the past. Cartoonists are often at their best when they are critical, exaggerating a physical feature of a political figure or capturing anti-government sentiment.

The emergence of the United States as a world power and the rise of Theodore Roosevelt both as president and main architect of U.S. foreign policy in the early twentieth century gave cartoonists plenty to draw about. The proliferation of cheap newspapers at the turn of the century, most notably those of publishing magnates William Randolph Hearst and Joseph Pulitzer, provided cartoonists with ample space for their caricatures. When the Spanish-American War broke out, the Hearst and Pulitzer papers whipped up public sentiment by having artists draw pictures of "lustful" Spaniards stripping American women at sea and encouraging cartoonists to depict the Spanish as "brutes." Hearst, in particular, used such cartoon portrayals of the Spanish to increase his papers' daily circulation to one million copies. However, by the time of the Philippines debate, to the imperialists' dismay, many previously supportive cartoonists had reversed their attitude toward this particular manifestation of American colonialism, and used their creative talents to criticize the government's Philippine policy. One such rendition had "Liberty" stopping "American Butchery in the Philippines" (1899). A year earlier, cartoonists supported the war against Spain, and thus released such classics as "The Spanish Brute Adds Mutilation to Butchery." Both cartoons condemned the "butchery" of native populations, but by 1899, Uncle Sam had become the killer, although not as menacing a figure as the Spaniard who was shown to be an ugly gorilla. However, both cartoons shared a similarity of stance: blood-covered swords with a trail of bodies behind.

Only a handful of U.S. presidents have provided cartoonists with as rich a potential for caricature as Theodore Roosevelt. His physical appearance and personality made him instant fodder for the cartoonists' pens. His broad grin, eye-glasses, and walrus moustache were the kind of features that fueled the cartoonist's imagination. A man of boundless energy, TR's style was as distinctive as his look. Other factors, such as the "Rough Rider" nickname, the symbol of the "big stick," and policies like "gunboat diplomacy" made him the perfect subject for caricature.

the doctrine with impunity. By the time of Roosevelt's presidency, the economic and military condition of the United States had changed dramatically. America was no longer a second-rate power. Roosevelt's policy asserted the right of the United States to intervene in the domestic affairs of Western Hemispheric nations in order to prevent European intrusion. The European nations would no longer be allowed to use the collection of debt or any other excuse to disrupt the government of Western Hemisphere countries.

Events in Venezuela and the Dominican Republic hardened TR's resolve to establish intervention as a necessary component of American policy in Latin America. The governments of both nations were controlled by corrupt dictators who had defaulted on loans owed to German and British banking houses. Their reneging led to a German-led European naval blockade and bombardment of their capital in 1902 and a threatened invasion of the Dominican Republic by Italy and France in 1903. In response, TR issued a statement to Germany threatening military action if they did not withdraw from the Venezuelan coast, which they finally did in 1903. In the Dominican Republic, after an insurrection overthrew the dictator, the U.S. assumed control of the nation's customs bureau.

To prevent further European actions against Latin American countries, Roosevelt made it clear that henceforth the United States would assume the responsibility of policing the hemisphere. All future issues between the Europeans and Latin American nations would be arbitrated by the United States. In effect, TR declared American predominance over the entire hemisphere—any attempt by the European powers to ignore or violate the policy would be met by a military reprisal.

As far as the Latin Americans suffering under such oppression were concerned, TR dismissed their plight as simply confirmation of their inherent incapacity for democratic government and socioeconomic progress. Roosevelt's only interest was asserting and sustaining U.S. authority. When the Cubans revolted in 1906 in an attempt to liberate themselves from a repressive U.S.-backed puppet government, Roosevelt sent in the Marines to crush the uprising. American troops remained in Cuba for three years to ensure there would be no further populist insurrections against the American-supported regime.

The Panama Canal

Without question the construction of the **Panama Canal** marked the high point of Roosevelt's agenda in establishing the United States as a recognized world power. Influenced by his reading of Alfred T. Mahan's seminal works on the importance of naval power, Roosevelt agreed more strongly than ever that the United States needed a swifter way of moving its ships between the Pacific and Atlantic Oceans than the only alternative—navigating around the tip of South America. Such a journey now could result in the U.S. not being able to protect its new distant possessions. Thus, Roosevelt concluded that for reasons of national security, the United States needed to gain access to a canal route across Central America, preferably at its narrowest width across the Colombian province of Panama. During the 1880s, a French company had attempted such an undertaking, but a host of technological difficulties, logistical problems, rampant outbreaks of malaria and yellow fever, and mounting financial costs ended the effort.

Despite the French failure, Roosevelt was determined to see the U.S. make an attempt to organize and build an isthmian canal. He first needed to convince the British government to approve the United States building its own canal because the two nations had agreed back in 1850 that any canal project in the region would be a joint undertaking. The Hay-Pauncefote Treaty signed with Great Britain in 1901 released the United States from the previous arrangement. Although initially intending to build the canal across Nicaragua, Roosevelt decided that the Panamanian route already started by the French and 40 percent completed was shorter and would therefore be cheaper to build and would be completed much faster. After long negotiations with Secretary of State Hay, the French construction company accepted a reduction from $109 million to $40 million in order to relinquish its rights to the route. Hay then quickly negotiated an agreement—the **Hay-Herrán Treaty**—with Tomás Herrán, the Colombian *charge d'affaires* in Washington, giving the United States the right to build a canal across Panama. For this privilege, the United States was to pay Colombia a one-time payment of $10 million and annual rent of $250,000.

Much to Roosevelt's subsequent outrage, the Colombian Senate reneged on the arrangement, asking instead for an initial payment of $25 million. Roosevelt felt deceived even though the Colombians were acting within their rights as a sovereign nation. Infuriated he worked behind closed doors with Philippe-Jean Bunau-Varilla, the chief engineer for the French company, and representatives of Panamanian rebels to plan an uprising, with the president promising the Panamanians that he would provide American military assistance and recognize their independence from Colombian rule. With such assurances, the Panamanians revolted in 1903. Roosevelt sent the gunboat *U.S.S. Nashville* to prevent Colombian troops from entering Panama. U.S. Marines then came ashore to aid the rebellion. The Roosevelt administration

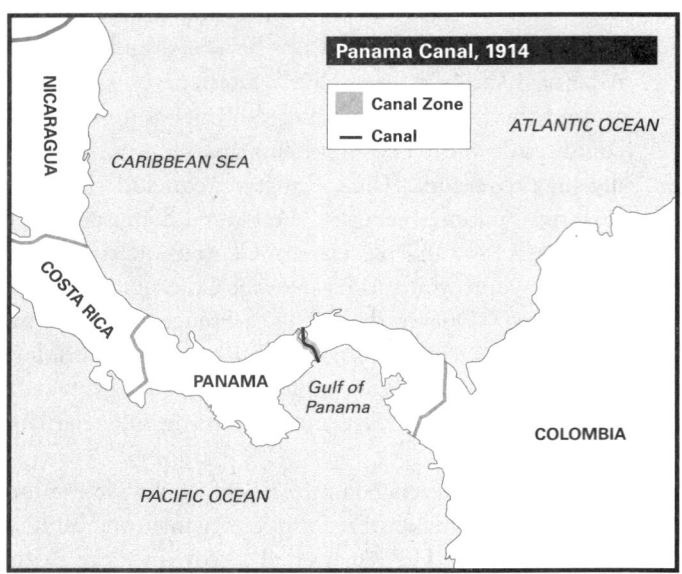

Map 19.4 The Panama Canal Zone and the Panama Canal

formally recognized the sovereign state of Panama only two days after the revolt began.

The provisional Panamanian government named Frenchman Bunau-Varilla to the post of temporary envoy to the United States. Roosevelt accepted him and asked Secretary Hay to quickly negotiate a canal treaty. The resulting **Hay-Bunau-Varilla Treaty** formalized the United States' right to a ten-mile wide canal zone in return for the package that Colombia had rejected—a $10 million down payment and a $250,000 annual leasing fee. Thus, by rather dubious means, Roosevelt secured American access to the canal region.

Roosevelt turned the canal into a showcase of superior American technology, ingenuity, and perseverance. Engineers overcame every physical obstacle; doctors developed drugs and mosquito eradication techniques to combat malaria and yellow fever; and some 30,000 West Indian workers labored for a 10-year period, for 10 hours a day, for six days a week, for ten cents an hour. Roosevelt visited his project in 1906, becoming the first American president to travel outside the United States while in office.

When the canal opened with great fanfare in 1914, it shortened the voyage from the West Coast to the East Coast by 8,000 miles, greatly enhancing the United States' international prestige. The Panama Canal became the perfect venue for Roosevelt to impress the great powers that the United States and the American people possessed the moral and physical character essential to accomplish such an undertaking.

In 1921, the United States paid the Colombian government $25 million as compensation for having, in effect, stolen the Canal Zone. In 1977, the U.S. Senate ratified a treaty negotiated by the administration of President Jimmy Carter that transferred control of the canal to Panama by the year 2000.

Roosevelt's Policies toward Asia

With respect to Asia, President Roosevelt withheld his aggressive policy of asserting United States authority with military force. The realization that a more militaristic posture would not endear him to the great powers heavily involved in the region (Russia, Japan, and the United Kingdom) affected Roosevelt's attitude. Instead, he pursued a policy of acceptance of the Open Door Policy in China while seeking to maintain a balance of power in Asia. However, the thwarting of Russian and Japanese expansion proved more difficult. Both nations coveted Manchuria and Korea. For Russians sought control of a warm water port in the Pacific Ocean while Japan desired access, if not complete control, of the rich ore deposits of Manchuria to aid in their country's industrialization.

Competition between Russia and Japan for territory in the region in 1904 escalated into a major conflict—the **Russo-Japanese War.** Much to the surprise of the European powers who still regarded the Japanese as an "inferior yellow people" incapable of defeating a great, white European power such as Russia, the Japanese routed the Russians on both land and sea with its superior forces and military leadership. The conflict revealed that Russia was still essentially an industrially backward nineteenth-century country, incapable of fighting, let alone winning, a modern war. Roosevelt feared that a defeat in Asia would end Russian presence in the region, disrupting the precarious balance of power, allowing the Japanese to gain ascendancy over the other great powers, especially in China. Japanese preeminence in the region would also establish Japan as a potential threat to United States' interests in Asia and the Pacific. Sensing such an outcome, the president entered into secret negotiations with both belligerents, seeking to end the war before Russian annihilation became complete.

Roosevelt invited representatives from both belligerent nations to Portsmouth, New Hampshire, hoping to secure a negotiated compromise. Despite all of his cajoling and browbeating, the Japanese diplomats refused to relinquish the territory that their military recently secured: Korea, the southern portion of Sakhalin Island (located to the north of the Japanese home islands), and Port Arthur (or Lüshun, located on the southern tip of the Liaodong Peninsula adjacent to northern Korea.) However, thanks to Roosevelt's intercession, Russia did not have to pay Japan a huge indemnity, and it retained Siberia (a "wasteland" in Japanese eyes), thus preserving its image (albeit a significantly diminished one) as an East Asian power. The president's only coup at Portsmouth was his persuading of both Russia and Japan to leave Manchuria, thus maintaining China's territorial integrity and simultaneously the United States' Open Door agenda. For his peace initiative, Roosevelt became the first American to win the Nobel Peace Prize in 1906.

As Roosevelt worked to craft agreements with Japan that respected that nation's sphere of influence in Asia, an event occurred at home that tested his skills in international relations. In California, another outbreak of anti-Japanese hysteria engulfed the state. White Californians had long resented the presence of Asians within their state, and for several decades the federal government capitulated to such nativism. In 1882, Congress passed the Chinese Exclusion Act, which ended most Chinese immigration to the United States but Japanese immigration had soon replaced the Chinese influx. By 1906, the Japanese population in California had reached 24,000. In that year, the San Francisco school board ordered the removal of all Asian schoolchildren from the city's public school system so they would not intermingle with white children. In 1907, the California legislature seriously considered passing a law that would stop all future Japanese immigration into the state. Violent anti-Asian riots erupted in San Francisco and Los Angeles. Most of the outbreaks were caused by the press, whose editorials about the "Yellow Peril" whipped white Californians into such a frenzy.

The Japanese government was outraged by the treatment of its citizens. Militarists began talking about a possible war with the United States. Roosevelt assured the Japanese government officials that he did not agree with the Californians' behavior. To resolve the matter, he reached the so-called "**Gentleman's Agreement**" whereby Japanese government officials agreed to halt the further immigration of adult male laborers to the United States in return for the president's pledge to bring an end to anti-Japanese discrimination in California. In return, Roosevelt pressured the San Francisco school board to retract its segregation ordinance. However, de facto segregation of Japanese citizens continued, as did occasional violent attacks upon them and their property.

WILLIAM HOWARD TAFT AND DOLLAR DIPLOMACY

Roosevelt's successor, William Howard Taft, brought solid foreign policy experience to the presidency, having served as the first governor-general of the Philippines, as well as Roosevelt's Secretary of War. In 1905, he negotiated the Taft-Katsura Agreement whereby the United States recognized Japanese control over the Korean peninsula in exchange for a Japanese promise to respect U.S. authority over the Philippines. Despite having learned much about international politics under Roosevelt, Taft lacked Roosevelt's understanding and appreciation of balance-of-power geopolitics. He also chose to be much less personally involved in foreign policy, preferring instead to delegate authority to his Secretary of State, the corporate lawyer Philander C. Knox. Reflecting his years of defending the excesses of American corporate capitalism, Knox believed that the main focus of U.S. foreign policy should be expanding American corporate investment abroad—a disposition that prompted critics to deride his agenda as "**Dollar Diplomacy**." Both Taft and Knox believed that American investments would not only greatly benefit the U.S. economy, but also offer a more peaceful way of winning new international friends while maintaining stability than reliance on the use of military action.

The inability of Taft and Knox to grasp the complexities of power politics led to diplomatic reversals, upsetting the delicate balance of power that Roosevelt had established in East Asia. Prodded by his Wall Street friends, Knox sought to expand American investment in China, even into Manchuria—an area that Roosevelt had previously accepted as within the Japanese sphere of influence. In 1911, Knox put together a consortium of European bankers to buy the South Manchuria Railway (then under Japanese control) for the purpose of opening up North China to international trade. The Japanese naturally viewed Knox's scheme as an unwelcome attempt to undermine their privileged position in the area.

In response, the Japanese signed a friendship treaty with their former adversary, Russia, allowing that country's goods into Manchurian markets while preventing the penetration of American, French, and British products into the region. The Japanese knew they could not stand alone against such a powerful Western power. They were thus willing to engage in détente with Russia, which desperately needed markets for its industrializing economy. If Russia joined with Japan in such an arrangement, perhaps the Western powers would back off, for they would not want to alienate future potential allies, as tensions in Europe among the great powers mounted. As a result of the Russo-Japanese cordial relations, Knox's syndicate idea collapsed, dealing a serious blow to America's Open Door Policy. Most important, in 1912, the foreign-controlled puppet government of China fell, precipitating ten years of revolution and civil war, resulting in the loss of millions of American investment dollars. The zealous devotion of Taft and Knox to the value of the U.S. dollar in determining foreign policy initiatives had backfired.

Dollar diplomacy fared somewhat better in the Caribbean and Central America. Knox encouraged American investment in the hemisphere, both to provide corporations with opportunities for profit and to supplant the European investors already there or to beat them to the punch in acquiring new ventures. During the Taft administration, over half of all U.S. dollars invested abroad were found in various Latin American enterprises, ranging from oil to public utilities to railroads and agriculture. Most important, U.S. conglomerates became such powerful economic entities in these host countries, especially in the more vulnerable countries of Central America, that they not only controlled the country's economy but politics as well. Such was the power of the United Fruit Company of Boston, Massachusetts. By controlling the majority of the banana plantations of Costa Rica and Honduras, (bananas were the main export crop of both countries), the company virtually owned both nations. Taft and Knox were so driven by their devotion to dollar diplomacy that they assured American corporations that if at any time their enterprises were threatened by political opposition or turmoil in the countries where they had such a presence, the U.S. would simply send troops to protect their interests.

Such a provocation occurred in 1910 when the Nicaraguan dictator, Jose Santos Zelaya, began considering negotiations with a European government to build a second isthmian canal through his country. Upon hearing of the rumors, Taft sent a force of U.S. Marines to overthrow his regime. U.S. troops arrived again in 1912 to support Zelaya's successor, Adolfo Diaz, who alienated his people by his pro-American policies. Except for a brief period in 1925, American forces remained in Nicaragua until 1933. With his willingness to send troops to safeguard his dollar diplomacy approach, Taft engaged in the same militarism that his predecessor readily employed in order to sustain puppet governments friendly to the United States and maintain order in Latin America.

UNITED STATES EXPANSION

Americans living at the end of the Civil War who were still alive by the outbreak of World War I in 1914 witnessed a monumental transformation of their country. Most aspects of life from their early days were gone, replaced by technological advancements changing the ways that they worked and lived. As a nation, America's place in the world as a global power was also far beyond the country's previous experiences just 60 years earlier. In the Pacific, the United States forged a chain of far-flung possessions into a confederated empire—from Alaska in the north to Samoa in the south; from Hawaii in the central Pacific to Guam and the Philippines in eastern Asia. In Latin America, the other region of immediate importance to the U.S., America secured direct control of Puerto Rico, an island base in eastern Cuba, and most significantly, the Panama Canal Zone. Indirectly, the United States through the implementation of the Roosevelt Corollary to the Monroe Doctrine reserved the right to intervene (and often did) in the domestic affairs of Caribbean nations.

In both regions, traditional American ideals were challenged, and often evolved to fit the new circumstances. The values of democracy, freedom, and self-determination touted by the United States were tested as American government leaders aggressively sought to prevent European encroachment and extend U.S. influence in Latin America. In the cases of Panama and Nicaragua, American military interventions occurred purely for national self-interest (as defined by Theodore Roosevelt and William Taft, respectively). In Asia, the United States engaged in a four-year-long conflict against Filipino rebels seeking to rule their country after centuries of Spanish occupation had been removed by U.S. forces. Though imperialists justified control of the Philippines as the legitimate spoils of war, other Americans, including President McKinley, were not eager to extend U.S. control over a land occupied by millions of non-English-speaking people spread out across an archipelago of hundreds of islands but paternalistically justified U.S. annexation in the belief that the Filipinos were "not ready" for self-government. In the process of spreading "the benefits of civilization" to the Philippines, American troops committed a host of atrocities and utilized brutal tactics to suppress the guerilla fighters and any civilians they suspected of aiding the rebels. Such a beginning in empire building for the United States begs the question: in what tangible ways did the United States behave differently than the expanding empires of Europe and Japan?

Table 19.1   Major U.S. Territorial Acquisitions, 1867-1917

Territory	Date Acquired	How Acquired	Significance to the U.S.
Alaska	1867	Purchase from Russia	Northern Pacific ports
Midway Islands	1867	Annexation	U.S. naval station in the Central Pacific
Guam	1898	Peace treaty following the Spanish-American War	Naval base + coaling station in the western Pacific
Philippine Islands	1898	Peace treaty following the Spanish-American War	Naval base + coaling station in the western Pacific
Puerto Rico	1898	Peace treaty following the Spanish-American War	Naval base + coaling station in the Eastern Caribbean
Hawaii	1898	Annexation treaty with the "Republic of Hawaii"	Naval base + coaling station in the Central Pacific
American Samoa	1899	Annexation	Naval base + coaling station in the South Pacific
Guantanamo Bay	1903	Lease provision written into Cuban constitution	Naval base + coaling station in eastern Cuba
Panama Canal Zone	1903	Hay-Bunau-Varilla Treaty with Panama	Construction route for the Panama Canal
U.S. Virgin Islands	1917	Purchase from Denmark	Naval base in the Eastern Caribbean

Chronology

1875	U.S. agrees to allow Hawaii to export sugar to America duty-free.
1878	U.S. gains treaty rights for base at Pago Pago in Samoa.
1887	U.S. gains treaty rights for base at Pearl Harbor in Hawaii.
1889	First Pan-American Congress.
1890	Alfred Thayer Mahan publishes *The Influence of Sea Power on History.* U.S. ends favored status of Hawaii in sugar trade.
1893	U.S. sugar planters in Hawaii foment rebellion against weak native king. Cleveland rejects attempt to annex Hawaii.
1894	Wilson-Gorman tariff on Cuban sugar.
1895	President Cleveland defends Monroe Doctrine in border dispute between Venezuela and Guiana.
1896	William McKinley elected president.
1898	William Randolph Hearst, publishes de Lôme letter. U.S. battleship *Maine* explodes in Havana harbor. Congress declares war on Spain. Dewey destroys Spanish fleet in the Philippines. U.S. troops defeat Spanish forces in Cuba. Treaty of Paris ends war with Spain and cedes Puerto Rico, Philippines, and Guam to the U.S. United States annexes Hawaii. Anti-Imperialist League formed.
1898-1902	Philippines revolt against American rule.
1899	Senate ratifies Treaty of Paris. Hay releases "Open Door notes" on China.
1900	Foraker Act establishes civil government in Puerto Rico. Hawaii granted territorial status. Boxer rebellion breaks out in China. McKinley reelected president.
1901	American forces capture Filipino rebel leader Emilio Aguinaldo. U.S. establishes civil government in Philippines. Platt Amendment.

SUGGESTED READINGS

Robert L. Beisner, *From the Old Diplomacy to the New, 1865-1900* (1986).

————, *Twelve Against Empire: The Anti-Imperialists, 1898-1900* (1968).

James E. Bradford, *Crucible of Empire: The Spanish American War and Its Aftermath* (1993).

Michael Blow, *A Ship to Remember: The Maine and the Spanish-American War.* (1992)

Warren J. Cohen, *America's Response to China* (1971).

Graham A. Cosmas, *An Army for Empire: The United States Army in the Spanish-American War* (1971).

William B. Gatewood Jr., *"Smoked Yankees; Letters From Negro Soldiers 1898-1902* (1971).

David F. Healy, *U.S. Expansionism: Imperialist Urge in the 1890s* (1970).

Walter R. Herrick, *The American Naval Revolution* (1966).

Walter LaFeber, *The Cambridge History of Foreign Relations: The Search for Opportunity, 1865-1913* (1993).

Gerald F. Linderman, *The Mirror of War: American Society and the Spanish-American War* (1974).

William E. Livezey, *Mahan on Sea Power* (1981).

Thomas J. McCormick, *China Market: America's Quest for Informal Empire, 1890-1915* (1971).

Ernest R. May, *Imperial Democracy: The Emergence of America as a Great Power* (1961).

Stuart Creighton Miller, *"Benevolent Assimilation:" The American Conquest of the Philippines, 1899-1903* (1982).

Joyce Milton, *The Yellow Journalists* (1989).

H. Wayne Morgan, *America's Road to Empire* (1965).

Edmund Morris, *The Rise of Theodore Roosevelt* (1979).

Ivan Musicant, *Empire by Default: The Spanish-American War and the Dawn of the American Century* (1998).

Louis A. Perez, *Cuba Under the Platt Amendment, 1902-1934* (1986).

William A. Russ Jr., *The Hawaiian Republic, 1894-1898 and Its Struggle to Win Annexation* (1961).

Peter Stanley, *A Nation in the Making: The Philippines and the United States, 1899-1921* (1974).

E. Berkeley Tomkins, *Anti-Imperialism in the United States, 1890-1920: The Great Debate* (1970).

David F. Trask, *The War With Spain* (1981).

Richard E. Welch, Jr. *Response to Imperialism: The United States and the Philippine War, 1899-1902* (1979).

William Appleman Williams, *The Tragedy of American Diplomacy* (1959).

Marilyn B. Young, *The Rhetoric of Empire: American China Policy, 1895-1901* (1968).

Review Questions

1. Discuss the factors leading to the United States becoming a major world power by the end of the 1800s.

2. Discuss the arguments used by American imperialists to justify gaining possession of overseas territories in the years after the Civil War.

3. Assess the causes and consequences of the 1898 Spanish-American War.

4. Why were American imperialists interested in Asia, especially China? What were the short-term and long-term consequences of the United States' attempts to establish influence in that region of the world?

5. What foreign policy legacy did Theodore Roosevelt leave for his successors?

Glossary of Important People and Concepts

Battle of Manila Bay
Emilio Aguinaldo
Boxer Rebellion
de Lôme Letter
"Dollar Diplomacy"
Foraker Act
Gentlemen's Agreement
Hay-Bunau-Varilla Treaty
Hay-Herrán Treaty
Queen Liliuokalani
William McKinley
Alfred Thayer Mahan
Open Door Policy
Panama Canal
Platt Amendment
Roosevelt Corollary
"Rough Riders"
Russo-Japanese War
Samoa
Josiah Strong
Teller Amendment
Treaty of Paris
U.S.S. Maine
Valeriano Weyler
Yellow journalism

Horse-drawn fire engines in the street on their way to the Triangle Shirtwaist Company Fire, New York City. March 25, 1911

Chapter Twenty

The Progressive Reformation of Industrial America

On March 25, 1911, New York City experienced a horrific industrial fire at the Triangle Shirtwaist Company, a manufacturer of popular ladies' blouses. Beginning late on a Saturday afternoon among one of the many piles of discarded fabric clippings, the inferno spread rapidly across the upper floors of the ten-story Asch Building where the factory was located in the heart of Manhattan's Garment District. Workers on the eighth and tenth floors were able to escape, but those on the ninth floor found themselves trapped. Though the floor had many exits, only a few lucky ones were able to catch an elevator while it was still in operation in order to reach the ground floor. A few others used a stairway to reach the roof. Flames prevented large numbers of workers from using another stairway while the main exit was useless because its doors had been illegally locked by guards who were told to screen employees from walking off their jobs to prevent them from stealing cloth. Increasingly desperate, many ran to the single fire escape, which was poorly maintained and thus quickly collapsed from the overload of weight, dropping victims over a hundred feet to the pavement below. Fire engines soon arrived on the scene, but their ladders reached no higher than the sixth floor. Eventually, in an action to be replicated ninety years later at the World Trade Center on 9/11, sixty-two desperate women horrified onlookers as they jumped to the street below. None of them survived. As one reporter later related the details of the terrible scene that he witnessed:

. . . [A] young man helped a girl to the windowsill on the ninth floor. Then he held her deliberately away from the building, and let her drop. He held out a second girl the same way and let her drop. He held out a third girl who did not resist. They were all as unresisting as if he were helping them into a street car instead of into eternity. He saw that a terrible death awaited them in the flames and his was only a terrible chivalry. He brought around another girl to the window—I saw her put her arms around him and kiss him. Then he held her into space—and dropped her. Quick as a flash he was on the windowsill himself. His coat fluttered upwards—the air filled his trouser legs as he came down. I could see he wore tan shoes.

In all, 146 victims, most of them young Jewish and Italian immigrant women, had perished in the city's worst workplace disaster.

The incident and subsequent outpouring of emotion, which included a Fifth Avenue procession of grief in which over 100,000 took part and another 400,000 witnessed, led to demands for a full investigation. The state legislature responded by creating a Factory Investigating Commission, which completed a broad survey of factory safety and health that included recommendations to improve the protection of workers. Thirteen bills based on the Commission's suggestions became law, leading to improvements in fire safety, factory

**Triangle Shirtwaist Co.,
New York City,
March 26, 1911.
Crowd outside of
the pier morgue.**

ventilation, sanitation, machine guarding, and other special measures for specific industries.

The fire reinforced arguments made by many reformers during the Progressive Era—that business could not go on as usual. In the early days of the Industrial Revolution, many Americans were reluctant to embrace a wide range of intrusions on corporations lest the industrialization process be hindered, but opinions of a majority of Americans had changed by the turn of the twentieth century. Reformers argued that the processes of industrialization and urbanization could be greatly improved and made more efficient if the country would adopt a more ordered approach. As America entered a new century, an increasing number of citizens began to listen to those who professed that the means existed to maintain the benefits of industrialization without the sometimes appalling human cost such as occurred that terrible day in 1911.

Contemporaries and later historians have used the term "**progressivism**" to describe the reform impulse that surged in American political and social life at the turn of the twentieth century. A significant response to the tremendous changes that marked America's transition to an urban-industrial nation, the effort marked the end of unbridled laissez-faire capitalism. Progressive activists did not desire to dismantle big business or the rise of large metropolises by "turning back the clock" to a simpler time, but, rather, sought to bring rational order to a significantly altered society. They wished to keep the more positive benefits brought about by industrialization while seeking to limit its least desirable aspects.

Diversity remains one of the Progressives' salient characteristics. Though particularly strong among the urban middle class of the Northeast, reformers came from all walks of life (as did their opponents). Progressives not only could be found among the recently emerging middle class but also among the old-money elite, some wealthy businessmen, members of the industrial working class, and residents of small towns and rural areas. Progressivism crossed party lines—there were Republican reformers, Democratic reformers, and even some Socialists who supported progressive causes. Though its nature changed with geography, reform leaders and their supporters showed strength across the country—in the Northeast, the Midwest, the Far West, and the South.

Progressives were united in their desire for constructive changes in response to the new realities of twentieth-century life. They also tended to share common approaches to problems, believing strongly in the tools of science, the value of mass publicity, and the powers of government to investigate problems, educate the public, and provide solutions through legislation. Certainly no Progressive supported all the proposals being offered during the period. Many vehemently opposed some suggestions. Perhaps the best way to understand the nature of Progressivism is through the concept of "shifting coalitions." Diverse groups and individuals such as doctors, women's activists, certain religious organizations, and businessmen, for example, might come together for different motivations to strongly support the prohibition of alcohol, yet when the issue turned to factory regulation, the businessmen might balk at the notion and refuse to ally themselves further with the previous coalition because they might perceive the proposal as working against their interests. These types of revolving alliances appeared frequently during the era.

THE MUCKRAKERS

The efforts of determined investigative journalists greatly helped to spread awareness of problems and proposed solutions. A true phenomenon of the age, new ten-cent national magazines such as *Collier's*, *McClure's*, and *Cosmopolitan* regularly carried exposés (often later published as books) designed to elevate subscription sales while arousing the public on a variety of issues. Some writers, such as Lincoln Steffens in his *McClure's* series "The Shame of the Cities," described the power of urban political machines. Others focused on corporate power and influence, such as Ida Tarbell, whose damning *McClure's* articles on John D. Rockefeller's ascent to power by crushing honest competitors through immoral and illegal actions and the use of special privileges were later published as *The History of the Standard Oil Company*. Some reporters used the power of photography to illustrate their findings, such as newspaperman Jacob Riis who used photographic images to clearly display the misery of New York City slum life in *How the Other Half Lives*. Many writers also used fiction to dramatize a real-life issue. In Frank Norris's novel *The Octopus*, the author used drama based on fact to demonstrate the power of the Southern Pacific Railroad over the citizens of California, especially its farmers.

While the work of the investigative reporters re-

Ida M. Tarbell, c. 1922.

ceived a wide audience, not everyone was pleased with the constant tone of confrontation that often coincided with the latest revelations. In a 1906 speech designed to please many Washington politicians whose support he needed for aspects of his domestic program, President Theodore Roosevelt coined the term **"muckrakers"** to characterize the era's probing journalists. Referring to a character in John Bunyan's *Pilgrim's Progress* who became so focused on his job of raking up the muck that he did not look up to see the beauty and goodness there was in the world, Roosevelt decried those individuals who solely focused on the negative aspects of American life, or spread untruths in an effort to promote the greater good, while acknowledging that there were many evils in the world that needed to be exposed and eradicated.

LOCAL URBAN REFORMS

Energetic urban reform during the Progressive Era emanated from those active "in the streets," endeavoring to solve everyday problems produced by modern urban-industrial life. Publicity surrounding the labors of the nation's first generation of social workers focused increased attention on the myriad of problems produced by the sprawling industrial cities. Inspired by British students from Oxford University who founded Toynbee Hall in a London slum during the mid-1880s, some Americans similarly sought to establish so-called **"settlement houses"** to live and work amongst the immigrant poor. Often but not always consisting of college-educated middle- and upper-class women wishing to do useful work beyond the limits of acceptable roles dictated by traditional society,

Lincoln Steffens, 1914.

settlement house workers sought to reduce class antagonisms through the establishment of close personal contact with neighborhood residents—seeking to earn their trust through the sponsorship of a variety of educational, cultural, and social activities designed to improve their living environment. Stanton Coit first brought the settlement idea to the United States in 1889 when he and several friends from several women's colleges helped to establish the College Settlement in a tenement area of New York City's Lower East Side. Later that same year, Rockford College classmates Jane Addams and Ellen Gates Starr established the most famous settlement house—Chicago's Hull House. From their South Halsted Street base, Addams, Starr, and their fellow social workers sponsored lectures, exhibits, and festivals designed to reinforce pride in the immigrants' cultural heritage. Simultaneously, they taught classes ranging from homemaking to American history while establishing nurseries, day care centers, kindergartens, and playgrounds for urban youth. They also investigated social conditions, lobbied for changes with local government authorities, joined municipal reform campaigns, and did much to educate the general public about the need for concrete changes in numerous aspects of American city life. By 1910, hundreds of young men and women had followed their lead, operating approximately 400 settlement houses across the country.

The club movement offered another avenue for middle- and upper-class women to engage in urban reform efforts. Though unable to vote or hold public office in most regions of the country, many women during the Progressive Era influenced local political battles by using their social clubs to lobby for a host of reforms designed to improve city life. Ever mindful of societal limits regarding what was deemed women's proper place, these women often characterized themselves as "**municipal housekeepers**" to overcome these gender expectations by asserting that their activism reinforced their role as protector of family and home. In this manner, progressive women claimed that their campaigns strengthened families by producing a healthier and safer environment through such efforts as city beautification projects, library and hospital construction, and establishment of juvenile courts for youth offenders.

A cadre of reform-minded mayors also contributed to important urban changes often emulated elsewhere in the country. Elected the mayor of Detroit, Michigan, in 1890, Republican Hazen S. Pingree, sponsored efforts to create municipally-owned competitors to the electric and gas company monopolies that existed in an effort to drive down utility prices. During the Depression of 1893, he aggressively expanded local welfare programs through the creation of public works programs for the unemployed

Jane Addams, c. 1912.

and opening up city-owned land for use by the poor to grow food crops. During his tenure as mayor of Toledo, Ohio from 1897 to 1905, Democrat Samuel L. "Golden Rule" Jones also made a name for himself nationally by pressing for city control over utilities and arranged for funds to be allocated for the construction of recreational facilities and places for the city's homeless to live.

Nonpartisan efforts to provide "honest, effective, businesslike government" in order to root out corruption and the perceived inefficiency of urban political machines also occurred across the nation. After being elected mayor on a reform platform supported by Republicans and anti-Tammany Hall Democrats in 1894, Republican merchant William L. Strong reorganized many city departments, established a Board of Education, created a series of municipal parks, and appointed Theodore Roosevelt as Police Commissioner who energetically transformed the New York Police Department into a modern urban force through a series of reforms much emulated across the country—new disciplinary rules, creation of a mobile bicycle squad, direct communication among all precinct headquarters via telephones, standardized use of pistols by officers with requisite firearms training, annual physical exams, establishment of meritorious service medals, and appointment of new recruits based on their physical and mental qualification rather than political affiliation.

In other cities, reformers sought additional means to correct "structural defects" in the organization of municipal governments. After a devastating hurricane destroyed Galveston, Texas, for example, residents approved a massive overhaul of the city government to speed up rebuilding efforts. The Texas state legislature allowed Galveston to cast aside its mayor-city council form of local government in favor of a **commission-style government** whereby five individual commission members undertook personal responsibility for one of the key departments of city governance, such as police, fire, housing, and utilities. As the town slowly recovered, the appeal of the "Galveston Plan" rose across the country. Other cities sought to bring about changes in their localities without the interference of partisan political rancor and self-interest. Des Moines, Iowa, adopted also a commission-style government in 1908, followed by hundreds of other middle-sized cities over the next decade.

The inherent challenges presented by the emerging urban-industrial order offered numerous opportunities for many professionals eager to apply their training in an effort to solve them. While social workers involved themselves in settlement work, city planners began to ply their trade in many cities across the country. Not an entirely new concept, city planning began to be taught as a field of intense study in the nation's universities during the Progressive Era, producing recent graduates wishing to reorganize American city life. Zoning became the primary means of accomplishing their task. By advocating the segregation of various city districts by function, planners hoped to create a much safer and efficient urban environment. Whereas previously the cities had grown in an unrestrained and unregulated manner, planners sought the passage of laws that would limit the use of land in a given area. Junkyards and industrial plants, for example, would now be kept some distance away from parks and schools. Residential areas would now be located away from heavy commercial districts. Medical doctors also sought to improve the health of the nation's cities and rural areas. Physicians actively supported political campaigns and education drives that championed sanitation reforms, creation of local health boards, construction of hospitals, the eradication of diseases, and improvement in medical school standards through which the nation's doctors were produced.

STATE-LEVEL REFORMS

Labor Reforms

Even before the Progressive Era, many state governments in the Northeast during the first decades of the Industrial Revolution responded to strong pressure from organized labor and were already investigating working conditions in factories and mines, publishing findings through annual reports of state bureaus of labor statistics. The information gathered, often highlighting the number and nature of industrial accidents, led labor groups to further push for the passage of factory inspection legislation modeled after the pioneering laws in this field implemented in England.

Progressives worked aggressively to strengthen these safety laws and their enforcement as well as to secure additional labor reforms that they believed were necessary to humanize the Industrial Revolution. Ending child labor, for example, became the passionate calling for many social progressives who viewed the practice as a resident evil in need of eradication. Historically, American children, as youths elsewhere in the world, were an important part of the pre-industrial work force. Children performed a variety of tasks on family farms plus many were apprenticed at a young age to learn a trade. The expansion of industry after 1880 led to a tremendous increase in native-born children working in Appalachian coal mines and southern textile mills. (In 1899, 25 percent of all workers in southern cotton mills were under the age of 15.) In addition, the huge influx of immigrants from southern and eastern Europe led to a large number of children working in the cities of the Northeast and Midwest as factory workers, shoe shiners, newspaper sellers, and product peddlers on the streets. Statistics from the 1900 Census, which underestimate the extent of the problem, show that at the very least, 1.75 million children aged 10-15 (26 percent of boys, 10 percent of girls, and 18 percent total) were employed.

The large number of children working in factories, mines, farms, or on the streets alarmed many progressives, as did the often rough working conditions for the youths. After 1900, progressives began to organize efforts to regulate or end child labor. Settlement house workers, women's clubs, and local reform groups led the way by forming state child labor committees. In 1904, the National Child Labor Committee was established to arouse public indignation and target state legislatures for effective changes. Utilizing expert investigators to gather data, effective use of photography to document and publicize the plight of child workers, mass mailings of pamphlets and leaflets to alert the public, and a heavy dose of political lobbying, the committee successfully convinced two thirds of the states to enact some form of child labor legislation by 1907 such as minimum wages, maximum hours, and the prohibition of children working in certain occupations, though many loopholes remained in terms of excluded trades and lax enforcement procedures. Acknowledgement of these limitations led many child labor advocates to seek federal remedies.

Social progressives also sought to regulate the wages and hours of working women. **Florence Kelley**, the daughter of a Pennsylvania Quaker businessman and congressman, led the crusade. After graduating from Cornell University and studying for a time in Europe, she arrived in Chicago in 1891 to work at Hull House and pursue a law degree at Northwestern University. After Kelley persuaded the Illinois legislature in 1893 to pass a factory labor law that limited women to eight-hour work days and banned the use of children under the age of fourteen (overturned by the state supreme court two years later), Governor John P. Altgeld named her to be the state's chief factory inspector. She remained at Hull House working alongside Jane Addams for the remainder of the decade until she moved to New York City's Henry Street Settlement where she tirelessly collected data and published articles on the ill effects of long hours on the health and safety of female workers. In 1899, Kelley became the general secretary for the National Consumers' League, an organization which coordinated the efforts of local groups seeking to educate the public about women's and children's working conditions and to organize consumer boycotts of goods produced by employers who exploited their workers.

As a result of a mobilized electorate, many states began to pass laws limiting the working hours of women in certain occupations. Opposition from employers often led to legal challenges, none as significant as *Muller v. Oregon* argued before the Supreme Court in 1908. In 1903, Oregon passed a law restricting women to work no more than ten hours per day. When Portland laundry owner Curt Muller refused to obey the law, he was fined ten dollars. The businessman appealed to the state supreme court, but the tribunal upheld his conviction. The U.S. Supreme Court agreed to hear Muller's federal appeal during which his lawyers brought up the High Court's ruling in *Lochner v. New York* (1905) whereby a New York general labor statute limiting working hours under such terms was thrown out as a violation of the right to contract between employer and employee. Defenders of the Oregon law retained the services of constitutional lawyer Louis D. Brandeis whose famous "Brandeis Brief" (with data assembled by Florence Kelley and actually written by her friend Josephine Goldmark) used sociological, medical, and other scientific evidence to document the point that women's "physical structure and the performance of her maternal functions" placed them at such a disadvantage that their physical well-being became an object of public interest. Brandeis proved to the Court's satisfaction that long working hours were harmful to the well-being of women and affirmed the overall principle that governmental interest in public welfare outweighed any absolute freedom of contract. Progressives generally cheered the ruling, though many feminists voiced displeasure that the basis of the ruling relied heavily upon the separation of the sexes into stereotyped gender roles. Nevertheless, in the decade following the decision, most states began to pass laws limiting the working hours of women.

Improving general occupational health marked another important concern of progressives. Not just limiting their efforts to reducing industrial accidents, many reformers also concentrated on common health dangers in the workplace. In 1909, a team of researchers led by Alice Hamilton for the Illinois Occupational Disease Commission produced a pioneering report on the subject, highlighting the detrimental effects upon workers of exposure to toxic chemicals. The most significant section of the report publicized the dangers of lead poisoning in numerous trades. Another campaign led by John B. Andrews sought to outlaw the use of white phosphorous in matches because repeated exposure to the chemical by workers led many of them to develop phosphorous necrosis or "phossy jaw," a disfiguring disease that eroded the teeth and jaw bones of laborers in the match factories. Already banned in many European countries, Congress finally acted in 1912 when it placed a large tax on white phosphorous matches. Meanwhile, the Diamond Match Company waived its patent on a harmless substitute for white phosphorous that allowed competitors to begin using them in the manufacture of matches. The efforts of progressives such as Hamilton and Andrews focused national attention on the issue of occupational safety and led to an entirely new field of study for social scientists and members of the American medical profession.

Prohibition

Efforts to curb or eliminate alcohol from American life had existed since colonial days. In 1851, Maine became the first state to prohibit alcohol within its borders. During the 1870s, women's groups, most notably the Woman's Christian Temperance Union, actively sought to close down saloons and promote individual moral reform. By the turn of the twentieth century, efforts to prohibit alcohol had become a reform supported by a large number of progressives who viewed the availability of cheap mass-produced alcohol as a societal danger in need of removal. Alcohol was viewed by many women's groups as a family-wrecking evil, by doctors as the source of countless health problems, by businessmen as a factor contributing to inefficiency, and by urban political reformers as a lifeblood of saloons that functioned as centers of

Members of the Anti-Saloon League at the White House, January 16, 1924.

moral degeneracy promoting drunkenness, violent crime, prostitution, and police corruption. (Many progressives also opposed Prohibition efforts for a variety of reasons.)

By the mid-1890s, the **Anti-Saloon League (ASL)** emerged as a major special interest group promoting Prohibition. Enlisting the support of many Protestant congregations, ASL members pledged only to support "dry" Democratic or Republican candidates for public office. The ASL pressured legislators for community "local option" laws and statewide prohibition statutes. In states that allowed referendums, the ASL succeeded in placing proposed Prohibition measures before local and statewide voters. Some of these efforts failed (such as in Texas where referendums held in 1908 and 1911 barely failed to pass), while many others proved successful. By 1917, 21 states had banned saloons entirely and three-fourths of Americans lived in a legally dry county. While achieving many state-level successes, prohibitionists still desired passage of a proposed federal constitutional amendment to outlaw liquor and would pursue that goal vigorously after the outbreak of World War I.

Woman Suffrage

Similar to Prohibition, the woman suffrage movement had its origins in the antebellum era but evolved into a Progressive era crusade. Organized efforts to promote female voting in America had existed since the 1840s, with a main line of argument being that men were denying civil rights to women. While that approach continued into the twentieth century, many pragmatic suffragists in the early 1900s began to gain crucial support by persuading reformers that their endeavors to end child labor, prohibit

alcohol, and even limit the voting strength of immigrants would be greatly bolstered with the addition of qualified women voters. (In the South, some feminist groups argued openly that adding women to the voter rolls would increase white voting power over African Americans due to their larger numbers.)

After the Civil War, the suffrage movement experienced internal divisions over tactics and priorities, leading to a factional split. In 1890, a major reconciliation among suffragists led to the formation of the **National American Woman Suffrage Association (NAWSA)**, which revitalized the movement. The organization sponsored state-level educational activities, well-financed referenda drives, and brisk lobbying of legislators. In its first six years of operation, NAWSA's work bore some fruit with the admission of Wyoming and Utah into the Union with woman suffrage written into their state constitutions and voters in Colorado and Idaho granting unrestricted female voting by referendum. The next fourteen years, however, proved disappointing. Despite the launching of 480 separate petition campaigns to give women the vote in states across the country, only a few succeeded in getting the measures on the ballot, and none passed. Starting in 1910, former NAWSA President Carrie Chapman Catt's renewed efforts to organize effective state-level campaigns began to pay off. Seven western states granted unlimited female suffrage by 1914, with Oklahoma and South Dakota following suit by 1918. Nevertheless, the failure to gain the franchise in most central and eastern states (except for the allowance in some states to participate in local or presidential elections only) led not only to a wave of congressional petitions to introduce a proposed federal constitutional amendment but also to an increase in deliberately abrasive tactics by

Woman Suffrage
Headquarters in
Cleveland, Ohio, 1912.

so-called militant suffragists to use more aggressive tactics employed by British suffragists to bring about the desired change at the national level.

Political Reforms

The arguments of woman suffragists to allow female voter participation worked well among Progressives who concerned themselves with reforming politics and government. Motivated by a desire to reduce corruption and improve the efficiency of government, reforms that they adopted democratized the political process for many common citizens while other changes actually restricted access to participation for members of certain groups. Nevertheless, the perceived need to adapt to changed times unified them to seek alterations in the nation's political system.

By the 1890s, most states had moved to the so-called Australian ballot system, whereby voters cast their votes in secret on publicly printed ballots (in English) with all candidates listed available only at official polling places. Other states went further to limit potential corruption by outlawing vote-buying and corporate donations while limiting acceptable uses of campaign funds. Though many hailed these and other reforms, they often contributed to a decline in excitement at election time and decreased voter turnout.

Most Progressives did not mind an overall reduction in voter participation—their goals were often to "improve the quality" of the electorate rather than to expand its numbers. Such thinking guided more open

disfranchisement efforts in the North and South at the turn of the century. In the South, Democrats alarmed by the Populist challenge of the 1890s sought to greatly reduce black and poor white involvement in elections through a variety of devices including poll taxes, literacy tests, "civics" exams, and other restrictions. Meanwhile, Republicans in the North and West used similar devices to reduce the influence of potential voters from recent immigrant groups. While these efforts disregarded the spirit of the Fifteenth Amendment, they did not violate the letter of the amendment, which stated only that a citizen could not be denied the right to vote on grounds of race or color.

The **direct primary** became a quintessential Progressive reform. Activists often found their efforts stymied by conservative political bosses and their corporate allies in both major political parties who arranged for the nomination of candidates who usually held anti-reform views at state conventions. In an effort to break down these barriers, Progressives across the country sought to take the power of nominations away from the party bosses and place them in the hands of responsible citizens. Over a dozen states allowed for the direct primary by the 1912 presidential election. Most states had the device by 1920. Riding on the heels of the direct primary's popularity, three-quarters of the states ratified the Seventeenth Amendment to the U.S. Constitution in 1913, which allowed for the direct election of U.S. senators by popular vote rather than state legislatures.

Further efforts to limit the power of conservative Democratic and Republican party bosses under the sway of corporate influence involved the inclusion of eligible citizens in the legislative process. Among these "direct democracy" provisions adopted by a growing number of states by 1920, the referendum also allowed voters to express their opinion and advise the legislature how to act on a controversial issue. Meanwhile, the initiative allowed activists to gather signatures to qualify legislation for approval by the voters. If passed, the proposition would become law without approval needed by the state legislature. Some states adopted the recall, allowing disgruntled citizens to gather enough signatures on a petition to call for a special election to seek the removal of certain officeholders.

AFRICAN-AMERICAN RESPONSES TO JIM CROW

Despite the end of Reconstruction leading to the establishment of second-class status for African Americans in southern society, black voting had not been entirely eliminated. With their economic clout, conservative members of the new upper class thought that they could effectively manage the black vote. In the late 1880s and early 1890s, however, growing agricultural unrest led to the formation of the Populist Party which, for a while, seemed capable of merging oppressed black and marginal white farmers into an effective coalition to challenge conservative rule. Southern Democratic politicians responded by reviving racist propaganda and returning to warnings about "Negro domination" and "revival of black Reconstruction" to discredit the Populists. After successfully maintaining their power, these leaders soon undertook a major effort to disfranchise black and poor white voters in the name of "good government." Rather than expanding the electorate, "election reform" advocates argued that reducing the number of eligible voters to those "better qualified" to participate in the process would improve the overall quality of government and reduce corruption. Between 1890 and 1910, the southern states imposed poll taxes, literacy requirements, and other creative means to suppress the vote. Four states even instituted "grandfather clauses" into their voting laws, allowing men to vote only if their ancestors had voted before 1867 (when blacks had been first granted the vote). The Supreme Court eventually overturned this obvious violation of the Fifteenth Amendment, but not until 1915. Combined, these measures succeeded in an almost total elimination of black voting in the South. As late as 1896, over 130,000 blacks continued to vote in Louisiana. By 1904, only 1,342 were able to do so. Although loopholes and lax enforcement permitted whites to vote far more often than blacks, poll taxes

and literacy laws did reduce the number of poor illiterate white voters in many southern localities.

Booker T. Washington

African Americans responded to the imposition of segregation and disfranchisement, along with the threat of violence to sustain the system, in a variety of ways. Large numbers accepted the accommodationist philosophy of **Booker T. Washington**—the principal of Alabama's Tuskegee Institute who, by the turn of the twentieth century, had emerged as the most well-known black leader in the nation. Educated at Virginia's Hampton Institute, one of many new black colleges founded by sympathetic white Northerners after the Civil War, Washington brought Hampton's emphasis on manual training for teachers to the Alabama Black Belt when he founded Tuskegee in 1881. His students did not receive an advanced education in subjects deemed "impractical" in the current environment. Instead, they learned the basic skills necessary to return to their communities and teach others how to become a better farmer or tradesman.

In political matters, Washington refused to agitate for change. Though publicly expressing his hope many times that segregation and disfranchisement would eventually end, Washington refused to protest openly for change, choosing to accept the status quo rather than threaten a white backlash that he believed would only lead to violence and the closing of his school. Instead, he often commented on his belief that whites would ultimately accept blacks in southern society and grant them equal rights. Washington most famously expressed his public views in his 1895 Cotton States and International Exposition Address in Atlanta before a large predominately white audience. Calling for interracial cooperation, he asked whites to aid industrious African Americans by giving them gainful employment. Meanwhile, he reminded blacks that the chance "to earn a dollar in a factory just now is worth infinitely more than the opportunity to spend a dollar in an opera house." He then bowed to Jim Crow segregation by using a famous metaphor: "In all things that are purely social we can be as separate as the fingers, yet one as the hand in all things essential to mutual progress." Such public positions made Washington acceptable to southern leaders while allowing the educator to channel money from northern and southern philanthropists to simultaneously build up Tuskegee and his personal reputation. Privately, however, Washington worked behind the scenes to subvert the system by funding legal challenges to segregation and supporting campaigns to thwart the implementation of the grandfather clause in Louisiana. While this covert activity has led some modern critics to label Washington a hypocrite, the "Wizard of Tuskegee" viewed himself as a pragmatist—a practical realist who sought tangible benefits within a harsh environment.

W.E.B. Du Bois

A growing number of black intellectuals strongly disagreed with Washington's public approach. In Boston, William Monroe Trotter began publishing *The Guardian*, a newspaper dedicated to constant agitation for complete acceptance of African Americans as equals, laying intense criticism not only on Jim Crow and disfranchisement, but also on Booker T. Washington for his appeasement of white supremacy. Initially supportive of the educator and his accomplishments, **W.E.B. Du Bois**, the first African American to receive a Ph.D. from Harvard University, came to reject Washington's narrow focus on material well-being at the expense of equality. In education, Du Bois argued for increased opportunities for African Americans beyond manual training. A classical education would foster the emergence of qualified black leaders—the "talented tenth"–while expanding curiosity and intellectual development for African Americans with a desire to learn more about the world. "Is not life more than meat?" Du Bois asked in his 1903 seminal work *The Souls of Black Folk.*

Du Bois also looked with disgust at Booker T. Washington's contention that African Americans should wait for their rights to be bestowed by whites. Mocking Washington's 1895 Cotton Exposition Speech as the "Atlanta Compromise," he believed that blacks should settle for nothing less than immediate social and political equality. Before 1906, Du Bois generally limited his complaints to writings and his lectures at Atlanta University, but after a bloody race riot in Atlanta that year claimed dozens of black lives, the professor became radicalized, determined to become a proactive force for change. Along with William Trotter and 27 other black leaders, Du Bois convened a conference in Niagara Falls, Canada (hotels in nearby Buffalo, New York barred blacks) to formally renounce Washington's accommodationism and form a new organization—the "Niagara Movement"—to promote their goals. Three years later, they merged with white allies (including Florence Kelley and Oswald Garrison Villard, a grandson of abolitionist William Lloyd Garrison) to form the National Association for the Advancement of Colored People (NAACP). Eschewing grass-roots protesting, the early NAACP pursued a strategy of legal challenges to Jim Crow statutes while educating the public and generating publicity through its journal *The Crisis* (edited by Du Bois). Though decades would pass before these efforts produced results, Du Bois and his devotees had accepted the challenge of overturning centuries of entrenched racial prejudice in America.

NATIONAL REFORM UNDER ROOSEVELT

The Rise of Theodore Roosevelt

The death of William McKinley by an anarchist's bullet at the 1901 Pan American Exposition in Buffalo, New York elevated **Theodore Roosevelt** to the presidency, culminating a remarkable political rise. Born into a New York "old money" family on October 27, 1858, young Teddy received encouragement from his father to overcome his childhood bouts with asthma by building up his body through rigorous physical activity. While engaging in athletics and other outdoor activities, he also exercised his mind through voracious reading, especially books on history, politics, and natural science. Roosevelt's application of this life philosophy, which he called the pursuit of the "strenuous life," came to dominate his personality. While attending Harvard, he met and married his first wife, Alice Hathaway Lee. After graduation in 1880, Roosevelt studied law while writing a naval history of the War of 1812, the first of many books that he authored in his lifetime.

Unlike others within his social class, Roosevelt desired to formally enter the political arena, and in 1881 he won election as a Republican to the New York Assembly. With his youthful energy and idealism, Roosevelt won over many of his colleagues and earned the position of minority leader before resigning the post when, on the same day in 1884, his young wife Alice died after giving birth to the couple's only child, followed by his mother who succumbed to typhoid fever. Leaving his young child temporarily with family members, he journeyed to the Badlands of the Dakota Territory to oversee two cattle ventures and to forget his personal troubles by immersing himself in the western lifestyle that he had read so much about. Though he lost heavily on his monetary investment, the experience boosted his physical and mental condition while adding to the life narrative that benefited his subsequent political career. Upon his return from the frontier in 1886, Roosevelt remarried and made a failed run for mayor of New York. As he started a new family life, Roosevelt gained his first federal government post when President Benjamin Harrison appointed him to the Civil Service Commission. After six years, he returned to New York City to serve a two-year term as president of the police commission.

With the city's police force modernized in numerous ways that proved to be influential on municipalities across

JACK JOHNSON (1878-1946)

Boxing legend Jack Johnson, the first African American to win the world heavyweight boxing championship, was born in Galveston on March 31, 1878. He left school in the fifth grade to help support his parents, both former slaves, and their nine children. He swept out a barbershop, worked as a porter in a gambling house, and later labored as a dockworker. Johnson began his boxing career as a sparring partner and participant in "battle royals," where several black youths would fight each other at the same time with the winner receiving money thrown to him from the white spectators. He started fighting in private clubs in the Galveston area, finally becoming a professional prizefighter in 1897.

Johnson left Galveston in 1899 and did not return. He spent his time traveling the country, fighting, and gaining increasing recognition. By 1902 he won over 50 fights against white and black opponents. In 1903 he won the Negro heavyweight championship, but the reigning white heavyweight champion, Jim Jeffries, refused the challenge to fight him. Johnson had to wait until after Jeffries's retirement for his opportunity. In 1908, he defeated the Canadian world champion Tommy Burns in Australia. The boxing community did not recognize Johnson as the actual champion until 1910 when Jim Jeffries came out of retirement to fight Johnson in Reno, Nevada, but was soundly defeated. Race riots broke out in many parts of the country, including Texas, as a result of Johnson's triumph.

Jim Jeffries was the first of many recruited "great white hopes" charged with the task of defeating Johnson, who infuriated the majority of whites because of his color, his taunting and trash-talking of opponents, and his non-conformist behavior, especially scandalous public relationships with white women. He was easily the most famous (and in many circles the most hated) African American in the country. Johnson's propensity for white women (usually, but not always prostitutes) made him a constant target for authorities. In 1913 he fled a conviction for violation of the Mann Act, a federal law designed to combat prostitution by forbidding the transportation of women across interstate lines for "immoral purposes." In practice, authorities during the Progressive Era often used the law as a weapon to prosecute individuals engaging in premarital, extramarital, or (as in the case with Johnson) interracial relationships. Facing a fine and prison time if he remained in the country, Johnson left the United States for an extended tour in Europe, Mexico, and Canada.

Johnson finally lost the heavyweight championship to a white man, Jess Willard, in Havana, Cuba, in 1915. Despite his age (he was 37 by then) and the extreme tropical heat, he was not knocked out until the 26th round. In 1920, Johnson returned to the United States and was arrested for his Mann Act conviction and served over a year in Leavenworth Prison. Upon his release, he returned to boxing, but he was well past his prime. He gave up professional fighting in 1938. During the last decade of his life he promoted fights, refereed bouts, and occasionally managed and trained boxers. Johnson's raucous life ended the way he lived it—in a high-speed car crash near Raleigh, North Carolina in 1946.

the country, Roosevelt returned to Washington, D.C. to serve as Assistant Secretary of the Navy under President William McKinley. Always interested in naval history and possessing a strong belief (reinforced by his readings of Alfred Thayer Mahan) that the country needed a large, modern navy, Roosevelt enjoyed promoting his ideas in the years leading up to the Spanish-American War. When the conflict arrived, he convinced himself that he could not just support the war from the sidelines—to remain true to his principles, he volunteered to fight. Growing up enamored with books that touted the gallantry of military struggle, Roosevelt also wanted to experience combat personally. After organizing a volunteer regiment that trained outside of San Antonio, Texas, "Roosevelt's Rough Riders" saw extensive fighting in the heights surrounding Santiago, Cuba. Colonel Roosevelt emerged from battle alive and, thanks to his journalist friends in the press corps, a war hero.

In 1898, Roosevelt gained the Republican nomination for the governorship of New York and narrowly defeated his Democratic opponent. For the next two years, he earned the reputation of an able administrator who would frequently rankle leaders within his party by openly differing with them on political appointments, regulation of corporations, and other public policies. After the death of McKinley's first vice president, public pressure grew (encouraged by many Republican Party leaders in New York who wanted Roosevelt out of the

state) for the governor to join the ticket with McKinley as the vice presidential nominee in the upcoming election of 1900. Given the weakness of the vice presidency and temperamentally opposed to taking the back seat to anybody, Roosevelt preferred to remain as governor and seek the presidency in 1904. Nevertheless, not wishing to disappoint party members who might feel snubbed if he turned down the popular clamor for his candidacy, Roosevelt accepted the honor. Though conservative Senator Mark Hanna prophetically chided his colleagues by exclaiming, "Don't any of you realize that there's only one life between that madman and the presidency?", the McKinley-Roosevelt team proved unstoppable in 1900, handily defeating the Democratic nominee William Jennings Bryan.

Roosevelt Takes Command

Upon McKinley's death, 42-year-old Theodore Roosevelt became the youngest president in U.S. history. His youthful energy, leadership style, and precedent-setting actions reinvigorated the executive branch, paving the way for the transformation of the presidency to its modern empowered position in the federal government relative to its declining status during the Gilded Age. Understanding the power of publicity since his days as New York City police commissioner and governor of New York, President Roosevelt created a strong bond with the national

President Theodore Roosevelt, his wife Edith, and their children, c. 1903.

press corps. While making himself accessible to reporters in an unprecedented fashion, he also used the media to channel his message by purposefully leaking stories with selected information, issuing press releases and giving press conference timed for maximum exposure, and punishing reporters who criticized him or betrayed his confidence by releasing information he wished to remain out of public view. Roosevelt also endeared himself to the national media because he could always be relied upon for a good story, such as occurred when the president, though an avid sportsman with the rifle, refused to kill a small bear while on a hunting trip in Mississippi. The resulting news coverage of the incident led executives at a toy company to start issuing the first stuffed "Teddy Bears." The new president's independent streak also became readily apparent, perhaps with no better example than his October 1901 dinner invitation to the African American leader Booker T. Washington. While members of the southern press lambasted the president for committing in their minds an outrageous inherent acceptance of racial equality, Roosevelt never apologized (though he never repeated the gesture).

More than a recognizable change in style, Roosevelt's presidency marked a considerable change in substance. During his first term, he overcame the lack of a mandate due to his elevation to the presidency through non-electoral means by positioning himself on the popular side of many key progressive issues. He also avoided potential clashes with conservative opposition in Congress by often pursuing foreign and domestic policy agendas that did not necessitate congressional involvement.

The Northern Securities Company Case

The question of how the nation should respond to the rise of large dominant corporations, or "trusts," that controlled numerous sectors of the national economy became the primary domestic issue of Roosevelt's presidency. As a result of the unprecedented growth and size of big business, many Americans felt threatened by the notion of corporations wielding unaccountable economic and political power. On this matter, Roosevelt's ideas were clear: the people, through the power of the federal government, should establish its supremacy by passing and enforcing laws that established proper rules of conduct and regulated corporate behavior. Initially, the young president sought to use publicity to praise corporations who acted properly while lambasting those that acted in a socially irresponsible manner. In the bill creating the Department of Commerce that Roosevelt signed into law in early 1903, the president reveled in an amendment attached to the measure that created a Bureau of

Corporations empowered to assemble data on national businesses for the purposes of allowing the president to make recommendations to Congress, which also gave him the power to selectively release such information to the public.

Roosevelt's main effort to assert the power of the federal government over corporations came with his administration's suit in federal court against the **Northern Securities Company**, a recently established railroad monopoly that had the potential to dominate the nation's railroad traffic from Chicago to the West Coast. Created to settle a potentially bitter competitive dispute among railroads controlled by magnates James J. Hill, E. H. Harriman, and J.P. Morgan, the Northern Securities Company was a holding company possessing the stock of the Great Northern and Northern Pacific Railroads whose appearance greatly alarmed farmers, businessmen, newspaper editors, and politicians across the Northwest. Sensing the popular mood, and strongly against the combination personally, Roosevelt asked his attorney general, Philander C. Knox, to seek the breakup of the monopoly for violation of a section of the 1890 Sherman Antitrust Act, which outlawed monopolies determined to have used their dominant market position to restrain trade. In March 1904, the Supreme Court laid down a landmark 5-4 decision in favor of the Justice Department's position that the Northern Securities Company violated the Sherman Act and must be dismantled—the first business entity to be broken up by a federal court order. As the decision reverberated throughout the corporate world, Roosevelt would continue to dissolve other perceived illegal combinations. But while the national press often referred to the president as "The Trust Buster," Roosevelt did not seek to dissolve every monopoly in the country. He did not believe that the size of a company mattered as much as its behavior. Roosevelt left other monopolies alone, such as J.P. Morgan's U.S. Steel Company, and more often sought to cajole the trusts into proper legal and moral behavior with the combination of information gathered by the Bureau of Corporations and the threat of a lawsuit from the Justice Department. It was an uneven and unpredictable approach but perhaps the best Roosevelt could do with the tools available under existing statutes.

The Anthracite Coal Strike

The 1902 **Anthracite Coal Strike** presented another opportunity for Theodore Roosevelt to seize upon a popular issue while also seeking to expand the powers and responsibilities of the presidency. In May 1902, over 100,000 Pennsylvania coal miners walked off the job to protest low pay, poor working conditions, and the non-acceptance of their union by management. By late September, many began to fear the onset of a nationwide coal shortage as the winter months approached. Instances of hoarding commenced, and coal prices doubled.

Roosevelt responded by inviting mine owners and the president of the United Mine Workers Union, John Mitchell, to a tense White House meeting. The president left the conference believing the owners acted unreasonably, preferring that the administration stay out of the affair if federal troops would not be sent to handle the strikers. Roosevelt soon unveiled a plan calling for the mine owners and workers to accept the rulings of a special arbitration commission that would hear both sides of the case and seek a settlement. To pressure the mine operators to accept the offer, the president let it be known that he had drawn up plans to declare a national emergency and was preparing to send federal troops into the mining areas to extract the coal without profit for the mining companies. While doubting the courts would ever sanction such an action, the mine owners believed Roosevelt to be serious and knew that favorable public opinion bolstered his resolve, so they eventually submitted to the creation of the commission. In the meantime, the striking laborers agreed to go back to work and await the commission's findings.

Ultimately, the commissioners determined that the coal miners should receive a 10 percent pay increase, a 9-hour working day, and the establishment of an arbitration system to resolve work-related disputes. The mine owners, however, benefited from the commission's avoidance of other worker complaints, most importantly, the non-recognition of the union as the members' legitimate bargaining agent. While the results were mixed for the dueling parties, the resolution of the coal strike clearly benefited Theodore Roosevelt and his efforts to elevate the power and prestige of the presidency. Unlike previous chief executives, Roosevelt injected the White House directly into a major labor dispute in a way other than sending in troops to break a strike. The president resolved the potential economic crisis by employing the arbitration principle—though a commonly used device today, the move was an unprecedented action at the time. In the process, Roosevelt bolstered the organized labor movement in the country by elevating the representatives of workers to an equal basis with business executives. Rather than assuming a pro-union stance, Roosevelt believed he acted out of fairness for the workers (providing them a "Square Deal," as he came to call his domestic agenda) while seeking to end the crisis for the good of the country as a whole.

Roosevelt's Reelection

Despite misgivings among conservatives in his party, Roosevelt experienced little difficulty securing the Republican Party nomination in 1904. After pleasing them by accepting one of their own, Senator Charles W. Fairbanks of Indiana as the vice-presidential nominee, Roosevelt enjoyed unanimous renomination at the Republican National Convention and awaited his Democratic opponent. After William Jennings Bryan's defeat in 1900, conservative Democrats regained power within the party and achieved the nomination of New York state judge Alton B. Parker. Given the party's hold on the southern states, Democrats believed Parker could triumph by carrying his sizeable home state (which also happened to be Roosevelt's), and then picking up a few modest-sized northern and border states. They portrayed Parker as a candidate with a calm, judicious, conservative mind to be contrasted against Roosevelt's alleged brash, reformist tendencies. The strategy backfired. By presenting themselves as the more conservative party, Democrats miscalculated the temper of the times. By trying to make Roosevelt's personality a major campaign issue, they gave the popular president a political gift. In comparison, Parker seemed dull, aloof, and uncharismatic. Though worried about his reelection chances to the very end, Roosevelt achieved an overwhelming victory over Parker who was only able to carry the southern states. Roosevelt's 336-140 win in the Electoral College and almost 20-percentage point margin in the popular vote (56.4 percent to 37.6 percent) provided him with a strong affirmation of his foreign and domestic policies and convinced him that he had received a mandate to press for further progressive reforms.

On election night, Roosevelt issued a statement thanking the nation and informing the citizenry that he would only serve one full term before retirement. Though some believed that he acted out of impulse in appreciation for the incredible endorsement that he had just received from the public, Roosevelt had pondered the issue and truly believed at the time that even though he had not been elected the first time, he had filled out most of William McKinley's term and no person should serve for more than two terms (term limits for presidents did not come until the 1950s by constitutional amendment). While a noble gesture that he did not have to make, the pledge worked to undermine Roosevelt's ability to govern during his second term. Instead of keeping the public and Congress guessing about whether he would run again, and thus using that uncertainty as a source of political capital, the anti-third-term-pledge instantly made him a "lame duck" president. Though still able to achieve some solid accomplishments during his second term, his power with respect to Congress eroded and limited his ability to achieve many items on his agenda.

Railroad Regulation

Regulation of the nation's railroads became a major priority for Roosevelt early in his second term. Two years earlier, the president had supported the Elkins Act, which had banned the practice of railroads giving rebates to shipping businesses. That legislation, however, was not controversial—few members in either house of Congress opposed the bill. In fact, the railroad companies largely welcomed the law because it eliminated a practice used by many large shippers to apply pressure in order to receive preferential rates.

During his second term, Roosevelt threw his weight behind the growing movement in the country to regulate the rates that railroad companies charged for the shipment of goods. For years, many citizens had called for federal government oversight of railroad rates, preferably by the Interstate Commerce Commission (ICC), as a means of curbing inflated charges and eliminating price discrimination. Roosevelt did not create the movement for railroad rate regulation—he joined an already popular effort and fought for its success by his typical means of generating publicity and actively working with members of Congress to enact the best bill possible. Eschewing an alternative that would have empowered the ICC to set specific rates, Roosevelt endorsed a bill sponsored by Representative William Hepburn of Iowa that called for the ICC to have the authority to set maximum rates that a railroad could charge. When Senate resistance stiffened, the president backed an amendment supported by many conservatives (and opposed by many progressives including Robert La Follette who had been elected to the Senate in 1905) that allowed for federal courts to review and overturn ICC rate decisions, though the burden of proof would rest with the carriers rather than the shippers or the ICC to supply evidence to challenge those rate determinations. With that legislative addition, further opposition crumbled. Shepherding the **Hepburn Act** through Congress was one of Roosevelt's signature achievements. The new law not only empowered the ICC to fix maximum railroad rates, subject to court review, but also vastly improved government oversight of the railroad industry by prescribing uniform bookkeeping procedures of company records and allowing ICC officials to review these company records in order to better render its decisions. The law would have lasting significance, not only for railroad regulation but also for government supervision of the national economy as a whole. The Hepburn Act marked the first time that a federal law authorized inspection of any national business's financial records and marked the first time that the rates and prices of a company would be subject to federal government review.

Regulation of the Nation's Food and Medicine

Soon after passage of the Hepburn Act, Roosevelt quickly joined another growing regulatory cause, this time, the desire for supervision of the food processing and medicine-producing industries. For years, muckrakers had been delivering a steady drumbeat of revelations detailing ways in which food manufacturers altered spoiled products to make them palatable or added harmful ingredients to preserve them longer. Pharmaceutical companies frequently made claims about the curative powers of their medicines without the science to back them up, often including compounds in their products that were far more harmful than beneficial to a patient's health. Published in 1906, Upton Sinclair's novel on the Chicago meatpacking industry, ***The Jungle***, became the most powerful work of this genre. A journalist with strong socialist beliefs, Sinclair wrote the exposé after spending weeks working undercover in meatpacking plants and interviewing laborers. Though Sinclair's main purposes were to publicize the lives and working conditions of the immigrants while promoting socialism as an alternative to capitalism, the novel's sections detailing the unsanitary processing of meat resonated far more with the public and President Roosevelt than the portions highlighting the harshness of life in the slums or the exploitation of workers. Sinclair's descriptions of how meatpackers employed such practices as incorporating the meat of cows suffering from tuberculosis, added chemicals to spoiled meat to alter their appearance, and tried to contain rats by laying out poisoned bread amongst unguarded meat, just to name a few, struck a powerful chord with consumers who demanded action. Roosevelt responded to the growing public pressure by sending investigators to Chicago who verified Sinclair's descriptions of abysmal processing conditions at the plants in a damning two-part report. When recalcitrant lawmakers continued to drag their feet, Roosevelt released the first part of the report to the public and threatened to reveal its entire contents. By this time, the large meatpacking firms had already determined that regulation was in their best interest, not just because of the public clamor in the United States but also due to threatened boycotts of American meat products by the governments of many European nations. The new rules would actually place the larger firms at a relative advantage to their competition—these large companies could now afford the additional expense of maintaining sanitary conditions if their smaller competitors were forced to do the same. Meanwhile, the reputation of the quality of American meat exports would be bolstered. When the industry secured a provision, with Roosevelt's approval, calling for the federal government to cover the cost of inspections, opposition soon dissipated. The subsequent **Meat Inspection Act** empowered the U.S. Department of Agriculture to establish regulations for the sanitary processing of meat products and to provide for regular inspections of meat processing facilities. While the president and much of the nation greeted the reform law with satisfaction, Upton Sinclair displayed indifference to the measure. In noting how the nation fixated on the meat processing aspects of his book rather than the plight of industrial workers or the message of the Socialist Party, Sinclair wryly reminisced: "I aimed at the public's heart, and by accident I hit it in the stomach."

Passed into law on the same day as the Meat Inspection Act, the **Pure Food and Drug Act** addressed the safety of other foods intended for human consumption as well as medicines. This law created a new federal government agency, the Food and Drug Administration, to test and approve drugs before being allowed for sale on the market. The legislation also banned, for the first time in the nation's history, certain items from being included in a food or drug. For years, cocaine had been used as a stimulant in products, including Coca-Cola. Heroin had been sold over-the-counter as a mood relaxer. Crude petroleum was sometimes used in laxatives. These and other ingredients found to have no medicinal value, too addictive, or better served by otherwise safer alternatives could no longer be legally sold in the country. The law also targeted untruthful labeling by manufacturers. For the first time, labels had to specify if certain ingredients on a government-approved list were included in the product, and it was now unlawful to state that an ingredient was included in a product when, in fact, it was not. Together with the Hepburn Act, passage of the Meat Inspection Act and the Pure Food and Drug Act marked the apex of Roosevelt's regulatory agenda seeking to bring the nation's corporations under federal supervision.

The First Environmental President

Of all his endeavors as president, Theodore Roosevelt took most pride in his conservation efforts. Already possessing a strong affinity for the outdoors, Roosevelt shared the views of many outraged citizens who felt strongly that existing federal land policy sanctioned wasteful practices that despoiled the landscape and threatened to deplete the nation's resources. He believed that uncontrolled

development of federal lands during the late-nineteenth century led to exploitation of forests, mineral resources, and public grazing lands, potentially leaving little for future generations of Americans. Though many progressive reformers agreed on the problem, they characteristically disagreed on proposed solutions. Two general reform camps emerged by the early twentieth century. Led by Sierra Club founder John Muir, the "preservationists" represented the most radical supporters of a new direction in land management. They sought to keep as much pristine wilderness away from development as possible in order to preserve the natural landscape. Though a close friend of Muir, Theodore Roosevelt typically sided with U.S. Chief Forester **Gifford Pinchot** and other "conservationists" who favored resource development guided by federal regulation based upon scientific management. In their opinion, trees on public lands could and should be cut down, for example, but the amount should be strictly regulated and supplemented with increased plantings to ensure that the nation had ample supplies of lumber. While many citizens sympathized with these early environmentalists, tough opposition frequently had to be overcome from many Westerners who generally resented eastern meddling in their affairs and believed federal

President Theodore Roosevelt and Chief Forester Gifford Pinchot on a trip down the Mississippi River in October 1907.

limitations hindered economic development, as well as smaller stockmen and lumber companies who believed that government regulations worked against their interests (Larger cattle and timber businesses operators, by contrast, tended to support rational land use as the best policy for the long-term stability of their industries).

Roosevelt made government supervision of federal land use his own personal crusade. In the process, he became the first president to make conservation of the nation's resources a national priority. Early in his first term, the new president supported the National Reclamation Act sponsored by Nevada Senator Francis G. Newlands, which allocated money from the sale of public lands to build dams, reservoirs, and irrigation canals to aid in reclaiming desert lands in the West for agricultural use. On his watch, Roosevelt also initiated a system of licenses and fees for those wishing to use the public domain for the grazing of cattle and sheep or the extraction of mineral resources.

Chief Forester Gifford Pinchot proved to be Roosevelt's closest advisor and primary advocate on conservation issues. Similar to the president, Pinchot came from a wealthy old-money New York family and believed strongly in the great outdoors. Educated at Yale, he pursued his interest in forestry by studying in Germany before returning to the United States to lead the U.S. Forest Bureau under President McKinley. In 1905, Roosevelt arranged for Congress to transfer jurisdiction over the nation's forest reserves from the Interior Department to Pinchot's agency (which would be renamed the United States Forest Service) in the Agriculture Department. Pinchot recruited a new force of agents he labeled Forest Rangers, designed their distinctive badges and green uniforms, and provided the charismatic force that motivated the agency's employees to perform their best while managing the reserves. Together, Roosevelt and Pinchot worked to regulate, but not eliminate, use of the nation's publicly-held timberlands. While Roosevelt tripled the size of national forest reserves to be excluded from public use to over 170 million acres (including a single 16 million-acre designation in 1907 just before a congressional deadline), the federal government during Roosevelt's presidency regularly collected large sums for timber use fees. From 1905 to 1906 alone, the government received $800,000, equal to the entire congressional appropriation for the Forest Service. A much-publicized quarrel between Pinchot and the preservationists took place over the chief forester's support for San Francisco, California's plans to damn the beautiful secluded Hetch Hetchy Valley, located adjacent to the popular Yosemite Valley, for the purpose of building a reservoir to act as the city's water supply after a devastating 1906 earthquake. While Roosevelt stayed out of the fracas, Muir threw himself into a desperate publicity campaign to arouse the nation's conscience. In the end, Muir succeeded only in delaying the valley's flooding. Construction of the reservoir finally commenced in 1913 during the Woodrow Wilson administration.

Though Roosevelt more often sided with Pinchot's views than Muir's, the president nevertheless performed many acts that elated the preservationists. Besides authorizing the creation of five new national parks, 150 national forests, and over 50 wildlife refuges, Roosevelt also established the nation's first national monuments, including the Grand Canyon, under power granted by the 1906 Antiquities Act, designed to preserve areas of important historical and archeological significance from economic development.

Roosevelt Chooses a Successor

At fifty years of age in 1908, Theodore Roosevelt prepared to become the youngest former president in American history—not a moment too soon for many conservatives in his own party who often displayed a façade of unity while privately disdaining his positions. Still energetic after seven and a half years in the White House, Roosevelt nevertheless honored his election night pledge and prepared to step aside but actively sought to choose a successor who would continue his policies and fight for what had not yet been achieved. Immediately ruling out Vice President Charles Fairbanks and other conservatives, Roosevelt also found most of the leading Republican progressives, such as Wisconsin's Robert La Follette, to be unpalatable because of personal differences or the belief that they were simply too radical in their views. His two favorite choices, Massachusetts Senator Henry Cabot Lodge and Secretary of State Elihu Root, took themselves out of the running. Ultimately, Roosevelt settled on his good friend **William Howard Taft**. A former federal judge and U.S. Solicitor General from a prominent Ohio family, Taft served as governor of the Philippines before Roosevelt appointed him to be Secretary of War in 1904. The two men had known each other since the early 1890s and enjoyed a warm relationship. Though Roosevelt believed that they held similar views, he would later find Taft's progressivism to be more limited.

Roosevelt secured the Republican presidential nomination for Taft and campaigned hard for his friend in the general election against the Democratic nominee, William Jennings Bryan, making his third attempt to win the presidency. Taft needed the help. While a likeable man with a large six-foot, 300-pound frame who exuded confidence, the presidency was the first elective office that Taft ever sought. He leaned heavily on Roosevelt's campaign experience, and it paid off. Despite Bryan's superior energy and oratorical talents along with a Democratic Party platform that mirrored many of Roosevelt's positions on the major issues of the day, Taft won 29 states (sweeping the Northeast, Midwest, and much of the West) with 321 electoral votes compared to Bryan's 17 states (mostly in the Solid South) with 162 electoral votes. The popular vote tally matched McKinley's victory over Bryan in 1900, with Taft securing 52 percent of the roughly 14 million votes cast.

THE TAFT PRESIDENCY

William Howard Taft experienced a rough time as president. Any individual following Theodore Roosevelt would have found themselves under incredible scrutiny and relentless comparison, but Taft bore the additional burden of being Roosevelt's chosen successor. He found it very difficult to emerge from Roosevelt's shadow positively in the eyes of the former president's rabid supporters who wished he had run for a third term. While personally affable, Taft lacked Roosevelt's dynamism and political skills. Truly disdaining the everyday give-and-take of politics, his main aspiration in life was never to be president but, rather, to be Chief Justice of the U.S. Supreme Court (a goal finally achieved when President Warren Harding appointed him to the post in 1921). Further complicating his tenure, Taft's main advisor and confidante, his wife Helen, suffered a debilitating stroke two months after becoming First Lady, thus limiting her ability to aid her husband.

Though the new president agreed with Roosevelt on many progressive issues, Taft differed philosophically on the proper role of the president in the legislative process. While Roosevelt never cowered from the prospect of wrestling with members of Congress over issues, Taft believed the president should propose items for consideration rather than guide legislation through each house. He also believed in restrained presidential power as opposed to Roosevelt's broad assertions of executive authority. Whereas Roosevelt often asked: "Is there a specific law that would keep the president from performing this action?" Taft would often ask: "What law authorizes the president to do this?"

Progressive congressmen in Taft's own party made life difficult for him even before he took office when they opened a controversy over limiting the power of conservative Republican House Speaker Joseph G. Cannon of Illinois. Angered by his seemingly autocratic rule, insurgent Republicans such as George W. Norris of Nebraska sought to restrict Cannon's authority over committee appointments and parliamentary procedures. Taft initially expressed sympathy for the cause but then quickly backed away after Cannon and other conservatives threatened to thwart all of the president's legislative proposals. The speaker later returned the favor by supporting Taft's call for tariff reform. Though only a few imported products received a direct reduction in tariff rates, Taft found satisfaction with a provision he supported that allowed the president to reduce rates further if a reciprocity agreement could be reached with individual countries that agreed to reduce their tariff rates on American exports. Flustered when the president retracted his public support for their efforts, progressive Republicans and Democrats continued to push for further tariff reductions and to reduce Speaker Cannon's power. Ultimately, they got nowhere on additional tariff changes during Taft's presidency, but they succeeded in adopting new rules that expanded House Rules Committee membership from five to fifteen members, made membership elective rather than appointed by the Speaker, and excluded the Speaker himself as a member.

Another rift between Taft and the progressives took place over conservation policy and the so-called **Ballinger-Pinchot Affair.** The root of the conflict involved Chief Forester Gifford Pinchot's strong dislike for Taft's choice of Richard Ballinger as Secretary of the Interior. A former mayor of Seattle, Washington and U.S. land commissioner, Ballinger strongly favored western economic development. During his tenure, he would open more than a million acres of public land for commercial use. Pinchot soon opened a campaign against the secretary using speeches and other publicity-generating techniques that Roosevelt often employed to place doubts in conservationists' minds about Ballinger. When the secretary came under suspicion of engaging in corruption while serving as Roosevelt's land commissioner, Pinchot leaked information to the press about the subsequent congressional investigation. Believing Ballinger to be innocent of the charges, Taft ordered Pinchot to desist from the attacks, but the chief forester only increased them when he became aware of a private deal arranged with the secretary's approval for a group of Ballinger's Seattle business associates and New York banker J.P. Morgan to develop previously-reserved Alaskan coal lands. Taft then fired Pinchot for insubordination, raising the ire of many progressives.

Taft's political blunders obscured a series of progressive achievements during his presidency. In four years, Taft oversaw the withdrawal of more public land for forest and oil reserves than Roosevelt had done in almost twice the time. He also accelerated the pace of antitrust prosecutions under the Sherman Act, most notably against the John D. Rockefeller's Standard Oil Company and

James Buchanan Duke's American Tobacco Company, which were both ordered to be broken up and reorganized into smaller independent operations. In all, Taft's Justice Department instigated 90 such cases versus 57 during the Roosevelt presidency. Taft's support of the Mann-Elkins Act enabled its passage, which strengthened the ICC by allowing it to initiate freight rate changes and gave the agency regulatory jurisdiction over telephone and telegraph companies. The president also succeeded in getting congressional approval for an eight-hour work day for federal employees, the first mine safety standards, and creation of a federal Children's Bureau empowered to investigate and publicize upon all matters pertaining to the welfare of children but in practice specialized in highlighting child labor issues.

Roosevelt vs. Taft

Though Taft viewed his accomplishments with satisfaction, he found himself constantly embroiled in inter-party divisions that were imploding the Republican Party. Whenever he made moves favorable to reform-minded Republicans, he alienated members of his party's Old Guard. When he pleased conservative Republicans, progressive Republicans inevitably cast him as a tool of the entrenched conservative political establishment. Viewing it all from the sidelines was Theodore Roosevelt. Though he had left the country for an extended jaunt through Europe capped by a hunting safari in Africa, the former president kept tabs on current events back home (and received constant updates from Gifford Pinchot and others who complained often about Taft's quiet progressivism when they believed that the times called for Roosevelt-style exuberance and action). After Roosevelt's lively return to America in June 1910 capped by a New York City ticker-tape parade, he largely kept quiet in order to promote party unity. The mid-term elections in 1910, however, proved to be disastrous for the Republicans. In primary elections, Taft made the decision to side with conservatives that he personally favored over reformers he disliked, but in most cases the voters supported the progressives. Democrats took advantage of the rift, adding 12 Senate seats and gaining 58 seats in the House of Representatives to seize solid control of that body.

Even before the mid-term elections concluded, Roosevelt began delivering a series of speeches calling for the acceptance of further reforms promoting social justice and direct democracy. He argued that his advocacy for change was not radicalism, but reforms meant to avert significantly radical ideas from gaining traction in the country. Privately, he tried to coax Taft to be more assertive with progressive causes, but that only irked the president who began to resent his friend's meddling in his administration's affairs. The final breaking point between the two men occurred when Taft's Justice Department announced the filing of an anti-trust suit against J.P. Morgan's United States Steel Corporation, specifically citing its 1907 takeover of the Tennessee Coal, Iron and Railroad Company. In fact, Roosevelt had personally allowed Morgan to merge the two companies without any trouble from his Justice Department as a means of helping to avert a growing crisis on Wall Street. At the time, a major brokerage firm, which had invested heavily in the stock of the Tennessee Iron and Coal, found itself on the brink of bankruptcy. In an early twentieth century example of a corporation being deemed by the government to be "too big to fail," Roosevelt allowed Morgan to swallow up Tennessee Iron and Coal to preserve the brokerage house, helping to alleviate the panic. While a subsequent congressional investigation provided much impetus for the creation of the Federal Reserve System in 1913 to enable the federal government to have greater control over the nation's credit so such deals would not have to be made in the future, the immediate impact of the lawsuit (which U.S. Steel ultimately won) was to irritate Roosevelt and end his friendship with Taft. For the first time, the former president publicly criticized Taft for excessively filing anti-trust measures. Rather than seeking to break up monopolies, the best approach in Roosevelt's mind would be for the federal government to strictly monitor corporate behavior and use the threat of dissolution to guarantee proper moral and legal behavior. By early 1912, the estrangement between Roosevelt and Taft was complete. The two men were no longer on speaking terms, and Roosevelt finally announced in February that he would seek the Republican Party nomination for an unprecedented third term as president.

The Election of 1912

The 1912 presidential election was a monumental affair in American political history, presenting multiple candidates delivering impassioned but disparate messages to the voters regarding their visions of the proper direction for the country. Theodore Roosevelt campaigned hard to win 9 of the 12 states that held Republican Party primaries (Robert La Follette won two states and Taft won only one), but the thirty-six remaining states had yet to adopt the primary system. Thus, a majority of delegates to the Republican national convention were selected at state conventions directed by leaders loyal to the president. As a result, Taft secured enough delegates to take the nomination. Roosevelt and his supporters responded by bolting the convention with plans of forming a third

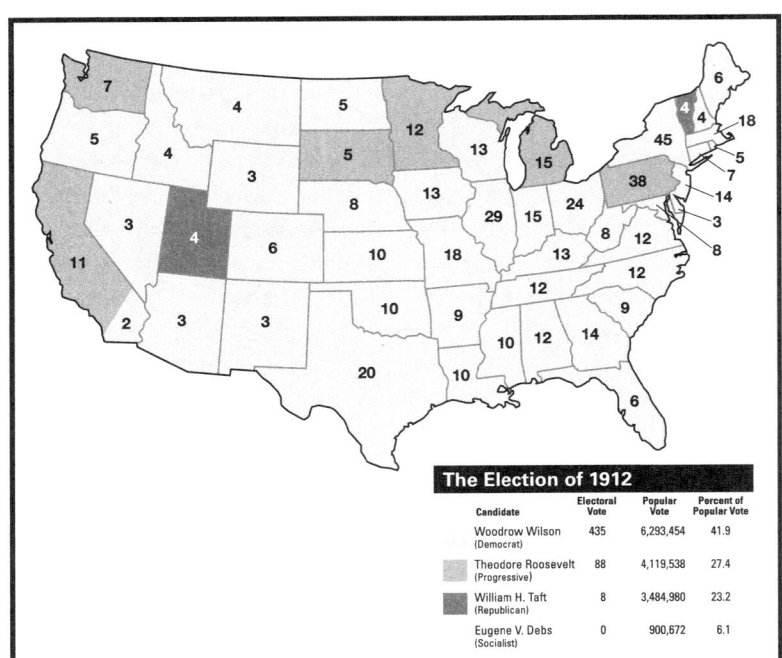

Map 20.1   The Election of 1912.

The Election of 1912			
Candidate	Electoral Vote	Popular Vote	Percent of Popular Vote
Woodrow Wilson (Democrat)	435	6,293,454	41.9
Theodore Roosevelt (Progressive)	88	4,119,538	27.4
William H. Taft (Republican)	8	3,484,980	23.2
Eugene V. Debs (Socialist)	0	900,672	6.1

party based on reform principles that they hoped would transform American politics. Knowing he would probably not be reelected, Taft only gave a few speeches in the coming campaign and remained in the contest largely to ensure Roosevelt's defeat. His main support derived from Republican Party loyalists, mostly conservatives. All hope for Roosevelt's success depended upon who won the Democratic nomination. If they selected a conservative or a candidate without national appeal, Roosevelt would have had a significant chance by appealing to progressives across party lines.

Three Democratic candidates dominated the presidential field—House Majority Leader Oscar Underwood of Alabama, Speaker of the House Champ Clark of Missouri, and New Jersey Governor Woodrow Wilson. The fact that the party held onto its archaic rule requiring two-thirds of the assembled delegates to agree upon a candidate promised a raucous meeting at the party's national convention in Baltimore. Speaker Clark held the lead in delegates entering the convention, but, after days of effort, his supporters failed to control the requisite number for the nomination. Eventually, the work of Wilson's convention floor managers and the endorsement of William Jennings Bryan produced victory for the governor on the forty-sixth ballot, much to Roosevelt's chagrin. Though generally acceptable to conservative Democrats, Wilson made a name for himself by supporting numerous state-level progressive measures while governor of the Garden State. His call for major national economic reforms promised to keep enough progressive Democrats within the party as they sought to win the White House for the first time since Grover Cleveland's victory in 1892.

Wilson's selection dismayed Roosevelt but did not deter him or his supporters from organizing their third party. In August, they met in Chicago to hold a national convention and launch their "**Progressive Party**." After Roosevelt told a reporter that he felt "fit as a bull moose" for the coming fight, the Bull Moose soon became the party's symbol. Ever since, most Americans have usually referred to the Progressive Party as the "Bull Moose Party" rather than by the organization's official name.

Yet a fourth candidate vying for the presidency gave voters an additional choice. **Eugene Debs**, a former Democratic state legislator and national labor leader from Indiana, accepted his third bid as the nominee of the Socialist Party of America. A dynamic orator, the Socialists had no better messenger to spread their alternative to both laissez-faire capitalism and corporate regulation. Seeing the major problems of the Industrial Revolution caused by capitalism, not industrialization itself, Debs and the Socialists sought to awaken Americans to a path they believed would end the exploitation of labor and consumer price gouging; namely, government ownership of major banks, industries, and utilities managed on a non-profit basis in the public interest.

Ultimately, the race boiled down to a contest between Roosevelt and Wilson. The Bull Moose Party platform endorsed most of the major social justice, direct democracy, and campaign reforms championed by progressives that exist today but had yet to be enacted. In addition to calls for active government regulation and supervision of big business, the platform also included demands for social insurance for the elderly, unemployed, and the disabled, minimum wages and maximum weekly hours for workers, compensation for work-related injuries, an end to child labor, a constitutional amendment to allow the collection of income taxes, woman suffrage, direct election of U.S. senators, primary elections for all state and national offices, acceptance of the initiative and referendum, the recall of elected officials, and limits to campaign contributions. Throughout the race, Roosevelt used the label "New Nationalism" (borrowed from a book by supporter Herbert Croly) to tout the party's message, which he believed was a "corrective to socialism and an anecdote for anarchy."

For his part, Wilson endeavored to maintain Democratic Party unity while proposing many reforms of his own. Though the Democratic platform included calls for a workers' compensation law, extension of the presidential primary system, and a constitutional amendment providing for a federal income tax, Wilson's "New Freedom" agenda concentrated on national economic reforms designed to restore competition in the marketplace. Believing that high protective tariffs contributed to the high cost of living, he desired a lower, revenue-only tariff. Wilson agreed with those who believed that the time had come for an overhaul of the nation's banking system to free up credit and overturn the national economy's reliance on New York bankers. Finally, the governor favored strong antitrust legislation, stating that, unlike Roosevelt who preferred regulating behavior, he wished to limit the actual size of corporations. By establishing thresholds in the marketplace that a corporation could not legally exceed, Wilson hoped that monopolies would dissipate and other companies would fill the void, thus returning competition to the American economy for the benefit of all.

The election received a severe jolt on October 12 when a deranged man with a pistol shot Roosevelt in the chest as he left a Milwaukee, Wisconsin hotel to deliver a speech. Seriously wounded from the bullet that tore through his heavy coat, eyeglass case, and speech notes, he nevertheless assessed that vital organs were missed and demanded to be taken to his engagement. Upon his arrival, Roosevelt explained that he had just been shot but that it would take "more than that to kill a Bull Moose." Though he stated that given the circumstances he would not be talking long, he spoke for over an hour and a half to the concerned but adoring crowd about the principles for which he was fighting. After the speech, Roosevelt spent the next nine days in the hospital as the other candidates suspended their campaigns until doctors released him for the final two weeks of the race.

As most everyone expected, Wilson took full advantage of the Republican split to triumph on election night. Receiving almost 6.3 million popular votes, he carried 40

states with 435 electoral votes. Roosevelt finished second with 4.2 million popular votes, winning six states with 88 electoral votes. Taft became the only president seeking reelection to finish in third place, tallying only 3.5 million popular votes and winning only two small states with eight electoral votes. Eugene Debs collected no electoral votes, but garnered over 900,000 popular votes—the high water mark for the Socialist Party in any presidential election with 6 percent of the popular vote. Wilson and the Democrats were elated. Not only had their party won the White House after a twenty-year drought, they also picked up enough seats to gain a majority in the Senate, giving them complete control of Congress.

NATIONAL REFORM UNDER WILSON

Wilson's Background

A government professor by training, **Woodrow Wilson** spent much of his adult life in academia before his meteoric rise to the governorship of New Jersey in 1910 followed soon by his ascent to the presidency in 1912. Born in Staunton, Virginia, on the eve of the Civil War, Wilson spent much of his early life in Georgia and the Carolinas. Though a deeply religious man whose father served as a Presbyterian minister and seminary professor, he decided against a life in the ministry. Instead, Wilson attended Princeton University in New Jersey before studying law for a year at the University of Virginia. After withdrawing due to health reasons, he continued his studies at home, passed the Georgia bar exam, and briefly practiced law in Atlanta. Bored with the law and realizing that it was not aiding his growing interest in politics, Wilson attended graduate school at Johns Hopkins University in Baltimore, eventually earning a PhD in history and political science. Hoping to become a force in politics as an observer and known author, the young professor began to make a name for himself in the scholastic world through his publications, public lectures, and holding political science professorships, eventually landing a tenured position at Princeton. After his election to the presidency of his alma mater in 1902, Wilson soon became a nationally known university leader through his expansion of campus facilities, recruitment of noteworthy individuals for the faculty, and especially for a highly-publicized but failed effort to transform campus culture by seeking to abolish the school's exclusive social clubs.

As Wilson failed in other ways to reform social life at Princeton, he prepared to resign his post when New Jersey Democratic Party bosses presented him with the opportunity of a lifetime. Viewing the college president as a political conservative with name recognition who might help them resist the efforts of progressives in the state legislature from enacting various reforms, the bosses approached Wilson about the possibility of accepting their party's nomination for governor. In the past, Wilson had written essays critical of Theodore Roosevelt and William Jennings Bryan while touting a traditional, Jeffersonian states' rights and limited government viewpoint that was consistent with his southern upbringing. However, by 1910 Wilson knew which way the political winds were blowing. After securing the nomination, he quickly pivoted to a pro-reform stance during the campaign, a move that the bosses interpreted as mere grandstanding. But, after Wilson's victory in the general election, they soon discovered their miscalculation. The new governor not only failed to become the naïve political rookie dependent upon the bosses' advice to perform his duties, he also linked up with progressive-minded Democrats and Republicans in the legislature to enact a broad reform agenda that included the establishment of primary elections, enactment of campaign spending limits, a workers' compensation system, and the regulation of public utilities. Wilson's moves garnered national attention and propelled him to the short list of potential Democratic Party presidential candidates. Just two years later, he would enter the White House.

Wilson's Economic Reforms

Viewing himself as a party leader as well as president, Wilson assumed a primary role in mapping out the Democratic Party's legislative agenda. Moving quickly, he called a special session of Congress to enact his measures. In a major break from tradition, Wilson became the first president since John Adams to appear before a joint session of Congress. Theodore Roosevelt recognized the maneuver as a masterful political stroke designed to dramatize the moment and generate publicity while showing members of Congress that the president wished to work directly with them on the important issues of the day. (Roosevelt wondered openly why he had never thought of performing such a perfect act of political theatrics.) Thus began the regular Wilsonian practice of appearing personally at the Capitol to deliver State of the Union addresses and other speeches on important issues in which the president desired that Congress act decisively. By the end of his presidency, he would appear before Congress more times than any other chief executive before or since.

Wilson's first congressional appearance dealt with the subject of tariff reform. Since the Democrats historically opposed high tariffs, their newfound majority status seemed to dictate that downward revisions would soon become a reality. On the House floor, Majority Leader Oscar Underwood easily produced the votes needed for passage. Trouble occurred in the Senate, however, when industry lobbyists and their senatorial allies slowed down the process and attempted to dilute the effort through a serious of crippling amendments. Wilson directly interjected himself into the fray when he publicly criticized the obstructionist senators while shining the spotlight on the power of the countless lobbyists engulfing the capital, at one point complaining that a brick couldn't be thrown in Washington without hitting one of them. In the Senate, Robert La Follette also turned up the heat when he denounced the lobbyists and began a public investigation of their influence on legislation. Ultimately, the president and pro-reform forces in the Senate prevailed. The resulting **Underwood-Simmons Tariff Act** became law, leading to a 25 percent average reduction of tariff rates on almost a thousand imported items while adding 100 items (including important consumer goods and raw materials such as sugar, wool, cement, coal, and iron ore) to the free-entry list. To offset the loss of government revenue due to the reduced import duties, the law levied the first income taxes since passage of the Sixteenth Amendment, which authorized their collection. Mainly impacting wealthy Americans, the tax started at a rate of 1 percent for individuals earning at least $3,000 annually then increased on a graduated scale (2 percent for citizens making at least $20,000 per year up to a maximum of 7 percent for annual incomes over $500,000).

Wilson next sought to work with Congress on enacting the first banking and currency reforms since the Civil War. While all the major industrializing nations of Europe had some form of central banking system, the United States lacked such an institution. Many Americans saw the positive benefits of a national banking structure, but great disagreement existed on its proper configuration, especially if it should be a centralized or decentralized organization and whether control should lay with private bankers or government bureaucrats. After allowing the matter to stalemate in Congress, Wilson delivered his second address before the body to dramatize the issue and lay down the general principles he wished the legislation should possess, including his endorsement of public control. The resulting **Federal Reserve Act** ultimately bore the characteristic marks of compromise. The law established Federal Reserve Banks in twelve regions of the country to be owned by member banks within their districts but under the general supervision of a Federal Reserve Board appointed by the president. The member banks allocated a portion of their capital to the district banks, which could then loan money to other banks within their regions. Despite this decentralized structure, the federal government now possessed an important tool to promote economic stability. The new system enabled the Board to influence the national money supply through various mechanisms at its disposal, including the ability to impact interest rates that banks charged, as well as setting the percentage of capital that banks were required to keep in reserve. In times of low business activity, the Board could stimulate the economy by pursuing policies that freed more capital and credit into the marketplace. In times of high inflation, the Board's policies could also tighten credit to slow the pace of economic activity in order to reign in prices. Though the new system could not guarantee prosperity, the national dependence upon the decisions and actions of New York bankers for economic growth and stability began to lessen as financial power in the country shifted from Wall Street to Washington.

As Wilson tackled the antitrust portion of his agenda, the president deviated for the first time from positions that he articulated during the campaign. Upon determining that his proposal for limiting the size of corporations held only lukewarm support in Congress, Wilson embraced Theodore Roosevelt's idea of a potentially powerful government agency to regulate corporations by resolutely enforcing the antitrust laws. He also favored new legislation that would more specifically define what constituted "restraint of trade" and "unfair competition" under the law. In the fall of 1914, Congress passed the Federal Trade Commission Act, which replaced the Bureau of Corporations with a five-member **Federal Trade Commission (FTC)** appointed by the president. The new agency had the power to initiate investigations of corporations suspected of violating the nation's antitrust and unfair competition laws. Upon determining the existence of unlawful behavior, the FTC could issue "cease-and-desist" orders, though much to the chagrin of progressives, Wilson allowed conservative legislators to attach an amendment providing corporations with the ability to appeal the Commission's orders in federal court. Also in the fall, Congress approved the Clayton Antitrust Act, which improved the Sherman Act by detailing numerous prohibited practices including price discrimination (companies charging different prices for goods and services), exclusive dealings (corporations preventing companies from dealing with their competitors as a condition of doing business), interlocking directorates (members of board of directors serving on the board of a competitor), the formation of cartels to control markets, and companies buying the stock of competitors. The new law also aided organized labor by specifically stating that labor unions were not an unlawful combination in restraint of trade subject to court injunctions (the Supreme Court had ruled to the contrary in a 1894 case involving the Sherman Act).

In his first 18 months in office, Wilson displayed fine leadership in guiding significant national economic reforms through Congress. Nevertheless, on the social justice front, his record left much to be desired. Though distracted by the death of his wife, Ellen, in August 1914 (within a year Wilson became the only president to remarry while in the White House), his latent belief in states' rights on social reform matters explains much of his disinterest. In other instances, Wilson's racist beliefs inculcated by his upbringing in the postbellum South, account for his terrible record on civil rights issues. (Earlier he had praised the Ku Klux Klan in a history of the United States he authored. While president, he enthusiastically endorsed D.W. Griffith's epic film *The Birth of a Nation*, which presents an openly racist and decidedly pro-Confederate view of the Civil War and postwar Reconstruction). He supported the passage of the Smith-Lever Act of 1914, which created the Federal Extension Service to provide vital services to aid farmers with their agricultural operations and home life and also consented to the establishment of a separate Negro Division that offered inadequate assistance to southern black farm families (due to the unequal allocation of resources, not the energetic efforts of its black county agents). This decision paralleled Wilson's acquiescence to southern members of his cabinet who established strict segregation within their departments. Not very concerned with racial issues, however, most social progressives began to show disfavor with the president because of his obvious disinterest in their reform efforts. Wilson made no effort to endorse the movement for a federal woman suffrage amendment or to support the call for a restriction of child labor, believing both to be under the purview of the states. With the next presidential election looming, social progressives began to communicate their displeasure to Wilson in order to spur him into action, threatening to withhold support for him by either staying home on election day or casting their lots with his opponent.

The Pinnacle of National Progressivism—Wilson's Acceptance of Social Reform

The 1914 mid-term elections gave Wilson reason to take stock of the political landscape. Across the country, Republican conservative candidates defeated many noteworthy insurgents during party primaries followed by victories against Democrats and Bull Moosers in the November general elections. While Democrats maintained a slim majority in Congress, Theodore Roosevelt appeared as a wild card, reading the results and contemplating a return to the Republican Party. The former president's displeasure with Wilson's desire to remain neutral since

President Woodrow Wilson (holding the American flag) marching in a parade on Flag Day, June 14, 1916.

the outbreak of World War I in 1914 (Roosevelt favored U.S. intervention on the Allied side) guided his thinking along with a growing belief that many who had joined the Progressive Party were too radical for his liking.

Wilson sought to openly convert these progressives in 1916 as he set aside his previous objections to federally-sponsored social reforms for the sake of political expediency in order to keep himself and his party in power. To the delight of social progressives, Wilson signed the **Keating-Owen Child Labor Act**, which prohibited the interstate shipment of goods produced in whole, or in part, by children younger than 14 years of age. Though the Supreme Court ruled against its constitutionality three years later, Wilson probably gained a few hundred thousand votes in the coming election the moment that he signed the bill into law. By signing the Adamson Act, which established an eight-hour workday for railroad laborers, he approved the first federal legislation setting maximum hours for workers of private companies. Wilson accepted creation of a workers' compensation system covering all workers performing work under a federal government contract. To aid rural areas, Wilson signed the Federal Farm Loan Act, which extended federal credit to farmers for the first time, the Warehouse Act allowing growers to store their crops and use them as loan collateral, and the Federal Highways Act, which provided funds to the states for road construction, helping to diminish the degree of rural isolation. In addition to these and other tangible actions, Wilson also made a significant symbolic gesture designed to garner political support of social progressives. When a vacancy on the Supreme Court appeared, Wilson nominated social justice champion Louis Brandeis for the post and actively lobbied for his eventual acceptance by the Senate. A major

advisor to Wilson during the campaign and throughout his first term, Brandeis became the first Jewish person to serve on the High Court.

The Election of 1916

President Wilson's endorsement of key social reforms greatly aided his reelection, as did his acceptance of a notable increase in the size of the nation's military forces. In an effort to blunt the criticism of Theodore Roosevelt and others on the "preparedness" issue, Wilson called for, and received from Congress, a tripling in the number of active army personnel to increase to almost 250,000 men and a large naval expansion program. To pay for this expansion that they opposed, progressive congressmen enacted the Revenue Act of 1916, which increased taxes on the wealthy and munitions makers by increasing the top income tax rate on those earning over $2 million annually to 15 percent, added a 10 percent estate (inheritance) tax on large fortunes, and established a 12.5 percent levy on the income of defense industries.

At their national convention, the Democrats excitedly renominated Wilson for the presidency by affirmation. In the process, the keynote speaker, former New York governor Martin Glynn, unintentionally developed a major campaign theme when he detailed Wilson's steps toward maintaining American neutrality in the bloody conflict raging in Europe at the time, culminating with the cry: "We didn't go to war!" The peace message from the speech resonated so well with the delegates that other speakers worked it into their addresses until it became the major theme of the conclave and the subsequent campaign. After the meeting ended, party activists molded Glynn's yell into the slogan: "Vote for Wilson. He kept us out of war!"

For their part, the Republicans hoped they could rebound from the previous election by nominating a candidate acceptable to members of the sagging Bull Moose Party, eventually selecting Charles Evans Hughes—a progressive former governor of New York from 1907 to 1910 until being nominated to serve on the Supreme Court. As the Progressive Party officially disbanded, Roosevelt returned to the Republican fold and brought some prominent Bull Moosers with him (though many more flocked to Wilson). On foreign affairs, Hughes tried a difficult balancing act. While sometimes criticizing Wilson for not being tough enough with the Allies, he did not want to appear pro-German, so he refused to accept the endorsement of German-American organizations and Irish nationalist groups with strong anti-British views, nor did he criticize Roosevelt when the ex-president made strong public statements mocking the Kaiser, Germany's leader. Though a lackluster campaigner, Hughes tried his best to hammer Wilson on two main domestic matters, the Revenue Act and the Adamson Act. The increased income and estate taxes led wealthy conservatives to solidly back Hughes, but they would have supported the Republican candidate anyway. Hughes's assault on the Adamson Act was more promising, as he shaped his argument to convince voters that the law was a sell-out by Wilson to organized labor. Though Hughes made headway with some voters with such attacks, Wilson support for union exemption from antitrust prosecutions and passage of the Adamson Act guaranteed solid support from organized labor. Ultimately, the election may actually have all turned on a highly-publicized snubbing of California's Bull Moose governor Hiram Johnson (Roosevelt's running mate in the 1912 contest) by Hughes. Though both men were briefly staying in the same Los Angeles hotel, the Hughes campaign made no effort to arrange a meeting. Hughes's opponents pounced on the rebuff—a costly gaffe given the eventual closeness of the election.

Both candidates went to bed on election night not knowing who had won. After sweeping the Northeast and Midwest, Hughes held the upper hand, needing

---

The Adamson Act and the Eight-Hour Work Day

Many Americans today reap the benefits, and often take for granted, the standard eight-hour work day. For much of this nation's history, large numbers of workers in factories, workshops, mines, and farms toiled every day from sunrise to sunset. Labor unions during the Industrial Revolution effectively used the eight-hour day as a rallying cry to recruit more members while seeking to pressure companies to reduce the number of daily hours that their employees worked. For some, the motivation was the dignity of labor; for others, a desire to spread the available jobs around to a larger pool of workers.

During the Progressive Era, many reformers joined the movement for reduced daily hours, either out of a sense of moral decency or simply to improve business efficiency. While some successes had been won for government workers and union laborers in certain trades before 1916, that year saw passage of the first federal law to establish an eight-hour work day for workers in the private sector—the Adamson Act—which applied specifically to the nation's railroad workers.

The Adamson Act resulted from a combination of public concern over the frequency of railroad accidents linked to worker fatigue, steadfast labor union agitation on the issue, and the desire of President Woodrow Wilson and Democratic congressional leaders to keep their party in power during a pivotal election year. In August 1916, railway workers across the country voted to authorize a strike if their employers did not act upon their demands for an eight-hour day. When the railroads refused to comply, the president and Congress intervened. Signed into law by Wilson on September 3, the Adamson Act imposed a standard work day of eight hours for railway workers across the United States. Employers could still make workers take longer shifts, but overtime compensation at 1.5 times the amount of regular pay was established. The Supreme Court approved the constitutionality of the law by a narrow margin the following year.

In the following decades, the Adamson Act, along with continued labor union agitation, helped to generate momentum for the adoption of the eight-hour day and overtime pay in other occupations, culminating in the Fair Labor Standards Act of 1938, which included a major provision establishing an eight-hour workday and (originally) a 44-hour work week with "time and a half" overtime pay for non-salaried employees. Though a major exception carved out for farm workers and domestic servants, both the Adamson Act and the Fair Labor Standards Act represented success of the vision of progressive reformers for positive change through legislation, but the primary motor behind the movement remained the dedicated activism of the nation's labor unions.

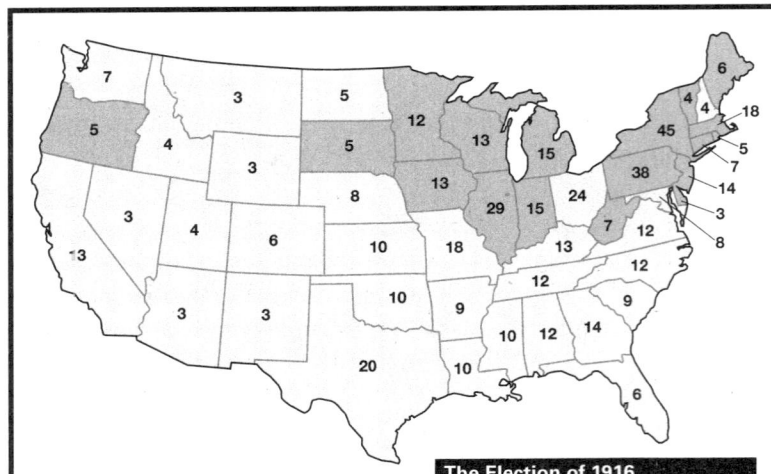

Map 20.2 The Election of 1916.

only Republican-leaning California's 13 electoral votes to win. Over the next couple of days, however, revised tallies culminated with Wilson being certified the winner in the Golden State by less than 4,000 votes. With the president's solid showing in the South and most of the western states, Wilson eked out a 277-254 victory in the Electoral College (with 9.1 million popular votes versus 8.5 million votes for Hughes).

The supreme irony of the 1916 campaign became the fact that Wilson's triumph meant that the candidate whose main slogan was "He Kept Us Out of War!" would be asking Congress for a declaration of war just one month after being inaugurated. For his part, Wilson disliked the mantra, though he did nothing to stop his people from using it. As he once prophetically stated concerning the possible sinking of American ships on the high seas by German submarines (the eventual cause of U.S. entry into the First World War): "I can't keep this country out of war. Some damned little German lieutenant can plunge this nation into war through a calculated outrage."

THE LEGACY OF PROGRESSIVISM

Reform efforts reached their pinnacle at the end of Wilson's first term. With U.S. entry into World War I in 1917, progressivism began to wane but never disappeared from American life. The nature of progressivism would evolve over time as fresh generations of reformers emerged to tackle new issues. The battles between reformers and conservatives would characterize much of the country's political story for the remainder of the century and beyond.

Americans living today may recognize certain reforms that originated during the Progressive Era while also noting their limitations. Regulatory legislation, for example, like all other laws, can only be as potent as they are enforced. Political scientists often take note of the phenomenon of "agency capture," whereby a government regulatory unit acts more in the interest of the industry that it is supposed to be monitoring rather than the public interest due to the particular philosophies of the regulators or the possibility of a lucrative private sector job within the industry when their public service tenure ends. The inability of the Federal Reserve Board to enact policies providing a quick economic recovery following the arrival of the "Great Recession" that began in 2008 at the end of the George W. Bush administration also displays the limits of that important reform (while reinforcing the notion that the federal government does not have complete control over the American economy). Primary elections may have made the political process more democratic, but they still have not negated the power of money in elections.

Taken as a whole, however, the reforms enacted during the Progressive Era impacted a majority of Americans for the better. By the 1930s when the United States entered a new phase of reform with Franklin Roosevelt's New Deal, the nation had state and national laws in place that improved the political process, provided some important protections for workers and consumers, aided farmers and organized labor, brought more orderly business operations, and even focused attention on the environment. To be sure, not all benefited immediately from these efforts, especially African Americans. Those who objected to limits placed on individual freedoms by such progressive measures as the prohibition of alcohol could find much fault with the goals of certain reformers. Nevertheless, there can be no doubt, that the aspirations of the progressives provided an important corrective to the direction of the country at the turn of the twentieth century as they pushed for the realization of what progressive author Herbert Croly dubbed "The Promise of American Life."

Table 20.1   Some Notable National-Level Progressive Era Reforms

Reform	Date	Significance
Hepburn Act	1905	Allowed the Interstate Commerce Commission (ICC) to set maximum railroad rates pending court approval
Meat Inspection Act	1906	Authorized federal supervision of meat processing
Pure Food and Drug Act	1906	Banned the manufacture, sale, or transportation across state lines of fraudulently labeled or adulterated food or drugs; banned foods and drugs containing certain ingredients
Mann-Elkins Act	1910	Extended ICC regulatory powers to the telecommunications industry
16th Amendment	1913	Allowed Congress to levy an income tax
17th Amendment	1913	Allowed voters to vote directly for U.S. senators
Federal Reserve Act	1913	Established the Federal Reserve System to influence the nation's money supply
Federal Trade Commission Act	1913	Established the Federal Trade Commission to oversee regulation of economic competition in interstate commerce
Clayton Antitrust Act	1914	Outlawed price discrimination, corporate tying agreements, interlocking directorates, and companies owning stock of their competitors
Adamson Act	1916	Established the 8-hour work day for railroad workers
Keating-Owen Act	1916	Outlawed the interstate sale of goods made in a factory, shop, or cannery that employed workers under 14 years of age (later ruled unconstitutional)
18th Amendment	1919	Banned the manufacture and sale of alcoholic beverages (repealed 1933)
19th Amendment	1920	Banned the denial or abridgement of the right to vote on account of a voter's sex

Chronology

1900	Robert La Follette elected governor of Wisconsin.
1901	William McKinley assassinated. Theodore Roosevelt becomes the 26th U.S. President.
1902	Anthracite Coal Strike.
1904	Northern Securities Company dissolved. Theodore Roosevelt reelected president.
1906	Hepburn Act; *The Jungle* published. Meat Inspection Act; Pure Food and Drug Act.
1908	*Muller vs. Oregon* decision. William Howard Taft elected the 27th U.S. president.
1909	Ballinger-Pinchot Affair.
1910	Woodrow Wilson elected governor of New Jersey.
1911	Triangle Shirtwaist Fire.
1912	Woodrow Wilson elected the 28th U.S. president.
1913	16th Amendment (income tax) ratified. 17th Amendment (direct election of U.S. senators) ratified. Federal Reserve Act.
1914	Federal Trade Commission Act. World War I begins (Wilson declares U.S. neutrality).
1916	Adamson Act; Keating-Owen Act. Federal Farm Loan Act; Wilson reelected.
1917	U.S. entry into World War I.
1918	World War I ends.
1919	18th Amendment (Prohibition) ratified.
1920	19th Amendment (Woman Suffrage) ratified.

SUGGESTED READINGS

H.W. Brands, *TR: The Last Romantic* (1997).

Douglas Brinkley, *The Wilderness Warrior: Theodore Roosevelt and the Crusade for America* (2009).

John D. Buenker, *Urban Liberalism and Progressive Reform* (1973).

Kendrick A. Clements, *The Presidency of Woodrow Wilson* (1992).

Paolo E. Coletta, *The Presidency of William Howard Taft* (1973).

John Milton Cooper, Jr., *Pivotal Decades: The United States, 1900-1920* (1990).

——, *The Warrior and the Priest: Woodrow Wilson and Theodore Roosevelt* (1983).

Allen F. Davis, *American Heroine: The Life and Legend of Jane Addams* (1973).

——, *Spearheads for Reform: The Social Settlements and the Progressive Movement, 1890-1914* (1967).

Lewis L. Gould, *The Presidency of Theodore Roosevelt* (1991).

Samuel P. Hays, *Conservation and the Gospel of Efficiency: The Progressive Conservation Movement, 1890-1920* (1975).

Gabriel Kolko, *The Triumph of Conservatism: A Reinterpretation of American History, 1900-1916* (1967).

Aileen S. Kraditor, *The Ideas of the Woman Suffrage Movement, 1890-1920* (1981).

Arthur S. Link and Richard L. McCormick, *Progressivism* (1983).

Judith N. McArthur, *Creating the New Woman: The Rise of Southern Women's Progressive Culture in Texas, 1893-1918* (1998).

Edmund Morris, *The Rise of Theodore Roosevelt* (1979).

Thomas R. Pegram, *Battling Demon Rum: The Struggle for a Dry America, 1800-1933* (1998).

Jacob Riis, *How the Other Half Lives* (1997).

Patricia A. Schechter, *Ida B. Wells-Barnett and American Reform, 1880-1930* (2001).

Upton Sinclair, *The Jungle* (1906).

James H. Timberlake, *Prohibition and the Progressive Movement, 1900-1920* (1970).

Robert Von Drehle, *Triangle: The Fire That Changed America* (2003).

Robert H. Wiebe, *Businessmen and Reform: A Study of the Progressive Movement* (1962).

——, *The Search for Order, 1877-1920* (1967).

Review Questions

1. Describe the many similarities and differences among Progressive Era reformers.

2. Describe the ways in which progressivism impacted the cities and states before the advent of national-level reform.

3. What do you believe was Theodore Roosevelt's most significant domestic achievement as president? Why?

4. Describe the achievements and failures of William Howard Taft as president.

5. What do you believe was Woodrow Wilson's most significant domestic achievement as president? Why?

Glossary of Important People and Concepts

Anthracite Coal Strike
Anti-Saloon League (ASL)
Ballinger-Pinchot Affair
Direct Primary
W.E.B. Du Bois
Federal Reserve Act
Federal Trade Commission
Hepburn Act
The Jungle
Keating-Owen Child Labor Act
Florence Kelley
Meat Inspection Act
"Muckrakers"
"Municipal Housekeeping"
National American Woman Suffrage Association (NAWSA)
Northern Securities Company
Gifford Pinchot
Progresssive ("Bull Moose") Party
Progressivism
Pure Food and Drug Act
Theodore Roosevelt
Settlement houses
William Howard Taft
Booker T. Washington
Woodrow Wilson

SURE!
We'll
Finish
the Job

VICTORY LIBERTY LOAN

Chapter Twenty-one

THE "GREAT WAR": World War I

From the outbreak of World War I in August 1914, the fighting in Europe had been bloody and intense. The initial five-week engagement fought along France's borders with Belgium and Germany, known as the Battle of the Frontiers, presaged how brutal and ruthless the war would be, as both the French and Germans lost over 300,000 men. The German assaults were finally stopped at the First Battle of the Marne in northeastern France at the outskirts of Paris. The combined casualties of that five-day battle in September were more than 500,000, with almost 200,000 dead. The extent of the death and destruction proved only one thing: this would be a long war, potentially lasting several years. The primary cost would be the deaths of some of the best and brightest young men of every major nation involved.

After the Germans fell back and stabilized their position in the Aisne Valley, the war degenerated into an extended stalemate with neither side able to push through the others' defenses as each side built a massive series of trenches. By November, the landscape was marked by parallel lines of opposing troughs running from the North Sea all the way to the Swiss border. In between lay "no man's land," and it was truly a killing field. The holiday season of 1914 certainly did not appear that it would be the traditional time promoting "peace on earth and good will toward men."

These trench lines were not separated by great distances, and most of the soldiers from the armies could shout and send greetings to each other, which happened more often than one would believe. In 1914, the armies generally stopped fighting when cooks and supply personnel brought food rations to the front. If no offensive operations were taking place, soldiers from either army would occasionally meet on the middle ground, usually at dusk, and exchange pleasantries, though officers on both sides discouraged such meetings and tried to ban them. Then, beginning in the first part of December, an unofficial evening truce began so that each side could venture out of their trenches and collect their dead; some Allied and German soldiers even exchanged newspapers, and conversation about football (soccer) was common. If a group of soldiers on one side began to sing, it was not uncommon for troops on the other side to join in. Nevertheless, the fighting would resume the next day with the same intensity.

The notion of a Christmas truce was not unique to World War I, and the idea in 1914 did not originate solely with the soldiers in the trenches. Benedict XV had begun calling for a Christmas truce almost immediately after he became the new pope in September, but both sides quickly rejected any such overtures. Thus, any official "Christmas Truce" was out of the question, but as previous events had proven, an unofficial celebration was certainly a possibility.

On Christmas Eve, 1914, the phenomenon began as over 100,000 British and German troops in the Ypres and Saint-Yves area began what has become known as the Christmas Truce of 1914. German troops decorated their trenches with candles and small Christmas trees, and then began to sing carols. The British joined in with their own carols. Each side soon delivered Christmas greetings to their adversaries in "No Man's Land," exchanging small gifts and food, and playing friendly soccer games against each other in some sectors along the front lines. On Christmas Day, the interactions continued, with even the officers taking part by sharing cigars.

There would be later attempts at such seasonal truces, but after 1915, the movement faded. The fighting never paused during Christmas in 1916 and 1917, and the bitter feelings between the combatants would grow more intense. Still, some of the veteran soldiers for each side fondly recalled the Truce of 1914, lamenting the length of the war with its corresponding horrific loss of life.

No war would directly affect world history as extensively as World War I. Called the "Great War" at the time, it would tremendously change the map of Europe and bring to a halt the "Age of Imperialism," signaling the beginning of what some historians would call "The American Century," as the United States would emerge as the predominant nation in world affairs. World War I also had lasting significance because it failed to resolve tensions between the great European powers, leading just two decades later to an even larger global conflagration.

When the war began in 1914, most Americans thought of it as just another European entanglement, and President Woodrow Wilson would work hard to keep the United States out of the affair for as long as possible. However, as the fighting dragged on, and the horrific casualty lists mounted, much of this isolationist sentiment began to change. Eventually, Wilson and other American leaders concluded that the U.S. could not remain neutral, especially if they hoped to play a role on the world stage and influence the new world order when the war ended. The United States finally entered the war in April 1917, and when the peace negotiations began in Paris in 1919, their president would become the central figure in determining the conditions for officially concluding what was at that time the worst and deadliest conflict in which humans had ever engaged. Because of the failure to secure a lasting peace in Paris, that distinction would not last long.

WILSONIAN "MISSIONARY DIPLOMACY"

Woodrow Wilson entered the presidency with no experience in conducting foreign affairs. He had spent his life before entering politics as a professor and college president, with his only elective office being the governorship of New Jersey. Wilson's presidential campaign had barely mentioned international relations, and his entire focus had been on promoting his particular brand of progressivism. When he took office, those domestic affairs received the bulk of his attention, but eventually events in his own hemisphere forced him to at least attempt to make decisions on conditions outside the American borders.

Wilson may not have initially dedicated much attention to diplomatic affairs, but, like almost anything else connected with Wilson, that did not mean he did not have self-assured opinions about foreign policy matters. Much like how he had approached domestic issues, the president envisioned a "new world order," one that was shaped by morality and "self-determinism." However, his view of diplomacy was also a reflection of his personality and beliefs. Wilson was temperamentally stubborn in the

sense that he often believed that only his thoughts and considerations had any validity, and his outlook toward other nations was often tainted with his personal racism. While some of his rhetoric reflected a soaring moral idealism, such as when he touted the spreading of democracy and freedom, Wilson's "Missionary Diplomacy" often degenerated into paternalistic and racist dogma. At one point, he famously said to a British Foreign Service officer, "I am going to teach the South American republics to elect good men."

Wilson sought to alter the course of his predecessors, particularly the implementation of President Taft's "Dollar Diplomacy," by denouncing the practice of "forcible interference" in order to collect foreign loans—a scheme that he called "obnoxious to the principles upon which the government of our people rests." He also declared that the United States would begin to deal with Latin American nations with "terms of equality and honor."

The president's statement about honor toward Latin America represented, at best, the often contradictory aims of his "Missionary Diplomacy" and, at worst, his often outright hypocrisy when it came to his words and deeds, particularly involving "non-white" nations. Wilson claimed that the strategic importance of the Panama Canal, which he officially opened in 1914, meant that the United States would claim the right to suppress any "unrest" in Latin America. He considered much of Central America to be essentially an American "protectorate," exerting almost complete control of Nicaragua in the interest of "regional security." Interference in Nicaragua meant that Wilson kept Adolfo Dìaz in power, just the sort of brutal dictator that Wilson claimed to oppose. Wilson also sent Marines into Haiti in 1915 and the following year into the Dominican Republic. In both instances, the president believed American military forces were necessary to bring stability to the hemisphere by ending the civil war and violence that seemed to plague both countries, but American intervention in the long run failed in both countries as Haitians and Dominicans would continue to live under corrupt and brutally oppressive dictatorships, suffering through decades of constant civil war.

The best example of the failure of Wilson's "Missionary Diplomacy" involved his relations with the United States' southern neighbor, Mexico. The Mexican nation had been plagued by chaos since its founding in 1821, much of it resulting from European interference and American intrigues. After a short period of democratic promise under Benito Juárez in the late 1860s and early 1870s, Mexico once again came under the control of a dictator, Porfirio Díaz, in 1876. Dìaz absolutely until 1910, allowed the Mexican upper class and foreign capitalists to virtually divide up the wealth of the nation. As Dìaz aged, however, his grip on power began to fade, leading to a struggle among several contenders and eventually a revolution, which caused Dìaz to flee the country in 1911.

Francisco Madero, a native of northern Mexico who financed a rival political movement against Dìaz, assumed power as the new president of Mexico in 1911 with the idea of establishing a liberal democracy, but the unstable conditions wrought by the Mexican Revolution made it impossible for him to govern. One of his military generals, **Victoriano Huerta**, drove Madero from power, seized power, then ordered Madero murdered. Huerta began to once again establish a dictatorship, which delighted the European powers who had made extensive investments in Mexico under Dìaz and potentially faced the loss of their assets. But Wilson, angered and appalled by Madero's murder, refused to recognize the legitimacy of Huerta's government and began to actively work to undermine the general. He successfully lobbied the British to withdraw recognition for Huerta's regime in 1913, and began to demand that Huerta hold free elections before the United States would even consider any sort of regular diplomatic relations. Huerta loudly and publicly refused, leading to a tense diplomatic standoff between the two governments that grew worse when Wilson expressed support for a new revolutionary faction seeking to oust Huerta led by Venustiano Carranza.

The tensions between the U.S. and Mexico turned violent in April 1914 after a small shore party of American sailors was arrested in the Mexican port of Tampico for allegedly entering a restricted area. Mexican officials quickly released the sailors, but the American naval commander demanded a formal apology and a 21-gun salute for the American flag as a sign of respect. The Mexican commander complied with the apology but refused to provide the salute. Wilson then used the incident, as well as the impending arrival of a German cargo ship bearing arms for Huerta's army at the port of Veracruz, as an excuse to send American troops ashore in Mexico. On April 21, 1914, a force of marines landed at Veracruz and occupied the town after a battle costing over two hundred Mexican and 19 American lives. The ensuing crisis led to a diplomatic cry from nations throughout Central and South America condemning both the American actions and the Huerta government. Soon, however, Huerta was forced from power leading to a takeover by Carranza.

The new president promised democratic reforms, but he proved to be about as brutal and oppressive as Huerta, so much so that one of his own supporters in northern Mexico, **Francisco "Pancho" Villa**, rose up against him. Villa had been a player in most of the intrigues taking place in Mexico since the end of the Dìaz dictatorship. He had a penchant for playing both sides and emerging with

more power after each power struggle. When he declared against his former commander Carranza, Villa indicated at the same time that he would welcome American support. Wilson, also growing exasperated with Carranza, gave him rhetorical support but nothing else, and Carranza's forces quickly drove Villa's men back to their northern base. Wilson finally decided that he would back Carranza and recognized his government, which angered Villa, who now resolved to punish the Americans while creating incidents that would compel the United States to invade Mexico and help him to overthrow Carranza. Thus, Villa and his forces stopped a train in northern Mexico and murdered 16 young American mining engineers, then crossed the border and attacked Columbus, New Mexico, killing nineteen more American civilians.

Wilson responded to these outrages by sending a force of 11,000 men under General **John J. Pershing** into Mexico to hunt for Villa, but the American army could not locate the Mexican revolutionary. For almost a year, the American army chased Villa and his men all over northern Mexico but only engaged his forces (and Carranza's) in a few small skirmishes. As tensions with Germany mounted, Wilson realized that potential war with that country represented a more urgent crisis than having the United States Army senselessly roaming northern Mexico so he finally decided to abandon the effort in January 1917. However, with Villa focused on the U.S. troops, Carranza was able to consolidate his power and succeeded in getting a liberal constitution approved for Mexico. Wilson declared that his "missionary diplomacy" had worked, but the reality was that the U.S. had made things more unstable in Mexico instead of helping. The nation continued to be plagued by violence and instability into the 1920s. His interventions, bungling, and heavy-handed diplomacy and military responses produced ill feelings between most of the nations of Central America and the United States for decades to come.

THE OUTBREAK OF THE GREAT WAR

While Woodrow Wilson was engaged in Central American interventions, Europe, and much of the rest of the world, soon plunged into what would become the largest and deadliest war up to that time in human history. The precipitating event for the war was the assassination of the heir to the throne of the Austro-Hungarian Empire, **Franz Ferdinand**, by a Bosnian Serb nationalist named Gavrilo Princip—a member of the "Black Hand" terrorist organization that had ties to radical anti-Austrian members of Serbia's government and who desired an end to Austrian rule over the province of Bosnia. The death of the archduke at the hands of an assassin in Sarajevo, Bosnia's capital, would seem a poor reason to cause a global conflict, but the fuel for the combustible tinderbox of war had been building in Europe for years, and Ferdinand's death was just the spark necessary to cause the continent—and eventually much of the world—to explode.

Causes of the War

Imperialism, the pursuit of power and possessions, had dominated the actions of many European governments during the late nineteenth century. During the 1800s, Great Britain had built the most expansive empire in world history, one upon which it was proverbially said "the sun never sets," and the other European nations had scrambled, in the last few decades of the century, to catch up. Germany, particularly, had begun to make great leaps in acquiring territory, emerging as Britain's chief rival after the previously separated German kingdoms had united in 1871 following the end of the Franco-Prussian War. After Kaiser Wilhelm II ascended to the throne in 1882, Germany began to advance a more imperialistic foreign policy, gobbling up colonies in Africa and islands in the western Pacific Ocean. Germany's aggressiveness led to conflict with its neighbors, particularly France and Britain, but also with Russia. Eventually, Germany aligned with Austria-Hungary and Italy and formed what they called the Triple Alliance (which would become the Central Powers, minus Italy but with the Ottoman Empire of the Turks added during World War I). The western powers, France and Great Britain, would form their own alliance—the Triple Entente—with Russia, as a countermeasure to preserve a balance of power in Europe to discourage the possibility of war among the imperial rivals. The Russians also pledged to protect Serbia in the Balkans region from any attacks by Austria-Hungary, and the British and French agreed to check any German aggression toward Belgium and the Netherlands. Both alliances began to build great armies and navies, and diplomacy took on an aggressive tone throughout the early twentieth century.

The Balkans region of southeastern Europe had already witnessed unrest and violence as the Slavic Christians living in several countries engaged in wars of national liberation from the Muslim Ottoman (Turkish) Empire. As soon as these Slavic peoples freed themselves, they found a new potential oppressor in the form of the Austro-Hungarian Empire, whose Habsburg rulers had long wanted to expand their empire into southeastern Europe. (In 1908, Austria formally annexed the Balkan province of Bosnia on the Adriatic coast, which had been previously held by the Ottomans.) For protection, the leaders of Serbia turned to Russia, a fellow Slavic country

whose Romanov rulers were more than willing to offer the Balkan Slavs security because they were just as territorially ambitious in the region as the Habsburgs. Meanwhile, many Serbs wished to expand their country and create a greater Pan-Slavic state in the Balkans at the expense of Austria-Hungary. By 1914, the tensions between the Austrian, Serbs, and Russians in this most volatile part of Europe had reached the point where each nation anticipated a future showdown. When Princip assassinated Franz Ferdinand, the continent would soon be engulfed in a destructive war, as human emotions replaced all efforts at diplomacy, and all the deterrents to armed conflict were ignored.

Austria-Hungary quickly began to mobilize against Serbia as a reprisal for Ferdinand's death, which, in turn, led Russia to mobilize in preparation for moves to threaten Austria-Hungary. Germany demanded that Russia cease its mobilization, and when the Russians refused, Germany declared war on Russia on August 1, 1914, and then France—Russia's ally—two days later. Germany's intentions, however, were not to rush into Russia or even to protect Austria-Hungary, which they proved with their immediate invasion of Belgium with the intention of moving on to France before the French could fully mobilize. The German strategy was based on their long-practiced **Schlieffen Plan**, which in the case of war called for a quick knock-out of the French before the British could come to their rescue and before the Russians could fully mobilize in the east. For the strategy to be effective, the Germans had to reach Paris as quickly as possible, which meant invading through neutral Belgium. Much to the Germans' surprise, however, the Belgians put up stronger than expected resistance. When coupled with the arrival of British troops, the French had time to mobilize enough forces to hold the line at the First Battle of the Marne outside of Paris.

Though the invasion of Belgium was the official reason that Britain entered the conflict on August 4, the British leaders worried that a German victory would upset the balance of power on the continent and thus threaten England itself. Meanwhile, in the western Pacific, Japan, eager to build its own empire, took advantage of the occasion and declared war on Germany on August 23. As if that was not enough, the Ottoman Empire, who wanted to end any British influences and designs on the Middle East, joined in on the German-Austrian side in October. Italy would stay out of the war until 1915, when they finally revoked their alliance with Germany and joined with Britain and France against the Austro-Hungarian Empire in the hope of acquiring new territory in southeastern Europe.

German forces made quick offensive advances into both Belgium and France in the early days of the conflict until British and French troops stopped the advance in the fall of 1914. After that, the Germans were forced to abandon the Schlieffen Plan and peel away entire divisions to protect their eastern border with Russia. The war along the eastern front with soon stabilized into a stalemate. Meanwhile, along the western front in northeastern France, the war degenerated into "trench warfare" as both armies dug themselves into trenches that stretched hundreds of miles through the length of the front. The area between the trenches became known as "no man's land," the zone in which any advancing forces were met with a hail of weaponry and artillery that made progression nearly impossible, resulting in astronomical levels of casualties. Men often crawled over the ground in an effort to escape gunfire, hand grenades, as well as the miles of barbed wire strung across the fields. If the death and destruction of the battles was not enough, the trenches themselves were pits of squalor and disease, often flooding leading to men spending days at a time with their feet immersed in putrid standing water. That, in turn, led to infection ("trench foot"), and other illnesses that killed almost as many soldiers as enemy fire.

New technology and weapons made World War I a conflict unlike any other previously fought. When the war began, many of the commanders, trained in nineteenth-century tactics, sent their troops forward in flanking and marching positions but were met with machine gun fire, high-range and high-velocity rifles, as well as accurate and deadly artillery, poison gas, flamethrowers, and a new particularly deadly weapon, armored tanks. The result was massive carnage and ghastly numbers of casualties. As one military commentator noted, "the generals planned tactics and strategies, but all they accomplished was the death of young men." When the war ended over nine million of those soldiers were dead, and another almost twenty million suffered wounds.

American Neutrality

Woodrow Wilson declared soon after World War I began that the U.S. government would remain neutral. As the reports from Europe reached the United States, many Americans were shocked but also strengthened in their resolve to stay out of the conflict. President Wilson echoed these sentiments when he decried the conditions that had led to war, imploring the warring nations to solve their differences. He also publicly and stridently stressed that the United States would remain "neutral in thought as well as in action."

Remaining neutral as 1914 became 1915, and then 1916 would be difficult. When accounts such as those from the Battle of the Somme in July 1916 made their way across the Atlantic and Americans heard figures like 60,000 British casualties in one day of fighting, their resolve was tested. The United States was a land of immigrants, and many retained ties to their homelands. Some German Americans felt a connection to the German Empire, but even more seemed to support the British and French. British propaganda that portrayed the German military as savage beasts who threatened freedom and democracy only increased that support, with the implication that if Germany were to win the war in Europe they would then become a direct threat to the United States. Other supposedly "legitimate" newspapers and magazines

German soldiers on horseback viewing a captured trench abandoned by the British. The presence of horses reveals that this photo was taken early in the war.

published lightly edited pieces from British governmental offices that depicted the Germans as ruthless barbarians who regularly slaughtered civilians, raped innocent women, and brutally stormed through the nations in their zeal to conquer Europe. It had a powerful effect on the citizens of the United States.

The English Blockade and German Submarine Warfare

Threats and hindrances to U.S. neutrality came not just from propaganda but also on the high seas. International law granted neutral nations the right to trade with any party in a war, and the U.S., in 1914, was prepared to do just that, but the might of the British Navy made that very difficult. The British followed typical maritime wartime strategy and declared their intention to place an almost full blockade on goods entering Germany; any foreign flagged ships had to enter British or French ports to be searched for anything that was deemed to allow Germany to wage war; if any such items—including goods as seemingly innocuous as food, furniture, or clothing—were deemed "contraband," the cargoes were immediately confiscated and usually with no payment to the owner.

The British tactics on the seas angered Wilson and he protested through diplomatic channels, but the British refused to budge, and even declared that their "fight for survival" made it necessary for them to break international law. Privately, Wilson expressed admiration for the British cause, and even went so far as to tell a British ambassador that a German victory "would be fatal to our form of Government and American ideals." Another reason that the president failed to press the British further involved his worries that a protracted European conflict could negatively impact the American economy. To prevent such a possibility, Wilson asserted that Americans should be allowed to trade with all combatants. This would prove to be easier said than done because the British government had no intention of allowing neutral vessels to enjoy unfettered trade with its enemies if their navy had anything to say about the issue. As a result, American trade with the Central Powers was effectively shut down, leading the United States to trade only with England and its Allies for most of the war. The sheer volume of American commerce with Britain and France, as well as massive loans that U.S. banks began to give the Allies in 1916-1917, seriously strained the notion that the U.S. was being "neutral in thought" as Wilson had declared.

Neutral in thought was one thing, but as the war dragged on and the stalemate in Europe became a reality, a change in German tactics on the seas began to test the American resolve to remain on the sidelines. The

Germans could not hope to defeat the massive British Navy in direct battle, and to even try would mean the decimation of their surface fleet, thus giving the British a decided advantage in the war. Their solution was to incorporate a new weapon into their fleet—the submarine, which they called a **U-Boat** (short for *Unterseeboot*). The U-boats could sail underwater largely undetected, but the very nature of their conditions meant that they operated differently than traditional surface ships. A submarine became most vulnerable when it surfaced, so it fired its torpedoes at unsuspecting ships, and the results were often deadly. Such tactics were frowned by most students of war when used against warships, but they were considered downright hideous and barbaric when deployed against unarmed cargo vessels.

In early 1915, the Germans began a new chapter in naval warfare when they announced that U-boats would sink any enemy ships, not just warships, on sight without warning. The consequences of the new German policy became a stark reality when on May 7, 1915, a German U-boat sank the British passenger liner **Lusitania** off the coast of Ireland, killing over 1,100 passengers and crew, 128 of them Americans. Wilson was appalled at the German action, and asserted forcefully in a note to the German foreign minister that there was no justification for such an act. When the Germans responded with the assertion that the *Lusitania* was carrying munitions (which it was) and thus a viable target, Wilson rejected their explanation and demanded that Germany had attacked innocent citizens and must immediately desist from such a policy in the future or he would sever diplomatic relations.

Eventually, because Germany did not want to risk the U.S. entering the war against them at that time, its leaders agreed to end U-Boat attacks on merchant vessels. The German acquiescence in using their vital weapon lasted for less than a year. When Britain and France announced in early 1916 that they would begin to arm their merchant ships with guns designed to sink submarines, Germany announced that it would once again begin to fire upon any vessel that flew an Allied flag. They proved their point when they sunk the French cargo steamer *Sussex* a few weeks later. Wilson once again denounced the German tactics, and, once again, Germany temporarily abandoned its "unrestricted submarine warfare."

THE UNITED STATES ENTERS THE WAR

Woodrow Wilson entered the election year of 1916 with a great deal of uncertainty about his chances for reelection.

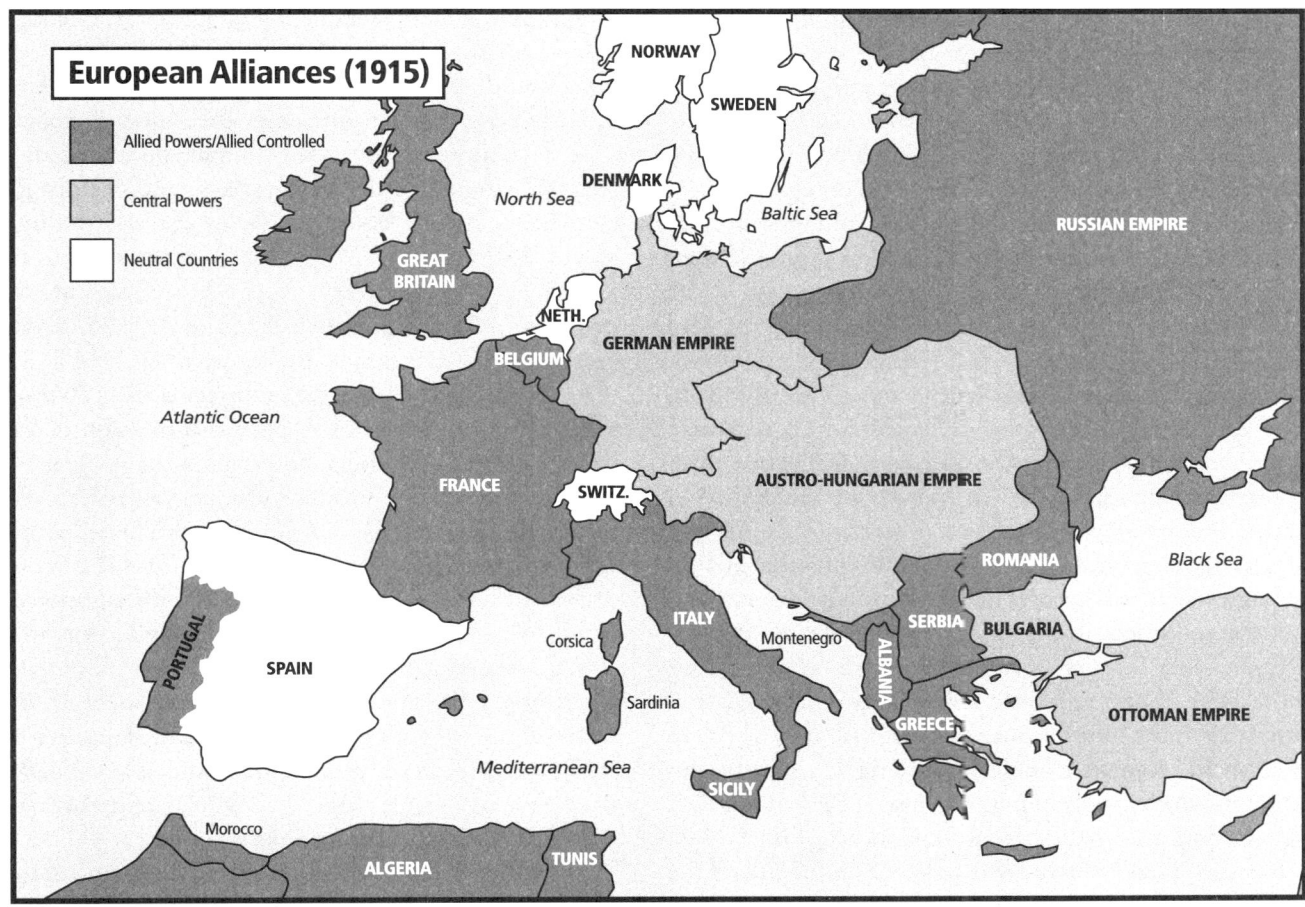

Map 21.1 European Alliances (1915)

He had been the beneficiary of a split in the Republican Party in 1912, and the Republicans remained the majority party in the U.S. "The Great War" and, in particular, the continued American avoidance of entry into the war dominated the campaign. Isolationists in both parties sounded the alarm of continued neutrality, though a growing faction led by former president Theodore Roosevelt began to make a case for American intervention. Wilson deftly walked the line between both sides by gradually building up American forces as a precaution against entry into the war, while at the same time campaigning on the slogan "He Kept Us Out of War." It was an effective strategy, and Wilson won a slim victory over Republican Charles Evans Hughes, but he knew that his second term would be dominated by questions of the war in Europe.

The Return of Unrestricted Submarine Warfare and the "Zimmermann Telegram"

By 1917, Wilson had no doubt that the U.S. would not be able to avoid entry into the war for much longer. The diplomatic tensions between the U.S. and Germany were high, especially after Germany announced in January that it would once again begin employing "unrestricted submarine warfare," this time against neutral as well as Allied ships. The resumption of their naval initiative coincided with preparations for a major assault against the Allied troops on the Western Front in an attempt to end the war once and for all, with an eye toward winning quickly before U.S. forces could fully aid Britain and France.

In disgust, Wilson broke off diplomatic relations with Germany and addressed Congress, laying the groundwork for American entry into the war. The president needed a reason to join a war that a majority of Americans believed was not their country's fight, and he found one when he began to speak about using war as a way to construct a "new world order," one that would stress freedom and democracy, and "self-determination." In his address, Wilson stressed that the United States needed to be a leader in a postwar world, a "peace without victory" he called it, something that could only be accomplished through a permanent "league of nations," that the United States must lead. Germany could see that the U.S. was inching closer to joining the fight.

Tensions grew more intense in February of that year when the British government passed along to the Wilson administration a copy of a German diplomatic cable that they had intercepted intended for the government of Mexico. The telegram, which became known as the **"Zimmermann Telegram"** named after its sender, German Foreign Minister Arthur Zimmermann, proposed to Mexico that if war broke out between the U.S. and Germany, Mexico should immediately join the Germans and attack the United States. Germany promised that, if they were to win the war, they would insist in the peace settlement that Mexico should receive all the land that it had lost during the U.S.-Mexican War in 1848. When Wilson made its contents public in early March, the Zimmermann Telegram inflamed American public opinion. Later that month, Germany torpedoed three American ships and that was enough for the president. Appearing before a joint session of Congress on April 2, 1917, Wilson formally asked for a declaration of war. Congress debated the issue for four days as isolationist and pacifist sentiment in the nation still had strong support. Nevertheless, Congress responded with an affirmative vote. The Senate approved the war declaration 82 to 6 on April 4; the House concurred on April 6 by a vote of 373 to 50. Jeannette Rankin of Montana, a pacifist and the first woman to serve in the House of Representatives, was among those who voted against the war. The United States had finally entered World War I on the side of the Allies.

THE WAR AT HOME

World War I's greatest impact on the United States would occur at home. When the U.S. entered the war, the country was hardly ready to become engaged in such an extensive military operation. The United States had no real tradition in fighting a foreign war, and its commitment to not allowing a large standing army meant that the nation would have to mobilize its military and the national economy for the major fight seemingly from scratch, and do so quickly. Ultimately, the U.S. succeeded by proceeding in ways unimaginable in previous decades. In the process, they would introduce Progressive economic concepts, as well as massive propaganda, to serve as a model for future administrations throughout the remainder of the twentieth century.

Propaganda and Hysteria

Wars are often won not just on the battlefield, but also at home, especially in a society that depends on democratic support for credibility and power. The most strategic plan and the most organized economy alone cannot overcome a free public that does not fully support a war effort. Wilson and his administration knew that the American people were divided about entering the conflict in Europe, so they faced the task of convincing the American people that intervention was necessary. To that end, the administration inaugurated a massive propaganda campaign designed to instill a commitment to the war through ideas of patriotism and nationalism. At the same time, Congress, at Wilson's behest, would pass a series of acts calculated to oppress any dissent to the war and federal government policies supporting those efforts.

To organize and oversee the propaganda effort, Wilson created the **Committee on Public Information (CPI)** through an executive order, and named the progressive journalist George Creel to head the new agency. Creel urged Wilson to run the campaign much like an advertising effort, which he called creating a "propagation of the faith." The Committee supervised the distribution of more than 75 million pieces of printed material, primarily destined to appear in newspapers and magazines across the country. The government designed posters, flyers, and "news pieces," following the earlier British pattern of depicting the Germans as barbarians and savage killers, with the war as a whole often depicted as an effort to "save the world" from brutal authoritarianism.

The CPI was able to help spur greater support for the war, but Wilson and his supporters in Congress thought such efforts needed additional help, specifically, laws to suppress dissent against the war. If successful, such legislation would destroy both the isolationist tendencies that had originally kept the U.S. out of the war, as well as silence some growing political movements, such as the Socialist Party, that might threaten the political hegemony of the two mainstream political parties. Outside of the public opinion endeavors, the CPI encouraged the public to report "subversive behavior," or any instances of "disloyalty."

More chilling was Congress' passage of the **Espionage Act** of 1917 and the Sedition Act of 1918. The Espionage Act made it a crime to disrupt military operations, including the promotion of insubordination in the military or interference with recruitment or drafting of soldiers and sailors. To shore up this law, Congress passed the Sedition Act, expressly prohibiting anyone from using "disloyal, profane, scurrilous, or abusive language" about the United States government, the American flag, or the U.S. armed forces. (In addition to these congressional actions, U.S. Attorney General Thomas Gregory wanted to do more to curb internal dissent and thus instructed the Postmaster General, Albert Burleson, to censure and, if necessary, discontinue delivering any anti-American or pro-German newspapers and magazines through the mail.)

Eugene Debs leaving the White House on December 23, 1921, three days after the commutation of his 10-year prison sentence by President Warren Harding for violating the Sedition Act by publicly speaking out against the military draft. Photo credit: Library of Congress.

Although of questionable legality, the Espionage and Sedition Acts became law with no interference from the courts, and the Wilson administration used them more for silencing political opponents than looking for foreign efforts to disrupt the war effort. Labor unions, especially the radical Industrial Workers of the World (IWW), and the Socialist Party came under the most scrutiny and prosecution under the legislation. Socialists opposed involvement in the conflict on the grounds that it was a war to benefit capitalism rather than to guarantee freedom from authoritarianism. In Europe, socialist groups had begun to form real opposition to their governments on the continent, and Wilson was determined to make sure that the same thing did not happen in the U.S. Using the new laws as cover, Wilson's Justice Department arrested, convicted, and sentenced Socialist Party leader Eugene V. Debs to a ten-year prison sentence in 1918, and only a pardon by the new president, Warren Harding, in 1921 kept him from serving his full penalty. Officials also prosecuted a number of members of the IWW, including its leader William Haywood, who avoided prison only by fleeing to the Soviet Union. In the end, the government prosecuted almost 20,000 from 1917 through 1919 utilizing some aspect of these laws.

After the war, in its 1919 *Schenck v. United States* decision, the Supreme Court upheld the constitutionality of the Espionage and Sedition Acts. Just the year before, Charles Schenck, a leader of the Socialist Party who oversaw his organization's anti-draft pamphleteering campaign, was charged with sedition, found guilty, and imprisoned. In a unanimous decision, thrice-wounded Civil War veteran Chief Justice Oliver Wendell Holmes, Jr., stated "The question in every case is whether the words used are used in such circumstances and are of such a nature as to create a clear and present danger that they will bring about the substantive evils that the United States Congress has a right to prevent. It is a question of proximity and degree. When a nation is at war many things that might be said in time of peace are such a hindrance to its effort that their utterance will not be endured so long as men fight, and that no Court could regard them as protected by any constitutional right." In other words, in Holmes's opinion, the needs of the state, especially in times of crises, superseded those of the individual, and dissent of any form could be determined by government officials to be illegal.

The actions of the CPI and the Congress helped to create a dangerous atmosphere on the home front during World War I, producing what could be termed "super-patriotism" in society—the idea that any sort of opposition, disagreement, or even difference with mainstream views could be termed radical or subversive. Mobs in many municipalities attacked unionized workers as "agents of subversion," and community leaders used the guise of patriotism to root out any element that they dubbed "radical." Some of the efforts in local places were almost silly, such as the banning of using the name "sauerkraut" for fermented cabbage, instead calling it "liberty cabbage." Others, however, were alarming, such as prohibiting the teaching of German or the playing of German music, Bach, for example, since it demonstrated just how pervasive and widespread forced compliance with social and cultural norms could become. Violence against people of German dissent, or anyone who expressed opposition to the war, became if not common still disturbingly more frequent.

Manpower (and Womanpower) Mobilization

When the United States entered the fighting in April 1917, it was in no way prepared to wage such a vast war fought on an overseas continent. The United States had a tradition of not having a large standing army, and that was certainly the case in 1917. Wilson named **John J. Pershing** (the former leader of the force that entered Mexico to try and capture Pancho Villa) as the commanding general of what would become known as the American Expeditionary Force (AEF). Pershing knew

Sergeant Alvin York

World War I is often used as a demarcation point for the true beginning of the twentieth century, largely because the war swept away many of the "old arrangements" and, as Woodrow Wilson believed, ushered in a "new world order." Emblematic of such change was the most famous American foot soldier of World War I, Sergeant Alvin York of Tennessee.

York was born in Pall Mall, Tennessee in 1887. He grew up not only in the Jim Crow South, but in a part of it that time and modern advancement rarely touched. His experience growing up was a rural life that differed very little from that of his grandfathers in the years after the Revolutionary War. He grew up one of eleven children in a family that farmed on a small plot of barely arable land, an existence that often failed to provide enough subsistence for them to survive on farming alone. That life led to one of the skills that made York such a valuable soldier; because the family often had to supplement their meager diet with hunting, Alvin York became a skilled marksmen. His hard upbringing also played a role in how he lived as a young man. York ran with a "hard crowd" that was rowdy and frequently drunk. He gained a reputation as a man that had no goals and few chances to succeed.

Such a lifestyle came to an abrupt end for Alvin York in 1914. After his closest friend was killed in a drunken brawl in a bar, York attended a revival organized by the Churches of Christ in Christian Union, one of many strictly fundamentalist Christian sects that was sweeping the South in those early years of the twentieth century. Grief stricken over the death of his friend and resolved not to follow the same path that he did, York converted to the church and began to lead a new life of abstinence from alcohol, swearing, dancing, and, most importantly, a very strict and moral avoidance of violence of any kind.

When the U.S. entered World War I and instituted a draft to fill the ranks of its forces, York's new religious doctrine would be severely tested. He was drafted into the Army, but according to the theology of the Churches of Christ in Christian Union, the taking of a life in a war was immoral, so York's pastor counseled him to apply for conscientious objector status. York told his local and state draft boards that he "didn't want to fight," but they denied his appeal because the Churches of Christ in Christian Union was not yet recognized as a "legitimate" religious denomination.

So, Alvin C. York went to war as a member of Company G in the 328th Infantry, part of the U. S. Army's 82nd Division. York's fellow soldiers regarded him as odd; he was the best shot in the unit, but he hated the thought of battle. Finally, after his company commander convinced him that the American cause was moral and approved by God, he agreed to fight, and at the Argonne Forest he performed one of the greatest feats of courage in American war history. York, then a corporal, and sixteen other soldiers were sent to capture a railroad behind a hill. Because no one in the company could read a map, they became lost behind German lines. They skirmished with a larger German force, forcing their surrender, but when the Germans realized that the Americans' numbers were so small, a nest of their machine gunners opened fire on York and his fellow soldiers. Nine men were killed instantly, and the sergeant leading the unit was severely wounded. York was then ordered to take out the machine gunners. Although he did not act alone, all accounts were that York, the keen marksmen, was the reason that the small unit was able to silence all the machine gun nests, killing twenty-five Germans, and then taking 132 prisoners. For his bravery, the former rowdy turned devoutly religious Tennessean was awarded the Congressional Medal of Honor.

that he needed to rapidly build up the AEF before they would be able to perform their assigned task in France. In early 1917, there were only about 200,000 Americans in uniform. They were ill equipped, lacking sufficient quantities of the modern weapons of war—machine guns, tanks, and long-range artillery.

Although many in Congress clamored for calling for volunteers, Wilson decided that conscription was the best method for quickly raising an army large enough to fight in the trenches of Europe. In May 1917, Congress passed the **Selective Service Act**, which called for all men between the ages of 21 and 30 (later changed to 18-45) to

register for a military draft, the first since the Civil War. Within a month, almost 10 million men had registered, and by the end of the war approximately 25 million would do so. Eventually, almost 3 million men would be drafted, approved, and inducted into the armed forces. Congress soon provided the funding for vast expenditures in modern guns, ships, tanks, and other implements needed by these soldiers for the coming fight.

On the home front, women also joined in the war effort. Large numbers took jobs in weapons factories; sold Liberty Bonds at church, school, and social functions; led clothing drives for soldiers; ran canteens for American service men in England; and over 10,000 volunteered for service as Red Cross nurses in France. Women's organizations put their work on the back burner in order to help in the war effort. The National American Woman Suffrage Association (NAWSA), for example, sponsored mobile field hospitals in France and England. Some NAWSA leaders were concerned that Jeannette Rankin's "no vote" would taint their organization. (Congresswoman Rankin had been one of the movement's stalwarts for years.) Much to NAWSA's relief, their efforts lessened any reservations that citizens may have had about the association's devotion to the war effort. Even Rankin participated in some of the more humanitarian programs sponsored by the group. In addition to patriotism, NAWSA leaders hoped that devotion to the grand cause would help them in their suffrage efforts. Indeed, female contributions did succeed in changing public attitudes, leading to the passage of the Nineteenth Amendment granting women the vote within two years of the end of the war.

Mobilization of Resources

Modern wars are not won by the nations that have the bravest soldiers or the most able commanders. Those factors help, along with good strategy and a willing public, but the most overwhelming advantage in winning a modern war is to possess an economy that can build, ship, and, most importantly, pay for the resources needed to wage a war. The United States would emerge as a preeminent world power during World War I precisely because it could marshal all of these forces quickly and efficiently. The American mobilization of its resources would become one of its primary contributions to the war and perhaps the most decisive determinant in the eventual Allied victory.

In the terms of funding and governmental involvement in the economy, World War I transformed how the United States approached federal intervention in the nation's economy. Mobilization and equipping the armed forces to fight such a war took an unprecedented amount of money, and the quick and efficient allocation of those resources would call for the establishment a new federal bureaucracy unthinkable in the nation just a few years earlier. Progressivism had laid a foundation for such programs, but World War I would establish the continued need for such initiatives.

The first problem the Wilson administration faced was how to pay for the war. Congress had passed legislation authorizing more than $30 billion to fight the war, but since the entire federal budget before the war was less than $1 billion, officials had to come up with some way to raise the additional funds. An increase in taxes, primarily by subjecting more Americans to the new income tax, as well as new taxes on corporations, raised close to $10 billion. The remainder of the money to finance the war came from the sale of "Liberty Bonds," a direct campaign to convince the American people to essentially loan the government the money it needed to pay for the war. Through a deft use of advertising, entertainment campaigns, and appeals to patriotism, the United States by 1920 had sold almost $25 million worth of these bonds.

Finding the money to pay for the war was a daunting challenge, but even more formidable was organizing the nation's entire economy around producing for the war. Wilson, who had anticipated the coming of war before he hinted at such to the public, saw the need for such an approach as early as 1916, when he established the Council of National Defense. The council then organized local defense councils in states and even municipalities, which in turn began to come up with their own concepts of preparing for war according to their local preferences and traditions. The result was a disorganized, ad hoc mess with no central structure and no overarching idea of how to proceed. As the war drew closer, the council urged Wilson to centralize the process, in other words, make the federal government in charge of streamlining and organizing the nation's entire economy to better promote war preparation and efficiency.

The next step for the Wilson administration and Congress was to divide the economy into specific sectors and functions, and then have a government planning commission oversee the supply, production, and price of each segment. Congress adopted the Fuel and Food Control Act in 1917, for example, creating the Fuel Administration to control the production, distribution, and price of the nation's main fuel sources, such as oil, gas, and coal. Food production and consumption, which also worried the Wilson administration, led the president to issue an executive order creating the U.S. Food Administration. Headed by future president Herbert Hoover, this agency worked to assure the supply, distribution, and conservation of food during the war primarily through appeals to patriotism rather than by government dictate. The results of such efforts were mixed; the boards were able to meet basic needs, but often lacked efficiency and coordination, resulting in delays getting the supplies where they needed to go. The president thus decided that a different approach would be required.

Wilson and Congress then created the **War Industries Board (WIB)** in July 1917 with the mission to consolidate and coordinate the purchase of military supplies in a manner more proficient than the "war boards." The same problems that had beset the earlier apparatus also plagued the WIB until Wilson placed Wall Street financier Bernard Baruch in control. Baruch almost wholly centralized the entire scope of war production by using the WIB to decide what factories would be producing which war materials. In addition, Baruch also had the WIB set production quotas as well as prices. Rather than openly demanding obedience, Baruch preferred to use a combination of persuasion and threatened negative publicity in order to cajole corporate compliance on all aspects of war procurement and production, from the distribution of raw resources to the placing of price controls on finished goods, which included chemical, steel, textile, rubber, and leather products. In a way, Baruch formed a direct partnership between the government and military contractors, all in the name of efficiency and the war effort.

Coordinating and organizing production within the economy was a way to control costs and promote efficiency, but those goals could not happen without some sort of concession and rights for those who toiled in the factories. Congress and Wilson sought to remedy the situation with another federal agency, the National War Labor Board (NWLB), which began in April 1918. The NWLB operated as the final arbiter in all disputes between capital and management, and, after pressure, convinced the businesses producing war materials to grant workers an eight-hour work day, higher wages, and equal pay for women. Also, for the first time in American history, the agency granted labor in those industries the right to organize into unions and to bargain collectively. In return, the NWLB received promises that workers would not strike for the duration of the war. These would prove to be special wartime exemptions not continued after the war.

When viewed collectively, these major agencies actually represented only the tip of the regulatory iceberg. Nearly 5,000 government-created agencies supervised home front activities. Others of note include the Shipping Board, which regulated the transportation of goods by water, and the Railroad Administration, headed by Treasury Secretary William McAdoo. When railroad lines refused to allow their competitors to use their tracks to transport goods, a stoppage occurred in the flow of supplies to Europe in the winter of 1917-1918. McAdoo's agency intervened and soon consolidated the thousands of miles of track owned by the competing companies into an efficient national rail system under his board's control. McAdoo (with the approval of the president and Congress) semi-nationalized the nation's rail system, bringing all major carriers under direct government regulation for the war's duration. Although tightly monitoring the railroads' shipments of goods, the federal government did not take the revenue for such services. Significant profits continued to flow into the coffers of the railroad magnates.

African Americans and the War

When Congress passed the Selective Service Act, African Americans as well as whites became eligible for the draft. Over 400,000 African-American males entered the ranks of the United States military during World War I. However, only a small percentage of African-American soldiers saw combat despite having the desire to prove that blacks were as intelligent, honorable, dedicated, and courageous as their fellow white citizens. The American military at the time of the Great War reflected the segregated nature of American society. All branches of the armed services were separated into all-white and all-black units, with white officers in charge of African-American enlistees and draftees. The overwhelming majority of African American military personnel worked in non-combat support roles such as mess attendants, laborers, and stevedores (ship cargo handlers). The relegation of the majority of black soldiers and sailors to menial, often demeaning, work reflected the white military establishment's belief that African-American men were incapable of holding up in combat, certain they would run at the first sign of a fight or danger because of their supposed inherent character defects such as cowardice. Although assigned to often menial tasks, some jobs proved indispensable to the war effort. Sometimes working 24 hours non-stop, black stevedores, for example, unloaded vital supply ships with incredible speed and efficiency. Surprisingly to both black and white Americans, black AEF soldiers were welcomed by the French military and were treated with respect. Such displays of humanity initially shocked the African-American troops, but as they interacted with the French people, they came to realize that not all white societies were like the United States; there were predominantly white countries in which they could live free from prejudice and discrimination. No surprise that after the war hundreds of black veterans chose to remain in France for the rest of their lives, enjoying a quality of life as an expatriate that they sadly could only dream about having back home.

When given the opportunity to fight, African-American soldiers distinguished themselves, such as the all-black 369th Infantry Brigade, known as the "Harlem Hell Fighters." Under the command of Colonel William Hayward, the Hell Fighters became one of the most decorated U.S. military units of the war. Among their accolades, the unit became the first American combat outfit to be awarded the French Croix de Guerre after being "loaned" to the French army and participating in some of the war's most vicious fighting.

Many African Americans had hoped that the war, which President Wilson promoted as necessary to "save democracy," would be an impetus for instituting full civil rights, with an end to Jim Crow segregation and oppression in the United States. After all, they would argue, why would we fight for freedom in Europe if we were not willing to provide full freedom in our own nation? While many of them held such high hopes, their aspirations were once again dashed by discrimination at home. When the war ended, despite their service, African-American soldiers were denied the right to participate in marches and other celebrations as well as being excluded from numerous art projects that touted the nation's victory.

More significant was the effect that the war had for African Americans at home. Blacks had been greatly concentrated in the South since the end of the Civil War where they had become one of the primary cogs in the region's sharecropping system while being subject to ongoing Jim Crow segregation. The First World War would provide a way for many blacks to escape such conditions. Beginning in 1914 with the great increase in northern manufacturing, especially in those industries that provided war materials to the European nations at war, and then greatly accelerating in 1917 when the United States joined the war and hundreds of thousands of men went off to fight, African Americans embarked on one of the largest physical movements in American history. Since dubbed the "Great Migration," approximately 500,000 southern African Americans would leave the South for northern states in the years between 1914 and 1920. This great movement, mostly to northern urban areas, would transform the social, political, and cultural landscape of those cities in a short period of time as these industrial centers filled with large numbers of African-American migrants. The Great Migration also altered African-American society and culture. In the South, blacks had been largely a rural people, but in the northern cities they began to build a culture that was fundamentally urban.

When African Americans migrated north, they had hoped that they would find a home that eschewed the oppression of the Jim Crow South, offer great economic opportunity, and also promise political freedom and participation. Those dreams quickly died as they discovered that racism was not endemic to the American South, and oppression was universal. They tended to endure substandard living conditions, lower wages, and unequal political freedom. The federal government under Woodrow Wilson was not interested in bringing about any impetus for civil rights, and in many ways they traded one method of oppression for another. Blacks would have to wait another generation for any sort of momentum toward providing equality under the law and in society.

African Americans returning from the war, like those who had migrated to northern cities, thus faced a sobering reality: it was not just southern social construction that treated anyone of African descent—or of any ethnic origin other than European—as second-class citizens, but rather, a national problem. The migration of blacks out of the South also exacerbated racial tensions in the nation as a whole. When combined with the growing antagonistic response of many blacks toward the new realization of racial attitudes in the nation, the United States' experienced a wave of racial tension and violence during and immediately after the war. Instances of lynching, already a staple in the nineteenth century, skyrocketed in the South during the 1910s. In the North, when white veterans returned from military service, many African Americans who had once filled their jobs were fired, and those who remained on the job had to endure lower wages and white anger, fueled by the cry from whites that African Americans were "stealing their jobs."

The new racial animosity spilled over into the streets of a number of cities during the later stages of the war and into 1919. Black soldiers who faced discrimination from whites in Houston while they guarded the construction of an army camp rioted against whites when a rumor of a white mob marching to their barracks swept their encampment. Whites rioted against blacks in St. Louis and Chicago. In Chicago, the violence lasted an entire week and before it was quieted 38 people were dead. Racial violence during the summer of 1919 alone led to 120 deaths throughout the nation.

Racial violence in the United States was, of course, nothing new, but in the past it had primarily involved whites attacking African Americans. However, the situation this time was different: African Americans had fought back or even instigated some of the violence. The newly formed National Association for the Advancement of Colored People (NAACP) encouraged such a stance, explaining that if blacks were waiting on the government to protect them, they would most likely wait forever. Governments—North and South—were predominantly on the side of the white majority.

THE UNITED STATES AND THE WAR IN EUROPE

Before the United States entered World War I in the spring of 1917, the Allies faced a real danger of losing the war. The Germans were inflicting great damage to Allied shipping on the seas, and a British offensive in Flanders had stalled with a huge loss of life. Most significantly, a democratic revolution in Russia had ended the rule of the Tsars, soon followed by a second communist revolution leading to a negotiated separate peace with Germany, allowing the Germans to concentrate all their efforts on the Western Front. Thus, the Americans would provide critical manpower and resources at a crucial point in the war.

The Bolshevik Revolution

Russia, whose pact with Serbia was a key factor in starting the war and had also kept the German Army occupied on the Eastern Front by reducing the pressure on the British and French in the West, became a different kind of flashpoint in 1917. Ruled by an absolute monarchy under the Romanov Dynasty for over 300 years, Russians by the early twentieth century had begun to chafe and resist the regime of Czar Nicholas II. An attempted revolution in 1905 had almost ended the Tsar's rule, leading to reforms that were supposed to keep the Tsar from exercising autocratic power. However, when Russia joined World War I, the inefficient and incompetently led Russian Army suffered serious setbacks and extreme levels of casualties fighting the Germans. At the same time, the economy cratered, leading to food shortages that spurred a number of riots among the people, with almost all of the anger directed toward the Tsar.

A large riot broke out in the capital of St. Petersburg in early March 1917. The rioting lasted for weeks, and when most of the army garrison in the city defected and joined the revolutionaries, the move forced the tsar to abdicate his throne. When his brother refused to take his place, the Romanov Dynasty came to an abrupt end. Russia's legislative body, the Duma, quickly appointed a provisional government headed by **Alexander Kerensky**. When Kerensky and his coalition of anti-Bolshevik socialists, constitutional monarchists, and other factions seized power, their tenure was destined to be short-lived. Although his government faced a multitude of domestic crises, Kerensky's refusal to withdraw Russia from the war fatally weakened his regime. By that time, especially the nation's soldiers, had grown weary of the war. The conflict had brought them nothing but miseries, ranging from starvation to the slaughter of hundreds of thousands of poorly clad and equipped peasant conscripts on the battlefronts. By succumbing to the Allies' relentless pressure to have Russia remain in the war, Kerensky sealed the fate of the country's brief experiment in parliamentary government.

Kerensky was opposed by a growing Marxist movement, the Petrograd Soviet of Workers' and Soldiers' Deputies. The two sides jockeyed for position over the course of the spring, but it quickly became apparent that the Soviet had more power and influence than the provisional government, particularly as numerous other soviets, based on the Petrograd model, organized in cities throughout Russia. The provisional government was reorganized four times, but the nation was still in chaos with collapsing morale within the army on the Eastern Front, and nationalist uprising plaguing the non-Russian areas of the nation.

Eventually, by the autumn of 1917, the two strongest groups with the soviet parties, the **Bolsheviks** and the Left Socialist Revolutionaries, under the leadership of **Vladimir Lenin**, had gathered the most power among the various movements and their "peace, land, and bread" slogan had gained widespread appeal, not only among the industrial workers of the cities and the rural peasants, but also the soldiers at the front. The Bolsheviks staged a nearly bloodless coup in November 1917, and with the convening of the Second All-Russian Congress of Soviets in St. Petersburg they took control of the government. Lenin ascended to power and began to establish a communist government. While urging workers in Europe and the United States to rise in revolt against the "capitalist-imperialist war," Lenin's regime negotiated a separate peace with Germany and withdrew from the war. Thus, in November 1917, shortly after the vast majority of the American forces arrived in France, the Germans could now transfer the bulk of their army that had been fighting against the Russians in the East to the Western Front.

For his part, Woodrow Wilson reacted negatively to the events in Russia. Although supporting liberal-capitalist reform movements throughout the world, the president opposed anti-capitalist revolutions, not only in Russia but in China and Mexico as well. He wanted to reform capitalism; the Bolshevik leader Lenin wanted to destroy it. Until the end of his presidency, Wilson would try to isolate Lenin and the Bolsheviks. In August 1918, even before the Great War had ended, Wilson sent 15,000 American troops into Russia as part of a multinational force to help defeat the Bolsheviks, who at the time were engaged in a bloody civil war against various Russian anti-Bolshevik factions, known collectively as the "Whites." Despite this aid, the efforts of Wilson and the other Allies (including Japan) failed. By 1920, the Red Army, under the leadership of Leon Trotsky, had crushed the Whites. With their defeat, all foreign mercenaries left the country.

"Over There": The U.S. Military in World War I

The United States' lack of full preparation for war meant that the full impact of American troops in Europe would not come until the winter of 1917 at the earliest, with the bulk of U.S. forces not arriving until the spring of 1918. In the meantime, the United States could immediately

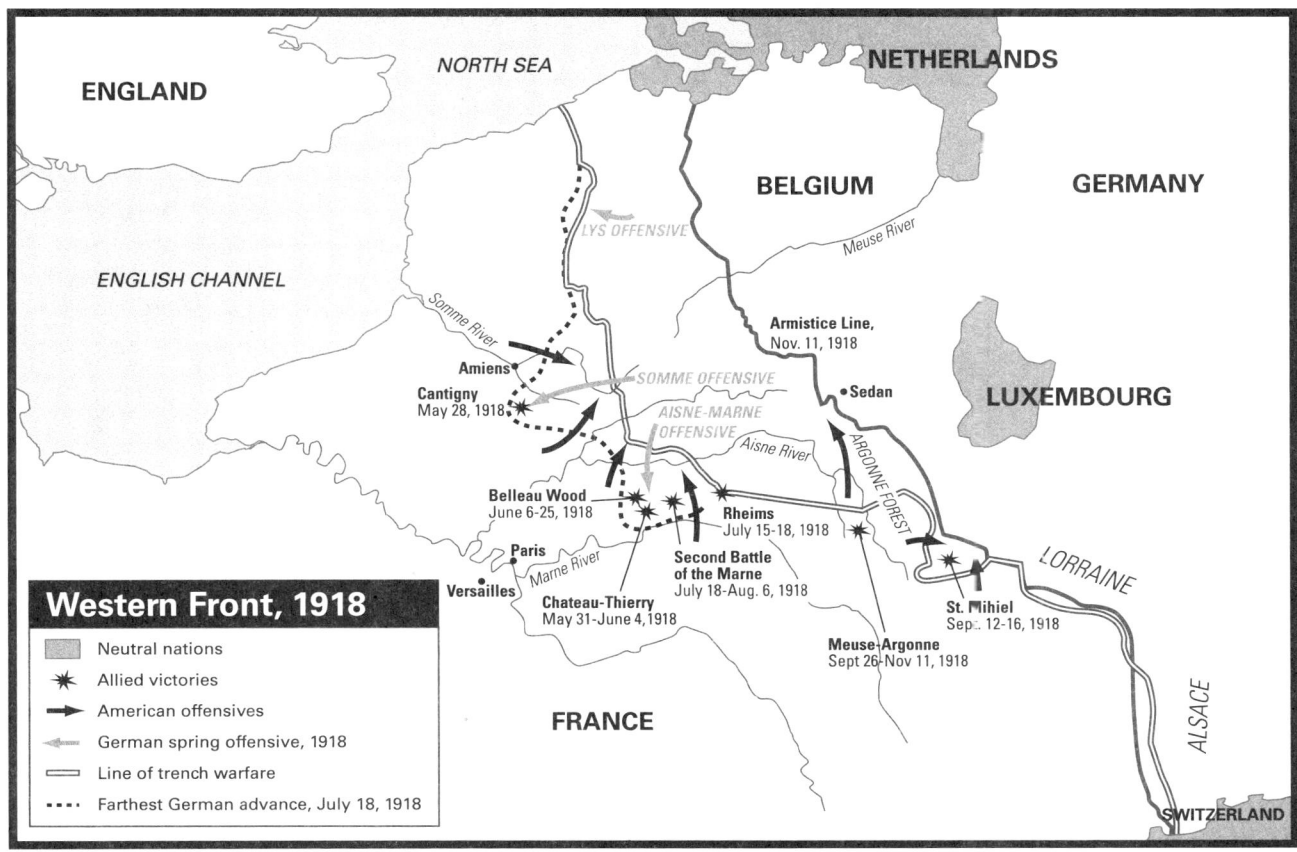

Map 21.2 Western Front, 1918

provide aid on the seas. Great Britain's Royal Navy, the mightiest in the world at the outset of the war, had been stretched thin by 1917 protecting the shipment of vital supplies across the Atlantic. The United States Navy almost immediately began to join the British in limiting the damage caused by U-Boats by escorting merchant ships across the ocean.

The pressing need for U.S. ground troops in Europe became even more necessary when Russia, after the Bolsheviks seized power, withdrew from the war. When the full commitment of American troops arrived in April of 1918, they provided an immediate impact, playing a significant role in beating back a huge German offensive at Château Thierry and winning a key battle at Belleau Wood. The Germans launched another assault on Allied forces at Rheims, located to the south of Paris, but once again were repelled. At the Marne River, the Allies ended the large German summer offensive designed to finally win the war once and for all for the Central Powers, clearing the way for Allies to launch a counteroffensive against the Germans.

The Allies began their massive counterattack in September 1918, when 500,000 American and about 200,000 French troops assaulted German positions from their stronghold at St. Mihiel near Verdun. American soldiers then lead a massive offensive against the Germans in the Argonne Forest, driving rapidly toward a key German supply line. The Allies finally broke fully through the German lines in October, driving the entire German army back toward its border. At this point German leadership knew that the war was all but over. By early November 1918, Germany's allies had already quit the war. With its Arab possessions in open revolt and British troops in the Middle East approaching the borders of Turkey itself, the Ottoman Empire had sued for peace on October 30. Meanwhile, Italian armies finally gained the upper hand against Austria-Hungary and began advancing while multiple declarations of independence within the empire proclaimed by Czechs, Hungarians, and Croatians finally forcing the Austrians to capitulate on November 3. With its allies deserting them and the French and British bolstered by the arrival of large numbers of American troops, the German High Command understood that their grand gamble had failed. Faced with the prospect of a devastating invasion of Germany and the potential corresponding loss of life, German ministers contacted Woodrow Wilson to ask for help in brokering a cease-fire. Negotiations quickly gained momentum, and on November 11, 1918 the guns went quiet along the front. The fighting in Europe was over. The United States' brief

The Battle of Belleau Wood

About fifty miles northeast of Paris is the small village of Belleau. Today it is a peaceful landscape of trees, small hills, and green as far as the eye can see. Visitors to the spot usually come to visit a 42 acre cemetery and memorial that commemorates a time about a hundred years ago when the panorama was not as bucolic. Instead, it was the scene of a great battle, one in which United States Marine Corps and Army soldiers repelled a German force and began the beginning of the end of the World War I. The fighting at the Battle of Belleau Wood was brutal and often at close-quarters, and the cemetery at the spot recognizes the sacrifice of almost 2,000 Americans in their largest engagement of the "Great War."

The United States had been in the war for more than a year by the spring of 1918, but because the nation was ill-prepared for an overseas fight the bulk of U.S. troops did not arrive in France until the late winter/early spring of 1918. American Expeditionary Force commander John J. Pershing had, thus far, refused to allow American troops to become intermingled with French or British regiments, so the lack of numbers meant the U.S. had played only a token part in the war up to that point. However, that was all about to change in May 1918 when U.S. soldiers would experience their first real test in a large-scale pitched battle.

When the United States joined the war in April 1917, German leaders understood that American numbers could tip the balance of the war in the Allies' favor, but fighting in Russia had prevented them from mounting an effective offensive in France. However, when Russia negotiated an end to their participation in March 1918, Germany could then shift more than fifty divisions to the Western Front. The Germans hoped that their planned offensive could knock out the French and British troops before the Americans could be fully mobilized, which would ensure a German victory. They launched two assaults against the Allied troops, and while so far the lines had held, it was a tenuous clasp. Germany was sure a third wave would lead to victory.

The Germans began their third offensive on the Western Front against French troops between Soissons and Reims in late May, and by May 27 they had pushed the French back and reached the north bank of the Marne River at Château-Thierry, only sixty miles from Paris. However, what the Germans had feared then happened: The United States Army 3rd Division advanced to the Marne and stopped the German advance. The Germans thus turned right along the north side of the river towards Vaux and Belleau Wood. The Germans took Château-Thierry and Vaux on June 1, and now turned their attention toward Belleau Wood. If they could take Belleau, they would have punched a hole in the Allied lines and have a real possibility of moving toward Paris.

The United States 2nd Division, which included a brigade of Marines, marched to the front, with the 5th Marine and 23rd regiment serving as reserve troops, all to confront the German assault. The Germans relentlessly advanced toward Belleau, but despite being outnumbered and outgunned Army General James Harbord refused to listen to French advice to retreat, and he ordered the Marine regiments to "hold where you stand." Marine Captain Lloyd W. Williams defiantly answered the French treatises to retreat with the now famous retort: "Retreat? Hell, we just got here!" The Marines did hold, and then after support from the Army arrived the Americans stopped the German offensive.

The Americans halted the German advance, but the battle was not over since the Germans remained in Belleau Wood. Battalions of the 5th and 6th Marines, along with the 23rd Infantry advanced on the Germans on June 6. The Germans had established a defensive position and inflicted terrible casualties on the U.S. troops, but despite the horrible bloodshed, the American troops pushed forward again the next day, and then the day after that. They rested for a day as artillery assaulted the German position, and then they charged the German position once again. The 7th Army Infantry arrived on June 10 to help, but the fighting in Belleau Wood continued for three weeks, often in hand-to-hand combat. The American troops methodically moved through the German ranks, and finally, on June 26, Marine Major Maurice Shearer sent the following message: "Belleau Wood now U.S. Marine Corps entirely." The war did not end with the conclusion of the Battle of Belleau Wood, but the end was now in sight.

involvement in war had not been without a price; they counted 53,402 combat deaths, over 3,000 missing, and more than 200,000 wounded. Disease and other non-combat-related fatalities claimed another 63,000 American soldiers.

Wilson's Fourteen Points

Woodrow Wilson had led the U.S. into war with the promise of not only saving democracy, but also the establishment of a "new world order" and a stable peace throughout the war. He had aspirations of taking his ideas of efficient progressivism to the entire world, so even before the war ended, he began to formulate a plan to accomplish his goals. Addressing Congress on January 8, 1918, he presented his ideas and overall vision, and also to justify the war that Americans were fighting.

The president explained that the United States would have certain aims for the war, and grouped them under fourteen headings, hence they would be known as the "Fourteen Points." They also fell into three broad categories. His first eight points constituted the first category, and they were concerned specific proposals for determining postwar boundaries—in Poland, for example—and for also establishing new nations mostly in the Middle East from the remnants of the Ottoman Empire, a scheme that eventually create the countries of Iraq, Syria, and Saudi Arabia, among others. The second set was a series of five strictures that would govern international relations in the future, specifically such concepts as freedom of the seas, an abrogation of secret treaties between nations, arms reduction, and an opening of trade. But it was his last proposal that would become the centerpiece of his plan, and the mechanism that would make all the others possible. Wilson called for the creation of a **League of Nations** to serve as an international body overseeing and implementing the other principles of his plan, most significantly, the call to resolve disputes between nations before they lead to war.

Wilson's Fourteen Points were celebrated by many Europeans in that war-ravaged continent, but also by peoples still feeling the yoke of colonialism from European powers who hailed him as a savior of freedom and self-determination. In many respects, Wilson became the most popular person in the world. His proposals, however, combined with his arrogant bravado in suggesting a plan for the whole world while at the same time formulating policies that bypassed his own Congress angered two powerful constituencies: the leaders of his European allies and Republicans in the United States Senate who would be needed to ratify any negotiated treaty. In the end, the president's difficulties with both

groups would prove costly to his efforts. As the end of the war came into sight, the leaders of both Britain and France balked at Wilson's desire that any peace treaty be non-punitive to the Central Powers, specifically Germany. They viewed German actions as responsible for beginning the war, and with their casualty numbers unprecedented in world history, they were in no mood to treat Germany benevolently. At home, Wilson took his appeal directly to the American people by indicating that support for his plan meant votes for Democrats in the congressional elections of 1918. His plea backfired when Republicans took full control of Congress. Wilson then openly challenged Republicans when he refused to include a member of their party in his delegation that would negotiate the peace treaty. The president also refused to consult with the Republican leadership in the Senate about any aspect of his proposals that would shape the coming peace treaty despite the necessity of Senate approval.

THE SEARCH FOR A LASTING PEACE

The fighting in Europe and the rest of the world had ended on November 11, 1918, but the process to negotiate and formulate a peace treaty did not begin until December 13, 1918 in Paris. When Wilson arrived in France and began his trip to Paris, the scene took on the appearance of a political campaign, with throngs of cheering crowds and gatherings that saluted him almost like a conquering hero. In many ways, it was the wrong approach at the wrong time; Wilson should have entered he negotiations with humility and deference if he wanted his proposals to carry the day, but that was not the "Wilson way." His hubris would, in the end, cloud the process, especially when he returned home and had to face the wrath and recalcitrance of Senate Republicans.

The Versailles Peace Conference

Resentment, animosity, and differences in opinion were the prevailing moods when the leaders of the Allies sat down at the Versailles Palace outside of Paris to discuss the parameters of a peace treaty with Germany and its allies. Wilson and the prime ministers of the three main allied powers (David Lloyd George of Great Britain, Georges Clemenceau of France, and Vittorio Orlando of Italy) began the arduous back-and-forth process that would form a treaty with generally one axis of agreement—none of the three European leaders really favored Wilson's peace plans. The prime ministers did not share Wilson's idealism, and they certainly feared the growing power of the Russian communists who had been excluded from

Railroad car in which the Armistice was signed, November 11, 1918.

attending the conference. (At that very moment, American, British, French, and Japanese troops were aiding the anti-Bolshevik forces fighting against the Bolsheviks.)

Despite Wilson's vehement opposition, the Allies dealt harshly with the losing side, and the president was unable to prevent George and Clemenceau from placing blame for the war squarely on Germany, forbidding the Germans from building a military any larger than a token defense force, and assessing high reparation payments upon them in the amount of $33 billion to be paid to France, Great Britain, Italy, and Belgium—outlays that would eventually cripple that nation's economy for years to come. The Allies also successfully carved up German and Austrian lands for themselves. For abandoning neutrality and joining the Allies in 1915, Italy received the promised seaport on the Adriatic (Trieste) and the South Tyrol from Austria. The Rhineland, one of Germany's most vital natural resource areas, was demilitarized and designated a French protectorate for fifteen years. The **Treaty of Versailles** would also allow the French to occupy the coal-rich Saar region for a similar period and returned the province of Alsace-Lorraine (taken by Germany in 1871 at the conclusion of the Franco-Prussian War) back to France. To add further insult, the treaty cut eastern Germany into two parts by giving the newly independent Poland access to the Baltic by way of the eastern Prussian city of Danzig, which now became a Polish city despite close to one million Germans living there. Another 500,000 Germans of the Sudetenland became Czech citizens when that territory was given, along with former Austrian territory, to the newly created country of Czechoslovakia. Ultimately, the peace accord dismantled the Austro-Hungarian Empire while stripping Germany of one-eighth of its territory, one-tenth of its population, and all of its colonies. The treaty humiliated

and enraged the Germans, fueling a desire for revenge.

The victorious Allies also grabbed territory outside of Europe as the spoils of war. Great Britain acquired control over Palestine, Jordan, and, most importantly, oil-rich Mesopotamia (present-day Iraq) from the Ottoman Empire as well as all of Germany's African colonies. France received Syria and Lebanon from the Turks. Japan obtained all of Germany's islands in the Pacific and its sphere of influence in China, Shantung Province. To his credit, Wilson tried to prevent such reprisals, though he did not object too strongly because he feared pushing Clemenceau to demand even harsher peace terms on Germany. All the while, the president warned the victors that if they imposed such a harsh and dishonorable settlement upon the Germans, they might be sealing their own future fate by ensuring another European conflagration. In 1939, Wilson's prediction would certainly come true.

Not all of Wilson's entreaties fell on deaf ears. Wilson was able to convince the Allied leaders to agree to some of his Fourteen Points. He did prevail on some new conditions for former German and Ottoman colonies, as well as the establishment of new boundaries and the creation of new European nations—such as Czechoslovakia, Poland, and Yugoslavia. Most importantly to him, the president also secured approval of his crowning achievement, the creation of the League of Nations to oversee international affairs and relations between nations and which he hoped would make all wars a thing of the past, ensuring that the Great War would truly be the "war to end all wars." The most significant component of the League's charter was Article 10, which established the concept of collective security, whereby each member nation would pledge to respect and preserve each other's independence and territorial integrity against aggressors, and to use whatever means appropriate or necessary—economic sanctions or military intervention—to stop the invader and restore peace. In an attempt to avoid future wars, members agreed to submit for arbitration all disputes that created tensions between countries that could lead to war. They also agreed to address the arms race issue and to create a permanent court of international justice, popularly known as the World Court. Though the Allies agreed to the provisions of the Treaty of Versailles on January 29, 1919, Wilson now had to return home and convince the Senate to ratify the agreement.

Ratification and the Fight for the League of Nations

Ratification of the Versailles Treaty in the Senate faced an uphill battle. The Senate objected to the treaty on many levels, but two groups were most prominent. One faction became known as the "**Reservationists**." These senators accepted parts of the treaty but wanted to amend the United States' role within the League of Nations. Many of them were Republicans, such as **Henry Cabot Lodge** of Massachusetts, the chair of the Senate Foreign Relations Committee, who wanted to wound Wilson politically and give Republicans a victory that might translate to an electoral advantage. Lodge and his followers adopted a strategy of crafting amendments to the treaty (or "reservations") that would weaken American commitments abroad as well as the American role in the League of Nations. Senator Lodge especially objected to the concept of collective security, which he believed would not be a practical deterrent to war, leading to the U.S. to join other nations in an endless series of interventions abroad in countries where the United States had no direct interest. Thus, he supported an amendment calling for a vote of Congress being necessary before American troops were sent anywhere on a collective security mission.

Another powerful group opposed to the treaty, consisting mostly of Republicans but which included some Democrats, believed that the United States should refrain from all involvement in European and world affairs since such entanglements so often led to war. Led by Republican senator William Borah of Idaho, they were determined to sink both the treaty and the League of Nations, allowing the United States to return to the security of isolationism. Much to Wilson's surprise and eventual dismay, these senators rejected U.S. membership in the League and called instead for a return to isolationism. Many of them worried that the League would be exploited by nations like Britain and France to promote further colonialism around the world. These senators who were steadfastly opposed to the treaty became known as the

"**Irreconcilables**." Together, the Reservationists and the Irreconcilables presented Wilson with an unanticipated battle for ratification.

The most prudent strategy for the president at that point may have been to yield on a few points and negotiate some sort of settlement, but again that was not the 'Wilson way." He was so convinced about the absolute need for American (and other countries') devotion to collective security as a deterrent, for example, that he refused to contemplate any sort of compromise on that important provision. Instead, he dug in his heels and insisted that the senators accept the whole package or nothing at all. The ratification became a force of will between Senate Republicans and President Wilson.

Furious at both Lodge and Borah for their obstructionism, and convinced that he could rally public support for the Versailles Treaty, Wilson decided to take his case directly to the American people. Much like a campaign for office, the president departed Washington on a train on a planned 8,000 mile journey to speak to gathered crowds and implore them to tell their senators that they wanted the treaty ratified. For three straight weeks, he spoke three to four times a day, and it seemed as if he might be making progress and putting pressure on the Senate, but Wilson was setting a grueling pace for himself. The schedule would have been demanding on a young man, but was strenuous past the point of fatigue on a person of Wilson's age (he was 60 years old) and with his history of health problems (he suffered from complications due to arteriosclerosis). Finally, after delivering a speech in Pueblo, Colorado on September 29, 1919, Wilson reached the point of utter exhaustion, canceled the rest of his tour, and went back to the White House. When he arrived back in Washington, he suffered a major stroke and was near death for more than a week. Through the end of 1919, he was so ill that he could not conduct his official duties. Wilson's doctor and his wife, Edith, hid the president's illness from all but his inner circle. He recovered somewhat by the spring of 1920, but his infirmity seemed to strengthen his resolve to get all he wanted and to have the treaty ratified with no changes. Ultimately, Henry Cabot Lodge and his Foreign Relations Committee sent to the full Senate a version of the treaty that Wilson refused to consider. Since the president was intractable in his desire to have only the version he wanted, the Treaty of Versailles died without ratification by the Senate. American diplomats would later negotiate a separate peace with Germany, but the major damage was done. The League of Nations would be formed, but without the membership of the United States, greatly weakening the effectiveness of that body moving forward.

The Red Scare

Given their traditional notions of individual initiative and adherence to capitalism, the majority of Americans had long regarded the organization of labor and collective action by workers as harbingers of radicalism and inimical to the concepts of freedom on which the nation was founded. Mixed with natural ideas of wariness toward industrialism and cities, this majority tended to oppose any actions by organized labor. When World War I ended, many of the protections guaranteed to labor by the WIB ended with it, and in 1919, numerous strikes and violence both in support of and against labor strikes roiled the nation. When labor leaders in Seattle, Washington in February 1919 united in a general strike for higher wages, the politically ambitious conservative mayor of the city, Ole Hanson, contrary to all evidence, immediately colored the striking workers "red," ensuring that he would have universal support in crushing the strike because it "duplicated the anarchy of Russia." The mayor had no problem requesting federal troops to maintain public order, even though there was no need for such heavy-handedness. In Boston, even the police struck, walking off their beats when the police commissioner suspended nineteen officers for attempting to establish a patrolmen's union affiliated with the AFL. Unfortunately for the striking officers, a wave of rowdy behavior, theft, and violence hit the city, which in turn enraged Massachusetts governor Calvin Coolidge, who denounced the policemen for their dereliction of duty and declared that none of the strikers would be rehired. To restore law and order in Boston, Coolidge mobilized state troopers while he recruited unemployed veterans for an entirely new police force. Mayors, governors, and the general public applauded Coolidge's stand. Such unrest, combined with the racial violence that also gripped the country during and immediately after the war, gave many Americans a sense of unease about what they perceived as growing "radicalism." That discomfort was exacerbated by the rise of communism in Russia after the Bolshevik Revolution and the recent ascension to power of Vladimir Lenin.

After the Bolsheviks seized power, forming the Union of Soviet Socialist Republics (USSR), the concept of communism was no longer a theory but, instead, a reality, with a form of government and society that seemed, to many Americans, utterly inimical to the founding beliefs of the United States. One of the primary tenets of Marxist-Leninist thought is the prediction that communism would spread around the globe and free the workers who suffered under the yoke of capitalist oppression. The Soviet Union hoped to speed that process when, in 1919, they announced the formation of the Communist International (Comintern), which was designed to export the peculiar Soviet revolution and forms of Marxism throughout the world. Such developments bred a feeling of dread about the growth of communism in the United States, and when, in the spring and summer of 1919, rumors about radical plots, combined with a series of bombings attributed to radicals (one mail bomb blew off the hands of a senator's maid while another explosive device placed inside a package destroyed the front of the home of the attorney general), many Americans began to believe that a nationwide conspiracy existed, designed to take over the U.S. government and institute a communist regime. The nation became obsessed with its first "**Red Scare.**"

In response to these real but also imagined threats, close to thirty states passed sedition acts that resembled those passed by the federal government during the war. Incorrectly, organized labor became associated with communism, and workers and other members became targets of violence and recrimination. Universities tried to expel students suspected of "radicalism" and fired professors who even seemed to sympathize with communism. The most visible and spectacular contribution to this fear came from the United States Justice Department under the leadership of Attorney General **A. Mitchell Palmer.** Palmer organized a series of "raids" ("The Palmer Raids") on New Year's Day, 1920, on groups and individuals that he suspected of being radicals, communists, or anyone associated with dissent. Before he was through, Palmer and his agents had arrested over 6,000 people. Most of those were never charged, and the majority of the rest were acquitted. However, Palmer did have over 500 noncitizens deported by charging them with subversion and revoking their visas.

Eventually, the most strident aspects of Red Scare subsided, particularly as it became apparent that Attorney General Palmer was instigating more of a "witch hunt" against organized labor and Socialist Party members than real communist infiltrators. Palmer's political career came to an abrupt end. However, the perception of "radicalism" as adverse to American principles persisted among many, and any association with a group that did not adhere to the supposed virtues of capitalism and democracy was often enough to taint one with the moniker of subversive. One positive development coming out of the Red Scare, however, was that it led to the formation of the American Civil Liberties Union (ACLU), a "watch dog" group whose mission became to protect the civil liberties of all Americans, no matter their political, social, or cultural beliefs.

Map 21.3   Europe after World War I

POSTWAR NORMALCY

War, racial violence, labor unrest, and the political back-biting between the two major parties, had advanced on the heels of over a decade of Progressive reform. Major social changes had taken place, but many Americans began to grow weary of the seeming fast-paced changes. The passage and ratification of the Eighteenth and Nineteenth Amendments—Prohibition and Woman Suffrage—signaled to many that Progressivism had accomplished all that it could, and that it was time to "return to normal."

A "Return to Normalcy" became a key component of Republican Warren Harding's 1920 election campaign, promoting the desire to put the previous decades behind them by rejecting any further changes along the lines of Wilsonian progressivism. The powerful two-term tradition, combined with his ill health, meant that Woodrow Wilson no longer stood for the presidency, so the Demo-crats turned to Ohio Governor James Cox and his young running mate Franklin Delano Roosevelt who both supported joining the League of Nations. Meanwhile, the Republicans nominated another Ohio native, Senator Warren G. Harding, a generally unspectacular politician who opposed membership in the League and whose primary appeal was that he was just that—average.

Woodrow Wilson viewed the election for his successor as a referendum on the League and his vision for the world. He would be sorely disappointed. Americans agreed with Harding and the Republicans campaign slogan of "Return to Normalcy," and gave Harding a comfortable victory, as well as returning the Republicans to power in Congress. Many Americans wanted to turn a page and, in some ways, forget that the last two decades had happened. They wanted to retreat to isolationism and to a less hectic lifestyle, welcoming not having to solve problems, often by just pretending that they did not exist.

Chronology

1914 Archduke Franz Ferdinand assassinated.
World War I begins in Europe.
Panama Canal opens.

1915 U.S. marines occupy Haiti and the Dominican
Republic.
Lusitania sunk by German U-boat.
Women's Peace Party formed.
Wilson begins preparedness program.
Italy joins Allies.

1916 Battle of Verdun.
Woodrow Wilson re-elected.

1917 Germany begins unrestricted submarine
warfare.
Zimmermann telegram becomes public.
United State declares war on Germany (April 6).
Selective Service Act.
War Industries Board and Committee on
Public Information.
Espionage Act.
Sedition Act.

1918 Bulk of U.S. troops arrive in Europe.
Battle of Argonne Forest.
Wilson issues his Fourteen Points, Jan. 8.
Armistice begins on November 11.
Paris Peace talks begin in December.

1919 U.S. Senate rejects Treaty of Versailles.
Race riots break out in Chicago, St. Louis, and
other cities.
Wave of labor strikes begins across the U.S.

1920 Justice Department launches Palmer Raids.
"Red Scare" hits nation.
Nineteenth Amendment (Women's Suffrage)
ratified.
Warren G. Harding elected president.

SUGGESTED READINGS

Arthur E. Barbeau and Florette Henri, *The Unknown Soldiers: Black American Troops in World War I* (1947).

Richard D. Camp, *The Devil Dogs at Belleau Wood: The U.S. Marines in World War I* (2008).

Edward Coffman, *The War to End All Wars: The American Military Experience in World War I* (1998).

Justus D. Doenecke, *Nothing Less Than War: A New History of America's Entry into World War I* (2011).

Ernest Freeberg, *Democracy's Prisoner: Eugene V. Debs, The Great War, and the Right to Dissent* (2008).

Frank Freidel, *Over There* (1964).

Lettie Gavin, *American Women in World War: They Also Served* (2006).

Martin Gilbert, *The First World War: A Complete History* (1994).

Maurine W. Greenwald, *Women, War and Work* (1980).

Ellis W. Hawley, *The Great War and the Search for a Modern Order: A History of the American People and Their Institutions* (1992).

Jennifer Keene, *World War I: The American Soldier Experience* (2011).

David M. Kennedy, *Over Here: The First World War and American Society* (1980).

Celia Malone Kingsbury, *For Home and Country: World War I Propaganda on the Homefront* (2010).

Arthur S. Link, *Woodrow Wilson: Revolution, War, and Peace* (1979).

Carole Marks, *Farewell—We're Good and Gone: The Great Black Migration* (1989).

William H. Thomas, Jr., *Unsafe for Democracy: World War I and the Justice Department's Covert Campaign to Suppress Dissent* (2008).

William Tuttle Jr., *Race Riot: Chicago and the Red Summer of 1919* (1970).

Chad Louis Williams, *Torchbearers of Democracy: African American Soldiers in the World War I Era* (2010).

Robert H. Zieger, *America's Great War: World War I and the American Experience* (2001).

Review Questions

1. Describe Wilson's Mission Diplomacy and how it impact U.S. relations with Latin America before World War I.

2. How was the American mobilization of the economy and production in order to fight World War I representative of the tenets of Progressivism? What is meant by the term "command and control" in regards to the economy?

3. Racial tension and rioting was a significant feature of the years of World War I and immediately afterward. What developments brought about such racial tension? What was different about the tenor and nature of racial violence and riots during this era?

4. Woodrow Wilson had a certain vision of how the world should be ordered at the end of World War I. How did his "Fourteen Points" lay the groundwork for such a vision? What were the guiding principles of his Points?

5. Why was there a "Red Scare" in the United States at the close of World War I? What were some of the key events and results of this unique circumstance?

Glossary of Important People and Concepts

Bolsheviks
Committee on Public Information (CPI)
Espionage Act
Franz Ferdinand
Victoriano Huerta
Irreconcilables
Alexander Kerensky
League of Nations
Vladimir Lenin
Henry Cabot Lodge
Lusitania
Francisco Madero
A. Mitchell Palmer
John J. Pershing
Red Scare
Reservationists
Schenck v. United States
Schlieffen Plan
Selective Service Act
Treaty of Versailles
U-Boats
Pancho Villa
War Industries Board (WIB)
Woodrow Wilson
Zimmermann Telegram

1921 MODEL T

Chapter Twenty-two

THE CONTENTIOUS TWENTIES

Perhaps no American had a more profound impact on the decade following the First World War than Henry Ford. Though he did not invent the automobile, Ford's contribution lay with improving the assembly-line technique of manufacturing cars by utilizing moving conveyor belts. This innovation led to the mass production of the vehicles, reducing their price to affordable levels for millions of middle-class families. By the 1920s, the automobile not only gave the country expanded transportation opportunities, but also transformed many elements of American social life. In the opinion of Ford and other Americans, however, these changes were not always desirable.

In many ways, Ford retained the mentality of a rural mechanic born on a small Michigan farm during the Victorian Age who only had eight years of formal schooling. He often railed against many aspects of the modernizing world of which the automobile had become an integral part. While he hoped that citizens would frequently use the automobile to escape urban areas in order to experience the beauty of nature, cars also led to pollution, suburban sprawl, and the withering away of many formerly pristine rural areas across the country. In the media, Ford extolled many of his personal views, such as his strong opposition to cigarettes, alcohol, jazz music, wild dancing, and looser sexual morals. Yet, the automobile provided an easier means for many to avoid Prohibition laws by attending secret "speakeasies" where smoking, drinking, and wild dancing took place, not to mention the greater ease that autos allowed individuals to sneak away to engage in sexual escapades.

Still, Henry Ford continued to promote the dominant values of an earlier time. His sense of nostalgia sometimes served noble purposes, such as spending large sums of money to build re-creations of small eighteenth- and nineteenth-century towns. Other times, his lack of education and worldliness showed a dark side, such as when he evoked his blatantly anti-Semitic views in his **Dearborn Indepen-** **dent** newspaper, blaming Jews for everything from labor unrest to the spread of communism. (Ford also sponsored the publication of 500,000 copies of the **Protocols of the Elders of Zion**—a fraudulent work originating in Russia that purported to reveal a secret Jewish plan to dominate the world—thus greatly increasing its visibility and further inciting anti-Semitic views domestically and internationally.) In many ways, these internal divisions within Ford symbolized the new era of American history. Like the nation itself, Ford kept one foot in the old world and one foot in the new.

THE POSTWAR ECONOMY

"Sick Industries"

The cessation of wartime government contracts, the removal of price controls and minimum pay requirements, and the passage of anti-strike legislation led to a period of high inflation and widespread labor unrest (discussed in the previous chapter) as well as a severe postwar recession. While the overall economic situation improved greatly by mid-1920s, certain sectors of the economy—agriculture and the so-called "**sick industries**"—continued to languish throughout the decade. When the Great Depression arrived, the downturn merely made worse what these producers had already been experiencing for several years.

Coal mining, textile manufacturing, and railroads were among the most notable "sick industries" plagued by excessive productive capacity with declining demand and labor conflict. Competition from rival industries—electricity for the coal producers, synthetic rayon for cotton mills, and motor trucks for the railroads—caused further problems resulting in low financial returns and high unemployment. The passage of the Prohibition Amendment also hurt the nation's breweries during the

1920s, leading most to close and the remainder to weather the storm through diversification. As a result, the nation saw the former producers of Budweiser, Schlitz, Miller, and Pabst beer turn to the manufacturing of near beers, root beers, colas, and malt extract (syrup) in an effort to stay in business.

American agriculture, which had been booming during wartime, went into a sharp decline following the end of hostilities. Many farmers borrowed heavily to buy additional land and equipment as they took advantage of increased prices. On average, farm prices rose 82 percent from 1913 to 1917, leading to a 150 percent net increase in farm income. Once the war ended, however, the termination of government purchases and the revival of European agriculture led to a sharp decline in domestic prices and income. Wheat prices dropped from $2.50 per bushel to less than $1. Wool prices fell from 60 cents per pound to 19 cents. Similar declines took place across the board, affecting the nation's cotton, tobacco, beef, and dairy producers especially hard. The collective response to the burst price bubble, however, was not decreased production. To the contrary, as farmers received less income, many tried to make up the difference by raising more crops. Along with the increased efficiency created by more widespread use of mechanization, fertilizers, high-quality seeds, and improved farming techniques, the maintenance of high production levels contributed to further price declines and income stagnation. By the end of the decade, average per capita income for American farmers was only 25 percent the level for urban dwellers, leading many rural residents to leave the land in order to seek better employment opportunities.

Economic Boom

The postwar revival in the American economy began to take place in 1922. Corporate profits rose and unemployment began to drop as many old and new industries saw a marked uptick in demand and more efficient production. In terms of aggregate profits and high employment, the American economy during the 1920s enjoyed its best performance to date. Average corporate profits rose 62 percent from 1923 to 1929 while the national unemployment rate never topped 3.7 percent. Workers' incomes rose 30 percent during the decade while inflation remained low (the annual average increase in prices remained below 1 percent). This increase in purchasing power (along with the inauguration of installment buying that allowed consumers to make extensive purchases on credit) helped to fuel a vast consumer spending binge that lasted until 1929.

During this unprecedented economic boom, **Henry Ford** led the way by transforming the automobile indus-

try from a maker of luxury vehicles for the rich into an economic sector that manufactured affordable transportation for millions of middle-class families. Ford began production of his "Model T" in 1909, producing over 1,700 cars for $950 each. His greatest contribution to the industry would be his modification of Ransom Olds's use of the assembly line by introducing moving conveyor belts in 1914. With workers specialized in performing one or two specific operations of the total of forty-five needed, the vehicle began to take shape more quickly and efficiently. A Model T could be produced every 90 minutes and sold profitably for less than $500. By 1920, 1.25 million rolled off the assembly line as one car could be produced every 60 seconds and sold for as low as $350. Fifty-seven percent of all cars in America were Fords by 1923, making the company's owner a billionaire.

Despite relatively high pay compared to other industrial jobs (many line workers could earn as much as $5 per day), work on a Ford assembly line could be quite dehumanizing. Employee tasks involved much repetitive motion throughout each working hour. In addition, Ford demanded that his employees remain so focused on their assigned task that he forbade talking, singing, and even whistling on the job. Ford's behavioral edicts also extended to his workers' personal lives. Any employee found to have used tobacco or consumed alcohol (on or off the job) would be immediately terminated. Because Ford did not hire any workers who belonged to a labor union, there was no avenue for appeal. Indeed, one major reason why Ford paid higher wages was to undercut potential union activity in his factories. Ford also hired company spies to monitor his employees, especially looking for signs of union organizing.

Though Ford controlled a majority of the industry's market share in the early 1920s, he did not completely dominate the market. His major rivals—General Motors, Chrysler, Studebaker, Packard, and Hudson – continued to eat away at Ford's market share through creative innovations. In 1925, General Motors introduced the K Model Chevrolet, which included among its features a convertible roof, wider leg room, and a windshield with automatic wipers. Hudson began producing its closed-roof Essex coach, which offered consumers a car with a sturdier frame and a sportier look than the Model T. When Ford's market share dropped below 50 percent, he decided to shut down his massive River Rouge plant in Detroit for an entire year to revamp his entire operations in order to begin production of his new car—the Model A, which incorporated many features begun by Ford's competitors: a sleeker look, availability in multiple colors (the Model T had only been available in black), and installment buying for the first time. By 1929, Ford once again produced a majority of cars in the American market.

The impact of Ford and his rivals on the American economy went far beyond the benefits to the auto companies, their workers (during the 1920s, 7 percent of all industrial workers labored in automobile factories), the economies of the towns and cities where automobile plants were located, or the financing and marketing apparatuses behind vehicle sales. The American automobile industry was simply the largest driver of the national prosperity during the decade as the demand for cars greatly stimulated other sectors of the economy. The providers of raw materials for automobile manufacturing benefited tremendously as massive orders came in from the auto companies for steel, glass, rubber, and paint, not to mention the huge demand for gasoline that the cars' internal combustion engines required. The need for repair and maintenance services provided many new jobs for mechanics and repair specialists. The necessity for various forms of assistance to the increased number of road travelers offered an untold number of employment opportunities for service station attendants, motel employees, workers in the booming tourist industry, and road construction laborers.

While the automobile industry was king during the 1920s, many other sectors of the economy also performed well. In addition to cars, large numbers of upper- and middle-class Americans purchased a host of new electrical household appliances including washing machines, dishwashers, refrigerators, vacuum cleaners, flat irons, and toasters that promised to relieve many (usually female) home dwellers from the toils of domestic upkeep. Americans began mass consuming copious amounts of other new products that have become commonplace in homes today, everything from new food items such as freeze-dried vegetables, candy bars, and frozen popsicles to new sundries in the form of disposable handkerchiefs (Kleenex), disposable blades, and Listerine mouthwash.

Among the many additions to American homes during the 1920s, perhaps the most significant was the radio. In 1920, KDKA in Pittsburgh became the first station in the country to broadcast regularly scheduled programming as it transmitted popular music, news bulletins, and sporting events. Over 3 million radios were in use by 1923 when Americans could tune in to over 500 stations nationwide. By the middle of the decade, the National Broadcasting Company (NBC) and the Columbia Broadcasting System (CBS) emerged as the leading networks of affiliated stations. Money derived from commercial advertisements sent over the airwaves soon became the major revenue stream for broadcasters.

THE MYTH OF THE "ROARING 20s"

An enduring myth about social life during the 1920s is the notion that most Americans broke away from their traditional values and celebrated the end of the war and postwar economic prosperity by partaking in a binge of hedonistic excess characterized by attending wild parties, consuming copious amounts of alcohol, gyrating to the latest wild dance crazes, obsessing over relatively superficial events making headlines, discarding the old time religion, and generally loosening their moral standards. A majority of women presumably basked in the achievement of suffrage and enjoyed the liberation provided by new modern household appliances by going out and having fun while dressed in the new provocative styles touted by New York City fashion designers.

This image of the decade as the "**Roaring Twenties**," however, is only a caricature based on the activities of some Americans. Serious historians now discard such stereotypical depictions of the 1920s as a means of describing what a majority of Americans were thinking and doing at the time, arguing that the activities of these individuals recounted in the media at the time, and since, have been blown out of proportion. The Roaring Twenties stereotype has two main origins. First, there were, in fact, some individuals during the 1920s who did partake in rowdy behavior deemed unacceptable by traditional standards. After the First World War, a minority of largely middle- and upper-class urban youth who had the time, money, and inclination to pursue these new behaviors, modes of dress, and popular fads adopted a more carefree lifestyle in an effort to put the negativity of the war behind them, take advantage of new freedoms provided by technological advances such as the widespread availability of the automobile, and follow the latest trends publicized in mainstream magazines and movies. Second, during the 1920s, and since, popularizers of the Roaring Twenties myth have crafted enduring depictions of the era in books and film. Writing in the early 1930s, journalist Frederick Lewis Allen produced a best-selling reflection of the just-concluded decade entitled *Only Yesterday: An Informal History of the 1920s*, in which he devoted much attention to the new modes of dress, the fads and crazes that made the news, and examples of individuals who discarded old thoughts and beliefs to further the notion that these activities were the norm for most people living during these times. Allen's book, along with F. Scott Fitzgerald's popular novels *The Great Gatsby* and *This Side of Paradise*, not to mention many Hollywood films have done much to solidify the view that wildness and excitement dominated the years between World War I and the Great Depression. Allen and the others have erred, however, by taking the new behaviors exhibited by a minority of the population and applying them to explain the mentality and lifestyle of the majority. Nevertheless, many important modernizing influences crept into American life during the 1920s, foreshadowing much of what would later become commonplace. Though a growing number of Americans embraced certain aspects of this social and economic change, others were rabidly determined to contain and reverse these trends, lest the traditional way of life that they understood and provided them with comfort be lost to an age of uncertainty and moral confusion.

"Ballyhoo" and Record-Breaking

One of Frederick Lewis Allen's major themes in *Only Yesterday* was the misplaced notion that most Americans did not care about "important issues" during the 1920s. As evidence, he cited the country's apparent obsession with various crazes, fads, stunts, record-breaking, and publicity-grabbing incidents that continuously made headlines in the print media of the day. While Allen overemphasized the importance of such sources in determining the national mood (he was, after all, editor of *Harper's Magazine*), there is no doubt that many Americans became interested in such "Ballyhoo" phenomenon that has been strongly linked to the 1920s ever since.

A stunt actor named Alvin "Shipwreck" Kelly inaugurated the decade's flagpole sitting fad. Though his initial

foray lasted half a day, Kelly continuously pushed the boundaries as others got into the act. In 1927 he spent an entire week on a stool affixed to a 50-foot pole atop the St. Francis Hotel in Newark, New Jersey, living off milk, broth, coffee, and cigarettes hoisted to him. For this effort he received national fame along with $1000 promised to him by a promoter plus extra money that the "Flagpole Rooster" received for holding up advertisement banners. His crowning achievement occurred in 1929 when he spent a record 49 days on a pole at a pier in Atlantic City, New Jersey.

While flagpole sitting events made the news because they were unknown in the United States before the 1920s, such stunts served more as publicity-generating devices rather than elements of a craze that lured huge numbers of active participants. The same could not be said for marathon dancing, however, which attracted many more devotees. Originally beginning as fun competitions for individuals or couples to win small prizes and gain some local notoriety, the phenomenon of **dance marathons** soon evolved into commercial ventures pushed by promoters across the country as a way to make money. Formal contests began to charge admission to spectators, pay a growing number of professional marathon dancers who traveled the country to compete, and doled out cash prizes to the winners. Established rules were developed for each contest, dictating how long the participants could take breaks and governing such behavior as eating, napping, bathing, and using restrooms. Though organizers occasionally instructed contestants to perform such popular dances as the Charleston and the Fox Trot, they were never graded on technical ability—what mattered was endurance, to be the last dancer standing with their feet still moving. As some competitions continued into days and weeks, the physical and emotional exhaustion among the remaining dancers entered an element of drama that promoters often exploited for effect. This early example of

"Where there's smoke there's fire" This 1920s illustration captures the style of a fashionably dressed "flapper," with a cigarette indifferently hanging from one hand, leaving a seductive, curving line of smoke. Flappers represented the sexual rebellion of the so-called "New Woman" in the post-war decade.

Marathon dancers, April 20, 1923.

George Herman "Babe" Ruth, started his professional baseball career with the Boston Red Sox but was traded to the New York Yankees in time for the 1920 season. Ruth established himself as one of the game's all-time homerun kings.

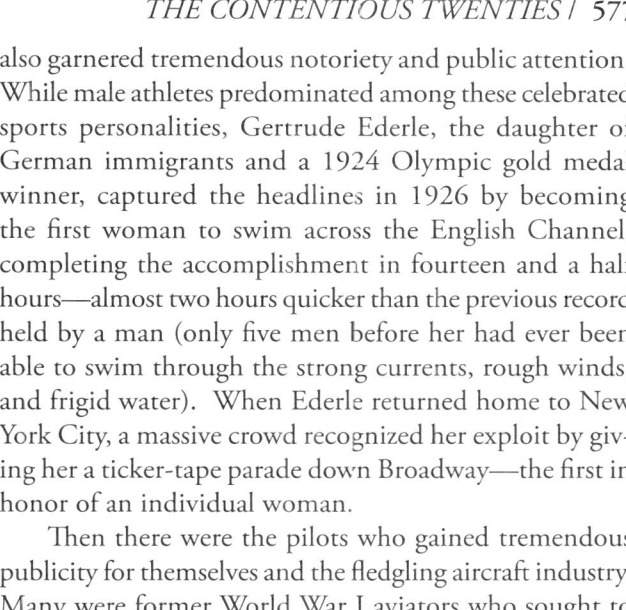

a "reality show" involving normal people entertaining an audience by their dancing as well as their struggles to stay in the competition remained popular well into the 1930s as contestants sought prize money in the midst of the Great Depression. Although dance marathons continue to take place today, usually as fundraisers for charity, the modern versions are a pale comparison to the exploitive spectacles from which they evolved.

During the 1920s, the American media also fixated on individual feats of athletic prowess. Baseball fans marveled at the exploits of Babe Ruth who popularized the home run by producing record numbers of them, helping to revive baseball's popularity after the 1919 "Black Sox Scandal" in which some Chicago White Sox players accepted money from gamblers in return for throwing the World Series. Football fans cheered Harold "Red" Grange—the "Galloping Ghost"—as the elusive University of Illinois and Chicago Bears running back broke countless records at the collegiate and professional level. Champions in boxing (Jack Dempsey), tennis (Bill Tilden), golf (Bobby Jones), and many other sportsmen

also garnered tremendous notoriety and public attention. While male athletes predominated among these celebrated sports personalities, Gertrude Ederle, the daughter of German immigrants and a 1924 Olympic gold medal winner, captured the headlines in 1926 by becoming the first woman to swim across the English Channel, completing the accomplishment in fourteen and a half hours—almost two hours quicker than the previous record held by a man (only five men before her had ever been able to swim through the strong currents, rough winds, and frigid water). When Ederle returned home to New York City, a massive crowd recognized her exploit by giving her a ticker-tape parade down Broadway—the first in honor of an individual woman.

Then there were the pilots who gained tremendous publicity for themselves and the fledgling aircraft industry. Many were former World War I aviators who sought to make a living after the war while honing their flying skills. The term "barnstormer" began to be applied to those pilots who flew from place to place around the country to thrill crowds with daredevil flying demonstrations and to charge passengers for rides. By the latter end of the 1920s, aviators tended to operate from just one airfield (so-called "fixed-base operations") while they continued to make a living by performing stunts and charging for rides, in addition to training new pilots and occasionally flying advertisement banners over local areas.

Those pilots who sought to gain fame and wealth by setting or breaking records gathered the most attention. By far the most popular aviator of the era was **Charles A. Lindbergh**. The son of a Swedish immigrant who became a Minnesota congressman, Lindbergh dropped out of the mechanical engineering program at the University of Wisconsin in 1920 to pursue his interest in flying. After completing his initial flight school, he barnstormed for a while to gain flying experience and earn money before beginning a year of flight training with the United States Army Air Service. Upon his graduation in 1925, Lindbergh served as an Army reserve officer while returning to civilian aviation as an air mail pilot covering the route between Chicago and St. Louis. In 1927, though only 25 years old and a trained pilot for only five years, Lindbergh sought to claim the elusive Raymond Orteig Prize offered up by a French hotelier for the first person to pilot a non-stop solo transatlantic flight between New York and Paris. In pursuit of this prize and the accompanying notoriety, six aviators had already died and three injured (including Richard Byrd, who claimed to be the first to fly across the North Pole in 1926 though that assertion has been doubted by many critics).

Financed by loans from St. Louis businessmen and his personal savings, Lindbergh oversaw the construction of a custom-built single-engine, single-seat monoplane dubbed *The Spirit of St. Louis*. To boost fuel efficiency with an improved center of gravity, the plane's large fuel tank was placed in the forward section of the fuselage. This design, however, dictated that there would be no windshield in front of the pilot. Besides a small retractable periscope, his visibility would be limited to side windows only. To maximize space, Lindbergh had to sit in a cramped cockpit so small he could not stretch his legs and only carried with him a map, his passport, four sandwiches and a couple of canteens of drinking water.

Taking off from Long Island's Roosevelt Field in a morning rainstorm on May 20, 1927, Lindbergh stayed airborne, sometimes at 10,000 feet, sometimes just above the ocean's waves, for the next thirty-three and a half hours. Along the way he battled poor visibility caused by icing and fog. He also combated his own body's resistance. Fatigue caused him to hallucinate, fall asleep, and occasionally lose track of his bearings (what pilots today refer to as "spatial disorientation"). Adrenaline kicked in twenty-six hours after take-off, however, when the aviator spotted a small group of fishing boats indicating that he was nearing land (the Irish coast). Adjusting his course, Lindbergh reached France as darkness fell for the second time during his epic flight. He landed at Paris's Le Bourget Airport at 10:22 p.m. on May 21. A crowd of over 100,000 enthusiastic spectators charged the airfield and triumphantly carried Lindbergh on their shoulders while souvenir hunters tore at the *Spirit's* fabric-covered fuselage. Lindbergh's flight made him an instant celebrity, gave further publicity to the budding aviation industry, and revived the belief of many Americans and others throughout the world in the ability of mankind to push the boundaries of achievement in the spirit of past pioneers. While other pilots over the next couple of decades would catch the public's attention, including Amelia Earhart who became the first woman to duplicate "Lucky Lindy's" accomplishment the very next year, Charles Lindbergh's feat was the most celebrated by the era's pilots and came to symbolize the adventurous energetic spirit so synonymous with the Roaring Twenties image.

The "New Woman"

The beginning of the 1920s witnessed a tremendous advance for women in the form of the ratification of the **Nineteenth Amendment** to the U.S. Constitution barring the denial of voting rights for citizens on the basis of gender. Though states could still restrict the vote by means of poll taxes, literacy tests, and other means that continued to deny large numbers of African Americans from voting in the South, the Nineteenth Amendment nevertheless retained large symbolic importance while marking a huge practical gain for middle- and upper-class white women. Passage of the Nineteenth Amendment resulted from the determined efforts of multiple generations of woman suffragists, culminating with successful agitation by female and male activists during the Progressive Era. While some turn-of-the century reformers continued to lobby for suffrage on the basis of simple justice and ending the denial of basic civil rights, many began to utilize more innovative lines of reasoning to promote their cause. Among the most powerful new arguments in favor of woman suffrage was the notion of "municipal housekeeping," which suffragists used to overcome gender expectations by reinforcing the traditional ideals of domesticity and maternalism. In this manner, they justified activism for the vote by emphasizing the need for women to participate within the political process. Thus, suffrage would not destroy the traditional family but, rather, would strengthen the institution by helping civic-minded women better protect their homes by voting for proper candidates and supporting essential reforms. Some suffragists also reflected the racial biases of their times by claiming the vote was necessary in order to allow Anglo women to better protect their families by negating the negative influences of foreign-born radicals and black males.

While an important achievement, passage of the woman suffrage amendment did not completely satisfy the most outspoken radical feminists. Led by **Alice Paul**, activists within the National Woman's Party (NWP)—an offshoot of the National American Woman Suffrage Association (NAWSA)—had been among the most vociferous of the suffragists, employing aggressive publicity-generating tactics learned from the British suffrage movement. Though often described as "militant suffragists" because of their vociferous activism, Paul and other members of the NWP used only nonviolent means to garner attention, such as picketing the White House (some chained themselves to the gates), allowing themselves to be arrested for disturbing the peace, and undertaking hunger strikes (where they were often force-fed by authorities) while incarcerated.

After passage of the Nineteenth Amendment, Paul sought acceptance of a new constitutional amendment that would end gender discrimination by eliminating all legal distinctions between men and women: "Men and women shall have equal rights throughout the United States and every place subject to its jurisdiction." Many female Progressive leaders such as Florence Kelley and Jane Addams balked at Paul's proposal, arguing correctly that the Equal Rights Amendment (ERA) would result in the end of protective legislation for women. Kelley

The Black Sox Scandal

During the early twentieth century, professional baseball players joined factory laborers as an exploited group, often mistreated by unscrupulous employers desiring to squeeze production out of their workforce. This case was certainly true for the 1919 Chicago White Sox, a talented assortment of ballplayers on a team controlled by parsimonious owner Charles Comiskey. An ex-professional player himself, Comiskey garnered the hatred of his players for such practices as underpaying them, sitting players near the end of the season to deprive them of achieving performance bonuses based on their yearly statistics, and even deducting the cost of laundering their uniforms from their paychecks. Upset with their treatment and lured by greed, some White Sox players became enticed to purposely lose the 1919 World Series against the underdog Cincinnati Reds in exchange for payoffs equal to many times their annual salaries and, of course, the ability to place bets against their own team.

After the Series loss, rumors circulated that the White Sox had thrown the Series—eventually corroborated with evidence gathered by an energetic sportswriter. A Chicago grand jury indicted eight White Sox players for active participation in the conspiracy, or knowing about the scheme but failing to report the malfeasance. Though convicted in the national "court of public opinion," the local jury in Chicago acquitted all eight players of wrongdoing. Still, baseball owners knew that the "Black Sox Scandal" could potentially threaten the integrity of their business. In response, Major League Baseball created the office of Commissioner of Baseball to police the sport, appointing respected federal judge Kenesaw Mountain Landis to the post. Landis' first action was to ban the eight White Sox players for life, citing his granted power to act in the best interest of baseball.

The commissioner's move did much in the short term to address the issue of corruption in baseball, but the game's return to prominence during the spectator-sport-crazy decade of the 1920s coincided with the excitement generated by George Herman "Babe" Ruth, who revolutionized the game with his ability to hit long and frequent home runs. In 1919, the same year that the White Sox won the American League pennant and earned the right to play in the World Series, Ruth set a new major league record by swatting 29 home runs for the Boston Red Sox (the previous record of 27 had been set in 1884). During the off season, not wishing to accede to Ruth's pay demands, the Red Sox owner infamously sold Ruth's contract to the New York Yankees. Ruth rewarded his new team by slugging an astounding 54 home runs. The following year, he clubbed 59 round-trippers—a feat thought never to be broken until he hit 60 home runs in 1927 as part of the Yankees' famous "Murderers' Row" lineup that included future Hall of Famers Lou Gehrig, Tony Lazzeri, and Earle Combs. In that year alone, Ruth's epic performances helped Major League Baseball draw over 20 million people—a definite sign that for most sports fans, the Black Sox scandal had already faded into distant memory.

and Addams had been working for such laws for most of their adult lives and believed that they were not only important reforms for women but also served (along with their efforts to end child labor) as a vital starting point in an extended campaign to win protections for all workers. Paul, however, countered that laws such as limiting work hours or preventing women from working at night or in certain occupations stigmatized women and reduced their economic opportunities, not to mention the separate status they assigned for women in the workplace and society in general. While the infighting in the women's movement raged, members of Congress introduced Paul's ERA for debate in 1923. The merits and drawbacks of the ERA would continue to divide feminists and the major political parties alike for the next 50 years. In 1972, an amendment based on Paul's initial proposal ("Equality of rights under the law shall not be denied or abridged by the United States or by any State on account of sex") passed both houses of Congress but ultimately fell short

of ratification by the required three-quarters of the states.

While Paul and the NWP sparred with old progressives and members of the new League of Women Voters (formerly NAWSA) over many issues, they tended to fall into agreement that many young women of the postwar generation were squandering their hard-fought achievements through self-indulgent actions and behavior that simply fed into prevailing stereotypes of women as non-intellectuals overly concerned with physical appearances, reliant upon men for stability and happiness, and obsessed with obtaining the latest highly-desired consumer goods. In their minds, the only notion worse than women seeking satisfaction through finding a husband, raising a large family, and living in material comfort were those young women increasingly referred to as "**flappers**" who sauntered around as gadflies flaunting social convention by their outrageous dress and behavior before settling down. While the origin of the term "flapper" is in dispute (some believe it derived from the movement of unfastened galoshes that were popular at the time, while others point to much earlier uses in England referring to young birds who furiously beat their wings as they learn to fly), the appearance of these young women who wore short skirts, bobbed their hair, listened to jazz music, danced to the latest popular wild dances, drank alcohol, smoked in public, drove automobiles, treated sex in a more casual manner, and generally displayed disdain for accepted social standards regarding acceptable female public behavior caused quite a stir among those raised during the Gilded Age. While condemned by many preachers on Sunday mornings, the flapper image was popularized in national magazines, newspapers, novels, and many Hollywood films as the most vibrant manifestation of the "new woman" who was not beholden to past societal norms. In the ensuing decades, the iconic flapper image endured whenever Americans thought of the 1920s. Though certainly a new phenomenon worth noting, in reality only a minority of young middle- and upper-class women adopted such a lifestyle.

THE IMPACT OF THE GREAT BLACK MIGRATION

Begun during the First World War, the vast movement of African Americans from the rural South into northern industrial cities continued unabated during the 1920s. From 1920 to 1930, an estimated half-million blacks packed their bags to head north. Though not experiencing legal segregation as existed in the South, prevailing customs in the North led to *de facto* segregation in all-black neighborhoods. Despite these limitations, life in the northern urban enclaves proved to be generally less oppressive while being more emotionally and materially rewarding. As black enterprises catered to the public and cultural pride flourished, African Americans also became a growing political force as many took part in participatory democracy for the first time in their lives.

The growing popularity of **jazz** music among mainstream (white middle-class) Americans during the 1920s is directly linked to the spreading of that unique blending of African and European musical styles from its native South by recent black migrants to northern cities spread within nightclubs and broadcast over radio stations. Writers during the decade and since have described early jazz music, with its characteristic liveliness, syncopated rhythms, and often improvisational presentation as synonymous with the mood of the 1920s. F. Scott Fitzgerald labeled the 1920s as the "Jazz Age" because of his connection of the art form's style to the wild behavior of the nation's youth that he often described in his novels. Though not an accurate description for the majority of Americans during the time, Fitzgerald's observation captured the spirit of the minority of youth, whose gyrating dancing to the Charleston, the Black Bottom, and the Fox Trot, not to mention their carefree lifestyle, upset the nation's moral guardians.

The profusion of jazz music into the public consciousness proved to be the most salient example of a great explosion in African-American culture and racial pride to appear during the 1920s. Though Chicago, Philadelphia, Detroit, St. Louis, and many other northern cities experiencing large black population gains displayed elements of the new profusion of music, literature, visual arts, theater, and intellectual works, the Harlem neighborhood of New York City's Upper West Side became the center of the phenomenon leading to the label "**Harlem Renaissance**" being applied to the entire movement that signaled a new era of thought and expression for African Americans. In Harlem, artists of various types attempted to create a new black identity so the country would be forced to no longer view all blacks as mere southern rural peasants incapable of displaying creativity and sophistication. Playwrights produced theater pieces in which the African-American characters displayed complex human emotions rather than stereotypical portrayals frequently appearing in vaudeville and minstrel shows. (Minstrel shows featured white artists who wore makeup and wigs to create an exaggerated caricature of African-American features. Such shows were a popular form of entertainment with white audiences from the 1840s to the mid-twentieth century and included comedy sketches delivered in a crude imitation of black dialect and music meant to mimic black styles.) Poets and novelists such as Langston Hughes sought to create original written works that celebrated his race while often protesting existing social conditions. Musicians including Duke Ellington and Jelly Roll Morton and a large host of singers showcased their talents before crowds dancing excitedly to the artists' lively compositions. Within the pages of Harlem-published *Crisis* magazine, the official journal of the NAACP edited by W.E.B. Du Bois, enthusiastic readers found the nation's leading forum for exhibitions of African-American poetry, essays, novel excerpts, and works of art.

The most radical expression of black racial pride during the 1920s proved to be **Marcus Garvey**'s "Negro Nationalism" movement. A well-read Jamaican immigrant who traveled to America in 1916, Garvey applied his experience as a printer and editor to the promotion of his United Negro Improvement Association (UNIA), which he created to unite and uplift all individuals of African ancestry. Garvey's approach entailed not only glorification of the race but also racial separation from whites in a manner that placed him directly at odds with Du

Bois and other black leaders who were fighting for racial integration and acceptance by whites. Garvey exhorted African Americans to maintain racial purity by avoiding interracial contact and to build a strong economic base by only patronizing black-owned businesses, especially the grocery stores, laundries, and restaurants operated by UNIA, as well as the Black Star steamship line—the organization's main business effort designed to foster unity and trade between blacks in Africa and the Western Hemisphere. In exchange for monthly dues, UNIA members received health insurance and death benefits, the option to buy stock in the group's subsidiaries, and the emotional contentment derived from expressing racial solidarity in a common venture. At its height in the early 1920s, UNIA boasted over two million members in over 800 chapters in the U.S. and abroad.

While earning the wrath of Du Bois and other NAACP leaders for his separatist ideas (Du Bois once referred to Garvey as "the most dangerous enemy of the Negro race in America"), Garvey's activities garnered the attention of J. Edgar Hoover, the general intelligence division director of the Justice Department and future head of the Federal Bureau of Investigation, who came to believe Garvey was a potential fomenter of social unrest. With the encouragement of the NAACP, Hoover spent two years investigating UNIA's business dealings by paying spies to infiltrate the group and gather evidence. Prosecutors found little trouble in securing an indictment of Garvey on mail fraud charges (Black Star Line stock sales had taken place after the image of a ship appeared on a mailed brochure even though UNIA had not yet purchased the ship). A jury convicted Garvey, sentencing him to five years in a federal prison. Upon his release, he was deported to Jamaica thus ending the American branch of UNIA. Despite Garvey's removal, the notions of black nationalism and Pan-Africanism endured with the founding of the Nation of Islam in 1930 and experienced a more popular revival during the "Black Power" Movement of the 1960s.

THE DEFENDERS OF TRADITION

As new modes of dress, behavior, and expression became acceptable to those who viewed such social changes as positive elements of modernization, large numbers of Americans during the 1920s, especially a majority of those reared in rural areas, clung to their familiar ways of life stronger than ever. In part, this attitude reflected the natural tendency to adhere to what is known in uncertain times, but it also represented a definite reaction to the Roaring Twenties lifestyles swirling about them. As a result, these Americans culturally retrenched and resisted change in a host of ways that belies the commonly-held notion that most wholeheartedly accepted the advent of a new modern America.

In his classic book on American thought covering the 1917-1930 period titled *The Nervous Generation*, historian Roderick Nash makes a vital point concerning the 1920s when he noted that most of the authors commonly associated with the decade in textbooks were largely avoided by the general public at the time. Later generations of Americans read F. Scott Fitzgerald and Ernest Hemingway rather than those living in the immediate years following World War I. The most popular contemporary author of the 1920s in terms of the number of books sold, in fact, was an Ohio dentist-turned-western writer named **Zane Grey**. From 1917 to 1924, Grey was never off national bestseller lists, writing novels that were often converted into full-length motion pictures, helping the writer become a millionaire and a major force in shaping many commonly-held myths about the Old West. While possessing only basic literary talent, Grey succeeded because his stories reaffirmed traditional values, striking a chord with millions of readers who much preferred to read books confirming their beliefs rather than challenging them.

Restrictions on Dress, Dancing, and Movies

Bathing suits became a hot topic of conversation during the 1920s when many areas of the country banned certain new styles from being worn in public. Until the turn of the twentieth century, most public beaches were segregated by gender (as well as by race). As authorities began to lift those limits, women began to intermingle with men along the shorelines but were still expected to wear cumbersome outfits with bloomers and heavy flowing skirts that resembled streetwear. Some women began to fight back against these regulations. During the summer of 1921, Louise Rosine, a Los Angeles resident visiting Atlantic City, New Jersey, was arrested for refusing to roll up her stockings above her knees. Other women caused similar uproars when they donned the new one-piece suits that many in the public found immoral or objectionable, considering them to be "men's suits." Countless similar episodes of protest by women can be found in contemporary newspapers, as well as the strong efforts to crack down on such new modes of dress, signifying how much of the country had not converted to the Roaring Twenties lifestyle.

Numerous government and church authorities made concerted efforts during the 1920s to clamp down on dancing, perceiving the activity as inherently immoral or leading to other forms of decadent behavior. In 1918, the

Vatican prohibited Catholics from dancing the Tango, the Fox Trot, and other "modern dances." Baptists forbade dancing of any kind because of the "long train of attendant evil" that supposedly accompanied the practice. Most Methodist leaders agreed not only to a ban on dancing but also theater attendance and circus going. Newly elected governors Pat Neff of Texas and Jason Fields of Kentucky both cancelled inaugural balls because of their personal distaste for dancing.

Hollywood motion pictures also fell under intense scrutiny in many sections of the country during the 1920s. After a U.S. Supreme Court decision found that free speech guarantees did not apply to film, many states and localities began to institute censorship boards to oversee the content of movies shown in their jurisdictions. The large Hollywood studios also responded to the decision, naming **William H. Hays** to be the first president of the newly formed Motion Pictures Association of America (MPAA). Before heading the MPAA in 1922, Hays served as chairman of the Republican National Committee, Warren Harding's campaign manager in the 1920 presidential campaign, and Postmaster General in the Harding Administration. Studio executives chose Hays to lead the MPAA because he was an elder in the Presbyterian Church who could help Hollywood clean up its image with the public and avoid federal government regulation.

Hays endeavored to develop a standard voluntary code for filmmaking designed to produce films without objectionable material that would also save the studios money by not having to constantly edit their movies to comply with the desires of the myriad of local censors around the country. Hays began with a list of suggested

Col. Sherrell, Supt. of Public Buildings and Grounds, issued an order that bathing suits at the Washington D.C. bathing beach must not be over six inches above the knee. Bill Norton, the bathing beach policeman, is measuring the distance between the knee and the bathing suit on a woman. 1922.

"Don'ts and Be Carefuls"—a set of general rules based on the most frequent objections of local censorship boards. The 11 "Don'ts" to be avoided completely included profanity, nudity, miscegenation, acts of childbirth, ridicule of the clergy, and "any inference of sex perversion." The 26 "Be Carefuls" in which special care was to be exercised in the depiction of certain subjects included crime, violence, use of firearms, sympathy for criminals, seduction of females, drug use, and "excessive or lustful kissing." This list became the basis for the future Motion Picture Production Code (often referred to as the "Hays Code"), which began to be enforced by the motion picture industry's Production Code Administration (PCA). After 1934, all films had to be approved by the PCA before they could be released to the general public. (The Hays Code governed the content of Hollywood films for the next 35 years until replaced by the Movie Ratings System used in modified form today.) The MPAA's decision to hire Hays reflects the film industry's necessity to respect the prevailing national attitudes to avoid government regulation but also to curry favor with a public that did not completely adapt to the changing times. If the majority of the country had converted to the tenets of the Roaring Twenties, the Hays Code would certainly not have been necessary.

Prohibition

The prohibition of alcohol proved to be the most notable nationwide restriction to personal liberty during the 1920s while also providing the greatest challenge to the argument that the decade was a period in which the majority cast aside their previous inhibitions and undertook a radical change in their lifestyle and behavior. Advocates seeking to reduce alcohol consumption had existed in the country for over a hundred years, but at the turn of the twentieth century, Prohibition turned into a Progressive social reform in response to the increased availability of cheaper alcohol provided by the processes of the Industrial Revolution as well as the conspicuous drinking of many foreign immigrants. Protestant organizations such as the Woman's Christian Temperance Union and the Anti-Saloon League pushed for state and federal restrictions against alcohol, forging a coalition among those who believed that outlawing alcohol would "clean up society" in a myriad of ways: businessmen would have a more sober workforce, women would have less violent husbands who would not squander hard-earned money on drink, and doctors would witness the justification of research showing that the elimination of alcohol would lead to a healthier populace.

American entry into World War I aided Prohibition forces. By 1917, eighteen states, with nearly two-thirds of the country's population, had already banned the manufacture and sale of alcohol. As wartime need for grain plus vehement patriotism (many breweries were owned by German Americans) arose, reduced production and consumption of alcohol ensued. After the war's end, on January 16, 1919, the requisite number of states finally ratified the **Eighteenth Amendment** to the U.S. Constitution, outlawing the manufacture, sale, or transportation of intoxicating liquors. The amendment's enforcement legislation passed by Congress in October 1919, the Volstead Act, made it illegal to make, ship, or sell beverages with alcohol content greater than 0.5 percent beginning on January 16, 1920.

The most immediate effect of Prohibition was the closure of bars, saloons, and other public drinking establishments. While many estimates place the reduced consumption of alcohol at 50 percent (especially among urban working-class ethnic groups who could not afford to consume as much illegal alcohol because of the higher prices), large numbers of Americans certainly did not stop drinking. Instead, the activity went underground. In cities across the country, secret "speakeasies" arose where patrons illegally consumed alcohol. The hip flask became a common item among those who ignored the law and wished to have a personal stash of their elixir of choice near them at all times. Those with access to alcohol took many trips into secluded rural areas, even caves, to drink.

The type of alcohol consumed during Prohibition varied between bottles of wine and hard liquor made before the law went into effect to more recently-made beverages, either smuggled from outside the country or domestically manufactured drinks from an assortment of stills and hidden manufacturing facilities (sometimes producing liquor with very harmful health effects). The reduced supply of alcoholic beverages led to increased prices for "bootleg liquor," luring many criminals to get into the action. In the South, alcohol runners began to modify their vehicles to enable them to outrun law officials. (Some creators of these modified "stock cars" later started racing their vehicles in the 1930s, leading to the eventual formation of NASCAR). In the northern industrial cities, organized crime syndicates previously involved in gambling, prostitution, and narcotics (most famously, the empire led by Chicago's Al Capone) sought to dominate the illicit trade in booze. Gang violence became a more frequent occurrence as rival bands fought highly-publicized turf battles that led to many deaths and public calls for more resources dedicated to their suppression. Failing to receive adequate resources to deal with Prohibition-related issues, local, state, and federal officials constantly had their hands full trying to enforce the law. The increased focus on Prohibition offenses also diverted police attention away from other crime-related activities.

Though leading to reduced consumption of alcohol, Prohibition failed in terms of the goal to eliminate drinking completely from American society and led to a whole slew of new problems unforeseen by its advocates. The failure of Prohibition, along with the arrival of the Great Depression, would lead to the eventual repeal of the Eighteenth Amendment (by ratification of the Twenty-first Amendment in 1933). Though often referred to as the "Noble Experiment," most of its supporters did not view Prohibition as a mere test. Instead, they doggedly held onto their belief that the effort to eliminate alcohol would improve society and caused more good than harm even after a majority of Americans determined otherwise.

Immigration Restriction

Many old-stock Americans during the 1920s felt threatened by the renewed influx of immigrants coming into the country after the conclusion of the First World War. After a four-year hiatus during the war when the flow of foreigners slowed to a trickle, starting in 1919 nearly a million new arrivals per year (two-thirds from Southern and Eastern Europe) entered the United States, renewing the belief of many that radical political ideas, not to mention Catholicism and Judaism, would spread unabated across the land. The popularity of this insular, anti-foreign nativist viewpoint, especially among rural folk and migrants from the countryside residing in the bustling cities, found expression in a new drive to restrict foreign immigration.

Congress responded to the public clamor in 1921 by passing the Emergency Quota Act of 1921, legislation that introduced numerical limits on the number of legal immigrants entering the country and used a quota system for the first time. The law set the maximum number of legal immigrants at 350,000. Further, the number of new immigrants entering the U.S. from any given country was limited to 3 percent of the number of each nationality residing in the United States in 1910, thus favoring immigrants from Northern and Western Europe. Three years later, Congress passed the **National Origins Act**, which further tightened the flow of legal immigration by reducing the cap level to 150,000 while altering the nationality quotas to 2 percent of the number of each nationality residing in the United States in 1890—a choice deliberately made to further drop the number of Southern and Eastern Europeans arriving because the majority of individuals from those groups had arrived after that base year. For the next four decades, the number of people legally entering the U.S. from Southern and Eastern European countries would be reduced to no more than

15 percent of the total immigration pool. In addition to addressing the concerns of Protestant Northeasterners and residents of the Midwest, these laws also showed the influence of political pressure applied by representatives of the western states. While the Emergency Quota Act and the National Origins Act placed complete bans on immigrants from Japan and other East Asian countries (with the notable exception of the U.S.-held Philippines), neither law placed limits on immigration from Latin American countries to continue to allow agribusinesses access to an ample supply of low-wage labor.

Fundamentalism

The rise of religious **fundamentalism** proved to be another strong reaction to modernizing influences within American society. In the late nineteenth century, many scientists and intellectuals built upon scientific developments and new theories to present secular challenges to many aspects of organized religion. In response, some liberal theologians began applying historical and scientific methods to examine the Bible with a critical eye. Countless religious conservatives responded negatively to any updating of orthodox Christianity. Eventually, many evangelicals began to label themselves "Fundamentalists," with the name derived from the title of a noted series of essays— *The Fundamentals*—published from 1910 to 1915 by the Bible Institute of Los Angeles. Written by an assortment of conservative theologians and edited by evangelical pastor A. C. Dixon (the brother of Thomas Dixon, Jr. who wrote the novel *The Clansman*, which served as the inspiration for D.W. Griffith's film *The Birth of a Nation*, which glorified the Reconstruction-Era Ku Klux Klan), the authors stated their beliefs about the fundamentals of Christian faith (including the virgin birth, the resurrection of Jesus, and the Bible as the inspired word of God to be read literally) while attacking liberal theology, atheism, and Catholicism, as well as evolution and other modern scientific theories. Financed by California oil man Lyman Stewart, millions of copies of the essays were sent free to ministers and other active Christians, helping to spread the views presented in the *Fundamentals* and unifying like-minded believers.

In addition to being fueled by resentment toward secular challengers, liberal theologians, Catholics and Jews, fundamentalism also spread rapidly across the country during the first three decades of the twentieth century because of the dynamic efforts of many flamboyant and charismatic preachers who attracted multitudes to their campaigns. Among the myriad of evangelists to emerge, the most famous was **Billy Sunday**. An ex-major league baseball player from Iowa (whose father came from a family of German immigrants named Sonntag who anglicized their name to "Sunday" upon their arrival to America—a fortunate decision for the future preacher), Sunday began attending a Presbyterian church in Chicago in the middle of his career and became a convert. After his playing days ended, Sunday began working for the YMCA in Chicago where he became an assistant to J. Wilbur Chapman, a renowned Presbyterian minister who taught him the fine arts of preparing and delivering sermons while reinforcing the tenets of fundamentalism.

Starting in 1896, Sunday began his career as a minister of the old-time religion, taking advantage of his notoriety as a baseball player to generate publicity. Preaching with a classic fear-of-damnation style across the country, he delivered his messages in a loud booming voice, often filling his sermons with animation as he would contort his face, flail his arms, run across the stage and dive as a ballplayer, and even smash chairs to assert his points. His message reflected all the tenets of fundamentalism, including the existence of a Devil, attacks on modernism, and an affirmation of a literal reading of the Bible.

From the Pentecostal strand of fundamentalism, **Aimee Semple McPherson** presented a fresh face during the Twenties. Born Aimee Elizabeth Kennedy on a Canadian farm, she spent much of her youth with her religious mother who worked for the Salvation Army. She met her first husband, a Pentecostal missionary from Ireland named Robert Semple, while attending a revival. Soon after getting married, the couple traveled to China to perform missionary work, but Robert died of malaria in 1910, forcing Aimee and her newborn daughter to return to the United States. She later married her second husband, a grocer named Harold McPherson, in 1912. The couple had a son the next year, but Aimee soon rebelled against the life of domesticity her traditional husband planned for her. With her children in tow, she left McPherson to become an itinerant Pentecostal minister, travelling in her "Gospel Car," a Packard touring vehicle adorned with religious slogans written along the chassis. Though some were uncomfortable with a woman preaching the Gospel, McPherson attracted large crowds as she hosted revivals across the eastern United States. As she honed her oratorical skills, McPherson delivered deeply conservative messages that resonated with the crowds—constantly railing against numerous aspects of modernity and demanding that people remain true to the fundamentalist faith of the old time religion.

Seeking a permanent home for her family, McPherson moved in 1918 to Los Angeles, California—a city undergoing rapid population growth (from 575,000 in 1920 to over 1.2 million by 1930), with many of the newly arriving migrants coming from midwestern and southern rural areas holding strong fundamentalist beliefs. After establishing her new "International Church of the Foursquare Gospel," she made frequent trips across the country to raise money for the construction of a large structure to house her growing congregation. On January 1, 1923, the nation's first "megachurch" opened when McPherson dedicated the new 5,300-seat Angelus Temple, which often filled to capacity. Besides the sense of community provided by the large crowds attending the Temple, devotees flocked to the church because of McPherson's personal charisma and her sense of dramatic flair. Arriving in grand fashion (often in a deluge of bright light surrounded by bouquets of roses, though one time she entered on a motorcycle down the main aisle), she always produced immaculate stage presentations with orchestral accompaniment to drive home her messages and keep the audiences entertained. Unlike Billy Sunday and many other fundamentalist evangelists, McPherson preached optimism rather than fire and brimstone. Though tending to avoid using the Pentecostal label, she occasionally spoke in tongues and performed dramatic faith healing demonstrations in the Pentecostal tradition as part of her sermons. In addition to showing a gift for oratory and theatrics, McPherson also displayed a keen awareness of the potential of new media outlets to reach new potential converts. In 1924, she purchased a radio station and began preaching over the airwaves to the entire city.

McPherson's fame began to wane after a month-long disappearance from a Southern California beach in 1926 that ended when she was discovered alive in Douglas, Arizona, claiming to have been drugged and held for ransom by Mexican kidnappers. Doubters were probably correct that the incident was designed to be part-publicity stunt and partly an effort to hide her affair with her married radio station manager. Nevertheless, her Foursquare Gospel Church endured the scandal, and McPherson continued preaching with less public fanfare until her death in the early 1940s.

Riding the success of a growing movement, fundamentalists during the 1920s sought to put their ideas into action to shape the direction of society. The largest *bête noir* for fundamentalists was the spreading of Charles Darwin's theory of evolution, especially in public education. For those who unquestioningly believed the story of creation of mankind presented in the Book of Genesis, Darwin's proposition that humans descended from primates was a blasphemous doctrine that had to be crushed. If the story of creation were to be disregarded, the entire Bible would then become disputed ground. Three-time former Democratic presidential nominee **William Jennings Bryan**, himself a devout fundamentalist, led the effort in the various states to pass laws removing the teaching of Darwinian theories from public education. A politician with strong reform credentials, Bryan believed that Darwin's views enhanced political conservatism by justifying a "survival of the fittest" mentality. He also believed that acceptance of evolution removed the consciousness of God's presence in people's daily lives, leading one to conclude that "no spiritual force has touched the life of man and shaped the destiny of nations."

Though a national effort, the anti-Darwin movement achieved its only successes in the South where several states banned textbooks with any mention of Darwin and made it a crime to teach evolution in public schools. In 1925, Tennessee fundamentalists, whipped into a frenzy by a recent Billy Sunday crusade, pressured members of their legislature to pass a law making it a misdemeanor "to teach any theory that denies the story of the Divine Creation of man as taught in the Bible, and to teach instead that man had descended from a lower order of animal." When some in the state decided to challenge the constitutionality of the new law, the stage was set for the biggest clash of the decade between secularists and fundamentalists.

The American Civil Liberties Union (ACLU), a free speech organization originally formed to defend those being punished for opposing American involvement in World War I, announced that it was willing to defend any teacher arrested for violating the Tennessee statue. Seeking a test case to appeal to the U.S. Supreme Court, ACLU lawyers found a group of collaborators in the form of some local leaders in the small town of Dayton, located midway between Knoxville and Chattanooga in eastern Tennessee. There, businessmen and attorneys concocted a plan to bring a show trial over evolution to Dayton to boost the town's sagging economy. Calling upon their high school's young and easygoing part-time general science instructor and football coach John T. Scopes to seek his participation in their scheme, the men got the 24-year old teacher's concurrence that biology could not be taught properly without addressing Darwin's theory of evolution and his consent to be arrested for violating the state's new antievolution statute.

The carnival-like atmosphere that would characterize the **Scopes "Monkey Trial"** developed quickly with the publicity being generated soon exceeding that for a Jack Dempsey boxing match. Though ACLU officials hoped for a simple, quiet test case to bring through the appellate courts, the Dayton leaders had other priorities. To increase the trial's notoriety, they invited William Jennings Bryan to take part in the court proceedings as an assisting prosecuting attorney. Upon hearing of Bryan's acceptance to participate, Chicago defense attorney Clarence Darrow—the most famous lawyer in the country and an evolution supporter – offered his services to aid the ACLU in defending Scopes. Though ACLU officials did not desire Darrow's help out of fear that his rabid agnosticism and gruff demeanor would present the wrong image to the public, Scopes wanted Darrow's counsel and retained him for his defense team. Dayton's residents, especially the town's merchants, welcomed the crush of out-of-town journalists, peddlers, hucksters, and curiosity-seekers who arrived to spend their time and money during the eleven-day trial. More than 200 newspaper reporters from across the country covered the trial and a live radio feed allowed Americans to listen to the first broadcasted trial in U.S. history from the comfort of their homes.

Inside the hot, poorly-ventilated courtroom, the opposing sides battled each other, not over the details of the case for the jury (Scopes freely admitted he was guilty of violating the law), but over the merits of the larger issues of evolution and acceptance of a literal interpretation of the Bible for the newspaper-reading and radio-listening national public. On the final full day of the trial, the judge moved the proceedings outdoors due to the stifling heat. Darrow then dramatically called Bryan to the witness stand. Over the lead prosecutor's objection, the judge allowed the questioning to proceed when Bryan stated that he wished to defend his beliefs as long as he would be allowed to question Darrow afterwards. In an effort to ridicule Bryan's views and to suggest that Bible stories were unscientific and therefore inadmissible in a science class, Darrow aggressively interrogated the aging politician about the veracity of numerous Bible passages, including God acceding to Joshua's request to make the sun stand still, Jonah being swallowed by a whale, the story of Adam and Eve, and the creation of the world in six days. Bryan steadfastly stated that while he could not explain many contradicting passages or glaring omissions in the Bible (such as where Cain--Adam and Eve's son-- found his wife if they were the first human beings, and how there could have been a first, second, or third day if the sun was not created until the fourth day), he nevertheless believed it all unequivocally. At one point Bryan potentially upset many followers when he admitted under rigorous questioning to the possibility that the seven days of creation might refer to long epochs of time. Exhausted with the two-hour long exercise, the judge finally ended the session. On the next day he did not allow Bryan the opportunity for rebuttal and instead called for closing arguments. The jury then took only nine minutes to deliberate, finding Scopes guilty as the defense team expected and hoped. The judge ordered Scopes to pay a $100 fine.

In the days that followed, Bryan died of a heart attack (becoming a martyr in the eyes of fundamentalists, though there was no direct link between the trial and his death), and ACLU lawyers filed their appeal. In 1927, members of the Tennessee state Supreme Court who feared that the U.S. Supreme Court would overturn the anti-evolution law, however, set aside Scopes's conviction on the technical grounds that under Tennessee law the jury should have decided such a high fine, not the trial judge. The prosecution refused to retry the case. Though the anti-evolution movement stalled after the Scopes Trial, evolution continued to remain separate from the scientific curriculum of numerous southern public education systems for decades until the U.S Supreme Court ruled in the 1968 *Epperson v. Arkansas* case that such bans stood in violation of the Establishment Clause of the First Amendment (Tennessee had repealed its anti-evolution statute the previous year.) Nevertheless, anti-evolution sentiment would remain within America's conservative Christian subculture, thriving in church-affiliated education and home schooling.

Though much has been made over the years about how the Scopes Trial pitted "the two Americas" against each other, the majority of Americans during the 1920s were in between the two extremes of Darrow's rabid agnosticism and Bryan's devout fundamentalism. Nevertheless, the trial stands as one of the great symbolic experiences of the decade, clearly displaying that Americans were far from united in terms of their social and cultural views. Modernists (whether those with secular or liberal Christian viewpoints) viewed Bryan and his followers as backward, superstitious bumpkins out of tune with the discoveries of modern science. Fundamentalists, regardless of their denomination, believed that the supporters of Darwin were atheists or misguided Christians seeking to undermine the foundation of their religious beliefs.

The Second Ku Klux Klan

During the 1920s, a revived **Ku Klux Klan** became the embodiment of the most extreme defenders of the old social order. Not only proclaiming to be the regulators of the color line, Klansmen during the decade set out to stem the tide of foreign immigration and stamp out the teaching of evolution while maintaining the sanctity of marriage, supporting Prohibition, and enforcing a proper Victorian Era code of public dress and conduct, by force if necessary.

In 1915, an unsuccessful former Methodist minister named William J. Simmons founded the Second Ku Klux Klan as a fraternal organization with membership limited to white, Protestant, native-born adults. Taking advantage of the popularity of the recently released film *Birth of a Nation*, which glorified the original Klan of Reconstruction days, Simmons borrowed the dress and many rituals from the hooded order to create a living memorial to the old group while focusing on new issues that were supposedly destroying American society. The Klan grew at a glacial pace over the next five years, largely reflecting Simmons's lack of organizational and promotional ability. By 1920, the group had only 5,000 members in Georgia and Alabama when Simmons entered into a business deal with Edward Clarke and Elizabeth Tyler—two Atlanta-area publicists with promotional and fundraising experience. Using corporate publicity techniques and a trained staff of one thousand recruiters (or "kleagles," as they were called by the Klan), Clarke and Tyler added greatly to Klan membership rolls by exploiting fear and prejudice against blacks, Mexicans, Catholics, Jews, and immigrants while championing support for Prohibition, patriotism, and traditional moral standards. They also got rich in the process. For every $10 "klectoken" (initiation fee) collected, Clarke and Tyler pocketed $4, the kleagle received $4, and the remainder went to Klan national headquarters in Atlanta. Kleagles received instructions to take a top-down approach when recruiting in a locality, first contacting local business, religious, and political leaders in order to gain credibility, then working down to the middle-class, and finishing by convincing those at society's bottom to join. These techniques proved to be very successful. By the end of 1922, the Ku Klux Klan boasted 700,000 members nationally.

A major misconception about the 1920s Klan is that the order was primarily an anti-black organization. While many Klansmen held strong white supremacist views and some performed acts of violence against African Americans, other motivations accounted for the Klan's rise. Beyond fears of blacks crossing the color barrier, the majority of Klan members tended to view those issues as lesser aspects of the overall goal of controlling the rapidly modernizing world. Even more important to them were signs of moral decay and the breakdown of traditional societal norms represented by new "scandalous"

forms of entertainment and dress, rampant lawlessness exhibited by evasion of the Prohibition laws, challenges to traditional Christianity, and decrepit moral behavior displayed by gamblers, prostitutes, and individuals who engaged in premarital and extramarital sex. In the end, devout Klansmen wanted to use their organization as a device to take the country back to an alleged time when these behaviors were rare. Many did not mind using violence and other extralegal means to enforce their models of social conformity. Many females also agreed with the Klan's efforts so strongly that they organized "Women of the Ku Klux Klan" auxiliaries in 36 states. Most were religious women who rejected the modernistic elements of the Roaring Twenties.

While the Klan provided a sense of community for its members through grand parades, dramatic initiation ceremonies, casual social events, and even occasional charity work, the hooded order became an outlet for others who wished to impose their desires through vigilantism. They spied on neighbors, issued threats to suspected wrongdoers, and took part in brutal acts of violence against their adversaries. Newspaper stories of Klan violence during the 1920s abound. Though many attacks were directed against African Americans, large numbers of Klan victims were white. Klansmen escaped prosecution for these and other offenses because eyewitnesses were too afraid to testify, grand juries refused to indict offenders, and law enforcement officials (many of whom were Klansmen themselves) often looked the other way.

The Klan moved into the realm of politics starting in 1922 after a faction led by Hiram Wesley Evans, a Dallas dentist who had served as leader of the Dallas klavern, gained control of the national organization. Unhappy with Simmons's leadership, Evans and his supporters supplanted the Klan's founders, eventually buying out

Those Who Joined the Klan

Though researchers have shown that some people joined the 1920s Ku Klux Klan for simple business reasons, as the group's leaders preached a message of "vocational Klanishness" whereby members were expected to trade with each other at the expense of nonmembers, the vast majority connected with the group because the Klan seemed capable of providing a strong counterforce to the many aspects of life appearing in 1920s America which greatly upset them. While providing a link to a glorified and mythologized past, the 1920s Klan attracted bewildered people, many of whom were bored or otherwise disgruntled with their mediocre lives, and promised to make them part of a cause greater than themselves. Others who disliked the Klan's many hate-filled statements and acts of violence nevertheless supported the order because they sympathized with its concerns, if not all of their deeds.

Regarding class membership of the Klan, a popular myth exists that this second manifestation of the Klan was primarily dominated by the "lower orders" of society. While the Klan did have lower-class members, scholars have shown that not only did the "klaverns" (local chapters) have modest numbers of upper-class individuals, the Klan's base also consisted largely of middle-class membership. Though many middle-class Americans would have nothing to do with the Klan, the fact remains that men with such varied occupations as store owners, dentists, druggists, realtors, salesmen, bookkeepers, clerks, skilled tradesmen, and farm owners joined the group in large numbers.

Simmons and banishing Edward Clarke and Liz Tyler. Afterwards, Evans pushed for Klan entry into Democratic Party politics across the nation. He also sought to change the Klan's image as a violent organization (somewhat ironic since he led the group of Klansmen who brutally attacked and branded a Dallas bellhop accused of crossing the color line during the previous year). Klan-supported candidates achieved notable successes in many states, winning control of the legislatures of Texas, Oklahoma, Oregon and Indiana, and helping to elect six governors and three U.S. Senators, not to mention thousands of candidates for local offices.

Reaching its pinnacle of support by the mid-1920s (symbolized by thousands of Klansmen triumphantly marching down Washington, D.C.'s Pennsylvania Avenue in 1926), external and internal forces eventually overwhelmed the Klan. Judges and district attorneys began to press grand juries for indictments against Klansmen for violent acts. Major state newspapers and national magazines published anti-Klan editorials and articles detailing Klan violence (especially against whites) and continuous accusations of political corruption. Many local chambers of commerce started to speak out against the Klan's lawlessness, and average citizens questioned the organization's growing political clout. Finally, many scandals involving prominent Klan leaders forever tarnished the group's image in the public's eyes. Some of the incidents involved financial impropriety while others involved personal failings or political corruption. The scandal that enveloped the Indiana Klan, however, included all these elements. After a jury convicted its leader, David Stephenson, of raping a woman while in a drunken rage—an incident that eventually led to her suicide by poisoning, but not before penning a detailed description of the attack that directly led to his arrest and conviction. The Klansman expected a pardon from the governor who he helped to get elected. When the anticipated clemency was not forthcoming, Stephenson released evidence of bribery and other illicit forms of corruption that disgraced the governor and many other state politicians. Demoralized as a result of such scandals and disillusioned with its growing number of electoral defeats, the Klan began a rapid descent. Continuous negative press about these events and ongoing citizen disgust with continuing acts of violence by renegade Klansmen delivered the final blows as prominent men began to depart from the organization. Eventually, the negative sentiment reached the point where the Klan itself began to become a victim of violence. In a sign of the changing times, unknown assailants detonated two bombs at the 4,000-seat klavern hall of Fort Worth (Texas) Klan No. 101, completely destroying the building.

RESURGENT POLITICAL CONSERVATISM

If as commonly portrayed, nontraditional and carefree attitudes characterized the 1920s, this reality would have been reflected in the successful election of countless unorthodox and even radical candidates for public office. Instead, the decade marked the resurgence of political conservatism and the waning of progressivism. To be sure, echoes of progressivism remained as indicated by efforts to enforce Prohibition, ratification of the woman suffrage amendment, creation of the Federal Extension Service to spread agricultural research and home economics information to the nation's farmers, and the passage of the Sheppard-Towner Maternity and Infancy Protection Act in 1921 providing federal funds to help states establish clinics providing instruction in pre-natal and infant health care (though Congress ended the program in 1929). Nevertheless, conservatism reigned, as reflected in Old Guard Republican control of Congress throughout the decade and three successive Republican presidents in the White House.

Election of 1920

With the infirmed Woodrow Wilson not seeking another term, both political parties sought to overcome internal divisions to select a winning candidate to succeed the president. The Democrats divided over three main candidates. William Gibbs McAdoo, a former Treasury Secretary and Wilson's son-in-law, enjoyed solid support from Prohibition supporters in the South and West. Opponents of Prohibition in the Northeast and Midwest supported two candidates—governors James M. Cox of Ohio and Al Smith of New York. After three days and 44 rounds of balloting at the Democratic National Convention in San Francisco, deals were struck to ensure Cox's nomination. Delegates then rallied behind Assistant Secretary of the Navy Franklin D. Roosevelt (a Wilson loyalist with the added benefit of being Theodore Roosevelt's cousin) for the vice president's slot.

The Republicans also were divided among three major candidates, though none of the contenders were able to win over the Republican National Convention to gain the nomination. General Leonard Wood, a former Army Chief of Staff who served as Teddy Roosevelt's superior officer in Cuba during the Spanish-American War, garnered support among those delegates who appreciated his bellicose stands on foreign policy and constant criticism of Woodrow Wilson. Frank Lowden, a popular governor from Illinois, enjoyed support from Midwestern states but was not very popular away from his native region. California Senator Hiram Johnson, Teddy Roosevelt's Bull

Moose running mate in the 1912 election, had the support of the party's progressive wing, but that faction was now definitely in the minority. Going into the convention, Wood and Lowden each had the support of a third of the delegates, with Johnson lagging behind followed by lesser candidates from states who hoped that their man would rise from the crowded field as the convention's compromise choice. One of these favorite-son candidates, Senator **Warren G. Harding** from the key state of Ohio, followed this path to emerge victorious after ten rounds of balloting. For the vice presidential nomination, the delegates chose Governor Calvin Coolidge of Massachusetts, a politician probably more well-known to the nation than Harding because of his anti-union stance during the Boston police strike of 1919.

Handsome and rather shallow, Harding did not have a hard time playing up to the part of a steady and modest Midwesterner running as an anti-Wilson candidate. Relying on his sizable advantage in funding, Harding spent most of the campaign in his hometown of Marion, Ohio, issuing press releases and giving occasional "front-porch talks," allowing him to control his message and avoid any slip-ups. The former small-town newspaper editor and his campaign manager, William Hays, correctly sensed that the nation after World War I wished to move away from grand idealistic crusades, both foreign and domestic. During a rare campaign appearance, Harding famously stated that the country's greatest need "was not nostrums but normalcy, not revolution but restoration"—Harding's way of calling for an end to reform and the return of calmer times at home as well as isolationism from troubles abroad. (He opposed the U.S. joining the League of Nations.) By contrast, Cox and Roosevelt, knowing that they were the underdogs, campaigned vigorously across the country making multiple speeches a day in an effort to outhustle the Republicans. Despite the prevailing national mood, the Democratic nominees favored continued domestic reform efforts and joining the League. Ultimately, Harding and Coolidge routed their opponents, winning just over 16 million votes (60 percent of the total) and 37 states for 404 electoral votes. Cox and Roosevelt received only 9 million (34 percent) and 11 states, all in the South. Socialist Party candidate Eugene Debs (still in prison) picked up 920,000 votes, his party's highest vote tally ever, but the Socialists' percent share of the total electorate was less than half of its 1912 peak performance. The Republicans picked up 61 House seats to hold a solid majority, in addition to gaining 10 Senate seats allowing the party to have a 59-37 edge—the largest majority held by any party in that chamber in over 100 years.

The Failed Harding Presidency

Harding made reduced government spending and the curtailment of business regulation top priorities for his administration. He supported passage of the Budget and Accounting Act of 1921, which gave presidents authority over the federal budget. The law created the Bureau of the Budget whose director was responsible for working with the president to develop a yearly budget to be submitted to Congress. The act also established the General Accounting Office to oversee and audit budget expenditures. During the course of his three-year presidency, Harding approved budgets that reduced federal government spending by almost 50 percent. He also supported lax regulation of corporations by appointing conservative administrators to the Federal Trade Commission, the Interstate Commerce Commission, the Federal Reserve Board, and other important government agencies. Harding appointed four new Supreme Court justices friendly to business interests, including Chief Justice William Howard Taft—the only ex-president ever to serve on the High Court. The Taft Court invalidated federal child labor laws and a state minimum wage law for women, issued numerous injunctions against labor unions, and made many pro-business rulings. To fill his Cabinet positions, Harding made some choices that the contemporary press generally celebrated. In addition to selecting Charles Evans Hughes to handle foreign affairs as Secretary of State, the president made two notable appointments who forcefully guided economic policy.

Banker and businessman **Andrew W. Mellon**, then the third-wealthiest man in America, became Secretary of the Treasury and immediately made an imprint on administration monetary policy. While advocating reduced government expenditures, he famously called for marked reductions in corporate and high-income taxes. On Mellon's suggestion, Congress eliminated excess-profits taxes from the war, lowered the estate tax, and ended a federal gift tax. With the support of Harding (and Coolidge after he became president), Congress gradually reduced the maximum marginal income tax rates from 73 percent in 1921 to 25 percent by 1926. Mellon supported these tax reductions in the belief that more money in the hands of businesses and wealthy individuals would spur investment by corporations and members of the upper class, leading to employment that would benefit the middle- and lower classes (what later became known as "trickle-down economics"). In the final analysis, while some sound investments occurred during the boom years of the mid-to-late 1920s, investors squandered much wealth on real estate booms, stock market speculation, and chasing elusive investment schemes, which contributed to financial instability by the end of the decade and helped spur the arrival of the Great Depression.

Commerce Secretary Herbert Hoover provided an element of business progressivism to the Harding Administration. A self-made millionaire who made his fortune as a mining engineer and consultant, Hoover served with distinction as Food Administrator and director of Belgian Relief during World War I before Harding asked him to lead the Commerce Department. Believing that unbridled laissez-faire capitalism led to inefficiency and waste, Hoover used his position to promote the idea of "associationalism," or cooperation between business and government via the establishment of trade associations. Through those private agencies, Hoover hoped that companies would standardize elements of their industries and share information on sales, production, and prices in an effort to set prices, reduce costs, and lessen the atmosphere of cutthroat competition. Hoover also sought to use the associations to spread information about business conditions and make recommendations on ways companies could produce more efficiently and pursue policies beneficial to the public interest. He hoped that government partnership with industry would help stabilize the American economy by ending boom-and-bust cycles. Overseeing the creation of hundreds of trade associations during the 1920s (he retained the Commerce post through Coolidge's administration), Hoover found himself often fighting efforts by businessmen to use the trade groups as a means of collusion to fix prices and allocate markets rather than the higher purposes that he sought.

Ultimately, most scholars view Harding's presidency negatively, one of the worse in history, and for good reasons. Though amiable and sympathetic to the plight of others (he freed Eugene Debs from prison, for example, supported anti-lynching legislation in Congress, spoke out against racial segregation, and signed the Sheppard-Towner Act into law), he possessed many flaws that have tarnished his legacy. Despite the Prohibition law, he drank heavily with friends at White House affairs. He also enjoyed many mistresses over the years—a practice that did not stop while president. In addition to these personal imperfections, his main trouble proved to be his intellectual limitations and his trusting nature. Harding was simply overwhelmed by the immensity of the job and heavily delegated responsibility to others. No harm was done when those he chose rose to the occasion and showed themselves to be exceptional administrators, such as Hughes and Hoover. Many other selections, however, proved to be selfish individuals who used their White House connections to engage in criminal activities that forever damaged Harding's presidency. While not condoning or encouraging such illegal activities, Harding bears much responsibility for naively selecting many trusted cronies and associates for high office and for lax oversight of his people.

Harding showed pride when he signed the bill creating the Veteran's Bureau to aid returning soldiers from World War I. Charles Forbes, the friend who the president entrusted to direct the new agency, however, proved to be a crook worthy of the two-year jail sentence he eventually received. Forbes was a construction company executive who Harding named to head the agency because of his war service and successful efforts to swing the Washington state delegation to his side at the Republican National Convention. Soon after his appointment, Forbes began to disgracefully line his pockets at every opportunity—selling

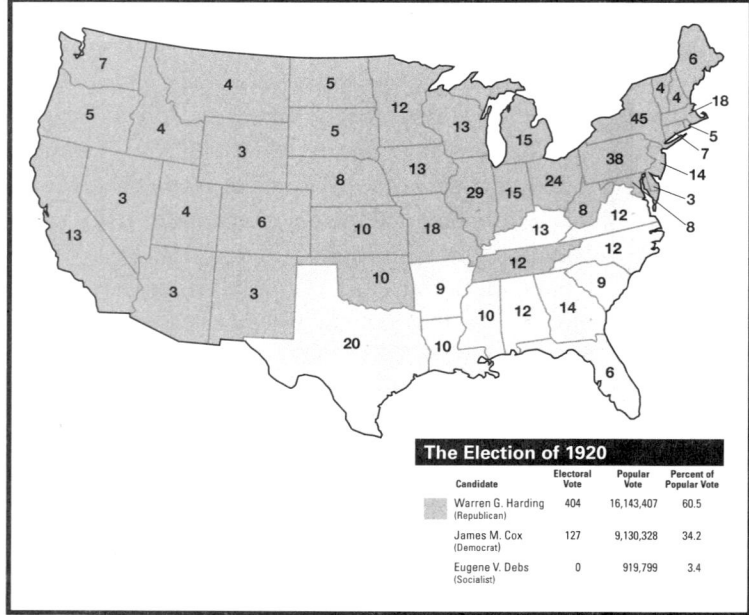

Map 22.1 The Election of 1920.

off medical supplies intended for veterans and pocketing the proceeds, receiving kickbacks from contractors for awarding them contracts to build veterans hospitals, and overbilling taxpayers for expensive jaunts across the country under the guise of hospital inspection trips. When he found out about the accusations, Harding demanded Forbes's resignation. The director obliged but not before bystanders had to pull Forbes away from Harding's choking grasp for embarrassing his administration.

One of Harding's closest associates, Harry Daugherty, also let the president down. The Ohio Republican Party operative received the post of Attorney General as a reward for managing Harding's efforts to receive the presidential nomination at the national convention. Along with his aide, Jesse Smith, Daugherty used his position to peddle influence for cash, receiving gifts and bribes in exchange for settling various government matters including pardons and disposing of confiscated German property from World War I. When rumors of investigations and indictments began to swirl, Smith shot himself. Daugherty remained at his post until fired by Harding's successor, Calvin Coolidge. He twice avoided conviction at trials when juries failed to reach definitive verdicts, probably due to his thoroughness in destroying evidence plus Smith no longer being alive to testify against him.

The **Teapot Dome Affair**, soon to become the most famous of the Harding administration scandals, led to the first ever conviction and imprisonment of a cabinet member. Harding's choice for Secretary of the Interior, Senator Albert Fall of New Mexico, sought to profit directly from his position by receiving money ($100,000 cash plus $200,000 in war bonds) from two oil company executives. In return, Fall arranged for control of government-owned petroleum reserves at Elk Hills in California and Teapot Dome in Wyoming to be transferred from the U.S. Navy to his department, before leasing the lands to the oil companies. When rumors swirled that lavish improvements had been made to Fall's New Mexico ranch, Senator Burton Wheeler of Montana began to investigate and eventually uncovered evidence of bribery. A jury convicted the Secretary, sentencing him to a year in prison with a $100,000 fine.

"Keeping Cool" With Coolidge

While in San Francisco on an exhausting speaking tour of the West Coast during the summer of 1923, the 57-year old Harding suffered a heart attack and died just two and a half years into his term, before the full extent of the crimes committed by members of his administration became public knowledge. In the middle of the night, Vice President **Calvin Coolidge** heard the sorrowful news while visiting his childhood home in Vermont. His father, a former state legislator, administered the oath of office under the light of a couple of kerosene lamps.

Early in his life, Coolidge had followed a political path similar to his father's before moving to higher office. Educated at Massachusetts' prestigious Amherst College, he studied law, serving in a series of local offices before being elected as a state legislator, lieutenant governor, and finally governor. Coolidge's sole claim to national fame occurred when he presented strong resistance to the Boston police strike of 1919, famously remarking: "There is no right to strike against the public safety by anybody, anywhere, any time." To the delight of conservatives across the country, he refused to rehire any of the policemen who picketed after the walkout ended. More than anything else he did as governor, his firm stand propelled his name for consideration for the vice presidency when Republicans convened for their 1920 national convention.

A staunch ideological conservative, Coolidge believed that the basic foundation of American social and political structure to be sound. In his mind, those who sought change were dangerous radicals who must be resisted. His belief that the role of government should be limited was unwavering, especially with regard to the regulation of business. Personally frugal and honest, he expected the same from government. He favored reduced expenditures and won over many in the public when he fired Harding's cronies from his administration while keeping respected members of the cabinet such as Mellon, Hoover, and Hughes.

Coolidge's removal of the tainted Harding personnel, the improvement of the American economy, and division among his opponents helped the new president in his bid to win a full term in 1924. Democrats divided between two of the major candidates from the 1920 campaign—William Gibbs McAdoo and Al Smith. McAdoo received substantial support from the still-powerful Ku Klux Klan and his delegates strongly objected to Smith's Catholicism. After ten days of debate and 103 rounds of balloting, party leaders negotiated a settlement—the respected Wall Street lawyer John W. Davis of West Virginia, Woodrow Wilson's solicitor general and a former ambassador to England, would receive the presidential nomination and Nebraska governor Charles W. Bryan (brother of William Jennings Bryan) would be the vice presidential nominee. Disgusted by the nomination of two pro-business conservatives by both major parties (Davis was a senior partner in a law firm whose most important client was J.P. Morgan and Company), progressive Wisconsin Senator Robert La Follette attempted to rally like-minded citizens into a grand campaign. Rather than creating a third party, which might hurt progressive Democrats and Republicans in congressional races, he entered the race as an independent candidate, hoping to attract progressives, old Populists, union members, and farmers through a program denouncing monopolies and corporate power, ending injunctions against labor unions, making the judiciary more responsive to public will through the election of federal judges, and government aid for the ailing agricultural sector of the economy. Coolidge easily won a term in his own right, with over 15 million popular votes and 382 electoral votes compared to Davis's 8 million popular votes and 136 electoral votes (all coming from the South.) La Follette's underfunded campaign finished a distant third, earning 4.8 million popular votes and only securing the electoral votes of his home state of Wisconsin. With the progressive spirit in check, the Republicans were ascendant, not only solidifying control of both houses of Congress but also continuing their state-level dominance of politics in states outside of the old Confederacy.

"The Business of America"

For all his faults and limitations, Warren Harding had sought to educate himself on many issues and otherwise learn the ropes of being president. Calvin Coolidge, however, exuded a self-confidence that bordered on smugness and often strove to do as little as possible in the White House. Embodying this attitude, he prided himself on sleeping twelve hours every night as well as finding time to take an afternoon nap. Reiterating his philosophy in characteristically simple terms, Coolidge once stated that "The chief business of the American people is business." To that end, Coolidge scaled back executive actions, not only deferring to Congress but also to the large corporations who could now expect little trouble in the form of "burdensome government regulations."

In an effort to scuttle the advances of regulatory reform, Coolidge appointed anti-progressives to head numerous government agencies. To serve on the Federal Trade Commission (FTC), for example, the president appointed former congressman William E. Humphrey, a lumber industry attorney who had previously made numerous speeches attacking the FTC. On Humphrey's watch, FTC commissioners greatly reduced the degree of corporate oversight, promoting private settlements with business rather than issuing cease-and-desist orders against law violators. In other agencies, the Coolidge administration's budget cuts led to greatly reduced staff and fewer investigations of questionable corporate activities. This phenomenon of agencies empowered under the law to oversee business activities being led by advocates for the very industries they are supposed to regulate—known as "agency capture" by political scientists—continues to exist to the present day and displays the limits of the progressive faith in regulation as the primary means of checking corporate power.

Coolidge's defense of free market capitalism and his belief in limited government led naturally to his resistance to efforts by farm representatives to develop plans to aid agriculture, the weakest sector of the economy throughout the decade. Though the war increased demand for products across the agricultural spectrum, the boom ended by 1920. The return of world agricultural production and domestic overproduction led to a dramatic drop in farm prices. In Washington, congressmen from agricultural states formed the "farm bloc" to promote the interests of their constituents. Farm organizations and spokesmen lobbied tirelessly for many proposals to aid the nation's farmers and agribusinesses. The most dynamic agrarian advocate during the 1920s proved to be George N. Peek, president of Illinois's Moline Plow Company. For many years a Midwestern leader in the sale of plows and other farming implements, Peek's company collapsed after the war because of declining sales. Arguing "You can't sell a plow to a busted farmer," Peek developed a plan that proposed to help the nation's farmers improve their incomes. His scheme would be developed into legislative form in the proposed **McNary-Haugen bills** first introduced in 1924. Rather than encourage decreased production of farm commodities to lower domestic supply and boost prices, Peek proposed that the U.S. government use its financial resources to buy up crop surpluses in order to remove them from the domestic market. The government could then dump the surplus overseas into global markets for whatever prices they could receive. The difference between the price that the government paid and the price sold in world markets would be made up by charging farmers an "equalization fee" in order to prevent the government from having to incur any losses. Peek convinced many farmers and their representatives that growers would see substantial increases in their incomes to offset the surcharges.

Despite passing both houses of Congress in 1927 and 1928, the McNary-Haugen bills never became law, having been vetoed twice by Coolidge who believed the proposals expanded the role of government beyond its just limits and were probably unconstitutional. Many farmers resented Coolidge's rebukes, leading some northern and western producers to start rethinking their political allegiance to the Republican Party. Though they failed to become law, the effort to pass the McNary-Haugen bills became a strong catalyst to the formation of the farm bloc and its subsequent efforts to aid agriculture in the 1930s and beyond.

The money flowing to the country's corporations and upper classes as a result of the tax cuts advocated by Treasury Secretary Mellon spurred some sound investment by businesses and rich investors during the mid-to-late Twenties, but the flood of funds to the wealthy also led to wild speculation in real estate and the stock markets, eventually destabilizing the entire economy by the end of the decade. The greatest example of rampant real estate gambling took place in Florida, a state lightly populated before World War I (Miami had only 5400 residents in 1910). As investors spent billions developing areas of coastal Florida in the early 1920s and began publicizing the benefits of warm water and sunshine to chilled middle-class Midwesterners and residents living in the Northeast, a flood of migrants arrived via the automobile. Land prices skyrocketed as Florida's population swelled from 968,000 in 1920 to 1.2 million in 1925 (with Miami growing to over 130,000). The boom led many to participate in the action without ever going to the state, choosing instead to gamble by purchasing residential and commercial lots from agents soliciting the sales as a sound investment with huge potential profits. In a practice to be replicated in the stock markets, many salesmen enticed buyers to place only a portion of the purchase price down with subsequent monthly installments and interest paid later. This so-called "margin buying" allowed more investors to participate in the mania, with the enlarged pool of available money leading to land prices being bid even higher. The bubble finally burst when the high level of funds necessary to maintain the speculation began to recede. Already declining, the *coup de grace* to the Florida land boom occurred in September 1926 when a powerful hurricane slammed into Miami, killing 400 people, leaving 50,000 homeless, and destroying in the public's mind the illusion that the Florida peninsula was a pristine paradise. Thousands of investors lost their fortunes as the number of tourists and investors dried up.

As the Florida economy declined in the late-Twenties, the New York Stock Exchange surged with stock prices reaching record high levels. During the first two-thirds of the 1920s, stock prices displayed steady growth matching the rise in corporate profits. From 1928 through most of 1929, however, the massive gains did not reflect company performance and completely lost track of rational justification. Similar to the tremendous rise in Florida land prices, the sharp increase in stock prices mostly reflected the influx of funds into the market as investors simply bid up prices based on their belief that they would continue to rise, leading to amazing profits. Investors entered the fray with low margins, securing loans from brokers who charged them 20 percent interest and received commissions for each share bought or sold. (Buyers did not mind

such charges if, for example, they bought Montgomery Ward stock at $117 per share in January 1928 and still held it in January 1929 when its value had risen to $440). Bankers poured billions into the stock markets, lending funds to brokers and purchasing stocks themselves. Though some began to call for more restraint, these pleas mostly fell on deaf ears. The consequences of Andrew Mellon's policies, heartily endorsed by Coolidge, would not become fully evident until the end of 1929 when the chickens came home to roost during the presidency of his successor, Herbert Hoover.

THE ELECTION OF HOOVER AND THE GREAT CRASH

Calvin Coolidge surprised many in 1927 when he announced that he would not seek another term as president. Rather than having foresight that the economy might start sinking and he wished to jump ship before that occurred, Coolidge simply believed he had led the country in the proper direction and wanted to enjoy life with his family. Commerce Secretary **Herbert Hoover** quickly emerged as the leading candidate for the Republican nomination. More progressive in his thought than Harding and Coolidge, many party leaders hoped another more conservative candidate would emerge, or perhaps Coolidge could be persuaded to run again. When neither occurred and Hoover clearly showed popularity with the voting public, most resistance to his candidacy evaporated. Hoover was nominated on the first ballot at the Republican National Convention.

On the Democratic side, the urban northeastern faction of the party finally succeeded in promoting their favorite candidate, New York's four-term governor Al Smith, to the presidential nomination at the party's national convention held in Houston, Texas. A New York City politician who opposed Prohibition, Smith's candidacy troubled the party's rural, southern, and western elements, but lacking a sound alternative they fell into line and elected him on the first ballot. Smith made history by becoming the first Catholic to win a major party's nomination. Arkansas Senator Joseph Robinson, a Prohibition supporter, balanced the ticket by securing the vice presidential slot.

Hoover's popularity drove the race. Benefiting from his reputation as a sound administrator and humanitarian through his direction of the Food Administration and aid to war refugees, his organization of relief for victims of the early-1920s Russian famine and Mississippi River Flood of 1927, and his supervision of the Commerce Department under Harding and Coolidge convinced a

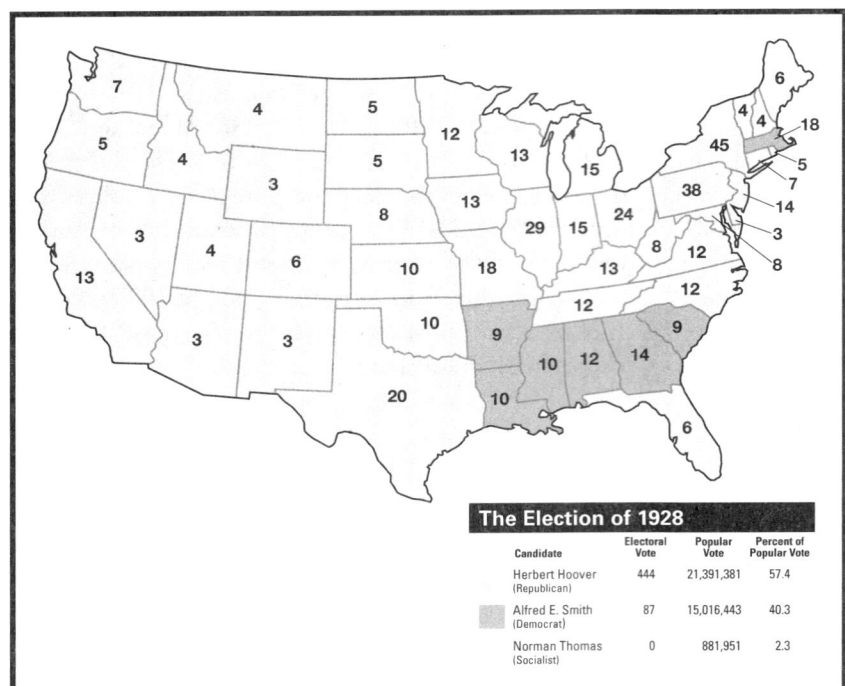

Map 22.2 The Election of 1928.

The Election of 1928			
Candidate	Electoral Vote	Popular Vote	Percent of Popular Vote
Herbert Hoover (Republican)	444	21,391,381	57.4
Alfred E. Smith (Democrat)	87	15,016,443	40.3
Norman Thomas (Socialist)	0	881,951	2.3

majority of Americans that he was simply the most qualified man for the job. Though known as a progressive who supported many state-level reforms while serving as governor of New York, Smith chose to run a conservative campaign, wooing corporate donors by promising a more pro-business administration than Hoover would provide. With the regulation of business not an issue in the campaign, Smith's adversaries focused their fire on his Catholicism, opposition to Prohibition, and background as a Tammany Hall politician in New York City. Hoover ultimately prevailed handily, providing Republicans with their third consecutive presidential victory by securing 21 million popular votes and dominating the map with 444 electoral votes. Though the Republican brand name was still largely tarnished in the South, Hoover's reputation, when coupled with general prosperity plus the Prohibition and Catholic issues, helped him carry Texas, Florida, North Carolina, Virginia, and Tennessee. Smith did well in northern urban areas and among discontented western farmers but managed to only win 15 million popular votes, with his 87 electoral votes coming from the Deep South, Massachusetts, and Rhode Island.

Hoover enjoyed a nine-month honeymoon period as president before the bottom fell out of the economy. To be sure, warning signs were already evident even before the stock market crash of late-October 1929. By the summer of 1929, consumer spending declined to the point that economists noted the country was entering a recession. Producers of many items began to experience a condition known as "saturated markets," whereby the pool of potential buyers for products that had helped sustain

prosperity during the boom period of the decade (such as cars, homes, household appliances, and radios) had begun to dry up, at least for levels necessary to sustain economic growth. Certainly not all Americans possessed these items, but those who had the funds and were inclined to buy them (even with installment buying plans in place) had already done so, pointing to an even larger structural problem with the American economy—the chronic maldistribution of wealth. Simply stated, too much of the nation's wealth had accrued to the top and not enough reached the workers (who were also the consumers) to keep the economy going. With unsold inventories beginning to rise, companies began to lay off workers, adding to the severity of the situation. Meanwhile, average stock prices continued to set records for a few more months.

The infamous stock market "crash" finally came in the last week of October, 1929. As more brokers began to place sell orders for their clients, the general consensus among dealers on the New York Stock Exchange was that speculators who had created the bubble were fearing it was about to burst and wanted to get out while they were still ahead. On October 24 —"Black Thursday"—sell orders rained down from the moment trading commenced, leading to plunging prices. By the closing bell, stockholders had lost $3 billion. Major banks and brokerages purchased several millions of dollars worth of stocks in an effort to instill confidence and quiet the panic, but the effort calmed the situation for only a few days. On "Black Tuesday," October 29, the bottom fell out as the torrent of selling continued, leading to a $10 billion loss for investors. Within three weeks, average stock prices had dropped 50 percent. The decline would continue unabated for the next four years—with average stock prices declining to one-fifth their pre-crash value by early 1933. Investors lost billions; many banks and corporations went out of business. As a crisis mentality soon overwhelmed the economy, those banks still solvent refused to lend funds to companies and individuals, adding to the strain. Businesses that had not gone bankrupt began to shut down production and lay off workers in an effort to stay afloat, contributing to the economy's downward spiral.

Though the stock market crash did not cause the Great Depression, the extreme market correction smashed confidence, ruined many institutions, and accelerated the downturn by exposing the severe fundamental flaws in the structure of the 1920s economy. In ordinary times, the nation would have benefited greatly from the diverse experiences and exceptional organizational skills of Herbert Hoover, who might have gone down in history as an above-average president with many noteworthy accomplishments. The Depression, however, defined his presidency. Though far from a supporter of laissez-faire (as Calvin Coolidge, who would have done nothing with his office to correct the economic decline), Hoover's reliance on the tenets of voluntary cooperation to combat the Depression (to be detailed in the next chapter), instead of mobilizing the resources of the federal government, would prove to be inadequate to the task. After four years of failure, the nation was ready for bolder efforts under the auspices of Franklin Roosevelt and the New Deal.

Table 22.1

Emerging Modernity and Persistent Traditionalism during the 1920s

Elements of Modernity	Elements of Tradition and Reaction
"Ballyhoo" behavior/Record-breaking	Restrictions on dress, dancing, and movies
Jazz music	Zane Grey novels
The "flapper" lifestyle	Religious fundamentalism
The Charleston and tango; freestyle dancing	Prohibition of alcohol
Expressionism and Surrealist art	Immigration restrictions
Freudian psychoanalysis	Political conservatism at the national level
Promotion of African American pride	Rise of the Second Ku Klux Klan
Art Deco architecture	Red Scare raids

Chronology

1918 World War I ends.

1919 18th Amendment (Prohibition) ratified.
KDKA in Pittsburgh becomes the first U.S. radio station to broadcast regularly scheduled programming.

1920 Warren Harding elected president.
19th Amendment (Woman Suffrage) ratified.

1921 American Birth Control League is organized.
Emergency Quota Act passes Congress.

1922 Secretary of the Interior Albert Fall begins secretly leasing oil reserves at Teapot Dome, Wyoming.
William Hays begins his leadership of the Motion Picture Association of America.

1923 Aimee Semple McPherson opens the 5,300-seat Angelus Temple in Los Angeles, CA.
Equal Rights Amendment is proposed in Congress.
Marcus Garvey convicted of mail fraud.
Warren Harding dies.

1924 Calvin Coolidge elected to a full term as president.
National Origins Act passes Congress.

1925 The Scopes "Monkey Trial" takes place in Dayton, Tennessee.
Indiana Klan leader David Stephenson convicted of murdering his secretary.

1926 Gertrude Ederle becomes the first woman to swim across the English Channel.
Maximum federal income tax rate reduced to 25 percent.
Major hurricane hits Miami, Florida commencing the decline of the Florida land boom.

1927 Charles Lindbergh becomes the first pilot to fly solo across the Atlantic Ocean.
Marcus Garvey deported.
Sacco and Vanzetti executed.

1928 McNary-Haugen bill vetoed for a second time by Calvin Coolidge.
Herbert Hoover elected president.

1929 Shipwreck Kelly sits atop a flagpole in Atlantic City, New Jersey for a record 49 days.
Stock Market Crash.

SUGGESTED READINGS

Charles C. Alexander, *The Ku Klux Klan in the Southwest* (1995).

Frederick Lewis Allen, *Only Yesterday: An Informal History of the 1920s,* (1931).

A. Scott Berg, *Lindbergh,* (1998).

David M. Chalmers, *Hooded Americanism: The First Century of the Ku Klux Klan: 1865 to the Present,* (1965).

Kendrick A. Clements, *The Life of Herbert Hoover: Imperfect Visionary, 1918-1928* (2010).

Edmund David Cronon, *Black Moses: The Story of Marcus Garvey and the Universal Negro Improvement Association,* (1955).

Paula S. Fass, *The Damned and the Beautiful: American Youth in the 1920s,* (1977).

John Kenneth Galbraith, *The Great Crash: 1929,* (1988).

John D. Hicks, *Republican Ascendency, 1921-1933* (1960).

Kenneth T. Jackson, *The Ku Klux Klan in the City, 1915-1930,* (1992).

David M. Kennedy, *Birth Control in America: The Career of Margaret Sanger* (1970).

Aileen S. Kraditor, *The Ideas of the Woman Suffrage Movement, 1890-1920,* (1981).

Edward J. Larson, *Summer for the Gods: The Scopes Trial and America's Continuing Debate over Science and Religion,* (1997).

David Levering Lewis, *When Harlem Was in Vogue,* (1989).

Nancy MacLean, *Behind the Mask of Chivalry: The Making of the Second Ku Klux Klan,* (1994).

Donald R. McCoy, *Calvin Coolidge: The Quiet President,* (1967).

Roderick Nash, *The Nervous Generation: American Thought, 1917-1930,* (1990).

Michael E. Parrish, *Anxious Decades: America in Prosperity and Depression, 1920-1941,* (1992).

Thomas R. Pegram, *Battling Demon Rum: The Struggle for a Dry America, 1800-1933,* (1998).

Andrew Sinclair, *Era of Excess: A Social History of the Prohibition Movement* (1964).

Review Questions

1. Describe many aspects of the Roaring Twenties lifestyle. How widespread were these behaviors among Americans during the decade?

2. How did life change for American women during the 1920s and how did life remain the same when compared with the previous two decades?

3. Describe the impact of the Great Migration on African Americans and the United States.

4. Describe ways in which many Americans attempted to defend traditional values during the 1920s.

5. In what ways did Warren Harding and Calvin Coolidge promote business interests during the 1920s?

Glossary of Important People and Concepts

William Jennings Bryan
Calvin Coolidge
Dance Marathons
Eighteenth Amendment (Prohibition)
"Flappers"
Henry Ford
Fundamentalism
Marcus Garvey
Warren G. Harding
Harlem Renaissance
William H. Hays
Herbert Hoover
Jazz
Ku Klux Klan
Charles A. Lindbergh
Aimee Semple McPherson
Andrew W. Mellon
National Origins Act
Nineteenth Amendment (Woman Suffrage)
Alice Paul
"Roaring Twenties"
Scopes "Monkey Trial"
"Sick industries"
Billy Sunday
Teapot Dome Scandal

In a rare photograph showing the president in a wheelchair,
Franklin Roosevelt enjoys a moment of relaxation with his dog Fala and
Ruthie Bie, the granddaughter of the caretaker of FDR's estate in Hyde Park, New York.
Photo by Margaret Suckley

Chapter Twenty-three

THE GREAT DEPRESSION AND THE NEW DEAL

On the night of October 30, 1938, many Americans who tuned in late for the NBC radio network's national broadcast of Orson Welles's **Mercury Theater on the Air** suddenly became transfixed by an absolute horror their minds could not comprehend. Was it really true? Had Martians really landed in the United States? Yet, the unbelievable seemed to be unfolding right before their ears. The orchestral music show they turned on was being constantly interrupted by "news reports" that strange gas eruptions on Mars had earlier been observed by "famous Princeton astronomer Richard Pierson" who had been monitoring the red planet. Soon thereafter, a space vessel that had been spotted entering the Earth's atmosphere landed near Grovers Mill, New Jersey. As police and onlookers gathered, a reporter described the ship opening up, followed by the emergence on an alien who soon began firing heat rays killing most of those around. Military personnel arrived on the scene, but they too were vaporized. A slew of "journalists" and "government representatives" sporadically broke into the show to report that other landings were taking place near major metropolitan areas. New York City was under direct attack, as relayed by eyewitnesses who described the Martians laying waste to everything in their path as thousands of citizens plunged into the East River in a desperate attempt to escape the onslaught.

Forty minutes into the show (which had no commercial interruptions), the network broke for station identification followed by the show's producer Orson Welles, playing the role of Professor Pierson, giving a twenty-minute soliloquy summarizing events that he explained had led to the demise of the alien invaders. After destroying much of New York City, it turns out that the Martians had no protection against bacteria and other earthly pathogens. Welles then reminded his audience that it was Halloween eve and that the play—a modern adaptation of H.G. Welles's classic novel **War of the Worlds**—was the Mercury Theater's way of "dressing up in a sheet and saying Boo!"

Though it had not been his intention, the combination of Welles's creative use of real-life radio news techniques and the reaction of those not understanding the show's premise (many of whom made frantic calls to others not listening to the radio) generated a brief panic in many parts of the country. Police departments across the United States later reported getting inundated with phone calls from concerned citizens seeking confirmation of the invasion or reassurance that all was well. Some citizens armed themselves with a determination to defend their homes, while others hopped into their cars and headed for the hills. One motorist rode through Baltimore, Maryland honking his horn as he desperately tried to sound the alarm. A Broadway play ended abruptly in New York City as word spread among the theater's audience who soon fled for the exits. In Minneapolis, Minnesota, a woman reportedly ran into a church yelling that Armageddon had arrived—she heard it on the radio. A squad of New Jersey state troopers hastily dispatched to the invasion's initial landing site, Grovers Mill, found nothing astir.

Though the scare abated a few hours after the end of the broadcast, news of the previous night's fright became a national news story over the next few days, helped by a front-page story in **The New York Times**. Many historians and sociologists now believe a panic no doubt occurred among *many people in different parts of the country, but that the extent of any true hysteria has been very much overblown. Later studies estimated that only 2 percent of the national public listening to the radio at the time tuned into the show, or about 6 million people. Of that number, maybe a million initially believed the broadcast to be real, though most did no more than call local police or their neighbors. The researchers argue that the print media is to blame for greatly exaggerating its magnitude in a concerted effort to discredit radio as a medium of communication. Feeling the effects of competition cutting greatly into their already-shrinking advertising revenue due to the Great Depression, newspapers and magazines tried to impart the sense that radio networks were run by irresponsible people who sensationalized their programming to attract audiences. By contrast, print was supposedly a bedrock institution employing professionals that the public could trust.*

Much has been written by historians of the large role played by radio and film to provide Americans affordable entertainment as they struggled to get by during the Great Depression. Weekend attendance at the theaters as well as daily radio broadcasts helped millions temporarily escape from the demoralizing impact of the economic downturn. In this instance, however, for some at least, even that medium provided no comfort.

The stock market crash of October 1929, followed by a prolonged decline in stock prices and real estate values and a profound rise in the unemployment rate, quickly evaporated the economic growth and prosperity generated during the 1920s, however unequally distributed that wealth may have been. The 1930s would become one of the most critical eras in American history, as the nation grappled with the unprecedented economic downturn. Faith in the country's economic system and its government was rattled to its core as the nation faced its most challenging crisis since the Civil War.

In early 1929, Herbert Hoover, the incredibly popular incoming president, seemed the most qualified man in America to lead the country to unprecedented heights of prosperity. During his March 1929 inaugural address, he confidently expressed the prevailing faith in the ability of modern industrial capitalism to provide for all citizens as he extolled: "We in America today are nearer to the final triumph over poverty than ever before in the history of any land. The poorhouse is vanishing among us." Though acknowledging that the nation had not yet achieved that lofty goal, he proclaimed, "given a chance to go forward with the policies of the last eight years, we shall soon with the help of God be in sight of the day when poverty will be banished from this nation." Those words would surely

come back to haunt Hoover—within eight months of his speech, the American economy began its rapid descent, ultimately collapsing into the worse financial crisis in the country's history.

Within four years, Hoover's active but limited efforts to turn the economic tide led to his transformation into a much-maligned figure with little chance at re-election. The previously-patient but now disillusioned electorate in 1932 would reject Hoover and turn the reins of government over to Franklin Delano Roosevelt, the Democratic governor of New York and distant cousin of former progressive Republican president Theodore Roosevelt, who promised a more active federal government response—a "New Deal" for the American people. After the 1930s, the American people would often look to their national government to stabilize the economy and correct downward turns if they should occur, as well as blame the party in power if the economy failed to be corrected. The New Deal would lay the foundation for postwar liberalism, which replaced the laissez-faire business attitude of the post-Civil War era as the dominant ideology in American political culture for the next 50 years.

THE PRESIDENCY OF HERBERT HOOVER

The Technocrat as President

Though the presidency was his first elected political office, **Herbert Hoover** seemed poised and ready to overcome any difficult challenges that he and the nation might encounter on his watch. Born into a devoutly Quaker family in rural Iowa, both of his parents died by the time he was 10 years old. The orphan moved to Oregon to be raised by his maternal uncle who later sent him to the newly opened Stanford University in California where he graduated with a degree in geology. Hoover began a successful career as a world-respected mining engineer by working for companies in California, Australia, and China before starting his own consultation firm and publishing a popular textbook on mining principles. A millionaire by the age of forty, Hoover was overly proud of his accomplishments, stating at one point "If a man has not made a million dollars by the time he is forty, he is not worth much." Still, he longed to do more with his life and received his opportunity with the arrival of the First World War. Before the United States' entry into the conflict, Hoover gained notoriety for heading a private relief agency that fed over ten million civilians living in German-occupied Belgium. After American entry into World War I, President Woodrow Wilson appointed Hoover to direct the U. S. Food Administration. Under his directorship, Hoover oversaw the nation's food supply and was able to increase agricultural production while decreasing domestic consumption by appealing to voluntarism rather than asking Congress to impose rationing by law as would occur during World War II. Upon the conflict's conclusion, Hoover added to his reputation as an efficient organizer and great humanitarian by leading a series of relief efforts to provide food for millions of civilians across war-ravaged sections of Europe. The Republican victor in the election of 1920, Warren Harding nominated Hoover to the position of Secretary of Commerce. Remaining at the post through the Coolidge Administration until he sought the presidency in 1928, showed his connection to the strain of progressivism that promoted efficiency by endeavoring to work with the business community to eliminate waste, reduce accidents, lessen conflict with organized labor, encourage the standardization of products within various industries, and promote American exports. Because he championed efficiency, Hoover thought of himself as a progressive, but his reluctance to use the government as an agency of change and reform would inevitably alienate him from pre-war social progressives.

Hoover's initial responses to the Great Depression were consistent with his firm belief that Americans could come together and organize cooperatively to overcome the economic downturn. This view included a limited but active role for government. Unlike those who held to the laissez-faire ideology of non-government involvement in the economy (his predecessor Calvin Coolidge would have done nothing to attempt to counter the downward spiral), Hoover believed that the government, without assuming direct responsibility, nevertheless possessed the means to bring private groups and individuals together in ways that could stabilize the economy and return the nation to prosperity. He sought to utilize his position as president to encourage businessmen, workers, farm groups, charities, and ordinary citizens to volunteer their energies, resources, and time in a variety of ways to work for the common good and generate economic recovery.

During the first three years of the crisis, Hoover turned to these principles of **voluntary cooperation** that he had first practiced as head of the Food Administration and later as Secretary of Commerce. Because his efforts seemed to pale in comparison with his successor, Franklin Roosevelt, historians and Americans in general for many years came to associate Hoover with ineffectiveness and inaction. Though the former conclusion was true (the economy only got worse as Hoover's presidency continued), the latter certainly was not, as the president spent long hours every day seeking new ways within his constrained philosophy to turn around the downward trajec-

Herbert Hoover

tory of the economy. To help stop the decline and spur recovery, Hoover sponsored forums such as the National Business Survey Conference, hoping to convince the heads of the major corporations to maintain production and refrain from further wage cuts and job layoffs despite piling inventories of unsold goods. Cutting back, he argued, would only drive the economy further down. Initially, the president was successful in receiving promises from corporate leaders to give his approach a chance. From union leaders, he received further voluntary pledges not to go on strike or demand wage increases until the economy righted itself. Additionally, governors and mayors of large cities vowed, despite declining tax revenues, not to reduce or end work projects in the hope of not adding to the growing national unemployment problem. Hoover convinced a group of New York bankers to form the National Credit Corporation—a pool of $500 million of the private financial institutions' own money to be used to aid smaller banks in distress. For agriculture, a new agency, the Federal Farm Board, issued credit to growers so they could form commodity cooperatives to reduce costs as well as create so-called "stabilization corporations" to store crops in order to temporarily keep them off the market in a desperate effort to halt the decline in farm prices.

Hoover saw one of his roles as being the nation's cheerleader, charged with maintaining the nation's morale. He delivered numerous speeches with optimistic themes and became the first president to experiment with radio addresses to the public to disseminate information and elevate spirits. It was Hoover who popularized the term "depression" to imply the up-and-down cyclical nature of economic activity rather than the more popular expression "panic" to describe an economic downturn, because he felt the term unnecessarily promoted fear. Hoover also made the president's office a major publicity agency for private relief efforts as he exhorted his fellow Americans to help those in need by donating money and volunteering their time to churches, charity organizations, and local soup kitchens. Between 1929 and 1932, donations for relief increased eightfold, a remarkable accomplishment by any previous standard, but ultimately not enough to aid more than a small fraction of the destitute.

Viewing the economy as a national system, Hoover was the first president in history to attack a national economic slump systematically. Thus, he has been characterized by many historians as the "last of the old presidents and the first of the new." Unfortunately for Hoover and the nation, his reliance on voluntarism proved to be a woefully inadequate approach given the size of the emergency. As the economic climate deteriorated, businessmen and bankers began to disappoint Hoover by failing to maintain their voluntary pledges. Their refusal to fully accept his ideas helped to plunge the economy ever deeper into disaster.

The Deepening Depression

Along with the economy, President Hoover by mid-1931 seemed to experience a grim personal decline. As his sense of control began to slip, he became more isolated, disillusioned, and frustrated by the lack of sustained positive movement in the economy as home and farm mortgage foreclosures, business bankruptcies, and bank collapses only increased. Particularly disturbing was the abandonment of his cooperative approach by corporate leaders. As a consequence, unemployment in the industrial sector continued to rise as corporations continued to cut costs by laying off workers. By 1932, Hoover had become so overwhelmed and filled with despair that the White House seemed to some observers to resemble a funeral parlor. Never a charmer, the president looked, as one visitor remarked, as if a rose would wilt at his touch. Reluctantly, Hoover began to accept the necessity of direct government intervention to aid some desperate corporations and banks in order to prevent their failure, which he feared would trigger a huge ripple effect that would further damage the fragile economy. In January 1932, Hoover asked Congress to establish the **Reconstruction Finance Corporation (RFC)** to provide $1.5 billion in low-interest government loans to ailing banks and corporations—the largest peacetime intervention ever by the federal government in U. S. history. In addition, the Home Loan Bank Board, also established in 1931, offered funds to savings and loans, mortgage companies, and other financial institutions that lent out money for home construction projects. Meanwhile, to ease the pressures on international finances, Hoover issued a moratorium on the payment of debts owed to the United States by its former allies in the war against Germany.

Despite these breaks with his reliance on voluntary cooperation, Hoover refused to offer the same generosity to suffering Americans. He detested the notion of offering direct federal relief to citizens in dire need. The idea of creating a welfare state never crossed the president's mind. Every American, he believed, must ultimately rely for survival on his or her own efforts. To give money to the poor, he insisted, would destroy their desire to work. Nevertheless, in the summer of 1932, during the midst of his re-election campaign, he succumbed to political pressure and signed the Emergency Relief and Construction Act, which provided $2 billion in federal emergency loans to the states for the creation of work relief projects, most notably Boulder (later Hoover) Dam in the Black Canyon of the Colorado River along the Arizona-Nevada border. Viewing the law as a temporary measure to provide short-term relief, he remained firmly opposed to large-scale and permanent expenditures for government relief.

By 1932, the president's policies lay in shambles. The exceptionally high Hawley-Smoot Tariff, which Hoover had signed into law in 1930, only intensified a growing global depression by contributing to the curtailment of international trade through the virtual locking-out of foreign manufactured goods from American markets, leading countries to enact retaliatory policies that greatly hurt American exporters. Employers discarded their programs for spreading the workload, leading to over 12 million people walking the streets (over 25 percent of the working population). Local relief agencies, both public and private, were overwhelmed by the immensity of the crisis. As commodity prices fell, the Federal Farm Board's stabilization corporations simply ran out of funds, leading farmers to dump their crops on an already-glutted market, which drove prices down to record lows. In some Midwestern county seats, men with shotguns closed local courts so that their neighbors' mortgages could not be foreclosed. By early 1932, a large groundswell of resentment toward the president had emerged.

Occupying Washington: The Bonus Army

In the spring of 1932, a group of unemployed veterans sought to bring pressure upon the government to redress their grievances. In 1924, Congress had authorized a

The Bonus Expeditionary Force encamped on the Anacostia Flats, southeast of the Capitol, in Washington, D.C. 1932.

$1,000 pension payment (popularly called the "bonus") for World War I veterans in the form of compensation certificates that would mature in 1945. Desperate for help and fearing that they may not be alive in a dozen more years to see these payments become a reality, the former soldiers organized to demand payment immediately, even in discounted form, to help them get through their current hard times. Spearheaded by a group from Portland, Oregon, veterans organized and started out on a cross-country trek to Washington, D.C. Harkening back to the American Expeditionary Force of the Great War, they called themselves the Bonus Expeditionary Force, but the media preferred to label them the "**Bonus Army**," as a comparison to Coxey's Army of unemployed laborers who marched to the nation's capital in 1894 to demand government work projects for the nation's unemployed during the last major depression to hit the country from 1893-1897. As the destitute veterans traveled eastward, many surviving on handouts from sympathetic citizens, their ranks grew to over 20,000 protesters. Upon their arrival in Washington, D.C., the Bonus Marchers held a rally on the steps of the Capitol and petitioned Congress for early payment of the promised bonus. The House of Representatives voted to support a bill with such a provision sponsored by Representative Wright Patman of Texas, but the Senate rejected the legislation. President Hoover, who had refused to meet with any of the protesters' leaders, agreed with the Senate's decision. To him, the gathering represented not a plea for help but a sign that potential revolution was on the horizon.

Some veterans and their families left the capital, but the majority of them decided to stay and keep their protest alive by setting up a make-shift encampment at Anacostia Flats along the Potomac River and occupied abandoned government buildings within the city. By July 1932, after

two months in Washington, D.C., the Bonus Army was becoming desperate for help. Hoover, however, refused to budge. Finally, after a group of veterans staying in the buildings resisted eviction and scuffled with local police (most of whom were actually sympathetic to the veterans' plight), Hoover used the incident to call on federal troops led by Army Chief of Staff Douglas MacArthur to remove the troublemakers. Given vague orders on how to accomplish the mission, General MacArthur (who believed that all the protesters were communists when in fact only a handful were) chose to send a strong message to other potential agitators by attacking the veterans' Anacostia encampment with a large show of force that included the deployment of tanks. In the process of brutally razing the tents and dispersing the veterans, more than fifty were wounded, over one hundred arrested, and one infant died after inhaling tear gas.

Though some media outlets and private citizens approved of the provocative act, the news that impoverished veterans and their families had been attacked in the nation's capital intensified an already growing anti-Hoover sentiment. Those who suspected that the president simply did not care about the plight of the poor and dispossessed were now convinced that Hoover was a callous man, willing to use force to suppress cries for help. His days in the White House were numbered.

The Election of 1932

By 1932, the majority of Americans were desperate and ready to move on from Herbert Hoover, often blaming him for their troubles in bitter, personal ways. Homeless families who set up groups of makeshift hovels in major cities across the country began calling their shantytowns "Hoovervilles." Penniless individuals walked around town

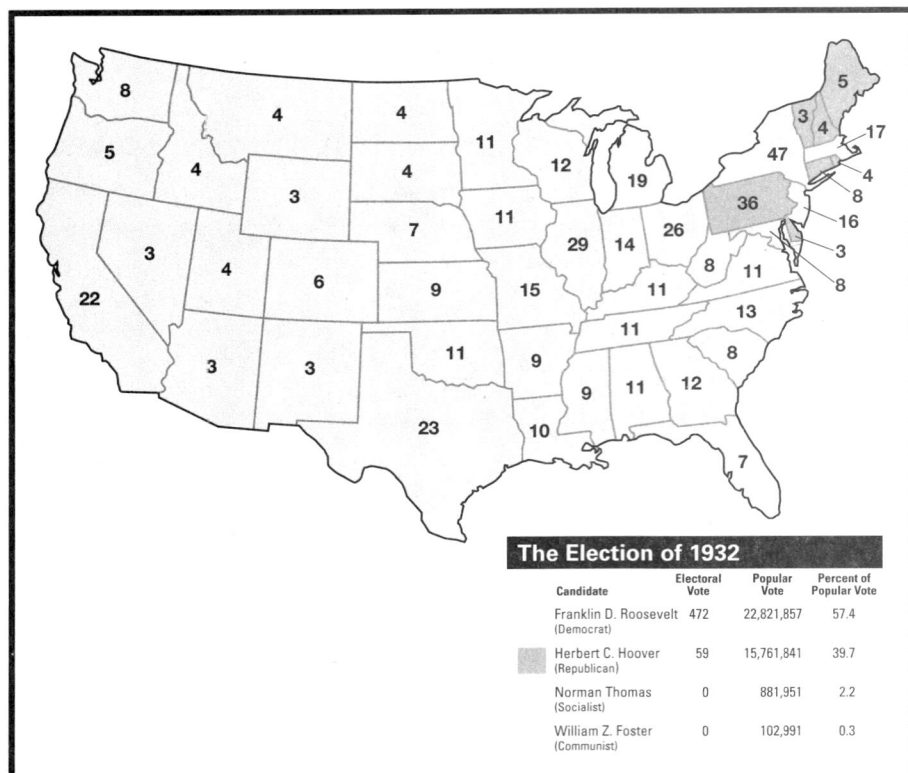

Map 23.1 The Election of 1932.

The Election of 1932

Candidate	Electoral Vote	Popular Vote	Percent of Popular Vote
Franklin D. Roosevelt (Democrat)	472	22,821,857	57.4
Herbert C. Hoover (Republican)	59	15,761,841	39.7
Norman Thomas (Socialist)	0	881,951	2.2
William Z. Foster (Communist)	0	102,991	0.3

with their pockets pulled out to display their "Hoover flags." A humane man with great administrative skills who probably would have been an above-average president in quieter times, Hoover lacked the political instincts, flexibility, and inspirational leadership necessary to rally the nation and its resources to combat the Great Depression. Further, after four years of halfway measures, Hoover opened the door for a more activist approach by a successor who might rise to defeat his re-election bid. In 1932, the American electorate indeed turned completely against the Republicans and their president. Hoover received only 39.6 percent of the popular vote and just 59 (of 531) electoral votes. The Democratic Party nominee, Governor Franklin D. Roosevelt of New York, won a resounding victory by promising government help for unemployed laborers and hurting farmers as well as the nation's bankers and businessmen. Ahead in the polls throughout the race, Roosevelt refused to be pinned down on too many specifics, preferring to keep his options open and to focus on building confidence in his ability to lead the nation out of the morass. At the Democratic National Convention in Chicago, Roosevelt broke precedent by flying to the Windy City to accept his party's nomination in person. In the conclusion of his acceptance speech, the nominee proclaimed: "I pledge you, I pledge myself, to a new deal for the American people. Let us all here assembled constitute ourselves prophets of a new order of competence and of courage. This is more than a political campaign;

it is a call to arms. Give me your help, not to win votes alone, but to win in this crusade to restore America to its own people." Many news outlets quickly latched onto the phrase "new deal," and soon the moniker would become synonymous with Roosevelt's activist domestic agenda seeking to pull the nation out of the depths of the Great Depression

FDR: THE LORD OF THE MANOR

From their disparate backgrounds and varied life experiences to their markedly different personalities and public demeanors, **Franklin Delano Roosevelt** was the polar opposite of Herbert Hoover. As his fifth cousin Theodore Roosevelt, FDR was born in 1882 into a patrician Anglo-Dutch family in New York whose pedigree on both sides dated back to the colonial period. Their Hudson River Valley manor provided young Franklin with countless opportunities for exploring nature, inculcating within the young boy a lifelong fascination with forests and wildlife, especially birds. An only child, Roosevelt was doted on by his adoring parents who fostered his youthful curiosities. He grew up among people convinced of their superiority in terms of ancestry, intelligence, and leadership but who felt that their elite status obliged them to public service and to give back to society through a variety of philanthropic endeavors. Like his cousin Theodore (and probably because of his success), Franklin Roosevelt would later extend this belief into running for political office, following an astonishingly similar path. After receiving his education at Groton Academy, Harvard College, and Columbia Law School, he planned to follow the tracks laid down by Teddy, first envisioning a seat in the New York State Assembly, then appointment as Assistant Secretary of the Navy, a successful bid for the governorship of New York and the vice presidency, culminating finally in his election as President of the United States. Incredibly, this is almost exactly what happened (except that he became a state senator rather than an assemblyman, and he lost his 1920 bid for the vice presidency).

The New York governorship and the presidency might have eluded FDR had he not been transformed by personal calamity. In 1921, at the age of 39, he was stricken by the polio virus. Although it did not kill him, the disease ultimately took away the use of his legs. Before this life-altering event, Roosevelt's career, both professionally (the practice of law) and politically, was not that outstanding. Mostly he owed his political success to his famous last name. Always the pleasure-seeker, a playboy in many ways, he devoted more time and energy to his outdoor hobbies and to socializing (especially partying

Franklin D. Roosevelt and Herbert Hoover in a convertible on their way to the U.S. Capitol for Roosevelt's inauguration. March 4, 1933.

and womanizing) than he did developing a devotion to career and family. While spending the next two years of his life mostly bedridden, he seemed to experience a reformation of character and spirit, a desire to eschew his past life, and strive to forge a new one with a seriousness of purpose absent from his earlier years. He also developed a sense of humility and compassion for the downtrodden that allowed him to empathize with the millions of Americans suffering during the Depression—an understanding which Hoover never seemed to grasp—that sometimes bad things happen to people and it is not their fault.

FDR's infirmity also transformed his relationship with his wife, Eleanor. After discovering Franklin's affair with her secretary near the end of World War I, she had agreed to stay married to him for the sake of the children when he agreed never to see the other woman again. Her dedication to nursing him back to health healed their marriage, though by that point it was based more on mutual respect than romantic love. A naturally shy woman not used to the public spotlight, Eleanor worked with FDR's political adviser Louis Howe to keep her husband's name floating in Democratic Party circles by writing letters and making speeches to prepare for a potential political comeback. Their hard work paid off in 1928 when Roosevelt won the governorship of New York.

In his four years as governor, despite limited resources, FDR did what he could to address the needs of hard-pressed New Yorkers while promoting his name as a viable presidential candidate. State-sponsored work projects aided some of the unemployed while more out-of-work laborers simply received a relief stipend to help make ends meet. Roosevelt's activism as governor allowed him to contrast his approach successfully with Hoover's reliance on voluntarism. After winning the presidency, Roosevelt had to wait five months until inauguration day, spending the time meeting with advisors, political leaders, and representatives from business and labor groups to work on the details of his proposals for Congress to undertake. Then, three weeks before his inauguration, FDR was almost assassinated in Miami by an unstable unemployed bricklayer who fired a pistol at Roosevelt from close range at a park after the president-elect gave a brief word of thanks to a crowd that showed up to greet him following a fishing vacation. Roosevelt was unharmed, but four others were hit by bullets including the mayor of Chicago who was standing next to the president and later succumbed to his wounds. One can only wonder at how differently the nation would have fared over the next four to eight years if Roosevelt had also died that evening and his conservative running mate, John Nance Garner of Texas, became the new incoming president.

LAUNCHING THE NEW DEAL

Saving Capitalism: Banking and Stock Exchange Initiatives

Roosevelt's most pressing priority upon assuming office was to repair the nation's banking system, which had all but collapsed. By inauguration day, with many reputable banks going bankrupt, several governors had already closed the banks in their states as panic spread. FDR famously addressed this anxiety head on early in his inaugural address in his demand for action: "First of all, let me assert my firm belief that the only thing we have to fear is fear itself—nameless, unreasoning, unjustified terror which paralyzes needed efforts to convert retreat into advance." The new president's first action was to issue an executive order closing all remaining banks in the country for an indefinite period, declaring a national "Bank Holiday." Administration officials, congressmen, and representatives of the banking industry then met to quickly draft emergency legislation to help ailing financial institutions while bolstering public confidence in the banking system as a whole. Within 48 hours, the bank relief bill reached Congress, passed both houses, and received the president's signature. Known as the **Emergency Banking Act**, the law authorized an extension of the bank holiday indefinitely until expert teams of analysts investigated a particular bank's assets and liabilities. Those institutions found to be in sound financial shape received government approval to reopen immediately. Banks on the verge of collapse were closed forever with any remaining assets used to pay off creditors. In this manner, the relatively small number of institutions that had most damaged the reputation of the American banking system (and would soon be bankrupt anyway) were eliminated. A large number of banks that government agents considered weak but savable became eligible for government aid in the form of low-interest loans from the RFC and short-term government purchase of bank stock in order to quickly infuse the institutions with cash (actions largely duplicated 75 years later by the George W. Bush and Obama administrations under different circumstances during the severe economic downturn of 2008). Overall, the RFC initiated a transfusion of over a billion dollars into the banking system.

Roosevelt soon delivered his first Fireside Chat to the American people in a warm conversational tone, explaining what the government was doing, why the actions were undertaken, and to encourage citizens to make deposits in their banks where the funds would be safe and would contribute to the national economic recovery. When

First Lady Eleanor Roosevelt played an active role in her husband's administration. This was a sharp change from the roles of previous First Ladies. Eleanor had an unwavering commitment to social justice. She became the eyes and ears for her wheelchair-bound husband and traveled extensively, touring the depression-scarred nation.

Gabriel over the White House

When Franklin Roosevelt finally assumed office in early 1933, the reversal in presidential personality and outlook between Herbert Hoover and his successor could not have been more striking. While Hoover, as one associate remarked, "didn't like the human element." Roosevelt reveled in it. He mixed easily with all kinds of people, many times on only a superficial basis, but he made them feel that he sympathized with them. A master of popular phrasing, simple analogies, and, most importantly, the media, the president had a strong, warm voice that would reach into millions of American homes through his famous "Fireside Chats" over the radio, which began soon after his inauguration. Over the airwaves, Roosevelt projected the image of a kindly grandfather, gathering his children around him. He spoke in a plain, friendly voice that went far to calm the fears and anxieties of the forlorn and discouraged.

The country's citizens nevertheless wanted more than reassuring words—they also wanted action. Anecdotal evidence of this feeling exists in the appeal of a then-popular, but now largely-forgotten, Hollywood film financially backed by the publishing titan William Randolph Hearst titled **Gabriel over the White House**. In the movie, a boring and conservative president named Judson Hammond (played by Walter Huston) is transformed by an auto accident, which somehow results in a 180-degree turn in temperament. The new President Hammond emerges with a dynamic series of proposals that he demands Congress adopt immediately in order to combat a severe economic downturn, counter government corruption, and fight a national crime wave, exhorting at one point: "You have wasted precious days and weeks and years in futile discussion. We need action—immediate and effective action!" This plea would have resonated with many Depression Era-movie audiences, but Hammond concludes with another demand that, given events going on in Nazi Germany, took on fascist overtones: "I ask you gentlemen to declare a state of national emergency, and to adjourn this Congress until normal conditions are restored. During this period of adjournment, I shall assume full responsibility for the government." After the Congress accedes to Hammond's request, Hammond zealously tackles national and international problems: organized crime is defeated by a ruthless national police force; disgruntled unemployed citizens are placated with promises to organize a government-sponsored "construction army" to put them back to work; his strength at global peace conference forces all the nations of the world to disarm their militaries, and so on. At the height of his power, with all his major goals accomplished, President Hammond finally succumbs to the infirmity that he received in the car accident resulting in this burst of dictatorial activity.

The idea of a benevolent dictator appealed to a growing number of Americans as the country continued to languish during the Depression—something that Franklin Roosevelt and other political leaders were well aware at the time. It remained to be seen if the nation could weather the storm using the instruments of democracy or if the combination of fear and disillusionment with the status quo would lead to the acceptance of more radical options.

Policemen reporting to depositors during a "run" in early 1933 that the bank was closed.

banks began reopening across the country, the public began returning their money, which had been hidden in their mattresses and attics or buried in their backyards. As the level of deposits greatly exceeded the amount of withdrawals, the panic subsided. The government's moves proved to be an exemplary performance that saved the free-enterprise system. Wall Street joined Main Street in cheering the president. "In one week," journalist Walter Lippmann declared, "the nation, which had lost confidence in everything and everybody, has regained confidence in the government and itself."

Only after the financial crisis eased did President Roosevelt and Congress turn to the structural reform of Wall Street to restore public confidence and thus aid the economic recovery. The Glass-Steagall Act (1933) contained provisions to separate commercial banking from high-risk investment banking and created the **Federal Deposit Insurance Corporation (FDIC)** to oversee the manda-

FERA, CWA, and WPA Director Harry Hopkins

tory insurance fund that banks were now required to financially support in order to protect depositors to a level set by law (originally $5,000 but now up to $250,000). Interestingly, FDR initially opposed this reform because of the failed history of similar attempts by several state governments. Over time, government guarantee of bank deposits became one of the most popular of all New Deal reforms. To bring order to the stock markets and commodities exchanges, the Securities Act (1933) and the Securities Exchange Act (1934) imposed long overdue regulations such as requiring truthful and accurate information be provided to investors and forbidding insider trading, and established the Securities and Exchange Commission (SEC) to enforce them. The SEC, first led by Massachusetts millionaire Joseph P. Kennedy (father of future president John F. Kennedy and someone well aware of many of the now-illegal actions that took place in the exchanges since he had partaken in many of them himself), began the task of overseeing the stock markets' daily operations empowered to investigate improprieties and punish violators with fines, loss of licenses, and criminal prosecution for was especially egregious infractions.

INITIAL RELIEF AND RECOVERY EFFORTS

Major Relief Programs

Although a fiscal conservative at heart, Roosevelt understood the need to temper financial prudence with compassion. Congress responded swiftly in 1933 to the president's request to establish the **Federal Emergency Relief Administration (FERA)**, granting it $500 million for direct relief to the poor. Upon receiving aid requests from state and local relief organizations, the new agency channeled approved funds back for disbursement. To head the FERA, Roosevelt appointed the liberal social worker Harry Hopkins, who had run FDR's state-sponsored relief efforts in New York while serving as governor.

To help the unemployed survive the winter of 1933-34, FDR launched the Civil Works Administration (CWA) also headed by Hopkins. This expensive temporary work program focused on providing work-relief jobs and before it disbanded in March 1934 to save money the agency's laborers laid over 10 million feet of sewer pipes, built over a quarter of a million miles of roads, constructed or improved 40,000 schools, and began work on over a thousand airports.

For middle-class Americans threatened with the loss of their homes, Roosevelt won congressional approval to create the Home Owners' Loan Corporation (HOLC) to refinance mortgages. The HOLC provided interest-bearing government bonds to creditors in exchange for defaulted home mortgages. The agency then offered homeowners lower monthly payments with longer pay-out periods. Although the agency eventually foreclosed on over 200,000 homes nationally, the HOLC brought stability to the national housing emergency by refinancing one-fifth of the mortgages in the country and actually returned a slight profit to Congress when it ceased its operations in the early 1950s.

True to his Rooseveltian heritage, FDR was as much a conservationist as his cousin Theodore (in some ways, such as his strong desire to preserve the nation's beauty and wildlife, even more so). He thus became deeply interested in expanding the national park system from the early years of his presidency. The creation of the **Civilian Conservation Corps (CCC)** served as a logical and natural complement to this interest. Concurrently, FDR and his advisers were also concerned about the possible rise in juvenile delinquency and crime among unemployed young men, especially in the urban areas. After their recruitment by the U.S. Department of Labor, over 2.5 million Americans from families receiving FERA relief (primarily in the 18-25 years old age bracket, though Roosevelt issued an executive order allowing a quarter million older veterans of the Spanish-American War and World War I to serve) joined the program. The Corps provided free room and board as well as a paycheck—enrollees received $30 per month, with $25 of the amount sent home to needy family members. They labored in rural camps operated by the U.S. Army on projects usually supervised by the Interior and Agriculture Departments. Most of the work involved building or maintaining state and national

These Civilian Conservation Corps boys are weeding pine seedlings at the Tennessee Valley Authority nursery, Wilson Dam, Alabama. The CCC planted over 80 million trees for soil conservation and flood control in the Tennessee Valley. June 1942.

parks and forests. Corps members built roads, erected small dams, developed campsites, constructed lodging facilities, created swimming pools and recreation halls, planted millions of trees, and fought forest fires. The CCC also provided educational opportunities for off-duty enrollees. In addition to trade school training, enrollees could take on-site classes or correspondence courses from the remedial stage up to college level. The Corps was probably the most popular of all New Deal measures as the nation celebrated the hard work of these young men that built up their bodies and maintained their morale during hard times. Though some enrollees got homesick and either asked to be released or simply deserted, most enjoyed the experience to work at a challenging job some distance from home for the opportunity to provide their dollar-a-day salary to their families.

Industrial Recovery Measures

Two programs formed the heart of the early New Deal's efforts to generate economic recovery—the **National Recovery Administration (NRA)** and the Agricultural Adjustment Administration. During his first year in office, Roosevelt was confident that he could promote economic recovery through industrial and agricultural cooperation. He regarded the **Agricultural Adjustment Act**, which created the Agricultural Adjustment Administration in May 1933, and the National Industrial Recovery Act (NIRA), which created the NRA in June, to be the most important legislation of his first term. Because overproduction in both economic sectors had contributed to the depression, each law aimed to curtail production in order to restore

balance to the markets. Prices were then expected to rise, but also, in theory, would workers' wages, company profits, and farmers' incomes. Once they earned profits again, industrialists and farmers could then increase their purchases, invest in new technology, and hire more workers, leading to the return of prosperity.

The NIRA's most important provisions authorized every major industrial sector to prepare a code of "fair competition" to eliminate price cutting and overproduction while establishing basic labor standards for all businesses within their sector to follow, and established the NRA as the agency to supervise the process. To direct the NRA, FDR appointed Hugh Johnson, a brash army general with experience in public relations who previously served on the War Industries Board during World War I. Johnson immediately launched a campaign with much fanfare to rally all Americans behind the program. Through parades (including a massive march down New York City's Fifth Avenue), public rallies with patriotic speeches, and other assorted hoopla, the general created massive publicity to convince businessmen and consumers to join the crusade. Johnson made the NRA's logo, which he designed, a Native American Thunderbird-like image named "The Blue Eagle," synonymous with cooperation in the collective national endeavor to restore economic prosperity. Only business owners who voluntarily complied with the code for their particular sector of the economy could legally display the symbol in their stores, on their products, or in their advertisements. Meanwhile, the government openly encouraged consumers only to purchase goods and services from establishments displaying the Blue Eagle. The NRA's symbol soon sprouted everywhere—on placards

The Blue Eagle was a symbol used in the United States by companies to show compliance with the National Industrial Recovery Act.

Secretary of the Interior Harold Ickes

in storefront windows, at factory entrances, on company stationery, and newspaper ads, usually accompanied by the slogan "We Do Our Part."

Johnson brought together the largest producers in every business sector of the economy and in the NRA's first four months, over seven hundred codes were written to govern their affairs. Where one or more large firms dominated an industry, the agency relied on them to prepare the regulations; where no company controlled an industry, the NRA turned to a trade association. When some code-making efforts stalled, Johnson asked business leaders in an industry to accept a standard "blanket code" that would guarantee a minimum wage between 20 and 45 cents per hour (to raise consumer purchasing power), limit workers' hours to a maximum of 30 to 45 hours per week (to spread the number of employable workers), and abolish the use of child labor. Although the codes varied, they all were expected to include agreements on increased prices and wages, as well as a series of limits on competition for the benefit of the businesses (and theoretically its workers) as a whole. Where properly enforced, the NIRA's Section 7a enhanced the ability of workers to organize and bargain collectively through labor unions.

In the summer and fall of 1933, the NRA codes drawn up for steel, textiles, coal mining, and other industries seemed to be working as economic activity improved. By the spring of 1934, however, economic indicators plunged downward once again, and critics from all sides appeared.

Many industrialists blamed the NRA's labor provisions and complained about the high level of paperwork and general interference with their business practices. Small business owners railed against the big businesses that dominated the code making and code enforcement authorities, believing that wage and price provisions were written for the benefit of the corporate entities at their expense. Workers charged the NRA with failing to accept their unions of choice. Consumers complained that the rise in prices was not offset by a corresponding increase in wages and job opportunities. All began to believe that the oversight committees set up to enforce the codes were powerless to punish violators. By early 1935, it was clear that the NRA had failed. When the Supreme Court declared that the agency's codes were unconstitutional in May 1935, even FDR was relieved that the NRA experiment was over.

In addition to establishing the National Recovery Administration, the NIRA also had launched the **Public Works Administration (PWA)**. Placed under the direction of Secretary of the Interior Harold Ickes—an old Bull Moose progressive political reformer from Chicago—the PWA spent over $6 billion sponsoring internal improvements to refurbish and expand the nation's infrastructure of roads and bridges, as well as other necessary construction projects including sewage systems, hospitals, airports, port facilities, and even warships for the U.S. Navy. The

President Franklin Roosevelt at the Grand Coulee Dam in Washington, October 2, 1937.
Photo credit: FDR Presidential Library.

required labor for PWA projects, Roosevelt administration officials hoped, would shrink the relief rolls and reduce unemployment, while the demand for materials would stimulate a myriad of industries far away from the construction sites. The projects themselves were expected to be sound economic investments for the long-term benefits of a community or the nation as a whole. State and local governments were expected to contribute close to 50 percent of the cost with the PWA making up the difference plus guaranteeing that private companies winning contracts adhered to certain labor standards including minimum wages for laborers.

Progress on getting many projects approved was often notoriously slow, however, because to Secretary Ickes's meticulous personal oversight due to his obsession with avoiding any sign of favoritism or corruption in the dispensing of contracts. Nevertheless, the PWA eventually provided the funds necessary for the completion of three major Western dams (Grand Coulee, Boulder, and Bonneville), the construction of major thoroughfares, such as the Pennsylvania Turnpike and the 100-mile causeway linking the Florida Keys, and lasting infrastructure projects such as New York City's Lincoln Tunnel and San Francisco's Golden Gate Bridge.

Agricultural Recovery Efforts

Beside the NIRA, the other cornerstone of the early New Deal was the **Agricultural Adjustment Act**, which established the Agricultural Adjustment Administration (AAA). The fundamental objective of this program was to increase farmers' incomes by reducing production in an effort to relieve the glutted agricultural markets. By decreasing supply through the inducement of government subsidies, Roosevelt administration officials hoped that incomes would rise to a level of parity, or equality, with the farmers' purchasing power just before World War I—the supposed golden years of farm production and income. The act included a grab bag of alternatives seen in almost every farm program proposed during the early twentieth century: marketing agreements, commodity loans, export subsidies, government purchases, and even currency inflation. To these familiar devices, the government added production restrictions, promoted by agricultural economics professor M.L. Wilson as the best means to reduce agricultural surpluses at the source. During its first months of operation, the AAA used production cutbacks as a way of infusing emergency funds to the countryside. In the case of two agricultural commodities, desperate measures were employed. In mid-season of 1933, the AAA's first year of operation, the government paid southern cotton farmers to plow under a portion of their already-growing crops. Meanwhile, government agents paid hog producers to slaughter six million baby pigs in order to boost pork prices by removing the piglets from the national market. Though this latter action provoked much criticism in a time of want, the government justified the move as a necessary expedient to remove the burdensome market glut. (Some of the meat eventually made it to canneries for distribution to aid families on relief.)

The AAA aroused opposition from some farmers who mistrusted the government and valued their independence over their financial security, but the agency also garnered significant support from growers across the country and ultimately acted as a successful holding operation allowing millions of landowners to weather the storm of the depression and hold onto their farms. Nevertheless, the AAA made few provisions for southern sharecroppers, tenant farmers, and farm workers, white and black, hundreds of thousands of whom were subsequently thrown out of work due to the reduced need for agricultural labor as a result of the agency's crop reduction policies. For them, less land in production meant less demand for agricultural labor and fewer opportunities to stay on the land.

A 1935 Supreme Court ruling against the AAA's processor taxes and production control payments forced the Roosevelt administration to work with Congress to find a quick replacement. Congress soon passed the Soil Conservation and Domestic Allotment Act (SCDAA). Under this law, signed by FDR on February 29, 1936, the government would continue to make payments to farmers (from the Federal Treasury rather than from processor taxes as the AAA had previously done), but for soil conservation practices rather than solely for production control. Growers would receive checks for diverting acreage formerly used to raise soil-depleting crops such as cotton to soil-building crops such as grasses and legumes, and for implementing approved soil conservation practices. The SCDAA proved to be an inadequate production control measure. In the case of cotton, drought conditions kept agricultural production low in 1936, but the return of good weather in 1937 coupled with the absence of planting restrictions led to a record southern cotton crop and the return of low prices. On February 16, 1938, Congress passed the Agricultural Adjustment Act. This law was the culmination of efforts undertaken to create a long-term price-support scheme for American farmers based on a combination of the administration's previous efforts: acreage restrictions, production quotas, conservation payments, and price-support loans. This system provided the basis for the federal government's agricultural programs for decades after World War II.

Farmers on the Southern Great Plains experienced additional hardship during the Great Depression, partly due to Mother Nature and partly due to the excesses of agricultural capitalism. Always an area subject to periodic drought, high winds, and small-scale dust storms, the 1930s experienced something quite different as the result of several years of land exploitation without sound conservation measures. Since World War I, an increasing number of growers had arrived to raise wheat, including a large number of "suitcase farmers" who were not full-time farmers. These itinerant growers planted crops and left the area, returning only at harvest time hoping for a nice payoff if the weather was good. When the rain stopped falling, the land, stripped of its native grasses that had previously held the soil in place, and subjected to high heat and a dearth of moisture literally dried up, turned to dust, and blew away. Dust became a fixed feature of daily life on the Plains, but the area of most severe activity centered on northwest Texas, eastern New Mexico, southeastern Colorado, western Kansas, and western Oklahoma—an area that soon became known as the **Dust Bowl**. Mammoth storms frequently raged through the region, some reaching hundreds of feet in the air as they blackened the sky, suffocated livestock, covered crops with sand dunes, dumping tons of clay soil on farms, homes, and roads, and forcing people indoors for the duration. The remnants of the storms often affected areas hundreds of miles away. In 1934, the residue from one storm covered the skies over Washington, D.C.

Over a third of the residents left the Dust Bowl region, never to return. The remainder stayed and received government relief in the form of AAA crop reduction payments and SCDAA payments for adopting approved soil conservation practices such as terracing the land and planting cover crops. The situation finally improved during the 1940s when the rains returned, but also the result of a slew of government programs designed to save the soil, including the continuation of paying farmers for soil conservation, grazing regulations on public land for livestock, and the purchase of over a million acres of submarginal land that was retired from commercial use and converted into national grasslands and wildlife refuges.

The Tennessee Valley Authority

In many ways, the most ambitious piece of legislation passed during the early New Deal to promote economic recovery proved to be the Tennessee Valley Authority Act, which established the **Tennessee Valley Authority (TVA)** to supervise a massive government effort to directly foster economic development in one region of the country—the vast watershed area of the South known as the Tennessee River Valley. Encompassing parts of six southern states, this vast river basin served as the home of a large number of residents experiencing widespread poverty due to their inability to control the region's river and tributaries, espe-

An ominous dust storm blankets Spearman, Texas. April 14, 1935.
Photo credit: FDR Presidential Library

cially during the rainy season. Flooding was endemic, and thus the towns and farms along the river were frequently damaged or destroyed by the surging waters. The primary objective of the TVA became to control the flooding of the Tennessee River while simultaneously harnessing its water power to generate electricity, develop local industry (such as fertilizer production), improve river transportation, and, in the process, ease the poverty and isolation of the region's inhabitants. The bold project reflected the influence of presidential advisers who were committed to large-scale government planning as a solution to society's problems.

The TVA built or refurbished twenty-five dams, including the massive Wheeler Dam near Muscle Shoals in Alabama. Many of these dams included hydroelectric generators, which provided low-cost electricity for the region's population for the first time. Indeed, many residents never before had the possibility of obtaining electric power at any price because private companies had not deemed the much of the region to be profitable. In areas that private power companies did serve, the low rates charged by the TVA forced the utility companies to reduce their rates to more affordable levels. As it undertook its efforts, the agency also purposefully flooded some areas in the region leading to the removal of submarginal farmland (and even some small towns) and taught local farmers how to prevent soil erosion, especially through the planting of trees—a practice always championed by Franklin Roosevelt.

The TVA improved the region in several ways. In the short-term, a large number of jobs were created to build the dams, channel water from impassable areas, plant trees, and lay down power lines. Over the long run, agricultural practices were improved through the application of sounder soil conservation techniques and cheap electric power transformed the lives of rural residents. In 1933, only 2 percent of the homes and farms in the region had electricity. By 1945, 75 percent had electric power enabling them to have access to a variety of domestic luxuries that other Americans took for granted--home lighting, water heaters, and electric-powered appliances.

The TVA marked the first time that the federal government intervened on a massive scale to bring prosperity to an impoverished region. Although the agency was one of the New Deal's most touted successes and boldest experiments in government planning, it generated little enthusiasm for more ambitious programs elsewhere in the country, let alone large-scale national planning of the American economy. The majority of Congress and the American people disapproved of any further extension of governmental power. Nevertheless, when FDR was asked what he believed his proudest domestic achievement, he often cited the Tennessee Valley Authority.

POPULIST OPPOSITION TO THE NEW DEAL

In their desire to rally popular support for such New Deal programs as the NRA, Roosevelt and the New Dealers unleashed new political forces that they would have to reckon with by the middle of the president's first term. Though opposition to the New Deal emerged from the Far Right (most notably in the form of the American Liberty League—a conservative organization bankrolled by the DuPont family and other wealthy industrialists angered at FDR's support for the regulation of business), various groups of left-leaning dissidents who argued that the New Deal did not go far enough to address the needs of the needy ultimately posed the greatest political threat to Roosevelt. The great fanfare created to boost popular support for key programs, such as the NRA, raised the people's expectations that recovery was on its way and freed many from their apathy, as they now demanded significant changes in the way that the economy operated. This politicized electorate also made it clear to the New Dealers that if they could not achieve economic recovery, then they might turn to others who promised to do so.

Radicalism in the States

Some states during the early 1930s witnessed the emergence of left-leaning third-party movements. In Wisconsin, for example, Philip La Follette, son of "Battling Bob" La Follette of Progressive-era fame, was elected governor in 1934 and 1936 as the candidate of the radical Wisconsin Progressive Party, which advocated unemployment compensation and farm loans. In Minnesota, the Farmer-Labor Party, a fusion of discontented farmers and urban laborers led by Governor Floyd Olson, rose to challenge the major party establishment and came to dominate state politics. Their party echoed that of Wisconsin's Progressive Party, with Olson using the same radical rhetoric of La Follette, declaring that capitalism was "on trial for its life." Olson's relief agenda for his citizens far outstripped FDR's modest early approaches, with the governor threatening conservatives in the legislature that he would declare martial law if they did not enact his relief bills. As the rise to power of both La Follette and Olson indicated, the overwhelming majority of Minnesotans and Wisconsinites wanted more drastic change than the New Deal was producing.

The same message emanated from California. Instead of forming a third party, discontented Californians tried to take over the Democratic Party. In the Golden State, famous Socialist author Upton Sinclair led the anti-New Deal charge. In a book titled *I, Governor of California, And*

How I Ended Poverty: A True Story of the Future, Sinclair outlined his plan. The novelist described how he would be elected governor, leading to the adoption of a production-for-use economy in the midst of capitalist California. Sinclair predicted that he would totally eliminate poverty in the state in less than four years. The central feature of his plan, entitled "End Poverty in California" (EPIC), was the concept of production-for-use. The profit system, the writer argued, had produced itself into a Depression, as workers were not paid enough to buy what they made. To remedy this situation, Sinclair proposed that California take over idle land and factories, permitting the unemployed to use them to provide for their needs. Sinclair also advocated the establishment of land colonies to produce food for the hungry and state-owned factories to meet other needs. Sinclair's brand of socialism terrified California conservatives. Opposition became vicious in its falsehoods and accusations, labeling Sinclair an atheist and a communist. Eventually, the massive propaganda campaign took its toll on the public's views of EPIC and became too much for its supporters to overcome, though Sinclair was defeated by a closer-than-anticipated margin.

The Rise of the Demagogues: Huey Long and Father Charles Coughlin

One of the most alarming critics of the Roosevelt administration proved to be Senator **Huey P. Long** of Louisiana, who had risen to power by engaging in demagoguery; that is, by exploiting the fears, prejudices, and general feelings of alienation and hostility of middle- and lower-class Louisianans toward the conservative political oligarchy that controlled the state. This powerful group of bankers, oilmen, sugar planters, and utility company owners primarily located in the southern part of the state ruled Louisiana with an iron grip. Long's strident attacks on these interests won him the governorship in 1928. From that office, he launched a successful war on these individuals and their various enterprises. Many claimed, and rightfully so, that Long had become a virtual dictator. Nevertheless, he remained popular with the electorate because of his flamboyant, charismatic personality his bombastic oratory, and his ability to deliver the goods. He arranged for the building of new roads, schools, and hospitals; got the legislature to revise the tax codes and distributed free textbooks; and provided for the lowering of utility rates. To pay for his progressive programs, which he boasted were for the benefit of the common people, Long taxed wealthy Louisianans heavily. Barred by law from succeeding himself as governor, Long ran for a seat in the United States Senate in 1930 and won easily. He then began to take his ideas to Washington, D.C. and the national stage.

Long supported Roosevelt for president in 1932 but broke with FDR within six months, railing against the growing size of government and bureaucracy. As an alternative to the New Deal, he advocated something he had introduced as governor: taxing the wealthy to force a redistribution of wealth. He named his program the "Share-Our-Wealth Plan." The government, he claimed, could end the depression easily by using the tax system to confiscate the surplus fortunes of over $5 million and distribute them to the rest of the population. Such action would allow the government, he claimed, to guarantee every family a minimum homestead of $5,000 and an annual income of $2,500. Long's mastery of the radio helped to create a membership of 8 million Americans in his Share-Our-Wealth Clubs. Regardless of whether or not his plan was fiscally sound, Long's idea was popular with millions of unemployed, suffering, and disillusioned Americans searching for a scapegoat for their woes.

By 1935, FDR considered Long to be the most likely challenger to his Democratic renomination bid. Further, in the spring of 1935, a poll by the Democratic National Committee showed that Long might attract as much as 10 percent of the national vote if he ran as a third-party candidate. That outcome would be enough to allow a Republican challenger to win if the election was close. Before that campaign took place, however, Long was assassinated in the Louisiana State Capitol building in early September 1935, by Dr. Carl Weiss, the son-in-law of a judge who Long had arranged to be redistricted out of a job.

In the Midwest, Father Charles Coughlin, also gained popularity deriding the alleged shortcomings of the New Deal. A known figure whose weekly sermons

Louisiana politician Huey Long

were broadcast nationally to over 30 million Americans from his home parish in Royal Oak, Michigan (a suburb of Detroit) in which he denounced communism while espousing gospel homilies, Coughlin at first supported Roosevelt and the New Deal, which he initially called "Christ's Deal." By late 1934, however, the "radio priest" had become a harsh critic and began proposing a series of monetary reforms—remonetization of silver and the end of the banker-dominated Federal Reserve. Coughlin came to believe that the New Deal was a conspiracy hatched by Wall Street to aid the bankers, which he increasingly hinted were heavily influenced by Jews within the Roosevelt administration. He also advocated a redistribution of wealth, lending support to Huey Long. After Roosevelt's reelection in 1936, an embittered Coughlin moved even further to the right, denouncing both Jews and the New Deal with incredible vehemence. His ravings became so extreme that many radio stations refused to air his program. Despite his fanaticism, millions of ordinary citizens continued to listen to the radio priest.

THE "SECOND NEW DEAL"

As President Roosevelt began to plan his re-election campaign in early 1935, he proposed a new wave of reforms and government programs to be considered by Congress. While many of these proposals had been under policy development for some time, the populist insurrections of 1934-35 (and his increasingly perturbed attitude toward criticism of his policies) no doubt concerned FDR and led him to unveil many of them sooner rather than later. The president certainly began to adopt some of the elements of the oratorical style used by many of the populist leaders. His rhetoric suddenly took on an anti-corporate tone as he attacked the wealthy for their selfish ways while calling for new programs to aid the poor and the downtrodden, culminating in his acceptance speech at the 1936 Democratic National Convention where he railed against the forces of business and financial monopoly who "had begun to consider the Government of the United States as a mere appendage to their own affairs." Holding firm, Roosevelt bellowed: "Never before in all our history have these forces been so united against one candidate as they stand today. They are unanimous in their hate for me—and I welcome their hatred. I should like to have it said of my first Administration that in it the forces of selfishness and of lust for power met their match. I should like to have it said of my second Administration that in it these forces met their master."

Electricity for All

Among Roosevelt's first actions of the Second New Deal were proposals for legislation to greatly increase taxes on the wealthy and to break up the eight great utility holding companies, which at the time controlled almost 75 percent of the nation's electric power and unpopular throughout the country because of the high rates they charged consumers. Eventually, Congress passed only moderate increases on high incomes and inheritances as well as the Public Utility Holding Company Act of 1935, which increased competition by reducing utility company operations to either a single state or a single integrated system serving a limited geographical region. (Congress repealed the law in 2005).

More significant proved to be the establishment of the **Rural Electrification Administration (REA)**, which oversaw the distribution of electricity at reasonable rates to hundreds of thousands of rural households. Created by executive order in 1935 and made permanent by an act of Congress the next year, the REA helped to usher in a new age in the American countryside where only 10 percent of the nation's rural areas possessed electric power. The REA contributed to the wiring up of non-urban America by providing low-interest loans to communities that established electrical cooperatives owned and operated by rural residents. The loans paid for the placement of

Rural electrification in the San Joaquin Valley, California. November 1938.

power lines in localities that private electric companies had previously ignored. The cooperatives' customers would then retire the loans over a 30-year span. With the rural markers shown to be profitable, private power companies eventually began to step in and provide additional electric service to the countryside.

The lifestyle changes brought about by rural electrification were revolutionary. Radio (and later television) use broke down cultural isolation. Electric pumps provided indoor plumbing, resulting in immediate access to hot water for cooking and cleaning. Indoor toilets and hot water tubs led to increased sanitation. Electric kitchen appliances eased the burden of cooking, while refrigeration improved diets and overall health for farm families. Reduced time from chores freed up more time for relaxation, recreation, and entertainment, increasing the quality of rural life. Simply stated, electrification provided rural Americans with an escape from the pre-industrial age.

New Relief Programs

In 1935, Congress passed the Emergency Relief Appropriation Act, a $5 billion measure that dwarfed similar relief legislation passed during the first New Deal. While diverting some funds to the CCC to continue that popular youth work program, FDR used a portion of the new appropriation to create another work program for youth—the National Youth Administration (NYA), which in Texas was directed by future president Lyndon Baines Johnson. The agency provided jobs for eligible youth who either could not or would not enlist in the CCC. Some joined the NYA instead of the CCC because they were reluctant to distance themselves from home. Other NYA enrollees were female, and therefore, ineligible to join the CCC.

The NYA had two main programs to offer. The most well-known NYA program provided part-time jobs for high school and college students on their campuses, eventually employing two million young men and women to perform such jobs as landscape maintenance, library work, office work, and teacher assistance. The other, lesser-known NYA program aided an equal number of out-of-school youth through work programs that later served as the inspiration for the Job Corps (a Great Society program initiated during Johnson's presidency). Over two and a half million youths worked for wages and gained marketable skills learning a trade by training at established work centers and undertaking on-the-job training projects in the field.

Most of the new congressional funds, however, were used to form a new work-relief agency in May 1935, the **Works Progress Administration (WPA)**. Although

NYA Project: **Men working on metal bridge project in Texas, 1936.**
Photo credits: FDR Presidential Library

Roosevelt terminated the Civil Works Administration in early 1934, the idea of work relief rewarded with quickly placing dollars in unemployed hands to help stimulate the economy lived on through the WPA. Headed by Harry Hopkins, the WPA focused a considerable amount of its energy and money on infrastructure projects, usually on a smaller scale than the jobs performed by the Public Works Administration. More typical, WPA workers labored on country roads, city streets and sidewalks; courthouses, post offices, city halls, libraries, and other public buildings; and a host of school and zoo improvements as well as city beautification projects.

The WPA also channeled funds into non-construction employment projects in order to aid women and men less suited for construction work, about 25 percent of the WPA's total workforce. Creativity marked the agency's non-construction programs, which included work such as running day care centers, sewing blankets for the poor, running bookmobiles, preserving and cataloguing library books, and surveying historic sites. Many arts projects created by the WPA are the most famous of these non-construction programs. The WPA created Theater Projects in major cities that provided jobs for unemployed actors, directors, and stagehands. These men and women

Poster for the WPA encouraging laborers to work for America

produced plays for paying customers in their cities and other communities while on tour. The WPA Music Project paid unemployed musicians to perform concerts and teach music classes in schools who had laid off their music teachers. The WPA Art Project paid approved artists to display their work and also to teach art classes in school districts. (A famous New Deal project that paid artists to produce murals to be displayed in post offices and other public buildings across the country has often been associated with the WPA Arts Project, but was actually managed by the U.S. Treasury Department). The WPA Writers' Project hired unemployed writers to produce, among other items, state travel guides and books promoting tourism.

The WPA became the largest work relief program in history. Before its termination in 1943, the agency employed over 8.5 million Americans and helped to transform the urban and rural landscape of the country in ways still noticeable to this day.

Social Security

Without question, the most momentous piece of legislation to come out of the Second New Deal was the 1935 **Social Security Act**—a crucial first step in building the nation's most important social safety net for the elderly,

disabled, and the unemployed. Work relief agencies such as the WPA could do nothing for those who could not support themselves such as the old, the deaf, the blind, and the crippled. Further, only Wisconsin had a functioning state-run unemployment insurance system to aid heads of households who remained out of work. Because Congress had produced a myriad of conflicting proposals addressing these matters, Roosevelt early in the New Deal asked Secretary of Labor Frances Perkins (the first woman appointed to a Cabinet position) to head a committee charged with researching the subject and suggesting the best way to create a system of federally-sponsored social insurance for the elderly and the unemployed of the United States—then the only industrialized nation not to have a national retirement system. By 1934, grass-roots pressure had begun to attract his attention when **Francis Townsend**, an elderly California physician, produced a plan to aid the elderly that garnered much publicity. The doctor claimed that the way to end the Depression was to give every citizen over the age of 60 a monthly stipend of $200, provided that they retired (to open more job opportunities for the unemployed) and spent the money in full within 30 days (pumping needed funds into the economy). By 1935, the Townsend Plan had attracted the support of more than 5 million older Americans. While the plan itself made little progress in Congress, the idea's popularity helped build support for the Social Security Act based on the Perkins Committee's suggestions and passed in 1935.

The Social Security Act in many ways laid the foundation of the modern welfare state. The legislation established several distinct programs, including a federal-state unemployment insurance system and federal aid to the disabled. For the elderly, the law provided monthly assistance for those destitute at the time, and also, more importantly for the future, Americans presently working were incorporated into a pension system to which they and their employers would contribute via a mandatory payroll tax. Those funds would provide workers with a basic income upon their future retirement. Whereas some supported financing the pensions from general revenues with benefits fixed by the government (as existed in most European systems), Roosevelt sided with those advocating the payroll tax, primarily for political reasons. Not only was this method more popular in Congress, he also came to believe that this approach was the best way to make people feel like they had a larger stake in their retirement. "We put those payroll contributions there so as to give the contributors a legal, moral and political right to collect their pensions and their unemployment benefits," he once explained. "With those taxes in there, no dam politician can ever scrap my social security program."

The Townsend Plan

Dr. Francis Townsend was a critic of the New Deal who felt that FDR's program did not do enough to address the problems of the elderly during the Great Depression. He devised a plan to provide every retired American with a pension contingent upon the recipient spending the money within thirty days. Townsend believed that the retirement of elderly citizens would make room for younger people in the workforce while the pension that they received would stimulate the economy through consumer spending, thus creating full employment. Most historians concur that support for the doctor's proposal, as evidenced by the two million people who joined one of the new "Townsend Clubs" appearing across the country to promote the plan, played an important role in pressuring the Roosevelt administration and Congress to create the Social Security system in 1935.

This cartoon, from the **Townsend Weekly,** a newspaper published by the movement's national organization, expresses the group's main objection to Social Security—that it was not generous enough in the benefits that it offered. The Townsend Plan promised every senior citizen $200 per month, regardless of past earnings. Under the social insurance program of the Social Security Act a worker whose earnings averaged $100 per month for 40 years would collect a Social Security retirement benefit of only $35 per month. (Most economists, however, estimated that it would have required one-half of the nation's total income to fund the level of benefits promised by Townsend).

Source: Web Pages of Social Security Administration
http://www.ssa.gov/history/townbrief.html

THE RISE OF ORGANIZED LABOR

Organized labor received a tremendous boost during the 1930s, becoming one of the most important political and social developments of the decade. The Great Depression rapidly changed working-class sentiment toward unions and labor militancy. Occurring partly in response to government overtures to unions, the growth of organized labor resulted more from the collective efforts of American laborers and their leaders, demanding a seat at the bargaining table in order to receive improved working conditions, more adequate pay, and recognition of their right to be at the bargaining table in the first place.

Impatience with the NRA

Section 7(a) of the NIRA had granted workers the right to bargain collectively, leading to increased union organizing efforts, but in practice the NRA code authorities failed to prevent widespread malfeasance by management using tactics such as forming company unions to circumvent the law indirectly when they were not openly violating the law directly by ignoring wage and hours provisions or recognizing unions of their workers' choice. In 1934, workers began to take matters into their own hands, staging over 2,000 strikes across the country. While many of the walkouts were peaceful and attracted little attention, some escalated into violent, bloody confrontations between workers and police. In May, 10,000 workers at the Electric Auto-Lite plant in Toledo, Ohio, surrounded the factory and blocked all entrances and exits in the hope that the company would shut down operations and negotiate a union contract. Management refused and called out the police to remove the strikers, leading to a seven-hour battle that failed to disperse the workers despite the use of fire hoses, tear gas, and gunfire. Only after the governor called out the National Guard were the strikers disbanded, but not before more gunfire was exchanged and two workers lay dead. Similar scenes took place throughout the year, against striking truck drivers and warehousemen in Minneapolis, as well as striking longshoremen in San Francisco, culminating in the fall when 400,000 textile laborers from Maine to Alabama came together to strike. Workers previously unwilling to unite because of ethnic and religious differences bonded together against the mill owners. In the first two weeks of September, they brought cotton production to a virtual standstill. When mill owners in Rhode Island tried to bring in replacement workers and hired private security forces to protect them, they only caused greater anger among the strikers leading to further violent confronta-

tions, causing several deaths scores of injuries. Similar encounters took place in the South, where local vigilante groups, claiming workers to be communists, sided with the police and National Guardsmen to beat up strikers, kill union organizers, and help to incarcerate hundreds of strikers in barbed-wire camps.

The Wagner Act

Although FDR was front and center as a driving force behind much of the New Deal, there were some elements of his agenda where true credit belongs elsewhere even if Roosevelt later received much of the credit for the achievement. As already stated, the guarantee of bank deposits through the FDIC was one example. Another is the National Labor Relations Act, or **Wagner Act**, which resulted primarily from the efforts of its author, the progressive Democratic Senator Robert F. Wagner of New York. Roosevelt held an ambivalent attitude concerning workers' rights, adopting a paternalistic and rather naïve approach that laborers' lives would probably best be improved by the passage of laws benefiting the general population. Senator Wagner, an immigrant son of a German janitor, felt he knew better and crafted a new bill designed to boldly assert workers' rights. The legislation would prohibit companies from engaging in a wide range of enumerated "unfair labor practices," such as blackballing workers for union activity or forming company unions. The law would also create a National Labor Relations Board empowered to supervise employee elections for union representation with which employers were bound to bargain in good faith. If a majority of workers at a work site voted to join a particular union then all of them would be represented by that organization. Business leaders and groups such as the National Association of Manufacturers condemned the proposal as an unconstitutional intrusion of the government in the workplace and had the support of some southern conservative Democratic leaders in the Senate, including Majority Leader Joseph T. Robinson of Arkansas. At a White House meeting with the senators, FDR was non-committal, not wishing to offend his conservative or progressive supporters within his party, but Wagner was able to get a vote on his measure in both houses where it passed and Roosevelt signed the bill into law.

The Emergence of the CIO and the Sit-Down Strike

The often brutal suppression of strikes and other labor protests made workers more determined than ever to organize to combat management's refusal to accept their right to join unions. Soon after passage of the Wagner Act, John L. Lewis of the United Mine Workers, Sidney Hillman of the Amalgamated Clothing Workers, and the leaders of six other unions separated from American Federation of Labor (AFL) when they failed to receive AFL support to organize millions of unskilled workers along industrial lines rather than the federation's traditional reliance of organization by craft, which favored a relatively smaller number of white skilled workers. The new consortium initially called itself the Committee for Industrial Organization, and later renamed itself the **Congress of Industrial Organizations (CIO)**, whose priority was to organize the millions of workers, regardless of skill level, gender, or race, into effective unions by industry in order to strengthen their economic and political power.

In early 1936, members of the United Rubber Workers (a CIO affiliate) at a Goodyear Rubber plant in Akron, Ohio, went on strike to protest wage cuts and longer work hours. Rather than following the routine of walking off the job and allowing strikebreakers to be hired while they faced police harassment outside the gates of the facility, the workers occupied their factory and refused to leave until they received company recognition of their union. Thus, the "**sit-down strike**," was born. Caught off guard, executives initially thought that they could wait the workers out, but after a month they agreed to most of the strikers' demands. During the winter of 1936, members of the United Auto Workers (UAW), another CIO affiliate, copied the tactic at their General Motors plant in Flint, Michigan. Refusing to leave the premises until management recognized their union, the workers endured extreme cold conditions for over a month as the factory's heat was turned off and fought back furiously with fire hoses, bottles, bolts, and hinges when armed police stormed the plant in an effort to dislodge them. Fourteen workers were shot, but they survived and held their ground with their comrades. When that operation failed, followed by the unprecedented decision by the Democratic governor Frank Murphy, to call out the National Guard to protect the workers rather than to take over the plant, General Motors capitulated.

Many Democratic and Republican politicians condemned the sit-down strikes and criticized the president for not coming out forcefully against the workers. For his part, FDR publicly expressed displeasure with the strikes, but he refused to send federal troops to break them up. Though the Supreme Court ruled in 1939 against the legality of sit-down strikes, by then great successes had already been achieved. CIO membership had already soared to over 3 million members by 1937 as Chrysler, United States Steel, and other corporations agreed to allow their employees to join a union of their choice. Roosevelt and his party reaped the benefits from the mobilized workers who increasingly supported Democrats in local, state, and national elections and became a reliable part of the growing New Deal political coalition.

THE SOCIAL IMPACT OF THE GREAT DEPRESSION

The Depression and the American Family

Hard economic times greatly impacted the American family during the 1930s, and inevitably, affected the outlook and behavior of most Americans who lived through the experience for the rest of their lives.

The uncertainty of employment not only affected family budgets but also created great stress and anxiety. In 1932, the national unemployment rate stood at 25 percent, but that figure by itself fails to register the dire state of the economy. Many areas had unemployment rates vastly above the national average, especially manufacturing cities such as Chicago (40 percent), Cleveland (50 percent), Detroit (50 percent), Pittsburgh (40 percent), and Toledo (80 percent). Such basic statistics also do not take into account the number of underemployed who worked fewer hours than before the Depression, not to mention the reduced wages for which laborers who found a job were paid. Also, many Americans living on farms were employed, but their incomes were greatly reduced as the result of plummeting crop prices.

Not only did the bleak employment prospects weigh heavily on the minds of Americans, but also many who lost their life savings when their bank went out of business had nothing to fall back on. Families skimped and "lived lean" in a variety of ways. They ate less, canned food, and raised vegetables in backyard gardens. Family members wore out their shoes, made some of their own articles of clothing, and often reduced purchases to bare necessities. They occupied their time with cheap forms of entertainment and spent more time at home. To help make ends meet they took in boarders so they could charge them a little rent, accepted odd jobs for extra cash, and condemned wasteful practices that might cost the family money needed to pay their bills.

The economic strains inevitably shaped the makeup of countless American families. Marriage and birth rates plummeted, less fortunate members of the extended family moved in, and while the Depression strengthened the resolve of many families, an increasing number of men buckled under the pressure of failing to provide for their brood and simply deserted their wives and children, or committed suicide.

A great rise in the number of displaced Americans wandering the cities and countryside occurred. An estimated one to two million men often referred to as "hoboes" moved about looking for work and subsistence. Quite a few intact families who lost their farms or homes also migrated to cities or other states in search of a better life.

Women and the Depression

The Great Depression fell especially hard on American women. Men of all classes experienced a degree of emasculation during the Depression years because so many had lost their identity as the breadwinner and provider for their families. For such men, being unemployed and then having to accept relief unleashed feelings of inadequacy. The unemployment rate for men, especially among the ranks of blue-collar workers, tended to be higher than those of women, many of whom worked in white-collar occupations, and thus were less vulnerable to job cutbacks. Resentment toward women with jobs intensified as most men were not yet ready to accept the possibility that a woman could be a family provider, especially if there was another man, capable or not, being kept from aiding his family due to her employment. Women, were laid off jobs at a much higher rate than men if a man was capable of doing the work and the task was not viewed as a "woman's job." This male anxiety led several states to pass laws forbidding the hiring of married women. The labor movement, even the CIO, made the protection of the male wage earner one of its principal goals.

While government programs helped many women survive during the Depression, the New Deal also left women out of countless opportunities. The Social Security pension system, for example, did not cover waitresses, domestic servants, and a host of other female-dominated occupations. Relief agencies were especially reluctant to authorize aid for unemployed women. In screening job applicants, WPA administrators often discriminated against women, giving preferences for jobs to unemployed male family heads at the expense of unemployed single females or married women. Women were barred from performing any type of heavy outdoor labor, channeled instead into work projects such as sewing, food processing, child care, health care, and (especially for black and Hispanic women) domestic service.

African Americans in the Roosevelt Era

No other ethnic groups suffered more during the Great Depression than African Americans. In 1932, the unemployment rate for blacks was over 50 percent, or twice the national average, as employers tended to lay them off first. The situation was the same across the country—in Memphis, Tennessee and Philadelphia, Pennsylvania, 75 percent of the black population was unemployed.

The New Deal proved to be a mixed blessing for African Americans, who, like women as a whole, received some tangible benefits by participation in government programs but also experienced stark episodes of discrimination in the dispensing of aid. State relief administrators typically determined that the amount of their FERA aid should be markedly less than that received by whites. African Americans were hired to perform work for the CWA and WPA but at less pay than non-blacks. Across the South, planter-dominated committees working for the AAA routinely allowed black sharecroppers to be cheated out of their half of the agency's crop reduction payments. African-American youth benefited from the CCC, though racial prejudice impacted that agency's operations as well. Initially, the Army chose to scatter small numbers of black enrollees into integrated camps throughout the country. When the director of the Corps, Robert Fechner, found out about the practice, however, he ordered the camps located in the South to be immediately segregated. Broad categories of workers (including domestic servants and agricultural laborers, occupations overwhelmingly dominated by African Americans and women) were excluded from Social Security. Black homeowners failed to receive mortgage relief from the HOLC or low-interest loans from the Federal Housing Administration (FHA), a new government agency created to jump-start the construction of homes in the country through loans to the general public. Through the practice of "redlining," the HOLC and FHA drew up survey maps of various residential areas in American cities and rated them based upon racial and ethnic lines—houses within districts within redlines, typically those with heavy African American populations, received negative ratings killing their chances of receiving government financing.

Few liberals in the government were ready or willing to address the nation's deep-seated social issues. Their priority remained saving American capitalism. FDR repeatedly refused to endorse a federal anti-lynching measure debated throughout the decade for fear of alienating powerful southern conservative members of Congress who might scuttle more valued elements of his agenda. The main exception to the administration's seeming lack of empathy was **Eleanor Roosevelt,** who often wrote and spoke out, both to the general public and privately to her husband and government administrators, against prejudice and promoting the inclusion of African Americans within New Deal programs and American society as a whole. She wrote letters to USDA officials in 1939 when over a thousand displaced Missouri Bootheel sharecroppers staged a highly publicized roadside demonstration, inquiring as what the government could do for them. When Secretary of Agriculture Henry Wallace casually replied that what was going on in the countryside was the result of mechanization and the continuing movement of people from rural areas to the cities, the First Lady sarcastically replied: "Should we be developing more industries and services? Should we practice birth control or drown the surplus population?" Her most famous display of support for African Americans occurred in 1939, when she relinquished her membership in the Daughters of the American Revolution when the organization refused to allow renowned black opera singer Marian Anderson to perform at Constitution Hall in Washington, D.C. With the support of her husband, Eleanor persuaded another civil rights sympathizer, Secretary of the Interior Harold Ickes, to sponsor a concert featuring Anderson on the steps of the Lincoln Memorial. On Easter Sunday, 1939, 75,000 people gathered at the memorial to hear Anderson sing while demonstrating their support for racial equality. FDR did not attend.

Despite the rampant prejudice inherent in the implementation of New Deal policies, African Americans began to support FDR and the Democrats in ever increasing numbers. Getting some government help during such dire economic times seemed by most blacks to be much better than no help at all. In the 1936 presidential election, northern blacks began to say "farewell to the party of Lincoln" and voted Democratic in large numbers, becoming important swing voters in some key northern states such as New York, New Jersey, Illinois, Ohio, and Pennsylvania. Blacks could no longer be ignored at election time leading to significant shifts in policy by the national Democratic Party in the coming years.

Hispanic Americans during the Great Depression

The poor economy and lingering racism combined to make the Depression years especially harsh for Hispanics in the United States. The most devastating manifestation of racial prejudice toward Mexicans and Mexican Americans proved to be the policy of **repatriation**, or the policy of returning immigrants and their family members to their land of origin, which actually began during the Hoover administration but was continued during the early New Deal years. As the Great Depression worsened and white Americans in certain regions looked for scapegoats for their woes, the Hoover administration announced a plan in 1931 to repatriate illegal aliens in order to open more job opportunities for white citizens. This policy focused on Mexican immigrants in California and Texas, the two

western states with the largest Hispanic populations at the time. Local government officials there were willing to enforce the policy because of their eagerness to eliminate the minority poor from their relief rolls. Between 1929 and 1935, the federal government repatriated 82,000 Mexican immigrants after raids on businesses and homes. California and Colorado authorities went even further. Threatening to remove them from the relief rolls, officials persuaded tens of thousands of unemployed Mexicans to leave, offering them free railroad tickets to Mexico as a further inducement. Such a dragnet by federal, state, and local governments created a climate of fear within the Hispanic community and consequently 500,000 more returned to Mexico voluntarily. This total equaled the number of Mexicans who had come to the United States during the 1920s. Most revealing was the fact that within the ranks of the repatriated were a significant number of legal immigrants unable to produce their immigration papers, the American-born children of illegals, and most egregious, thousands of Mexican Americans who had lived in the Southwest for generations.

Life grew more difficult for those immigrant Mexicans who stayed behind. Harassed by government officials, Mexicans sought to escape public attention and scrutiny. In Los Angeles, where their influence had been felt and accepted in the 1920s, they now retreated into the separate community of East Los Angeles. To many, they became the invisible minority. Mexican Americans did receive some benefit from the New Deal, especially from the program's pro-labor legislation. Those Hispanics living in urban areas and who worked in blue-collar industries, such as in the cannery and garment sectors, joined CIO-affiliated unions in large numbers and won concessions from their employers, but most were agricultural workers living in rural areas and therefore excluded from the original provisions of the Social Security Act.

In some instances, Hispanic Americans organized to push for change. Led by 21-year-old activist Emma Tenayuca, workers for the Southern Pecan Shelling Company of San Antonio, Texas, engaged in a well-publicized strike in 1938. Tenayuca convinced 12,000 mostly Hispanic pecan shellers to walk off the job in protest against a proposed 50 percent wage reduction. On multiple occasions police fired tear gas on the picketers and arrested Tenayuca along with over a thousand strikers, but they pressed on with their demands. The walkout finally ended when management agreed to arbitration. After Congress passed the National Labor Relations Act later that year, the new national minimum wage raised the workers' wages to twenty-five cents an hour, but thousands started losing their jobs in 1939 when companies began the process of mechanizing their shelling plants to counter rising labor costs.

A New Deal for Native Americans

Native Americans were one minority group to benefit significantly from New Deal policies. From the 1880s to the 1930s, the federal government had largely pursued a policy of relegating them to reservations, with nearly half of those by 1933 becoming landless because they had been swindled out of their land by greedy land speculators. Most with land lived in desert regions and other marginal land that no white person or resource corporation desired. Additionally, white assimilationists during the 1920s continued to exert pressure on the Bureau of Indian Affairs (BIA) to outlaw all native religious ceremonies and frequently took children from tribal communities to place them into federal boarding schools.

Such policies finally ended during FDR's presidency due to the devoted efforts of John Collier, Roosevelt's new BIA commissioner. No sooner did he assume his office than he pursued a policy of relentless pressure upon other New Deal agencies to include Native Americans in their programs. Due to his exertions, all-Native American CCC companies were created and they worked for numerous other agencies on projects to improve reservation land. In 1934, Congress passed the Johnson-O'Malley Act, allocating federal money for states to provide for Indian health care, welfare, and education. Collier also pushed for the repeal of the once-mandatory federal boarding schools for Indian children and instead promoted their enrollment in local public schools. One of his most important accomplishments was allowing Native Americans to once again practice their traditional religions.

The centerpiece of Collier's agenda was the **Indian Reorganization Act of 1934**, which revoked the allotment provisions of the Dawes Act (See Chapter 18) by restoring tribal lands and granting Native Americans the right to establish constitutions and bylaws for self-government. The legislation also provided support for new tribal corporations that would regulate the use of communal lands

and appropriate funds for the economic development of the reservation. The law ended the assimilationist policy pursued by previous administrations by recognizing the principle that Native American groups possessed the right of self-determination and self-government, as well as the right to control their own cultural and economic well being. Collier hoped that his policies would invigorate and sustain traditional Indian culture.

Collier encountered opposition on multiple fronts—from Protestant missionaries and cultural conservatives wanting to continue the assimilationist policy, as well as from white farmers and businessmen who feared that the new legislation would protect Indian lands from their acquisition. Collier even received criticism from some Indian groups who had already embraced assimilation. The Navajo (the nation's largest Native American group) was one such tribe whose members believed the Indian Reorganization Act was another white conspiracy against Native Americans and voted to reject its terms. Many other Native groups also rejected the law's terms. Nevertheless, 181 Native peoples (nearly 70 percent of the total) supported Collier's agenda and organized new tribal arrangements under its auspices. Thanks to Collier and the BIA, many Native American tribes gained significant measures of freedom and autonomy with the New Deal showing considerably more sensitivity to the needs of Native Americans than previous administrations.

ROOSEVELT'S REELECTION AND SECOND TERM

The Election of 1936

Despite the thunder from the left and the anxiety it caused Roosevelt and the New Dealers, by election time, the president had little to fear from the populist activists. By

Bureau of Indian Affairs Commissioner John Collier

shrewdly moving the New Deal to the left, he neutralized the populists and ensured a victory for himself and his party. Efforts by the Far Right members of the American Liberty League to influence the outcome proved to be ineffective. During his re-election campaign, FDR labeled the conservatives and corporate moguls "economic royalists" and called on citizens to strip them of their power and "save a great and precious form of government for ourselves and the world." Voters responded to such rhetoric and the improved (but far from recovered) economy by giving Roosevelt the greatest popular mandate in the history of American politics up to that time. FDR received 61 percent of the popular vote. His Republican challenger, Governor Alf Landon of Kansas (who even lost his own state) received only 36 percent. Only Maine and Vermont, with a combined total of 8 electoral votes, went for Landon.

Roosevelt's landslide represented not only overwhelming endorsement for the president and his New Deal but also the beginning of a liberal Democratic ascendancy. From 1936 forward, the Democratic Party became the party of reform and aid to the "forgotten American." FDR had skillfully assembled various interest groups into a coalition that would become the majority party for the next five decades. One of the party's key voting blocs became northern urban African Americans who deserted the "Party of Lincoln" *en masse* to vote for Roosevelt and the Democrats. African Americans calculated that their interests would best be served by the "Party of the Common Man." Ethnic, urban, working-class Americans, especially those of Italian, Irish, and Jewish heritage, voted overwhelmingly Democratic. To this largely urban contingent, rural farmers in the West and North increasingly joined Southerners in supporting the Democrats in appreciation of the administration's agricultural policies.

Stalemate, 1937-1940

In the euphoria of Roosevelt's landslide victory, the president and his advisers interpreted the result as a popular mandate for their ideas and devised new plans to expand the government's role in the nation's economic affairs. In 1937, Congress created the Farm Security Administration to help improve life for tenant farmers, sharecroppers, and farm laborers, but due to scant funding, the agency only helped a limited number of better-off tenant farmers who received modest rural rehabilitation loans for farm improvements. That same year, Congress established the U.S. Housing Authority to undertake slum clearance and build low-income housing projects. In 1938, New Dealers drafted and lobbied successfully for passage of the Fair Labor Standards Act, which finally outlawed child labor, set minimum wages and maximum hours for adult workers, and established the principal of overtime pay for non-salaried workers.

Republican Party presidential nominee Alf Landon arriving at the White House for a luncheon with President Roosevelt. 1936.

Despite these successes, the New Deal began to lose momentum and popularity by 1938. Though initially supportive of the working class, organized labor's increasing militancy, exemplified by the CIO's rise to prominence via sit-down strikes, began to alienate many in the middle class who became disturbed by labor's growing power and apparent radicalism. To them, Roosevelt had taken the New Deal too far to the left. This was the moment that conservatives had been waiting for. With middle-class support for the New Deal waning, the Right resurrected itself and began to aggressively challenge the president and his programs. Though the conservatives' criticisms found receptive ears, ultimately forcing FDR to move back to the center and curtail the more ambitious, left-leaning social reform programs of the New Deal, at no time was the president ever in jeopardy of losing favor with the American people.

The "Court Packing" Furor

One year after receiving the greatest electoral landslide in American political history, the president committed one of the greatest political blunders of his career: his attempt to increase the size of the Supreme Court—"**court packing**," his critics derisively charged—by proposing to add a new justice for each sitting justice who, having served at least ten years, did not resign or retire within six months after reaching the age of 70 (with a proviso that no more than six additional justices would be appointed). FDR's public reason for his plan was that the current justices were too old and feeble to handle the large volume of cases coming before them, but it soon became apparent that FDR believed that for the New Deal to move forward, he had to find a way of removing the last obstacle to that end. He believed that the most effective way was to propose the idea of simply adding more justices to the bench in order to dilute conservative power. Naturally, his nominees for the High Court would be liberals, and no further New Deal legislation would go the way of the NIRA, the Agricultural Adjustment Act, the Guffey Coal Act, and also some state laws that were all ruled unconstitutional by an obstructionist coalition of conservatives on the Court in 1935-36.

Much to Roosevelt's amazement, many Americans did not agree with his arguments for judicial reform. Though some supported him, quite a few citizens perceived the move as a high-handed attempt to concentrate even greater power in the executive branch, removing the last check on the president's already immense control of the government. In their eyes, Congress had become a rubber stamp for FDR's agenda. Members of the Senate, some of them quite old themselves, objected to the president'

bringing up the age issue. Other lawmakers feared a breakdown of the separation of powers among the three branches of government if the Court was reorganized, effectively making the judicial branch a puppet of the executive branch. Southerners were especially aroused by the plan, for they read into it a conspiracy by Roosevelt and his Yankee New Deal liberals, led by "That Woman," Eleanor Roosevelt, to appoint liberal justices who would upset their region's racial order.

FDR was stunned by the widespread opposition to his plan in Congress but kept fighting with a cadre of congressional supporters including Senate Majority Leader Joseph Robinson. Though Chief Justice Charles Evans Hughes had given congressional opponents some much-needed ammunition when he issued a letter refuting the president's reform claims, at the end of March 1937, Hughes and fellow conservative Justice Owen Roberts broke away from the four reactionary justices on the Court to vote with three liberal justices to uphold a Washington state minimum wage law almost identical to a New York law that a majority had struck down as unconstitutional just six months earlier. Two weeks later, the same combination of justices produced a 5-4 majority to uphold the constitutionality of the Wagner National Labor Relations Act.

This shocking course of events seemed to imply that Roosevelt's attempt at judicial reform had frightened Hughes and Roberts to change their vote (famously referred to as the "switch in time that saved nine") in order to undercut the president and his supporters' efforts to press FDR's scheme. Closer analysis, however, reveals a broader picture. Though the decisions were not released to the general public until March and April 1937, the Court had actually voted on these cases in December 1936—a month after Roosevelt's landslide reelection and three months before the president surprised the Court, and the nation, with his court-packing proposal. Thus, the extent of FDR's triumph, not reform proposal, jolted Hughes and Roberts into rethinking their opposition to the president's policies. As historian Michael Parrish has written: "Hughes and Roberts, both loyal Republicans who distrusted many of the New Deal's innovations, had played a high-stakes political game against the president in 1935-36. Voting with the Four Horsemen (as the Court's four reactionary, ultraconservative justices were often nicknamed) on crucial issues, they hoped to mobilize popular opposition against the administration by portraying it as dangerously radical, a threat to constitutional norms. When the voters rejected this interpretation and gave FDR an overwhelming mandate, the Chief Justice and Roberts had little choice but to temper their opposition, especially after February, when most observers predicted a quick presidential victory on the court-packing bill."

In the coming weeks, High Court approval of the Social Security Act (again, by a 5-4 majority) along with the retirement of reactionary Justice Willis Van Devanter doomed the chances that the court-packing plan would survive. The final blow came when the bill's most energetic champion, Senator Joseph Robinson, suffered a heart attack and died. Nevertheless, while Roosevelt lost the political battle, most historians have concluded that he won the larger war. After 1937, the Hughes Court upheld the constitutionality of New Deal measures, and, as retirements occurred over the next six years, FDR would appoint nine vacancies to the Supreme Court.

The Recession of 1937-1938

Whatever hope Roosevelt may have had for a quick recovery from the court-packing battle was dashed by a sharp recession that hit the country beginning in late 1937. Roosevelt had mostly himself to blame for the downturn. The expanded work program of the Second New Deal helped stimulate the economy to the degree that in 1937 production surpassed the highest level of 1929, and unemployment dropped to 14 percent. Confident that the depression was easing, he made the mistake of cutting back on federally sponsored work relief programs that sustained the supposed recovery. The Federal Reserve tightened credit, and new payroll taxes took $2 billion from wage earners' income to subsidize the Social Security pension fund. That withdrawal would not have hurt the economy had the money been returned to circulation as pensions for retirees. Instead, the money was held with no pensions scheduled to be paid until 1941. Once again, the economy lacked a sufficient money supply, leading to a sharp stock market decline. By October 1937, the market fell by almost 40 percent from its August high. By March 1938, the unemployment rate soared back to 20 percent.

The widespread distress resulting from the 1938 recession badly hurt Democrats in the 1938 mid-term elections. Republicans won a smashing victory, gaining 81 House seats and 8 seats in the Senate. The Congress that assembled in January 1939 was the most conservative of the New Deal years. Since all the Democratic losses had taken place in the North and West, particularly in such key states as Ohio and Pennsylvania, Southerners were now once again in a strong position, and they were in no mood to see any further extension of the welfare state now that the economic emergency of early 1933 had subsided. The House contained 169 non-southern Democrats, 93 southern Democrats, 169 Republicans, and 4 third-party representatives. For the first time, the president could

not form a majority without the help of Southerners and Progressive Republicans. Most observers agreed that the president could, at best, hope to consolidate but certainly not extend the New Deal.

By the end of 1938, it had become clear that any new ambitious goals faced an uncertain future. The New Deal had essentially come to an end as congressional opposition now made it difficult, if not impossible, for FDR to enact any major new programs. More important, perhaps, in ending the New Deal was the threat of world crisis caused by the rise of fascism, which hung heavy in the political atmosphere during the president's second term. Roosevelt gradually became more concerned with persuading a reluctant nation to prepare for war than with pursuing new avenues of reform. With such retrenchment at the national level, the way was now open for conservatives in both parties to unite and mount an all-out attack on New Deal liberalism. By this time, most believed that the New Deal had run its course.

NEW DEAL LEGACY

Elected in 1932, Franklin Roosevelt dominated much of the nation's political history for the next thirteen years. He had few qualms about using the powers of the federal government to combat the Great Depression. Dire economic problems gave him unprecedented opportunities to redefine the federal government's relationship with the American people.

Nevertheless, FDR faced serious constraints. Crisis or not, there were political limits to what the president could do. Many on the political left saw Roosevelt's election as a chance to reform society, to achieve social justice for all, and to restructure American capitalism in order to make it more humane and responsive to the needs of the common people, but FDR had no intention of abandoning corporate capitalism or remaking American society. His choices were shaped by public expectations and political limitations as they intersected with the economic and social needs caused by the Depression. The result was the New Deal, a three-part barrage of government activity designed to bring about relief for the Depression's victims while generating economic recovery and enacting long-standing structural reforms to better regulate the economic sector.

In the end, the New Deal did not end the Depression but served as a mighty holding operation until the massive government borrowing and spending during America's involvement in World War II (what Keynesian economists had long been advocating) finally produced the much-desired economic recovery. One of the most significant legacies of the New Deal lay in the emergence of the federal government, especially the executive branch, as the most powerful and important level of government in the nation. Before the 1930s, people had looked to local, county, and state governments for help. After the New Deal, people looked to Washington for assistance, with government and politics forever changed. Because of the New Deal's extension of public relief to millions of desperate citizens during the most jarring economic calamity in the nation's history, Americans have come to accept the legitimacy of the welfare state. Though they may continue to argue over details, most have come to recognize that many individuals in our society need such assistance to survive. The same voters who returned Roosevelt to office for unprecedented third and fourth terms remained wedded for the next forty years to FDR's central idea: that a powerful state could enhance the pursuit of liberty and equality while preserving its basic economic and political institutions.

Table 23.1

Major New Deal Agencies

Agency	Purpose
Agricultural Adjustment Administration (AAA)	Offered subsidies in exchange for reduced agricultural production to reduce surpluses and boost crop prices
Civilian Conservation Corps (CCC)	Work relief program for youth and war veterans primarily to develop state/national parks and forests
Federal Deposit Insurance Corporation (FDIC)	Established to guarantee depositors' accounts in national banks up to a maximum amount set by Congress
Federal Emergency Relief Administration (FERA)	Worked with state relief agencies to channel funds to the unemployed at the beginning of the New Deal
Federal Housing Administration (FHA)	Attempt to stimulate the construction industry through loans to the general public for home purchases
Home Owners Loan Corporation (HOLC)	Worked with lenders to refinance mortgages to ensure repayment while allowing borrowers to keep their homes
National Labor Relations Board (NLRB)	Supervised employee elections for union representation authorized by the Wagner Labor Relations Act
National Recovery Administration (NRA)	Attempt to generate economic recovery by approving business-created codes setting higher wages and improved working conditions as well as profitable prices for business
National Youth Administration (NYA)	Work relief agency for youth that paid high school and college students to perform jobs on their campuses while providing work skills training for graduates and dropouts
Public Works Administration (PWA)	Work relief program focusing primarily on large-scale infrastructure projects.
Resettlement Administration (RA)	Sought to resettle poor farmers on improved land, issue rehabilitation loans to growers remaining on their land, and provide aid to migratory farm workers
Rural Electrification Administration (REA)	Made loans to local cooperatives to promote accessibility to electricity in rural areas
Securities and Exchange Commission (SEC)	Established to regulate the nation's stock markets and commodities exchanges
Social Security Administration (SSA)	Supervised the new social insurance program established to provide old-age pensions and aid to dependent children and the disabled.
Tennessee Valley Authority (TVA)	Oversaw the construction of dams and hydroelectric plants to end chronic flooding, generate electricity, and foster economic development in the impoverished Tennessee Valley region.
Works Progress Administration (WPA)	Work relief program created in 1935 to greatly expand work opportunities for the unemployed.

Chronology

1929	Herbert Hoover assumes the presidency. Stock Market crashes on "Black Tuesday," October 29.
1930	Hawley-Smoot Tariff.
1932	Unemployment rate reaches 25 percent. Reconstruction Finance Corporation established. Bonus Army marches on Washington. Franklin D. Roosevelt defeats Hoover for presidency.
1933	Hundred Days legislation defines First New Deal. Good Neighbor policy toward Latin America launched. "Bank Holiday."
1934	Charles Coughlin and Huey Long attack New Deal. Indian Reorganization Act.
1935	Committee for Industrial Organization (CIO) founded. Supreme Court declares NRA unconstitutional. Social Security Act. Wagner Act. Emergency Relief Administration Act. Rural Electrification Administration established.
1936	Franklin D. Roosevelt elected to a second term. Supreme Court declares AAA unconstitutional. Soil Conservation and Domestic Allotment Act.
1937	United Auto Workers defeat General Motors in sit-down strike. Supreme Court upholds constitutionality of Social Security and National Labor Relations Acts. Economic recession slows recovery.
1938	Second Agricultural Adjustment Act. Fair Labor Standards Act.
1939	75,000 gather to hear black opera singer Marian Anderson perform at Lincoln Memorial.
1940	FDR reelected for unprecedented third term.

SUGGESTED READINGS

Anthony Badger, *The New Deal: The Depression Years* (1989).

Alan Brinkley, *The End of Reform: New Deal Liberalism in Recession and War* (1995).

Lizabeth Cohen, *Making a New Deal: Industrial Workers in Chicago, 1919-1939* (1990).

Blanche Wiesen Cook, *Eleanor Roosevelt*, vol. 1 (1992).

Cletus E. Daniel, *Bitter Harvest: A History of California Farmworkers, 1870-1941* (1981).

Roger Daniels, *The Bonus March* (1971).

Melvyn Dubofsky and Warren Van Tine, *John L. Lewis: A Biography* (1977).

Sidney Fine, *Sitdown: The General Motor's Strike of 1936-1937* (1969).

Frank Friedel, *Franklin D. Roosevelt: A Rendezvous With Destiny* (1990).

Ellis Hawley, *The New Deal and the Problem of Monopoly* (1967).

Abraham Hoffman, *Unwanted Mexican Americans in the Great Depression: Repatriation Pressures, 1929-1939* (1974).

Lawrence C. Kelley, *The Assault on Assimilation: John Collier and the Origins of Indian Policy Reform* (1983).

David Kennedy, *Freedom From Fear: The American People in Depression and War, 1929-1945* (1999).

Nelson Lichtenstein, *The Most Dangerous Man in Detroit: Walter Reuther and the Fate of American Labor* (1995).

Richard Lovitt, *The New Deal and the West* (1984).

William F. McDonald, *Federal Relief Administration and the Arts* (1968).

Robert S. McElvaine, *The Great Depression* (1984).

George T. McJimsey, *Harry Hopkins: Ally of the Poor and Defender of Democracy* (1987).

Michael E. Parrish, *Anxious Decades: America in Prosperity and Depression, 1920-1941* (1992).

Albert V. Romasco, *The Poverty of Abundance: Hoover, the Nation, the Depression* (1965).

Harvard Sitkoff, *A New Deal for Blacks* (1978).

Keith J. Volanto, *Texas, Cotton, and the New Deal* (2005).

Geoffrey Ward, *Before the Trumpet: Young Franklin Roosevelt, 1882-1905* (1985).

Susan Ware, *Holding Their Own: American Women in the 1930s* (1982).

Nancy J. Weiss, *Farewell to the Party of Lincoln: Black Politics in the Age of FDR* (1983).

Ahmed White, *The Last Strike: Little Steel, the CIO, and the Struggle for Labor Rights in New Deal America* (2016).

Review Questions

1. Assess the Hoover presidency and discuss why Hoover became a one-term president. What were Hoover's views regarding the government's role during a national economic crisis?

2. Describe Rooseveltian liberalism and how FDR's political and economic philosophy differed from that of Hoover, thus allowing FDR to more effectively deal with the Great Depression.

3. Discuss what you believe to be the most important New Deal programs and why.

4. As the New Deal unfolded and its various programs implemented, critics and opposition to such an unprecedented government intervention and assistance emerged. What were some of the opposition's arguments?

5. After the Great Depression and the New Deal, the relationship between the federal government and the American people would never be the same. Why?

Glossary of Important People and Concepts

Agricultural Adjustment Act
Bonus Army
Civilian Conservation Corps (CCC)
Congress of Industrial Organizations (CIO)
Court Packing
Dust Bowl
Emergency Banking Act
Federal Deposit Insurance Corporation (FDIC)
Federal Emergency Relief Administration (FERA)
Herbert Hoover
Indian Reorganization Act of 1934
Huey Long
National Recovery Administration (NRA)
Public Works Administration (PWA)
Reconstruction Finance Corporation (RFC)
Repatriation
Eleanor Roosevelt
Franklin Delano Roosevelt
Rural Electrification Administration (REA)
Social Security Act
Tennessee Valley Authority (TVA)
Francis Townsend
Voluntarism (Voluntary Cooperation)
Wagner (National Labor Relations) Act
Works Progress Administration (WPA)

USS ARIZONA at Pearl Harbor

Chapter Twenty-four

Democracy, Fascism, and Communism at War, 1921-1945

Born into a large farm worker family in northern Mexico, three-year-old Macario García moved to Texas in 1923 with his parents and siblings. Together, they made a living by tending crops on a ranch near Houston. In late 1942, the U.S. Army drafted García, who became an infantryman in the Fourth Infantry Division. Wounded during the Normandy invasion, he recovered and rejoined his unit in time to participate in the final push against Germany. On November 27, 1944, he bravely distinguished himself in battle in western Germany when he singlehandedly assaulted two enemy machine-gun emplacements blocking his company's advance. Though wounded in the shoulder and foot, he crawled toward the machine-gun nests and destroyed the position with grenades, killing six German soldiers and capturing four others. President Harry S Truman personally awarded García the Medal of Honor at a White House ceremony on August 23, 1945. He also received the Purple Heart, the Bronze Star, and the Combat Infantryman's Badge. The government of Mexico later awarded García the Mérito Militar, the Mexican equivalent of the U.S. Congressional Medal of Honor. Receiving an honorable discharge from the army with the rank of sergeant, he returned to Texas with great fanfare as a war hero and was often asked to speak at meetings and banquets.

Despite his elevated status, García attracted media attention in September 1945 when the Anglo owner of a restaurant near Sugar Land, Texas, outside of Houston refused to serve him because he was Hispanic. Upset with his treatment as a second-class citizen despite his military service, García quarreled with the proprietor. Local police arrested the veteran, who was subsequently charged with assault. García's case immediately became a symbolic rallying point for the Tejano community. Many groups, including the League of United Latin American Citizens, and individuals rallied to his aid by sponsoring fundraisers to pay for his defense. Well defended by two fine Tejano attorneys, García was acquitted by a local jury. In 1947, he became an American citizen.

Macario García's experiences were not uncommon for Hispanics and other minority groups before, during, and after World War II. Before the war, García worked hard despite his limited economic and social opportunities. The war provided an avenue for him to show loyalty to his adopted country and to contribute to America's ultimate victory. García's war experiences also changed the veteran, who became less tolerant of segregation and other indignities. As the United States emerged from World War II, the social forces unleashed by the conflict began to alter the country in significant ways.

The United States entered the years after the First World War inwardly confident but unsure of the future. During the 1920s, the nation emerged as an active player on the world stage promoting global stability while expanding its economic reach. With the advent of the Great Depression and the rise of totalitarian regimes in Europe and Asia, however, the U.S. shied away from foreign diplomatic conflicts and focused on domestic matters in an effort to isolate itself from potential involvement in another great cataclysm. With the outbreak of renewed war, however, President Franklin Roosevelt led the United States into a fragile neutrality period that fell just short of open belligerency until the Japanese attack on Pearl Harbor in December 1941.

AMERICA AND THE WORLD DURING THE 1920S

Contrary to a commonly held perception, the United States did not stay aloof from international affairs during the first decade after World War I. During the 1920s, America became involved in foreign issues at an unprecedented level for peacetime. The nation flexed its economic muscles as it maintained a growing trading empire and worked with other countries to promote global stability, pursuing these efforts without military commitments or becoming involved in formal alliances. As historian Warren Cohen described American foreign policy during the decade, the nation's leaders sought to create an "empire without tears," benefiting from a predominant role in a stable postwar world without risking being drawn into another major conflict.

Emerging from the First World War as the world's wealthiest nation, U.S. business and government leaders sought to leverage America's new economic power in an effort to supplant England's historic dominance over global investment and trade. Before World War I, the United States was a debtor nation, owing foreign investors close to $4 billion more than the amount that American investors lent abroad. By the war's end, however, reduced investment by foreign counties in the United States plus large loans by American banks to the Allied nations resulted in a reverse situation whereby the U.S. became a creditor nation with an almost $4 billion favorable balance. During the 1920s, Wall Street bankers greatly expanded financial investments to Europe, Canada, Latin America, Africa, and Asia. By 1929, the value of American exports tripled from pre-war levels, reaching over $7 billion.

Stabilizing the European Economy

European nations found it difficult to repay their American lenders after the war. The U.S. government's high tariffs on foreign goods, a consequence of legislation passed in 1922 and 1930 designed to reverse the previous reductions of the Wilson era, complicated Europe's financial problems. The victorious Allies sought to have much of their $10 billion debt to American bankers canceled, but Woodrow Wilson refused to listen, as did the Republican presidents of the 1920s. Germany experienced great difficulty paying the burdensome war reparations dictated by the Versailles Treaty. After a German default in 1923, French and Belgian troops occupied the heavily industrial Ruhr region of western Germany to extract coal and steel resources, sending a message that non-payment was not an option. The Weimar Republic (Germany's new democratic government established after the war) responded by printing a vast amount of paper money, devaluing its currency, and producing a situation of grave hyper-inflation. The crisis stabilized only after the creation of an international commission headed by Chicago banker Charles G. Dawes, which formulated a plan calling for the flow of private capital (with a majority of the funds coming from American banks) to Germany in exchange for the removal of French and Belgian occupation forces and the resumption of German reparations payments. Approved by the Coolidge administration, the Dawes Plan established a system whereby American financiers made loans to Germany, which used the money to make reparations payments to the victorious Allies, who then began paying back their war loans to the United States (often to the same bankers making the original loans to Germany.) This triangular flow of capital brought financial stability but only as long as the Germans could secure American credit. In 1929, a new commission developed the Young Plan, calling for a sizeable reduction in reparations payments, but the Stock Market Crash and arrival of the Great Depression led American bankers to pull their loans to Germany with devastating economic and political consequences.

Toward the Good Neighbor Policy

The United States remained actively involved in Latin American affairs during the 1920s. While continuing to exert dominance in the region through the traditional means of trade, financial investment, and occasional military intervention, the U.S. also employed new efforts to extend good will. President Harding sought to improve relations with Latin America by recognizing the government of General Alvaro Obregón after the Mexican Revolution and encouraged the U.S. Senate to ratify a treaty authorizing a $25 million payment to Colombia as compensation for America's role in the Panamanian Revolution, which allowed the United States to receive the Panama Canal Zone. In 1924, President Coolidge withdrew marines from the Dominican Republic (under U.S. occupation since 1916), though American representatives remained to manage the revenues of the country and ensure payments of debts to U.S. banks. The American military also organized and trained Dominican forces to replace the departing American troops. (Their leader, General Rafael Trujillo, later overthrew the government and established a brutal thirty-year dictatorship). Coolidge also ordered the removal of American troops from Nicaragua in 1925, but he sent them back a year later when civil war broke out, and they remained until 1932. (The leader of U.S.-trained National Guard forces in Nicaragua, Anastasio Somoza, eventually centralized power under his control in 1936 and ruled by force for the next twenty years.)

President-elect Herbert Hoover signaled a further desire to seek a new relationship with the region when he embarked on a tour of ten Latin American nations in late-1928 and also reversed Woodrow Wilson's policy of not recognizing governments led by individuals who gained power by force. The U.S. government began to recognize any regime in control of its country as long as the new regime met its foreign debt obligations and promised to hold future elections. Hoover also approved public release of the Clark Memorandum, a policy statement written by an undersecretary of state that specifically repudiated the Roosevelt Corollary's reliance upon the to the Monroe Doctrine as a basis to justify American military intervention in the Western Hemisphere.

Hoover's actions laid the groundwork for his successor, Franklin Delano Roosevelt (FDR), to pursue the more assertive **Good Neighbor Policy** during the 1930s. Seeking increased trade with Latin American nations in the midst of the Great Depression, as well as cooperation on mutual defense issues in light of the rise of totalitarian regimes in Europe and Asia, Roosevelt condemned America's past imperialist actions in Latin America. In 1933, Secretary of State Cordell Hull approved a resolution at the Pan-American Conference stating that no country had the right to intervene in the internal affairs of another. The next year, Hull signed an agreement with Cuba renouncing the Platt Amendment to Cuba's constitution, which had given the U.S. government the exclusive right to intervene in the island nation's affairs if its independence or internal order were threatened—a device by which America troops were twice sent to Cuba. In 1936, Roosevelt traveled to Buenos Aires, Argentina, to open the Pan-American Conference with a speech reiterating his administration's desire to stay out of the internal affairs of Central and South American countries. By the end of that year, Roosevelt withdrew the last remaining U.S. troops from Latin American soil. The president's actions resulted in two major benefits to the United States by the end of the 1930s: a quadrupling of trade with Latin America and an increased desire by Western Hemispheric nations to join in a collective security alliance with the United States against potential aggression by Germany and Japan.

Active Global Diplomacy

After World War I, many Americans, including some influential members of Congress, became involved in a growing "peace movement," which sought proactive ways to prevent another horrendous modern war from befalling humanity. American leaders not participating in the movement also favored efforts to preserve global peace, believing that stability best served the interests of the country and its growing economic empire. The major manifestations of the 1920s peace movement were efforts to cooperate with the League of Nations, global armaments reduction, and the seeking of pledges from world governments to renounce war as an instrument of foreign policy.

Though American membership in the League of Nations was a dead issue after Warren Harding's election, the U.S. government still maintained contact with the League through correspondence and by sending diplomats to observe the global organization's meetings in Switzerland. American public opinion strongly supported United States membership in the World Court. Nevertheless, despite all three Republican presidents during the decade and a majority of Congress favoring American participation, the United States did not become a member of the World Court. Key opposition by Senators Henry Cabot Lodge and William Borah led to the Senate only approving the U.S. joining if the Court agreed to avoid addressing matters involving American interests. The Court's members refused the condition, and the United States never joined.

Through Secretary of State Charles Evans Hughes, the Harding administration took an active role in seeking to eliminate a postwar arms race, specifically focusing on the reduction of capital warships (battleships and carriers) held by the major world powers. A majority of Americans agreed with those in the peace movement who believed if nations had reduced armaments they would be less likely to engage in war. Hughes and other government leaders favored arms reductions for more nuanced reasons, specifically, cost savings from reduced defense budgets and significant limits on the naval growth of England and Japan. They also favored meeting with the world's powers to discuss ways to reduce ongoing tensions between them over China. Both Great Britain and Japan had been engaging in massive expenditures for naval construction and signaled a desire to engage in talks toward the goal of arms limitation if they could receive certain assurances that their security would still be protected.

In 1921, Harding invited eight powers to attend an arms limitation conference in the nation's capital. Secretary Hughes opened the **Washington Naval Conference** without obligatory diplomatic clichés expressing hope for success. Instead, he boldly expressed his desire to reach serious agreement on naval reductions and laid out a detailed plan calling for the destruction of specific ships currently in the navies of the invited nations. Over the course of the next several months, the conferees signed three major treaties. The first agreement, the Four-Power Treaty, accepted by the U.S., England, Japan, and France, allowed for a major arms reduction settlement by replacing the existing Anglo-Japanese defense alliance (greatly upsetting to American officials) with a pledge to respect each nation's island possessions in the Pacific. A Nine-Power Treaty, signed by delegates from the nations who agreed to the Four-Power Treaty plus Belgium, Italy, the Netherlands, Portugal, and China sought to reduce commercial rivalries in East Asia. Each nation agreed to adhere to the United States' coveted Open Door Policy in China, thus promising to respect China's territorial integrity while giving each foreign nation an equal opportunity for investment and trade rather than seeking to carve out monopoly privileges in certain regions of the country. The most important accord reached at the conference, however, was the Five-Power Treaty signed by the U.S., Great Britain, Japan, France, and Italy, which provided tonnage limits for each nation's battleships and aircraft carriers (at a ratio of 5:5:3:1.67:1.67 for the above nations, respectively) and a ten-year respite from further battleship construction. Though the agreement did not include smaller combat ships, such as cruisers, destroyers, and submarines, the deal temporarily slowed a growing arms race, at least with regard to capital ships. Japan's government accepted a lower tonnage limit than England and the United States because it would remain the predominant naval force in the Western Pacific (the U.S. also sweetened the pot by agreeing not to build new Pacific bases or to further fortify Guam and the Philippines). Meanwhile, the U.S. gained limits on England and Japan that ensured American predominance in Western Hemispheric waters and British leaders were satisfied that their navy would reign over the high seas everywhere else.

At the time, the Washington Conference seemed to be a significant achievement. Secretary Hughes and American diplomats had led the way to treaties that increased global security by reducing the size of fleets and came to agreement on divisive international issues such as the China trade. Despite the meeting's great promise, however, the deals all lacked tangible enforcement mechanisms beyond the goodwill of the participants. In the early 1930s, Japanese actions in East Asia soon led to the unraveling of all of the diplomats' hard work.

THE RISE OF TOTALITARIANISM IN ASIA AND EUROPE

By the mid-1930s, the world witnessed the rise of dictatorships in Japan, Italy, and Germany—nations that held strong grievances after World War I whether they fought on the losing side (Germany) or contributed to the Central Powers' defeat (Japan and Italy). During the 1930s, the leaders of all three nations chose to pursue aggressive foreign policies with ultimately catastrophic results for their countries as they endeavored to undermine the efforts of the previous decade's peacemakers.

Japanese Militarism and the Takeover of Manchuria

Japan emerged from the nineteenth century as the only industrializing nation in Asia. Its leaders, both civilian and military, sought access to the natural resources needed for its factories that the island nation lacked, though they disagreed on how best to secure these resources. While both groups resented the continuing existence of American and European colonies in Asia, the military leaders who gained increasing control of the Japanese government throughout the 1920s and 1930s favored using force if necessary to acquire the materials that would enable Japan to become the dominant economic and military power in eastern Asia. The reduction of trade and high unemployment that followed the arrival of the Great Depression in Japan only further solidified the leaders' aggressive mindset.

In 1931, Japan became the first nation to abrogate the Nine-Power Treaty and the Kellogg-Briand Pact when its forces took over the loosely-governed Chinese province of **Manchuria**. Long invested commercially in the territory, Japan received half of its food and pig iron from Manchuria, which also served as an outlet for emigrants leaving their overpopulated home islands. Japanese leaders also viewed the region strategically as a vital buffer against Soviet expansion in eastern Asia. Increasingly concerned by the assertion of authority over the region by Chinese Nationalist leader Chiang Kai-shek (Jiang Jièshí), Japanese military leaders staged an incident to justify sending in troops to "restore order." Army units already stationed in the province to guard the Japanese-built South Manchuria Railway—a major thoroughfare from the resource-laden interior to ports on the southern coast—dynamited a section of the line then blamed renegade Chinese soldiers for the action. Japan soon converted Manchuria into a puppet state renamed "Manchukuo" under the control of Puyi, the last emperor of China who had been toppled after the Revolution of 1911. Though Secretary of State

Henry Stimson strongly protested, President Herbert Hoover did not allow him to press American complaints beyond moral objections and a policy of non-recognition of the new regime, soon to be known as the "Stimson Doctrine." After members of the League of Nations followed suit, Japan formally withdrew from the global organization in 1933.

The Rise of Mussolini and the Invasion of Ethiopia

After World War I, Italy came under the domination of **Benito Mussolini**. A former Socialist Party editor and war veteran, Mussolini became the champion of the country's growing **fascist** movement—an extreme right-wing ideology characterized by ultra-nationalism, corporatism, militarism, rabid anticommunism, opposition to democracy, and submission to the state. He capitalized on the suffering postwar Italian economy and discontent with the relatively small amount of spoils that the country received from the Versailles Treaty. Demanding order and the restoration of Italian national pride,

Benito Mussolini

Mussolini led a march of tens of thousands of supporters on Rome in 1922 that turned into a political coup d'état when the king forced out the sitting prime minister and handed Mussolini the reins of power. Within a year, he received dictatorial powers by the national assembly and strengthened control over the country's economy, media outlets, and education system.

Mussolini advocated an expansionist foreign policy for Italy, seeking to create a modern Roman Empire. His initial efforts focused on East Africa where Italy already had a foothold in Somaliland and Eritrea on the eastern border of Ethiopia (which, with Liberia, was one of the last two African nations not under European control). In 1896, Italy had attempted to subjugate Ethiopia but suffered a humiliating military defeat at Adowa. Seeking to avenge that setback and finally bring Ethiopia under Italian control, Mussolini used a skirmish between Italian and Ethiopian forces along the Ethiopia-Somaliland border in late 1934 to justify an all-out attack in October 1935. When the emperor of Ethiopia, Haile Selassie, called for assistance from the League of Nations (of which Ethiopia was a member), he found Great Britain, France and the other major countries distracted by the global economic depression and unwilling to risk another major war. Instead, they filed official protests and enacted minor economic sanctions but fell short of embargoing oil shipments to Italy or taking further steps to force an Italian withdrawal. At one point, the British and French foreign ministers secretly proposed a partition of Ethiopia that was retracted after French journalists revealed the plan to the public. By mid-1936, Italian forces using planes, tanks, and chemical weapons completed their conquest against the outgunned Ethiopian resistance, forcing a dejected Selassie into exile. As historian Robert A. Divine wrote about the lack of will demonstrated by the Western European countries that dominated the League of Nations: "Collective security, the Wilsonian formula for world peace, proved unworkable. No great power was willing to risk war to preserve peace."

The Rise of the Nazis

In Germany, **Adolf Hitler** took notice of the League's impotence. An ethnic German born in Austria, the sociopathic Hitler became chancellor of Germany in 1933 after his fascist, anti-Semitic Nazi Party gained a plurality of seats in the Reichstag (the German Parliament). A small and insignificant fringe group for many years after World War I, the Nazis increasingly took advantage of popular discontent with the Weimar Republic's inability to stem the tide of massive unemployment and business failures caused by the Great Depression and fears generated by the growth of German communist groups. Like other German political parties, the Nazis gained adherents by denouncing the humiliating conditions of the Versailles Treaty, but their ideology and rhetoric went much further, espousing a sinister racism that guided much of their future actions. Touting the racial superiority of the German people, Hitler and other Nazi leaders demanded that all Germans in Europe reside under one government—a belief that justified annexing former German lands that had been taken away by the Versailles Treaty. Hitler also complained that postwar Germany was too small for its burgeoning population and needed to enlarge its borders, in order to survive. Thus, the Nazis justified expansion in the name of *lebensraum*, or "living space," for the German people, especially into the lands of Eastern Europe, which were currently held by racial inferiors. The Nazis also pushed a belief system that called for the elimination of all political and racial undesirables who might weaken their ideal German state. Hence, the later Nazi practice of establishing concentration camps and death camps for communists, Jews, and everyone else they despised. Their hatred of Jews, which was especially virulent, tapped into a longstanding prejudice in German society, making it easier for the Nazis to make scapegoats out of the Jewish people, blaming them for a myriad of problems in postwar Germany.

The Nazis gained more support as Hitler and other party leaders continually blamed the victorious Allied Powers from World War I, Jewish financiers, and communists for the country's ills and promised a restoration of national pride by establishing order, creating a bustling economy, and renouncing the Versailles Treaty. Within three years of assuming power, Hitler received dictatorial powers from the Reichstag, withdrew Germany from the League of Nations, began rebuilding the country's military, and sent troops into the demilitarized Rhineland along the border with France and Belgium with no ramifications.

The Spanish Civil War

After the bloody three-year **Spanish Civil War**, Spain also witnessed the specter of fascism as right-wing rebels finally seized power in 1939. Eight years earlier, a combination of economic hardship caused by the Great Depression and ongoing popular resentment against a dictatorial general serving as prime minister led to the non-violent overthrow of King Alfonso XIII. A republic established to replace the monarchy brought to power many politicians whose liberal and anticlerical reforms appalled Spanish traditionalists. A new constitution called for the absence of religious involvement in government and educational affairs while allowing the possibility of the nationalization of many public services. Further, the new government allowed home rule for the province of Catalonia, upsetting those who believed that such action would lead to national disunity and the breakup of the Spanish state. In July 1936, after national elections won by left-leaning political parties were followed by a series of political assassinations and street fighting incidents conducted by extremists on both sides of the political spectrum, army units based in Spanish-held Morocco under the command of fascist General Francisco Franco revolted against the republican government. Though supported by monarchists, Catholic clergy and religious conservatives, large landowners, wealthy urban elites, and army troops based in several regions of the country, Franco's move initially met with strong resistance from large segments of the population, especially the country's liberals, labor unions, socialists, and communists.

Both sides received foreign military aid. The rebels received generous support from Mussolini and Hitler who sought to test out new military equipment and tactics while currying favor with their ideological counterparts in Spain, possibly acquiring a valuable future ally if Franco could emerge victorious. The German "Condor Legion" consisting of air and ground forces directly aided Franco, beginning with twenty transport planes used to ferry Franco's forces from Morocco to southern Spain. German bombers also attacked Republican military positions and

Adolf Hitler

occasionally terrorized the civilian population (one such raid on a Spanish town inspired Pablo Picasso's famous painting *La Guernica*), as did Italian air forces based on the island of Majorca. For a time, Italian submarines sank Spanish loyalist ships in the Mediterranean Sea. Eventually over 50,000 Italian and 15,000 German troops entered Spain to equip, train and fight alongside the Spanish fascists. While the governments of England, France, the United States, and other major nations stood idly by in hopes of avoiding escalation into a major European war, the Soviet Union sent several hundred men and pilots along with money and military equipment to aid the Spanish loyalists. An additional 30,000 volunteers from other countries (including 3,000 Americans) formed various "international brigades" to fight for the republican cause.

Ultimately, the fascist forces gained the upper hand and drove the republicans from power. Though sympathetic to Germany and Italy, Franco never formally allied with Hitler or Mussolini, focusing instead on rebuilding the country and establishing a right-wing dictatorship that would control Spain until his death in 1975. Many conservatives hailed the general as the nation's savior who stamped out the forces of anti-clericalism, socialism, communism, and anarchism. For republicans and their allies outside of Spain, Franco's triumph was a victory for reactionary forces who favored the status quo that benefited the privileged classes at the expense of social reforms that would aid a broader spectrum of the population. For students of history, the Spanish Civil War represents a precursor of the much larger and bloodier European war yet to come.

AMERICAN ISOLATIONISM

During the 1930s, the United States turned inward and largely retreated from the global arena. Supporters of American **isolationism** believed that the rise of aggressive militarist regimes in Europe and Asia threatened world peace. Abstaining from involvement in the affairs of those continents might avert the United States being drawn into another bloody conflict matching or surpassing the carnage of the First World War. Not all Americans held this sentiment. Many internationalists believed it foolhardy to think that the U.S. had no stake in what took place in Europe or Asia, or that the nation could remain aloof from global affairs and be guaranteed that its security would not be endangered. Non-interventionists won the debates of the early-to-mid 1930s, however, because the Great Depression simply dominated the public's attention. As historian Robert Divine described the prevailing attitude:

"Most Americans in the 1930s were neither isolationists nor internationalists. Rather than adhering to any dogmatic views of foreign policy, they simply ignored the world." Isolationist politicians in Congress tapped into this sentiment to drive American foreign policy during most of the 1930s until the outbreak of the Second World War caused many Americans to rethink their country's role as an innocent bystander.

The Neutrality Acts

Beyond the renewed threat of war, the 1930s spirit of non-involvement had much to do with a reassessment of World War I. Popular novels such as Erich Maria Remarque's *All Quiet on the Western Front* fed into the public's growing repugnance to the glorification of war. Historians began to re-examine Woodrow Wilson's role in a negative light, blaming the president for policies that linked the United States inexorably closer to the Allies, making American involvement all but inevitable. Corporations also came under heavy fire for profiting heavily from the conflict. As calls rang out to investigate "the merchants of death," isolationists in Congress responded by probing the actions of businesses and their possible connection to U.S. entry into the war. Senator Gerald Nye of North Dakota headed a two-year special Senate committee investigation of armaments manufacturers, the shipbuilding industry, and investment bankers such as J.P. Morgan and Company. In addition to publicizing the huge profits reaped by bankers and munitions makers, the Nye Committee uncovered evidence of collusive bidding for government contracts and other nefarious practices but could never concretely substantiate the assertion that American businessmen used their power and influence to draw the country into the European war in order to garner huge profits.

The Nye Committee's findings led isolationist senators to sponsor neutrality legislation specifically designed to insulate the nation from repeating the steps that led the United States into the First World War. From 1935 to 1937, Congress passed three separate **Neutrality Acts** making the selling of arms or the issuance of loans to nations at war, regardless of circumstances, a criminal offense. American citizens could only legally trade non-military items to nations at war on a "cash and carry" basis, meaning without credit and only if the belligerents hauled away the items on non-American ships to avoid their potential sinking in a war zone leading to an international incident. Though President Franklin D. Roosevelt preferred language that would allow him to exercise discretion with regard to applying the legislation's terms, he reluctantly signed the Neutrality Acts into law. Understanding the prevailing political mood and needing the support of isolationist members of Congress to get key provisions of his New Deal program passed, FDR bowed to the pressure while reserving the idea of seeking revisions in the future. The president showed much more rigor in 1938 when he mobilized supporters in Congress to defeat the so-called Ludlow Amendment—a proposed constitutional amendment sponsored by an isolationist Indiana congressman that would have required a majority vote of the American people in a nationwide referendum before Congress could authorize U.S. involvement in any war.

THE COMING OF WORLD WAR II

Despite Roosevelt's dilemma of facing the threat to world peace posed by Germany, Italy, and Japan while isolationist sentiment remained strong in the United States, the president continued to speak out in an effort to influence public opinion. In October 1937, FDR gave his famous "Quarantine Speech" in Chicago in which he called on nations to rise up and contain the world's aggressors (which he refused to mention directly). Rather than issuing a specific plan of action, Roosevelt characteristically used a simple metaphor to make his point, describing war as a "contagion" and expressing his belief that the world must react to the "epidemic of world lawlessness" as the public would respond to a medical crisis: "When an epidemic of physical disease starts to spread, the community approves and joins in a quarantine of the patients in order to protect the health of the community against the spread of the disease." Though the isolationist press soundly criticized the address as unnecessarily provocative, a majority of editorials in American newspapers supported the president's stance and choice of words. Nevertheless, the western European democracies and the United States government continued to avoid taking a firm stand in the direct path of the aggressor nations.

The Japanese Invasion of China

In July 1937, the Japanese army took advantage of an ongoing civil war between Nationalist forces under Chiang Kai-shek and communist rebels led by Mao Zedong to commence an all-out invasion of China. Though civilian leaders in Japan had long sought to extract the wealth of China through diplomatic maneuverings and favorable trade deals, militarists within the government who assumed power by the mid-1930s determined to use force to exert their nation's dominance. The move into China culminated a series of recent actions by the Japanese government signaling the implementation of a more ag-

gressive foreign policy. In the prior four years, Japanese leaders had withdrawn from the League of Nations, chose not to renew the Five-Power Treaty, and signed the Anti-Comintern Pact with Germany as a sign of mutual hostility against communism and to form the basis of a defensive alliance against the Soviet Union. Despite these moves, the American government was caught off guard as Japanese forces pressed deeply into northern China. Upset at the unprovoked attack and believing that the neutrality legislation's provisions concerning arms and loan bans would favor Japan, President Roosevelt chose to use Japan's failure to formally declare war against China as a pretense for not applying the Neutrality Acts to the conflict.

As Japan's forces brutally dominated China's coastal regions and sacked its largest cities (killing an estimated 200,000 civilians in Nanking alone), Chiang and Mao declared a temporary cease fire and withdrew into the country's vast interior to wage a long fight against their common foe. Americans within China occasionally came under fire, most notably in December 1937 when overzealous Japanese pilots attacked the *Panay*, a U.S. Navy gunboat serving in a squadron stationed on the Yangtze River near Nanking to protect American nationals and oil tankers trading along the waterway. After a thirty-minute bombing and strafing run, the *Panay* and three nearby tankers sank to the bottom of the Yangtze. The attack killed three American sailors and wounded forty-three others. Though U.S. State Department officials loudly protested, most Americans did not see the incident as the equivalent of the sinking of the *Maine* or the *Lusitania*. Many agreed with Senator William Borah's view that the incident was a regrettable consequence of the presence of Americans in a war zone. Japanese leaders quickly moved to resolve the matter by formally apologizing and agreeing to indemnify the United States government and families of the victims, though they continued to hold to the false assertion that the attack had been merely a case of mistaken identity. Though Americans soon forgot the *Panay* episode, they continued to sympathize with the Chinese as Japan solidified its hold over China. Nevertheless, the United States continued to supply Japan with oil, scrap iron, and other materials used for military purposes.

The High Water Mark of Appeasement: Austria and Czechoslovakia

In Europe, the people and governments of Great Britain and France feared the outbreak of another continent-wide war. Both countries assumed a defensive posture during the late-1930s by continuing a passive foreign policy while rearming their militaries. France spent considerably on its Maginot Line, a massive network of fixed fortifications along the French-German border stretching from Switzerland to Belgium, begun in 1930 as a deterrent to German aggression. In the two years since moving troops into the Rhineland, Adolf Hitler quietly rearmed the German war machine, aided Franco's forces in the Spanish Civil War, and formed an alliance with Italy (creating the Berlin-Rome "Axis") but did not make any belligerent moves for territory. This dormancy changed in early 1938 when Hitler began amassing troops on the Austrian border, demanding the union (or *anschluss*) of his homeland with Germany—something Austria's fascists (and some non-fascists) had been advocating for years. Not receiving support from England and France (or Italy, which had previously opposed Austro-German unification), Austrian chancellor Kurt Schuschnigg sought to avoid bloodshed by resigning and allowing the leader of the Austrian Nazis to replace him. Hitler soon received an invitation to send troops into Austria. The next day, German storm troopers arrived, followed by Hitler himself who triumphantly returned to Vienna, the old Austrian capital where he lived as a young man before leaving to fight in the German army during World War I. Though forbidden by the Versailles Treaty, Germany soon formally annexed Austria with nary a protest from English and French leaders. The first phase of Hitler's expansionist agenda had succeeded.

Hitler soon made new territorial demands in Central Europe, this time upon the newly-formed nation of Czechoslovakia. In the Sudetenland, a mountainous region formerly part of Austria-Hungary that the Versailles agreement gave to the Czechs in order to create a militarily strong western border, the province's 3.5 million ethnic Germans (out of a total Sudeten population of 5 million) continually sought autonomy. Sudeten fascists went further, demanding annexation by Germany. Though Czech leaders reluctantly agreed to grant local autonomy, Hitler intervened and advocated the turnover of the entire province to German control or face invasion. Shrouding himself under a veil of Wilsonian self-determination as a champion for the rights of a supposedly oppressed German minority, the dictator's real desire was to dismantle the rigid fortifications constructed in the mountain ranges along the border with Germany, which the large and well-equipped Czech army could use to severely hamper a potential attack.

Czech president Eduard Beneš appealed to France, which had a defense treaty with his country. The French government refused to act alone (nor did the Soviet Union, which had a conditional defense agreement with Czechoslovakia based on French action) but asked British Prime Minister Neville Chamberlain to intervene. In late-September 1938, Chamberlain traveled to Bavaria to meet personally with Hitler in order to resolve the crisis. Hitler continued to press for annexation of the Sudetenland, claiming its German majority were being grossly mistreated. Hoping to forestall war, Chamberlain accepted Hitler's demands in principle and informed the Czechs that they would eventually have to turn over the province to Germany as the price for peace. After Beneš reluctantly agreed to the conditions, Chamberlain relayed the Czech government's acceptance only to discover that Hitler now demanded the transfer of the Sudetenland to take place by October 1 or German troops would march.

French, British, and Czech public opinion bristled at Hitler's arrogance, while in the United States the mood soured as the specter of war appeared. Franklin Roosevelt then sent a message to Beneš, Hitler, Chamberlain, and President Edouard Daladier of France urging the leaders to meet and settle the matter peacefully. At no point, however, did Roosevelt suggest that he would personally take part in the proceedings. Hitler soon invited Chamberlain, Daladier, and Mussolini (but not Beneš) for a conference in Munich. When Roosevelt heard that Chamberlain accepted Hitler's invitation, the president sent a two word telegram to the prime minister: "Good man."

The **Munich Conference**, which took place September 29-30, marked the high water mark for the failed efforts of the British and French governments to contain Hitler's ambitions through the policy of appeasement, or the continuous granting of concessions in the hope that violence would be averted. At Munich, Chamberlain agreed to German occupation of the Sudetenland by mid-October in return for his promise not to invade Czechoslovakia, but he truly believed that he scored a major diplomatic achievement in the form of a signed agreement by Hitler affirming that the dictator had no further territorial aspirations in Europe. Returning to London, the prime minister famously told a friendly crowd while holding the signed document that he had in his hand "peace in our time." Ultimately, the Munich Conference proved to be Hitler's greatest diplomatic victory because he had no intention of honoring the deal.

As German troops entered the Sudetenland, Hitler began to plan his next moves during the ensuing winter. On March 15, 1939, he largely expected to start the next major European war when he crassly ordered troops to invade Czechoslovakia. As German forces swept down from the Sudenland, the Czechs put up little resistance. The next day, Hitler proclaimed the creation of the Protectorates of Bohemia and Moravia out of the country's remaining Czech-majority western provinces. Fascists in the eastern Slovakian provinces soon proclaimed their independence and formed an alliance with Germany. To these actions, the shocked Chamberlain and Daladier filed formal diplomatic protests, ordered a quickened rearmament, and made pledges to Poland on Germany's eastern border regarding its territorial integrity—a German invasion of Poland would mean war with England and France.

The Nazi-Soviet Partition of Poland

Having basically torn up the Munich agreement with no ramifications, Hitler did not fear the British and French threats and prepared to attack Poland. The dictator did, however, feel unsure about the Soviet reaction to such a move. If England and France declared war against Germany, Hitler did not yet wish to become involved in a fight with the Russians (though he planned to attack the Soviet Union to acquire more lebensraum for Germany at a later date), so he sent diplomats to Moscow to negotiate an understanding over Polish territory. For his part, the Soviet leader Joseph Stalin wished to delay a war with Germany. Having seized power after the death of Vladimir Lenin, the ruthless Stalin spent much of the 1920s and 1930s creating a police state while expanding the country's industrial base and building up the Russian military. Ever fearful of being overthrown, the paranoid dictator added generals and other top army officers to his long list of real and imagined opponents that he ordered imprisoned or killed. Aware that his purge greatly weakened the leadership of his armed forces, Stalin proved willing to strike a deal with Hitler in order to buy more time. The announcement of the resulting **Nazi-Soviet Non-Aggression Pact** on August 20, 1939, shocked many throughout the world. The leaders of Fascist Germany and Communist Russia, two countries with polar opposite ideologies (though both controlled by dictators), publicly pledged mutual peace and promised neutrality if the other became engaged in a war with other nations. Privately, the two sides also agreed to divide Poland along stipulated boundaries—the Germans would occupy the western two-thirds of the country while the Russians would move into the eastern third.

WORLD WAR II BEGINS IN EUROPE

On September 1, 1939, German forces stormed into Poland. Though England and France could do nothing immediately to stop the onslaught, their governments carried out their threat to declare war on Germany. Stalin ordered Russian troops to occupy its prescribed zone, ostensibly to protect the western border of the Soviet Union. The valiant Polish resistance lasted three weeks. By the end of September, the Germans had captured the capital of Warsaw and dominated the western and central regions of the country. Meanwhile, Russian troops and secret police secured control of the eastern sector. Stalin ordered political leaders, army officers, and the Polish intelligentsia to be rounded up and imprisoned. The next year, he ordered over 20,000 to be executed, including 5,000 members of the officer corps in the Katyn Forest Massacre—an atrocity that the Nazis uncovered in 1943 and publicized for propaganda purposes.

Neutrality Revision

The outbreak of war in Europe led Franklin Roosevelt to immediately declare U.S. neutrality. Unlike Woodrow Wilson, Roosevelt did not ask the American people to be neutral in thought as well as action. In a fireside chat to the nation, the president stressed his desire to keep the United States at peace but stated clearly that neutrality did not necessarily mean impartiality. Seeking to aid the western allies and sensing public reaction shifting toward sympathy with England and France, the president soon called a special session of Congress to consider revision of the Neutrality Acts. The isolationists rallied in protest. While opposition congressmen organized a voting bloc, a flurry of celebrities from diverse backgrounds, such as the aviator Charles Lindbergh, Socialist Party leader Norman Thomas, and former President Herbert Hoover delivered mass appeals to pressure Congress to maintain the Neutrality Acts. Though still a potent force not to be ignored, the spirit of isolationism began to wane in the face of the Nazi juggernaut. Both houses of Congress passed a new Neutrality Act in early November 1939 that ended the arms embargo on nations at war provided that they adhered to the cash and carry system. Because the British navy could easily prevent any German merchant ships from traveling to the United States and returning with cargo, the revisions clearly benefited England and France.

The Fall of France

With the exception of the Soviet Union's costly but successful fight against neighboring Finland to secure territory around its vital port city of Leningrad, inactivity characterized the immediate winter months after the fall of Poland. This period of relative calm ceased in April 1940 when Germany began offensive operations in Western Europe by attacking Denmark and Norway. The following month, German ground troops supported by tanks and dive bombers employing new *blitzkrieg* ("lightning war") tactics emphasizing speed and concentrated power at the point of attack, sliced through the Netherlands and Belgium to press into northwestern France where they outflanked the Maginot Line defenders. Within a week, British forces sent to aid the French found themselves cut off and forced to retreat to the port city of Dunkirk along the English Channel. Miraculously, almost 340,000 British and French troops were able to evacuate via a combination of Royal Navy vessels and private craft, including fishing boats, yachts, and merchant ships. Italy entered the fight late by launching an attack on southern France in mid-June. Within six weeks, Nazi forces reached Paris—a goal that had eluded Germany in four years of fighting during World War I. The French government soon surrendered, leaving Germany in control of Western Europe. To conserve military resources, Hitler struck a deal with French leadership—German troops would occupy only the northern and western regions of the country while French fascist and reactionary collaborators led by 84-year old Philippe Pétain, the famed World War I marshal who defeated the Germans at Verdun, would establish a government in the south known as Vichy France (named after the city which served as its administrative center). The 100,000 exiled "Free French" forces based in England under the command of General Charles de Gaulle refused to recognize the legitimacy of Pétain's regime.

With his requests for a ceasefire rebuffed by England's new Prime Minister, Winston Churchill, Hitler made plans for an invasion of the British Isles. The Royal Air Force and Royal Navy, however, stood in his way. The first phase of the attack, begun in mid-July 1940, involved an attempt to destroy England's air forces. To this end, German Luftwaffe (air force) commander Hermann Goering ordered daily sorties of bombers over England to hit military and industrial targets. This action would draw out British fighter planes, which he hoped to eliminate with escorting fighter squadrons. For the next four months, the **Battle of Britain** raged in the British skies. During the fight, German bombers struck airfields, port installations, and factories, but also deliberately targeted cities, especially London. While both sides suffered tremendous losses, the British began to seize the upper hand. Helped out by the new technology of radar, ground technicians tracked the arrival of raiding planes, allowing scrambling pilots to concentrate their defenses with maximum efficiency. Eventually, Hitler called off the air assault, not wishing to lose most of his air forces in a grinding battle of attrition. Confident that he neutralized England, the dictator chose to conserve his air forces for his planned invasion of the Soviet Union. That offensive, codenamed "Operation Barbarossa," would be Hitler's boldest move yet as he carried out the Nazi desire for *lebensraum*. The

breaking of the Non-Aggression Pact with Stalin, however, also proved to be the beginning of his downfall.

THE AMERICAN REACTION TO WAR

The swiftness of France's defeat and the ferocity of Germany's subsequent air attacks on English cities during the Battle of Britain generated much fear and anxiety in the United States. Hitler's rapid victories meant that Americans could not simply rely on the latest round of European fighting to become the long grueling stalemate that occurred during World War I. Congress soon voted for a five-fold increase in the 1940 military budget (from $2 billion to over $10 billion), producing a tremendous increase in defense-related jobs that largely ended the Great Depression by early 1941. In September 1940, Congress approved FDR's request for the nation's first-ever peacetime draft. Noting the shift in American public opinion concerning the situation in Europe, Roosevelt became bolder in issuing executive orders. Following a request for additional aid from Winston Churchill, the president authorized the transfer of fifty aging destroyers to England in order to be outfitted with modern equipment to help the British navy fight off German U-Boats. In exchange for these submarine hunters, the United States would take over British air and naval bases in the Western Hemisphere from Newfoundland to the West Indies. Though beneficial to American defense, the destroyers-for-bases deal was yet another move clearly designed to benefit Germany's enemies.

The Election of 1940

The war in Europe loomed heavily over the political landscape in the 1940 presidential race. Not wishing to hand the reins of government to a new leader in a time of global crisis (especially when that leader might be a Republican), Franklin Roosevelt decided to seek an unprecedented third term. Isolationists who pinned their hopes on like-minded politicians such as Senator Robert Taft of Ohio or Senator Arthur Vandenberg of Michigan were gravely disappointed when Republicans nominated utility company executive Wendell Willkie of Indiana. Though an ardent opponent of New Deal business regulations, Willkie supported the president's policy of aiding England and endorsed both the destroyers-for-bases deal and the peacetime draft. Despite favoring aid to Britain, both Roosevelt and Willkie relentlessly sought to reassure voters that they favored staying militarily out of the European conflict. Near the end of the campaign, Willkie began to openly question Roosevelt's commitment to remain out of the war. The president responded in a speech delivered in Boston by famously declaring: "Your boys are not going to be sent into any foreign wars." When an adviser pointed out before the address that the statement might be misleading because it left out the possibility of America retaliating if directly attacked, Roosevelt replied: "Of course we'll fight if attacked. If somebody attacks us, then it isn't a foreign war is it?" Ultimately, with both candidates supporting aid to England while keeping American troops at home, a majority of voters chose the more popular and experienced leader, not wishing to change horses midstream. Though the energetic Willkie outperformed previous Roosevelt opponents, the president made American electoral history by securing his third term with a solid reaffirmation from the electorate, winning by a 27,307,819 (54.8 percent) to 22,321,018 (44.8 percent) popular vote margin and a 449-82 electoral vote tally.

Lend-Lease

A month after FDR's victory, Prime Minister Churchill penned a long letter to the president explaining Britain's dire financial condition. Due to run out of cash reserves within six months, England would no longer be able to purchase American war supplies. Churchill implored Roosevelt to find new ways to maintain the lifeline of supplies to help defeat Hitler. A few weeks later, the president explained the situation to a group of assembled reporters and announced his decision to ask Congress to authorize the leasing of American war materiel to Great Britain, likening the circumstances to loaning a garden hose to a neighbor whose house was on fire and then later taking back the hose free of charge. Isolationists who believed Roosevelt's proposal was both unnecessary and wasteful because war equipment loaned out for combat service would never be useful again preferred Senator Taft's analogy better, comparing the leasing of war supplies to lending out chewing gum—once used, "you don't want it back."

Despite isolationist criticism, FDR's opponents faced an uphill battle in their effort to stymie the president's plan and were soundly routed by large margins in both houses of Congress. Signed into law on March 11, 1941, the **Lend-Lease Act** authorized a $7 billion appropriation and empowered the president "to sell, transfer title to, exchange, lease, lend, or otherwise dispose of" any American defense articles to the government of any country whose defense the president deemed vital to the protection of the United States. The intention was clear: the United States government would no longer be merely allowing American manufactures to sell munitions to England.

Though still expected to be hauled away on British naval vessels, weapons and other military equipment would now simply be purchased by the U.S. government (or taken directly from its military stockpiles) and given to the British with no expectation of repayment. When Hitler finally broke the Non-Aggression Pact with Stalin and foolishly launched Operation Barbarossa against Russia in June 1941, Roosevelt authorized the extension of Lend-Lease aid to the Soviet Union.

The Undeclared Naval War vs. Germany in the Atlantic

Always desirous of establishing trust with those he worked with closely, Roosevelt invited Winston Churchill to attend a secret conference so the two leaders could converse about the latest war developments and form the basis of a personal friendship. For four days in early August, Roosevelt and Churchill convened onboard British and American warships off the coast of Newfoundland. After discussing ways to aid the Soviet Union and agreeing to give Japanese leaders a vague warning about the potential for war if their aggression in East Asia did not cease, Roosevelt and Churchill worked out a set of jointly held moral principles. Known as the Atlantic Charter, the joint statement announced that the two nations agreed to the principles of self-determination, equal access to raw materials, and freedom of the seas, while condemning Nazi tyranny and promoting a new system of international security. Though Churchill wished to have more definite commitments from Roosevelt, the prime minister understood the president's position. Until the American public signaled a willingness to enter the fight, he would have to be satisfied for the moment with Roosevelt's symbolic show of support.

After his meeting with Churchill, Roosevelt stepped up U.S. naval aid to the British. At the start of the war, the president had established a 300-mile neutrality belt in the western Atlantic. By the autumn of 1941, American forces occupied Greenland and Iceland. Further, Roosevelt authorized U.S. naval ships to escort British convoys heading from America as far as Iceland's shores. The president also allowed American ships to assist British planes and ships in locating German submarines in the North Atlantic.

Provocative incidents were bound to occur. On September 4, 1941, a German U-Boat fired upon the *Greer*, an American destroyer that had been helping a British patrol plane track the submarine. After the plane dropped four depth charges, the U-Boat fired two torpedoes at the *Greer* (both missed) before escaping. Reporting the event to the American public before the details were completely known, Roosevelt deliberately whipped up public outrage in an effort to portray the incident as a completely unprovoked act of aggression by the German submarine, which he famously dubbed a "rattlesnake of the Atlantic." He then warned German and Italian ships that they entered the U.S. defense perimeter at their own peril. Hitler scoffed at Roosevelt's proclamations, but with the invasion of Russia still in doubt, he ordered German submarine commanders to avoid attacks on American vessels. Nevertheless, confrontations in the undeclared naval war continued to take place. On October 17, the U.S. destroyer *Kearney* responded to reports that several U-Boats were attacking a nearby Canadian convoy. Upon its arrival at the scene, the destroyer began dropping depth charges before being struck by a torpedo. The blast killed eleven sailors before the ship limped back to port in Iceland. Two weeks later, another U-Boat sunk the *Reuben James* while the U.S. destroyer escorted British merchant vessels. Though 115 sailors perished, only a quarter of Americans surveyed in a national poll favored war with Germany over the incident. In response to these hostilities, Congress (by a close vote in each house) revised the 1939 Neutrality Act by authorizing the arming of American merchant ships and allowing American merchant and naval vessels to enter war zones (thus ending cash-and-carry). Though the isolationists showed that their viewpoint could not be ignored, the internationalists once again retained the support of a majority of Americans and secured the necessary votes in Congress to continue their piecemeal stripping away of neutrality short of U.S. entry into the fight. At the time, most Americans believed that if their country entered the conflict it would result from a provocative act by Germany rather than Japan.

Worsening Relations with Japan

The outbreak of war in Europe presented opportunities for the Japanese in Southeast Asia. The region's French, English, and Dutch colonies stood virtually defenseless against any move by the Japanese military to secure control of their vital oil, rice, tin, and rubber resources. Only the United States stood in the way of these ambitions. Immediately after the fall of France, Japanese leaders made demands upon the Vichy French government to cut off an important aid route for Chiang Kai-shek's forces in southern China by shutting down a railroad link from North Vietnam. After the French acquiesced, England reluctantly gave in to Japanese demands to close the Burma Road being used to funnel supplies from British-held Burma into southern China.

Concerned about the possibility of a Japanese takeover of Southeast Asia, FDR implemented a series of cautious moves designed to send warnings to the Japanese leaders without unnecessarily provoking them into action. In May 1940, the president transferred the headquarters of the Pacific Fleet from California to Pearl Harbor in Hawaii. This relocation placed the nation's naval forces much closer to American possessions in the Western Pacific. Though justifiable as a defensive measure, the order sent a definite signal to Japan that Roosevelt was aware of the geopolitical situation and would not ignore further Japanese advances in Asia. He also began to advocate the use of limited economic sanctions against Japan. Though some of his advisers believed that trade embargoes would drive Japan to aggression, Roosevelt agreed with those who wished to see if economic pressure might persuade the Japanese leaders to alter their policies, beginning with aviation fuel and high-grade steel. When Japan demanded and received from Vichy France the right to place troops and airbases in the northern Vietnam portion of French Indochina in August 1940, Roosevelt banned all scrap iron and steel exports to Japan. Though Japan relied heavily on the United States for oil (90 percent of its imported petroleum came from America), the president chose to hold that card in his deck for the time being.

In late-September 1940, Japanese leaders responded to the American embargoes by signing the Tripartite Pact with Germany and Italy. The treaty members pledged "to assist one another with all political, economic, and military means" if one of the nations were to be attacked "by a power at present not involved in the European War or in the Sino-Japan conflict." In case there was any doubt that the agreement was directly aimed at the United States, the treaty included a section specifically exempting the Soviet Union from its provisions. Thus, Japanese and German leaders hoped to dissuade the United States from military involvement against them by conjuring up the logistical nightmare of a two-front war to be fought on opposite ends of the globe. If Japanese leaders thought their action would allow them to pursue a free hand in Southeast Asia, however, they were mistaken. The Tripartite Pact irked Roosevelt and other American leaders, hardening their attitudes toward Japan. The treaty fed into the narrative that Japanese aggression in Asia had to be resisted not just because of the economic problems that a Japanese-dominated Asia would pose to American interests, but also because of the very real military threat that an empowered Japan in control of Asian resources and in league with the Berlin-Rome Axis would pose to American security.

Roosevelt responded to the announcement of the Tripartite Pact by adding pig iron, iron ore, and copper to the list of embargoed items while stepping up American aid to China. In addition to authorizing a $100 million loan to Chiang's government, the president allowed American military pilots to resign their commissions and volunteer to fight in China in squadrons under the command of Colonel Claire Chennault. Using American planes but flying Chinese Nationalist insignia, the "Flying Tigers" provided some semblance of a Chinese Air Force and helped to bog down sizeable numbers of troops and planes that the Japanese could have better utilized elsewhere.

The Road to Pearl Harbor

In an effort to warm relations, Japan sent a new ambassador to the United States in February 1941, the amiable Admiral Kichisaburo Nomura—a man with many prominent American friends who professed an honest desire to reach an understanding between the two countries. Nomura met over forty times throughout the year with Secretary of State Cordell Hull, but the talks eventually stalled. Japanese leaders would not settle for anything less than American acceptance of their country's dominance over eastern Asia while the United States continued to press for Japanese withdrawal from China and Indochina.

While negotiations continued, the Japanese government continued plans to expand into Southeast Asia. After Germany attacked the Soviet Union in June 1941, Japanese leaders felt secure about the northern flank of their empire. With the Russians preoccupied, they could now focus attention on the European colonies to the south of China. Hitler desired a Japanese attack on the Russians in eastern Siberia, but Japan refused—a

"Flying Tigers"

clear sign that while Japan and Germany faced common enemies, they selfishly took advantage of each other's actions against their opponents without closely coordinating their moves. Ignoring Nomura's pleas to grant some concessions to the American position, Japanese leaders made plans to take over all of Indochina. This decision became quickly known to U.S. government officials because cryptographers with Naval Intelligence had recently broken the Japanese diplomatic codes. All messages sent to, and transmitted from, the Japanese embassy were routinely intercepted and deciphered. Before the Japanese invaded southern Indochina in late-July, Roosevelt had already prepared an executive order declaring an oil embargo plus a freeze of Japanese assets held in American banks, effectively severing all trade between the countries. Though the president realized his decision might provoke the Japanese to seize the Netherlands East Indies leading to war with the United States (a scenario he wished to avoid because of the perceived greater threat posed by Germany), he refused to stand by idly while Japan continued its aggression with tacit American government approval. Determined to try one last round of economic coercion with the major commodity that Japan's industry and war machine truly relied upon, FDR placed the ball in Japan's court—if aggression continued, they would be the instigators and America would have no choice but to intervene in order to prevent all of East Asia falling under Japanese control.

Saddled with only a year's supply of oil in reserve and committed to expansion by force if necessary, Japan's leaders decided to seize the Dutch East Indies. Concluding that war with the United States was probably inevitable, they approved plans to get the upper hand in the coming fight by attacking the American Pacific fleet at **Pearl Harbor.** The strike would precede a larger series of moves designed to seize control of Southeast Asia and much of the Western Pacific. In mid-October, hardliners in the government forced the resignation of Prime Minister Prince Fumimaro Konoye (who had supported continued diplomacy with the United States) and installed General Hideki Tojo, a militant expansionist. After a final round of proposals and counterproposals led nowhere, a Japanese fleet headed for Pearl Harbor on November 26 under strict radio silence to carry out a mission that had been planned and practiced for several months. From intercepted diplomatic dispatches, American officials sensed the outbreak of hostilities at any moment but did not know where the Japanese would strike. Sightings of Japanese naval troop transports heading southward from the island of Formosa convinced many analysts that Japanese aggression would commence at one of the British or Dutch-held colonies in Southeast Asia. American forces in the western Pacific were placed on high alert. Hawaii also received such warnings, but a combination of complacency by local commanders and a lack of sufficient patrol resources limited the ability of the American fleet to provide ample protection for the fleet.

The Japanese attack on Pearl Harbor caught the American forces completely by surprise. In the early Sunday morning hours of December 7, 1941, two waves of over 350 fighters, bombers, and torpedo planes launched from six aircraft carriers assailed the docked American ships in the port as well as the American planes parked at adjacent airfields. The two-hour attack sunk three battleships, capsized a fourth, grounded another trying to leave the harbor, and damaged three others. Ten other ships, including cruisers and destroyers were sunk or damaged. Additionally, the Japanese destroyed 188 aircraft and damaged 155 planes. The human toll was heavy—more than 2,400 servicemen (and some civilians) killed and over 1,100 wounded.

Though devastating, a closer analysis reveals the Pearl Harbor raid's significant tactical shortcomings. Foremost, the attack failed to eliminate any of the American Pacific Fleet's three aircraft carriers—the ships that would become the true source of naval power in the Second World War. All three carriers were away from Pearl Harbor at the time of the attack (one was delivering combat planes to Midway Islands, another was returning from delivering a squadron to Wake Island, and a third was in San Diego, California being repaired.) The failure of the Japanese to destroy the U.S. Navy's oil storage tanks & repair docks at the port looms as another major deficiency. Had these facilities been razed, Pearl Harbor would have been taken out of commission as an effective base for over a year. Japanese planners had made contingency for a third wave of planes whose purpose was to eliminate such vital support installations, but the plan left discretion for this phase of the attack to the fleet commander who decided against it due to the unknown whereabouts of the American aircraft carriers.

The decision to attack the United States also proved to be a monumental strategic mistake by Japanese leaders. Thinking that the assault would deal a crippling blow to the American military while subsequent attacks in the Western Pacific would allow the establishment of an extensive defense perimeter, the leaders underestimated the ability of the United States to quickly replace their losses and their own ability to maintain control of such a wide expanse of territory. America would soon replace the short-term loss of men, planes, and ships. (Two of the sunken battleships were actually raised and refitted for duty). Once reaching maximum capacity, the American industrial base produced thousands of ships and tens of thousands of aircraft. Tojo and the other Japanese militarists also blundered in believing that a crippling sucker-punch to the United States would smash the morale of the American public. In fact, the raid on American soil and subsequent attacks against U.S. forces in the Pacific unified the country against Japan like nothing else.

Remaining isolationist sentiment was swept away in the national furor and demands for revenge. A shocked Franklin Roosevelt appeared before Congress the next day seeking a formal declaration of war against Japan. The Senate voted unanimously for war, while in the House, the first woman elected to the U.S. Congress, pacifist Representative Jeannette Rankin of Montana (who in 1917 voted against American entry into World War I) cast a lone dissenting vote. The president and the American people did not immediately know what war against Japan would mean for the conflict in Europe. As a defensive treaty protecting members against attack from the United States, the terms of the Tripartite Pact did not apply. Nevertheless, on December 11, Germany and Italy announced declarations of war against the United States. Already irked by America's supplying of his enemies, Hitler predicted that the United States and Germany would fight each other eventually. Though he believed that the United States had the industrial might and superior racial makeup to defeat a smaller Asiatic country like Japan in a one-on-one fight, stretching American resources to support a two-front war with theaters of action separated half a world away would give both the Japanese and Germans their best chance of success. This failed gamble ranks as one of Hitler's biggest blunders, only outdone by his decision to attack the Soviet Union six months earlier.

HALTING THE AXIS, 1941-1942

A series of defeats at the hands of the Japanese created a pronounced sense of gloom in the United States during the first six months after the Pearl Harbor attack. Before May 1942, Japanese forces moved relatively unimpeded as they invaded American Pacific islands and European colonies in Southeast Asia to establish their defense perimeter, from the Thailand border with India in the west looping around the Dutch East Indies to the south and sweeping up through the islands of Micronesia to the east. On December 10, 1941, over 5,000 Japanese troops easily overran Guam's 500 defenders. At Wake Island, located over 2,000 miles west of Hawaii, the post's 500 defenders drove off an initial Japanese task force on December 7, but succumbed to a stronger second assault group two weeks later. Elsewhere, the Japanese moved into Thailand and defeated British forces in Burma, Hong Kong, and Singapore.

American and Filipino forces on the main Philippine island of Luzon under the command of General Douglas MacArthur held out the longest despite the general's inadequate defense preparations. Though MacArthur received word of the Pearl Harbor raid as early as 3:30 a.m. local time, American planes remained parked in the open at Clark Field located 50 miles northwest of Manila when Japanese planes arrived at noon to bomb the base. The general lost half his aircraft in one strike, crippling his chances of defending the Philippines. Outflanked on the beaches by Japanese amphibious troops, MacArthur fell back to the Manila area, eventually settling his men on the jungle-infested Bataan Peninsula and nearby Corregidor Island, which guarded the mouth of the harbor. Short on food, medicine, and military supplies, the 15,000 American and 65,000 Filipino troops held out for several months against rampant malaria and frequent Japanese air and ground attacks. In the process, they temporarily denied the enemy use of Manila Bay and bought crucial time for Australia to beef up its defenses. In early March 1942, President Roosevelt ordered MacArthur and his family to leave the area. Sneaking out by torpedo boat before flying to Australia, the general famously proclaimed: "I shall return." Mindful of MacArthur's popularity with Republicans and knowing that the nation needed heroes at this desperate time, Roosevelt refused to reprimand the general for his many blunders and would soon accede to placing him in command of leading the counterattack against the Japanese in the South Pacific.

American and Filipino forces at Bataan finally surrendered on April 9, while those on Corregidor endured continuous bombardment until their surrender on May 6. During the subsequent Bataan Death March, Japanese soldiers forced their prisoners to walk 65 miles northward to prison stockades, murdering any who could not keep up because of wounds, starvation, disease, or exhaustion. Over 7,000 POWs died along the way to slave labor camps where almost half did not survive the war. The Japanese troops who committed these atrocities succumbed to the hateful preaching of their officers who constantly reinforced the notion that surrender was not an option, nor should any soldier who dishonored themselves by surrendering be treated with anything but repugnance. Often brutally beaten by their officers since their days in training camp, many Japanese soldiers internalized the violence and reflected their treatment back upon their prisoners. Similar incidents occurred wherever the Japanese military triumphed.

The Battle of the Coral Sea marked the first time that an American battle fleet stopped a Japanese offensive in the Pacific. Moving beyond simply consolidating their considerable gains in the six months following the Pearl Harbor attack, Japanese leaders succumbed to what many of them later described as "victory disease"—the prevailing belief that they were unstoppable. As a result of this arrogance, they began to make careless moves as they sought further glory. Seeking to capture Port Moresby in southeastern New Guinea (a island larger than France located just to the north of Australia) as a preliminary move before controlling the air and sea lanes to Australia, a Japanese task force entered the Coral Sea only to be intercepted by an American flotilla led by two aircraft carriers. By that time, Naval Intelligence had broken the Japanese naval code, allowing the new Pacific Fleet commander, Admiral Chester Nimitz, to react quickly to thwart the offensive. The ensuing battle on May 7, 1942, became the first naval engagement in world history involving fleets not in sight of each other. The combat took the form of planes launched from aircraft carriers pounding away at their enemy's ships. Of its two carriers in the fight, the U.S. Navy lost the *Lexington* while the *Yorktown* suffered severe damage. Nevertheless, the Japanese were forced to turn back due to heavy damage to one carrier and another carrier losing most of its planes.

A month after the Battle of the Coral Sea, the Japanese launched another major offensive directed at the Midway Atoll, the westernmost of the Hawaiian Islands located 1,000 miles from Pearl Harbor. In addition to providing the Japanese with an advanced base relatively close to the major Hawaiian Islands, the thrust would draw out the American Pacific Fleet for a grand showdown to eliminate the carriers not destroyed during the Pearl Harbor raid. Once again, Naval Intelligence provided Nimitz with advanced knowledge of Japanese plans, allowing him to ignore a diversionary move against the Aleutian Islands in southern Alaska in order to concentrate on the main battle group led by four large Japanese aircraft carriers with experienced flight crews. Nimitz ordered the two American carriers then located at Pearl Harbor to head immediately toward Midway. When the damaged *Yorktown* finally arrived from the Coral Sea, Nimitz gave the ship's captain 72 hours to patch up the carrier, take on additional planes, and start heading for Midway. In the upcoming battle, Japanese planners expected at worst a 4-to-2 advantage in carriers. In addition to the early arrival of the *Enterprise* and the *Hornet*, the unexpected appearance of the *Yorktown* (only possible because of the Japanese failure to destroy Pearl Harbor's repair docks)

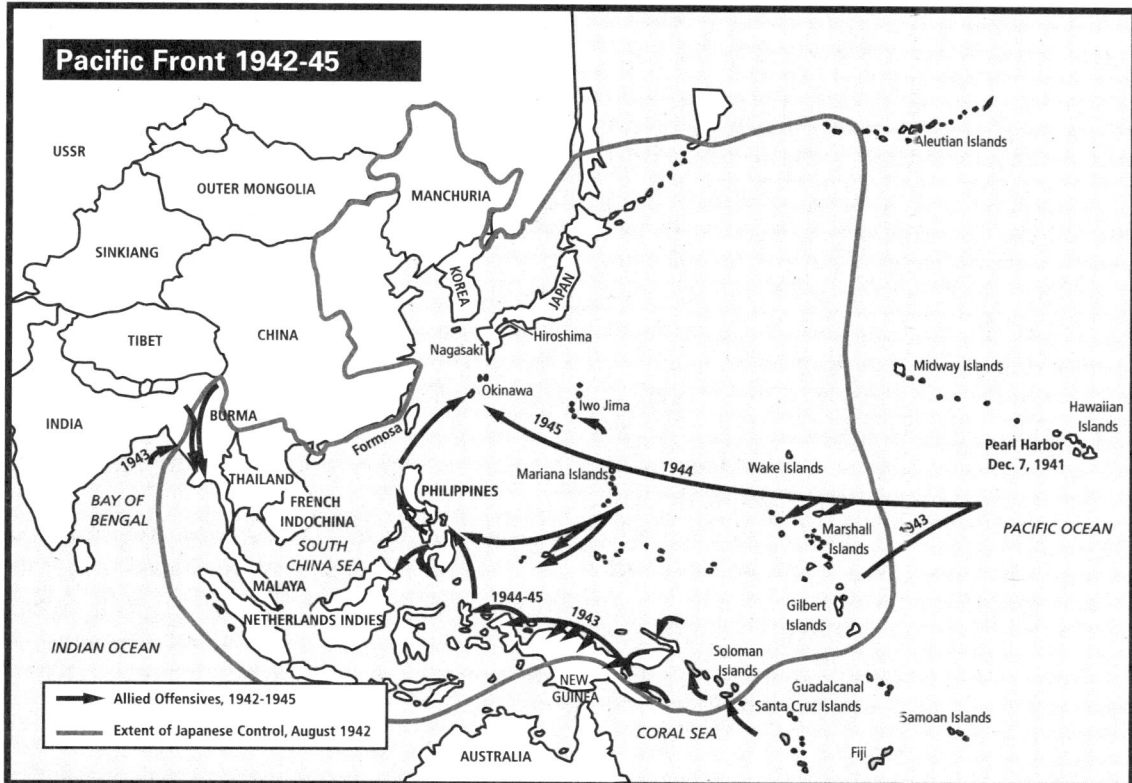

Map 24.1 World War II in the Pacific

added another element of surprise. Though the fighting began with Japanese planes pummeling Midway Island, the main battle took place in a similar manner to the Battle of the Coral Sea—both fleets dispatched scout planes over the horizon to locate the enemy fleet then sent scores of dive bombers and torpedo planes to eliminate the targets, focusing on enemy carriers. At the **Battle of Midway**, the Americans located the enemy first, and despite attacking in a haphazard and uncoordinated manner that resulted in the loss of entire squadrons of planes, the pilots eventually broke through enemy defenses to destroy all four Japanese carriers. (The Japanese were only able to sink the already heavily-damaged *Yorktown.*) The Battle of Midway proved to be a turning point of the war in the Pacific. Though the conflict was far from over, the Japanese were no longer capable of mounting major offensive naval operations.

Despite their defeat at Midway, many Japanese military leaders refused to give up the initiative, wishing to expand their perimeter of control and neutralize Australia as an American base of operations. Having failed to capture the vital air and naval base of Port Moresby in southern New Guinea because of the setback at the Battle of the Coral Sea, the Japanese attempted to seize the port by ordering troops overland from their holdings in northern New Guinea. The Japanese also landed troops at Guadalcanal, located at the southeastern tip of the Solomon Islands, in an attempt to set up an air base

that would sever Allied supply lines to eastern Australia. Standing in the way of the Port Moresby attack force, however, was the imposing 10,000-foot Owen Stanley Mountains whose brutal conditions hampered supply lines and greatly weakened their numbers before determined Australian defenders finished them off. Meanwhile, the U.S. Navy reacted to the Japanese move on Guadalcanal by hastily landing marines who quickly seized the partially-constructed airfield but became embroiled in a six-month-long fight on the heavily wooded island. While the Navy fought five major engagements against the Japanese offshore, the undersupplied marines valiantly held on against the harsh environment and reinforced enemy troops until February 1943 when Japanese leaders admitted defeat and ordered a withdrawal. The twin defeats in southern New Guinea and at Guadalcanal ended Japanese offensive operations in the Pacific, forcing them to hunker down on the hundreds of islands under their control spread out over thousands of square miles, waiting to see if the Americans would risk the vast casualties necessary to dislodge them.

Allied Victories in Egypt and Russia

The Axis nations continued to make tremendous gains of territory in Europe throughout 1941 and most of 1942 before Allied forces finally stopped their momentum.

An initial attempt by the Italians in the fall of 1940 to conquer Greece failed miserably, but after German forces quickly secured control of Yugoslavia in April 1941, Hitler invaded Greece and the nearby island of Crete. Both fell within a month. Meanwhile, in North Africa, the British stymied an Italian thrust into Egypt launched from neighboring Libya in October 1940 and then counterattacked. Once again, Hitler reluctantly sent reinforcements to bail out Mussolini, ordering General Erwin Rommel in February 1941 to create an *Afrika Korps* consisting of armored divisions to take over North African operations. Though perpetually short on supplies, Rommel eventually restored German and Italian control over eastern Libya before pressing forward into western Egypt. In early November 1942, however, British General Bernard Montgomery succeeded in smashing through Rommel's positions at El Alamein, just 150 miles to the west of the vital Suez Canal, forcing the *Afrika Korps* into headlong retreat back into Libya, never to regain the initiative. Coupled with the recent British capture of Ethiopia, Eritrea, and Somaliland from the Italians, the Allies held firm control over eastern Africa.

In Eastern Europe, the advance into the Soviet Union also began well for the Axis forces, only to be met with disaster by early 1943. In June 1941, over 3.5 million German troops, supplemented with another million fascist soldiers from Italy, Hungary, and Romania, attacked the Soviet Union and advanced along a 1,000-mile front deep into Belorussia and Ukraine. The Russians fell back, moving civilians and even entire factories safely to relocation centers east of the Ural Mountains where war production resumed. The Axis forces threatened the capital of Moscow and the strategically important northern city of Leningrad before winter set in to shut down offensive operations. Expecting victory before the arrival of winter, the unprepared Germans suffered heavy losses in the extreme cold and experienced great difficulty maintaining long supply lines under frequent attack by partisans. After the grueling winter, Hitler ordered his forces to concentrate on **Stalingrad** along the Volga River in southern Russia, which served as the gateway into the petroleum-rich Caucasus. If captured, the Germans would deny the Soviets the use of their main oil-producing region. Stalin ordered his namesake city to be held at all costs. Both sides devoted massive resources in the fight for control of Stalingrad, which began in late-August 1942. Though greatly undersupplied, the Russians used their manpower advantage to great effect, albeit at tragic cost. Soviet troops without bullets in their rifles were often ordered to charge German positions and to use the ammunition of fallen comrades when it came available. After several months of brutal fighting, the Soviets began to turn the tide, surrounding German forces and cutting them off from supplies and reinforcements. Though Hitler ordered his forces to fight to the last man, Field Marshal Freidrich Paulus thought otherwise and surrendered on January 31, 1943. The Germans lost over 200,000 troops at Stalingrad, including 90,000 prisoners. Though victorious, the Russians suffered much higher casualties—close to half a million killed and over 600,000 wounded (more than the United States incurred during the entire war.) After Stalingrad, the Germans lost the initiative on the Eastern Front, and were forced to fall back, regroup, and assume a defensive posture for the remainder of the war.

The Battle of the Atlantic

In the Atlantic Ocean, U-Boats turned loose on American shipping exacted a heavy toll within a few weeks of U.S. entry in the war. With little preparation given by the American military to antisubmarine warfare, German submarines had a field day destroying merchant ships, especially oil tankers, off the eastern coast of the United States and the Gulf of Mexico. Many attacks, such as one taking place in June 1942 near Virginia Beach, Virginia, occurred in broad daylight. Though Admiral Karl Doenitz, commander of the U-Boat forces, only sent a dozen U-Boats to American waters, half of Allied shipping sunk in the early months of 1942 took place there. Coastal defenses eventually improved, however, as the country instituted mandatory seaside blackouts to prevent submarine crews from using the silhouettes of merchant ships against brightly-lighted shorelines and civilian-piloted Civil Air Patrol planes coordinated with military aircraft to monitor the nation's seaboards.

On the high seas of the North Atlantic, German submarines wreaked havoc on Allied shipping throughout 1942, threatening to sever the American supply line to Great Britain. Admiral Doenitz estimated that his submarines needed to sink an average of 700,000 tons of Allied shipping each month to weaken England effectively. German U-Boats reached Doenitz' threshold by June 1942, but effective Allied countermeasures began to slowly reduce the damage. Allied aircraft began to use radar and high-intensity searchlights to locate surfaced submarines at night. American and British escort ships also began to utilize radio detectors to locate U-Boats by intercepting transmissions to their home bases.

Two major developments ultimately contributed to the eradication of the U-Boat menace in the North Atlantic. The first involved effective use of ULTRA, the designation for the breaking of the German military code (made possible by the British retrieval of a German deciphering machine from a captured U-Boat). ULTRA allowed the Allies to decode and analyze intercepted German military dispatches. In the **Battle of the Atlantic**, ULTRA intercepts allowed the Allies to anticipate U-Boat movements and to deliver telling blows upon their discovery. The other major boost to anti-submarine warfare proved to be the deployment of light escort carriers. Capable of carrying up to thirty planes, the carriers' pilots could patrol wide zones around convoys and undertake search-and-destroy missions against enemy subs. By mid-1943, U-Boats ceased to be a threat in the North Atlantic. The Germans sunk over 250,000 tons of shipping in April 1943, but two months later that figure plummeted to a mere 18,000 tons. Though U-Boats remained active away from the North Atlantic, German submarine crews found themselves in increasing peril. Of the 1,162 U-Boats deployed during the war, 941 were eventually sunk or captured. The Allied victory in the Battle of the Atlantic ranks alongside the great land battles of Stalingrad and the Normandy invasion in terms of overall contribution to the Axis defeat in Europe.

THE AMERICAN HOME FRONT

The Japanese attack on Pearl Harbor awoke a sleeping economic and military giant. Though it would take time for the groggy behemoth to become fully alert as the United States initially struggled to efficiently mobilize men and materiel, the Axis powers would soon bear the brunt of America's enormous industrial output and manpower resources. As the war raged, daily life became as profusely impacted by the conflict as by the Great Depression. Though wartime demands generated near-full employment, shortages of consumer goods and forced rationing disrupted everyday life. Despite these inconveniences, the war opened opportunities for women and minorities, not only to demonstrate their loyalty to their country but also to showcase their abilities and value to the nation. Though the full social impact of World War II would not be seen until decades after the war's conclusion, the groundwork for the modern equal rights movements had been laid with these groups' wartime service.

Industrial Mobilization

During the American neutrality period, FDR addressed war preparation issues by creating a series of advisory boards to study and make recommendations about prioritizing production and manpower resources. These agencies lacked coercive powers, however, relying instead on seeking the voluntary cooperation of business leaders to emphasize future military needs over civilian desires

for consumer goods. In early 1942, Roosevelt centralized these boards into one agency, the War Production Board (WPB), under the direction of former Sears Roebuck executive Donald Nelson. As the case with the previous boards, however, the WPB lacked any means of coercion, leading to its ineffectiveness as a means to provide central economic direction to the war effort. Since the WPB could only cajole businesses to direct production in certain directions, the agency would only be as assertive as its leader and Nelson proved to be far more conciliatory than aggressive. He often deferred to the purchasing bureaus of the separate military branches, allowing them to pursue their own needs rather than acting in the best interest of the nation as a whole. Ultimately, the president rectified the situation in May 1943 by creating the Office of War Mobilization (OWM) under former South Carolina senator and Supreme Court justice James Byrnes, granting him considerable authority to control and coordinate the mobilization effort and to serve as a court of final appeal to resolve any differences among defense industries or government agencies involving the allocation of defense-related materials or labor resources.

Though setting priorities (and finally enforcing them through the OWM), the Roosevelt administration and Congress never dictated to business what must be produced. Instead, the federal government lavished business with an incredible array of incentives to ensure that the military received what it needed to prosecute the war while still providing the necessities for the civilian population on the home front. As Secretary of War Henry Stimson recorded the administration's mindset in his diary: "If you are going to try to go to war, or to prepare for war, in a capitalist country, you have got to let business make money out of the process or business won't work." Companies enjoyed generous tax breaks and low-interest loans that covered the costs for defense-related plant expansion and equipment investments. The federal government also constructed many defense plants which it then leased to corporations, such as the Consolidated Vultee aircraft factory in Fort Worth, Texas and the Bell Aircraft facility in Marietta, Georgia. Most beneficial to business, the military negotiated contracts on a "cost-plus" basis whereby the price that companies charged the government guaranteed a profit. (Agricultural producers similarly benefited by a government guarantee of high prices at 110 percent of "parity," or the favorable price ratio of agricultural prices to industrial prices received by farmers during the prosperous 1909-1914 period. During the war, farm prices doubled.) For its part, the military gravitated toward the large corporations to fill out a majority of its requisitions, a practice the Roosevelt administration did not challenge. The production levels that American industries eventually reached during the war were truly astounding: 300,000 planes, 100,000 tanks and armored vehicles, 80,000 landing craft, over 5,000 merchant ships, and 1,500 vessels for the U.S. Navy, not to mention the millions of small arms, tons of bombs, and the billions of rounds of ammunition manufactured as the national Gross Domestic Product doubled from 1939 to 1945.

The rapid development of wartime industry affected all geographic regions of the country, from the traditional manufacturing areas of the Northeast and Midwest to the agriculturally-dominated South and West. In Michigan, after the manufacture of new cars had been outlawed, Henry Ford constructed the massive Willow Run aircraft plant outside Detroit. The 67-acre complex with a mile-long assembly line eventually built over 9,000 B-24 Liberators and employed over 40,000 workers. To make up for the loss of access to natural rubber (Japanese-held Southeast Asia accounted for 90 percent of the U.S. pre-war rubber supply), the federal government spent close to a billion dollars building fifty synthetic rubber factories, which it leased to private rubber companies. The largest facility in Institute, West Virginia, operated jointly by U.S. Rubber and Carbide and Carbon Chemicals (a subsidiary of Union Carbide) encompassed 77 acres and produced 90,000 tons per year. From 1942 to 1944, American synthetic rubber production increased from 8,000 to over 750,000 tons, enough to meet national wartime needs. In the South, southern builders produced one quarter of American shipping, from torpedo boats and landing craft along the Gulf Coast to massive aircraft carriers at Newport News, Virginia. In Texas, oil producers stepped up production and the proliferation of military bases invigorated the state's economy. In the West, giant plants such as those operated by Boeing Aircraft in Seattle, Douglas Aviation in Los Angeles, and Consolidated Vultee in San Diego employed hundreds of thousands of workers and accounted for half of the country's wartime production of planes. At his Portland, Oregon and Richmond, California shipyards, Henry J. Kaiser used prefabricated materials and other mass-production techniques to vastly reduce the time necessary to construct the vital 10,000-ton transport vessels known as "Liberty Ships." In 1941 it took a full year to build a Liberty Ship, but within a year Kaiser reduced the production time to less than two months. Two years later, his workers built a complete Liberty Ship in two weeks.

Manpower Mobilization

The mobilization of American armed forces began a year before the Pearl Harbor attack in September 1940 when Congress passed the Selective Training and Service Act creating the Selective Service System to implement the nation's first peacetime draft. The law authorized the initial conscription of 900,000 men between the ages of 21 and 27. Though isolationists railed against the measure, the draft did not become an election issue in 1940 because of Republican nominee Wendell Willkie's strong approval. After Pearl Harbor, the U.S. armed forces swelled as a result of the draft's expansion and citizen volunteering. Draft boards staffed by local leaders administered the system by overseeing registration, handling requests for exemptions or deferments, and listening to appeals of their decisions. Of the 50 million men that the Selective Service System registered, 10 million were drafted for active service. (Over six million serving in uniform volunteered.) About 10 million received an exemption or deferment from service on the basis of medical condition, family hardship, religious conscientious objection to war, or laboring at an "essential" industrial or agricultural occupation.

In addition to mobilizing manpower for the military, the federal government also oversaw the mobilization of the civilian workforce. Created in early 1942, the War Manpower Commission (WMC) became the main government agency involved in civilian workforce mobilization. The WMC recruited and trained male and female laborers for specific tasks, worked with the Selective Service System to classify occupations as essential and nonessential to the war effort, and coordinated the placement of workers into jobs that most optimized their skills. In an effort to prevent wartime strikes, Roosevelt brokered a no-strike pledge from the nation's leading labor unions and a no-lockout agreement with the country's leading corporations. The president also created the National War Labor Board to set wages and hours, promote collective bargaining, and negotiate labor disputes that might endanger production. Union membership soared during the war, rising from 9 million in 1939 to over 15 million by 1945.

Though Congress passed (over FDR's veto) the Smith-Connally War Labor Disputes Act making it a crime to advocate work stoppages and empowering the president to seize any factory or mine vital to the war effort if its workers engaged in a strike, hundreds of walkouts nevertheless occurred. Most of these protests were brief "wildcat" strikes unauthorized by union leaders, usually to highlight a particular grievance concerning workplace conditions. The largest exception was the series of United Mine Workers strikes in 1943 led by the flamboyant John L. Lewis. The actions embittered the public to the union and infuriated Roosevelt, who seized the mines and publicly threatened to draft the striking workers before eventually negotiating a deal that reopened the mines after granting Lewis's demands for higher wages to offset the dangerous but valuable work his union's members contributed to national defense.

The war brought about the end of many New Deal programs created during the Depression to provide work for the unemployed. With Americans pouring into the armed forces and defense plants, the national unemployment rate almost evaporated as work could now be readily found. During the 1942 midterm congressional elections, Republicans gained 46 House seats and 9 Senate seats. Forming a coalition with southern Democrats, they successfully dismantled the Works Progress Administration, Farm Security Administration, National Youth Administration, and the Civilian Conservation Corps.

Financing the War

Eventually costing over $300 billion, the Second World War was the largest expense for the federal government in American history. The Roosevelt administration worked with Congress to finance the war through a combination of increased taxation and deficit spending covered by war bonds. Taxes paid for almost half of wartime government outlays (compared to one-third for World War I), with terms largely laid out by the Revenue Act of 1942. This significant legislation greatly increased the number of citizens eligible to pay income taxes. In 1939, fewer than 4 million Americans earned the minimum income level of $1,500 necessary to file an income tax return. By 1943 that number had soared to over 40 million—a consequence of the increased revenues produced by wartime prosperity but also the lowering of the tax-exemption level to $624. Individual tax rates also increased, leading to the amount of revenue received by individual income taxes to rise from $1 billion in 1939 to over $19 billion in 1945, surpassing the level of corporate taxes for the first time. The Revenue Act also authorized the new withholding system whereby employers were required to deduct taxes from worker paychecks and collect the revenues on behalf of the government. Government borrowing financed approximately 55 percent of the war's cost, largely achieved through the sale of bonds. By including small-denominations to allow more citizens to participate, bond drives proved to be an effective means to boost patriotism and "sell the war" to the public. Nevertheless, three-quarters of the money raised through bond purchases came from banks and other financial institutions.

Though increased taxes and bond sales soaked up much consumer income during the war, the unprecedented levels of government spending energized the economy and largely legitimized the economic theories of British economist John Maynard Keynes who had long advocated national government spending programs and tax reductions during economic downturns to generate recovery by stimulating consumer demand. When the private sector lacks vigor and confidence to invest, preferring to sit on its wealth until the general economic climate improves, Keynes argued, a government should stimulate its country's economy by providing tax relief and bankrolling investments in infrastructure in an effort to put more money in consumers' hands. Their subsequent purchases would provide the fuel necessary to jumpstart a stalled economy. Though Roosevelt increased government spending to unprecedented levels during the Great Depression, his (and Congress') lack of total devotion to Keynesian principles meant that while the economic climate began to improve, general recovery had yet to be achieved by 1939. With the arrival of hostilities, however, FDR and Congress threw aside their aversions to budget deficits and spent lavishly to produce what was needed to win the war. The end result was not only victory on the battlefield, but nearly total employment and record-high profits for American business.

Civilian Sacrifice

While Americans on the home front saw the return of employment opportunities and substantially higher incomes than during the Depression, the military's insatiable demand for raw materials created huge shortages of consumer goods that risked inflation and profiteering. The government created the **Office of Price Administration (OPA)** to implement price controls, which in April 1942 capped most non-farm prices at the highest level reached by March 1. In July 1942, the National War Labor Board implemented a maximum 15 percent wage increase (based on average 1941 wages) to coincide with the 15 percent rise in prices over the same period. In April 1943, Roosevelt issued a "hold-the-line" order which froze all prices and wages at current levels for the duration of the war.

Beginning in 1942, the OPA also created a rationing system to guarantee equal distribution of several civilian items in short supply. Meat, sugar, coffee, butter, and shoes all made the OPA's list of rationed goods initially drawn up by the War Production Board (WPB). Gasoline found its way on the list, not due to a petroleum shortage, but as part of a greater effort to conserve rubber tires. Likewise, canned goods were rationed to reduce the use of tin. Shortages sometimes led to many items, especially meat, coffee, cigarettes, and canned goods, to become simply unavailable for significant lengths of time. Many nonessential civilian items disappeared completely, including refrigerators, silk stockings, tinfoil, cellophane, tennis balls, and bobby pins. The WPB also ordered restrictions on the "wasteful" use of materials found in numerous items, especially clothing. The agency impacted menswear by banning the manufacture of vests, cuffs, patch pockets, and extra pairs of pants with suits to save wool. Likewise, women's clothing saw the elimination of ruffles, pleats, and long skirts. Though some resorted to the black market for access to meat and other desired items, and many grumbled at the shortages of goods and the OPA's stamp books and changing point system to carry out its policies, the majority of citizens patriotically adhered to the agency's regulations.

Women during World War II

World War II greatly impacted the lives of American women. Whether raising a family at home or joining the workforce (or trying to do both), most women felt the strains and inconveniences of the war on a daily basis. Rationing, food shortages, and the absence of many common consumer goods complicated efforts to provide the basic comforts of home life. Many devoted valuable time volunteering as a nurse, participating in scrap drives, aiding government agencies in explaining civil defense programs, monitoring local grocery prices, and entertaining troops at the new United Service Organizations (USO) canteens created to maintain the morale of service men and women.

Some women actively served in the military during the war providing valuable support services for their country. About 200,000 American women served in the Women's Army Corps, or WACs, under the command of Colonel Oveta Culp Hobby (the wife of former Texas governor William Hobby). WACs performed 239 important support roles, ranging from secretarial duties to motor vehicle maintenance, freeing up men for other assignments including combat duty. Over 100,000 American women performed similar duty in the Navy as "Women Accepted for Volunteer Emergency Service," or WAVES. Close to 20,000 women served in the Marine Corps Women's Reserve while an additional 10,000 performed duties as members of the Coast Guard Women's Reserve (nicknamed SPARs after the motto Semper Paratus – "Always Ready").

Created to overcome the shortage of pilots and to free up more male pilots for combat duty, the **Women Airforce Service Pilots (WASPs)** provided another valuable contribution to the war effort. Commanded by aviator Jacqueline Cochran, the WASPs trained at Sweetwater, Texas's Avenger Field before its graduates transferred to flying assignments across the country. Though the federal government refused to grant the civilian WASPs any recognized military status (let alone use them in combat), they played vital support roles throughout the war ferrying all types of military aircraft (including heavy bombers), providing instrument instruction and towing targets for male trainee pilots, testing damaged planes, and transporting cargo. Ultimately, over 25,000 women applied to be WASPs, 1,830 were accepted, 1,074 graduated, and 38 died while performing their duties.

The war altered the roles of women in American society in countless ways, but nowhere more than in the workplace. Before World War II, women were systematically excluded from many jobs, with 90 percent of the nation's 12 million working females laboring in ten categories. While working white women tended to gravitate to retail trade, teaching, and secretarial jobs, a majority of black and Hispanic women were relegated to domestic service. Following the prevailing custom, most working women were young and single (only 15 percent of married women worked). A 1936 Gallup poll revealed that 82 percent of men and 75 percent of women surveyed believed that wives with employed husbands should not work.

Defense industry leaders initially excluded women from factory employment, not having much faith in their ability to perform the required work in addition to naively believing that the male labor supply would not soon be depleted. From late 1942 on, however, female laborers were in peak demand. The War Manpower Commission and private corporations began to actively recruit women for war work. The response was overwhelming, with the number of employed increasing from 14.6 million in 1941 to almost 20 million (over a third of all adult American women) by 1944. The biggest change occurred among married women who outnumbered single women in the work force for the first time. Women poured into manufacturing jobs, especially defense-related employment, eventually making up a third of all war industry workers. Though many took clerical positions, large numbers also labored as welders, riveters, and steelworkers. While the male-dominated unions tended to be lukewarm about the presence of female workers, they doggedly fought to protect the principle of equal pay for equal work, if for no other reason than to prevent employers from undercutting the salaries of male workers.

For the most part, women welcomed their war work. Though some clearly wanted to prove they could do traditional "male work," most had more practical motivations than trying to make a social statement. Single and married women alike enjoyed the additional money they were able to earn for themselves and their families while often doing work that they would never have been allowed to perform during peacetime. Most married women especially enjoyed the challenge provided by their new jobs when compared

Oveta (Culp) Hobby, ca. February 1953.

to their domestic chores. Patriotism also played a role in deciding to work, especially in the defense industry, by allowing women the opportunity to show that they were "doing their part" to help the nation achieve victory. Large numbers had loved ones in uniform overseas and believed their work would help bring them home sooner.

Even before the war ended, women in the war industries were gradually relieved of their duties. Employers, in tandem with the government, began to initiate campaigns preparing the country for women to return to their

homes, allowing male war veterans to return to work in the factories. Women at the time expected this development and most complied without much protest, mostly being happy that the war would soon be over. Regardless, the war experience of women did help to produce a steady shift in attitudes among males and females about women's roles in the workplace and society in general. While most women of the war generation gladly returned to domesticity, many later raised their daughters to challenge the prevailing beliefs about a woman's proper station in society, establishing the basis for a growing women's movement during the postwar period.

The African-American Experience

World War II allowed a record number of African Americans to serve in uniform and work in the industrial sector, though discrimination continued to limit opportunities. Before the war, fewer than 4,000 blacks served in the peacetime army of 230,000 soldiers, with only five African Americans holding officer rank (of which three were chaplains). All black soldiers served in segregated units under the command of white officers. The military completely excluded blacks from service in the Marine Corps and Army Air Corps. In the Navy, African Americans could only serve as cooks and mess men. Meanwhile, in the civilian workforce, very few of the 5 million employed blacks labored in the well-paying defense industry.

Glaring manpower needs, President Roosevelt's desire to gain African-American votes, and political pressure applied by black activists, however, began to effect notice-

Female factory worker Virginia Davis, Corpus Christi, Texas, August 1942.

OVETA CULP HOBBY FORMS THE WAC

Oveta Culp Hobby, the commanding officer of the Women's Army Corps (WAC) during World War II was born in Killeen, Texas on January 19, 1905. The daughter of a Texas state legislator, she graduated from Temple High School before attending Mary Hardin Baylor College. In 1925, the speaker of the Texas House of Representatives asked young Oveta Culp to serve as legislative parliamentarian, which she performed until 1931 while continuing her education at the University of Texas. In 1928, she helped to organize the Democratic Party Convention held in Houston. After helping a Houston candidate's successful mayoral campaign, she agreed to serve as assistant to the city attorney.

*Oveta Culp knew former governor William Hobby (then editor and publisher of the **Houston Post**) through her father. They resumed their friendship when she was the Houston city attorney's assistant, and though she was only twenty-six and he was fifty-three, they married in 1931. Oveta Culp Hobby then began to learn the newspaper publishing business, reviewing books for the **Post**, writing editorials, and acting as a personal assistant to her husband. In the summer of 1936, the Hobbys both survived a private plane crash after their flight from Dallas to Houston encountered mechanical difficulties. Unharmed, Mrs. Hobby pulled her unconscious husband from the burning wreckage.*

In June 1941, the U.S. Army contacted Mrs. Hobby about possibly serving as organizer of women's activities for the military. The War Department was receiving numerous requests from women after Congress passed the Selective Service Act asking how they could do their part to serve their country. She refused, citing her work load and family obligations, but agreed to create an organizational chart with recommendations on ways women could serve. Eventually, she was convinced to come to Washington in order to implement her plan. At General George Marshall's request, she studied the role of women in the British and French armies and prepared a plan by which the United States could learn from their experiences.

Hobby was heading home to Houston when she learned of the Japanese attack on Pearl Harbor. She returned to Washington, where General Marshall placed her in charge of the new Women's Army Auxiliary Corps (WAAC). Because Congress had been unwilling at first to make the WAACs an integral part of the army, the Corps served an ambiguous role in the War Department requiring forceful action by Hobby and others so as not to be ignored. Though never a militant feminist, she perfectly understood the numerous barriers to women that existed at the time. Hobby worked diligently to ensure proper treatment in every imaginable situation from salary issues to uniform design to basic respect from career military officers who despised the thought of women soldiers in the army. All volunteers, the WAACs soon proved their value to the military, performing vital support functions from secretarial work and kitchen patrol to parachute folding and automobile engine repair. When the Corps was first organized, Congress reluctantly agreed to allow women to perform fifty-four army jobs. Hobby (who attained the rank of colonel) eventually arranged for the number of responsibilities for women be increased to 239. In July 1943, President Franklin D. Roosevelt signed legislation formally incorporating the WAAC into the U.S. Army and changing its name to the Women's Army Corps.

*Exhausted from her duties, she resigned in July 1945 and resumed her career as director of the family-owned KPRC radio and TV stations, as well as executive vice president of the **Houston Post**. In 1953 she became the first Secretary of the new Department of Health, Education, and Welfare. Continuing her lifelong commitment to public service, she served on numerous boards, including the American Red Cross and the American Cancer Society, and special committees until her death in 1995.*

able changes. A month before the 1940 election, Eleanor Roosevelt urged FDR to meet with NAACP executive director Walter White and **A. Phillip Randolph**, the leader of the Brotherhood of Sleeping Car Porters (the largest African-American labor union in the country). After the meeting, Roosevelt arranged for the Army to add enough new black enrollees to reflect the African-American proportion of the total population (about 9 percent), the promotion of Colonel Benjamin O. Davis, Sr. to the rank of Brigadier General (making him the Army's first black general), and for the Marines and Army Air Corps to begin accepting African-American recruits.

Black combat units, however, would remain segregated. After the election, Randolph began to organize a planned 10,000-man march on Washington to protest continued discrimination in the defense industry. Franklin and Eleanor Roosevelt both opposed the proposed march, fearing the protest would embarrass the administration and might lead to violence. Undaunted, Randolph continued with his plans, threatening to mobilize up to 100,000 to rally in Washington's Capitol Mall. After a personal meeting with Randolph in June 1941, Roosevelt capitulated. In return for Randolph calling off the march, FDR issued Executive Order 8802, which forbade discrimination by defense industry employers or government agencies based on race, color, creed, or national origin.

To investigate discrimination complaints, Roosevelt created the Fair Employment Practices Commission (FEPC), an agency which soon had its hands full trying to enforce Executive Order 8802. Discrimination persisted as the FEPC suffered from lack of sufficient funds and staff members. The agency was reactive, responding only to complaints rather than pursuing independent investigations. The FEPC did not have the power to coerce compliance if its agents found evidence of discriminatory practices, relying on publicity and moral suasion to produce a change in behavior. Despite its limitations, the FEPC alerted the country to the existence of various forms of discrimination and served as a precursor to future federal civil rights agencies.

Despite the persistence of discrimination by employers (as well as many unions), African-American employment in war production work greatly increased due to wartime necessity. The proportion of blacks employed in the defense industry rose from 3 percent in 1942 to 8.6 percent in 1945. More than 100,000 labored for the first time in iron factories and steel mills. Another 200,000 began to work in the federal civil service, close to half in good-paying clerical positions. Almost a half million black women moved away from domestic service positions to labor in industries for larger paychecks than they had ever received. Overall, average annual wages for African Americans increased from $500 to $2,000

Tuskegee Airmen at their base in Ramitelli, Italy, March 1945.

(compared to an increase from $1000 to $2,600 for whites.)

The availability of industrial employment triggered the movement of one million African Americans from the rural South to urban areas across the country, especially California, Illinois, Michigan, and New York. Over a third of the Deep South's young African Americans left for jobs in northern cities. Violent clashes with whites who were also flooding into high-employment urban areas occurred in all regions of the country. The largest racial clash during the war took place in Detroit where competition for housing and jobs, racial animosity, hot summer weather, and a steady increase of hostile incidents finally escalated to full-scale violence in June 1943. For two days, whites and blacks roamed the streets attacking and counterattacking each other before federal troops arrived to restore order. Nine whites and 25 blacks were killed with over 1,000 citizens injured.

As the case for industrial employment, Roosevelt's moves to boost African-American strength in the military resulted in noticeable changes, though limitations remained. Though the number of blacks serving in the U.S. Army increased from 100,000 in late 1941 to 700,000 by 1944, over half remained stationed in the United States due to the reluctance of Army commanders to use them overseas. At home or abroad, African-American soldiers were an underutilized resource, often performing support roles such as bridge building and road construction. Though the Navy began to organize black Marine units, a majority of blacks continued to serve as mess men, laundry hands, and dock workers. Nevertheless, some black combat units distinguished themselves when given the opportunity. Trained at Fort Hood, Texas, the all-black 761st Tank Battalion known as the "Black Panthers" served under General George Patton, earning distinction for its courageous fighting during the Battle of the Bulge in late 1944 and later helping to spearhead the final advance into Germany. The most famous African-American fighters of the war proved to be the "**Tuskegee Airmen**"—black military pilots who trained in Tuskegee, Alabama. Initially assigned outdated "hand-me-down" aircraft to perform ground support roles that prevented them from engaging in air-to-air combat, the African-American aviators for the 99th Pursuit (Fighter) Squadron were first deployed in the invasions of North Africa and Sicily before being assimilated into the 332nd Fighter Group based in southern Italy under the command of Colonel (later General) Benjamin O. Davis, Jr. The "Red Tails," as the pilots of the 332nd were known because of the distinctive red-painted tails on their P-47s and P-51s, achieved fame escorting B-29 Super Fortresses of the Fifteenth Air Force during strategic bombing raids on

Germany and other enemy targets in Central Europe with minimal losses to the heavy bombers. Of the 1,000 pilots trained at Tuskegee, 445 were shipped overseas. One hundred and fifty died in combat or accidents while 32 were shot down and captured. By the war's end, the 99th and the 332nd earned three Distinguished Unit Citations, 150 Distinguished Flying Crosses, a Silver Star, and 14 Bronze Stars. They were credited with destroying 112 German planes in combat and another 150 on the ground while eliminating hundreds of enemy trucks and rail cars, and even sinking a naval destroyer. (In 2012, George Lucas released the film *Red Tails* to retell the Tuskegee Airmen's story to a new generation of Americans unaware of their contribution.)

Hispanics and the War

With over 350,000 serving in the military, Mexican Americans played a significant role during the war. Tens of thousands of Latinos also left agricultural work in the countryside to labor in shipyards, aircraft factories, and other war industries where they previously had been excluded. In Los Angeles, a city containing the largest Hispanic population outside of Mexico, certain Latino youths known as *pachucos* grew increasingly discontented with local prejudice, segregation, and poverty by expressing racial pride in numerous ways, the most noticeable being the wearing of the "zoot suit"—a men's clothing style actually originating in Harlem noted for its long jackets with padded shoulders and baggy pants accessorized with a long key chain and felt hat. Anglo civilians associated the suit wearers with increased violent gang activity and believed the amount of material used to create a zoot suit was an extravagant waste of material in wartime. White servicemen stationed in Los Angeles occasionally engaged in altercations with Latino youths who they tended to view negatively as draft dodgers and juvenile delinquents. On June 4, 1943, a group of sailors who fought with some *pachucos* earlier in the evening began a rampage against any Mexican-American youths they encountered, beating them while stripping off their zoot suits. With a supportive local press, police stood idly by over the next four nights as a few thousand sailors, marines, and private citizens proceeded to enter Latino neighborhoods and randomly attack *pachucos* during these so-called "Zoot Suit Riots" until military authorities finally ordered the soldiers and sailors back to their bases and ships. Though local newspapers praised the servicemen for clearing the streets of "hoodlums" and the city council soon banned the wearing of zoot suits, a governor's commission later attributed racism as the main cause of the riots.

As large numbers of Latinos left farms in favor of work in war factories, an agricultural labor shortage ensued. In addition to using German POW labor, the federal government responded by arranging the Mexican Farm Labor Program Agreement (also known as the *bracero* program) to provide Mexican laborers to work legally for American farmers and ranchers for the duration of the war. The agreement guaranteed a minimum wage of 30 cents an hour and humane treatment in the form of adequate shelter, food, and sanitation. Two hundred thousand *braceros* eventually worked in the United States during the war, with over half laboring in California. When Texas farmers balked at the terms of the agreement, however, the Mexican government refused to allow temporary work visas for migrant farm workers to enter Texas. Nevertheless, farmers in South Texas benefited during the war from access to undocumented Mexican labor.

Native American Contributions

Twenty-five thousand Native Americans served in the armed forces (some were drafted, some volunteered), mostly in the U.S. Army serving in fully integrated units. Ira Hayes, a Pima from Arizona, earned fame as one of the Marines raising the American flag atop Mount Suribachi during the Battle for Iwo Jima depicted in Joe Rosenthal's famous Pulitzer Prize-winning photo. The most well-known contribution of Native Americans came from 400 Navajo "code talkers" who served in the U.S. Marine Corps in the Pacific and relayed coded messages in their rare language, making it impossible for the Japanese to decipher their transmissions. (The Army successfully used some Choctaw code talkers in Europe during World War I and also used a few other non-Navajo code talkers during WW II). Another 50,000 Native Americans left their reservations to perform war work, primarily on the West Coast.

The Internment of Japanese Americans

One of the most shameful episodes for the United States during the war involved the nation's treatment of ethnic Japanese residents living on the West Coast. Almost 50,000 were "Issei," or first generation aliens who often could not vote and endured other restrictions by state and federal law. Another 80,000 were "Nisei," or American-born Japanese who were legal citizens who nevertheless found themselves subject to the century-old prejudices often found in the western United States against all Asians. Despite the climate of legal discrimination and a myriad of restrictions based on local custom, many Japanese prospered in California, Oregon, and Washington as small truck farmers and fishermen.

Japanese-Americans transferring from train to bus at Lone Pine, California, bound for the war relocation authority center at Manzanar. April 1942.

After the attack on Pearl Harbor, fear and hysteria reigned on the West Coast as politicians, editors, and many in the general public feared that the Japanese residents would undertake espionage and sabotage missions for the enemy. Government officials did nothing to stop that perception even though the Federal Bureau of Investigation found no basis for such fears. The region's long-standing anti-Japanese racism explains much of this thinking—in Hawaii, home to a much larger Japanese population than existing on the West Coast and the location of the Pearl Harbor attack, few questioned the loyalty of the islands' Japanese Americans. Some on the West Coast also coveted Japanese-American property.

In February 1942, President Roosevelt bowed to the public clamor and signed Executive Order 9066, which authorized the U.S. military to remove any and all people from designated "military exclusion zones." Ultimately, the West Coast became the only declared zone and only people of Japanese descent were excluded. Without any legal due process, ethnic Japanese men, women, and children (including Nisei who were U.S. citizens) were ordered to report to "assembly centers," often located at fairground facilities and horse stables at racetracks, for processing and to await completion of the ten internment camps (officially known as "war relocation centers"), which would become their ultimate destination. Given less than a week to dispose of property that they could not take with them, Japanese Americans lost millions of dollars of property as they sold land, homes, and businesses at prices far below market value. Many had to simply abandon property they could not sell, returning after the war to find strangers living in their homes or farming on their lands.

Camp conditions were generally poor. Mostly located in desert or mountain areas of six western states (two were placed in Arkansas), internees were often subjected to extreme hot and cold. Some died due to inability to acclimate. Individuals and families lived in barracks with little to no privacy. Though the term "concentration camp" would be associated for generations in the public mind with the Nazis, American internment camps were also concentration camps in that they forcibly kept people inside against their will with a combination of barbed wire fences and armed guards.

Some internees challenged their imprisonment in federal court, including California native Fred Korematsu, who police arrested for refusing to report to his designated assembly center. In 1944, a majority of Supreme Court justices ruled in the *Korematsu v. United States* case that the government's internment policy was constitutional, thus continuing the tradition of allowing the executive and congressional branches of the government much leeway in defining "military necessity" in times of war. During the 1980s, a government commission determined that "race prejudice, war hysteria, and a failure of political leadership" were the main factors behind the forced relocations. This admission led Congress in 1988 to issue an official apology to Japanese Americans and to grant $20,000 compensation to each of the 80,000 surviving members of the camps. Ten years later, the healing process continued when Fred Korematsu received the Presidential Medal of Freedom from President Bill Clinton.

Despite being forcibly relocated by their government, 26,000 Nisei, determined to prove their loyalty, left the camps and served in the U S. Army, with over half serving in the 442nd Regimental Combat Team—an all-Japanese-American infantry regiment assigned to combat duty in Europe. The 442nd became the most decorated U.S. regiment of the entire war (21 of its members earned Congressional Medals of Honor) while sustaining the

Frank Fujita, Jr.—A Japanese-American Prisoner of the Empire of the Rising Sun

Due to his unique situation of being the only Japanese-American combat soldier captured by Japanese forces during World War II, Frank Fujita's wartime experiences differed from those of any other American. Fujita's father arrived in America from Nagasaki, Japan in 1914, a traveling private chef for railroad company officials. While on a layover in Illinois, he met Fujita's future mother, a white woman from Oklahoma working as a waitress in a local hotel, and they eventually married. Fujita attended Abilene High School where he stood out among his peers because of his ethnicity and his incredible drawing ability.

In 1938, Fujita joined an artillery battalion of the Texas Army National Guard's 36th Infantry Division. Three years later, as hostilities with Japan seemed more imminent, the U.S. Army separated Fujita's battalion from the already-activated 36th Division and shipped his unit to the Pacific to bolster American defenses in the Philippines. Eight days after embarking from California, Fujita's convoy received word of the Japanese attack on Pearl Harbor. Diverted initially to Australia, Fujita's unit was ordered to the Dutch East Indies in January 1942 to help defend Java. Japanese forces invaded the island on March 1, 1942, and overwhelmed the Allied forces within a week, resulting in Fujita's capture.

The first half of Fujita's 42-month long incarceration mirrored the experiences of other Allied POWs. On Java, guards brutally mistreated Fujita and his comrades while demanding immediate compliance to their orders. The Japanese forced the prisoners to labor on the island while being crowded in squalid camps with horrendous sanitation issues. The prisoners' quarters were constantly infested with bedbugs, fleas, and lice while the food provided was meager and of poor quality, often consisting of small quantities of rice, bread, and soup infested with worms.

After six months on Java, the Japanese crammed Fujita and other chosen prisoners into the holds of cargo ships and transported them to Changi prison camp in Singapore, a larger facility containing over 15,000 British and Australian prisoners. Living conditions there proved to be no better than on Java. In December 1942, Fujita and a contingent of men from his unit were again loaded into cargo ships, this time to be transported to Nagasaki, Japan—his father's former home—for hard labor at local shipyards.

Fujita toiled in the shipyards for four months until a Japanese guard who could read English discovered his heritage while skimming over the prison roster. This was the moment Fujita had long feared, convinced that the Japanese would single him out and kill him for being a racial traitor. Instead, enemy officers tried in vain to teach him the Japanese language and indoctrinate him to their cause. One day in August 1943, however, hateful guards took out their anger on Fujita. When their officers left the base to attend important meetings, the guards brought him into a room where they took turns beating him senseless. Despite the thrashing he received, Fujita refused to fall to the ground, partly out of spite, but also because he had seen beaten prisoners who fell down receive even worse treatment, sometimes resulting in death.

In October 1943, Fujita was sent to Tokyo and informed that he would deliver propaganda messages over the radio or "his life would not be guaranteed." A dozen other coerced POWs joined Fujita in the broadcasts but there were also a couple of Americans who willingly collaborated with the enemy and were greatly despised by Fujita and the other prisoners. For the remainder of the war, Fujita passed the time delivering lackluster radio messages, observing the Allied bombings of Tokyo, and making entries into a secret diary he had kept since being captured on Java despite the Japanese military's threat to shoot any POWs caught possessing a journal.

As the war drew to a close, Fujita greatly feared that he and the other prisoners would be executed, but the war's abrupt end negated such thoughts. Instead, Fujita and the other prisoners' morale soared as American planes identified their camp and dropped packages of food and medical supplies. The next day, U.S. Navy ships were spotted in Tokyo Bay with small boats heading for the prison camp located along the coast. Though weakened from years of mistreatment and malnourishment (his pre-war frame of 145 pounds had been reduced to 90 pounds), Fujita was so elated at the sight of American ships that he joined other POWs who foolishly jumped into the bay to swim out to the incoming boats, almost drowning in the process before being plucked out of the water by the shocked sailors.

After the war, Fujita's secret war diary served as evidence in various war crimes trials before being returned. Though partially disabled due to his wartime treatment, Fujita eventually used his artistic talents to work as an illustrator for the Air Force. Before his death in 1996, Fujita published his memoirs based on his diary, which include many drawings and intricate maps he created to powerfully relay to his readers many important aspects of his brutal incarceration.

highest casualty rate (57 percent) of any similar-sized American combat unit.

VICTORY IN EUROPE, 1943-1945

Despite the common goal of defeating the Axis, a significant degree of mistrust characterized the uneasy alliance between the United States, Great Britain, and the Soviet Union during World War II. The three powers not only brought different strengths to the inevitable winning coalition—the Soviet Union had seemingly endless manpower, England had its superior navy, and the United States possessed vast natural resources and industrial capacity—they also had contrary national temperaments and interests. The Soviets sought to drive the Germans and their allies out of Russia and to establish a strong security zone in Eastern Europe while maintaining a desire to export communist ideology abroad. The English wished to defend their island and overseas empire while preventing Soviet expansion and the spread of communism in Europe. The Americans sought to defeat the Germans and Japanese, to end totalitarianism, and extend its economic reach throughout the world.

The Debate Over Strategy in Europe

One of the earliest manifestations of the potentially tense alliance involved the development of an effective strategy to defeat Germany. Bearing the brunt of Axis forces driving deep within western Russia in 1941 and 1942, the impatient Joseph Stalin demanded the western Allies open up a major **second front** against the Nazis in France as soon as possible. Such an offensive would draw away a significant number of German divisions from the Eastern Front, guarantee the survival of the USSR, and allow the Russians to counterattack. The Soviet dictator, prone to bouts of paranoia, believed western allied leaders privately hoped that the communists and fascists would kill each other off on the Russian steppes. Determined not to have the Soviets take the bulk of the punishment from German aggression, Stalin occasionally dangled the possibility of a cease fire with Hitler in order to spur American and British decision makers to action.

For their part, American military leaders generally concurred with Stalin's sentiment albeit for different reasons. Not favoring a long, drawn-out conflict, and trained since the Civil War to amass forces and hurl overwhelming firepower at the enemy's strength, American generals such as Roosevelt's Army Chief of Staff George C. Marshall wished to gather significant U.S. and British troops in England before ordering an invasion across the English Channel to hit the Nazis in northern France. Such a move would force Hitler to divert forces from Russia and keep the Soviets in the fight. After liberating Paris, the western Allied forces would drive into the heavily industrial Ruhr region of Western Germany and knock the Nazis out of the war. Marshall made plans, tentatively approved by Roosevelt, for a sizeable military buildup in England throughout 1942. Ideally these forces would not go into action until early 1943, but he also authorized a contingency for a desperate late-1942 attack if the USSR appeared to be on the verge of collapse.

British Prime Minister Winston Churchill wholeheartedly opposed the idea of a cross-Channel invasion. Stung by the heavy troop losses that Britain endured during World War I and the early stages of World War II, he favored a patient, less direct approach. Adopting the traditional viewpoint of a naval power's leader, Churchill preferred to blockade Axis ports and pick at the enemy's weak points along its overextended periphery. Not believing that sufficient American and British forces could be accumulated for a successful cross-Channel strike for many years, he tried to convince Roosevelt that an attack upon Vichy-controlled Northwest Africa showed more promise for initial success. Such a move would support English troops in their struggle against Rommel's Afrika Korps and allow the British to control the Mediterranean Sea, freeing England to resume use of the Suez Canal in Egypt to channel supplies and troops into North Africa from India. General Marshall strongly dissented against Churchill's proposal, arguing that an attack on northwestern Africa would be a mere sideshow interfering with the buildup of forces in England. If Roosevelt accepted the plan, Marshall warned that the U.S. should commit to a purely defensive posture in Europe and send all nonessential resources to the Pacific for offensive operations against the Japanese.

Roosevelt set aside Marshall's complaints and ultimately accepted Churchill's North Africa proposal, hoping that the first American ground forces would get into action against Axis troops before the midterm congressional elections set for early November 1942. Though the president also concurred with the plans for a cross-Channel invasion, the date for that attack would be pushed back until mid-1944. Stalin was furious when informed of Roosevelt's decision. Though Churchill personally traveled to Moscow to visit the dictator in August 1942, Stalin received him coldly. The seeds of mistrust had been planted anew.

Operation Torch

The attack on northwestern Africa, code-named Operation TORCH, involved 65,000 American and English troops at three landing sites in Morocco and Algeria under the overall command of U.S. General Dwight Eisenhower. Plans to land troops as far to the east as Tunisia were scrapped due to fears over German air power in the central Mediterranean and possible Spanish entry into the war disrupting Allied supply lines through the Strait of Gibraltar. French forces initially resisted all three landings and hundreds of American soldiers were killed before negotiators quickly struck an agreement with the local Vichy military commander, Admiral Jean François Darlan. In return for ordering a cease fire, the admiral was allowed to assume administrative control over French North Africa. Though many in the United States criticized the military for generously dealing with a Nazi sympathizer, the move saved additional American soldiers' lives plus Darlan was soon killed by an anti-fascist Free French assassin.

The successful Allied landings in Northwest Africa initiated a chain of responses by the Axis. While Italian forces moved into the French island of Corsica in the western Mediterranean, Hitler ordered Nazi forces to move into Vichy France to protect the southern coast from potential attack. German troops also began to pour into Tunisia where they linked up with scattered Vichy French forces trekking eastward from Algeria and over 200,000 German and Italian soldiers fleeing Libya after the defeat at El Alamein. The initial Allied decision not to attack Tunisia assured a hard fight against strong defensive positions taken by Rommel in the eastern Atlas Mountains before all of North Africa could be secured. The first assaults by green American troops against Rommel's veteran *Afrika Korps* ended horribly, most notably at Kasserine Pass in February 1943, but time and logistics worked against Rommel who eventually had to leave North Africa due to illness. After Hitler questionably reinforced Tunisia (weakening the effort on the Russian Front in the process), Axis forces eventually found their supply lines cut off by the British Royal Navy and American air superiority. While U.S. forces under General George Patton renewed their attacks against their weakened foes from the west, British General Bernard Montgomery finally succeeded in breaking through the German and Italian lines from the east. In May 1943, over 250,000 Axis forces in North Africa, over half of them German troops, capitulated to the Allies.

The Allied Invasions of Sicily and Southern Italy

Stalin reluctantly accepted the fact that Operation TORCH meant there would be no second front established in northern France during 1942. He soon discovered that the Western Allies would not attack there in 1943 either. Before the German and Italian defeat in North Africa, the British and American high commands were already pondering their next moves. Churchill and Roosevelt agreed to a summit to take place in recently-captured Casablanca, Morocco, in January 1943 to hammer out an agreement for joint action. Churchill and his military staff came to the Casablanca Conference prepared to argue for a move against Sicily as the first step to knock Italy out of the war. As a result of dogged British determination for their viewpoint and divisions among Roosevelt's commanders about how to proceed, Churchill convinced the president to authorize an attack on Sicily. In an attempt to placate Stalin's assumed anger from the further delay of establishing the Second Front in France, Roosevelt and Churchill decided to commence a strategic bombing campaign against Axis targets and publicly announce unconditional surrender as a declared Allied war aim. Stalin seethed, however, when he learned that northern France would not be the next location for a major American and British offensive, threatening to conquer Germany himself and establish a puppet state there without consulting the western Allies.

Preparations for the Sicilian invasion included an elaborate ruse designed to confuse the Germans about the location of the next Allied Mediterranean offensive (later depicted in the novel and movie *The Man Who Never Was*.) Acquiring the cadaver of a drowned Englishman, British agents handcuffed a suitcase filled with fake documents to the body, which was dumped along the Spanish coast to give the illusion that he was an important courier who had been lost in a plane crash. After the corpse's discovery, Spanish authorities gave copies of the satchel's contents to the Germans who considered them authentic. Hitler became so convinced that the next Allied move would be against Sardinia and Greece that he ordered reinforcements there but not to the real target of Sicily where over 150,000 American, British, and Canadian troops came ashore in mid-July 1943, soon followed by 300,000 more. The Italians had close to 300,000 soldiers in Sicily, but most began to reconsider their allegiance to Mussolini and showed little desire to fight. Over 60,000 German defenders provided the bulk of the resistance, benefiting from the rocky terrain to slow the Allied advance and inflict heavy casualties before evacuating the island after a five-week confrontation.

As the fighting in Sicily raged, King Victor Emmanuel ordered Mussolini's arrest (though German commandos soon rescued the deposed dictator, transporting him to northern Italy) and named Marshal Pietro Badoglio to be the new prime minister. Badgolio publicly announced Italy's continued support for the Axis but soon began secret negotiations with the Allies, finally surrendering in early September 1943 as British and American troops began to invade southern Italy. Hitler built up German strength on the Italian peninsula, ordered the occupation of Rome, and demanded the deactivation of Italian forces. German soldiers imprisoned Italians who had been fighting alongside them in Russia and massacred over 5,000 Italian soldiers in Greece when they refused the order to disarm (an episode dramatized in Louis De Bernières's novel *Captain Corelli's Mandolin*). While the Allies encountered stiff resistance securing a beachhead at Salerno, German forces under Field Marshall Albert Kesselring dug into the rough terrain of the Italian countryside and prepared for a grinding war of attrition. Though gradually driven back over the next 18 months, Kesselring succeeded in protecting Germany's southern flank for the remainder of the war. When Germany finally surrendered in May 1945, the Allies had only reached the Italian border with Austria.

Strategic Bombing

The origin of high-altitude **"strategic bombing"** can be found in the prewar writings of air power advocates who garnered the enthusiastic support of British and American air marshals wishing to distinguish their branch of the service within their countries' respective military apparatuses. In addition to advocating the combat use of aircraft for such tactical objectives as ground support attacks, the air marshals came to believe that victory in modern war could be achieved through the strategic bombing of economic targets (factories) and infrastructure facilities (such as dams, bridges, and rail stations). The marshals argued that large numbers of thickly armored bombers armed with multiple machine gun turrets and flying in tight formations without fighter escort could adequately defend themselves while dropping heavy payloads with precision from very high altitudes to deliver crippling blows to the enemy's ability to prosecute a war while receiving relatively light casualties. At the very least, they wished to try. Looking for another sign of commitment to show Stalin in lieu of opening the Second Front in 1943, Roosevelt and Churchill agreed at the Casablanca Conference to implement a combined bombing offensive against the Axis.

Prior to 1943, Germany and Great Britain had undertaken high-altitude bombing attacks against the other with minimal results. During the Battle of Britain, German bombers killed hundreds of civilians and destroyed portions of London and other English cities but did little damage to industrial targets while suffering heavy losses. Churchill ordered retaliatory strikes against German industrial cities. These counterattacks also killed many civilians and damaged many neighborhoods but failed to destroy the intended targets and resulted in significant losses to air crews. Nevertheless, in their desire for revenge and to take the horrors of war directly to the German people, Churchill and his air marshals authorized frequent "area bombings" of German cities designed primarily to kill civilians and break the morale of the survivors. To reduce the loss of planes, these raids primarily took place at night. In one notable instance, British pilots armed with incendiary devices firebombed Hamburg in late-July 1943 resulting in over 40,000 civilian deaths and the destruction of over a quarter million homes.

During the Combined Bomber Offensive of 1943, the U.S. Eighth Air Force joined the British Royal Air Force (RAF) in hitting enemy targets for the first time utilizing B-17 "Flying Fortresses." Generally opposed to nighttime area bombing (mostly on military grounds rather than moral objections), American commanders preferred to focus on daytime precision bombing of selected industrial targets even though the German and British failure to produce consistent results should have dissuaded them from the attempt. The U.S. air marshals professed more faith in the B-17s than the British Lancaster bombers and the German equivalents, plus they wanted to see how the Flying Fortresses would perform. Subsequent experience would show that American high-altitude bombing did little directly in 1943 to slow the German war effort. High-altitude "precision bombing" was, in practice, not very precise at all. A U.S. military survey estimated that only 3 percent of bombs dropped by American air crews hit their intended targets. The remaining ordinance landed on scattered fields, forests, churches, and houses across the countryside. Far from contributing to the breakdown of German public morale, resentment among civilians only stiffened as they felt unfairly targeted by enemy planes. Though the bombing campaign contributed to the Allied achievement of complete air superiority over Europe by mid-1944 (due to the great reduction of Luftwaffe numbers as German fighter pilots were shot down at unsustainable rates), that result would have occurred anyway due to the massive buildup of American air forces from 1942 to 1944. The Nazis largely maintained industrial production through 1944 while inflicting heavy losses upon Allied bomber crews. With some raids producing 20 percent losses, the B-17 proved not to be a "flying fortress." Efficient aerial attacks against Axis strategic targets began to take place in mid-1944, resulting from the achievement of complete Allied air supremacy, the development of the P-51 Mustang to provide effective long-range fighter escort, and a shift to lower-altitude strikes by medium-sized fighter-bombers.

French General Henri Geraud, President Franklin Roosevelt, Free French military commander Charles DeGaulle, and British Prime Minister Winston Churchill discuss the course of the war against the Axis Powers at an conference of the Allies at Casablanca, January 24, 1943.
Photo credit: FDR Presidential Library.

Only then did German manufacturing and transportation facilities suffer consistent destruction. Still, the RAF continued to undertake terror raids against enemy population centers, joined by American squadrons in a controversial February 1945 fire-bombing of Dresden in eastern Germany, which killed over 30,000 civilians for no apparent purpose other than the city had not yet been attacked.

The Combined Bombing Offensive has received intense criticism from military personnel and historians alike. While some question the morality of sinking to the level of the enemy by deliberately targeting civilians (over 300,000 German civilians were killed by Allied air raids), most have noted the tremendous cost in manpower and materiel needed to wage such a campaign for such relatively moderate returns. The British Bomber Command lost over 50,000 airmen in the skies over Europe. U.S. bomber crews suffered comparable combat losses in addition to losing over 35,000 in accidents. (By comparison, the entire U.S. Navy suffered only 16,000 fatalities during the war). Further, the ground personnel and resources necessary to build and maintain the heavy bomber bases in England, if diverted to support ground units, could have provided the Allies with forces comparable to an extra field army in Europe. Though easy to point out the inadequacies of the Allied air marshals' bold predictions for "victory through air power," such condemnation can only be delivered through the luxury of hindsight. Never before deployed in combat, high-altitude strategic bombers represented a genuine hope that they could be used to defeat the enemy with greatly lower casualties than witnessed in the First World War. Experience eventually showed this to be an overly optimistic illusion.

The Tehran Conference

In late-November 1943, the "Big Three" Allied leaders (Roosevelt, Churchill, and Stalin) met jointly for the first time in Tehran, Iran, to discuss plans for the long-awaited cross-Channel invasion of northern France and the establishment of the Second Front. Churchill remained in favor of a postponement of the offensive (now code-named OVERLORD) in favor of continued attacks on Axis positions in the Mediterranean. Holding many strong cards at the conference as his troops continued to drive the Germans back along the Eastern Front, Stalin pressed for firm commitments on OVERLORD and would not discuss much else until they finalized its particulars. Roosevelt also strongly desired a cross-Channel attack in mid-1944, believing it important to satisfy Stalin in the short term and hopefully usher in a spirit of cooperation for the postwar years. Ultimately, the Big Three chose May 1944 as the first possible date for the invasion, which would be led by Dwight D. Eisenhower, the American general who had previously overseen the attacks on North Africa and southern Italy. Stalin received assurances that the Soviets would be able to annex the Baltic States and portions of eastern Poland (areas soon to be under Russian military control) as well as some island territories from Japan in East Asia. In exchange for these concessions, Stalin satisfied FDR by agreeing to launch a major offensive on the Eastern Front coinciding with OVERLORD, vowing to enter the war against Japan after Germany's defeat, agreeing to partition Germany upon its defeat, and promising to join a new postwar global organization.

D-Day

The buildup of men and materiel in England for **Operation OVERLORD** continued throughout the first

Map 24.2 World War II in Europe

months of 1944. Knowing from ULTRA intercepts that the Germans expected the cross-Channel invasion to take place at Pas de Calais, located only 20 miles from southern England, Eisenhower and the British generals did everything they could to reinforce that notion. Their deception included allowing the Germans to intercept fake radio transmissions and planting fraudulent documents to be captured, which implied that Calais would be the target zone. Eisenhower also created a faux army base in southeast England to convince Hitler that armored divisions under the command of General George Patton were assembling there for a quick strike on Calais. Such ruses ultimately paid off, helping OVERLORD's success and saving many lives as Hitler kept valuable reserves in the area of Calais rather than the real attack point chosen by Eisenhower: five beaches in Normandy on the north-central French coast.

Weather considerations postponed "D-Day" until June 6, but six Allied divisions (three American, two British, and one Canadian) of 100,000 men finally came ashore in the largest amphibious invasion in world history. The attack involved 5,000 ships transporting troops

and vehicles across the Channel and providing offshore bombardment. Eight hundred planes dropped American, British, and Free French paratroopers inland to support the landings while an additional 300 planes strafed German positions. Most Allied soldiers came ashore with little difficulty, the major exception being American forces on "Omaha Beach" that encountered rough seas and tenacious resistance by German defenders who pinned them down with withering artillery and machine-gun fire from cliffs overlooking the landing zone for much of the day until being finally dislodged (Steven Spielberg re-created the carnage that took place on Omaha Beach in the beginning of his 1998 film *Saving Private Ryan.*)

The Allies suffered 10,000 casualties to secure the Normandy beaches, which soon became the staging area for a massive buildup of men, vehicles, and equipment allowing for the breakout that would establish the Second Front. Within ten days, over 500,000 men came ashore. By July 1, over a million soldiers occupied the beachhead. Allied forces advanced slowly southward as they encountered strong resistance from German troops using the terrain of Normandy's *bocage* to their advantage. In this region, high earthen banks topped by thick hedgerows lined the roads and pastures, providing the Germans with natural walls of defense that neutralized the ability of Allied armored units to maneuver. Improvising American soldiers, however, eventually developed ways to cut through the hedgerows, setting the stage for a major breakout into the French countryside.

As Allied forces drove off the Normandy beachhead, events taking place in Germany almost ended the war sooner than many had expected. On July 20, Colonel Claus von Stauffenberg, chief of staff for the Reserve Army, planted a suitcase bomb under a table at a conference attended by Hitler at his "Wolf's Lair" military headquarters in East Prussia. The explosion killed four men but only wounded Hitler and twenty others. Sensing the war was lost and that Hitler planned to destroy Germany in the process, Stauffenberg and his fellow conspirators had planned the dictator's assassination as the first step in a greater effort to seize control of the government and negotiate a peace settlement with the Allies. Hitler's survival, however, ruined the plot. In an effort to cover up his knowledge of the conspiracy, General Friedrich Fromm, commander of the Reserve Army, ordered the colonel's arrest and quick execution by firing squad. Nevertheless, Fromm and many others involved in the conspiracy, or with knowledge of it, were subsequently put on trial and executed.

A week after the attempt on Hitler, the Allies launched a major offensive, finally breaking out into the French interior. American forces under General Patton and British troops under General Montgomery now moved swiftly westward into Brittany, southward toward Paris, and eastward toward the Belgian border. On August 15, American and Free French forces landed in southern France, capturing valuable ports before driving northward. Ten days later, Allied troops entered Paris. As enemy resistance crumbled, American and British forces pressed eastward toward Germany, occupying most of Belgium and Luxembourg by mid-September. Eisenhower authorized a bold plan devised by Montgomery to swing around German defenses by striking quickly into the Netherlands, followed by a drive southward into the Ruhr region, Germany's industrial heartland. Montgomery called for 30,000 paratroopers to capture key bridges behind enemy lines, followed by the arrival of supporting armored divisions, which would secure the bridges that would serve as major pathways into the Ruhr. The operation (code-named Market-Garden) failed, however, due to a combination of bad weather, the complicated logistics of capturing bridges over 50 miles behind the front lines, and the tenacious defense of two German armored divisions in the area. The failure of Market-Garden meant the war would not end in 1944.

As winter settled on the new Western Front, Allied forces made preparations for a final spring offensive into Germany. Hitler used the lull to organize a massive counterattack through the densely wooded Ardennes Forest area of Belgium. Pulling crucial forces from the crumbling Eastern Front, Hitler gambled that a large mobile attacking force thrown against the unsuspecting Allies could drive a wedge between the British and American armies, forcing a grand Allied retreat, and providing a tremendous morale boost for Germany. The surprise attack began on December 16, taking advantage of fog and snow that neutralized Allied air supremacy. Over a quarter of a million men assisted by armored divisions punched a "bulge" 60 miles deep and 50 miles wide into the front lines. Initially caught off guard, Eisenhower quickly mobilized over 200,000 reinforcements to stabilize the Allied position. After a week of fighting, fair weather returned, allowing Allied planes to pound German forces. Soon, General George Patton led a counterstrike that shrank the bulge and eventually compelled Hitler to order a retreat by mid-January. With almost 90,000 casualties (19,000 killed, 47,500 wounded, and 23,000 captured or missing), the United States suffered more casualties in the "Battle of the Bulge" than in any single fight during the entire war. Hitler nevertheless squandered most of his remaining reserves, losing 100,000 men. France and Belgium remained in Allied hands as Eisenhower prepared for the final thrust into Germany. Meanwhile, the Soviets continued to drive westward along the Eastern Front. By the end of January 1945, Russian forces had not only expelled the Germans from the Soviet Union, but also controlled most of Poland, Slovakia, Hungary, and Romania.

The Yalta Conference

In February 1945, Franklin Roosevelt made the long laborious trip to Yalta on the Crimean Peninsula in southern Russia to have his final Big Three summit with Winston Churchill and Joseph Stalin. Having recently defeated Thomas Dewey, the Republican governor of New York, to win an unprecedented fourth term, Roosevelt arrived with a determination to get firm commitments from Stalin on the final phase of the war and to establish the structure for postwar cooperation. At the **Yalta Conference**, the Big Three finalized many agreements that had been initially discussed at the Tehran Conference. Prescribed zones in Germany and Central Europe for American, British, French, and Russian troops to occupy for an indeterminate amount of time were established, with the German capital of Berlin (well within the Russian zone) also to be subdivided among the four Allies. Germany would be disarmed and any captured Nazi war criminals prosecuted in a postwar tribunal. Roosevelt and Churchill reluctantly allowed Stalin to annex eastern Poland. Stalin promised (though he never followed through with his pledge) to include non-communists in a new Polish coalition government and to allow free elections in Eastern European countries under Soviet occupation. Roosevelt exacted a pledge from Stalin to enter the war against Japan three months after the conquest of Germany. In return, the Soviets could take possession of the Kurile Islands and the southern half of Sakhalin Island located to the north of Japan. Finally, Stalin reaffirmed his commitment to join the new global organization that would become the United Nations.

Critics later accused FDR of "giving away" too much to Stalin at Yalta, possibly because of his obviously failing health (he died two months after the visit). In reality, the president was still in charge of his mental faculties and while Stalin got much of what he desired, Roosevelt did exact some concrete agreements from the Soviet leader. With Russian troops in control of Eastern Europe and pouring into Germany, the strategic situation greatly favored Stalin. Further, not willing to rely on the possibility of successfully developing the atomic bomb in time to make a difference in the war, Roosevelt felt it was imperative to receive Russian assistance against Japan in East Asia.

End of the War in Europe

By the spring of 1945, the end of the war in Europe was a foregone conclusion—the only questions that remained were how long would it take for the Allies to complete the task, how many more casualties would each side have to endure, how many Axis leaders would be captured alive to be brought to justice, and what would be Europe's condition when it was all over. As Allied forces pressed into Germany, the horrors of the **Holocaust** were revealed to American and British forces as they already had been exposed by the Russians in Poland. Allied troops not only liberated prisoner-of-war camps, but also the Nazi death camps where six million Jews and an equal number of other "undesirables" such as gypsies, homosexuals, mentally and physically handicapped, and various political prisoners met their fate. Only a relatively small number of emaciated victims survived to be freed. Unable to dispose of the remaining corpses in time, German guards left piles of bodies stacked like firewood several feet high. Hardened Allied veterans of modern war could barely believe that such places existed. As one soldier wrote his family: "Every day for the rest of my life, what I've witnessed here will be the first thing I remember and the last thing I forget." While the American public had heard stories of

Map 24.3 Prescribed zones for a divided Berlin

Nazi atrocities and death camps, many discounted what they heard as wartime propaganda in the same vein as they discredited stories about the Germans spread by the British during World War I. Many American military and political leaders knew better—that these camps did exist, the main purpose to efficiently kill all who entered, either immediately in gas chambers or gradually through brutal forced labor. Anti-Semitism and simple indifference explain much of the nonexistent effort to act more decisively to aid Jewish refugees or disrupt the rail lines to the death camps. While military officials contended that attacking the rail lines (or even the gas chambers themselves) would divert resources from more efficient missions designed to speed up the end of the war, targets located only a few miles away from death camps were hit multiple times in 1944 and 1945, not to mention the fact that the military occasionally took other nonmilitary considerations under advisement when determining missions.

By the end of April 1945, Allied troops in Italy finally defeated General Kesselring's forces, captured the major northern cities of Genoa, Milan, and Venice, and forced Kesselring's successor to surrender the remainder of his army group. In the end, 60,000 Allied soldiers and 50,000 German troops died fighting on the peninsula. On April 27, Italian communist partisans captured Benito Mussolini, his mistress, and staffers as they attempted to escape to Switzerland. They were all shot the next day and brought to Milan where their bodies were displayed in the city square—a place where anti-fascists had been executed during the dictator's regime. After the corpses of Mussolini and the others received significant abuse, they were hanged upside down to the delight of jubilant onlookers.

Meanwhile, American and British forces pressed into western Germany, capturing the Ruhr region by mid-April as German forces surrendered en masse. On April

16, Russian forces attacked Berlin. Over a two-week period they suffered 100,000 casualties driving into the central district of the German capital against diehard Nazi fighters. Wishing to avoid Mussolini's fate, Adolf Hitler committed suicide in his private bunker on April 30. Two days later, Berlin fell to the Soviets. Though sporadic fighting continued for another week away from the capital, the war in Europe was finally over.

The victory over Germany not only revealed the atrocities of the Holocaust but also the full extent of Nazi technical prowess. Though Hitler did not allow much funding on atomic research, preferring instead to develop more "practical" weapons, by the war's end German scientists created a whole new generation of destructive technological innovations that the dictator had hoped would miraculously turn the tide of the war. Beginning in mid-June 1944, the Germans fired almost 10,000 V-1 cruise missiles on southern England (causing over 20,000 civilian casualties) and over 3,000 short-range ballistic missiles (V-2 rockets), which killed approximately 7,000 Londoners. In the final months of the war, the Germans deployed the C-2, the world's first surface-to-air guided missiles, and a small number of crude but effective jet fighters (the ME-262s). Further, German scientists had developed prototypes for air-to-air missiles as well as long-range ballistic missiles and submarine-launched missiles capable of hitting targets in the United States.

Table 24.1   **Noteworthy European and North African Theater Operations, 1942-1945**

Battle/Campaign	Date	Significance
Operation TORCH	November 1942	Successful American and British landings in NW Africa
El Alamein	November 1942	Stopped Axis advance upon Egypt/Suez Canal
Stalingrad	August 1942- February 1943	Stopped German advance into Southern Russia; beginning of Russian counterattack
Kursk	July 1943 – August 1943	Last German offensive on the Eastern Front stopped
Operation Husky	July 1943 – August 1943	Successful Allied invasion of Sicily
Salerno and Anzio landings	September 1943 and January 1944	Allied beachheads established in southern Italy
D-Day/Normandy Invasion	June 1944	Second front established by western allies in northern France
Battle of the Bulge	December 1944	Failed counterattack by Germans on the Western Front
Battle of Berlin	April – May 1945	Russian capture of the Nazi capital

VICTORY IN THE PACIFIC, 1943-1945

Before focusing on an effective strategy to defeat the Japanese, President Roosevelt first had to overcome the intense inter-service rivalry between the Army and the Navy. General Douglas MacArthur strongly desired to become the supreme commander of American forces in the Pacific. FDR balked at the idea, not only to avoid upsetting top Navy brass but also to prevent elevating MacArthur's status to a level that might make him a formidable Republican presidential candidate. Roosevelt also dismissed the notion of naming Chester Nimitz, the head of the Pacific Fleet, supreme commander because of his relative lack of prestige. Ultimately, Roosevelt decided upon a compromise—command in the Pacific would be divided. MacArthur would direct operations against the Japanese in the South Pacific. From Australia, the Army would attack New Guinea and advance westward toward the Philippines. Meanwhile, Nimitz and the Navy were charged with attacking the Japanese in the Solomon Islands located to the east of New Guinea as well as advancing upon the major enemy-held island chains in the Central Pacific. Though politically satisfying, the arrangement proved to be an inefficient way of conducting a major war effort against a tenacious foe. While a strongly coordinated strategy would have maximized resources, the two military branches often worked independently of each other in their separate theaters of operation, possibly prolonging the conflict and adding to the war's cost in men and materiel. Nevertheless, beginning in late 1942, American forces prepared for the grim fight ahead. Though the Japanese suffered major defeats at Midway and Guadalcanal, hundreds of thousands of soldiers remained entrenched on islands across the western Pacific prepared for a grinding war of attrition. In consultation with MacArthur and Nimitz, Army and Navy war planners in Washington ultimately developed a strategy to drive westward effectively, despite the limitations of the split command, and force a Japanese surrender within three years.

The South Pacific Campaign

After forcing the Japanese withdrawal from Guadalcanal in February 1943, the U.S. Navy began a steady drive up the narrow central gap within the Solomon Islands known as "the Slot" by American military personnel. The heavily defended air and naval base at Rabaul on the island of New Britain located to the north of the Solomons was the ultimate goal. After a series of successful air assaults on the Japanese stronghold, however, military leaders in Washington called off plans to attack the base. Since the 100,000-man garrison had been neutralized, American lives and resources would be spared by simply sidestepping the base and moving on to the next strategic objective in the South Pacific—the Philippines.

Simultaneous to the effort in the Solomon Islands, Douglas MacArthur led an American and Australian counterattack against Japanese forces on New Guinea. With limited sealift capacity, the general ordered his troops to cross the brutal Owen Stanley Mountains in order to capture a major Japanese position on the northeastern portion of the island. From there, MacArthur's forces spent the first half of 1944 rapidly driving westward along New Guinea's northern coast. Finally given adequate landing craft for amphibious movement, MacArthur skillfully employed a bypassing strategy to avoid strongly-held Japanese positions while infusing a strong element of surprise in his attacks deep behind enemy lines. By the summer, his forces advanced a thousand miles to the western side of New Guinea, setting the stage for his promised return to the Philippine Islands.

The Central Pacific Campaign

Even more significant to the defeat of Japan than MacArthur's push to the Philippines, the U.S. Navy's successful drive through the Central Pacific island chains provided the means for the American military to hit the Japanese home islands with long-range heavy bombers. Before such bombing could commence, the Navy first had to gain control of the Gilbert, Marshall, Caroline, and Mariana Islands. Rather than attempting to dislodge the enemy from every island enclave, Admiral Nimitz used an "island hopping" strategy to limit the number of engagements with the Japanese. Similar to MacArthur's bypassing operations in New Guinea, Nimitz ordered specific islands to be assaulted that would yield air bases to allow American patrol planes to neutralize the remaining islands in a chain before moving on to the next objective closer to Japan. Though this approach minimized the amount of potential casualties and spent resources, brutal engagements nevertheless took place when the key islands in a chain were invaded and entrenched Japanese defenders fought tenaciously, rarely surrendering.

The Navy's first attack in the Gilberts took place in November 1943 when marines stormed the tiny atoll at Tarawa. In three days of intense fighting on Tarawa's Betio Island (which covered less than three square miles), over a thousand marines lost their lives struggling to push off the landing beaches against 5,000 Japanese defenders fighting to the death. Only 17 prisoners were taken. On nearby Makin Atoll, an assault force of 6,500 U.S. Army troops attacked a much smaller force of 800 Japanese defenders.

President Franklin Roosevelt (center) confers with his top Pacific commanders, Army General Douglas MacArthur and Navy Admiral Chester Nimitz at Pearl Harbor, Hawaii, July 26, 1944.

Because effective enemy sniper fire delayed completion of the task for four days, a Japanese submarine had enough time to infiltrate the supporting fleet offshore, firing torpedoes that sunk the escort carrier *Liscome Bay* at the cost of 650 sailors—one of the largest single losses for the U.S. Navy in the entire war.

Success at Tarawa and Makin allowed Nimitz to order a leapfrogging thrust at Kwajalein Atoll in the central Marshall Islands, and Eniwetok located at the western edge of the chain. In early February 1944, intense air and offshore bombardment allowed over 40,000 marines to come ashore unmolested at the northern and southern islands at Kwajalein, setting the stage for a successful four-day fight against 8,000 Japanese defenders with less than 400 marines dead—far fewer than the costly fight on Tarawa. Because Eniwetok lay within the range of Japanese ships and aircraft based at their extensive anchorage at Truk in the central Caroline Islands, Nimitz ordered massive air assaults on the bastion from carrier-based planes before advancing further. The mid-February raids destroyed over 200 aircraft and sank multiple warships, effectively neutralizing Truk as a major base of operations. The attack on Truk not only greatly aided the conquest of Eniwetok but also allowed Nimitz to safely bypass all Japanese garrisons in the Carolines to undertake operations a thousand miles to the west of the Marshalls against the Japanese in the Marianas—large islands with airstrips long enough to support long-range bombers capable of hitting the Japanese home islands.

As American forces landed troops onshore at Saipan, the first major island in the Marianas to be seized, Japanese naval leaders vainly tried to disrupt the invasion by sending a fleet based in the Philippines to intervene. On June 18, 1944, with most of their veterans lost by this stage of the war, the outnumbered and relatively inexperienced Japanese pilots fell in droves to their American foes who had not only grown more experienced since the beginning of the war but were now flying superior F6F Hellcats. The Japanese lost 275 of the 373 aircraft engaged compared to the United States losing 29 planes in the Battle of the Philippine Sea, known by American pilots as "the Great Marianas Turkey Shoot." On Saipan, marines with army support fought over three weeks to clear out the 30,000 Japanese defenders doggedly resisting through a series of tunnels and reinforced bunkers, at the cost of 14,000 American killed and wounded. Near the battle's conclusion, hundreds of Japanese soldiers sacrificed themselves in fruitless "banzai" charges. Meanwhile, two-thirds of the island's 12,000 Japanese civilians (mostly women and children), convinced by their military that the American soldiers would rape and kill all survivors, congregated at the northern tip of the island and killed themselves by blowing themselves up with grenades or jumping off cliffs. The Marianas campaign concluded on August 1 with the end of enemy resistance on Tinian and Guam. As the Japanese stubbornly and pointlessly fought on, many Americans openly speculated about the potentially high level of casualties that an invasion of Japan would entail.

The Fight for the Philippines

After securing control over northern New Guinea, General MacArthur focused on the recapture of the Philippines, which would not only fulfill his promise to Filipinos to return after his flight in early 1942, but also cut off Japan from its vital oil supplies in the Dutch East Indies. MacArthur made plans for a joint operation with the Navy to attack the archipelago with the largest force yet assembled in the Pacific. Choosing to bypass the large southern island of Mindanao, the general favored first landing troops on the east-central island of Leyte in preparation for a grand thrust at the major northern island of Luzon (on which Manila resides). On October 20, 1944, after troops secured a beachhead on Leyte, MacArthur waded ashore in front of newsreel cameras and boldly announced that his pledge to return had been fulfilled. The main fight on land and offshore, however, had yet to occur.

Japanese leaders decided to contest the Leyte landing by desperately deploying their remaining naval forces in a complex series of maneuvers designed to surprise the Americans and destroy the fleet supporting the landing. The last remaining four carriers of the Imperial Navy with its support ships bore down from southern Japan. Because the carriers only possessed a total of 100 planes with novice pilots, this fleet served as a decoy to hopefully lure the American carriers away from the Leyte area. Meanwhile, two separate Japanese naval task forces consisting of large surface ships were to converge on Leyte Gulf from the west, with one group of battleships, cruisers, and destroyers taking a route around the north of the island and another taking a southern route.

On October 23, two American submarines spotted the northern fleet and seemingly drove it off with the help of supporting aircraft. When Admiral William "Bull" Halsey received word of the decoy enemy carrier force coming from the north, the characteristically aggressive commander took the bait and ordered his carriers and major surface ships to intercept them. With the remaining battleships and cruisers sent to the south to fend off the Japanese southern attack force, the admiral left the Leyte landing zone to be defended by only five small escort carriers, three destroyers, and four destroyer escorts under the command of Rear Admiral Clifton Sprague. As Halsey chased the decoy fleet (eventually sinking all four of its carriers), the Japanese fleet which had initially been turned away swung around under cover of darkness and continued its advance to the north of Leyte. Greatly outnumbered and outgunned, Sprague's light force performed the seemingly impossible task of holding off the massive Japanese battlewagons and cruisers by executing a series of intricate diversionary maneuvers. Sprague's pilots, trained only in ground-support combat, slowed down the Japanese ships by dropping the few torpedoes they had, along with non-armor piercing bombs. When their ordinance ran out, they simply made multiple dry runs with no ammunition. Meanwhile, Sprague's destroyers and destroyer escorts laid smoke screens and made swift attacking runs with their torpedoes and deck guns. So tenacious was the defense of the Gulf that the Japanese commander, who believed he was actually facing Halsey's large carriers and capital ships, finally called off the attack. The four separate engagements from October 23-25 collectively known as the **Battle of Leyte Gulf** was the largest naval battle in world history. The victorious Americans lost a light carrier, two escort carriers, two destroyers, one destroyer escort, and 3,000 men. Meanwhile, Japanese losses were staggering: four large carriers, three battleships, ten cruisers, nine destroyers, and over 10,000 men.

U.S. forces gained control of Leyte by December, though sporadic Japanese resistance continued for several more months. MacArthur finally landed troops on Luzon in January 1945 as Japanese pilots desperately flew their bomb-laden aircraft into American ships, sinking one escort carrier, damaging another, and also hitting two battleships and five cruisers. Initially used at the end of the Battle of Leyte Gulf, these suicidal kamikaze attacks could occasionally be devastating to American ships. (Named after the Japanese phrase "divine wind," kamikaze pilots deliberately dove their planes into targets like American ships.) Though the majority of kamikazes were shot down, enough penetrated American naval defenses during the waning months of the war to do significant damage to American vessels and morale. By February, American ground forces reached Manila and proceeded to spend the entire month clearing out Japanese defenders in street fighting that resulted in the deaths of almost 100,000 Filipino civilians.

The Bloody Fight for Iwo Jima and Okinawa

While the fight for Manila commenced, the U.S. Navy landed marines on the small volcanic island of Iwo Jima. Despite its size (5 miles long and 2 ½ miles across), located halfway between the Marianas and Tokyo, Iwo Jima held strategic value to the Japanese as a fighter base along the flight path for American heavy bombers, which had already begun hitting the home islands. The U.S. military wished to capture the island to eliminate its ability to serve as a Japanese fighter base, to use the airfields to house American fighter escorts, and to serve as an emergency landing strip for disabled bombers. Though small, the island's topographical features greatly aided the island's 20,000 defenders who were well supplied with artillery and machine guns. Iwo Jima possessed several rocky high points, including the 550-foot Mount Suribachi, which dominated the southern tip of the island. On the beaches, volcanic ash rather than sand covered the coastline making it difficult for men and vehicles to maneuver. The island also contained countless caves, which the Japanese used to connect with underground tunnels, reinforced bunkers, and blockhouses.

Landing on Iwo Jima's southern shore on February 19, 1945, marines fought their way off the beaches for three days before capturing Mount Suribachi. The most famous American photograph of the war was soon taken when Associated Press photographer Joe Rosenthal snapped a picture of five marines and a U.S. Navy corpsman raising a large American flag over the position. The fight for Iwo Jima, however, was far from over—three of the flag-raisers would be killed before the battle ended a month later. For the next four weeks, marines fought their way northward across the grueling terrain under withering enemy fire, helped out with tanks using flamethrowers to clear out the enemy defenders. As was the case in Saipan, when the last remaining Japanese soldiers realized that hope was lost, they sacrificed themselves with suicidal banzai charges. The final human cost of the battle to wipe out the entire Japanese garrison was 6,821 dead marines with over 17,000 wounded. Of all U.S. Marines killed in the Pacific, one-third died at Iwo Jima.

On April 1, 1945, the U.S. military conducted its final amphibious operation of the war, landing 180,000 marines and army personnel on the island of Okinawa. Located only 350 miles south of Kyushu, the southernmost of the main Japanese home islands, Okinawa contained airfields and anchorages that could serve as an excellent base for close-range bombings of Japan as well as a staging area for a direct attack invasion. Japanese military leaders were well aware of the island's importance and planned to hold it at all costs, reinforcing its garrison to 100,000 men – the largest force that American troops would ever face during the entire Pacific war. Over fifty times larger than Iwo Jima, Japanese soldiers used defensive networks imbedded in the rough terrain similar to the earlier fight to exact high casualties and continued to fight with tenacity and desperation. Offshore, the U.S. Navy endured the largest series of kamikaze attacks of the war, losing 35 ships with 350 damaged. Ultimately, the battle for Okinawa, the bloodiest that the Americans fought in the Pacific, took six weeks to complete. The United States lost over 7,000 army soldiers and marines on the ground and another 5,000 sailors at sea due to the kamikazes. The Japanese lost 95,000 men (including 1,900 kamikaze pilots) while over 7,000 defenders (mostly recent local civilian conscripts) surrendered.

Naval Blockade and the Fire Bombing of Japan

While the fight for Okinawa raged, the nation learned of Franklin Roosevelt's death on April 12 from a cerebral hemorrhage. By the time Harry Truman assumed the presidency, Japan was a defeated nation, even if its leaders refused to accept that fact. In China, large numbers of occupation soldiers garrisoned the large cities in the eastern coastal areas, but ceded much of the countryside to the nationalist forces of Chiang Kai-Shek and communist rebels under Mao Zedong. In the western Pacific, American forces were pressing against the home islands. Japanese forces still held on to a large number of islands in the central and southern Pacific, but their troops were left to "die on the vine"—isolated and cut off from their supply lines by American patrol planes and surface ships. By mid-1945, the main Japanese islands were virtually cut off from the outside world by American minelayers and submarines. Half of Japan's merchant fleet had been destroyed with the remaining ships clinging to the shores, abandoning the high seas. Most food importation from China and Manchuria ended. As oil imports from the Dutch East Indies ceased, Japanese air and naval units suffered greatly and Japanese industry ground to a halt.

Meanwhile, Japan began to be relentlessly pummeled from the air by B-29 Super Fortresses—new heavy bombers that were larger and faster than the B-17s used in Europe with much greater range and payload capacity. Originally launched against Japan from China in June 1944, the B-29s initially followed the same high-altitude strategic bombing tactics used in Europe—with equally ineffective results. Even after the bombers were redeployed to the Marianas for missions over Japan starting in late November and placed under the command of General Curtis LeMay, an innovative veteran commander who led strategic bombing attacks over Germany, the poor results continued. Though the American pilots had to contend with few enemy fighter planes, strong winds from the jet stream and frequent heavy cloud cover limited the success of the missions. LeMay then shifted to incendiary attacks using Napalm-B—a new flammable jelly developed by Dupont and Standard Oil designed to spread fires rapidly. For greater precision, the bombing runs would take place at a much lower altitude (5,000 feet). To avoid heavy antiaircraft fire, the general ordered the removal of most machine gun turrets and crew for increased flight speed and to attack at night. The first mission under the new guidelines took place over Tokyo on March 9, 1945. The raid destroyed 16 square miles (about a quarter of the capital city) and killed approximately 100,000 civilians by incineration or suffocation—by far the most deadly bombing of the entire war. Heartened by his success, LeMay ordered similar attacks over the next several months against 60 other Japanese cities, wiping out over half their size and killing another 400,000 Japanese civilians. While the attacks destroyed some industrial targets, they were morally indefensible—the clear purpose of the raids was to break the will of the Japanese public through terror bombing. After the war, LeMay admitted the immorality of targeting civilians but consoled himself with the basic belief that all war was immoral and if one worried about such matters he would not be a good soldier. He then added: "I suppose if [we] had lost the war, I would have been tried as a war criminal."

Despite the blockade and continuous aerial bombing, Japanese leaders still refused to surrender unconditionally as the Allies demanded. While some diehards in the government would never surrender under any circumstances, many held on to the vain hope that a negotiated settlement could be reached because the Americans wished to avoid the massive casualties an invasion of Japan would deliver. The Japanese sent inquiries to Joseph Stalin to ascertain if the Soviet leader was interested in brokering a peace deal, but the dictator turned away the diplomats' request for a meeting. Aware of the overture, the Truman administration nevertheless refused to deviate from the demand for unconditional surrender. Meanwhile, November 1, 1945 was set as the preliminary date for the invasion of Kyushu. With entrenched enemy forces supported by a hostile civilian population fighting fanatically in defense of their homeland, the U.S. military estimated that American casualties would exceed a quarter of a million killed and wounded. While these figures weighed on President Truman's mind, the president hoped for positive news coming from the government's top-secret atomic research program.

The Defeat of Japan

The origins of the Allied atomic weapons development program, code-named the **Manhattan Project**, trace back to 1939 when a small group of scientists including Albert Einstein brought the possibility of an atomic bomb being created in the near future to Franklin Roosevelt's attention. Fearing such a weapon of mass destruction in Hitler's hands, Roosevelt and Churchill decided in 1940 to secretly work together on its development (though Stalin was never told of the Manhattan Project before the bomb's use, he became aware of its development through his spy network.) Military officials informed President Truman of the first successful detonation near Alamogordo, New Mexico on July 16, 1945, while he was meeting with Winston Churchill and Stalin at the Potsdam Conference outside Berlin. Truman used the occasion to inform Stalin that the U.S. now had a bomb of immense destructive capability. Feigning ignorance of the atomic program, Stalin simply told Truman to use the weapon against Japan as soon as possible, which was indeed Truman's intention. At Potsdam, Truman, Stalin, and Clement Atlee (the new British Prime Minister who replaced Churchill after the first parliamentary elections after the collapse of Nazi Germany) issued the Potsdam Declaration, which reiterated the demand for Japan to surrender unconditionally or face "complete and utter destruction."

Though some historians have argued that Truman's primary motivation in using the atomic bomb was to keep the Soviets in line after the war's conclusion, the president and his advisors largely viewed that possibility as a side benefit. In the end, Truman believed, correctly or not, that the bomb would save American lives by ending the war sooner without the need for an invasion of Japan. In making the decision, he pushed aside strong objections raised by a cadre of scientists who had developed the weapon as well as some top military brass. Though Army Chief of Staff George Marshall concurred with Truman that the atomic weapon had to be used, Fleet Admiral William Leahy, the Chief of Staff to the Commander in Chief (equivalent of the Chairman of the Joint Chiefs of Staff today) strongly objected on moral grounds, later writing in his memoirs: "It is my opinion that the use of this barbarous weapon . . . was of no material assistance in our war against Japan. The Japanese were already defeated and ready to surrender because of the effective sea blockade and the successful bombing with conventional weapons. . . . My own feeling was that in being the first to use it, we had adopted an ethical standard common to the barbarians of the Dark Ages. I was not taught to make wars in that fashion, and that wars cannot be won by destroying women and children." General Dwight Eisenhower, the Supreme Allied Commander in Europe, also objected. In his published recollections after the war, he related details about a meeting with Secretary of War Henry Stimson in which he was informed of the bomb's existence and the government's plans to use it. "During his recitation of the relevant facts," the general wrote, "I voiced to him my grave misgivings, first on my belief that Japan was already defeated and that dropping the bomb was completely unnecessary, and secondly because I thought that our country should avoid shocking world opinion by the use of a weapon whose employment was, I thought, no longer mandatory as a measure to save American lives. It was my belief that Japan was, at that very moment, seeking some way to surrender with a minimum loss of 'face.' The Secretary was deeply perturbed by my attitude."

On the morning of August 6, 1945, a B-29 named the *Enola Gay* took off from its base on Tinian in the Marianas to drop an atomic bomb codenamed "Little Boy." Hiroshima, a port city of 340,000 located on the southern coast of Japan's largest island of Honshu, headed a list of potential targets that consisted of large urban centers with military value that had escaped firebombing. At 8:15 a.m., Little Boy detonated 2,000 feet over the city center, immediately producing an immense fireball emitting radiation and a powerful shock wave that destroyed all buildings within a mile radius of the blast point. Seventy to one hundred thousand men, women, and children (including at least 10 American prisoners-of-war) were killed directly as a result of the bombing, with the death toll reaching near 200,000 due to the effects of radiation poisoning within a few years.

After the Hiroshima bombing, Japanese diplomats renewed their efforts to involve Stalin in peace negotiations, but the Soviet leader not only demurred, he also declared war on Japan, fulfilling his promise to Roosevelt at Yalta. Sensing the war was nearing its conclusion, Stalin ordered Russian troops to attack Manchuria and to seize as much land as possible—a very demoralizing development for Japanese leaders. While they debated the merits of a

(L) Hiroshima after the bomb
(R) Second atomic bombing of Nagasaki, Japan. August 1945

possible surrender, Truman authorized the dropping of a second atomic bomb. Not only had the Japanese government failed to surrender unconditionally, but an earlier decision dictated that the second bomb should be used relatively quickly after using the first one—since the U.S. had initially only developed three bombs and it would be weeks before additional bombs would be available, Truman concurred with advisors who suggested that quick use of two bombs would have added shock value, giving the impression that the first bomb was no fluke and that the United States had the capability of immediately destroying Japan. Hence, the crew of a B-29 named *Bockscar* left Tinian on August 9, headed for Kyushu. Their target was the city of Kokura, but with reports of bad weather, the commander decided to divert the mission to its secondary target—the port city of Nagasaki with a population of a quarter million. The hills surrounding the city limited the extent of the cataclysm, but the blast destroyed the town center and killed 40,000 immediately with an equal number succumbing by the end of the year.

The dropping of both atomic bombs and Russian entry into the war convinced many Japanese leaders that they must surrender, though most did not wish to do so unconditionally. Even after the atomic attacks, they desired guarantees for the life and position of their emperor. Emperor Hirohito's supreme war council became deadlocked between such peace advocates and the radical military elements who wished to fight on. The ruler finally interceded to break the impasse by relaying his desire to accept the Potsdam Declaration if the institution of the emperor would be retained. The council relayed this proposal to the Truman administration, which accepted the proviso with the understanding that the emperor's authority would be subject to the dictates of the Allied commander of occupation forces (General Douglas MacArthur). As Japanese leaders debated this proposal, rogue army officers desperately sought to take over the government to prevent the possibility of surrender, but their coup attempt failed. After three days of discussion, Japan accepted the modified conditional surrender terms on August 14, unofficially ending the war. Some historians later asserted, as did General MacArthur, that the war might have ended weeks earlier without the use of atomic weapons if the U.S. had agreed, as it later did anyway, to the condition of retaining the emperor and giving him immunity from prosecution for war crimes. Regardless, Japanese officials formally signed the surrender agreement aboard the deck of the battleship *Missouri* in Tokyo Bay on September 2, thus ending the most bitter and destructive war in the history of the world.

TO THE COLD WAR

In the final analysis, World War II should be viewed as the culmination of clashing ideologies unleashed by the disappointments created by World War I and the extreme economic hardships of the Great Depression. On the one hand, the Soviet Union, formed in the aftermath of the First World War, emerged as the world's first communist power. Ostensibly elevating the working man to cast off the chains of capitalist oppression by confiscating excess wealth and private property, diehard Bolsheviks sought to spread their ideology beyond Russia's borders. At the other extreme, the 1930s witnessed the rise of fascism in Italy, Germany, and Japan—an ideology that manifested itself differently in various countries but shared such common characteristics as militancy, ultra-nationalism, vehement anticommunism, and a strong aversion to the "inefficiency" of democracy. Between the extremes of communism and fascism lay the democracies of the United States, Great Britain, and France, which incor-porated progressive (and occasionally socialistic) reforms to moderate its capitalist systems in order to promote efficiency and social justice while undercutting more radical proposals. While the Second World War ended the threat of militant fascism to world peace, the conflict also set the stage for a new global struggle between democratic capitalist nations led by the United States and communist countries guided initially by the Soviet Union, soon to be joined by the People's Republic of China.

Table 24.2

Noteworthy Pacific Theater Operations, 1942-1945

Battle	Date	Significance
Coral Sea	May 1942	First halting of a Japanese military advance
Midway	June 1942	Severe defeat for Japanese navy, ending ability to undertake major offensive naval operations in the Pacific
Guadalcanal	August 1942 – February 1943	First successful counterattack against Japanese ground forces in the South Pacific
Tarawa	November 1943	First successful counterattack against Japanese ground forces in the Central Pacific
Saipan/Guam	June 1944 – August 1944	Capture of the Mariana Islands; establishment of air bases to launch bombing raids upon Japan
Leyte Gulf	October 1944	Largest naval battle of WW II; failure of Japanese navy to stop American landings in the Philippines
Iwo Jima	February 1945 – March 1945	Capture of island base used by Japanese fighter planes to intercept American bombers
Okinawa	April 1945 – June 1945	Largest amphibious assault of the Pacific Theater; capture led to establishment of U.S. bomber bases close to Japanese home islands

Chronology

1921	Washington Conference first meets.
1922	Mussolini assumes power in Italy.
1923	France and Belgium occupy the Ruhr.
1928	Kellogg-Briand Treaty signed.
1931	Japanese occupation of Manchuria.
1933	FDR inaugurated president. Hitler becomes chancellor of Germany.
1935	First U.S. Neutrality Act passed. Italy invades Ethiopia.
1936	German troops occupy the demilitarized Rhineland.
1937	Japan attacks China.
1938	Germany annexes Austria. Germany occupies the Sudetenland.
1939	German takeover of Czechoslovakia. Nazi-Soviet Non-Aggression Pact signed. Germany attacks Poland.
1940	Tripartite Pact signed. Japan occupies Indochina. FDR re-elected to 3rd term.
1941	Germany attacks Russia. Japan attacks Pearl Harbor.
1942	Battles of Coral Sea, Midway, El Alamein, and Stalingrad. U.S. forces land in North Africa.
1943	Allied forces invade southern Italy. Italy quits the war. Battle of Tarawa.
1944	Invasion of Normandy. Battle of Leyte Gulf. FDR elected to fourth term. Battle of the Bulge.
1945	Yalta Conference. FDR dies. Germany and Japan defeated.

SUGGESTED READINGS

Thomas A. Bailey and Paul B. Ryan, *Hitler vs. Roosevelt: The Undeclared Naval War* (1979).

John Morton Blum, *V Was for Victory: Politics and American Culture during World War II* (1976).

Warren I. Cohen, *Empire without Tears: America's Foreign Relations, 1921-1933* (1987).

Matthew Ware Coulter, *The Senate Munitions Inquiry of the 1930s: Beyond the Merchants of Death* (1997).

Robert Dallek, *Franklin D. Roosevelt and American Foreign Policy, 1932-1945* (1979).

Roger Daniels, *Prisoners without Trial: Japanese Americans in World War II* (1993).

Robert A. Divine, *The Reluctant Belligerent: American Entry into World War II*, 2nd ed. (1979).

Justus D. Doenecke and John E. Wiltz, *From Isolation to War, 1931-1941*, 3rd ed. (2003).

Sherna Berger Gluck, *Rosie the Riveter Revisited: Women, the War, and Social Change* (1987).

Waldo Heinrichs, *Threshold of War: Franklin D. Roosevelt and American Entry into World War II* (1988).

Saburo Ienaga, *The Pacific War, 1931-1945* (1978).

Akira Iriye, *The Origins of the Second World War in Asia and the Pacific* (1987).

John Keegan, *The Second World War* (1989).

David Kennedy, *Freedom from Fear: The American People in Depression and War, 1929-1945* (2001).

Warren F. Kimball, *Forged in Battle: Roosevelt, Churchill, and the Second World War* (1997).

Michael J. Lyons, *World War II: A Short History*, 3rd ed., (1999)

National Park Service, *World War II and the American Home Front: A National Historic Landmarks Theme Study* (2007).

William L. O'Neill, *A Democracy at War: America's Fight at Home and Abroad in World War II* (1998).

Richard Polenberg, *War and Society: The United States, 1941-1945* (1972).

Richard Rhodes, *The Making of the Atomic Bomb* (1995).

Martin Sherwin, *A World Destroyed: Hiroshima and Its Legacies*, 3rd ed. (2003).

Review Questions

1. Describe America's international relations during the 1920s. Was the United States aloof and isolationist, or actively engaged in foreign affairs during the decade? Explain with examples.

2. Describe the challenges that Franklin Roosevelt faced at home and abroad during the period of American neutrality before U.S. entry into World War II. How did he react to these challenges?

3. Identify and describe three turning points during World War II that culminated in the defeat of Germany, Italy, and Japan.

4. Describe the contributions of women and minority groups to the American war effort during World War II.

5. Describe the development and use of the atomic bomb during World War II.

Glossary of Important People and Concepts

Battle of the Atlantic
Battle of Britain
Battle of Leyte Gulf
Battle of Midway
Battle of Stalingrad
Fascism
Good Neighbor Policy
Adolf Hitler
Holocaust
Lend-Lease Act
Manhattan Project
Munich Conference
Benito Mussolini
Nazi-Soviet Non-Aggression Pact
Neutrality Acts
Office of Price Administration (OPA)
Operation Overlord
Pearl Harbor attack
A. Phillip Randolph
Spanish Civil War
Strategic bombing campaign
Tuskegee Airmen
Washington Naval Conference
Women Airforce Service Pilots (WASPs)
Yalta Conference

HARRY S TRUMAN

Chapter Twenty-five

THE ORIGINS OF THE COLD WAR

Loud knocks on a door early in the morning would unnerve anyone, but the knocks heard by Hans-Peter Spitzner and his family in their small apartment in Karl-Marx Stadt in the German Democratic Republic (GDR) especially terrified them. Hans-Peter was frightened and panicked because he knew who was on the other side of the door—members of the Stasi, the state security police. As he began to open the door, four men who never formally identified themselves themselves burst through and in a loud and authoritarian voice announced, "House Search!" The men proceeded to tear apart drawers, cushions, and anything else they pleased. They even, almost with glee, destroyed some of his daughter Peggy's toys. After wrecking the apartment and finding nothing (Hans-Peter was sure they were not actually looking for anything), he was told to get dressed before being forcibly taken to Stasi headquarters where he was interrogated for hours. Why was all this happening? The teacher had refused to vote for the names on his trade-union election ballot because they were all members of the Communist Party.

After his ordeal, Hans-Peter Spitzner made a decision: he and his family would try to flee to West Germany. It was not a decision that anyone in the GDR made lightly. Since the Soviet Union had sealed the borders and succeeded in helping to establish the Communist client state in East Germany after World War II, officially almost 1,000 people had been killed by border guards or soldiers trying to escape to the West, but Hans-Peter also knew that "official" number was not accurate. He also knew that countless other victims had never made it to the border to be killed because informants exposed their plans and were either sent to prison or exterminated by the Stasi. Thus, just deciding to plan to escape put him and his entire family at risk.

Ingrid, his wife, had an aunt who lived in Austria on the other side of the "Iron Curtain." She had recently asked for and received permission to visit her on her birthday in July 1989. The authorities did not worry much about allowing travelers such as Ingrid to leave because they knew that they could make hostages out of the family left behind. Hans-Peter saw an opportunity, so he planned to take Peggy and escape to meet Ingrid in Austria, but ever fearful of reprisal and informants he told no one, not even Ingrid or Peggy.

He loaded Peggy and drove the one hundred miles to Berlin, where he went to the Allied bus station and begged the drivers to let him and Peggy become stowaways. All refused; after all, if they were caught smuggling escapees, the consequences would be severe. Finally, Hans-Peter convinced a young U.S. military enlisted man to place them in his trunk and drive them across the border. Hans-Peter's greatest moment of anxiety and fear came when the car stopped at infamous "Checkpoint Charlie," the primary crossing point between East Berlin and West Berlin. He finally felt relieved when the car started and was allowed to continue. As soon as they were safely in West Berlin, the soldier let them out of the trunk and said that they could now go anywhere they wished. He got a message off to Ingrid, and she flew to West Berlin to reunite with her family.

Hans-Peter, Ingrid, and Peggy Spitzner were some of the last people to escape to the West. The Berlin Wall, a symbol of the Cold War divide in Europe, which had lasted for over forty years would soon be coming down after great pressure *from its people and the world in November 1989. Shortly thereafter, the East German government fell, and the two Germanys (and the two Berlins) once again became one. The Cold War had finally ended. After unification, the Spitzners moved back to what used to be Karl-Marx Stadt (now known as Chemnitz), where Peter still teaches.*

World War II had brought together an uneasy alliance among Great Britain, the Soviet Union, and the United States. The Americans, as well as the British, had warily viewed the Soviets as a threat to their concepts of the world before the war began. Only the immediate need to defeat Fascist Germany and Italy had made the U.S. and the U.S.S.R. cast aside their differences, but even during the war, tensions arose that never truly subsided. British Prime Minister Winston Churchill mistrusted and intensely disliked Soviet Premier Josef Stalin. For his part, Stalin had mistrusted the western Allies, believing, among other things, that they had delayed their offensive on Germany in order to allow the Germans and Russians to weaken themselves and each other on the Eastern Front. When World War II ended, these old conflicts and previous suspicions returned. Those strains, in turn, became a part of the diplomatic maneuvers after the war that opened a dangerous rivalry between the former allies that would be the most integral factor in determining American foreign relations over the next five decades, what American journalist Walter Lippmann famously described as a "Cold War."

THE EMERGING COLD WAR

The primary cause of the **Cold War** proved to be the great differences in how the Soviet Union and the two Western powers—the United States and Great Britain—viewed the world after World War II. Franklin Roosevelt and Winston Churchill had articulated their vision of the world with the signing of the Atlantic Charter in 1941, imagining a world in which all nations ended the traditional diplomatic mechanisms such as military alliances and "spheres of influence," and their relations became governed by democratic processes, with an international organization serving as the arbiter of disputes and the guarantor of self-determination for all nations. It was a decidedly American vision, one born during the Progressive Era, and reflected the primary policy goal of President Franklin Roosevelt. The British were less sanguine about such a view, as Churchill and his party took a more cynical view of the world and, particularly, the Soviets. British leaders also saw how a strict interpretation of the

charter could affect the governance and control of their own vast empire. Still, World War II had made the U.S. the premier power among the Allies, and Great Britain had little choice but to acquiesce to the American vision.

The Soviets, naturally, had an entirely different view. Twice since 1914, Germany had invaded Soviet territory, and in both world wars the Soviet casualty totals were horrendous. Most importantly, the Soviets wanted security from aggression, and in Stalin's mind, the best way to achieve such a goal was to carve out a "sphere of influence" in central and Eastern Europe, territory that would serve as a "buffer" to potential attack from the West. The Soviets also desired to spread communism outside its borders.

The differing world views eventually caused the great schism that brought forth the Cold War. One of the biggest debates among historians concerns who was most responsible for the beginning of this fight. One view that finds the most credence among more "traditional" interpretations of the Cold War is that Soviet dictator, Josef Stalin, was a paranoid leader whose insecurity led him to seek to dominate and control the entire world. "Stalinism," in their eyes, was a particularly retrograde form of communist thought, one that sought to establish a communist world through any method, including by force, if necessary. Such a stance, they argue caused the U.S. during the late 1940s, under President Harry Truman, to begin to oppose Soviet moves in every arena and in every diplomatic exchange. This position led to a confrontation in foreign relations that established two spheres of influence in the world: East and West, Soviet and American, communism and democracy.

The analysis from revisionist historians blames both sides for the struggle. In order to advance their agendas, both sides engaged in intense rhetoric, counter-diplomatic initiatives, and introduced the dangerous specter of nuclear holocaust. Such actions created a condition of hostility not only between nations but also between cultures and lifestyles. The result was a world divided between two ideologies, each one intent on superseding the destruction of the other.

THE TRUMAN PRESIDENCY

Harry S Truman ascended to the presidency upon the death of Franklin Roosevelt in April 1945 with very little knowledge of what had occurred at the Yalta Conference (see Chapter 25), or how other aspects of diplomacy had been conducted during the last years of the war. He was more staunchly anti-communist than Roosevelt had ever been, and like Winston Churchill, Truman mistrusted and

British Prime Minister Winston Churchill, U.S. President Harry Truman, and Soviet Premier Joseph Stalin at the Potsdam Conference, July 23, 1945
Photo credit: Truman Library.

personally disliked the Soviet leader. Churchill had sent a message to the new American president in May 1945, exhorting him to press the Soviets for concessions, writing at one point that an "iron curtain is drawn down upon" Eastern Europe. The prime minister would repeat that phrase at a speech at Westminster College in Fulton, Missouri almost a year later, giving to the world the famous moniker describing the division between East and West. The president agreed with Churchill and resolved to be "tough" on Stalin in talks. Truman's views, as well as his personality, would greatly shape the next discussion over Europe at a meeting in Potsdam, Germany, in July 1945.

Truman began his presidency insisting that the Soviets honor the Yalta Accords and allow free elections in Poland. The Soviets conceded nothing, and Truman was not in a position of strength since the U.S. was still fighting the Japanese, and the Red Army fully occupied Poland. When Stalin made a superficial conciliation of including some of the Free Polish leaders in minor positions in the Polish government, Truman had no choice but to acquiesce and recognize the Soviet puppet state. Thus, the president headed to the Potsdam meeting with less leverage than Roosevelt had at Yalta. Churchill also joined the talks, but he learned while he was there that he was no longer the Prime Minister of Great Britain after his party lost

the parliamentary elections. Truman had no choice but to accept reality regarding Poland—the borders as set by the Soviets and the government installed by Stalin. He did refuse to back down on reparations, telling Stalin that he would collect nothing from the Germans in the American, French, and British occupation zones. Truman was, in effect, dividing Germany into two nations: one allied with the Western powers, and the other oriented toward the Soviet Union, assuring that the western half would follow a Western-style form of government, while the eastern half would become a communist state.

THE TRUMAN DOCTRINE AND THE POLICY OF CONTAINMENT

Aid to Greece and Turkey

Potsdam and further events on the world stage would eventually lead Truman to directly confront the Soviets, leading to the first real crisis of the emerging Cold War. The result would be a new direction in American foreign policy, a diplomatic and military strategy known as the **containment policy** or "The Truman Doctrine." Containment was based upon acceptance of the presence of communism within its current areas of control, but with the commitment to oppose any attempt to spread the Marxist-based ideology to the rest of the world. The doctrine would guide and direct almost every American foreign policy decision for the next four decades, and would lead the nation into two direct military actions in Korea and Vietnam.

The policy emerged out of a confrontation with the Soviet Union over Greece and Turkey in the years immediately after World War II. Greece had been under the control of the Nazis since 1940. When the war ended, two rebel factions remained and were soon engulfed in a civil war: one group that wanted to establish a pro-Western, republican style of government and another that favored the Soviets and wanted to establish a communist regime. The Soviets, who viewed Greece as a strategically important seaport country that could allow them access to the Mediterranean Sea, actively favored the communist group. In the years before the war, Greece had been in the British "sphere of influence," and they were backers of the pro-Western group. However, World War II had greatly weakened the British and reduced their ability to influence affairs throughout the globe, so they announced that they would no longer be able to provide support for the pro-Western faction. Meanwhile, the Soviets were trying to gain influence and favors in nearby Turkey, a nation

George F. Kennan

A native of Milwaukee, George F. Kennan was a career foreign policy officer who became known as the architect of the "Policy of Containment." Kennan had seen, up close, the rise of Adolph Hitler and totalitarianism in Europe while he served as a diplomat. He was briefly detained by the Nazis before he was allowed to return to the United States, where he became intensely committed to making sure that no nation, or single leader, was ever able to plunge the world into such an intense war. After the war, Kennan became the Chargè d'Affaires in the Soviet Union, and while in that position he wrote, anonymously as "Mr. X," what became known as the "long telegram" that laid out his ideas on how to confront communism. In the missive, Kennan wrote "the main element of any United States policy toward the Soviet Union must be that of a long-term, patient but firm and vigilant containment of Russian expansive tendencies." He further called for defying "Soviet pressure against the free institutions of the Western World" with "adroit and vigilant applications of counter-force at a series of constantly shifting geographical and political points, corresponding to the shifts and maneuvers of Soviet policy." He predicted that following such a policy would eventually result in "either the break-up or the gradual mellowing of Soviet power."

President Harry Truman used Kennan's ideas when he gave his speech before Congress asking for aid to Greece and Turkey in 1947. Furthermore, he used the notions of containment in formulating American policy toward the Soviets for the rest of his term, which in turn laid the foundation for American diplomatic relations with the Soviet Union for the administrations that would follow. When he heard the speech, Kennan reportedly objected to how Truman had made his policy idea an "open-ended commitment" to contain communism; he had intended for his concept of containment to be used discriminately and selectively, not one that could be used to involve the U.S. in every confrontation with communism throughout the world. In his later years, he became a critic of many of the American policy ideas undertaken under the guise of his original notions.

Kennan would eventually leave the State Department in the 1950s and become a professor at Princeton University (he did serve briefly as Ambassador to Yugoslavia in the 1960s), where he became a prolific author on foreign policy issues and won two Pulitzer Prizes for his work. He died in Princeton, New Jersey in 2005.

in the midst of trying to become a more integral part of Europe and less tied to the Middle East. Thus, by 1947, if the communists were to be defeated and thwarted in both nations, it would fall to the United States to provide the leadership, material, and assistance.

Truman responded with a forceful new policy, one in which he drew on the ideas articulated by **George F. Kennan** (see insert) in a speech delivered to a joint session of Congress on March 12, 1947. He appealed for an aid package of $400 million for the two nations to counter the communist threat, announcing the core beliefs of what would become the Truman Doctrine. The president warned the Soviets that the United States would actively support the Greek pro-Western faction and told Congress "it must be the policy of the United States to support free peoples who are attempting subjugation by armed minorities or by outside pressures." Truman was declaring that it would be the official policy of the United States to counter the Soviets anywhere in the world if they tried to spread their influence. Implied in much of the containment policy was that the U.S. was prepared to use not only financial and diplomatic assistance, but also military aid—up to and including the use of nuclear weapons.

Congress provided the aid to Greece and Turkey, which led to stability in the region. The Greek Civil War ended with the non-communist faction in control. Moving forward, American government officials looked favorably upon the results of the first application of the Truman Doctrine and believed that they had found a winning formula.

The Marshall Plan

By 1945, six years of constant war had devastated Europe. While the physical destruction of World War II was massive, it had also destroyed economies and disrupted governments. Amidst such damage, communist activists in a number of countries saw an opportunity to gain a foothold in power, their credibility enhanced by their participation in the resistance against the fascists. At the same time that the Soviets were consolidating their control of Eastern Europe, the U.S. seemed powerless to stop the Soviet movements, much less exert any influence. If Eastern Europe were to fall behind Churchill's proverbial "Iron Curtain," there was the possibility that other countries of Europe would follow.

Former General George C. Marshall, chief of staff of the U.S. forces in World War II under President Roosevelt, became Secretary of State in January 1947. He used the opportunity of the commencement address at Harvard University that year to announce what became known as the "**Marshall Plan**," a massive program of economic aid to Europe. The Marshall Plan was designed not only to reconstruct the countries overwhelmed by the wreckage of war, but also to give them a firm economic grounding. This would keep them from being a drain on the U.S. economy while also making them profitable trading partners and helping the people of those nations reject the promises of communism.

The Soviets and their allies in Eastern Europe had been initially invited to participate, but as American policy makers correctly anticipated, Stalin rejected any program whose intent was to foster American capitalism anywhere in Europe. One of his long-term objectives was certainly to keep Eastern Europe economically in submission and subservient to Soviet needs. Stalin also balked at numerous terms and conditions that American officials had deliberately imbedded into the plan to compel Soviet refusal, such as the use of funds to purchase American products and the need for U.S. officials to personally investigate and assess the amount of aid rather than the "blank check" Stalin would have preferred to receive.

Truman called a special session of Congress to act on the package in December 1947, but Republican leaders (Republicans had taken control of the body in the 1946 elections), many of whom still had isolationist tendencies, delayed any acceptance of the plan for two months. In February 1948, the Communist Party of Czechoslovakia (KSC), backed by the Soviets, instigated a coup and took control of the nation. Czechoslovakia had been one of the few nations liberated by the Soviets that had held free elections with minimal Soviet influence. While the KSC had gained a plurality in those elections, they did not hold complete power and had actually fallen from favor with the Czech electorate. The U.S. and other Western nations had hoped that the Czechs could be a shining example for the rest of Eastern Europe, but the brutal coup dashed such aspirations. It also confirmed the threat of communism in Europe and led Congress to pass the Marshall Plan in late March. President Truman signed the bill on April 2, 1948, and it would eventually disperse more than $13 billion (the Truman administration had originally asked for $50 billion) in economic recovery efforts in Europe.

The Marshall Plan eventually proved to be a stunning success. Though conservatives believed that the plan was a waste of taxpayer money, Truman pointed out that the plan opened up both markets and investment opportunities in Western Europe to American business. Moreover, it helped stabilize the European economy by quadrupling industrial production within its first few years. Improved standards of living enhanced political stability, which helped undermine Western European left-wing political parties from gaining control. Congress later approved a separate allocation of $2.5 billion for the rebuilding of Japan.

The Berlin Crisis

The Marshall Plan "saved" Western Europe from falling under the influence of communism and the Soviet Union, but it worsened relations between the U.S. and the U.S.S.R. Stalin was incensed that the U.S. was trying to blunt his influence in a region that he viewed, in many ways justifiably so, as vital to the security of the U.S.S.R. Stalin's anger would color his decisions on the next arena of the emerging "Cold War" between the two nations, the plans to organize a still-occupied Germany.

All four of the Allied nations continued to occupy Germany in 1947. The capital, **Berlin**, also remained divided into four zones of occupation—American, British, French, and Soviet. The lack of a central direction for the nation meant that the economy lagged, and the uncertain future hindered any efforts to make economic, social, or political plans. Eventually, in 1948, the three Western powers—the U.S., Great Britain, and France—combined their zones into one region and began to develop plans for a unified government, a common currency, and financial stability, becoming the Federal Republic of Germany, commonly referred to as West Germany. Leaders began to form state governments and also wrote a federal constitution that ensured that the nation would adopt a Western-style government.

Stalin had held out hope that he could orchestrate a united Germany that would be a firm Soviet satellite state, but the formation of West Germany dashed such aspirations. Still undecided in Germany was the ultimate fate of Berlin, which sat in the middle of the Soviet zone, eventually becoming the German Democratic Republic (GDR) or East Germany. But like the nation, Berlin was divided into four zones of occupation controlled by the four powers. The three Western-controlled sections of the city were in a precarious position, surrounded by over a million Soviet troops and an increasingly hostile regime.

Stalin decided to make a statement about the Marshall Plan and his former allies' actions in West Germany by completely cutting off West Berlin from West Germany. West Berlin was slated for shipments of the new West German currency, which Stalin wanted to block, forcing an economic crisis. Furthermore, he could then isolate the city from any supplies and aid, forcing the three Western powers to withdraw and leave the capital of Germany solely in East German—and thus Soviet—hands. The Soviet leader cut all rail and road traffic through East Germany to Berlin on June 23, 1948, and the next day he cut electrical power to the western half of the city.

Truman faced a momentous decision. He could cut his losses and allow the Soviets to have all of Berlin, which would abandon the people of West Berlin to Soviet control, but its loss would not be much more than symbolic. The other course was to defy the Soviets, breach the blockade, and risk outright war with the Soviet Union over one city. In the end, Truman decided that he had to risk Stalin's wrath if he hoped to make the Truman Doctrine have any teeth. So, with the roadways blocked, the U.S. and Great Britain began what became known as the "Berlin Airlift," a massive operation of round-the-clock air deliveries of food and supplies to West Berliners. The president essentially dared the Russian military to shoot down the American and British cargo planes, once again with the implied threat that the United States could respond with nuclear weapons. The Berlin Airlift lasted for eleven months until May 1949, when Stalin called off his blockade, realizing that he was losing the public relations battle, plus he needed Western food aid due to a poor Soviet agricultural harvest. West Berlin became a symbol of defiance of communism, and the two halves of the city developed into an iconic symbol of the Cold War, much amplified a dozen years later when the Soviets began construction of the Berlin Wall.

The National Security Act of 1947

The menace of nuclear weapons made the United States a formidable foe at the end of World War II. President Truman recognized this potential, but he also acknowledged the great possibility for the abuse of power and destabilization if such a destructive weapon remained in the hands of one nation. He approached the Soviets and offered to share American nuclear technology with the world by creating an international agency that would control all nuclear weapons. The Soviets, who were in the verge of developing their own nuclear weapons, rejected Truman's overtures. Thus, the U.S. president moved to make atomic research a central part of American military might. He oversaw the creation of the Atomic Energy Commission in 1946, which would direct U.S. nuclear research for both civilian and military use.

Historically the United States had always fully demobilized its military forces at the end of a major war. When World War II ended, Truman and military leaders prepared to take similar action, but the continued occupa-

tion of Europe and the ongoing conflict with the Soviets caused a change in traditional policy. A conventional drawdown of the military was impractical when threats of warfare seemed imminent. Also, the containment policy involved the imminent threat of American military intervention all over the globe. Truman's first response was to ask Congress to institute the first peacetime draft in American history. Congress responded with a bill that revived the Selective Service Act. He next proposed a restructuring of the nation's military, diplomatic, and intelligence apparatuses, leading to congressional passage of the **National Security Act of 1947**, creating the Department of Defense to oversee the nation's armed forces, replacing the Department of War and the Navy Department. The U.S. also created a new branch of the military—the United States Air Force—which would take over the responsibility of the former Army Air Corps. (The Navy retained its own aviator corps separate from the Air Force.) The act also established the National Security Council, consisting of the vice president, military and intelligence leaders, and high-ranking Cabinet members who advise the president on national security and foreign policy matters. The legislation also created the **Central Intelligence Agency (CIA)**, responsible for collecting and analyzing intelligence (spying) outside the borders of the United States and directing covert operations throughout the world.

The National Security Act gave the greatest amount of concentrated power in the nation's history to the President of the United States. The executive branch would now become the storehouse and interpreteFr of intelligence data, as well as the formulator of American military responses across the globe. Truman, and those who followed him in office, claimed that such concentration was necessary to fight the Cold War and counter Soviet designs around the world.

The Formation of NATO

The twin crises in Czechoslovakia and Berlin, as well as the potential for conflict in a divided Germany, convinced Truman and his advisers that the Western nations needed to form a defense arrangement to counter any potential Soviet moves to seize European territory. Diplomats met and constructed a framework for a defense agreement between the United States, Canada, and most western and southern European countries (Great Britain, France, the Netherlands, Belgium, West Germany, Iceland, Norway, Italy, Denmark, and Luxembourg). On April 12, 1949, those nations established the **North Atlantic Treaty Organization (NATO)**, a collective security alliance based on the principle that an attack on any member nation would

Map 25.1 The New Europe. Greece and Turkey joined NATO in 1952, West Germany became a member in 1955, and Spain would later enter the alliance in 1982. France withdrew from NATO in 1966, and Albania would leave the Warsaw Pact communist bloc in 1968.

lead to an immediate military intervention from all the other allied countries. (Greece and Turkey joined NATO in 1952, followed by West Germany in 1955.) NATO would also maintain a combined force in Europe whose primary responsibility would be to counter and respond to a Soviet invasion. Finally, the U.S. agreed to place all the nations of NATO under their nuclear umbrella, with the threat of nuclear reprisal a clear part of its response policy. The Soviets reacted to the formation of NATO with the creation of the Warsaw Pact (not formalized until 1955) that promised the same type of response from all the communist nations of Eastern Europe (U.S.S.R., Poland, East Germany, Czechoslovakia, Hungary, Rumania, Bulgaria, and Albania), with the notable exception of Yugoslavia under Josip Broz Tito, which had a communist government but remained unaffiliated. NATO and the Warsaw Pact essentially formalized the division between East and West.

DOMESTIC POLITICS DURING THE TRUMAN YEARS

The United States faced almost as many quandaries and questions on the home front after World War II as it did overseas. World War II had caused the United States

to build the largest and most powerful military force in its history, and it had also converted almost its entire economy to supplying that massive war effort. The end of the war meant that the nation had to undergo almost an equally massive reduction, a demobilization of its military and a return to the domestic industrial economy. However, that alone did not end the problems of the nation moving forward. The United States still faced the issue of racial apartheid in one section of the nation—the South—and a lack of full racial equality in the remainder. There were also serious political differences over the role of organized labor, as well as serious disparities between the parties on governmental responsibility in shaping the direction of the economy. Harry Truman would become besieged on all sides during his first few years as president.

Truman and Civil Rights

World War II had certainly affected the world in profound ways, but it also began the process of transforming the United States' long practiced tradition of racial separation and institutional racism. One of the persistent themes of American propaganda during World War II had been the need to combat the state-supported racism of Nazi Germany. However, despite a policy in ending racial disparity abroad, the United States fought World War

II with a segregated military, and allowed the continued practice of Jim Crow separation in the South, and racial segregation by custom and practice elsewhere. It seemed to be an incongruous existence, a condition that the Soviet Union made sure to highlight in its anti-American propaganda. The Soviet Union emphasized that under communism the races were equal, while capitalism and American-style governmental policy seemed to promote racial division. U.S. diplomats faced such criticism when trying to counter Soviet policy abroad.

At the same time, African-American servicemen, who had to fight in segregated units, still bled and died to supposedly end inequality from taking over the world. They then returned home to a nation that practiced some of that same inequality. Black veterans began to take leadership roles to combat such policy, and spoke out against the continued injustice. Many of their efforts were met with violence, especially in the South. For some Americans, fighting social inequality was acceptable in Europe and Asia, but not at home. As a member of an Alabama "White Citizen's Council" remarked in 1946, "Our heroes didn't die in Europe to give Negroes the right to marry our wives."

Harry Truman grew up and lived in a Jim Crow society in Missouri, so he was certainly aware of the inequality of such a system. Indeed, such an environment influenced his thoughts and his speech during his early years. In a 1911 letter to his future wife Bess, Truman expressed his belief that he thought "one man is as good as another so long as he's honest and decent and not a nigger or a Chinaman." Referring to an uncle, he wrote candidly "He does hate Chinese and Japs. So do I. It is a race prejudice, I guess. But I am strongly of the opinion that negros ought to be in Africa, yellow men in Asia, and white men in Europe and North America."

Truman's thoughts on race, nevertheless, did evolve over time. A former World War I veteran himself, he was especially appalled by stories of acts of violence perpetrated against African-American soldiers in uniform upon their return home. In 1947, he became the first president to address the National Association for the Advancement of Colored People (NAACP), declaring his support for African American civil rights. That same year, he appointed a Committee on Civil Rights to document and investigate lynching and voter intimidation in the South. His commission recommended preventive measures, as well as federal legislation to make lynching a federal crime and to end the poll tax. Truman supported such measures, but Southerners from his own Democratic Party kept any civil rights legislation bottled up in Congress.

While Truman was becoming the first president to move forward in any significant way on civil rights, an important social advancement occurred that would eventually prove to be one of those transformational tremors in American history, even though not recognized until much later. Baseball had long been known as the "national pastime." During the 1940s professional baseball was by far the nation's most popular sport, but it was also for whites only, as its teams enforced an informal agreement to keep African Americans out of the major leagues, relegating them to the all-black Negro Leagues. One man who itched to end that practice was Brooklyn Dodgers General Manager Branch Rickey. A devout Methodist with strong beliefs regarding social justice, Rickey was opposed to such racial practices. He had also observed the talented ballplayers who toiled in the Negro Leagues, knowing that such players could instantly make his Brooklyn team contenders for the World Series. He also believed that he needed a person who could handle the pressure of being the first black player in baseball, facing intense bigotry every day. He found such a man in Jackie Robinson.

Born in rural southern Georgia, Robinson grew up in urban southern California, where he attended UCLA on an athletic scholarship. He was a three-sport star—football, baseball, and track. Upon graduation, he entered the army as an officer in 1944. While he was stationed at Fort Hood, Texas, Robinson refused to conform to the Texas Jim Crow practice of segregated buses, and subsequently arrested for insubordination. At trial, a military tribunal acquitted the young officer, and noteworthy was how Robinson had quietly, but with resolve and dignity, dealt with his predicament. Rickey hoped he would do the same in baseball.

Rickey signed Robinson to the Dodgers AAA minor league team in Montreal. Then, in 1947, Robinson joined the Dodgers and became the first man to cross baseball's color line in the modern era. (Some black baseball players had played alongside whites in the professional game as late as the 1880s.) Robinson endured racial taunts, threats of violence, mutinous teammates, and retaliation from fans and opposing players, as well as the denial of service from hotels and restaurants while on the road, but he withstood it all with the same dignity that he possessed during his military trial. He was also a very good ballplayer, winning Rookie of the Year honors and helping the Dodgers become one of the best teams in baseball.

Harry Truman would not have taken subsequent action on the military without the example of Jackie Robinson. His success in crossing baseball's color line gave added impetus to Truman's next civil rights initiative. The segregation of the military was one of the most glaring examples of American racial policy, which Truman was determined to end. On July 30, 1948, he issued an executive order gradually ending all segregation in the U.S. armed forces. Truman claimed afterward that this was "the greatest thing that ever happened to America."

The Fair Deal

Civil Rights were not the only issue that caused Truman great consternation. World War II had not only ended the Great Depression, it also triggered an economic boom for those industries that supplied the military, as well as good wages for the people working in those factories. Rationing and the directing of materials to the military had caused consumers to curtail their spending during the war years. When the war ended, Americans were ready to spend some of their savings on a vast array of goods that they could not purchase during the war.

Consumer spending kept production at a high pace but also produced the unintended consequence of high inflation as domestic prices rose as much as 15 percent annually. While prices increased, industrialists and other employers were slow to raise wages, leading to labor unrest. Unions had conceded to business owners on a number of issues during the war in the spirit of defeating the Axis, but they believed that when the war was over, many of their concessions—particularly on wages—would be restored. When the war ended, many companies and firms did not follow that line. When combined with inflation, workers experienced losses in lifestyle and income. Thus, in late 1945 and in 1946, a number of workers in the automobile, steel, and electrical industries went on strike.

One group that went on strike was the United Mine Workers in April 1946. Led by John L. Lewis, the coal miners' walkout threatened the nation's vital supply of coal, the primary fuel for electrical plants and other industrial machines. For forty days, the miners struck for better safety conditions and higher wages, but mine owners refused to meet such demands. Truman grew frustrated with the lack of progress and the potential that the strike had for dragging down an already fragile economy, so he made a bold move, asking the mine owners to make concessions. When they refused, he threatened to send in the army to take control of the mines in the interest of national security in a move reminiscent of Theodore Roosevelt's threat to anthracite mine owners in 1902 (see Chapter 21). The owners then acquiesced to almost all demands, although their enmity toward Truman's actions was apparent. Truman took the same action during a railroad strike. When the rail leaders balked, he threatened to draft the workers into the military, which forced an end to the strike.

Truman had tried to revive the economy with an extension of the New Deal that he termed the "**Fair Deal**."

The president had presented to Congress, in the fall of 1945, a domestic agenda that not only expanded but also made permanent many of the most significant portions of his predecessor's initiatives—programs that World War II had interrupted. He proposed a large expansion of Social Security, a raise in the minimum wage, and unprecedented peacetime federal spending to accomplish "full employment." He also advocated a huge increase in federal public housing and "slum clearance" for the nation's cities, as well as greater federal expenditures on education. One of his boldest, and most controversial, projects was to offer government-funded medical care.

Labor dissension with Truman's Fair Deal played a huge role in the congressional elections of 1946. The same coalition that had thwarted most of FDR's New Deal legislation in the final days—southern Democrats and a majority of Republicans—also bottled up almost every facet of the Fair Deal through 1946. Truman faced opposition not only from the Republicans and southern Democrats, but also from the more liberal elements of the Democratic Party who viewed the president as too soft in labor disputes as well as not expanding and supporting progressive causes with enough vigor. The Congress of Industrial Organizations (CIO) called Truman "the No. 1 strikebreaker," while other more left-leaning elements in the party howled in protest when the president forced out Secretary of Commerce Henry A. Wallace, a darling of the most progressive elements in the party. The constant drumbeat of opposition took its toll as Democratic enthusiasm lagged, and the Republicans scored a key victory in November, winning both houses of Congress for the first time since before the beginning of the Great Depression.

The Republicans quickly embarked on the primary component of their agenda: thwarting the growing power of labor unions. Republican ideology had opposed many of organized labor's goals for decades. The most conservative, pro-business elements of the party, a key bloc since the formation of the party in 1854, opposed any legislation that gave labor an equal footing with business management. The less powerful progressive faction, the remnants of Theodore Roosevelt's influence in the party, still followed TR's ideas. While some concessions to labor were palatable, even necessary, labor organization and recognition were to be avoided as detrimental to efficiency. One of their first actions was to pass the Taft-Hartley Act in 1947, which slashed many of the rights that the Wagner Act of the New Deal had granted to labor, most significantly prohibiting what was known as the "closed shop," which barred the hiring of non-union members in a company that had formed and recognized a union. States were free to pass "closed shop" laws, but the federal government could not mandate such laws. Almost immediately, some states, predominantly in the South, passed these "right-to-work laws" that outlawed "closed shops," while the industrial states of the upper Midwest and the East allowed the "closed shops" to continue. The law also made secondary strikes illegal, as well as any work stoppages by federal employees. Truman vetoed the bill—to the delight of organized labor—but support in Congress was strong enough to override the president's objection.

The 1948 Election

The confrontation between President Truman and the Republican-controlled Congress became the most visible issue of the 1948 presidential election. Truman was determined to make Congress his key opponent in the race, calling it the "Do Nothing Congress"—but also run a somewhat populist-tinged campaign by taking his case directly to the American people. The Republicans, secure in the unpopularity not only of Truman's policies but also him personally, came into the election confident of victory.

The Republicans nominated New York governor Thomas E. Dewey, and their platform was generally benign. It endorsed the more moderate elements of the New Deal, the continued fight against communism, and the increased American role in Europe. The biggest difference that Dewey offered between his presidency and Truman's was that he promised to be more efficient and avoid squabbles with Congress. The Democratic National Convention turned out to be more contentious than anyone had predicted. Most observers expected the Democrats to do what they had always done at their last three conventions: placate the South and the conservative elements, work out differences in the back rooms, and then proceed with a fairly united program, but this was not the intention of the more liberal elements in the party. Already in trouble with the southern contingents due to his desegregation of federal offices and the military and another executive order ending segregation in the civil service, Truman had hoped to place only a vague, general plank on civil rights in the party platform. The liberal faction had other ideas, and they insisted on a convention resolution calling for a more vigorous pursuit of civil rights for African Americans. When a young mayor from Minneapolis, Hubert H. Humphrey, gave a speech that implored Democrats to "get out of the shadow of states' rights and walk forthrightly into the bright sunshine of human rights," at least half the delegates erupted in an enthusiastic display. Others—the southern representatives—sat in stunned silence. The proposed plank passed and became the official policy of the Democratic Party. Truman had little choice but to accept the new policy,

President Truman waving from the rear platform of a train. June 3, 1948
Photo credit: Truman Library

although privately he supported the action. The implication was clear: many Democrats were ready to directly confront the southern system of racial apartheid that had kept the nation hostage to racial disharmony since at least the end of the Civil War.

The southern delegates wasted little time responding. The Alabama and Mississippi delegations immediately left the convention, meeting later in Birmingham, Alabama with a group of southern Democrats to form a new presidential ticket—The States' Rights Democrats, which soon gained the moniker of the "Dixiecrats." They nominated South Carolina governor Strom Thurmond, for president on a platform declaring full support for Jim Crow segregation. The Dixiecrats knew they had no chance to win the election outright, but they hoped that by denying Truman the usual reliable southern electoral votes, the election would be turned over to the House of Representatives where their power among committee chairmen and party leaders might allow them to make a deal. At the very least, they could deny Truman reelection and send a message to future Democratic nominees that they would take action against segregation at their own political peril.

Southern Democrats were not the only faction of the party unhappy with the president and his policies. A further blow to Truman's electoral chances, one week

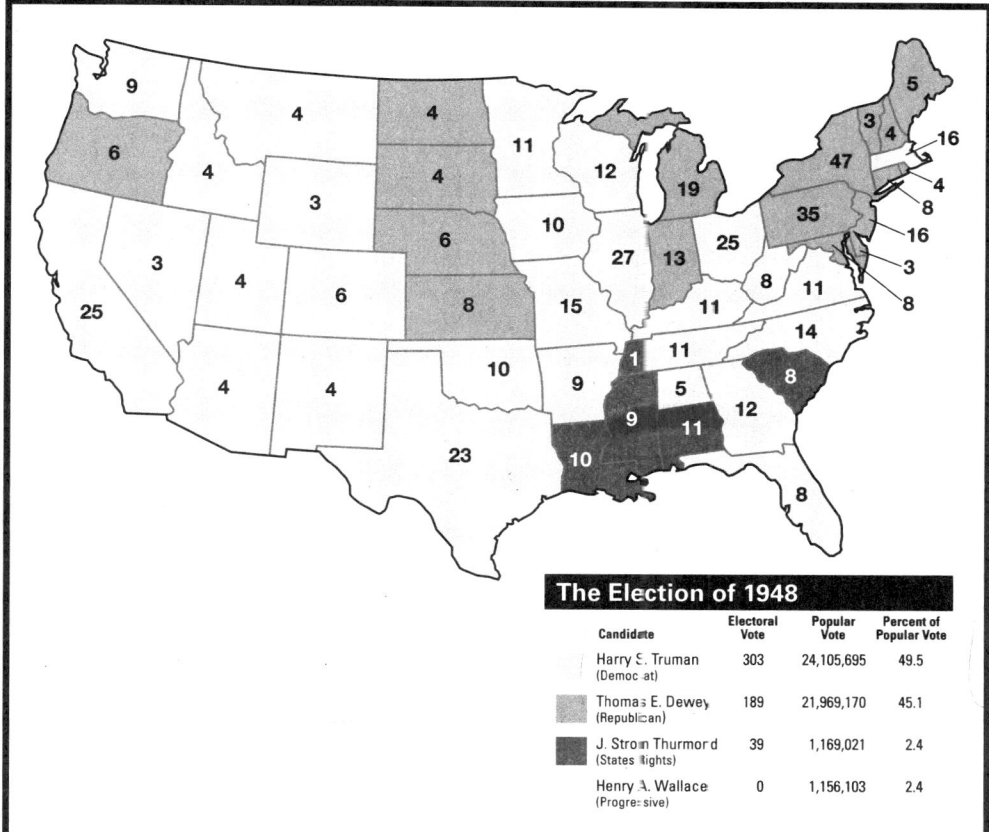

Map 25.2 The Election of 1948

	The Election of 1948			
	Candidate	Electoral Vote	Popular Vote	Percent of Popular Vote
	Harry S. Truman (Democrat)	303	24,105,695	49.5
	Thomas E. Dewey (Republican)	189	21,969,170	45.1
	J. Strom Thurmond (States Rights)	39	1,169,021	2.4
	Henry A. Wallace (Progressive)	0	1,156,103	2.4

after the Dixiecrats created a dissident ticket, the more left-leaning elements in the party met in Philadelphia to form the Progressive Party. They nominated former vice president Henry A. Wallace for president and vowed to press for a greater expansion of the New Deal, to instigate a "progressive agenda" at the federal level, and a less belligerent stance against the Soviet Union.

Truman's chances seemed doomed. His party was split in three parts, and the Republicans had nominated a competent, if somewhat bland, candidate. The president, however, was not discouraged, and he followed his campaign strategy to the end. He ran what came to be called a "whistle-stop campaign," traveling the country in a special train car, where at each stop he would rail against Congress and his opponents in Washington. Truman's basic stump speech was one that combined good-natured populism with indignant anger, an emotional appeal that seemed to connect with voters. Playing on the president's reputation as a man who was often prone to utter a profane word or two, some in the crown began to yell, "Give 'em Hell, Harry!" Truman took to responding with, " I don't give 'em hell. I just tell them the truth and they think it's Hell." He also benefited tangibly from the black vote in some key northern states for his civil rights initiatives, from Jewish voters in appreciation for his quick recognition of Israel, and from large swaths of Americans for his

continued support of the ongoing Berlin Airlift. Left for political death after the convention, Truman began to gain momentum as the summer turned to fall, but most polls showed that while he had closed the gap, it was just too little, too late to come out with a win.

Harry Truman pulled off one of the most dramatic electoral surprises in American history. Almost everyone had predicted a Dewey victory, but when the votes were counted, Truman was not only reelected, but he won by a comfortable margin—49.5 percent to 45.1 percent in the popular vote, and 303 electoral votes to 189 for Dewey and 39 for Strom Thurmond. (The Democrats also regained control of Congress.) The Dixiecrat revolution had failed. Though winning Louisiana, Mississippi, Alabama, and Thurmond's home state of South Carolina, in the rest of the South the ticket had fizzled. Meanwhile, Wallace and the Progressives were barely a blip on the political radar screen.

Truman's second term would begin as an attempt to return to his Fair Deal policies, but it would end in a morass of foreign entanglements and disillusionment. The new Congress gave Truman some small legislative victories, but for the most part it rejected a large part of his agenda. It did raise the minimum wage to seventy-five cents, increased benefits to Social Security—although not as high as Truman had asked for—and passed statutes for greater public housing, but they rejected his national health insurance initiative and his civil rights proposals.

THE SOVIETS GET THE BOMB AND THE COMMUNIST TAKEOVER OF CHINA

During the last years of his presidency, Truman had to deal with some serious foreign policy headaches. When the United States dropped the first two atomic bombs on Japan to the end of World War II, a new element entered world diplomacy and geopolitics. Nuclear weapons were so destructive that the fear of their use would ultimately transform the way that nations interacted with one another. Although Harry Truman had tried to make an international body responsible for all applications of nuclear technology—including weapons of war—when the Soviets rejected his proposition, the possession and potential use of atomic weapons became a key facet of American military and diplomatic response to the U.S.S.R. during the early stages of the Cold War. As long as the United States and its allies remained the lone nuclear power, they held a distinct strategic advantage.

The nuclear balance of power shifted in August 1949. The Soviet Union, on August 29, at a test site in Kazakhstan, successfully tested a nuclear device. The United States and the West no longer exclusively possessed nuclear weapons, which meant that any use of atomic bombs by the United States had the potential of nuclear reprisal by the Soviets. The specter of wholesale destruction of the world had become a reality, an existence that would now be a factor in every decision of the Cold War.

On the heels of the news from the Soviet Union came another shocking foreign development. Even before the Japanese invaded China in 1937, the nation had been in the grips of a civil war between the forces of **Chiang Kai-shek**, known as the Nationalists and supported by the United States, and the Communists under **Mao Zedong**. The two armies ceased fighting and combined to battle the Japanese during World War II, but in 1945, the war between the competing armies resumed.

Chiang and his Nationalist government collapsed in the late fall-early winter of 1949. Mao's forces swept the Nationalists from the field with both speed and efficiency. Chiang could never gain the support of China's peasantry, who found his regime elitist and authoritarian, and the control of the countryside proved decisive for the Communist forces. Chiang and the remaining Nationalists fled to the island of Taiwan, and the mainland fell to Mao's communist forces. Republicans blamed Truman for "losing China," although their earlier policies of isolationism had kept aid from the Nationalists. The United States refused to recognize the new communist regime and allow Zedong's representatives to take the Chinese seat on the United Nations Security Council. The most populous nation in the world was now under communist rule.

COLD WAR HYSTERIA: ### The Second Red Scare

The Cold War campaign against communism did not just have diplomatic and military ramifications. It also caused a great upheaval and new "hysteria" within American society. The constant rhetoric of war, subversion, and imminent loss fueled a feeling among many Americans that the nation was under siege from communism and that a communist takeover of the government was possible, involving high officials working for the other side. The result was a campaign of "finding and ridding" the nation of "communist agents," according to the words of one anti-communist pamphlet from the period. Some politicians, most notably Richard Nixon and **Joseph McCarthy**, would use such hysteria to further their political aspirations, while others would use the specter of "reds" to ruin the careers of people in many walks of life. Somewhat ironically, revelations found after the fall of the Soviet Union discovered that the frenetic and feverish campaign against suspected communists served to provide cover for some actual communist agents operating in the United States.

Richard Nixon, Alger Hiss, and the House Un-American Activities Committee (HUAC)

Because Republican Herbert Hoover presided over the beginning years of the Great Depression, he and his party became inextricably tied to the horrendous business downturn. It did not help that the Republicans had been in control of the presidency and Congress for much of the previous decade, and while they had promised an end to poverty during the 1920s, the Depression put a harsh end to such thinking and soiled the party's reputation for a generation. Thus, with the election of FDR, the Democrats became ascendant and the Republicans were marginalized on the fringes of political power. At the end of World War II, they needed an issue with which to attack the Democrats, and they found it in anti-communism.

When Republicans gained control of Congress after the 1946 elections, they used the **House Un-American Activities Committee (HUAC)** to attack Democrats for allegedly being "soft on communism." They held investigations of Democratic officials and activities that they claimed either supported or actively aided communist agents infiltrating the U.S. government, especially the executive branch. The HUAC also turned to filmmakers in Hollywood, who they accused of using the medium as propaganda to influence American movie audiences. Committee members accused actors, directors, and writers of being members of the Communist Party. Some of the victims of these allegations were no more than supporters of progressive politics, although there were some who had been active members of the Communist Party during the 1920s and 1930s. Although the HUAC never proved that any of the accused were active members or had used their positions to influence movie messages, the allegations alone were usually enough for movie executives to fire or stop hiring anyone called before the committee, a process that became known in Hollywood as "blackballing."

Hollywood was not the HUAC's only target. The committee gained even greater attention when they decided to go after members of the government. The most notorious of their marks was **Alger Hiss**, a former State Department official who had served under FDR and was a key part of formulating the Yalta Accords. Hiss became a focus of the committee after he became involved in a lawsuit with Whitaker Chambers, an editor for *Time* magazine. Chambers was a self-confessed former communist turned zealous anti-communist, accused Hiss of being a communist agent. Chambers stated that he had been Hiss's "contact," the person to whom Hiss passed classified State Department documents. Hiss sued Chambers for slander, but at the civil trial Chambers produced the alleged documents that Hiss had passed, which allowed him to prevail in the case, although Hiss continued to protest his innocence.

The purported incident had occurred during the 1930s, so the statute of limitations prevented Hiss from being tried on espionage charges, but because he had denied engaging in the conduct at the trial and before Congress, he could be tried for perjury. Hiss was called before the HUAC, largely due to the insistence of freshman California Representative Richard M. Nixon, who was in political peril in his district and looking for an issue upon which to capitalize and thus keep his career alive. Nixon persistently grilled Hiss at the hearing, and Hiss was eventually convicted of perjury and sentenced to prison. He continued to deny the charges until his death in 1996, and many people believed the dictum that Hiss was an innocent victim of an anti-communist witch-hunt. Recent studies of material located in the archives of the former Soviet Union and other evidence has led to an emerging scholarly consensus that Hiss was at least a part of some sort of Soviet espionage scheme, if not an actual Soviet agent.

Truman's "Loyalty" Program

The Truman administration bore at least partial responsibility for the outrages that would occur in the name of anti-communism over the next several years. The Hiss case, the Hollywood blacklist, and the growing public anxiety over domestic communism led the president to take action to try to lessen the political fallout for Democrats and his administration. In 1947, he ordered a probe to investigate the loyalty of all federal employees. The inquiry eventually caused more than 2,000 employees to resign, although it exposed no actual members of the Communist Party. To further placate the rabid anti-communists in Congress who had been ranting about supposed communists in the federal government, Truman issued an executive order creating the **Federal Employee Loyalty Program**. The order gave government security officials authorization to screen two million federal employees for any hint of political deviance and also authorized the Attorney General to draw up a list of "totalitarian, fascist, or subversive organizations." Membership, or even sympathy with such groups, would then be used as a basis for proclaiming a person to be disloyal and subject to job termination.

Truman also tacitly approved a Justice Department initiative led by FBI Director J. Edgar Hoover to investigate, expose, and eradicate "subversive organizations" in the country. Hoover and his agents harassed and accused any group that they thought even hinted at "radicalism," including civil rights groups and labor unions. Hoover used the anti-communist purge to attack his enemies more than to actually find any suspected communists. Anticommunist zeal also led Congress to pass the McCarran Internal Security Act in 1950, placing restrictions on "subversive" activity, which was never really defined and left to the interpretation of men like Hoover. Communist organizations were ordered to register with the Justice Department and publish their records. Truman vetoed the constitutionally borderline legislation, but Congress overwhelmingly overrode the veto.

The Rosenberg Case

One of the most spectacular of the anti-communist public displays of the era came in the trial of **Julius and Ethel Rosenberg**. The Soviet acquisition of the nuclear bomb in 1949 not only terrified many Americans, it left a number of American diplomats and intelligence officers wondering how they could have acquired the technology so quickly. Many concluded that the Russians must have had help, which meant that they had stolen information or somehow acquired American atomic technology. Their

Julius and Ethel Rosenberg are separated by a heavy wire screen as they leave the U.S. Court House after being found guilty by a jury. 1951

suspicions were confirmed when Klaus Fuchs, a British scientist, admitted that he had given the Soviets the schematics and techniques to make an atomic weapon.

But where had Fuchs received such material? The answer came from a most unlikely place: Julius and Ethel Rosenberg, an obscure New York couple and members of the Communist Party. The claim was that the Rosenberg's had received the information from Ethel's brother, who had worked in a minor position on the Manhattan Project, and they in turn passed it to Soviet agents. Both Julius and Ethel were convicted of treason and espionage.

Sentenced to death, they were executed on June 19, 1953. Contemporary studies into the Rosenbergs reached a general consensus that Julius Rosenberg was most likely guilty of the charges brought against him, but Ethel was probably not.

The Rise of McCarthyism

Hiss, HUAC, the Rosenbergs, "blacklists," and loyalty oaths were all some of the paranoid products of the anti-communist hysteria of the years immediately after World War II. But no anti-communism fanaticism or rise to popular appeal could compare to the spectacular rise and fall of Joseph McCarthy. In 1950, Wisconsin Senator McCarthy was an obscure, politically impotent, and most likely a one-term phenomenon. Elected during the Republican wave of 1946, McCarthy had proved to be particularly ill-suited for the office. A natural loner who suffered from an alcohol problem, McCarthy had been in many ways an embarrassment to his constituents and fellow Republicans. If he was going to survive politically, he needed an issue, and the most expedient one at the time was anti-communism. Thus, while giving a speech to a women's group in Wheeling, West Virginia, in February 1950, McCarthy dramatically lifted a piece of paper in the air and claimed that he had a list of 205 "known communists" currently in the State Department. On the heels of the Hiss case, this was disturbing—and in many ways believable—news. It was an explosive charge, one that made newspaper headlines across the nation.

The paper that McCarthy held up that day was blank. That did not matter to a voracious public, and McCarthy quickly became one of the most requested and popular politicians in the country. In speech after speech, he

Senator McCarthy talking to reporters after a session of his Senate Investigations Subcommittee. August 15, 1949. Credit: Dwight D. Eisenhower Library

repeated his accusations. The Republicans, largely due to their exploitation of the anti-communist issue and anger over the Korean War (see below), had captured control of the Senate. McCarthy became the chair of a sub-committee investigating subversive activity in the government. He had no evidence of any officials who had any ties to communism but that did not stop him from launching baseless investigations, subpoenaing blameless individuals to testify before his committee as to their ties to communism (which generally served to ruin their careers), and blustering his accusations across the country. Instead of questioning his tactics and authenticity, the public made him perhaps the most popular politician in the country. However, McCarthy made a mistake when he decided to go after the U.S. Army and accuse them of "harboring communists." After a televised hearing in which he attacked army officials, and when it became obvious that McCarthy had no real proof, his reputation was badly damaged. He was eventually condemned by the Senate in 1954, and died of complications from alcoholism in 1957 without serving out the end of his second term.

THE KOREAN WAR

During the late 1940s, the Cold War had been mostly a diplomatic stalemate, with tense but non-violent (except for in Czechoslovakia) actions. However, the Cold War spawned its first actual "shooting" war when the communist forces of North Korea, supported by the Chinese and Soviets, attacked South Korea—allied with the United States—on June 24, 1950. The United States responded immediately with military force to aid the South Koreans, and the war became an early test of the effectiveness of the new United Nations.

North and South Korea

Japan annexed Korea in 1910 and controlled the peninsula as a colony until the end of World War II when American forces occupied the southern half of the region, and Soviet troops, in one of their only campaigns against Japan, seized the northern half. Just as they did in Europe, the United States and Soviets established governments that reflected their ideology in their occupied areas. The Soviets set up a communist government under Kim Il-Sung with its capital at Pyongyang, and the Americans left the South in the hands of Syngman Rhee, who had established an authoritarian regime, but his redeeming quality was that he was no communist. The communist North built a huge military force with a goal of one day uniting the two Koreas, while Rhee (who also wished to unify the peninsula, though under his control) used most of his military power to subvert and oppress his internal political opponents. The U.S., busy with problems in Europe, further declared that Korea was not part of its "defense perimeter" in the spring of 1950.

North Korea Invades the South

The U.S. statement that South Korea was not part of their defense strategy was all the impetus the North Koreans needed to invade the South. They launched a massive assault across the border on June 27, 1950. The small South Korean army was not much more than a token impediment to the North Korean advance. Truman, despite the earlier assertion, immediately ordered military assistance to the South Koreans, and he appealed to the United Nations to intervene. The Soviets would have naturally vetoed any UN aid, but at the time they were boycotting the U.N. because the U.S. would not recognize Mao's regime in China. The U.N. passed a resolution calling for international military assistance to South Korea.

Truman sent American troops into South Korea on June 30, and he appointed General **Douglas MacArthur** to command the U.N. operations (in total, sixteen nations sent combat troops under the U.N. flag to South Korea, but the vast majority of the fighting troops were American). The first American troops in the region were a small force and could not stem the tide of the North Koreans. American and South Korean forces were pushed all the way to the extreme southeastern end of the peninsula near Pusan by September. MacArthur, however, executed a bold plan on September 15 when he landed forces at Inchon, along the west-central coast, behind the main North Korean army. He then rolled back the invaders, entered North Korea, captured Pyongyang on October 19, and drove the North Koreans all the way back near the Chinese border on the north. MacArthur assured Truman that he would secure a victory by Christmas.

Chinese Intervention

One of the fears of Truman, the U.N., and the entire world was that the Korean action might trigger a larger conflict between the United States and China, the United States and the U.S.S.R., or both. The Chinese had watched anxiously as the U.N. forces moved up the peninsula, and on November 4, they decided to act. The Chinese sent eight full divisions consisting of hundreds of thousands of men across the Yalu River, the border between the two countries. The Chinese offensive fought in the bitter cold of the Korean winter when temperatures plunged to near or below zero and took the American troops by

**President Truman
and
General MacArthur.
October 15, 1950.
Photo credit:
Truman Library**

surprise. Brutal combat raged throughout December, but the Americans could not stem the tide of the huge combined Chinese/North Korean armies. In January the Chinese and North Koreans had re-captured the South Korean capital of Seoul, but the American forces launched a counter-offensive. By spring 1951, Americans had taken back Seoul, and pushed the two combined armies back across the 38th Parallel (the border of the two countries). At that point, the Chinese regrouped, and the war essentially became a stalemate.

Truman Fires MacArthur

Harry Truman remained concerned that the war could spread after the Chinese joined the fighting. He preferred a negotiated settlement that would restore the borders to their pre-war status, but to open negotiations he needed the cooperation of the Chinese. Douglas MacArthur, however, was making such an agreement difficult. The general saw the Chinese as the major enemy in the conflict, and he pressed Truman to be allowed to directly attack China. At the very least, he wanted to bomb Chinese supply roads north of the Yalu River, but he was also open to using the threat of the atomic bomb in order to force the Chinese to stop aiding the North Koreans. MacArthur openly expressed his frustrations, challenging Truman's policies. He wrote a letter to a Republican Representative that criticized the president. Truman was probably looking for a reason to dismiss the popular military leader, and the letter gave him that opportunity. Citing insubordination, Truman removed MacArthur as the commander on April 11, 1951. Truman appointed General Matthew Ridgway, who followed orders and

did not advance into North Korea, but instead kept the Chinese out of South Korea. American, Chinese, and North Korean diplomats opened negotiations to end the war in July 1951, but could not come to any agreement and the war dragged on through the presidential election year of 1952.

The Election of 1952

Harry Truman could have run again for president in 1952 despite the ratification of the Twenty-Second Amendment the year before which limited a person to two terms because the amendment exempted the current officeholder at the time of ratification. Truman, however, chose not to seek another term. If he had run again, he probably would not have won. The president's second term was burdened by an unpopular war in Korea, public anxiety, and a nation seemingly tired of reform.

The country was looking for someone new and former General Dwight David Eisenhower fit that role. He was not a career politician, but a military man. Promising efficiency and moderation, as well as a solution to the situation in Korea, Eisenhower vowed to "take a broom and clean up Washington D.C." His opponent, Illinois Governor Adlai Stevenson, by contrast, had a reputation as an "intellectual." Though liberal Democrats admired him, he had a difficult time connecting with the common people in the party and the nation as a whole. He never really stood much of a chance against the affable Eisenhower, whose campaign portrayed him as a calm but stern man, someone everyone could trust and admire. He gained over seven million more votes than did Stevenson, and won the Electoral College in a landslide. For the first

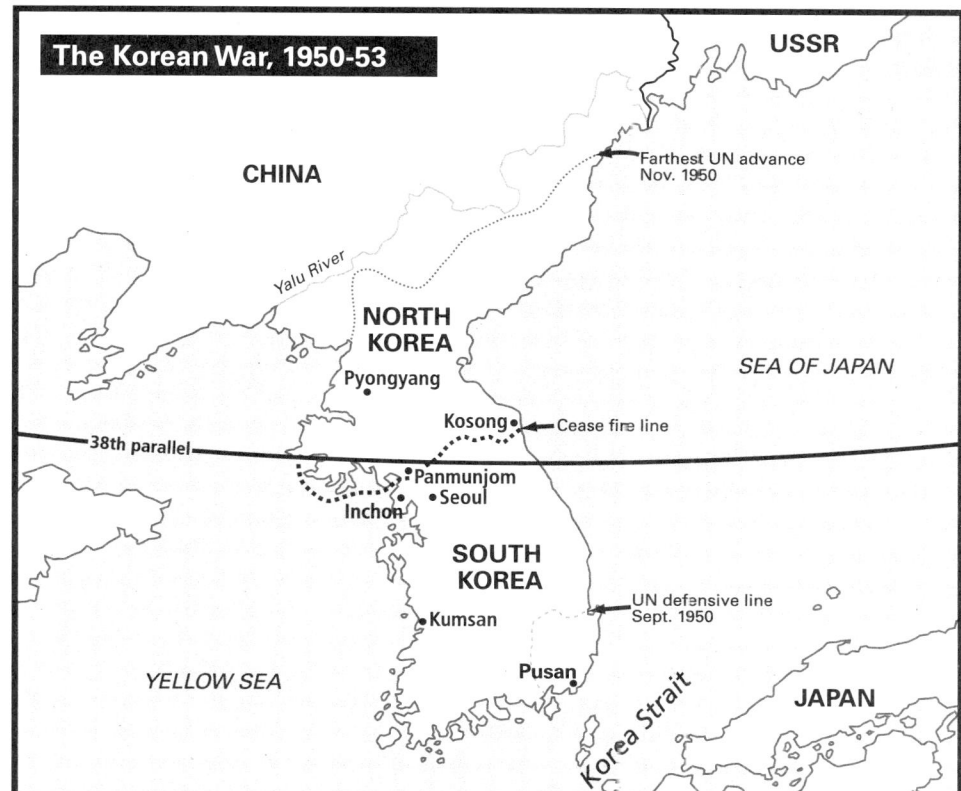

Map 25.3 The Korean War

time since 1928, the United States had elected a Republican president.

AMERICA TURNS TO EISENHOWER

The 1950s in the United States was a decade of prosperity, and in many ways the celebration of a nation that was dominated by young people. While an illogical fear of communism and the constant threat of nuclear war permeated society, it was also a time when the nation looked to the future with optimism. The man who served as the chief executive during the bulk of that decade, Dwight David "Ike" Eisenhower, did nothing to discourage such an outlook. For many, President Eisenhower was like a grandfather, a reassuring figure who promised an era that would not be radical but instead stable. Eisenhower's political stance assured his fellow Americans that he would retain the efficient parts of the New Deal, but at the same time restrain the growth of federal power. He would end the war in Korea, but stand up to the Soviets without plunging the world into another catastrophic world war. Eisenhower was someone who would restore traditional values.

Certainly, such outcomes were unrealistic and mostly symbolic, and many of Eisenhower's policies and rhetoric served more to mask the nation's ills and shortcomings

than to solve problems. The nation remained one that had a divided, bi-racial society, and prosperity had not solved the issue of generational poverty. The Cold War meant that there were "hot-spots" all over the world, a situation that even a superpower like the United States could not fix. But, after two decades of Depression, war, and unrest, Americans were ready for a president and a mood that at least promised stability and calm, even if much of it was an illusion.

The End of the Korean War

Peace talks to end the Korean stalemate had been ongoing since 1951, but they had made little progress. Truman's Secretary of State Dean Acheson had proposed a cease-fire in the summer of 1951, which permanently divided the peninsula along the 38th parallel, a compromise that North Korea and China accepted. The negotiations dragged on, however, with no agreement on POW exchanges, the regional role of China and the Soviets, and South Korea's continued insistence of a unified Korea under the rule of Syngman Rhee. Truman left the White House with no peace, and the war continued with casualties but no solutions and no concrete "end game," which frustrated and angered American voters.

The failure to end the fighting in Korea was one of the primary reasons behind Eisenhower's victory in the 1952 election. Eisenhower vowed that he would "go to Korea," and bring an end to the war. Eisenhower's Secretary of State, **John Foster Dulles**, joined the negotiations and began to use his policy of "brinkmanship" at the table, implying that if China and North Korea did not soon agree to an agreement, the United States might use nuclear weapons. The threat was enough for a cease-fire, with the final border drawn a little north of the 38th parallel with a demilitarized zone of approximately two and a half miles. The nations exchanged prisoners and the fighting stopped, though no formal peace agreement or treaty was ever signed. The United States had over 30,000 war dead, and more than 100,000 casualties, and the result returned the peninsula to the exact condition it had been in June 1950. In many ways, it was the perfect metaphor for the policy of containment. Because no peace treaty has ever been signed, a state of war officially exists to this day between the two Koreas.

Initial U.S. Involvement in Vietnam

While U.S. troops were fighting in Korea, other developments in Asia would eventually have long-range ramifications and transform the nation as few other events ever had. The southeastern Asian nation of Vietnam had long been the object of a number of different imperialist actions. The Chinese had controlled the region for centuries, and after a brief period as an independent entity, the French began to colonize and control Vietnam along with neighboring Laos and Cambodia in the late nineteenth century, grouping the entire area into one colony known as French Indochina. The Japanese Empire took control before the start of World War II (see Chapter 25), but when the war ended, the French came back, once again trying to establish hegemony over the region.

Even before Japanese control during World War II, a nationalist movement under Ho Chi Minh expanded in Vietnam. Ho and his forces had fought the Japanese, and when the war ended, they were angered to see the French try to reestablish control. Ho had actually appealed to the U.S. for support, citing American language of self-determination in the Atlantic Charter. However, American officials were blinded by the anti-communist rhetoric at the time, and Ho Chi Minh was a communist. Thus, the U.S. threw their support behind the French.

Ho and the nationalists continued to resist French rule, and by 1954—with help from the Soviets and the Chinese—he was winning. French troops were surrounded at the village of Dien Bien Phu in northwest Vietnam during the early winter of 1954, and it became apparent to the Americans and the British that the French could not remain in control of Vietnam. President Dwight

Eisenhower faced a choice: allow Vietnam to fall to Ho, intervene with direct military action—something his Secretary of State John Foster Dulles urged—or find another solution. Eisenhower chose to let the French fail. Ho and his forces broke the French lines and defeated them at Dien Bien Phu in May 1954.

France agreed to negotiate a settlement in the summer of 1954 at Geneva, Switzerland. France signed the **Geneva Accords**, which the U.S. was not a direct party to, that divided Vietnam along the 17th parallel. Ho Chi Minh would rule North Vietnam, and South Vietnam would set-up a pro-Western government. The agreement called for unifying elections in 1956, with the winning party controlling Vietnam. The French did not have the resources—or the inclination—to aid South Vietnam, so Eisenhower and the U.S. helped to launch the government. They installed **Ngo Dinh Diem**, a member of the Catholic Vietnamese elite. He was no supporter of democracy, but he also was not a communist, which was good enough for American government officials. The U.S. also promised military support should South Vietnam ever be attacked by the North.

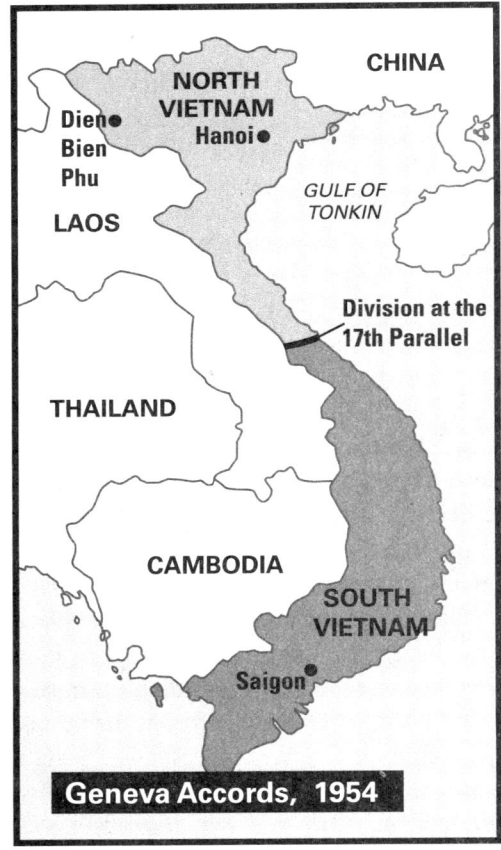

Map 25.4 The Geneva Accords

EISENHOWER AND THE COLD WAR

Dwight Eisenhower took office during a time of heightened tension in world affairs. The presence of opposing nuclear power seemed to presage not a question of "if" a nuclear holocaust would take place, but "when." Eisenhower and John Foster Dulles had another plan for the military uses of nuclear power. In their minds, atomic power could serve as a deterrent for war, allowing the United States to restructure their armed forces and rely less on standing ground troops, which would cost less money. Their "**New Look**" plan would lead the United States into the next decade, but they would have to confront a number of Cold War crises along the way.

John Foster Dulles, the "New Look," and "Massive Retaliation"

John Foster Dulles had spent his career preparing to oversee the United States' foreign affairs operation. He had been a part of the U.S. delegation at the Versailles Peace Conference to end World War I, had helped to draft a plan to reduce German reparations after the war during the 1920s, and served as an advisor to prominent Republicans throughout World War II. When Eisenhower tapped him to become his chief of the State Department after his election, Dulles had a clear vision what he wanted to accomplish.

Eisenhower had a definitive goal on foreign policy, specifically, allowing the United States to fulfill its Cold War responsibilities, but also practicing fiscal restraint. He thought that the U.S. should emphasize the use of strategic nuclear weapons as a deterrent to check any Soviet moves, which would allow the United States to reduce its reliance on large deployments of ground troops in Europe and reduce the military budget. Dulles and the president agreed on these ideas, with Dulles calling it "more bang for the buck." Eisenhower left it to his Secretary of State to work out the details of the policy, which came to be known as the "New Look."

The "New Look" relied on a shift in defensive strategy. The nation would depend on the threat of nuclear destruction to keep Soviets from launching an attack, or—if an invasion did occur—the U.S. would respond with a strike of "massive retaliation." The U.S. would use a three-pronged strategy and develop the capability to launch nuclear strikes from the ground (missiles), from the air (strategic bombers), and from the sea (ships, most menacingly, submarines). The approach would allow the nation to cut its conventional forces by at least a third, and also reduce expenditures on conventional weaponry.

Critics of Massive Retaliation

What Dulles and Eisenhower were promising was to ensure the peace by countering any major Soviet military threat in the world with a nuclear strike upon the Soviet Union itself. If the Soviets were to invade South Korea, for example, the U.S. response would be to launch nuclear missiles at Moscow. Of course, Moscow would then launch strikes at the United States, ensuring worldwide devastation, a concept known as "MAD:" Mutually Assured Destruction. Many critics pointed out that the policy had the potential to destroy the world, and it reliance on solving crises by bringing the globe to the brink of disaster was one that was dangerous and foolish. Other detractors, such as prominent diplomatic historian John Lewis Gaddis, saw a serious flaw in the approach. While such a policy might deter a direct invasion that pitted Soviet troops against American or Western European forces, it was not a credible way to deter smaller actions, such as the 1956 Hungarian Revolution that the Soviets brutally suppressed, and the U.S. was helpless to stop.

During World War II, the popular image of General Eisenhower depicts him wearing a well tailored, short-waisted, smart-looking jacket, designated officially as the "Wool Field Jacket, M-1944." To the troops it was known as the ETO (European Theater of Operations) Jacket, or even more popularly as the "Ike Jacket."
Credit: of Dwight D. Eisenhower Library

Soviet Repression in Hungary

Eisenhower retained the concept of direct confrontation and resistance to the spread of Soviet influence that had begun with his predecessor. He accepted the containment policy, and it guided many of his foreign policy decisions. Europe remained the primary area of concern, but in 1956, in Hungary, the world saw the limits of American resolve to stop the Soviets from exerting their influence in their "backyard" of Eastern Europe.

Hungary had been one of the most resistant of the Eastern European nations to Soviet control since the end of World War II. The Hungarians had chafed under the boot of the Soviets, and there had been a simmering opposition to the communist government that the Soviets had instituted for years. Dissident elements finally felt confident to launch an uprising against the communist regime in November 1956, primarily because they thought that they could count on American support, but that did not happen. Almost immediately, Soviet tanks and troops poured into Hungary to support their puppet government. The Eisenhower administration did nothing in response without risking a full-scale war with the U.S.S.R. The containment policy accepted that Eastern Europe was firmly under the control of the Soviet Union for the foreseeable future.

Covert CIA Operations in Iran and Guatemala

One of the most significant changes in Cold War strategy for the two world superpowers in the 1950s was the shift in focus from confrontation in Europe to open competition in other areas of the world. After the Cold War tensions had carved Europe into halves—East and West—the conflict between communism and democratic-capitalist republics moved on to what was then often referred to as the "Third World," and today is known as "emerging countries." Like so much else in this era, the ideology present at the end of World War II was responsible for much of the tension. The U.S. diplomatic focus in the immediate postwar years of advocating "self-determination" had helped to bolster the growing anti-colonial independence movements throughout the world. It became uncomfortable for American policy and leaders when in some places those nationalist movements came against their allies—like in Vietnam against the French—and when some of those nationalists leading the movements at least leaned toward, if they not out right advocated—communism. Indicative of two of these awkward settings for the U.S. came in Iran and Guatemala.

When World War I ended in 1918, France and Great Britain had divided the old Ottoman Empire of the Middle East into "spheres of influence," places where even if they did not directly rule as a colonial power they manipulated the puppet leaders who directed policy that benefitted the Europeans, not the natives of the nation. The presence of massive petroleum deposits in many of the Middle Eastern countries made the control of those nations even more important to the two European powers.

Britain had exerted control over Iran. The British had pioneered the oil industry in the country after the first discovery in 1908, and by the late 1940s Iran held the largest known oil reserves in the world at that time. British officials ran Iran as if it was a subsidiary of British Petroleum (BP), and Iranian oil was an important component of not only British fuel needs, but also the health of the huge national oil conglomerate. However, the emerging anti-colonial movements sweeping the globe influenced Iran, and in 1951 elected as Prime Minister Mohammad Mossadegh, a committed nationalist whose primary agenda was the ending of European, specifically British, influence in his nation. In October 1952, Mossadegh took the fateful step of severing all diplomatic relations with Great Britain and nationalizing the Iranian oil fields. The potential loss of their oil investments alarmed British officials, but the toll of World War II had so drained British resources that there was little they could do, so British diplomats reached out to the American government for help.

Eisenhower agreed to intervene, primarily to allow U.S. firms access to the potentially rich oil deposits in Iran, and to extend American influence in the Middle East to use against any potential Soviet designs on the region. The president approved a bold plan hatched by the CIA and its director Allan Dulles, the brother of the Secretary of State. Called "Operation Ajax," Dulles's plan called for the CIA to bribe Iranian Army officers to begin an anti-Mossadegh movement in Iran. The Iranian CIA clients paid people to stage riots, creat propaganda attacking the prime minister, and then hired mercenaries to arrest and detain Mossadegh and remove him from office. The now former head of the Iranian government was tried and convicted of treason in a largely show trial, locked away in prison for three years, and then released only under house arrest, which he remained until his death in 1967. The U.S. then placed an heir to the throne ("Shah") Mohammed Reza Pahlavi, whose father had ruled Iran (for the Ottomans) until he was deposed, ironically, by the British after World War I. The new Shah of Iran essentially turned over the Iranian oil fields to American and British firms.

The success of CIA designed coups to accomplish American diplomatic goals led Eisenhower to begin to

Did The "Policy of Containment" Work?

The "Truman Doctrine" initiated the "policy of containment" toward Soviet Union designs to extend their influence in Europe specifically, but it became more broadly prescribed in subsequent years by every presidential administration from Eisenhower to Reagan as a counter to the spread of communism throughout the world. It became the foundation of American foreign policy for almost fifty years, a philosophy that guided American decisions regarding how to conduct diplomacy. The Soviet Union collapsed in 1991, and with it the specter of communist domination throughout the globe, so in the minds of many historians, commentators, and political observers, the policy worked as it was intended: it kept communism from spreading and it allowed for the growth of liberal political ideas in places outside those influenced by traditional western enlightenment philosophy. Such a statement may be accurate in an abstract sense, but by measuring the real application of events can we categorically decide if the policy of containment "worked"?

The first dimension of the efficacy of the policy came in Greece and Turkey, and in that instance it did work as intended. Both nations were able to resist internal communist insurgencies, and the Soviets did not gain a strategic foothold in the Mediterranean. Truman used the philosophy of containment to once again stare down the Soviets in Berlin by re-supplying the beleaguered city to defeat the USSR's blockade. However, both of those "victories" came when the United States was the lone nuclear power in the world. Those events also occurred in Europe, where the U.S. had the direct cooperation of its allies on the continent. The application of containment—resisting expansion only when it was outside its previous existence—also allowed the U.S. to yield in any attempts to quell Soviet interference during the coup attempt in Czechoslovakia in 1948 and the uprising against the government in Hungary in 1956.

It was when the policy of containment moved outside of Europe that the results become much more circumspect. Containment led the United States directly into war in Korea in 1950. The stated goal of the Truman Administration was to resist North Korea's attempts to conquer South Korea—a pure containment objective—and in that sense it was successful. However, almost 36,000 Americans died in a three-year war that did little more than establish the status quo of June 1950, and today Korea remains one of the most volatile regions of the world.

Containment led the U.S. to begin a series of misadventures in the Middle East. The CIA, with the approval of President Eisenhower, planned and helped to carry out a coup in Iran against the democratically elected government of that nation. Certainly, the installation of Reza Pahlavi on the Peacock Throne in Iran kept the Soviets from gaining influence in Iran, but it also sowed seeds of discontent that would lead directly to the formation of Islamic fundamentalism in that nation, a movement that would name the United States as its mortal enemy. Such developments, combined with the Suez Crisis, growing American support of Israel, and aid to corrupt governments in the region caused many young Arabs and other residents of the Middle East to think of the United States as opposed to their aspirations, another factor in the flourishing rise of Islamic fundamentalism.

Cuba became the second test of the policy of containment, and the consequences there are also murky. American diplomatic blunders and miscalculations led Cuba, and its leader Fidel Castro, to turn to the Soviet Union for support and subsequently led Castro to establish a communist regime in the American hemisphere. The presence of Cuba at America's doorstep first led to the disastrous Bay of Pigs incident, which played a huge role in the biggest crisis involving Cuba: the missile crisis of 1962. For two weeks the world stood on the brink of nuclear war between the superpowers, and while Kennedy and Khrushchev eventually avoided direct confrontation, American attempts to quell "another Cuba" in the Americas led it to support brutal dictators and regimes in Chile, El Salvador, and Nicaragua, all actions that may have kept communism from spreading at the time, but also led to ill-will toward the U.S. in a number of Central and South American nations.

The most direct failure of the American policy of containment was, of course, Vietnam. The policy of containment led Dwight Eisenhower to inaugurate initial U.S. involvement in Vietnam as a counter to Ho Chi Minh. John F. Kennedy increased American participation, and then direct U.S. combat began during the Johnson Administration. All three presidents, citing containment, led the U.S. into another Asian war that cost almost 60,000 American deaths. In the end, South Vietnam fell, and communism took over all of Vietnam.

When the Soviet Union imploded in 1991, many celebrated the success of a five-decade policy of opposing communism at every turn. However, communist governments remain within the world, and many of the American stratagems against the spread of communism have caused consequences that continue to reverberate for American diplomats. So, did the policy of containment work? The imperfect answer is perhaps, but only imperfectly.

favor a number of such schemes to undermine governments in the emerging world that might govern counter to American wishes. The president set his sights on Guatemala in 1954. Guatemala had staged a revolution against an American-backed dictator in 1944, and had begun a series of liberal reforms that threatened the profits of the mostly American-owned agricultural firms in the nations, the most powerful and largest being the United Fruit Company (UFC), which today operates under the Chiquita brand. Former Defense Minister Jacobo Arbenz Guzmán was elected president in 1950, and he continued the reform program. Guzmán raised the ire of the Eisenhower administration when he nationalized the property and facilities of all American-owned firms in his country, most importantly those of UFC.

John Foster Dulles, with input from his brother in the CIA, convinced Eisenhower that Arbenz was turning toward communism and would pose a threat to the entire region. Eisenhower approved a covert CIA operation to get rid of the Guatemalan president. The CIA assembled and trained an army in Honduras of mostly mercenaries and former Guatemalan army officers, who then invaded Guatemala on June 18, 1954, defeated Arbenz's surprised troops, and forced the president into exile in Mexico. The new American-backed president, Carlos Castilla Armas, returned the UFC's confiscated lands and instituted a police state in Guatemala, eliminating all political opposition until his assassination by a palace guard in 1957. After Castillo's murder, Guatemala continued to be controlled by a series of authoritarian rulers, though openly resisted by an assortment of guerilla bands in the countryside, until the United Nations brokered an end to the civil war in the mid-1990s.

The coups in Iran and Guatemala represented a disturbing new trend in American foreign policy. The Cold War had led the U.S. government to actively seek the overthrow of foreign governments that did not support the Americans, using the specter of communism to justify such actions. In many cases the result was the support of a brutal, dictatorial regime whose only saving grace in American policymakers' eyes was that it did not fall into the communist sphere.

Trouble in the Middle East

Iran was not the only problem the United States faced in the strategically important Middle East. The region's resources, access to sea-lanes, and central location along numerous overland trading routes had made it a center of conflict between empires since ancient times. In the mid-twentieth century, largely due to its vast oil deposits, the Middle East now became the center of a number of Cold War confrontations. The Soviets wanted to extend their influence in the region, while the U.S. and its allies were just as intent on keeping them out.

The diplomatic focus in the Middle East was drastically changed in 1948 with the formation of the nation of Israel. Since at least the late nineteenth century, Jews throughout the world had engaged in a Zionist campaign to restore a nation for Jews in the Middle East. Palestine was the ancient homeland of the Jewish people, but following the Jewish Diaspora over the centuries, the region fell under the control of Palestinian Arabs. After World War I, Palestine came into the British "sphere of influence," and many committed Zionists moved there to engage in a political, and sometimes violent, movement to force the British to establish a Jewish state.

World War II and Hitler's Holocaust changed the views of many in the world toward the Jews. With the memory of the slaughter of Jews in Europe fresh in their minds, the leaders of the new United Nations partitioned Palestine and established Israel in May 1948. President Truman immediately recognized the new nation, followed closely by the Soviets. However, the presence of Israel surrounded by Arab nations created new problems. The Arab nations launched an attack against Israel in 1948, and while they were not successful in defeating the Jewish nation, the Arab-Israeli conflict would continue to cause foreign policy headaches for the United States.

Israel's neighbor, Egypt, also became the focus of tension for Eisenhower in 1956. Like so many other nations riding the wave of nationalism unleashed by World War II, Egypt came under the leadership of a charismatic nationalist, Gamal Abdel Nassar, who decided that the best path for Egypt was to play to Cold War tensions. He began to make overtures to the Soviets, who were all too happy to gain influence in Egypt given its vital spot between the Mediterranean Sea and the Red Sea, with access via the **Suez Canal** to the Indian Ocean. Nassar knew that his friendship with the Soviets would alarm the United States, but he thought he could then obtain concessions from the U.S. in return. However, he did not count on Eisenhower's reaction. The U.S. had already committed to aiding the Egyptians in building a massive dam project on the Nile, the Aswan High Dam, that was vital for flood control and irrigation in the largely desert nation. When Nassar began to become friendly with the U.S.S.R., Eisenhower, at the insistence of John Dulles, canceled the aid.

Nassar responded a week later with one of the few retaliatory options he had. The Suez Canal had been under the control of the British since the nineteenth century; they considered it vital to the maintenance of their empire and to efficiently ferry military troops throughout the world. Nassar nationalized the canal and ordered the British out under the pretense that he now needed the income of the canal to pay for building the dam.

The British were determined to take the canal back and planned a multi-layered scheme to make it happen in October 1956. They first convinced the Israelis to invade Egypt in the north, followed the next day by French and British paratroopers who landed in the Suez Peninsula and recaptured the canal. However, the British had not informed their American allies of their plan, and Eisenhower—besides being angry—feared that such a move would drive Egypt even closer to the Soviets. He made a surprising decision, refusing to support the action and joined in a United Nations censure of the British invasion. Eisenhower then used diplomatic pressure to force the British, Israelis, and French to withdraw. Ultimately, these maneuvers did no good as Nassar signed a lease with the Soviets allowing them to base warships in Egypt.

Sputnik

During the Cold War, even the dream of space exploration became a contested arena. The developing military missile technology of World War II promised expectations of allowing men to explore the great beyond. The United States had begun to work on such an initiative in the early 1950s, but it was not a priority and often seemed more like science fiction than reality.

The rivalry with the Soviets changed such an approach. The nation that could dominate space might have an advantage in the Cold War, and the Soviets had launched a much larger program than had the Americans. Their efforts paid off in 1957 when they launched ***Sputnik***, the world's first orbiting satellite. Eisenhower and his advisors were caught off guard, and the fact that the Soviets had beaten the U.S. to space was a huge blow to American pride. The government placated the American public's anxiety about "being behind" the Russians with the passage of the National Defense Education Act to encourage scientific education in American schools and the establishment of the National Aeronautics and Space Administration (NASA), a civilian bureaucracy to coordinate missile development and future space exploration, to be headquartered in Houston, Texas. The U.S. finally blasted off its own satellite, *Explorer I*, in January 1958.

The U-2 Incident

Josef Stalin had died in 1953, and after a power struggle, **Nikita Khrushchev** rose to the leadership of the U.S.S.R. Khrushchev had begun a "de-Stalinization" of the Soviet Union, releasing some political prisoners. While still committed to expanding communism, the new leader projected the impression that he was open to a less contentious relationship with the U.S. He suggested that the two superpower leaders engage in direct talks, what became known as "summits," with Khrushchev visiting the U.S. in 1959, followed by another conference between the two in Paris in 1960, with a reciprocal Eisenhower meeting to the Soviet Union to be planned for later that same year. Eisenhower agreed, and when Khrushchev visited the U.S., he used much of his visit as a propaganda tool to the rest of the world and back home. While nothing productive came of the visit, no harm had been done either, so the 1960 Paris summit remained on each leader's schedule.

Days before the Paris meeting, however, the Soviets announced that they had shot down an American **U-2 high-altitude spy plane** that the U.S. had been flying over Soviet air space to monitor the U.S.S.R.. They had captured the pilot, Francis Gary Powers, who they displayed on Soviet television. Khrushchev arrived at the Paris meeting and bitterly castigated the U.S. policy of spying—although the Soviets certainly did the same—and abruptly ended the Paris meeting and canceled Eisenhower's later visit. The promised thaw in the Cold War did not materialize.

Eisenhower Warns of a "Military-Industrial Complex"

Eisenhower had entered office with a promise of a new direction in American foreign policy, and he did succeed in transforming how the U.S. practiced defense in the new age of nuclear technology. What he did not do was lessen the conflict of the Cold War. In fact, in many ways, he expanded the fight, brought it into new areas, and assured Americans that he would confront the Soviets in any corner of the globe. In the process, he also demonstrated that there were limits to American power, and that this would be a conflict not easily won or quickly concluded. The president also left the U.S. with a legacy of commitments—such as in Vietnam—that would hinder later administrations and complicate foreign policy for decades to come. When Eisenhower delivered a farewell address to the nation in January 1961, he explicitly warned of the "unwarranted influence" of what he called a "vast military-industrial complex," one that had the potential of usurping American freedom and asserting undue power on the nation's politics and society. Somewhat ironically, many of Eisenhower's Cold War policies had allowed that "complex" to rise to power, and they would also make his successors' jobs much more difficult.

Chronology

1945   United Nations founded.
Yalta and Potsdam Conferences.

1947   Truman Doctrine announced.
National Security Act passed.
Marshall Plan initiated.
Jackie Robinson breaks the MLB "color barrier."

1948   Israel founded.
Berlin Blockade and Airlift.
Truman desegregates of U.S. armed forces.
Alger Hiss case
Truman reelected president.

1949   NATO established.
China falls to Mao and Communists.
U.S.S.R. acquires nuclear weapons.

1950   Korean War begins.

1951   Truman fires General MacArthur.
Rosenbergs convicted of espionage (executed in 1953).

1952   First hydrogen bomb exploded.
Eisenhower elected president.

1953   Korean War fighting ends.
CIA-supported coup in Iran.

1954   Army-McCarthy hearings.
CIA intervention in Guatemala.

1956   Suez Canal Crisis.
Eisenhower re-elected.
Hungarian Crisis.
Eisenhower supports Diem in Vietnam.

1957   *Sputnik* launched.

1958   NASA created.

1960   U-2 incident.

1961   Eisenhower's farewell address.

SUGGESTED READINGS

Stephen E. Ambrose, *Eisenhower: Soldier and President* (1990).

Walter La Feber, *America, Russia, and the Cold War, 1945-2006* (2008).

Richard F. Freeland, *The Truman Doctrine and the Origins of McCarthyism: Foreign Policy, Domestic Politics, and Internal Security, 1946-1948* (1972).

John Lewis Gaddis, *Strategies of Containment: A Critical Appraisal of National Security Policy During the Cold War* (2005).

____, *We Now Know: Rethinking Cold War History* (1998).

Alonzo Hamby, *Man of the People: A Life of Harry Truman* (1995).

Max Hastings, *The Korean War* (1988).

George F. Kennan, *American Diplomacy, 1900-1950* (1951).

____, *Memoirs 1925-1950* (1967).

Michael L. Krenn, *Fall Out Shelters for the Human Spirit: American Art and the Cold War* (2005).

Ralph B. Levering, *The Cold War: A Post-Cold War History* (2005).

Ernest R. May, *American Cold War Strategy: Interpreting NSC-68* (1993).

David McCullough, *Truman* (1992).

John Ranleagh, *The Agency: The Rise and Decline of the CIA from Wild Bill Donovan to William Casey* (1986).

Richard Rhodes, *Dark Sun: The Making of the Hydrogen Bomb* (1995).

Lisle A. Rose, *The Cold War Comes to Main Street: America in 1950* (1998).

Stanley Sandler, *The Korean War: No Victors, No Vanquished* (2000).

Sam Tannehaus, *Whittaker Chambers, A Biography* (1997).

Warren A. Trest, *Air Commando One: Heinie Aderholt and America's Secret Air Wars* (2000).

Stanley Weintraub, *MacArthur's War: Korea and the Undoing of an American Hero* (2000).

David Wise and Thomas B. Ross, *The Invisible Government* (1962).

Review Questions

1. What were the major developments and events of the Cold War through 1960? Through an analysis of these developments, can you determine if the United States was actively pursuing conflict with the Soviets, or was it more of a reaction to Soviet actions?

2. What was the "Red Scare?" What caused it? What were its major effects in American society and politics?

3. What led President Truman to declare the "Policy of Containment" (Truman Doctrine)? How did such a policy lead the U.S. to conduct foreign affairs in a certain manner?

4. What was the Fair Deal? What did Truman hope to accomplish through such a program?

Glossary of Important People and Concepts

Berlin Crisis
Central Intelligence Agency (CIA)
Chiang Kai-shek
Cold War
Containment Policy (Truman Doctrine)
Ngo Dinh Diem
John Foster Dulles
"Fair Deal"
Federal Employee Loyalty Program
Geneva Accords
Alger Hiss
House Un-American Activities Committee (HUAC)
George F. Kennan
Nikita Khrushchev
Douglas MacArthur
Joseph McCarthy
Mao Zedong
Marshall Plan
National Security Act of 1947 "New Look"
North Atlantic Treaty Organization (NATO)
Ethel and Julius Rosenberg
Sputnik
Suez Crisis
U-2 Incident

The entrance to the "Negro Waiting Room" at the Katy Depot in San Antonio, Texas, in 1956.

Chapter Twenty-six

AMERICAN CULTURE FROM 1945 to 1960

During World War II, the American public knew that under Adolf Hitler, Germany exterminated Jews and other supposed racial inferiors. Not until the end of the war could Americans imagine the scope of the Nazi genocide. The George Gallup polling organization in November 1944 asked, "Do you believe that the Germans have murdered many people in concentration camps?" While 76 percent of respondents believed that mass murder had occurred in the Nazi empire, Americans badly underestimated how many victims died as a result of the German race war against Jews, Poles and other groups the Third Reich deemed inferior. According to the poll, 36 percent of those who believed people had been killed in concentration camps placed the number of victims at 100,000 or less. Slightly more than 50 percent placed the death toll at one million or less, while only 16 percent guessed the number to be two to six million.

American soldiers received a shocking lesson in the dangers of racism and intolerance. They could not anticipate the hellish landscape that greeted them as they advanced into the heart of Germany. On April 12, 1945, in Gotha, Germany, the Supreme Commander of the Allied Forces in Europe, General Dwight D. Eisenhower, and two other top officers, General Omar Bradley and General George S. Patton, toured the Ohrdruf Concentration Camp. "The smell of death overwhelmed us even before we passed through the stockade," Bradley later recalled. "More than 3,200 naked, emaciated bodies had been flung into shallow graves. Others lay in the streets where they had fallen. Lice crawled over the yellow skin of their sharp, bony frames." Shaken, Eisenhower ordered American soldiers in the region to view the remains of Ohrdruf. "We are told that the American soldier does not know what he is fighting for," Eisenhower said. "Now, at least, he will know what he is fighting against."

Black, brown and Anglo soldiers brought face-to-face with the horrors of Nazi genocide returned to America as changed men. The concentration camps, after all, represented the logical conclusion of racist thought popular not just in Germany, but also in America and Great Britain, before the war. Nazis gave racism a bad name. Even though American culture still included deep elements of bigotry, a perceptible change in American attitudes toward race took place after the war. More northern whites, at least, seemed ready to support the African-American campaign for desegregation in the South. **Anti-Semitism**, widely shared among even educated Americans, clearly declined partly as a reaction to the Nazi death camps. Asked in August 1945 by the U.S. Army's **Yank** magazine, "What changes would you like to see made in post-war America?" a majority agreed that they wanted, "above everything else [the] . . . wiping out [of] racial and religious prejudice." In a series of surveys conducted by the American Jewish Committee (AJC) between 1946 and 1951, the number of Americans reporting that they had overheard anti-Jewish remarks during the previous year declined from 64 percent to 16 percent. The AJC also asked American Gentiles if there were "any nationality, religious or racial groups in this country that are a threat to America." In 1946, 18 percent named Jews. By 1954, the number was down to 1 percent.

In addition to shock over the crimes of the anti-Semitic Nazi regime, another factor that pushed anti-Semitism from *the mainstream to the American fringe was that by 1950, 75 percent of Jews in America had been born in the United States. Jewish celebrities, such as Bess Myerson, who won the "Miss America" beauty pageant in 1945, and Detroit Tiger Hank Greenberg, who blasted a ninth-inning grand slam homer to capture the World Series for his team the same year, won legions of Gentile admirers in the post-war years.*

A new America was born inside the gates of Nazi death camps. The diminishing of American anti-Semitism would be only one of a legion of convulsive changes that would rock America in the 15 years from 1945 to 1960. If anti-Semitism declined after the war, the struggle against anti-black and anti-Latino discrimination and the struggle to end sexism proved more intractable. Nevertheless, the 1950s proved to be a revolutionary decade in terms of race, gender, and sexual politics, the media, and entertainment. Millions of black and Mexican-American veterans returned home from the war doubly determined not to accept a return to a status quo of racial violence, segregation, low wages, and dilapidated schools. Millions of women who worked in factories to replace their soldier husbands and boyfriends would no longer accept domestic confinement as housewives. Stereotypically portrayed as a sleepy, conservative, introspective time, the 1950s instead saw the rise of protest movements, and redefinitions of the family, sexual morality, and popular culture. Rather than a placid time, the Beat poet Allen Ginsberg saw the era as an epoch in which the best were destroyed by madness. More accurately, it became a time in which a growing number of Americans began to confront the insanity of racism, sexism, militarism, and the ugly endurance of American poverty.

RACISM BEFORE WORLD WAR II

Before the war, numerous American college professors and bestselling authors embraced the idea of white supremacy. Madison Grant, who received a law degree from Columbia University, authored *The Passing of the Great Race: or The Racial Basis of European History* (1916), and Lothrop Stoddard, who received a Ph.D. in history from Harvard, wrote *The Rising Tide of Color Against White World-supremacy* (1920). Both became best sellers. These books claimed that African Americans possessed less intelligence and a greater tendency toward crime than Americans of European descent. Allowing African Americans any degree of political power, Grant and Stoddard argued, would destroy the American political system. Blacks, however, did not represent the only demographic category threatening the future of the country.

The Persistence of Eugenics

Grant, Stoddard and other scholars in the fields of anthropology, biology and history argued that Jews, Italians, Greeks, Poles and other immigrants from Southern and Eastern Europe represented racially inferior groups that, because of their supposed lower intelligence and lack of moral character, could never become productive citizens. Grant became the leading voice of the **eugenics** movement, which held that biological inheritance, rather than environment, determined not only a person's physical characteristics, but also intelligence and moral outlook. American and British eugenicists also divided Europeans into several "races," of which so-called Nordics from Northern and Western Europe were rated the best and most valuable. Southern and Eastern Europeans ranked under Nordics, and eugenicists ranked Jews even lower. Eugenicists theorized that breeding between superior and inferior races produced offspring inferior to either parent.

Eugenicists misused Stanford-Binet IQ tests to prove America was amidst a racial crisis, a genetic meltdown that would destroy the country. To investigate the alleged impact of mass immigration to the United States from the 1880s through the first two decades of the twentieth century, eugenicists persuaded the military to submit Army recruits, many of them recent immigrants with limited command of English, to Army IQ tests during 1917-1918 when America became involved in the First World War. The tests required soldiers to do addition and other math problems, answer questions about American history, and identify characters associated with advertising or answer other culturally based questions. The Army subjected 1.75 million recruits to IQ testing during the war, and the results were published in 1921. Assuming that the recruit's test results indicated the intelligence of the general population, the Army reported that the average American had a mental age of 13. According to the Army tests, Russian immigrants possessed an average mental age of 11.34; the Italians, 11.01; and the Poles, 10.74. Blacks supposedly held a mental age of 10.41, the lowest of all groups.

Groups like the American Eugenics Society (AES) sounded the alarm against American "race suicide." Hoping to reverse what was perceived as a national decline in intelligence, state legislatures and the U.S. Congress passed a series of laws aimed at improving the country's racial stock. Between 1905 and 1922, fifteen states passed bills allowing institutionalized people to be sterilized without prior consent. Doctors eventually carried out 3,233 such procedures. By 1931, twenty-eight states had such laws, and the rate of operations surged dramatically. Doctors not only performed involuntary tubal ligations and vasectomies on mental patients but also on many African-American men and women simply unfortunate enough to go to eugenically minded physicians. By 1941, 38,087 people had been legally sterilized involuntarily across the country because of sterilization laws. Such U.S. legislation strongly influenced Nazi Germany's 1933 edict under which 3.5 million people deemed insane, epileptic, or mentally deficient were forcibly sterilized, a program publicly praised by American eugenicists throughout the decade.

Racism crossed boundaries between North and South and between the political left and right. Feminist and socialist birth control advocate Margaret Sanger battled enthusiastically to limit the birth rates of blacks, working class whites, and the mentally disabled. "More children from the fit, less from the unfit—that is the chief issue of birth control," Sanger said. Allying with Dr. Clarence J. Gamble, a philanthropist, she later helped develop the so-called "Negro Project" encouraging birth control among southern African Americans.

As Nazis forcibly sterilized epileptics, alcoholics, and others deemed racially unfit and as persecution of Jews intensified and became more ruthless in the late 1930s, a backlash brewed against ideas associated with the Third Reich, such as eugenics. A sterilization bill proposed in the Alabama state legislature stalled because, as one opponent to the law put it, "In my judgment, the great rank and file of the country people of Alabama do not want this law; they do not want Alabama, as they term it, Hitlerized." Politicians stopped openly advocating involuntary sterilizations, but the practice continued quietly for two decades. As part of the eugenics crusade, doctors sterilized an estimated 62,000 Americans in thirty states from the 1920s until the early 1960s, according to a study sponsored by the United States Holocaust Memorial Museum.

By 1945, however, it had been two decades since the restrictive 1924 immigration law took effect, and Anglo-Saxons no longer felt threatened by immigration from Eastern and Southern Europe. Films addressing the evils of anti-Semitism, such as *Gentleman's Agreement*, reached wide audiences. The undeniable debt that the Nazi regime owed to American and European eugenicists became a public relations nightmare for eugenicists after the liberation by American soldiers of German concentration camps.

In 1945, the United Nations Educational, Scientific and Cultural Organization (UNESCO), blamed World War II on the "doctrine of the inequality of men and races." By 1950, UNESCO issued its "Statement on Race," which announced that "[s]cientists have reached general agreement that mankind is one; that all men belong to the same species, *Homo sapiens*." Humanity could not be properly divided into types, but into populations where small differences occurred based on variation of one or more genes, but these differences were small in comparison to the vast genetic similarity. UNESCO proposed replacing the term "race," which it described as hopelessly vague, with the phrase "ethnic group." The changing social climate led Anglo Christian Americans to more readily accept Jews, Italians, and Greeks as white people. Asian Americans eventually benefited from the new atmosphere. In 1952, the Walter-McCarran Act allowed Japanese immigrants to become American citizens for the first time. Generally discrimination against the Japanese declined, though it remained the strongest in the Pacific Rim. Young internees who experienced life in the Japanese internment camps during the war, and the children of internees, would lead an Asian American civil rights movement in the 1960s and 1970s.

The humor magazine *Puck*, on the cover of its June 18, 1913, issue, satirically suggests that eugenics—the pseudo-science that aimed at breeding racially superior humans—had become so dominant in Western thought that by the second decade of the twentieth century it, like gravity, "made the world go around."

THE COLD WAR AND RACE RELATIONS

The Cold War proved as important as any event in changing how white American elites thought about race. The political leadership perceived the Soviets, armed with nuclear weapons shortly after World War II, as set on world conquest. As the colonial empires of Britain and France fell apart, several presidential administrations eagerly pursued alliances with and sought to establish bases in newly born countries across Africa and Asia. Locked in a bitter ideological war with the Soviets for hearts and minds in new independent states, the Truman and Eisenhower administrations both realized that southern lynchings of black men and women, segregation, and the disenfranchisement of African-American voters gave the United States a bad image in countries governed by people of color. With the Soviet Union presenting an image of both anti-imperialism and anti-racism, the United States found itself in a public relations bind.

The paradox of America presenting itself as the land of the free while African Americans faced segregation and violence, particularly in the South, did not escape the attention of even conservative publications like *Time* magazine, which observed "in Washington, the seated figure of Abraham Lincoln broods over the capital of the U.S. where Jim Crow is the rule." Cases of racial discrimination received wide attention not only in the Soviet press, but also in newspapers and radio broadcasts in recently independent nations like India and Ceylon, and in sub-Saharan Africa. The Truman and Eisenhower administrations fretted over losing a global public relations war with the Soviets.

BLACK POLITICAL ACTIVISM

Whether or not they had the support of the Washington political establishment, the African-American community did most of the hard work of the freedom struggle themselves. In October 1946, four hundred African-American children in Lumberton, N.C., staged a walkout from classes to protest the shoddy, unsafe conditions at segregated black campuses. The students held signs sadly asking, "How Can I Learn When I'm Cold?" and noting "It Rains On Me." Such grassroots protests enjoyed surprising, if still limited, success. Spending on black education increased in the South in the immediate post-war years, but that improvement was relative since allocations for African-American schools in the former Confederacy before the war had been minuscule. Nevertheless, the increased industrialization of the South as a result of the world war and the post-war economic boom gave the poorest states in Dixie more money to spend on black students. The per capita spending in Louisiana on African-American pupils rose from an almost non-existent $16 in 1940 to a still meager $116 in 1955.

White-run southern legislatures did this because, against all odds, African Americans applied pressure to the southern power structure. The NAACP's anti-lynching campaigns had substantially reduced the number of black men, women and children murdered for racial reasons each year. White mobs murdered almost sixty African Americans annually in the five years starting with the end of World War I, from 1918 through 1922. As a result of NAACP lobbying, the Civil Rights Section of the Justice Department in the late 1930s increased federal prosecutions for police brutality and began investigating lynchings. Between 1937 and 1946, lynch mobs murdered 42 African Americans, but as a result of federal pressure, law enforcement rescued 226 potential victims. Whites lynched six African Americans in 1946, but local authorities prevented twenty-two murders.

Black political power increased as the number of African-American voters inched up across the South. American prosperity after World War II made southern blacks more impatient for improvement in their material lives, while many returning black veterans, who had fought to defeat the racist Nazi regime, insisted on change at home. Although most southern African Americans still lacked access to the ballot, the total number of registered blacks in the former Confederacy had increased from a few thousand to approximately one million by 1952. In close elections, African Americans could determine the outcome.

Nevertheless, by the early 1950s the economic, political and academic inequalities faced by African Americans in the South remained glaring and tragic. During an NAACP inspection of white and black schools in Clarendon County, S.C., for instance, Howard University associate professor Mathew J. Whitehead found that white schools had water fountains but black students had to use a dipper to scoop water from open buckets. The school system provided white students with buses but black students living far from campuses had no access to transportation. Each white campus employed a janitorial staff, but black teachers and students had to serve as uncompensated custodians at Jim Crow schools. White schools provided seating for every student, while one black school in the county did not possess a single desk.

Desegregation in Higher Education

Beginning in the 1940s, the NAACP launched a legal offensive aimed at step-by-step desegregation of American education. **Heman Marion Sweatt** forced open the doors of the University of Texas law school to African Americans in 1950. An NAACP activist in Houston since the early 1940s and a columnist for the local black-owned newspaper the *Informer*, Sweatt plunged into fundraising drives for the NAACP's lawsuit against the so-called "white primary." Democratic Party rules in Texas barred blacks from voting in primaries, which, given the party's almost complete monopoly on elective office in the first half of the twentieth century, left African Americans with no voice in partisan political races. The NAACP successfully persuaded the United States Supreme Court to declare the white primary unconstitutional in the 1944 *Smith v. Allwright* case.

A postal carrier, Sweatt fought against discriminatory policies that blocked African Americans in Texas from higher paying positions as clerks. His work on that issue sparked his growing personal interest in a law career. At the urging of Dallas NAACP attorney W.J. Durham, Sweatt applied to the UT Law School, aware that the school was legally vulnerable to litigation since the state of Texas had failed to provide a law school for African-American students. Sweatt was turned down, and on May 16, 1946 filed the **Sweatt v. Painter** case.

In order to avoid a federal desegregation order, the University of Texas regents set aside a basement in a building south of the campus on Thirteenth Street where black students could receive law instruction from the most junior members of the faculty, although African Americans would not have direct access to the law library or other resources. Only one black student, Henry Doyle, attended the Jim Crow classes. Sweatt and the NAACP refused to accept this fraud.

After years of financial hardship while waiting for the case to wind through the courts, Sweatt prevailed in his lawsuit against UT in 1950. The same day as its *Sweatt v. Painter* decision, the Supreme Court ruled in *McLaurin v. Oklahoma State Regents* that Oklahoma State University had erred when it admitted a black student to a graduate program but then required him to sit apart from white students.

After the *Sweatt* decision, the University of Texas admitted 22 African Americans out of a total enrollment of 12,000, with six of the black students enrolled in law classes. The state of Texas began allowing African Americans to attend other graduate programs besides the UT law school but only if those programs were not available at Prairie View A&M, a segregated black college. According to Texas NAACP historian Michael Gillette, the reactions of whites to Sweatt and the five other African Americans in the program were mixed. Most were agreeable, Sweatt said, and he and the other integration pioneers encountered few problems as they sought access to water fountains, restrooms, school dining facilities, lounges and football games. The Friday of his first week at UT, however, Sweatt discovered, after studying late at the law library, that a large white crowd had gathered across the street and was burning a cross. Accompanied by a white friend, Sweatt made it safely to his car, only to discover that the tires had been slashed. Although a few campus liberals offered condolence, UT officials largely ignored the incident, and Austin police never made an arrest in the case.

The intense scrutiny of the press, the racism of faculty and students, and financial pressure destroyed Sweatt's marriage during his two years at UT and undermined his academic performance. Poor health added to Sweatt's difficulties as he battled a painful ulcer and missed seven weeks of classes after suffering appendicitis. He failed courses in his first year, audited the classes he failed in the fall of 1951, and re-enrolled in the spring semester of 1952, but he subsequently dropped out. Nevertheless, the *Painter* case laid the groundwork for the more famous *Brown v. the Board of Education* school desegregation decision in 1954.

The Brown Decision

During a 1950 NAACP legal strategy session, lawyers decided to challenge public school segregation head-on. The civil rights organization represented African-American parents who filed lawsuits against segregated school districts in Delaware, Kansas, Louisiana, South Carolina, Virginia, and Washington, D.C. These suits reached the United States Supreme Court in 1952, the Court consolidating the cases under the title **Brown et al v. Board of Education of Topeka, et. al.** The Court announced its decision on May 17, 1954. In overturning the 1896 *Plessy v. Ferguson* decision, Chief Justice Earl Warren spoke for a unanimous court in declaring "In the field of public education, the doctrine of separate but equal has no place. Separate educational facilities are inherently unequal."

Unfortunately, the Supreme Court delayed its implementation of *Brown* for a year. The May 31, 1955, implementation order, known as *Brown II*, set no firm deadline for school districts to achieve integration, only urging local authorities to proceed with "all deliberate speed." The Court failed to define the threshold at which a school district achieved desegregation, leaving that matter to the federal district courts. Finally, the Court provided a list of reasons school districts could use to delay implementation, such as administrative difficulties.

The Court also unintentionally gave opponents of integration a chance to organize what came to be known as "**massive resistance**" to the *Brown* decision. In July 1954, plantation manager Robert P. Patterson organized the first "**White Citizens Council**" in Sunflower County, Mississippi. Labeled by NAACP attorney and future Supreme

Court Justice Thurgood Marshall as the "uptown Klan," these organizations drew segregationist lawyers, doctors, bankers, merchants and other influential citizens to their ranks, and they used legal and illegal methods to prevent enforcement of *Brown*. Byron De La Beckwith, who assassinated civil rights campaigner Medgar Evers in 1963, belonged to a chapter of the White Citizens Council. These groups used their financial and political influence primarily to minimize integration. African Americans who filed integration lawsuits lost jobs and could find no further employment in the white community because of boycotts organized by the councils. Furthermore, these groups raised millions of dollars to establish private "white academies" where parents wishing their children to attend segregated campuses could send their children. At the movement's peak, about 1 million belonged to White Citizens Councils across the South.

Under pressure from pro-segregation groups to take a more defiant stand against *Brown*, southern legislatures tried various ruses to avoid integration. Faced with integration orders, school officials in Little Rock, Arkansas, and Norfolk, Virginia, completely shut down their public schools. Prince Edwards County, Virginia, closed its public schools for eight years to avoid admitting African-American students. Some southern states provided white parents vouchers to pay for tuition at private, non-integrated schools.

Attorneys general in several southern states began a coordinated legal assault on the NAACP, hoping to harass the organization into bankruptcy and to frighten its members into silence. African-American teachers made up a large percentage of the group's membership rolls, so states like South Carolina passed laws prohibiting educa-tors from publicly advocating integration, forcing twenty-four teachers at Elloree Training School in Orangeburg County who belonged to the NAACP to step down.

In Texas, State Attorney General John Ben Shepperd pressured the state NAACP by forcing the group to cough up unpaid franchise taxes. He also insisted that the NAACP publicly file its membership list. Settling out of court, the NAACP agreed to pay the franchise taxes in return for the state agreeing not to challenge the civil rights organization's nonprofit status. Resentment over the Texas NAACP's decision to settle and the publication of membership lists prompted resignations across the state, with the number of branches plummeting from 76 to 46 and overall membership declining from almost 17,000 in 1956 to under 8,000 the following year. This followed the pattern across the South. In Alabama, the NAACP refused to hand over its membership lists and state Judge Walter B. Jones issued an injunction prohibiting the group from operating anywhere in the state, an order that stood for eight years.

The Murder of Emmett Till

The beating death of a 14-year-old African-American boy named **Emmett Till** in Money, Mississippi, August, 28, 1955, horrified much of the world and did much to mobilize the Civil Rights Movement in the second half of the 1950s. A Chicago native, Till traveled south to visit his extended family in the Mississippi Delta when, one week into his trip, he and several friends were standing outside a white-owned grocery in the tiny town of Money. Till told his unbelieving friends that he had several white friends in the North, including friendships with white

Holding a poster against racial bias in Mississippi are four of the most active leaders in the NAACP movement, from left: Henry L. Moon, director of public relations; Roy Wilkins, executive secretary; Herbert Hill, labor secretary, and Thurgood Marshall, special counsel. 1956

girls. The friends dared him to go inside the store and flirt with Carolyn Bryant, a white woman who worked at the cash register. Accounts conflict on what happened next, with some claiming he whistled at Bryant, others that he reached for her hand and asked her out, while according to a third version, he said, "Bye, baby," as he left the store. The cashier's husband, Roy Bryant, returned from a road trip three days later and vowed that he would "teach the boy a lesson."

Just after midnight August 28, 1955, Bryant and his step-brother J.W. Milam arrived at the house of Moses Wright, where Till was staying. They threw Till in the back of a pickup truck and drove him to nearby Sunflower County, where they beat him until his face was unrecognizable and shot him. Tying a seventy-pound weight to his body, Bryant and Milam threw Till's body into the Tallahatchie River. After three days, authorities discovered Till's bloated body and later arrested Bryant and Milam.

Till's mother, Mamie Till Bradley, had her son's body brought to Chicago for the funeral. After seeing her son's mutilated face, she insisted on an open-casket funeral. "I wanted the world to see what they did to my baby," she said. Photographs of Till in his casket, with his face visible, appeared in *Jet*, an African-American-owned magazine, and soon shocked viewers around the world. In spite of the fact that Wright bravely identified one of the killers in the courtroom, an all-white jury took little more than an hour to acquit the defendants. Bryant and Milam, protected from further prosecution for Till's murder by the constitutional ban on double jeopardy, later admitted to the killing in a *Look* magazine interview in return for $4000.

Rosa Parks and the Montgomery Bus Boycott

As a child attending the Montgomery Industrial School for Girls, an institution founded in the Alabama city in 1886 by two New England missionary women, **Rosa Parks** learned a principle that would guide her entire life. "What I learned best," she recalled, "was that I was a person with dignity and self-respect, and I should not set my sights lower than anybody else just because I was black." Joining the NAACP at the age of 30, Parks became secretary of the Montgomery, Alabama branch. Parks earned a reputation as a quiet but hard worker guided by strong beliefs.

African Americans in Montgomery had planned for some time to challenge segregated seating on the city's buses. Black riders were made to sit in the back. Each bus had a "moving barrier" that divided the races. If the white section filled up, blacks were expected to move farther back and, if necessary, surrender seats to just-boarding white passengers. On December 1, 1955, Parks left her job as a seamstress at the Montgomery Fair department store and entered the bus that took her home each afternoon. A white man stood at the front of the bus and driver J.P. Blake demanded that four black passengers sitting just behind the back of the white section

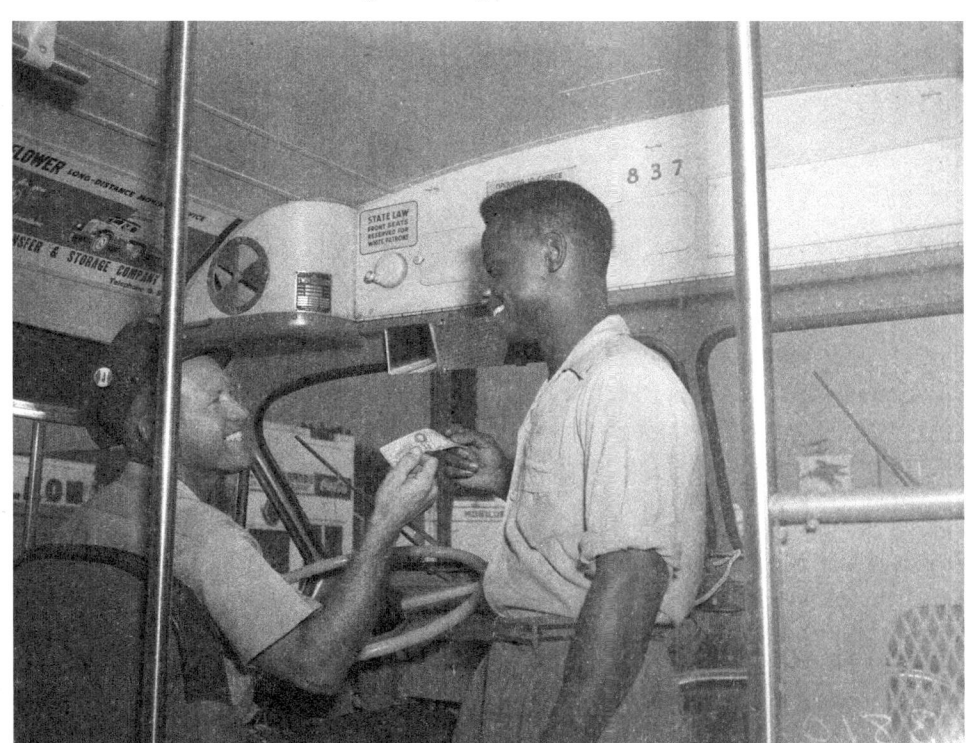

This bus in San Antonio, Texas, 1949, has a sign above the driver's seat that states
"STATE LAW: Front Seats Reserved for White Patrons"
Credit: Institute of Texan Cultures

move to seats farther down. The African-American riders did not budge. After a threat from Blake, three of them relented. The fourth, Parks, told Blake that she was not in the white section and would remain in her seat. Blake replied that he had the authority to determine where the white section ended and the black section began and to arrest Parks if she refused to move. She refused, and Blake told her she was under arrest. She remained seated until Blake returned with Montgomery police officers, who fingerprinted her and placed her in jail. The police charged her with violating Alabama's bus segregation laws.

The African-American community in Montgomery, who all shared humiliating experiences coping with the city's Jim Crow ordinances, quickly mobilized as word spread of Parks's arrest. The Montgomery Improvement Association (MIA) led a boycott of the city bus system with a 26-year-old Baptist minister, Martin Luther King, Jr., selected as its president. A one-day black boycott of the city's mass transit turned into a more than yearlong campaign.

During the **Montgomery Bus Boycott**, the MIA arranged transportation for the African-American domestic servants, sanitation workers, and janitors participating in the bus boycott to help them travel the often long distances to their jobs. Montgomery police began arresting drivers participating in the MIA carpools. Police arrested Dr. King for allegedly speeding, and four days later someone ignited dynamite at the homes of King and of E.D. Nixon, another boycott leader. Montgomery's white leadership hoped to break the spirit of the boycotters, but the King arrest and the terrorist attacks had the opposite effect. One maid vowed she would crawl before she got back on the city buses.

The MIA vowed to continue the boycott until the city desegregated the buses. In spite of the poverty of its supporters, the MIA raised $2,000 a week to continue its carpools, pay legal expenses, and carry on the boycott. By February of 1956, the story made headlines around the world and donations to the cause poured in from other countries. The boycott lasted 381 days and began to adversely affect white businesses in downtown Montgomery. A federal court in June 1956 ruled that Alabama's and Montgomery's bus segregation laws violated the Constitution, a decision affirmed by the U.S. Supreme Court's *Browder v. Gayle* decision. Even though segregated public transportation remained the rule in the South for years to come, the Montgomery Bus Boycott made King a national civil rights leader and set the precedent for sit-ins and other mass protests that would mark the Civil Rights Movement. Other southern cities, such as Tallahassee and Baton Rouge, would witness similar bus boycotts.

The Little Rock Crisis

Such protests required much physical bravery and commitment, and very often the youngest Americans paid a high price in the struggle for civil rights. African-American children breaking the color bar often suffered horrendous verbal and physical abuse from white students, as was the case of the nine students sent to integrate Central High School in Little Rock, Arkansas, in 1957. Arkansas Governor **Orval Faubus,** who had earned a reputation as a racial moderate, faced a tough re-election battle and decided to exploit the racial tensions sparked by a court order to desegregate the Little Rock campus. On September 2, 1957, the night before the school term began, Faubus appeared on Arkansas television and announced that it would "not be possible to restore or maintain order if forcible integration is carried out tomorrow." Faubus dispatched the Arkansas National Guard to Central High to bar the entrance of the African-American students who volunteered to integrate the high school. The black students did not attempt to enter the campus the next day, but a federal judge ordered integration to proceed. As the black students approached the following day, a large white mob gathered around Central High and yelled, "Niggers! Niggers! They're coming. Here they come!" National Guardsmen turned back the Little Rock Nine, as the black students came to be called.

Dwight Eisenhower then occupied the White House, and he had no appetite for getting involved in the **Little Rock Crisis.** The Republican president, who in 1952 had won four southern states against the liberal Democrat Adlai Stevenson, believed that the GOP had a chance of making electoral headway in the South, and he did not want to alienate segregationist voters. Eisenhower himself sympathized somewhat with white southern racial atti-

President Dwight Eisenhower has a special broadcast on the Little Rock situation. September 24, 1957. Credit: Eisenhower Presidential Library

tudes. After the *Brown* decision, he told Supreme Court Chief Justice Earl Warren, "These [white Southerners] are not bad people. All they are concerned about is to see that their sweet little girls are not required to sit in schools alongside some big black bucks." At a press conference the week the Little Rock Nine tried to enroll at the high school, Eisenhower said, "You cannot change people's hearts merely by laws."

Eisenhower's actions the year before gave civil rights supporters little hope that the president would intervene to protect the Little Rock Nine from physical danger. In 1956, a federal court mandated school desegregation in Mansfield, Texas, a small town between Dallas and Fort Worth. With the support of Texas Governor Allan Shivers, enraged white mobs surrounded Mansfield High School on August 30 and 31 in order to block the enrollment of three African-American students. Whites hanged three black-faced effigies, which dangled in front of the Mansfield High campus for days with no action from school officials. Rather than calling for Mansfield residents to respect the law, Shivers disobeyed court orders, dispatching Texas Rangers to keep the three African-American students from entering the campus.

Facing re-election in 1956, and hoping to win votes in Texas, Eisenhower took no action to enforce the desegregation order. The president allowed Governor Shivers to illegally maintain segregation, which did not end at the campus until the high school faced the loss of federal funds in 1965. Inspired by events in Mansfield, Arkansas Governor Faubus expected a similar result in Little Rock in 1957.

Ordered a second time on September 20, 1957, to implement desegregation, Governor Faubus withdrew the National Guard and predicted bloodshed as he left the state to avoid responsibility. A large, unruly crowd gathered at Central High School by Monday, September 23. The mob chanted, "Two, four, six, eight, we ain't gonna integrate!" and "Niggers, keep away from our school—go back to the jungle." This time the Little Rock mayor ordered the black students withdrawn.

Concerned about the rising national and international criticism of his inaction, Eisenhower federalized the Arkansas National Guard and dispatched a thousand troops of the 101st Airborne Division to Central High to escort the Little Rock Nine safely to the campus. Armed soldiers would accompany the African-American students for several weeks, but the black students would face danger upon the withdrawal of the federal troops.

The coming months proved hellish for the small black contingent. One student, Melba Pattillo, suffered racial slurs and was pushed, hit, and tripped by white students. One white student squirted acid into her eyes, almost causing permanent blindness. "If someone called me names or spat on me, or kicked me in the shin, or walked on my heel, I thought I couldn't make it one more moment," said Pattillo, who nevertheless persisted to the end of the school year. Terrorists fired bullets into her home and the school district threatened her mother, a teacher at a black school, that her job would be eliminated. A National Guardsmen felt compassion for Pattillo and advised her not to reveal her emotional pain to her tormentors. "Warriors don't cry," he told her.

One of the nine, Minnijean Brown, could take the harassment no more and poured chili on a group of white boys who were tormenting her in the school cafeteria. School officials did nothing to the boys but suspended Brown for six days. After another incident, officials suspended Brown for the remainder of the school year. Her parents transferred her to a high school in New York. Faubus, meanwhile, continued his resistance by closing down all of Little Rock's high schools in the 1958-59 school year. Federal courts intervened to reopen the schools. That year, the Arkansas governor was named one of the most admired men in America in a Gallup Poll.

The Sit-in Movement

Even though the United States Supreme Court had ruled school segregation unconstitutional in the *Brown v. Board of Education* decision in 1954, by 1959 more than 99 percent of black and white students in the South still attended Jim Crow campuses. Across the former Confederacy, states denied African Americans the right to vote in spite of a 1957 Civil Rights Law passed by Congress that reaffirmed the Fourteenth and Fifteenth Amendments to the U.S. Constitution. These amendments guaranteed voting rights regardless of race or color. Throughout the South, blacks who asserted their constitutional right to vote, or to sit near white people in movie theaters or on buses, faced getting fired or physical violence.

Tired of continued discrimination, four African-American students at North Carolina A&T College in Greensboro, N.C., Ezell Blair, Franklin McCain, Joseph McNeil, J.R. David Richmond, and white NAACP member Ralph Johns planned a direct blow against local segregation laws. After buying school supplies to establish that they were paying customers, the five staged a "**sit-in**" at the segregated lunch counter at the town's F.W. Woolworth Company department store February 1, 1960. "We believe, since we buy books and papers in the other part of the store, we should get served in this part," one of the students told a wire service reporter from United Press International. The demonstrators asked for coffee. C.L. Harris, the store manager, chose to ignore the five protestors. "They can just sit there. It's nothing to me." The five protestors sat at the lunch counter for hours as some white customers, assuming the men did not know any better, told them that they were at a "whites only" counter. Others cursed them while a small number patted them on the back and expressed support.

Protestors proved much harder to ignore the next day. Twenty-five participated in a second sit-in. On the third day, 85 showed up. The fourth straight day of sit-ins included white students from the University of North Carolina's Women's College in Greensboro. Soon, North Carolina students staged sit-ins at theaters, drugstores, and other businesses in a dozen towns across the state. Sit-ins bedeviled Jim Crow businesses outside of the state in Hampton, Virginia, and in Chattanooga and Nashville, Tennessee. On the seventh day of the campaign, civil rights demonstrators held 54 sit-ins in fifteen cities and nine states across the former Confederacy. Eventually 70,000 Americans would participate in the sit-in movement of 1960, and 3,000 would be arrested, with the demonstrations breaking out even as far away as Nevada.

If the first sit-ins were spontaneous, as the movement spread, such demonstrations became more organized with students trained in the non-violent techniques established by civil rights leaders like **Martin Luther King, Jr.**, and his allies in the 1950s. The Student Nonviolent Coordinating Committee (better known as the SNCC or "Snick") formed and launched a national sit-in campaign.

As the non-violent sit-ins spread, whites often responded with brutality. At Nashville lunch counters, angry local whites burned the backs of black women with lit cigarettes, while in Biloxi, Mississippi, whites shot and wounded ten African Americans gathered at a public beach. At one sit-in, as newspaper photographers snapped pictures and television cameras rolled, whites hit well-dressed, well-behaved black students, poured ketchup and mustard on their heads and pulled them off of stools.

Such scenes had a profound impact on newspaper and magazine readers and television viewers across the country, with African-American activists winning sympathy from white audiences in the North, Midwest, and the West Coast. In the North, blacks and whites organized boycotts of chain stores that practiced segregation in the South such as Walgreen's, Woolworth's and S.H. Kress. Yolande Betbeze Fox, a white former Miss America, protested at Woolworth's stores in New York City, telling reporters, "I'm a Southern girl, but a thinking girl."

The sit-in movement represented a shift in the civil rights leadership from an older establishment to their children and grandchildren. It also established a precedent for more "direct action" protests, which became the focus of the movement instead of the reliance on lawsuits that marked the NAACP strategy in the 1940s and 1950s.

MEXICAN-AMERICAN ACTIVISM

From 1941-1945, close to 500,000 Mexican Americans served in the United States military out of a Hispanic population of about 2.7 million. In Los Angeles, Hispanics accounted for one-tenth of the total population but comprised one-fifth of the metropolis' wartime casualties. Hispanics made up 25 percent of the victims of the "Bataan Death March" (in which Japanese soldiers beat, shot and marched to death captured British and American prisoners of war in the Philippines), and Mexicans and Mexican Americans earned more medals of honor than any other demographic group.

The Mexican population in the United States increased dramatically during the post-World War II period, with Mexican immigrants increasing from 5.9 percent of all newcomers to 11.9 percent at the end of the 1950s. Part of this increase resulted from the *bracero* program, in which American landowners imported Mexicans as low-paid agricultural workers. The number of *braceros* brought in from Mexico jumped from about 35,000 in 1949 to 107,000 in 1960. Many *braceros* remained in the United States after their year-long contracts expired.

Responding to Anglo panic about the rising number of immigrants who supposedly crossed the border illegally by swimming across the Rio Grande River, the federal government launched a crackdown on undocumented workers called "**Operation Wetback**," the name derived from an anti-Mexican slur. During the next five years, the government seized and deported nearly four million people whom authorities claimed were illegal immigrants, with Mexican-American legal residents sometimes included in the sweeps. Immigration would heavily politicize the Mexican-American community after the war. Many Hispanic political organizations battled to improve working conditions for migrant workers. They fought what they saw as harassment of the Mexican-American community, including repeated FBI investigations of Hispanic labor unions that Anglo law enforcement accused of being communist fronts.

As with African Americans, Mexican-American veterans of World War II returned from a war against racist fascist regimes impatient with the intolerance they still encountered at home. Passage of the G.I. Bill of Rights meant that more Mexican Americans attended college than ever before, and with increased enrollment at colleges and universities came rising expectations for a better life. Hispanic veterans in particular played a major role in the two primary Latino civil rights organizations of the post-war years: the **League of United Latin American Citizens (LULAC)** and the **American GI Forum (AGIF)**. Well-educated, often prosperous, and urban Mexican-American elites formed LULAC in Texas in the late 1920s. LULAC's founders saw assimilation with the Anglo majority as a path toward winning acceptance in American society. They embraced a "Mexican American" identity that combined respect for Mexican traditions and pride in American citizenship. A major focus was "Americanizing" Latinos who still spoke Spanish. These groups sought an end to discrimination against Hispanics, but avoided entanglement with the African American civil rights struggle.

The Anglo response to Mexican Americans and immigrants in states like Texas and New Mexico varied widely, with discrimination more common and harsher in places with large Spanish-speaking populations. The law in Texas and other Southwestern states did not define Mexican Americans and Mexican immigrants as non-whites, so segregation of Latino students resulted from custom rather than statute. In such communities, authorities denied Mexican Americans access to public parks and swimming pools, and restaurants either would not serve Mexican American and Mexican patrons or would force them to take their food through a back window and eat outside. Though no formal law segregated Mexican and Mexican-American children from Anglos in Texas schools, in districts with large Latino populations, school officials routinely assigned Hispanic children to separate, crowded and poorly funded schools.

Hispanic students rarely finished their public school education with a high school diploma. Many non-native speakers of English ended up assigned to remedial classes. In San Antonio in 1920, 11,000 students attended the district's elementary schools, but there were only 250 high school graduates. In 1928, only 250 Mexican students attended colleges and universities in the entire state of Texas.

In 1946, a U.S. District court in Southern California ruled in *Méndez v. Westminster School District* that segregating Mexican school children violated their constitutional rights, a decision later upheld by the Ninth Circuit Court of Appeals. The dismantling of segregation in Texas began with the 1948 ***Delgado v. Bastrop ISD*** decision, in which a lower federal court banned school boards from placing Mexican-American students in different schools than Anglo children. The court's rationale rested on Texas's legal definition of Mexican American as white. These cases provided two of many precedents for the *Brown* decision.

Dr. Hector Garcia formed the American GI Forum (AGIF) in Corpus Christi, Texas, in 1948 to serve Mexican-American veterans who frequently did not receive Veterans Administration benefits on time. Shut out by the Anglo-run American Legion, Garcia and others decided to form their own veterans' group. The AGIF grabbed national headlines in 1949 when it led protests against a Three Rivers, Texas, funeral home that denied the use of a chapel to the family of Army Private Felix Longoria, who died in combat in World War II. The AGIF launched an intense lobbying campaign. Lyndon Johnson, at the time a U.S. senator from Texas, successfully persuaded authorities to grant a full funeral service for Longoria at Arlington National Cemetery. Angered by the treatment of Longoria, Mexican-American veterans

LULAC meeting at Aztec No. 3 club on Main Street, Victoria, Texas, 1940s. Source: Tensy Quinbar, San Antonio, Texas. Credit: Institute of Texan Cultures

Leaders of the Latino civil rights struggle gather outside the Casa Blanca restaurant in San Antonio, Texas, during a celebration of victory in the landmark 1948 *Delgado v. Bastrop ISD* decision that outlawed segregation against Latino students. Pictured, from left to right: Dr. Arthur Campa, a University of Denver professor; Dr. George I. Sanchez, a professor at the University of Texas at Austin; Joe Castanuela, president of a local LULAC chapter; and Ramon Galindo, president of local Mexican-American Chamber of Commerce.
Credit: Institute of Texan Cultures

across the country flocked to the GI Forum, and by the end of 1949, there were 100 AGIF chapters in 23 states across the country.

Groups like LULAC and AGIF focused their legal strategies not on fighting segregation on principle, but on securing a consistent legal definition of Mexican Americans as whites who therefore had the right to attend better-funded white schools. Nevertheless, Mexican-American politicians like Henry B. Gonzalez of Texas threw his support behind the NAACP and black desegregation efforts. The Chicano movement of the late 1960s would bring increased efforts to unite blacks and browns in a common battle against racism.

ROSIE THE RIVETER AFTER THE WAR

During World War II, millions of women filled industrial jobs left by men serving in the military and played a critical role in producing military equipment and other products needed by the troops in Europe and Asia. Between 1940 and 1945, the number of women workers climbed by 50 percent. About 75 percent of women workers were married and most had school-age children. By 1944, the year before the war ended, 36.5 percent of women worked outside the home.

After the war, however, employers laid off female workers en masse, with the percentage of women earning wages outside the home dropping to 30.8 percent in 1947. Among women who stayed in the workplace, those who had enjoyed higher wages in manufacturing jobs during the war often found themselves consigned to lower-paid, more traditional positions as secretaries. Nevertheless, by the beginning of the 1950s, the number of women earning salaries began to inch upward again. In 1952, there were two million more women in the workplace than

at the peak of wartime production. A decade later, 40 percent of women aged 16 and older held jobs. Driving increased female employment, at least in part, was a rise in consumerism, created in turn by a vast expansion of mass media and advertising in the late 1940s and 1950s. Purchases of household appliances and furniture spiraled 240 percent between 1945-50. The dazzling array of household products paraded in newspapers, magazines, and nightly on television shows and the radio put pressure on family incomes. Women worked so families could keep up with what came to be called the "rat race." However, even women who returned to a domestic life were influenced by their wartime experiences, and many taught their daughters that they could do whatever men could do. These women laid a foundation for the feminist movement of the 1960s.

Dr. Hector P. Garcia, founder of the American G.I. Forum. Credit: Institute of Texan Cultures

Representative Henry B. Gonzalez, Austin, Texas, 1950s

Women in 1950s Popular Culture

Assertive women, however, were demeaned by American culture from the late 1940s to the early 1960s, and blamed for a supposed rise in juvenile delinquency, homosexuality, and other alleged social ills. Movies like **Rebel Without a Cause** (1955), *Psycho* (1960), and *The Manchurian Candidate* (1962) depicted children raised by domineering mothers with no strong male in the house as liable to become at best dysfunctional and at worst homicidal monsters.

The popular situation comedy *I Love Lucy* portrayed the ditzy title heroine's dreams of a show business career as laughable. Lucy carried a mixed message. The title character, like many real 1950s women, desperately wanted a career and success outside of the boring housewife role the male-dominated culture thrust upon them. All of Lucy's attempts to become an actress, a novelist, or a singer, however, ended in comic failure. In most family-centered comedies, however, women were portrayed as happy and fulfilled homebound wives and mothers. Shows like *Father Knows Best* and *Ozzie and Harriet* featured men as the wage earners and decision makers of the family and adult women as perfectly dressed and bejeweled housewives with no life outside of keeping house and fretting about the children. In such programs, housewives did not come up with solutions to the problems facing the family but instead meekly deferred to their presumably smarter and wiser husbands.

In movies, unconventional women were portrayed in more sinister hues. In *Rebel Without a Cause*, the tragic hero of the film, Jim Stark, (played by teen idol James Dean) descends into juvenile delinquency in large part because of a weak father dominated by a bossy wife. At one point, Stark bitterly complains that his mother bullies his father, who in one scene wears a kitchen apron. She

"eats him alive and he takes it," Stark complains, later insisting that "if he had guts to knock Mom cold once, then maybe she'd be happy and then she'd stop pickin' on him, because they make mush out of him."

Heavily influenced by the overt sexism of Freudian psychology, bestsellers like *Modern Woman: The Lost Sex*, by Ferdinand Lundberg and Marynia F. Farnham published in 1947, suggested that women who sought careers or higher education sought to symbolically "castrate" men. Psychiatrists regularly diagnosed women who defied the gender norms of the time by delaying childbirth, pursuing careers, or being insufficiently subservient to their husbands as neurotic or even as suffering from schizophrenia. According to historian Stephanie Coontz, the medical records of women hospitalized as "schizophrenic" in the San Francisco Bay area in the 1950s reveal that most of these women were subjected to forced commitment and electro-shock therapy in order to get them to accept their domestic roles and the authority of their husbands. Doctors also used electro-shock to "cure" women who sought abortions, which doctors interpreted as a sign of mental illness.

FAMILY LIFE AND THE BABY BOOM

Few women experienced the lives portrayed on popular TV shows, but that was not for lack of effort. The median age for women marrying for the first time dropped to just over 20 years in mid-decade (the median age for men was around 22.5.) It became common for couples to marry shortly after high school graduation. No generation married at higher rates than those Americans who reached maturity during World War II. About 96 percent of the women and 94 percent of the men in that group married, with the average family having between 3.2 and 3.7

children during the course of the 1950s. The so-called "**Baby Boom**" years from 1946 to 1964 saw the birth of 79 million children. Births per year soared from around 2.5 million in the 1930s and the early 1940s to a peak of 4.3 million in the late 1950s.

Sadly, marriage and children often failed to bring the emotional and material rewards to men and women as promised on television comedies. As in other eras, family life in the 1950s featured tragically frequent incidents of child and spousal abuse, infidelity, chemical dependency, and poverty. Under state laws of the 1950s, wife-beating was not considered a crime, and psychologists and sociologists largely overlooked issues like child abuse. In Colorado, where in one year police recorded 302 cases of battered children, 33 died from beatings.

Family Troubles

Even though the father of psychoanalysis, Sigmund Freud, came to conflicting conclusions about the prevalence of incest and the sexual abuse of children by family members, Freudian psychiatrists in the 1950s tended to dismiss female patients accusing their fathers of rape, claiming that such women were indulging in sexual fantasies. Not believing their abuse claims, doctors often sought to sedate their female patients. A multi-million dollar industry manufacturing tranquilizers and sleeping pills underwent explosive growth in the 1950s, and females became the major consumers. Consumption of anxiety medications climbed from 462,000 pounds nationally in 1958 to 1.15 million pounds only a year later.

Educated women in particular felt they were not free to express themselves intellectually. About 40 percent of Barnard College women in one survey admitted to "playing dumb" in order to attract men, but once in such relationships, they often experienced anger and frustration. In 1957, Betty Friedan began the research that led to her groundbreaking 1963 book *The Feminine Mystique*, and she found legions of thoughtful middle- and upper-class women who spent their years after college graduation with nothing more mentally taxing to do than housework. A study of young female college graduates found that those who became full-time housewives after school suffered from a more intense fear of growing old, enjoyed less confidence, were more critical of themselves, and had greater doubts about their skills as mothers than women who had paying jobs. Male doctors at the time saw frustrated women as suffering from mental illness but did not perceive as sick a society that denied smart, educated women a professional outlet.

SEX DURING THE 1950s

Other women found themselves trapped into marriage by premarital pregnancy. According to John D'Emilio and Estelle B. Freedman, historians of American sexuality, the period after World War II saw an increase in sexual permissiveness that had actually begun in the 1920s and 1930s when young people first began in large numbers to select their own mates instead of letting their parents arrange courtships and choose their marriage partners. By mid-century, it became common for girls and boys in high school to "go steady," a commitment to a relationship that allowed these couples a greater degree of sexual exploration. Sexual contact short of intercourse became more commonplace, particularly with the great availability of automobiles.

The Double Standard

As sexual activity became more common, American society gave boys greater permission to pursue sexual contact, but women who engaged in sexual acts lost social standing and became less attractive to boys as long-term partners. Boys often shunned girls with whom they had engaged in premarital sex. "How are you supposed to know what they want?" a sixteen-year-old girl complained in the 1950s. "You hold out for a long time and then when you give in to them and give your body they laugh at you afterwards and say they would never marry a slut, and that they didn't love you but were testing because they only plan to marry a virgin and wanted to see if you would go all the way."

Regardless of the stated sexual standards of the day that condemned homosexuality, adultery, and premarital sex for women, the work of Alfred Kinsey, a zoologist from Indiana University, made it clear that many Americans lived in secret defiance of those standards. Kinsey's dry 1948 scientific tome, *Sexual Behavior in the Human Male*, spent 27 weeks on the *New York Times* bestseller list, eventually selling 250,000 copies. The 1953 follow-up, *Sexual Behavior in the Human Female*, joined its predecessor at the top of the book charts. Kinsey and his staff questioned 5,300 white men and 6,000 women before drawing his conclusions. Interview subjects would be questioned in great detail on up to 521 items on his survey.

Among his controversial findings: 90 percent of men had engaged in premarital intercourse; 50 percent had engaged in extra-marital affairs; about 37 percent of males and 13 percent of females had at least one "homosexual experience"; nearly all men had found a "sexual outlet" by the age of 15; and 95 percent reported they violated a law at least once while achieving orgasm (by, for instance, violating state statutes against oral sex or homosexual acts, or by sexual acts with an underage partner). Fewer women violated supposed American sexual standards, but the Kinsey results still startled the media and the average reader. According to Kinsey, more than 62 percent of women masturbated, 90 percent engaged in petting, 50 percent had sex before marriage, and 15 percent had participated in extramarital affairs. According to Kinsey, Americans were more sexual than was publicly acknowledged and also more hypocritical about sex than was commonly admitted.

The Cost of Sexual Hypocrisy

Even though American teenagers had greater knowledge of and made more use of contraceptives in the 1950s, unwanted pregnancies still haunted many adolescent girls. In 1957, 97 out of every 1,000 girls from age 15 through 19 gave birth for the first time, in contrast to 52 of every 1,000 girls 26 years later. As Stephanie Coontz writes, "A surprising number of these births were illegitimate." To avoid scandal, parents often sent their daughters to homes for unwed mothers and urged them to put their children up for adoption. Overall, the period from 1944 to 1955 saw an 80 percent climb in the adoption of children born outside of marriage.

Many women forced into early marriage or to raise children as single parents experienced poverty, but they were hardly alone. After World War II, women who continued to work outside of the home found it hard to get the type of high-wage, challenging jobs they held in the early 1940s. Men returning from the war took back manufacturing jobs in the defense, steel, and automobile industries. Women once again could only find low-wage jobs as secretaries and domestics. In any case, a high number of men and women did not enjoy the economic boom time of the period from 1945 to 1960. One out of four Americans met the official definition of poverty in the 1950s, including one-third of children. African-American women and their children faced a double bind, and by 1959, 55 percent of the black population lived in poverty, one more instance of how real American family life in the 1950s differed from the fantasy projected in popular culture.

Oppression and the Birth of the Gay Rights Movement

During the war, millions of gay men and women left their small towns and farming communities where they had lived lonely lives of isolation and entered the military where for the first time they met large numbers of other gays. After the war, many homosexuals from middle America settled in cities that already had substantial, established gay communities like New York, San Francisco and Los Angeles. Gay men turned to YMCA dormitories and public parks along with the more traditional gathering places like bathhouses and gay bars to find sexual and romantic partners and to connect with a larger community. Kinsey's report on the prevalence of homosexual behavior among men, and his estimate that gays constituted between 4 to 10 percent of the population, bolstered the confidence of the community even as positive images of lesbian relationships appeared in the paperback novels of Ann Bannon and Paula Christian.

The Cold War, however, sparked a new wave of anti-gay oppression. Some allies of the red-baiting Wisconsin Senator Joseph McCarthy claimed that homosexuality represented part of a communist conspiracy to undermine American masculinity, the family, and the country's military resolve. Government officials claimed that gay government workers posed a security risk because they were weak and vulnerable to blackmail by Soviet agents. In 1950, a State Department official revealed that his office had fired dozens of employees for suspected homosexuality. Republican members of Congress charged that gays had infiltrated President Truman's administration. In June 1950, the Senate authorized an investigation into the prevalence of homosexuality in the federal workforce.

In December 1950, the government issued a report, "Employment of Homosexuals and Other Sex Perverts in Government" that charged, "The lack of emotional stability which is found in most sex perverts and the weakness of their moral fibre makes them susceptible to the blandishments of foreign espionage agents . . . [and] easy prey to blackmailers." A purge of gay government workers ensued. Investigators warned the targets of the gay witchhunt that their lifestyles would be publicly revealed and they could face criminal prosecution if they did not provide names of other homosexuals working in federal agencies. The number of government employees sacked during the "gay scare" increased by twelve times in the period between 1950 and 1953. Shortly after being sworn in as president, Dwight Eisenhower issued an executive order barring any gay man or woman from working for the federal government. A gay purge happened in the military, with annual discharges doubling through the 1950s. Even companies doing business with the federal government began screening employees for "homosexual tendencies."

The federal gay purge probably inspired increased harassment of homosexuals by local police departments, which increased raids on gay bars and bathhouses. Police frequently beat gay suspects. Washington, D.C. police arrested more than 1,000 suspected gays a year in the early

1950s, with other police sweeps of gay hangouts taking place in cities like Baltimore, Miami, New Orleans, and Dallas. The psychiatric profession, meanwhile, defined homosexuality as a mental illness, and many gays found themselves involuntarily committed to mental hospitals where, like unconventional women, they found themselves subjected to electro-shock therapy or to insulin injections aimed at causing "curative" seizures.

Watching a climate of fear settle over the gay community, Henry Hay created what could be described as the first gay civil rights organization in the United States, the **Mattachine Society**. The Mattachine Society derived its name from the Italian word mattachino, which referred to medieval court jesters who risked telling the king painful truths. The first chapter of the society formed in Los Angeles in 1950, with affiliates soon popping up in Boston, Philadelphia, Chicago, Denver and Washington, D.C. In its founding statement of principles, the group sought to consciously imitate other "minority" groups like "the Negro, the Mexican, and the Jewish people," in developing an "ethical homosexual society" and to campaign against "discriminatory and oppressive legislation" and assist "our people who are victimized daily as part of our oppression." Yet, it would not be until the Stonewall Riot in New York City in 1969 that the gay civil rights movement would make significant headway.

THE INTERSTATE HIGHWAY SYSTEM

During World War II, the American military worried about attacks on the American Pacific coast by the Japanese and on the Atlantic coast by the Germans. A highway bill had passed in 1944, but Eisenhower, who had been impressed by the German autobahn highway system that had been constructed by the Nazis, wanted superhighways for America. In 1956, the U.S Congress passed the **Interstate Highway Act**. President Eisenhower supported the bill as an aid to national defense. Automobile manufacturers lobbied for highway construction as well. Crews built 46,000 miles of road with $130 billion in federal funds as a result of the 1956 law. The country's new highway system proved to be one of the most transformative forces in American life from 1945 to 1960.

Americans quickly came to prefer driving their own cars to being passengers on public transportation. Tragically, the spread of highways and America's infatuation with cars also increased pollution and the country's dependence on oil. At the same time, a new industry, fast food, grew with the spread of the highway system. The spreading high-speed road network of the 1950s provided a marketing strategy for the fast food emporiums rising

in the next decade. Located strategically on off-ramps, these restaurants offered quick, cheap, predictable meals to harried and wearied travelers who increasingly drove long distances from their downtown jobs to the suburban homes or who trekked across the ever more accessible breadth of the country in search of sales opportunities and business contacts. McDonald's, Kentucky Fried Chicken, and other national fast food chains began to conquer the American landscape by the 1960s. The explosion of fast-food restaurants contributed to an epidemic of American obesity by the late twentieth century.

The year 1956 saw not just the beginning of highway construction across the nation but also the opening of America's first indoor shopping mall in Edina, a suburb of Minneapolis, Minnesota. With more and wider roadways available and car ownership on the increase, retail outlets increasingly moved from urban downtowns to outlying suburbs. The prototypical post-war suburb, with blocks of affordable, modest-sized, look-alike homes, arose in Levittown, New York, a 17,500-home community designed by William Levitt specifically for veterans returning from World War II and their wives and children. Increasingly, Americans moved from large cities to nearby suburbs, with the suburban population doubling from 36 million to 72 million from 1950 to 1970. Part of this population shift resulted from "white flight," as Anglo families sought neighborhoods farther from the growing African-American and Mexican-American communities within

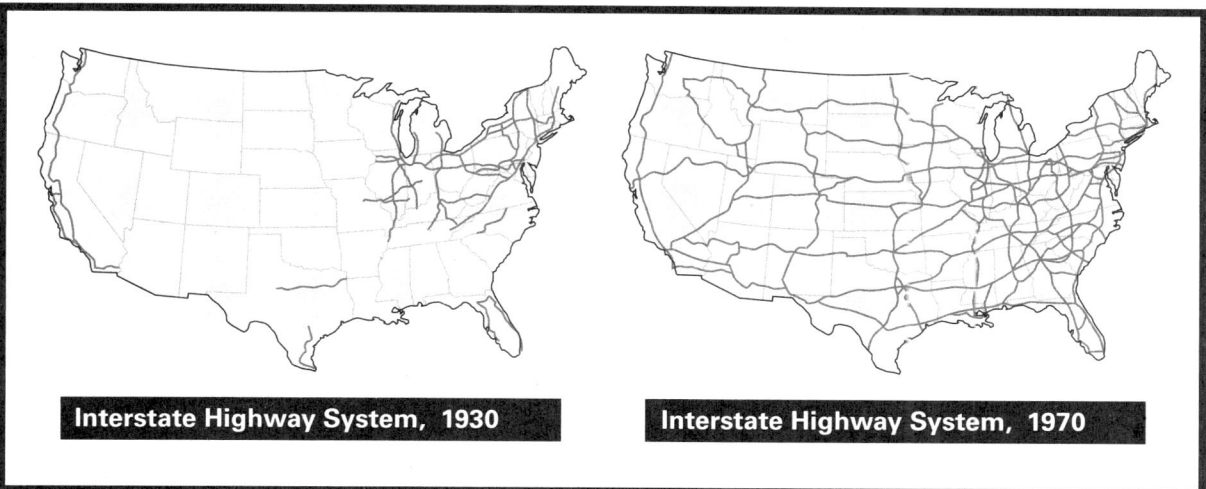

Map 26.1 **The Interstate Highway and Defense System Act of 1956 authorized federal funds to build the highways that crisscrossed the nation.**

the major cities. The move of so many Americans farther from the urban core led to the economic deterioration of inner cities. Corporations, manufacturers and retail outlets soon also fled to suburbs offering lower taxes. The combined effect would be increased traffic, higher highway fatalities, and urban sprawl.

TV NATION

Americans grew addicted to television in the 1950s. The number of households with television sets grew from a few thousand in 1946 to 15 million six years later. By 1955, two-thirds of American households owned a TV. Television served as the most effective medium for advertising to date. Soon, "Marlboro Men"—handsome cowboys riding horses on the American plains—made cigarette smoking appear masculine and glamorous, while sales of other products ranging from cars to aftershave and mouthwash soared because of the new medium. Hygiene products suddenly acquired sex appeal through the use of attractive male and female actors. Advertisers spent only $170 million on television advertising in 1950, but just five years later, TV's advertising revenues surpassed $1 billion. The success of television dramatically affected radio programming, as the soap operas, police dramas and comedies that had appeared on the older medium became staple TV fare. Radio increasingly became a medium for music, news, and talk shows.

A few serious programs, such as Edward R. Murrow's CBS news program *See It Now,* graced the airwaves. A series of 1954 *See It Now* broadcasts investigating the unethical behavior and unsubstantiated charges of Senator Joseph McCarthy contributed to the Wisconsin politician's fall. Another CBS series, *Playhouse 90,* featured

serious dramas starring respected actors, including episodes such as "The Miracle Worker," about teacher Anne Sullivan's education of the deaf, mute and blind Helen Keller, and "Judgment at Nuremburg" about Nazi war crimes. Both episodes later became acclaimed movies. However, broadcasters preferred what they considered the "least objectionable" content, airing dramas and comedies that steered clear of controversial subjects.

Rod Serling, writer of a *Playhouse 90* episode, "Requiem for a Heavyweight," recalled scripting a drama for the *United States Steel Hour* about an elderly Jew murdered by a bigot who is acquitted of the crime by a small-town jury. Asked by a reporter if the script was a comment on the Emmett Till murder, Serling said, "If the shoe fits . . ." Hearing this and afraid of offending southern audiences, sponsor U.S. Steel demanded several script changes, including making the murder victim an unspecified foreigner, removing the word "lynch" from the script and requiring characters to repeatedly say, "This is a strange little town," so it would not seem the program was criticizing any specific American community.

Frustrated, Serling decided he would enjoy more creative freedom if he disguised discussion of contemporary issues by masking them as science fiction and horror stories, creating the series **The Twilight Zone,** a show first airing in 1959. The innovative program dealt with many controversial themes such as McCarthyism, nuclear weapons, the Holocaust, racism and other issues but often in a disguised manner that avoided the detection of wary censors or advertisers.

Most airtime became relentlessly bland. Critics soon called television the "idiot box." As Newton Minow, the controversial chair of the Federal Communications Commission in the early 1960s, put it, "When television is good, nothing is better. But when television is bad, nothing is worse. I invite you to sit down in front of your TV set and keep your eyes glued to that set until the station signs off. I can assure you that you will observe a vast wasteland."

Almost all programs lacked African American, Mexican American and Asian actors. The only program on the TV schedule with an all-black cast in 1951-1952 was the CBS comedy *Amos 'n' Andy*, a spin-off of a long-popular radio series that had starred two white actors in black face. In spite of the lack of other black performers on network television, the NAACP led a campaign for the cancellation of the show, which catered to white-held stereotypes of African Americans. In spite of good ratings, the show eventually could find no sponsors. CBS cancelled the program after its second season, and black people almost completely disappeared on the networks until the 1960s.

Television and Professional Sports

Before television became a feature of most Americans' homes, professional baseball reigned as the country's favorite sport. With its intricate strategy, slow pace and long pauses between action, baseball represented a perfect sport for radio. The integration of professional baseball after World War II, however, made its debut on television a culturally significant event. The National League and American League had segregated in the late nineteenth century through an informal "gentleman's agreement." As a result, up until the end of World War II, talented African American professional players spent their careers in several black baseball associations that came to be known as the "**Negro Leagues**."

Just after World War II, **Jackie Robinson** became the first African-American ball player to break major league baseball's color barrier. A child of sharecroppers, Robinson attended UCLA and lettered in four sports, but lacking financial resources, he left college just short of graduation. After the Japanese attacked Pearl Harbor, he enlisted in the Army, earning the rank of second lieutenant. Robinson, however, was arrested by military police and court martialed after he refused to move to the back of a bus while in Texas. Robinson eventually faced charges of insubordination but was acquitted and received an honorable discharge. After the war, he played for the Kansas City Monarchs in the Negro Leagues, but his talent caught the attention of the Brooklyn Dodgers organization. Robinson first played for the Dodgers on April 15, 1947 and stayed with the team until his retirement in 1956. During his career, he endured verbal abuse from fans and fellow players who called him "nigger." Some racist players deliberately injured him, and the St. Louis Cardinals at one point said they would refuse to play against him.

Nevertheless, Robinson's talent and courage allowed him to outlast his detractors, and he opened the door for other future Hall of Fame black players in the National League, such as Ernie Banks, Hank Aaron, and Willie Mays. The American League took longer to desegregate, but the sight of black professional players on television in broadcast markets often far removed from professional franchises and playing such a commanding role in what had long been considered the "national pastime" erased white myths about black physical inferiority.

No sport benefited more from the popularity of television in the 1950s than professional football. The National Football League began play in the 1920s, but had taken a distant back seat not only to professional baseball but to college football as well. Pro games rarely sold out and were usually played at college stadiums or professional baseball fields converted for football use. The biggest baseball stars like Joe DiMaggio pulled salaries of $100,000 a year or more. In contrast, most pro football players earned less than $6,000 a year, barely above the average American worker's $5,000 annual income, and had to supplement their income with jobs at car dealerships, grocery and liquor stores, or with furniture movers to pay their bills.

Football, however, with a larger ball and faster pace than baseball, proved an ideal match for television. When televised NFL games appeared on Sunday afternoons, the audience for the game grew, and by the late 1950s, 37 percent of the American public watching TV in that time slot tuned in to pro football games. A turning point in American sports history happened on December 28, 1958, when the New York Giants played the Baltimore Colts in the NFL title game. Seen in black-and-white across the nation, the championship became the first game in NFL history to go into overtime and it thus extended into prime time—the peak hours of television viewing. With the game tied 17-17, the Colts reached the goal line in the first overtime period when a fan accidentally tripped over a cable and darkened TV screens across the country. The NBC broadcasting crew sent someone onto the field to delay the game while an engineer discovered the source of the broadcast interruption and reconnected the cable. The game went back on air just in time for the audience to witness the Colts score a game-winning touchdown.

The dramatic game vastly expanded pro football's television audience, which had grown to the point that by 1960 football fans could support an NFL rival, the American Football League. Competition between the leagues created a salary arms race that brought NFL wages closer to baseball standards. Both leagues took a gamble by creating franchises in the South, where college football remained the region's favorite sport. Competitive pressures led the Dallas Cowboys of the NFL, the Dallas Texans of the AFL (a team that would become the Kansas City Chiefs in 1963), and the AFL's Houston Oilers to sign black players even though those Texas cities still enforced segregation laws. The American Football League, uncertain of its financial future, desperately searched for stars and drafted players from previously ignored historically black colleges like Grambling University. The AFL soon had a higher percentage of black players than the NFL and the arrival of star black players like Abner Haynes of the Texans helped hasten the demise of Jim Crow in the state. This process accelerated as the NFL in the mid-1960s opened franchises in New Orleans and Atlanta and the AFL in Miami. From the Civil War to the early 1960s, the South had been culturally isolated from the rest of the nation, but the arrival of professional sports helped bridge the regional distance. Southern sports fans, it turned out, could cheer for black players as long as they helped their favorite teams win games. Meanwhile, football became the new national pastime. By the end of the 1960s, pro football eclipsed baseball as the nation's most popular sport, and NFL teams, by the end of the century, could demand millions from cities for the right to host a franchise.

THE BEATS: SUBTERRANEAN REBELS

"Beatniks" eventually became an icon of the 1950s, but they inspired fear and derision in their own era. Decades later, the leaders of the **Beats** could not agree where the label applied to their generation came from. Jack Kerouac said it came from the phrase, "beat it!" meaning "leave me alone." Others suggested "beat" referred to the rhythms of the jazz music Beatniks admired. One Beat author, John Clellon Holmes, claimed it referred to being exposed, suffering raw nerves or being "beat," or exhausted in a world of nuclear threat, political crisis and painful social conformity. Whatever the origin of the term, the Beats embraced sexual rebellion, a sometimes condescending admiration of black culture, experimentation with marijuana and other drugs, and a rejection of the materialism and blandness of 1950s culture.

Four major authors defined the Beat movement: Kerouac, who authored the seminal novel *On the Road*; William S. Burroughs, writer of the disjointed and nightmarish novel *Naked Lunch*; and the openly sexual poets Gregory Corso and Allen Ginsberg, the latter whose collection of poems *Howl* celebrated homosexuality and

sparked an obscenity case. The quartet's careers blossomed in the late 1940s and early 1950s.

The four became close companions, with Kerouac, Ginsberg and Burroughs first meeting in the early 1940s and Corso joining the gang by 1950. These authors became characters in each other's novels and poetry and critiqued each other's writings. To this quartet and the Beat writers who followed, American culture in the 1950s smothered individualism and creativity. Dim-witted TV comedies, frozen foods, maddeningly repetitive and depersonalized neighborhoods such as Levittown, and the constant hypocritical praise for the "nuclear family" represented a living death for Beat novelists and poets.

The Beat writers celebrated brutal self-honesty, merging the personal and the political even as they painfully confessed sexual anxiety and self-doubt, politically incorrect thoughts, homosexual crushes, and moments of petty violence and criminality. Their lives often proved as chaotic as their writing. Such was the case with Allen Ginsberg, a gay Jew whose mother was an institutionalized schizophrenic and who was sent to a mental institution himself, and William Burroughs, a heroin addict who accidentally killed his wife trying to shoot an apple off her head in imitation of William Tell during a drug binge in Mexico. Ginsberg only had to look to his friends for inspiration when he wrote the opening lines of "Howl," his groundbreaking 1956 poem in which he described his generation as "destroyed by madness," driven by addictions and in an eternal, obsessive quest for authenticity in a plastic, phony world.

The mostly white Beats idealized African Americans as living genuine lives as an oppressed people alienated from mainstream culture. They could be maddeningly unaware of black suffering. Kerouac, author of works like *The Subterraneans* and *The Dharma Bums*, achieved fame with his epic novel *On the Road*, which followed the aimless wanderings of Salvatore Paradise and Dean Moriarty as they drive across America, get drunk, read poems, and make love. Marked by unrealistic and condescending depictions of African Americans, *On The Road* in one scene features the narrator thinking as he strolls through the streets of Denver that he wishes he "could exchange worlds with the happy, true-hearted, ecstatic Negroes of America." Kerouac reduces African Americans to childlike noble primitives and never acknowledges the violence, poverty and political marginalization experienced by such "happy Negroes."

The pace of the book, alternating between languid and frantic, derived from the art of African-American bebop musicians. Bebop artists broke the mold of the big band jazz music dominant in the early 1940s. As rebels, they earned the adoration of Beats like Kerouac. Exempli-

THE "SICK HUMOR" OF LENNY BRUCE

Comedian Lenny Bruce got arrested eight times in his 40-year-life, four times for obscenity. Yet much of the language that got him in so much trouble during his tumultuous career in the 1950s and 1960s can be heard regularly today on basic cable TV programs like South Park. **Time Magazine** in 1959 may have derided him as a "sick comic," but, as always, Lenny had an answer. "The kind of sickness I wish **Time** had written about, is that school teachers in Oklahoma get a top annual salary of $4000, while [singer] Sammy Davis Jr. gets $10,000 for a week in Vegas."

What really angered the authorities, however, was Bruce's attacks on hypocritical moralists who would get upset over four-letter words while segregation still reigned in the South and women and children got burned by bombs in Vietnam. In an age when comics usually told simple-minded, sexist jokes about their wives and mothers-in-law, Bruce pushed buttons mocking the cynicism of religious leaders, the hypocrisy of politicians, and sexual double standards. His fearlessness made him a legend but also a target of law enforcement.

Born Leonard Alfred Schneider on October 13, 1925, the future comedian was raised by a smart-alecky divorced show business mother, Sally Marr, in a working-class neighborhood in New York. "I won't say ours was a tough school, but we had our own coroner," he joked with characteristic hyperbole. "We used to write essays like: What I'm going to be if I grow up."

He joined the Navy in 1942 at the age of 16 and served on the **USS Brooklyn** during World War II, but, perhaps tiring of the rigid discipline of military life or desiring an early exit from the war, he got into trouble for wearing a dress on board the ship and then, as a joke, telling the ship's medical officer that he was experiencing homosexual urges. This led to a dishonorable discharge.

After the war, he married a stripper and showgirl named Honey Harlow who, unfortunately, was one of the close associates who introduced him to heroin. In 1955, Bruce would have a daughter with Harlow named Kitty. Moving to California, he adopted his famous stage name, made some ultra-low-budget films like Dance Hall Racket, and wrote material for his first comedy album, The Sick Humor of Lenny Bruce. One routine, about Louisiana Governor Earl Long, who spent some time in a state mental hospital, lampooned politicians who kept poor whites and blacks at each other's throats even as they robbed the state treasury. Such sophisticated jokes caught the attention of Tonight Show host Steve Allen, who featured Bruce as a guest on his television show.

Bruce's drug use gained the notice of the law. The heavily Catholic Chicago Police Department did not care for his parodies of the church. He was subjected to numerous arrests for drug possession and public obscenity, including a bust during a routine on October 4, 1961, at the Jazz Workshop in San Francisco. After describing the stupidity of the arrest and firing of a teacher for engaging in sodomy, he used a term for a person engaging in oral sex with a male. This inspired one of his most famous routines in which he parodied lawyers and the judge at his subsequent obscenity trial who kept repeating the word Bruce got arrested for. To not get arrested again, Bruce substituted the questionable word with the phrase, "blah-blah-blah." After imitating the judges, the lawyers, and even the bailiff saying the supposedly offending word, Bruce said, "And then I dug something: they sort of liked saying blah-blah-blah."

The arrests would pile up, and he would find it increasingly difficult to find nightclubs that would book him. Legally declared a pauper by a California court because of his inability to perform, two courts—one in Chicago and one in New York—convicted him of obscenity. The fear of spending time in prison seized him. Before that happened, he died of a morphine overdose in the bathroom of his dilapidated Los Angeles mansion on August 3, 1966. In 2003, he would receive, at the behest of his wife Honey Bruce, a posthumous pardon for his obscenity conviction from New York Governor George Pataki.

Lenny Bruce represents one of the most important cultural figures in the twentieth century, a fact verified by the cover of the Beatles' "Sgt. Pepper's Lonely Hearts Club Band." Lenny's face can be seen on the cover, the humorist honored by the most important rock band of the twentieth century as one of their chief inspirations. The careers of later gifted comedians, such as George Carlin, Richard Pryor, Bill Hicks, Bill Maher, and Margaret Cho, would be unimaginable if Bruce had not first blazed the trail. "Lenny Bruce dead at 40," one friend said, "Now that's obscene."

fied by artists such as Charlie Parker and Dizzy Gillespie, Bebop focused on individual performers who rejected the limits of conventional tonality. Bebop influenced other art forms. Jackson Pollack brought a Bebop sensibility to his paintings, a series of wild color splashes that led some critics to dismiss him as "Jack the Dripper."

Many new Hollywood actors in the 1950s took their cues from the Beat movement and became major youth culture idols along the way. The acting technique of stars such as James Dean, Marlon Brando, Paul Newman, and Montgomery Clift derived much from the attitude of characters in novels like *On the Road*. Movies such as *The Man with the Golden Arm* (1956), that starred popular singer Frank Sinatra as a jazz-playing junkie, and *All the Fine Young Cannibals* (1959), featuring Robert Wagner, aimed to capture the romance of the Beat hipster scene. Films like *Rebel Without a Cause* and *The Wild One* (1953) drew on Beat nihilism and rebelliousness. Not surprisingly, many of these films won a large audience of alienated teenagers eager to escape neighborhoods of look-alike homes and conformist values. Dean, who died in a car crash in 1955 at age 24 after starring in just three major films, and Brando both became major idols for a generation of frustrated and bored suburban kids.

ROCK 'N' ROLL

Few cultural innovation of the 1950s thrilled more teenagers and dismayed more parents than the rise of **rock 'n' roll**. The ultimate origins of rock music can be found in the ring shouts of West Africa. A form of praying, singing, and dancing performed as participants stood in a circle, ring shouts broke out during weddings, funerals and other religious rituals throughout West and Central Africa, the ancestral homeland of most African Americans.

Over the 200-plus years of American slavery, African music forms blended with European folk melodies and structure as the inspiration for work songs used by blacks to keep time, raise spirits, and make moral comment on their slave masters as they worked in the fields. Slave songs also led to black gospel music while the West African call-and-response style formed the structure of jazz and blues songs composed by black artists in the early twentieth century along the Mississippi River from Chicago to Memphis to New Orleans. Another source for rock music came from the boogie style of piano-playing inspired by the hectic pace of life in African-American urban neighborhoods. With the structure of a blues band centered on a lead singer backed by the guitar, drums, bass, and piano in various combinations, the way was paved for the rise of rock music.

As the music evolved, a new invention—the electric guitar—entered the sound mix. By 1940, pioneer blues artists like T-Bone Walker regularly played electric guitar riffs as part of stage performances. If rock primarily derived from African heritage, however, rural southern white and black musicians fed off of and challenged each other, with Bob Wills and the Texas Playboys playing white backwoods country and western music blended with urban African-American blues and the sophisticated big band sounds from the East Coast to create a new genre called western swing music.

The cross-pollination of diverse musical styles accelerated with the development of sound recording in the late nineteenth and early twentieth century and the wider distribution of 78 rpm music "records" by mid-century. As radio formats changed from comedy and drama programming to music, white children in the late 1940s and early 1950s saw a chance to rebel and experience greater sexual expression as they danced to "race records"—blues songs recorded by black performers like Big Mamma Thornton and Fats Domino.

Memphis became an incubator for rock music by the early 1950s. Guitar masters like B.B. King stretched the boundaries of urban blues. Record producer Sam Phillips meanwhile assembled a stable of artists that would dominate American youth music for the next decade first at the self-named Phillips Records, which opened for business in 1950, and then at Sun Records starting in 1952. Over the years, Phillips would polish raw talents like Jerry Lee Lewis, Carl Perkins, Roy Orbison, and Johnny Cash at tiny studios, launching them into national stardom.

Phillips acted as B.B. King's producer and in 1951 worked with musician Ike Turner on a recording of "Rocket 88," a number in praise of the American automobile and highlighted by a fuzzy, highly amplified electric guitar playing to a boogie rhythm. The lyrics and the arrangement have led many music historians to label "Rocket 88" as the first rock 'n' roll single. "Rocket 88" would soon also be recorded by Bill Haley and the Comets. Haley later released the hit "Rock Around the Clock," a top-seller featured on the sound track of the juvenile delinquency-themed movie *The Blackboard Jungle*.

Haley would be one of many white artists who made hit versions of songs originally written and performed by black musicians and composers. Most African-American performers remained uncompensated when white singers recorded hits based on their compositions. Nevertheless, the rapid rise of rock music opened the door for black performers like Fats Domino, Little Richard, and Chuck Berry to win an army of young white fans and to reach an even larger audience through variety programs like *The Ed Sullivan Show*. No black or white artist, however,

The Comic Book Wars

Many of the American soldiers in World War II entered military service while still in their teens, and they brought youthful reading habits with them to the front. Sensing an opportunity for good publicity and to create new readers, comic book publishers provided free copies of **Superman***,* **Batman***, the detective series* **Dick Tracy***, and science fiction fare to appreciative servicemen during the war. Many of these young men continued to feed their new comic book habit when they returned to the United States after 1945.*

Following the war, many comic books took a more sexual and violent turn. Perhaps frightened and deeply marked by the horrors of the Second World War, the Holocaust, the atomic bombings of Hiroshima and Nagasaki, and the mayhem that broke out in Korea in 1950, young readers enjoyed escaping into the fantasy bloodshed regularly featured in the popular new "horror comics" like **Tales from the Crypt***,* **The Crypt of Terror***,* **The Vault of Horror** *and* **Weird***, many published by EC, a company run by William M. Gaines.*

The content of the horror comics reflected the youthful distrust of the phony pieties surrounding institutions such as marriage and the family. In these stories, weaklings turn the tables on the strong, thus appealing to youths coping with schoolyard bullies or the random dictates of their parents. In one story, a housewife can no longer stand the tyranny of her obsessively neat, orderly husband. She murders him and when police arrive, they see jars containing body parts labeled "kneecaps (2), toes (10), heart (1)." The wife, Eleanor, tells a detective, "I remember wanting to show him I could be neat! I wanted it to be a neat job! I cleaned up everything when I finished!"

Gaines's horror comics also published illustrated versions of budding science fiction writers like Ray Bradbury. His artists intentionally defied convention, drawing villains to resemble the pope and heroes to bear a striking resemblance to Soviet dictator Joseph Stalin. Gaines also published **Mad Magazine***, founded in 1952, which in its early years parodied other comic books like* **Superman** *and even Walt Disney's* **Mickey Mouse***.*

With the horror comics adding to the violent content common on television police dramas and Westerns, Dr. Fredric Wertham, a famous Freudian psychiatrist, warned parents that popular culture threatened the mental health of their children. Wertham's 1954 book **The Seduction of the Innocent: The Influence of Comic Books on Today's Youth** *attacked comic books like* **Batman** *for the supposed subliminal homosexual relationship between the title hero and his youthful sidekick, Robin. Wertham claimed that comic books glorified violence as a solution to all problems, and thus promoted juvenile delinquency.*

Fearing public backlash, the possibility of boycotts, and the threat that Congress or the states might pass laws censoring content, comic book publishers formed the Comics Magazine Association of America, which in turn created the Comics Code Authority. The CCA would give or withhold a seal of approval from each issue of each comic book. To earn the seal, comic book stories could not in any way create sympathy for criminals; cause disrespect for police, judges, or other government officials; had to always present good as triumphing over evil; and could never use lurid or gory images to accompany the content. The code forbade the words "terror" or "horror" in comic book titles, as well as scenes of bloodshed, cannibalism, or sadism.

With bland content now mandated voluntarily by the industry, comic book sales plummeted. For instance, in 1955, DC Comics (which published **Superman** *and* **Batman***) sold 10.5 million copies of all its publications. Two years later, sales had dropped by more than 50 percent. Meanwhile, Gaines switched his focus to* **Mad** *magazine, which expanded its focus to satirize politics, television programs, popular music, social movements, and advertising. Publishing* **Mad** *as a "magazine," Gaines would not have to worry about compliance with the comic books code.* **Mad** *became far more rebellious and anti-establishment than any of the horror comics had ever been.* **Mad** *became a major inspiration for later comedy television programs such as* **Saturday Night Live** *and* **The Simpsons** *and the online newspaper parody* **The Onion***.*

matched the popularity or fame of **Elvis Presley,** born to a dirt-poor Tupelo, Mississippi, family in 1935.

Sam Phillips would produce and engineer a custom-made record for anyone who came into his studio for $2 a side. In 1954, Elvis Presley appeared at the studio to record a pair of songs for his mother. Presley lobbied Phillips to record him for a professional release and the collaboration produced a single of the old blues number, "That's All Right." Phillips delivered a tape of the session to a Memphis radio station where a friendly disc jockey played the song six times in a row to an enthusiastic listening audience. By the time the record was finally released, there was a back order of 5,000 copies in the Memphis area, before the recording reached number one on the city's country and western sales charts. By mid-1955, Presley enjoyed his first national country and western hit.

Signed by the flamboyant agent "Colonel" Tom Parker, who would over the years cheat his protégé out of millions of dollars, Presley would become the first rock 'n' roll superstar. He recorded a remarkable string of number one hits such as "Heartbreak Hotel," "Hound Dog," and "Jailhouse Rock." Presley's curling upper lip, untamed bangs and erotically charged dance moves led teenage girls in his audience to scream and weep. His openly sexual approach to music stirred controversy and attracted gigantic audiences when he appeared on the *Milton Berle* and *Ed Sullivan* television shows. Parents worried that Presley's music would inspire sexual promiscuity among excited teenage girls. Alarmed by the clear influence of black music on white performers like Presley and other rock stars, the secretary of the North Alabama White Citizens Council warned in a 1956 television message that "Rock and roll is a means of pulling the white man down to the level of the Negro. It is part of a plot to undermine the morals of the youth of our nation."

In 1950s, adults also perceived rock 'n' roll as "children's music," as comedian Tom Lehrer put it. Newspapers and magazines disparaged youth culture and paid it scant attention. When an airplane crash in 1959 killed rock stars Buddy Holly, Ritchie Valens, and J.P. Richardson, famous as the "Big Bopper," many newspapers ran the story on inside pages. But rock 'n' roll would be influenced by politically oriented folk-music recorded by singer-songwriter Bob Dylan and others in the early 1960s, and would exercise a profound effect on the adult politics of war and civil rights in the coming decade. Young whites who eagerly bought rock records featuring songs written by or first performed by black musicians or released by black artists themselves developed an appreciation for African-American culture that deeply influenced the attitudes of the Sixties generation.

THE LASTING INFLUENCE OF THE 1950s

In 1971, singer-songwriter Don McLean released an epic hit song, "American Pie," which traced in symbolic language the journey of American politics and culture from the time of the plane crash that killed Buddy Holly and his fellow rock stars in 1959 to the assassinations and climate of fear that menaced society by the end of the 1960s. In McLean's lyrics, Buddy Holly's death is characterized as the "day the music died," but more broadly the songwriter suggested that America passed from a more innocent time just after World War II to an epoch of disillusionment and division during the Vietnam War.

Gauzy nostalgia apparently distorted McLean's memories of the 1950s. The reality was more tumultuous. The expectations, frustrations, and dreams that fueled the Women's Movement of the 1960s and 1970s—what Betty Friedan would call "the problem with no name"—were in place by the early 1950s. The African American Civil Rights Movement, meanwhile, had already reached full tilt, and blacks had already scored some of their most important legal victories in their campaign for equality before 1960, starting with the 1954 *Brown v. Board of Education* decision. Mexican-American politics remained largely shaped by conservatism, but young Mexicans had before them the model of black protestors. The triumphs and tragedy of the African American civil rights campaign in the Fifties inspired a more radical Chicano generation a decade later. Turmoil marked the Fifties, with only some of the ferment under the surface.

American sexual attitudes had always been more varied than the myth promoted by the decade's situation comedies. Most did not live the tame, bland, conformist existence portrayed on programs like *The Donna Reed Show*. Behind the walls of those suburban homes, Americans experimented with premarital sex, adultery, homosexuality, and alternative family structures. If the 1960s would be characterized as the "Sexual Revolution," the first shots of that rebellion had been fired in the late 1940s and the 1950s. The popular culture reflected this more open sexuality in advertising. Movies, suffering a loss of audience because of the growing ownership of television sets, also became more frankly erotic in content.

Behind a sexual opening up of the culture loomed a growing awareness of the mass market provided by those millions of children born during the Baby Boom. In the earliest days of television, children's programs rapidly expanded, and advertisers realized they could go over the heads of parents and aim their commercials for toy guns, Barbie Dolls, and G.I. Joe soldiers directly at children. As these children reached a rebellious adolescence, they wanted music, magazines, and movies that pushed the cultural envelope, that pierced the veil of the hypocritically Victorian middle class.

By the late twentieth century, conservatives would hail the 1950s as the "anti-1960s," in other words a golden age of sexual discretion, intact nuclear families, patriotism, traditional values, and a respect for authority. Hollywood movies of the era, however, reveal a wide array of anxieties haunting what one 1970s television sitcom called *Happy Days*. The plots of movies from 1945 to 1960 reflect fears not just about the role of men in the post-war world, the impact of more assertive women on society, and the menace of juvenile delinquency. Movie audiences in the 1950s also shared with Hollywood screenwriters worries about the dangers of conformity and McCarthyism (the subtext of the 1956 science fiction classic *Invasion of the Body Snatchers*), and the threat to human survival posed by nuclear weapons (an anxiety evident in a flood of movies about monsters created by radiation such as 1954's *Godzilla and Them!*, and 1955's *It Came From Beneath the Sea*). Monsters ranging from giant ants to masculinized, ambitious women terrified Americans, many of whom had only to glance at their backyard bomb shelters to be reminded of how fragile their suburban world had become.

The 1950s served as the necessary prelude to the decade of hippies, war protestors, and youth rebellion that would shortly follow. Teenagers who engaged in "heavy petting," who idolized movie stars like James Dean and rock stars like Elvis, had already walked away from the worldview of their parents. Many youths in the 1960s would conclude that Auschwitz and Hiroshima consumed one world and that a new one must rise from its ashes, but doubts about America's religious values and cultural priorities, its Cold War politics, about the media and the country's leaders, sank deep roots in the fifteen years from 1945 and 1960.

TABLE 26.1 Key Moments in the Civil Rights Movement, 1945-1960

Event	Date(s)	Significance
Executive Order 9981	July 26, 1948	President Harry Truman orders the United States military to desegregate.
Delgado v. Bastrop ISD decision	November 1, 1948	A U.S. District Court orders Texas school districts to stop segregating Mexican American school children, with an exception for first-grade language instruction.
Sweatt v. Painter decision	June 5, 1950	The U.S. Supreme Court orders the University of Texas law school to admit an African American applicant, Heman Sweatt.
Brown v. Board of Education decision	May 17, 1954	The U.S. Supreme Court rules that segregation of public schools is unconstitutional.
Montgomery Bus Boycott	December 5, 1955-December 20, 1956	Prompts an accelerating wave of protests against segregation, contributes to a December 20, 1956 U.S. Supreme Court decision ordering desegregation of Montgomery's buses, and catapults Martin Luther King, Jr. to national civil rights leadership.
Little Rock Crisis	September 2- 25, 1957	Arkansas Gov. Orval Faubus uses the National Guard to prevent nine African American teenagers from starting classes at all-white Central High in Little Rock but President Dwight Eisenhower later nationalizes the troops to ensure the students begin classes.
Civil Rights Act of 1957	September 9, 1957	Establishes a Civil Rights Commission and prohibits intimidation of voters.
Sit-in Movement	February 1, 1960	Beginning with four African Americans who sit in at a whites-only lunch counter in Greensboro, N.C., this event inspires a wave of "direct action" protests against segregation that continues for several years.

Chronology

1944   *Smith v. Allwright* decision.

1946   President's Committee on Civil Rights issues its report, "To Secure These Rights."
Post war "Baby Boom" begins.

1947   Jackie Robinson breaks Major League Baseball's color barrier.

1948   Executive Order 9981 ordering desegregation of the military.
Delgado v. Bastrop ISD ruling.
Alfred Kinsey's *Sexual Behavior in the Human Male* becomes a bestseller.

1950   United Nations Educational, Scientific and Cultural Organization issues its "Statement on Race."
Sweatt v. Painter decision.

1951   The Mattachine Society forms.

1952   Walter-McCarran Act.

1953   *Playboy Magazine* begins publication.

1954   *Brown v. Board of Education* decision.
The first "White Citizens Council."
Fred Werthem's book *The Seduction of the Innocent: The Influence of Comic Books on Today's Youth* is published.

1955   Emmett Till beaten to death.
Montgomery Bus Boycott begins.

1956   Interstate Commerce Act.
Allen Ginsberg's *Howl* and *Other Poems* is published.
Elvis Presley makes television performances.

1957   The Little Rock school desegregation crisis.
Jack Kerouac's novel *On The Road* is published.

1959   Buddy Holly, Ritchie Valens and J.P, "The Big Bopper" Richardson, die in a plane crash.

SUGGESTED READINGS

Robert H. Abzug. *Inside the Vicious Heart: Americans and the Liberation of Nazi Concentration Camps* (1985).

Rodolfo Acuña. *Occupied America: A History of Chicanos* (1988).

Elazar Barkan. *The Retreat of Scientific Racism: Changing Concepts of Race in Britain and the United States between the World Wars* (1993).

Taylor Branch. *Parting The Waters: America in the King Years, 1954-63* (1988).

Stephanie Coontz. *The Way We Never Were: American Families and the Nostalgia Trap* (2000).

John D'Emilio and Estelle B. Freedman. *Intimate Matters: A History of Sexuality in America* (1997).

Rachel Devlin, *A Girl Stands at the Door: The Generation of Young Women Who Desegregated America's Schools* (2018).

Neil Foley. *Quest for Equality: The Failed Promise of Black-Brown Solidarity* (2010).

Byrne Fone. *Homophobia: A History* (2000).

Edward Halsey Foster. *Understanding the Beats* (1992).

Risa L. Goluboff, *The Lost Promise of Civil Rights* (2010).

Sherna Berger Gluck. *Rosie the Riveter Revisited: Women, the War and Social Change* (1988).

David Halberstam. *The Fifties* (1993).

Elaine Tyler May. *Homeward Bound: American Families in the Cold War Era* (1988).

Daniel Okrent, *The Guarded Gate: Bigotry, Eugenics, and the Law That Kept Two Generations of Jews, Italians, and Other European Immigrants Out of America* (2019).

Sean Patrick O'Rourke and Lesli K. Pace, *Like Wildfire: The Rhetoric of the Civil Rights Sit-Ins* (2020).

Eric Schlosser. *Fast Food Nation: The Dark Side of the All-American Meal* (2002).

Amilcar Shabazz. *Advancing Democracy: African Americans and the Struggle for Access and Equity in Higher Education in Texas* (2006).

William Karl Thomas. *Lenny Bruce: The Making of a Prophet* (1989).

Timothy Tyson, *The Blood of Emmett Till* (2017).

Review Questions

1. What factors led to the decline of scientific racism and to President Harry Truman's support for Civil Rights for African Americans after World War II?

2. What legal cases led to the overturn of segregation at public schools and colleges and in what ways did white Southerners resist implementation of these decisions?

3. What changes happened in the lives of American women after World War II and how were women portrayed in the culture?

4. What themes did the Beats explore in their novels and their poetry and what impact did they have on the broader American culture?

5. How did American adults view youth culture—comic books, science fiction, and rock 'n' roll—in the 1950s?

Glossary of Important People and Concepts

American GI Forum
Baby Boom
Beats
Brown v. Board of Education of Topeka
Delgado v. Bastrop ISD
Eugenics
Orval Faubus
Interstate Highway Act of 1956
Alfred Kinsey
League of United Latin American Citizens
Little Rock Crisis
"Massive Resistance"
Mattachine Society
Montgomery Bus Boycott
Negro Leagues
On The Road
"Operation Wetback"
Rosa Parks
Elvis Presley
Rebel Without a Cause
Jackie Robinson
Rock 'n' Roll
Sweatt v. Painter
Emmett Till
The Twilight Zone

**Harry Truman and Lyndon Baines Johnson
(day of Medicare Bill Signing).
July 30, 1965**

Chapter Twenty-seven

KENNEDY & JOHNSON AND THE VIETNAM WAR

In Liberty, Mississippi, on September 25, 1961, a member of the all-white state legislature, E.H. Hurst, murdered an African-American man and former childhood friend, Herbert Lee, when the latter tried to register as a voter. In front of a cotton gin, Hurst shot Lee in the head as he sat in the cab of his truck. Lee fell out of the vehicle, and his body was left lying in an expanding pool of blood for two hours before a black undertaker picked up the body.

A farmer and father of nine, Lee had been active in the voter registration drive conducted in the black community by the Student Nonviolent Coordinating Committee (SNCC). He acted as a chauffeur for the group's leader, Robert Parris Moses, a Harlem native who moved to the rural community to head the campaign. Even though Hurst murdered Lee outdoors in broad daylight in front of several witnesses, a coroner's jury ruled the death a justifiable homicide. Hurst claimed that Lee owed him money and became threatening when the politician demanded payment. Hurst also told the jury he had accidentally pulled the trigger on his .38 pistol. One African-American witness, Louis Allen, had been threatened and out of fear testified before the jury that the five-foot-four Lee had tried to strike Hurst, who stood more than six feet, in the head with a tire iron.

*By October, a federal grand jury had convened to consider indicting Hurst for violating Lee's civil rights. Allen told Moses that he was willing to recant his earlier statements and would testify that Hurst killed Lee without provocation. Moses called the U.S. Department of Justice (DOJ) and tried to get protection for Allen, but the DOJ turned him down. Later, an FBI agent tipped off the local sheriff's department that Allen was planning to testify against Hurst. Allen was attacked, the assailant breaking the witness's jaw with a flashlight. Shortly thereafter, on January 31, 1964, an as-*sassin killed Allen with three shotgun blasts. That killer also was never punished.*

THE 1960 PRESIDENTIAL ELECTION

Presidential candidates largely overlooked the civil rights struggle in the 1960 election. Several signs pointed to a favorable year for the Democrats, out of power in the White House for the eight years of Dwight Eisenhower, but the party still relied heavily on its southern segregationist wing. Senator **John F. Kennedy** of Massachusetts, who waged an unsuccessful campaign to win the party's vice presidential nomination in 1956, opened the race as a top contender because of family money, a highly publicized war record, his personal attractiveness, and the glamour of his wife, the former Jacquelyn Bouvier. Kennedy feared alienating key white southern politicians as he fought an uphill primary battle with two-time presidential nominee Adlai Stevenson, the favorite of the liberal wing, and Senate Majority Leader **Lyndon Johnson** of Texas, who expected to draw heavy support from southern and western states. Kennedy avoided discussing civil rights issues as much as he could during his primary battle, and he actively courted and won an early endorsement from arch-segregationist Alabama Governor John Patterson.

Kennedy had essentially run for the presidency since 1957. That year saw publication of his second book, *Profiles in Courage*, a series of biographical sketches of eight senators who defied the wishes of their party or risked political popularity because of principle. The book, reportedly ghost-written by Kennedy family friend and speechwriter Ted Sorensen, became a bestseller and established Kennedy's intellectual credentials. However, the Massachusetts senator had to fight to win over liberals in his own party. His wealthy father, Joseph P. Kennedy, a former ambassador to England, had been seen as an appeaser of Hitler's Germany in the days leading to World War II. The elder Kennedy was a close friend of red-baiting Senator Joseph McCarthy. Finally, during debates on a 1957 Civil Rights Act, John Kennedy had sided with southern segregationists on some issues. Liberals did not trust him because they felt that during his Senate career, as Eleanor Roosevelt said, he had shown "more profile than courage."

Kennedy's obvious intelligence, charm, humor and good looks, however, proved to be potent political weapons. The big challenge came in the West Virginia primary contest against Minnesota Senator Hubert Humphrey. Many expected Kennedy's Catholicism to be a problem with West Virginia's overwhelmingly Protestant voters. The only other serious Catholic candidate for president in American history had been Democratic nominee Al Smith in the 1928 presidential race, and Smith lost badly, to a large degree because Protestant voters believed that a Catholic president would be subservient to the Pope and would weaken American independence.

In speeches Kennedy told voters, "I refuse to believe that I was denied the right to be president on the day I was baptized." During a television broadcast in West Virginia, he said, ". . . [W]hen any man stands on the steps of the capitol and takes the oath of office of president, he is swearing to support the separation of church and state . . . And if he breaks that oath, he is not only committing a crime against the Constitution, for which the Congress can impeach him—and should impeach him—he is committing a sin against God." Kennedy beat Humphrey in the West Virginia primary by a comfortable margin and convinced Democratic Party elders that a Catholic could win the general election. Humphrey dropped out of the race and at the Democratic National Convention that summer, Kennedy captured the Democratic nomination on the first ballot. In a controversial move protested even by his brother and campaign manager Bobby, John Kennedy selected Johnson as his running mate. The move was aimed to comfort southern Democrats but antagonized party liberals who questioned Johnson's commitment to civil rights.

Civil Rights and the 1960 Campaign

The Republican Party platform included planks friendly to civil rights, but the party's nominee, Vice President Richard Nixon, tripped over himself trying not to alienate black voters while at the same time hoping to carry white southern voters as successfully as Eisenhower had in 1952 and 1956. Kennedy, meanwhile, realized that the black vote could swing six of the eight most populous states his way in the November elections. Liberal advisors persuaded him to reach out to African Americans. Kennedy soon promised that with a "stroke of the pen" he would end discrimination in federally funded housing. An incident in Georgia, however, provided an important, lucky opportunity for the Democrat to win over African-American voters.

On October 19, less than a month before the election, police arrested civil rights leader **Martin Luther King, Jr.**, along with 53 other African-American protestors at Rich's Department Store in Atlanta, for refusing to leave tables at the segregated Magnolia Room Restaurant. King was sentenced to four months' hard labor for supposedly driving with a suspended license and was transferred to Reidsville State Prison. Members of the King family feared that the minister would be murdered while in custody.

Nixon instructed aides to tell the press that the vice president would offer no comment on the issue. The Kennedy campaign, however, saw an immediate opportunity to gain ground with African-American voters. "They're going to kill him—I know they're going to kill him," King's wife Coretta, who was six months pregnant, said in an urgent call to Harris Wofford, the Kennedy campaign's civil rights advisor. Wofford sent an urgent message to Kennedy, who was campaigning in Chicago and in Michigan. Kennedy placed an immediate call to Mrs. King and told her he would see if he could assist the family. Campaign manager Bobby Kennedy phoned the judge who had sentenced King. Within days, authorities released the minister from jail.

The civil rights leader's father, the influential minister Martin Luther King, Sr., said, "I had expected to vote against Senator Kennedy because of his religion. But now he can be my president, Catholic or whatever he is. It took courage to call my daughter-in-law at a time like this." A blue-bound election pamphlet distributed to African-American church congregations quoted the elder King's endorsement and spread among black congregations in the days leading to the presidential election. Kennedy had won over black voters worried about his Catholic background, but his religion continued to be an issue with white Protestants.

The Catholic Issue Returns

As it became increasingly possible that Kennedy might win the November election, several prominent Protestant ministers, such as evangelist Billy Graham, bestselling author Norman Vincent Peale, and W.A. Criswell (head of the largest Southern Baptist congregation in the world, First Baptist Church of Dallas) warned that a Catholic president represented a threat to religious freedom in America. Kennedy had in fact split with the Catholic Church on numerous issues, for instance backing bills that provided federal funds for public schools but not funding for parochial schools, and opposing the appointment of an American diplomat to Vatican City. Kennedy concluded he had no choice but to directly address the issue as he had in the West Virginia primary, and the forum he chose was the Greater Houston Ministerial Association on September 12.

Many historians, journalists and political scientists rate it as the future president's finest performance in the campaign. "I believe in an America where the separation of church and state is absolute—where no Catholic prelate would tell the president (should he be a Catholic) how to act, and where no Protestant minister would tell his parishioners for whom to vote," Kennedy said. The press covering the event interpreted this as the moment when Americans grew comfortable with the idea of a Catholic president. For the rest of the campaign Kennedy largely focused on Eisenhower's handling of the Cold War and the sluggish economy, and tried to shift blame for these failings to Richard Nixon.

Television and the Kennedy-Nixon Debates

Television news came of age during the 1960 campaign, and the signal moment arrived with the four **Kennedy-Nixon Debates**—the first time ever that presidential nominees directly debated each other, let alone on national television. A champion college debater, Nixon had judged Kennedy's acceptance speech at the Democratic National Convention during the summer as a failure and, in a moment of overconfidence, agreed to appear on a television stage with the junior senator from Massachusetts. Exhausted from an effort to keep a campaign promise to appear in all 50 states, ill, and still suffering from a knee injury suffered shortly after he became the Republican nominee, Nixon arrived at the CBS television studios in poor shape for the critical first debate.

An estimated 70 million Americans watched the first debate, which marked a shift in American culture in which Americans increasingly got their information from television rather than newspapers. Following their first TV face-off, the consensus of the media and the political world was that a cool-headed Kennedy had triumphed and achieved his primary goal of attaining presidential stature standing next to nervous Richard Nixon. Nixon, stumbling over his words, directed his comments toward his debate opponent, often did not look at the camera, and appeared to be talking down to the Democrat. Kennedy, with a better understanding of television, appeared calm and self-assured as he spoke directly to the TV audience.

There was scarcely any distance between the two candidates on the issues. The sharpest difference came over Fidel Castro's regime in Cuba. Kennedy had been briefed by the State Department about CIA plans to overthrow Castro, who was moving toward an alliance with the Soviet Union. During the debates, Kennedy pushed for a more aggressive stance toward Castro. Not wanting to tip off the secret CIA planning to the Russians, Nixon attacked Kennedy's posture as reckless, but ended up making himself, in the intense Cold War climate of the day, look weak and vacillating.

The election was a squeaker. Kennedy carried only 49.7 percent of the popular vote as opposed to Nixon's 49.5 percent, a raw vote difference of 118,550 ballots out of nearly 69 million votes. Nixon would suggest that Kennedy won the Electoral College 303 to 219 because corrupt Democratic political boss Richard Daley, mayor of Chicago, stuffed ballot boxes. In Illinois, Kennedy's margin was 8,856 out of a total of 4.75 million. Voting results in Chicago were suspicious. In Chicago's 50th Ward, 222 registered voters somehow cast seventy-four votes for Kennedy and three for Nixon. Regardless, even if one accepts Nixon's later claims that Kennedy stole Illinois' 27 Electoral College votes, that would not have been enough for Nixon to win the Electoral College.

Kennedy did extremely well among Catholic voters, carrying 80 percent as opposed to the usual 67 percent carried by Democratic presidential candidates. In the industrial Midwest states, his gains among Catholics offset losses from anti-Catholic voters. Meanwhile, even though at the start of the Democratic Convention Kennedy was the least popular among the party's major candidates among African Americans, on Election Day he carried 70 percent of black votes. This constituency provided his margin of victory in South Carolina and Texas, and also may have pushed him over the top in nine other states, including electoral-vote rich Michigan, New Jersey, and Pennsylvania. Whatever his emotional distance regarding the civil rights struggle, Kennedy probably owed his presidency to African Americans.

THE "NEW FRONTIER"

At the time, John Kennedy's opening words as president struck the audience in Washington, and the larger television audience around the world, as an eloquent promise of American resolve to make the world a better place.

On a day when eight inches of snow fell and the temperature was 22 degrees (which felt like 7 degrees when the wind chill was considered) Kennedy still stirred his heavily bundled inaugural audience on January 20, 1961, with this bold notice: "Let every nation know, whether it wishes us well or ill, that we shall pay any price, bear any burden, meet any hardship, support any friend, oppose any foe, in order to assure the survival and the success of liberty."

The words proved sadly prophetic. The audience could not know it, but in their drive to pay any price and bear any burden, Kennedy and his two successors would commit American prestige, money, and troops in increasing numbers to oppose what was seen as a global communist menace in Cuba, Vietnam, Cambodia, and Laos. A decade after Kennedy's inaugural speech, with its promise of an aggressive foreign and military policy, Americans would tire of both the price and the burden of extending what Kennedy called the "**New Frontier**" around the globe. The first act in a tragic drama would unfold within weeks in Cuba.

The Bay of Pigs Fiasco

During the Eisenhower administration, the CIA formulated a plan for the invasion of Cuba and the overthrow of Fidel Castro. The agency informed Kennedy that the plan was ready for implementation soon after he took office. Kennedy, a fan of the *James Bond* spy novels written by British author Ian Fleming, liked the boldness of the scheme and signed off on the operation. On April 17, 1961, a force of 1,400 CIA-trained and armed Cuban exiles landed at the **Bay of Pigs** in Cuba. The CIA had failed to notice the presence of coral reefs in the bay. The reefs tore the undersides of several landing craft. Swamps surrounded the landing site, trapping the invaders. Castro responded quickly, and Cuban ground forces and attack planes routed the invaders. As the invasion instantly went awry, Kennedy cancelled a planned air strike for fear it would reveal the degree of American complicity in the invasion. The incident would foster in Kennedy a strong distrust of the military and intelligence leadership that had assured him that Cubans would support the invasion and that the invasion would succeed. Publicly, a shaken president took responsibility for the failure. "Victory has a hundred fathers and defeat is an orphan," he told a press conference.

The botched invasion inspired a Cuba obsession within the Kennedy administration. In the coming months, the CIA concocted a variety of schemes to overthrow Castro. The agency's "Operation Mongoose," involved plans to sabotage the Cuban economy and concocted outlandish plots for killing Castro. Knowing that the Cuban leader liked to scuba dive, the CIA drew up an assassination scheme that involved planting explosives in a colorfully painted shell in hopes it would draw Castro's attention. Castro liked to smoke cigars, so CIA planners discussed planting in Castro's possession an exploding cigar with enough firepower to kill him. The CIA knew that Mafia kingpins wanted to get even with

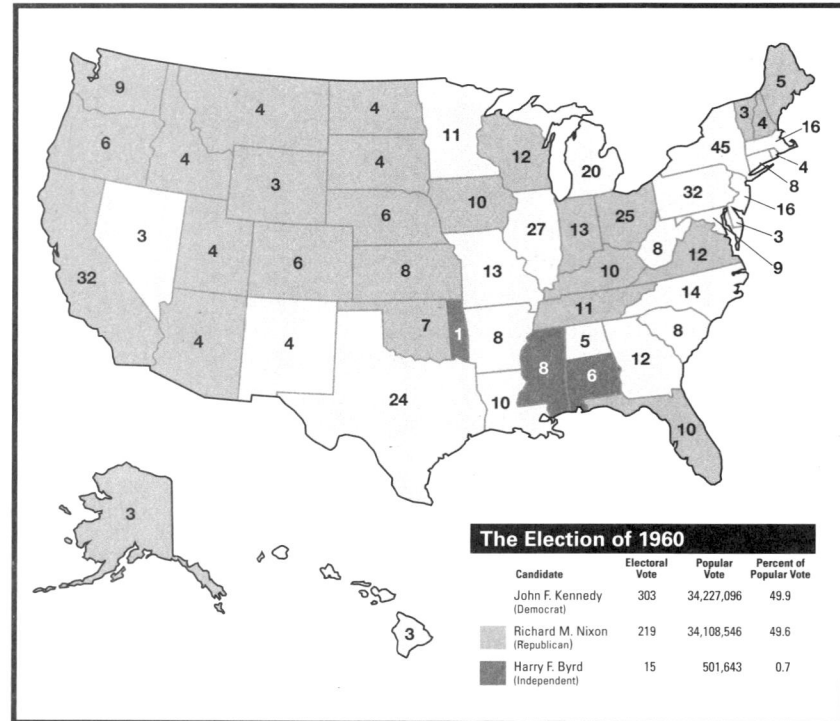

Map 27.1 The Election of 1960

The Election of 1960			
Candidate	Electoral Vote	Popular Vote	Percent of Popular Vote
John F. Kennedy (Democrat)	303	34,227,096	49.9
Richard M. Nixon (Republican)	219	34,108,546	49.6
Harry F. Byrd (Independent)	15	501,643	0.7

**President and Mrs. Kennedy
arrive at the National Guard
Armory in Washington for the
Inaugural Ball.
Jan. 20, 1961
Photo credit: Abbie Rowe,
National Park
Service/JFK Library**

Castro because he had closed down lucrative casinos in Havana and eliminated mob-run drug and prostitution rings in the island capital. The intelligence agency offered $150,000 to mob leaders Sam Giancana, Santos Trafficante and Johnny Roselli in return for a successful assassination of Castro, but none of these attempts succeeded. Meanwhile, the failed Bay of Pigs invasion and the plots against Castro worsened U.S.-Soviet relations and set the stage for the Cuban Missile Crisis.

The Berlin Wall

Kennedy and Soviet leader Nikita Khrushchev faced off against each other in a summit in Vienna in June 1961, just two months after the Bay of Pigs disaster. Many Kennedy advisors wanted the president to cancel the meeting, expecting it would result only in escalating tensions, but Kennedy wanted to present himself as a strong, resolute leader willing to stand up to his adversaries face-to-face. The meeting proved to be another embarrassment. Khrushchev berated Kennedy, whom he saw (in the wake of the Cuban incident) as weak and indecisive. Kennedy wanted Khrushchev to back down in his support of communist insurgencies in Southeast Asia, but the Soviet leader insisted that the USSR had a moral obligation to support what he called "wars of liberation." The two leaders butted heads on the issue of Berlin. The city had been divided since the end of World War II, with American allies controlling the western part of the city and the Soviet Union and its allies controlling the east. At various times, the Soviets had cut off access to West Berlin, which was surrounded by East Germany.

Kennedy declared that the United States would defend West Berlin at all costs.

Kennedy returned home worried that the Soviets were contemplating starting a nuclear World War III. He went on national television, called up the reserves, and asked the public to support doubling the size of the military draft, the mass construction of bomb shelters, increased funds for civil defense, and a boost in the military budget by $3 billion. Meanwhile, through the summer 6,000 East Germans fled to West Berlin every day. In response, the East German government constructed a 12-foot wall, complete with sniper nests, which would divide the city until the fall of the communist regime in 1989. After a year had passed, the Berlin Wall was more than seven miles long and fences were placed around the remaining almost 92 miles of East Berlin. Over the years at least 163 men and women died attempting to cross from East to West Berlin. Meanwhile the Soviet Union resumed testing nuclear weapons, and Kennedy responded in kind.

The Cuban Missile Crisis

The Bay of Pigs misadventure had a terrifying sequel. Alarmed by America's attempts to unseat him, Castro pleaded for more visible support from the Soviet Union. Khrushchev ordered the installation of Soviet nuclear missiles in Cuba capable of striking any major city on the American East Coast. By the fall of 1962 American spy planes had photographs of the missile sites under construction. That October, during the **Cuban Missile Crisis**, the world came as close as it ever did to a nuclear holocaust.

Kennedy's military advisers proposed a wide range of options, including bombing the missile sites or an invasion of Cuba. Kennedy opted for a naval blockade of Cuba, what he called a "quarantine," which would intercept Soviet ships carrying missile parts. Four missile sites in Cuba were fully operational, and nuclear warheads were already on the island. Nineteen American ships stood between Cuba and a fleet of 25 Soviet vessels. Ship captains were ordered to stop any vessel with a cargo hold large enough to contain a nuclear warhead. Soviet vessels approached the American ships, but half turned back while the other half stopped their advance. "Doomsday didn't happen that day because we were lucky," a Kennedy advisor later recalled.

On October 26-27, the White House received two very different teletype messages from Khrushchev. In one, the Soviet leader insisted that the missiles in Cuba were for defensive purposes only and that the Russian ships that approached Cuba did not carry weapons. Khrushchev urged Kennedy to ratchet down the tension so as to not ". . . doom the world to the catastrophe of thermonuclear war." Khrushchev suggested that Kennedy promise that he would not invade Cuba. In return, the Soviet Union would withdraw military advisors from the island. The next day, the White House received an angrier message from Moscow. This time, the Soviet leader insisted that the United States withdraw nuclear warheads from Turkey before the Kremlin would consider removing missiles from Cuba. Presidential advisers argued over how to respond to the mixed messages coming out of Moscow. Meanwhile, a plume of smoke wafted from chimneys at the Soviet Embassy as staff, worried about the likelihood of war, began burning secret documents.

The president's brother, Attorney General Robert Kennedy, proposed that the president ignore the angry second message and respond positively to the more friendly and conciliatory first teletype. A positive response was sent, but the Soviets were warned not to reveal the American agreement to pull missiles out of Turkey. (Kennedy had already planned this course of action anyway.) Meanwhile, Bobby Kennedy warned Soviet ambassador Anatoly Dobrynin that unless the missiles were removed, a bombing raid would be authorized.

For several hours the Cabinet awaited what they feared would be Armageddon. Then, on Sunday morning, October 28, a radio bulletin announced that Khrushchev had accepted Kennedy's terms for ending the standoff. Many in the Cabinet felt they had won a major showdown with the Soviets after embarrassing diplomatic defeats at the Bay of Pigs and the Vienna Summit. Upon hearing the news, Secretary of State Dean Rusk exclaimed, "We were eyeball to eyeball and I think the other fellow just blinked."

In the coming year, the United States dismantled the missiles in Turkey, a telephone "hotline" to the Kremlin was installed in the Oval Office to facilitate instant communication between the American and the Soviet leaders, and the two countries began hammering out an agreement on ending atmospheric testing of nuclear weapons. A new tone had been set in American-Soviet relations.

"Both the United Sates and its allies have a mutually deep interest in a just and genuine peace and in halting the arms race," Kennedy said in a speech to graduating students at American University on June 10, 1963. ". . . For, in the final analysis, our most basic common link is that we all inhabit this small planet. We all breathe the same air. We all cherish our children's future. And we are all mortal."

The Space Race

The rivalry between the United States and the Soviet Union extended even into outer space. Fear had spread across the country in 1957, when the Soviets successfully launched *Sputnik I*, the first artificial satellite into orbit around the earth. Americans immediately worried about the military implications of the Soviet scientific achievement, terrified that a fleet of spacecraft far beyond any American defense system could bombard the United States with nuclear warheads.

Concerned not just about the military aspects of Soviet space flight but also the blow to the prestige of the United States, the Eisenhower administration inaugurated a crash space program to catch up with the Soviets. The United States put an unmanned craft of its own, *Explorer I*, into orbit on February 1, 1958. This first American spacecraft sent data back to Earth, producing

The crew of *Apollo 1* who died after an electrical spark ignited the pure oxygen piped into their command module during a launch rehearsal test on January 27, 1967.

A gathering at the White House to watch the liftoff of the *Friendship 7* spacecraft that will make John Glenn the first American in outer space. (From left to right): Vice President Lyndon Johnson, presidential advisor Arthur Schlesinger, Admiral Arleigh Burke, President John Kennedy and the First Lady, Jacquelyn Kennedy. Photo credit: Cecil Stoughton, White House/JFK Library.

an important scientific discovery, the Van Allen Radiation Belts. By July 29, 1958, President Eisenhower had signed legislation creating the National Aeronautics and Space Administration (NASA), which would plan future space missions, design new spacecraft, and determine priorities in what was already being called a "space race" with the Soviet Union.

NASA soon announced the beginning of the *Mercury* space program, which would culminate in manned flights in space. Always romantically attracted to adventure, Kennedy approved the **Apollo program,** which aimed to land humans safely on the moon. American scientists felt even more pressure when the Soviets sent the *Vostok I* into Earth orbit carrying cosmonaut Yuri Gagarin, who on April 12, 1961, became the first human in outer space.

American astronaut Alan Shepard became the second man in space on May 5, flying onboard the first of the *Mercury* program rockets. Kennedy now felt confident enough to announce even bolder plans for NASA. During a May 25, 1961 speech before Congress, he announced, "I believe that this nation should commit itself to achieving the goal, before this decade is out, of landing a man on the moon and returning him safely to the earth." Kennedy accelerated the *Mercury* program. By February 20, 1962, astronaut John Glenn became the first American to orbit Earth, making the round trip three times and spending what was then a record 34 hours in space. Soon the United States launched the Telstar TV satellite, which made live worldwide television broadcasts possible for the first time.

THE CIVIL RIGHTS MOVEMENT DURING THE KENNEDY YEARS

The Freedom Rides

Events in Cuba, the confrontation with the Soviets, and the mounting communist guerilla war in Vietnam consumed the Kennedy administration. Even the space race was part of a "twilight struggle" with the Soviets. The president quickly lost his enthusiasm for domestic matters and believed that foreign policy afforded him more freedom of action. Segregationist Democrats from the South served as chairs of the important House and Senate committees, and they allied with conservative Republicans to block much of the president's agenda. Civil rights issues, therefore, proved particularly vexing since the Kennedy administration did not want to alienate powerful Southerners in the Congress. Civil rights leaders, however, refused to make their cause subservient to Kennedy's long-term strategic interests. Recent federal court orders had mandated desegregation of interstate transportation terminals. In the spring of 1961, James Farmer, executive director of the Congress of Racial Equality, announced that black and white "**Freedom Riders**" would test the willingness of the federal government to enforce these Court decisions by boarding buses and traveling across the South.

Seven African Americans and six whites boarded two buses in Washington, D.C., in May 1961, headed for the dangers of violently segregated Alabama and Mississippi. Future Congressman Lewis paid a heavy cost early in the odyssey. As he attempted to enter a whites-only restroom in Rock Hill, South Carolina, a gang of whites blocked Lewis's entry and clubbed and beat him. Physical injury became a regular feature of the journey, and white police and sheriff's deputies refused to provide the Freedom Riders any physical protection or to prosecute those guilty of assault. The federal government had still not intervened as the buses headed toward Alabama.

Angry whites carrying sticks and metal bars lined the streets of Anniston, Alabama as the Freedom Rider buses entered town. With local police nowhere to be seen, the mob slashed two tires on the lead bus. When the tires flattened, the bus stopped and the crowd shattered the bus windows. A southern white man who boarded the bus in Atlanta, Eli Cowling, went to the door, pulled a gun, and held the mob back for 15 minutes. Later it turned out that Cowling was an undercover police officer sent by Alabama Governor John Patterson, who worried about the damage to the state's image if one of the protestors were murdered.

Cowling, however, was unable to prevent one man from thrusting a bomb into a broken window. The passengers ran out of the bus and crawled out of the shattered windows, only to be beaten by the frenzied throng. The beatings stopped when Cowling fired his handgun in the air and threatened to kill the next person who hit anyone. The mob also attacked the second bus, which nevertheless reached the Birmingham terminal where another gang beat the riders with lead pipes, baseball bats, and bicycle chains. After the pummeling, one rider needed 53 stitches on the head. Birmingham Police Commissioner **Eugene "Bull" Connor** claimed that none of his officers arrived to rescue the Freedom Riders because they had taken the day off for Mother's Day. In fact, an informant had passed word to J. Edgar Hoover that Connor had promised the local Ku Klux Klan a free 15 minutes to beat the protestors. Hoover, the head of a deliberately segregated agency who was convinced that Martin Luther King, Jr. and other civil rights leaders were communist agents, sat on the information.

As news coverage of the civil rights campaign increased, the president sent John Seigenthaler, a top aide to the attorney general, to Alabama to persuade officials there to protect the Freedom Riders. Seigenthaler escorted the battered demonstrators from Birmingham and onto a plane that flew them to New Orleans. James Farmer then announced that more Freedom Rides would follow. Frightened of violence, Greyhound bus drivers refused to transport the Freedom Riders. Bobby Kennedy, resigned to the fact that the rides would continue, called the Greyhound Company superintendent and insisted that the company comply with recent Court decisions. "Somebody better get in the damn bus and get it going

and get these people on their way." The following morning a Greyhound bus carried the riders to Montgomery, Alabama. Streets appeared abandoned when the bus arrived at the city's depot. Residents had been notified in advance of the travel itinerary. When riders stepped out of the bus, whites poured out of surrounding buildings, shouting, "Niggers, kill the niggers." A member of the mob beat one rider until he suffered a spinal cord injury. The mob also attacked an NBC television network cameraman, smashing him in the head with his equipment until he passed out. John Doar, an attorney with the Justice Department's Civil Rights Division, desperately phoned Bobby Kennedy from the scene while Seigenthaler was struck in the head, a protective helmet dented, as he tried to escort two women bus riders from the scene. Through all the violence, the police took no action.

The Freedom Riders pressed on to Jackson, Mississippi. The Kennedy brothers secured a promise from Mississippi Senator James Eastland that the Riders would be safe on their journey across the state as long as the administration did not object if the protestors were arrested and jailed for traveling "with the avowed purpose of inflaming public opinion." Hellish conditions awaited the Freedom Riders in the Jackson jails. Police packed as many as 14 prisoners in cells meant to accommodate only two. Some prisoners were forced to do outside labor in sweltering heat. The blankets smelled of urine. Guards intentionally sealed windows when temperatures soared to triple digits to increase the stifling heat. Guards and inmates beat the Riders whenever they started singing "freedom songs."

With a certainty that the Freedom Rides would continue until segregation ended on public transportation, and the equal certainty that the Freedom Rides would embarrass the president before the world, Robert Kennedy prodded the Interstate Commerce Commission and pressured the operators of bus terminals to quietly take down the "whites only" signs across the South. Worried about the economic repercussions of continued violence, several southern communities removed the Jim Crow signs without news coverage or protestors.

Integrating "Ole Miss"

John Kennedy's inaugural speech deeply moved an African-American veteran of the Air Force, James Meredith, who attempted to register at the all-white University of Mississippi at Oxford. In spite of his excellent grades and his service in the military, the university's admissions office turned down his application. Meredith filed a lawsuit and a federal court ruled that the university had to admit him as a student. On September 20, 1962, Mississippi

KENNEDY & JOHNSON AND THE VIETNAM WAR / 739

Governor Ross Barnett personally blocked Meredith's way as he attempted to register at the admissions office. Angry over Barnett's obstruction of a federal order, Robert Kennedy sent 500 federal marshals to "Ole Miss," as the campus was known. Meredith registered and checked into his dorm room without violence.

However, on September 30, an agitated mob of students and non-students from across the South gathered to chant, "Two, four, one, three, we all hate Kennedy." The mob began throwing rocks at the federal marshals, and the marshals responded by firing tear gas canisters into the crowd. The crowd grew into the thousands.

Soon a riot broke out with the white mob throwing rocks, bricks, and Molotov cocktails while gunmen fired shotguns. As a result of the mêlée, 160 marshals were wounded, with 28 hit by bullets. Two men were killed, a jukebox repairman who happened to be at the wrong place at the wrong time and a French news cameraman. Monitoring events through the night, Kennedy ordered 5,000 army troops to the campus before dawn. In the end, Meredith attended Ole Miss for two semesters, enduring anger, threats and harassment from fellow students.

"Bombingham"

Martin Luther King, Jr., and other civil rights leaders knew it would take more dramatic direct actions to keep the administration focused on the issue. They planned a series of boycotts aimed at department stores in downtown Birmingham, where the Freedom Riders had received their worst beatings and where city officials shut down all parks rather than comply with a Department of the Interior order to desegregate them. King deliberately started the campaign during Easter time, knowing that the city's African-American community spent a substantial sum every year buying holiday clothes at the city's segregated department stores. These stores would not allow black customers to try on clothes and made them buy any product they touched. Activists began their sit-ins and picketing on April 3, 1963.

After eight days of protests, a state court ordered King to stop the campaign. King was arrested on April 12, on Good Friday. Eight southern ministers and rabbis issued a statement praising Birmingham officials for enforcing the law. They criticized King and other civil rights leaders for increasing racial tensions, called their boycott "unwise and untimely," and urged black leaders to wait until southern society was ready to accept the type of changes the freedom movement demanded. The statement provoked King to write his "**Letter from a Birmingham Jail**," a masterpiece of American literature that would later be included in his book, *Why We Can't Wait*. A black trusty lent him a pen and scraps of paper, and King composed his letter in a dimly lit cell. In the April 16, 1963 letter, King explained to southern moderates that the movement could afford no more patience. He described the long history of broken promises made by the federal government to African Americans, the psychological damage inflicted on children locked into second class status by segregation, and the life-destroying poverty created in the black community because of discrimination. He also called out the hypocrisy of white "moderates" who were forever willing to delay freedom for other people and expected black people to wait for freedoms they expected for themselves.

King's letter was published and quoted in newspapers and church bulletins across the country. He was finally released on April 20. King and his top lieutenants then agreed to recruit high school students to participate in the protests. By May 2, more than 900 children had gone to jail for participating in the protest. On May 3, police officers stormed the Sixteenth Street Baptist Church, where more than 1,000 boycotters had gathered. As the protestors left the church, police aimed fire hoses at the congregants with sufficient force to knock both children and adults to the ground and tear skin from their bodies.

**James Meredith walking on the campus of the University of Mississippi accompanied by U. S. marshals.
October 1, 1962**

Vivian Malone, one of the first African Americans to attend the University of Alabama, walks through a crowd that includes photographers, National Guard members, and Deputy U.S. Attorney General Nicholas Katzenbach to enter Foster Auditorium to register for classes. June 11, 1963

Sales at downtown Birmingham stores dropped to almost nothing during what traditionally had been a profitable season. Local merchants were also facing pressure from northern suppliers who were appalled by the televised violence and the possibility that the boycott movement might spread to affect their businesses. The downtown merchants hammered out a compromise with King on May 10. In return for desegregation of the stores, the protestors would end the boycott. Alabama Governor George Wallace and Sheriff Connor attacked the agreement, with Connor urging whites to boycott stores that had integrated.

In the aftermath of the Birmingham campaign, two dynamite explosions blasted the home of King's brother, a Birmingham minister, while another dynamite blast destroyed part of the Gaston Motel where the movement leadership had set up headquarters. African Americans again took to the streets and hurled rocks and other weapons at police who responded by again clubbing the protestors. Birmingham became known as "Bombingham."

The University of Alabama Integrates

Even as the administration wished the civil rights issue would fade from public attention, protests against segregation broke out across the country. In 1963, civil rights activists marched not just for desegregation but also for better jobs and better schools, not just in southern cities like Jackson, Mississippi and Raleigh, North Carolina, but also in cities like Los Angeles and Philadelphia. Approximately 75,000 Americans participated in civil rights marches in May 1963 alone.

Alabama Governor George Wallace stood blocking the entrance to Foster Auditorium at the University of Alabama as two African-American students, Vivian

Malone and James A. Hood, armed with a court order mandating their admission, attempted to enter the building. Wallace won election the previous year promising to resist integration. During his inaugural speech on January 14, 1963, he declared, "Segregation now! Segregation tomorrow! Segregation forever!" The Kennedys negotiated with Wallace, who agreed he would step aside to let the students inside the building once he had finished making a speech. President Kennedy nationalized the Alabama National Guard to guarantee Wallace's compliance. That night in a national broadcast, the president made his strongest statement ever in support of civil rights. "We are confronted primarily with a moral issue," Kennedy told his audience. "It's as old as the Scriptures and is as clear as the American Constitution . . . If an American, because his skin is dark, cannot eat lunch in a restaurant open to the public, if he cannot send his children to the best public school available, if he cannot vote for the public officials who represent him, if, in short, he cannot enjoy the full and free life which all of us want, then who among us would be content to have the color of his skin changed and stand in his place?

The same evening as this dramatic speech, the field secretary of the Mississippi NAACP, Medgar Evers, was shot to death in the driveway of his Jackson, Mississippi home. On June 19, 1963, the president submitted to Congress a sweeping civil rights bill that strengthened voting rights laws, empowered the attorney general to file school desegregation lawsuits, gave the president the power to end federal funding of state programs that racially discriminated, and outlawed segregation in public accommodations such as restaurants, movie theaters, hotels and motels, stores, and stadiums. Civil rights leaders wanted more, such as a ban on job discrimination, but Kennedy told movement leaders that the bill went as far as it could if it were to have any chances to pass the Congress.

The March on Washington

To put pressure on Congress to pass the bill and perhaps strengthen it, King organized a "**March on Washington**" to be held in late August. The Kennedys strongly opposed the rally, fearing wavering members of Congress might resent the show of force, that violence might break out, or that a small turnout might undermine momentum for the legislation. When it became clear that the march would take place, the Kennedy team essentially stage-managed the event, insisting that speeches be cleared with them beforehand.

About 250,000 people showed up for the August 28 event. The world listened as national TV broadcast King's famous "I Have a Dream" speech. In ministerial cadences, King mesmerized the marchers in Washington and the vast television audience with his most famous words. In the twenty-first century, this speech might now seem over-familiar, and in public memory it has been reduced to a bland call for a future in which black and white children might live and thrive together side-by-side. The speech in its entirety, however, was far bolder, calling for an immediate end to segregation, police brutality, and black disenfranchisement in the South, and a cynical political system in the North that gave African Americans there nothing to vote for.

Kennedy declined to speak at the event but agreed to meet the organizers after the successful march. He greeted King with words echoing the civil rights leader's earlier speech: "I have a dream." Rather than provoke a backlash, the march gave momentum to the civil rights bill, which was approved by the House Judiciary Committee and referred to the full House on October 23, 1963.

Kennedy had feared that support of civil rights would lose him the critical support of southern Democrats, but polling by Louis Harris in November 1963 indicated he had gained more support than he lost by backing the legislation.

Four Little Girls

Whatever euphoria civil rights activists might have felt in the wake of the March on Washington gave way to bitter tears on September 15, 1963. That Sunday an explosion rocked the Sixteenth Street Baptist Church in Birmingham during services. A bomber had tunneled under the church basement and set off a bundle of dynamite underneath the girls' restroom, killing four young girls dressed in white, three 14-year-olds named Cynthia Wesler, Carole Robertson and Addie Mae Collins, and one 11-year-old named Denise McNair. The explosion during the church's annual "Youth Day" injured 20 other worshippers. McNair's father, upon discovering her body, stood holding one of her white dress shoes and screamed, "I'd like to blow the whole town up." The United Klans of America targeted the church because it had served as a meeting place for civil rights leaders. Alabama Governor Wallace had been exploiting racial tensions to enhance his popularity with white voters, and one week before the explosion *The New York Times* published an interview in which Wallace said that the state needed a "few first-class funerals" to stop the civil rights protests. It took until November 1977 for the bomber, Robert Chambliss, to be found guilty and sent to prison. Juries eventually convicted three accomplices and sentenced them to prison terms as well. King, however, blamed Wallace for instigating murder with his violent words. Sorrow and anger over the Sixteenth Street Baptist Church Bombing did, however, intensify the effort to pass major civil rights legislation in 1964.

Governor Wallace, attempting to block integration at the University of Alabama, stands defiantly at the door while being confronted by Deputy U.S. Attorney General Nicholas Katzenbach. June 11, 1963

THE KENNEDY ASSASSINATION

By the early 1960s, Dallas, Texas had acquired the reputation as the home of right-wing political extremists. Uncertain of carrying Texas in the 1960 presidential campaign, Kennedy sent his running mate Lyndon Johnson to make an appearance in the city in the closing days of the race. On November 4, Johnson and his wife Lady Bird appeared at the Adolphus Hotel in downtown Dallas for a speech. After the speech, the pair was assaulted by a well-dressed mob led by rightwing Republican Congressman Bruce Alger. Calling LBJ "Late Blooming Judas" because of his role in passing the 1957 civil rights bill, the hostile throng spat upon the Johnsons and pulled on Lady Bird's hair and clothes. Another reactionary mob spat upon United Nations Ambassador Adlai Stevenson after he made an October 26, 1963, speech to the Dallas Council on World Affairs marking United Nations Day.

Kennedy arrived in Dallas on November 22, 1963. Riding in a limousine with the top removed so onlookers could get a better view of the president and the first lady, Kennedy smiled broadly at the crowd and waved right up until the moment the car passed the School Book Depository in downtown Dallas' Dealey Plaza. Three shots rang out, with bullets hitting Kennedy in the neck and, fatally, in the head. Rushed to Parkland Hospital, Kennedy was soon declared dead. Instead of a right-winger, police arrested Lee Harvey Oswald, an employee of the Book Depository and a self-styled leftist who supported Fidel Castro's regime in Cuba and defected briefly to the Soviet Union before returning to a life of loneliness and frustration in Texas. Oswald himself would be murdered by a local nightclub owner with organized crime ties, Jack Ruby, who claimed he killed the suspect out of respect and sorrow for the president's widow, Jackie Kennedy.

The president's murder, and the rapid killing of his suspected assassin, spawned a host of conspiracy theories that blamed the Russians, the Cubans, the Mafia (angered by Bobby Kennedy's work as a lawyer for a Senate committee investigating organized crime in the 1950s), Teamsters Union boss Jimmy Hoffa (jailed for corruption after prosecution by the Kennedy administration), and even Vice President Johnson. The new president, seeking to quell suspicions, appointed a blue-ribbon panel chaired by Supreme Court Chief Justice Earl Warren and including future President Gerald Ford, then a congressman from Michigan, to investigate the assassination. The Warren Commission concluded that Oswald acted alone, but a large percentage of the population continued to doubt the official government version of events. In the decade that followed Kennedy's death, a period that would see government lies about the Vietnam War exposed and the revelations about the Watergate scandal during the Nixon administration, the assassination in Dallas ushered in an era of cynicism.

LBJ: A POLITICAL FORCE OF NATURE

Lyndon Johnson might have been the most complicated figure in American political life in the mid- and late-twentieth century. Often crude, he nevertheless proved to be perhaps the greatest political tactician of his era. The graduate of Southwest Texas State Teachers College, a small Central Texas campus, he often suffered from an inferiority complex in the company of the Ivy Leaguers peopling the Kennedy administration, yet his ambitions bordered on the grandiose. A small-town Southerner, Johnson would use the word "nigger" in private conversation but still devoted much of his public life to promoting civil rights and fighting poverty. An inveterate compromiser, Johnson would also propose some of the boldest reform legislation in American history.

Johnson's early career as a grade-school teacher would shape his political worldview. During the 1928-29 school year, he taught fifth-, sixth- and seventh-graders at a tiny, segregated Mexican-American school in Cotulla, Texas, just south of San Antonio. Three-quarters of the Mexican population in the town, according to Johnson biographer Robert Dallek, lived in "hovels or dilapidated shanties without indoor plumbing or electricity." The parents worked at area ranches and farms for "slave wages." Johnson would later recall that his heart broke looking at students "mired in the slums . . . lashed by prejudice . . .

Swearing in of Lyndon B. Johnson as president, Air Force One, Love Field, Dallas, Texas.
November 22, 1963
Photo credit: LBJ Library Photo

Mrs. Kennedy and her children leave the Capitol building.
(L-R) actor and Kennedy in-law Peter Lawford, Attorney General Kennedy, Patrica Kennedy Lawford, Caroline Kennedy, Mrs. Kennedy, and John F. Kennedy Jr.
November 24, 1963
Photo credit: Abbie Rowe, National Park Service/JFK Library

buried half-alive in illiteracy." He remembered looking at their eyes and seeing "a quizzical expression on their faces" as they wondered, "Why don't people like me? Why do they hate me because I am brown?" Johnson was often harsh and sometimes intolerant as a teacher, using corporal punishment if he caught students speaking Spanish, but he also felt empathy for his young charges' poverty.

Johnson carried his conflicted personality, which was both bigoted and empathetic, to his job as director of the New Deal-created National Youth Administration (NYA) in Texas from 1935 to 1937. Though he sometimes accommodated local anti-Mexican prejudice in his hiring of unemployed youths on projects such as constructing roadside parks, he was more assertive in recruiting and promoting African Americans. Under Johnson, the NYA created Freshman College Centers for students who had received a high school education but could not, with their small NYA salaries, afford tuition at local colleges. Under this program, students could take a pair of college courses tuition-free, improving their education and their resumes at the same time.

An Unlikely Civil Rights Ally

In 1937, when James P. Buchanan, the longtime congressman in Johnson's home district died, the young NYA director decided to run for the open seat as a supporter of Franklin Roosevelt and the New Deal. A close friend of House Speaker Sam Rayburn, Johnson remained in the House for 11 years and was named head of the Democratic Congressional Campaign Committee in 1940. He ran unsuccessfully for the Senate in a special election in 1941. Johnson served in the Navy in 1942 but returned to his House seat at the insistence of President Roosevelt.

Johnson ran for the Senate again in 1948 in a heated and controversial race against the archconservative and segregationist former Texas Governor Coke Stevenson, winning the Democratic primary by only 87 votes. Johnson earned the ironic nickname "Landslide Lyndon" as a result of this election and charges of voter fraud dogged him the rest of his political life, although Stevenson himself certainly engaged in ballot box stuffing in the same election.

Early in his Senate career, Johnson intervened in the controversy surrounding Private Felix Longoria, who had been denied a funeral in Texas, because of racial prejudice. Johnson helped arrange a funeral for Longoria with full honors at Arlington National Cemetery on February 16, 1949. In 1955, Johnson's peers selected him as Senate Majority Leader. With a White House bid in mind, in the late 1950s Johnson positioned himself as a racial moderate. He was pointedly not asked to sign the so-called "Southern Manifesto" circulated among and supported by 101 members of the House of Representatives and the United States Senate. The 1956 document condemned the Supreme Court's 1954 *Brown* school desegregation order.

Lyndon Johnson also gave his critical support to the 1957 Civil Rights Act, the first voting rights law passed by the Congress since Reconstruction. Under this law, Congress established the Justice Department's Civil Rights Division. The law empowered this division to investigate claims of voter harassment and racial discrimination by election officials. The Justice Department now could prosecute individuals conspiring to deny voting rights. The law also established a six-member United States Civil Rights Commission, which examined cases where voters were denied the ballot because of race.

Johnson entered the 1960 Democratic presidential primary campaign, losing to Kennedy. He was selected as running mate because the party faithful worried about their prospects in Texas, a state that had gone for Eisenhower twice in the previous two presidential elections. Kennedy and Johnson proved a mismatch. The president and his brother Bobby saw Johnson as unsophisticated, and they underestimated his political skills. Johnson bridled at serving as junior partner to the younger Kennedy; Johnson had previously held seniority in the Senate.

Nevertheless, when Johnson spoke up, it could be with force. Johnson later recounted an anecdote: He was vice president and he asked his African-American cook and her husband to drive him from Washington, D.C., to Texas. Their route took them through Alabama, Mississippi, and Louisiana, and the entourage could find no restaurants or restrooms open to two of the three passengers. "Two people who worked for the Vice President of the United States peeing in a ditch . . . That's not right," Johnson would later drawl.

The Great Society

Because of his origins in a highly conservative and segregationist state like Texas, many liberals worried about Johnson's political intentions when the Kennedy assassination thrust him into the presidency. Johnson, however,

pushed through at breakneck speed a torrent of legislation unmatched since Franklin Roosevelt's famed first 100 days in office. Johnson skillfully used the memory of the widely mourned Kennedy to win support for civil rights, anti-poverty legislation, and government investments in education and health care to create what he called "**The Great Society**."

Boldly declaring a "War on Poverty," Johnson aimed new government programs at the 20 percent of the American population still living below the poverty line. The Job Corps (based in part on his work with the NYA), for example, provided skilled employment training for low-income youth. Head Start provided preschool educations for children living in poverty allowing them an opportunity to catch up with students from more advantaged backgrounds. The Food Stamps program, which provided tax-supported stipends to supplement the diets of low-income families, also benefited farmers, food processors, and grocery stores by providing an expanded market for domestically-produced food commodities. Collectively, these government initiatives contributed to the reduction of the poverty rate by almost half by the end of the 1960s despite the gradual withdrawal of significant funds to fight the war in Vietnam.

In addition to the anti-poverty programs, Congress sent $1.5 billion to aid the states with education and

The "Johnson Treatment" is displayed here with Louis Martin (top-L) at a reception for the Democratic National Committee delegates on April 20, 1966, in the Red Room of the White House, Abe Fortas (R), associate justice of the Supreme Court in July 1965, at the White House, and with Senator Richard Russell (bottom) on December 17, 1963, in the Cabinet Room of the White House. Photo credit: LBJ Presidential Library

created the National Endowment for the Arts and the National Endowment for the Humanities, in addition to establishing the Public Broadcasting System (PBS) and National Public Radio (NPR). Medicare and Medicaid became the most important domestic programs created since the establishment of the Social Security Administration three decades earlier. Medicare provided health insurance coverage for Americans aged 65 and older, while Medicaid, which shared administration by the federal government and the states, provided access to health care for the poor. Johnson believed that Kennedy's death lent momentum for these programs, but most of all for civil rights.

THE CIVIL RIGHTS MOVEMENT DURING THE JOHNSON YEARS

The 1964 Civil Rights Act

Johnson frequently invoked his martyred predecessor as he pushed, needled and cajoled the Congress toward passage of his top legislative priority, the **1964 Civil Rights Act**. The law banned segregation at public facilities and racial discrimination in the work place, empowered the attorney general to initiate lawsuits against segregated school systems, and allowed the federal government to withhold funds from schools refusing to comply with desegregation orders. In the Senate, Richard Russell of Georgia launched a filibuster, relying on a team of 18 colleagues who attempted to talk the bill to death, claiming the proposed law would lead to "amalgamation and mongrelization of the races."

Meanwhile, in the House of Representatives, Democratic leaders joined by liberal Republicans defeated more than 100 "poison pill" amendments that would have gutted the legislation or made it unacceptable to a congressional majority. Attempting to kill the bill, Congressman Howard Smith of Virginia introduced an amendment banning employment discrimination against women as well as African Americans. Mistakenly thinking that adding women's rights to the civil rights bill would kill the legislation, southern segregationists joined with feminists to approve Smith's amendment. One critic said that Smith "outsmarted himself," and the bill passed by an overwhelming 290-130 vote.

Senator Hubert Humphrey of Minnesota, soon to become Johnson's vice president, urged Senate Minority Leader Everett Dirksen, not previously a supporter of civil rights legislation, to join the cause. On June 10, 1964, Dirksen announced his support for a cloture vote, which would end the filibuster and allow a vote on the bill. The cloture motion passed 71-29, with four votes more than needed to close debate. The front lines of the battle for social justice, however, would not be found in Washington, D.C., but in the backwoods of Mississippi.

Freedom Summer

A younger generation of black protestors was not content to wait upon the slow workings of the United States Senate. The NAACP, representing an older generation, fought segregation through a series of lawsuits. Martin Luther King Jr.'s Southern Christian Leadership Conference (SCLC) sought to defeat Jim Crow through political lobbying, negative publicity about southern discrimination, and acts of non-violent resistance, such as sit-ins at segregated lunch counters. With a younger membership, the Student Nonviolent Coordinating Committee (SNCC) favored direct action against injustice, led by local civil rights campaigners. SNCC's membership resented King and other civil rights "celebrities" they accused of swooping in at the end of a campaign and claiming credit for the hard grassroots work of locals.

Seen as reckless by the older peers, SNCC members marched directly through the gates of fire, continuing their voter registration campaign in Mississippi in spite of past bloodshed. Even though the Kennedy brothers had been lukewarm in their support of past civil rights campaigns, the administration hoped that increasing black voter registration in the South would offset white votes lost because of hostility to the civil rights bill President Kennedy sought in the last year of his life. Bobby Kennedy arranged $870,000 (about $5.5 million in today's dollars) in funding from groups like the liberal Taconic Foundation, the Stern Family Find, and the Field Foundation for black voter registration drives in the old Confederacy. With this aid, SNCC, the NAACP and CORE (Congress of Racial Equality) launched the Voter Education Project in April 1962. Over the next two years, the project registered for the vote more than a half-million African Americans in the South, but the overwhelming majority of these voters lived in big cities. A significant number of rural southern blacks remained unregistered, and in Mississippi, the project had added only 4,000 new voters.

Having seen so many African Americans injured or killed over civil rights, and a victim of an attempted murder himself, civil rights leader Bob Moses in the fall of 1963 invited the participation of white students from colleges like Harvard, Yale and Stanford. Moses moved ahead with plans for a "Freedom Summer" in 1964, in which hundreds of white volunteers would join black activists to increase the number of African American voters across Mississippi. Most of the 900 student volunteers who arrived from out of state for the campaign were well-off white students from elite universities.

The Schwerner, Chaney, and Goodman Murders

Civil rights dominated the headlines in 1964. The Twenty-fourth Amendment to the U.S. Constitution, banning poll taxes, had been submitted to the states in 1962 and was ratified January 23, 1964. Meanwhile, during Mississippi's "Freedom Summer," volunteers not only registered black voters but set up 30 "Freedom Schools" to offer children an alternative to the state's dilapidated, underfunded Jim Crow schools. CORE and other groups also helped organize the Mississippi Freedom Democratic Party (MFDP) as an alternative to the white supremacist state Democratic Party. The MFDP, which held its own primaries, elected a competing slate of delegates. The MFDP would challenge the credentials of the all-white, segregationist delegation during the convention and demand that the national Democratic Party recognize its integrated slate as the legitimate representatives of Mississippi.

Michael Schwerner, 24, was among the white men and women who responded to Bob Moses's call to bring democracy to Mississippi. A native of Manhattan's Lower East Side and a CORE volunteer, Schwerner had already registered African Americans in Meridian, Mississippi, when he returned to that state for Freedom Summer. Schwerner was joined by a local African-American man, James Chaney, a 19-year-old high school dropout drawn to the civil rights movement in spite of his family's fears, and Andrew Goodman, a Queens College anthropology major from New York who had never before been in Mississippi.

On June 21, the three traveled to investigate a report that Mount Zion United Methodist Church in Philadelphia, Mississippi had been torched by white supremacists. The local Ku Klux Klan and White Citizens Council closely monitored the trio's movements, and Neshoba County Deputy Sheriff Cecil Price, a Klansman, arrested them for supposedly speeding. Price arranged for Klansmen to ambush the activists after they were released from jail. After the three crossed the town limits, Price pulled them over. Klansmen then yanked Schwerner, Chaney and Goodman out of the car. When Schwerner was pulled from the car, a man with a pistol said, "You still think a nigger's as good as I am?" before shooting the civil rights worker in the chest. The Klansmen savagely beat Chaney and fatally shot all three activists before burying their bodies in an earthen dam. After being paid $25,000, an FBI informant told agents to look for the bodies in the dam at the Bogue Chitto Swamp. Navy divers and FBI agents found not only the bodies of Schwerner, Chaney and Goodman, but also the corpses of seven other black men murdered by whites and dumped there over the years.

State and local authorities refused to charge the perpetrators with murder, so the U.S. government secured federal indictments against Price, Neshoba County Sheriff Lawrence Rainey and 16 other defendants. They were charged with depriving Schwerner, Chaney and Goodman of their civil rights. A jury found seven of the defendants, including Price and Klan Imperial Wizard Samuel Bowers, guilty on October 20, 1967. Authorities released all those convicted within six years. After an investigation by a Mississippi journalist and by high school students competing in a National History Day contest, enough evidence was uncovered to lead to the arrest and conviction for murder of another killer, preacher Edgar Ray Killen, in 2005. Killen, then 80, received a sentence of

Martin Luther King, Jr. talks with President Lyndon B. Johnson in the Oval Office, White House. December 3, 1963 by Yoichi R. Okamoto. Photo credits: LBJ Library Photo

three consecutive 20-year sentences. He died in prison in 2018 just before his 93rd birthday.

The Election of 1964

Lyndon Johnson had long felt like an unwanted interloper, and was rankled that some Democrats saw him as an illegitimate heir to the Kennedy throne. Thus, Johnson hoped that the 1964 Democratic National Convention that summer in Atlantic City would be his coronation, an untarnished celebration of that year's many legislative accomplishments. Unfortunately, in spite of movement in the direction of expanded black civil rights, the signs loomed of a national white backlash against reform legislation. George Wallace, the segregationist governor of Alabama, entered the Democratic presidential primaries and carried 34 percent of the vote in Wisconsin, 30 percent in Indiana, and a shocking 43 percent in Maryland. When Wallace's insurgent campaign failed to unseat Johnson, many of these voters began drifting to Republican nominee **Barry Goldwater**, a libertarian who portrayed civil rights laws as the intrusion of a growing and increasingly tyrannical federal government into states' rights. Rioting in Harlem and other American cities in the summer of 1964 provoked white anger and increased Johnson's fear of a challenge on the right. Until November, Goldwater hammered the Democrats for being soft on communism, arguing that past Democratic presidents like Franklin Roosevelt had handed over domination of Eastern Europe to the Soviet Union, that Harry Truman had "lost" China to the communists and failed to "win" the Korean War, and that the Kennedy-Johnson team had bungled the liberation of Cuba at the Bay of Pigs.

The president, however, perceived a more direct challenge from southern African Americans seeking to put a stop to the all-white segregationist delegations from the South that had been a feature of Democratic Conventions since the 1830s. Using a black panther as its symbol, the Mississippi Freedom Democratic Party (MFDP), which had been organized during Freedom Summer, planned to challenge the credentials of Mississippi's all-white delegation on the floor of the 1964 convention. The delegates would charge that the Mississippi regulars conducted primaries that ignored black voting rights and were thus in violation of federal law and could not be legally seated.

President Johnson did not want a credentials fight at his convention. Seeking to not embarrass the president, liberals proposed seating both the all-white Mississippi regulars and the Freedom delegation. A compromise was offered that would allow two Freedom delegates to sit with the regulars while sixty-six other Freedom Party members could sit as non-voting observers with other delegations.

Unwilling to accept even this watered-down proposal, and a demand that they pledge loyalty to the Democratic presidential ticket, the all-white regular delegation walked out of the convention along with the Alabama delegates. The walkout did not spread, however, which Lyndon Johnson declared as victory. The convention voted to insist that the 1968 Mississippi delegation had to be integrated.

The Democratic ticket overwhelmingly defeated GOP nominee Goldwater that November. The Arizona senator frightened off mainstream voters with a convention nomination speech in which he declared, "I would remind you that extremism in the defense of liberty is no vice! And let me remind you also that moderation in the pursuit of justice is no virtue!" Later, Goldwater dismissed the hydrogen bomb as "merely another weapon." On September 7, the Johnson campaign ran a television ad in which a young girl pulled petals from a daisy and counted them. Then, a voiceover counted down to a missile launch and the screen filled with footage of a mushroom cloud. Though it only ran once, the now-famous "Daisy Ad" (and the subsequent buzz it generated in the news media) effectively reminded voters of the dangers of nuclear weapons and helped the Democrats depict Goldwater as a dangerous man to have in the White House.

On election night, Johnson carried 61 percent of the popular vote and beat Goldwater 486-52 in the Electoral College. Goldwater's sweep of the Deep South states of Louisiana, Mississippi, Alabama, Georgia and South Carolina, where he carried the votes of whites angered by Johnson's support of civil rights legislation, seemed to represent the only dark cloud on the political horizon for the Democrats.

"Bloody Sunday" in Selma

Lyndon Johnson might have gotten his way regarding the Mississippi Freedom Democratic Party at the 1964 Democratic convention, but Martin Luther King Jr. would force the president's hand regarding passage of a voting rights act in 1965. For his next ballot access campaign, King targeted Selma, Alabama, where only 383 of about 15,000 African Americans were registered. King chose Selma not only for the obvious suppression of black voting but because he could count on an overreaction by Dallas County Sheriff Jim Clark. This man had acquired a reputation for out-of-control anger and violence.

The push started in January 1965. King announced that the campaign would climax with a 54-mile march on March 7 from Selma to the statehouse in Montgomery, the one-time capital of the Confederacy. That day, 600 marchers led by John Lewis crossed the Edmund Pettus Bridge onto state Highway 80 before state troopers, who arrived in squad cars adorned with Confederate flags, halted the march. The state police charged into the crowd wielding billy clubs and firing tear gas canisters. State police chased the marchers back across the bridge with Sheriff Clark shouting, "Get those goddamned niggers!"

Deputies carried on what was essentially a police riot in Selma's black neighborhoods, seizing a young black man from inside a church and throwing him through a stained-glass window decorated with an image of Jesus. The event came to be known as "Bloody Sunday."

King announced a second march. Johnson worked out a deal with Wallace. King could bring the marchers to the bridge, but they would halt when ordered to by the state troopers. The protestors would then bow in prayer and leave. Sadly, violence still broke out the night of the second march on March 9, when thugs beat to death James Reeb, a white minister from Massachusetts who had participated in earlier protests.

Johnson had wanted a "cooling off" period for civil rights legislation and hoped to focus on Medicare and other parts of his "Great Society" agenda, but the scenes on Bloody Sunday outraged him, and he made a voting rights bill a priority. Johnson would also step in to allow King and his fellow marchers to complete their symbolic trek from Selma to Montgomery. Johnson federalized the Alabama National Guard for the third march, which began on March 21. With 1,900 guardsmen shielding them from violence, by the fourth day the marchers numbered 25,000 protestors and included entertainers like the musical group Peter, Paul and Mary, United Nations Ambassador Ralph Bunche, and longtime activists such as A. Philip Randolph. On March 25, King spoke from the steps of the Alabama State Capitol, where Jefferson Davis had been sworn in as president of the Confederacy in 1861.

The protestors happily sang freedom songs at the end of the long journey to Montgomery. Again, the sense of celebration was short-lived. The night of March 25, Viola Liuzzo, a white woman from Detroit, volunteered to help transport marchers. The mother of five was driving with a black passenger on Highway 80, the main route to Montgomery, when a car occupied by four Klansman pulled alongside her and fatally shot her in the head.

The Voting Rights Act of 1965

"Bloody Sunday," followed by the Liuzzo murder, gave momentum to passage of the **Voting Rights Act of 1965**. The act prohibited devices employed by southern legislatures to keep African Americans from voting, such as literacy tests, which were supposedly equally enforced for black and white voters but were manipulated to systematically deny African Americans the ballot. The law also empowered the U.S. Justice Department to monitor elections in order to prevent intimidation and harassment of black voters in districts with a history of such behavior.

On August 3, the House passed the measure by a 4-1 margin, and the next day the Senate passed the legislation 79-18. Johnson signed the bill into law August 6. A jubilant atmosphere attended the signing ceremony, but Johnson knew the political dangers of pushing for such revolutionary change. "I have signed away the South for a generation," he is said to have commented after he signed the bill into law. Johnson had no way of knowing if African Americans would vote in significant numbers after the bill's enactment. He could count on, however, an angry southern white backlash.

As a result of this law and the 1964 Civil Rights Act, segregation slowly faded across the South. Restaurants, hotels, and other public facilities opened to African Americans, most rapidly in southern cities, though Jim Crow lingered for years in rural areas. School desegregation did not keep pace with integration of public accommodation, and decades later many students across the country would still attend overwhelmingly white or predominantly black and brown schools. But in terms of black voter registration, the impact of the 1965 Voting Rights Act was dramatic. In the states of Virginia, South Carolina, Georgia, Alabama, Mississippi and Louisiana, black registration overall went from 31 percent to 57 percent by the late 1960s. Black registration climbed from 32 to 60 percent in Louisiana, 19 to 53 percent in Alabama, and from 6 percent to 44 percent in Mississippi. The number of black elected officials in the South also sharply climbed. In the six states mentioned above, the number of black elected officials grew from 70 to about 400.

The Life and Death of Malcolm X

Even with these gains, the frustrations of watching Martin Luther King Jr.'s non-violent campaign against segregation and racism so frequently encounter murderous violence from powerful southern whites led many African Americans to question King's tactics and to embrace the concept of self-defense. The leader of this alternative approach to black resistance was a man born Malcolm Little, who would later achieve international fame as Nation of Islam Minister **Malcolm X.**

In his bestselling book *The Autobiography of Malcolm X* (1965), Malcolm describes how, in spite of making high grades through his eighth year of public school, he became bitter and rebellious when a previously supportive white English teacher asked him what he wanted to do for a living. When Malcolm said he wanted to become a lawyer, the teacher told him "that's no realistic goal for

Upstaging the President: Fannie Lou Hamer and the 1964 Democratic Convention

Millions of Americans watching television coverage of the Democratic National Convention August 22, 1964, for a change, heard the voice of someone who was not one of the rich, powerful, white men who always dominated such proceedings. They were riveted instead by the words of Fannie Lou Hamer, the granddaughter of slaves and the youngest of 20 children in a poor Mississippi family. Since her youth, she had toiled as a sharecropper.

The Democratic Party had gathered in Atlantic City, New Jersey, to crown Lyndon Johnson as its nominee for president. Television cameras rolled while a Democratic Party committee considered the credentials of a segregated slate of Mississippi delegates to the Democratic National Convention. Hamer spoke out against the racism and violence experienced by African Americans who attempted to exercise their constitutional rights as citizens. Johnson, who wanted the convention to be an uncontroversial celebration of his nine months in office and the programs he promised for the future, raged as he watched "that illiterate woman," as he called her, grab the limelight. The president hastily called a press conference to get Hamer off the air. Networks cut away from Hamer's testimony, but Johnson's ploy did not work, as the evening news broadcasts that night featured her testimony.

Born October 6, 1917, Hamer may have seemed to strangers as the unlikeliest person to upstage a president. Because of her family's poverty, Hamer dropped out of school in the sixth grade and began the exhausting work of picking cotton at a Sunflower County, Mississippi plantation, picking up to 300 pounds a day. Without her consent, a doctor sterilized her at age 44 as part of the state's longstanding eugenics program that aimed to reduce African-American reproduction, a procedure so commonly forced on black women in the state that it was called a "Mississippi appendectomy." She did not become active in the movement until, in the same year, she attended a meeting hosted at a local church organized by the Student Nonviolent Coordinating Committee (SNCC) and other activist groups.

Funded by liberal foundations, SNCC was launching a major voter registration drive in Mississippi aimed at African Americans. Hamer and seventeen others put their safety at risk as they volunteered to register to vote in Indianola that August 31. She was harassed by police and her landlord fired her when she returned to her plantation. Sixteen bullets were shot into the window of a house where she had lived. Hamer continued her crusade and became famous among her fellow civil rights workers for her joyful singing of hymns like "Go Tell It On The Mountain." On June 9, 1963, when she returned from civil rights work in South Carolina, police arrested her in Winona, Mississippi, and subjected her to a torture she would make famous during her testimony to the Democratic Party credentials committee. A state highway patrolmen threw Hamer in jail and ordered her black fellow prisoners to beat her. "The first Negro began to beat, and I was beat until I was exhausted . . . After the first Negro was exhausted, the State Highway Patrolmen ordered the second Negro to use the blackjack. The second Negro began to beat . . . I began to scream, and one white man got up and began to beat me on my head and tell me to hush." Hamer suffered lifelong disabilities afterward, including vision problems and the worsening of a limp originally caused by polio.

In spite of the risks, the next year Hamer became vice-chair of the Mississippi Freedom Democratic Party (MFDP). Segregationists in Mississippi's Democratic Party used violence and intimidation to keep African Americans from voting or participating in party caucuses and sent an all-white delegation to the 1964 Democratic National Convention. The MFDP, which held its own primaries, elected its own slate of delegates. The MFDP delegates travelled to Atlantic City and insisted that they, not the segregationist party regulars, were the legitimate representatives of the state's party. "When we went to Atlantic City, we didn't go there for publicity, we went there because we believed that America was what it said it was, 'the land of the free.'" Hamer later said. The credentials committee held its hearings to make recommendations to the full convention on which delegation should be seated.

Hamer embarrassed the party into enacting reform. A compromise was offered that would have allowed two MFDP members to sit as non-voting members of the Mississippi delegation, but this was too much for the Mississippi regulars, who walked out. The full convention voted to require integrated delegations for the 1968 convention. Hamer served as a Mississippi delegate in 1968 and later ran twice unsuccessfully for Congress. An activist against the Vietnam War, she died of cancer in 1977.

a nigger" and advised him to become a carpenter. Disillusioned, he became a petty criminal. Malcolm's problems prompted his move in 1941 to Boston, where he lived with his half-sister Ella. He soon drifted to the fringes of Boston's underworld, remaking himself as "Detroit Red," a zoot-suited con artist, dope dealer, burglar and pimp. He was arrested in February 1946 and given a seven-year sentence on several felony charges including illegal breaking and entering.

Surprisingly, his arrest gave Malcolm an opportunity for self-education, with the future minister copying by hand a dictionary word for word and voraciously reading at the prison library. At this time, his brothers Philbert and Reginald exposed him to the teachings of the Nation of Islam (NOI), a religious sect founded around 1930 in Detroit and led by Elijah Muhammad. According to the NOI, whites were an inherently evil race created in ancient times by a sinister black scientist named Yacub. On judgment day the NOI deity, Allah, would destroy whites and save the black race. Until then, blacks should win the favor of Allah by surrendering vices such as alcohol, avoiding impure foods such as pork, and educating themselves about the past achievements of the black race. Rather than integrate into a racist white society, blacks should embrace complete segregation from white society and dedicate themselves to establishing a financially and politically independent black homeland.

Upon his release from prison in 1952, Malcolm replaced his last name with an "X" to represent the African family name lost under slavery. He soon rose as a full-time NOI minister and distinguished himself as Elijah Muhammad's most effective recruiter and spokesman.

Malcolm X denounced middle-class black leaders as "Uncle Toms" and labeled Martin Luther King, Jr. a "chump" for advocating integration, declaring that "an integrated cup of coffee was insufficient pay for 400 years of slave labor." Malcolm also ridiculed King's "I Have a Dream" speech, insisting that independence, not integration, represented the only true path to African-American freedom.

Malcolm later wrote that he became disillusioned with the Reverend Elijah Muhammad after learning that the chief NOI minister had affairs with several secretaries and fathered six illegitimate children. In December 1963, when Malcolm described the recent assassination of President John F. Kennedy as a case of "chickens coming home to roost." Muhammad, for all his rhetoric about black assertiveness and self-defense, feared a white backlash and suspended Malcolm from his ministry for ninety days. On March 8, 1964, Malcolm publicly severed his ties with the Nation of Islam. He now wanted to work more closely with King, stating that both men sought black freedom.

Malcolm began receiving death threats from his former colleagues in the NOI. On February 21, Talmadge Hayer repeatedly shot Malcolm at the start of a speech at the Audubon Ballroom in New York. A grand jury indicted Hayer, Norman 3X Butler, and Thomas 15X Johnson, all members of the NOI, for Malcolm's murder. On the day after the assassination, Elijah Muhammad denied involvement with the killing. Malcolm's influence increased after his death with the publication of *The Autobiography of Malcolm X*. Members of the Student Nonviolent Coordinating Committee (SNCC) increasingly came under the posthumous influence of Malcolm and radicalized, even throwing white members out of the group in the name of black independence.

Signing of the Voting Rights Act. President Lyndon B. Johnson moves to shake hands with Dr. Martin Luther King while others look on. LBJ Library photo by Yoichi Okamoto.

Martin Luther King and Malcolm X waiting for a press conference. March 26, 1964

Long Hot Summers

For Lyndon Johnson and the Democratic Party, the era of peaceful reform ended with shocking abruptness in the mid-1960s. Rather than a racial millennium, the immediate aftermath of the landmark civil rights legislation from 1964 to 1965 brought explosive urban uprisings across the country and angry backlash from the white working and middle classes. A mere five days after Johnson signed the Voting Rights Act, a riot exploded in the Watts neighborhood of Los Angeles. The riot started when Lee Minikus, a white police officer, arrested Marquette Frye, an African American who had just consumed two beers with his brother Ronald, for speeding.

As a possibly intoxicated Frye began to resist arrest, a rumor spread rapidly through the crowd that police had beaten Frye's mother and pregnant girlfriend. Tempers rose on the hot summer day and the crowd, which included many who had been roughly treated by Los Angeles police, began throwing rocks and bottles. About 5,000 Watts residents, chanting "Burn, baby, burn," began torching buildings, looting stores, and firing handguns.

The Watts Riot lasted for six days and took the lives of 34 people (32 of them black), injuring another 900, leaving hundreds homeless, and destroying neighborhood businesses. The months of June through August 1967 became known as the "long, hot summer," as riots in 127 cities claimed at least 77 lives and a total of a half-billion dollars in property. The worst urban upheaval exploded in Detroit on July 23, where again a history of police brutality served as the spark. A total of 33 African Americans and 10 whites died in the melee, which caused $250 million in damages to homes and businesses. Much

of Detroit turned into a burned-out shell. Michigan Governor George Romney described Detroit as looking like it "had been bombed on the west side."

THE WARREN COURT

During the 1960s, civil rights marchers sought to revolutionize American race relations as they assaulted the citadels of segregation. Kennedy dramatically energized the office of the presidency, transforming it into the dynamic center of the federal government after what he saw as the long eight-year slumber of the Eisenhower years. Scientists, meanwhile, shattered humanity's bondage to planet Earth through the space program. Yet, ironically, one of the most revolutionary forces in the decade was a collection of nine mostly elderly, wealthy white men: the United States Supreme Court as led by Chief Justice Earl Warren.

President Eisenhower appointed Warren, the Republican governor of California and the GOP's nominee for vice president in 1948, as chief justice in 1953. Eisenhower saw Warren as a middle-of-the-road personality like himself who would preside over a cautious court. Warren proved talented in winning over justices to his legal viewpoints and in presenting to the world an image of a united Supreme Court in even the most controversial cases. The year after his appointment, Warren provided the leadership that led to the historic *Brown v. Board of Education* school desegregation decision.

Warren had missed the initial arguments in the case but was on hand for the second round of arguments. After that session, the justices discovered that a 5-4 majority favored overturning the *Plessy v. Ferguson* "separate but equal" decision. Warren, however, said that the authority of such an important decision would be undermined if the Court remained almost evenly split. He insisted on a unanimous decision and gradually persuaded the remaining four justices that segregation could be justified only on the assumption that African Americans were intellectually inferior. Through a slow process, Warren won over the entire court. Warren himself delivered the Court's unanimous decision.

Brown was just the beginning of a long, remarkable and controversial string of decisions. Under Warren, a previously conservative Court shifted sharply in a liberal direction. Eisenhower later said that appointing Warren as chief justice was "the biggest damned-fool mistake I ever made."

The **Warren Court** outraged social conservatives with a pair of 1963 rulings regarding school prayer. In 1960, after discovering that her son William was compelled to participate in daily group prayers at his junior high school, outspoken atheist Madalyn Murray brought a lawsuit against the Baltimore school district. A Maryland district court and the state appellate court rejected her arguments that the school prayers violated the United States Constitution's ban on government "establishment" of religion. Murray's appeals eventually reached the Supreme Court, which combined *Murray v. Curlett* with the similar *Abington School District v. Schempp* case. Murray argued that the Constitution provided an "unalienable right to freedom from religion as well as freedom of religion." In an 8-1 opinion, the Court ruled that mandated school prayers indeed violated the Constitution's establishment clause.

Sexual freedoms also expanded under the Warren Court. In the 1965 *Estelle v. Griswold* case, the Court ruled a Connecticut law that outlawed the use of contraceptives to be unconstitutional. By a 7-2 vote, the justices ruled that the statute violated the right of privacy indirectly provided by the Constitution through the Ninth and the Fourteenth Amendments and the penumbras of other rights provided under the national charter. The Court's reasoning would later provide the basis for the *Roe v. Wade* decision that legalized abortion in the first two trimesters of pregnancy. Meanwhile, several states had repealed laws deeming publications providing information on contraception as obscene. In 1960 the Federal Food and Drug Administration approved the marketing of the birth control pill, an event many feminists hailed as a moment of liberation. With the pill, many argued, adults could decide when to have children and how many, and women could be freed to have an active sex life and pursue a career.

The Warren Court also greatly upset conservatives by expanding the rights of criminal defendants with its 1963 *Gideon v. Wainwright* and 1966 ***Miranda v. Arizona*** decisions. In *Gideon*, the Court held that under the Sixth Amendment to the Constitution, which guarantees the right of those accused of a crime to have "the assistance of counsel," impoverished criminal defendants have to be provided lawyers if they cannot hire one on their own. In the *Miranda* decision, the Supreme Court ruled that any person interrogated while in police custody had to be informed of his/her rights, including the right to not speak without a lawyer present.

BEARING ANY BURDEN IN VIETNAM

No bigger shadow falls on Kennedy's and Johnson's legacies than the Vietnam War. Numerous flawed assumptions shaped that disaster. Kennedy saw the communist regime in Moscow, like the Nazi regime in Germany, as engaged in an aggressive campaign to dominate the world. Appeasement of the communists, he argued, would only encourage more aggression from the Soviets. The United States must back anti-communist regimes wherever they stood, even in small corners of the world like Southeast Asia, to prevent "the onrushing tide of Communism from engulfing all Asia," even if this meant supporting oppressive dictators who nevertheless opposed communism, like South Vietnamese dictator Ngo Dinh Diem.

The 1954 Geneva Peace Accords ending France's brutal colonial regime in Indochina split Vietnam into a communist north and a pro-American south. Diem could hardly have been a worse choice to lead South Vietnam. Diem was a wealthy man in a country of poverty. He was a Catholic in a land with a Buddhist majority and a man with poor political skills for a badly divided nation. Nevertheless, the United States chose to back him against **Ho Chi Minh**, widely regarded as a patriot and a hero in the wars of independence against the Japanese and French in the 1940s and 1950s. Ho's popularity in the North only grew during the 1950s as he implemented badly needed land reform.

In South Vietnam, land remained in the hands of the few. Bureaucrats in the Diem government became infamous for greed. Incompetent South Vietnamese government officials routinely demanded bribes, and Diem personally controlled drug trafficking in the country. The dictator shut down newspapers that criticized him. Dissidents who spoke out against the Diem dictatorship faced arrest and torture, and some simply disappeared. By the time Diem and his brother Ngo Dinh Nhu, the head of the South Vietnamese secret police, were killed during a 1963 military coup, 50,000 languished in prisons on political charges.

When Diem cancelled an election scheduled in 1956 that would have unified North and South Vietnam, the communists began a guerilla war. In 1960, the war escalated with the formation of the National Liberation Front (NLF), or the "Viet Cong (VC)," as they were labeled by the Diem regime. The North Vietnamese regular army amply supported the NLF.

Buddhist Protests and Deeper American Involvement

One of Kennedy's top advisors on Vietnam, General Maxwell Taylor embraced the so-called "**domino theory**"—the argument that if South Vietnam fell to the communists, neighboring countries would be swallowed by the "red tide" until, as Vice President Johnson said, American troops would have to fight "on the beaches of Waikiki" in Hawaii. To stop this feared communist onslaught, Taylor pushed for a dramatic increase in the number of American troops in South Vietnam. In late 1961, the number of American military advisors had grown to 3,000 and would reach 16,000 by the time of the American president's murder in 1963.

President Diem, however, continued to lose support from his own people. No group felt more alienated under Diem than South Vietnam's Buddhist majority. In government appointments, Diem heavily favored fellow Catholics, and his police violently suppressed Buddhists during the lead-up to celebrations of the Buddha's 2,527th birthday on May 8, 1963. Nine Buddhists celebrating the birthday died when fired upon by South Vietnamese troops. Ten thousand Buddhists marched two days later to protest the killings, and Diem responded in a typically heavy-handed way, ordering the mass arrests of outspoken Buddhist monks and their backers.

The Buddhist clergy captured world attention on June 11, 1963. On that day, a monk named Thich Quang Duc exited a car and sat in the lotus pose at a busy Saigon intersection in front of the Cambodian embassy. Other monks chanted while two doused the 66-year-old with gasoline. Quang Duc lit a match and burned to death while a man with a microphone declared, "A Buddhist priest burns himself to death. A Buddhist priest becomes a martyr." Only his heart remained unburned, and this became a sacred relic and symbol of the rightness of the Buddhist protests against Diem. As the shocking images of this public suicide reached the United States, Americans realized how deep the opposition to Diem ran and how badly they had been misled by the Kennedy administra-

tion about Vietnamese support for American policies. The monk's death sparked a summer of demonstrations at public schools and colleges, and five more Buddhists set themselves ablaze by the end of October 1963.

By September, Nhu and his brother Diem had completely outlived their usefulness to the administration. Nhu sent word to Ho Chi Minh that the Diem government was interested in negotiating a possible ceasefire with North Vietnam, directly contradicting the U.S. position. Kennedy officials signaled to top South Vietnamese generals that they would not object to a military overthrow of President Diem. On November 1, the South Vietnamese military overthrew Diem's government, murdering the president and Nhu the following day in the back of an armored personnel carrier. After shooting both, soldiers vented their rage at Nhu, stabbing his body multiple times after his death. General Duong Van Minh briefly led a new South Vietnamese government.

JOHNSON ESCALATES

John Kennedy died 20 days after Diem, leaving the war in the hands of the new president, Lyndon Johnson. A clear transition took place in President Kennedy's thinking about Vietnam in the final days of his administration. Kennedy asked his commanding officers to draw up contingency plans for a withdrawal. Maxwell Taylor, the chairman of the Joint Chiefs of Staff, issued a memo on October 4, 1963, which called for the removal of 1,000 military personnel by the end of the year. Additionally, Kennedy's budget for the fiscal year ending June 30, 1964,

Buddhist monk Thich Quang Duc, burning himself to death to protest persecution of Buddhists in Vietnam, as other monks look on, Saigon, 1963.

envisioned no major expansion of troop levels, thereby suggesting no plans existed for an escalation of troops in Southeast Asia.

Unfortunately, Diem's regime had reduced South Vietnamese agriculture to a shambles. Saigon's political chaos since the coup added to American troubles. Ten men held the South Vietnamese presidency between the 1963 coup and June 14, 1965, when Nguyen Van Thieu began his decade-long autocratic leadership, which would last until the waning days of the South Vietnamese Republic. Subsequently released taped White House conversations from the first half of 1964 show that **Secretary of Defense Robert McNamara** repeatedly urged Johnson to consider withdrawal of American forces from Vietnam within two years. Johnson shot back that Kennedy and McNamara had hurt the war effort and soldiers' morale in late 1963 by openly discussing such a possibility. Johnson, meanwhile, felt torn between two contradictory impulses, which he believed to be inextricably entwined. The future of the Democratic Party, he believed, depended on the success of his "Great Society" programs, such as the "war on poverty" and Medicare. But the United States would lose face and its influence in the world if he were perceived to be the first president to "lose a war."

Unable to choose between contradictory demands, Johnson made what proved to be a very expensive choice: he opted for both guns and butter. The increasing use of North Vietnamese regular troops in South Vietnam made the task more difficult for the Army of the Republic of Vietnam (ARVN). Johnson made General **William Westmoreland,** an advocate for an increased U.S. military presence in Vietnam, the new commander of the U.S. military advisory group as he relied on an inner circle more hawkish (pro-war) than Kennedy's.

The Gulf of Tonkin Incident

Increasing numbers of North Vietnamese Army troops fought alongside the Viet Cong to gain control of South Vietnam and end the American presence there. Ho Chi Minh anticipated that the Americans would try to inflict damage on the North and had convinced the Soviet Union and the Chinese government to provide sophisticated anti-aircraft batteries, radar, missiles and other defensive weapons. The American military conceived a plan in which South Vietnamese commandos would attack and activate North Vietnamese radar transmitters, allowing the signals to be inte rcepted by American intelligence ships, which could then pin down the location of these defense installations. American aircraft could then destroy communist radar sites and anti-aircraft guns, enabling American bombers to destroy larger targets within North Vietnam.

This would require the Americans and the South Vietnamese to patrol the waters near North Vietnam's coastline, considered vulnerable to attack by the communist military command. The naval destroyer *USS Maddox* became one of the first ships dispatched to conduct intelligence probes in late July 1964. Superiors instructed Captain John J. Herrick, the ship's commander, to maneuver no closer than eight miles from the coast or four miles from its islands. North Vietnam had never declared the limits of its territorial waters. When they ruled the region, the French had set the limit at three miles from its coast, but Hanoi followed China's lead and regarded 12 miles as the line of demarcation.

The afternoon of July 30, four swift boats manned by South Vietnamese commandoes attacked the North Vietnamese island of Hon Me, seven miles off the coast, then Hon Ngu, an island just three miles from the busy port of Vinh. The *Maddox* intercepted radar signals and transmitted the information to the CIA. The vessel stayed in the area and, in the early morning of August 2, 1964, the crew encountered three North Vietnamese patrol vessels armed with torpedoes ("PT craft") along with scores of unarmored North Vietnamese vessels. On high alert, Captain Herrick radioed to the Seventh Fleet Command that he expected an imminent attack by the North Vietnamese PTs.

A technician on board the *Maddox* informed Herrick that he had intercepted a North Vietnamese message suggesting the enemy vessels were preparing for "military operations." Herrick requested permission to withdraw, but instead his superiors ordered him to remain, and the *Maddox* moved within 10 miles of the Red River Delta. Technicians intercepted new orders from the North Vietnamese ships to attack the destroyer after refueling. Herrick told his crew to fire if enemy craft came within 10,000 yards. Soon the *Maddox* unleashed repeated salvos on the North Vietnamese torpedo boats.

After a twenty-minute battle, the *Maddox* barely suffered a scratch but seriously damaged two North Vietnamese vessels and sank a third. The *Maddox* withdrew from the Gulf of Tonkin, but Johnson gave the Navy orders to send the ship back, this time accompanied by a second vessel, the *Turner Joy.*

As the *Maddox* approached its objective on August 4, thunderstorms played havoc with the ship's equipment. Sonar and radar operators signaled to the captain that North Vietnamese vessels had fired 22 torpedoes at them, even though no enemy ships had been seen and none of the charges hit their supposed targets. The *Maddox* opened fire. Technicians then warned of more torpedoes on the way.

Captain Herrick dispatched pilots to find the attacking ships. Commander James Stockdale, who would later be shot down over North Vietnam and spend 1965-1973 as a prisoner of war before being promoted to admiral, flew one of the planes. (Independent presidential candidate Ross Perot would tap Stockdale as his running mate in 1992.) Flying over the Gulf, Stockdale radioed back, "Not a ship, not the outline of a ship, not a wake, not a reflection, not the light of a single tracer bullet. Nothing." The captain sent a report to naval command, cautioning that an error may have been made in reading the sonar.

McNamara later said that Johnson reacted to the Gulf of Tonkin incident "on the belief that it was a conscious decision on the part of the North Vietnamese political and military leaders to escalate the conflict and an indication that they would not stop short of winning." As the Pentagon spoke of "a second deliberate attack," the president addressed the nation on television, declaring "Repeated acts of violence against the armed forces of the United States must be met not only with defense, but with positive reply."

That positive reply came in the form of the first major American bombing raid against North Vietnam. American aircraft bombed four North Vietnamese patrol bases and an important oil storage depot, destroying or damaging twenty-five North Vietnamese vessels. The North Vietnamese downed two American planes in the engagement, including one carrying Everett Alvarez, Jr., of San Jose, California, who would become the first American prisoner of war in the Vietnam conflict and would remain in Communist custody for another nine years.

The guns aboard the *Maddox* had barely cooled when a war powers resolution giving the president a free hand in Vietnam was introduced in the Congress. Known popularly as the "**Gulf of Tonkin Resolution**," the document declared "the Congress approves and supports the determination of the President as Commander in Chief, to take all necessary measures to repel any armed attack against the forces of the United States, and to prevent further aggression." President Johnson would behave as if the resolution, passed on August 7 by a 414-0 vote in the House of Representatives and opposed only by Senators Wayne Morse and Ernest Gruening of Arkansas in the upper chamber, represented a virtual declaration of war. Congress surrendered its constitutional prerogative to decide on matters of war and peace, and for nine years the House refused to shape war policy through its power of the purse for fear of being accused of not supporting the troops.

DIRECT U.S. MILITARY INTERVENTION

Operation Rolling Thunder

Armed with a mandate from the voting public in the 1964 presidential race and the Gulf of Tonkin Resolution, Johnson felt politically strong enough to push a more aggressive approach in Indochina. He spent early 1965 relying on a heavy bombing campaign in North Vietnam aimed at breaking the communists' will to fight and the Hanoi regime's ability to supply men and arms to the South. Called "Operation Rolling Thunder," the bombing of North Vietnam lasted from March 1965 until November 1968, involving two million sorties in which more than one million tons of bombs were dropped. In all, 7,078,032 tons of bombs would be dropped by Americans on North and South Vietnam from 1964 until 1973, as compared to a total of 2,057,244 tons dropped by American pilots in all theaters of World War II. This came to about 1,000 pounds for every Vietnamese man, woman, and child.

Bombing raids on an almost entirely rural country like North Vietnam, however, produced meager military results, and the South Vietnamese military continued to perform poorly. The communists, meanwhile, seemed poised for an offensive in the South's Central Highlands. Johnson reluctantly gave approval to an expanded air campaign with fewer restrictions.

Two battalions of Marines waded ashore at Da Nang on March 8, 1965, along with tanks and howitzers, to protect the airbase there—the first American combat units dispatched to Vietnam. The administration decided to lengthen the bombing campaign to a year (it would be extended to more than three years) and to put 40,000 combat troops "in country."

Search and Destroy Missions

American ground troops felt unprepared for the physical demands of fighting in Vietnam, where temperatures often soared as high as 120 degrees Fahrenheit, the heat enhanced by high humidity. Salt tablets became part of a soldier's necessary survival tools. Meanwhile, fire ants and leeches tormented soldiers, leaving the surface of the skin painfully itchy and fiery red. Abrasive elephant grass growing as tall as eight feet also tore at the troops' skin. Rubber and bamboo trees so densely crowded the jungle landscape that the sun at times could not be seen in broad daylight. Soldiers often could move no more than 100 feet in one hour, even as they were overwhelmed by the smells of gunpowder, sulfur, diesel fuel and rotting corpses.

In the cities, soldiers had to watch out for hidden explosives in abandoned toys and even in the bodies of

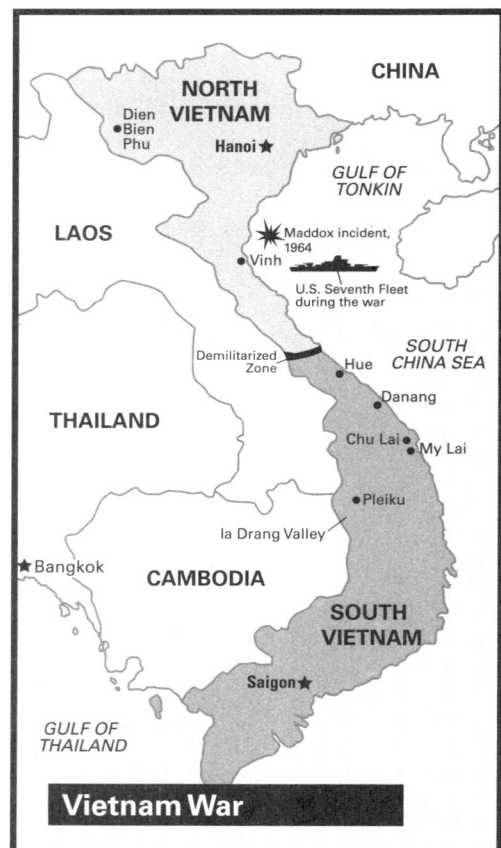

Map 27.2 Vietnam

an angry, hungry and homeless population. The Viet Cong use of traps, as well as women and young children as soldiers, increased the paranoia of American troops. Seeing potential assassins everywhere, American soldiers frequently shot neutral and friendly Vietnamese, which greatly increased the support for the communists.

THE WAR AT HOME, 1965-67

The "Television War"

For the first time, America fought a war in which the overwhelming majority of the country's households included at least one television set. Two years after the end of the Korean War, in 1955, 64.5 percent of homes had access to television. A decade later, 92.6 percent did. Starting in the mid-1960s an ever-growing number of homes could watch war coverage in color. The mid-1960s also marked the first time that more Americans told pollsters that they received news primarily from television than from radio or newspapers. Also by the mid-1960s, evening network news broadcasts had expanded from the 15-minute format used by CBS and NBC in the 1950s to a full half-hour. The expanded time provided more opportunities to cover the war.

These factors converged to make Vietnam the first "television war" or the "living room war." President Johnson obsessed over network coverage of Vietnam and had three televisions in the Oval Office set to ABC, CBS, and NBC when the news came on every evening. Johnson called network anchors to praise them when their coverage pleased him but would give them obscenity-strewn tongue-lashings when the coverage was critical.

In the beginning, most coverage of the war supported the American military's point of view uncritically. A *Boston Globe* survey of the 39 largest daily newspapers' editorials revealed that as late as 1968, not one advocated withdrawal from Vietnam. Criticism focused mostly on tactics. To war critics, far too many reporters relied exclusively on military spokesmen and official press releases for their stories. Some covered the war from the relative safety and comfort of Saigon hotels, rarely following troops into the field. The American media, with notable exceptions, gave little coverage to how the war affected the Vietnamese.

The cozy relationship between the press and the Defense Department began to unravel, however, as the war dragged on and reporters tired of hearing about a "light at the end of the tunnel" that receded ever farther in the distance. Told repeatedly that the Viet Cong and the North Vietnamese would soon collapse, reporters instead saw an enemy that seemed highly motivated and

dead Vietnamese. On top of these dangers, soldiers and Marines witnessed women and small children tossing hand grenades at Americans and sometimes discovered that Vietnamese to whom they had grown close were secretly fighting for the Viet Cong. It became increasingly difficult to distinguish friends from foes.

Underestimating the North Vietnamese and Viet Cong level of commitment, U.S. commanders assumed that the American technological advantage would mean they would prevail in a war of attrition, forcing the outgunned communists to sue for peace. To accomplish this, Westmoreland asked for more troops, a total of 450,000 by the end of 1966. The Viet Cong and NVA proved willing to suffer large numbers of combat deaths and injuries and quickly adapted to American combat tactics and strategies. The Americans expended huge amounts of ammo and often had little to show for it.

Such fighting proved unnerving to 18- and 19-year old soldiers, more and more of whom were draftees in dark, unfamiliar and heavily wooded terrain. Search and destroy missions based on rooting out Viet Cong bases of operations often put Americans in the position of destroying entire villages. The Americans would use Zippo cigarette lighters to burn down huts, destroy chickens and water buffalo that could be used to feed communist soldiers, and then moved on, leaving behind

A South Vietnamese woman and her children sit with an American military adviser among the ruins of her village burned by South Vietnamese government troops who believed its inhabitants were harboring Viet Cong rebels there. 1963.

determined even as the South Vietnamese military seemed increasingly dispirited, corrupt, and incompetent. Many reporters, however, risked their lives to experience the war as lived by the American soldiers, with sixty-three journalists killed during combat action in Vietnam.

Public Opinion and the War

A commonly believed post-Vietnam legend suggests that a politically liberal press opposed the Vietnam War from the start and unfairly portrayed the military as filled with drug-crazed baby killers, and that this undermined public support of the war. In reality, not only did newspapers back America's military involvement in Vietnam on the editorial pages, both the print and the electronic media sat on stories that would have increased opposition to it. A broad consensus developed among elites in support of the Vietnam War, encompassing leading Democrats and Republicans, much of academia, newspaper publishers, television executives, and business leaders.

The American public at large did not share this sentiment. As of March 1966, most Americans still supported Johnson's actions in Vietnam, but this support was soft. A majority told pollsters they would approve of a withdrawal of troops and free and fair elections in South Vietnam even if that meant a political victory by the Viet Cong. Johnson's advisors opposed both of these options, as did most newspaper editorial boards. By August 1968, the broader American public had turned against the war. That month, a Gallup poll showed that 53 percent of the American public thought American involvement in Vietnam had been a mistake. The gap between elites and the rest of the country on the wisdom of American intervention grew deeper up to the American withdrawal in the early 1970s.

Opposition to the war ran inversely to educational attainment. According to a Gallup Poll taken in January 1971, 73 percent of the American public favored withdrawal from Vietnam. The percentage favoring withdrawal was highest, 80 percent to 20 percent, for those with only a grade-school education. Among high school graduates, 75 percent favored withdrawal. The most educated remained the most supportive of the war. Among college graduates, only 60 percent favored withdrawal while 40 percent backed continued military involvement.

Class Divisions

The Vietnam War deepened the class divide in American society. About 80 percent of the 2.5 million American men who served in the Vietnam War came from the poor or working class. Meanwhile, as author Christian G. Appy put it, ". . . America's most unpopular war was fought primarily by the nineteen-year-old children of waitresses, factory workers, truck drivers, secretaries, firefighters, carpenters, custodians, police officers, sales people, clerks, mechanics, miners and farmworkers . . ."

Enlistees from blue-collar families ranged from a low of 52 percent in the Vietnam-era Air Force to a high of 57 percent for the Marine Corps. From 1966 to 1971, 79.7 percent of servicemen had 12 years or less of education. High school dropouts outnumbered college graduates in the military by 3-1. For most of the war, soldiers fighting and dying in Vietnam were also disproportionately African American.

America's Racial Divides Come to Vietnam

Racism shaped the Vietnam War in two ways: how American soldiers treated each other, and how they saw and treated the Vietnamese. Growing up in a culture saturated with white supremacist ideas, American soldiers often brought their racist baggage with them to Vietnam. Many black veterans reported being called "nigger" and being singled out for punishment as early as boot camp. In Vietnam, closer relationships developed between whites and blacks on the front, where soldiers depended on each other for survival, than in the rear where whites and blacks segregated in housing and in friendships.

African-American soldiers, who suffered death rates out of proportion to their share of the U.S. forces, suspected that white officers singled them out for dangerous combat duty. For this and other reasons, early on the Vietnam War became controversial in the African-American community. In the early 1960s, Malcolm X saw the war as white America's imperialism against people of color.

For years, the mainstream civil rights organizations held back, not wanting to antagonize allies in the Kennedy and Johnson administrations. Dr. Martin Luther King, Jr., however, attacked the war in accordance with his pacifist beliefs. By 1967, his words became sharper as he expressed fears that programs he favored, such as the War on Poverty, would be sacrificed to feed the ever-costlier war in Southeast Asia. Johnson's anti-poverty initiatives had raised people's hopes, King said, but the war was "an enemy of the poor."

As had others, King pointed to the irony of black men fighting for the freedom of others while being denied basic dignity at home. "We were taking the young black men who had been crippled by our society and sending them 8,000 miles away to guarantee liberties in Southeast Asia which they had not found in Southeast Georgia and East Harlem," King said. "So we have been repeatedly faced with the cruel irony of watching Negro and white boys on TV screens as they kill and die together for a nation that has been unable to seat them together in the same schools."

In an April 1967 speech at the Riverside Church in New York, King said that he struggled with how to answer young men condemned for participating in urban uprisings in cities like Los Angeles when the U.S. created such mayhem in Vietnam. "Their questions hit home, and I knew that I could never again raise my voice against the violence of the oppressed in the ghettos without having first spoken clearly to the greatest purveyor of violence in the world today—my own government," King said.

When white American soldiers arrived in Vietnam, they often brought their country's legacy racist culture with them. American soldiers often perceived a deep racial divide between themselves and their Vietnamese hosts. Drawing on America's mythology of the Old West, their minds filled with scenes from movies in which the cavalry mowed down droves of murderous "redskins," troops in Vietnam often called themselves "cowboys" and the natives "Indians."

As in the Asian theater of World War II, American soldiers were more likely to shoot soldiers who had surrendered than were their peers fighting in Europe during the First and Second World Wars. Like Anglo soldiers fighting the Japanese, American soldiers also sometimes collected and even mailed home "trophies" of their Vietnamese killed, such as severed ears. The longer the war dragged on, the bigger the gulf between the supposed liberators and the intended beneficiaries. "Too many of us forgot that Vietnamese were people," one soldier said. "We didn't treat them as people after a while."

In the early years of the war, African Americans, often coming from poor backgrounds, were more likely to volunteer for the military or to lack college deferments or other means of avoiding the draft. They made up 20 percent of combat deaths. (African Americans in the mid-1960s comprised 11 percent of the American population.) Part of the working class opposition to the war stemmed from the fact that their children disproportionately had to serve in Vietnam and casualties from Vietnam more often came from poor and working class neighborhoods. A firefighter who lost a son in Vietnam told interviewer Robert Coles, "I'm bitter. You bet your goddamn dollar I'm bitter. It's people like us who give up our sons for the country. The business people, they run the country and make money from it. The college types, the professors, they go to Washington and tell the government what to do . . . But their sons, they don't end up in the swamps over there, in Vietnam."

Until 1971, the American draft laws granted deferments for those attending college. College students disproportionately came from the middle and upper classes. Future political leaders like President Bill Clinton, Vice President Dick Cheney, Deputy Defense Secretary Paul Wolfowitz—an architect of the American invasion of Iraq in 2003—and House Speaker Newt Gingrich all received college deferments during the Vietnam War. Another recipient of a college deferment, future House Majority Whip Tom DeLay, claimed, "So many minority youths had volunteered . . . that there was literally no room for patriotic folks like myself."

Placement in the reserves and the state National Guard units became another way elites with political connections avoided combat duty in Vietnam. Only 15,000 National Guard and reserve soldiers actually served in Vietnam, out of a total of more than a million men. The National Guard became such a popular means of avoiding Vietnam that by 1968, the waiting list for enlistment reached 100,000 names. Future political leaders who avoided Vietnam service through this means included Vice President Dan Quayle and President George W. Bush.

Anti-War Protests Emerge

The leaders of the anti-war movement did come from college campuses rather than assembly lines. Risking accusations of undermining America's struggle against the Soviet Union in the Cold War, the "New Left," as it came to be known, rejected what it saw as American militarism. The Students for a Democratic Society (SDS) originated as a youth chapter of the League for Industrial Democracy, a socialist group that once claimed the authors Upton Sinclair and Jack London as members. Whites overwhelmingly made up the New Left, which drew its inspiration from African-American groups like the Student Nonviolent Coordinating Committee (SNCC.) The SDS consciously imitated SNCC's community organizing programs, which trained the poor in how to obtain assistance for food and for utility payments, taught the needy how to deal with landlords, and informed parents about pre-school and other programs available for needy children.

SDS members travelled South to risk their lives in civil rights sit-ins, freedom rides, marches, and protests. White members wanted to employ the direct-action tactics of groups like SNCC to address a wider range of issues, including the Vietnam War. A small core of peace activists, made up mostly of Unitarians and pacifist Quakers, had protested American foreign policy since the beginning of the Cold War. Protests against the Vietnam War at first drew little media attention. In New York on May 12, 1964, a dozen men burned their draft cards during a rally held by the Student Peace Union.

The SDS organized the first mass protest against the war on April 17, 1965. About 20,000 protestors assembled for an SDS-sponsored anti-war rally in Washington, D.C. Folk singers such as Joan Baez and Judy Collins performed as civil rights veterans such as Robert Moses denounced the American war effort. As a result of the April protest,

SDS chapters formed at 300 campuses across the nation, with more than 100,000 students joining the cause.

The SDS and similar groups picketed Central Intelligence Agency recruiters visiting colleges and protested against companies like Dow Chemical that manufactured war materials such as napalm and Agent Orange. These chemicals, often dropped by American war planes, burned human skin and caused injury, sickness and death among Vietnamese civilians. They also rallied against university science, chemistry and engineering departments conducting weapons research and development for the Pentagon. Other forms of anti-war activism included letter-writing campaigns aimed at newspapers and the Congress, withholding of taxes owed, and acts of civil disobedience such as blocking the movement of trains carrying troops.

The March on the Pentagon

The anti-war movement during the Johnson era reached a crescendo in 1967. A new draft policy launched that year ended the deferments granted for postgraduate education. Aimed at making the controversial conscription program fairer to working class constituents, this policy frightened and radicalized the previously apathetic middle class and affluent white students who enrolled in graduate school programs. A new contingent of young people suddenly felt they had a personal stake in ending the war.

That spring, the National Mobilization Committee Against the War, known by members as "The Mobe" and made up of pacifists, leftist radicals, and more conventional liberals, staged anti-war events in New York and San Francisco. Momentum steadily built toward the year's climax, the March on the Pentagon on October 21. The rally, attended by 70,000 protestors called "armies of the night" by the novelist Norman Mailer, opened at a cultural touchstone, the Lincoln Memorial, where Martin Luther King, Jr., had delivered his "I Have a Dream Speech" four years earlier. Popular chants—such as "Ho, Ho, Ho Chi Minh/The NLF is gonna win"—supported the North Vietnamese and Viet Cong forces still seen as the enemy by many in middle America. Some protestors rhythmically asked the Commander in Chief, "Hey, hey, LBJ/How many kids did you kill today?"

The protestors moved from the Lincoln Memorial to the Pentagon. As he nervously watched from his office window, McNamara insisted that none of the 3,000 troops and 1,800 Guardsmen load their rifles without his authorization. Some protestors placed flowers in the barrels of soldiers' M-14 rifles. Picketers pushed back against the defensive perimeter, with about 3,000 attempting to break through police lines. A small group eventually succeeding in entering the Pentagon, provok-

Protest vigil for peace taken outside the Alamo, San Antonio, Texas, Feb. 4, 1967.

ing nervous and angry building security to rough up the intruders. Eventually, authorities arrested 681, mostly for charges ranging from disorderly conduct to breaking police lines.

1960-1967: THE BEST OF TIMES

The curses of poverty, unemployment, crime, poorly funded and understaffed schools, and malnutrition still haunted African-American communities. Nevertheless, it would be wrong to assume that the voting rights laws, legislation requiring access to public accommodations regardless of race, anti-poverty programs and anti-discrimination mandates passed by Kennedy and Johnson had no impact.

For instance, during the 1960s, black unemployment dropped 34 percent. From 1959 to 1967, the poverty rate among African Americans dropped from a staggering 55.1 percent to a still much too high but significantly better 39.3 percent. (By 1970, the poverty rate among African Americans dropped further to 33.5 percent.) The poverty rate for all Americans in that time period dropped from 22.4 to 14.2 percent. Before the 1960s, a large percentage of African Americans held low-paying custodial or domestic jobs, or worked as under-compensated farm labor. During the 1960s, the number of blacks holding jobs in higher-paid technical, professional and clerical fields doubled, and the length of time African Americans stayed in school increased by an average of four years.

Largely because of civil rights laws and the Voting Rights Act of 1965, African Americans gained unprecedented clout in local, state and national politics during the Kennedy-Johnson era. Between 1960 and 2000, the number of African-American officeholders sharply climbed from just 300 to nearly 9,040. African Americans have been elected mayor of many of the nation's largest cities, including New York, Los Angeles, Chicago, Washington, D.C., Dallas, Atlanta, Philadelphia, and Detroit. Without the 1965 Voting Rights Act, it is highly unlikely that Barack Obama, whose mother was white and whose father was a black native of Kenya, could have been elected president in 2008. In a matter of weeks after passage of the landmark 1964 Civil Rights Act, "whites only" restrooms, water fountains, and seating in theaters, sports stadiums and restaurants disappeared across the South. Between 1964 and 1974, the United States Justice Department filed suits against 500 school districts and more than 400 gas stations, hotels and motels, restaurants and lunch counters, bars and truck stops that still segregated black patrons.

It was not just African Americans who benefited from Kennedy's New Frontier and Johnson's Great Society. Increased government spending on both defense and domestic projects helped create 8.4 million new jobs from 1960 to 1966. Spending on health and education increased 59 percent and on urban development by 76 percent. The average family saw a 30 percent gain in real income from 1960 to 1968. Counting all racial categories, at the beginning of the 1960s, 40 million Americans lived in poverty. A decade later, the poverty rate dropped to

A peace moratorium at Trinity University, San Antonio, Texas, Oct. 14, 1969.

24 million, a decline from 20 percent of the population to 12 percent.

The Kennedy-Johnson years saw the development of a more equitable criminal justice system. Johnson established public television and public radio, which gave Americans access to information, music and news not subject to the pressure of commercial popularity or pressure from sponsors. Laws passed in this era provided greater protection for privacy, increased rights for women, a sharper division between church and state, and an explosion of scientific and technological innovations. Literacy rates rose dramatically. In addition to space travel, the era saw the rapid improvement in the power and efficiency of computers, and better prospects for patients with cancer and other lethal diseases. Life spans lengthened and the population generally enjoyed better health from the 1940s until the late 1960s, an age of political liberalism.

1960-1967: THE WORST OF TIMES

In spite of all these achievements, the problems faced in the 1960s proved maddeningly hard to solve. Johnson's programs to fight poverty and racial discrimination proved the least popular initiatives of his presidency among white voters who began to feel they were too highly taxed for the benefit of racial minorities. A July 1966 poll revealed that a majority of Americans favored cuts in anti-poverty and urban renewal programs, rent subsidies and welfare expenditures, and showed that they wanted the savings to be used to increase spending on the Vietnam War. Most Americans, according to polls, approved spending on the space program and programs to curb pollution, but an astonishing 90 percent were against further civil rights legislation. A Gallup survey indicated that 88 percent of Americans thought that more hard work and effort would solve black poverty, rather than additional government assistance. By 1967, after another round of urban riots, 52 percent of Americans believed that Johnson had moved "too fast" on the issue of integration. By 1966, President Johnson despaired that Americans were more excited about the prospects of humans landing on the moon than they were about any successes of the war on poverty.

According to George Lipsitz, a professor of ethnic studies at the University of California at San Diego, much of the celebrated civil rights and anti-poverty legislation of the Kennedy and Johnson years foundered because of white bureaucrats' unwillingness to enforce anti-discrimination laws. The newly established Equal Employment Opportunity Commission lacked enforcement powers such as the ability to issue cease and desist orders against discriminating employers. The EEOC could do no more than offer its services as a non-binding arbitrator between discriminated against individuals and discriminating employers. Underfunding, understaffing and a lack of administrative will to tackle entrenched job discrimination made the EEOC a paper tiger. By 1967, the agency received an average of 23 discrimination complaints a day. By 1972, only about half of the 80,000 cases referred to the EEOC had ever been investigated.

Even after the Kennedy-Johnson reforms, African Americans still suffered significantly higher poverty rates than whites. This is attributable in part to a sharp increase in the number of single-parent homes in black America. In 1950 single women headed only 17 percent of black homes. By 1970, the percentage of black homes headed by single women stood at 34.5 percent.

Protesting the Vietnam War: The March on the Pentagon. Washington D.C., October, 21, 1967

According to the federal government, most absent fathers in recent decades have ended up paying no child support or less than the splitting couple had agreed upon. Black women were particularly hard hit by the absence of the father's income. Even with an increase in black wages from 1960 to 1970, African-American men climbed from $669 earned for every $1,000 earned by whites in 1960 to only $704 per each $1,000 earned by whites in 1970. Black women experienced a much more dramatic growth in wages but still lagged considerably behind whites. In 1960, black women earned $696 per $1,000 paid to whites and only $851 per $1,000 for whites in 1970.

After the Kennedy-Johnson initiatives, white flight aggravated the poverty of black neighborhoods. The United States Census Bureau reported that about 900,000 whites moved from cities to the suburbs each year between 1965 and 1970. This mass movement started in part in reaction to the riots in the larger cities. Whites concluded it was no longer safe to live inside the nation's metropolises. White parents also feared sending their children to the same schools as black and Latino children. The sad irony was that once schools were legally mandated to desegregate, the schools re-segregated because of the white

migration. With the fleeing whites went white-owned businesses and white money, and urban school districts, now with a minority majority population, would struggle to make up the decrease in tax revenues.

In the end, Lyndon Johnson's dream of winning the war on poverty and ending racial strife was sacrificed on the altar of the Vietnam War. The war consumed an ever-larger percentage of the budget. Total American military expenditures grew from more than $295 billion in 1964 to over $354 billion in 1967. With major increases in both domestic and military spending, inflation began to rise each year, from 1.28 percent in 1964 to 4.27 percent in 1968, Johnson's last full year in office. Johnson steadily lost interest in battling poverty and discrimination as he became obsessed with avoiding the onerous fate of being the "first" American president to lose a war. By 1967-1968, Johnson began cutting domestic programs in order to support a deepening war effort in Southeast Asia. Dr. King would come out against the war, seeing in it the defeat of his campaign for social justice.

"A few years ago there was a shining moment in [the civil rights] struggle," King said in a New York speech April 4, 1967, exactly one year before his assassination. "It seemed as if there was a real promise of hope for the poor, both black and white, through the poverty program . . . Then came the buildup in Vietnam"

The Vietnam War not only diverted funds from needed social programs, but opposition to the war provoked an assault on civil liberties by the Johnson administration. Fearing the anti-war movement's apparent momentum, Johnson tried to disrupt it by dispatching CIA agents, in violation of U.S. law, to spy on peace advocates. The agency compiled dossiers on more than 7,000 citizens. Grand juries indicted draft resisters while the FBI infiltrated the peace movement and attempted to discredit its leaders by spreading false information about alleged sexual affairs, crimes, and other fabricated misdeeds that reached family members, friends, and sometimes the media. Undercover FBI agents provocateur incited activists to commit illegal acts just so they could be arrested. These illegal activities of the FBI, part of its COINTELPRO (Counter Intelligence Program), were not uncovered until Senate investigations in the mid-1970s.

Whites resented African American civil rights gains they perceived as coming at their expense. Continued poverty, racism, and police violence outraged African Americans. These resentments, mixed in with mounting public anger over the Vietnam War, created a volatile political atmosphere. Unbelievably, after the heartaches of the Kennedy, Medgar Evers and Malcolm X assassinations, the Schwerner, Chaney and Goodman murders, the Sixteenth Street Baptist Church bombing, and the holocausts that consumed Watts, Detroit and scores of other cities, the frustrated dreams of Americans would explode in 1968, creating terrifying chaos and violence that would dwarf the murderous previous three years. In a matter of months, Martin Luther King, Jr. and Bobby Kennedy would die violently, and American cities once again went up in flames. Meanwhile, Vietnam would enter its bloodiest period, consuming at unprecedented levels the lives of American soldiers and demolishing Lyndon Johnson's hopes for a Great Society.

Table 27.1   **Major Reform Programs Under Kennedy and Johnson**

Reform	Date Legislation Passed	Significance
Equal Pay Act of 1963	June 10, 1963	Made it illegal to set different wage scales based on sex and also gave the Secretary of Labor increased power to set wage and hour standards for children in the workplace.
Abolition of Poll Taxes	January 23, 1964	The 24th Amendment abolished poll taxes, state taxes that disenfranchised millions of African Americans.
Civil Rights Act of 1964	July 2, 1964	Prohibited discrimination based on race, color, religion, sex or national origin in terms of accommodations, hiring and firing; strengthened enforcement of voting rights; and allowed the U.S. attorney general to sue schools still practicing segregation.
Economic Opportunity Act	August 20, 1964	Created VISTA (a domestic version of the Peace Corps) and the Job Corps to promote economic development, provide job training, and reduce poverty.
Elementary and Secondary Education Act	April 11, 1965	Provided funding for schools serving low-income students and launched Head Start, a program preparing disadvantaged preschool children for education.
Medicare and Medicaid	July 30, 1965	The Johnson administration created Medicare and Medicaid under the Social Security Amendments of 1965. Medicare provided health insurance for those over 65 while Medicaid provided health care access for the poor.
Voting Rights Act	August 6, 1965	Banned literacy tests used to disenfranchise African Americans and empowered the Justice Department to monitor elections to prevent voter intimidation.
Environmental reforms	October 3, 1964 – November 21, 1967	The Wilderness Act of 1964, The Water Quality Act of 1965, and the Air Quality Act of 1967 aimed at preserving nature and reducing the harmful health effects of industrialization.

Chronology

1960 Sit-ins at lunch counters begin.
John Kennedy elected president.

1961 Peace Corps created.
Alliance for Progress established.
Bay of Pigs Invasion.
Berlin Wall erected.
Kennedy dispatches 100 Special Forces troops to South Vietnam

1962 Cuban Missile Crisis.
James Meredith enrolls at Ole Miss.

1963 Civil Rights demonstrations in Birmingham.
March on Washington.
Test Ban Treaty signed.
Diem assassinated.
Kennedy assassinated.
Betty Friedan publishes *The Feminine Mystique*.
By the end of the year, 16,000 American troops are stationed in South Vietnam.

1964 Job Corps established.
Head Start created.
Mississippi Freedom Summer declared.
Civil Rights Act sighed into law.
Gulf of Tonkin incident.
War on Poverty declared.
Johnson-Goldwater election.

1965 U.S. combat troops deployed to Vietnam.
Assassination of Malcolm X.
Medical Care Act passed.
Civil Rights March: Selma to Montgomery.
Voting Rights Act signed into law.
Watts Riot.
Grape strike in California.
Operation Rolling Thunder.

1966 National Organization of Women (NOW) founded.

1967 Anti-war demonstrations spread.
A race riot erupts in Detroit.
Thurgood Marshall, first African-American appointed to the U. S. Supreme Court.
March on the Pentagon.

SUGGESTED READINGS

Christian G. Appy, *Working-Class War: American Combat Soldiers and Vietnam* (1993).

Taylor Branch. *Parting the Waters: America in the King Years, 1954-1963*. 1988.

Roger Bruns. *Martin Luther King, Jr.: A Biography*. 2006.

Clayborne Carson. *In Struggle: SNCC and the Black Awakening of the 1960s*. 1981.

Dan T. Carter. *The Politics of Rage: George Wallace, The Origins of the New Conservatism, and the Transformation of American Politics*. 1995.

Robert Dallek. *An Unfinished Life: John F. Kennedy, 1917-1963* (200.

_____,*Lone Star Rising: Lyndon Johnson and His Times, 1908-1960* (1991).

_____,*Flawed Giant: Lyndon Johnson and His Times, 1961-1973* (1998).

George Q. Flynn, *The Draft: 1940-1973* (1993).

Todd Gitlin. *The Sixties: Years of Hope, Days of Rage* (1987).

Andrew Hacker. *Two Nations: Black and White, Separate, Hostile, Unequal* (1992).

David Halberstam, *The Best and the Brightest* (1969).

William M. Hammond, *Reporting Vietnam: Media and Military at War* (1998).

Maurice Isserman and Michael Kazin. *America Divided: The Civil War of the 1960s* (2000).

Stanley Karnow, *Vietnam: A History* (1983).

Martin Luther King, Jr. *Why We Can't Wait* (1964).

Richard Kluger. *Simple Justice: The History of Brown v. Board of Education and Black America's Struggle for Equality* (1975).

Mark Hamilton Lytle. *America's Uncivil Wars: The Sixties Era From Elvis to the Fall of Richard Nixon* (2006).

Allen J. Matusow. *The Unraveling of America: A History of Liberalism in the 1960s* (1984).

Robert McNamara, *In Retrospect: The Tragedy and Lessons of Vietnam* (1995).

Anne Moody. *Coming of Age in Mississippi* (1968).

Rick Perlstein. *Nixonland: The Rise of a President and the Fracturing of America* (2008).

Harvard Sitkoff. *The Struggle for Black Equality, 1954-1980* (1981).

Robert Weisbrot. *Freedom Bound: A History of America's Civil Rights Movement* (1990).

Theodore H. White. *The Making of the President: 1960* (1961).

Tom Wolfe. *The Right Stuff* (1979).

Malcolm X (as told to Alex Haley). *The Autobiography of Malcolm X* (1964).

Review Questions

1. How did the sit-in movement mark a change in strategy for the Civil Rights Movement and where else did leaders use the tactic of "direct action"?

2. What major events marked the American relationship to the communist world during the Kennedy and Johnson administrations?

3. What were the most important domestic initiatives that comprised the "Great Society," including civil rights reforms?

4. What underlying factors caused the urban unrest of the mid- and late-1960s?

5. By what steps did the United States get involved in the Vietnam War, and what assumptions, such as the "Domino Theory," drove this process?

Glossary of Important People and Concepts

Apollo Program
Bay of Pigs Invasion
Civil Rights Act of 1964
Cuban Missile Crisis
Domino Theory
Freedom Riders
Barry Goldwater
Great Society
Gulf of Tonkin Resolution
Ho Chi Minh
Lyndon Baines Johnson
John F. Kennedy
Kennedy-Nixon Debates
Martin Luther King, Jr.
"Letter from a Birmingham Jail"
John Lewis
Robert McNamara
Malcolm X
March on Washington
Miranda v. Arizona
"New Frontier"
Voting Rights Act of 1965
Warren Court
Watts Riot
William Westmoreland

ROBERT KENNEDY

Chapter Twenty-eight

THE NIGHTMARE YEAR, 1968

As the first major Democratic showdown loomed in the Indiana primary on May 7, Robert Francis Kennedy (RFK) drew large crowds that responded to his appearances with frightening intensity. The multiple tragedies of 1968 and the dreams that his supporters projected upon Kennedy delicately balanced the candidate at a thin intersection of hope and doom. Friends warned Kennedy that someone would kill him. The question for some was whether he would be slain by someone who despised him or someone motivated by a twisted sense of love.

Kennedy's fans screamed and wept at his appearances, their faces marked by and their voices touched with pain over past losses and a despairing, wounded desire for a better tomorrow. Bobby's older brother, President John Kennedy, had been assassinated five years earlier. The recent murder of civil rights leader Martin Luther King, Jr., as well as the bloodshed in Vietnam and a series of race riots that had ripped apart American cities had taken their toll on the emotions of the younger Kennedy's followers. His audiences reached out to the New York Senator as a refuge from the madness.

"The crowds were savage," recalled RFK adviser John Bartlow Martin. "They pulled his cuff links off, tore his clothes, tore ours. In bigger towns, with bigger crowds, it was frightening." Kennedy would stand in his open top car as it slowly inched through admiring, emotional throngs, briefly touching the hands, arms and faces of grasping admirers while his aide Bill Barry desperately held him from behind, trying to keep him from being pulled away. "Not so tight, you're going to break my back," Kennedy was once heard pleading. Nevertheless, on one occasion a woman yanked his head down by pulling on his tie while another woman pulled him off the car completely.

These were violent scenes in a violent year. Two political murders darkened the year, as did the slaughter by American soldiers of the civilian residents of a Vietnamese village named My Lai. In 1968, nearly 16,000 American soldiers died in Vietnam and another 99,000 suffered injuries, the bloodiest year yet of the war in terms of American casualties. The war also came home. The United States turned on itself, with the conflict between whites and blacks, pro-war "hawks" and anti-war "doves," between college students and the working class, and between rich and poor often punctuated with bloodshed.

In 1920, the Irish poet William Butler Yeats looked back at another time of multiple horrors, the First World War, and composed one of the landmarks of modern literature, a poem called "The Second Coming." Looking at Europe's post-war landscape, Yeats wrote:

Things fall apart; the centre cannot hold;
Mere anarchy is loosed upon the world,
The blood-dimmed tide is loosed, and everywhere
The ceremony of innocence is drowned;
The best lack all conviction, while the worst
Are full of passionate intensity.

Yeats's words perfectly describe 1968. It was a year in which the bullet carried more power than ideas. This epic year was a time when political heroes became martyrs, idealism turned to rage, and cities in Vietnam and the United States became funeral pyres.

CAMPUS UNREST

The Columbia Occupation

In 1968 political disputes over topics ranging from the seemingly trivial (the construction of a gymnasium) to the essential (the Vietnam War) at times appeared to shake the very foundations of Western society. Nowhere was this more the case than on college campuses around the world. There, revolution seemingly joined "readin" and "'ritin" and "'rithmetic" as one of the four "R's." The year 1968 saw student rebellions at Columbia University in New York; in Paris, France; and in Mexico City. These youthful uprisings aimed at greater academic freedom, genuine democracy, socialism, and an end to imperialist wars.

Protests at Columbia and Harlem

A **student revolt at Columbia University** in New York City captured 1968 in a microcosm. There the students protested against capitalism, the Vietnam War, the university's involvement in developing war technology, and institutional racism. Mostly affluent and overwhelmingly white, a majority of the students at the school did not care that the university had broken ground for a new gymnasium that would intrude on the largely poor and African American Harlem neighborhood next to the campus. Morningside Park, an undeveloped 30-acre plot on the eastern side of the campus, had always served as the border between Columbia and Harlem.

Planned since 1959, the gym would cost $8.4 million ($52.6 million in 2010 dollars), and Columbia promised to construct public facilities, including a swimming pool, open to Harlem residents. Proposed spending on the gym, however, outstripped planned university spending on the local community by five to one. By the time of its ground-breaking in February 1968, the project had become a target of discontent for Black Power advocates in Harlem, who derided it as "Gym Crow." White anti-war activists attending Columbia took a longer time to notice the dispute. Student activism focused on the on-campus recruitment conducted by Dow Chemical, the manufacturer of Napalm-B (the cancer-causing, flammable chemical agent used to burn communist troops and destroy villages in South Vietnam) and the Central Intelligence Agency. The campus chapter of the leftist Students for a Democratic Society (SDS) also objected to Columbia University's participation in the Institute for Defense Analyses (IDA), which developed weapons and "counter-insurgency" strategies against guerrilla forces such as the Viet Cong. Finally, campus SDS leader Mark Rudd and other members of the anti-war group objected to a campus-wide prohibition on indoor demonstrations as a violation of free speech.

On March 27, students protested against Columbia's contribution to war technology by occupying part of Low Library, the location of university administration offices, in open defiance of the ban against indoor demonstrations. Students occupied the building and demanded to meet Columbia President Grayson L. Kirk, who sat on the board of the IDA. Kirk's reign as campus president bordered on autocratic.

A student occupation of Hamilton Hall began on April 23. Henry Coleman, the Columbia College acting dean, went to his office in Hamilton and promptly became a hostage of the protestors. By the fourth day, demonstrators controlled five buildings. Students decorated the occupied buildings with pictures of Cuban revolutionary Ernesto "Che" Guevara, Soviet revolutionary leader Vladimir Lenin, and Malcolm X.

The university suspended construction of the new gymnasium, which was never completed at the Morningside Park site. A different one would eventually be built inside the campus. The students made five other demands before they would leave the buildings they controlled: the end of Columbia's affiliation with the IDA; the reversal of the ban on indoor demonstrations; the dropping of criminal charges against the student demonstrators; the release of six prisoners already arrested for protests against the IDA; and amnesty from suspensions and other discipline for the protest participants. The university rejected amnesty for the protestors, and on April 30, the New York City police gathered in military formation and stormed the occupied buildings, ejecting the protestors. Police beat protestors with nightsticks and blackjacks. They forced one group of protestors to run a gauntlet, with officers raining down blows with clubs and other weapons. Several hundred were injured, and police reported that 720 had been arrested.

In response, a general strike paralyzed the campus. About 350 students once again occupied Hamilton Hall. Events unfolded as they had on April 30, with 68 students injured and 177 arrested. Nevertheless, the protesting students got most of what they wanted. Columbia University ended its affiliation with IDA, and the prohibition against indoor demonstrations was reversed. The university dropped trespassing charges against most of the students. The school also dropped the attempt to expel Linda LeClair, a student enrolled at the affiliated Barnard College, because she had been caught living in off-campus housing with a male student enrolled at Columbia. LeClair was allowed to stay at Barnard, though she was banned from the Barnard cafeteria and all campus social events.

Revolution in the Air

Student revolts rocked politics around the world in 1968, with the occupation by students in Columbia University inspired by and serving as an inspiration for other youthful insurrections. Many of these students embraced the slogan coined by Jack Weinberg, a leader of the Free Speech Movement at the University of California at Berkeley, who once said in an interview, "You can't trust anybody over 30."

The worldwide student rebellions began in October 1967 in Prague, capital of the communist nation of Czechoslovakia. There, 2,000 students attending the city's Polytechnical University and angered by the lack of reliable lights and heat in their cold dormitory rooms marched to the Presidential Palace. The Czech government sent in riot police who beat the demonstrators with clubs and fired tear gas into the crowds. The students continued their bold protests throughout the winter, persuading the Communist Party leadership to dump the conservative First Secretary Antonin Novotný and replace him with the smiling, cheerful reformer Alexander Dubcek who ushered in a period of political idealism that spring and summer.

The non-violent revolution, in which Dubcek tried to open up the totalitarian government's decision-making process and to allow a broad range of artistic freedoms, displeased the Soviet Union, which had dominated Czechoslovakia since the end of World War II. On August 20-21, 1968, the Soviet Union sent its troops, along with soldiers from other communist Warsaw Pact countries, to crush what amounted to a Czech independence movement. The Soviets arrested Dubcek and his allies and installed a more subservient, and more oppressive, pro-USSR government. The American debacle in Vietnam made it easier for the Soviets to successfully crush the "Czech Spring" with few international repercussions, and depressed many activists in the United States.

In Paris, students began their revolt for relatively pedestrian reasons. Students protested at first against severe overcrowding at university campuses. Protests began on March 22 when students, artists and left-leaning political activists took control of an administration building at the University of Nanterre. Protests soon swept the country. A general strike, largely by workers in state-owned industries, on May 13 brought one million protestors into the streets of the French capital. Other demonstrators, more broadly, called for the overthrow of capitalism across the West. Protestors set the stock exchange building on fire.

For a time, it appeared that the government of French President Charles De Gaulle might fall. But by the time of parliamentary elections on June 23, public support for the strikers had faded. De Gaulle's conservative party won a huge majority in the election.

In Mexico, students chafed against the corrupt, autocratic domination by the Institutional Revolutionary Party, which by 1968 had ruled the country for almost a half century. The International Olympic Committee had selected Mexico City to host the 1968 summer games and the government, in spite of the widespread poverty in Mexico, spent lavishly to prepare athletic venues for the games. On August 27, a half million people staged an anti-government rally, the largest such demonstration in Mexican history.

Eager to end the uprising before the arrival of the international press covering the Olympics, President Gustavo Diaz Ordaz dispatched 10,000 combat ready troops to crush a demonstration of about 5,000 men, women and children at the Plaza de Tres Culturas on October 2 in the District of Tlatelolco. Government troops fired machine guns into the crowd even as helicopters dropped flares from above. Up to 400 died in the violence, though the government admitted no more than 43 deaths.

More political controversy unfolded at the Olympics. Two African-American track stars, Tommie Smith and John Carlos, respectively the gold and bronze medalists in the 200-meter dash, bowed their heads and gave a "black power" salute as the "Star Spangled Banner" played during the medal ceremony. Speaking later to reporters, Smith added, "It is very discouraging to be in a team with white athletes. On the track you are Tommie Smith, the fastest man in the world, but once you are in the dressing rooms you are nothing more than a dirty Negro."

The United States Olympic Committee immediately kicked both athletes off the team and sent them home early. Both received death threats and the American press described their gesture as a "Nazi-like salute" and called them "black-skinned storm troopers." The year 1968 ended with the elites in power in January still largely in charge in December.

VIETNAM IN '68

During the summer of 1967, congressional leaders confronted Lyndon Johnson about the immense costs of both the Vietnam War and Johnson's beloved "Great Society" social programs. By this point, the war cost $20 billion a year (more than $132 billion a year in 2014 dollars). To pay the bills for these expensive projects, the president would have to propose tax increases and/or budget cuts. Johnson opted for a 10 percent tax surcharge to be assessed on all corporate and individual taxpayers. "Until that moment, most Americans had not been asked to do anything or pay anything to support the war," journalist Dan Oberdorfer wrote.

The Tet Offensive

Disturbing signs abounded that the war would take a more violent turn. By the summer of 1967, American military commanders received intelligence indicating a buildup of North Vietnamese forces in Khe Sanh in the far northwestern corner of South Vietnam, not far from the Demilitarized Zone (DMZ) dividing the two countries. Commanders dispatched Marines to reinforce the base against an anticipated North Vietnamese Army (NVA) assault. The North Vietnamese and National Liberation Front (Viet Cong) troops began bombarding Khe Sanh January 21, 1968 and laid siege to the base. American air superiority allowed the military to keep Khe Sanh supplied. The siege lasted 77 days and resulted in 703 American and South Vietnamese deaths and 2,642 wounded.

Many journalists, politicians and historians later agreed that the **Battle of Khe Sanh** was an intentional distraction, aimed at forcing American commander General William Westmoreland to divert resources to an unimportant corner of South Vietnam as part of a grand strategy. Such analysts believe that the communists intended to draw American troops away from multiple cities across South Vietnam in preparation for a campaign launched on January 30 that came to be known as the **Tet Offensive**.

Americans had negotiated a ceasefire with the North Vietnamese during Tet season, a Vietnamese Lunar New Year celebration. The Americans anticipated a quiet holiday. Instead, close to 70,000 communist soldiers launched a surprise attack at the beginning of Tet. The North Vietnamese and their NVA allies attacked more than 100 cities and towns, including 39 of South Vietnam's 44 provincial capitals. The North Vietnamese and their NLF allies also startled the Americans with their abrupt change of tactics. The communists had always tried to avoid direct confrontation with the better-armed U.S. military, preferring ambushes and hit-and-run attacks. For the Tet Offensive, suddenly the communists fought as an effective conventional army.

When the Viet Cong seized control of the South Vietnamese city of Hue, they carried with them a detailed enemies list that included top South Vietnamese soldiers and residents who had collaborated with the American-supported regime in Saigon. During the weeks communists held the city, they massacred between 3,000 and 6,000 supporters of the "puppet regime" in Saigon.

Four thousand communist troops struck the South Vietnamese capital of Saigon. Ho Chi Minh, the North Vietnamese leader, and his officers displayed a keen awareness of the importance of press coverage to their military campaign. They launched the offensive in the dead of night, including the all-but-doomed assault on and occupation of the American embassy by 19 guerillas, in sufficient time for film to be shot, processed and transmitted from Japan just in time for the evening news broadcasts in America. The battle at the embassy captured the attention of the world press.

"One of the Great Pictures of the Vietnam War"

One searing image from the Tet Offensive fixed in the American mind the brutality of the Vietnam War. On February 1, General Nguyen Ngoc Loan, the chief of South Vietnam's national police, conducted a spontaneous street execution of a communist guerilla. Images of the killing reached newspaper readers and television viewers around the world. Loan had ruthlessly crushed a dissident Buddhist movement in Hue two years before. During the Tet Offensive, communist soldiers had killed several of his men, including a major who was a close friend, along with the major's wife and children. That day, Associated Press photographer **Eddie Adams** and Vo Suu of the National Broadcasting Company cruised around the gun-blasted South Vietnamese capital, eventually approaching the An Quang temple. They spotted South Vietnamese marines who held in custody a man in black shorts and a checkered shirt, with his hands tied behind him. They led the prisoner to General Loan, who carried a pistol.

Loan used the gun to wave away a gathering crowd, stretched his right arm towards the prisoner's temple, and pulled the trigger. Adams's camera had captured the moment when the bullet from Loan's gun first struck the prisoner's temple. Adams had photographed one of the iconic and most devastating images from the Vietnam War. "Everyone knew it was a prizewinner," author Don Oberdorfer wrote, "one of the great pictures of the Vietnam War." The next day, Adams's photograph appeared

Vietcong prisoner, Nguyen Van Lém, being executed by police chief General Nguyen Ngoc Loan in Saigon. February 1, 1968 Credit: Library of Congress

on the front pages of newspapers around the world. NBC broadcast film of the incident shot by Vo Suu in color as part of *The Huntley-Brinkley Report*. No pictures did more to underscore the violence of Vietnam and the ruthlessness of the South Vietnamese regime, even if viewers did not understand the brutality of the North Vietnamese and Viet Cong during the Tet Offensive.

The Johnson administration's efforts to manage the news from South Vietnam suffered more damage on February 7. The American military organized a field trip for reporters to Ben Tre, the capital of Kien Hoa province, which had been home to 35,000. The town lay in ruins and the battle there produced a high number of civilian casualties. One major told AP reporter Peter Arnett, "It became necessary to destroy the town to save it." If Adams's and Suu's photography captured the savagery of the Vietnam War, the quote reported by Arnett captured the war's insanity. The tremendous technological advantage the United States brought to the war obviously had failed to crush the North Vietnamese and the Viet Cong's will to fight, but the advanced weaponry clearly had inflicted much pain and suffering on America's South Vietnamese ally.

Years of empty assurances from President Johnson and Secretary of Defense Robert McNamara about success in Vietnam lay in ruins. The Tet Offensive can be considered the death knell of Johnson's credibility with the American voting public. A substantially larger percentage of Americans believed that the United States was losing

the war in Vietnam in late February 1968 than had the previous November. The number saying America was losing went up from 8 to 23 percent in that four-month period, according to a Gallup organization poll, while the number believing that America was making military "progress" dropped from 50 percent to 33 percent.

Losing "The Most Trusted Man
in America"

From a pure tactical standpoint, the Tet Offensive represented a disaster for the North Vietnamese military and its NLF allies. Ho Chi Minh and other North

Secretary of Defense Robert McNamara on the telephone January 10, 1964 Credit: LBJ Library

Vietnamese leaders had hoped that the offensive would spark a popular uprising against the Saigon regime, but they were sorely disappointed. The communists were unable to hold positions they had taken and were forced, bloodied and disappointed, to melt back into the jungles. While the Americans had lost about 2,000 men between January 30 and early March, the highest death toll in a single campaign yet for the United States in the war, and the South Vietnamese lost 4,000, the North Vietnamese and Viet Cong suffered almost a mortal wound. Credible estimates put communist deaths at 50,000 in one month.

Westmoreland described the offensive to reporters as a failed "go for broke" move similar to the German Ardennes Offensive in 1944-1945 that led to the Battle of the Bulge. The American general celebrated a victory on the ground, but the communist leadership had additional objectives that Tet season. North Vietnamese military strategist Võ Nguyên Giáp hoped the offensive would demoralize the American public and increase impatience in the United States for an end to the conflict. As Ho had warned the French twenty years earlier, "You can kill ten of my men for every one I kill of yours. But even at those odds, you will lose and I will win."

Considered the most trusted man in America, CBS News anchor **Walter Cronkite** traveled to South Vietnam in February 1968 with the objective of measuring how close the United States was to truly winning in Vietnam or whether victory was any longer possible. In the days before the internet, in which only three television networks competed for national news audiences, an anchor such as Cronkite enjoyed enormous influence. On February 27, CBS broadcast *Report from Vietnam by Walter Cronkite*. The Nielsen ratings service later estimated that nine million Americans watched the report. Among them was a nervous Lyndon Johnson who dreaded a critical broadcast. Johnson's worst fears were realized as Cronkite editorialized at the program's conclusion:

> It now seems more certain than ever that the bloody experience of Vietnam is to end in a stalemate . . . To say that we are closer to victory today is to believe, in the face of the evidence, the optimists who have been wrong in the past. . . To say we are mired in stalemate seems the only realistic, yet unsatisfactory, conclusion . . . [I]t is increasingly clear to this reporter that the only rational way out then will be to negotiate, not as victors but as an honorable people who lived up to their pledge to defend democracy and did the best they could.

The anchor's words thunderstruck President Johnson, who said, "If I've lost Cronkite, I've lost Middle America."

In fact, a substantial percentage of Americans had grown skeptical of the war before Cronkite's broadcast. Support for the president dropped, but there was no significant increase in opposition to the war, or a decline in support for the war. The tone of news coverage, however, permanently changed. Before Tet, war supporters appearing on network news broadcasts outnumbered critics by more than 6-1. It was only after Tet that critics and war supporters achieved parity on the evening news.

The My Lai Massacre

The Tet Offensive provided the most memorable photographic image of the Vietnam War and after the Battle at Ban Tre, its most ironic, unforgettable quote. The mass murder by American soldiers of approximately five hundred unarmed women, children and elderly at **My Lai** provided the war's great moment of infamy. In many ways, My Lai simply represented the cold, logical conclusion of General Westmoreland's decision to fight a war of attrition, in which the communists supposedly would flinch as casualties mounted. As Philip Caputo, a Marine who later wrote extensively and critically about the American experience in Vietnam, observed:

> Our mission was not to win terrain or seize positions, but simply to kill: to kill Communists and kill as many of them as possible. Stack 'em up like cordwood. Victory was a high body count, defeat a low kill ratio, war a matter of arithmetic. The pressure on unit commanders to produce enemy corpses was intense, and they in turn communicated it to their troops . . . It is not surprising, therefore, that some men acquired a contempt for human life and a predilection for taking it.

Nevertheless, the men of Charlie Company, who carried out the four-hour massacre at the village the Americans called My Lai 4, went above and beyond that homicidal imperative. Of the most infamous murderers in the company, Lieutenant **William Calley**, historians of the My Lai Massacre Michael Bilton and Kevin Sim said, "His averageness had made him so invisible at one college he had attended that all anyone could remember about him was that he paid his rent regularly." A post-massacre study by the Army documented that Charlie Company had a 20 percent higher ratio of high school graduates than the Army as a whole, and that in other aspects—such as IQ test scores and amount of training—these men matched Army norms. The **Peers Report**, commissioned by the Army, analyzed the causes of the My Lai Massacre and concluded that the perpetrators of the atrocity were "generally representative of the typical cross section of American youth assigned to combat units throughout the Army."

Soon after it arrived "in country" Charlie Company found itself in Quang Ngai Province, which, the men had been briefed, represented a hotbed of NLF resistance. Commanders sent the newest, greenest wave of American soldiers on "search and destroy" missions in the Quang Ngai countryside. Lieutenant Calley, filled with stories about the North Vietnamese and Viet Cong using children as soldiers, saw local youths as killers in waiting. "All the men loved them," Calley later told investigators. "Gave the kids candy, cookies, chewing gum, everything. Not me. I hated them. I was afraid of Vietnamese kids." One soldier later described Calley as a "glory hungry person . . . the kind of person who would have sacrificed all of us for his own personal advancement." Calley grew so despised by the men of Charlie Company that a price was put on his head.

A pattern was set where soldiers committed human rights abuses that were ignored or even praised by superior officers. Paranoia overcame the soldiers, particularly after the launch of the Tet Offensive. On February 11, one of Charlie Company's radio operators, Ron Weber, died after a shot ripped a kidney from his body, the first death experienced by the unit. On February 13, nearby Bravo Company came under fire in a battle resulting in one soldier's death and wounds for five others. Charlie Company had yet to find one Viet Cong soldier, much less inflict one confirmed casualty. Any remaining restraints unraveled in one incident when Calley and a G.I. named Herbert Carter interrogated an old man, beat him, and threw him down a well before Calley shot him with an M-16. One soldier, Dennis Conti, became infamous for raping Vietnamese girls. After one assault, Conti cut braided hair off one of his victims and used this "trophy" to decorate his helmet. Bitterness among the Americans deepened with the explosion of a mine that killed three members of Charlie Company on February 25. The American soldiers blamed the locals for not warning them about the mines.

On March 15, Task Force Barker, which included Charlie Company, received the assignment to clear out local villages of suspected Viet Cong fighters. The task force was named after Lieutenant Colonel Frank A. Barker, the commander of the operation. The men of Charlie Company were primed for vengeance. Task force officers later claimed that Barker ordered the destruction of the "houses, dwellings, and livestock" in the My Lai area. Many officers, including Captain Ernest Medina, told their men that anyone they found in the village the morning of the operation was probably a Viet Cong fighter.

"He [Medina] stated that My Lai . . . was a suspected VC stronghold and that he had orders to kill everybody that was in the village," Max D. Hudson, a weapons squad leader, told the Army Criminal Investigation Unit later.

The operation started at sunup on March 16. One soldier, Michael Bernhardt, reported later that when the men stepped off helicopters they began firing the minute any Vietnamese were spotted, and the victims were left on the ground wounded or dying. An old Vietnamese man stood in a field next to a water buffalo and put his hands in the air to indicate he was a non-combatant. Lieutenant Calley passively watched as several in the unit shot the elderly man to death. Conti forced a woman about 20 years old to have oral sex with him, coercing her by putting a gun to the head of her four-year-old child.

A group of soldiers assigned to the First Platoon gathered about 60 Vietnamese villagers. The group included children ranging in age from infancy to around 12 and 13, as many as 15 old men, and 10 younger women, along with a group of very elderly women. Calley yelled at a group of soldiers, "I want them killed." Calley and another soldier fired into the civilians from ten feet away. "The Vietnamese screamed, yelled and tried to get up," authors Michael Bilton and Kevin Sim wrote.

> It was pure carnage as heads were shot off along with limbs; the fleshier body parts were ripped to shreds . . . Mothers had thrown themselves on top of the young ones in a last desperate bid to protect them from the bullets raining down on them. The children were trying to stand up. Calley opened fire again, killing them one by one.

Calley moved on. The lieutenant stood near a ditch filled with children. A two-year-old climbed away from his mother and got to the top of the ditch. Calley spotted the toddler, yanked up the child, flung him back into the ditch and shot him. Elsewhere, soldiers sodomized women with their rifles, sometimes before shooting them in the genitals, while others joined Conti in rape. In four hours as many as 500 villagers in My Lai 4 and the immediate surrounding area had been butchered. The Army's newspaper, *Stars and Stripes*, initially reported that Charlie Company and other units involved in the massacre had encountered enemy resistance and made the patently false claim that 128 enemy fighters had been killed by Task Force Barker. The story of My Lai would remain hidden from the American public for more than a year.

THE WAR AND DOMESTIC POLITICS

RFK

The tragedies and failures of Vietnam created opportunities for the president's political enemies. No Johnson foe stood taller in the public mind than **Robert F. Kennedy**, the younger brother of slain President John Kennedy. The two never liked each other, and this mutual antagonism became harsher when Johnson took control of the White House. Robert Kennedy resented Johnson as a crude, uncultured interloper. The new president, meanwhile, raged at the condescension shown to him by the attorney general and others belonging to the late president's circle of friends.

Bobby, as he was known to intimate associates, was haunted by JFK's assassination. He "seemed devoured by grief," biographer Evan Thomas wrote. "He literally shrank, until he appeared wasted and gaunt . . . he appeared to be in physical pain, like a man with a toothache or on the rack. Even walking seemed difficult to him, though he walked for hours, brooding and alone."

Once the most powerful member of his brother's cabinet, Kennedy continued as attorney general under a new president who did not trust him. Kennedy resigned, moving to New York to run for the United States Senate in 1964. A lifelong resident of Massachusetts, Kennedy had to deal with accusations that he was an opportunistic "carpetbagger." Much to his chagrin, he depended on Johnson's considerable coattails to win the race. He won the Senate seat by 700,000 votes, 2 million fewer votes than the president carried in New York.

Kennedy did not enjoy his time in the Senate. During his three-plus years in that body he was unable to pass a single major piece of legislation he had authored. As early as April 1965, he doubted that the Vietnam War could be won in conventional military terms. In February 1966, Kennedy made a bold break with Johnson, declaring during a press conference that the United States should seek a negotiated settlement with North Vietnam and perhaps even include the National Liberation Front, the political arm of the Viet Cong, in a coalition government.

Having grown up in a family in which he felt like an underdog, Bobby believed he understood the desperation of impoverished African Americans and Latinos. Invited to speak in South Africa, where the ruling white supremacist regime had imposed apartheid, a rigidly enforced system of racial separation and oppression of the black majority, Kennedy visited the poverty-stricken

(Left) Senator Robert Kennedy and Donald Benjamin (Central Brooklyn Coordinating Council for Bedford-Stuyvesant) join kids at a playground. (Right) Senator Kennedy discusses school with a young boy. February 4-5, 1966.

black townships lying on the outskirts of South Africa's major cities. A crowd of approximately 15,000 attended his speech at the University of Cape Town. Realizing his audience was filled with activists committed to justice but afraid of their authoritarian government, Kennedy urged his listeners not to feel powerless. As he told the assembled:

> Few will have the greatness to bend history itself; but each of us can work to change a small portion of events and in the total of all those acts will be written the history of this generation . . . It is from numberless diverse acts of courage and belief that human history is shaped. Each time a man stands up for an ideal, or acts to improve the lot of others, or strikes out against injustice, he sends forth tiny ripples of hope, and crossing each other from a million different centers of energy and daring these ripples build a current which can sweep down the mightiest walls of oppression and resistance . . .

Hunger and deprivation became personal issues for the wealthy and privileged politician. In 1967, serving on the Senate Labor Committee's Subcommittee on Poverty, Kennedy attended hearings in rural Mississippi. "Appalled by the testimony, he went out into the fields," Thomas wrote. "Kennedy was hardly new to scenes of want and deprivation, but he was still shocked by the living conditions of poor blacks in the Delta. The stench and vermin

Senator Eugene McCarthy at a meeting in the Cabinet Room. October 3, 1966 Credit: LBJ Library

in the windowless shacks overwhelmed his senses. He sat down on a dirty floor and held a child who was covered with open sores. He rubbed the child's stomach, which was distended by starvation. He caressed and murmured and tickled. No response. The child was in a daze."

Kennedy, who mocked himself as someone who had made a D in his college economics class, struggled for an answer to poverty. He launched an experiment in the neighborhood of Bedford-Stuyvesant in Brooklyn. Poor and with a population that was 82 percent African American and 12 percent Puerto Rican, "Bed-Stuy," as it was known, became the scene of a riot in 1964 after a police shooting of a black teenager. After a February 1966 tour of the neighborhood, Kennedy met with business leaders and the wealthy heads of charitable foundations to see if a program combining government incentives such as tax breaks and grants with private investment capital could be marshaled to create quality jobs in the neighborhood.

Along with his fellow New York Senator Jacob Javits, Kennedy secured passage of an amendment in November 1966 to the Economic Opportunity Act originally passed in 1964. The new provision created the Special Impact Program. This law allowed the creation of the Bedford-Stuyvesant Development and Service Corporation. The agency included one board made up of members of the local community that would determine which projects were most needed while another board sought corporate investment dollars and provided management expertise. In the last four decades, the program has provided job placement services, opened an arts academy and the Billie Holliday Theatre (named after the legendary jazz singer), constructed 2,200 housing units, and provided $60 million in mortgage financing to about 1,500 Bed-Stuy residents.

"Clean for Gene": Surprise in New Hampshire

The Kennedy family had always placed a high premium on action and courage, but as the 1968 presidential campaign opened, and anti-war activists tired of waiting for Robert to announce his candidacy, war critics began to accuse him of political cowardice and began looking for someone else to pick up the mantle. Minnesota Senator **Eugene McCarthy** had become one of the early skeptics of the Vietnam War. McCarthy and only four other senators voted for a motion to repeal the Gulf of Tonkin Resolution, which had given Johnson the authority to pursue the Vietnam War. A quiet, deeply religious Catholic and a published poet, he could not have had a more different personality than Lyndon Johnson, the backslapping, larger-than-life president. He spoke with the cool, detached air of an intellectual and often irritated his campaign staff with what seemed his lack of passion. However, his opposition to the Vietnam War, and his resentment over the increase of executive power that came in the Johnson years, pushed him into the unlikely arena of presidential politics.

With no other Democrat willing to mount a credible challenge to Johnson's misadventure in Vietnam, McCarthy announced his entry into the primaries on November 30, 1967. McCarthy benefited from lucky political timing. During the month leading up to the campaign season's opening New Hampshire primary, the news was filled with reports on the Tet Offensive. As the only man standing up to Johnson within the Democratic Party, McCarthy received the enthusiastic support of anti-war college and high school students from all across the country.

Unpaid campaigners knocked on nearly every door in the state and spoke to virtually every person who intended to vote in the Democratic presidential primary. An incumbent president would be expected to win by a landslide in his party's primaries, so all McCarthy needed was a respectable showing in order to be seen as the victor. McCarthy's election night tally on March 12 exceeded

President Lyndon Johnson reads a story about the bombing halt in *The Evening Star*. November 1, 1968

any television and newspaper pundit's highest expectations. The Minnesota senator won 42.4 percent of the New Hampshire primary vote, with President Johnson receiving only 49.5 percent.

The New Hampshire results gave Bobby Kennedy the opening he had been looking for. Kennedy announced he was entering the presidential sweepstakes four days later, on March 16. The New York senator received flack from some Democrats who accused him of splitting the peace vote, but Kennedy was certain that McCarthy had no realistic chance of capturing the Democratic nomination, much less of defeating the likely Republican nominee, former Vice President Richard Nixon.

LBJ Bows Out

Even before thee New Hampshire primary in November 1967, Lyndon Johnson despaired about the war. He had convened a meeting of longtime friends, advisers, and political insiders—a group dubbed the **"Wise Old Men"**—to Washington, D.C., to discuss the future plan of attack. Included in the discussion was Clark Clifford, an attorney soon to be appointed McNamara's replacement as defense secretary, former national security advisor McGeorge Bundy, and Supreme Court Justice (and, like Clark, a longtime Johnson confidant) Abe Fortas. The

President Lyndon Johnson listens to a tape sent by Captain Charles Robb, his son-in-law, from Vietnam.
July 31, 1968

President Lyndon B. Johnson addresses the nation, announcing a bombing halt in Vietnam and his intention not to run for re-election. March 31, 1968. Credit: LBJ Library

men received typically glowing reports from military officers on the progress being made in the war. Only Bundy raised an objection and that only as the meeting was breaking up. "I've been watching you across the table," Bundy said. "You're like a flock of buzzards sitting on a fence, sending the young men off to be killed. You ought to be ashamed of yourselves." No one responded to Bundy.

That was before the embarrassment of the Tet Offensive. Meanwhile, the budget office placed the cost of 206,000 more troops that General William Westmoreland, the commander of the Vietnam mission, had recently requested at $2 billion for the last four months of the fiscal year and up to $12 billion for the following fiscal year. In the wake of the Tet Offensive, Johnson asked the Wise Old Men to gather again at the State Department on March 25. Once again, they received glowing reports from the military. The Wise Men, however, had become skeptics. Clifford, for instance, had been told by generals he questioned that there was no real plan to end the war. As historian Taylor Branch observed, Bundy "chilled the Cabinet Room" with his first words. "Mr. President, there is a very significant shift in most of our positions since we last met." Bundy bluntly told the president, "We must begin steps to disengage."

Johnson realized that he no longer had the confidence of his own cabinet. The negative feedback from the Wise Men and McCarthy's showing in New Hampshire moved the president towards making a decision he had contemplated at least since the fall of 1967. The president had been scheduled to make a televised speech in prime time about the Vietnam War on March 31. Clifford got the president to change the first line of his speech from "I want to talk to you about the War in Vietnam" to "I want to talk to you about peace in Vietnam." The final draft of the speech included a bombing halt in North Vietnam. Johnson told his speech writers that he would provide the concluding remarks himself.

During the speech, the president told his audience that the United States would end bombing of North Vietnam as part of an effort to kick-start peace talks. At the end, he looked up from the paper copy of his speech and said directly into the camera that he "did not want the presidency to become involved in the partisan divisions that are developing this political year." Johnson continued:

> With our hopes and the world's hopes for peace in the balance every day, I do not believe that I should devote an hour or a day of my time to any personal partisan causes or to any duties other than that of the awesome duties of this office—the presidency of your country. Accordingly, I will not seek, and I will not accept, the nomination of my party for another term as your President.

Some of Johnson's most sharp-tongued critics now praised the president's statesmanship. Even the president's chief nemesis, Bobby Kennedy, spoke highly of the speech, describing the president's decision as "truly magnanimous" and offering to meet with Johnson to discuss "how we might work together in the interest of national unity during the coming months." That Wednesday, North Vietnam finally agreed to start peace talks with the United States.

MARTIN LUTHER KING, VIETNAM, AND THE POOR PEOPLE'S CAMPAIGN

By early 1968, **Martin Luther King, Jr.**, battled deepening depression. He knew the FBI was harassing and spying on him, and he felt increasingly isolated from some former white supporters and from many younger people in the black community. Men like **Stokely Carmichael** began to mock King's non-violent approach to protest. Carmichael led the Student Nonviolent Coordinating Committee (SNCC), a black civil rights group that had expelled white members in order to chart a course free of white domination. Carmichael, who coined the phrase "Black Power!" as a rallying cry, belittled King's Southern Christian Leadership Council, which financially relied on donations from sympathetic white liberals.

By 1968, King also faced verbal assaults and harassment from law enforcement because of his decision to expand his crusades from assaults on discrimination to the problem of poverty and the tragedy of the Vietnam War. He not only charged that the Southeast Asia conflict drained badly needed money from the president's avowed war on poverty but said that the violence used by the American government in Vietnam spawned a general social sickness that manifested in urban riots. King urged his listeners who objected to the war and got snared in the military draft to claim conscientious objector status. For the first time, northern liberal editorialists blasted King with the venom he usually received from southern segregationists.

The FBI War on MLK

By 1968, FBI Director **J. Edgar Hoover** had spent almost 14 years trying to destroy King. Hoover had led the agency, originally known as the Bureau of Investigation, since 1924. Hoover had grown up in segregated Washington, D.C., and his racist attitude towards blacks reflected a white southern cultural background.

King obsessed Hoover. The director focused on King's relationship with Stanley Levinson, who in the early 1950s had given the Communist Party USA financial advice. Both with and without the legal authorization of the Kennedy and Johnson administrations, the FBI director ordered the wiretapping of Levinson's phones and those of the SCLC. Agents also tapped the phones in the hotel rooms occupied by King and other civil rights leaders.

Hoover had remained director of the FBI in spite of abundant evidence of his incompetence. The director was slow to respond to the rise of gangsters like Bonnie and Clyde and John Dillinger in the 1930s, had insisted that the Mafia did not exist even as organized crime took over several cities in the 1940s and 1950s, and had spent the McCarthy era wasting agency resources chasing a mass communist conspiracy that proved to be a phantom. Part of the secret of his survival was his exploitation of the FBI to spy on the sexual habits of the most powerful figures in Washington, D.C., information that ended up in Hoover's "Obscene File," a compilation of erotic dirt on those who could cause the director trouble. This was one way that Hoover convinced Bobby Kennedy to agree to wiretapping King. The attorney general's brother President Kennedy had numerous affairs. One girlfriend, Judith Exner, was also the mistress of Mafia boss Sam Giancana. More seriously, another mistress, Ellen Rometsch, was a suspected East German spy. Though he disliked and distrusted the FBI director, Robert Kennedy thought it best to keep Hoover happy.

This made the Kennedy administration the unwilling partner in Hoover's private crusade against King, a persecution that continued after Johnson took office. On January 5, 1964, King and his lieutenants checked into the Willard Hotel in Washington, D.C., and FBI agents planted a microphone in his suite. The FBI recorded King, other officials from the SCLC and two women drinking and having sex. According to author Richard Hack, Hoover listened to parts of the tape in his office and, in a celebratory mood, declared, "This will destroy the burr head."

After Hoover briefed President Johnson on the matter, LBJ suggested that the information should be made available to the press "for the good of the country." To Hoover's frustration, however, the press did not take the bait. Unable to smear him publicly, Hoover sought to frighten King out of politics. With the director's approval, the FBI anonymously sent a package to King that contained an edited audiotape of King's extramarital sexual encounters with a threatening letter, calling the civil rights leader a "fraud" and a "moral imbecile." Unless King stopped his activism, the letter warned, "The American public . . . will know you for what you are—an evil, abnormal beast." The letter then darkly suggested that suicide was the civil rights leader's only real option. "King, there is only one thing for you to do. You know what it is."

Meanwhile, feeling pressure from all sides, deeply sad and tired, King had every incentive to withdraw from public life in the spring of 1968. Instead, he pressed on.

The Poor People's Campaign

As part of his "**Poor People's Campaign**" to seek justice for all impoverished Americans, King spent the early months of 1968 planning a Poor People's March, based on his triumphant 1963 March on Washington. King conceived of the march as a means of responding to a noticeable white backlash to the African American freedom struggle. Across the country, white voters reacted angrily to the urban uprisings in places like the Watts neighborhood of Los Angeles, in Detroit, and in Newark. White voters who had backed liberal, or at least moderate, Democrats began in 1966 to support conservative "law and order" Democrats and Republicans who promised to crack down on lawless inner city youths and drug-taking anti-war protestors.

King hoped that by focusing on poverty he would be attacking an issue that transcended race. About 13 percent of all Americans lived in poverty in 1968, including 3.6 million whites, with poor whites heavily concentrated in deep southern states like Mississippi and the hills of Kentucky and Tennessee. Poverty, King suspected, lay behind the white resentments that fed anti-black racism. Details of the planned march remained vague even as a humble strike by sanitation workers created what became an enormous distraction.

Mostly African American, Memphis sanitation workers lived below the national poverty line even though they worked full-time. About 40 percent received such low wages that they qualified for welfare. These collectors carried heavy, leaky garbage containers, which often showered them with rotting food, dirty diapers and maggots. Tragedy struck on February 1 as compressors crushed to death two sanitation workers, Echol Cole and Robert Walker. Galvanized by the tragedy, 930 of the city's 1,100 sanitation workers launched the **Memphis Sanitation Workers' Strike** on February 12, 1968, demanding safety equipment, paid days off during rain, better pay, benefits and recognition of their American Federation of State, County, and Municipal Employees Union.

King saw that the fight of the Memphis sanitation workers fit perfectly into his Poor People's Campaign, and though advisors—worried about the ugly atmosphere in Memphis—urged him not to get involved, he supported their cause and agreed to appear there. King arrived in town on March 28. Events soon spun out of control.

A group of thirty black students with rocks and clubs marched down Beale Street, heart of the city's blues district. Suddenly the protestors heard loud pops that sounded like gunshots. The sound, instead, marked the cascade of shattered storefront windows being broken by angry marchers along Beale and Main Streets. A confrontation between protestors and police turned violent. The day saw nine police officers injured, including one beaten by five enraged teenagers with sticks used to support protest placards. In addition, two hundred protestors would be arrested and sixty injured. One police officer backed a 16-year-old suspected rioter into a stairway and blasted him point blank with a sawed-off shotgun.

King considered canceling the Poor People's March. The rioting was a gift to the movement's enemies in the FBI, he said. "Maybe we just have to admit that the day of violence is here," he said in a tone of resignation. "And maybe we just have to give up and let violence take its course." Eventually, he overcame his defeatism and said he had to try to organize a peaceful rally in Memphis before he could successfully lead one in Washington, D.C.

The King Assassination

A bomb scare delayed King's return to Memphis on April 3. When King arrived, an army of uniformed and undercover Memphis police and FBI agents followed him. He should have been the safest man in America. Hoover, however, violated normal FBI policy, refusing to inform the civil rights leader of death threats. King checked into the Lorraine Motel, a location advertised in the local press.

King was scheduled to speak to sanitation workers that night at the city's Mason Temple but, as tornados and harsh thunderstorms struck the region, he received a report that only 2,000 were at that night's massive speaking venue that could hold up to 14,000. King asked his aide, the Reverend **Ralph Abernathy,** to speak in his place. Abernathy sensed upon arrival the crowd's disappointment when they did not see King enter the hall as well. Abernathy called King and told him the Mason Temple was "a core crowd of sanitation workers who had braved a night of hellfire to hear him and they would feel cut off from a lifeline if he let them down."

Cheers rattled the building when the audience spotted King, who would treat them to one of the most prophetic speech of his career. King recalled significant highlights of the civil rights struggle. He then compared himself to Moses, who according to the Bible led the Israelites out of slavery in Egypt but was allowed by God to see the Promised Land only from the summit of a mountain.

The night of King's epic speech at the Mason Temple, an escaped convict named **James Earl Ray** also arrived in Memphis after driving from Atlanta. Ray, a small-time crook previously convicted of armed robbery targeting gas stations and liquor stores, broke out of a Missouri prison April 23, 1967. Living in hiding, he heard rumors of southern businessmen who would pay a bounty to anyone who killed King. Reading in the newspapers that King was staying at the Lorraine Motel, Ray rented a cheap room at Bessie Brewer's flophouse, conveniently across a parking lot from where King was staying. Among Ray's few belongings was a .30-06 Remington Gamemaster rifle.

ROBERT KENNEDY ON THE DEATH OF MARTIN LUTHER KING, JR.

Riots raged across the United States the night on April 4, 1968, as news spread of Martin Luther King, Jr.'s murder. At the corner of 14th and U Streets in Washington, D.C., activist Stokely Carmichael spoke to a mob of 400. "Go home and get your guns," he said. "When the white man comes he is coming to kill you. I don't want any black blood on the street. Go home and get you a gun and then come back because I got me a gun." The next day, Friday, fires roared just two blocks from the White House. Riot troops gathered on the White House lawn. Across the country, 39 died and 2,500 suffered injuries.

One city remained quiet April 4. Senator Robert Kennedy spent that afternoon flying from Washington, D.C., to Indiana, where an important presidential primary loomed. Kennedy enjoyed enthusiastic support among black and poor voters, and he could expect a friendly audience that night in the Indianapolis ghetto. On the campaign plane, reporter Johnny Apple of **The New York Times** *leaned toward the candidate with the shocking news that King had been shot. Apple later said that Kennedy "sagged. His eyes went blank."*

Bobby Kennedy and Martin Luther King had shared a tense relationship. As his brother's attorney general and chief political captain, Kennedy had resented the spotlight King had often placed on America's ugly race relations, which Robert believed placed President Kennedy in an embarrassing political light. Sadly, the two often saw each other as antagonists.

When the plane landed in Indianapolis, reports of riots in other cities began to filter in. The city's police chief feared unrest and advised Kennedy to cancel his appearance. Around one thousand people had shown up to hear the presidential candidate speak. The crowd, about 70 percent African American, had not yet heard the terrible news. It would be Kennedy's job to tell them.

He would speak off the cuff and from the heart. "Ladies and gentlemen, I'm only going to talk to you just for a minute or so this evening because I have some very sad news for you all, and I think sad news for all our citizens and people who love peace all over the world," Kennedy said, gingerly feeling his way toward the awful truth. "And that is that Martin Luther King was shot and was killed in Memphis, Tennessee." The audience screamed and many murmured in disbelief, "No, no." Kennedy then improvised the best speech in his tragically brief political career.

The New York Senator reminded the crowd of the tragedy his family had experienced with the murder of President John Kennedy. "For those of you who are black and are tempted to be filled with hatred and distrust at the injustice of such an act, against all white people, I can only say that I feel in my own heart the same kind of feeling," he said. "I had a member of my family killed, but he was killed by a white man . . . What we need in the United States is not division; what we need in the United States is not hatred; what we need in the United States is not violence or lawlessness; but love and wisdom . . ."

Kennedy latter called King's widow, Coretta Scott King, and provided a plane to fly King's body back to Atlanta. After Robert Kennedy's performance in Indianapolis, black leaders asked him to make speeches to African-American audiences to calm the waters. Suspending his campaign schedule, he spoke on the King assassination in Cleveland on April 5.

Kennedy noted, "[T]here is another kind of violence, slower but just as deadly, as the shot, or the bomb in the night. This is the violence of institutions: indifference and inaction and slow decay . . . It is the slow destruction of a child by hunger, and schools without books and homes without heat in the winter."

Kennedy used his Cleveland speech to prophetically condemn the American addiction to gunplay. "This is a time of shame and sorrow," Kennedy said. ". . . I have saved this one opportunity, my only event today, to speak briefly to you about this mindless menace of violence in America which again stains our land and every one of our lives . . . It is not the concern of one race. The victims of violence are black and white, rich and poor, young and old, famous and unknown. They are most important of all, human beings whom other human beings loved and needed. No one—no matter where he lives, or what he does—can be certain who will suffer from some senseless act of bloodshed. And yet it goes on, and on. Why?" Bobby Kennedy would be shot by an assassin 62 days later.

The afternoon of April 4, King was in a jolly mood, swapping good-natured jokes with several fellow ministers and activists about each other and women they knew and about their past together. The group planned an early supper before a mass meeting to discuss the upcoming Memphis March. The Reverend Jesse Jackson's civil rights group Operation Breadbasket had a band scheduled to perform that night. From the balcony of the Lorraine Motel, King shouted to the band's saxophonist, Ben Branch, that he wanted the group to play the black spiritual "Precious Lord, Take My Hand." The song's lyrics powerfully evoked King's recent life.

> Precious Lord, take my hand,
> Lead me on, let me stand
> I'm tired, I'm weak, I'm alone
> Through the storm, through the night
> Lead me to the light.

"Play it real pretty," King told Branch. "O.K., Doc, I will," Branch promised. King turned back toward his room to get a topcoat. It was 6:01 p.m. In seconds, the sharp report of a rifle cracked through the sky. From across the street, Ray had put in his sights a man called a spiritual leader, a modern Moses, a revolutionary, winner of the 1964 Nobel Peace Prize, an agitator, and a subversive—and pulled the trigger. The bullet sailed through the air and passed through King's jaw and neck, leaving an enormous wound. King collapsed. His closest friends ran to be with him, stood next to his lifeless body sprawled on the balcony, and pointed in the direction of the dingy flophouse across the parking lot where the rifle blast had erupted. King was 39 years old.

That night, as news spread that the leader of the most successful non-violent reform movement in American history had died, riots exploded in 110 American cities. In Minneapolis, a man seized with disbelief declared he would kill the first white man he saw. He then shot his neighbor six times. Fires erupted in Boston, the birthplace of the American Revolution, and Winston-Salem, the scene of peaceful sit-ins in an earlier, now-distant era. One quiet exception was Indianapolis, where Robert Kennedy made a campaign stop and delivered an off-the-cuff speech, one of the most important in his political career. He informed a largely African-American audience of King's death. Sensing their shock and grief, he reminded them that he too had lost a loved one to a murderous act by a white man. He urged his audience to forgo rage and to battle to make the country a better place. While America burned that night, Indianapolis stayed calm. Kennedy's life and career, meanwhile, careened to its heartbreaking climax.

Bobby Kennedy's Doomed Crusade

During his 85-day presidential campaign, a previously halting and unsure Bobby Kennedy finally found his political voice. Facing a tough primary challenge campaigning in conservative Indiana, he did not pander, but often defied his audience, at the risk of angering them, to sacrifice the privileges of a middle-class existence for the sake of their country. During one April 26 campaign stop, he addressed doctors and medical students at the University of Indiana. In spite of his well-off, all-white, conservative audience, Kennedy chose that evening to call for government-provided health care for the poor. "Where are you going to get all the money for these federally subsidized programs you are talking about?" one irritated student asked. "From you," Kennedy answered bluntly, provoking boos and hisses from the crowd. Unfazed, Kennedy reminded the audience that those who have received much from their country should give much in return. "If you do not do this, who will do this?" The candidate pushed even harder. "You sit here as white medical students, while black people carry the burden of the fighting in Vietnam."

He prevailed in Indiana, but the path to the Democratic nomination hit a bump when Kennedy lost the Oregon primary on May 28. It marked the first time a son of Joseph Kennedy had lost a political race since the first time John Kennedy ran for a position in student government at Harvard. With Vice President Humphrey enjoying the support of Johnson and lining up a multitude of party regulars who would serve as delegates at that summer's Democratic Party Convention, the next primary, in California, was a must win for Kennedy's campaign.

Throughout his campaign, Kennedy had had trouble winning over Jewish voters. Bobby's father, Joseph Kennedy, was widely known as an anti-Semite who, as American ambassador to Great Britain, had urged President Franklin Roosevelt to avoid war with Adolf Hitler's Germany. To reassure these voters, Kennedy endorsed the sale of more weapons to Israel during the campaign.

Just the year before, the State of Israel had defeated Egypt, Jordan and Syria in a lightning-quick attack that came to be known as the Six-Day War. As a result of the war, Israel now occupied a large swath of what used to be Jordanian territory on the West Bank of the Jordan River, including the eastern half of Jerusalem. A Jordanian living in California named **Sirhan Sirhan** had already been angered by a news photo of Bobby Kennedy wearing a Jewish head covering called a yarmulke. Now, he heard that the candidate called for further American military support for Israel. Sirhan bought a box of ammo for his small .22 caliber handgun and committed to take grim action.

The night of the California primary, Kennedy won 46 percent of the vote to McCarthy's 42. Late that night, the senator reached the Ambassador Hotel in Los Angeles to be interviewed by reporters and to thank supporters. Shortly before midnight, Kennedy went down to the ballroom, the crowd erupting in joy when he emerged. He spoke under the stifling hot lights of the TV cameras. "What is quite clear [is] that we can work together in the last analysis, and that what has been going on within the United States over a period of the last three years—the divisions, the violence, the disenchantment with our society; the divisions, whether it's between blacks and whites, between the poor and the more affluent, or between age groups or on the war in Vietnam—that is we can start to work together. We are a great country, an unselfish country and a compassionate country." Then, referring to the site of the coming Democratic National Convention, he told the joyful crowd, ". . . My thanks to all of you, and now it's on to Chicago and let's win there."

Kennedy's handlers guided the candidate out of the ballroom and through the kitchen corridor. At about 12:13 a.m. June 5, Sirhan was standing on a low tray-stacker when Kennedy passed. The young man stepped off the tray stacker, raised his pistol-bearing right hand over a cluster of Kennedy staffers, and aimed at the senator's head. He fired one shot, then after a brief pause, several more quick shots. Kennedy "threw his hands up to his face, then staggered back, falling to the grey concrete floor on his back—his eyes open, his arms over his head, his feet apart," a reporter, Jules Witcover said. ". . . He was alive, but grievously wounded; blood flowed from behind his right ear. In back of him, others were hit and fell."

Kennedy still lived as his wife Ethel stroked her dying husband's face and chest. Still conscious, he asked, "Is everybody else all right?" Meanwhile, the audience in the ballroom heard the news and let out a terrible scream. Doctors pronounced Kennedy dead at 1:44 a.m., June 6, 1968. His body lay in state at St. Patrick's Cathedral in New York and would be buried at Arlington National Cemetery in Washington, D.C., next to his slain brother John.

News coverage of the service switched to breaking news that King's assassin, Ray, had been arrested in London. Somehow, the almost penniless unemployed drifter, after killing King, successfully crossed the border and reached Toronto, Canada, and with a forged passport flew to London and then reached Lisbon, Portugal, where he purchased a second fake Canadian passport. Flying back to London's Heathrow Airport, Ray carried a loaded pistol as he tried to board a plane to Brussels, Belgium. Law officials there had photos of King's wanted assassin provided by the FBI. Ray was spotted by Scotland Yard and arrested.

The rituals that Americans observed to say goodbye to prominent political figures—those enacted for John Kennedy, Medgar Evers, Malcolm X, and Martin Luther King, Jr., now marked the passing of Robert Kennedy. As with services for Abraham Lincoln 103 years earlier, a train bore Kennedy to the nation's capital. "As they had for Lincoln, many thousands—perhaps, for RFK, a million people, lined the tracks," Thomas wrote. ". . . [A]long the route of the train, Boy Scouts and firemen braced at attention; nuns, some wearing dark glasses, stood witness; housewives wept. Thousands and thousands of black people waited quietly in the heat . . ."

THE 1968 PRESIDENTIAL CAMPAIGN

Former Vice President Richard Nixon had been nursing personal grudges and mining white resentment since he lost his presidential contest against John Kennedy in 1960. Born in 1913 in Yorba Linda, California, the child of two intensely religious Quakers, Nixon was described by authors Maurice Isserman and Michael Kazin as a "solitary and unsmiling child." The family suffered numerous tragedies, including the deaths of two of Nixon's brothers before he finished college. "Early on he concluded that life was a grim and no-holds-barred struggle, in which success came only to those who persevered at any cost," the authors said.

Nixon always felt insecure about his poor parents and his education, attending small Whittier College in California rather than the prestigious, expensive Ivy League schools favored by the affluent. Nevertheless, through hard work he won a scholarship to Duke University in North Carolina, where he earned a law degree. After serving in the Navy in the South Pacific during World War II, he returned to Whittier and practiced law with a small firm. Always ambitious, Nixon challenged incumbent liberal Congressman Jerry Voorhis, whom Nixon characterized with great inaccuracy as a supporter of "Communist principles." Already, Nixon had acquired a reputation as a dirty campaigner, but to the young congressman this was the only way to challenge the unfair advantages of wealth and prestige enjoyed by his political opponents.

Nixon was named to the House Un-American Activities Committee, where his flair for red-baiting would get a choice platform. He achieved fame serving on a committee investigating charges of communist influence at the State Department under presidents Franklin Roosevelt and Truman. He revealed to the public documents hidden in a pumpkin patch purportedly showing that a former Roosevelt adviser, Alger Hiss, spied for the Soviet Union and had passed copies of secret government documents to the Moscow regime.

Nixon exploited his newfound fame in 1950 when he ran for the United States Senate against liberal Democrat Helen Gahagan Douglas. Again, he smeared his opponent as a communist sympathizer, calling her a "pink lady." Nixon won again. When he ran for president in 1952, the moderate Eisenhower picked as running mate the conservative Nixon to broaden his appeal and to help him earn California's electoral votes.

Nixon had his first of many political near-death experiences during the 1952 campaign when news stories revealed that Nixon had received possibly illegal contributions from wealthy supporters to reimburse the California senator for his campaign expenses. He defended himself on national television, delivering his "Checkers Speech" misleadingly characterizing his income as meager. Critics began calling him "Tricky Dick." Nevertheless, Nixon's performance won support from the public and ensured he would remain on the Eisenhower ticket.

Nixon took his loss to Kennedy in the 1960 presidential election as a personal repudiation and he desperately wanted to win back public approval. In 1962, he ran for California governor against the Democratic incumbent, Edmund "Pat" Brown. A moderate on civil rights during his Senate career and a supporter of some social programs, Nixon had fallen out of touch with the right-wing drift of the California Republican Party during his sojourn in Washington. Right-wingers were less than enthusiastic about Nixon, and many did not turn out on Election Day. Pat Brown, meanwhile, charged that Nixon had no interest in serving as governor and that he would exploit the office in order to run for president again. Nixon lost to Brown by approximately 52 percent of the vote to 47 percent.

Nixon held a bitter press conference upon losing the California governor's race. "And as I leave the press, all I can say is this: for sixteen years, ever since the Hiss case, you've had a lot of fun—a lot of fun—that you've had an opportunity to attack me, and I think I have given as good as I have taken," he told a crowd of reporters. ". . . [A]s I leave you I want you to know—just think of how much you are going to be missing. You won't have Nixon to kick around anymore, because, gentlemen, this is my last press conference."

Across the country, journalists panned Nixon's performance at the press conference, which they said showed the man to be resentful and unpresidential. Nixon stayed in the background during the 1964 presidential campaign. When the GOP nominated Senator Barry Goldwater of Arizona, Nixon alone among prominent Republicans campaigned across the country for the party's standard-bearer, making 156 speeches on his behalf. Nixon realized that the conservative delegates who supported Goldwater at the 1964 Republican National Convention would be in charge for the 1968 convention. Having campaigned for both conservative and liberal Republican candidates across the country in 1964, and again in 1966, Nixon would soon collect his chits.

Wallace Enters the Race

Nixon found political gold in tapping white anger against African Americans. As part of his comeback plans, the former vice president already implemented what would come to be known as the 'Southern Strategy" during his presidential administration. Nixon watched with intense interest and fear the career of segregationist Alabama Governor **George Wallace**, who had performed surprisingly well in northern Democratic primaries in 1964. Politicians like Wallace, Nixon and former Hollywood actor Ronald Reagan perceived the growing white backlash in the United States, even in places as far from the South as California, where 65 percent of voters in 1964 approved Proposition 14, a measure that overturned a previously passed fair-housing law prohibiting home sellers from discriminating against racial minorities.

As the 1968 presidential season dawned, Wallace sought out disaffected whites across the country as he launched the American Independent Party, a third-party vehicle for his presidential ambitions. A Detroit newspaper columnist derided Wallace's constituency, which included Klansman and Neo-Nazis, as "kooks." Wallace scoffed. "The other side's got more kooks than we do," he insisted, adding, "kooks got a right to vote too."

Former Governor George Wallace of Alabama during the news conference in which he announced his candidacy for the presidency on a third-party ticket.
February 8, 1968   Credit: Library of Congress.

The race riots that had wracked the country, Wallace claimed, were the product of a sinister plan to destroy America launched by "pointy-headed" bureaucrats in Washington who were taking their orders directly from communist leader Fidel Castro in Cuba. He spoke in racial code, of lazy people on welfare, and the collapse of law and order. "You people work hard," he told a white, blue-collar California audience, "you save your money, you teach your children to respect the law." Yet, Wallace said, when someone burns down a city and murders someone, "'pseudo-intellectuals' explain it away by saying the killer didn't get any watermelon to eat when he was 10 years old."

While the Northeast press derided Wallace for his simple-minded and often crude rhetoric, voters found the renegade candidate refreshingly blunt. "You don't have to worry about figuring out where he stands," a steelworker in Youngstown, Ohio, told one reporter. "He tells it like it really is."

Nixon's Comeback Conpleted

Nixon saw Ronald Reagan as his chief obstacle. In California, Reagan had handily defeated Pat Brown, the man Nixon lost to in 1962, in the 1966 gubernatorial contest. As the top elected official in the state with the most electoral votes, he immediately became a presidential contender. During his gubernatorial campaign, he sounded many of the same themes as Nixon and Wallace, though in a more appealing, Hollywood star fashion. Always an advocate of tax cuts for the rich, Reagan still resonated with working-class audiences by appealing to their resentments against supposedly spoiled, unapprecia-tive college students who burned the flag and rioted rather than taking advantage of going to college and learning.

Within 10 days of his election as governor, Reagan gathered his advisors at his Pacific Palisades home and discussed a presidential campaign for the first time. Reagan's first two years as governor, however, let the air out of his ambitions. When tax cuts he pushed for created a deficit, he then presided over the largest tax increase in state history. A so-called homosexual scandal broke out. The newspaper columnist Drew Pearson revealed the presence of gays on Reagan's staff, and in this intensely homophobic era the story tarred Reagan's reputation. Reagan purged gays from the state government, but as journalist and author Theodore White wrote, "From this blow, the Reagan campaign never recovered."

Nixon won the nomination at the Republican National Convention in Miami on the first ballot, August 7, 1968. He gave one of the best speeches of his career when he accepted the nomination the next night. "As we look in America, we see cities enveloped in smoke and flame. We hear sirens in the night . . . We see Americans hating each other, fighting each other; killing each other at home." Little did Nixon know that night that his words would be an apt description of the Democratic National Convention in Chicago, August 26-29. The nation would watch in horror as police rioted, demonstrators bled, and a major political party committed suicide in front of television cameras.

The Chicago Convention Riot

Like Nixon, Vice President **Hubert Humphrey** had sought the presidency for eight years. Unlike Nixon, however, Humphrey had to answer for the unpopularity of Johnson's war in Vietnam. Choosing to avoid the party's primaries, he preferred to campaign behind the scenes, lining up the support of party bosses who controlled a majority of the delegates attending the Democratic Party Convention in August. Approximately 80 percent of Democratic primary voters had supported the major anti-war candidates, Bobby Kennedy and Eugene McCarthy. However, the only math that mattered was that in 33 states, pro-administration party officials chose who would attend the convention. Throughout the 1968 campaign, Humphrey would not clearly break with the president on Vietnam.

A bad atmosphere pervaded Chicago even before the Democratic National Convention started. The corrupt and almost dictatorial Democratic Mayor **Richard J. Daley** turned the International Amphitheatre, where the Democrats convened, into a war zone. Barbed wire that could be electrified surrounded the building, as did a literal army of 12,000 police officers working 12-hour shifts, 6,000 National Guardsmen as well as another 6,000 soldiers whose arsenals included not only rifles and sidearms but also bazookas and flamethrowers.

Anti-war activists planned a confrontation in Chicago during the convention. The **Youth International Party, or Yippies**, and other activists anticipated that the Chicago Police under Daley would respond with violence to anti-war protestors outside the Democratic Convention. A bloody clash, Yippies like Jerry Rubin and Abbie Hoffman hoped, would prove that the United States had become a police state.

Daley had given his police department "shoot to kill orders." The city banned any permits for groups wanting to camp at city parks. Protestors ignored the order and occupied Lincoln Park. Late on the Sunday night before the convention opened, the police charged into the protestor encampment determined to clear the anti-war protestors from the area. Yippies and others yelled,

"Pigs!" and cried "Oink, oink," prompting many officers to shout, "Kill the Commies!" as they cracked the heads of young people with nightsticks. A Chicago police officer shouted an obscenity at a *Newsweek* magazine reporter when he displayed his press credentials and clubbed him on the head and body. Police injured ten journalists that evening.

While pro-Johnson delegates at the convention shot down a Vietnam peace plank, around 10,000 protestors gathered in nearby Grant Park. One demonstrator donning an army helmet attempted to remove the American flag from a flagpole at Grant Park and was mauled by police. Another group took the flag down and replaced it with a red T-shirt, provoking what a later investigative commission would call a "police riot." Swinging nightsticks and pelting the protestors with tear gas and Mace, Chicago police launched a full-scale crackdown. TV broadcasts gave viewers a close-up look as police bloodied protestors and innocent bystanders as well. Police pushed onlookers, reporters and demonstrators on the sidewalks of Michigan Avenue through plate-glass windows fronting the Hilton Hotel. Meanwhile, protestors repeatedly chanted, "The Whole World Is Watching!"

Humphrey's inevitable nomination defined the term "Pyrrhic victory." More relevant than the nomination was the image fixed in the minds of the voters of the Democrats as a party of violence and anarchy. In contrast, the relatively calm Republican convention projected an image for Nixon and the GOP as the forces of law and order. During the Democratic convention, more than 12,000 had been arrested. A total of 65 journalists covering the convention had been assaulted and/or arrested. Area hospitals reported treating 111 demonstrators, while volunteers with the Medical Committee for Human Rights reported treating more than 1,000 at the scenes of protests. Polls afterwards showed that a clear majority of Americans supported the actions against the protestors taken by the mayor and his police department. At a press conference on September 9, Daley, famous for being tongue-tied, announced, "The policeman isn't there to create disorder, the police is there to preserve disorder."

Nixon Victorious

A year that often seemed to presage a revolution ended instead in a counter-revolution. The luck Nixon enjoyed in the race for the Republican nomination held up during the fall. Remembering painfully his fall in the 1960 debates with John Kennedy, the Republican avoided sharing a stage with Humphrey and relied instead on a sophisticated media strategy that foreshadowed the style of presidential candidates ever since. Meanwhile, Humphrey struggled to dig himself out of the hole created by the Chicago convention.

By September 27, a Gallup poll placed Humphrey fifteen points behind Nixon and a mere seven points ahead of Wallace. Desperate, the Humphrey campaign spent $100,000 to buy 30 minutes on national television TV time. Humphrey made a conditional promise that, if elected president, he would halt bombing in North Vietnam if the communists would "restore" the Demilitarized Zone separating North and South Vietnam that had been repeatedly violated in recent months. "As president, I would be willing to stop the bombing of the North as an acceptable risk for peace," he told the audience. When the vice president spoke soon thereafter at the University of Tennessee for the first time in weeks, he did not have to deal with protestors and some students held a sign that said, "IF YOU MEAN IT, WE'RE WITH YOU."

More important, labor unions finally leapt into the campaign, providing volunteers and money when Humphrey most needed it. Humphrey received a big boost from mistakes by the Wallace campaign. The former Alabama governor had trouble getting someone to agree to run with him. Wallace approached Ezra Taft Benson, the former Secretary of Agriculture under Dwight Eisenhower to be his running mate and was turned down and also considered asking Harland Sanders, better known as "Colonel Sanders" of Kentucky Fried Chicken fame. The nod for the vice presidential candidacy instead went to Air Force General Curtis LeMay, who had directed the air war against the Japanese in World War II, and became commander of operations during the Berlin Airlift in 1948 when the Soviet Union cut off West Berlin from NATO.

In his public statements, LeMay had expressed his frustration with America's "phobia" about using nuclear weapons. Wallace held an October 3 press conference alongside LeMay broadcasted by the three television networks. *Los Angeles Times* reporter Jack Smith asked the general if the United States could win the Vietnam War "without nuclear weapons." "We can win this war without nuclear weapons," LeMay said, but added, "I think there may be times when it would be most efficient to use nuclear weapons."

Humphrey benefited from the LeMay gaffe, with some Wallace supporters concluding that the American Independent Party and its top two candidates were irresponsible and dangerous. Many of these voters drifted back to the Democratic Party, and Humphrey had erased most of Nixon's lead going into the last days of the campaign.

Nixon's strategy, meanwhile, focused on avoiding mistakes. In addition to not debating Humphrey, where he might slip, he avoided press conferences where he might be tripped up by a question from a skeptical reporter.

Nixon instead taped a series of ten television programs in which he answered questions from pre-screened voters before an audience of around 200 committed supporters. The audience and the pre-selected questioners sat in a semi-circle around Nixon. Audience members were told beforehand to applaud when Nixon answered and to get up and surround him at the end of these taped encounters so the last thing the television audience would see was Nixon shaking hands with a friendly crowd. Worried about the tendency of his upper lip to sweat when he was hot, Nixon ordered the air conditioner in the studio to run at full blast.

In front of a friendly audience, Nixon did not sweat, he smiled often enough, did not lose his temper, and he handled the rare tough question with relative calm and grace. During the campaign, Nixon also promised he had a secret plan to end the war. The campaign successfully re-branded Nixon as a steady, tough and experienced potential president who would pursue a tough course with Vietnamese communists but would soon end the war, and who would not tolerate the lawlessness that had marked recent years.

Nixon's approach proved to be a winning one, though it barely succeeded. The networks did not call the November election until 9 a.m. the next morning. Nixon won 43.4 percent of the vote, and 301 Electoral College votes, and Humphrey carried 42.7 percent of the popular vote, with 191 Electoral College votes.

Wallace waged one of the most successful third-party campaigns in U.S. history. He carried 13.5 percent of the popular vote and received 46 votes in the Electoral College, but he won states only in his Deep South home base—Alabama, Arkansas, Louisiana, Mississippi and Georgia. Adding the Wallace and the Nixon votes, together, which represented 57 percent of the electorate, the results represented a firm rejection of Johnson policies which were blamed for creating an atmosphere of dangerous permissiveness. Many white voters in particular had grown tired of the revolution in civil rights and the indecisive results in Vietnam and wanted a return to what they saw as normality.

1968: THE "WHAT-IFs"

Few years in American history inspire as many of what historians call "counter-factual propositions" as the year 1968. For instance, what would have happened if Lyndon Johnson had not dropped out of the Democratic presidential race and decided to run for a second full term? Bobby Kennedy would never have directly challenged a sitting Democratic president and most likely would have lived to run for president in 1972, leaving McCarthy alone in a quest to challenge the Johnson juggernaut. Clearly, because of the president's continued control over about

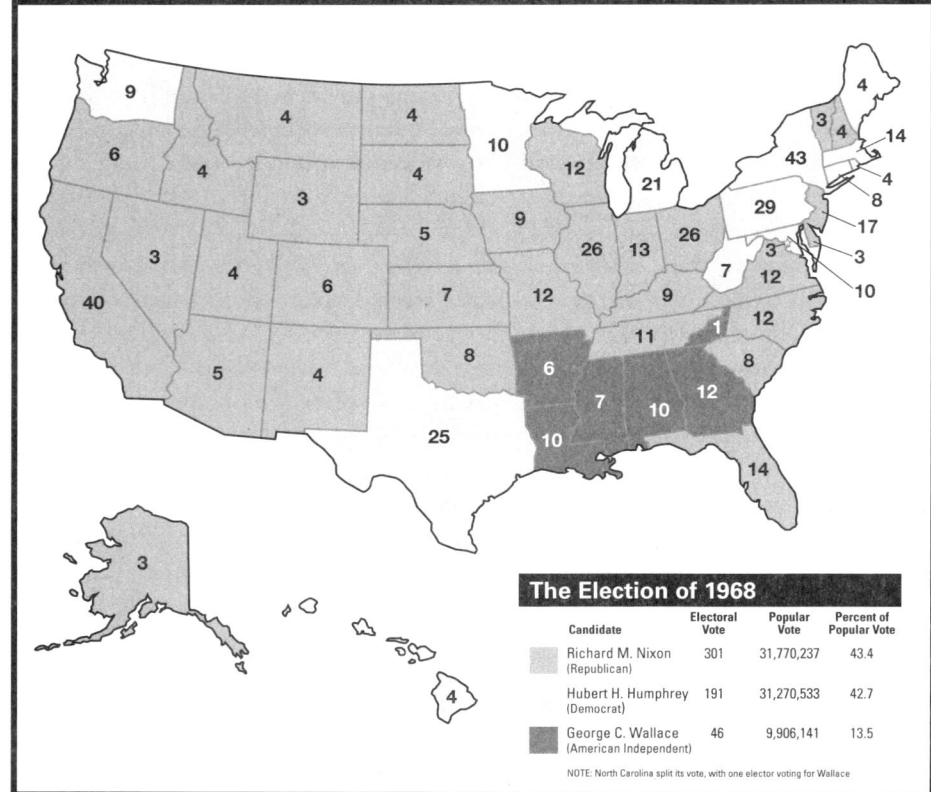

Map 28.1   The Election of 1968

The Election of 1968			
Candidate	Electoral Vote	Popular Vote	Percent of Popular Vote
Richard M. Nixon (Republican)	301	31,770,237	43.4
Hubert H. Humphrey (Democrat)	191	31,270,533	42.7
George C. Wallace (American Independent)	46	9,906,141	13.5

NOTE: North Carolina split its vote, with one elector voting for Wallace

66 percent of the delegates who would have attended the Democratic convention, Johnson would have easily won re-nomination. After that, the speculation gets murkier, but given the mood of the time, it is hard to imagine Johnson triumphing in November.

What if Johnson had dropped out, and Kennedy had entered the primaries, but had not been murdered in California? Back in 1988, on the twentieth anniversary of Bobby Kennedy's assassination, historian Arthur Schlesinger, a close friend of the New York senator, speculated that Bobby would have catapulted from his victory in the California primary to the Democratic nomination. He then would have beaten Richard Nixon in the November presidential election. Winning the White House, Kennedy would have ended the Vietnam War much sooner, cutting in half the number of names now on that tragic Vietnam Memorial in Washington.

President Robert Kennedy, Schlesinger Jr., speculated, would have continued the reform tradition of the New Deal and New Frontier, might have achieved racial reconciliation between whites and blacks and, by defeating Nixon, would have prevented the national malaise ushered in by Watergate and the later failed presidencies of Gerald Ford and Jimmy Carter. That's a huge, messianic burden for a one-term U.S. attorney general and four-year senator from New York to bear, a similar one that has been thrust upon the shoulders of Bobby's similarly-martyred brother John F. Kennedy. The idolization of both Kennedys represents prime exhibits of what historians refer to, usually with derision, as the "Great Man" theory of history—the notion that the times are shaped not by larger forces like industrialization or racism but by bold individuals of unique vision who rise above the moment and bend the world to their will.

There's reason to think that the world would have changed less dramatically had Bobby Kennedy lived. If he had reached the White House and fulfilled his campaign promise to withdraw from Vietnam, South Vietnam likely still would have fallen to the communists. Republicans and conservative Democrats would have pilloried him as the man who "lost Southeast Asia," much as Harry Truman had been condemned as the man who supposedly lost China in 1949. There likely would have been a postwar recession, as happened under Nixon, when defense spending inevitably declined. White Americans still would have been frightened by the rise of assertive black nationalist groups like the Black Panthers, and liberal judges probably still would have ordered school busing in places like Boston, sparking a white backlash that has defined American politics for nearly four decades.

In any case, the deindustrialization of the Northeast would have eroded the strength of the union vote so essential to the Kennedy family's national political ambitions. Bobby Kennedy would have been a more progressive president than Nixon, and may have been less divisive, but he likely would have had as mixed a record in the White House as his older brother.

What if Martin Luther King had survived 1968? Although he was overwhelmingly admired by African Americans, by 1968 signs abounded that his influence within the left wing of the black community had ebbed. He could not have prevented continued violence by various white-controlled police departments and white supremacists acting alone or as part of an underground. Likely, he could not by himself turn back the embrace by some African Americans of more violent action in response. More radical alternatives to King, like the Black Panther Party, had risen by the time of his death.

King had taken on a far more difficult crusade than southern desegregation at the end of his career. During his campaign against poverty, he called for a massive redistribution of wealth, a solution controversial even among the liberals who normally would have been his allies. In any case, solving poverty would have been a much more difficult feat than getting "whites only" signs taken down from water fountains. Alienated from at least some more radical African Americans, he likely would have lost white support as well.

In the end, this is all speculation. We can be certain only about what actually happened. The year 1968 marked a triumph not of reform or liberalism but of retrenchment and conservatism. As president, Nixon proved as reluctant as Johnson to be the "first president to lose a war." As a result, the war dragged on for four more years, and about 30,000 more Americans died in the conflict. Johnson's last year in office marked the last time that the federal government recorded a balanced budget until Bill Clinton's second term in the late 1990s. The start of the Nixon years would launch three decades of debt that would leave the funding for federal budget dependent on China's purchase of U.S. bonds.

Nixon's insecurities and fears would infect his presidency, leading to the Watergate scandal. Even before burglars working for the Nixon re-election campaign broke into Democratic Party headquarters on June 17, 1972, the deception of the Gulf of Tonkin Resolution, and the constant lies surrounding American progress in Vietnam had pushed Americans into greater skepticism of and alienation from the federal government.

The twin assassinations of Martin Luther King, Jr. and Bobby Kennedy in 1968, joined with the earlier murder of John Kennedy, led many Americans to doubt the official finding of guilt and to suppose that the federal government, up to the highest offices, played a hand in the murders. The public increasingly concluded that corruption in government was business as usual, leading them to doubt the likely benefits of heroic reform programs that had been promised as part of The New Frontier and The Great Society. Fueled in part by white anger against what was seen as the excesses of the 1960s, and particularly the near-anarchy of 1968, America entered a long political period of conservative dominance starting with Nixon's election to the White House. Conservative Republicans would control the White House for 30 of the next 50 years and both houses of Congress for 16 of the 24 years from 1995 to 2019.

Humphrey's defeat and Democratic nominee George McGovern's crushing loss at the hands of Nixon in 1972 convinced Democrats as well that the days of big government liberalism had ended. The next three Democratic presidents – Jimmy Carter, Bill Clinton, and Barack Obama—would try to rule from the center-right of American politics, and spend much of their political lives criticizing the party's left wing. Meanwhile, King's life and words would be whitewashed. His birthday would become a holiday and his most provocative and radical statements would be forgotten. Conservatives would distort the meaning of his words during the March on Washington, in which he wished for men to be "judged not by the color of their skin, but by the content of their character," to mean that King would have been opposed to affirmative action programs that favored people of color, even though King had supported such initiatives. Safely dead, King was remade by white America as a non-threatening figure whose innocuous dream of equality, white America falsely claimed, had been already achieved.

Author Charles Kaiser once interviewed folk/rock star Bob Dylan and asked him about the events in 1968. "All those things like that deaden you," Dylan said. "They kill part of your hope. And enough of those blows to your hope will make you deader and deader and deader, until a person is existing without caring any more . . ." America left 1968 sad, exhausted and a little bitter, feeling not hope but a nostalgia for a largely fictitious and presumed Golden Age of Innocence. In the 1970s, Americans came to believe they lived in a declining empire.

Table 28.1

1968: A World in Crisis

Crisis	Date(s)	What Happened
The Pueblo Incident	January 23-December 23	The North Korean Navy captures an American vessel on an espionage mission, *The Pueblo*, seizes surveillance equipment and intelligence, and holds 82 crew members hostage.
The Tet Offensive	January 30-September 23	The North Vietnamese Army and its allies, the National Liberation Front, launch surprise attacks across South Vietnam, eroding U.S. confidence in the war effort.
Martin Luther King, Jr. assassination	April 4	The United States loses its most important civil rights leader, and violent urban uprisings break out across the country.
Columbia University Protests	March 27-April 30	Students occupy five buildings, protesting the college's involvement in developing war technology, recruitment of students by defense industries, and the construction of a university gym in a nearby African American neighborhood.
"May '68"	May 2-June 23	A wave of strikes and protests by students and union members spreads across Paris over American imperialism and the Vietnam War, conditions for workers, and male domination of French society.
Robert Kennedy Assassination	June 5	Kennedy, younger brother of slain president John F. Kennedy and a leading contender for the 1968 Democratic Party presidential nomination, is murdered the night he wins the California primary.
Soviet invasion of Czechoslovakia	August 20	The Soviet Union and several of the its Eastern Europe allies invade Czechoslovakia to overthrow a reformist and more open Communist regime.
Democratic National Convention Riot	August 28	Approximately 10,000 anti-war protestors face off against Chicago Police, who respond with widespread violence.
Tlatelolco Massacre	October 2	After months of protests over the Mexican government's suppression of labor unions, farmers, teachers and students demanding greater democracy and more focus on ending poverty, the Mexican military massacres about 400 demonstrators in Mexico City just before the start of the Olympic Games.

Chronology

January 23	North Koreans seize the *USS Pueblo*.
January 30	Tet Offensive.
February 27	*Report from Vietnam by Walter Cronkite.*
March 12	Eugene McCarthy wins 42.4 percent of the vote in the New Hampshire Democratic Primary.
March 16	My Lai Massacre. Bobby Kennedy announces he is entering the Democratic race for president.
March 27	Student occupation of Columbia University.
March 31	Lyndon Johnson announces that he will not seek another term as president.
April 4	Martin Luther King, Jr., is assassinated.
June 6	Bobby Kennedy is assassinated in the Ambassador Hotel in Los Angeles.
June 8	Arrest of James Earl Ray, the assassin of Martin Luther King. Bobby Kennedy is buried.
August 20-21	The Soviet Union, and most of its Warsaw Pact allies, invade Czechoslovakia.
August 26-29	The Democratic National Convention becomes a scene of chaos. Hubert Humphrey wins the nomination of the Democratic Party for president.
November 6	Richard Nixon is elected president.

SUGGESTED READINGS

David L. Anderson, ed., *Facing My Lai: Moving Beyond the Massacre* (1998).

Michael Bilton and Kevin Sim. *Four Hours in My Lai* (1992).

Taylor Branch. *At Canaan's Edge: America in the King Years, 1965-1968* (2006).

Dan T. Carter. *The Politics of Rage: George Wallace, The Origins of the New Conservatism, and the Transformation of American Politics* (1995).

Michael A. Cohen, *American Maelstrom: The 1968 Election and the Politics of Division* (2018).

Robert C. Cottrell and Blaine T. Browne, *The Rise and Fall of the New American Revolution* (2018).

Robert Dallek. *Flawed Giant: Lyndon Johnson and His Times, 1961-1973* (1998).

Brian Dooley. *Robert Kennedy: The Final Years* (1996).

Michael Eric Dyson. *April 4, 1968: Martin Luther King Jr.'s Death and How It Changed America* (2008).

Carole Fink, Philipp Gassert, and Detlef Junker, *1968: The World Transformed* (1998).

Richard Hack. *Puppetmaster: The Secret Life of J. Edgar Hoover* (2007).

Charles Kaiser. *1968 in America: Music, Politics, Chaos, Counterculture, and the Shaping of a Generation* (1988).

Mark Kurlansky, *1968: The Year that Rocked the World* (2005).

Don Oberdorfer. *Tet: The Turning Point in the Vietnam War* (1984).

Rick Perlstein. *Nixonland: The Rise of a President and the Fracturing of America* (2008).

Mark Rudd. *Underground: My Life With SDS and the Weathermen* (2009).

Evan Thomas. *Robert Kennedy: His Life* (2000).

Richard Vinen, *1968: Radical Protest and Its Enemies* (2018).

Jules Witcover. *85 Days: The Last Campaign of Robert Kennedy* (1969).

Review Questions

1. How did perceptions of Martin Luther King, Jr. change in the black and white communities in 1967-1968?

2. What factors possibly led to the My Lai Massacre?

3. What challenges did the Democratic Party face in the 1968 presidential race?

4. Why did J. Edgar Hoover seek to undermine Martin Luther King, Jr., and his movement?

5. What strategy did Richard Nixon follow in winning the presidency in 1968?

Glossary of Important People and Concepts

Ralph Abernathy
Eddie Adams
Battle of Khe Sanh
William Calley
Stokely Carmichael
Columbia University Student Revolt
Walter Cronkite
Richard J. Daley
J. Edgar Hoover
Hubert Humphrey
Robert F. Kennedy
Martin Luther King Jr.
Curtis LeMay
Eugene McCarthy
Memphis Sanitation Strike
My Lai Massacre
Peers Report
Poor People's Campaign
Pueblo Crisis
James Earl Ray
Sirhan Sirhan
Tet Offensive
George Wallace
"Wise Old Men"
Youth International Party ("Yippies")

Chapter Twenty-nine

AMERICAN FRUSTRATION AND DECLINE IN THE 1970s

Books predicting stock market crashes, death-dealing ecological disasters, and even the imminent Second Coming of Jesus sold in the millions in the early 1970s. Observing the cultural landscape in California, **New York Times** reporter Steve Roberts noted in 1971, "Prophets of doom are as common as girls in bikinis (there are even a few prophets of doom in bikinis). Some predict the whole state will break off and sink into the Pacific—probably this month."

Twentieth-century Protestants increasingly embraced "pre-millennial dispensationalism"—the belief that soon Christians will be taken up to heaven in an event called "the Rapture" so they would not suffer a seven-year series of natural disasters and wars causing millions of deaths (a period believers call "the Tribulation"). The Tribulation would end, such evangelicals believed, with the emergence of a satanic figure called the Antichrist who would become a dictator of the world before being defeated by Jesus and his angels. Hal Lindsey, a former tugboat captain and graduate of the Armageddon-oriented Dallas Theological Seminary, brought these ideas to a broad audience and became one of the 1970s' most successful prophets of doom, writing that decade's bestselling non-fiction book, **The Late, Great Planet Earth**. Formerly an evangelist for the Campus Crusade for Christ, Lindsey grew sideburns, a moustache and longer hair and filled his book with the language of the 1960s youth counterculture, using a popular term for LSD hallucinations when he described the Rapture as "the ultimate trip" and calling the Antichrist "the weirdo beast." Lindsey frightened his audience, insisting that images of fire and blood in the Biblical Book of Revelation were predictions of nuclear war.

California cult leader Charles Manson led his followers on a killing spree that claimed seven victims in the summer of 1969. Their intention was to produce a race war between blacks and whites that he believed the Bible predicted. Religion did not inspire all late-1960s and early 1970s doomsday prognosticators. A novel, **The Andromeda Strain,** by Michael Crichton depicted the human race as threatened with extinction by a killer virus delivered to the planet by a fallen space satellite. A bestselling non-fiction book called **The Population Bomb** by Paul Ehrlich predicted a human population explosion leading to mass famine and warfare over diminishing resources. "While you are reading these words, four people will have died from starvation," the back cover grimly proclaimed, "most of them children."

Dread of religious or secular Armageddon haunted movies and music as well. One hit film, **The Planet of the Apes**, takes place after a nuclear war has allowed mutant apes to take over Earth and enslave a human race that has lost the power of speech. Daily newscasts and the morning headlines in the 1960s and 1970s fed this dread of the future. Political assassinations, the American military failure in Vietnam, the decline in the American economy starting in the late 1960s, urban uprisings, the loss of manufacturing jobs overseas, and the scandals engulfing the Nixon administration reinforced a feeling many Americans had that they were witnessing the end of the world as they knew it.

In the early 1960s, the more idealistic members of the Kennedy administration hoped to usher in an America freed from segregation and poverty. Meanwhile, counterculture youths saw a world poisoned with militarism and corrupted by the undemocratic dominance of wealthy, straight, Protestant, English-speaking Anglo men. Both sets of idealists looked outward to make the world a better place rather than inward for self-justification. Two nearly overlapping journeys in the summer of 1969 illustrate these separate quests for a better world: the *Apollo 11* moon landing on July 20, 1969, and the Woodstock Music and Arts Festival in upstate New York, August 15-18. For millions of Americans the manned moon landing marked the emotional highlight of a difficult, often depressing decade, a rare moment of unity in a divisive time. A party atmosphere surrounded Cape Kennedy in Brevard County on Florida's east coast on the morning of July 16. About 1 million visitors flocked to the launch site. Families and tourists gathered in house boats or camped out in tents or camper vans, sipping beer and soda as they waited for the launch.

Inside the space center, officials set up bleachers for establishment celebrities and important officials, including former President Lyndon Johnson, Charles Lindbergh, the first man to fly solo across the Atlantic, and *Tonight Show* host Johnny Carson. About 600 million people around the world, 20 percent of the Earth's population, watched on television or listened on the radio when Mission Commander Neil Armstrong announced at 4:18 p.m. EST on July 20 that "The Eagle has landed." ("The Eagle" was *Apollo 11*'s landing craft, the so-called lunar module.) When an announcer at Yankee Stadium in New York informed the fans of the Eagle's touchdown, the crowd of 16,000 let out a whoop of celebration, belting out "The Star-Spangled Banner." In Britain, television networks provided their first all-night broadcast, allowing audiences there to see the landing live. For two and a half hours, the world stood amazed, viewing Armstrong and fellow astronaut Edwin "Buzz" Aldrin as they planted an American flag, walked on the Moon's surface, and gathered rocks to be transported back to Earth.

Almost simultaneously with the *Apollo* launch, about 400,000 gathered in upstate New York for a journey of a different sort. Promoters organizing the Woodstock Music and Art Fair had rented 600 acres of farmland from Max Yasgur to see one of the most storied music lineups in history, including longtime folk music legend Joan Baez; the English rock band, The Who; blues-inspired, scorching Texas vocalist Janis Joplin; the band most associated with extended musical LSD raves, the Grateful Dead; and emerging guitar legends Carlos Santana and Jimi Hendrix.

In spite of a fierce thunderstorm, a shortage of outdoor toilets, and a rash of bad LSD trips, the sprawling audience proved peaceful. No fights broke out. There were only two drug-related deaths. A tractor driver also accidentally fatally ran over a person dozing in a sleeping bag. In spite of these incidents, a police official described the "Woodstock Nation," as it came to be called, "the most courteous, considerate, and well-behaved group of kids that I have ever been in contact with in my twenty-four years of police work." Woodstock came to symbolize for many young Americans the hope for a more peaceful future, one based on sharing, mutual respect, equality, and the joy of living in the minute. These two events in the summer of 1969 represented in many ways a timeout—an all-too-brief pause—before one of the most bitter, disillusioning decades in American history.

THE NEW PRESIDENT

Richard Nixon preferred to work in solitude. He hated the handshaking, the backslapping, and the give-and-take essential to any political career. Nixon once described himself as an introvert in an extrovert's business. Much of his discomfort came from his embarrassment over economic hardships during his childhood, the trauma

Richard M. Nixon flashes the "V" for "victory" sign.
Photo credit: Nixon Presidential Library.

he shared with his parents when two of his brothers died of tuberculosis, and his resentment at what he saw as an easier life enjoyed by others, such as the family he came to obsessively hate—the wealthy and glamorous Kennedys. He left nothing to chance and memorized what he was going to say when he was going to meet people.

Henry Kissinger, who served as Nixon's national security advisor and then as his Secretary of State, did not have kind words for his former boss after both men had left public office. "He was a very odd man," Kissinger said. ". . . He is a very unpleasant man. He was so nervous. It was such an effort for him to be on television. He was an artificial man in the sense that when he met someone he thought it out carefully so that nothing was spontaneous, and that meant he didn't like people. What I never understood is why he became a politician. He hated to meet new people. Most politicians like crowds. He didn't."

Nixon was to a large degree a product of his times. One of the most perceptive politicians of his era, he quickly recognized shared grievances. Nixon called his culturally conservative political base the "Silent Majority," a group involving "millions of people in the middle of the American political spectrum who do not demonstrate, who do not picket or protest loudly." Nixon and his aides sought to walk a tightrope, wanting to appear moderate compared to explicit racists like Alabama segregationist governor and presidential candidate George Wallace, while still appealing to Wallace's resentful southern white constituency. This approach came to be known as the "Southern Strategy."

During his career in the United States House and the Senate, Nixon acquired the reputation of a racial moderate, so much so that for a time he was seriously competitive for the African-American vote in his presidential race against John Kennedy. While vice president, Nixon supported the United States Supreme Court decision *Brown v. the Board of Education*, a step further than President Eisenhower was willing to take. He backed civil rights bills introduced in the Congress in the 1950s and the 1965 Voting Rights Act, and met publicly with Civil Rights leader Martin Luther King, Jr., in 1957. Nixon, nevertheless, "thought, basically, they [African Americans] were genetically inferior . . . He thought they couldn't achieve on a level with whites," said John Ehrlichman, White House counsel and assistant to the president for domestic affairs.

Audiotapes Nixon made in the Oval Office when he was president revealed he frequently used the word "nigger" and other slurs to refer to blacks. Nixon told his personal secretary, Rosemary Woods, that it would take 500 years for African Americans to catch up with whites.

Nixon also harbored a deep distrust of Jews, whom he described as "disloyal" and out to get him. "The Jews voted 95 percent against me," he complained. Nixon, however, to a large degree kept these explicit prejudices close to his vest, even as he sought to take advantage of white anger against African Americans. Hoping to build Republican support in the South, Nixon and Attorney General John Mitchell in 1969 asked the courts to delay enforcement of the desegregation of Mississippi schools. "Do only what the law requires," Nixon wrote in a memo. "Not one thing more."

DOMESTIC AFFAIRS UNDER NIXON

Affirmative Action

Nixon did pursue one policy that seemed, on the surface, to be friendly to the civil rights movement, supporting federally enforced guidelines regarding the hiring of African Americans and other "minorities" in private employment. This policy came to be known as "**affirmative action**." Under affirmative action, starting in 1970, all federal agencies and contractors had to meet "numerical goals and timetables" in hiring a proportionally representative number of African Americans, Mexican Americans, women and other groups that had been historically discriminated against. Many on the right criticized this program as creating a quota system that would reward less qualified applicants with jobs based on their race or gender.

Nixon liked affirmative action because it would cost the federal government very little, as opposed to a jobs program for instance. Nixon also liked the prospect of forcing Democrats to choose between their white working class voters who would see affirmative action as an assault on the privileges of union seniority, and their African-American supporters who might benefit from affirmative action. Compared to later Republican presidents, such as Ronald Reagan and George W. Bush, much of Nixon's domestic agenda was relatively liberal. He signed laws increasing welfare spending in programs such as Social Security, Aid to Families with Dependent Children (AFDC) and food stamps, creating the Occupational Safety and Health Administration (OSHA) and the Environmental Protection Agency (EPA). However, he also implemented cost-benefit reviews of all environmental regulations, watering down their effectiveness, and tried to eliminate the Office of Economic Opportunity, which had been the agency charged with implementing President Johnson's War on Poverty.

Nixonomics

Nixon faced a major political challenge with the economy. Lyndon Johnson's spending on domestic programs and the Vietnam War had sparked inflation in the Democrat's later years in office. By 1968, Johnson's last year in office, inflation quadrupled to 4 percent. In Nixon's first year in office, 1969, inflation rose to 7 percent. While incomes for Americans improved steadily for 25 years from 1945 to 1970, the long boom began to ebb. To curb inflation, Nixon cut spending on both domestic programs and the military, increasing unemployment, which reached 6 percent by 1971. For the first time, the economy experienced both rising joblessness and inflation. Baffled economists combined "stagnation" and "inflation" to term the phenomenon "stagflation."

Even worse for American workers, the European and the Japanese economies began to expand faster than the United States' in the 1970s, and the United States started running trade deficits, meaning it bought more products overseas than it sold to the rest of the world. As Americans made fewer products for the international market, and Japanese cars and electronics took a larger share of the American market, the number of manufacturing jobs began a sharp decline that would continue in the early twenty-first century. One million American manufacturing jobs in the auto, steel, electronics and garment making industries disappeared between 1966 and 1971. A recession began in 1970.

In August 1971, Nixon issued executive orders imposing a three-month freeze on wages and prices, a 10 percent tax on imports (a policy designed to boost sales of American-made goods), and he took American currency off the gold standard. At the same time, the Democratic-controlled Congress boosted spending on Social Security and military veterans while Nixon accelerated government purchases of goods such as trucks, office supplies, and even toilet paper. A mild recovery began. Unemployment dropped to below 5 percent by 1972 while earnings again rose by about 4 percent in both 1971 and 1972.

Nixon never cared for the wage and price controls he implemented in his first term and, with his re-election secured, he lifted these caps in January 1973. Unfortunately, he unleashed another devastating round of stagflation. The overheated consumer demand boosted wholesale prices by an incredible 20 percent in the first half of the year, resulting in an 8 percent spike in consumer prices. In June, Nixon relented and placed a 60-day freeze on all prices. Not wanting to sell at artificially low prices, some producers responded by holding back goods from the market. This created shortages. To prevent events from spinning out of control, the Federal Reserve Board

Map 29.1 Israel, Six-Day War 1967

increased the prime interest rate from 10 to 12 percent, which cooled down the economy. The good news did not last. Americans did not know it, but they were at the dawn of a new and harder economic reality dominated by de-industrialization, the rise of America as a lower-wage service-sector economy, increasing workplace automation that reduced the number of jobs available, and a decline in union membership along with a deterioration of the average family's standard of living.

The First Energy Crisis

On shaky ground, the American economy took another major hit in late 1973 when the Arab members of the Organization of Petroleum Exporting Countries (OPEC) staged an oil boycott of the United States following that year's Arab-Israeli War. The second Middle Eastern conflict in six years, the so-called Yom Kippur War, began on October 6 during the Jewish holiday when Egypt, Jordan and Syria (along with military units provided by Iraq and Libya) attempted to retake land (the Sinai Peninsula, the West Bank and the Golan Heights) occupied by Israel since the overwhelming defeat of the Arabs in 1967's Six-Day War.

While the Arab states initially caught Israel ill-prepared, American jets delivered more military equipment and ammunition to the Israelis in 1973 than they had brought to the besieged city of West Berlin during the 1948-1949 airlifts. The tide of the war turned. The

United States and the Soviet Union brokered a truce. A cease-fire was signed November 11. In retaliation for American aid to the Israelis, Saudi Arabia, Kuwait, Iraq and Libya cut off all oil shipments to the United States and reduced their shipments to the rest of the world by 5 percent. About 35 percent of American oil supplies in 1973 came from foreign sources. Gas prices at the pump quadrupled from 30 cents a gallon to $1.20 (or from $1.70 to $6.81 in 2018 dollars) at the height of what was widely called "**The Energy Crisis.**" Shortages forced a rationing system on service station owners. Owners of vehicles with license plates ending in even numbers could buy gasoline only on even-numbered days while those with plates ending in odd numbers could refuel only on odd days. Many gas stations limited purchases to ten gallons per customer. Violence broke out at some gas stations.

Nixon tried a patchwork of temporary fixes. At Nixon's prompting, the Congress banned gasoline purchases on Sunday and extended daylight saving time from January 6, 1974 to February 23, 1975, controversial because this forced many school children to wait at bus stops in the dark or for their parents to drive them to campuses before sunrise. Furthermore, in 1974 the Congress set a national maximum highway speed limit of 55 miles per hour.

OPEC lifted the embargo on March 18, 1974, but the damage to the economy had been done. OPEC set oil prices at $11.65 a barrel, up from $1.80 in 1970. (In 2018 dollars, the increase was from $9.20 to a barrel to $59.56). High gasoline prices rippled through the economy. Wholesale prices jumped by 18 percent in 1973, and then consumer prices increased an average of 12 percent the following year. Meanwhile, from January 1973 to December 1974, the Dow Jones Industrial average dropped 45 percent.

FOREIGN AFFAIRS UNDER NIXON

The 1973 Energy Crisis revealed the limits of American global power, as did the continued U.S. frustrations in Southeast Asia. Nixon's foreign policy centered on how to deal with reduced American power and influence. From the beginning, the key player in Nixon's foreign policy team was national security advisor **Henry Kissinger**. Later elevated to Secretary of State by Nixon and kept on by Nixon's successor, Gerald Ford, Kissinger saw himself as a hard-bitten pragmatist. His Jewish family had fled Nazi Germany in 1938. Highly intelligent, Kissinger received a Ph.D. from Harvard University in 1954, and became a professor of government and international affairs there the same year. He impressed Nixon with his sharp mind and the sweep of his vision for American foreign policy.

Nixon saw a clear American victory in Vietnam as already impossible by the time he took office in 1969. Early on, the White House unveiled the so-called "Nixon Doctrine" in which the United States would rely on allies such as Japan, and unsavory regimes such as the white supremacist apartheid government in South Africa, the dictatorship ruling Pakistan, and the Shah's ruthless monarchy in Iran to bear more of the responsibility for checking the spread of communism. A balance of power between the Americans and the Soviets became Nixon

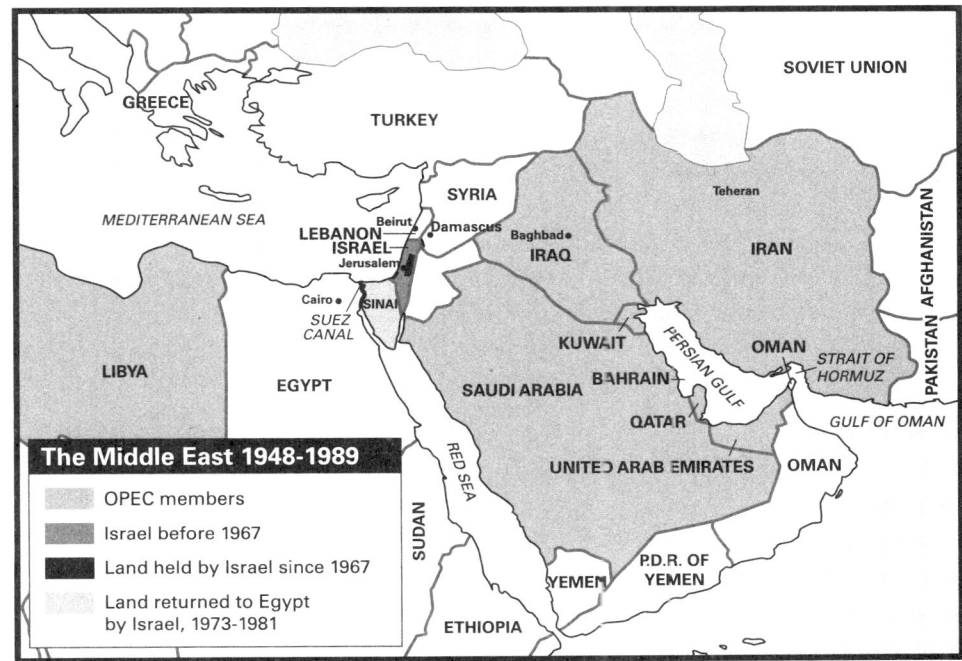

Map 29.2 The Middle East
1948-1989

The Shah of Iran, President Nixon, and Mrs. Nixon in formal attire for a state dinner in the White House. October 2, 1969 Photo credit: Nixon Presidential Library

and Kissinger's obsessive priority. Human rights and self-determination in the developing world did not enter into their calculations.

As part of the Nixon Doctrine, American sales of fighter planes, tanks, radar, anti-aircraft weapons, and other military hardware to American allies escalated by billions. In the early 1970s, with Washington's encouragement the Shah of Iran spent $35 billion of that nation's oil revenues upgrading and expanding the military, mostly on American-manufactured weapons, even though life expectancy in Iran was only 50, childhood mortality remained high, and 6 out of every 10 Iranians remained illiterate. In many American client states, health and education took a back seat to the larger needs of the Cold War.

A Coup in Chile

The Nixon Doctrine would claim human rights victims around the globe. Chile represents one heart-breaking case in point. On September 4, 1970, a Marxist, Salvador Allende, won a democratic election for the presidency of Chile, a mineral-rich nation whose border snakes along more than half of South America's Pacific coast. Chile was of interest to the United States primarily because of its rise as the world's leading producer of copper, used in building motors, generators, cables, and wires. By the late twentieth century, two American mining companies dominated Chile's copper industry and International Telephone and Telegraph controlled Chile's phone services. In spite of its wealth of natural resources, millions of Chileans lived in poverty.

Allende, the leader of Chile's Socialist Party, rose to political prominence in the 1960s. He advocated peaceful revolution through democratic elections. IT&T

and other companies that gave money to Nixon's 1968 campaign asked for the president's help in preventing Allende from taking power, and Nixon obliged, asking the CIA to instigate a coup. The CIA successfully recruited General **Augusto Pinochet** to lead a military overthrow, which toppled the Allende regime on September 11, 1973. Using American weapons and money, soldiers seized control of police stations, government buildings, and radio stations. Rebel airplanes believed to have been flown by American pilots fired rockets into the presidential palace. Pinochet's military dictatorship later claimed that Allende committed suicide rather than surrender, while others say he was murdered.

In the days immediately after the coup, over 10,000 prisoners were rounded up and taken to the two main soccer stadiums in the capital of Santiago. There, soldiers brought collaborators to point out "subversives" who were subsequently taken to nearby locker rooms, which had been converted into torture chambers. In all, the Pinochet regime executed 3,200 citizens, imprisoned another 80,000, and forced over 200,000 to flee. By the year after the coup, 1974, Chile's economy shrank by 15 percent and unemployment, which had been 3 percent under Allende, skyrocketed to 20 percent. By 1988, Chile's economy stabilized but 45 percent of the population had fallen below the poverty line. This was the Nixon Doctrine in action. Allies were rewarded for being anti-communist, even if they were brutally anti-democratic and poorly served their people.

Détente

Kissinger and Nixon sought to reduce the overwhelming pressure on the American military by easing tensions

**President Nixon meets with China's Communist Party Leader, Mao Zedong.
February 29, 1972,
Photo credit: Nixon Presidential Library**

with the Soviet Union, a chief supplier of weapons to North Vietnam. Nixon's pursuit of warmer relations with Moscow came to be known by the French term **détente**. Nixon and Kissinger quickly exploited a dangerous conflict that developed in the communist world in 1969. The Soviets and the Chinese almost came to war, exchanging gunfire along the Ussari River that separated the two nations near Vladivostok in far East Asia. The Nixon White House sought to play both nations off of each other.

The White House realized that if the U.S. cultivated a friendlier relationship with China, the Soviet Union—suffering from consumer shortages and feeling the economic strain of the long Cold War—would feel threatened on two fronts. The Kremlin might become more attentive to American foreign policy concerns, such as pressuring the North Vietnamese to make peace. The American president also saw China as an ascending power.

Since the triumph of the communists in the 1949 Chinese Revolution, the United States had never diplomatically recognized the Beijing regime. Defeated in the revolution, the forces of deposed Chinese anti-communist dictator Chiang Kai-shek retreated to the island of Taiwan and separated from the communist mainland, establishing a rival government. Ever since, the United States had recognized the Taiwan leadership as the legitimate government of China. Nevertheless, on December 8, 1970, Chinese Premier Zhou Enlai (the second most powerful man in the country after communist party chairman Mao Zedong) sent Nixon a letter seeking better relations. The first sign of a thaw came on April 6 of that year when, at the end of the World Table Tennis Championships in Japan, the American team captain received an invitation by the Chinese captain to play a week of exhibition matches in Beijing. The invitation came from Chairman Mao. The American team was the first official U.S. delegation in the country since the 1950s.

Kissinger arranged for a weeklong visit in China by President Nixon, from February 21 to 28, 1972, the first appearance by an American leader in that nation since the 1949 revolution. The United States established full diplomatic relations with China under President Jimmy Carter on January 1, 1979, and recognized Taiwan as just part of a single Chinese nation, even though Americans continued to give aid to the anti-communist regime on the island. The opening to China, as Nixon and Kissinger expected, inspired the Soviets to move toward détente. Nixon visited Soviet leader Leonid Brezhnev in Moscow in May 1972, striking a deal that allowed the Soviets, suffering from inefficient farming, to buy American wheat and leading to the Strategic Arms Limitation Treaty (SALT I). The United States and the USSR agreed to cap the number of intercontinental ballistic missiles either side could install. Under SALT, both the Americans and the Russians pledged not to develop new anti-ballistic missiles, which could have provoked an expensive arms race.

"Peace With Honor"

Nixon's evolving relationship with the Soviets and the Chinese had less impact on the Vietnam War than he hoped. The Russians wanted the war to end. The Chinese, at the same time, were worried about the massive buildup of Soviet troops along its border and sought a closer relationship with the Americans as a protection against Russian aggression. The Beijing government knew support of North Vietnam would complicate that objective.

Yet, the worries of the Russians and the Chinese were of no concern to North Vietnam. The North Vietnamese saw themselves as fighting a war of national independence, not as serving as pawns for communist super-states. The relationship between North Vietnam and Russia strained badly as the Kremlin increasingly urged a settlement. The Vietnamese, furthermore, had a difficult and often hostile relationship with China stretching back centuries.

Nixon had no grand scheme to cut this Gordian knot. He said repeatedly that he was seeking "peace with honor." To the outside world, this meant that the United States would not withdraw until it had guaranteed the survival of a non-communist South Vietnam. To Nixon's inner circle, this meant getting out of Vietnam without making Nixon appear like he was "the first president of the United States to lose a war." By the time he was sworn in as president, Nixon believed that a clear military victory in Vietnam was impossible but hoped he could

President and Mrs. Nixon at the Great Wall of China. February 24, 1972. Photo credit: Nixon Presidential Library

leave behind a stable, adequately strong South Vietnam as American forces withdrew. He wanted to achieve this through what the White House called "**Vietnamization**." Nixon planned to replace American soldiers in Vietnam with South Vietnamese troops heavily armed with U.S.-provided weaponry.

By April 30, 1969, the number of American military personnel in Southeast Asia reached a record 543,000. Troop levels would drop from this peak for the rest of the war. American hopes for an end to the war briefly rose when North Vietnamese leader Ho Chi Minh died on September 2, 1969, but the communist leader's successors instead vowed to continue the struggle until "there is not a single aggressor in the country."

Operation Menu

Within weeks of the president's 1969 inauguration, generals convinced Nixon to launch an intensive bombing campaign aimed at destroying North Vietnamese "sanctuaries," supply routes and weapons depots the communists had created in neighboring, neutral Cambodia. Nixon kept the bombing campaign, dubbed "Operation Menu" secret from the public and even the Congress. From its launch in February 1969 until 1973, Operation Menu resulted in 3,600 missions dropping 500,000 tons of bombs on eastern Cambodia. Bombers also attacked communist positions in Laos as well. The Cambodian government led by Prince Norodom Sihanouk had been fighting a low-intensity war with communist forces that called themselves the "Khmer Rouge." (The Khmers are Cambodia's largest ethnic group while "Rouge" is French for "red," the symbolic color of the international commu-

nist movement.) The Khmer Rouge represented one of the most fanatical communist forces in the world. Their leader, Soloth Sar, went by the *nom de guerre* "Pol Pot."

American planes began to follow and attack Viet Cong and North Vietnamese soldiers as they crossed into Cambodia, but sometimes they hit civilians. As American bombers caused approximately 150,000 deaths of mostly unarmed peasants during Operation Menu, from March 1969 to May 1970, the Khmer Rouge enjoyed more support and began to control more territory.

In May 1969, the *New York Times* revealed the bombing campaign in Laos and Cambodia. Angered and wanting to know who revealed the secret military operation to the press, Nixon ordered FBI wiretaps of four reporters and thirteen government officials. Without court authorization, these illegal wiretaps started the Nixon White House pattern of law-breaking and violations of civil liberties, which would continue and expand until the Watergate scandal forced Nixon's resignation in August 1974.

Irritated by Cambodian Prince Sihanouk's neutrality, the Americans supported General Lon Nol when he overthrew the government in 1970 and launched a more aggressive war against the Khmer Rouge forces. The Americans provided Nol with more weapons but did not respect him enough to consult him before the United States launched a series of ground raids into Cambodia in March. The American public was informed of the invasion on April 30, 1970. On May 2, *The New York Times* informed the public of a secret bombing campaign that had begun in North Vietnam, the first such bombings in the North since Johnson had suspended the attacks in 1968. The bombing, and the invasion of Cambodia, angered senators and members of the House who believed that the president, by not consulting with the legislative branch before taking military actions, was essentially suspending the part of the Constitution that gave the power to declare war exclusively to the Congress.

Four Dead in Ohio

Shortly after Nixon announced that U.S. forces had invaded Cambodia, anti-war protests opened at **Kent State University** in Ohio. The protestors set fire to the ROTC (Reserve Officer Training Corps) building and burned an American flag. Students then tried to set fire to the campus library. On May 2, Governor James Rhodes ordered National Guard units to the campus and pledged to use "every force possible" to quell the disorder. Close to noon on May 4, Guardsmen faced a hail of rocks thrown by the protestors. They fired canisters of tear gas and advanced on a crowd of angry students. At around 12:24 p.m.

several of the troops dropped to one knee and fired in the direction of a group of students getting off 67 rounds in 13 seconds. Thirteen students, "mostly bystanders," fell with one paralyzed and four (Allison Krause, William Schroeder, Jeffrey Miller and Sandra Lee Scheuer) killed. Two of the deceased were 19 years old; the other two were 20. Many of the victims were not in any way involved with the protests and were simply walking to class.

Later that week to prevent protests, 448 campuses closed. Demonstrations took place at more than 1,100 schools with an estimated 2 million students going on strike. On May 14 at Jackson State College in Mississippi, an historically black college, two African-American students died during an uprising when police fired into a dormitory. A Gallup poll indicated that 58 percent of Americans blamed the students for their deaths. Angry that Mayor John Lindsay of New York lowered flags at half-staff in honor of the Kent State dead, 200 construction workers, so-called hardhats, charged into an anti-war rally, beating the protestors with fists, pipes and hammers. Many of the blue-collar workers shouted, "Kill the Commie bastards" and "Love it [America] or leave it."

A picture of a 14-year-old girl, Mary Ann Vecchio, kneeling beside the body of a dead student at Kent State and lifting her arms as if in prayer, won a Pulitzer Prize for the photographer John Filo. Printed in newspapers around the world, the picture became an iconic image of America at war with itself. In October, a grand jury cleared the Guardsmen involved in the shooting, though it indicted students for arson and other offenses prior to the massacre.

The Pentagon Papers

Richard Nixon deeply believed in secrecy and felt threatened whenever White House discussions became public knowledge. This extended even to awareness about debates within previous administrations. His volcanic temper exploded, therefore, with *The New York Times'* 1971 publication of what came to be known as "**The Pentagon Papers**," a huge collection of government memos on Vietnam from the period just after World War II to the Kennedy and Johnson administrations that had been archived and analyzed by the Defense Department under the order of former Defense Secretary Robert McNamara in 1967. The documents spanned 47 volumes, complete with 3,000 pages of commentary by unnamed government historians. The papers revealed that several Democratic and Republican administrations had intentionally misled the American public about the military's success in Vietnam and the stability and strength of the United States' ally South Vietnam.

The Nixon administration rushed to the federal courts to halt publication of the documents after the *Times* published three installments. The Justice Department won a temporary restraining order to stop further publication by the *Times* and the *Washington Post*, which had begun to publish its own series. On June 30, 1971, the United States Supreme Court lifted the order, holding that freedom of the press stood paramount over administration concerns about secrecy.

Nixon's secret investigation revealed the source of the leak, Daniel Ellsberg, a Pentagon official during the McNamara era. Egil "Bud" Krogh, a White House assistant, sought to damage the reputation of Ellsberg and prevent further press leaks. "Anyone who opposes us, we'll destroy," Krogh said. "As a matter of fact, anyone who doesn't support us, we'll destroy." The team Krogh assembled to "plug" leaks became known as the "White House Plumbers." The Plumbers, which included White House Special Counsel Charles Colson, former CIA Agent E. Howard Hunt, and retired FBI agent G. Gordon Liddy, would play a key role in the Watergate scandal.

The Plumbers put Ellsberg under surveillance and in one of their many illegal acts, burglarized the office of his psychiatrist hoping to find damaging evidence about his mental health. A grand jury had indicted Ellsberg for theft of the *Pentagon Papers,* and he went on trial in January 1973, but all charges were dropped on May 11 after news broke about the Plumbers' burglary.

The Christmas Bombing

By the start of 1972, the president could correctly point out that he had withdrawn more than 400,000 troops from Southeast Asia. Now, combat deaths were down to about 10 a week. Kissinger was secretly negotiating with the government committee that had run North Vietnam since Ho's death. Yet, the war was going to take one more bloody turn that year.

The North Vietnamese launched their "Easter Offensive" on March 30, with more than 120,000 North Vietnamese Army and Viet Cong soldiers initially overwhelming South Vietnamese forces in the northern provinces, the Central Highlands and the area just north of the capital, Saigon. Politically unable to re-introduce combat troops, Nixon pounded North Vietnam and communist positions in South Vietnam with bombs, American B-52s flying about 50,000 sorties south of the demilitarized zone that separated the two countries. By the time "Operation Linebacker" ended in October, North Vietnam had suffered 100,000 casualties. At the end of 1972, the Americans could not "win" with air power alone, and the North Vietnamese could not protect themselves from bombers. Hanoi signaled it was ready to talk again.

The combat in 1972, however, produced one more shocking image preserved forever on film. On June 8, South Vietnamese pilots accidentally dropped napalm on a South Vietnam village and Nick Ut photographed a young girl, Kim Phúc, who had torn off her burning clothes and was running down a road near Trang Bang screaming as the chemicals seared her flesh. The napalm incinerated her skin at almost 1,500 degrees Fahrenheit. Phúc, who eventually defected to Canada, underwent 17 surgeries to overcome her injuries. Ut won a Pulitzer Prize for his photo, another scarring image from a long, divisive war. As it was published around the world, even more Americans questioned the sanity of continuing the conflict.

One last act remained in the almost 30-year drama. Talks between Kissinger and the North Vietnamese representative to the peace talks, Le Duc Tho, resumed on August 1. Kissinger told the American public that peace "was at hand" just before the November election showdown with McGovern, but the talks stalled again. Nixon responded with the so-called "Christmas Bombing" in December, in which U.S. planes dropped more ordnance than in the first two years of the Nixon administration. By now, both sides were exhausted. The North Vietnamese no longer demanded the removal of South Vietnamese President Nguyen Van Thieu as a pre-condition for a peace agreement. All remaining differences between Le Duc Tho and Kissinger were resolved, and a truce was signed January 27, 1973, which allowed Nixon to declare, "We have finally achieved peace with honor."

"Nothing More to Say After That": Aftermath of the Vietnam War

Under the peace terms, the Americans agreed to remove all troops, including military advisers, from South Vietnam. The U.S., South Vietnam, and the North also agreed to exchange prisoners of war. North Vietnamese troops could maintain their positions in South Vietnam, as could Viet Cong guerillas. In essence, the truce was a surrender document, not much different from what the president could have gotten from Hanoi when he first took office in 1969. In all, 58,193 Americans died in Vietnam, almost 21,000 under Nixon's watch, as well as close to 2 million Vietnamese. At least 150,000 soldiers and medical personnel suffered injuries. The United States spent $138 billion in military aid plus $8.5 billion in economic aid, a total of about $948 billion in 2018 dollars.

Henry Kissinger and Le Duc Tho received Nobel Peace Prizes for the truce in 1973, in spite of Kissinger's key role in invasions of Cambodia and Laos and his likely involvement in the Chilean coup the same year. The comedian and musical satirist Tom Lehrer supposedly retired from performing upon hearing the news. "It was at that moment that satire died," Lehrer reportedly said. "There was nothing more to say after that." Kissinger and Le Duc Tho's Peace Prize became even more ironic since the Vietnam War did not actually end until two years later.

The Democratic Party-dominated Congress in November 1973 passed the **War Powers Act**, overriding Nixon's veto. Congressional leaders knew that the free hand given several consecutive administrations, culminating in the Gulf of Tonkin Resolution in 1964, had resulted

Photograph showing Vietnamese children, including Kim Phúc, running and crying after napalm was dropped from South Vietnamese Skyraider airplanes on their village of Trang Bang. June 8, 1972

The Hanoi Hilton

A perception of American cruelty may have contributed to, or at least provided a rationale for, the inhumane treatment suffered by American GIs languishing in North Vietnamese prisons. Downed bomber pilots and flight crews made up most of the 591 prisoners of war released as part of "Operation Homecoming" at the end of the war. In April 1993, Harvard economist Stephen Morris discovered North Vietnamese documents indicating that Hanoi held 1,205 American prisoners as late as September 1972, a short time before prisoner releases began. Whether the discrepancy between the number of American prisoners released through Operation Homecoming and the number mentioned in the report represents a clerical error, a translation mistake, or evidence of the mass killing of American POWs remains a mystery. When the United States pulled combat forces out of Vietnam in 1973, about 2,000 servicemen remained unaccounted for. A larger number of Vietnamese soldiers remained missing.

Released prisoners, including future Arizona senator and 2008 Republican presidential nominee John McCain, reported being tortured. North Vietnamese guards beat prisoners with rifle butts, clubs and fists, deprived them of sleep and adequate nutrition and mocked them when news arrived of tragedies in the prisoners' families. Many were forced to sit through interminable "re-education" sessions and were told 5,000 years of Vietnamese history through the Hanoi regime's perspective. Withholding medicine became a common method of weakening prisoner resistance. Interrogators sometimes sought intelligence, but just as often they simply wanted to shatter the spirit of their hostages. The POW camp at Hao Lo gained particular infamy and was given the sarcastic name "Hanoi Hilton."

Porter Halyburton served as pilot in a two-man Navy F-4 Phantom that was shot down while bombing a bridge on a road connecting the North Vietnamese capital, Hanoi, to China. Parachuting over hostile territory, he quickly fell into the hands of North Vietnamese soldiers who put him in an animal shed, giving him rice, water, and cigarettes until a jeep arrived to carry him to Hanoi. "They told me, 'If you cooperate with us, and repent for your crimes, we will move you to a nice camp, a really nice place. You'll be with all your friends. You'll have nice food and you can play games and write to your family. But if you refuse, we'll move you to a worse place.'"

The North Vietnamese forced POWs to march through Hanoi, handcuffed two-by-two. Made to bow as they stumbled forward, the prisoners suffered a blow to the back of their heads every time they looked up. At the urging of the guards, the crowds screamed, "Yankee imperialists! Air pirates! Murderers!" The North Vietnamese then confined Halyburton in a remote prison nicknamed "The Briarpatch." The guards wanted him to write a confession. "First, they just beat the crap out of you to soften you up," he said. Or they made you sit on a little wooden stool for days . . . After that, the torture began. The method they used on me we called "max cuffs." Your arms were pulled up behind your back and then they put these handcuffs on the upper part of your arm. Then they tied a rope on your wrists and pulled it up. I could actually see the fingertips over the top of my head when they did that. It pressed the nerves against the bone. It was like molten metal flowing through your veins—just indescribable "pain."

This last round of abuse broke Halyburton's resistance. He signed confessions, gave biographical information and listed all his flights over North Vietnam. They asked him to write the same information over and over. "Psychologically, I think this was more damaging than the physical torture because you felt like you completely failed," he said. "You had given up. You had capitulated. You had violated the code of conduct. You let everybody down." It was only after the war that he found out that his breakdown had been universal.

in the Vietnam quagmire. Alarmed particularly by Nixon's unauthorized invasion of Cambodia and bombing campaigns there, members of the House and Senate sought to reassert their voice in military policy. Under the War Powers Act, the president has to notify Congress within 48 hours of any military deployment where battle conditions prevail or where combat was likely to take place. If the Congress does not sign off on the military action, the president has to withdraw troops within 60 days.

The Hanoi government clearly saw the peace agreement as merely a pause in the action. Fighting between the North Vietnamese and Viet Cong and South Vietnam began almost immediately after the American departure. North Vietnam launched a new full-scale offensive in 1975. By then, North Vietnam boasted the fifth largest military in the world. It anticipated that the last phase of the war would take two years, but final victory came in only 55 days.

The advance of North Vietnamese troops in early 1975 triggered a panic as South Vietnamese soldiers, police, and other government officials fled in droves, struggling to flee on clogged roads and arriving as refugees

FRAGGING

By the early 1970s, many military officers worried that the armed services in Vietnam were in a state of mutiny. A new word, "fragging," had ominously entered the military vocabulary. Fragging referred specifically to the murder of commanding officers in combat, usually when the officer made an unpopular decision, was inept, demeaning to soldiers, or put his men unnecessarily in harm's way.

The term comes from the small percussion fragmentation hand grenades often used in such homicides. In one such incident, Private Gary Hendricks had been ordered to stand guard at night near the Da Nang Airbase. Sergeant Richard Tate discovered Hendricks asleep while on duty and "gave the private a tongue lashing, but took no further action," according to historian Peter Brush. Around midnight the following day, Hendricks threw a fragmentation grenade into a bunker occupied by Sergeant Tate. "The grenade landed on Tate's stomach and the subsequent blast blew his legs off, killing the father of three from Asheville, North Carolina, who had only three weeks left on his tour of duty," said Brush. Hendricks confessed to the murder and was convicted by general court-martial. His death sentence was reduced to life in prison.

Hendrick's case was but one of 209 fragging incidents resulting in 34 deaths in 1970. By July 1972, Army officials believed 551 fraggings had killed 86 and injured more than 700. By the last years of the Vietnam War, the military command uncovered numerous cases of "bounty hunting" in which soldiers raised money to pay someone to murder an unpopular and/or dangerous officer. Soldiers also began to openly defy orders. In 1971 in Laos, a captain ordered two platoons to charge into withering enemy fire. The soldiers said no. "A lieutenant colonel pleaded, then ordered," author Rick Perlstein wrote. "Fifty-three still refused. They also refused to give their names. No disciplinary action was taken. The brass also feared that the mutiny would spread brigade-wide."

As it became clear that the Nixon administration intended to withdraw from Vietnam, soldiers increasingly resisted being put at risk for a cause the government had apparently given up on. The American army was collapsing in the field. "I just work hard at surviving so I can go home and protest the killing," explained one GI.

At Fort Bliss, soldiers violated military rules and addressed their commanding officers by their first names. The rate of soldiers who went absent without leave (AWOL) increased by five times between 1966 and 1971. Toward the end of the war, soldiers openly mocked clueless commanders and expressed their frustrations with sarcastic slogans scrawled on their helmets ("Make peace, not war" or "The unwilling, led by the unqualified, doing the unnecessary, for the ungrateful . . ."). One soldier, called on the carpet for a rules infraction, asked his superior officer, "What are you going to do about it, send me to 'Nam?'"

Drug use spiraled among soldiers, according to one official report, and contributed to violence between American soldiers. The American command in Saigon estimated that 65,000 soldiers operating in the theater were on drugs in 1970. An American helicopter pilot, Fred Hickey, reported that entire units —from privates to the commanding officers—were "doing heroin."

Unit cohesion collapsed as American units turned not only on their officers but also on each other. Hickey told journalist Stanley Karnow that in his unit, GIs split into factions, "the rednecks from Texas and the Deep South who hated the California and New York liberals, and vice versa . . . The blacks were moving into their black power thing, and they got militant . . . Everybody seemed to be at everybody else's throat. You had to speak softly, mind your own business, sleep with a weapon at all times, and only trust your closest buddies, nobody else. I had a knife attached to my boot." As the war wound down to its sad conclusion, American soldiers sometimes found that the enemy within was as dangerous as the enemy without.

in Saigon, which became virtually the last government stronghold by April 1975. Gerald Ford, who assumed the American presidency when Nixon was forced to resign August 9, 1974, authorized "Operation Frequent Wind," which eventually evacuated more than 7,000 American personnel and 150,000 South Vietnamese officials and family members who feared retribution from the North Vietnamese government. The morning of April 30 the last American personnel, 10 Marines, departed and North Vietnamese forces poured into Saigon, which they quickly renamed "Ho Chi Minh City" after the late communist leader.

The collapse of Saigon marked the start of a mass Vietnamese diaspora. Some fled by foot to nearby countries. Thousands who came to be known as "boat people," those who had worked for or supported the South Vietnamese government or served in its military or its intelligence services, put together rickety sea craft. They sailed until they met friendly vessels and were placed in refugee camps and tent cities across East Asia. Some eventually reached the United States.

About a quarter million Vietnamese-born refugees made it to the United States between 1975 and 1980, settling in large numbers in California and Texas. Reminders of a lost war, the refugees often received a harsh reception in the United States. In 1981, armed Klansman led by Vietnam War veteran Louis Beam harassed the new Vietnamese community, burned crosses, hanged effigies and torched boats owned by Vietnamese fishermen near Galveston, Texas. A Gallup Poll taken in 1975 showed that Americans opposed admitting the refugees by a margin of 54 percent to 36 percent. The House of Representatives rejected a bill that would have provided $327 million in aid to the refugees. "Those sons of bitches," President Gerald Ford said when he heard about the vote.

In the nearly four decades since the war ended, 40,000 Vietnamese have died or have been injured by land mines and unexploded bombs left behind in Southeast Asia. Meanwhile, digging up the explosives cost Vietnam about $1,000 each and disturbing the soil exposed the local population to the cancer-causing defoliant Agent Orange. Until a 1970 lab study demonstrated that Agent Orange caused birth defects in animals, American planes dropped 12 million gallons of the chemical compound, created by Dow Chemical, on the Vietnamese countryside to strip trees as a means of exposing communist fighters. Up to one million Vietnamese children have suffered birth defects as a side effect of the chemical, with another half-million injured during the initial chemical drops. Since then, cancer rates in Vietnam exploded and soldiers and servicemen from the United States, Australia and other countries that fought there have reported skin rashes, cancers of the skin, lung, brain and prostate, non-Hodgkin lymphoma, Hodgkin's lymphoma, and unusual rates of handicaps in their children.

The Killing Fields of Cambodia

There was no more tragic aftermath to the Vietnam War than the rise of the Khmer Rouge in Cambodia. During the Operation Menu bombing campaign that began in 1969, Cambodian President Lon Nol noted a sharp increase in the number of communist guerillas operating in his country. At the same time, Lon Nol's government proved ineffective, corrupt and cruel. Cambodia's economy began to collapse, which added to the Khmer Rouge's momentum. Food prices escalated wildly. Nixon's invasion of Cambodia created 700,000 refugees by the end of 1970. Eventually 540,000 tons of bombs fell on the tiny country, and the number of refugees by the end of 1971 reached a staggering two million people out of a total population of about seven million. By March 1973, American bombing raids encompassed the entire country, with 3,000 civilians dying in just three weeks. Armed by the North Vietnamese, the Khmer Rouge became a tightly disciplined, dedicated and ruthless fighting force. On April 17, 1975, the remnant of Lon Nol's forces collapsed. The Khmer Rogue marched into Phnom Penh and took control of the nation they renamed Democratic Kampuchea. Pol Pot declared the start of "Year Zero." Cambodia would be rebuilt from the ground up and become an almost entirely agricultural society in which all private ownership was banned and the family abolished. The Khmer Rouge closed down newspapers and television stations, prohibited the use of money, and shuttered schools. Small children as well as adults became part of a mass agricultural work force. Pol Pot ordered all of the 2 million persons living in Phnom Penh to evacuate. Soldiers went through hospitals, shot patients too weak or ill to move, and forced the rest to join a mass march to the countryside.

In mass agricultural camps, men and women lived separately and ate meals communally. Children were separated from parents and casual conversation was suppressed, and some were executed for laughing. Workdays, beginning at 4 a.m., lasted 18 hours, followed by mandatory lectures on communism. Overwork, combined with paltry food rations (amounting to 90 grams of rice a day) caused starvation and death from exhaustion.

About 2 million Cambodians died during less than four years of rule by the Khmer Rouge. Democratic Kampuchea became, as the North Vietnamese regime described it, "a land of blood and tears, hell on earth." The Khmer Rouge remained in power until a series of Cambodian border raids provoked Vietnam to invade on December 25, 1978. The Vietnamese took control of Phnom Penh in January 1979. They set up a puppet government with the Khmer Rouge losing control of the majority of the country. The Khmer Rouge continuing a guerilla war against the new government from remote outposts mostly in the western part of the country for 17 years. The Vietnamese withdrew in 1990. The Khmer Rouge collapsed in 1997-1998, with Pol Pot placed under arrest by his own forces. He died in April 1998, 23 years after launching his brief, nightmarish reign.

NIXON'S RE-ELECTION

The year 1972 did not bring a return to boom times, but for a while the economy improved enough to no longer be a major political handicap for Nixon. Nevertheless, Nixon approached his re-election campaign with dread. Chaos within the Democratic Party made Nixon's task easier. After the disastrous 1968 presidential nominating convention in Chicago, liberals (led by presidential contender and South Dakota Senator George McGovern) rewrote party rules to ensure that women, young people, African Americans and other traditionally disenfranchised constituencies would get fair representation in the 1972 convention to nominate the party's presidential ticket. These changes would prove to be a big advantage for McGovern in that year's Democratic nomination contest. The leading Democratic contender, the moderate environmentalist Senator Edmund Muskie of Maine (who had served as Hubert Humphrey's running mate in 1968), collapsed due to his poor performance in the New Hampshire primary. The highly conservative *Manchester (New Hampshire) Union Leader* newspaper printed two harsh articles that accused Muskie of using an anti-French-American slur, "Canuck," on one occasion. The Nixon re-election campaign faked the evidence for that charge, an explosive accusation in a state with a large French-American community. The newspaper also smeared Muskie's wife Jane as an alcoholic. Just before the New Hampshire primary, Muskie held a press conference in front of the *Union-Leader* offices and then appeared to break down in tears. (Muskie later said that the moisture on his cheek was melting snow.) New Hampshire voters questioned whether Muskie was tough enough to be president. Muskie won the primary, beating McGovern by 46 to 37 percent of the vote, but he was expected to do much better in a state next to his native Maine. The press interpreted Muskie's numerical win as a strategic loss. Later, when Muskie finished a disappointing fourth in Florida, the man many believed to be the strongest Democratic candidate against Nixon in November, dropped out of the race.

The false stories about Muskie's wife constituted part of what Nixon's re-election campaign called "dirty tricks." The Committee to Re-elect the President (or, as it was called, "CREEP") spied on other candidates and stole confidential campaign files. These tactics would culminate in the wiretapping of the Democratic National Headquarters at the Watergate Hotel in Washington, D.C., causing the scandal that would come to be known simply as "Watergate."

The result of the Democratic primary campaign pleased Nixon operatives as the candidate the Republicans regarded the weakest potential rival, McGovern, won the nomination. Seen as sincere and idealistic, McGovern certainly was the favorite of those new Democratic voters between the ages of 18 and 21 who were drawn to his strong opposition to the Vietnam War. Unfortunately for the Democrats, the McGovern campaign fell apart almost as soon as it was clear that McGovern would be the nominee. Sensing that McGovern's presidential quest was doomed, the best-known and most popular Democrats, such as Massachusetts Senator Edward Kennedy, Humphrey, and Muskie turned down McGovern when he asked them to serve as his running mate. McGovern eventually went through 24 names of possible running mates before finally selecting the little-known freshman Senator Thomas Eagleton of Missouri.

Almost immediately, McGovern's nomination was overshadowed by the news that, unknown to McGovern, Eagleton had received repeated electroshock therapy as a treatment for chronic depression. It turned out later that Eagleton had been the source of an anonymous quote reported by conservative columnist Robert Novak that the Democratic nominee was "for amnesty [for Vietnam draft dodgers], abortion, and legalization of pot."

The Nixon campaign picked up on this phrase, and McGovern was labeled the candidate of "acid [LSD], amnesty, and abortion." Eagleton would be replaced on the Democratic ticket by Kennedy in-law Sargent Shriver, the first director of the Peace Corps. After this incident, voters doubted McGovern's competence. McGovern probably made his already hapless campaign hopeless when he made a speech in October promising the immediate withdrawal of U.S. forces from Vietnam without even setting as a pre-condition the return of hundreds of American prisoners of war from the North. Then, before Election Day, Secretary of State Henry Kissinger hinted at an end to the war, announcing "We have now heard from both Vietnams and it is obvious that a war that has been raging for ten years is drawing to a conclusion . . . We believe that peace is at hand."

Election Day 1972 resulted in one of the biggest landslides in American history, with Nixon winning 61 percent of the vote and losing only Massachusetts and the District of Columbia in the Electoral College. Nixon even won 35 percent of Democratic voters. Young people did not turn out in the numbers expected and were not as solidly Democratic as many had predicted. In spite of Nixon's overwhelming success, the president had no coattails. Republicans lost a pair of seats in the Senate, giving the Democrats a 57-43 majority, and picked up only 12 new seats in the House of Representatives, where the Democrats still claimed a commanding 243-192 edge.

A CANCER CLOSE TO THE PRESIDENCY:
The Watergate Scandal

The cluster of scandals that became known by the shorthand phrase **Watergate** started well before the morning of

June 17, 1972, when Washington, D.C., police arrested five men employed by Nixon's Committee to Re-Elect the President after they broke into the Democratic National Committee headquarters located in the Watergate Hotel (just one mile from the White House). By the time of the break-in, Nixon had already violated the law by authorizing illegal wiretaps to determine who had leaked the information on American bombing in Cambodia and Laos and had formed the "Plumbers Unit," initially to plug such internal leaks. Soon enough, however, the Plumbers became involved in the operation at the Watergate Hotel to repair bugging devices planted there during an earlier break-in.

Nixon wanted the Plumbers to reveal what he thought was a criminal relationship between Democratic National Chair Lawrence O'Brien and the reclusive billionaire Howard Hughes, who also had contributed money to Nixon. Police nabbed the five Watergate burglars, including former CIA agent Bernard Barker and James W. McCord (a security coordinator for the Republican National Committee and CREEP). The Plumbers wore business suits, carried the bugging equipment, and held $2,300 in cash in a series of $100 bills with sequential serial numbers.

White House Press Secretary Ron Zeigler dismissed the incident as a "third rate" burglary. Bob Woodward and fellow *Washington Post* reporter Carl Bernstein, however, turned Watergate into a full-time beat. The pair of investigative journalists, receiving tips from a source they identified only as "Deep Throat" (who three decades later was revealed to be Mark Felt, the deputy director of the FBI) demonstrated that the Nixon campaign had created an illegal $350,000 election "slush fund" in which money from donors was "laundered" through Mexican bank accounts to conceal the source of the money. The money was then used to pay for dirty tricks. Though Woodward and Bernstein proved a connection between the break-in and the president's re-election campaign, Watergate had no effect on the 1972 election.

The scandal grabbed the public's attention in January 1973 when a Washington jury convicted the Watergate burglars, Howard Hunt and G. Gordon Liddy, of conspiracy and burglary charges. Threatened with a long prison term, McCord began to provide the court details about the Plumbers and other illegal White House operations. The Senate empaneled a Select Committee on Presidential Campaign Activities chaired by the colorful, story-telling, longtime segregationist North Carolina Senator Sam Ervin. The Watergate suspects began to talk to investigators. White House Counsel John Dean warned Nixon on March 21, 1973, "We have a cancer within, close to the presidency, that's growing. It's growing daily.

It's compounding. It grows geometrically now, because it compounds itself."

Speaking with the president, Dean laid out the financial demands in return for silence from the Watergate burglars. "Hunt is now demanding another $72,000 for his own personal expenses: $50,000 to pay his attorney's fees . . . wanted it by the close of business yesterday," Dean said. The White House lawyer hoped to alert Nixon to the dangers of the White House submitting to blackmail. Instead, Nixon asked, 'How much money do you need?" Hoping to scare the president off from committing bribery, Dean said, "I would say that these people are going to cost a million dollars over the next two years." Nixon did not blanch. "We could get that . . . If you need the money, you could get the money. I know where it could be gotten."

The president eventually authorized his legal advisor to raise $75,000 in "hush money" to ensure Hunt would remain silent about criminal acts and White House involvement. Unknown to Dean and others, Nixon had been secretly audiotaping his Oval Office conversations. Convinced that he was making history, Nixon had requested systematic taping of his conversations so he could retrieve every word he uttered in the Oval Office. The secret taping indeed preserved his place in history but not in the way Nixon imagined. The recordings had just caught the president ordering an aide to bribe witnesses in a criminal case.

Federal Judge John Sirica pressured McCord to cooperate with investigators, and McCord accused Dean and others of ordering a cover-up to conceal the White House connection to Watergate. Dean, in turn, implicated more White House officials including top Nixon lieutenants Haldeman and Ehrlichman. Sadly for the country, the drama dragged on for more than another year. Hoping he could convince the public that he wanted to get to the bottom of the matter, Nixon appointed Archibald Cox as special prosecutor to investigate the Watergate matter. That summer, Ervin's committee held televised hearings. Commercial networks broadcast five hours of the hearings each day. About 85 percent of the American public told pollsters that they watched some part of the hearings. A turning point came in July 1973 when former White House staffer Alexander Butterfield revealed the existence of the White House tapes.

An unrelated scandal involving Vice President Spiro Agnew further tarred the administration. Agnew had been the administration's conservative lightning rod, making fiery speeches attacking the supposedly liberal media, war protestors, and black radicals. But now he faced charges that while Baltimore County executive and governor of Maryland he had accepted $147,500 in bribes, sometimes delivered to the governor's mansion in brown paper bags, from businesses seeking state contracts. He continued to accept the bribes when he assumed the vice presidency. He had also failed to report the illegal income on his tax forms. Shortly after pledging in a speech that he would not "resign if indicted," Agnew stepped down on October 10, 1973, after pleading no contest to one count of tax evasion.

For the first time ever, the Twenty-Fifth Amendment to the United States Constitution, ratified in 1967 and adopted in the wake of President Kennedy's assassination, required a president to appoint and the Senate and House to confirm a replacement vice president. (Previously, if a vice president vacated the office through death, succession to the presidency or some other reason, the office remained open until the next presidential election.) Nixon sought a non-controversial replacement and selected House Minority Leader Gerald Ford of Grand Rapids, Michigan, to serve as the next vice president. Bland but pleasant and not heavily ideological, Ford struck many as a feasible president, and he was approved by the Senate 92-3 and the House by a 387-35 margin.

"The Saturday Night Massacre"

The Senate and Special Prosecutor Cox demanded that the White House turn over the tapes, but Nixon refused, citing "executive privilege," the legal argument that presidents need candid advice from their advisors in order for the Executive Branch to function and that the Constitution's "Separation of Powers" doctrine allows presidents to keep certain conversations from public scrutiny. Angered by Cox's persistence regarding the tapes, Nixon on the evening of October 20, 1973, ordered his Attorney General Elliot Richardson to fire the special prosecutor. Richardson resigned rather than comply. William D. Ruckelshaus stood next in line in the Justice Department, and Nixon fired him minutes later when he also refused to follow orders. Finally, the Solicitor General, Robert Bork (later unsuccessfully nominated by Ronald Reagan to the United States Supreme Court) carried out Nixon's command. The incident became known as the "Saturday Night Massacre" and deepened the growing public perception that Nixon had something to hide.

On November 1, Nixon was forced to name a new special prosecutor, Leon Jaworski, who continued to press the White House to release the tapes. On March 1, 1974, a federal grand jury returned indictments against seven former top White House officials, including one-time Attorney General Mitchell, Haldeman, Ehrlichman, and special counsel (and later Christian evangelist) Charles Colson, on charges of conspiracy to obstruct justice. The grand jury named Nixon as an "unindicted co-

Members of the White House staff watch as Richard Nixon, who announced his resignation as president the night before, leaves the White House August 9, 1974, with his wife Pat and accompanied by his successor, Vice President Gerald Ford and his wife Betty.

conspirator." With increasing evidence gathering against Nixon, who was also charged with ordering IRS audits of political opponents, the House Judiciary Committee began impeachment hearings in March, the first such event since Andrew Johnson's impeachment proceedings just after the Civil War.

The Supreme Court ruled unanimously in 1974 in *United States v. Nixon* that the president must release 42 tapes of discussions Nixon held with his cabinet and aides. Included among the recordings was a June 23, 1972 conversation that revealed that, in contradiction to his public statements, Nixon knew that the Watergate burglars were tied to the re-election campaign and that former Attorney General Mitchell had helped plan the break-in. Stories circulated during Nixon's last week in office, from August 2-9, 1974, that the president was drinking to the point of intoxication. Son-in-law Edward Cox told frightened listeners that Nixon was "up walking the halls last night, talking to pictures of former presidents—giving speeches and talking to the pictures on the wall."

Between July 27 and 30, the Judiciary Committee approved three articles of impeachment—abuse of powers, obstruction of justice and defiance of House Judiciary Committee subpoenas. Nixon's voter approval rating had dropped to 24 percent. With Democrats controlling more than two-thirds of the votes in the chamber, it was clear that the House of Representatives would vote to impeach the president, leaving the matter in the hands of the Senate where a two-thirds vote was necessary for conviction. Nixon would be the first president to stand trial in the Senate in 106 years.

Complying with the Supreme Court, on August 5 Nixon released three tapes containing damaging conversations demonstrating his hands-on management of a criminal cover-up. The president's remaining support in the Senate vanished. Nixon announced his resignation—the first by an American president—during a televised speech the next night, August 8, from the Oval Office. Before retreating to his home in California the next day, he said goodbye to his cabinet as the live television cameras looked on. The August 9 farewell speech was classic Nixon, at different times eloquent, self-pitying and defiant. "Always remember," he told his staff, "others may hate you—but those who hate you don't win unless you hate them, and then you destroy yourself." It was advice Nixon never took to heart.

A FORD, NOT A LINCOLN

A generally quiet man who spoke in a slow monotone, **Gerald Ford** was born Leslie Lynch King in 1913, but renamed himself later in life in honor of his stepfather. An All-American football center at the University of Michigan, Ford received contract offers from two National Football League teams, the Detroit Lions and the Green Bay Packers but decided instead to attend Yale Law School. There, he worked as an assistant football and boxing coach and graduated in the top third of his class before seeing combat duty in the United States Navy during World War II. He won his first race for the United States House in 1948 and never carried less than 60 percent of the vote in his home district.

By 1950, he won a spot on the House Appropriations Committee. Ford voted against Lyndon Johnson's Medicare and public housing programs. Genial, well liked, and seen as honest, he nevertheless acquired a reputation among liberals as someone out of touch with the poor and as being sub-par intellectually. Lyndon Johnson famously put him down as someone who played "too much football without a helmet." Nevertheless, Johnson appointed him to serve on the Warren Commission that investigated President Kennedy's assassination, and Ford became a vigorous defender of its controversial conclusions. In 1965, he rose to the position of House Minority leader and from that point on his ambition was to become House Speaker,

which he described as the "greatest job in the world." By 1973 he gave up hope that Republicans would ever gain a majority in the House and decided that he would run for only one more term and return to Michigan. Then, Nixon selected him to be vice president.

Ford won easy confirmation as vice president from Congress in December 1973. When Nixon resigned and he was sworn in as president, he jokingly contrasted himself with a luxury car, saying he was, "a Ford, not a Lincoln." Exhausted by Vietnam and Watergate and the lies that surrounded both issues, Americans responded with relief when Nixon stepped down and Ford assumed the presidency. He asked the Marine Corps Band to not play "Hail to the Chief" at his swearing-in, saying that he would prefer the University of Michigan fight song. His words were also winningly humble. "My fellow Americans, our long national nightmare is over," he said. "Our Constitution works; our great Republic is a government of laws and not of men. Here, the people rule." With a few short words and simple gestures, Ford generated a lot of support. His first major act as president, however, would inspire cynicism and anger.

"A Full, Free, and Absolute Pardon"

Ford worried that the continuing controversy surrounding Nixon, and the prospect of a criminal trial for the former president, would consume the country and make governing a nation already buffeted by scandal, high inflation, and the continued conflict with the Soviet Union even more difficult. Ford's honeymoon with the press and the American public came to a crashing halt on September 8, 1974, on a Sunday morning when he announced on television that he had granted Nixon a "full, free, and absolute pardon" for "all offenses against the United States" Nixon "has committed or may have committed."

The reaction was immediately angry and harsh. Ford faced accusations that he had agreed to pardon Nixon in return for gaining the White House. In October, Ford appeared before a House Subcommittee on Criminal Justice to deny any corrupt deal had been made related to the Nixon pardon, but the damage was done. After the pardon, Ford's approval rating seldom climbed over 50 percent. His political problems deepened with the fall elections in 1974. The Democrats picked up 43 seats in the House where they would hold a better than 2-1 margin, 291-144, and picked up three more seats in the Senate, which they now commanded by a 61-39 edge. Democrats now served as governors in 36 states. It was the Republican Party's worst performance since the 1932 landslide when Franklin Roosevelt crushed Herbert

Hoover. Even Ford's old congressional district went to the Democrats.

An athletic man, Ford's image took another hit in June of 1975 when during a trip to Europe and following a mostly sleepless night, Ford slipped down the metal steps leading from Air Force One, falling to the tarmac. Photographs and film footage of the event filled newspapers and television coverage, and soon every Ford stumble caught media attention. By the time Ford fell while skiing in Vail, Colorado, the president's alleged clumsiness added to his reputation as an intellectual lightweight, became a running joke and a staple of a popular new TV variety series that debuted in the fall of 1975, *Saturday Night Live*.

The Reform Congress

The new heavily Democratic Congress believed it had won a mandate to reform government, and it focused on limiting what it saw as presidential powers run amuck. The Congress had already passed the War Powers Act while Nixon was still in office. More directly addressing the abuses of Watergate, the 93rd Congress passed the Federal Election Campaign Act of 1974 that, in an attempt to limit the influence of special interests, allowed for the first time public financing of presidential campaigns. The Congress also amended the Federal Election Campaign Act of 1971 that placed limits on the size of political contributions in federal elections, put in place stricter requirements on candidates to report the source of their campaign funds and the details of their expenditures, and created the Federal Election Commission (FEC), which was given the job of enforcing campaign finance laws.

These reforms suffered fatal flaws. Over the years, the FEC has been reluctant to enforce rules, and the limits on corporate, union and personal donations simply inspired the creation of so-called "third party" groups that operated under no limitations in fundraising and spending as long as they supported "positions"—for example, support of free trade—and not particular candidates. The Republican Party became particularly adept at creating so-called "PACs" or political action committees in the 1970s and 1980s, such as the National Conservative Political Action Committee (NCPAC) that raised record amounts of money from big business to support Ronald Reagan and other right-of-center candidates in presidential elections.

Even as they tried to prevent future corruptions of the political process, Democrats uncovered past misdeeds. Already accustomed, after the Johnson and Nixon administrations, to distrusting the government, the public received another round of shocks with the Church Committee Hearings in 1975. In late 1974, investigative reporter Seymour Hersh, the man who had revealed the My Lai Massacre, reported that the CIA had illegally spied on American citizens. This prompted the U.S. Senate in 1975 to empanel an 11-member committee chaired by Idaho Democrat Frank Church that would investigate past abuses by the CIA, the FBI, the National Security Agency and the Internal Revenue Service.

The committee exposed the existence of the FBI's COINTELPRO (Counter-Intelligence Program) in which undercover agents infiltrated protest groups such as the Black Panthers and attempted to disrupt them through spreading false rumors about leaders and encouraging members to violate the law so the agency could justify a crackdown. Investigators further discovered that in the 1950s, the CIA had experimented with the use of the hallucinogenic drug lysergic acid diethylamide (LSD), first developed in 1938 as a truth serum that could be used to get information from Soviet and other communist prisoners. The agency gave LSD to 1,000 soldiers without their knowledge in the 1950s. In one case, Dr. Frank Olson, a civilian employee of the U.S. Army, unknowingly drank a potion that contained LSD. Olson panicked when he started exhibiting what he thought were symptoms of paranoia and schizophrenia, and in 1953 fatally jumped from a ten-story window while awaiting treatment.

The panel released a two-foot-thick report, without the endorsement of Republican committee members, in May 1976. The hearings resulted in the creation of the Senate's permanent Select Committee on Intelligence, charged with monitoring the actions of intelligence agencies, and also added to the sense of many Americans that the government was out of control and often acted as an enemy rather than a protector of ordinary citizens.

The Ford Interlude

A foreign policy crisis gave Ford a brief bump in his popularity. On May 12, 1975, Khmer Rouge forces seized control of the American merchant ship, the *SS Mayaguez*. The Cambodian government held the 39-person crew hostage for 65 hours before Ford ordered a military rescue mission. The crew was safely removed, but at the cost of 41 American military deaths. Ford's approval ratings shot up 11 percent after the costly rescue, but this political gain quickly faded.

Fatal to Ford's long-term prospects was a sinking economy. By 1974, American automakers were losing sales because of the availability of cheaper Japanese cars that recorded better gas mileage. The auto industry laid off about half its workforce that year, and the unemployed found few replacement jobs to match their experience

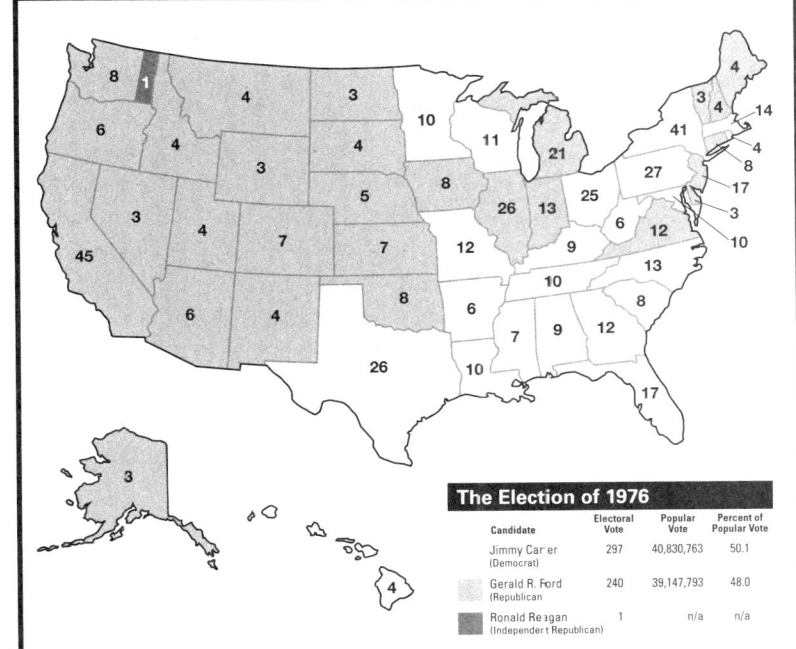

Map 29.3 The Election of 1976

The Election of 1976			
Candidate	Electoral Vote	Popular Vote	Percent of Popular Vote
Jimmy Carter (Democrat)	297	40,830,763	50.1
Gerald R. Ford (Republican)	240	39,147,793	48.0
Ronald Reagan (Independent Republican)	1	n/a	n/a

and skills. America's industrial dominance in the world was crumbling. Factories with a high-paid union work force in so-called "Rust Belt" states in the Northeast and Midwest shut down so owners could take advantage of the low wages in the so-called "Sun Belt"—the stretch of states from Georgia to California—where so-called "right-to-work" laws and police harassment had kept union membership at a minimum.

A low point in the Ford years came in 1974 when inflation cracked double digits, hitting a painful 12.2 percent, the highest level that Americans had experienced since 1946. Americans who had rarely experienced significant price increases in the 1950s and 1960s underwent sticker shock. "Things went up not just a few cents, or gradually," one Seattle woman complained, "but whole dollars and seemingly all at once."

As under Nixon, inflation combined with high unemployment to further stagger Americans. Unemployment soared from 5.3 percent when Ford first took office in August 1974 to 8.3 percent a year later. Industrial workers with or without high school diplomas suffered more in an economy in which American manufacturing increasingly became a thing of the past. Ford tried to curb inflation by encouraging Americans to voluntarily cut back on consumption. In imitation of the "Blue Eagle" National Recovery Administration logo during the New Deal, the administration released "WIN!" ("Whip Inflation Now!") buttons. His formerly warm relationship with the Congress grew bitter as he set a modern mark for presidents in exercising the veto to stop Democratic job bills and other economic stimulus programs he saw

as too expensive and inflationary. Ford vetoed 66 bills during his two-and-a-half years as president, the fourth highest per-year average in American history. Congress was able to override only 18 of the vetoes, meaning that the government was often in gridlock during the economic crisis.

THE 1976 ELECTION

Thunder from the Right

The president had never won an election in an area larger than a congressional district, and the economy and his media image seemed to be working against him. The right wing of the Republican Party, which temporarily retreated after the debacle of the Barry Goldwater campaign in 1964, had been slowly and surely taking over the GOP in the Nixon years, and the movement's leader, Ronald Reagan, smelled blood. In spite of Ford's clear record of fiscal conservatism, Reagan objected to the president's continuation of détente towards the Soviet Union. Following the expiration of his term as California governor in 1975, he confidently launched a full-time rebel campaign against his party's incumbent president.

Many did not take the former Hollywood actor, who had once co-starred with a chimpanzee in the movie *Bedtime for Bonzo*, seriously. The economy began to improve as 1976 approached, and Ford sought to enhance his prospects with conservatives by convincing his liberal vice president, Nelson Rockefeller, to step down as running mate. However, Ford underestimated the ideological commitment of the Republican right. After losing in early primaries like New Hampshire, Reagan scored an upset in North Carolina and began attacking Ford as part of the liberal establishment, weak on defense, and an appeaser towards the Soviet Union who let the United States slip to a "second-rate power." Reagan also accused Ford of failing to rein in the excesses of the liberal welfare state and made numerous, repeated false claims on the campaign trail. A favorite, racially-charged tall tale of his concerned a "welfare queen" who supposedly used 80 false identities, had a dozen Social Security cards and allegedly cashed in on veteran's benefits from four husbands.

Reagan went on to win primaries in Texas, Alabama, Georgia, and Indiana before Ford regained his stride. Ford did not seal his win until the Republican National Convention in Kansas City, and he eked by 1,187 delegates to 1,070. The primary campaign had been brutal and expensive, and the president started deep in the hole.

The Democratic Challenge

"Washington" was a dirty word by the time of the 1976 presidential election. The Democratic nominee, **James Earl "Jimmy" Carter**, started a tradition whereby White House hopefuls ran not on their diplomatic or executive experience but on their status as "outsiders" and their zeal to clean out the corruption and dysfunctions of the capital city. Born on October 1, 1924 in Plains, Georgia, a small community of only 500 people, Carter was the son of a successful businessman who operated a peanut warehouse and owned considerable real estate. Carter entered the United States Naval Academy where he excelled, finishing 16th out of a class of 822 midshipmen. He graduated in 1951 and spent seven years in the Navy, serving on the *Seawolf*, the prototype of the Navy's nuclear-powered submarine. After his father's death, Carter spent years rebuilding the family's peanut business.

Carter proved to be a good businessman and the peanut warehouse flourished, but politics fascinated him. He served two terms in the Georgia state senate from 1963-1967 and established a reputation as a moderate who emphasized the need to help the poor. He attacked the corrupt relationship between the state's politicians and special interests. Jimmy Carter became famous for his toothy smile and for his commitment to human rights, but when competing, he occasionally could be hardnosed. He won the Georgia gubernatorial race in 1970. He appealed directly to segregationists, attacking mandatory school busing to achieve racial balance, and making a campaign stop at an all-white private academy. Carter served as Georgia governor from 1971-1975.

In spite of his toying with racists, Carter behaved differently as governor. Carter famously ordered a portrait of the late civil rights leader Martin Luther King, Jr., to be displayed in the Georgia statehouse and said that segregation had no future in Georgia politics. During his one term as governor, the number of African Americans holding state jobs grew from 4,850 to 6,684. In addition, he modernized Georgia's services for the mentally ill and passed some of the state's most progressive laws on the environment.

Carter campaigned for the 1976 nomination promising to bring "a government as good as its people." Carter worked hard to appeal to women and African-American voters, and conducted a door-to-door campaign in early caucus and primary states like Iowa and New Hampshire. The African-American vote was key for Carter. He won 90 percent of the African-American vote in North Carolina. Black voters would be a significant part of Carter's coalition in November. Carter had the Democratic nomination locked up before the summer.

"No Soviet Domination of Eastern Europe"

During the Republican National Convention, Ford dramatically challenged Carter to a series of debates. None had been held since the famous Kennedy-Nixon debates in 1960. Carter agreed, and the two nominees debated three times, with a fourth faceoff held by Carter's running mate, Senator Walter Mondale of Minnesota, and Ford's vice presidential nominee Senator Robert Dole of Kansas. As the debates approached, Ford had pulled even with or passed Carter in some public opinion polls.

In the second debate, Ford made a mistake that may have cost him the election. The Ford administration had recently signed the Helsinki Accords, a 1975 agreement in which the United States, Canada, the Soviet Union and 32 other nations committed to recognize European boundaries established just after World War II, to cooperate in scientific research and economic development, and to respect human rights such as free speech and freedom of religion. Not a formal treaty, the agreement was nonbinding on the signatory nations, but many conservatives in the United States saw this accord as surrendering Eastern Europe to permanent Soviet occupation. During the second debate, on October 6, 1976, a reporter asked Ford what the United States had gained in return for "an agreement that the Russians have dominance in Eastern Europe?" Ford said, "There is no Soviet domination of Eastern Europe, and there never will be under a Ford administration . . ."

Ford had recently visited Eastern Europe and had been impressed by what he saw as the determination of

**President Jimmy Carter and Rosalynn Carter at the
Inaugural Ball. January 20, 1977 Photo credit: Jimmy Carter Library**

Poles, Czechs, and others living under the military control of the Soviet Union to achieve political independence. It was the will of the people there to not live under Russian control that Ford referred to, not the present-day control the Soviets exercised in the region. Nevertheless, the remarks reinforced the perception that Ford was not very smart or competent. Ford's remarks also angered voters of Eastern European descent who longed for their homelands to overthrow Soviet occupation.

Ford's performance in the debates stalled the major comeback the Republican ticket had made. In spite of their mistakes, however, Ford almost pulled off an upset. Carter won only 50.1 percent of the popular vote to Ford's 48 percent and the Electoral College was also close, with Carter carrying 297 votes to Ford's 240. Carter owed his victory to African Americans (he carried 5/6ths of the black vote). Blue-collar voters had turned on McGovern, but Carter carried 60 percent of this important Democratic constituency. Carter also won 54 percent of the white southern vote, the highest percentage for a Democrat since 1948. (McGovern had won just 27 percent of white Southerners.)

THE CARTER PRESIDENCY

Crippled with a weakened economy, high energy costs, and the unexpected rise of a militant anti-American regime in Iran, Carter faced immense challenges to his leadership throughout his term. He was philosophically at odds with many members of his own party. "He didn't fit neatly into the existing wings of the party," said Carter's chief domestic policy advisor, Stuart Eizenstat. "He was neither a typical southern conservative nor a Kennedy liberal." This odd position between the wings of the party often left him with few allies, a situation made worse with his personality.

Meanwhile, the economy was particularly vulnerable due to America's continuing dependence on expensive foreign oil. Carter directed his Secretary of Energy, Ford's former Defense Secretary James Schlesinger, to draft a comprehensive energy plan that aimed at reducing American dependence on Middle Eastern petroleum, expanded natural gas production, increased use of alternative energy sources such as nuclear energy and coal, and encouraged conservation. Carter and Schlesinger had not consulted Congress when the administration revealed its complicated 100-point plan, which raised the ire of both environmentalists (because of its support for increased coal and nuclear energy use) and the oil industry (because of its advocacy of federal gasoline taxes as a means of reducing consumption). Congress rejected the plan, and the United States again would suffer serious energy shortages in 1979 after a revolution in Iran.

The near meltdown of a nuclear reactor at Three Mile Island near Harrisburg, Pennsylvania, on March 28, 1979, also thwarted Carter's push for increased use of nuclear energy. A failure of a pump and valve caused

Menachem Begin, Jimmy Carter, and Anwar Sadat during one of the Camp David Summit meetings.
September 7, 1978 Photo credit: Jimmy Carter Library

one of the reactors to overheat, and clouds of radiation appeared in the skies. The area around Harrisburg was evacuated. Just before the accident, American audiences had seen the movie *The China Syndrome* in which a nuclear power plant experienced a similar malfunction. (The title refers to the theory that a nuclear meltdown in America would cause a chain reaction that would blow a radioactive hole in the Earth's crust from the United States to China.) The movie, the incident at Three Mile Island, and another incident July 16, 1979, when a dam burst near Church Rock, New Mexico, flooded uranium mines and filled the Rio Puerco River Valley with ninety million gallons of radioactive waste water, proved politically fatal to advocates of nuclear energy like Carter.

Like Nixon and Ford, Carter faced unusually high inflation yet had to combat unemployment at the same time. Inflation climbed from 5.2 percent when Carter first took office to 7 percent in 1978. Because of escalating energy costs, certain commodities rose in price more sharply. In 1978, for instance, meat prices shot up a stunning 18 percent. Economists have called the period "the Great Inflation." Carter focused on balancing the budget. At the same time, he persuaded the Congress to increase spending on Social Security, Medicare, and Medicaid. His policies were a muddle, and many of the weaknesses in the American economy were beyond his ability to control.

In spite of the rising price of gasoline, American auto manufacturers in Detroit continued to build big gas guzzlers, driving consumers to buy imports. The American steel industry also began to collapse. Many steel plants, such as in Youngstown, Ohio, had not updated technology in decades while by the 1970s European and Japanese industry had completely recovered from World War II and were using cutting-edge machinery. Because of technological improvements, Japanese steel cost 15 to 20 percent less than American steel, allowing them to sell under the price set by American producers. Tens of thousands of jobs in the American steel industry would disappear during the 1970s.

The Panama Canal Treaties

Seeking a more moral foreign policy and improved relations with Latin America, President Carter supported efforts to hand over control of the Panama Canal to the government of Panama by the year 2000. The negotiations were a continuation of talks dating back to when Panamanians had staged anti-American protests outside the 10-mile-wide Canal Zone in 1964. Panamanians and others in Latin America saw the canal as a symbol of American bullying and imperialism. Carter and Panamanian President Omar Torrijos signed two treaties in 1978, one guaranteeing the neutrality of the Canal Zone (meaning that use of the canal could not be blocked to international vessels for political reasons) and another that provided for joint U.S.-Panamanian control of the canal until December 31, 1999, when full control would pass to the government of Panama. The treaty outraged many conservative leaders. Already running for president, former California Governor Ronald Reagan belittled Torrijos as a "tin-horn" dictator and proclaimed to cheering audiences, "We built it! We paid for it! It's ours and we're going to keep it!" The U.S. Senate ratified the treaties in March and April of 1978. Though the agreement greatly improved the United States' relationship to Latin America, Reagan cited the treaty as a sign of American retreat and weakness under Carter, and the issue would help fire up the conservative base in the two years leading up to the 1980 presidential elections.

The Israeli-Egyptian Peace Agreement

Carter earned broader plaudits for his role in securing what came to be known as the "**Camp David Accords**." Egypt had borne the brunt of Arab-Israeli wars in 1948, 1956, 1967, the unofficial so-called "War of Attrition" from 1967-1970, and in 1973, suffering greater casualties (more than 15,000) than any other Arab state. Military expenses put a strain on the weak Egyptian economy and that of their more prosperous enemies next door, the Israelis. Egyptian President Anwar Sadat believed that the greatly improved performance of his military in the 1973 Yom Kippur War (as opposed to the humiliation of the Six-Day War in 1967) gave him enough prestige and credibility to resolve the Arab-Israeli conflict. In a November 9, 1977 speech to the Egyptian Parliament, he declared he would do anything to achieve peace. "I am ready to go to the Israeli parliament itself and discuss it with them," Sadat proclaimed.

Five days later, Walter Cronkite interviewed Sadat on his primetime CBS News broadcast and the Egyptian president repeated his offer, saying that he could make the trip to Jerusalem within days. "I'm just waiting for the proper invitation," Sadat said. Cronkite then interviewed Menachem Begin, Israel's newly elected prime minister and head of the right-wing Likud Party, who extended the invitation. On November 20, Sadat became the first Arab leader to visit Israel and, as promised, he made a speech to the Knesset, the Israeli Parliament, and spoke with other Israeli leaders.

Carter invited Begin and Sadat to Camp David, a presidential retreat in Maryland built during the Eisenhower administration, for peace negotiations. Under pressure at home, Sadat pressured Begin for some concessions to the Palestinians who had been forced from their homes during the Israeli War of Independence in 1948 and were living in squalid refugee camps in the Israeli-occupied West Bank of the Jordan River, and in Arab nations like Jordan and Lebanon. Unable to resolve the conflict over the Israeli-occupied West Bank, the Golan Heights (in Syria) and the Gaza Strip (adjoining the Sinai Peninsula), the Camp David agreement became simply an accord between Egypt and Israel that Carter would declare a "framework of peace" in the entire Middle East.

The Israelis agreed to return the Sinai Peninsula to Egypt, and in return Egypt would diplomatically recognize Israel. Begin and Sadat said they would continue negotiating the Palestinian issue. The two Middle Eastern leaders signed a formal peace treaty in 1979. The state of war that had existed between Egypt and Israel officially ended after 30 years. Carter played a major role in achieving this breakthrough, but it would be Begin and Sadat who would be awarded the Nobel Peace Prize.

The agreement made Sadat a marked man in the Arab world. The Palestinians felt abandoned by the largest Arab nation. Several Arab countries withdrew their diplomats in Cairo and hit the poverty-stricken nation of Egypt with economic sanctions. To make up for these losses, Egypt and Israel became the two largest recipients of American foreign aid. Enraged Egyptians assassinated Sadat while he viewed a parade honoring troops on the anniversary of the Yom Kippur War in October 1981. In spite of the promise for peace Camp David represented, the final status of the Golan Heights, the West Bank and the Gaza Strip remained unresolved as of 2019, and most Palestinians live in poverty with few opportunities.

The Iranian Revolution

The United States had been deeply involved in Iranian politics since 1953 when the CIA, at the direction of the Eisenhower Administration and at the urging of the British government, overthrew the democratically elected government of Prime Minister Mohammad Mossadegh. The Iranian leader had angered the West when he seized control of the Anglo-Iranian Oil Company. Mossadegh wanted Iranians to profit from their own oil and for the money to be invested in Iranian schools, colleges, agricultural projects and hospitals. He also wanted to limit the power of the Shah, the nation's strongly pro-Western emperor Mohammed Reza Pahlavi.

Pahlavi had ascended the so-called "peacock throne" in Iran in 1941 and achieved absolute power in 1953, when the CIA engineered a coup against Mossadegh. He crushed dissent and spent huge amounts of money on weaponry—$10 billion in the United States alone—between 1972 and 1976. His secret police force, SAVAK, tortured and killed dissidents or had them deported.

There was no more ferocious critic of the Shah, of his closeness to the United States, and his support for the state of Israel than Iran's extremely conservative religious leader, the Ayatollah Ruhollah Khomeini. The Shah ordered Khomeini arrested, and he was expelled from the country. By 1978, the dissident had settled in Paris. Opposition to the Shah came not just from mullahs—individuals trained in Muslim religious law—but also from secular intellectuals who wanted a more democratic government. In spite of American support, the Shah's regime began to unravel in the late 1970s when an economic slowdown produced rising unemployment and inflation, which reached a catastrophic 50 percent. Starting in January 1978, riots broke out with protestors in the large cities, like the capital Tehran, numbering in the millions. The Shah ordered a crackdown, and police killed some 8,000 demonstrators, including 700 at one protest in Jaleh Square in Tehran. The Shah then imposed martial law, and Khomeini responded by calling a general strike. When soldiers refused to follow orders to shoot at protestors, the Shah realized his life and his family's lives were in danger, and he fled into exile.

The Ayatollah arrived at the airport in Tehran on February 1, 1979, as a returning hero. Khomeini soon ruled by religious decree, making his interpretation of Islam the law of the land. Music was banished, women were forced to wear traditional head coverings, supporters of the Shah were executed, and religious minorities like Zoroastrians and Christians were persecuted.

Carter's "Malaise Speech"

The chaos surrounding the Iranian Revolution caused a drop in the world's supply of oil by 2 million to 2.5 million barrels of oil a day between November 1978 and June 1979, causing crude prices to more than double from $14 to $35 a barrel. Gasoline prices at the pump climbed to an unprecedented 90 cents a gallon (about $3.12 in 2018 dollars), and drivers sometimes spent hours in line at the gas stations during the Energy Crisis of 1979. Violence broke out. In Los Angeles, one person attacked a pregnant woman accused of cutting in line. Some carried guns when they went to fill up.

By January of 1980, inflation roared at a devastating 18.2 percent, the highest in six years. The prime interest rate stood at 18.5 percent in April of that year, causing home sales to drop by 6 percent and higher unemployment in the construction trades. Unemployment reached 7.8 percent in 1979, and most economists expected it to go higher in 1980.

Religious in his orientation, Carter believed he detected a crisis in the American spirit. He shared his thoughts with the public in a televised broadcast June 15, 1979. It would be the most prophetic speech of his career. "All the legislation in the world can't fix what's wrong with America," he said. Americans, he said, had found themselves in a new age of limits. Carter urged Americans to think of future generations and conserve energy. He pledged to limit oil imports, and to increase funding for research into alternative energy sources such as solar power. He called on Americans to approach the energy crisis with the same spirit that suffused the *Apollo* mission that placed the first humans on the lunar surface just a decade earlier.

Initial reaction to the address, which began to be known as the "Malaise Speech" even though the president never specifically used that word in his remarks, was strongly positive. Unfortunately, Carter quickly squandered what he gained from the speech. Just two days later, he impulsively fired and asked for the resignation of five cabinet officers. It made Americans again think the administration was clueless, lurching from one action to another with no grand plan. The Carter years seemed like a parade of crises. The economy continued to be shaky and by that November events in Iran would overtake the White House.

After 444 days, the Iranian hostage crisis ended, but it destroyed Carter's chances for re-election.

America Held Hostage

Foreign affairs took an ugly turn on December 24, 1979, when the Soviet Union invaded Afghanistan to prop up a friendly communist regime, starting a decade-long war that would hasten the fall of the Soviet government. It would also mark the first appearance on the world stage of Osama bin Laden, who later became the mastermind of the September 11, 2001, terrorist attacks on New York City and Washington, D.C. He was an anti-Soviet fighter in the mountainous nation of Afghanistan. American-Soviet tensions rose sharply, and in retaliation for the invasion, Carter decided to cancel America's participation in the summer Olympics scheduled to take place in Moscow the next summer.

Clouds appeared elsewhere in the Middle East. Distracted by his Egyptian-Israeli diplomacy, Carter was slow to react to the Iranian Revolution. The new "Islamic Republic of Iran" demanded that the Shah be returned to government custody to stand trial for his human rights abuses and put pressure on other governments to not give him sanctuary. Students began holding angry demonstrations in Iranian cities, shouting, "Death to America!" and burning the American flag.

The Shah shuttled with his family from Egypt to Morocco to the Bahamas and then to Mexico. In Mexico, doctors diagnosed him as suffering from cancer. Carter allowed the Shah to enter the United States to receive medical treatment. In response, on November 4, 1979, more than 3,000 student radicals, at the behest of the Iranian government, took over the American embassy in Tehran and held those inside hostage. The Iranians also seized control of most of the embassy files.

Khomeini said there would be no release of the 66 hostages until the Shah was sent back to Iran to stand trial, thus beginning the 444-day **Iranian Hostage Crisis**. Two weeks after the initial embassy takeover, the Iranians did release five women and eight African-American men. Another hostage was let go in July 1980 when he began to suffer symptoms of multiple sclerosis. Carter for a long time retreated to the White House, eager to let Americans know that he was focused on winning the release of the hostages and had no time for ordinary politics. In fact, he created the impression of being besieged, an image reinforced by a TV news show on ABC that debuted in 1979, *America Held Hostage*. Hosted by Ted Koppel, the show focused on each day's developments concerning the hostage drama. Each episode was labeled by the number of days since the crisis began—for instance, "Day 100." As the number of days the hostages remained captive grew higher, already low approval ratings for Carter dropped even further.

The Iranian government demanded reparations for the nation's suffering during the Shah's rule and the handover of the Shah himself. The Shah left the United States on December 15, 1979, and stayed in Panama, where Omar Torrijos was repaying a debt to Carter for the canal treaties. With negotiations hopelessly deadlocked, patience running thin, and Carter aware of the political damage being done to him, the president authorized a military mission to rescue the hostages on April 24-25, 1980. Malfunctioning helicopters forced Carter to abort the mission. Eight Marines died in the rescue attempt and five suffered injuries, a failure that seemed to symbolize the powerlessness of the Carter administration and of America in the 1970s. The hostages remained captive even after the Shah died in Egypt on July 27, 1980.

The Moral Majority

Some Americans drew a religious message from America's troubles. Religious conservatives believed that the various recent social revolutions, such as feminism, gay rights, the experimentation with drug use and open sexuality, and the legalization of abortion had brought the wrath of God upon the nation. A majority of people who called themselves born-again Christians had voted for Carter in 1976, but they were disillusioned with him by 1979. Throughout the second half of the 1970s, the Reverend Jerry Falwell of Virginia held "I Love America!" rallies that featured the flag, gospel songs and political preaching. Falwell had opposed ministers getting involved in politics when Martin Luther King, Jr., and other ministers had led the African-American civil rights movement. But since then, Falwell had been angered by the Supreme Court's 1973 *Roe v. Wade* decision that legalized abortion in the first two trimesters. He also fiercely opposed the ongoing campaign for the Equal Rights Amendment (ERA) to the United States Constitution, which would have federally outlawed gender discrimination.

Falwell formed a group called the **Moral Majority**, dedicated to electing candidates who supported what Falwell and other Christian Right activists called "family values." The Moral Majority registered conservative Christian voters, bought ads attacking the positions taken by liberal candidates on issues like school prayer and abortion, and issued "report cards" for members of Congress and presidential candidates on "moral" issues, including their support for weapons systems like the B-1 bomber. It delivered votes almost exclusively for the Republican Party.

Ronald Reagan, opposed to abortion and gay rights and sharing the TV preacher's enthusiasm for a big defense budget, openly sought the support of Christian

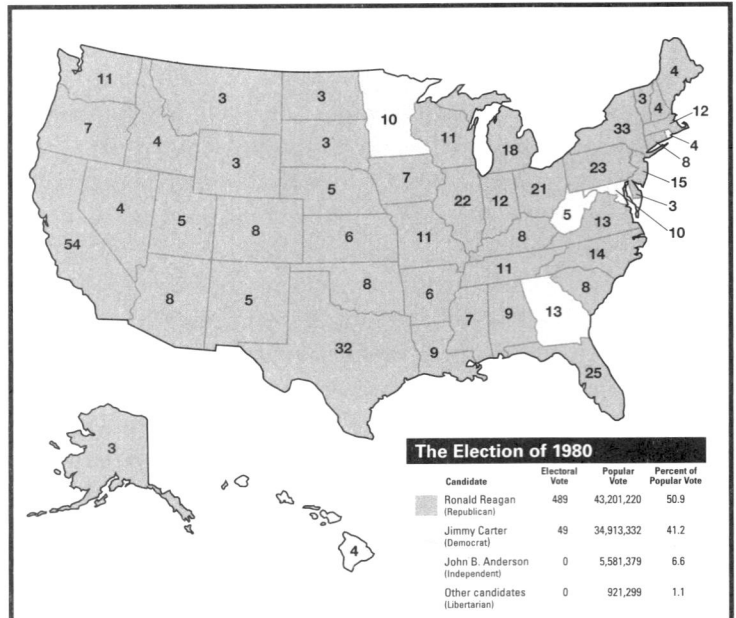

Map 29.4   The Election of 1980

The Election of 1980

Candidate	Electoral Vote	Popular Vote	Percent of Popular Vote
Ronald Reagan (Republican)	489	43,201,220	50.9
Jimmy Carter (Democrat)	49	34,913,332	41.2
John B. Anderson (Independent)	0	5,581,379	6.6
Other candidates (Libertarian)	0	921,299	1.1

conservatives after he won the Republican nomination in the summer of 1980. Reagan appeared at the Religious Roundtable National Affairs Briefing in Dallas, Texas, in August 1980, and at a press conference expressed doubt concerning the theory of evolution. In a speech to the large assembly, which included Falwell, television evangelist Pat Robertson, and anti-ERA activist Phyllis Schlafly, Reagan said, "I know you can't endorse me, but I endorse you."

The 1980 election would mark the marriage of the Religious Right with the Republican Party. It helped the Republican Party and candidates like Reagan that most of the Christian Right was not just culturally conservative but economically conservative as well. White voters had increasingly opposed welfare programs and, slammed by high oil prices and growing tabs at the grocery store, they also became increasingly impatient with high taxes. Anti-tax sentiment was a powerful force going into the 1980 elections. The Republican nominee, Reagan, was able to unite both fiscal and religious conservatives that year, and reshaped his party for decades to come. The GOP remained in favor of low taxes and against government regulations, but opposition to abortion, and gay rights, and support for legalizing directed school prayer and tax support for church schools increasingly became litmus tests for hopeful Republican candidates.

"There You Go Again":
The Election of Ronald Reagan

Inflation, high unemployment, and the Iranian hostage crisis turned out to be too much for Jimmy Carter to overcome as he ran for re-election in 1980. The Demo-

cratic president first had to battle a challenge from Massachusetts Senator Edward Kennedy that lasted until the party's national convention. Kennedy was unable to overcome the suspicions regarding the 1969 Chappaquiddick incident in which he left a party where he had been drinking and drove off a Massachusetts bridge near the Chappaquiddick ferry, killing his passenger, 28-year-old Mary Jo Kopechne. Kennedy left the scene before police arrived. Kennedy lost but left Carter badly damaged politically. During the August 11-14, 1980 Democratic National Convention at Madison Square Garden in New York City, Kennedy's rousing concession speech got more applause than Carter's acceptance speech. At the end of the convention, red, white and blue balloons failed to release at the right moment, an unfortunate omen for Carter's fall campaign.

Carter faced not just Reagan, but moderate Republican Congressman John Anderson of Illinois who dropped out of the GOP primaries when it was apparent he could not win the party's conservative base; Anderson instead ran as an independent. The Carter campaign ignored Anderson, and the race tightened as the Carter campaign called attention to the many fact errors Reagan made on the campaign trail, such as when he claimed that "80 percent" of pollution comes from "plants and trees." Once again, as happened in 1960 and 1976, a televised presidential debate played a decisive role. Carter and Reagan faced off in Cleveland on October 28, and Carter showed a command of facts, but many voters saw the president as grim and aggressive. Reagan, meanwhile, appeared warmer and showed a sense of humility and humor, asking viewers, "Are you better off than you were four years ago?" Whether or not it was his fault, it was impossible for Carter to deny that most Americans were worse off economically in 1980 than they had been in 1976.

Reagan won in a landslide, receiving 51 percent of the popular vote to Carter's 41 percent and Anderson's 7 percent. Carter won only the states of Georgia, Maryland, Minnesota, Rhode Island, and West Virginia and the District of Columbia as Reagan beat him in the Electoral College 489 to 49. Carter made his concession speech early in the night, which caused Democratic voters in the West to not show up at the ballot box, a mistake that helped lose the Democratic Party's control of the Senate. The election was held on Day 365 of the hostage crisis. After the election, Carter worked with determination to finally secure the release of the hostages, but even with the issues resolved, the Iranians waited until minutes after Reagan was sworn in on January 20, 1981, to free them after 444 days of captivity. It was salt in Carter's psychic wounds, and he would retreat into depression for months, until he re-emerged as a leader of numerous humanitarian causes.

YOUTH PROTEST
FROM THE MID-1960S TO 1980

Continued racism, sexism, homophobia, and failed American imperialism from the Kennedy administration to the end of the Carter years propelled myriad social justice movements that advocated everything from reform to revolution. The African-American civil rights movement influenced all other struggles for equality. Until the mid-1960s, the "Movement," as it was known, had been biracial. However, in 1966 some African-American civil rights leaders such as Stokely Carmichael who had coined the phrase "Black Power!" believed that white people within the movement held black people back. To black radicals, the white philanthropists who supported the NAACP and other groups were just trying to stave off a real revolution against a capitalist system that was inherently racist. The African-American freedom struggle took a more independent turn in the late 1960s and through the 1970s.

Black Nationalism

Inspired by Malcolm X, so-called Black Nationalists rejected what they saw as the hopelessly idealistic dream of a just, multi-cultural America. They concluded that African-American freedom would come when black people lived under black leaders, were served by black institutions, and supported black businesses. Some Black Nationalists went as far as the Nation of Islam, advocating the creation of a separate black homeland within the United States. Turning away from Martin Luther King Jr.'s non-violent approach to civil disobedience, many Black Nationalists embraced self-defense as a necessity in a violent white supremacist society.

In 1966, Bobby Seale and Huey Newton, two southern-born African-American students who had attended Merritt College in the Oakland area in Alameda County in Northern California, formed the **Black Panther Party** for Self Defense on October 15, 1966, to counter police abuse and killings of black youths in ghetto neighborhoods. Seale and Newton were moved to arm themselves after an April 1, 1967 incident in which a black child named Denzill Dowell was shot to death by police in the nearby town of Richmond. Police claimed Dowell who suffered from a painful hip injury had fled from arrest. Seale, Newton, and the other Panthers armed themselves and began to shadow police officers operating in their neighborhood, directly confronting them when they believed police overstepped their authority. The Panthers also provided books and free breakfast programs for children, programs that received a lot less attention from the media.

The Panthers, bearing firearms and exhorting their followers to "Off a Pig!" (kill a cop), provoked a white overreaction. Don Mulford, a conservative California Republican in the state assembly, introduced a gun control measure prohibiting citizens from carrying loaded weapons in public places. The Panthers arrived at the California state capitol on May 2, 1967, carrying loaded shotguns and rifles in protest before police forced them out of the building. The California legislature passed the law, and Governor Ronald Reagan, later hailed by conservatives as a defender of gun owner rights, signed the measure into law.

Law enforcement declared war on the Panthers. Chicago police in coordination with the FBI, on December 4, 1969, assaulted the home of Panther leader Fred Hampton. Officers fatally shot Hampton, 21, and his body guard Mark Clark, 22, multiple times even though both apparently were unarmed at the time of the raid. It was later revealed that an FBI spy within the Panthers had slipped Hampton a drink laced with sedatives that would make it harder for him to defend himself. The violence of the raid was so excessive that the Cook County district attorney, his assistant, and eight Chicago police were indicted by a federal grand jury, but all were gradually acquitted. Overall, 26 Black Panthers died violently, mostly at the hands of police, between April 1968 and December 1969.

LATINO ACTIVISM

The African American civil rights movement profoundly inspired Latinos after World War II. Latinos represented one of the fastest-growing populations in the United States after the war, with approximately 6 million people of Mexican descent living in the Southwestern United States from California to Texas. A large cluster of Cuban immigrants had settled in Florida, and the major urban centers in the Northeast now included a large number of residents of Puerto Rican descent. Many Mexicans had settled in the United States as a result of the *bracero*, or agricultural guest worker program, between Mexico and the United States from 1942 to 1964. After World War II, Latinos of all ethnicities became increasingly aware that their larger numbers could translate into greater political power.

Mexican Americans primarily voted for the Democratic Party. During the 1960s, *Viva Kennedy!* clubs formed all over the Southwest as the largely Catholic Mexican American population rallied behind their co-religionist. After Kennedy's election, older Latino civil rights organizations such as the League of United Latin American Citizens (LULAC) and *Viva Kennedy!* joined together, following a 1961 meeting in Victoria, Texas to form the Political Association of Spanish-Speaking Organizations (PASO), which would shake the political world with local elections in the small town of Crystal City, Texas.

The Crystal City Protests

Crystal City was an agricultural community in South Texas where Mexican Americans made up 80 percent of the population. Many lived in poverty and attended poorly funded schools. The city council was entirely Anglo in 1963. Juan Cornejo, a member of the local Teamsters Union at the Del Monte cannery in Crystal City (a politically powerful local business), and a PASO organizer, launched a successful campaign to get Mexican Americans to pay the poll tax and register to vote. As a result of the drive, Mexican Americans constituted almost 70 percent of voters.

Cornejo then helped boost the city council candidacies of five Mexican-American candidates, who came to be known as *los cinco*. The Mexican-American slate won the election and held all seats on the new Crystal City Council. The PASO faction lost control of the city government by 1965, but Anglos would never again hold a monopoly on power in Crystal City. Events taking place there politically energized Latinos across the United States.

César Chávez and the United Farm Workers

Among Latino leaders, **César Chávez** uniquely was able to build a large following among people on the left and the political center, eventually gaining support from the Anglo anti-war and the black civil rights movements. Chávez first achieved notice when Filipino workers in the Agricultural Workers Organizing Committee (AWOC) on September 8, 1965, organized a strike against grape growers in the Delano region of California's San Joaquin Valley. Earlier that year, the U.S. Labor Department had ordered that *braceros* working in the Coachella Valley receive pay of $1.40 an hour ($10.40 an hour in today's dollars.) The grape pickers were receiving 30 cents, or $2.15 an hour less in today's dollars. Filipino and Mexican workers walked off the job, demanding the same pay as the *braceros*.

Chávez became a champion of the grape pickers' cause. Born in Yuma, Arizona, in 1927, Chávez was the child of a union activist and a member of the United Farm Labor Union. He recalled being abused by teachers who punished students who spoke Spanish. One teacher made him wear a sign that said, "I am a clown. I speak Spanish." He was deeply influenced by Pope Leo XIII's 1891 papal encyclical *Rerum Novarum* in which the Catholic leader urged church members to support workers' rights and fight for social justice. In 1962, he moved to Delano to work as a union organizer, focusing on recruiting Mexican field hands. By 1964, the National Farm Workers Association (NFWA), the grape pickers' union, had a membership of 1,700.

To protest the low wages and long working hours grape pickers were subjected to, NFWA started a boycott that hurt growers, grocers, and wine manufacturers. The boycott eventually persuaded some of the biggest grape growers and wine manufacturers such as Gallo, Christian Brothers, and Paul Masson to sign multi-year contracts with higher pay for the grape pickers. The boycott spread to Canada and Europe, and by 1970, the strike in its fifth year, major growers in the San Joaquin and the Coachella Valley signed contracts with the NFWA.

Chicanismo

By the late 1960s, Black Nationalism became a model for younger Latinos who had tired of the more modest goals of assimilation and desegregation sought by groups like LULAC. Younger activists began to adopt the term **Chicano** to refer to their community. *Chicano* historically was a term of abuse aimed at poor Mexicans, but a younger generation wore the label with pride. Linking themselves to the poor, *Chicanos* rejected the materialism of their elders and declared their solidarity with African Americans, Cubans, the Viet Cong and others they saw as victims of *Gringo* (Anglo) imperialism and capitalism. *Chicanos* rejected the approach taken by older Mexican-American political groups like LULAC and the GI Forum.

This embrace of cultural difference, which came to be known as *Chicanismo*, found a following among young Houston, Texas Latinos in the mid-1960s. When the Anglo-run Houston school board attempted to dodge sending white children to desegregated schools by designating Mexican-American children as white and grouping them with African Americans, *Chicano* youths resisted. *Chicanos* launched a two-and-a-half-week strike involving 3,500 students who refused to attend Houston schools in August and September 1970. *Chicanos* set up *huelga* or strike schools, so Mexican-American children could continue their lessons and learn more about their culture and history. As a result of the strikes, more bilingual Mexican-American teachers were hired by the Houston district, the curriculum was rewritten so students would be exposed to positive portrayals of Mexican Americans and physical improvements were made at some minority-majority schools. The Houston school board, however, never recognized *Chicanos* or Mexican Americans as a separate racial category, and brown and black children continued to bear the burden of desegregation. Houston *Chicanos*, however, deeply influenced the future shape of Mexican-American politics across Texas and the country for the next four decades. Similar student walkouts occurred in the late 1960s and early 1970s in California, Colorado, New Mexico and in major cities across the country.

BACK TO WOUNDED KNEE:
The American Indian Movement

Beginning in the late 1960s, and continuing through the 1970s, Native Americans emerged from the political shadows and launched a "Red Power" movement to protest poverty, lack of jobs and poor health care on reservations, the disrespect shown Indian history and culture in American movies and television, and the lengthy list of treaties with Indian nations signed and broken by the federal government. In the early 1960s, as the historian James Wilson wrote, conditions in "most Indian communities were appalling . . . more than 90 percent of their housing was substandard; their infant mortality rate was more than twice the national average; their incidence of preventable diseases such as tuberculosis, meningitis, and dysentery exceeded the general population's by anything

up to a hundred times; their average age of death was 43 years [as opposed to almost 70 for the general population]; and, with unemployment running between 40 percent and 80 percent, their average family income was only around 20 percent of their Anglo-American neighbors."

The American Indian Movement (AIM), founded in 1968 by two members of the Chippewa Nation, George Mitchell and Dennis Banks, became perhaps the most influential and powerful "Red Power" group among Native Americans. Formed in Minnesota, AIM organized "patrols to protect Indians from police brutality" and used federal funds to "establish 'urban alternative' schools, where Native American children who had dropped out of the school system could develop greater cultural awareness and self-respect and learn how to survive in both the Indian and non-Indian worlds."

Native American groups in the late 1960s and early 1970s sought to speak not just for individual tribes but for all indigenous people victimized by white oppression. Such was the approach when a force that called itself "Indians of All Tribes" on November 20, 1969, gained control of Alcatraz Island, a closed federal prison in San Francisco Bay. The force included 300 Native Americans from 50 different Indian nations. The occupiers held Alcatraz for 19 months, demanding that the government turn the property back over to its proper Indian owners and calling for the construction of an Indian cultural center on the site that would include an Indian college, museum and ecology center. Federal marshals ousted the last 15 Native American protestors on June 11, 1971.

A dynamic new leader of AIM, Russell Means, continued to raise the visibility of the Indian cause by staging protests at two sites cherished by white America: Mount Rushmore, the sculpted tribute to four American presidents (George Washington, Thomas Jefferson, Abraham Lincoln and Teddy Roosevelt) created on a mountain on Indian land in South Dakota, and at the *Mayflower II*, the replica of the Pilgrim ship in the harbor at Plymouth, Massachusetts.

Indian pride fueled another protest action at Wounded Knee, South Dakota, scene of a late-nineteenth-century massacre of Native Americans by the U.S. Army. On February 27, 1973, about 200 Native Americans armed themselves and took over the Pine Ridge Indian Reservation in Wounded Knee to overthrow a corrupt Indian leader enjoying white support who tried to crush AIM. "The young kids tied eagle feathers to their braids, no longer unemployed kids, juvenile delinquents or winos," recalled one participant, Mary Crow Dog. More than 300 National Guardsmen and U.S. marshals surrounded Wounded Knee village. This siege lasted 71 days. Across America, Native American and *Chicano* protestors rallied in support of the Indians, and some were killed by police violence. Shootouts at Wounded Knee killed two Indians, with one federal marshal injured. In May, the Indians agreed to lay down their weapons.

THE ENVIRONMENT MOVEMENT

Silent Spring

A 55-year-old woman became the unlikely inspiration to an emerging, youth-oriented environmental movement. The year 1962 saw the publication of *Silent Spring* by **Rachel Carson**, a zoologist who charged that the chemical pesticides used in American agriculture killed birds and left their eggshells dangerously thin. The problem worsened markedly in 1942 when farmers started spraying fields with DDT, a chemical that killed insects on contact. The United States Department of Agriculture's 1957 fire ant eradication program, involving intense use of DDT, provoked Carson's scientific investigation of pesticides. "Chemicals are the sinister and little-recognized partners of radiation in changing the very nature of the world—the very nature of life," Carson said. Such chemicals as were used in pesticides, she said, exterminated whole species, disrupted delicate food chains and could eventually endanger all life.

In May 1963, President Kennedy's Scientific Advisory Committee issued a report on pesticides that vindicated Carson's warnings. Dr. Jerome B. Wiesner declared that the unregulated use of pesticides represented "potentially a much greater hazard" to survival of life on the planet than radioactive fallout from atomic weapons. Carson's efforts led to a nationwide ban on DDT and other chemical pesticides and helped inspire the environmental movement of the late 1960s. Scientific investigation after Carson's death from breast cancer in 1964 demonstrated that chemicals such as DDT found their way inside humans and caused soft-tissue cancers.

Earth Day and Ecological Consciousness

Awareness of the dangers of pollution increased throughout the 1960s. The public in large numbers celebrated the first "Earth Day" April 22, 1970. The initial push for Earth Day came from Democratic Senator Gaylord Nelson of Wisconsin who believed the health of the planet to be "the most critical issue facing mankind" and who, borrowing an idea from the anti-Vietnam War movement, encouraged a nationwide "teach-in" about the environment in which Americans would be educated about the harm of industrial pollutants, the devastation of wildlife, and related issues.

When April 22 arrived, about 10 million Americans, plus millions more across the globe, celebrated Earth Day by hiking, planting trees, and picking up litter. Earth Day became an annual event and promoted the growth of grassroots environmental activism. Sensing the popularity of the issue, President Richard Nixon signed into law the Clean Air Act of 1970, which for the first time established national air quality standards and set caps on harmful emissions by automobiles. Privately, Nixon had little interest in the environment. "I think interest in this will recede," he wrote in an internal memo.

Nixon badly underestimated the concern over pollution. One in four Americans named the environment as the most serious problem facing the nation. Responding to public pressure, Congress passed an outpouring of environmental laws in the early 1970s, including the statute that created the Environmental Protection Agency (EPA) in 1970. The Endangered Species Act in 1973 protected not only endangered animals but also the habitats they depended on that were threatened by economic development. The Safe Drinking Water Act of 1974 gave the EPA the power to set standards in terms of chemical content for water across the United States.

The movement remained mostly white and middle- and upper-class, but environmentalists learned much from the sit-ins and non-violent protest tactics of the African American Civil Rights Movement. Organizations like the Abalone Alliance in California used civil disobedience, using up to 2,000 activists to occupy and block entrances of work crews at the Diablo Canyon nuclear power plant located near a fault line by San Luis Obispo, California. The protestors, however, failed to stop the opening of the plant. Such defeats did not dim the idealism of committed environmentalists. According to the *New York Times*, the spontaneous "back-to-nature movement" had created 2,000 communes and 5,000 collective farms by the beginning of the 1970s.

Two incidents in the 1970s dramatized the need for environmental regulation. In Niagara Falls, New York, the Hooker Chemical & Plastics Corporation had poured 22 tons of toxic chemicals into a dry channel called Love Canal between 1947 and 1952 and concealed the dump with layers of clay soil. The local school district, short of cash and experiencing a local population boom requiring construction of new campuses, bought the land from Hooker for $1 and built an elementary school on top of the poisonous underground stew. Other schools were rapidly constructed nearby. As the community later grew to a population of 75,000, residents complained of bad smells in their basements and of chemicals leaking to the surface that sometimes caught fire. Heavy rains and melted snow following a blizzard exposed more of the waste. EPA investigators would later find higher-than-normal rates of miscarriages and birth defects, elevated levels of toxic chemicals in the milk of breast-feeding mothers and increased cancer rates in the neighborhood.

New York Department of Health Commissioner Robert Whalen proclaimed the Love Canal site a threat to human health in 1978. The New York state government purchased the entire neighborhood and evacuated around 800 families. In response to the crisis, Congress in 1980 passed the Comprehensive Environmental Response Compensation and Liability Act, better known as the "Superfund" law. The law set aside federal money to aid states in cleaning up toxic waste sites near residential areas. Love Canal became the first Superfund-designated site. The Love Canal area was not declared clean by the federal government until 2004. The publicity surrounding Love Canal and the near meltdown of the Three Mile Island nuclear power plant near Harrisburg, Pennsylvania, on March 28, 1979, deepened the public distrust of American corporations and increased awareness of the immense dangers posed by industrial capitalism to the natural world.

THE WOMEN'S RIGHTS MOVEMENT

"The Problem with No Name"

Women played a major role in the African-American freedom struggle and some applied the lessons they learned in that movement to battle sexism. What came to be known as "Second Wave Feminism" (the first wave was the suffrage campaign from 1848 to 1920) can trace its origins to the 1963 publication of the bestseller book *The Feminine Mystique*. Author **Betty Friedan** described the frustration and boredom felt by many educated suburban housewives as the "problem with no name." Friedan's book described a generation of feminists who battled employment and wage discrimination and challenged society's expectations of what women could accomplish physically, intellectually, and politically.

Conducting an extensive survey of middle class and affluent women similar to herself, Friedan blamed the "feminine mystique"—which glorified only women who played a traditionally subservient role to men—as the cause of an outbreak of depression, anxiety, emotional withdrawal, anger and infantilization of adult women and their daughters. The book found an understanding audience, and *The Feminine Mystique* became a bestseller with more than a million copies purchased.

"The Bunny Law"

The women's movement scored a major legislative triumph partly as a side effect of the African American civil rights movement. The Equal Pay Act and the anti-sex discrimination provisions of the 1964 Civil Rights Act had a dramatic impact on women's experiences in the workplace. The law empowered the newly created Equal Employment Opportunity Commission (EEOC) to enforce provisions against racial and sexual discrimination. At first EEOC administrators laughed at the concept of gender discrimination, an insensitivity reinforced by the male-dominated press that frequently scoffed at the idea of male and female equality. Editorialists railed that men and women were biologically suited for different kinds of work. Would feminists protest, they joked, if a man were refused a job as a Playboy bunny, a waitress dressed in what was basically a one-piece bathing suit adorned with a fluffy bunny tail and bunny ears who served drinks at the nightclubs owned by Hugh Hefner, the publisher of *Playboy*, a popular men's magazine? Newspapers caustically dubbed the anti-sexual-discrimination provisions of Title VII of the Civil Rights Act as the "bunny law."

Feminists did not find such condescending attitudes from men amusing. Women still faced substantial legal obstacles. State laws in the 1950s and 1960s did not take spousal abuse seriously. Several states placed barriers to women serving on juries. Connecticut prevented women from obtaining birth control. Through the early 1960s, it was typical for classified ads to specify, "Help Wanted: Male." In Texas, until 1967, a woman technically could not sign a contract to work without her husband's permission.

Women activists realized that they would have to form their own civil rights group to be heard. In 1966, feminists formed an organization named, at Betty Friedan's suggestion, the National Organization for Women (NOW). Overwhelmingly white, NOW at first catered primarily to older, more affluent, professionals—lawyers, government workers, and women working in the media. Like the NAACP, NOW primarily battled gender discrimination through lobbying Congress and state legislatures and litigation rather than through "direct action" protests.

The Failure of the Equal Rights Amendment

The continued barriers to women in the workplace sparked a movement to add an **Equal Rights Amendment (ERA)** to the United States Constitution. "Equality of rights under the law shall not be denied or abridged by the United States or by any state on account of sex," said

Activist Phyllis Schlafly wearing a "Stop ERA" badge, demonstrating with other women against the Equal Rights Amendment in front of the White House, Washington, D.C.,

the first section of the brisk, 56-word proposed amendment. A version of the ERA had been written by Alice Paul in 1923 and had been introduced in every session of Congress since, until the modern version passed both houses of Congress in 1972. A seven-year deadline was placed on ratification, and the amendment went to the states. Within five years, the ERA had been ratified by 35 states, just three short of the 38 needed for it to become part of the Constitution. Majority opinion supported the ERA, with the amendment winning the backing of as much as 74 percent of voters polled in 1974. Opponents never represented even a third of voters.

Momentum had undeniably slowed by 1977. The ERA was partly a victim of feminism's successes. With laws already on the books banning discrimination in hiring and pay, some Americans found the need for the amendment less urgent. The states that had not passed the ERA were heavily concentrated in the highly conservative and religiously fundamentalist South and Western Mormon areas, which saw the proposed amendment as a threat to the traditional "God-mandated" role of women as mothers and homemakers. A conservative woman who had campaigned for Barry Goldwater for president in 1964, **Phyllis Schlafly**, led the group STOP ERA and would battle the entire feminist agenda. Schlafly was conservative across the board, supporting the war in Vietnam, and opposing gay rights, social welfare programs and federal involvement in education.

Schlafly warned that the ERA would end special protections for women who might become eligible for the draft and placed in combat. Men would no longer be forced to pay alimony if they left their wives. Schlafly also warned that the ERA would result in unisex restrooms

in public buildings and the legalization of gay marriage. Congress extended the deadline for ratification until 1982, but no more states passed the amendment. Support for the ERA had been on the platform of both major parties, but the Republican Party—at the behest of conservative presidential candidate Ronald Reagan's supporters—removed its pro-ERA plank in time for the 1980 national convention.

Roe v. Wade

Many feminists insisted that it was not enough to fight wage and job discrimination and to confront a popular culture that demeaned women's intelligence and character. Abortion was a felony in 49 states and the District of Columbia as of 1967. Activists said these laws endangered women's lives, prompting between 200,000 and 1.2 million illegal abortions a year. Some of these illegal abortions were performed by doctors with shady credentials or by the pregnant women themselves and the women often died or suffered serious injury as a result. A poll taken by *Modern Medicine* revealed that almost 87 percent of American doctors supported liberalizing abortion laws. The American Law Institute proposed a "model abortion law" that allowed abortions if the mother's life or health were at risk, when the women became pregnant as a result of rape or incest, or if the fetus was seriously malformed. Colorado adopted the institute's recommendations in 1967. Other states followed suit by 1969, such as Arkansas, Delaware, Georgia, Kansas, Maryland, New Mexico, Oregon, and California, where the reform measure was signed by Governor Ronald Reagan, later touted as a hero by the anti-abortion movement.

In the early 1970s, Norma McCorvey said she was in Dallas, pregnant a third time after giving up one child for adoption and having another taken away by her mother. Suffering from substance abuse and money problems, she did not want another child but was turned down for an abortion by a doctor who told her the procedure was illegal in Texas. She went to an illegal clinic in Dallas, but the police had shut it down just before McCorvey's visit. She agreed to talk to two lawyers she had been told were seeking to challenge the Texas anti-abortion law. Those lawyers, Linda Coffee and Sarah Weddington, filed a class action suit against Dallas District Attorney Henry Wade claiming that the Texas anti-abortion law, which allowed the procedure only to save the patient's life, violated the constitutional right of privacy.

The case worked its way up to the United States Supreme Court, which on January 22, 1973, ruled by a 7-2 margin in ***Roe v. Wade*** that the Constitutional right to privacy was "broad enough to encompass a woman's

A coalition of gay and lesbian activists gather for a parade in downtown Des Moines, Iowa on June 28, 1983,
to kick-off the start of National Gay and Lesbian Pride Week.
Credit: Library of Congress

decision whether or not to terminate her pregnancy" during the first two trimesters (or first six months.) Judge Harry Blackmun, who wrote the majority opinion, held that a woman had an unqualified right to an abortion in the first trimester, and the states could only require the abortion be carried out by a qualified person. The states could only regulate the practice to protect the life and health of the mother in the second trimester. In the final trimester, Blackmun wrote for the Court, the fetus is viable (able to survive outside its mother's body). At that point, states could regulate or even ban the practice. Strict abortion laws in Texas and most other states were overturned.

THE BEGINNING OF THE GAY LIBERATION MOVEMENT

The Stonewall Uprising

During the 1950s and 1960s a focus of the gay rights movement was to challenge stereotypes such as that all gay men were effeminate. Promoting tolerance of sexual orientation became secondary to changing the image of the gay community. By the late 1960s, however, a new generation of gay activists wanted to move on from confronting stereotypes. The rise of the "Gay Liberation Movement," which sought acceptance of homosexuality as an example of human diversity, was greatly aided by the development of large gay communities with thriving subcultures in places like San Francisco's Castro District.

Perhaps the most critical moment in the history of gay activism happened on June 27, 1969, when New York City police conducted a raid on a local tavern, the **Stonewall Inn**, on Christopher Street in the heart of the metropolis'

gay community. Police routinely harassed patrons at gay nightspots, with customers rounded up and arrested, but on this night something different happened. The usual arrests were unfolding as police seized control of the Stonewall and loaded up the patrons into a police van when a lesbian began to struggle against arresting officers.

Upwards of 1,000 protestors arrived on the scene. Gay men, who had been routinely beaten and humiliated by police, fought uniformed officers and covered buildings on Christopher Street with graffiti that read, "Gay Power!" The police department dispatched a riot squad to quell the disturbance, but demonstrations continued in New York for days. Within a short time, gay men in New York had formed the Gay Liberation Front, a group that modeled itself on groups like the Black Panthers. Similar organizations calling for not just acceptance of homosexuals but political power for gays spread throughout the country.

Gay bars had long been gathering spots for the community, but after Stonewall, restaurants, legal clinics, newspapers, churches and synagogues aimed at the gay public opened in cities across America. Gay rights advocates won one of their most significant political victories in 1974. Until that year, the American Psychiatric Association defined homosexuality as a mental illness in its *Diagnostic and Statistical Manual of Mental Disorders* (DSM). In pursuit of curing this so-called disease, doctors subjected gay patients to castration, overdoses of insulin, electro-shock and "aversion" therapy. Activists demanded the profession provide objective evidence that gays were less well adjusted than heterosexuals or drop the designation. A committee could find no scientific evidence that gays were not mentally healthy. In 1974, the psychiatric group voted to drop homosexuality from the DSM. The following year, the United States Civil Service Commission dropped its prohibition on the hiring of gays in the federal government. City governments in Boston, Detroit, Houston, Los Angeles, San Francisco, and Washington, D.C., included a ban on anti-gay discrimination in their civil rights ordinances.

Harvey Milk

Harvey Milk's political career captured the triumph and tragedy of gay politics in the 1970s. A Navy veteran and former Wall Street investment banker, he moved to San Francisco and opened a camera shop on Castro Street in 1972. Milk organized the Castro Village Association, a merchants' organization in the neighborhood famous for its large gay community. A mayor and a County Board of Supervisors governed both the city and the county of San Francisco. After losing three times as an openly gay candidate in races for the Board of Supervisors when elections were held on a city-wide basis, the "Mayor of Castro Street" finally won an election on January 8, 1977, when the county races were broken into individual districts.

Milk received letters of admiration, as well as ugly threats from across the country. "I thank God," read one letter from a 68-year-old lesbian, "I have lived long enough to see my kind emerge from the shadows and join the human race." More sinister was another note that said, "Maybe, just maybe, some of the more hostile in the district may take some potshots at you—we hope!!!" Milk took such threats in stride. One of his biggest accomplishments was passage by the board of an anti-discrimination ordinance that prohibited businesses from firing individuals based on sexual orientation.

Milk was assassinated just nine days later by Dan White, a mentally imbalanced man who had recently resigned from the Board of Supervisors over the issue of pay and then became enraged when San Francisco Mayor George Moscone would not reinstate him. On November 27, White, a conservative Catholic and former police officer, firefighter and military veteran, arrived at city hall, sneaked into the building with a handgun, fatally shot the mayor and then killed Milk, shooting him five times. Insult was added to injury at Dan White's trial when defense attorneys successfully kept gays and people of color off the jury and argued that at the time of the murders White suffered from "diminished capacity" mentally from eating too much junk food, the so-called "Twinkie defense." The jury convicted White of voluntary manslaughter, rather than first-degree murder, and he was sentenced to only seven years and eight months in prison. A mob of 3,000 gay men and women rioted on the night of the verdict, May 21, 1979, leaving more than 160 hospitalized, including 61 police officers, and more than $1 million in damages across the city.

AMERICANS GET ANGRY

Americans got angry during the 1970s. They expressed this rage in ways great and small. In 1980, they voted out an incumbent president, and the Democrats lost 12 seats in the United States Senate. A more meaningful statistic might be the number of voters who expressed disgust at both Republicans and Democrats and indifference to the political process by declining to vote. About 63.1 percent of registered voters participated in the presidential election between John F. Kennedy and Richard Nixon in 1960. The percentage declined slightly to 60.6 in 1968. By 1980, barely over half—52.6 percent—cast a ballot in the election between Carter and Reagan.

The Vietnam War and the Iranian hostage crisis told Americans in the 1970s that the United States could no longer impose its will on the world. Watergate and the Church hearings proved that Americans could no longer trust their government. According to surveys, the percentage of Americans who trusted their government to "do the right thing" fell sharply from 75 percent in 1964 to only 36 percent by the time Nixon resigned in 1974. This had a profound effect on American politics as voters no longer trusted the government to accomplish big things like the moon landing or the kind of massive public works projects that characterized the New Deal. Skepticism of government served a conservative agenda as both Republicans and Democrats moved further right after the 1970s.

Americans' distrust deepened as they were battered by successive waves of inflation, unemployment, and the disappearance of decent wages and benefits. Writers like the journalist Tom Wolfe ridiculed the 1970s as "The Me Decade," but narcissism was a luxury of the well-to-do, those pampered enough to be frivolous. For working Americans, the decade marked the start of the Great Squeeze, an age in which they could not find enough hours in the week or earn enough money to guarantee their children a college education, or themselves a secure job and a comfortable retirement. Working class Americans began to sense that the social contract had been broken. Many white working class Americans in particular felt they had sacrificed over and over again, in coping with a depression in the 1930s, battling against fascism in the 1940s, serving in Korea in the 1950s, and losing their sons in the Vietnam War in the 1960s and 1970s. In return, they watched their hopes for a better life evaporate due to technology and deindustrialization even as wealthy elites exported their jobs overseas. The resentments that boiled over beginning in the late 1960s paved the way to a conservative backlash that would last more than three decades.

Table 29.1   Key Milestones for American Women in the 1970s

Event	Date	Significance
Women's Strike for Equality	August 26, 1970	To mark the centennial of the 19th Amendment which gave women the right to vote, 50,000 women in New York City marched against job discrimination, and in favor of free childcare and abortion rights. Protests were held in other cities as well.
Reed v. Reed decision	November 22, 1971	In a case involving who can administer estates, the U.S. Supreme Court ruled that the equal protection clause of the 14th Amendment prohibits discrimination based on sex.
Equal Rights Amendment Sent to the States	March 22, 1972	The House Approved the Equal Rights Amendment, which would have prohibited discrimination based on sex, on October 12, 1971. The Senate approved it on March 22, 1972. The amendment fell three states short of ratification by the required 38 states needed for ratification on June 30, 1982.
Roe v. Wade decision	January 22, 1973	Following a 1972 ruling, *Eisenstadt v. Baird,* that gave unmarried women a legal right to birth control, in *Roe* the U.S. Supreme Court ruled that women have an unqualified right to an abortion in the first trimester of pregnancy though states can impose certain restrictions in the second and third trimesters.
Fair Housing Act of 1974	August 22, 1974	Amended the 1968 Fair Housing Act to prohibit discrimination in housing based on sex and marital status.
Taylor v. Louisiana decision	January 21, 1975	Prohibited the exclusion of women from juries.
Publication of *Against Our Will*	1975	Author Susan Brownmiller detailed the history of rape and documented its pervasiveness.
Planned Parenthood v. Danforth	July 1, 1976	The United States Supreme Court ruled that a state may not require the consent of a spouse before having an abortion during the first 12 weeks of a pregnancy.
National Women's Conference in Houston, Texas	November 18-21, 1977	A pivotal event drawing 2,000 delegates, the conference adopted a plan of action calling for increased participation of women in politics, access to lower-cost reproductive health services, an end to job and wage discrimination based on sex, and equal access to credit regardless of sex.

Chronology

1968 My Lai Massacre.

1969 Richard Nixon sworn in as 37th president.
Nixon begins bombing campaign in Cambodia.
The Moratorium takes place across the nation.

1970 American troops invade Cambodia.
Protests are held at Kent State University.

1971 Twenty-Sixth Amendment giving 18-year-olds
the right to vote is ratified.
The *New York Times* publishes *The Pentagon Papers*.

1972 Nixon visits China and the Soviet Union.
SALT I treaty is signed.
Break-in at Watergate.
Nixon wins re-election.
Christmas Bombing of North Vietnam.

1973 Peace accords in Vietnam take effect.
Senate Watergate hearings begin.
The CIA instigates a coup in Chile.
Vice President Spiro Agnew is forced to resign.
The Yom Kippur War.
"Saturday Night Massacre."

1974 Richard Nixon resigns as president.
Gerald Ford becomes the 38th president.
Ford pardons Nixon.

1975 The South Vietnamese government surrenders.
The Khmer Rouge takes over Cambodia.
The *Mayaguez* incident.

1976 Jimmy Carter is elected president.

1978 Panama Canal Treaty is ratified.
Camp David Peace Accords.
The Iranian Revolution starts.

1979 The Shah of Iran is overthrown and Ayatollah
Ruhollah Khomeini becomes "Supreme Leader."
The United States formally recognizes China.
Egypt and Israel sign a formal peace treaty.
Three Mile Island accident.
American hostages are seized by militants in Iran.
The Soviet Union invades Afghanistan.
Carter cancels American participation in the
1980 Summer Olympics in Moscow.

1980 Ronald Reagan is elected the 40th president.

SUGGESTED READINGS

W. Carl Biven, *Jimmy Carter's Economy: Policy in an Age of Limits* (2002).

Peter Brush, "The Hard Truth About Fragging: Unprecedented Decline of Morale and Discipline Spawned a Phenomenon Forever Tied to the Vietnam War," *Vietnam* (July 28, 2010), http://www.historynet.com/the-hard-truth-about-fragging.htm. Accessed July 11, 2011.

William Bundy, *A Tangled Web: The Making of Foreign Policy in the Nixon Presidency* (1998).

David Frum, *How We Got Here: The 70s, The Decade That Brought You Modern Life – For Better or Worse* (2000)

Seymour M. Hersh, *The Price of Power: Kissinger in the Nixon White House* (1983).

Maurice Isserman and Michael Kazin. *America Divided: The Civil War of the 1960s* (2000).

Burton I. Kaufman, *The Presidency of James Earl Carter* (1993).

Stanley Karnow. *Vietnam: A History* 1983.

Ben Kiernan, *The Pol Pot Regime: Race, Power, and Genocide in Cambodia Under the Khmer Rouge, 1975-79* (1996).

Stephen Kinzer, *Overthrow: America's Century of Regime Change From Hawaii to Iraq* (2006.)

____, *All The Shah's Men: An American Coup and the Roots of Middle Eastern Terror* (2003).

Mark Hamilton Lytle, *America's Uncivil Wars: The Sixties From Elvis to the Fall of Richard Nixon* (2006).

Kevin Mattson, *What The Heck Are You Up To, Mr. President? Jimmy Carter, America's Malaise and the Speech That Should Have Changed the Country* (2010).

Yanek Mieczkowski, *Gerald Ford and the Challenges of the 1970s* (2005).

Rick Perlstein, *Nixonland: The Rise of a President and the Fracturing of America* (2008).

Bruce J. Schulman, *The Seventies: The Great Shift in American Culture, Society and Politics* (2001).

William Shawcross, *Sideshow: Kissinger, Nixon and the Destruction of Cambodia* (1979).

____, *The Shah's Last Ride: The Fate of an Ally* (1988).

Ronald H. Spector, *After Tet: The Bloodiest Year in Vietnam* (1993).

Bob Woodward, *Shadow: Five Presidents and the Legacy of Watergate* (1999).

Bob Woodward and Carl Bernstein, *All The President's Men* (1974).

____, *The Final Days* (1976).

Review Questions

1. In what ways did the Vietnam War prompt the Watergate Scandal?

2. What was the "Nixon Doctrine" and how was it applied in Vietnam, Iran, and Chile?

3. What were President Richard Nixon's objectives in improving relations with China?

4. What factors caused "stagflation" in 1973 and the economic slowdown in 1979-1980?

5. Describe how President Jimmy Carter applied and failed to apply his policy of "Human Rights" in his relationship with other world leaders.

Glossary of Important People and Concepts

Affirmative Action
Black Panther Party
Camp David Accords
Rachel Carson
James Earl "Jimmy" Carter
César Chávez
Chicano Movement
Détente
Energy Crisis (1973)
Equal Rights Amendment (ERA)
Gerald R. Ford
Betty Friedan
Iranian Hostage Crisis
Kent State Shooting
Henry Kissinger
Harvey Milk
Moral Majority
Pentagon Papers
Ronald Reagan
Roe v. Wade
Phyllis Schlafly
Stonewall Uprising
Vietnamization
War Powers Act
Watergate

A PERIOD OF TRANSITION: The Reagan Revolution, End of the Cold War, and the Gulf War, 1980-1992

The fall of the Berlin Wall, an event often viewed as the symbolic end of the Cold War, began as a miscommunication from an East German government spokesperson that quickly spilled out of control. A couple of months prior, several thousand East Germans had taken advantage of Hungary's decision to no longer guard its border with Austria by traveling to Hungary as tourists, then escaping to Austria. Though the East German government soon ended tourist travel to Hungary, authorities did nothing to stop the movement of people across their open border with Czechoslovakia, which quickly became the new route to freedom by travel into Hungary and then Austria. Demonstrations soon erupted as East German citizens called for political reforms, similar to protests taking place across Eastern Europe. Poland had recently established a democratic government, and movements were underway in nearby nations when it became known that Mikhail Gorbachev would not intervene with military force to end the protest movements as previous Soviet leaders had done in Hungary in 1956 and Czechoslovakia in 1968. In East Germany, a group of reform-minded communists had recently ousted the long-time communist hardline leader Erich Honecker, but so far no tangible difference had been noticed.

On November 4, 1989, over a half million people gathered in East Berlin's large public square to demand political change. In response, the new East German government authorities hastily made plans on November 9 for a program to allow travel to West Berlin and West Germany, but only for individuals who formally applied with the government, received permission, and received proper documentation in the form of exit visas. The changes were to be implemented starting the next day in order to print the required papers

and allow time to inform the border guards of the new policy. These details, however, were lost on Günter Schabowski, the government's spokesman, as he prepared to hold a press briefing and failed to closely read a memo that he had just received about the new policy. When he casually mentioned the recently developed program at the end of the news conference, a reporter asked him when the travel changes might come into effect. Unsure, Schabowski fumbled his papers a bit before responding, contrary to the government's plans: "As far as I know, immediately. Without delay."

The spokesman's answer quickly spread across both East and West Germany, and television and radio stations began reporting that the border between the two Germanys was now open. Thousands of people raced to the border checkpoints from both sides of the Berlin Wall. The border guards, who had not been informed of any change in government policy, initially refused to let anybody through their posts. At the Bornholmer Street crossing, Harald Jäger, an experienced guard who had worked at his post for over 25 years, frantically called his commander multiple times, but was told the same thing—not to let the people through to the other side. A police car showed up to blare over a loud speaker that visas were necessary for travel, and everyone should go home but nobody listened. East German television news anchors likewise began announcing that travel would require an application process starting the next day, but those details were also ignored as the people kept arriving at the wall demanding an end to all travel restrictions and limits upon their freedom in general.

Exasperated with the lack of support from his superiors, and concerned that some of his guards might lose patience and open fire on the crowd of several thousand people then congregating at his checkpoint, Jäger phoned his colonel one last time to inform him that he was opening the gate and letting the people into West Berlin unfettered. As the East Berliners joyously filed through his checkpoint, Jäger started to cry. Ducking inside a nearby building so his men would not see him like that, he found another guard already there weeping uncontrollably. At Checkpoint Charlie, the main crossing point in the divided city for foreign tourists, many West Berliners were defiantly climbing onto the wall and refusing orders to come down. Finally, as Jäger had done, the guards opened the barriers and stepped aside as the crowds of East Berliners poured in, most just wanting to see if they could actually step into the other side of their home city for the first time in their lives. They were met by huge numbers of the West Berliners, greeting them with smiles and warm hugs. At checkpoints all along the wall, a massive celebration had begun.

As some of the revelers that night broke out pick axes and hammers to snag souvenirs from the momentous occasion and begin the process of demolishing the wall that would later be completed by bulldozers several months later, thousands more heard the news and continued to flock to the scene to witness history. Among those celebrating that night was 35-year-old physical chemist Angela Merkel. After getting off work, she and a friend visited a local pub where a television was broadcasting the enormity of the situation occurring at the wall. They soon joined the action, crossing Harald Jäger's checkpoint at Bornholmer Street. After placing a phone call to her aunt who lived in Hamburg, West Germany, Merkel stayed up late sharing more beers with the other celebrants before heading back home so she could get some sleep before work the next day. Before long, Merkel would give up her job to pursue a career in politics, beginning an unlikely rise that would culminate in her being elected chancellor of a unified Germany.

In the United States, the news was greeted with astonishment and cheers. American network news broadcasts carried live pictures of the momentous occasion as it unfolded and for several days afterward as the partying continued. The most glaring symbol of Cold War animosity between East and West was finally coming down—a tangible sign that a new phase of American history was about to begin.

Ronald Reagan rode the crest of a rising political wave in 1980 to become not only the next president but also the leader of a movement that would revere him in conservative circles as a patron saint equal to the status held by Franklin Roosevelt among progressives. Those who made up the coalition of Reagan supporters—fiscal conservatives, low-tax advocates, evangelical Christians, aggressive foreign policy "neoconservatives," libertarians,

and members of the working class who traditionally voted for Democrats (so-called "Reagan Democrats")—were hopeful that he could deliver on his major campaign promises of lower taxes, a balanced budget, an enhanced military, and renewed respect for America abroad. By the end of the early 1990s, the results revealed a mixed bag. Business profits were up with reduced inflation, but the period also witnessed a vast inequality of wealth marked by increased poverty (from 26.1 million, or 11.7 percent in 1980 to 37 million, or 14.2 percent in 1992). Tax rates were reduced during the Reagan years, especially for corporate and high individual wealth, but the federal budget deficit ballooned. The military was larger and stronger than ever, but with an expanded role leading to its deployment to numerous hot spots around the globe. An ascendant Republican Party would win three straight presidential elections and gain control of the Senate in 1981, but proved incapable of preventing the Democrats from regaining the White House in 1992 when Bill Clinton defeated Reagan's successor, George H.W. Bush. Even the successful conclusion to the Cold War by the end of the Reagan-Bush era—a monumental development promising a brighter future with vast economic and foreign policy benefits—would soon be followed by American military involvement in the Middle East, leading within two decades to a massive commitment of resources to an exhausting global fight against militant Islamic fundamentalists that characterized much of the early years of the new millennium.

THE REAGAN PRESIDENCY

From Midwestern Youth to Hollywood Star

Growing up in small-town Illinois had a strong influence on the personality and outlook of young **Ronald Reagan**. Born in 1911 to a hard-working and hard-drinking father who peddled shoes for a living and a loving, religious mother who took care of him and his older brother, Reagan's family moved constantly until finally settling down in Dixon, Illinois. From his father, Reagan learned the value of hard work and patriotism, as well as an interest in storytelling, acting, and sports. His mother, meanwhile, inculcated her son with the faith of her church (the Disciples of Christ) and a positive outlook and belief in the goodness of people. After working as a lifeguard and other odd jobs, he attended Eureka College (a small local Disciples of Christ institution) where he studied economics and sociology while engaging in sports and theatrical activities. He also showed an interest in politics, serving as student body president before graduating in 1932. Seeking employment in the midst of the Great Depression, Reagan landed a job as a broadcaster for University of Iowa football games before going to Hollywood to pursue a movie acting career.

After passing a screen test, Reagan signed a contract with Warner Brothers Studios and starting in 1937 began appearing in a series of films, some noteworthy and many quite forgettable. He met and married the famous Hollywood actress Jane Wyman in 1940. A member of the U.S. Army Reserves, he was called up to active duty with the outbreak of World War II and served in various public relations capacities before joining the First Motion Picture Unit, which produced military training films. After the war, members of the Screen Actors Guild elected him to be president of their union from 1947 to 1952. During this period, Reagan, a fervent anti-communist, aided the FBI by providing the names of individuals that he suspected had communist sympathies. He also willingly testified before the House Un-American Activities Committee on the subject of communist influences in Hollywood.

After Reagan and Wyman divorced in 1949 (he would become the only U.S. president ever to have been divorced), he later met and married actress Nancy Davis. Experiencing a decline in the number and quality of film roles during the 1950s, television provided a chance to revive Reagan's career. His engaging personality served

him well as the host of *General Electric Theater*—a popular prime-time series of weekly dramas that appeared for eight years on CBS. He also became a spokesman for General Electric, touring the company's facilities and giving pro-business, morale-boosting speeches to employees and local business groups.

Though raised as a Democrat who admired President Franklin Roosevelt, Reagan's pro-business and strong anti-communist views began to change his political outlook. By the early 1960s, he joined the Republican Party and strongly supported the 1964 candidacy of Arizona Senator Barry Goldwater against Lyndon Johnson. Always interested in the possibility of serving in public office, Reagan decided to run for the governorship of California in 1966 and handily defeated the two-term incumbent Democrat Pat Brown. In 1970, he was re-elected to another four-year term. Though he worked with the Democrats who controlled the state legislature on many issues throughout most of his eight years in office, Reagan continued to promote his conservative ideas in noteworthy ways by cracking down on Vietnam War protesters, favoring lower taxes, supporting capital punishment, and frequently demanding that "welfare bums" go back to work. Growing in popularity among national Republicans, Reagan unsuccessfully challenged President Gerald Ford for their party's nomination in 1976 before his triumph four years later followed by his defeat of Jimmy Carter.

Nancy Reagan looks at her husband, Ronald Reagan, as he takes the oath of office as 40th President of the United States. January 20, 1981.
Photo credit: Reagan Presidential Library

The Eternal Optimist

Brimming with confidence in himself and his country, Reagan promoted hard work and unabashed patriotism as the ways for the nation to rise out of its current slump. His critics stated that his views were overly simplistic and often based on naïveté, but few doubted that Reagan truly accepted the ideals that he espoused and wanted his fellow citizens to feel similarly optimistic. Similar to Franklin Roosevelt, he used his inaugural address as a platform to raise national morale, asking the people to "believe in ourselves and to believe in our capacity to perform great deeds, to believe we can still resolve the problems which now confront us. Why shouldn't we believe that? We are Americans." His spokesmen would ensure that such positive messages would keep coming from the administration. As one advisor remembered, "We kept apple pie and the flag going the whole time."

While Reagan's faith in his words was devout, he lacked an interest, and frequently the capacity, to formulate actual policies. His style, therefore, was to delegate—instruct his subordinates what he wanted to be accomplished and left it for them to work out the details. For these endeavors, he relied upon a loyal cadre of advisors, the most important proving to be Chief of Staff James A. Baker, an experienced Texas political insider who knew how business worked in the capital, and two loyalists from his days as California governor—White House counselor Edward Meese and Baker's deputy chief of staff Michael Deaver. The First Lady, Nancy Reagan, also served as a trusted confidante inside the White House, dispensing her impressions to her doting husband, especially her opinions on administration personnel and the various individuals that they would meet during his tenure.

REAGAN'S FIRST TERM DOMESTIC AGENDA

Reaganomics

The first stage of Reagan's domestic agenda focused on jump-starting the economy through controversial and sometimes contradictory means that were nevertheless consistent with his economic and political ideology. Highly desirous of a balanced federal budget, he sought reduced social welfare programs but also wanted greatly to increase military spending while cutting taxes across the board. Soon labeled "**Reaganomics**," many economists and politicians questioned its practicality. During the 1980 campaign, Reagan's main rival who became his

vice president, George H.W. Bush, had even ridiculed the approach as "voodoo economics."

The targeting of social programs fit with the long-standing conservative desire to weaken, if not completely dismantle, the remnants of the New Deal and Great Society still existing in the 1980s. The desire to undercut social programs contradicted his fondness for Franklin Roosevelt. While paying lip service to FDR's leadership during the Great Depression and World War II, Reagan denounced modern liberal policies, believing they fostered idleness and dependency upon government.

To Reagan and like-minded conservatives, all of the country's socioeconomic ills since the late 1960s resulted from the continued expansion of the size and reach of government (except for the military) and the welfare state. If the federal government's presence in the daily life of the nation could be minimized, with all but the most essential social welfare programs or entitlements (such as Social Security) eliminated, then all would be right again in America as the private sector once again became responsible for the nation's economic well-being. Soon after entering the Oval Office, Reagan put administration officials to work developing the means to fulfill his vision. The White House ultimately asked Congress to cut tens of billions of dollars in domestic spending from social programs such as Food Stamps, Aid to Families with Dependent Children, and assistance to the states helping to support mental health services. To further satisfy social conservatives, Reagan made the ending of affirmative action initiatives one of his major efforts, ordering Attorney General William French Smith to challenge such programs in the federal courts while packing the Civil Rights Commission and Equal Employment Opportunity Commission with individuals dedicated to reversing the racial and gender policies of previous administrations.

Tax reduction was another primary goal for Reagan and his supporters as they sought to purge the economy of the Keynesian ideas that Democrats had implemented since the late 1930s. Inspired by British economist John Maynard Keynes, American liberals had used government spending to stimulate the economy during economic slowdowns. Such spending had often been financed by relatively high taxes on corporations and individuals in the upper-income brackets. These policies, conservatives argued, had caused the economic downturns of the 1970s and early 1980s. The president and his supporters believed that among their first corrective measures should be to sharply reduce personal and corporate income taxes by 30 percent over the next three years. Reagan fully embraced the fundamentals of supply-side economics, an anti-Keynesian approach that favored tax breaks to the business community and wealthy individuals in the belief that was the most efficient way to stimulate economic growth—an approach similar to what Secretary of the Treasury Andrew Mellon had advocated during the Coolidge administration of the 1920s (see Chapter 23).

Reagan named conservative Michigan congressman David Stockman to head the Office of Management and Budget (OMB). A devoted disciple of the supply-side theory, Stockman advocated sharp reductions in personal income taxes to encourage investments by entrepreneurs, who he believed would want to make more money by using their tax savings to expand their businesses, thereby creating more jobs. This increased commercial activity would theoretically spur rapid economic growth, hike personal incomes, and bring in greater tax revenues, even at the lower rates. Stockman would become increasingly troubled by the impact of the last major portion of Reagan's agenda—a large increase in defense spending—which the director believed placed undue demands on the budget without further offsets in the form of cuts to social programs.

As Reagan and his aides lobbied hard for the bill in March 1981, it became clear that the measure would not pass as easily as Reagan had hoped. Despite the defection of some Democratic stalwarts such as Senator Lloyd Bentsen of Texas, the majority of Democrats opposed the proposal, claiming that the tax cuts would benefit the rich more than the poor. While the impasse continued, fate dealt Reagan a cruel but politically auspicious hand. On March 30, 1981, a psychologically troubled twenty-five-year-old named **John Hinckley** tried to assassinate the president as he left a speaking engagement at the Washington Hilton Hotel. Firing six times with a .22 caliber pistol, Hinckley hit Press Secretary James Brady in the head, permanently disabling him. Other gunfire bloodied a Washington, D.C. policeman and a Secret Service agent. One of Hinckley's bullets ricocheted off the presidential limousine, hitting Reagan under his left arm. The bullet lodged in his lung close to his heart. An ambulance rushed him to the nearest hospital where doctors found him bleeding profusely. Surgeons operated on him for two hours to remove the bullet and save his life. Reagan's brush with death kept him in the hospital until April 11.

While Reagan recuperated, news releases informed a frightened public not only how close they came to losing their new president, but perhaps more important politically, how calm and good-humored he had been. When he saw his wife Nancy, Reagan quipped, "Honey, I forgot to duck." As doctors were about to put him under, he remarked, "Please tell me you are all Republicans." Polls recorded that his courage and joviality had caused his popularity to soar, with more than 70 percent of the people giving him favorable ratings. Upon his return to

Secret service agents rush an assailant who fired six shots at President Reagan as he was leaving the Washington Hilton on March 30. This photo released by the White House shows the door on the presidential limousine being closed (right) after Reagan was pushed in, and Press Secretary James Brady and patrolman Thomas Delahanty on the ground after being hit by gunfire.

the White House, Reagan kept a low profile until April 28, when he emerged to give an eagerly awaited television speech to a joint session of Congress. He seized the emotionally charged occasion to call upon the legislators to enact his economic program. For the next four months, the White House lobbied Congress extensively, with Reagan becoming personally involved, holding extensive meetings and telephone conversations with members of Congress. The president's persistence paid off. In July, Congress passed slightly modified tax and budget bills, thanks largely to the defection of conservative southern Democrats, who Reagan had won over during the preceding months. Eventually, Congress did not agree to a balanced budget, but obliged the president by cutting more than $25 billion from federal welfare programs while slashing taxes by $750 billion over the next five years, lowering the top marginal rate from 70 percent to 50 percent. Reagan also secured congressional approval for a staggering $1.2 trillion increase in defense spending over the same period. With this accomplishment, the so-called "Reagan Revolution" had secured its first victory in the ongoing conservative effort to alter the relationship of the people with their government.

The Air Traffic Controllers' Strike

Soon after the passage of the tax and budget bills, Reagan endeared himself further among the New Righters by adopting a tough stand against members of the **Professional Air Traffic Controller's Organization (PATCO)** who walked out on the job in their efforts to seek better pay and benefits. When the union members voted to strike, Reagan (the only president ever to have previously served as the head of a labor union) rejected its demands and threatened to fire the strikers if they did not return to work within 48 hours. Although Reagan believed in the basic right of workers to organize for better working conditions (he actually led an actors' strike in 1952 and also signed legislation extending workers' collective bargaining rights while governor of California), the president drew the line on what he considered to be an illegal federal workers' walkout, especially one that could potentially endanger the nation's safety. Many Americans agreed and supported Reagan's tough stance. When his 48-hour deadline passed, he announced that 38 percent of the strikers had returned to work and that military air traffic controllers would replace those still on strike. After firing more than 11,000 air traffic controllers, Reagan reassured the nation that air travel was safe and that flight schedules had returned to 80 percent normal.

Though Reagan's action devastated PATCO, his main intent was to take a stand against public workers using the strike as a negotiating tactic (similar to the actions of Calvin Coolidge—another hero of Reagan's—had done versus striking Boston police officers while Governor of Massachusetts in 1919) and not to challenge federal employees for organizing and bargaining collectively. In the long run, however, his move has been seen by supporters and opponents alike as an attempt to destroy public sector unions. Detractors point to the virtual end of voluntary work stoppages as a labor tactic by federal workers since 1981 out of fear of losing their jobs. Meanwhile, in the years that followed, conservative Republicans have increasingly obscured Reagan's stated beliefs regarding public sector unions, viewing his mass firings as a direct assault against such organizations rather than, as he saw it, a singular effort to thwart one union's effort to seek an upper hand by violating the law.

Taking on the Environmentalists

In addition to tax cuts and the deregulation of many sectors of the economy, Reagan proved equally passionate about giving corporations and ranchers more freedom to develop the nation's natural resources despite potential damage to the environment. He viewed federal environmental protection laws passed since the presidency of Theodore Roosevelt as one of the greatest handicaps to domestic economic expansion, believing they unnecessarily limited opportunities for growth by restricting business access to land and vital resources. Reagan appointed a pro-business Colorado state legislator, Anne Burford, to head the Environmental Protection Agency (EPA). During her two-year tenure before resigning over conflicts with Congress over her administration of a $1.6 billion Superfund to clean up toxic waste, Burford cut the EPA's budget by 22 percent, impacting enforcement of regulations and leading to a steep decline in the number of cases filed against polluters. Both Democratic and Republican supporters of environmental protections accused Burford of deliberately attempting to dismantle the agency's effectiveness.

Secretary of the Interior **James Watt** also received the ire of environmentalists. No one better reflected the Reagan credo relative to the environment than Watt, a pro-development attorney from Wyoming who worked tirelessly to open federal wilderness areas, forestlands, and coastal waters to oil and gas corporations. He undermined endangered species programs and cut initiatives to protect environmentally threatened regions. Before coming to Washington, Watt had headed the Mountain States Legal Foundation, an organization that spearheaded the so-called Sagebrush Rebellion of western conservatives seeking to open public lands to private development.

Watt's disdain for conservationists galvanized the environmental movement. In response to his extreme positions, membership in the Sierra Club, the Wilderness Society, and other environmental organizations skyrocketed. More than a million conservationists signed petitions demanding Watt's removal. Watt resigned in 1983, not because of his policies, but rather, a series of public relations gaffes. (He had first caused a public uproar when he famously banned the Beach Boys from performing an Independence Day concert on the Washington Mall because they supposedly attracted "the wrong element" and invited Las Vegas singer Wayne Newton to take their place. The incident that did him in, however, involved bigoted comments that he made while ridiculing affirmative action during a speech before the U.S. Chamber of Commerce.) Though the contentious Watt was gone, Reagan's policies continued under less controversial appointees.

The Reagan Recession

The economic recovery that President Reagan promised as a result of his policies was slow to materialize. The Federal Reserve Board under Chairman Paul Volcker aggressively attacked inflation with policies that raised interest rates in an effort to channel more money to savings accounts rather than purchases. With help from a drop in oil prices, the inflation rate fell from 14 percent at the end of Jimmy Carter's presidency to 4 percent by the end of 1982. The high interest rates necessary to curb inflation, however, soon brought on the worst economic decline to hit the country since the Great Depression of the 1930s, when the national unemployment rate rose above 10 percent. The industrial states of the Northeast and Midwest were hit especially hard as thousands of blue-collar workers were laid off when their plants closed their doors, continuing a general decline in heavy manufacturing. Agricultural producers suffered as well, with many growers losing their farms due to high interest rates and declining exports. Thousands of small businesses tied to greater economy also went bankrupt in large numbers, succumbing to what the press began to call the "**Reagan Recession.**"

Soaring federal deficits added to the economic muddle. Reagan's tax cuts reduced federal revenues without immediately producing the predicted business boom, while soaring military expenditures far exceeded domestic spending cuts. Members of the national media began to criticize the First Lady for wearing expensive designer dresses while hosting elaborate White House dinners on immaculate china as many in the nation were suffering. The electorate responded to the downturn in the 1982 mid-term congressional elections by voting 26 House Republicans out of office. Many analysts began to predict

that Reagan was on course to being a one-term president like his predecessor. When a Republican pollster in January 1983 told him that his approval rating was lingering at 35 percent, he quietly pondered the news for a while, then characteristically smiled and quipped: "I know just what I can do about it. I'll go out and get shot again."

An Uneven Recovery

By 1983, Reagan's popularity revived as many of the major national economic indicators began to trend positively. Encouraged by tax cuts, falling interest rates, and evidence that inflation had been tamed at last, many middle- and upper-class consumers felt better about their prospects and went on a buying binge. The automobile industry and the housing market saw increased sales once again, while buyers began to purchase large numbers of the latest and most expensive electronic gadgets, including VCR's, portable CD players, personal computers, and televisions with remote controls. The unemployment rate in 1984 declined to 7.5 percent.

The overall economic picture by the mid-1980s, though improved, was uneven. While wealthy individuals and the investor class prospered as never before, poverty increased and the real wages of full-time workers continued to stagnate. As during the 1970s, job seekers frequently complained that the fastest growing occupations were in the low-paying jobs of the service sector—waiters and waitresses, nurses, janitors, cashiers, and delivery drivers. As American manufacturing declined due to cheaper imported goods, or as increasing numbers of businesses moved their production facilities overseas to save labor costs, blue-collar American workers lost many good-paying jobs. If they wanted to continue working, they either had to learn a new skill or accept low-paying service-sector employment in order to put food on the table.

Better times for the wealthy led to a wave of stock-market speculation reminiscent of the 1920s. A "bull market" began in August 1982 and lasted for five years. Entrepreneurs such as Donald Trump, a Manhattan real estate mogul, and Ivan Boesky, a supposed genius at stock transactions, became millionaire celebrities by playing the market and engaging in a variety of other speculative ventures. The same mania to get rich quickly that affected Americans in the 1920s engulfed many during the 1980s. Banks and savings and loan companies, newly deregulated and flush with deposits of eager investors, ladled out billions to developers planning shopping malls, luxury apartments, condominiums, retirement communities, and office buildings.

REAGAN CONFRONTS THE WORLD

President Reagan's popularity stemmed not only from his views on domestic policy. His calls for a strong America projecting its strength in world affairs also garnered wide support. At the center of his belief system was the necessity to confront Soviet communism, which he often asserted bellicosely was the antithesis of freedom. He would frequently couch America's differences with the Soviet Union in stark good-versus-evil terms. In a June 1982 address before the British Parliament, Reagan expressed his hope that communism would wind up on the "ash heap of history" along with other discredited ideologies. A year later in a speech before a group of evangelicals, the president famously denounced the Soviet Union as the "Evil Empire." While active in pushing for a steep increase in defense spending to increase the size of the U.S. military, the president, as he did with most domestic matters, provided the vision but largely left the implementation to his trusted subordinates, in this case, to his Secretary of State George Schultz, Secretary of Defense Caspar Weinberger, and CIA Director William Casey. With self-righteous faith in the superiority of the "American Way," the United States government under Reagan sought the end of communism, supposedly not to promote the material or strategic interests of the nation, but for the benefit of all mankind.

Increased Tensions with the Soviet Union

To back up his belligerent rhetoric, Reagan asked for and eventually received congressional approval for a sizeable increase in defense spending. With such funding, he pledged to build 17,000 new nuclear missiles. Most controversially, Reagan lobbied Congress in 1983 to undertake a massively expensive **Strategic Defense Initiative (SDI),** which involved the attempt to development a defense shield capable of intercepting incoming Soviet missiles with lasers fired from satellites orbiting the Earth. Though deemed unfeasible by media pundits, reputable scientists, and even some high-ranking members of the administration, the planners of the audacious scheme (ridiculed as the "Star Wars" system by its staunchest critics) sought to ruin the Russian economy through Soviet efforts to match the American program as much as they hoped the project would actually work as designed. While the verdict is still out on whether the initiative

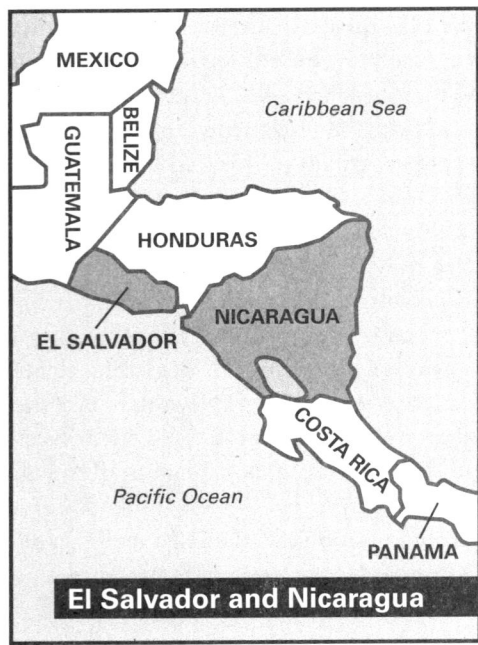

Map 30.1 El Salvador and Nicaragua

contributed in any significant way to Soviet economic problems during the 1980s, Congress did authorize over $17 billion in SDI funding (the most expensive defense system ever) over the course of the decade before finally terminating the program in 1989.

Relations with the Soviet Union worsened on September 1, 1983, when a Soviet fighter jet shot down a South Korean airliner when the civilian aircraft traveling from New York City (via Anchorage, Alaska) to Seoul, South Korea, accidentally veered into Russian airspace. All 269 people on board were lost, including a U.S. congressman from Georgia and 60 other Americans. The act was one of incompetence and confusion on behalf of the Soviets rather than one of wanton aggression as Soviet military officials genuinely believed the plane to be an intruder on a spy mission. Reagan ignored all evidence that the attack was a mistake, choosing instead to seize on the event to lead a worldwide condemnation of the Soviet Union, labeling the incident as a "crime against humanity," implying that the downing reflected the premeditated murder of innocent civilians.

Right-Wing Support in Central America

Reagan's obsession with stopping the spread of communism entangled the United States in two civil wars taking place in Central America as **El Salvador** and **Nicaragua** became fixations for the administration. Harkening back to the traditional Cold War "domino theory" that led to U.S. involvement in Korea and Vietnam, Reagan told a joint session of Congress in May 1983, "The national security of all the Americas is at stake. If we cannot defend ourselves there, we cannot expect to prevail elsewhere . . . and the safety of our homeland would be put at jeopardy." In El Salvador, the White House backed a right-wing military junta in its brutal suppression of all opposition. Certain the regime was fighting to preserve "democracy" in El Salvador, Reagan allowed the CIA to send advisors to help the Salvadoran army put down left-wing insurgents. With approval from Washington, the Salvadoran government unleashed a vicious reign of terror against suspected dissidents, with U.S.-trained paramilitary death squads roaming the countryside and slaughtering thousands over the course of several months. By 1984, the government claimed that El Salvador had been saved from communism. A U.S.-favored moderate, José Napoleón Duarte, won the 1984 presidential election, ending the junta's rule. Nevertheless, under Duarte the killing of political opponents continued.

In Nicaragua, the Carter administration, in an attempt to atone for decades of American support for the brutal Anastasio Somoza regime, had initially granted aid to the leftist Sandinista revolutionaries who overthrew Somoza in 1979. Fearing that the **Sandinistas** were turning Nicaragua into another Marxist state like Castro's Cuba, the Reagan administration began to make plans to subvert their government. Although they were socialists opposed to U.S. policy toward Central America, the Sandinistas had no desire to see their country become a Soviet puppet state. Nevertheless, Reagan's attitude and policies, which cut off all aid to Nicaragua, left the Sandinistas no choice but to turn to Cuba and the Soviet Union for assistance if their regime was going to survive. As the Sandinistas drifted deeper into the Cuban-Soviet camp, Reagan became more determined to overthrow them. In 1982, with his approval, the CIA organized and financed a 10,000-man anti-Sandinista guerrilla army based in neighboring Costa Rica and Honduras called the *Contras* with the avowed purpose of bringing down the government of Nicaragua.

Reagan and other conservatives frequently referred to the *Contras* as "freedom fighters" but as recently declassified documents have shown, the majority of the individuals comprising the force were ex-Somoza thugs and mercenaries, with many heavily involved in cocaine smuggling for Panamanian leader Manuel Noriega and large Colombian drug cartels. With full-fledged U.S. government support, the *Contras* conducted raids and carried out sabotage in Nicaragua, killing thousands of civilians in the process.

Many Americans grew alarmed as details of this secret war against the Sandinistas leaked out. Thus, in 1982, the House of Representatives passed the **Boland Amend-ment,** prohibiting the CIA and Defense Department from using funds to overthrow the Sandinistas. Some high-level Reagan administration officials, however, ignored the resolution and continued to funnel money contributed by foreign governments and right-wing groups in the United States to the *Contras.* Such covert operations increasingly came under the auspices of the National Security Council, which became the conduit for delivering the secret aid. The two men most responsible for the venture, National Security Adviser Robert MacFarlane and his overzealous staff assistant, Marine Lieutenant Colonel Oliver North, would be at the heart of the subsequent Iran-Contra Affair that would erupt during Reagan's second term when details of the clandestine operation became public.

Continuing Turmoil in the Middle East

The ongoing turmoil in the Middle East that had so frustrated the Carter presidency occupied the attention of Reagan administration officials. Determined to stop the spread of militant Islamic fundamentalism, with its call for jihad against Western corruption and imperialism in Muslim lands, the United States government sided with Saddam Hussein's Iraq in its eight-year war (1980-88) against Iran. The conflict resulted in an estimated 1.5 million Iraqi and Iranian deaths, devastated both nations' economies and created millions of refugees. American support for Iraq only served to embolden its dictator, Saddam Hussein, who believed that he would eventually dominate the Middle East.

As the Iran-Iraq war raged on, tensions between the Israel, the Palestinians, and their Arab allies continued to worsen. Since Israel was created in 1948 out of Arab-held lands in the British-held mandate for Palestine, millions of Arabs formerly living in Palestine had settled in refugee camps in nearby Arab countries, including the southern portion of Lebanon located to the north of Israel. Groups aiming at the establishment of a Palestinian state, such as the Palestinian Liberation Organization (PLO), had used the camps as a launching pad for guerilla strikes against Israel. Fighting had long taken place between the Israelis and the PLO along the Lebanese border. In 1981, Israel and the PLO concluded a cease-fire, but the PLO continued building up its forces. In June 1982, when an extremist within the PLO shot and critically wounded the Israeli ambassador to Great Britain, Israel retaliated by invading Lebanon. Upon the PLO's defeat, Yasser Arafat and the groups other leaders fled Lebanon.

The Israeli invasion only served to intensify an already bloody civil war in Lebanon between Christian and Muslim factions for control of the nation's government. Both the United States and Israel favored the Christian

The Reagans honor the victims of the bombing of the American Marines barracks, in Beirut, Lebanon, at Andrews Air Force Base, Maryland. April 23, 1983. Photo credit: Reagan Presidential Library

forces, believing that a Christian-dominated Lebanon would secure Israel's southern border with a friendly power while also giving the United States a non-Muslim ally in the region. With Israel's approval, a Lebanese Christian militia force entered two Palestinian refugee camps to disarm militant gunmen, but the raid's purpose turned into one of bloody revenge for the assassination of Lebanon's Christian president-elect, Bachir Gemayel. The partisans murdered hundreds of camp residents, including women and children.

In response to the massacre, Reagan offered two thousand marines to serve as part of a multinational peacekeeping force in Lebanon, oblivious to how Lebanon's Muslim militias would see his initiative. Starting in early 1983, extremists began using a new tactic in the Middle East—suicide missions using vehicles filled with explosives. On April 18, a car bomb destroyed the U.S. embassy in Beirut, killing many American foreign-service workers and Lebanese civilians. Then, on October 23, a Shiite Muslim on a suicide mission crashed a truck full of explosives into a U.S. Marine barracks, killing 241 soldiers.

The administration rebounded quickly from the Beirut disaster by invading the tiny West Indies island of **Grenada**, located to the north of Trinidad and Tobago, allegedly to protect the lives of American medical students after an internal power struggle led to the overthrow and murder of Marxist prime minister Maurice Bishop. In reality, very little evidence existed that the students were in any danger from the new regime, but Reagan administration officials felt the need for decisive action somewhere after the Beirut fiasco and invaded the island

U. S. Marines walk down a street of Greenville, Grenada, after landing near the town.

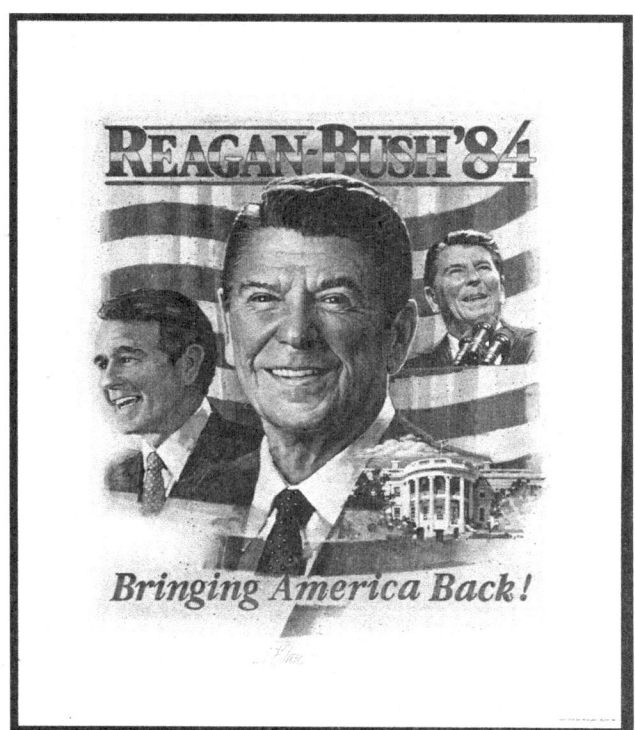

with 10,000 troops. After a day of skirmishing with seven hundred Cuban laborers constructing an airport (only one hundred of which were soldiers), Reagan declared a great American victory and the public generally displayed enthusiasm for the president over the relatively trivial affair. Reagan's public relations experts exploited the action to its fullest political potential, claiming to have restored America's military might by vanquishing a threat to national security.

THE ELECTION OF 1984

As the 1984 presidential election neared, liberal Democrats and many independents ramped up their criticism of Reagan for excessive military spending, Cold War belligerence, massive budget deficits, cuts in social programs, and assaults on the government's regulatory powers. The majority of Americans, however, dismissed such accusations, believing the president had redeemed America from its supposed malaise both at home and abroad. Helping Reagan was a booming economy with an end to the inflation that had wracked the country for several years. They applauded his tough stance with the Soviets and the rebuilding of America's military might. Many women voters welcomed his 1981 nomination of Sandra Day O'Connor as the first woman justice on the Supreme Court. The 1984 Republican convention held in Dallas, Texas, reinforced the themes of patriotism, prosperity, and, above all, the personality of Ronald Reagan—an individual they proclaimed to be most responsible for the nation's resurrection.

After Senator Edward Kennedy declined to enter the presidential campaign, former Vice President **Walter Mondale** emerged as the early favorite in the Democratic Party primary race, striving to show the reality of Reaganomics—that it had disproportionately benefited the rich. Senator Gary Hart of Colorado and the civil rights leader Jesse Jackson also entered the race and ran surprisingly strong campaigns. Receiving support from many young white Democrats, Hart often criticized unions and presented himself as a different type of Democrat who advocated new ideas that would free the party from New Deal-style, big-government liberalism in an effort to win back Democrats and independents who had voted for Reagan in 1980. Jackson, hoping to be the first African American to become a major party's nominee for president, promised to unite disaffected white liberals with blacks, Hispanics, displaced white-ethnic blue-collar workers, and all citizens negatively affected by Reagan's policies.

Democrats as a whole believed that voters had become alarmed by Reagan's militarism and Cold War belligerence. Polls revealed that more than 70 percent of Americans supported a nuclear freeze with the Soviet Union. Three-quarters of a million people had demonstrated in New York City on behalf of such disarmament. Reagan's increased production of weapons not only fueled out-of-control federal government budget deficits but also created the possibility of a military confrontation with the Soviets, not to mention fears of the possibility that the conflicts in Central America might turn into a new Vietnam.

Though Mondale lost many states to Hart and Jackson, he finally sewed up the Democratic nomination after the final round of primaries. Hoping to secure the party's liberal base, Mondale gave Jesse Jackson a primetime speaking slot at the Democratic National Convention in San Francisco then boldly chose New York Congresswoman **Geraldine Ferraro** as the first female vice-presidential candidate for a major party in American history. Mondale faced a near-impossible task trying to defeat Reagan in 1984. In addition to the economic turnaround, a new patriotism filled the country, and Reagan rode the wave to electoral victory. When Reagan asked at the close of one of the presidential debates "Are you better off than you were four years ago?" a large number of Americans agreed and voted accordingly. On Election Day, Reagan won in an overwhelming landslide, rolling to victory with 59 percent of the popular vote and taking 49 out of 50 states in the Electoral College for a total of 525 electoral votes to Mondale's 13.

REAGAN'S SECOND TERM DOMESTIC CHALLENGES

Tax and Immigration Reform

During Reagan's second term, Democrats and Republicans in Congress continued to work with him on many important issues dealing with the economy. Congress obliged the president's wishes by passing the 1986 Tax Reform Act to overhaul many aspects of the nation's revenue gathering. The law eliminated some personal deductions and corporate tax loopholes while raising corporate and capital gains taxes. The law reduced the number of tax brackets from fourteen to three, lowered the highest individual tax rate from 50 to 28 percent, and raised the lowest tax rate from 11 to 15 percent.

Another notable achievement for the president and Congress proved to be the **1986 Immigration Reform and Control Act**, which required most employers to verify their employees' legal status, outlawed the practice of knowingly hiring or recruiting illegal aliens, and offered legal status to aliens who had lived in the United States for five consecutive years and had not committed any crimes. Two million immigrants ultimately received legal status under the law's provisions, criticized by many conservative opponents as granting "amnesty" to illegal aliens. An optimistic supporter of the notion that America should remain the land of opportunity for those who wished to come and contribute to improving themselves while building up the nation, the president at one point stated: "I believe in the idea of amnesty for those who have put down roots and lived here, even though some time back they may have entered illegally." Despite the opposition, from many in his party's base, Reagan signed the bipartisan immigration bill into law.

Warning Signs

Despite the improved values of many economic indicators (low inflation, low interest rates, and rising employment), the inherent flaws of Reaganomics began to adversely affect the economy during the president's second term. Sky-high federal deficits grew worse, surging to over $200 billion in 1985 and 1986, and hovered at about $150 billion for the next two years. These huge deficits, coupled with the trade gap (which soared to $170 billion by 1987), made the United States the world's largest debtor nation. During the early 1980s, the wealthy diverted much of their additional windfall from reduced taxes into the stock market, contributing to bloated stock price increases. But later in the decade, despite rising stock prices, investors began to worry that the good times

would not last and continued high federal deficits might contribute to the return of high inflation, and massive sell-offs began to take place. On October 19, 1987 (soon to be known as "Black Monday"), as more orders to sell came in, computer trading programs with preset triggers at specific low price levels began to kick in, leading to a near collapse as the average price of stocks plunged a record 22.6 percent. To help quell panicked investors, President Reagan agreed to meet with congressional leaders to address the public's concerns over the federal deficit, stating that everything would be on the table for consideration (with the notable exception of Social Security) including modest tax increases.

Reagan-era deregulation policies in the savings and loan (S&L) industry also led to a financial crisis that ended up costing taxpayers billions of dollars to bail out depositors. The main cause of the S&L debacle proved to be the allowing of S&Ls to invest more heavily in real estate speculation. As the real estate market experienced a significant downturn, hundreds of S&Ls began to go bankrupt, creating a massive hole in the financial system that the federal government had to fill in order to avert disaster. As the volume of S&L defaults escalated, the Federal Savings and Loan Insurance Corporation (FSLIC, the S&L equivalent of FDIC) became overwhelmed leading the federal government to ultimately bailout the S&Ls in the amount of $100 billion by the mid-1990s. The bailout created a strain on the economy as taxpayers footed the bill for the failures, diverting billions from deficit reduction, tax relief, or spending on social and infrastructure programs, as well as the military.

The AIDS Epidemic

During the 1980s, the United States experienced the first mass outbreak of **AIDS (Acquired Immune Deficiency Syndrome)**—the potentially fatal disease caused by an individual's infection with a specific virus (HIV) that attacks the human immune system. Although originating as a sickness among primates in Africa, the disease crossed over to affect humans during the early twentieth century with the first known death of a person occurring in 1959 (the earliest acknowledged AIDS-related death in the U.S. to date has been traced back to 1969). In June 1981, the Center for Disease Control and Prevention (CDC) began reporting the first deaths linked to AIDS, though two years would pass before a team of French doctors would be able to isolate the HIV virus as the cause. Initially, the condition, which spreads by the direct transmission of bodily fluids, was viewed by most of the public solely as a "gay disease" because of its rapid spread in gay communities via homosexual sex, though as would become evident, anybody having unprotected sex with infected individuals, drug users sharing needles with infected individuals, and those receiving transfusions with infected blood were also highly susceptible populations.

Early on, officials in the Reagan administration adopted a casual attitude toward reports of a growing epidemic, with attitudes among the citizenry not significantly different according to contemporary public policy polls. In December 1985, 51 percent favored quarantining people with AIDS. A July 1987 poll revealed that 57 percent were not opposed to an employer firing an employee solely because they had AIDS. In November 1987, 43 percent of those asked stated that they believed that AIDS was "divine punishment for moral decline," 42 percent genuinely feared accidentally contracting the disease with 20 percent avoiding public restrooms completely due to such worries.

The AIDS epidemic had a particularly devastating impact in the arts and entertainment worlds, adding to the growing notoriety of the disease. Famous 1950s and 1960s screen star Rock Hudson, a Hollywood friend of the Reagans who hid his homosexuality, died of AIDS in 1985. The popular pianist Liberace, long suspected of being gay, succumbed in 1987. A large number of Americans began to take particular notice of AIDS as a national health issue when it began to impact mainstream America. Many were shocked to learn that African-American tennis champion Arthur Ashe revealed that he contracted the disease because of a blood transfusion with tainted blood during open heart surgery in the mid-1980s. Indiana teenager Ryan White gained notoriety in 1986 after being expelled from a public middle school after he became infected with the HIV virus after a blood transfusion in the treatment of his hemophilia. After a successful battle to be allowed to return to school, he became a national spokesperson and fundraiser for AIDS research before dying in 1990.

One of the most shocking revelations came in the early 1990s when NBA superstar Earvin "Magic" Johnson announced he was HIV-positive, the consequence of extensive heterosexual philandering.

The number of recorded deaths from AIDS continued to grow at a tremendous pace during the 1980s, from 234 in 1981 to 5,636 in 1985, and 14,544 by 1989. Though these figures would pale in comparison to the number who would die from the disease during the following decade (peaking at over 50,000 in 1995), by the end of the 1980s it could be noted at the very least that public awareness about the epidemic had greatly increased and calls for extensive AIDS research had become a salient public health and political issue.

Supreme Court Appointments

With his 1981 appointment of Sandra Day O'Connor, the first woman to serve on the Supreme Court, President Reagan had begun to reshape the Supreme Court into a more conservative institution. This trend continued during his second term. In 1986, with the retirement of Warren Burger, he elevated conservative Justice William Rehnquist to the position of Chief Justice. Further, after his choice of Robert Bork a legal reactionary with many political enemies, was rejected by the Senate, the president nominated another arch conservative, Antonin Scalia, to take Burger's vacated space on the bench. Two years later, Reagan made his final appointment when he nominated yet another conservative, Anthony Kennedy, to replace moderate justice Lewis Powell. Over the next two and a half decades, these Reagan appointees would tilt the Supreme Court's orientation to the right on many domestic issues. Though unable to completely overturn most of the Warren Court's landmark decisions, conservatives took solace in the newly refined Court's effectiveness in such endeavors as limiting gun control regulations and abortion access while hampering efforts to limit donations to political campaigns.

FIGHTING THE COLD WAR: BREAK-THROUGH AND SCANDAL

Monumental Changes in the Soviet Union

Changes in the leadership of the Soviet Union (USSR) during Reagan's second term provided fresh opportunities for a thawing in U.S.-Soviet relations. From 1982 to 1985, three separate Soviet leaders had died, leading to the ascension of **Mikhail Gorbachev**, an energetic 54-year-old Russian bureaucrat whose call for internal reforms would soon shake the foundations of the Soviet Union to its core. These developments would lead Reagan, one of America's most fervid anticommunists, to become the defender of open relations with the Soviet Union.

Spurring Gorbachev's actions were his knowledge that the Soviet system was collapsing, prompting the leader and his supporters in the government to seek a rapprochement with the United States. By the time that Gorbachev became the Soviet General Secretary, the decades of high levels of defense spending in Cold War competition with the United States (not just in response to the Reagan-era buildup) had finally taken its toll. The Russians simply could not keep pace with the more dynamic and abundant American economy to provide its

Ronald Reagan and the Challenger Disaster: The President as "Mourner-in-Chief"

One of the unofficial roles of modern presidents is to stand in as the country's "mourner-in-chief" during times of national tragedy. Especially in the television era, the sight of presidents grieving with them after a loss of life due to acts of violence, a natural disaster, or an unforeseen accident resonates strongly with Americans, as it does with the citizens of other nations in similar circumstances.

Perhaps no better example of a president performing this duty can be cited than Ronald Reagan's response to the space shuttle **Challenger** explosion. Americans were shocked on the morning of January 28, 1986, when they witnessed on live television, or soon heard the news, that the **Challenger** had broken up over the Atlantic Ocean 73 seconds after takeoff from Cape Canaveral, Florida, leading to the deaths of its seven crew members. Investigators later concluded that an O-ring seal in one of the rocket boosters failed, allowing hot gas from the rocket's motor to leak out and cause the adjacent external fuel tank to explode. Among the dead was Christa McAuliffe, a New Hampshire school teacher who won NASA's "Teacher in Space" competition to be the first civilian in space.

At the moment of the disaster, Ronald Reagan's mind was on the State of the Union Address that he planned to give later in the evening. As he was preparing remarks for the traditional State of the Union lunch with television network anchors, members of the White House staff rushed in with the breaking news. They turned on a nearby television and watched with horror and disbelief along with the rest of the country. He then convened a meeting with his advisers, and the decision was made to postpone his appearance before Congress. Instead, the president would address the nation via television and radio that night from the Oval Office. The job then fell to his main speech writer, Peggy Noonan, to quickly craft his words as he worked on the proper tone for his delivery. Reagan later recalled that it was one of the hardest days of his presidency.

Though brief (only 648 words delivered in four minutes), Noonan's words were beautifully crafted and the former actor's delivery was impeccable. In a fatherly tone reminiscent of the Fireside Chats of his childhood political hero Franklin Roosevelt, Reagan shared his grief with the nation while vowing to continue the nation's space exploration program, at one point stating: "I want to say something to the schoolchildren of America who were watching the live coverage of the shuttle's take-off. I know it's hard to understand, but sometimes painful things like this happen. It's all part of the process of exploration and discovery. It's all part of taking a chance and expanding man's horizons. The future doesn't belong to the fainthearted; it belongs to the brave. The **Challenger** crew was pulling us into the future, and we'll continue to follow them." He ended with the memorable lines: "We will never forget them, nor the last time we saw them, this morning, as they prepared for their journey and waved goodbye and slipped the surly bonds of earth to touch the face of God." Reflecting back on that day, former Democratic Speaker of the House Tip O'Neill, who earlier that morning had left the White House in a huff because of what he considered Reagan's callousness to the nation's unemployed, later recalled in his autobiography that he had seen the worst and best of the president in just a few hours' time. "It was a trying day for all Americans," he wrote, but in that moment "Ronald Reagan spoke to our highest ideals."

Three days later, the president and first lady Nancy Reagan traveled to Houston for a memorial service. On the plane to Texas, they sat between the widowed wives of **Challenger** commander Francis Scobee and crew member Michael Smith. "I found it difficult to say anything," Reagan recalled in his autobiography. "All we could do was hug the families and try to hold back tears." At the nationally-televised ceremony, he eulogized the crew members by name and continued with one of the themes from his brief Oval Office address: "Sometimes when we reach for the stars, we fall short. But we must pick ourselves up again and press on despite the pain. Our nation is indeed fortunate that we can still draw on immense reservoirs of courage, character, and fortitude; that we're still blessed with heroes like those of the space shuttle **Challenger**."

More so than the actual words that he spoke that day, the sight of Reagan's heartfelt attempt to comfort the families of the deceased was a high point of his presidency. Playing very well on television, it helped to soothe the nation's collective grief.

citizens with a high standard of living while simultaneously producing the most advanced nuclear and conventional military weapons. By the beginning of Reagan's second term, the old Soviet hardliners had either died (such as Gorbachev's predecessors Leonid Brezhnev, Yuri Andropov and Konstantin Chernenko) or had been replaced by a younger generation of leaders like Gorbachev, anxious to reform the USSR before it was too late.

Additionally, the Soviet Union was bleeding profusely from their invasion of Afghanistan, launched in 1979, which in many ways had become their own "Vietnam War." Just as American military proved unable to subdue the Viet Cong, neither could Soviet technological superiority defeat the Afghani insurgents fighting a guerrilla war with arms supplied by the United States and other countries. The Russians were not only losing a very costly war but also suffering from a multitude of deprivations at home as consumers waited in lines for hours for basic necessities such as meat, bread, and household supplies. While the government spent the equivalent of billions of American dollars on new rockets, planes and tanks in a failing effort to control Afghanistan, the majority of Soviet citizens believed that the conflict was a horrible waste of lives and resources. Gorbachev agreed and within a year of becoming premier, he withdrew all Soviet troops from Afghanistan, which later fell under the control of the Taliban, an Islamic fundamentalist faction that would create one of the most oppressive regimes in the world.

Gorbachev announced a commitment to the reform policies of ***perestroika*** ("restructuring" of the country's economic and political system) and ***glasnost*** ("openness," including greater freedom of speech and the press) while simultaneously approving massive cuts in Soviet arms production and a new policy of cooperation with the United States and its western allies.

The question now became how the Reagan administration would react to these startling developments. American conservatives were especially suspicious of Gorbachev's overtures. Radio host Rush Limbaugh warned against Americans falling for what he saw as a grand Russian ruse. The president was also initially skeptical, challenging Gorbachev to show with actions rather than words that events would be different on his watch. In a speech before the Brandenburg Gate section of the Berlin Wall, the president famously demanded before a huge crowd:

> We welcome change and openness; for we believe that freedom and security go together, that the advance of human liberty can only strengthen the cause of world peace. There is one sign the Soviets can make that would be unmistakable, that would

President Reagan and Vice President Bush meet with Soviet General Secretary Gorbachev on Governor's Island, New York. December 7, 1988
Photo credit: Reagan Presidential Library

advance dramatically the cause of freedom and peace. General Secretary Gorbachev, if you seek peace, if you seek prosperity for the Soviet Union and Eastern Europe, if you seek liberalization, come here to this gate. Mr. Gorbachev, open this gate. Mr. Gorbachev, tear down this wall!

Fortunately, Ronald Reagan rose to the occasion, having four summits with Gorbachev in two and a half years. In 1987, the two leaders signed the Intermediate Nuclear Forces Treaty (INF), providing for the removal of 2500 U.S. and Soviet missiles from Europe and provided for the destruction of all medium-range nuclear missiles, eliminating an entire class of existing nuclear weapons for the first time. The deal led to Reagan's historic visit to Moscow in May 1988, where the two leaders strolled and chatted in Red Square in front of the Kremlin. Historic in themselves, the INF Treaty and Reagan's trip to Moscow proved a mere prelude to more dramatic events to come. They marked, in fact, nothing less than the beginning of the end of the Cold War.

The Iran-Contra Affair

The most devastating blow to Reagan's credibility and popularity during his second term, the **Iran-Contra Af-**

When the Wall Came Tumbling Down

The Berlin Wall was in many ways the perfect symbol of the Cold War. The almost 100-mile concrete barrier wholly separated West Berlin—an official portion of West Germany—from the rest of communist East Germany. Although the most notable and infamous portion of the barricade was the part that directly divided East and West Berlin, the wall in fact encircled West Berlin, which made it one of the most isolated cities in the world. The end of World War II and the beginning of the Cold War had divided the city, but from 1948 through the summer of 1961, there was no "wall," although through the 1950s the communist government in East Germany heavily guarded and controlled the border between East and West. Despite such tactics, more than three million East Germans permanently left the nation and migrated to West Germany, with the majority of those taking up residence in West Berlin. To close this "hole," at the insistence of Soviet Premier Nikita Khrushchev, East German officials in August 1961 made the decision to completely close the border. Construction began in the middle of the night on August 12, 1961, and by the end of August 13 a rudimentary wall existed and the border was closed. Construction continued throughout the next year on the huge concrete barrier that the world would call "The Berlin Wall," standing as the premier symbol of division in Europe. Twenty-eight years later, no one could anticipate the wall vanishing overnight, but that is what practically happened.

The fall of the Berlin Wall was one of those historical events that seemingly happens quickly, but more accurately occurred through a sequence of interrelated circumstances that no one at the time could anticipate. The pressure to open the wall began not in East Germany, but in Hungary in June 1989. In an effort to quell unrest among its people, the Hungarian government announced a relaxation of its border fortifications with neighboring Austria. Almost immediately, in addition to Hungarians, almost 15,000 East German tourists began to pour over the border to make their way into West Germany to clamor for residency and asylum.

The East German government responded as most expected they would by ending any further travel to Hungary. But, they could not end the idea of migration, and a movement rippled in September 1989 throughout East Germany. Protesters began to demand access to the West, actions that East Germans came to call "The Peaceful Revolution." By the fall of 1989, the movement had swelled to almost half a million people agitating daily. The message had also changed. Now, instead of demanding a way to leave, people pleaded for regime change. The unexpected then happened: hardliner Erich Honecker, a man who had led East Germany since 1971, abruptly resigned on October 18, 1989.

Egon Krenz then took over, but the mass migration out of East Germany continued, now through Czechoslovakia and into Hungary, or by directly applying for asylum at the West German Embassy in Prague. Krenz tacitly allowed this to continue, but the East German Politburo knew they had a crisis on their hands. The ruling body agreed to allow refugees to exit directly through West Germany, but they would have to apply for passports and be given permission to do so. This method was thought to be orderly, and restricted, and they hoped this would ease the pressure, but chance entered into the equation.

Krenz and the Politburo gave instructions to spokesman Gunter Schabowski to announce the new policy. Schabowski had been briefed on what to say, but he was vague about the procedure. He read the change in policy and immediately reporters and anyone watching the proceedings began to buzz. It sounded as if the Politburo had just announced that East Germans could now travel, unhindered, to West Berlin. When he was asked by reporters when the new policy would begin, he said, "Immediately, straight away," which was not what the drafters had intended.

His words would have consequence as tens of thousands of East Germans descended on the Berlin Wall. The border guards had not been briefed and they had no idea what to do. Confusion reigned and eventually the gates opened. It was the beginning of the end of the Berlin Wall, the symbol of the Cold War divide in Europe. The wall came down completely by December 1989, and along with it all the communist governments of Eastern Europe. The Soviet Union lingered for a while longer, but by 1991, it ended as well, and so too, the Cold War.

fair, arose from his administration's effort to secure the release of seven American hostages in Beirut, Lebanon, while also wishing to control events in Latin America. Late in 1986, a Beirut newspaper reported disturbing news that a year earlier the United States had shipped, via Israel, 500 antitank missiles to the Iranian government in a series of arms deals in exchange for efforts on its behalf to work with pro-Iranian groups in Lebanon, such as Hezbollah, to free the hostages held there. While reluctantly acknowledging that the secret arms sale to Iran had taken place, the president initially denied adamantly that the United States negotiated with terrorists. Reagan had earlier accepted the advice of National Security Advisors Robert McFarlane and John Poindexter that selling defensive weapons to Iran might boost the standing of the U.S. among moderates within the Iranian government leading to the release of the hostages and more favorable relations between the two governments in the future. Under orders from McFarlane and Poindexter, a National Security Council (NSC) aide, Marine Lieutenant Colonel Oliver North, began to work on the logistics of the arms sales. Reagan ultimately admitted to the sales, claiming the administration had the best of intentions and that he had convinced himself that the arms deals were not directly connected to the payment of ransom for the release of the hostages, although the evidence concerning how the transactions were implemented pointed in that direction.

As remarkable as word of the Iranian arms sales had been, more explosive news emerged when a CIA cargo plane crashed in Nicaragua, revealing that the Reagan administration was secretly aiding the Contras *in direct violation* of the Boland Amendment. Soon the pubic would learn that Colonel North had masterminded a scheme to fund the Contras through the profits received from the Iranian arms sales. In November 1986, Reagan appointed the Tower Commission headed by former Republican Senator from Texas John Tower to investigate the growing scandal. Reagan testified before the commission, whose report, issued in February 1987, found no evidence of direct presidential knowledge of the diversion of funds from the Iranian arms sales to the Contras, but harshly criticized Reagan's failure to monitor the actions of his national security team and his detachment from day-to-day operations at the White House.

In May 1987, a joint congressional investigative committee opened televised hearings on the scandal. Perhaps most startling were the attitudes of Poindexter, North, and others who believed that they could work beyond the control of laws and institutions in pursuit of an agenda for the good of the country. During the hearings, Poindexter declared that he had the right to act on his own authority, without going to Reagan, because he knew what the

Lt. Col. Oliver North takes the oath before the House Foreign Affairs Committee. His vigorous defense of his actions in the Iran-Contra affair made him a cult hero to many on the political right, eventually leading to his unsuccessful campaign for the U.S. Senate in 1994.

president wanted. He stated his belief that it was more important not to inform the president of the details of the covert operations in order to guarantee Reagan "plausible deniability."

Even more outrageous was Oliver North's testimony, where the lieutenant colonel admitted that he, Poindexter, and CIA Director William Casey (who died of a cerebral hemorrhage the day before he was to testify) had planned from the beginning for the arms sales' funds to go to the *Contras*. With self-righteousness, North's attitude reflected obvious disdain toward the committee members for seeming to impugn his patriotism, which he believed his every action in the operation reflected. In 1989, after his indictment by a special prosecutor, North was ultimately convicted of obstructing a congressional inquiry as well as destroying and falsifying official government documents. The conviction was later reversed on the technicality that some testimony used against him had been given under a promise of immunity. Many Americans initially praised North as a national hero, more impressed by his expressions of patriotism than by his reckless disregard for the law. First Lady Nancy Reagan, however, felt otherwise. Years later, in 1994, she would get back at the man who damaged the credibility of her husband's administration by repeatedly speaking out against North when he ran for a U.S. Senate seat in Virginia, a race he eventually lost by a narrow margin.

Although less damaging than Watergate, the Iran-Contra scandal dogged the Reagan administration's final years as a gross abuse of executive power in a zealous campaign to overthrow a Latin American government that the White House found objectionable. Despite the magnitude of the crisis and the revelations about the inner workings within the White House and Reagan's managerial flaws, the president's approval rating, while weakened, remained relatively high.

George H.W. Bush Succeeds Reagan

As the time for the election of 1988 approached, Vice President **George H.W. Bush** was the clear favorite to receive the Republican nomination for president. Although not a conservative ideologue, Bush's identification with Reagan proved to be enough to overcome light opposition from conservatives within the party's ranks to become the Republican standard bearer. Upon accepting his party's nomination at the Republican national convention, Bush promised to carry forward the "Reagan Revolution" and placated his party's conservatives in two major ways: by repeating a popular campaign pledge during his acceptance speech—"Read my lips: no new taxes"—and by selecting a favorite among social conservatives to be his running mate, the bland junior senator from Indiana, Dan Quayle.

The Democrats had far more serious problems to overcome if they hoped to recapture the White House. First, and probably most important, was the loss of many of their party's blue collar, industrial, ethnic, Catholic workers—the "Reagan Democrats"—who had gravitated to the Republican Party in 1984. Also, by 1988, the transformation of the white South into a Republican stronghold in presidential elections was almost complete. Hurting the party was the loss to a sex scandal of its leading contender Senator Gary Hart of Colorado. The Reverend Jesse Jackson once again sought the nomination and for a while boasted the most delegates. To many pundits' surprise, however, a relative dark horse—Michael Dukakis, a dry, serious governor of Massachusetts—ended up the winner, owing his victory to a superior campaign organization. To balance his ticket in hopes of winning back at least some of the southern states, Dukakis chose a conservative Democrat, Texas Senator Lloyd Bentsen, to be his running mate.

In the race that followed both Bush and Dukakis at best paid only lip service to the profound issues facing the country, favoring TV-oriented photo opportunities and sound bites. Bush visited flag factories and military plants. Meanwhile, in one of the more ridiculous-looking staged press events, Dukakis tried to exude toughness on defense by posing in a moving tank but with only his head popping out of one of the vehicle's portals. Commentators noted that he looked like a jack-in-the-box.

Bush tried his best to identify himself with Reagan's achievements, while keeping his distance from the Iran-Contra Affair, which he repeatedly told the public, he was completely "out of the loop." Emphasizing peace and prosperity, he pointed to better Soviet relations, low inflation, and the 14 million new jobs created during the 1980s. In response, Dukakis emphasized his accomplishments as governor and downplayed ideology in an effort to bring back the Reagan Democrats. During the campaign, however, style often trumped substance. Dukakis often appeared dispassionate and rather lackluster, most notably when CNN anchor Bernard King famously opened the first presidential debate by asking the governor if he would favor the death penalty if someone raped and murdered his wife. His cool, reasoned response in the negative failed to resonate well with many voters. Meanwhile, many liberals chafed at Dukakis's centrist position on many issues and were especially upset by his less than enthusiastic support for social welfare legislation.

The Dukakis team did not have an effective response to the Bush campaign's running narrative that portrayed the governor as being weak on every issue that appeared to be important to voters, attacking him at his supposed strength as an effective governor. To highlight reports of water pollution in Massachusetts waterways, Bush snuck in a response line to a Dukakis answer during one of the presidential debates: "That answer was as clear as Boston Harbor." More effectively, the Bush campaign's attack ads on television painted the Democratic nominee as a cold, unpatriotic, anti-religious intellectual whose supposed opposition to the death penalty revealed an overall softness on crime while governor that was dangerous to public safety. One often-played ad, which showed a revolving door that allowed arriving inmates to quickly leave prison, implied that Dukakis pampered criminals and endangered law-abiding citizens. The most well known attempt to depict the governor as weak on crime, with latent racial undertones, proved to be an ad that focused on Willie Horton, a black inmate from Massachusetts who had been convicted of rape and assault. While on a weekend furlough (a state program to relieve prison overcrowding that Dukakis continued as governor), Horton had terrorized a white couple, raping the woman. Bush campaign strategist Lee Atwater boasted, "If I can make Willie Horton a household name, we'll win the election." On November 8, 1988, Bush carried forty states, giving him 426 electoral votes, while garnering 54 percent of the popular vote. Dukakis prevailed in only ten states plus the District of Columbia for 112 electoral votes. Although losing the White House once again, the Democrats retained control of both houses of Congress.

FOREIGN AFFAIRS UNDER GEORGE H.W. BUSH

George H.W. Bush's strength, experience, and clearly his interest lay with foreign policy rather than domestic politics. His years as a diplomat serving as a U.S. ambassador to China and the United Nations, as well as his time spent as America's chief intelligence officer when he directed the CIA, gave him a confidence that he could lead the United States during a time of epic change in Europe, Latin America, and the Middle East. Although criticized by liberals for being too aggressive and by the more hawkish hard-right members of his party for not being more aggressive on specific issues, the majority of Americans tended to agree with his stated foreign policy goals.

Bush and Latin America

During the Bush years, stability returned to Central America through a combination of brokered agreements, democratic elections, and, in one instance, an armed military Intervention by the United States. In Nicaragua, Bush proved to be much less of an evangelical anticommunist than his predecessor as the Reagan administration's failed policy of financing the *Contras'* war

against the Sandinistas was abandoned. By the time Bush became president, the Sandinista government was already in trouble. With its most important patron, the Soviet Union, increasingly focusing on its own internal crises, only Fidel Castro's government in Cuba could provide aid to sustain the Marxist regime. Bush's willingness to reach an accord with the Sandinistas paid off in that country's 1990 elections, which saw a multiparty coalition of anti-Sandinistas emerge victorious.

Open guerrilla warfare continued in Colombia, as government forces with American economic and military hardware sought to smash the powerful drug lords and their well-armed militias whose cocaine and heroin flowed into the United States with abandon. The Bush administration determined to stop the trade by getting rid of the individuals who served as the conduits. In December 1989, concern over the drug traffic led to a U.S. invasion of Panama to capture its dictator, General **Manuel Noriega**, who for years had been on the CIA's payroll while supporting various anti-communist efforts in the region, including aid to the Contras. (Critics later charged that Bush's true purpose in removing Noriega from power was the leader's knowledge of the former vice-president's supposed larger role in the Iran-Contra Affair.) Intelligence reports concluded that Noriega had been accepting bribes and kickbacks from the cartels to

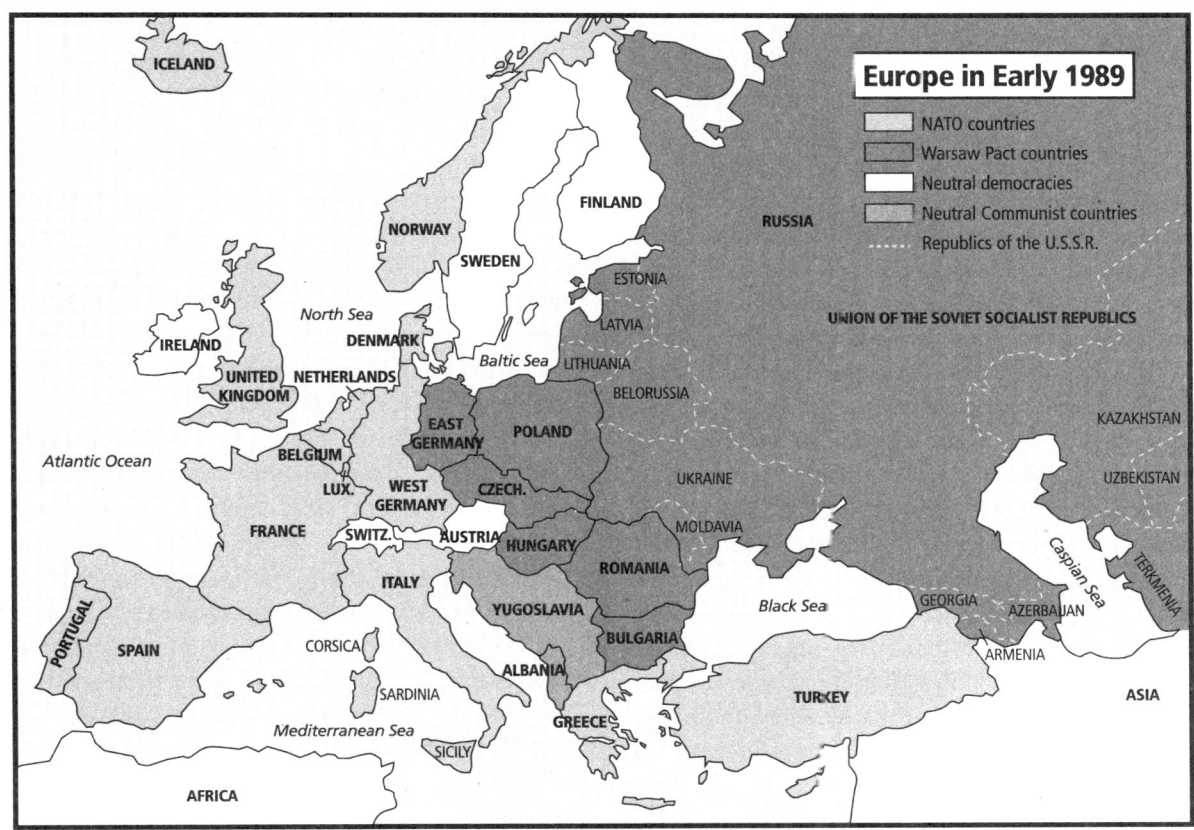

Map 30.2 Europe in Early 1989

permit drugs to pass through Panama on their way to the United States. Noriega had earlier annulled the results of an election in which an opposition candidate was victorious, leading Bush to worry about the turnover of the Panama Canal region in 1999 if someone like Noriega controlled Panama. After some of Noriega's men attacked a pair of American military officers in Panama City, killing one of them, Bush ordered over 25,000 paratroopers and Navy SEALs to secure the Canal Zone, take over Panama City, and capture Noriega. Brought to the United States for trial, Noriega was convicted of drug trafficking and given a 40-year sentence in 1992. After being extradited to France in 2007, he was found guilty of money laundering and murder charges before being returned to his native Panama to face more charges and remains held in a Panamanian prison.

The Cold War Ends

The American government's relations with China became increasingly problematic after that nation's communist government violently cracked down on a large group of pro-democracy demonstrators in Beijing during the summer of 1989. Tens of thousands of protestors consisting of college students, intellectuals, and other sympathizers inspired by changes taking place in the Soviet bloc and demanding freedom of speech, freedom of the press, and other reforms began occupying Tiananmen Square, much to the chagrin of government officials. When the occupiers refused to leave, troops cleared the large plaza by force on the night of June 4, killing and wounding thousands. International television news agencies covered the protest and subsequent massacre, leading to global condemnation of the Chinese government. The following day, foreign video crews and an Associated Press cameraman documented a lone man holding grocery bags blocking a tank column leaving the square by refusing to move out of its way. The video footage and photographs of the defiant "Tank Man" were soon seen around the world and made a lasting impression, becoming one of the most iconic images of the twentieth century. The Bush administration was especially embarrassed by this crisis. The president had recently negotiated a series of trade agreements with China, including the extension of "most favored nation" status allowing Chinese goods to enter U.S. markets after paying minimal or no tariffs. After lodging formal diplomatic protests condemning the violence, however, only a few symbolic gestures in sympathy with the protesters took place as Bush resisted calls for economic sanctions.

In contrast to Sino-American relations, major breakthroughs were happening within the Soviet bloc—developments inconceivable to most Westerners and largely unforeseen by expert analysts in the U.S. government. On the heels of a general crisis in the Soviet economy, the collapse of Russian power in Eastern Europe proceeded rapidly during Bush's presidency following a December 1988 announcement from Mikhail Gorbachev that the Soviet Union would no longer intervene in the domestic affairs of Eastern European countries to stymie political opposition. Soon thereafter, the Solidarity Party won free elections in Poland, leading to the establishment of a noncommunist government and a capitalist economy, followed soon by similar movements in Hungary, Bulgaria, and Czechoslovakia. In November 1989, workers rose up without interference to begin dismantling the Berlin Wall—a symbolic move that led the way to the end of communist government in East Germany and the reunification of Germany for the first time since the fall of the Nazis. The Baltic states of Estonia, Latvia, and Lithuania, forcibly annexed by the Soviet Union prior to World War II, also declared their independence. In Romania, regime opponents rose up and overthrew the harsh Stalinist dictator, Nicolae Ceausescu, who had brutally oppressed his people for decades, leading to his arrest and execution.

As these events transpired, Gorbachev was feeling pressure from reformers to move Russia more quickly toward greater democracy and privatization of the economy, as well as from hardline communists to suppress dissent and maintain the status quo. Bush cautiously bolstered Gorbachev from a safe distance, publicly applauding his every effort to change Russia. Through a series of summits, the two leaders arrived at stunning breakthroughs on arms control treaties that promised to reduce dramatically each country's nuclear arsenals. Bush's diplomacy was further tested in August 1990 when the irreconcilables within the Soviet government attempted a military coup in a last-ditch effort to retain power. The move was surprisingly thwarted by a spontaneous outpouring of support from citizens who rallied behind their nationalist leader Boris Yeltsin, who had recently won election as the president of Russia, the leading nation within the Soviet Union. Though unsuccessful, the attempted takeover greatly damaged Gorbachev's standing while bolstering popular support for Yeltsin and the further democratization of Russian society. Within weeks of the coup's defeat, the Soviet Union disappeared, dissolving into 15 different nation states loosely associated in a weak federation known as the Commonwealth of Independent States. Bush extended overtures to ally with Yeltsin, who traveled to Washington to request American economic support to sustain the movement toward democracy and a market economy.

While the end of communism took place relatively bloodlessly in the Soviet Union and most of Eastern Europe, this was not the case in Yugoslavia, where the nation's breakup was followed by years of ethnic violence. Since the end of World War II, the multi-ethnic and multi-religious nation consisting of Serbs, Croats, Slovenes, Albanians, Macedonians, and other ethnic groups that had been held together under the rule of Marshal Josip Tito—a communist who had led the wartime partisan resistance against the Nazis. Refusing to join the Warsaw Pact or otherwise be formally aligned with the Soviet Union, Tito charted an independent communist course until his death in 1980. By 1994, after sporadic fighting, Yugoslavia had disintegrated as Croatia, Slovenia, and Macedonia. Bosnia and Herzegovina had asserted their independence from the central government, which by then had been reduced to the old provinces of Serbia and Montenegro. Before long, violence broke out between different ethnic groups in the various former provinces, especially Bosnia and Herzegovina, where Bosnian Serbs began to assert control by undertaking an ethnic cleansing campaign against local Muslim residents that would receive world attention, leading to a military intervention by NATO during the presidency of Bush's successor, Bill Clinton.

The Gulf War

Just as events were portending an easing of tensions with Russia, the Middle East became a major concern for the United States and its western allies. More specifically, Iraq's dictator, **Saddam Hussein**, had become a general menace to many countries in the region, not to mention a ruthless leader within his own nation. A secular ruler and an ethnic Sunni, he clamped down on religious fundamentalists, especially members of the Shiite majority, as well as ethnic Kurds living in northern Iraq who desired their own government. Tens of thousands died under his oppressive regime, including 5,000 Kurdish civilians in the village of Halabja who died in March 1988 after a chemical weapons attack. Previously, the Reagan administration had been on cordial terms with Hussein, seeing his regime as a bulwark against both the expansion of communism from the Soviet Union located just to Iraq's northern border and Islamic fundamentalism from Iran lying just to Iraq's east. During the 1980-1988 Iran-Iraq War, begun when Iraq attacked Iran, the United States had favored Iraq and even assisted Hussein's military with hardware and satellite-based intelligence.

The Bush administration's posture towards Hussein radically changed when Iraqi forces moved southward in early August 1990 to invade the neighboring oil kingdom of Kuwait, one of the Western industrial powers' most important suppliers of oil. Though Bush placed his op-position in stark terms as an act of unprovoked aggression by a Hitler-like madman that would not be allowed to stand, the importance of Kuwaiti oil to the economies of the United States, Western Europe, and Japan cannot be ignored. Bush administration officials also feared the Kuwaiti oil wealth would further bolster Hussein's military capabilities, making him a further destabilizing force in the region. Hussein's public rants about destroying Israel could also never be tolerated by any American president.

When Hussein refused all demands to withdraw his forces, claiming that he was reclaiming an area that historically belonged to Iraq, Bush began to build a coalition in the United Nations, especially with European and Middle Eastern nations, for one clear goal—to drive Iraq from Kuwait; by economic pressure if possible, but by force of arms if necessary. In his call to arms, Bush received the support of Congress, the United Nations, and, most importantly, a majority of the American people. If the economic sanctions imposed by the United Nations failed to remove the Iraqis from Kuwait, Bush was ready to deploy more than 500,000 American troops to Saudi Arabia to prepare for an offensive to drive the Iraqis out of Kuwait. The United Nations mandated that Hussein withdraw from Iraq by January 15, 1991. On January 12, on divided votes, the Senate and the House endorsed military action against Iraq to commence four days later. Most Democrats voted against war, favoring continued economic sanctions. The air war portion of what the U.S. military named **Operation Desert Storm** began on January 16 as planned. For six weeks, B-52 and F-16 bombers pounded Iraqi troops, supply depots, and command targets in Baghdad, Iraq's capital.

In retaliation, Saddam fired Soviet-made Scud missiles against Tel Aviv and other Israeli cities, as well as against U.S. positions in Saudi Arabia. Americans watched transfixed as CNN and the major television news networks showed U.S. Patriot missiles streaking off to intercept incoming Scuds. (Most of the Scuds, and the Patriot interceptors, failed to reach their intended targets.) As portrayed on television, the war seemed to resemble a glorified video game. With CNN reporters broadcasting live from a Baghdad hotel room, the only fighting the American public saw on their television screens were the bombs exploding near their targets in Baghdad, as well as Pentagon news briefings in which the commanders displayed film footage taken from their aircraft giving the impression that every missile and bomb launched precisely hit their intended targets.

On February 23, 500,000 U.S. troops and 200,000 coalition soldiers under the command of U.S. General H. Norman Schwarzkopf moved across the desert from Saudi Arabia into southern Iraq and Kuwait. Within four days, Kuwait was liberated as Iraqi forces were crushed, losing between 75,000 and 100,000 men. Knowing they could not defeat the overwhelming military might of the United States, large numbers of Iraqi soldiers surrendered while others fled, though not before setting Kuwait's oil fields ablaze. U.S. casualties numbered 148 dead, including 35 killed by "friendly fire" and 467 wounded. With resistance quickly destroyed, Bush declared a cease-fire, resisting pressure from Schwarzkopf and other generals to push on into Iraq and remove Saddam Hussein, Bush refrained from such action. The purpose of the action had always been clear, as expressed in the United Nations mandate and the congressional resolution authorizing military intervention--the removal of Iraq's forces from Kuwait--and that goal had been achieved.

Despite some sporadic, half-hearted campus protests, the war enjoyed broad public support. After the victory celebrations, however, the outcome seemed less than decisive. Though weakened, Saddam Hussein still held power. . Bans on Iraqi imports of military goods as well as Iraqi exports of oil was imposed, in addition to the creation of "no-fly zones" over the Kurdish region in the north and the Shiite-majority area of southern Iraq. Nevertheless, these provisions did not stop Hussein's reconstituted army in the spring of 1991 from brutally suppressing uprisings by the Kurds and Shiites. Despite the stunning coalition military victory in the 1990 Gulf War, the Iraqi leader would remain a thorn in the side for the United States and its U.N. allies for years to come.

BUSH AND DOMESTIC POLITICS

Despite his foreign policy triumphs, domestic politics would prove to be George H.W. Bush's undoing, ultimately preventing him from serving a second term as president. During his acceptance speech at the 1988 Republican national convention, Bush called on Americans to donate their time and energy to help each other and their communities through volunteer work, shining like "a thousand points of light in a broad and peaceful sky." In asking America to become a "kinder, gentler nation," he seemed to be calling for a break from the harsh social policies of the Reagan years. Yet, conservative Republicans were just the constituency whose support he needed to secure if he was to win reelection.

Bush's Domestic Balancing Act

Though a supporter of conservative positions on many issues, Bush's politics reflected more of the attitudes and beliefs of the traditional Establishment wing of the Republican Party. Much to the dismay of his party's more doctrinaire conservatives, he did not overly pursue their interests. Instead, Bush chose to work with the Democratic-controlled Congress on several issues, signing into law the Americans with Disabilities Act in 1990—which prohibits discrimination on the basis of physical or mental disabilities in numerous aspects of daily life ranging from employment opportunities to public accommodations. That same year, he approved amendments strengthening

President Bush meets with the Emir of Kuwait, Jabir al-Ahmad al-Jabir al-Sabah to discuss developments September 28, 1990, after Iraqi dictator Saddam Hussein's troops invaded the Gulf State nation. Credit: George Bush Presidential Library

President Bush signing the Americans with Disabilities Act in the Rose Garden of the White House. July 26, 1990. Photo credit: George Bush Presidential Library

Environmental Protection Agency enforcement of the Clean Air Act by tightening regulations concerning air pollution. Bush also signed into law the Immigration Act of 1990, which led to a 40 percent increase in the number of legal immigrants allowed into the country.

In the afterglow of **Operation Desert Storm**, the president's popularity had reached an all-time high, reflected in a 91 percent approval rating. The lightning victory seemed to vindicate him, with many pundits suggesting that anyone who had opposed the war faced political extinction. Bush's monumental public acclaim in the early summer of 1991 made many prospective Democratic candidates reluctant to seek their party's nomination. Many potential candidates decided to give a pass on the 1992 campaign, assuming no one could even remotely challenge Bush. Such trepidation was based on a short-term perspective. An economic recession, caused by the final fallout of supply-side economics, inevitably would impact Bush's reelection chances, an ironic development given that it was George Bush who had labeled such policies as "voodoo economics" during his 1980 Republican primary campaign against Reagan.

Though it was Bush's good fortune to preside over the final dissolution of the Cold War and the unchallenged rise of the United States to military supremacy in the world, it was his greater misfortune to inherit an economy wasting away under bloated deficits (the national debt had tripled from $1 trillion in 1981 to $3 trillion by 1990). Bush's fiscal conservative instincts kicked in, leading him to enter negotiations with congressional Democrats on ways to reduce the deficit. He eventually approved a deficit reduction package that promised to gradually lower the government's liabilities by $500 billion but included a tax hike that would raise the top marginal tax rates from 28 to 31.5 percent, as well as increased taxes on the purchases of alcohol, tobacco products, automobiles, and yachts. In breaking his "read my lips, no new taxes" campaign pledge, the president raised the ire of diehard conservatives within his party and set himself up to sail in rough political waters in the future. By the fall of 1991, the inability of the economy to turn around caused Bush's approval ratings to drop below 50 percent. By January 1992, the unemployment rate was over 7 percent. New jobs that were created were largely concentrated in the low-paying service industries. Yet, instead of sounding the alarm, Bush administration officials responded with indifference, even complacency. The president had not entered the White House with a solid economic plan, eschewing what he called "the vision thing." Now, rather than devising new approaches, the president's advisors recommended standing pat.

The Bush administration thus ignored the change in the people's attitudes toward politics. Eight months after the Gulf War, fewer than 40 percent of the American people felt comfortable with the way that the country was moving. There seemed to be major problems for which no one in authority was proposing solutions, issues that for too long had been swept under the rug, first under Reagan and now with Bush. Encapsulating this frustration, anger, despair, and disillusionment, the **Los Angeles riots** exploded in April 1992 after a jury acquitted local police officers who had been shown on videotape beating black motorist Rodney King after a police chase even though King was not resisting arrest. For several days, the release of anger and pent-up frustration raged, leaving some forty persons dead and millions in dollars in property damage.

President Bush signs the Clean Air Act as William Reilly, administrator of the Environmental Protection Agency, and Energy Secretary James D. Watkin look on in the Rose Garden of the White House, July 21, 1989. Photo credit: George Bush Presidential Library

The 1992 Election

The recession following the Gulf War, along with Bush's broken tax pledge, lessened the president's chances for reelection in 1992. At first, only a couple of Democrats sought to challenge Bush, but other candidates entered the fray as the economy continued to weaken. Of the group, the 45-year-old governor of Arkansas, **William Jefferson Clinton**, emerged as the strongest candidate. Born after World War II ended, Clinton aspired to be the first Baby Boomer to win the presidency and had been working toward that goal most of his adult life. His father had died in an automobile accident before he was born, leading him to be raised by his mother and an abusive alcoholic stepfather. Focusing on his studies and a growing interest in politics kindled by a youthful idolization of John F. Kennedy, he left Arkansas to attend Georgetown University, won a Rhodes scholarship to Oxford, and then attended Yale Law School where he met his future wife Hillary Rodham. Returning to Arkansas, Clinton won election as state attorney general before winning his race for governor in 1978 at the age of 32. He lost his reelection bid in 1980 but went on to win five consecutive two-year terms. Claiming to be a "New Democrat," Clinton pushed a centrist agenda designed to establish better relations with the business community and the more upwardly mobile and affluent members of the middle class by promoting a new agenda stressing more fiscal restraint and tougher penalties for criminals while still valuing many social justice issues important to most liberals.

Unfortunately for Clinton, elements from his past would surface and threaten to derail his campaign. Reports of his alleged Vietnam War draft-dodging, involvement in antiwar protests while at Oxford, and youthful marijuana use dogged him. He attempted to counter these charges by explaining his principled opposition to the now-unpopular war in Vietnam and that the one time he was handed a marijuana joint he tried it but "didn't inhale," and never tried the drug again. Such political dancing seemed to deflate the matter but helped him to earn the moniker "Slick Willy" from his opponents. More troubling to Clinton's campaign were allegations of past sexual misconduct. Clinton, his politically savvy wife Hillary, and his campaign staffers knew such questions would arise and had prepared to address the inevitable, ultimately convincing the public that such indiscretions, such as claims from a woman named Gennifer Flowers that she had a 12-year affair with the candidate, were behind him. (Clinton later stated it was a one-time en-

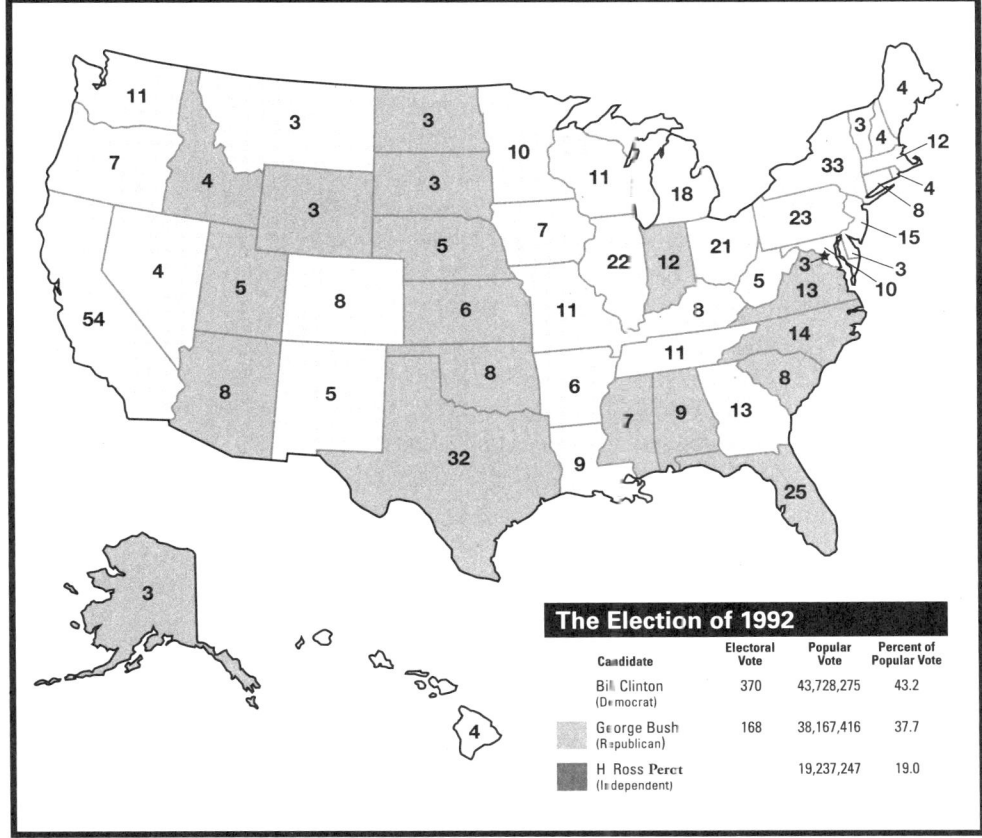

Map 30.3 The Election of 1992

The Election of 1992

Candidate	Electoral Vote	Popular Vote	Percent of Popular Vote
Bill Clinton (Democrat)	370	43,728,275	43.2
George Bush (Republican)	168	38,167,416	37.7
H. Ross Perot (Independent)		19,237,247	19.0

counter). Appearing on CBS' 60 Minutes, the Clintons confessed to past marital problems, but told viewers that those private issues had been worked out. To his campaign's great relief, Bill and Hillary's approach worked, as many voters forgave the candidate for his wandering. After a second-place finish in the New Hampshire primary, the Clinton campaign rolled, winning one primary victory after another. By the end of Super Tuesday in March 1992, the governor had wrapped up the Democratic nomination. Clinton further amplified his image as a moderate by choosing Tennessee Senator Al Gore, Jr., another politician in the New Democrat mold, to be his running mate. Clinton believed that by selecting Gore, he could win more southern states, essential to a Democratic victory.

Adding a further element of unpredictability to the campaign, Texas billionaire **H. Ross Perot**, announced that he would join the race as a third-party candidate. With a folksy Texas twang, Perot proved to have great populist appeal with uncomplicated, straight-talking views on every issue. He claimed to speak for Americans sick of big government and tired of both major parties' broken promises. The billionaire essentially articulated a libertarian political philosophy that was fiscally conservative and socially liberal, seeking less government involvement in most phases of people's lives. High on his priority list was balancing the federal budget by reducing government spending. Perot also heavily criticized President Bush for his support of the recently negotiated North American Free Trade Agreement (NAFTA), which, if passed by Congress, would establish a free-trade zone between the United States, Canada, and Mexico. A "giant sucking sound," he famously predicted, would be produced by American manufacturing jobs rapidly leaving the country as businesses quickly relocated to lower-wage Mexico.

The rapid unraveling of George H.W. Bush's presidency helped both Clinton and Perot gain growing support. Not only were real incomes declining for the lower middle-class and working class, but also Republicans around the country began expressing dissatisfaction with the administration's inertia. Compounding Bush's economic woes was the reemergence of a revitalized Republican Far Right led by individuals such as Patrick Buchanan. Such conservatives never saw Bush as one of them, and they constantly railed against him for eventually breaking his "Read my lips, no new taxes" pledge. The president tried to make peace with the right wing of his party by unwisely turning over the opening night of the Republican national convention in Houston, Texas, to Buchanan and the equally shrill fundamentalist minister Pat Robertson. Both men called for a cultural and religious war to cleanse the nation of feminists, homosexuals, pro-choice advocates, and other alleged deviants—all of whom, they claimed, were undermining the country's traditional moral underpinnings. To both men, diversity and multiculturalism, if not checked soon, would cause the end of an America they believed was meant to be a Judeo-Christian nation. Despite the combativeness displayed at the Republican convention, Bush continued to believe he could win. By invoking the pride of Operation Desert Storm, he would be returned to office. Reality set in, however, by mid-summer as Bush trailed Clinton in some polls by 15 points. Despite Perot's appeal with many devout followers, he proved to have a rather quirky personality. As his polls numbers began to his support dropping below 20 percent in national polls, Perot fired some campaign advisers as he resisted their efforts to widen the candidate's appeal by being more specific when talking in public about non-economic issues. He also appeared paranoid that Republican Party operatives were infiltrating his campaign. At one point, he even quit the campaign, citing his desire to prevent Republican dirty tricksters from smearing his daughter's reputation on the eve of her wedding. Though he returned to the race in time for the presidential debates after qualifying to appear on the ballot in all 50 states, Perot had no chance to win by that point.

Ultimately, Bush failed to resonate with the voters that Reagan had so skillfully cultivated, seeming unable to shed his blue-blood persona and image to connect with the average person. During a photo opportunity at an exhibit hall during a National Grocers Association convention, he famously stood in awe as a volunteer whirled some items past a price scanner, finally asking, "This is for checking out?" (Cashiers had been using the scanners at grocery stores across the country for over 10 years by that time.) Bush also didn't help his reelection chances when he showed disinterest during one of the presidential debates with Clinton and Perot by famously looking down at his wristwatch. On election night, Bush received only 37 percent of the national vote. In the end, Perot's candidacy hurt Bush more than Clinton. The Texas billionaire gained no electoral votes but did attract 19 million popular votes, or 19 percent of the total votes cast. Clinton won the electoral vote handily, 370-168, carrying 32 states and the District of Columbia, but with only 43 percent of the vote—the lowest amount for any presidential victor since Woodrow Wilson's 42 percent in 1912.

Ross Perot, January 24, 1990.
Photo credit: UTSA's Institute of Texas Cultures

A TRANSITIONAL DECADE

The 1980s proved to be a transitional decade in many regards. Americans celebrated the end of Cold War tensions with the Soviet Union. As the twentieth century neared its conclusion, the constant threat of a thermonuclear war was now part of history. Nevertheless, the Gulf War foreshadowed a new era of potential ongoing military involvement in the Middle East during the coming decades. At home, the 1980s marked the end of consistent Democratic control of the federal government as the Republican Party gained control of the White House for twelve consecutive years followed soon, despite Bill Clinton's election to the presidency in 1992, by the Republican takeover of both houses of Congress for the first time since a brief period during the 1950s. Technologically, as will be discussed further in the next two chapters, developments with computers and new forms of mass communication would greatly increase the ability of Americans to connect with each other while ironically creating the circumstances that would further isolate them and drive them apart.

Table 30.1

The End of the Cold War

March 1985	Mikhail Gorbachev becomes General Secretary of the Communist Party of the Soviet Union
1986	Gorbachev initiates a series of economic and political reforms (most notably *perestroika* and *glasnost*) to preserve the Soviet system
October 1986	Gorbachev and U.S. President Ronald Reagan hold initial summit meeting in Reykjavik, Iceland
December 1987	Gorbachev and Reagan sign the Intermediate-Range Nuclear Forces (INF) Treaty
May 1988	Soviet forces begin 9-month withdrawal of troops from Afghanistan
December 1988	Gorbachev announces that the USSR would no longer intervene in the domestic affairs of Eastern European countries
August 1989	Solidarity Party-led coalition government formed in Poland
October 1989	Noncommunist Republic of Hungary proclaimed
November 1989	Berlin Wall dismantled
December 1989	Overthrow of Ceausescu dictatorship in Romania
August 1990	Failed coup attempt against Gorbachev
October 1990	Reunification of Germany completed
November 1990	Noncommunist Republic of Bulgaria established
June 1991	Breakup of the Yugoslav Federation begins with declarations of Croatian and Slovenian independence
September 1991	USSR recognizes independence of the Baltic States
December 1991	Dissolution of the Soviet Union
January 1993	Czechoslovakia split into Czech Republic and Republic of Slovakia

Chronology

1981 Ronald Reagan takes office as president.
Hostages released from Iran.
Severe recession begins.
Researchers identify cause of AIDS.
Sandra Day O'Connor appointed first
female Supreme Court justice.
Reagan survives assassination attempt.

1982 U. S. supports contra war against
Sandinista government in Nicaragua.

1983 U. S. invades Grenada.
Terrorist attack in Beirut kills 239 American
Marines.
U. S. pulls out of Lebanon.
Reagan proposes Strategic Defense Initiative.

1984 Democrats choose Geraldine Ferraro to be
first female vice presidential candidate.
Reagan re-elected president.

1985 Mikhail Gorbachev becomes leader of the
Soviet Union.

1986 U. S. bombs Libya.
Challenger space shuttle blows up after takeoff.

1987 Congressional hearings held on the
Iran-Contra Affair.
Stock market suffers record decline.
Gorbachev comes to Washington.

1988 George H.W. Bush elected president.

1989 Berlin Wall is torn down.
Communism collapses in Eastern Europe.
U. S. invades Panama.
Chinese government crushes pro-democracy
demonstrations in Tiananmen Square.

1990 Bush and Congress agree on tax increases
to reduce budget deficit.
Iraq invades Kuwait.
Gorbachev wins Nobel Peace Prize as Soviet
troops withdraw from Eastern Europe.

1991 Soviet Union disintegrates.
U. S. ousts Iraqi army from Kuwait in
Operation Desert Storm.

SUGGESTED READINGS

Michael Beschloss and Strobe Talbott, *At the Highest Levels: The Inside Story of the End of the Cold War* (1993).

Lou Cannon, *President Reagan: The Role of a Lifetime* (1990).

Theodore Draper, *A Very Thin Line: the Iran-Contra Affair* (1991).

Lawrence Freedman and Efraim Karsh, *The Gulf Conflict, 1990-1991* (1993).

Andrew Hacker, *Two Nations: Black and White, Separate, Hostile, Unequal* (1992).

Haynes Johnson, *Sleepwalking Through History: America in the Reagan Years* (1991).

Michael Katz, *The Undeserving Poor: From the War on Poverty to the War on Welfare* (1989).

Jonathan Kozol, *Rachel and Her Children: Homeless Families in America* (1988).

Alex Kotlowitz, *There Are No Children Here: The Story of Two Boys Growing Up in the Other America* (1991).

Walter LaFeber, *America, Russia, and the Cold War, 1945-2002* (2002).

Nicholas Lemann, *The Promised Land: The Great Black Migration and How it Changed America* (1989).

Martin Lowy, *High Rollers: Inside the Savings and Loan Debacle* (1994).

James T. Patterson, *Restless Giant: The United States from Watergate to Bush v. Gore* (2005).

Kevin Phillips, *The Politics of Rich and Poor: Wealth and the American Electorate in the Aftermath of the Reagan Presidency* (1990).

Michael Schaller, *Right Turn: American Life in the Reagan-Bush Era, 1980-1992* (2005).

Arthur M. Schlesinger Jr., *The Disuniting of America* (1991).

Randy Shilts, *And the Band Played On: Politics, People and the AIDS Epidemic* (1987).

James B. Stewart, *Den of Thieves* (1991).

Gary Wills, *Reagan's America: Innocents At Home* (1987).

——, *Under God: Religion and American Politics* (1990).

James Graham Wilson, *Gorbachev's Adaptability, Reagan's Engagement, and the End of the Cold War* (2014).

Review Questions

1. Describe Ronald Reagan's background and how his life experiences influenced his personality and his presidency.

2. Why have many historians referred to the Reagan presidency as the "Reagan Revolution"?

3. Describe the theoretical assumptions behind "Reaganomics." What occurred to the economy and the government's financial situation, both good and bad, when it was applied during the 1980s?

4. Many Americans believe that Reagan's policies were responsible for ending the Cold War. Do you agree or disagree? Would the Cold War have ended regardless of Reagan's "tough talk" and policy decisions? Why or why not?

5. By the close of the Gulf War in the fall of 1991, George H.W. Bush had attained the highest popular approval rating of any president in modern history; a year later he was soundly defeated by Bill Clinton. What happened in that short time to cause the Bush presidency to unravel? What were some of the issues at the end of the Bush presidency (including those inherited from his predecessor, Ronald Reagan) that came to the forefront?

Glossary of Important People and Concepts

AIDS
Boland Amendment
George H.W. Bush
Bill Clinton
Contras
El Salvador
Geraldine Ferraro
glasnost and *perestroika*
Mikhail Gorbachev
Grenada
Saddam Hussein
Immigration Reform and Control Act of 1986
Iran-Contra Affair
Los Angeles Riots
Manuel Noriega
Oliver North
Operation Desert Storm
H. Ross Perot
Professional Air Traffic Controller's Organization (PATCO)
Ronald Reagan
"Reaganomics"/ supply-side economics
Sandinistas
Strategic Defense Initiative (SDI)
Tiananmen Square
James Watt

President Bill Clinton giving the 1999 State of the Union Address

Chapter Thirty-one

AMERICA DIVIDED AND UNITED, 1993-2008

Panic gripped the passengers of United Airlines Flight 93 on September 11, 2001 when, just 45 minutes into a transcontinental flight from Newark, New Jersey to San Francisco, California, four Al Qaeda terrorists seized control of the plane after killing the pilot, co-pilot, and a flight attendant. While three of the murderers guarded the cockpit, a fourth who had basic pilot training took the helm and turned the aircraft around and placed it on a new heading toward Washington, D.C.

After being herded to the back of the plane, many of the 37 passengers on board the Boeing 757 made desperate calls to friends, family, and phone dispatchers on their cellphones. They were able to ascertain that three other flights had been hijacked earlier that morning and crashed into the World Trade Center in New York City and the Pentagon Building in Washington. After correctly deducing that their flight was also part of an elaborate suicide mission, many of the passengers deliberated and quickly voted to act—they would rush the terrorists (who seemed to be armed with small knives and box cutters), break into the cockpit, and prevent them from achieving their goal, whatever that may be. (Though not conclusively determined, most agree that the intended target was either the White House or the Capitol).

Before hanging up on their calls, some of the passengers told those on the line that the decision had been made to attack the terrorists soon. One of them, Todd Beamer, asked a GTE phone operator to tell his family that he loved them. Before he hung up, the operator overheard him ask the others: "Are you ready? Okay. Let's roll."

The Flight 93 cockpit voice recorder, later recovered, captured the sounds of loud pounding and the shattering of glass, followed by shouts and screams coming from one of the hijackers posted outside the cockpit. Loud thuds are also discernible on the recording, probably from the passengers attempting to use a food cart as a battering ram against the cockpit door. More screams and yells can then be heard before the plane began to nosedive toward the Earth, crashing near Shanksville, Pennsylvania, about 65 miles southeast of Pittsburgh, just 20 minutes flight time away from Washington. Researchers have yet to determine conclusively whether Beamer and the other passengers were able to breach the cockpit or if the terrorist pilot simply decided that it would happen soon enough and put the plane down himself. Regardless of how it occurred, the result was the same—the White House or the Capitol were spared from destruction that day because courageous Americans with nothing to lose decided to end their lives on their own terms. In the process, their patriotic act preserved a national treasure and saved the lives of countless fellow citizens on the ground.

CLINTON'S FIRST-TERM DOMESTIC POLICY EFFORTS

During his campaign for president, **Bill Clinton** occasionally tried out the phrase "New Covenant" to explain his vision for policies that he would pursue as president. An ambitious politician who wanted a catchy label to be associated with his accomplishments as had been the case with other great presidents (Teddy Roosevelt pushed his "Square Deal" agenda, Franklin Roosevelt called for a "New Deal," Lyndon Johnson wished to promote the

"Great Society"), Clinton explained the New Covenant during his acceptance speech at the Democratic National Convention as a new approach "that offers more empowerment and less entitlement. More choices for young people in the schools they attend. . . And more choices for the elderly and for people with disabilities and the long-term care they receive. A government that is leaner, not meaner; a government that expands opportunity, not bureaucracy; a government that understands that jobs must come from growth in a vibrant and vital system of free enterprise." Though he dropped use of the phrase once elected, Clinton doggedly stuck to the centrist ideals behind these words.

Initial Successes

Contrary to George H.W. Bush, Bill Clinton engrossed himself in the details of domestic policy. With great command of a wealth of information on every domestic matter, he was known for being longwinded both in his lengthy speeches and many of his conversations, which tended to be one-sided. With a 258-176 Democratic margin in the House and a Senate advantage of 57-43, Clinton looked forward to pushing a domestic agenda in tune with his moderate, New Democrat philosophy. Initially, the new president garnered some noteworthy successes. He signed into law the Family and Medical Leave Act, which had been twice vetoed by Bush, which allowed for unpaid family leave up to twelve weeks for medical emergencies. Congress also agreed with the president's plan to establish AmeriCorps as an extension of LBJ's VISTA volunteer program to allow selected students the option of repaying college loans through community service. Clinton also secured passage of the **Brady Bill**, which instituted a five-day waiting period for the purchase of handguns. In conjunction, he also pushed through a ban on the manufacture, sale, or possession of nineteen different assault weapons.

Clinton had some difficulty getting a nominee for attorney general approved by the Senate. Wishing to make history for appointing the first female attorney general, his first two choices each succumbed to pressure to withdraw after revelations that both had hired nannies for their children "under the table," thus avoiding the payment of Social Security taxes. The president eventually turned to Florida prosecutor Janet Reno, who the Senate confirmed without difficulty to the post that she would hold throughout Clinton's time in the White House. Clinton was also able to name two justices to the Supreme Court during his first term, Ruth Bader Ginsburg and Stephen Breyer. By replacing a liberal and a moderate justice with another liberal and a moderate, these appointments did not disrupt the philosophical distribution of the High Court's membership.

Early in his term, Clinton struggled to carry out a campaign pledge to lift the longstanding ban on gays serving in the military. When Republicans and conservative Democrats in Congress drafted legislation designed to make it difficult for the president to carry out his campaign pledge, Clinton compromised, and in December 1993, issued a new directive banning the military from interrogating service members and recruits about their sexual orientation, but allowing the military to expel any soldiers and sailors if their homosexuality or bisexuality became known to superiors, a policy that came to be known as **"Don't Ask, Don't Tell."** Though conservatives often railed against the new policy, gays and their liberal allies also despised the system that left open the possibility of soldiers and sailors being blackmailed and otherwise taken advantage of, not to mention the humiliation of having to continue keeping their sexual identity a guarded secret in order to keep their jobs. Ultimately, the policy did not prevent the military from expelling over fourteen thousand servicemen and servicewomen because of their sexual orientation between 1993 and the repeal of the policy in 2011.

Senator Dick Durbin (D-IL) talks at the podium on the issue of handgun control. In the wheelchair to his left is James Brady, who was hit by gunfire when John Hinkley shot at President Reagan. The Brady Act is a congressional law mandating that state law enforcement agencies conduct criminal background checks prior to allowing an individual to purchase a handgun.

In an effort to further bolster his centrist credentials, Clinton pushed Congress for acceptance of a budget that included a significant attempt at deficit reduction. Under Reagan and Bush, the annual federal deficit had risen from $150 billion in 1987 to over $290 billion in 1992, an all-time high. Clinton's plan called for a budget package that would result in an estimated $500 billion reduction over the next five years. In the process, he upset liberals by dropping his campaign pledge for a middle-class tax cut and not pressing conservatives for acceptance of his request for emergency stimulus spending. By August 1993, he won congressional approval for many elements that he had desired: a 1 percent increase in the highest corporate tax rate, raising the individual tax rate to 39.5 percent for annual incomes over $250,000, expansion of the earned income tax credit for low-income working families, and some cuts in defense spending and social programs. Without gaining a single Republican vote, the measure passed by two votes in the House and by Vice President Gore breaking a 50-50 tie in the Senate. Ultimately, the plan worked largely as hoped—in 1998, the government enjoyed a $70 billion surplus, the first time that the government was "in the black" at the end of a fiscal year since 1969. Higher surpluses averaging over $150 billion per year occurred in 1999, 2000, and 2001.

After passage of his budget, Clinton sought success on major trade agreements that he hoped would solidify his standing as a moderate. A believer in lowering trade barriers to expand American exports, Clinton argued that such policies would help sustain prosperity while strengthening ties with foreign nations. Despite heavy opposition from labor unions who feared a huge loss of American manufacturing jobs, Clinton worked with many Republicans in Congress to secure narrow passage of the **North American Free Trade Agreement (NAFTA)**, which George H.W. Bush had just concluded negotiating in December 1992. The deal called for cutting tariffs and eliminating other trade barriers between the United States, Canada, and Mexico over a 15-year period.

Clinton also completed negotiations for the creation of the new World Trade Organization (WTO), a powerful multilateral group created to enlarge world trade by implementing new agreements and mediating disputes. Clinton moved to recognize the communist government in Vietnam but chose not to make such an overture to Cuba, apparently worried about the potential backlash against reaching any understanding with Fidel Castro's government from the fiercely anti-Castro Cuban American community in Florida, a critical state on the Electoral College map.

Failed Attempt at Health Care Reform

President Clinton's major goal during his first term was to reform the nation's health insurance system. By 1993, the U.S. was the only developed nation in the world without guaranteed coverage for all of its citizens. Nearly 40 million Americans had no health insurance, abhorrent to most liberals who came to believe that affordable health care was a fundamental right. Moreover, private expenditures for Americans who did have health insurance had exploded, from $250 billion in 1980 to almost $900 billion in 1993. For Clinton, economic reform and health-care reform were interrelated: any long-term effort to reduce deficits and promote sustained economic growth required harnessing the large increases in medical costs.

Clinton chose to place development of a workable plan to a team headed by his wife Hillary (an unprecedented role for a First Lady) and an old friend, Ira Magaziner. Relying largely on the input of academics and medical experts, the group worked without the input of Congress or the U.S. Department of Health and Human Services to create a complicated proposal over 1,000 pages in length. The overall goal of mandating employers to provide health insurance to their employees, nevertheless, was clear. The plan was based upon the creation of regional insurance-producing alliances that would rely on managed competition among private insurance companies to lower premiums while the government would pay for uninsured citizens to guarantee universal coverage. Many liberals were disappointed because they favored a single-payer system (such as Medicare for elderly Americans, and the system implemented in Canada for all of its citizens). Small insurers opposed the bill because they feared being pushed out by larger providers. Small business owners balked at the provision that they would have to pay for 80 percent of their employees' health premiums. Already philosophically opposed to the idea of government involvement in health care and not wishing to give Clinton a major political victory, congressional Republicans and conservative Democrats were determined to defeat his efforts, though they had no counterproposal of their own to offer as an alternative. Without a sustained groundswell of support from the grass roots, the measure eventually died in committee, not even making it to the floor of either house of Congress for a vote.

Republican Congressional Triumph

Republicans sought to build upon Clinton's failed health-care proposal by making a bold effort to gain control of Congress in the 1994 mid-term elections. Helping them was bad press coverage for the president regarding a failed real estate deal over a tract of land known as Whitewater involving the president and the First Lady while Bill Clinton served as the governor of Arkansas. Though the Clintons lost money on the investment, the Republican Congress launched an investigation, charging favoritism and criminal misconduct, and arranged for a special prosecutor, Kenneth Starr, to investigate the matter. When a White House lawyer and close friend of the Clintons, Vince Foster, then committed suicide, right-wing radio talk-show hosts such as Rush Limbaugh spread the false claim that Foster had been murdered because he knew something about Whitewater, even though repeated police investigations confirmed that the man's gunshot wounds were self-inflicted. Stories also still percolated once again about the president's alleged past marital infidelities, prompted in part by a sexual harassment lawsuit filed by an Arkansas woman, Paula Jones.

Looking to the impending congressional elections, Clinton once again tacked to the middle of the political spectrum by pushing a welfare reform proposal that failed to gain traction but found more success with a new federal crime bill. Passed by Congress in September 1994, the law allocated $30 billion for law enforcement by providing grants to communities to pay for an additional 100,000 local police personnel as well as new prison construction, and also instituted a controversial "three strikes and you're out" policy instituting mandatory life sentences for criminals convicted of three felonies in federal courts.

The Republican Right, led by Congressman Newt Gingrich of Georgia, sought to "nationalize" the 1994 congressional races by creating a "**Contract with America**,"—a party agenda that he hoped Republican candidates across the country would formally endorse. The plan consisted of ten objectives, but the most immediate and urgent were cutting taxes, passing a balanced budget amendment to the U.S. Constitution, reducing the size of the government bureaucracy, and welfare reform. The strategy worked, as the Republican Party gained nine Senate seats and 52 House seats to win control of both houses of Congress for the first time in 40 years.

BILL CLINTON AND THE WORLD

With the end of the Cold War, Bill Clinton felt inclined to focus primarily on domestic issues. "Foreign policy is not what I came here to do," he once stated soon after becoming president. Nevertheless, Clinton understood that foreign relations was an important part of the job of being president and worked hard to maintain America's position as the preeminent world power.

Relations with Asia: China and Vietnam

Clinton endeavored during his first term to improve relations with Asia's most important communist nations: the People's Republic of China and the Socialist Republic of Vietnam. Tensions emerged between the United States and China during Clinton's first year in office, as the president had inherited a strained relationship with China in the aftermath of the Tiananmen Square massacre (see Chapter 31) where troops killed an estimated 3,000 pro-democracy demonstrators in the summer of 1989. During the presidential campaign, Clinton had accused Bush of coddling China, but such rhetoric ceased after entering the White House. He came to believe, as had Bush, that the United States stood a better chance of advancing democracy in totalitarian countries such as China through cultural exchanges and by promoting free enterprise.

Similarly, in February 1994, the U.S. recognized the communist government of Vietnam and ended its 19-year-old trade embargo with that country after the fall of the South Vietnam to the North Vietnamese. American businesses began establishing trade relations with the regime, leading also to Nike footwear and other American products being manufactured in Vietnam. A steady flow of American tourists would also soon begin arriving to the country, spending money in a country that had been vilified over the previous decades as a major threat to the United States and its interests abroad.

The Israeli-PLO Agreement

In an attempt to foster peace in the Middle East, Clinton supported secret negotiations in Oslo, Norway between representatives of Israel and the Palestine Liberation Organization (PLO). Bringing together Israeli Prime Minister Yitzhak Rabin and PLO Chairman Yasser Arafat for a ceremony on the South Lawn of the White House, Clinton beamed as the two leaders famously shook each other's hands before signing the Oslo Accords in which the PLO renounced terrorism and recognized Israel's right to exist in exchange for Israeli withdrawal from the West Bank and Gaza Strip and acceptance of the creation of a Palestinian Authority to govern these Palestinian-occupied areas.

At the time, this "two-state solution" appeared to be a monumental step toward lasting peace in the Middle East, but when it came time for implementation, trouble remained. Israeli troops did finally withdraw, after an Israeli opposed to the peace process assassinated Rabin in 1995. Israel's government was soon replaced with hardliners favoring a more combative stance towards the

Palestinians. The Palestinian Authority was established, but after Arafat died in 2004, Palestinian extremists took control of the Gaza Strip, frequently firing rockets into Israel, often provoking violent responses from their antagonists.

Trouble in Africa

In the post-Cold War world, the president often found it difficult to balance concern for human rights with the nation's strategic and economic interests. Where should the U.S. intervene on humanitarian grounds and under what circumstances? The answers were indeed mixed and far from consistent. In the African country of **Somalia**, ravaged by famine and civil war, powerful and brutal warlords had taken over the country by the early 1990s. In the final days of the Bush administration, the president had ordered American troops, under the umbrella of a United Nations (UN) humanitarian mission, into Somalia to help deliver food and provide relief. As local warlords increased their attacks on the multi-national peacekeeping force, Clinton dispatched an additional 400 elite soldiers in an intensified effort to capture the main warlord. Unfortunately, the mission ended disastrously after what had been planned to be a one-hour raid turned into a two-day long melee with Somalian militia fighters after two American helicopters were shot down, leading U.S. soldiers to have to fight their way into the streets of the capital of Mogadishu to rescue the surviving downed crew members. (This event later became the basis for the 2001 film *Black Hawk Down*). Ultimately, U.S. forces prevailed, killing hundreds of Somalis and wounding many more, but the Somalis managed to kill eighteen American servicemen and wounded 84. For many Americans, seeing a dead U.S. soldier videotaped being dragged through the streets of Mogadishu by a jubilant mob in a country receiving the UN's good will was more than they could accept. In an increasingly isolationist mood, the public pressured Clinton to pull American forces out, which he did in the spring of 1994.

The unsatisfactory results in Somalia, and the subsequent public backlash, contributed to the Clinton administration's reluctance to intervene in a genocide taking place in the central African nation of Rwanda. Starting in April 1994 and lasting for 100 days, members of the Hutu ethnic group controlling the Rwandan government openly encouraged private militias of its people to attack the minority Tutsis. Over 800,000 people were slaughtered while two million people fled the country. The U.N. and France (Rwanda had once been a French colonial possession) ultimately intervened with troops, but only after the killing had decimated the country.

Peacekeeping in the Balkans

During his first years in office, Clinton failed to develop a consistent policy in the Balkans region of southeastern Europe. In the former Yugoslavia, violence between Serbs, Muslims, and Croats had led to the deaths of over 200,000 people, most of them Muslim civilians murdered by Bosnian Serbs undertaking ethnic cleansing operations to clear entire provinces of Bosnia and Croatia of non-Serbs. Neither the U.S. nor NATO intervened. Only 6,000 outnumbered U.N. peacekeepers stationed in Bosnia could provide temporary relief for a relative handful of residents.

The last straw took place in July 1995 when the Bosnian Serb fighters surrounded Dutch U.N. peacekeepers protecting Muslim refugees in the town of Srebrenica in eastern Bosnia. After women and children fled and the

Prime Minister of Israel, Yitzhak Rabin, President Clinton, and Yasser Arafat, chairman of the Palestine Liberation Organization, at the signing ceremony of the agreement between Israel and the PLO negotiated secretly in Oslo, Norway, and signed at the White House on September 13, 1993. Photo credits: Clinton Presidential Materials Project.

peacekeepers forced out, the Serbs proceeded to murder over 8,000 Muslim men and boys. Soon after the Srebrenica Massacre, Croatian military forces launched an offensive that successfully expelled Bosnian forces from Croatia and northern Bosnia. Sensing a breakthrough in the war, Clinton authorized American war planes to join NATO jets for targeted air strikes against Bosnian Serb forces. After two and a half weeks of heavy bombing allowing further gains by Croatian ground forces, NATO accepted a call for a cease-fire. After extensive peace talks held at Wright-Patterson Air Force Base near Dayton, Ohio, an agreement was finally reached. The 1995 Dayton Accords created a single state, the Federation of Bosnia and Herzegovina, with a dual government with power shared by Muslims and Croats. Displaced persons would be returned home while the U.S. agreed to send one-third of the 60,000 NATO soldiers charged with enforcing the terms of the agreement.

DIVISIVE CULTURAL ISSUES

Racial Polarization

During the 1990s, growing discontent among many citizens over the flow of Mexican immigrants into California led the state's Republican Party leadership to champion a state ballot initiative—Proposition 187—designed to halt access for illegal immigrant to vital social services such as prenatal and childbirth care, child welfare, public education, and non-emergency health care. The statute galvanized California's Hispanic population, leading them to take out their anger in the polls against Republican politicians. As a result, the Republican Party lost a majority of Latino voters in the Golden State, perhaps for multiple generations. Although the federal courts later overturned Proposition 187, illegal immigration would soon become one of the nation's most divisive issues.

Foreign immigration was not the only source of racial polarization in California, and the nation as a whole, during the Nineties. As the riots in south-central Los Angeles in the aftermath of the Rodney King trial (see Chapter 31) demonstrated, ongoing divisions between whites and African Americans were in the forefront of the country's consciousness. A new twist to this divide occurred in 1995, as millions of Americans watched or read about the lengthy trial of football legend **O.J. Simpson**, accused of murdering his former wife, Nicole (a white woman), and her white male friend, Ronald Goldman. Simpson's high-powered defense team led by legendary African-American trial lawyer Johnny Cochran skillfully echoed

memories of Rodney King to charge that the detectives who investigated the murder held racist views and set him up despite Simpson's celebrity status. Simpson's acquittal by a jury consisting of nine blacks, two whites, and one Hispanic bothered those who were convinced of Simpson's guilt and greatly dismayed with the notion that he was getting away with murder, they felt, largely because of his race. (Polls indicated that 60 percent of all African Americans believed Simpson innocent while 75 percent of white Americans believed him to be guilty.) To others, the justice system showed once again that it favored the wealthy who could afford the services of slick lawyers who could expertly plant the seeds of reasonable doubt in the minds of jurors in ways better than less-skilled attorneys for poor defendants.

Anti-Government Extremism

A slew of right-wing extremist groups emerged during the Clinton presidency to challenge the general direction of the country, both politically and religiously. Politically, some groups rejected the incoming administration because they viewed Clinton as a politician potentially threatening their ability to "defend their freedom" via gun ownership. Most members of the mainstream Religious Right disliked Clinton because they believed that he was a man of questionable moral character and opposed his liberal positions on abortion, but some of the more extreme religious sects held apocalyptic beliefs that skewed their world view into interpreting Clinton's election as possibly a sign that the end of days was near.

One such group of dissidents was the **Branch Davidians,** an offshoot from the Seventh-Day Adventists who formed in the 1950s and by the early 1990s were led by a fanatic named Vernon Wayne Howell who believed himself to be a prophet. Adopting the name "David Koresh," he preached that a forthcoming violent apocalypse was about to descend upon the Earth. In anticipation of the end of times, the Branch Davidians began collecting weapons at a compound located outside Waco, Texas. Outsiders soon became concerned about the group's stockpile of weapons, as well as rumors of other non-traditional religious practices that the sect practiced. It later became known that Howell had indeed committed statutory rape of many girls at the compound and also had started demanding that most adult female Davidians have sexual relations with him in order to procreate the group with special children of the prophet. (In all, Howell fathered at least 14 children with numerous female members.)

As they illegally stockpiled a large cache of firearms in preparation for Armageddon, the Davidians fell under suspicion by federal authorities who viewed them as a

Map 31.1 The Breakup of Yugoslavia

potentially dangerous para-military organization. The Bureau of Alcohol, Tobacco, and Firearms (ATF) soon obtained search warrants for a raid, expecting to secure the compound and arrest Koresh. The raid on February 28, 1993, however, proved to be a disaster. Forewarned by locals, the Davidians made extensive preparations. With Koresh at the lead, they defended their compound with gunfire, killing four ATF agents. Six Davidians were also killed. With the deaths of federal agents, the Federal Bureau of Investigation (FBI) assumed jurisdiction and established contact with Koresh as federal personnel moved to secure a wide perimeter around the compound and prepare for a prolonged siege. For the next 51 days, FBI negotiators sparred with Koresh in an effort to get the Davidians to surrender, all under the watchful eye of the national news media, which became fixated on an event that fascinated some and disgusted others. During the course of the siege, twenty children were released, but close to a hundred followers remained.

After interviewing many of the released children, the FBI, Attorney General Janet Reno, and President Bill Clinton determined that longstanding physical and sexual abuse continued to take place inside the compound. Authorities began to believe that he would never peacefully surrender. On April 19, 1993, an FBI assault came in the form of combat engineering tanks with plans to breach walls and then fire tear gas canisters to flush out and capture the occupants. However, fires soon broke out in different parts of the main Mt. Carmel building. Fewer than ten people escaped the building. In all, seventy-six perished; some from suffocation, some from falling rubble

as the building collapsed, and some from gunshot wounds that were either suicides or "mercy killings" as the flames and smoke filled the building. The event made headlines across the country and many were transfixed on the incident as it played out on national television broadcasts.

The official government commission's report on the assault demonstrated that the fires were started inside the complex, most likely under Howell's orders to fulfill the leader's apocalyptic teachings (surviving Davidians maintained that the government deliberately or accidentally ignited the tear gas). Some Americans, especially those espousing extreme right-wing political views, criticized the FBI's assault, blaming overzealous federal authorities for causing the deaths. For Far Right extremists, the Waco tragedy transformed Koresh into a martyr who had defended both gun ownership and Christian separatism (the belief of some extremists that Christians should withdraw from a supposedly anti-religious American society and create their own communities governed by Old Testament laws).

Tragically, it was only a matter of time before one of their militia groups would seek revenge. On April 19, 1995, precisely two years after the Waco incident, Timothy McVeigh and Terry Nichols, two ex-U.S. Army soldiers associated with right-wing militias, set off explosives packed into a rental truck parked in front of the Alfred P. Murrah Federal Building in Oklahoma City, killing 168 men, women, and children. At the time, the **Oklahoma City bombing** was the most deadly terrorist attack on U.S. soil. Though initial news reports of the tragedy openly speculated that the attack might have been the handiwork of a militant Islamic terrorist organization, authorities arrested McVeigh within hours of the bombing on a misdemeanor traffic violation and soon charged him in connection with the bombing just three days later. After a trial in federal court, a jury convicted McVeigh of capital murder and conspiracy to overthrow the government. He was given the death penalty (carried out in June 2001), while Nichols received a life sentence without the possibility of parole.

THE 1996 ELECTION

In the wake of the Oklahoma City bombing, Bill Clinton spoke out forcefully against extremism in an effort to position himself as a fair-minded politician opposed to the rhetoric of the Far Right members of the Republican Party, which he said contributed to a poisoned political climate and led to the senseless acts of violence that the country recently witnessed. When the president battled with Congress over the budget, congressional Republicans overplayed their hand, refusing to compromise and deciding not to authorize an interim resolution allowing for temporary funding in order to keep government agencies operational. Clinton called their bluff and allowed the federal government to shut down rather than authorize a series of sharp cuts to Social Security, Medicare, and other social programs. For 28 days in late 1995, all nonessential federal employees were furloughed from their jobs. After Republicans bowed to grass-roots pressure and capitulated, Clinton's standing with the public markedly improved.

The president continued with his centrist New Democrat positioning when he surprised Congress and the nation during his State of the Union Address in January 1996 with a declaration that "the era of big government is over" and then worked with Republicans to pass new legislation that was acceptable to them. He satisfied social conservatives by signing into law the Defense of Marriage Act, which defined marriage under federal law as a union between a man and a woman, and a new law designed to "end welfare as we know it." After vetoing two earlier versions of welfare reform measures that he believed were too conservative, Clinton finally approved one that ended the Aid to Families with Dependent Children (AFDC) program, part of Franklin Roosevelt's New Deal that provided federal aid to low-income families with children, usually single mothers with kids under the age of 18. In its place, the new system entitled Temporary Assistance to Needy Families (TANF) that authorized federal block grants to be sent to the states to determine eligibility and provide aid to needy families whose head of household needed to find work within two years. Further, the law established a five-year lifetime cap on the reception of benefits. By 2003, TANF provided support for 2 million families, markedly less than the almost 5 million who received AFDC aid in 1995.

To challenge Clinton for the presidency in 1996, the Republicans eventually nominated the long-time senator from Kansas Bob Dole, a World War II veteran with moderately conservative views, and chose Representative Jack Kemp of New York, a former professional quarterback, to be his running mate. Their campaign platform greatly satisfied conservatives by focusing on an abortion ban, a 15 percent across-the-board tax cut for all Americans, and a balanced federal budget. At 73 years old, Dole was the oldest person ever to run for president and was decidedly low energy, despite his good overall health, when compared to the more youthful Clinton. Dole appeared stiff on the campaign stump in part from his gruff personality but also because of war wounds that greatly limited his ability to use one of his arms. To many Americans, especially among the majority Baby Boom generation, he represented a step backward.

Winning almost 50 percent of the popular vote and over 70 percent of the Electoral College, Clinton centrist strategy succeeded brilliantly to cap an amazing political comeback from the depths of his party's trouncing in the 1994 congressional races when it looked as if the president's political days were numbered. Ross Perot also decided to run for president again, but in contrast to the previous election, his impact in 1996 was minimal (he garnered only 8 percent of the popular vote compared to 19 percent four years earlier), and his presence once again hurt the Republicans more than the Democrats. Although soundly defeating Dole, Clinton's victory was not a complete one for the Democrats. Despite some loss of seats in the House, the Republicans retained control of Congress and even gained a few seats in the Senate and won several new governorships. In a time of deep political rancor, Americans seemed to be directing their political leaders to stay the middle course.

SECOND TERM HIGHS AND LOWS

The Clinton Boom

Bill Clinton owed much of his popularity to the booming economy during most of his presidency, spurred on by unbridled consumer spending. By his last year in office, national unemployment was below 4 percent during a period of sustained low inflation. The "**Clinton Boom**" became the longest uninterrupted period of economic growth and general prosperity in the nation's history, leading to increased tax revenues that allowed for federal budget surpluses—a rare occurrence for post-World War II presidents.

To be sure, the United States was not a workers' paradise in the latter years of the twentieth century. Two-income households were becoming more of a necessity for families hoping for a better quality of life. Americans were working longer hours per week than most western Europeans, who enjoyed shorter work weeks and more frequent holidays. Though amazed at the work ethic of laborers in the United States, Europeans also noticed the elevated stress level of American workers. Adding to work-related anxiety was the growing insecurity that many Americans felt about their employment prospects. An increasing number of jobs were becoming automated. Other jobs were being lost to "outsourcing," when companies moved jobs to cheaper labor markets overseas. As the country neared the end of the century, a "knowledge economy" was evolving that rewarded those with access to more specialized education in order to better take advantage of the opportunities presented by globalization and computerization.

The Lewinsky Debacle

Despite the positive achievements of his first term and his political successes, including his re-election, much of Bill Clinton's second term was consumed with a personal scandal involving the president's physical relationship with an intern named **Monica Lewinsky,** a vivacious 23-year-old who had recently ended a five-year affair with her married high school drama instructor prior to landing her internship via a family connection. Beginning during the government shutdown in November 1995

and lasting a total of 16 months, Clinton and Lewinsky had nine separate physical encounters, though the contact apparently never went farther than oral sex. The two exchanged phone calls, notes, and a few gifts before staffers intervened, believing that Lewinsky simply was preoccupying too much of the president's time. Clinton abruptly ended the affair, though they remained in touch. Lewinsky's superiors arranged for her transfer to a post at the Pentagon, where she inexplicably shared knowledge of her affair with a co-worker, a disgruntled former White House employee named Linda Tripp. Unbeknownst to Lewinsky, Tripp began recording their conversations and later turned the tapes over to Kenneth Starr, the special prosecutor heading the Whitewater inquiry who then broadened the scope of his investigation with approval from a federal appeals court.

The Lewinsky story soon became a media sensation when the public began to learn some details about the matter in January 1998. In testimony under oath in the Paula Jones sexual harassment case, lawyers surprised the president by asking if he ever had sex with Monica Lewinsky. Clinton declared he had not. A few days later, Clinton again categorically denied the allegations, this time before live television cameras with this wife Hillary in the room, stating forcefully: "I did not have sexual relations with that woman." For her part, Hillary Clinton defended her husband, telling the press that the story had no validity and was all simply yet another manifestation of a "vast right-wing conspiracy" to destroy her husband.

While Clinton swore that no affair had taken place, evidence continued to mount that confirmed he was less than 100 percent truthful. After Starr threatened Lewinsky with a perjury charge because of a statement in a previous affidavit in which she denied having a relationship with the president, he granted her immunity

The president's daughter, Chelsea, walking with her parents down Pennsylvania Avenue in Washington, D.C., during Bill Clinton's second inauguration, January 20, 1997. Photo credits: Clinton Presidential Materials Project

from prosecution in exchange for testimony that she and Clinton had physical contact with one another, though no intercourse had taken place. For corroboration, she also turned over an unwashed blue dress with a semen stain on it. DNA analysis revealed that Clinton was indeed the source. Called to testify before a grand jury Starr had convened to consider the Whitewater-related allegations, Clinton finally admitted to an "improper relationship" and soon admitted the same to the nation in a brief television address, stating: "I did have a relationship with Miss Lewinsky that was not appropriate." Kenneth Starr reported to Congress that he had "substantial and credible information" that Clinton had committed offenses that constituted grounds for impeachment, including his supposed lying about the Lewinsky affair during his deposition in the Paula Jones lawsuit.

Since the Constitution states that impeachment and removal from office can occur for instances of bribery, treason, or "high crimes and misdemeanors," Republicans pursuing Clinton's removal would have to rely on Congress interpreting that latter vaguely written phrase from James Madison to determine if what Clinton had done rose to that level of impropriety. For the next three months, the nation watched as Congress heard and debated four different counts under which Starr wished Clinton indicted. On two of those four counts, most importantly the charge related to perjury, the House of Representatives voted for impeachment. Thus, for the first time since Andrew Johnson's presidency, the U.S. Senate would oversee the impeachment trial of a president. In the end, the Senate acquitted him of the charges, allowing him to remain in office. The majority of Americans agreed, believing that presidential lying about an affair did not constitute an impeachable offense, particularly when there were more serious national issues on which Congress should have been focusing.

The Rise of Al Qaeda

The threat of global terrorism became a growing concern for the United States during the Clinton presidency. The first breach in American security occurred on February 6, 1993, when a small group associated with **Osama bin Laden**, a Saudi Muslim fundamentalist who began his battle against the West as a guerilla fighter taking on the Soviets in Afghanistan (with CIA help) during the 1980s, bombed the World Trade Center in New York City. As Timothy McVeigh had done for the Oklahoma City bombing, the terrorists used a rented van loaded with explosives as their weapon of choice, parking the vehicle in an underground garage hoping to topple one of the Center's two towers. The blast killed six people and in-

jured more than a thousand, most from heart attacks and smoke inhalation during the evacuation after the explosion. The attack represented the most destructive act of foreign terrorism committed on U.S. soil up to that time.

Bin Laden was able to fund his terrorist activities in part from his family's riches but especially from wealthy patrons across the Middle East who agreed with his radical agenda of resistance to elements of Western culture seeping into Middle Eastern life, especially its commercialism, cosmopolitanism, more open sexuality, and general support for women's rights. By the mid-1990s, bin Laden and the senior leadership of his growing **Al Qaeda** terrorist organization were granted refuge in Afghanistan by the Islamic radicals known as the Taliban who had taken control there in 1989 after the Soviet withdrawal. From his bases in Afghanistan, bin Laden planned other lethal blows. On August 7, 1998, car bombs detonated outside of U.S. embassies in Kenya and Tanzania killing over 300 people and injuring over 4,000 people. Two years later, Al Qaeda operatives maneuvered an inflatable boat filled with explosives next to the *U.S.S. Cole*, an American guided-missile destroyer dock at the port of Aden in Yemen. In the aftermath of these attacks, the Clinton administration ordered aerial bombings of some suspected Al Qaeda bases and organized concerted efforts to track down the terrorist group's leaders, who managed to evade detection as they regrouped and began planning the most devastating strike on American soil in the nation's history, the attacks of September 11, 2001.

Meanwhile, the United States during Clinton's second term found itself once again in conflict with Iraqi leader Saddam Hussein, who began to renege on agreements he had signed at the end of the Gulf War, refusing to permit international inspectors to examine military and industrial sites in his country. Clinton responded by ordering a series of American bombing strikes at military targets inside Iraq and enforcing a "no-fly zone" over portions of the country in order to prevent Iraqi warplanes from attacking anti-Hussein Kurdish Iraqis in the northern part of the country and anti-Hussein Shiite rebels in the south.

The Kosovo Intervention

Another lingering foreign policy issue, ethnic cleansing taking place in the volatile Balkans region, forced the president during the latter half of his second term to face one of the most serious foreign policy crisis of his presidency. In 1999, massive retaliation by the Serb-dominated government of Yugoslavia against the independence-seeking Albanian Muslim inhabitants of the province of **Kosovo** threatened to devolve into genocide. Clinton and the world knew that the Serb president of Yugoslavia, Slobodan Milosevic, did not hesitate to use brutality against armed rebels and civilians alike in an effort to secure control over his vastly shrinking country in the face of the myriad of separatist movements that had formed since the early 1990s.

Clinton at first reacted tentatively, remembering the Somalia debacle and given that there was little public support in the United States for an intervention. There also did not seem to be united agreement in the United Nations (U.N.) either, especially with Russia and China who could use their veto as members of the Security Council to block U.N. involvement. A reluctance to intervene was also present among the NATO nations. The supreme allied commander of NATO forces, American general Wesley Clark, nevertheless joined Madeleine Albright, whom Clinton had appointed as the first woman U.S. Secretary of State, in seeking the president approval for some sort of intervention involving American troops. When negotiations failed and a new round of atrocities became public knowledge, Clinton still held off committing ground troops but did approve the deployment of American planes to conduct low-risk, high-altitude bombing of selected Serb targets. After a month and a half of ineffectiveness, the president approved an intensified bombing campaign over the next 80 days against Serb military positions in Kosovo as well as raids against the Yugoslavian capital of Belgrade. The strikes finally resulted in a cease-fire followed by the arrival of NATO peacekeeping forces and eventual withdrawal of Serb troops from Kosovo, though the province remained part of Yugoslavia. Meanwhile, Milosevic was voted out of office in 2000 and eventually prosecuted by a U.N. tribunal for war crimes, though he died of cardiac arrest in 2006 during his trial.

THE 2000 ELECTION

Despite much of the presidential campaign of 2000 itself being a lackluster affair, the political battle to determine Bill Clinton's successor in the White House ended with high drama caused by contested results for the first time since the disputed election of 1876. Both parties' nominees had dispatched their opponents fairly easily. Vice President **Al Gore** for the Democrats defeated a challenge from New Jersey Senator Bill Bradley, while Republicans chose Governor **George W. Bush** of Texas, the eldest son of former president George H.W. Bush, over Arizona Senator John McCain.

As the campaign progressed, Bush was better able to portray himself as likeable and relatable as a "regular dude," even though he came from a patrician family with immense wealth. Bush often claimed to be a "compassionate conservative" who wanted to be a "uniter, not a divider." For his part, Gore ran "as his own man," trying to distance himself from Clinton's personal scandals, but not having the president on the stump with him made it difficult for him to benefit from the economic boom then underway. He seemed to have an innate ability to come across as wooden and detached, even condescending, in his interactions with people. This trait became especially evident when the vice president performed disastrously at the televised debates, presenting himself in the opinion of many voters as a snarky know-it-all. During the first debate, his overconfidence showed when he repeatedly sighed audibly into his podium's microphone and rolled his eyes in response to many of Bush's answers. During a later debate, which used a town hall format, Gore wandered into Bush's personal space, employing a rather juvenile debate-class tactic to rile his opponent, which failed to do so but made him appear silly in the process. Still, Gore was only slightly behind in the polls when a last-minute "October surprise" rocked the Bush campaign when the candidate's previously-unknown arrest and conviction for drunken driving in Maine in 1976 became publicly known five days before the election, potentially shaking up the entire race.

The 2000 Post-Election Spectacle

By Election Day, the race appeared a toss-up. Few Americans were surprised that the election became one of the tightest in recent memory, but no one predicted how close the results eventually were, let alone the subsequent chaos and crisis that ensued. Out of 1000 million votes cast, Gore won the popular vote by 540,000, or 0.5 percent. Victory in the Electoral College, however, ended up hinging on which candidate won Florida. There, the Bush campaign claimed victory by a margin of 537 votes amid widespread confusion at the polls (paper ballots in some counties were constructed in a way that led some distressed voters to report that they may have voted accidentally for the wrong candidate), as well as claims of voter suppression and manipulation. In the days after the election, Gore refused to concede the election as Democrats focused their efforts on demanding a hand recount of the ballots in certain counties to ensure that machines properly determined each voter's choice. This legal challenge was based on the fact that ballots using a punch-out card system in these counties were susceptible to the machines undercounting votes whenever voters did not push the perforated "chads" all the way through their ballot to indicate their choices. The Florida Supreme Court agreed that such a request be granted, and soon Americans witnessed the spectacle on their television screens of local election officials holding ballots up in the air and squinting to determine a voter's intent on the ballots failing to have their chads punched all the way through.

As Republicans whipped up public efforts to portray the Democrats as sore losers, their lawyers sued in federal court to stop the recount, knowing that only the Democrats would benefit from updated returns coming in from Palm Beach, Broward, Miami-Dade, and Duval counties. Over a month after the election, on December 12, 2000, the U.S. Supreme Court ordered by a 5-4 vote a halt to the recounting of the disputed ballots. The High Court also allowed the state's secretary of state, Katherine Harris, to certify that Bush had carried the state and, therefore, won the presidency.

Legal analysts at the time, and since, have largely agreed that the **Bush v. Gore** decision represented one of the most politically biased verdicts in Supreme Court history. Historically, the Court had stayed out of determining winners and losers of elections taking place in the states. Further, by the late 1990s, the general tenor of the Court's conservative-majority in recent years had been to become much more federalist in its rulings, favoring more power being returned to the states at the expense of the federal government. Thus, in a move contrary to newly adopted stance, the Supreme Court's conservative majority members intervened at the state level to overturn the Florida Supreme Court decision regarding the proper interpretation of the state's own election laws.

Bush, Gore, and Bush supporters, as well as other outside observers, did not expect the Court to intervene at all due to historical precedent and because the matter did not seem to raise a federal constitutional question. The majority of the justices (all appointed by Republican presidents), however, defended their decision by invoking the "equal protection" clause of the Fourteenth Amendment, which they claimed required that all ballots within a state to be counted in accordance with a single standard—something impossible to accomplish given the wide variety of machines and paper ballots used in Florida. In effect, the Court's majority ordered the vote-counting process stopped because Florida voters were being treated unequally; only certain counties (Palm Beach, Miami-Dade, and Broward) had been singled out. This was done by the Gore campaign in part because those counties had Democratic Party majorities, but also because the certification date for the ballots in order to name presidential electors for the Electoral College vote was quickly approaching. Perhaps most disturbing about the Court's decision was a statement asserting that the ruling only pertained to this single case rather than a

Vice President Al Gore speaks at the 1997 dedication of the FDR Memorial, Washington D.C.

principle that could be applied universally.

The judges who dissented from the majority opinion objected with disdain. Justice John Paul Stevens declared that the ruling "can only lend credence to the most cynical appraisal of the work of judges throughout the land." Justice David Souter, a moderate Republican appointee, seconded Stevens' assessment, stating "there is no justification for denying the State the opportunity to try to count all disputed ballots now." Meanwhile, Justice Stephen Breyer, recalling the bitterness engendered in the nation by the *Dred Scott* decision before the Civil War, labeled *Bush v. Gore* another "self-inflicted wound—a wound that may harm not just the Court but the Nation." The Court had violated "the basic principle, inherent in our Constitution and democracy, that every legal vote should be counted." The Court had now become as bitterly divided as the country.

Subsequent reviews by news organizations revealed contradictory results. If the Supreme Court had allowed a recount of votes only in the four counties requested by the Gore campaign, the vice president would have narrowly lost the election. If all disputed ballots from Florida had been reviewed, then Gore could have managed an extremely narrow victory. In hindsight, a contributing factor behind Gore's loss in Florida was the disenfranchisement of over 600,000 ex-felons, mostly Latino and African-American males who tend to vote Democratic, who by state law could not legally vote. Nevertheless, both campaigns knew of the law before the race began. More troublesome to Gore proved to be the candidacy of Green Party presidential nominee Ralph Nader, who seriously hurt Gore's ability to win Florida. A life-long liberal social activist, Nader entered the presidential race

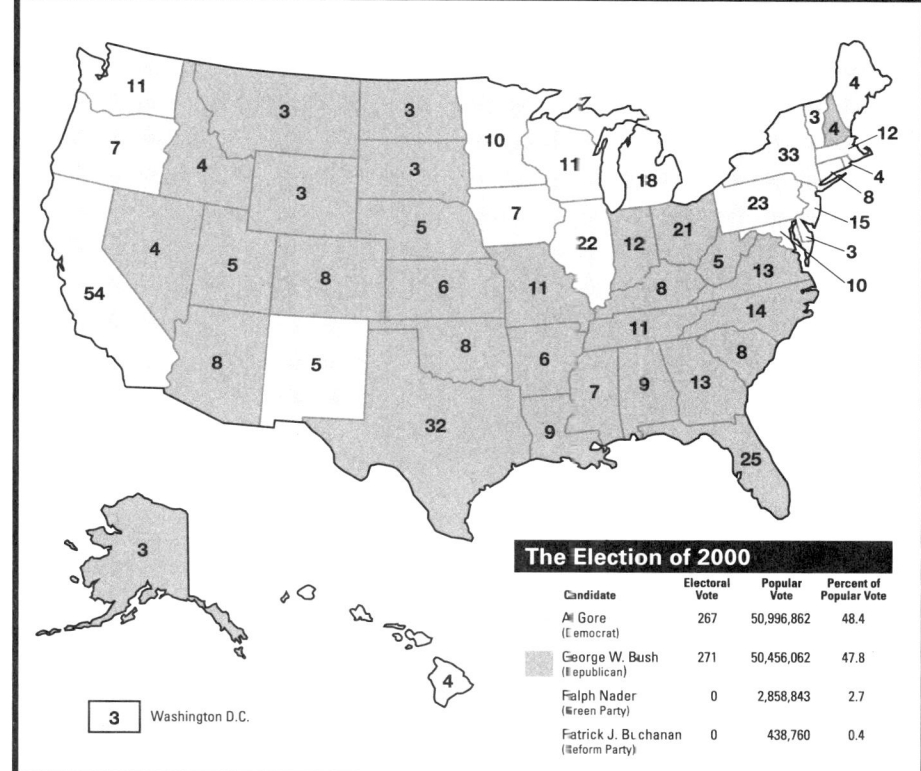

Map 31.2 **The Election of 2000**

The Election of 2000

Candidate	Electoral Vote	Popular Vote	Percent of Popular Vote
Al Gore (Democrat)	267	50,996,862	48.4
George W. Bush (Republican)	271	50,456,062	47.8
Ralph Nader (Green Party)	0	2,858,843	2.7
Patrick J. Buchanan (Reform Party)	0	438,760	0.4

3 Washington D.C.

to provide citizens with an alternative to the two major political parties that he believed were dominated by corporate special interests. Though lacking any chance to win, Nader campaigned, nevertheless, in an effort to publicize his views. Nationally, he garnered 2,882,995 votes, or 2.74 percent. In Florida, Nader received 97,421 votes. Because a sizeable majority of Nader's supporters would have voted for Gore rather than Bush if Nader was not on the ballot (though large numbers of them would have stayed at home rather than voting for either major party candidate), the conclusion is clear that Gore could have gained several thousand additional popular votes and gained Florida's electoral votes had Nader not run for president.

THE BUSH AGENDA

Neither an expert on domestic issues nor foreign policy, **George W. Bush** relied heavily upon the advice of Vice President Dick Cheney and other advisers who benefited the new president with their wide-ranging experience but also hampered his administration by providing faulty analysis and advice, ultimately leading the United States into a decades-long military engagement in the Middle East. Bush turned to one of his father's closest advisers, James Baker, for guidance in directing the start of his presidency. Baker urged him (as he similarly advised Ronald Reagan) to identify two or three major goals for his first year and

to pursue them doggedly. Bush soon made a major tax cut, a set of education initiatives, and a defense build-up as his priorities. Baker also assisted Bush in his Cabinet appointments, pushing for former head of the Joint Chiefs of Staff, Colin Powell, to be named Secretary of State. For Defense Secretary, Baker suggested that long-time Republican official Donald Rumsfeld would be the best choice.

Early Bush Domestic Policies

Though Bush during his campaign had made much of a desire for inclusion and bipartisan cooperation, such sentiments dissipated quickly as the president began to reveal policies appealing to the Republican Party's conservative base. In a rapid series of initiatives, Bush terminated U.S. government aid to international family planning agencies, satisfying anti-abortion groups. He rescinded prohibitions against logging on national forests in the West, greatly upsetting conservationists. He also proposed an energy package that favored large oil interests, including an endorsement for a proposal drilling in the Arctic National Wildlife Refuge, a sanctuary that most environmentalists and citizens in general wished to be protected. Most controversial proved to be Bush's support for the "privatization," via the nation's churches of the social welfare system. His so-called "faith-based" initiative would provide federal funds to religious groups that offered relief and care for local indigents. Liberals opposed the program, among other reasons, because they believed it would violate the separation of church and state.

Most upsetting to progressives, however, was Bush's tax plan, which planned to completely reverse President Clinton's policies by once again shifting the burden of taxation onto the middle class and the poor. Under Clinton, the tax rate on the rich went as high as 39 percent, while taxes for the majority of Americans—80 percent of the nation's population—went down. Bush's initiative reversed Clinton's structure by lowering taxes on all, but primarily benefiting the wealthy. The plan, commonly labeled the "**Bush tax cuts**," called for the biggest tax cut in history, giving back to taxpayers $1.3 trillion through 2010. When broken down by income of recipients, however, it became abundantly clear that the rich were the primary beneficiaries. The top 1 percent of taxpayers received 43 percent of the tax break. Most disturbing, the bottom 20 percent of taxpayers received on average only an additional $15 the first year and an extra $37 by the third year. By contrast, the top 1 percent received on average $13,469 in the first year, rising to $31,201 by the third year. One analyst estimated that by 2010 the Bush plan would return a "bonus" of $774 billion to the richest 1 percent of the nation.

With the economy slowing by 2001, Bush was able to convince Congress that his plan would stimulate new growth. The ideas behind the initiative were not new but instead a revised version of Reagan's trickle-down economics based on the assertion that taxes needed to be cut for the wealthy so that they could invest their tax savings in the economy. Such a result did not occur in the 1980s and, likewise, did not occur during the Bush years as relatively few wealthy individuals reinvested their funds.

Bush and Pre-September 11 Foreign Policy

George Bush's initial diplomatic actions sought to overturn certain foreign policies undertaken by recent presidents, including some pursued by his father. During the campaign, Bush criticized Al Gore for the Clinton administration's penchant for "nation building," or helping to stabilize countries in chaotic regions of the world with American dollars, which he and his advisers viewed as a waste of money. Bush also vetoed U.S. membership in an international criminal court being set up to prosecute violators of human rights, fearing that the court would assert jurisdiction over Americans. Bush also announced that the United States would not adhere to the 1997 Kyoto Protocol, a multinational agreement seeking to combat global warming—a slow rise in the earth's temperature caused by gases released by the burning of fossil fuels, such as coal and oil, that remain in the upper atmosphere and

trap heat reflected from the earth. Since the 1990s, when significant ice melting and glacier recession in Greenland and the Antarctic was discovered, scientists had been warning that such activity could have disastrous climatic, ecological, and environmental effects worldwide. Some 180 nations, including the United States, had agreed to accept the goals set in the Kyoto Protocol for addressing the emission of "greenhouse" gases. Because the United States burned far more fossil fuels than any other nation, Bush's repudiation of the treaty on the grounds that it would hurt the American economy infuriated much of the world, as well as environmentalists at home.

SEPTEMBER 11, 2001

Al Qaeda Strikes

The weather was excellent in the Northeast on the morning of September 11, 2001, so four commercial jets laden with fuel for transcontinental trips to California that morning—American Airlines Flight 11 and United Airlines Flight 175 from Boston, Massachusetts, American Airlines 77 from Washington D.C., and United Airlines 93 from Newark, New Jersey—would have no delays as they took off within an hour of each other. Unknown to the passengers and flight crew on board, each aircraft carried Al Qaeda terrorists, mostly from Saudi Arabia, Egypt, and Syria, who coordinated a diabolical plot to seize the planes and crash them into targets in New York City and Washington, D.C..

On each plane, the extremists seized control soon after gaining cruising altitude by breaking into the respective cockpits, killing the pilots, and steering the aircraft onward with the basic flight training that they had received. The first plane, American 11, struck the North Tower of New York City's World Trade Center at 8:46 a.m. Seventeen minutes later, as the national television networks began reporting the incident, with most anchors speculating that a small plane may have accidentally flown into the building, cameras picked up the image of United Airlines 175 as it slammed into the South Tower, revealing to all that this was no accident. As people in the lower levels of the towers frantically fled the buildings, those located above the planes' impact headed upward as first responders entered the building to rescue those in need of help. Within an hour, the South Tower collapsed, killing hundreds instantly. Thirty minutes later, the North Tower came down. As the drama in New York unfolded, American Airlines 77 was guided into the Pentagon, the headquarters of the Defense Department, located in northern Virginia just across the Potomac River from the nation's capital. Only United Airlines 93 remained aloft. On board, a heroic group of passengers—knowing from cell phone conversations what had happened in New York—refused to let their jet plane become another missile. Instead, they assaulted the terrorists, resulting in the plane crashing into a field near Shanksville, Pennsylvania, located 60 miles southeast of Pittsburgh.

Millions watched the rebroadcast of the television footage showing the second plane exploding as it blasted through the South Tower, as well as video showing each tower collapsing under its own weight as the supporting beams and girders failed due to the high temperatures generated by the burning jet fuel. In all, three thousand people died as a result of the **September 11 (or 9/11) attacks**, which included 265 on board the four planes, 2,606 people at the World Trade Center, and 125 on the ground at the Pentagon. Americans were shocked as they experienced "the Pearl Harbor of their lifetimes," but they also wanted to know who was responsible for the atrocities and most wanted revenge.

The CIA determined fairly quickly that the attack had been carried out by Al Qaeda members directed by Osama bin Laden who at the time was being protected by the **Taliban**, the Muslim fundamentalist extremist group who had seized control in Afghanistan after the Soviet withdrawal in 1989. From his base in Afghanistan, bin Laden built a network of terrorists from thousands of eager recruits who he indoctrinated and trained for attacks against the West, especially the United States, out of subservience to bin Laden who believed himself to be ordained by God to redeem the Muslim world from Western greed, secularism, and corrupting culture.

The possibility of a major terrorist attack on American soil had not been lost on American foreign policy experts and members of the intelligence community. There were individuals within the Clinton and Bush administrations who had warned about the likelihood of such an attack. William Cohen, Bill Clinton's Secretary of Defense, predicted a direct terrorist attack on the U.S. in an op-ed piece appearing in the *Washington Post* during the summer of 1999. A commission chaired by former Senators Gary Hart and Warren Rudman had also concluded that terrorism represented the most direst threat to the nation, but their report largely fell on deaf ears. Richard Clarke, one of Bush's national security advisors, also believed that an attack might be imminent. While on vacation in Texas, President Bush received a memo on August 6, 2001, entitled "Bin Laden Determined to Strike in U.S." The briefing specifically mentioned the possibility of terrorists hijacking airplanes to use as weapons, but Bush reportedly did not give the matter any special attention.

The "War on Terror" Begins

On the afternoon of September 11, President Bush appeared on national television to reassure the American people that the country would recover from the attacks of earlier that day and would bring the perpetrators to justice. Three days later, Bush famously appeared with a bullhorn on top of some rubble at the World Trade Center site, shouting encouragement to those digging for bodies at Ground Zero and reiterating his promise to punish those responsible. The following week, he appeared before a joint session of Congress to convey a clear sense of being up to the challenges before him. Bush declared in stark and rather simplistic terms, the country's enemies "hate our freedoms, our freedom of religion, our freedom of speech, our freedom to assemble and disagree with each other." (In later speeches, Bush repeated this theme, stating that the United States was disliked simply because "We love freedom, that's why. And they hate freedom.")

The heart of Bush's congressional address announced that the nation was involved in a "**war on terror**" unlike any conflict the nation had previously fought, with no decisive battlefield victories and few visible achievements to identify progress. Rather, this would be an unrelenting war involving a myriad of covert missions, high-tech operations, efforts to block terrorist financing, and new security legislation. Bush also made it clear that the war on terror might also demand American troops invading countries that supported terrorists. The American people largely approved of the president's words as they still tried to process the magnitude of the recent events. Throughout the country, citizens demonstrated sympathy for the victims as well as outbursts of intense patriotism, usually with good intentions but occasionally not, such as when some turban-wearing Sikhs were mistaken for Muslims and attacked for no reason other than their race or appearance.

After intelligence reports indicated that Osama bin Laden was still camped in Afghanistan, Bush demanded that the Taliban surrender the Al Qaeda leader. When the Taliban refused, Bush initiated hostilities on October 7, 2001, by launching an invasion of Afghanistan, code-named "**Operation Enduring Freedom**," hoping to kill or capture bin Laden as well as to overthrow the Taliban for harboring the terrorist leader and his minions. By December 2001, a combination of American bombing and ground combat operations undertaken by anti-Taliban Afghanis (known as the Northern Alliance) working with U.S. Army Special Forces and U.S. Marines had overthrown the Taliban government, whose members dispersed into the countryside to begin guerilla-style resistance efforts. Meanwhile, a new pro-American government was installed in the capital of Kabul. The new regime repealed Taliban laws denying women the right to attend school and prohibiting movies, music, and other expressions of Western culture but found it difficult to extend its control over the entire country, especially the remote mountain regions where the Taliban regrouped.

Bush insisted that the Taliban's overthrow marked only the beginning of the global war on terrorism. In his January 2002 State of the Union address, the president surprised many listeners by declaring three countries—Iraq, Iran, and North Korea—as forming an "Axis of Evil," being most responsible in his view for terrorism by providing safe sanctuaries for terrorists while also supposedly developing nuclear, chemical, and biological weapons of mass destruction posing the greatest threat to the United States. Despite Bush's forceful rhetoric, no evidence existed to support the notion that any of the three countries were involved in the 9/11 attacks. In the wake of his speech, the president followed advisers who favored the abandonment of the Cold War doctrine of deterrence, replacing that tradition with the concept of "preemptive war," whereby the United States reserved the right to attack a country first if the U.S. government believed that country was a possible future threat to its national security. Coupled with the "Axis of Evil" speech, the effort to justify preemptive war sent shock waves around the world, with many persons overseas fearing that the United States was claiming the right to act as a world policeman in violation of international law.

No sooner did the Bush administration announce the new policy than its real intention became readily apparent—the overthrow of Saddam Hussein—a move desired before 9/11 by many within Bush's inner circle of advisors, including Vice President Cheney, Defense Secretary Rumsfeld, and Deputy Defense Secretary Paul Wolfowitz. All three played key roles in developing a strategy and justification for a war against Iraq, asserting that such a conflict would illustrate the United States' commitment to freedom while bringing much needed stability to the region. They also convinced themselves that the Iraqis would openly welcome the U.S. troops as liberators, leading to the establishment of a democratic government. Initially, Secretary of State Powell opposed an invasion, asserting that the conquest and democratization of Iraq would require hundreds of thousands of American troops and that rebuilding Iraq would take more time than other cabinet officials believed. Powell's assessment fell on deaf ears, including those of the president.

Rumsfeld and other administration officials searched for a pretext to convince Americans and the global community that the overthrow of Saddam Hussein was necessary for both national security and world peace. Although definitely a brutal dictator, Hussein was not an Islamic fundamentalist, nor had any evidence linked him to the September 11 attacks. Nevertheless, to vilify the Iraqi leader, the administration stated that Hussein was developing chemical and bacterial weapons and was seeking to create "weapons of mass destruction," interpreted to mean nuclear arms that could be used by himself or some anti-American terrorist group. Hussein had started research programs into developing nuclear weapons and had used chemical weapons during the Iran-Iraq War of the 1980s as well as against the minority Kurds in northern Iraq. However, his efforts to develop weapons of mass destruction ended with Iraq's defeat in the 1991 Gulf War. The Bush administration's charges prompted the United Nations to send a team of weapons inspectors to Iraq. Soon after, the U.N. team reported that Hussein had no such weapons of mass destruction, but the White House labeled the inspectors' findings as inconclusive given Hussein's supposed ability to hide materials and industrial operations from the inspectors.

Early in 2003, despite his original misgivings, Secretary of State Powell delivered the administration's case before the United Nations Security Council, claiming that Hussein possessed a mobile chemical weapons laboratory, had hidden weapons of mass destruction in his many palaces, and was seeking to acquire uranium from Africa to build nuclear weapons. Every one of his assertions later proved to be false. Powell later felt duped and betrayed by the Bush White House, resigning soon after the president's reelection in 2004. Nevertheless, shortly after Powell's address, the president announced his intention to go to war, with or without U.N. approval, and soon received congressional authorization to use force against Iraq.

The Iraq War

As the patience of Bush administration officials with the U.N. inspections grew thin, antiwar protests emerged throughout the world. Although large-scale anti-war assemblies took place in the United States, the protests had little impact on the opinions of the majority of Americans who still supported the president and his policies. Other challenges came from several veteran foreign policy experts who believed that the administration's preoccupation with Iraq deflected attention from its real enemy, Al Qaeda, which remained capable of launching terrorist attacks. They doubted the ability of the United States to transform the Middle East into a bastion of democracy as the president and his advisers claimed was their long-term objective. Additionally, Afghanistan was still not stabilized, and an invasion of Iraq would force the United States to put the war against the Taliban and Al Qaeda in Afghanistan on the back burner, increasing their chances for survival.

Map 31.3 Afghanistan

Unable to obtain approval from the United Nations, the U.S. nevertheless attacked Iraq in March 2003, with Great Britain as its only substantial ally. President Bush called the war "**Operation Iraqi Freedom**." For all of Hussein's pre-war posturing about his nation's military might, Iraq's military forces once again proved to be no match for the overwhelming firepower of the United States. Within a month, American troops occupied Baghdad. American forces soon captured Hussein, who was subsequently put on trial before an Iraqi court for violation of human rights and other crimes against humanity. (Late in 2006, the court found Hussein guilty of ordering the deaths of many Iraqis during his reign and was executed by hanging.)

Bush jubilantly claimed victory in Iraq by personally landing a fighter jet onto an aircraft carrier off the coast of San Diego, California before delivering a televised address from its deck. The speech was most remembered for a large "Mission Accomplished" banner that served as a backdrop, as well as for the bold pronouncement: "Major combat operations have ended. In the battle of Iraq, the United States and our allies have prevailed." Both the visual of the banner and the president's statement would later come back to haunt the administration. Before long, it would become apparent that Bush's advisors had no sound reconstruction plans or nation-building agenda for Iraq, and no clear exit strategy. Rather than parades welcoming the American troops as liberators, looting and chaos mostly ensued following the fall of the Hussein's regime. Mobs routinely sacked military outposts, government buildings, and businesses with impunity, often seizing large stores of weapons in the process. An insurgency consisting of pro-Saddam Sunni fighters soon developed, targeting American soldiers and Iraqis who cooperated with the occupation forces. Sectarian violence soon swept

many parts of the country as a civil war emerged between Sunni and Shiite Muslims. The Shiite majority, who had always opposed Hussein, saw the developments in Iraq as an opportunity for revenge. Despite holding a number of elections, a stable Iraqi government could not be achieved. Most disturbing, American intelligence agencies revealed that Iraq had become a haven for terrorists seeking to attack Americans. The invasion of Iraq, contrary to the Bush administration's claims, achieved the capture and overthrow of Hussein but very little else, as guerilla fighters took advantage of the power vacuum that emerged in the country. By the end of December 2012, almost 4,500 Americans had been killed and another 33,000 wounded in the effort to maintain control. Ultimately, the U.S. invasion completely destabilized the region and disrupted the balance of power, leading to the emergence of Iran as a major player in the Middle East. As long as Saddam Hussein was in power in Iraq, the possibility of Iran becoming such a threat was less likely to occur. With Iraq embroiled in constant conflict, no counterbalance existed to contain the growing power of Iran, which as a Shiite Muslim nation, looked to spread its influence among the Shiite majority in Iraq and beyond.

The "Price of Freedom"

The war on terror presented some of the greatest challenges to American civil liberties in its history. In the aftermath of the attacks, Congress rushed to pass the **Patriot Act**, which granted unprecedented powers to law enforcement agencies charged with preventing domestic terrorism. Such agencies could now legally wiretap, perform surveillance, intercept and read e-mail, and obtain personal records from third parties all without a suspect's knowledge. Under the direction of Attorney General John Ashcroft, the Justice Department proposed the creation of military tribunals to hold trials, in secret, of suspected terrorists who were not American citizens.

As the Bush administration rounded up suspected terrorists abroad, a detention facility was opened for them at the American military base at Guantanamo Bay, Cuba. There, the captives of the war on terror were incarcerated with many forced to endure brutal interrogations, including "waterboarding" (in which someone being interrogated has water poured over their covered face to create the sensation of drowning) and other forms of physical and mental abuse to extract information. Bush stated that these so-called "enhanced interrogation techniques" were not torture, implying that inflicting pain to gather intelligence was completely different than inflicting pain for punishment or revenge, even though the United States executed Japanese military officers for waterboarding

Misplaced Patriotism: Post-9/11 Violence vs. American Sikhs

Born in Punjab, India, Balbir Singh Sodhi was doing his best to achieve the American dream as an industrious immigrant to the United States when the terrorist attacks of September 11, 2001 took place. Twelve years earlier, he had arrived in California and worked as a taxi driver, eventually saving enough money to buy a gas station in Mesa, Arizona. A devout member of the Sikh religion, he continued to follow the traditions of his faith, which included growing his hair long and wearing a traditional turban.

On the morning of September 15, Sodhi shopped at a local Costco to buy flowers for his station, before donating all of the $75 he had left in his wallet for a 9/11 victims' fund and calling his brother to ask him to buy some American flags to display. Sodhi and his landscaper were outside the gas station planting the flowers when 42-year-old Frank Silva Roque drove up in his Chevy truck. Seeking some sort of revenge for the 9/11 attacks and believing Sodhi was a Muslim because he was wearing a turban, Roque fired five shots at Sodhi with a .380 handgun, killing him. Roque, who had been overheard railing against immigrants at a local sports bar and talking openly about wanting to "go out and shoot some towel heads," drove away quickly and 20 minutes later fired his weapon from his speeding truck at a Lebanese-American man but missed. He then showed up at his former house that had been purchased by an Afghan family and fired multiple rounds at the exterior before driving to a local bar to brag about his deeds. Upon his arrest, Roque reportedly exclaimed: "I am a patriot! I stand for America all the way!" Though his lawyers tried to argue a diminished capacity defense, his co-workers at Boeing aircraft repair facility where Roque worked as a mechanic testified that he was simply narrow-minded and hated immigrants. A jury found him guilty of first-degree murder and sentenced him to death, though the Arizona Supreme Court changed his sentence to life without parole.

Sodhi's murder was hardly a unique occurrence in the aftermath of 9/11, as many Muslims and those perceived to be Muslims became the victims of violence across the country by self-proclaimed patriots seeking revenge for the September 11 attacks. While some violent acts took place within a few days of 9/11 when emotions were highest, hundreds more have occurred in the years since 2001. A sizeable number of these victims have been Sikhs, who have been targeted because their distinctive turbans, and many ignorant perpetrators simply assume that they are Muslim. The most outrageous act of such violence to take place occurred on August 5, 2012, in Oak Creek Wisconsin, when a white supremacist walked into a Sikh gurdwara, or temple, and killed a woman and five turban-wearing men.

In an effort to educate the public and hopefully reduce the level of violence, the Sikh Coalition was formed. The organization promotes civic engagement to foster mutual understanding and the appreciation of diversity through education. Rana Sodhi, one of Balbir Sodhi's brothers, devotes much of his time to speaking at local churches, schools, and community gatherings to encourage tolerance, refusing to be consumed by anger and bitterness over his brother's senseless death.

American POWs during World War II. Nevertheless, on this issue the Bush administration made it clear that the United States would not be bound by international law in prosecuting its war on terror. Government officials were especially eager to disavow the Geneva Convention and the International Convention against Torture, both of which regulate the treatment of prisoners of war and prohibit torture and other forms of physical and mental coercion. In January 2002, the Justice Department issued a memorandum stating that the convention's mandates did not apply to captured members of Al Qaeda because they were "unlawful enemy combatants," rather than soldiers of regular armies. White House counsel Alberto Gonzales advised the president that the Geneva Accords were obsolete in this new kind of war. A year later, February 2003, Bush issued a directive denying Al Qaeda and

Taliban prisoners any of the Geneva protections. In addition, the CIA set up a series of jails in foreign countries as part of an extraordinary "rendition" of suspects, some of whom were naturalized U.S. citizens of Arab-Muslim backgrounds, kidnapped and hauled to prisons in Egypt, Yemen, Syria, and Poland where they were tortured to obtain information. Once such activities became public, the image of the United States as a country adhering to high standards of civilized behavior and the rule of law became seriously damaged.

The 2004 Election

As a result of the protracted struggle to provide stability to Iraq and a limp economy, Bush's popularity had declined by 2004. Democrats believed that they might be able to retake the White House if they found the right candidate. A host of Democrats vied for the presidential nomination. Though Vermont Governor Howard Dean initially rallied the strongest antiwar advocates, it became clear after the first few primaries that Massachusetts Senator John Kerry would be the nominee. A decorated Vietnam War combat veteran who served as commander of a small coastal patrol craft known as a "swift boat," Kerry came home in 1969 after receiving his third Purple Heart and soon joined the antiwar movement. By nominating Kerry, Democrats hoped to put forth a candidate whose military experience would insulate him from Republican charges that Democrats were anti-military and too soft on terrorism. Simultaneously, the party believed his antiwar credentials would appeal to voters opposed to the invasion of Iraq.

No sooner did the campaign begin than a well-funded anti-Kerry organization emerged—the "Swift Boat Veterans for Truth"—which publicly questioned Kerry's heroism as a fabrication. Also hurting Kerry was his appearance before a congressional committee in 1971 in which he denounced the war in Vietnam, followed by his participation in an antiwar demonstration where he joined other disgruntled veterans in throwing their medals and ribbons over a fence erected at the steps of the Capitol. For many Vietnam War veterans, including those who opposed the war (as well as soldiers who served in other conflicts), the disparaging of such honors defiled the memory of those who served without being recognized

for their service. Indeed, these actions proved to be the major motivating factor behind the Swift Boaters' desires to thwart Kerry's candidacy.

Most important, Kerry proved an ineffective candidate. Aloof and lacking the common touch, he failed to generate the same degree of enthusiasm among his supporters that Bush maintained among his core followers. Kerry's inability to explain why he voted in favor of the Iraq War Resolution in the Senate only to denounce it later as a major mistake enabled Republicans to portray him as lacking resolve. Meanwhile, Karl Rove, Bush's political adviser, worked to mobilize the Republican Party's conservative base, believing they would turn out in large numbers to vote for Bush because the president agreed with them on social issues, such as opposition to gay rights, same sex marriage, and abortion. Indeed, the Republican Party sponsored a series of state ballot initiatives in Ohio and other states for the sole purpose of bringing out social conservatives to the polls in an effort to benefit Bush in the presidential race.

Polls predicting a very close election proved to be accurate as Bush won a narrow victory, with a margin of 3 percent of the popular vote and a difference of 286-251 in the Electoral College. In the end, only three states voted differently than four years before. Kerry carried New Hampshire while New Mexico and Iowa swung to the Republicans. Some pundits believed Kerry lost such a close race not because the Republicans dominated the

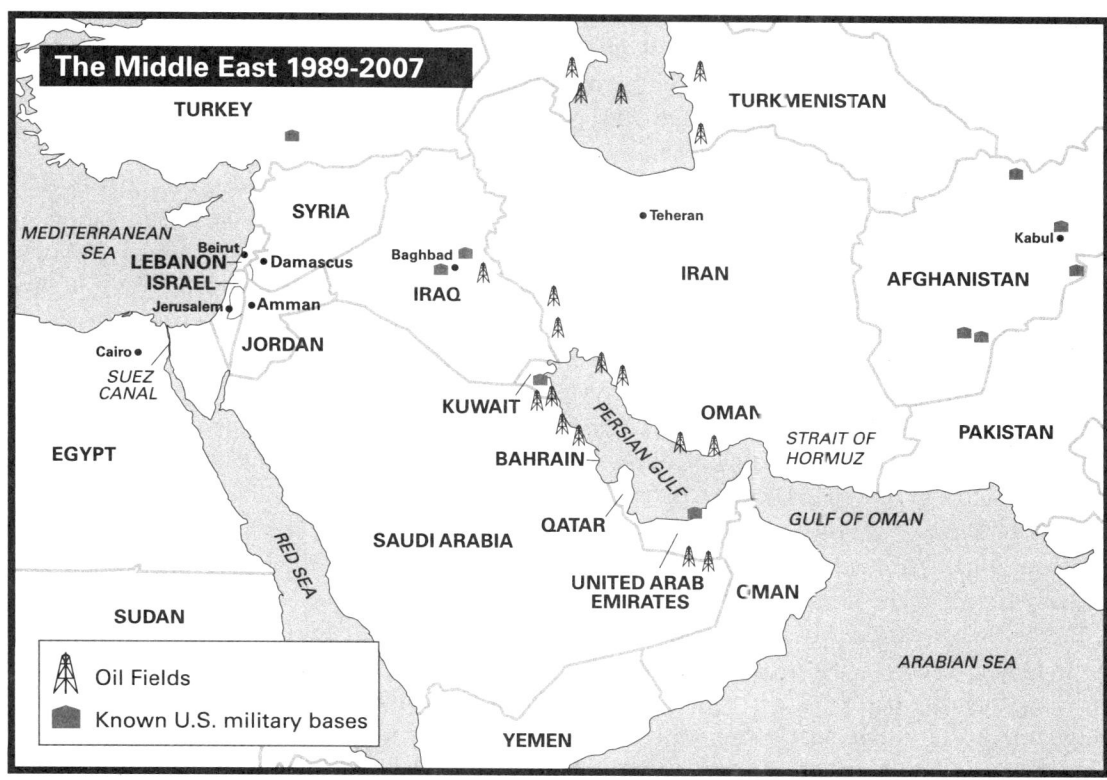

Map 31.4 The Middle East 1989-2007

evangelical Christian vote, but more important to the outcome proved to be the 9/11 attacks and the sense of being engaged in a global war on terrorism. No American president seeking reelection during wartime has ever been defeated and enough of the public agreed with the general course that Bush had taken. The president's popularity, however, would prove to be fleeting as the fighting in Iraq continued and second-term mishaps would lead to a sharp decline of support for Bush's foreign and domestic policies leading in two years to a Democratic takeover of Congress.

BUSH'S SECOND TERM

Bush believed his reelection was a "mandate" for the direction he wanted to move the country, both at home and abroad, stating that he had earned "political capital" that he intended to spend by pushing an aggressively for a conservative agenda during his second term. The president wanted to make his first-term tax cuts permanent and hoped that he could gradually transform Social Security from a public pension system into a privatized "401-K" form of retirement. Meanwhile, he would continue the Iraq War, believing that the United States had to persevere in Iraq until the fighting ceased and a regime friendly to U.S. influence was securely in place.

The president succeeded in moving the Supreme Court decisively to the right on social and civil liberty issues. In 2005, Sandra Day O'Connor, the first woman to be appointed to the Supreme Court, announced her retirement. O'Connor's decision to step down was followed shortly by the death of Chief Justice William Rehnquist. Bush now had the rare opportunity to appoint two justices at once. Bush wasted no time in filling the vacancies. The Senate confirmed two judges that he was confident would align themselves with conservative justices Antonin Scalia and Clarence Thomas. A 50-year old appellate jurist who had once worked in the Reagan Justice Department, John Roberts, succeeded Rehnquist as Chief Justice. Roberts proved to be a qualified choice but such was not the case for Bush's other nominee, Harriet Miers, his long-time family friend and White House counsel. Even right-wing pundits questioned Bush's selection because she possessed relatively meager qualifications for such a revered post. Bush eventually retracted the nomination and chose in her place Samuel Alito, a staunchly conservative federal district court judge, who was confirmed in early 2006 after a hard-fought Senate battle.

Although successfully moving the Supreme Court to the right, the rest of Bush's political agenda failed to materialize. Bush's attempt to partially privatize social security through private investment accounts paid with money diverted from the system's trust fund failed in Congress. The majority of Americans was already skeptical of the initiative and turned decisively against this proposed reform. Elderly Americans were especially wary since their modest but guaranteed monthly Social Security checks provided stability, often determining whether they would eat, pay their utility bills, and keep a roof over their heads.

Hurricane Katrina

The Bush administration's lackluster response to, **Hurricane Katrina**, which slammed into the Gulf Coast on the morning of August 29, 2005, added greatly to the president's decline in popularity. The storm inflicted tens of billions of dollars in property damage from the Florida Panhandle to Louisiana. The greatest damage took place when a storm surge breached the levees at New Orleans causing massive flooding in one of the nation's major metropolitan areas. Over 100,000 citizens, mostly poor, black, and working-class were stranded with no means to leave the city as water poured in from the broken levees. The majority of New Orleans' more affluent white residents who owned cars had been able to leave the city a few days earlier.

For many, the storm highlighted just how desperate the plight of the city's African-American population had been for generations. New Orleans had long been one of the nation's favorite cities to visit, with great cuisine and one of the nation's most exotic and carefree urban environments attracting hundreds of thousands of tourists annually. The majority of visitors, however, rarely ventured beyond the main tourist enclaves, never seeing the squalor, crime, and general destitution endemic among the city's majority black population. They were thus shocked at seeing such plight graphically covered by the television news cameras that arrived in New Orleans days before the Bush administration began to respond to the calamity, especially images of the thousands who rode the storm out packed inside the Superdome where some elderly and infirm people died. Hundreds of the city's inhabitants died during and after Hurricane Katrina made landfall, most of them residents of low-income neighborhoods who not only drowned but also fell victim to the heat, sickness, and dehydration due to an inept evacuation plan and to an excruciatingly slow response from National Guard units and the Federal Emergency Management Administration (FEMA). As a result of Katrina, more than 1.5 million Gulf Coast residents became homeless, eventually finding shelter in schools, sports arenas, hotels, and trailers in Houston, Baton Rouge, Memphis, and other southern and even northern cities.

For many Americans, like the ongoing troubles in Iraq, Katrina reinforced a growing narrative of the seeming incompetence and detachment of the Bush administration. Some even began to question whether such an inadequate response would have occurred if New Orleans was a majority white city. Bush's failure to respond swiftly and decisively resulted in the resignation of Michael Brown, FEMA's director, who in many ways became the scapegoat for the Bush administration's overall mishandling of the Katrina disaster. (Bush had initially expressed confidence in the FEMA director, famously telling him at a press conference: "You're doing a great job, Brownie.") Politically, the hurricane response caused a sharp decline in Bush's overall approval rating. A year after Katrina, corruption and continued mismanagement of the reconstruction process pervaded most facets of the recovery program. Less than half the money ($70 billion) that had been appropriated to assist victims had been spent. Over $2 billion had been lost to fraud and waste, and $900 million worth of mobile homes never got to individuals or went unused because of the determination that they were inappropriate for use in a flood plain. Due to the political and financial mistakes that ensued during the reconstruction effort, only 35 percent of the city's population returned to the Crescent City. The other 65 percent decided to relocate and live permanently elsewhere

The Unraveling of the Bush Presidency

By the close of 2005, the Bush administration's standing suffered as American people had grown increasingly tired of polarized politics and the ongoing conflict in Iraq, which appeared to have no end in sight. A growing number of Americans grew increasingly weary of the administration's talk about how the U.S. was winning over the Iraqi people to freedom and democracy, and how increased troop levels had the insurgents on the run, if not on the verge of defeat. Sectarian violence continued to wrack that war-torn country.

Still, for most Americans, the war was peripheral in their daily lives. They were more concerned with the state of the economy, which had become more inextricably tied to global markets, producing dynamics making some important aspects of life difficult to understand, let alone to predict. The continuing outsourcing of jobs and services continued to become the new order of the day, as increasing number of U.S. corporations, looking for greater profits and cheaper labor costs, moved many, if not all, of their company's operations overseas. In addition to being forced to consume products formerly made in America but now increasingly manufactured overseas, Americans frequently found that when they called a corporation on the telephone to inquire about the balance on their credit card, to negotiate a new rate on their insurance policy, or just to complain about a product they had recently purchased, that they were speaking with someone living and working in a foreign country. Such outsourcing of jobs greatly disturbed and angered Americans, reinforcing the view that corporations seemed to care more about maintaining profits than the long-term economic well being of the country as a whole.

Republicans Divided and Defeated

By the summer of 2006, there still appeared to be no end to the fighting in Iraq, leading many disillusioned Americans to take out their frustrations on the Bush administration and the Republicans in the upcoming congressional elections. Although the war's growing unpopularity would become the central issue of the 2006 campaign, scandals and legal issues would also prove to be devastating to the president's party. In April 2006, Texan Tom DeLay, the powerful House Majority Leader, resigned amid an indictment on campaign finance corruption charges. Other Republicans followed suit for similar malfeasance allegations, most notably those congressmen associated with Jack Abramoff, a notorious influence peddler and Republican partisan. Most appalling was the abrupt resignation of Republican Florida House member Mark Foley who had solicited former congressional pages for homosexual encounters. Finally, the vice president's office, through Dick Cheney's chief of staff, I. Lewis "Scooter" Libby, was responsible for the vindictive "outing" of a covert CIA operative, Valerie Plame, because she and her husband (also a former CIA agent) publicly disclosed many of the administration's lies about the presence of mass destruction in Iraq. Libby was found guilty of perjury and obstruction of justice and sentenced to 30 months in prison in June 2007 but never served a single day's confinement because President Bush commuted his sentence two weeks later.

The Iraq War perpetually plagued the Bush White House. Public opinion polls in 2006 revealed that more than two-thirds of the American people considered Bush's conduct of the war to be misguided. Among the chief critics were many from the military establishment—recently retired officers who fixed much of the blame for the war's debacle on Secretary of Defense Donald Rumsfeld, who they charged with failing to provide an effective exit strategy for U.S. troops. Secretary of State Colin Powell later discovered that he had been deceived by other members of the administration concerning Hussein's possession of weapons of mass destruction.

By November 2006, the majority of Americans no longer equated the conflict in Iraq with the war on terror.

Increasing numbers of initial supporters of the war within the Democratic Party moved decisively toward favoring the withdrawal of American troops. As Americans went to the polls that November, they vented their frustrations toward the Bush administration, resulting in the Democrats capturing both houses of Congress for the first time since 1994. Several Republican incumbents, including some from usually reliable states, lost their congressional seats largely the result of an unpopular president governing during an increasingly unpopular war. When Congresswoman Nancy Pelosi of California was chosen to be Speaker of the House, she became the first female ever to hold that powerful position.

THE COMPUTER AND TELECOMMUNICATION REVOLUTIONS

While the political battles were raging during the first decades of the twenty-first century, developments in the realm of electronics radically changed many core aspects of everyday life for Americans, and, indeed, people throughout much of the world. The electronics revolution created faster, more powerful, and extremely portable comput-ers providing vast benefits for researchers in a variety of fields, increased automation and improved efficiency for business and industry, and incredible gains in mass communication for the general public. The workplace for many professionals changed in notable ways, while friends and family members were now able to maintain contact like never before. Children growing up during these years would now often be treated to stories by their parents about trips to libraries being mandatory to pick up basic information that for them was now available with a few clicks on their computer's mouse. High school and college reunions were becoming less frequent occurrences as people no longer had to wait multiple years to stay in touch because of such developments as email, Skype, and online social networks. The wide diffusion of cell phones and smartphones also made it less likely that people who got separated from each other at amusement parks could not find each other, that those driving in an unknown part of town could not navigate their way to their ultimate destination, or someone whose car broke down on a lonesome stretch of highway would have to walk several miles to knock on someone's door to ask permission to use their house phone to call for a tow truck.

(clockwise from the top) Damaged by the 2005 Hurricane Katrina is a barber shop located in the Ninth Ward, New Orleans, Louisiana, (April 13, 2006) A Waffle House torn apart on the Gulf Coast, Biloxi, Mississippi, (April 12, 2006) and only steps left of a home (March 3, 2006). Credit: Library of Congress

Personal Computers

The capabilities of the latest generation of personal computer were truly remarkable. Now able to play compact discs, DVDs, and sophisticated video games with amazing graphics, they became excellent home entertainment centers. Skype technology now took video conferencing into the home, allowing parents and grandparents to see their kids and loved ones while chatting. Further, the increased availability of the mobile laptop computer provided great convenience for consumers who could now labor productively while away from their office computer, or for vast numbers of people, spend copious amounts of time watching DVD movies or videos on the Internet.

Not all homes had personal computers by the early twenty-first century, but their use was becoming increasingly pervasive. In 2001, 56.3 percent of all American households contained personal computers, up from 36.6 percent just four years earlier. The Census Bureau (which began tracking home computer use in the mid-1908s when only 8 percent of homes had them) has noted that while computer access continued to grow into the early 2000s, demographic differences indicate uneven distribution in ownership. Sixty-one percent of white households in 2001, for example, owned at least one computer, while only 37 percent of black families and only 40 percent of Hispanic households had home access to a computer. By 2011, 75.6 percent of American households had access to a computer, with use in white (76.2 percent) and Asian (82.7 percent) homes still topping Hispanic (58.3 percent) and African American (56.9 percent) households by notable margins.

The Internet

The Defense Department had developed the basic idea of the **Internet**, which allows computers to communicate directly with each other, back in 1969. The World Wide Web (created in the early 1990s) featuring images, movement, and sound, offering an even richer Internet environment than originally established, coupled with the vastly improved capacity of personal computers, made the mass use of the Internet possible by the early twenty-first century. In addition to facilitating the ubiquitous use of the electronic messaging system known as e-mail, the Internet allowed every major U.S. retailer to begin selling their products through their websites, while new businesses emerged to provide a vast array of services, from online dating to auction sites for merchandise. Among the new possibilities created by the Internet, various online social networks emerged, reuniting people from the past while maintaining contact among friends, family members, and acquaintances in the present. Launched in 2004 by Mark Zuckerberg, *Facebook* became the first major billion-dollar social network, generating massive ad revenue while connecting people across the country and around the globe.

Cellphones and "Smartphones"

Though cellular phone technology in the form of car phones and bulky hard-held devices had existed for a while, by the early twenty-first century the new generation of smaller, lighter, and more powerful cell phones at relatively affordable prices led to their mass acceptance by the public. Everyone from the elderly to pre-teens could be seen using them, and unlike personal computers, their relative affordability transcended race and often class lines.

Their popularity was further advanced by the Apple Corporation's release in 2006 of the iPhone, the first so-called "smart phone." A portable hand-held computer with telephonic capabilities, the smartphone became a part of life by the early 2000s, enabling people to utilize its capabilities to serve as an all-in-one portable computer, telephone, digital camera, and Internet searching device. As with cellphones, their utility and relative affordability also ensured their widespread use. Census data indicates that 50 percent of all Americans in 2011 used a smartphone in the everyday lives, with little difference noted by race or class. One noteworthy difference in smartphone use can be seen in the age of the user. While slightly over two-thirds of Americans under the age of 25 owned one in 2011, that number dropped to only 45 percent for those in the 45-54 year-old category, and only 23.3 percent of those 55 years of age and older that year reported owning a smartphone.

A POLITICAL PENDULUM

The partisan rancor and highly polarized electorate that characterized the early 1990s continued into the early twenty-first century. National politics became a roller coaster ride, as the nearly evenly-divided country moved back and forth, giving alternating control of the federal government to one party then the other as it reacted to a series of tumultuous internal and external events. George H.W. Bush was flying high in the early 1990s after the Gulf War, only to be consumed by a sharp recession and a broken tax pledge as the Republican president tried to shore up the huge budget deficit resulting from Ronald Reagan's economic policies. The country then gave Dem-

The World Wide Web

Did you register for this class electronically? Did you log on to the internet when you got up this morning, or perhaps began your day playing on online game? For the vast majority of people, utilizing the internet has become second nature, as much a part of their daily routine as eating meals. While many assume that the World Wide Web has been a part of the world as long as radios, televisions, and other modern means of communication, the internet is actually a very recent phenomenon, only being utilized by people since the 1990s.

The 1990s are remembered as a decade of great technological leaps, when digital hardware and software began to blossom, as cassette players gave way to CDs, and mobile phones first became ubiquitous in mainstream America. But the most remarkable and significant breakthrough of the decade by far was the development of the World Wide Web, a new form of "interconnectedness" among computers that would change daily life across much of the world.

The breakthrough responsible for creating the Web took place in 1990 through the brainstorm of a British computer scientist named Tim Berners-Lee, who proposed building a global informational system of hyperlinked documents and multimedia formats such as graphics, audio, and video. Berners-Lee christened the system a "web," since it depended on multiple platforms, formats, and documents all "spun" from intersected sources. An actual system of interconnected computer networks known as the "internet" was not new; in fact, one version had existed since the 1960s, within the United States military, and had grown to exchange data between government departments. Berners-Lee's idea built upon the existing structure and accentuated in a groundbreaking way. He envisioned technology in which data was relayed back and forth between a server and a client, from computer to computer, but also one that could utilize mobile devices.

The existing client-server infrastructure made it all possible, allowing content to be received and viewed on each end through the use of a software application that Berners-Lee named a "browser." Other essential components that he utilized were "Hypertext Markup Language (HTML) and Hypertext Transfer Protocol, both of which were brand new technologies developed in 1990. Berners-Lee wrote the code for the world's first web browser on a workstation called the NeXT Computer and published it on December 20, 1990, eventually calling the browser and web editor "Nexus." This first "Web" function, capable of displaying basic content, but also allowing the downloading of documents, video files, sound files, and graphics, revolutionized the industry.

Today, the Web has become an essential part of our lives, becoming the primary means by which we communicate socially, and has become the primary communication tool of business and commerce. We use it for research, to learn new information, to book travel, and to conceive new and innovative modes of business, play, and social interaction. Without the World Wide Web, entertainment today would be vastly different, education would remain in an often less accessible format, and our world would be, in a sense, "larger" and more distant than it is today. In many ways, electronic information delivered by Berners-Lee's idea has become the most significant force of "democratization" the world has ever known.

ocrat Bill Clinton two terms, but in spite of his adoption of many conservative positions on issues such as welfare reform, his efforts to reform health care, recognize the service of gays in the military, and his personal behavior energized his Republican opponents, leading to their seizure of the House and Senate for the first time in 40 years. After a bitterly contested election resulting in the Supreme Court voting along partisan lines, Republican George W. Bush assumed the presidency.

Political differences were temporarily put on hold after the terrorist attacks of September 11 brought unity to a horrified nation. The American people came together to support military operations in Afghanistan against Osama bin Laden and the Taliban leadership that protected him. The majority of Americans even supported President Bush when his administration tried to tie Saddam Hussein to Al Qaeda in order to justify toppling the Iraqi dictator's regime. Political control would swing back, however, after Bush was re-elected, as a result of public frustration with the long, drawn-out fight in Iraq after Hussein's removal and the administration's failed response to Hurricane Katrina. Democrats took back Congress in 2006 as the country continued to muddle through ongoing unpopular military conflicts in the Middle East. Within two years, America would witness the arrival on the national stage of Barack Obama—a fresh political figure whose place in history would be assured when he became the country's first black president in 2009, but his often-expressed hope to breach the nation's partisan divide would largely prove to be illusory.

Table 31.1

Arrival of Noteworthy Consumer Electronic Products and Services

Date	Development	Significance
1979	Sony Walkman	Portable cassette player
1981	Laptop Computer	Allowed mobile personal computing
1982	Compact Disc (CD) Player	Playback of digitally stored music
1983	Analog Camcorder	Portable video recording
1983	First Commercially Available Cellular Phone	Mobile phone communication
1984	Sony Discman	Portable CD Player
1985	CD-ROM	Disc storage of computer data
1989	Tablet Computer	Mobile computer with stylus input rather than mouse or keyboard
1990	Portable Digital Camera	Processing and development of photographic images via computer
1994	World Wide Web	Beginning of public internet services
1995	Digital Camcorder	Digital processing of camcorder videos
1996	High-definition Television	Vastly improved television imagery
1997	DVD Player	Improved digital video storage and playback (vs. analog VCR technology)
1998	MP3 Player	Playback of digital audio files
1999	High-speed Internet	Vastly increased speed of data delivery over the internet
1999	Bluetooth	Wireless headset
1999	Blackberry	Two-way paging communication
1999	Digital Video Recorder (DVR)	Digital recording of television programming
2000	Flash (Thumb) Drive	Extremely compact and mobile digital data storage device
2003	Skype	Voice, video, and text videoconferencing via the internet
2004	Facebook	First billion-dollar social network
2007	Apple iPhone	Handheld computer with telephonic, internet, and digital camera capabilities

Chronology

1992 Bill Clinton elected president.

1993 Janet Reno becomes first female attorney general.
Israel and the PLO sign Oslo Accords.
Branch Davidian siege in Waco, Texas.
U.S. soldiers killed in Somalia.
Congress approves NAFTA.
Terrorist bomb explodes in the World Trade Center.
Brady Bill signed into law.
North American Free Trade Agreement enacted.

1994 U. S. troops intervene in Haiti.
Genocide in Rwanda.
O.J. Simpson trial begins.
Republicans win both houses of Congress.

1995 Oklahoma City Bombing.
Israeli Prime Minister Yitzhak Rabin assassinated.
Srebrenica Massacre in Bosnia.
Dayton Accords signed.

1996 Personal Responsibility and Work Opportunity
Reconciliation Act
Clinton re-elected president.

1997 Madeleine Albright becomes first female
Secretary of State.

1998 Monica Lewinsky scandal.
Clinton impeached.

1999 Senate trial failed to approve articles of impeachment.
United States, with NATO, bombs Serbia.

2000 *U.S.S. Cole* damaged by terrorist bombing.
George W. Bush elected president.

2001 Bush tax cuts passed.
September 11. Terrorists destroy the World Trade
Center and damage the Pentagon.
United States attacks Afghanistan, driving out
Taliban government.
Patriot Act signed.

2002 Department of Homeland Security established.

2003 War with Iraq begins.

2004 Bush re-elected for a second term.

2005 Hurricane Katrina.

2006 Democrats gain control of both houses of Congress.

SUGGESTED READINGS

Richard Bernstein, *Out of the Blue: the Story of September 11* (2002).

George W. Bush, *Decision Points* (2010).

Richard Clarke, *Against All Enemies: Inside America's War on Terror* (2004).

Bill Clinton, *My Life* (2004).

Greg Critser, *Fat Land: How Americans Became the Fattest People in the World* (2002).

Alfred Eckes, Jr. and Thomas Zeilin, *Globalization and the American Century* (2003).

Lawrence Freedman and Efraim Karsh, *The Gulf Conflict, 1990-1991* (1993).

Gertrude Himmelfarb, *One Nation, Two Cultures* (1999).

Christopher Jencks, *The Homeless* (1994).

Haynes Johnson, *Divided We Fall: Gambling with History in the Nineties* (1994).

Joe Klein, *The Natural: The Misunderstood Presidency of Bill Clinton* (2002).

Alex Kotlowitz, *There Are No Children Here: The Story of Two Boys Growing Up in the Other America* (1991).

Jere Longman, *Among the Heroes: United Flight 93* (2002).

James T. Patterson, *Restless Giant: The United States from Watergate to Bush v. Gore* (2005).

Timothy Phelps and Helen Winternitz, *Capitol Games: Clarence Thomas, Anita Hill and the Story of a Supreme Court Nomination* (1992).

Kevin Phillips, *Wealth and Democracy* (2001).

Jeremy Rifkin, *The End of Work: The Decline of the Labor Force and the Dawn of the Post-Market Era* (1995).

Arthur M. Schlesinger Jr., *The Disuniting of America* (1991).

Eric Schlosser, *Fast Food Nation: The Dark Side of the All-American Meal* (2001).

Jeffrey Toobin, *Too Close to Call: The Thirty-Six Day Battle to Decide the 2000 Election* (2001).

Sanford J. Unger, *Fresh Blood: The New American Immigrants* (1995)

William Julius Wilson, *When Work Disappears: The World of the New Urban Poor* (1996).

Review Questions

1. What were some of Clinton's major policy and program accomplishments? What were some of his failures and why in both cases are they considered to be successes or failures?

2. Describe the basics of the Lewinsky debacle. How did President Clinton's behavior cause damage to the presidency? How did Republicans misread the attitude of Americans to the whole affair?

3. How have the terrorist attacks of September 11, 2001 changed America?

4. Discuss the challenges that the United States has faced in conducting its "war on terror." What have been some of its successes and notable shortcomings?

5. Describe how the administration's response to Hurricane Katrina contributed to Bush's decline in popularity during his second term.

Glossary of Important People and Concepts

Al Qaeda
Osama bin Laden
Brady Bill
Branch Davidians
George W. Bush
Bush tax Cuts
Bush v. Gore
Bill Clinton
Clinton Boom
Contract with America
"Don't Ask, Don't Tell"
Al Gore
Hurricane Katrina
Internet
Kosovo
Monica Lewinsky
North American Free Trade Agreement (NAFTA)
Oklahoma City Bombing
Operation Enduring Freedom (Afghan War)
Operation Iraqi Freedom (Iraq War)
Patriot Act
September 11 attacks
Somalia
Taliban
War on Terror

President Barack Obama delivers the State of the Union address in the House Chamber at the U.S. Capitol in Washington, D.C., January 24, 2012. (Official White House Photo by Pete Souza)

Chapter Thirty-two

BARACK OBAMA, DONALD TRUMP, JOSEPH BIDEN AND CONTEMPORARY AMERICA

*Beginning with his first presidential campaign, a group of conspiracy-minded right-wing opponents of Barack Obama who came to be known as the "Birthers" would initiate accusations that Barack was not born in Hawaii as he claimed, but rather, his mother gave birth to him outside of the United States, making him ineligible for the presidency under their reading of the Constitution, which states that presidents had to be 35 years of age at the time of election and a "natural born citizen"—a term never defined in the document. Even if one assumed the Birthers' facts that the candidate was born outside the U.S., most legal scholars believe that Obama was still a natural born citizen because his mother, a white woman named Ann Dunham, was an American citizen born in Kansas. Nevertheless, the truth remains that Obama was indeed born in the United States: his parents announced Obama's birth in a local newspaper—the **Honolulu Advertiser**—on August 13, 1961, a little more than a week after the future president was born. Still, the Birthers thought they smelled blood due to the fact that the candidate refused to release a long-form copy of his birth certificate to the public. It did not even occur to them that Obama and his advisers chose not reveal the document because they might be playing on the Birthers' paranoia to effectively paint his Far Right opponents as unreasonable fanatics.*

Helping to fuel the accusations and keep them alive were the rantings of Obama's future successor, New York billionaire Donald J. Trump. For his part, Trump began to use the Birther movement to grab headlines and further his own political aspirations. Though Obama largely ended any remaining controversy with the general public by finally releasing the long form of his birth certificate on April 27, 2011, Trump and others stated that they doubted its authenticity and tried to keep the story alive in the press. Three days later, the president was provided an opportunity to lampoon Trump in person when he famously ridiculed the mogul in front of a raucous crowd at the annual White House Correspondents' Dinner. Taking a break from his responsibilities (just an hour before the dinner, he authorized Navy SEALs to launch a raid in Pakistan that would result in the death of Osama bin Laden), Obama proclaimed to all in attendance: "Now, I know that he's taken some flak lately, but no one is happier, no one is prouder to put this birth certificate matter to rest than The Donald. And that's because he can finally get back to focusing on things that matter--like, did we fake the moon landing? What really happened at Roswell? And where are Biggie and Tupac?"

Through much of his 2016 presidential campaign, Trump continued to cast doubt on Obama's birth origin because it was such "red meat" for the party's base who loved hearing the candidate ridicule the president. After securing the Republican nomination and hearing from advisers that it would not be a wise issue to continue highlighting going forward in a general election, Trump dropped the matter by characteristically announcing a "news conference" that turned into a hour-long staged event promoting his new Washington, D.C. hotel followed by a salute to Trump by veterans who supported his candidacy. At the conclusion, he told the assembled reporters that his current opponent, Hillary Clinton, originally started the birther controversy during her primary fight against Obama back in 2008, before quickly reading a brief statement: "President Barack Obama was born in the United States. Period."

In the final analysis, while the Birther movement certainly included many unbalanced people who were willing to believe any conspiracy theory tossed their way, the force being the movement must be viewed for what it was: a rather crass political tactic advanced by crafty conservative political operatives seeking to further a false narrative in a blatant effort to discredit the popular African-American candidate, and later president, by placing doubts in the public's mind about his legitimacy. For his part, Obama largely accepted such political attacks as part of the job, but lectured reporters on the day that he released his long-form birth certificate: "I know there is going to be a segment of people for which no matter what we put out, this issue will not be put to rest. But I am speaking to the vast majority of the American people, as well as to the press. We do not have time for this kind of silliness. We've got better stuff to do."

Hillary Clinton

BARACK OBAMA AND THE ELECTION OF 2008

The Rise of Barack Obama

Though many individuals ascended to the American presidency under remarkable circumstances, the rise of **Barack Obama** to the highest office in the land is surely unique. Born in Honolulu, Hawaii, on August 4, 1961, Obama was the son of a white mother from Kansas (Ann Dunham) and an African father (Barack Obama, Sr.) who met each other while they attended the University of Hawaii at Manoa. While his parents were busy pursuing their education, Obama spent much of his early childhood being raised by his mother's parents in Hawaii. After his parents divorced and his mother married an Indonesian man who came to study at the University of Hawaii, the six-year-old Obama moved with his mother to Indonesia where she taught English and performed anthropology research. At age 10, he returned to Hawaii to attend a prep school while once again being cared for by his mother's parents. Obama eventually attended Columbia University, majoring in political science and international relations. Upon his graduation, he spent time as a community organizer in Chicago before attending Harvard Law School where he became the first African American to serve as president and editor of the prestigious *Harvard Law Review*. Obama then taught constitutional law at the University of Chicago for 12 years before winning election to the Illinois State Senate in 1997. Though he was defeated in a run for a U.S. House seat in 2000, he successfully gained election to the U.S. Senate in 2004.

While a candidate for that office, he gained the national notoriety by delivering a well-received keynote address at the Democratic National Convention. Though seen as a rising star in the party, most Democrats anticipated that he would not seek the presidency just four years into his first Senate term.

A Landmark Election

The 2008 election proved to be a momentous political event, producing not only a resounding victory for the Democratic Party in many key congressional races, but, most noteworthy, for Barack Obama as the nation's first African-American president. Senator Obama's campaign, culminating with his resounding victory over his Republican rival, Arizona Senator John McCain, was historic in many ways. The initial Democratic primary season was itself unprecedented, as Obama not only ended up defeating a host of experienced male party stalwarts, but also the woman who emerged as his main challenger, former First Lady **Hillary Clinton** (then serving as a U.S. Senator representing New York), who became the first woman to have a good chance of winning a major party's presidential nomination. (Maine Senator Margaret Chase Smith had previously sought the Republican nomination in 1964 and Congresswoman Shirley Chisholm also ran for the 1972 Democratic Party nomination.) After a hard-fought battle, Clinton finally acknowledged that Obama had won more delegates to win the Democratic Party's nomination on the first ballot and Obama graciously offered Clinton a high Cabinet post in his administration if he ended up winning the general election. For his running mate, Obama turned to Joseph Biden, a veteran senator from Delaware who had been one of the nominee's primary opponents. Biden provided Obama with an experienced member of Congress that he could lean on for advice, especially in foreign affairs (Biden served for decades on the U.S. Senate Foreign Relations Committee) as well as helping to secure support from wayward blue-collar voters who had been increasingly drawn to the Republicans since the days of Ronald Reagan.

On the Republican side, Senator **John McCain** of Arizona captured the nomination, defeating two conservative candidates, former Massachusetts Governor Willard "Mitt" Romney and former Arkansas Governor Mike Huckabee. As Clinton and Obama slugged it out from January to June, McCain moved ahead in the polls. McCain's campaign further received a jumpstart when he surprisingly selected first-term Alaska Governor Sarah Palin, a darling of the party's evangelicals, to be his vice-presidential choice. Choosing her only a few days before the national convention, a good number of Republicans, especially the moderates, were shocked by such a choice. Yet, for a few weeks after the Republican ballyhoo of the Republican National Convention in Minneapolis, Minnesota, the "Palin Factor" appeared to have a positive effect for the McCain campaign. Conservative Republicans celebrated her selection, proclaiming her to be the fresh, new, young, attractive look they needed to win. Moreover, Palin expressed support for the Far Right agenda, endearing her to that wing of the party.

As the presidential campaign rolled into the fall months, the economy continued its decline, forcing both candidates in October to return to Washington to vote on a $700 billion bailout package for the banks and major Wall Street brokerage firms that were going under due to a series of questionable practices (to be discussed later in this chapter). Such a financial calamity could not have been worse for McCain. Obama deftly tied him to George Bush (whose approval rating hovered near 30 percent) in every speech he delivered, declaring that McCain was no different than Bush in mentality and policy, and thus responsible for the present crises both at home and abroad. McCain would later regret declaring that the economy was "fundamentally sound," but perhaps the biggest mistake the candidate made was to allow the party's right wing to highjack his campaign. The senator had earned a reputation for being a "maverick" within his party, often expressing moderate views on many social issues such as immigration and campaign finance reform. As he began to slip in the polls, however, McCain allowed the right wing of his party to take control of his campaign and dictate the strategy, doubling down on conservative domestic and foreign policy issues in an effort to increase turnout among the Republican base. The majority of American voters, however, had become alienated and

disillusioned with George Bush, who they associated with the Republican right wing, and began to be turned off by the Republican campaign.

Compounding McCain's woes was the subpar performance of Sarah Palin as the vice-presidential candidate. Whenever she spoke in an unmanaged way, especially in press interviews, she constantly uttered inarticulate and uninformed thoughts. Palin's repeated gaffes and general inability to express coherent explanations of policy matters caused increasing numbers of Americans to fear the consequences if a President McCain should die in office. No matter how hard Republican spokespersons tried to bolster Palin as a viable running mate, their arguments fell on deaf ears.

As the economy worsened, it became increasingly clear as Election Day approached that Obama would win. Ultimately, he defeated McCain by winning 53 percent of the popular vote and the Electoral College by a 365-173 margin. His triumph, though aided by the deficiencies of his opponent's campaign, was grounded in his personal charisma, his well-honed oratorical skills, and his well disciplined, tech-savvy, and inspired campaign organization that was able to identify and mobilize supportive voters to the polls. To them, Obama promised change, moving away from the failed policies of the Bush years and looking forward to a brighter future. Though many Republicans feared that he was a liberal demagogue, Obama mixed support for New Deal-style programs with centrist pro-business appeals reminiscent of Bill Clinton's policies. In the end, the "Obama coalition" that his campaign was able to assemble—African Americans, Latinos, young "millennial" voters, single women, college-educated urban whites, and blue-collar workers—helped to ensure his victory.

OBAMA'S FIRST TERM DOMESTIC CHALLENGES

Though the state of the economy looked ominous in early 2009, Americans held high expectations as Barack Obama assumed office. Like Franklin Roosevelt, he sought to bolster citizens' spirits with a message of hope and change as he inherited an economic downturn that threatened the very fabric of the nation's stability. As Obama and his team of advisers scrambled to address what turned out to be the worse economic decline since the Great Depression, unlike FDR, he also would have to contend with two costly and prolonged wars overseas. The fact that he was ultimately successful in dealing with these challenges contributed to the president maintaining relatively high approval ratings guaranteeing his reelection.

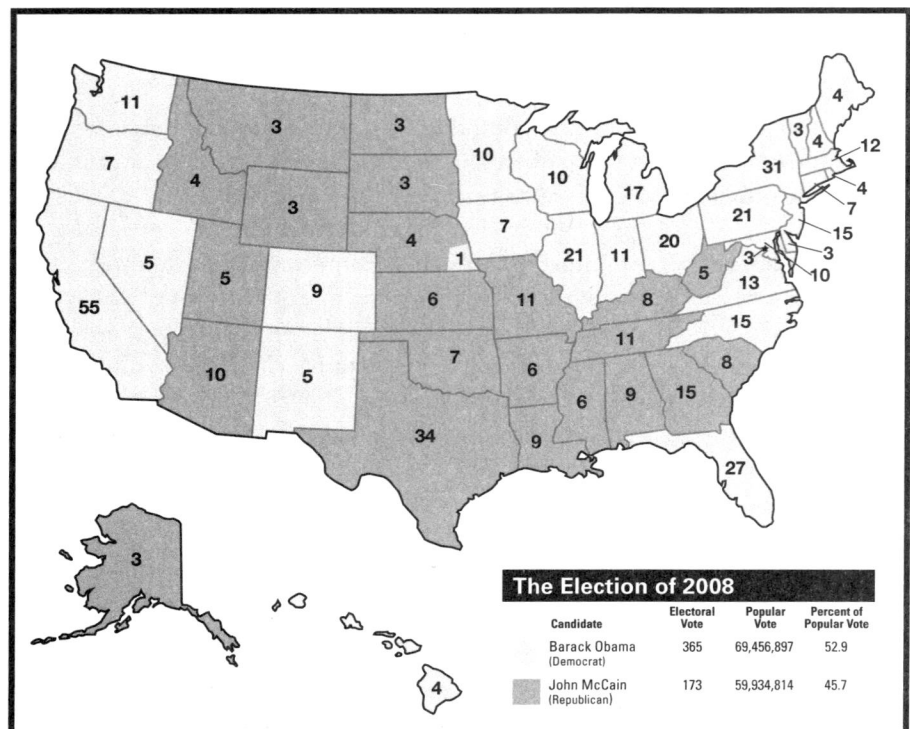

Map 32.1 The Election of 2008

The Election of 2008

Candidate	Electoral Vote	Popular Vote	Percent of Popular Vote
Barack Obama (Democrat)	365	69,456,897	52.9
John McCain (Republican)	173	59,934,814	45.7

From Recession to Crisis

During the summer of 2008, the failure of several major Wall Street brokerage firms, such as Lehman Brothers, Behr-Stearns, and Merrill-Lynch, as well as the real risk of collapse for Citibank, Bank of America, and the insurance giant AIG precipitated a genuine national economic crisis. Greatly contributing to the meltdown of these businesses was the development by the financial community of highly complicated speculative enterprises, most notably in the housing market with the arrival of **mortgage-backed securities**, that is, investments based on the cash flows derived from mortgage loans. Created by Wall Street, this device became an unregulated investment that was highly lucrative as long as borrowers continued to make their mortgage payments. The system collapsed, however, with devastating effects on investors and several key financial institutions when an unsafe number of homeowners defaulted. This occurred in some cases because borrowers simply failed to keep up with their payments due to over-borrowing. Many others, however, defaulted because their adjustable-rate loans, which had very low introductory interest rates for the first few years, rose dramatically based on formulas tied to various lending indexes, leading to outrageously high fixed rates (some as high as 16 percent). Still other borrowers had become victims of the deceptive "**predatory lending**" practices that lured unwary customers into mortgages they could never afford or with hidden terms they did not understand. When the previously booming housing market contracted, housing prices plummeted so fast that, seemingly overnight, homeowners found themselves "underwater" on their mortgages, meaning that they owed far more on their homes than they were worth. Such individuals tried to sell their homes, but as financially strapped banks and mortgage lenders (who before the recession had been extraordinarily lenient) began to tighten their credit requirements, fewer potential buyers could qualify for new loans. Thus, millions of Americans found themselves having to pay exorbitant interest rates on homes of steadily decreasing value, leading to leading to an exorbitant level of foreclosures not seen since the Great Depression. By the time of Obama's inauguration, thousands of once middle-class suburban neighborhoods, especially the huge new tract housing developments, became half-finished, abandoned, overgrown ghost towns. Particularly devastated by the recession were the states of California, Florida, Nevada (especially the Las Vegas area), and Arizona—states that had witnessed the most dramatic increases in new home construction and inflated home values over the previous decade.

The collapse of the housing market soon reverberated throughout the rest of the economy, causing hundreds of home-construction related businesses to close their doors, driving up unemployment. In the six months leading up to Obama's inauguration, the economy was shrinking at an annual rate of 9 percent. Since the recession began in December 2007, the United States had lost 8.4 million jobs, with millions more joining the ranks of the underemployed, which reached 17 percent by March

2010. Equally serious, job opportunities for recent college graduates greatly decreased with only a few occupations such as health care, engineering, and education providing employment possibilities on a full-time basis. The unemployment rate had reached 10 and 15 percent in California and Michigan, respectively. Because of the failing auto industry's concentration in the greater Detroit metropolitan area, the Motor City saw its unemployment skyrocket to 25 percent by spring 2009. By that time, both General Motors and Chrysler had gone bankrupt, with plant closings and related industries, including dealerships, shutting down across the nation, leading to thousands of more Americans becoming unemployed.

The Government Response

In response to the worst economic crisis to hit the country since the Great Depression, the incoming Obama administration and Congress intervened in ways that ultimately brought stability. The federal government had, in fact, already begun to address the financial crisis in the summer of 2008 during the presidential campaign. Then-Senator Obama had returned to Washington, D.C. to help pass emergency legislation, with President George W. Bush's approval, designed to shore up the nation's crumbling financial system. The intervention was in some ways reminiscent of the Roosevelt administration's approach soon after FDR assumed the presidency (see Chapter 24), specifically, through the government providing low-interest loans, the purchase of company stock, and other forms of bailouts overseen by the **Troubled Asset Relief Program (TARP)**. Congress initially allocated $700 billion for the effort, though ultimately less than $450 billion was utilized. The government eventually saw a small profit once the markets stabilized, and the government was compensated for the aid provided.

With respect to the auto industry, to prevent the collapse of General Motors and Chrysler, the Obama administration decided to bail out both companies in the form of a quasi-"receivership." Each corporation was placed under temporary government control in return for billions in bailout dollars. Further, the CEO's of each company were to restructure their corporations according to government guidelines in order to ensure future solvency and maintain employment. Free-market advocates and other conservatives criticized the president for his "government takeover" of GM and Chrysler, accusing Obama of being a big-government liberal if not a closet "socialist," but offering nothing in return other than the prospect of allowing GM and Chrysler to go bankrupt. Regardless of the criticism, the Obama administration's moves resulted in the preservation of thousands of workers' jobs.

In addition to dealing with the short-term crisis, the Obama administration sought to deal with the overall recession by making the creation of new jobs a high priority. Soon after entering the Oval Office, the new president urged Congress to pass a massive stimulus initiative designed to save and create jobs and promote economic recovery through a variety of means. The plan called for assistance in the form of the extension of unemployment benefits, tax relief for those most impacted by the recession, investments in infrastructure projects and others that would increase economic efficiency by supporting technological advances in science and health-related industries, and direct aid to state and local government budgets to help avoid tax increases or cuts in essential social services. The package, known as the **American Recovery and Reinvestment Act**, became the largest stimulus program in the nation's history, creating or saving approximately 640,000 jobs, though the final amount of $787 billion authorized by Congress fell far short of the much-higher level of spending that many liberal economists believed would be necessary to generate a completely robust recovery. In the end, the program had a minimal effect on reducing unemployment but did help to stabilize the growing national unemployment rate.

Many progressives at the time believed that Obama missed a prime opportunity at the beginning of his administration to reform the American capitalist system. The repeal of historic regulatory measures that had been supported by the Clinton administration (most notably the New Deal's Glass-Steagall Act) had opened the floodgates for Wall Street's later abuse of the nation's financial edifice. Upon his inauguration, Obama had public support to propose significant structural changes to the U.S. economy, but after a year in office he lost much of that momentum and failed to use his office to push for major systemic reforms. Obama's main effort with regard to addressing Wall Street's reckless behavior was to seek congressional passage in the summer of 2010 of the **Dodd-Frank Wall Street Reform and Consumer Protection Act**. The Dodd-Frank bill would establish an independent consumer bureau within the Federal Reserve to help protect borrowers against predatory lenders when seeking home mortgages, credit cards, and other situations. The legislation set up a council of federal regulators to watch for threats to the financial system, requiring large financial corporations to maintain comfortable levels of monetary reserves. The government could shut down a company's operations before their collapse could cause a ripple effect and bring down other banking houses, which the 2008 collapse revealed were more intimately connected than anyone realized. In the Senate, the bill passed by a vote of 60-39, with three Republican senators voting for the measure. Senator Russell Feingold of Wisconsin was the lone Democrat who opposed the bill, asserting that it did not go far enough in regulating Wall Street. Feingold was not alone in his criticism that Dodd-Frank was too weak in bringing Wall Street bankers and financiers to task for what they had done. Many liberals criticized Dodd-Frank for failing to more aggressively alter the structure of Wall Street and for leaving so many critical decisions to federal regulators who missed many of the warning signs before the 2008 crisis. Meanwhile, Republicans typically argued that the bill created bigger, more intrusive government, insisting that the new regulations would undermine the U.S. economy's competitiveness, stifle job growth, and kill jobs at a time when unemployment was still high. By 2012, none of the Republicans' dire forecast had come true.

The Health Care Debate

Early in his presidency, Obama refused to be overly confrontational, repeatedly presenting himself as a conciliator seeking to find common ground with his political opponents. Despite these well-intentioned attempts to work with the Republicans in a bipartisan fashion, it became clear that GOP leadership had no such desire to do so, instead vowing to pursue a dogged policy of obstructionism.

No issue of the early Obama administration more clearly demonstrated how the president and congressional Republicans would interact going forward than the debate over health-care reform. While the president tried to seek common ground, Republicans down the line refused to cooperate. A Democratic-sponsored bill proposed the most sweeping changes in the nation's health-care system since the mid-1960s when President Lyndon Johnson, along with fellow Democrats and some Republicans, created Medicare and Medicaid. At the time, the United States was still the only advanced nation without universal health care and had by far the world's highest health-care costs.

Though he deferred to Congress to work out the legislative details, the final product satisfied the major goals sought by the president. As finally drafted, the bill intended to eliminate medical discrimination, (such as denial of coverage due to pre-existing conditions) and mandated coverage for an additional 30 million Americans, leaving only 6 percent of the total population uninsured. Controversially, the proposed law attempted to control health-care costs by instituting an "individual mandate" on citizens by stipulating that all adults have health insurance coverage or be subject to tax penalties. This last provision had been demanded by insurance companies to help with the added cost of covering individuals with pre-existing conditions. (The bill did provide premium subsidies for low-income Americans to make their new health insurance affordable.) The Congressional Budget Office announced that the initiative would reduce the federal deficit by $138 billion in its first decade, amounting to approximately $1.2 trillion in its second decade in operation. The reform bill promised to be fiscally responsible while taking major steps toward dealing with rising health-care costs. In both houses of Congress, voting fell along strict party lines, with no Republicans in either chamber supporting the bill.

For President Obama, the fight over the health care reform bill began to impact his approach to governing. When he began his administration, he was hopeful that he could achieve needed reforms with some Republican support. His campaign pledge to work across party lines, however, became increasingly an unrealistic possibility due to determined Republican obstructionism. After months of enduring escalating vitriol about his policies, Obama began to give up on the bipartisan approach. Though he preferred the role of a consensus builder, he ultimately ignored his critics and secured passage of the legislation, known formally as the **Patient Protection and Affordable Care Act** (often casually referred to as the Affordable Care Act and derisively labeled "**Obamacare**" by its Republican opponents in an effort to directly link the president to what they hoped would become an increasingly unpopular reform measure).

No sooner did the health care reform bill pass than GOP leaders vowed to pursue its repeal, declaring that such action would be the major theme of their fall congressional campaign. The partisan struggle against the measure quickly shifted from Congress to the states and their federal courthouses. Led by several states' respective attorney generals, Republicans challenged the reform by declaring that its individual mandate violated both state sovereignty and individual rights. In mid-2012, the Supreme Court made its ruling on these legal challenges and surprisingly (given the conservative bent of the High Court) approved the individual mandate provision of the Affordable Care Act as a constitutional use of Congress' taxing power. Nevertheless, opponents continued to file lawsuits against other elements of the legislation and hampered implementation of portions of the law at the state level by such tactics as refusing to establish so-called "health insurance exchanges" where individuals shopped for insurance coverage by comparing available plans, forcing the federal government to develop such marketplaces for citizens residing in those states.

The Tea Party Movement

When the president first introduced his health-care initiative in early summer 2009, surprisingly shrill opposition appeared in town hall meetings throughout the country that were held to gauge the peoples' feelings about the proposed reform bill. Groups of individuals had already been gathering across the country to protest the Wall Street and automobile company bailouts and to vent outrage at perceived government handouts and entitlements, certain that such programs would inevitably lead to increased taxation. In its early phases, the **"Tea Party"** movement represented a simple tax protest, with members rhetorically connecting their cause against current government "tyranny" with that of colonial Americans against the alleged oppressive policies of the British government during the 1760s and 1770s. Colonial protests against Parliament's decrees had culminated with the 1773 Boston Tea Party, hence, the adoption of the name "Tea Party" by the new tax rebels. Many Republicans, particularly at the state level, joined in with the protesters, exhorting them in their tirades against the excesses of big government, which they ascribed to the Obama administration. The health-care bill simply galvanized this groundswell (helped along financially by wealthy reactionary donors) into a full-fledged nationwide protest movement, holding its first national convention in early February 2010. Over 600 people attended the conference, which also saw Sarah Palin and other right-wing notables show up to give rousing speeches endorsing the movement's crusade against big government, which to them meant the Obama administration and the Democratic Party.

Comprised mostly of ultraconservative Americans and libertarians, the Tea Partiers claimed to speak for those Americans supposedly fed up with excessive big government spending. They overwhelmingly favored Republicans over Democrats, but many challenged both parties and their respective leadership. They tended to be more secular-oriented individuals, although many also held anti-abortion views and opposed gay rights. The Tea Party movement was critical of the government in general. The country witnessed blatant disrespect, if not outright hatred for a president and his policies, at demonstrations, rallies, and conventions. Many Tea Party members were unabashedly malicious in their denunciations of the Obama administration, exhibiting shameless placards and slogans. The Republican Party establishment often quietly acquiesced to the Tea Partiers while many congressional Republicans and those aspiring to office openly pandered to the movement, believing that their party could use their support to sweep back into power. Some leaders within the Republican establishment, however, cautioned against giving the Tea Partiers too much influence within the party, fearing that their policy positions could affect the viability of Republican candidates in general elections against the Democrats, not to mention the possibility that their own less extreme candidates might find themselves challenged by Tea Party-backed challengers in the Republican primaries.

The 2010 Congressional Elections

Despite passage of the health-care bill, the Obama administration began to lose the confidence of a growing number of Americans, largely because the president's various economic stimuli and reforms had failed to immediately fix the economy, especially the high rate of unemployment, which by the November 2010 elections still hovered around 10 percent. Republicans and their Tea Party allies seized on this statistic, exploiting the growing despair among unemployed Americans and those

Tea Party gathering in Freedom Plaza (just off the Mall) Washington D.C. March 15, 2010. Credit: RTNews

in danger of losing their jobs, blaming the president's economic policies.

Despite the large amount of spending involved, the Obama stimulus (i.e., the American Recovery and Reinvestment Act) in retrospect was not enough to turn the economy around. Despite warnings from economists that a cautious approach would do little to ameliorate unemployment, the administration forged ahead while conservatives continued to obstruct his proposals and denounce Obama as a socialist. Unlike President Reagan and the Republican Party leadership of his era, who were willing to work with their Democratic counterparts to try to find ideological and policy common ground to ensure economic stability and security, the situation was now quite different. Because they did not wish to see the president succeed, and further, because they were in a stronger position electorally due to gerrymandered districts that allowed them to be comfortably elected despite holding unwavering views, Republican ideological stalwarts in Congress dug in and refused to compromise with Obama and congressional Democrats. By 2010, congressional Republicans had made it clear that they had no desire to engage in bipartisanship with the president and his party. House minority leader John Boehner and Senate minority leader Mitch McConnell hoped to discredit the president enough that by the 2010 congressional elections the Republicans would take over both houses of Congress. Once in control, they planned to continue to stymie the president's agenda until he could be defeated in the 2012 election. Thus, as the November elections neared, the Republicans pursued a policy of complete obstruction of any presidential or Democratic-sponsored legislation designed to try to address the economic recovery.

With a revived opposition and a non-energetic base, the president and his party took a "shellacking" (to use the president's words) in the midterm congressional elections, as Republicans swept back into control of the House of Representatives, picking up a net total of 63 seats and erasing gains achieved by Democrats in 2006 and 2008. Although the sitting president's party typically loses some congressional seats in a midterm election, the 2010 results witnessed the highest loss of a party in a House midterm election since 1938. Commanding 242 seats to the Democrats' 193, the Republicans gained control of the most House seats since 1946, when the American people repudiated Harry Truman. (The Democrats maintained control of the Senate by the narrow margin of 51 to 47.) Pundits generally concluded that three interrelated issues led to such a popular rejection of both the president and his party: frustration and anger with Obama's inability to fix the economy, opposition to the Affordable Care Act ("Obamacare"), and the rise of Tea Party opposition.

Representative John Boehner is the third representative from the state of Ohio to serve as Speaker of the House of Representatives. He served as the Republican House Minority Leader from 2007 until the election of 2010 gave the Republicans control of the House. Boehner was then elected Speaker. Credit: RTTNews

Occupy Wall Street

As Republicans continued to revel in their recent political victories, tens of thousands of citizens on the political left in the fall of 2011 initiated **Occupy Wall Street**—a nationwide protest movement not seen since the days of 1960s student activism. Initially, the demonstrators came from across a wide demographic, gender, age group, and occupation spectrum to rally along Wall Street in New York City for the purposes of letting bankers and financiers know that the people held them responsible for the nation's current condition. Indeed some activists wanted many of these corporate executives prosecuted for a litany of possible crimes. Also helping to fuel the outrage was the recent *Citizens United* decision of the Supreme Court, which held that freedom of speech prohibited the government from restricting political expenditures by organizations, leading protestors to predict the flooding of untold millions of dollars into political campaigns across the country, leading to a corrupted democracy.

From the moment that the first groups gathered in front of the headquarters of the Wall Street banks and brokerage firms, local police made their lives uncomfortable with constant harassment. Not to be intimidated, the Occupiers persevered for several months before finally being forced out. Similar protests emerged in a multitude of other American cities, where participants rallied under the same cause and banner, also being harassed by police until being forced to disband. The movement's purpose was simple enough: to make it clear to both political parties that the people had had enough of the corporate elites' nefarious ways and that they should be punished for having plunged the nation into its worst economic crisis since the Great Depression. Only a handful of politicians came out to support the movement. President Obama, who not only counted many Wall Street firms among his supporters but also included many pro-Wall Street economists among his closest economic advisers, refrained from making any substantive comments about the protests.

THE OBAMA ADMINISTRATION AND THE WORLD

Moving Away from Unilateralism

Few presidents inherited a tenser, more uncertain, and potentially volatile international scenario upon taking office than Barack Obama. None had ever assumed leadership of fighting two costly wars simultaneously, while seeking to repair the image of the United States abroad. As a result of the Bush administration's "first-strike" policy and disregard for the international community's concerns, global opinion of the United States had reached an all-time low. At no other time since the end of World War II had America's credibility been so universally questioned. By the close of the Bush administration, surveys of world opinion revealed that large numbers of people even in Western Europe viewed the United States as a threat to world peace. Obama thus made foreign policy a priority. He renounced President Bush's **unilateralism** with its de-emphasis of building coalitions with allies before undertaking military operations and reserving the right to launch preemptive strikes against any potential adversaries. Obama sought to return American foreign policy to the traditional post-World War II principle based on multilateral action and collective security pacts. The new president believed that the best way to show the world that his administration had no intention of continuing Bush administration's policies was to bring his new message of peace and multilateral cooperation through such organizations as the United Nations, as well as directly to those countries that had become the most suspicious and fearful of U.S. intentions. One of Obama's first sojourns out of the United States was to the Middle East, where in Egypt he assured the Arab-Muslim world that his administration wanted to cultivate better relations with them and did not see them as enemies of the United States, but rather as allies in the fight against the Muslim terrorist

extremists that had perverted an inherently peaceful faith.

Obama's overtures to the Muslim world naturally raised concerns that such a gesture would alienate Israel who might feel he was abandoning them in favor of developing stronger ties with Arab countries. The president visited Israel as a candidate in 2008, and since taking office, he repeatedly confirmed America's commitment to the U.S.-Israeli friendship. As every president before him since Truman, Obama assured the Israelis that he too considered them to be one of the United States' closest allies.

Obama also worked assiduously to repair America's relations with Europe, assuring European leaders that the days of the United States acting unilaterally were over and that the United States was ready to cooperate with the European nations on a variety of concerns, ranging from continued nuclear disarmament and talks with the Russians to acting in unison on the issue of **global warming**. On the latter topic, the Obama administration had high hopes that the United States could reclaim its leadership when it came to preserving the world's environment and addressing the effects of global warming. In December 2009, representatives from 193 nations met in Copenhagen, Denmark, to establish legally binding pacts toward limiting greenhouse gas emissions, which most scientists believe to be causing the earth's warming temperatures and climate change. Such was the commitment made by the United States in accepting the mandates of the 1997 Kyoto Protocol, though the Bush administration had declared that America would no longer abide by its provisions. Obama personally addressed the conference, telling its attendees that the United States was ready to do its part and support any initiatives established by the conference to reduce greenhouse gas emissions. The president's words, however, fell on largely deaf ears as the gathering failed to reach any sort of consensus or pact that would become a legally binding mandate among all the signatories.

Despite the Copenhagen Conference setback, President Obama's other international initiatives, especially his overtures toward peace and reconciliation with adversaries (such as Iran), and his reassertion that the U.S. was willing to negotiate and compromise rather than act wantonly and belligerently, earned the president the 2009 Nobel Peace Prize. Obama became only the third sitting president (Theodore Roosevelt and Woodrow Wilson were the first two) to win the award. Although recognized by the world for his leadership, many Americans, especially Republican critics, believed the president to be undeserving of such distinction, claiming he had done nothing substantive or extraordinary to earn the prize.

Winding down Two Wars

Obama inherited two separate wars in Iraq and Afghanistan and was determined to reduce U.S. involvement in each conflict. In his second month in office, he announced that all American combat troops would return home from Iraq by the end of 2011. A force of 50,000 men would remain until then to assist the Iraqi military in securing control of their country. In December 2011, the U.S. soldiers did finally come home, thus officially ending American military operations in Iraq, which ultimately cost the lives of over 4,300 GIs, the wounding of another 31,000 (the number of insurgents killed by U.S. or coalition troops was approximately 55,000), and roughly $900 billion from the government coffers.

Meanwhile, after several months of careful deliberation and consultation with his top military advisers, Obama decided in early December 2009 to send an additional 30,000 troops to Afghanistan. The president based his decision on his belief that in order to impress the Taliban combatants (which had increased in size and strength since being overthrown as a result of America's distracting invasion of Iraq in 2003) more American soldiers in the field would be required. Because of the Bush administration's preoccupation with Iraq, the Taliban had revitalized and become a threat to Pakistan, which the United States could ill afford to see fall to such a regime. Obama also believed that Osama bin Laden was still alive and operating out of the mountainous border region between Afghanistan and Pakistan. In his announcement during an impromptu visit to Afghanistan in late March 2010, Obama stated that the United States' objective was not only to ensure the survival of the pro-U.S. government led by Hamid Karzai by forcing the Taliban to the peace table, but in the process, hopefully finish off **Al Qaeda** and its leaders, especially bin Laden. By the summer of 2011, apparent military success led to a further announcement that phased withdrawals of American troops would begin to take place later that year, with the ultimate goal being the complete transfer of the fight against the Taliban to be in the hands of Afghan military forces by the end of 2014.

Narrowing the Struggle: The U.S. and Iran

While dealing with the struggles in Iraq and Afghanistan, Obama also had to monitor events in Iran where elections held in the summer of 2009 were completely rigged in favor of the country's ruling group of hardline leaders and President Mahmoud Ahmadinejad, resulting in widespread street demonstrations against the regime, which were viciously repressed. Moreover, there was little

doubt that Iran had nuclear aspirations, but whether the government intended to continue development for domestic energy purposes or to build weapons of mass destruction had yet to be determined. Despite tension between Iran and the United States over its nuclear program, the White House believed a continued cold war with Iran made little sense. Iran's Shi'ite theocrats had a mostly hostile relationship with Al Qaeda's anti-Shi'ite leaders. In both Iraq and Afghanistan, Iran had caused trouble for the United States largely out of fear that if the U.S. forces prevailed in both countries, Iran would be the next target for invasion and occupation. Obama believed, however, that if the U.S. could convince Iran's government that America had no intention of invading Iran, then the countries could cooperate to achieve their common objective in both Afghanistan and Iraq, which was smashing Al Qaeda.

Another problem facing the Obama White House was the fact that the United States was militarily distracted during the early 2000s making both the Iranian government and the Taliban less inclined to negotiate. With the U.S. mired in two wars, the Iranians were less afraid of American military power and continued their nuclear programs, while the Taliban had little incentive to break their ties with Al Qaeda. Thus, Obama felt compelled to initiate the surge in Afghanistan while pushing for new economic sanctions against Iran hoping that a diplomatic solution could eventually be achieved.

The Arab Spring

In addition to inheriting lingering global troubles, Obama's first term witnessed new historic developments as the Arab world became caught up in a wave of violent and nonviolent popular uprisings from North Africa to the Middle East known collectively as the "**Arab Spring.**" Though in many countries the unrests were stymied by a combination of minor changes in governmental structure, the firing of controversial officials, and the use of troops, in some cases the changes were truly revolutionary. Protests in Tunisia in late 2010 began the regional movement by ousting the nation's longstanding dictator, forcing him into exile in Saudi Arabia. In Egypt, the violent reaction to popular protests against the government of Hosni Mubarak led to the U.S.-supported dictator's fall when the military stepped in to restore order. After democratic elections led to the rise of a militant Islamist organization, the Muslim Brotherhood, the military intervened once again to quell new protests, this time by arresting the Brotherhood's leaders and outlawing the group. Meanwhile, in neighboring Libya, a civil war had broken out between supporters and opponents of the perennial American menace, Muammar Gaddafi. When NATO countries stepped in to aid the rebels through targeted air strikes, the tide turned against Gaddafi's forces, resulting in the eventual defeat of his forces, his capture, and murder.

Syria also descended into a vicious civil war. Bashar al-Assad (son of longtime dictator Hafez al-Assad) brutally suppressed an uprising that continued into Obama's second term. The Obama administration publicly condemned Assad's violent repression, which saw thousands of Syrian civilians and rebels killed. Although the president publicly denounced Assad's use of force and called for him to step down, the United States did not militarily intervene. The U.N. Security Council failed to unanimously approve sanctions against Assad, as both China and Russia, two of the council's permanent members who made money selling arms to Assad and saw the dictator's regime as their ally in the region, voted against any interference.

The End of Bin Laden

Americans breathed a deep sigh of relief, as did many people worldwide, and spontaneous patriotic rallies broke out in Washington D.C., New York City, and elsewhere when Barack Obama announced on the evening of May 1, 2011, that the CIA finally found the hiding place of **Osama bin Laden**, leading to a Navy SEALS raid that resulted in his death. American intelligence officials had long believed that bin Laden, after escaping U.S. forces who converged on his hideout in the Tora Bora cave complex within the White Mountains of eastern Afghanistan after the 9/11 attacks, fled to the rural areas of Pakistan to enjoy the protection of sympathetic local tribesmen. After a nine-year hunt, however, signs began to point to

a mysterious walled compound within the city of Abbottabad, an urban area in northern Pakistan with over 100,000 people.

After a lengthy surveillance, the president ordered the SEALS team to swoop down into the compound aboard stealth helicopters flown from a base in neighboring Afghanistan. To avoid possibly being tipped off by suspected Al Qaeda sympathizers within the Pakistani military and intelligence services, the government of Pakistan was not given advanced notice of the raid. After quietly landing at the site in the dead of night, the SEALS penetrated the largest building at the complex and killed several defenders before finding and killing bin Laden. Though one helicopter was badly damaged during the landing and had to be destroyed before leaving the site, the SEALS suffered no casualties and were able to carry away the terrorist mastermind's body as well as many computer files located at the scene.

Obama's Re-election

By early 2012, Obama started to more directly confront congressional Republicans by taking them to task for their obstructionism. Though he compromised on extending the Bush tax cuts, he did secure a Republican agreement to maintain middle-class payroll tax cuts and to extend the jobless benefits for several more months. Obama also succeeded in getting relief for homeowners by pressuring the nation's largest banks, such as Wells Fargo, Bank of America, and Citicorp to stop sitting on their billions of dollars in bailout money and to begin extending new loans to prospective homeowners, as well as to help Americans avoid foreclosure by refinancing their current loans at affordable rates. The Obama administration did not ag-

Members of Barack Obama's cabinet follow developments on May 1, 2011, as NAVY SEALS storm terrorist Osama bin Laden's compound in Pakistan and kill him. Vice President Joe Biden and President Obama sit on the left near Brigadier Gen. Marshall B. "Brad" Webb while Secretary of State Hillary Clinton and Defense Secretary Robert Gates sit on the right. Credit: Official White House Photo by Pete Souza.

gressively address the unemployment issue, although the president did ask for more funding from Congress for a new attempt to alleviate the problem. Perhaps most important for the Obama administration was the fact that the unemployment rate had begun to drop steadily by the opening months of 2012.

At the onset of the 2012 presidential election, unemployment hovered over 8 percent and consumer confidence remained flat. Combined with an international scene fraught with a multitude of uncertainties from a nuclear Iran to continued unrest in the Middle East, and a European economy that seemed to be contracting daily as the count of countries on the verge of economic collapse grew, Republicans seemed confident of recapturing the White House. They were determined to blame President Obama for a supposed lack of decisive leadership at home and abroad. Although much of the Republican criticism of the president's performance was blown greatly out of proportion, as often occurs during political campaigns, it did appear Obama had achieved less than had been hoped, but the president had a lot on his table to address, especially the financial crisis and auto industry collapse that had to be dealt with first. The modest stimulus passage had been passed, but other than health-care reform there were few other domestic accomplishments to show for the effort. To be sure, Republican congressional obstructions had a large hand in the lack of signal achievements, but the president's campaign would have to emphasize that point to the electorate. Obama's overall approval rating had plummeted below 45 percent—the lowest of his brief tenure—leading many to question whether he would be reelected.

Nevertheless, on Election Day, to the shock of overly confident Republicans who believed their candidate would win, the opposite occurred. Obama won 51.1 percent of the popular vote, while the Republican nominee, former Massachusetts governor Mitt Romney garnered only 47.2 percent. In the Electoral College, the margin of the president's victory was even greater: 332-206, with Obama winning all the battleground states but one, North Carolina. The president's "coattails" also proved longer than expected as his party picked up seats in both the Senate and the House; in the former, the Democrats enjoyed a 53-45 majority, increased by two independent New England senators who caucused with the Democrats, while in the latter, they narrowed the gap to 233-200 (with two seats vacant).

During the Republican primaries, Romney had abandoned his inherent moderate Republicanism, embracing instead the Far Right agenda of his party in order to secure his party's nomination. Romney's selection of Paul Ryan as his running mate confirmed this propensity, project-

ing the image (exploited by the Obama campaign) of being a "flip-flopper" on the major issues, whether it was foreign policy matters, domestic tax cuts, balancing the budget, or health care. (In the latter case, the structure of "Obamacare," including its use of individual mandates, was based on the model favored by Romney when Massachusetts instituted its own state-mandated health-care system while he served as governor.) Also contributing to Obama's victory was the strong endorsements from moderate Republican statesmen, including retired four-star general and former Secretary of State Colin Powell and New York City mayor Michael Bloomberg. Devastation brought to the East Coast in late October by Hurricane Sandy also helped the president by giving him an opportunity to demonstrate leadership in a time of regional devastation. One of Obama's biggest Republican opponents, New Jersey Governor Chris Christie, much to the horrible chagrin of fellow party members, praised the president for his unhesitating attention and non-partisan approach in helping his state. Finally, the October jobs report bolstered Obama's re-election bid as unemployment dropped to 7.8 percent—sanguine news for the president who had inherited an economy with an overall unemployment rate of over 10 percent.

CONTENTIOUS SOCIAL ISSUES

As Barack Obama settled in for his second term, the United States at home and abroad experienced the persistence of old problems and the emergence of new issues to challenge his leadership of the nation. While the economy showed signs of gradual but steady improvement from the depths of the "Great Recession" that dominated much of the president's first term, many societal issues began to once again assert themselves into the public consciousness.

Mass Shootings

Occasional outbreaks of mass shootings reignited the ubiquitous gun control debate during Obama's second term. Just six months after a schizophrenic college student killed 12 patrons and injured 70 more after opening fire at a movie theater in Aurora, Colorado, a twenty-year-old man with a history of mental problems entered Sandy Hook Elementary School in Newtown, Connecticut, with an assault weapon on December 12, 2012, and in just five minutes proceeded to murder 26 children and teachers. Predictably, gun control advocates renewed their calls for sensible gun control legislation, while the National Rifle Association and gun enthusiasts issued demands for the public to have more access to guns, not less, for protection.

President Obama weighed into the debate by endorsing efforts in Congress to establish a uniform background check system, a renewed ban on certain types of assault weapons (as were used in both attacks), and limiting the magazine capacity of weapons to ten cartridges. Ultimately, these efforts failed to receive congressional approval. Though some states instituted more gun limitation measures, many other states relaxed their gun restriction laws.

Mass shootings continued to take place sporadically across the country, most notably in Charleston, South Carolina on June 17, 2015, when a 21-year-old white supremacist entered the historic Emanuel African Methodist Episcopal Church and gunned down nine African American parishioners attending a Bible study group. Public outrage at the massacre led South Carolina officials to finally take down the Confederate battle flag from its prominent display on the state house grounds. President Obama attended the funeral and delivered a stirring eulogy but for the remainder of his term he felt demoralized that more could not be done on the issue of gun violence. In January 2016, Obama announced some limited executive actions that he was ordering to require more gun sellers to get licenses and more gun buyers to undergo background checks. Tears welled in his eyes and he expressed his wish to reporters that more could be done. Recalling the Sandy Hook murders, the normally even-keeled president let out his frustrations: "Every time I think about those kids, it gets me mad."

The specter of mass shootings would nevertheless revisit America again and again. In June 2016, an Afghan-American man claiming allegiance to the Islamic State terrorist group murdered 49 people and injured 53 others with semi-automatic weaponry at Pulse, a gay night club in Orlando, Florida, before being killed by local police officers. This event was the largest loss of life in a single mass shooting in United States history until the following year when on October 1, 2017, a 64-year-old man with a massive weapons cache fired over a thousand bullets into a Las Vegas, Nevada music festival from the vantage point of an upper-level room at the Mandalay Bay Hotel across the street from the venue. Sixty concert goers were killed and over 400 wounded before law enforcement officers reached the sniper's room and found the body of the perpetrator who had committed suicide.

"Black Lives Matter"

Instances of racially-tinged violence continued to make headlines, which along with the reaction to the cases among many in the general public, belied the notion that the election of the nation's first black president somehow meant that the country had entered a "post-racial" period of harmony. Protests erupted in Sanford, Florida, after a local district attorney refused to indict George Zimmerman, a white man who served as a self-appointed neighborhood watch volunteer, after he shot and killed Trayvon Martin, an African-American teenager who Zimmerman confronted after he grew suspicious of Martin as the youth walked home within the gated community in which they both lived. As the story began to receive nationwide attention, the public polarized, often along racial lines, with most blacks believing that Martin was accosted and murdered for no legitimate reason while a majority of whites seemed willing to believe Zimmermann's account that he acted in self-defense when Martin supposedly attacked him after resenting being followed. A special state prosecutor was brought in to try the case, resulting in a July 2013 trial in which the jury acquitted Zimmerman.

The acquittal of George Zimmerman led directly to a new grass-roots-based civil rights protest movement labeled "**Black Lives Matter**," whose name originated from a social media hashtag that became popularized among those greatly troubled by the verdict. Beginning as an online campaign, the group's leaders began to organize street demonstrations to protest an increasing number of police-killings of unarmed African-American men, most notably in August 2014, when mass protests erupted in Ferguson, Missouri, a suburb of St. Louis, after a district attorney refused to indict a white police officer who killed an unarmed black man in the middle of a public street. Once again, public opinion polls showed that a majority of whites interviewed sided with the officer's account that the officer felt threatened while most blacks found no justification for the killing. Many groups converged on Ferguson to engage in non-violent protests that were frequently broken up by police deploying tear gas and other crowd-disruption tactics that only further galvanized the demonstrations and increased the degree of press coverage that they received.

While a variety of traditional and newer civil rights organizations sought to highlight the issue of police brutality, Black Lives Matter emerged in the mid-2010s as the most visible (and most divisive) of the groups seeking to publicize instances of officer-involved killings of non-violent African-American offenders. Unfortunately, its members would have numerous cases to protest, including the November 2014 shooting of Tamir Rice, a 12-year-old boy in Cleveland playing in a park with an air pistol that was killed by policemen within seconds of arriving on the scene; the April 2015 shooting of Walter Scott in North Charleston, South Carolina, who was shot multiple times after running away from a policeman after a routine traffic

The Origins of a New Social Justice Movement: Black Lives Matter

During the summer of 2013, much of the nation's attention was focused on the courthouse in Sanford, Florida where George Zimmerman was on trial for murdering Trayvon Martin, a seventeen-year-old African-American youth visiting the apartment complex where his father lived and where Zimmerman served as a volunteer community watchman. Not recognizing Martin as a resident, Zimmerman confronted him, then shot him with his pistol during an ensuing struggle "out of fear for his life" after Martin allegedly attacked him. When the jury returned with a verdict of "not guilty," for many—and particularly among African Americans—such a rendering proved that the American justice system was not truly "just" when it came to judging white Americans who murdered citizens of color.

*The verdict sparked protests and anguish across the nation, as well as tension between those who felt the verdict was justified, and those who believed the decision was yet another example of "one law for whites, and another for non-whites." Almost three thousand miles away from Sanford, three activists—Alicia Garza, Patrisse Cullors, and Opal Tometi—all members of "Blacks Organizing for Leadership & Dignity" (BOLD), began corresponding through social media about the Zimmerman verdict. Though living in separate cities (Garza lived in Oakland, Cullers in Los Angeles, and Tometi in Phoenix), the three women all expressed anger at the Zimmerman verdict and began to discuss how they could possibly respond to what had transpired in Florida. Garza took to social media and, on BOLD's Facebook page wrote "A Love Note to Black People." Her text expressed the anger and heartbreak she felt at the Zimmerman verdict, and she called for those who felt as she did to "get active, get organized . . . and fight back." She ended with these words: "Black people. I love you. I love us. Our lives matter." Patrisse Cullors reposted Garza's note, and she added something else, a Twitter handle--#**BlackLivesMatter** and a movement was born.*

Garza, Cullors, and Tometi used social media to coordinate the movement. They naturally drew inspiration from the Civil Rights Movement of the 1960s, as well as campaigns for women's and LGBTQ rights. The activists also recruited hip-hop artists to penetrate popular culture, and social media allowed them to reach millions. Within a few months, activists in cities across the nation began to hold rallies and protests with the intention of spotlighting racial injustice, economic inequality, and the continued hegemony of white political, social, and economic power in a nation that professed to cherish diversity. However, while Black Lives Matter had a significant social media presence, it lacked a truly visible presence in circles outside its target audience. All that would change in the summer of 2014.

Ferguson, Missouri was typical of many inner-ring communities within the nation's urban areas. Ferguson lay within the St. Louis metropolitan region, a small community on the outskirts of St. Louis's Lambert International Airport. While it had once been a solidly mixed-race middle-class bedroom community, it had morphed into a predominantly working-class city, increasingly African American, and one that faced racial tension. African Americans in Ferguson felt shut out of political power, unfairly targeted by law enforcement, forced to live in "service deserts" devoid of necessary goods and services, and locked in poverty and oppression.

The city's anger boiled over when a Ferguson police officer, Darren Wilson, shot and killed an unarmed African-American teenager, Michael Brown, who he had detained for investigation of a minor crime. Wilson claimed that Brown attacked him, and that he shot him in fear of his life. However, Brown was shot in the back, and his lifeless body was allowed to lie in the street for hours, which for many Ferguson residents represented how callous white Ferguson viewed their lives. The new Black Lives Matter group helped to organize a protest on August 9, 2014, calling not just for justice for Brown, but for all victims of what they called an overzealous law enforcement culture that "targeted" African Americans. They initiated a nationwide campaign to highlight the many victims of police violence in the United States. When the grand jury in Ferguson refused to indict Officer Wilson, they took to the streets and chanted "Black Lives Matter!" and did the same when other cases of perceived unlawful aggression by police officers against African Americans began receiving increased media attention elsewhere in the country. Their protests sparked a symbol, "Hands up! Don't shoot," that spread across the country, and led to displays of public support by professional football and basketball players. Today, Black Lives Matter continues to press for social justice, calling attention to the pressing issue of unnecessary police violence against people of color.

stop; and the July 2015 killing of motorist Samuel DuBose by a University of Cincinnati policeman who stopped him for not having a front license plate and shot the driver when he started his car and attempted to drive away.

While many in the public became convinced that there was a new epidemic of police killings of unarmed blacks taking place, what these incidents and many others had in common was the presence of video cameras—a closed circuit camera at the park recorded Rice's shooting; a cell phone video taken by a passerby showed Walter Scott running away before being shot in the back multiple times; and the body camera on the officer who shot Samuel DuBose captured that killing. Activists argued that these events were not isolated incidents, nor the sign of any new behavior on the part of law enforcement. Instead, the widespread availability of digital video equipment was now simply displaying, for all the world to see, the routine brutal tactics that a minority of dangerous cops sometimes employed against black suspects, either because they were racially prejudiced and too easily disregarded the humanity of African Americans or because they were inadequately trained, leading them to resort to the use of lethal force far too quickly in order to protect themselves from perceived threats.

LGBT Equality under the Law

Significant achievements for LGBT (lesbian, gay, bisexual, and transgender) Americans took place during the mid-2010s resulting from continued activism, changes in public attitudes, and decisions made by officials in the legislative, executive, and judicial branches of the federal government. In 2010, Congress passed legislation leading to the end of President Clinton's "Don't Ask, Don't Tell" (DADT) policy (see Chapter 34) whereby the U.S. military had been barred from discriminating against closeted homosexuals and bisexuals serving in the armed forces while leaving the ban on their service intact if their orientation ever became public knowledge. (Over 13,000 service members were discharged from 1994-2010 under the terms of the policy). Congress passed legislation in December 2010 specifying that the DADT policy would remain intact until the president, Secretary of Defense, and Chairman of the Joint Chiefs of Staff certified that its repeal would not harm the military effectiveness of the U.S. armed forces. After receiving a clearance from the federal courts, President Obama initiated the process for the repeal of DADT in July 2011, and it went into effect in September of that year. Gays and lesbians could now serve openly in the U.S. military, with their sexual conduct placed under the same regulations as heterosexual service members.

Though the issue of marriage equality also continued to divide the country, the national trend was moving noticeably in favor of acceptance. As a growing number of states began to debate legalizing same-sex marriages, a host of legal challenges to existing bans took place and it looked increasingly as if the Supreme Court would become a major player in determining how the country would move forward on the issue. Although President Obama had been able to nominate two justices to the High Court, Sonia Sotomayor in 2009 and Elena Kagan in 2010, those liberal-leaning justices had replaced two liberals, so the Court's makeup still slightly favored the conservatives. Nevertheless, the Supreme Court ultimately made two significant rulings that delighted supporters of marriage equality across the country. First, in the 2013 *United States v. Windsor* case, the Court ruled against Section 3 of the federal Defense of Marriage Act passed in 1996, which had barred same-sex couples from receiving federal benefits granted to married heterosexual couples. Section 2 of the law, which had reaffirmed the rights of individual states to deny other states' acceptance of same-sex marriages, was unaffected. Two years after the *Windsor* decision, the Court issued its ruling in the landmark **Obergefell v. Hodges** case challenging the ability of states to continue outlawing same-sex marriages. By June 2015 when the Court decided the case, a majority of Americans already lived in a jurisdiction with marriage equality as a total of 37 states plus the District of Columbia had legally recognized same-sex marriages. In *Obergefell*, the Supreme Court ruled in a 5-4 decision that the Due Process and Equal Protection clauses of the Fourteenth Amendment requires all states to grant same-sex marriages and recognize all same-sex marriages registered in other states.

The Ongoing Immigration Debate

Illegal immigration continued to be a hot-button issue in the early twenty-first century, as it often was throughout the twentieth century during hard economic times. Whereas many Americans understood the symbolic, as well as practical, contribution of immigrants to American history and the national economy, many others found immigrants to be a convenient scapegoat for the loss of jobs, not to mention latent racial animosities felt toward so many of them looking differently than most other Americans and their speaking a multitude of foreign languages. While concern mounted among anxious Americans over Muslim immigrants and their possible ties to domestic terrorism, the largest apprehension over immigration dealt with the estimated 11 million illegal immigrants, mostly from Mexico and Central American countries, residing in the United States.

During his presidency, Barack Obama attempted to show compassion toward the large number of people coming to America seeking a better life for themselves and their families, balanced with legitimate public safety concerns and enforcement of the law. Primarily targeting immigrants who commit serious crimes or repeated misdemeanors, the Obama administration from 2009 to 2015 deported a record 2.5 million illegal immigrants, 91 percent of whom had a record of criminal activity in the United States. At the same time, the president supported passage of the DREAM Act, which proposed to give a path to citizenship for the 2 million children brought to the United States by parents who were illegal immigrants under the condition that they graduate from high school or serve two years in the U.S. military. After the law failed to pass Congress, Obama announced in 2012 that he would revise immigration enforcement policy by delaying deportation proceedings indefinitely and allow two-year work visas for such children who had clean criminal records and who attending high school, graduated high school, or served in the military. Republican politicians tended to criticize the program, labeled Deferred Action for Childhood Arrivals (DACA), as simply a crass effort by Democrats to curry the favor of Hispanic voters.

Early in Obama's second term, a bipartisan group of eight U.S. senators revealed a proposal for comprehensive immigration reform that would create a pathway to citizenship for all undocumented immigrants currently residing in the United States, streamline the legal immigration process, improve border security, and enforce employers' use of only legal workers. Though the bill passed the Senate, the measure languished in the Republican-led House and was never approved, once again leaving illegal immigration an important unsettled issue to be addressed by the next Congress and presidential administration.

FOREIGN POLICY SUCCESSES AND LIMITATIONS

While President Obama was able to oversee the end of the large-scale American military involvement in Iraq and Afghanistan begun during the Bush administration, military advisers and special forces units continued to be engaged on the ground in those countries helping government forces there secure control of their respective countries, in addition to their deployment in Syria to help rebel forces in their ongoing effort to topple the dictator Bashar al-Assad. In addition, although Al Qaeda had been

fairly minimized, a new threat from the self-proclaimed Islamic State in Iraq and Syria (ISIS) consisting of radical Sunni Muslim followers of the late Saddam Hussein, as well as newly-indoctrinated fanatical fighters, threatened the stability of the Middle East and occasionally terrorized Europe and the United States through acts of violence perpetrated by their members or their home-grown sympathizers who pledged allegiance to the organization. These and other foreign policy challenges kept Obama busy throughout his second term, although he would manage to keep up the fight against America's adversaries while scoring some notable diplomatic successes.

Whistleblowing or Treason? The Manning and Snowden Cases

Two significant security breaches occurring during Obama's tenure caused government officials great consternation as they worried that the information taken and revealed to the public might jeopardize many ongoing intelligence operations, though some of them were of questionable legality. In early 2010, Bradley Manning, a transgender intelligence analyst in the U.S. Army now known as Chelsea Manning, acquired access to hundreds of thousands of Army reports, diplomatic cables, and other classified military and diplomatic documents that she was able to duplicate and provide to WikiLeaks, an online organization that seeks to publish classified information from governments and corporations, it says, in the interest of transparency to ensure that such institutions are acting legally and morally in the public interest. WikiLeaks, in turn, revealed the material on its website, including U.S. military videos of airstrikes seemingly displaying the indiscriminate killing of civilians in Iraq and Afghanistan. Manning was eventually arrested and found guilty in July 2013 of violating the Sedition Act among other statutes. Acquitted of an aiding-the-enemy charge, which could have brought the death penalty, she received a 35-year sentence.

As the Manning trial was underway, another self-proclaimed whistleblower, **Edward Snowden**, fled the country to avoid arrest after copying tens of thousands of classified documents. While working as a computer professional for the private defense contractor Booz Allen Hamilton, Snowden had come across classified National Security Agency (NSA) documents that showed the extent of surveillance operations at home and abroad with the assistance of telecommunications companies. Snowden began releasing the material to American journalists, first from Hong Kong, and later from Russia, which granted him asylum. The more important revelations published in American newspapers have included: details on an NSA program to receive court-approved access to Americans' Google and Yahoo accounts; exposure of the existence of a daily-updated NSA database containing metadata on billions of phone call records handed over to the government by court order; information on the NSA practice of acquiring access to email accounts to search for content; and the disclosure that the NSA had spied on the leaders of over 100 nations, including Germany, France, Israel, and Great Britain.

More documents continue to be leaked by Snowden, who insisted that his actions reflected his shock and disappointment at the extent of NSA monitoring of citizens, leaders, and corporations at home and around the world undertaken by the Bush and Obama administrations. American government officials had a different take on his actions, describing them in treasonous rather than patriotic terms, arguing that he compromised programs vital to the effort to combat terrorism and guarantee national security in general. Snowden is currently under indictment for theft of government property and unlawful communication of national defense and classified intelligence information. In June 2015, President Obama signed into law the USA Freedom Act, which renewed some key provisions of the Patriot Act (see Chapter 34) while also instituting major surveillance reforms placing new restrictions on federal intelligence powers. The new law ended the NSA's bulk collection of Americans' telephone records and put limits on other ways that the government gathered large amounts of electronic data.

Dealing with Putin

In foreign affairs, remnants of old Cold War tensions with Russia seeped to the surface as the result of provocative actions undertaken in Eastern Europe by that country's leader, **Vladimir Putin**. Soon after Russia hosted the 2012 Winter Olympic Games, Putin reacted with hostility after a revolt ousted a pro-Russian government in neighboring Ukraine by taking over and annexing the Crimean Peninsula. Though Russia maintained a naval base in Crimea along the Black Sea, the rest of former Soviet territory had been ceded by Russia to Ukraine in 1991. Soon, Russia began to funnel arms and other aid to pro-Russian separatists in eastern Ukraine who began fighting their government. The Obama administration consulted with other Western powers and responded by initiating a series of economic sanctions designed to force Putin to change course. By the end of 2014, Russia maintained control of Crimea but had yet to annex eastern Ukraine.

American differences with Putin eventually spread to the ongoing civil war in Syria. After the reported use of chemical weapons by the government forces of Bashar al-Assad, the Obama administration announced in August 2013 that it was committed to regime change in Syria. American aid would now flow to the assortment of rebel forces that had aligned against Assad to overthrow his government after the dictator's troops began opening fire against peaceful Arab Spring protesters. When Assad's control seemed to be teetering and the dictator sought help from Russia, Putin ordered a military intervention in September 2015. Previously, the Russians had only been selling arms and other equipment to the Syrian regime, but now Russian airstrikes against Assad's enemies began to take place along with the arrival of Russian military advisors and special ground forces. In addition to helping turn the tide against the U.S.-backed Syrian rebels, the Russian intervention also aided efforts against ISIS—the mutual enemy of both the Assad regime and the anti-government rebels in Syria.

The ISIS Menace

Just as American combat troops were leaving Afghanistan, the **Islamic State in Iraq and Syria (ISIS)** emerged as a new threat to peace in the Middle East. The self-proclaimed Islamic State rose first in northern and western Iraq, where fighting had begun to subside compared to previous levels of violence, and in Syria where the bloody civil war continued unabated. Consisting of former supporters of Saddam Hussein and new Muslim recruits seeking to establish a Sunni Islamic caliphate in the region, ISIS grew in numbers and territory throughout 2014 as they fought all in their midst who happened to have different backgrounds and beliefs—Kurds, Shi'ite Iraqis, Syrian military forces, even Al Qaeda militants—terrorizing and murdering thousands of innocent people in their wake. A series of videotaped beheadings of Western civilians captured by the group were used by the U.S. government and its Western European allies to mobilize support for airstrikes against key ISIS military targets while Iraqi ground forces continued to be mobilized for operations against ISIS-held territory in their country. After Russia intervened in the Syrian civil war, its warplanes began to hit ISIS targets, though not as frequently as they launched attacks against the Syrian anti-government rebels.

The American and European-coalition air raids, joined by the Arab nations of Jordan and Saudi Arabia, spawned retaliatory terrorist attacks by ISIS agents and homegrown sympathizers in Europe and the United States. In November 2015, suicide bombers and gunmen killed 130 people in three attacks staged in Paris outside a soccer match, at restaurants, and at a concert hall. A month later, a Muslim American couple sympathetic to

ISIS shot and killed fourteen people in San Bernardino, California at a holiday party where the husband had worked. In March 2016, suicide bombers killed over 30 people at the international airport and a metro station in Brussels, Belgium. The most deadly mass shooting in U.S. history took place three months later, in June 2016, when an American-born Muslim swearing allegiance to ISIS entered a gay nightclub in Orlando, Florida and proceeded to murder 50 patrons with an assault weapon. The following month, in Nice, France, an ISIS terrorist attacked a large crowd on Bastille Day revelers along a beach promenade by plowing into them at full speed with a rental van, resulting in the deaths of 86 people and injuring over 400 more.

Such attacks were portrayed by Western governments as signs of desperation by ISIS as the allied bombing campaign had succeeded by 2016 in stymying the Islamic State's momentum in the region. Though ISIS continued to exist as 2016 closed, Iraqi ground forces aided by Kurdish fighters were nevertheless driving deep into Mosul, the fifth-largest city in Iraq, in an effort to dislodge them from the terrorist organization's largest-remaining stronghold in their country.

Some Diplomatic Successes

While dealing with the ongoing turmoil in many parts of the world, President Obama was able to achieve some noteworthy successes on the diplomatic front during his second term, potentially lessening tensions between the U.S. and its adversaries while working towards global consensus on threats to the environment.

In December 2014, Obama and Cuban president Raúl Castro announced the normalization of relations between the United States and Cuba for the first time since the late 1950s when Castro's brother Fidel overthrew the U.S.-supported regime of Fulgencio Bautista. Some travel restrictions were eased and efforts were underway to reestablish an American embassy in Cuba's capital of Havana. In March 2016, Obama became the first U.S. president to visit the island in 80 years.

For several years, the United States, the European Union, and the United Nations had enforced harsh economic sanctions against Iran in an effort to persuade that nation's government to refrain from advancing its nuclear program that Western leaders asserted would lead to Iran acquiring the capability of building nuclear weapons. In July 2015, the U.S., Germany, and the countries making up permanent membership of the United Nations Security Council—China, France, Great Britain, and Russia—announced an agreement with Iran calling for the easing of the economic sanctions in return for Iranian promises,

subject to rigid inspections by the United Nations via the International Atomic Energy Agency, to greatly reduce existing stockpiles of uranium (the element used for nuclear reactions) and strictly limit the ability to enrich uranium in the future.

The effort to combat climate change received a significant boost during the mid-2010s when representatives of 200 nations who accounted for over half of the world's total emission of greenhouse gases met in Paris, France to negotiate and sign a groundbreaking agreement in December 2015 designed to limit the impact of the human contribution to global warming. The signatory nations, and any others who would later sign the agreement, pledged to limit the emission of greenhouse gases by human activity to amounts that can be absorbed naturally by the planet (trees, soil, and oceans) beginning at some point between the years 2050 and 2100 in a concerted effort to keep global temperatures near pre-industrial levels. Each country would monitor the progress of other nations in achieving their pledged contributions, with wealthier countries providing financial assistance to poorer nations to help them meet their obligations.

AN ELECTION LIKE NO OTHER

By the end of his second term, Barack Obama had done much to stabilize the U.S. economy, reestablish America's leadership role in the world while rebuilding frayed alliances, and rebuild his popularity with a majority of the American people. Though certainly a large segment of the public (mostly Republicans) despised him, Obama's approval rating among the nation as a whole slowly ticked back up to positive territory, reaching over 55 percent as the election to choose his successor approached. Many began to look back on his two terms in office and grew nostalgic for Obama's steady hand as they pondered their less-than-thrilling choices in what would prove to be the strangest and most unpredictable election in modern memory.

A Raucous Primary Season

At first, the 2016 Democratic Party primary and caucus campaign looked to be a snoozer. All pundits expected former First Lady Hillary Clinton to walk away with the Democratic nomination relatively unchallenged. She had served as Secretary of State under President Obama during his first term, had previously served two terms in the U.S. Senate representing New York, and had extensive support from party insiders, noteworthy celebrities, and wealthy donors.

Donald Trump

Though a couple of other candidates entered the fray and quickly left, Clinton ended up becoming involved in a lengthy battle for the nomination with an unlikely adversary—Vermont Senator Bernie Sanders, a 75-year-old independent who caucused with the Democrats and wished to push the party in a more leftist direction than Clinton's more centrist positions on many issues. Though Sanders proclaimed himself to be a Socialist, his policy proposals during the campaign primarily reflected a desire to revitalize the old New Deal roots of the modern Democratic Party—a greatly increased (up to $15 per hour) minimum wage for workers, free college tuition, a call to break up the big Wall Street banks, and a renewed focus on the growing income equality between the super-rich and the rest of the country's population. Eschewing super PACs, or large political action committees that can legally pour millions into a campaign to support a particular candidate or denigrate their opponent, Sanders fueled his unlikely bid through small campaign donations, ultimately raising tens of millions of dollars from over a million contributors, which proved more than enough to wage an extensive battle against Clinton. His campaign also benefited from tens of thousands of rabid supporters, many of them young idealistic voters who used social media adeptly to promote Sanders's candidacy.

For her part, Clinton relied on larger donors and energized activists seeking to make her the first woman to win the presidency. She campaigned on her lengthy government experience and extending President Obama's policies, including equal pay for equal work, universal preschool, campaign finance reform, a path to citizenship for law-abiding undocumented immigrants, and making improvements to the Affordable Care Act. Sanders's early success helped push Clinton to modify and emphasize some of her economic positions, such as plans for regulating Wall Street banks and holding their executives accountable for illegal activity, support for a $15 minimum wage, and a promise to disavow free-trade agreements such as the Trans-Pacific Partnership (favored by President Obama), which would lower tariff barriers between the U.S. and 11 Pacific Rim nations but was opposed by Sanders and others who feared the deal would only help corporations grow wealthier by saving labor costs by moving large numbers of American manufacturing jobs abroad. Clinton ultimately prevailed by winning 34 primaries (Sanders prevailed in 23 primaries and caucuses), becoming the first female to win a major party's nomination. Despite many progressives wishing her to choose Sanders or another progressive to be her running mate, she instead chose another centrist Democrat, Virginia Senator Tim Kaine.

The Republican nomination process was chaotic from the beginning, with an assortment of 17 candidates, mostly senators and governors who were entrenched party establishment figures entering the fray. The major exception would prove to be Donald Trump, the New York billionaire who made his fortune in real estate and who more recently had been known as a reality television star through his long-running show "The Apprentice." From the beginning of the race, no one took Trump's candidacy seriously, believing it to be one big publicity stunt (which it originally may have been) because of his bombastic speaking style and obvious lack of familiarity with the major political issues of the day. Nevertheless, his rancorous style resonated with many Republican primary voters (and appalled many others) who began to see him as a political outsider unafraid to speak his mind as he condemned Democratic and Republican politicians alike, blaming them for many of the country's ills. He said his solution to illegal immigration was simply to round up all the illegal immigrants in the country and deport them while building a 3,000-mile wall along the U.S.-Mexico border. Responding to the threat of terrorism, he proposed banning all Muslims from entering the country, bombing ISIS into submission, and "bringing back a hell of a lot more than waterboarding."

Once the primary debate season began, Trump was still not taken seriously by his rivals who continued to point out many of his past outrageous statements and his shallow understanding of foreign and domestic issues. Trump tended to respond to the attacks by ridiculing and belittling his main rivals. The quiet-talking Jeb Bush (the former governor of Florida and brother of George W. Bush) became "Low Energy Jeb;" the slick Ivy League-educated Senator from Texas Ted Cruz became "Lyin' Ted Cruz;" Marco Rubio, the relatively diminutive Senator from Florida became "Little Marco," and so on. While hardly the type of behavior one would expect from a presidential candidate, a growing number of Republican voters were delighted, and the major television networks gave

Trump a tremendous amount of free publicity because he proved to be a solid ratings grabber. Ultimately, the inability of his opponents to counter Trump's appeal led them to drop out one by one. Despite a sizeable number of conservative writers such as George Will, political bloggers such as Erick Erickson, and radio personalities such as Glenn Beck joining a growing "Never Trump" movement, Donald Trump was able to defy the odds and become the Republican Party's nominee, eventually naming Indiana governor Mike Pence to be his running mate.

Clinton vs. Trump

Historians and political pundits will pore over the 2016 presidential election for decades, analyzing the events and ranking the important developments for their relative impact on the collective mindset of the voters and the end result of the campaign. The country is too close in time to the recently concluded election for a complete historical presentation, so a basic retelling of the major episodes will have to suffice.

Both parties solidified support behind their candidates after their respective national conventions. Clinton emerged from the Democratic National Convention with a solid lead in the polls. Helping her was Donald Trump's defiance of the conventional wisdom that nominees should pivot to the political center for the general election in order to win over the nation's independent voters. Instead, he continued to speak whatever entered his mind, flailing against President Obama and former Secretary of State Clinton as the "founders of ISIS," questioning the motives of a Muslim Gold Star father who lost his son in Iraq and spoke out against Trump's anti-Muslim views at the Democratic convention, and even thanked a veteran who gave him his Purple Heart by uttering "I always wanted to get the Purple Heart. This was much easier." (He had avoided military service during the Vietnam War by claiming a medical exemption for a foot condition.)

As Clinton continued to benefit from these unforced errors, Trump finally fired his campaign manager and brought in a new team that cleaned up the candidate in an effort to present him in a more disciplined manner. A key part of the transformation involved his rigid reliance upon a teleprompter for his campaign appearances, something that he had constantly ridiculed President Obama for employing.

Reading prepared remarks created by his staffers from the teleprompter, Trump stayed on script, and was able to more efficiently deliver his venom as he told many of his riled up listeners what they wished to hear—that he would tear up free trade agreements that took American manufacturing jobs away (though he marketed a Trump clothing line that made shirts and ties in Bangladesh and China), that he would build a great border wall and make Mexico pay for it while deporting millions of undocumented Mexican immigrants, and that "Crooked Hillary" Clinton was a corrupt establishment politician who would do nothing to make their lives better.

Trump continued these lines of attacks in his three presidential debates with Clinton. He made much use of the fact that the Federal Bureau of Investigation (FBI) had undertaken a serious investigation of her use of a private email server while serving as Secretary of State. He asserted that the FBI's findings of a total 30,000 emails from that server had been deleted demonstrated that she had something to hide and that he'd put her in prison if he was elected president. (FBI Director James Comey concluded that no criminal charges needed to be filed against Clinton, though he criticized her use of the private server as potentially harmful to national security if it had ever been breached by hackers.) Clinton performed well during the debates, displaying her knowledge and expertise of foreign and domestic policy details, plus she was able to score some points of her own against Trump for his various bombastic statements and for being the first presidential candidate in modern history not to release his tax records, asserting that he was the one who actually had something to hide.

Clinton's campaign thought that they had clinched the election when an archived 2005 audio tape of Trump talking lewdly about women with *Access Hollywood* host Billy Bush was leaked to the public. The clip, which had never aired, picked up the conversation between the men in which Trump relayed his failed effort to seduce a married host of Bush's show, as well as his observation that women were so impressed with his fame that he could just walk up and grope them and they did not care. The tape led to universal condemnation of Trump except from his most devout loyalists. Many Republican politicians proclaimed that their support for the nominee had ended. Speaker of the House Paul Ryan canceled a campaign appearance with Trump and stated that he would maintain his support but would focus solely on getting Republican House members elected. Over a dozen women came out over the next several days, claiming that he had made inappropriate advances upon them in the past and groped them without their consent. Trump attempted to excuse his words as being simply exaggerated "locker room talk," but then characteristically lashed out at his critics, bringing up former President Bill Clinton's past (not only Monica Lewinsky, but also other women who made accusations never proven to be true) and accusing Hillary Clinton of being his "enabler," who supposedly tried to destroy the women who brought up her husband's sexual indiscretions.

Despite the negative publicity, Trump continued to hold large rallies in the tossup battleground states as well as in Midwestern industrial states, such as Wisconsin, Michigan, and Pennsylvania that were viewed as longshots because Democrats had consistently won those states in recent presidential races and Clinton was ahead in the public polls there by close to double digits. It was at this point in the campaign that the political world was jolted to its core by a surprise announcement from FBI Director Comey that the FBI was reopening the investigation of Clinton's private email server because some emails from Clinton's server were found on the laptop computer of the estranged husband of her top aide who was under investigation for sexting with a minor. Trump and Republican operatives had a field day with the news, milking it for all it was worth. Even though Director Comey issued a statement a week later that most of the emails were duplicates of those already seen by the FBI and none of the others contained classified material, the political damage to the Clinton campaign may have been done as early voting had already commenced in several key states while the drama was unfolding that week, plus the affair may have left lingering doubts in the minds of some voters who planned on voting later. The relative impact of the "Comey announcement" on the election results is one aspect of the election that will surely be dissected and analyzed in the years to come.

Political pundits (and probably a majority of the voters) were expecting a Clinton victory on Election Night. The public polls were showing Clinton with a comfortable 4-percentage point popular vote lead in 4-way matchups that included Libertarian Party candidate Gary Johnson and Green Party candidate Jill Stein as well as Electoral College estimates of 280-330 electoral votes, with 270 needed to clinch the election. This result, however, failed to materialize as Donald Trump pulled off one of the most stunning upsets in presidential election history by not only winning the important battleground states of Florida, North Carolina, and Ohio, where polls had shown he had a good chance of emerging victorious, but quite stunningly he was able to eke out small wins in the "Rust Belt" states of Wisconsin, Michigan, and Pennsylvania to take their electoral votes—places that he had been seen as having little chance of success. In these states, Trump's relentless attacks against NAFTA, the Trans-Pacific Partnership, and other free-trade agreements resonated with white working-class voters. Reduced turnout among Democrats, either because of the Comey announcement or general complacency and overconfidence from viewing the positive poll numbers, also contributed to the

surprise result. In the end, Hillary Clinton won over 2 million more popular votes than Trump nationwide, and Democrats picked up five House seats and two additional seats in the U.S. Senate, but this was small consolation for the party whose members were decimated by the unexpected results. Not only had Republicans been able to retain control of both Houses of Congress, but now a man who many of them were firmly convinced was an unprincipled demagogue, completely unqualified to serve by experience and temperament, was about to become the 45th president of the United States.

THE CIRCUS BEGINS

Future historians will certainly be intrigued as they dissect and analyze the Trump presidency in an effort to understand the man's actions, his appeal to his robust supporters, the utter disgust that he elicited from his many detractors, and the various undercurrents that influenced the major issues of the period. Given the proximity of this writing to recent events, however, only a chronicle of the more noteworthy aspects of Trump's first two years in office will be related below.

During the 2016 Republican primary season, one of Donald Trump's opponents, former Florida governor Jeb Bush, asserted that the businessman's political inexperience and flippant nature made him a "chaos candidate" leaving no doubt that Trump would be a "chaos president" if ever elected. That prediction, about the only thing that Bush got right during his lackluster campaign, proved to be prescient. From the beginning, chaos, both by design and ineptitude, would characterize the first two years of the Trump presidency.

A Unique Inauguration

On the day of his inauguration, President-elect Trump's approval rating of 40 per cent ranked lower than any incoming president during the twentieth century. Though many enthusiastic supporters came to the capital for the inaugural ceremony, the overall size of 250,000 was average for such an event (television coverage showed many near-empty bleachers along the parade route following the venue). At the inauguration, Trump delivered a fairly stark address, invoking many campaign themes about ending a broken system in which the common people saw no benefit. "This American carnage," he asserted, "stops right here and stops right now." After painting a further bleak portrait of the country—allegedly withering away from uncontrolled immigration, bad trade deals, and expensive military commitments with other nations—the new president stated that going forward the overriding theme of his presidency would be putting "America first." The end result, he predicted, would be "America will start winning again, winning like never before."

Media coverage noted that, while many were in attendance to hear the address, the numbers paled in comparison to Barack Obama's inaugurations, especially his historic first ceremony where over 1.5 million attended. Further, the day after the inauguration, the nation's capital witnessed the "Woman's March on Washington"—a massive, unprecedented counter-demonstration in which an estimated half million women, men, and children (about twice the estimated size of Trump's inaugural audience) showed up to register their dissent to the election results and to announce that an organized political resistance was forming to temper the incoming president's excesses to the best of their abilities. Accompanying "sister marches" also took place in large cities and many small towns across the nation.

In an effort to counter the media narrative of a relatively small inauguration crowd, Trump deployed a tactic derived from his business experience—spreading misinformation. Whenever asked about his recollection of the inaugural crowd, Trump would recall the "millions" that showed up, occupying the National Mall "as far as my eyes could see." Further, Press Secretary Sean Spicer was soon sent out to address the Washington press corps with doctored photographs supposedly providing definitive proof that the crowd was "the largest audience to ever witness an inauguration. Period." The performance shocked the reporters and many Americans who viewed the display on television, but the episode was just the beginning of efforts to control the media narrative. Continuing with methods deployed during his campaign, Trump furthered his method of quick-line branding in order to disparage opponents and simplify complex issues. He would consistently, almost pathologically, refuse to take blame for anything negative appearing about him and his administration in the press, preferring instead to attack the media as habitually biased against him, reducing all criticism to the catch phrase "fake news," which he often repeated at press events, campaign rallies, and on Twitter, his social media platform of choice.

Though Trump promised during his campaign to "drain the swamp" in Washington, D.C. of corrupt influence peddlers, lobbyists, and establishment insiders, many of Trump's cadre of initial appointments to high posts within his administration were soon beset by scandals. Though appointing his son-in-law, Jared Kushner, to a high position as a presidential advisor and ersatz diplomatic envoy, as well as Trump's daughter Ivanka as a White House advisor, created nepotism concerns, the questionable actions of some Cabinet members led to their early departures: Secretary of Health and Human Services Tom Price left after media reports emerged of his use of private jets for personal business; Environmental Protection Agency Director Scott Pruitt resigned after government inspectors found substantial evidence of outlandish spending of public money, in addition to conflicts of interest involving receiving gifts and other benefits from energy company representatives; and Secretary of the Interior Ryan Zinke was forced to resign when government investigators documented his frequent use of expensive taxpayer-funded charter flights for government work and personal trips, in addition to reports detailing the merging official business with partisan politics, including a Virgin Islands trip to celebrate the 100-year anniversary of Denmark's sale of the islands to the United States that included an appearance at a Republican Party fundraiser where he posed for photographs in exchange for party donations. The earliest resignation of a Trump administration official, however, that of National Security Advisor Michael Flynn for not disclosing his secret lobbying efforts on behalf of the Turkish government and covert discussions with Russian officials before joining the administration, would prove to be the most significant scandal as it ultimately led to a wide-ranging investigation of the Trump campaign's activities, including the possible coordination of high-ranking campaign officials with individuals associated with Russian intelligence agencies.

Rolling Back Obama

During his first two years in office, Trump issued a flurry of executive orders to countermand many Obama administration policies. In the field of foreign relations, Trump withdrew U.S. participation from the 2015 Paris Climate Agreement, arguing that it was a bad deal that unfairly burdened American businesses. He also angered European allies by pulling the United States out of the nuclear deal with Iran and reinstituting economic sanctions, alleging that the Middle Eastern country was not adhering to its part of the arrangement.

With respect to the domestic economy, Trump issued executive orders to favor energy interests by authorizing the advancement of construction of the Keystone XL Pipeline through the northern Plains states, and greatly scaled back the expanse of area designated as national monuments to allow for increased mineral and oil resource exploration. The new president also actively pursued protectionist policies by withdrawing from the Trans-Pacific Partnership (a new trade barrier reduction deal involving many nations of North America, Latin America, and Asia), by renegotiating certain portions of the North American Free Trade Agreement with Canada and Mexico, and by greatly raising tariffs on goods imported from China and other nations.

Most divisively, Trump advanced his domestic agenda by using executive orders to promote the views of his core supporters on an array of controversial social issues. He provoked outrage among social liberals by imposing a ban on transgender men and women from serving in the U.S. military. The move lead to a direct legal challenge, resulting in a successful stay against implementation of the policy until properly adjudicated. (The case is still being litigated in the federal court system.)

Trump's opponents became apoplectic in response to his unilateral actions on immigration. In January 2017, the president issued an outright ban on people from Iran, Iraq, Libya, Syria, Somalia, Sudan, and Yemen from entering the United States, alleging that citizens from the seven predominately Muslim nations were inherently terrorist threats to the country. This "Muslim ban," as it became known, spurred spontaneous protests among activists at many major airports across the country and was immediately challenged in the federal courts. Citing discriminatory intent, plaintiffs used Trump's own campaign statements expressing a desire to ban all Muslims from entering the county for an indeterminate period. Though the administration initially suffered a serious of setbacks, a revised version of the ban with bland language pronouncing the general necessity of combating terrorist threats finally succeeded in receiving sanction by the U.S. Supreme Court in June 2018.

Trump signaled significant changes in immigration policy when he ended President Obama's deferred adjudication policy (DACA) for the children of illegal immigrants who had resided for several years in the United States. After failing to receive funding from Congress for his campaign-promised border wall (which he had continually insisted Mexico would pay for), Trump announced a "zero tolerance" policy at the Mexican border, generating a media firestorm when the public became aware that border patrol agents were being ordered to separate thousands of children of illegal immigrant and legal asylum seekers from their parents while their cases were being adjudicated, apparently as a form of deterrent for future entries into the country. The clamor over this **child separation policy** lasted from April to June 2018, when Trump finally bowed to intense political pressure and ended the practice, though to this day hundreds of infants and small children have not been reunited with their parents (and some may never be) because of the inability of government officials to gather and maintain information about the immigrants.

Trump's Judicial Impact

Trump's decision to avoid seeking consensus and to govern as a divisive leader who primarily catered to the voters who produced his electoral victory meant that he would never achieve a net positive rating in reputable public opinion polls. Nevertheless, his base of support—largely white Americans from diverse socioeconomic backgrounds who either agreed with his far-right political views or enjoyed how he irritated rival Democrats—continued to cheer on the president. Though some noteworthy establishment Republicans not currently holding political office declared themselves "Never Trumpers," most congressional Republicans played along with Trump in order to reap tangible benefits of having him in power.

This brand of transactional politics could be seen clearly in the realm of judicial appointments. Senate Majority Leader Mitch McConnell of Kentucky, whose parliamentary delay tactics against most of President Obama's judicial nominees led the then-Democratic Senate Majority Leader, Harry Reid, to orchestrate a change in Senate rules formally ending the filibuster for federal judicial nominees, took advantage of this change in order to shepherd a record number of Republican nominees through the Senate confirmation process.

Trump was also able to appoint two justices to the U.S. Supreme Court during his first two years in office. His first nominee, Neil Gorsuch, encountered resistance from Senate Democrats who deeply resented McConnell's successful efforts to stonewall the nomination of Obama appointee Merrick Garland to replace deceased conservative justice Antonin Scalia, but without the filibuster, they were unable to prevent Gorsuch's confirmation by a 54-45 vote. Trump's second nominee, to replace retiring justice Anthony Kennedy, proved to be more controversial. Kennedy had been a swing vote in favor of some liberal court victories, most notably the *Obergefell* decision that legalized gay marriage, and many Democrats feared that Trump's nomination of a conservative Republican ideologue, Brett Kavanaugh, would jeopardize many gains on social issues made over the past several decades. In addition to criticizing his politics prior to serving on a federal district court, Kavanaugh's opponents zeroed in on his personal life, assailing his privileged upbringing replete with heavy drinking. The high point of the challenge came from Christine Blasey Ford, an acquaintance from Kavanaugh's youth who accused the nominee of sexually assaulting her while in a drunken haze at a party during his wild private high school days. Though given the opportunity to speak at the confirmation hearing, Republican senators, citing a lack of direct evidence, pressed forward to advance Kavanaugh's nomination and he was approved by a 50-48 vote—an extremely narrow margin historically for an incoming Supreme Court justice.

Republican Legislative Reform Attempts

In addition to the Republican-controlled Senate cooperating with the president in placing conservative judges onto the federal bench, Trump also worked with congressional Republican leaders to advance longstanding Republican legislative goals, none more controversial than repealing the Affordable Care Act ("Obamacare") and significantly modifying the federal tax code. The rapid effort to discard Obamacare without holding hearings, plus the inability to agree on the details of an alternative proved to be problematic for Republicans, as no viable replacement for popular Obamacare features such as nondiscrimination for pre-existing conditions and extended insurance coverage for children were offered. After a lengthy fight, the effort failed when Democrats combined with a few Republicans up for reelection and Republican Senator John McCain of Arizona, then dying from an inoperable brain tumor, to kill the measure.

Efforts to revise the tax code caused additional troubles for congressional Republicans, but ultimately they received much of what they wanted in their final bill—the **Tax Cuts and Jobs Act**—which marked the first major revision in the federal tax code in 30 years. The legislation greatly reduced the corporate tax rate (from 35 to 21 percent), while providing a modest but temporary reduction in individual and family tax rates, though personal exemptions were eliminated. The standard deduction was doubled, but itemized deductions for state income, property, and sales taxes were capped. While corporations benefited greatly, it remained to be seen which individual filers gained and which ones lost from changes, as well as how the new law would affect the national debt.

Foreign Affairs under Trump

Donald Trump (and the American people) were fortunate that no major foreign policy crisis directly involving the United States emerged during the first two years of his presidency. Though he ordered a missile attack upon the forces of Bashar al-Assad in Syria after the dictator's military deployed chemical weapons against his opponents during his ongoing civil war, Trump otherwise ignored the conflict, satisfied that ISIS forces were in decline within the country.

Trump spent more time on the diplomatic front engaging in a series of photo ops to project American strength and enhance his personal prestige. He shocked the world by agreeing to meet personally with North Korean dictator **Kim Jong-un** in Singapore. The June 2018 summit provided memorable visuals of the two leaders shaking hands and speaking admiringly about each other, but nothing of consequence emerged from the initial meeting of the leaders beyond vague promises to work toward the ultimate goal of denuclearizing the Korean Peninsula.

In Europe, Trump attended a series of meetings with the leaders of NATO countries and provoked their ire by admonishing them to commit more funds for their countries' defense. None of Trump's diplomatic interactions generated more astonishment than his July 2018 summit with Russian Premier Vladimir Putin. Not only had the conversations taken place without transparency (only translators were present and any notes taken were not disclosed), but at a post-summit press conference, the president outraged many Americans, Democrats and Republicans alike, as well as European allies when he openly defended Putin after reporters asked questions related to potential Russian interference in the 2016 presidential election. These utterances by Trump convinced large numbers of his political opponents that, rather than being a simple gaffe, the president might well be acting on behalf of Putin's interests, thus it was imperative for Robert Mueller, the special counsel appointed by the Justice Department to investigate possible Russian ties to the Trump campaign, to work with due diligence in order to justify their suspicions or clear the president and his staff of potentially treasonous wrongdoing.

The Mueller Investigation

The **Mueller inquiry** into possible ties between Trump campaign operatives and Russian officials evolved out of an FBI investigation that had begun during the 2016 election, after being informed by an Australian diplomat that a Trump campaign foreign policy adviser, George Papadopoulos, let it slip during a night of heavy drinking with him that Papadopoulos had recently spoken to someone who told him that the Russian government had "dirt" in the form of stolen Clinton campaign emails. This tip led the FBI to explore whether Trump supporters or campaign personnel openly conspired with Russian agents to distribute the emails, which were later found to have been stolen by Russian hackers and distributed through the Wikileaks web site, and also uncovered Michael Flynn's secret contacts with Russian officials during the campaign and during the transition period before the inauguration.

The FBI investigation (which was never made public during the election) continued after Trump's inauguration, though the incoming president hoped it would cease and leaned on FBI Director James Comey to stop the investigation of Flynn. When Comey refused, Trump fired him, setting off obstruction of justice allegations. When the Justice Department opened an inquiry, Attorney General Jeff Sessions shocked many, including the president, when he announced that he was recusing himself because of his own admitted contacts with Russian officials during the election campaign. Deputy Attorney General Rod Rosenstein then decided to create a special counsel to investigate all election-related matters, appointing former FBI director Robert Mueller (pronounced "Muller") to the position. Outraged, President Trump railed against all the major figures involved—Comey, for not "letting the Flynn matter go" as he had asked; Rosenstein, for creating the special counsel; Sessions, for recusing himself from the investigation; and Mueller, for supposedly becoming a willing tool of his opponents. From the beginning, Trump denounced the investigation as a "witch hunt" designed to discredit his surprise electoral victory and to cast a long shadow upon his administration.

Despite the presidential attacks and veiled threats to rein in the investigation, Mueller's team continued their work well into Trump's term, in part because the work was tedious, in part because the scope was wide-ranging, and in part because the inquest continued to produce results. During its first two years, Mueller's team unearthed Russian internet "troll farm" operations that used fake personas while praising Trump and disparaging Hillary Clinton's campaign on Facebook, Twitter, and other on-line platforms, while also uncovering numerous crimes perpetrated by Trump campaign officials – most notably Michael Flynn's illegal lobbying efforts (to which he pled guilty), tax evasion and illegal lobbying undertaken by Trump's campaign manager Paul Manafort (to which he was convicted by two separate juries), and perjury by lower-level campaign officials trying to cloak their contacts with Russian government officials. Other findings leaked to the press by individuals with knowledge of the investigation revealed that Manafort, Jared Kushner, Donald Trump, Jr., and others held a meeting with Russians with ties to Putin's regime in New York's Trump Tower during the campaign for purposes yet to be revealed.

A Mid-Term Rebuke

A final Mueller investigation report will probably be released before the 2020 election, with its findings potentially having as great an impact on the final result as who the Democrats choose as their presidential nominee. Signs of impending trouble for Trump and his party were already seen in the results of the 2018 congressional races, as well as hundreds of state and local elections held across the country. In the lead-in to the 2018 mid-term elections, Democrats won many special elections for vacant U.S. House and state legislature seats, and competed very well to narrowly lose many contests in traditional Republican strongholds (and even won a special election to send a Democrat to the U.S. Senate from Alabama). This trend continued in the 2018 elections. The GOP was quite fortunate that most of the U.S. Senate seats in contention were in deeply conservative states that had voted for Trump in 2016. They dislodged four moderate Democrats who had been elected six years earlier by defeating lousy extremist Republican nominees, but also lost two seats in the Southwest as both Nevada and Arizona elected female Democratic candidates to hold previously-Republican seats. In addition to achieving great gains in state legislature and governors' races, the most impressive Democratic victories took place in the House of Representatives. Ultimately, the Democrats netted 41 seats to take control of the body, the largest gains for the party since the 1974 election held after the Watergate scandal. The results virtually assured the return of Nancy Pelosi as Speaker of the House, and definitely guaranteed additional inquiries into the activities of the Trump campaign and administration by newly empowered House Democrats.

The Mueller Report

The much-anticipated release of the Mueller Commission report occurred in the spring of 2019. On March 22, Robert Mueller formally delivered the 448-page document to President Trump's newly-appointed Attorney General William Barr. Two days later, Barr sent a four-page letter to House and Senate Judiciary Committee leaders in which he provided what he characterized as a summary of Mueller's principal findings, stating that there was no solid evidence of coordination on the part of Trump campaign officials with the Russian government nor proof that the president later engaged in obstruction of justice with regard to the investigation into the election probe. When Mueller became aware of Barr's characterization of his conclusions, he wrote to the attorney general to complain that his letter "did not fully capture the context, nature, and substance of this office's work and conclusions," leading to "public confusion" regarding some key points of the investigation. While a redacted version of the report released to the public on April 18 did indeed include the conclusion that there was insufficient evidence for the charge that the Trump campaign coordinated or conspired with the Russian government in its election-interference activities, such actions were

Hamilton and the Future of Modern Musical Theater

The smash Broadway hit **Hamilton** *caused a sensation in the world of musical theater as well as mainstream pop culture during the mid-2010s. Though the Founding Fathers had been covered before by Broadway in Sherman Edwards's 1969 Tony Award-winning musical adaptation of Peter Stone's book on the debate over the Declaration of Independence, the presentation was quite traditional in terms of musical style and the ways in which the main characters were portrayed. Besides occasional homages to certain earlier Broadway musicals, there is little traditional about Hamilton, which attempts to retell the story of the Founding Fathers for contemporary Americans using a diverse cast and an array of modern musical genres, especially hip-hop.*

Hamilton is the brainchild of Lin-Manuel Miranda, an American actor, rapper, composer, and writer of Puerto Rican descent who first scored Broadway success with the musical **In the Heights**, *a story based upon his upbringing in the Washington Heights neighborhood of his youth that won multiple Tony Awards including Best Musical. While on a much-needed vacation, Miranda picked up a copy of Ron Chernow's best-selling biography of Alexander Hamilton and became enthralled with the story. Reflecting his own background, he immediately began envisioning a grand drama with such recurring hip-hop-inspired themes as overcoming hardships and managing troubled relationships, as well as revolutionary, non-conformist behavior.*

Miranda soon began experimenting, conceiving a possible hip-hop album based on Hamilton's life. He debuted the first song for the project at the 2009 White House Evening of Poetry, Music, and the Spoken Word in front of President Barack Obama, his family, and a hundred invited guests. Decidedly different and skillfully executed (the video of his appearance is available on YouTube among other web sites), Miranda's performance was an immediate attention-getter. Inspired by the favorable reception, he plugged along and wrote more songs for the album over the next five years.

Eventually, Miranda was encouraged to think bigger than a concept album and visualize the work as a full-scale musical theater production. He began workshopping ideas with performers, unsure if this markedly different approach would translate to Broadway. After a successful season off-Broadway, **Hamilton** *premiered on Broadway in August 2015. Needless to say, the show has definitely resonated with audiences beyond Miranda's wildest expectations, selling out every show since its debut and nearly sweeping every Tony Award category—a testament to the vast popularity of Miranda's masterpiece.*

As with other great musical theater epics, those in attendance loved the music while laughing, crying, and generally bonding with the main characters who were interpreted and presented in a fresh manner that humanized them, made them relatable to modern audiences, used their stories as a running commentary on aspects of today's current racial and cultural climate. The show breaks down cast barriers by having an Hispanic actor portray the immigrant Founding Father Alexander Hamilton, black actors play the parts of Aaron Burr and George Washington, an Asian-American depict Hamilton's wife, and so on, with the cast members singing classic hip-hop-style numbers, Beyoncé-inspired tunes, traditional Broadway ballads, and even 1960s-era pop songs. As Miranda related in an interview about his effort to make the story more accessible to contemporary audiences: "Our cast looks like America now…It's a way of pulling you into the story and allowing you to leave whatever cultural baggage you have about the Founding Fathers at the door."

Experimental theater is not new. Orson Welles directed a version of **Macbeth** *for the Federal Theater Project in 1936, which included an all-black cast, and Andrew Lloyd Webber's counterculture-inspired rock opera* **Jesus Christ Superstar** *debuted on Broadway in 1971. Nevertheless, Broadway had never before embraced hip-hop, the music of today's youth, and it remains to be seen if* **Hamilton** *will be a noteworthy aberration or a bright torch lighting the way towards Broadway's creative future.*

determined to have been welcomed by the Trump campaign because of the resulting political benefits to their side. Further, Mueller did not exonerate Trump of the obstruction-of-justice accusation, instead concluding that such a determination was beyond his commission's charge. His team documented ten episodes in which Trump may have obstructed justice while attempting to control the course of the investigation, but they decided to provide the evidence to Congress and let that body determine if the president's actions constituted criminal levels of obstructing justice necessitating impeachment proceedings.

Impeachment Proceedings

While numerous congressional hearings were held in the wake of the Mueller Report, House Democrats did not initiate impeachment proceedings against Trump until another potential scandal broke later in 2019, this time involving the president's decision to withhold American military aid to Ukraine unless that country's leaders publicly investigated the business dealings in that country of Hunter Biden, the son of former Vice President Joe Biden, who Trump identified as his most likely challenger in his upcoming re-election campaign. In September, knowledge of a whistleblower complaint by a U.S. government official with knowledge of the details of a phone call between Trump and the president of Ukraine became public, in which the official accused Trump of abusing his office by openly soliciting foreign interference in the upcoming 2020 presidential race. Democrats in the House of Representatives launched an impeachment inquiry without cooperation from the White House, whose staff characterized the probe as "illegitimate and dangerous," with Trump accusing Democrats of generating a new false narrative to remove him from office after failing to do so with the Mueller investigation. Nevertheless, the president's stance was not helped by a public statement by his chief of staff, Mike Mulvaney, who acknowledged the substance of the allegation, stating "We do that all the time with foreign policy."

After a series of open and closed-door hearings, House Democrats moved to impeach the president on December 18, voting 230-197 in favor of indictment for abusing presidential power, and 229-198 for obstruction of Congress. For only the third time in American history, a president now faced a trial in the U.S Senate that could lead to his removal from office. With the basic facts of the case being known, the only question was whether any Senate Republicans would bolt their party and vote for a conviction, not a likely scenario. Senate Democrats pressed on regardless, stating that not acting upon such behavior would abdicate their congressional responsibili-

ties in checking unrestrained executive power. Meanwhile, Republican Party officials countered with the accusation that the Democrats were simply playing politics, over-exaggerating the circumstances for short-term political gain. After a two-week trial in early February 2020, the Senate failed to convict Trump by the requisite two-thirds vote. Fifty-three senators voted to convict on the abuse of power charge (including Mitt Romney of Utah, the only Republican to do so) versus 47 voting not guilty, while the vote was only 52-48 to convict on the obstruction of Congress charge.

As the trial ended, the nation began to turn its attention to the 2020 presidential and congressional elections which promised to be highly-polarized barnburners. Thus far, President Trump had proved to be fairly impervious to the multitude of slings and arrows thrust upon him by his political enemies, but just as his re-election campaign was heating up, his presidency would face its biggest challenge yet from a totally unforeseen source.

The Coronavirus Pandemic Strikes

In late-November 2019, COVID-19, a highly contagious respiratory disease caused by a coronavirus had erupted in Wuhan, a large provincial capital in central China. Though evidence would later show that numerous American travelers had brought the disease home from Wuhan before the end of 2019, the first recorded case in the United States was reported in Washington State on January 20, 2020. In response to a reporter's question about whether he was concerned about the case, President Trump responded: "No, not at all. We have it totally under control. It's one person coming in from China…. It's going to be fine." Four days later, he commended Chinese government authorities for their efforts to contain the virus, which had just included a total lockdown of Wuhan and its population of over 11 million people.

Despite continued public assurances that there was no imminent threat to the United States, on January 29 the White House announced the formation of a task force to advise the president on coronavirus matters and to relay updated information to the public. Less than a month later, the first reported American death took place in Washington State followed by two more deaths of elderly nursing home residents. (Later it was confirmed that the first U.S. death had actually occurred three weeks earlier in San Jose, California.) For the next few months, an increasing number of states began recording their first confirmed cases. At a task force press conference on March 9, President Trump continued to attempt to downplay the spread of the virus, at one point stating that the growing pandemic was "very much under control," that it was less deadly than influenza, and that there were indications that the number of positive cases would soon reach zero. (Trump later told journalist Bob Woodward that he did so to prevent causing a panic).

As an increasing number of states in early March began to announce their first confirmed COVID cases, many governors began to declare public emergencies. Many colleges soon followed the lead of Ohio State and Harvard Universities by ceasing face-to-face classroom instruction as the traditional spring break season approached, informing students that their soon-to-be frazzled professors would help them finish the semester by devising means of doing so online. Grammar schools and high schools across the country followed suit. By mid-March, with the number of confirmed cases and deaths significantly rising, the Center for Disease Control (CDC) issued guidelines that all gatherings of above 50 people should be avoided, and President Trump now urged citizens to avoid gatherings of more than ten people and also to restrict unnecessary travel. As state and local governments began to postpone primary elections and order "non-essential businesses" to close, California became the first of many states to issue a mandatory "shelter in place" order largely confining its residents to their domiciles (with some exceptions) until further notice in a frantic effort to lessen the spread of the virus.

Responding to the commercial shutdowns across the country and a plunge in the stock market (the Dow Jones Industrial Average had dropped by over a third in one month, from an all-time high of 29,400 points in mid-February to just over 19,000 in mid-March), Congress passed the Coronavirus Aid, Relief, and Economic Security (CARES) Act, which President Trump signed into law on March 27. The legislation authorized a $2 trillion economic stimulus package to be implemented in an effort to stabilize the economy, including one-time cash payments ($300 billion) to taxpayers, $260 billion in increased unemployment benefits, a forgivable loan program for small businesses ($350 billion) and corporations ($500 billion), and $340 billion in aid to state and local governments.

By the end of April 2020, as COVID-19 spread globally causing an extensive number of deaths in Asia, Europe, and Latin America, the number of cases in the United States had skyrocketed to over 1 million, with over 60,000 confirmed COVID-related deaths, a mortality rate of 6 percent for those unfortunate enough to have contracted the coronavirus. Despite such harrowing numbers, which would only increase as the months progressed and the federal government awaited the results of test trials undertaken by pharmaceutical companies for an effective vaccine against coronaviruses, pressure began to build for state and local governments to gradually relax existing restrictions on public gatherings and businesses that relied upon in-person patronage. Soon, organized pushbacks against requirements to wear masks in public, along with concerted campaigns questioning the science behind the mandates (blending with libertarian protests railing against alleged restrictions to "personal freedom") became increasingly visible, often given increased visibility by politicians wishing to piggyback onto the outcries for a "return to normalcy," while many others vociferously opposed such hasty responses as a danger to public safety until effective vaccines could be developed. Amid such an unprecedented backdrop, the rambunctious 2020 election cycle was soon underway.

The 2020 Campaign

With President Trump's renomination ensured, all political eyes were on the Democratic side as the party's announced candidates, many of whom had been running for close to a year, began to alter their campaign operations in response to pandemic concerns. Initially, liberal U.S. Senator Bernie Sanders of Vermont staked a lead among the large field of progressive and moderate candidates, but as Sanders took advantage of the widely divided field, the moderate candidates began to circle the wagons by increasingly dropping out, rallying behind former Vice President Joe Biden, who eventually ran away from the field to earn enough delegate support to clinch the nomination by June 5. To bolster support among blacks and progressive women, two core elements within the modern Democratic Party, he made a historic choice by inviting one of his primary opponents, Senator Kamala Harris of California—a woman with Jamaican and East Indian immigrant parents—to be his running mate.

The summer months before the national party conventions were rocked by the outbreak of protests in many cities across the country, the precipitating event being the May 25 death of George Floyd, an African American man detained by police in Minneapolis, Minnesota on the accusation of passing a counterfeit bill at a convenience store. As onlookers gasped in horror and pleaded for his life, a local policeman restrained Floyd, already handcuffed and lying face down on the pavement, for several minutes by leaning on his neck with the officer's knee. Floyd eventually lost consciousness, stopped breathing, and died before the arrival of medical personnel. Floyd's homicide (the officer was convicted of murder the following year) led to nationwide protests against police brutality, most remaining peaceful but many occasionally turning into mass destruction of private and public property with sporadic attacks on law enforcement officers by protesters releasing pent-up frustration with the lack of progress, along with the actions of some violent agitators seeking to take advantage of the protests for their own ends. The protests often became politicized, as Democrats often supported the stated police-reform goals of the protestors while Republicans tended to group all protestors with the violent ones.

With the pandemic raging, the two campaigns took divergent approaches. The GOP national convention was originally scheduled to take place in Charlotte, North Carolina, but the Republican National Committee withdrew the event when the North Carolina state government declined to allow the convention to proceed at full capacity and without required face masks and social distancing. The Republican presidential and congressional campaigns subsequently held regular rallies and canvassed neighborhoods in order to maintain interpersonal contact with voters. Meanwhile, the Democrats held their national convention in Milwaukee, Wisconsin, largely in name only, with greatly reduced personnel on site and most delegate deliberations taking place remotely from various locations across the country. The Biden campaign and Democratic congressional candidates chose to limit the degree of proximate personal contact by hosting drive-in rallies and reduced-size events while maintaining social distancing.

Both campaigns were impacted by the news of the death of long-time liberal Supreme Court Justice Ruth Bader Ginsburg on September 18. Republicans rushed to fill the seat with a conservative justice while President Trump was still in office, despite Republican Senate Majority Leader Mitch McConnell's highly-publicized denial to consider President Obama's nominee Merrick Garland one full year before the 2016 presidential race on the grounds that it was supposedly too close to the next election for the Senate to make such a move. Ten days after Ginsburg's death, Trump announced his nomination of conservative law professor and former federal jurist Amy Coney Barrett at an outdoor ceremony in the White House Rose Garden attended by more than 150 people, many of whom did not wear masks or practice social distancing. The Senate would confirm her a month later by a 52-48 vote with Democrats in unanimous opposition, but the greatest political impact in the short term proved to be the news that many attendees at the Rose Garden ceremony soon contracted the coronavirus, most notably President Trump himself, who began showing symptoms deemed severe enough to warrant a three-day trip to Walter Reed Hospital. A media circus ensued as Democrats lambasted the president and fellow Republican officials for flouting conventional anti-COVID protocols, while Republican leaders generally praised Trump for his

fortitude and quick positive response to the extensive treatments made available to him to counter the disease's effects. The second presidential debate was postponed one week to enable Trump time to recover, but once held the debate quickly devolved into a shouting match, often instigated by the president in an effort to unnerve Biden as well as to cover for Trump's obvious lack of preparation due to his illness. A third planned debate failed to materialize after the Trump campaign balked at holding the event virtually in response to the coronavirus.

While many polls predicted a solid Biden victory and a rout for the Democrats, putting faith in public polls for accurate predictions of election returns once again proved to be deceiving. While Trump won rather easily in some traditional battleground states like Iowa and Ohio where the results were expected to be much closer, the Biden campaign over-performed in a couple of key states that traditionally voted Republican in presidential races, Arizona and Georgia. Due to the effects of the pandemic, especially the move in some large states to mail-in ballots for the first time, results were sometimes slow in being processed. Because of the larger number of mailed-in ballots coming from urban areas that trended Democratic, Trump's early election-night lead in Pennsylvania, as well the aforementioned states of Arizona and Georgia, slowly but surely evaporated, leading the president and his supporters to declare their belief that many of the vote returns were being fraudulently tabulated. Nevertheless, within a few days of the election, it became apparent that Biden had triumphed with over 81 million popular votes (51.6%) and 306 electoral votes to Trump's 74 million popular votes (46.9%) and 232 electoral votes. In addition to winning the presidency, the Democrats gained control of both houses of Congress, but only by the narrowest of margins. In the House of Representatives, the Republicans picked up 15 seats but the Democrats held on to a mere 222-213 majority. In the Senate, Democrats had to wait another month for the results of two runoffs for seats in Georgia, where the polling again proved to be problematic, but this time in their favor as the party scored two unlikely upsets with the election of both Jon Ossoff and Raphael Warnock to gain control with a 50-50 split and the tie-breaking votes of the new Vice President, Kamala Harris.

The January 6 Election Riot

On the day after the Georgia runoffs, President Trump's hubris in refusing to concede the loss in his re-election bid, while continuing to feed hope to his supporters that there were still legal channels available to prevent Biden's victory being certified led to an unprecedented riot at the

U.S. Capitol building on January 6, 2021 as the Congress was meeting to confirm the Electoral College results. At a rally held several blocks away from the Capitol, Trump and several other speakers delivered speeches to thousands of gathered supporters, whipping many of them into a frenzy.

Whether the subsequent events took place spontaneously or as the result of prior planning is still the subject of an ongoing congressional investigation, but large groups of Trump supporters soon descended upon the Capitol and began engaging in a series of violent confrontations with the undermanned police force. After hundreds of rioters breached the police barriers and began entering the building (one female rioter was shot and killed inside), hundreds of other Trump supporters followed behind them, gleefully taking videos on the cellphones and roaming the corridors while members of Congress fled for safety. Many began entering and ransacking congressional offices while another group was able to enter the Senate chamber, sat down at desks, and generally dishonored the chamber with their presence before walking out.

For his part, Trump resisted sending in National Guard troops to drive out the mob. After several hours, he posted a video on Twitter reasserting his belief that the election results were fraudulent but told his supporters to "go home in peace." After the rioters left, the electoral vote tabulation resumed and was completed in the early morning hours the next day, with Vice President Mike Pence declaring Biden to be the president-elect. After some members of his administration resigned and others stated that they were planning to do the same, Trump finally committed to an orderly transition of power.

Furious at the turn of events that they soon characterized as an "insurrection" directly fomented by Trump's words and actions, congressional Democrats soon began planning an unprecedented second impeachment inquiry against the outgoing president. Within a week, House Democrats (along with 10 Republicans) voted to impeach Donald Trump for a second time, just before Joe Biden was inaugurated. Despite Trump no longer holding office, Senate Democrats decided to hold a second trial anyway, stating it was necessary to hold the former president accountable for his deeds, plus a conviction could have also led to the barring of Trump from holding federal office in the future. On the sole charge of incitement of insurrection, the Senate voted 57-43 in favor of conviction, ten votes shy of the two-thirds required. This time, seven Republican senators voted to convict Trump, the largest bipartisan vote for an impeachment conviction of an American president.

The Enduring Pandemic

By the end of 2020, COVID-19 had taken a devastating toll on the country. Over 19 million Americans (one in 22 Americans) had already tested positive for the coronavirus, with the death toll reaching 300,000 (an average of 1,000 per day since February). The death toll would reach 750,000 by the fall of 2021, or slightly more than one out of every 500 Americans. Some glimmer of hope emerged before Christmas, however, with the announcement that the Food and Drug Administration would issue emergency authorization for two anti-COVID vaccines for Americans 16 years of age and older. The Pfizer Corporation's vaccine, whose clinical trials demonstrated 91 percent effectiveness in preventing COVID-19 disease, was approved on December 11, with approval of the Moderna Therapeutics Corporation's vaccine coming a week later. With supplies initially limited, many Americans had to wait multiple months to receive word that they could receive their first shots, but distribution gradually ramped up.

While the arrival of workable vaccines were seen as a godsend by many Americans, 2021 would see a large amount of vaccine reluctance, not only from traditional "anti-vaxxers"—those on both the extreme political left temperamentally distrustful of large pharmaceutical companies as well as some on the extreme political right temperamentally distrustful of any large federal government initiatives—but also from a significant minority of mainstream Republicans who would come to believe that vaccines either were not scientifically proven to be effective or were unnecessary.

POLARIZATION: THE GREATEST CHALLENGE TO CONTEMPORARY AMERICA

The United States in the early decades of the twenty-first century experienced its latest manifestation of an ongoing theme in the nation's story—the persistent power of past traditions clashing with challenges brought forward by those championing new ideas. Politically, Barack Obama symbolized this dichotomy. While often acting in fairly traditional ways for modern chief executives, the mere fact that he became the country's first African-American president was a huge milestone in American political history. Many who grew up in the wake of the Civil Rights Movement, let alone those still alive who remembered the period before the Fifties and Sixties, never thought that they would live to see the day when a black person would be elected president. Yet, that day came.

In many ways, American society in the early twenty-first century also reflected this dual nature of the old mixed with the new. Though over half of Americans have divorced parents, and non-traditional relationships have become increasingly accepted, traditional family structures nevertheless endure. The much-acclaimed television comedy show *Modern Family* has resonated with multiple generations of Americans in part because of the affirmation of the view that one can still find comfort and familial love even if one's parents were not the "stereotypical" one-man/one-woman couple who only married once and stayed together forever. The show about three branches of an extended family not only includes a traditional suburban married couple with three children, but also the wife's father who divorced her mother and married a gorgeous (and much younger) Colombian woman, as well as the wife's gay brother who married his sweetheart and adopted an infant Vietnamese daughter. Despite encountering the trials and tribulations of modern life, often in hilarious melodramatic fashion, the diverse members of this extended American family all love and support each other just as more traditional families in earlier times had done.

Nevertheless, as always in American history, the keepers of the traditional order have not gone away quietly. Instead, they have challenged those touting such changes as progress and remain determined to hold back the tide, leading to an intense polarization of American life. Congressional obstruction of most reform efforts is just the most salient manifestation of the current divide. Beyond the long-existing urban-rural split in political representation, the country now regularly sees people watching separate news channels based on their partisan leanings. Growing numbers of Americans home-school their children or send them to private schools in order to better control the content of the curriculum taught to their kids. Long-time friends, and even family members, who have strong differences in ideology now often "unfriend" each other on Facebook because of their opinions, even though the original purpose of the social network was to bring people together.

In attempting to counter this trend, the links that currently binding contemporary America appear increasingly tenuous. The strongest bonds that now compel people to cross party lines and the racial divide are often holidays (especially secular ones such as Mother's Day, Thanksgiving, and the Fourth of July), television shows that avoid political controversy such as *American Idol* and *Dancing with the Stars*, and athletic events that allow people regardless of their backgrounds to don their favorite team's colors and cheer together in unison. Surely a nation that touts its exceptionalism and inherent greatness can construct stronger ties than these.

Table 32.1

Epidemic Outbreaks in the United States, 1918-2021

Date	Cause	Estimated U.S. Death Toll
1918-1919	"Spanish Flu" (H1N1) virus	675,000
1921-1925	Diphtheria bacteria	75,000
1947-1957	Polio virus	17,000
1957-1958	"Asian Flu" (H2N2) virus	116,000
1968-1969	"Hong Kong Flu" (H3N2) virus	34,000
1981-2000	HIV/AIDS	450,000
2009-2010	"Swine Flu" (H1N1) virus	12,500
2019-2021	COVID-19 virus	600,000 (as of June 2021)

Chronology

2008   **The Bush administration initiates bailouts of several major banks.**
Barack Obama elected president.

2009   The Obama administration bails out General Motors and Chrysler.

2010   Affordable Care Act enacted.
Obama announces troop withdrawal from Iraq by the end of 2011.
Obama increases U.S. troop levels in Afghanistan.
Passage of the Dodd-Frank Wall Street Reform and Consumer Protection Act.

2011   Arab Spring begins.
Osama bin Laden killed.

2012   Occupy Wall Street movement erupts.
Supreme Court approves most of the Affordable Care Act.
Mass shooting at an Aurora, Colorado movie theater.
Barack Obama re-elected for a second term.
Mass shooting at an elementary school in Newtown, Connecticut.

2013   President Obama announces new measures to prevent gun violence.
Edward Snowden leaks secret documents revealing NSA domestic and global surveillance programs.

2014   Russia annexes the Crimean Peninsula.
Emergence of ISIS in Iraq and Syria.
Emergence of "Black Lives Matter" movement following series of police killings of unarmed African American suspects.

2015   Supreme Court ruling in *Obergefell v. Hodges.*

2016   Donald Trump elected 45th President of the United States of the United States.

2018   Tax Cut and Jobs Act passes Congress

SUGGESTED READINGS

Ben S. Bernanake, *The Courage to Act: A Memoir of a Crisis and Its Aftermath* (2015).

Michel Chossoduvosky and Andrew Marshall, *The Global Economic Crisis: The Great Depression of the 21st Century* (2010).

Timothy F. Geithner, *Stress Test: Reflections on Financial Crises* (2015).

Fawaz A. Gerges, *ISIS: A History* (2016).

Michael Haas, *Mr. Calm and Effective: Evaluating the Presidency of Barack Obama* (2012).

Arthur Goldwag, *A History of Fear and Loathing on the Populist Right* (2012).

Amy Goodman, Denis Moynihan, and Michael Moore, *The Silenced Majority: Stories of Uprisings, Occupation, Resistance, and Hope* (2012).

Walter Isaacson, *Steve Jobs* (2011).

Jodi Kantor, *The Obamas* (2012).

Daniel Klaidman, *The War on Terror and the Soul of the Obama Presidency* (2012).

Marc Lynch, *The New Arab Wars: Uprisings and Anarchy In the Middle East* (2016).

Jill Lepore, *The Whites of Their Eyes: The Tea Party's Revolution and the Battle over American History* (2010).

Martin A. Levin, Daniel DiSalvo, and Martin Shapiro, *Building Coalitions, Making Policy: The Politics of the Clinton, Bush, and Obama Presidencies* (2012).

Barack Obama, *Dreams from My Father: A Story of Race and Inheritance* (1995).

——, *The Audacity of Hope: Thoughts on Reclaiming the American Dream* (2006).

Henry M. Paulson, Jr., *On the Brink: Inside the Race to Stop The Collapse of the Global Financial System* (2013).

Joseph A. Pika and John Maltese, *The Politics of the Presidency* (2012).

Raymond Sturgis, *His Love and Dream for America: A Presidency Rising Above Conflicts and Challenges* (2011)

Ron Suskind, *Confidence Men: Washington, Wall Street, and the Education of a President* (2011).

Bob Woodward, *Obama's Wars* (2012).

Review Questions

1. What factors contributed to Barack Obama's election victories in both 2008 and 2012?

2. What economic dynamics coalesced by 2008 to cause the financial crisis and subsequent economic downturn?

3. Why did the Affordable Health Care Act ("Obamacare") generate so much controversy?

4. What foreign policy issues did President Obama inherit from his predecessor, especially in the area of U.S. relations with the Middle East?

5. What factors contributed to Donald Trump's surprise election victory in 2016?

Glossary of Important People and Concepts

Al Qaeda
American Recovery and Reinvestment Act
Arab Spring
Child separation policy
Osama bin Laden
"Black Lives Matter"
Hillary Clinton
Dodd-Frank Wall Street Reform and Consumer Protection Act
ISIS
Kim Jong-un
John McCain
Mortgage-backed securities
Mueller investigation
Barack Obama
Obergefell v. Hodges
Occupy Wall Street
Patient Protection and Affordable Care Act ("Obamacare")
"Predatory Lending"
Vladimir Putin Mitt Romney
Edward Snowden
Tax Cuts and Jobs Act
Tea Party
Troubled Assets Relief Program (TARP)
Donald Trump
Unilateralism

APPENDIX A

Declaration of Independence

Congress, July 4, 1776

When, in the course of human events, it becomes necessary for one people to dissolve the political bonds which have connected them with another, and to assume, among the powers of the earth, the separate and equal station to which the laws of nature and of nature's God entitle them, a decent respect to the opinions of mankind requires that they should declare the causes which impel them to the separation.

We hold these truths to be self-evident: That all men are created equal; that they are endowed by their Creator with certain unalienable rights; that among these are life, liberty and the pursuit of happiness; that, to secure these rights, governments are instituted among men, deriving their just powers from the consent of the governed; that whenever any form of government becomes destructive of these ends, it is the right of the people to alter or to abolish it, and to institute new government, laying its foundation on such principles, and organizing its powers in such form, as to them shall seem most likely to effect their safety and happiness. Prudence, indeed, will dictate that governments long established should not be changed for light and transient causes; and accordingly all experience hath shown that mankind are more disposed to suffer, while evils are sufferable, than to right themselves by abolishing the forms to which they are accustomed. But when a long train of abuses and usurpations, pursuing invariably the same object, evinces a design to reduce them under absolute despotism, it is their right, it is their duty, to throw off such government, and to provide new guards for their future security. Such has been the patient sufferance of these colonies; and such is now the necessity which constrains them to alter their former systems of government. The history of the present King of Great Britain is a history of repeated injuries and usurpations, all having in direct object the establishment of an absolute tyranny over these states. To prove this, let facts be submitted to a candid world.

He has refused his assent to laws, the most wholesome and necessary for the public good.

He has forbidden his governors to pass laws of immediate and pressing importance, unless suspended in their operation till his assent should be obtained; and, when so suspended, he has utterly neglected to attend to them.

He has refused to pass other laws for the accommodation of large districts of people, unless those people would relinquish the right of representation in the legislature, a right inestimable to them, and formidable to tyrants only.

He has called together legislative bodies at places unusual, uncomfortable, and distant from the depository of their public records, for the sole purpose of fatiguing them into compliance with his measures.

He has dissolved representative houses repeatedly, for opposing, with many firmness, his invasions on the rights of the people.

He has refused for a long time, after such dissolutions, to cause others to be elected; whereby the legislative powers, incapable of annihilation, have returned to the people at large for their exercise; the state remaining, in the mean time, exposed to all the dangers of invasions from without and convulsions within.

He has endeavored to prevent the population of these states; for that purpose obstructing the laws for naturalization of foreigners; refusing to pass others to encourage their migrations hither, and raising the conditions of new appropriations of lands.

He has obstructed the administration of justice, by refusing his assent to laws establishing judiciary powers.

He has made judges dependent on his will alone, for the tenure of their offices, and the amount and payment of their salaries.

He has erected a multitude of new offices, and sent hither swarms of officers to harass our people and eat out their substance.

He has kept among us, in times of peace, standing armies, without the consent of our legislatures.

He has affected to render the military independent of, and superior to, the civil power.

He has combined with others to subject us to jurisdiction foreign to our constitution, and unacknowledged by our laws, giving his assent to their acts of pretended legislation:

For quartering large bodies of armed troops among us;

For protecting them, by a mock trial, from punishment for any murder which they should commit on the inhabitants of these states;

For cutting off our trade with all parts of the world;

For imposing taxes on us without our consent;

For depriving us, in many cases, of the benefits of trial by jury;

For transporting us beyond seas, to be tried for pretended offenses;

For abolishing the free system of English laws in a neighboring province, establishing therein an arbitrary government, and enlarging its boundaries, so as to render it at once an example and fit instrument for introducing the same absolute rule into these colonies;

For taking away our charters, abolishing our most valuable laws, and altering fundamentally the forms of our governments;

For suspending our own legislatures, and declaring themselves invested with power to legislate for us in all cases whatsoever.

He has abdicated government here, by declaring us out of his protection and waging war against us.

He has plundered our seas, ravaged our coasts, burned our towns, and destroyed the lives of our people.

He is at this time transporting large armies of foreign mercenaries to complete the works of death, desolation and tyranny already begun with circumstances of cruelty and perfidy scarcely paralleled in the most barbarous ages, and totally unworthy the head of a civilized nation.

He has constrained our fellow-citizens, taken captive on the high seas, to bear arms against their country, to become the executioners of their friends and brethren, or to fall themselves by their hands.

He has excited domestic insurrections among us, and has endeavored to bring on the inhabitants of our frontiers the merciless Indian savages, whose known rule of warfare is an undistinguished destruction of all ages, sexes, and conditions.

In every stage of these oppressions we have petitioned for redress in the most humble terms; our repeated petitions have been answered only by repeated injury. A prince, whose character is thus marked by every act which may define a tyrant, is unfit to be the ruler of a free people.

Nor have we been wanting in our attentions to our British brethren. We have warned them, from time to time, of attempts by their legislature to extend an unwarrantable jurisdiction over us. We have reminded them of the circumstances of our emigration and settlement here. We have appealed to their native justice and magnanimity, and we have conjured them, by the ties of our common kindred, to disavow these usurpations, which would inevitably interrupt our connections and correspondence. They, too, have been deaf to the voice of justice and of consanguinity. We must, therefore, acquiesce in the necessity which denounces our separation, and hold them, as we hold the rest of mankind, enemies in war, in peace friends.

We, therefore, the representatives of the United States of America, in General Congress assembled, appealing to the Supreme Judge of the world for the rectitude of our intentions, do, in the name and by authority of the good people of these colonies, solemnly publish and declare, that these United Colonies are, and of right ought to be, FREE AND INDEPENDENT STATES; that they are absolved from all allegiance to the British crown, and that all political connection between them and the state of Great Britain is, and ought to be, totally dissolved; and that, as free and independent states, they have full power to levy war, conclude peace, contract alliances, establish commerce, and do all other acts and things which independent states may of right do. And for the support of this declaration, with a firm reliance on the protection of Divine Providence, we mutually pledge to each other our lives, our fortunes, and our sacred honor.

JOHN HANCOCK

BUTTON GWINNETT
LYMAN HALL
GEO. WALTON
WM. HOOPER
JOSEPH HEWES
JOHN PENN
EDWARD RUTLEDGE
THOS. HEYWARD, JUNR.
THOMAS LYNCH, JUNR.
ARTHUR MIDDLETON
SAMUEL CHASE
WM. PACA
THOS. STONE
CHARLES CARROLL OF CARROLLTON
GEORGE WYTHE
RICHARD HENRY LEE
TH. JEFFERSON
BENJ. HARRISON

THOS. NELSON, JR.
FRANCIS LIGHTFOOT LEE
CARTER BRAXTON
ROBT. MORRIS
BENJAMIN RUSH
BENJA. FRANKLIN
JOHN MORTON
GEO. CLYMER
JAS. SMITH
GEO. TAYLOR
JAMES WILSON
GEO. ROSS
CAESAR RODNEY
GEO READ
THO. M'KEAN
WM. FLOYD
PHIL. LIVINGSTON
FRANS. LEWIS
LEWIS MORRIS

RICHD. STOCKTON
JNO. WITHERSPOON
FRAS. HOPKINSON
JOHN HART
ABRA. CLARK
JOSIAH BARTLETT
WM. WHIPPLE
SAML. ADAMS
JOHN ADAMS
ROBT. TREAT PAINE
ELBRIDGE GERRY
STEP. HOPKINS
WILLIAM ELLERY
ROGER SHERMAN
SAM'EL HUNTINGTON
WM. WILLIAMS
OLIVER WOLCOTT
MATTHEW THORNTON

APPENDIX B

The Constitution of the United States of America

PREAMBLE

We the people of the United States, in order to form a more perfect union, establish justice, insure domestic tranquility, provide for the common defense, promote the general welfare, and secure the blessings of liberty to ourselves and our posterity, do ordain and establish this Constitution for the United States of America.

ARTICLE I.—THE LEGISLATIVE ARTICLE

Section 1. All legislative powers herein granted shall be vested in a Congress of the United States, which shall consist of a Senate and a House of Representatives.

House of Representatives: Composition, Qualification, Apportionment, Impeachment Power

Section 2. The House of Representatives shall be composed of members chosen every second year by the people of the several States, and the electors in each State shall have the qualifications requisite for electors of the most numerous branch of the State Legislature.

No person shall be a Representative who shall not have attained to the age of twenty-five years, and been seven years a citizen of the United States, and who shall not, when elected, be an inhabitant of that State in which he shall be chosen.

Representatives and direct taxes shall be apportioned among the several States which may be included within this Union, according to their respective numbers, *which shall be determined by adding to the whole number of free persons, including those bound to service for a term of years and excluding Indians not taxed, three-fifths of all other persons.* The actual enumeration shall be made within three years after the first meeting of the Congress of the United States, and within every subsequent term of ten years, in such manner as they shall by law direct. The number of Representatives shall not exceed one for every thirty thousand, but each State shall have at least one Representative; *and until each enumeration shall be made, the State of New Hampshire shall be entitled to choose three, Massachusetts eight, Rhode Island and Providence Plantations one, Connecticut five, New York six, New Jersey four, Pennsylvania eight, Delaware one, Maryland six, Virginia ten, North Carolina five, South Carolina five, and Georgia three.*

When vacancies happen in the representation from any State, the Executive authority thereof shall issue writs of election to fill such vacancies.

The House of Representatives shall choose their Speaker and other officers; and shall have the sole power of impeachment.

Senate Composition: Qualifications, Impeachment Trials

Section 3. The Senate of the United States shall be composed of two Senators from each State, *chosen by the legislature thereof,* for six years; and each Senator shall have one vote.

Passages no longer in effect are printed in italic type.

Immediately after they shall be assembled in consequence of the first election, they shall be divided as equally as may be into three classes. The seats of the Senators of the first class shall be vacated at the expiration of the second year, of the second class at the expiration of the fourth year, and of the third class at the expiration of the sixth year, so that one-third may be chosen every second year; and if vacancies happen by resignation or otherwise, during the recess of the legislature of any State, the Executive thereof may make temporary appointments until the next meeting of the legislature, which shall then fill such vacancies.

No person shall be a Senator who shall not have attained to the age of thirty years, and been nine years a citizen of the United States, and who shall not, when elected, be an inhabitant of that State for which he shall be chosen.

The Vice President of the United States shall be President of the Senate, but shall have no vote, unless they be equally divided.

The Senate shall choose their other officers, and also a President *pro tempore*, in the absence of the Vice President, or when he shall exercise the office of President of the United States.

The Senate shall have the sole power to try all impeachments. When sitting for that purpose, they shall be on oath or affirmation. When the President of the United States is tried, the Chief Justice shall preside: and no person shall be convicted without the concurrence of two-thirds of the members present.

Judgment in cases of impeachment shall not extend further than to removal from the office, and disqualification to hold and enjoy any office of honor, trust or profit under the United States; but the party convicted shall nevertheless be liable and subject to indictment, trial, judgment and punishment, according to law.

Congressional Elections: Time, Place, Manner

Section 4. The times, places and manner of holding elections for Senators and Representatives shall be prescribed in each State by the legislature thereof; but the Congress may at any time by law make or alter such regulations, except as to the places of choosing Senators.

The Congress shall assemble at least once in every year, and such meeting *shall be on the first Monday in December, unless they shall by law appoint a different day.*

Powers and Duties of the Houses

Section 5. Each house shall be the judge of the elections, returns and qualifications of its own members, and a majority of each shall constitute a quorum to do business; but a smaller number may adjourn from day to day, and may be authorized to compel the attendance of absent members, in such manner, and under such penalties, as each house may provide.

Each house may determine the rules of its proceedings, punish its members for disorderly behavior, and with the concurrence of two-thirds, expel a member.

Each house shall keep a journal of its proceedings, and from time to time publish the same, excepting such parts as may in their judgment require secrecy; and the yeas and nays of the members of either house on any question shall, at the desire of one-fifth of those present, be entered on the journal.

Neither house, during the session of Congress, shall, without the consent of the other, adjourn for more than three days, nor to any other place than that in which the two houses shall be sitting.

Rights of Members

Section 6. The Senators and Representatives shall receive a compensation for their services, to be ascertained by law and paid out of the treasury of the United States. They shall in all cases except treason, felony and breach of the peace, be privileged from arrest during their attendance at the session of their respective houses, and in going to and returning from the same; and for any speech or debate in either house, they shall not be questioned in any other place.

No Senator or Representative shall, during the time for which he was elected, be appointed to any civil office under the authority of the United States, which shall have been created, or the emoluments whereof shall have been increased, during such time; and no person holding any office under the United States shall be a member of either house during his continuance in office.

Legislative Powers: Bills and Resolutions

Section 7. All bills for raising revenue shall originate in the House of Representatives; but the Senate may propose or concur with amendments as on other bills.

 Every bill which shall have passed the House of Representatives and the Senate, shall, before it become a law, be presented to the President of the United States; if he approve he shall sign it, out if not he shall return it with objections to that house in which it originated, who shall enter the objections at large on their journal, and proceed to reconsider it. If after such reconsideration two-thirds of that house shall agree to pass the bill, it shall be sent, together with the objections, to the other house, by which it shall likewise be reconsidered, and if approved by two-thirds of that house, it shall become a law. But in all such cases the votes of both houses shall be determined by yeas and nays, and the names of the persons voting for and against the bill shall be entered on the journal of each house respectively. If any bill shall not be returned by the President within ten days (Sundays excepted) after it shall have been presented to him, the same shall be a law, in like manner as if he had signed it, unless the Congress by their adjournment prevent its return, in which case it shall not be a law.

 Every order, resolution, or vote to which the concurrence of the Senate and House of Representatives may be necessary (except on a question of adjournment) shall be presented to the President of the United States; and before the same shall take effect, shall be approved by him, or being disapproved by him, shall be repassed by two-thirds of the Senate and House of Representatives, according to the rules and limitations prescribed in the case of a bill.

Powers of Congress

Section 8. The Congress shall have power

 To lay and collect taxes, duties, imposts and excises, to pay the debts and provide for the common defense and general welfare of the United States; but all duties, imposts and excises shall be uniform throughout the United States;

 To borrow money on the credit of the United States;

 To regulate commerce with foreign nations, and among the several States, and with the Indian tribes;

 To establish an uniform rule of naturalization, and uniform laws on the subject of bankruptcies throughout the United States;

 To coin money, regulate the value thereof, and of foreign coin, and fix the standard of weights and measures;

 To provide for the punishment of counterfeiting the securities and current coin of the United States;

 To establish post offices and post roads;

 To promote the progress of science and useful arts by securing for limited times to authors and inventors the exclusive right to their respective writings and discoveries;

 To constitute tribunals inferior to the Supreme Court;

 To define and punish piracies and felonies committed on the high seas and offenses against the law of nations;

 To declare war, grant letters of marque and reprisal, and make rules concerning captures on land and water;

 To raise and support armies, but no appropriation of money to that use shall be for a longer term than two years;

 To provide and maintain a navy;

 To make rules for the government and regulation of the land and naval forces;

 To provide for calling forth the militia to execute the laws of the Union, suppress insurrections, and repel invasions;

 To provide for organizing, arming, and disciplining the militia, and for governing such part of them as may be employed in the service of the United States, reserving to the States respectively the appointment of the officers, and the authority of training the militia according to the discipline prescribed by Congress;

 To exercise exclusive legislation in all cases whatsoever, over such district (not exceeding ten miles square) as may, by cession of particular States, and the acceptance of Congress, become the seat of the government of the United States, and to exercise like authority over all places purchased by the consent of the legislature of the State, in which the same shall be, for erection of forts, magazines, arsenals, dock-yards, and other needful buildings;—and

To make all laws which shall be necessary and proper for carrying into execution the foregoing powers, and all other powers vested by this Constitution in the government of the United States, or in any department or officer thereof.

Powers Denied to Congress

Section 9. *The migration or importation of such persons as any of the States now existing shall think proper to admit shall not be prohibited by the Congress prior to the year 1808; but a tax or duty may be imposed on such importation, not exceeding $10 for each person.*

The privilege of the writ of habeas corpus shall not be suspended, unless when in cases of rebellion or invasion the public safety may require it.

No bill of attainder or ex post facto law shall be passed.

No capitation, or other direct, tax shall be laid, unless in proportion to the census or enumeration herein before directed to be taken.

No tax or duty shall be laid on articles exported from any State.

No preference shall be given by any regulation of commerce or revenue to the ports of one State over those of another; nor shall vessels bound to, or from, one State, be obliged to enter, clear, or pay duties in another.

No money shall be drawn from the treasury, but in consequence of appropriations made by law; and a regular statement and account of the receipts and expenditures of all public money shall be published from time to time.

No title of nobility shall be granted by the United States; and no person holding any office of profit or trust under them, shall, without the consent of the Congress, accept of any present, emolument, office, or title, of any kind whatever, from any king, prince, or foreign state.

Powers Denied to the States

Section 10. No State shall enter into any treaty, alliance, or confederation; grant letters of marque and reprisal; coin money; emit bills of credit; make anything but gold and silver coin a tender in payment of debts; pass any bill of attainder, ex post facto law, or law impairing the obligation of contracts, or grant any title of nobility.

No State shall, without the consent of the Congress, lay any imposts or duties on imports or exports, except what may be absolutely necessary for executing its inspection laws: and the net produce of all duties and imposts, laid by any State on imports or exports, shall be for the use of the treasury of the United States; and all such laws shall be subject to the revision and control of the Congress.

No State shall, without the consent of Congress, lay any duty of tonnage, keep troops or ships of war in time of peace, enter into any agreement or compact with another State, or with a foreign power, or engage in war, unless actually invaded, or in such imminent danger as will not admit of delay.

ARTICLE II.—THE EXECUTIVE ARTICLE

Nature and Scope of Presidential Power

Section 1. The executive power shall be vested in a President of the United States of America. He shall hold his office during the term of four years, and, together with the Vice President, chosen for the same term, be elected, as follows:

Each State shall appoint, in such manner as the legislature thereof may direct, a number of electors, equal to the whole number of Senators and Representatives to which the State may be entitled in the Congress; but no Senator or Representative, or person holding an office of trust or profit under the United States, shall be appointed an elector.

The electors shall meet in their respective States, and vote by ballot for two persons, of whom one at least shall not be an inhabitant of the same State with themselves. And they shall make a list of all the persons voted for, and of the number of votes for each; which list they shall sign and certify, and transmit sealed to the seat of government of the United States, directed to the President of the Senate. The President of the Senate shall, in the presence of the Senate and House of Representatives, open all the certificates, and the votes shall then be counted. The person having the greatest number of votes shall be the President, if such number be a majority of the whole number of electors appointed; and if there be more than one who have such majority, and have an equal number of votes, then the House of Representatives shall immediately choose by ballot one of them for President; and if no person have a majority, then from the five highest on the list said house shall in like manner choose the President. But in choosing the President the votes shall be taken by States, the representation from each State having one vote; a quorum for this purpose shall consist of a member or members from two-thirds of the States, and a majority of all the States shall be necessary to a choice. In every case, after the choice of the President, the person having the greatest number of votes of the electors shall be the Vice President. But if there should remain two or more who have equal votes, the Senate shall choose from them by ballot the Vice President.

The Congress may determine the time of choosing the electors, and the day on which they shall give their votes; which day shall be the same throughout the United States.

No person except a natural-born citizen, *or a citizen of the United States at the time of the adoption of this Constitution,* shall be eligible to the office of President; neither shall any person be eligible to that office who shall not have attained to the age of thirty-five years, and been fourteen years a resident within the United States.

In case of the removal of the President from office or of his death, resignation, or inability to discharge the powers and duties of the said office, the same shall devolve on the Vice President, and the Congress may by law provide for the case of removal, death, resignation, or inability, both of the President and Vice President, declaring what officer shall then act as President, and such officer shall act accordingly, until the disability be removed, or a President shall be elected.

The President shall, at stated times, receive for his services a compensation, which shall neither be increased nor diminished during the period for which he shall have been elected, and he shall not receive within that period any other emolument from the United States, or any of them.

Before he enter on the execution of his office, he shall take the following oath or affirmation: —"I do solemnly swear (or affirm) that I will faithfully execute the office of President of the United States, and will to the best of my ability preserve, protect, and defend the Constitution of the United States."

Powers and Duties of the President

Section 2. The President shall be the commander in chief of the army and navy of the United States, and of the militia of the several States, when called into the actual service of the United States; he may require the opinion, in writing, of the principal officer in each of the executive departments, upon any subject relating to the duties of their respective offices, and he shall have power to grant reprieves and pardons for offenses against the United States, except in cases of impeachment.

He shall have power, by and with the advice and consent of the Senate, to make treaties, provided two-thirds of the Senators present concur; and he shall nominate, and by and with the advice and consent of the Senate, shall appoint ambassadors, other public ministers and consuls, judges of the Supreme Court, and all other officers of the United States, whose appointments are not herein otherwise provided for, and which shall be established by law: but the Congress may by law vest the appointment of such inferior officers, as they think proper, in the President alone, in the courts of law, or in the heads of departments.

The President shall have power to fill up all vacancies that may happen during the recess of the Senate, by granting commissions which shall expire at the end of their next session.

Section 3. He shall from time to time give to the Congress information of the state of the Union, and recommend to their consideration such measures as he shall judge necessary and expedient; he may, on extraordinary occasions, convene both houses, or either of them, and in case of disagreement between them, with respect to the time of adjournment, he may adjourn them to such time as he shall think proper; he shall receive ambassadors and other public ministers; he shall take care that the laws be faithfully executed, and shall commission all the officers of the United States.

Section 4. The President, Vice President and all civil officers of the United States shall be removed from office on impeachment for, and on conviction of, treason, bribery, or other high crimes and misdemeanor.

ARTICLE III.—THE JUDICIAL ARTICLE

Section 1. The judicial power of the United States shall be vested in one Supreme Court, and in such inferior courts as the Congress may from time to time ordain and establish. The judges, both of the Supreme and inferior courts, shall hold their offices during good behavior, and shall, at stated times, receive for their services a compensation which shall not be diminished during their continuance in office.

Jurisdiction

Section 2. The judicial power shall extend to all cases, in law and equity, arising under this Constitution, the laws of the United States, and treaties made, or which shall be made, under their authority;—to all cases affecting ambassadors, other public ministers and consuls;—to all cases of admiralty and maritime jurisdiction;—to controversies to which the United States shall be a party;—to controversies between two or more States;—*between a state and citizens of another state*;—between citizens of different States;—between citizens of the same State claiming lands under grants of different States, and between a State, or the citizens thereof, and foreign states, citizens or subjects.

In all cases affecting ambassadors, other public ministers and consuls, and those in which a State shall be party, the Supreme Court shall have original jurisdiction. In all the other cases before mentioned, the Supreme Court shall have appellate jurisdiction, both as to law and fact, with such exceptions, and under such regulations, as the Congress shall make.

The trial of all crimes, except in cases of impeachment, shall be by jury; and such trial shall be held in the State where said crimes shall have been committed; but when not committed within any State, the trial shall be at such place or places as the Congress may by law have directed.

Treason

Section 3. Treason against the United States shall consist only in levying war against them, or in adhering to their enemies, giving them aid and comfort. No person shall be convicted of treason unless on the testimony of two witnesses to the same overt act, or on confession in open court.

The Congress shall have power to declare the punishment of treason, but no attainder of treason shall work corruption of blood, or forfeiture except during the life of the person attained.

ARTICLE IV.—INTERSTATE RELATIONS

Full Faith and Credit Clause

Section 1. Full Faith and credit shall be given in each State to the public acts, records, and judicial proceedings of every other State. And the Congress may by general laws prescribe the manner in which such acts, records and proceedings shall be proved, and the effect thereof.

Privileges and Immunities; Interstate Extradition

Section 2. The citizens of each State shall be entitled to all privileges and immunities of citizens in the several States.

A person charged in any State with treason, felony or other crime, who shall flee from justice, and be found in another State, shall on demand of the executive authority of the State from which he fled, be delivered up, to be removed to the State having jurisdiction of the crime.

No person held to service or labor in one State, under the laws thereof, escaping into another, shall, in consequence of any law or regulation therein, be discharged from such service or labor, but shall be delivered up on claim of the party to whom such service or labor may be due.

Admission of States

Section 3. New States may be admitted by the Congress into this Union; but no new State shall be formed or erected within the jurisdiction of any other State; nor any State be formed by the junc-
tion of two or more States, or parts of States, without the consent of the legislatures of the States concerned as well as of the Congress.

The Congress shall have power to dispose of and make all needful rules and regulations respecting the territory or other property belonging to the United States; and nothing in this Constitution shall be so construed as to prejudice any claims of the United States, or of any particular State.

Republican Form of Government

Section 4. The United States shall guarantee to every State in this Union a republican form of government, and shall protect each of them against invasion; and on application of the legislature, or of the executive (when the legislature cannot be convened) against domestic violence.

ARTICLE V.—THE AMENDING POWER

The Congress, whenever two-thirds of both houses shall deem it necessary, shall propose amendments to this Constitution, or, on the application of the legislatures of two-thirds of the several States, shall call a convention for proposing amendments, which, in either case, shall be valid to all intents and purposes, as part of this Constitution, when ratified by the legislatures of three-fourths of the several States, or by conventions in three-fourths thereof, as the one or the other mode of ratification may be proposed by the Congress; *provided that no amendment which may be made prior to the year one thousand eight hundred and eight shall in any manner affect the first and fourth clauses in the ninth section of the first article*; and that no State, without its consent, shall be deprived of its equal suffrage in the Senate.

ARTICLE VI.—THE SUPREMACY ACT

All debts contracted and engagements entered into, before the adoption of this Constitution, shall be as valid against the United States under this Constitution, as under the Confederation.

This Constitution, and the laws of the United States which shall be made in pursuance thereof; and all treaties made, or which shall be made, under the authority of the United States, shall be the supreme law of the land; and the judges in every State shall be bound thereby, anything in the Constitution or laws of any State to the contrary notwithstanding.

The Senators and Representatives before mentioned, and the members of the several State legislatures, and all executive and judicial officers, both of the United States and of the several States, shall be bound by oath or affirmation to support this Constitution; but no religious test shall ever be required as a qualification to any office or public trust under the United States.

ARTICLE VII.—RATIFICATION

The ratification of the conventions of nine States shall be sufficient for the establishment of this Constitution between States so ratifying the same.

Done in Convention by the unanimous consent of the States present, the seventeenth day of September in the year of our Lord one thousand seven hundred and eighty-seven and of the Independence of the United States of America the twelfth. In witness whereof we have hereunto subscribed our names.

GEORGE WASHINGTON
President and Deputy from Virginia

New Hampshire
JOHN LANGDON
NICHOLAS GILMAN

Massachusetts
NATHANIEL GORHAM
RUFUS KING

Connecticut
WILLIAM S. JOHNSON
ROGER SHERMAN

Virginia
JOHN BLAIR
JAMES MADISON, JR

South Carolina
J. RUTLEDGE
CHARLES G. PINCKNEY
PIERCE BUTLER

New York
ALEXANDER HAMILTON

New Jersey
WILLIAM LIVINGSTON
DAVID BREARLEY
WILLIAM PATERSON
JONATHAN DAYTON

Pennsylvania
BENJAMIN FRANKLIN
THOMAS MIFFLIN
ROBERT MORRIS
GEORGE CLYMER
THOMAS FITZSIMONS
JARED INGERSOLL
JAMES WILSON
GOUVERNEUR MORRIS

Delaware
GEORGE READ
GUNNING BEDFORD, JR.
JOHN DICKINSON
RICHARD BASSETT
JACOB BROOM

Maryland
JAMES MCHENRY
DANIEL OF ST. THOMAS JENIFER
DANIEL CARROLL

North Carolina
WILLIAM BLOUNT
RICHARD DOBBS SPRAIGHT
HU WILLIAMSON

Georgia
WILLIAM FEW
ABRAHAM BALDWIN

THE BILL OF RIGHTS

The first ten Amendments (the Bill of Rights) were adopted in 1791.

AMENDMENT I.—RELIGION, SPEECH ASSEMBLY, AND PETITION

Congress shall make no law respecting an establishment of religion, or prohibiting the free exercise thereof; or abridging the freedom of speech, or of the press; or the right of the people peaceably to assemble, and to petition the government for a redress of grievances.

AMENDMENT II.—MILITIA AND THE RIGHT TO BEAR ARMS

A well-regulated militia being necessary to the security of a free State, the right of the people to keep and bear arms shall not be infringed.

AMENDMENT III.—QUARTERING OF SOLDIERS

No soldier shall, in time of peace, be quartered in any house without the consent of the owner, nor in time of war, but in a manner to be prescribed by law.

AMENDMENT IV.—SEARCHES AND SEIZURES

The right of the people to be secure in their persons, houses, papers, and effects, against unreasonable searches and seizures, shall not be violated, and no warrants shall issue but upon probable cause, supported by oath or affirmation, and particularly describing the place to be searched, and the persons or things to be seized.

AMENDMENT V.—GRAND JURIES, SELF-INCRIMINATION, DOUBLE JEOPARDY, DUE PROCESS, AND EMINENT DOMAIN

No person shall be held to answer for a capital, or otherwise infamous crime, unless on a presentment or indictment of a grand jury, except in cases arising in the land or naval forces, or in the militia, when in actual service in time of war or public danger; nor shall any person be subject for the same offense to be twice put in jeopardy of life or limb; nor shall be compelled in any criminal case to be a witness against himself, nor be deprived of life, liberty, or property, without due process of law; nor shall private property be taken for public use without just compensation.

AMENDMENT VI.—CRIMINAL COURT PROCEDURES

In all criminal prosecutions, the accused shall enjoy the right to a speedy and public trial, by an impartial jury of the State and district wherein the crime shall have been committed, which district shall have been previously ascertained by law, and to be informed of the nature and cause of the accusation; to be confronted with the witnesses against him; to have compulsory process for obtaining witnesses in his favor, and to have the assistance of counsel for his defense.

AMENDMENT VII.—TRIAL BY JURY IN COMMON LAW CASES

In suits at common law, where the value in controversy shall exceed twenty dollars, the right of trial by jury shall be preserved, and no fact tried by a jury shall be otherwise reexamined in any court of the United States, than according to the rules of the common law.

AMENDMENT VIII.—BAIL, CRUEL AND UNUSUAL PUNISHMENT

Excessive bail shall not be required, nor excessive fines imposed, nor cruel and unusual punishments inflicted.

AMENDMENT IX.—RIGHTS RETAINED BY THE PEOPLE

The enumeration in the Constitution, of certain rights, shall not be construed to deny or disparage others retained by the people.

AMENDMENT X.—RESERVED POWERS OF THE STATES

The powers not delegated to the United States by the Constitution, nor prohibited by it to the States, are reserved to the States respectively, or to the people.

PRE-CIVIL WAR AMENDMENTS

AMENDMENT XI.—SUITS AGAINST THE STATES
[Adopted 1798]

The judicial power of the United States shall not be construed to extend to any suit in law or equity, commenced or prosecuted against one of the United States by citizens of another State, or by citizens or subjects of any foreign state.

AMENDMENT XII.—ELECTION OF THE PRESIDENT
[Adopted 1804]

The electors shall meet in their respective *States*, and vote by ballot for President and Vice President, one of whom, at least, shall not be an inhabitant of the same State with themselves; they shall name in their ballots the person voted for as President, and in distinct ballots the person voted for as Vice President, and they shall make distinct lists of all persons voted for as President, and of all persons voted for as Vice President, and of the number of votes for each, which lists they shall sign and certify, and transmit sealed to the seat of the government of the United States, directed to the President of the Senate;—the President of the Senate shall, in the presence of the Senate and House of Representatives, open all the certificates and the votes shall then be counted;—the person having the greatest number of votes for President shall be the President, if such number be a majority of the whole number of electors appointed; and if no person have such majority, then from the persons having the highest numbers not exceeding three on the list of those voted for as President, the House of Representatives shall choose immediately, by ballot, the President. But in choosing the President, the votes shall be taken by States, the representation from each State having one vote; a quorum for this purpose shall consist of a member or members from two-thirds of the States, and a majority of all the States shall be necessary to a choice. And if the House of Representatives shall not choose a President whenever the right of choice shall devolve upon them, before *the fourth day of March* next following, then the Vice President shall act as President, as in the case of the death or other constitutional disability of the President.

The person having the greatest number of votes as Vice President shall be the Vice President, if such a number be a majority of the whole number of electors appointed; and if no person have a majority, then from the two highest numbers on the list the Senate shall choose the Vice President; a quorum for the purpose shall consist of two-thirds of the whole number of Senators, and a majority of the whole number shall be necessary to a choice. But no person constitutionally ineligible to the office of President shall be eligible to that of Vice President of the United States.

CIVIL WAR AMENDMENTS

AMENDMENT XIII.—PROHIBITION OF SLAVERY
[Adopted 1865]

Section 1. Neither slavery nor involuntary servitude, except as a punishment for crime whereof the party shall have been duly convicted, shall exist within the United States, or any place subject to their jurisdiction.

Section 2. Congress shall have power to enforce this article by appropriate legislation.

AMENDMENT XIV.—CITIZENSHIP, DUE PROCESS, AND EQUAL PROTECTION OF THE LAWS
[Adopted 1868]

Section 1. All persons born or naturalized in the United States, and subject to the jurisdiction thereof, are citizens of the United States and of the State wherein they reside. No State shall make or enforce any law which shall abridge **the privileges or immunities** of citizens of the United States; nor shall any State deprive any person of life, liberty, or property, without **due process of law**; nor deny to any person within its jurisdiction the **equal protection of the laws**.

Section 2. Representatives shall be apportioned among the several States according to their respective numbers, counting the whole number of persons in each State, excluding Indians not taxed. But when the right to vote at any election for the choice of Electors for President and Vice President of the United States, Representatives in Congress, the executive and judicial officers of a State, or the members of the legislature thereof, is denied to any of the male inhabitants of such State, being twenty-one years of age and citizens of the United States, or in any way abridged, except for participation in rebellion, or other crime, the basis of representation therein shall be reduced in the proportion which the number of such male citizens shall bear to the whole number of male citizens twenty-one years of age in such State.

Section 3. No person shall be a Senator or Representative in Congress, or Elector of President and Vice President, or hold any office, civil or military, under the United States, or under any State, who, having previously taken an oath, as a member of Congress, or as an officer of the United States, or as a member of any State legislature, or as an executive or judicial officer of any State, to support the Constitution of the United States, shall have engaged in insurrection or rebellion against the same, or given aid or comfort to the enemies thereof. Congress may, by a vote of two-thirds of each house, remove such disability.

Section 4. The validity of the public debt of the United States, authorized by law, including debts incurred for payment of pensions and bounties for services in suppressing insurrection or rebellion, shall not be questioned. But neither the United States nor any State shall assume or pay any debt or obligation incurred in aid of insurrection or rebellion against the United States, or any claim for the loss or emancipation of any slave; but all such debts, obligations and claims shall be held illegal and void.

Section 5. The Congress shall have power to enforce, by appropriate legislation, the provisions of this article.

AMENDMENT XV.—THE RIGHT TO VOTE
[Adopted 1870]

Section 1. The right of citizens of the United State to vote shall not be denied or abridged by the United States or by any State on account of race, color, or previous condition of servitude.

Section 2. The Congress shall have power to enforce this article by appropriate legislation.

AMENDMENT XVI.—INCOME TAXES
[Adopted 1913]

The Congress shall have power to lay and collect taxes on incomes, from whatever source derived, without apportionment among the several States, and without regard to any census or enumeration.

AMENDMENT XVII.—DIRECT ELECTION OF SENATORS
[Adopted 1913]

Section 1. The Senate of the United States shall be composed of two Senators from each State, elected by the people thereof, for six years; and each Senator shall have one vote. The electors in each State shall have the qualifications requisite for electors of (voters for) the most numerous branch of the State legislatures.

Section 2. When vacancies happen in the representation of any State in the Senate, the executive authority of such State shall issue writs of election to fill such vacancies: Provided, that the Legislature of any State may empower the executive thereof to make temporary appointments until the people fill the vacancies by election as the Legislature may direct.

Section 3. This amendment shall not be so construed as to affect the election or term of any Senator chosen before it becomes valid as part of the Constitution.

AMENDMENT XVIII.—PROHIBITION
[Adopted 1919; Repealed 1933]

Section 1. *After one year from the ratification of this article the manufacture, sale, or transportation of intoxicating liquors within, the importation thereof into, or the exportation thereof from the United State and all territory subject to the jurisdiction thereof, for beverage purposes, is hereby prohibited.*

Section 2. *The Congress and the several States shall have concurrent power to enforce this article by appropriate legislation.*

Section 3. *This article shall be inoperative unless it shall have been ratified as an amendment to the Constitution by the legislatures of the several States, as provided by the Constitution, within seven years from the date of the submission thereof to the States by the Congress.*

AMENDMENT XIX.—FOR WOMEN'S SUFFRAGE
[Adopted 1920]

Section 1. The right of citizens of the United States to vote shall not be denied or abridged by the United States or by any State on account of sex.

Section 2. The Congress shall have power to enforce this article by appropriate legislation.

AMENDMENT XX.—THE LAME DUCK AMENDMENT
[Adopted 1933]

Section 1. The terms of the President and Vice President shall end at noon on the 20th day of January, and the terms of the Senators and Representatives at noon on the 3rd day of January, of the years in which such terms would have ended if this article had not been ratified; and the terms of their successors shall then begin.

Section 2. The Congress shall assemble at least once in every year, and such meeting shall begin at noon on the 3rd day of January, unless they shall by law appoint a different day.

Section 3. If, at the time fixed for the beginning of the term of the President, the President-elect shall have died, the Vice President-elect shall become President. If a President shall not have been chosen before the time fixed for the beginning of his term, or if the President-elect shall have failed to qualify, then the Vice President-elect shall act as President until a President shall have qualified; and the Congress may by law provide for the case wherein neither a President-elect nor a Vice President-elect shall have qualified, declaring who shall then act as President, or the manner in which one who is to act shall be selected, and such persons shall act accordingly until a President or Vice President shall have qualified.

Section 4. The Congress may by law provide for the case of the death of any of the persons from whom the House of Representatives may choose a President whenever the right of choice shall have devolved upon them, and for the case of the death of any of the persons from whom the Senate may choose a Vice President whenever the right of choice shall have devolved upon them.

Section 5. Section 1 and 2 shall take effect on the 15th day of October following the ratification of this article.

Section 6. This article shall be inoperative unless it shall have been ratified as an amendment to the Constitution by the Legislatures of three-fourths of the several States within seven years from the date of its submission.

AMENDMENT XXI.—REPEAL OF PROHIBITION
[Adopted 1933]

Section 1. The eighteenth article of amendment to the Constitution of the United States is hereby repealed.

Section 2. The transportation or importation into any State, Territory, or Possession of the United States for delivery of use therein of intoxicating liquors, in violation of the laws thereof, is hereby prohibited.

Section 3. This article shall be inoperative unless it shall have been ratified as an amendment to the Constitution by conventions in the several States, as provided in the Constitution, within seven years from the date of submission thereof to the States by the Congress.

AMENDMENT XXII.—NUMBER OF PRESIDENTIAL TERMS
[Adopted 1951]

Section 1. No person shall be elected to the office of President more than twice, and no person who has held the office of President, or acted as President, for more than two years of a term to which some other person was elected President shall be elected to the office of President more than once. But this article shall not apply to any person holding the office of President when this article was proposed by the Congress, and shall not prevent any person who may be holding the office of President, or acting as President, during the term within which this article becomes operative from holding the office of President or acting as President during the remainder of such term.

Section 2. This article shall be inoperative unless it shall have been ratified as an amendment to the Constitution by the legislatures of three-fourths of the several States within seven years from the date of its submission to the States by the Congress.

AMENDMENT XXIII.—PRESIDENTIAL ELECTORS FOR THE
DISTRICT OF COLUMBIA [Adopted 1961]

Section 1. The District constituting the seat of Government of the United States shall appoint in such manner as the Congress may direct:

A number of electors of President and Vice President equal to the whole number of Senators and Representatives in Congress to which the District would be entitled if it were a State, but in no event more than the least populous State; they shall be in addition to those appointed by the States, but they shall be considered for the purposes of the election of President and Vice President, to be electors appointed by a State; and they shall meet in the District and perform such duties as provided by the twelfth article of amendment.

Section 2. The Congress shall have power to enforce this article by appropriate legislation.

AMENDMENT XXIV.—THE ANTI-POLL TAX AMENDMENT
[Adopted 1964]

Section 1. The right of citizens of the United States to vote in any primary or other election for President or Vice President, for electors for President or Vice President, or for Senator or Representative in Congress, shall not be denied or abridged by the United States or any State by reason of failure to pay any poll tax or other tax.

Section 2. The Congress shall have power to enforce this article by appropriate legislation.

AMENDMENT XXV.—PRESIDENTIAL DISABILITY, VICE-PRESIDENTIAL VACANCIES
[Adopted 1967]

Section 1. In case of the removal of the President from office or his death or resignation, the Vice President shall become President.

Section 2. Whenever there is a vacancy in the office of the Vice President, the President shall nominate a Vice President who shall take office upon confirmation by a majority vote of both Houses of Congress.

Section 3. Whenever the President transmits to the President pro tempore of the Senate and the Speaker of the House of Representatives his written declaration that he is unable to discharge the powers and duties of his office, and until he transmits to them a written declaration to the contrary, such powers and duties shall be discharged by the Vice President as Acting President.

Section 4. Whenever the Vice President and a majority of either the principal officers of the executive departments or of such other body as Congress may by law provide, transmit to the President pro tempore of the Senate and the Speaker of the House of Representatives their written declaration that the President is unable to discharge the powers and duties of his office, the Vice President shall immediately assume the powers and duties of the office as Acting President.

      Thereafter, when the President transmits to the President pro tempore of the Senate and the Speaker of the House of Representatives his written declaration that no inability exists, he shall resume the powers and duties of his office unless the Vice President and a majority of either the principal officers of the executive department{s} or of such other body as Congress may by law provide, transmit within four days to the President pro tempore of the Senate and the Speaker of the House of Representatives their written declaration that the President is unable to discharge the powers and duties of his office. Thereupon Congress shall decide the issue, assembling within forty-eight hours for that purpose if not in session. If the Congress, within twenty-one days after receipt of the latter written declaration, or, if Congress is not in session, within twenty-one days after Congress is required to assemble, determines by two-thirds vote of both Houses that the President is unable to discharge the powers and duties of his office, the Vice President shall continue to discharge the same as Acting President; otherwise, the President shall resume the powers and duties of his office.

AMENDMENT XXVI.—EIGHTEEN-YEAR-OLD VOTE
[Adopted 1971]

Section 1. The right of citizens of the United States, who are eighteen years of age or older, to vote shall not be denied or abridged by the United States or by any State on account of age.

Section 2. The Congress shall have power to enforce this article by appropriate legislation.

AMENDMENT XXVII.—VARYING CONGRESSIONAL COMPENSATION
[Adopted 1992]

No law varying the compensation for the service of the Senators and Representatives shall take effect until an election of Representatives shall have intervened.

APPENDIX C

PRESIDENTIAL ELECTIONS

Year	Name	Party Vote	Popular Vote	Electoral College Vote
1789	George Washington	Federalist		69
1792	George Washington	Federalist		132
1796	John Adams	Federalist		71
	Thomas Jefferson	Democratic-Republican		68
1800	Thomas Jefferson	Democratic-Republican		73
	John Adams	Federalist		65
1804	Thomas Jefferson	Democratic-Republican		162
	Charles C. Pinckney	Federalist		14
1808	James Madison	Democratic-Republican		122
	Charles C. Pinckney	Federalist		47
1812	James Madison	Democratic-Republican		128
	George Clinton	Federalist		89
1816	James Monroe	Dmocratic-Republican		183
	Rufus King	Federalist		34
1820	James Monroe	Democratic-Republican		231
	John Quincy Adams	Democratic-Republican		1
1824	John Quincy Adams	Democratic-Republican	108,740	84
	Andrew Jackson	Democratic-Republican	153,544	99
	William Crawford	Democratic-Republican	46,618	41
	Henry Clay	Democratic-Republican	47,136	37
1828	Andrew Jackson	Democrat	647,286	178
	John Quincy Adams	National Republican	508,064	83
1832	Andrew Jackson	Democrat	687,502	219
	Henry Clay	National Republican	530,189	49
	Electoral votes not cast		2	
1836	Martin Van Buren	Democrat	765,483	170
	William Henry Harrison	Whig	550,816	73
	Hugh White	Whig	146,107	26
	Daniel Webster	Whig	41,201	14
	Total for the 3 Whigs		739,795	113
1840	William Henry Harrison	Whig	1,274,624	234
	Martin Van Buren	Democrat	1,127,781	60
1844	James K. Polk	Democrat	1,338,464	170
	Henry Clay	Whig	1,300,097	105
1848	Zachary Taylor	Whig	1,360,967	163
	Lewis Cass	Democrat	1,222,342	127
	Martin Van Buren	Free-Soil	291,263	
1852	Franklin Pierce	Democrat	1,601,117	254
	Winfield Scott	Whig	1,385,453	42
	John P. Hale	Free-Soil	155,825	
1856	James Buchanan	Democrat	1,832,955	174
	John Fremont	Republian	1,339,932	114
	Millard Fillmore	Whig-American	871,731	8

1860	Abraham Lincoln	Republican	1,865,593	180
	John C. Breckinridge	Democratic	848,356	72
	Stephen Douglas	Democrat	1,382,713	12
	John Bell	Constitutional Union	592,906	39
1864	Abraham Lincon	Unionist (Republican)	2,206,938	212
	George McClellan	Democrat	1,803,787	21
	Electoral votes not cast		81	
1868	Ulysses S. Grant	Republican	3,013,421	214
	Horatio Seymour	Democrat	2,706,829	80
	Electoral votes not cast		23	
1872	Ulysses S. Grant	Republican	3,596,745	286
	Horace Greeley	Democrat	2,843,446	
	Thomas Hendricks	Democrat		42
	Benjamin Browns	Democrat		18
	Charles Jenkins	Democrat		2
	David Davis	Democrat		1
1876	Rutherford B. Hays	Republican	4,036,572	185
	Samuel Tilden	Democrat	4,284,020	184
	Peter Cooper	Greenback	81,737	
1880	James A. Garfield	Republican	4,453,295	214
	Winfield S. Hancock	Democrat	4,414,082	155
	James B. Weaver	Greenback-Labor	308,578	
1884	Grover Cleveland	Democrat	4,879,507	219
	James G. Blaine	Republican	4,850,293	182
	Benjamin Butler	Greenback-Labor	175,370	
	John St. John	Prohibition	150,369	
1888	Benjamin Harrison	Republican	5,447,129	233
	Grover Cleveland	Democrat	5,537,857	168
	Clinton Fisk	Prohibition	249,506	
	Anson Streeter	Union Labor	146,935	
1892	Grover Cleveland	Democrat	5,555,426	277
	Benjamin Harrison	Republican	5,182,690	145
	James B. Weaver	People's	1.029,846	22
	John Bidwell	Prohibition	264,133	
1896	William McKinley	Republican	7,102,246	271
	William J. Bryan	Democrat	6,492,559	176
	John Palmer	National Democratic	133,148	
	Joshua Levering	Prohibition	132,007	
1900	William McKinley	Republican	7,218,491	292
	William J. Bryan	Democrat	6,356,734	155
	John C. Wooley	Prohibition	208,914	
	Eugene V. Debs	Socialist	87,814	
1904	Theodore Roosevelt	Republican	7,628,461	336
	Alton B. Parker	Democrat	5,084,223	140
	Eugene V. Debs	Socialist	402,283	
	Silas Swallow	Prohibition	258,536	
	Thomas Watson	People's	117,183	

1908	William Howard Taft	Republican	7,675,320	321
	William J. Bryan	Democrat	6,412,294	162
	Eugene V. Debs	Socialist	420,793	
	Eugene Chafin	Prohibition	253,840	
1912	Woodrow Wilson	Democrat	6,296,547	435
	William Howard Taft	Republican	3,486,720	8
	Theodore Roosevelt	Progressive	4,118,571	86
	Eugene V. Debs	Socialist	900,672	
	Eugene Chafin	Prohibition	206,275	
1916	Woodrow Wilson	Democrat	9,127,695	277
	Charles E. Hughes	Republicn	8,533,507	254
	A.L. Benson	Socialist	585,113	
	J. Frank Hanly	Prohibition	220,506	
1920	Warren Harding	Republican	16,143,407	404
	James M. Cox	Democrat	9,130,323	127
	Eugene V. Debs	Socialist	919,799	
	P.P. Christensen	Farmer-Labor	265,411	
	Aaron Watkins	Prohibiton	189,408	
1924	Calvin Coolidge	Republican	15,718,211	382
	John W. Davis	Democrat	8,385,283	136
	Robert La Follette	Progressive	4,831,289	13
1928	Herbert Hoover	Republican	21,391,993	444
	Alfred E. Smith	Democrat	15,016,169	87
	Norman Thomas	Socialist	267,835	
1932	Franklin D. Roosevelt	Democrat	22,809,638	472
	Herbert C. Hoover	Republican	15,758,901	59
	Norman Thomas	Socialist	831,951	
	William Foster	Communist	102,785	
1936	Franklin D. Roosevelt	Democrat	27,752,869	523
	Alfred M. Landon	Republican	16,674,665	8
	William Lemke	Union	882,479	
	Norman Thomas	Socialist	187,720	
1940	Franklin D. Roosevelt	Democrat	27,307,819	449
	Wendell Willkie	Republican	22,321,018	82
1944	Franklin D. Roosevelt	Democrat	25,606,585	432
	Thomas E. Dewey	Republican	22,014,745	99
1948	Harry S. Truman	Democrat	24,179,345	303
	Thomas E. Dewey	Republican	21,991,291	189
	Strom Thurmond	Dixiecrat	1,176,125	39
	Henry Wallace	Progressive	1,157,326	
	Norman Thomas	Socialist	139,572	
	Claude A. Watson	Prohibition	103,900	
1952	Dwight D. Eisenhower	Republican	33,936,234	442
	Adlai Stevenson II	Democrat	27,314,992	89
	Vincent Hallinan	Progressive	140,023	
1956	Dwight D. Eisenhower	Republican	35,590,472	457
	Adlai Stevenson II	Democrat	26,022,752	73
	T. Coleman Andrews	States' Rights	111,178	
	Walter B. Jones	Democrat		1

1960	John F. Kennedy	Democrat	34,226,731	303
	Richard M. Nixon	Republican	34,108,157	219
	Harry Byrd	Democrat		15
1964	Lyndon B. Johnson	Democrat	43,129,566	486
	Barry Goldwater	Republican	27,178,188	52
1968	Richard M. Nixon	Republican	31,785,480	301
	Hubert H. Humphrey	Democrat	31,275,166	191
	George Wallace	American Independent	9,906,473	46
1972	Richard M. Nixon	Republican	47,170,179	520
	George McGovern	Democrat	29,171,791	17
	John Hospers	Libertarian		1
1976	Jimmy Carter	Democrat	40,830,763	297
	Gerald R. Ford	Republican	39,147,793	240
	Ronald Reagan	Republican		1
1980	Ronald Reagan	Republican	43,904,153	489
	Jimmy Carter	Democrat	35,483,883	49
	John Anderson	Independent candidacy	5,719,437	
1984	Ronald Reagan	Republican	54,455,074	525
	Walter F. Mondale	Democrat	37,577,137	13
1988	George Bush	Republican	48,881,278	426
	Michael Dukakis	Democrat	41,805,374	111
	Lloyd Bentsen	Democrat		1
1992	Bill Clinton	Democrat	43,727,625	370
	George Bush	Republican	38,165,180	168
	Ross Perot	Independent catdidacy	19,236,411	0
1996	Bill Clinton	Democrat	45,628,667	379
	Bob Dole	Republican	37,869,435	159
	Ross Perot	Independent catdidacy	7,874,283	0
2000	George W. Bush	Republican	49,820,518	271
	Albert Gore Jr.	Democrat	50,158,094	267
	Ralph Nader	Green Party	7,866,284	
2004	George W. Bush	Republican	62,040,610	286
	John Kerry	Democrat	59,028,439	251
	Ralph Nader	Green Party	463,653	
2008	Barack Obama	Democrat	66,882,230	365
	John McCain	Republican	58,343,671	173
2012	Barack Obama	Democrat	60,459,974	332
	Mitt Romney	Republican	57,653,982	206
2016	Hillary Clinton	Democrat	64,418,125	232
	Donald Trump	Republican	62,314,184	306
2020	Joe Biden	Democrat	81,268,924	306
	Donald Trump	Republican	74,216,154	232

APPENDIX D

Members of the Supreme Court of the United States

Chief Justices	State App't From	Appointed by President	Service
Jay, John	New York	Washington	1789-1795
Rutledge, John*	South Carolina	Washington	1795-1795
Ellsworth, Oliver	Connecticut	Washington	1796-1799
Marshall, John	Virginia	Adams, John	1801-1835
Taney, Roger Brooke	Maryland	Jackson	1836-1864
Chase, Salmon Portland	Ohio	Lincoln	1864-1873
Waite, Morrison Remick	Ohio	Grant	1874-1888
Fuller, Melville Weston	Illinois	Cleveland	1888-1910
White, Edward Douglass	Louisiana	Taft	1910-1921
Taft, William Howard	Connecticut	Harding	1921-1930
Hughes, Charles Evans	New York	Hoover	1930-1941
Stone, Harlan Fiske	New York	Roosevelt F.	1941-1946
Vinson, Fred Moore	Kentucky	Truman	1946-1953
Warren, Earl	California	Eisenhower	1953-1969
Burger, Warren Earl	Virginia	Nixon	1969-1986
Rehnquist, William H.	Virginia	Reagan	1986-2005
Roberts, John G., Jr.	Maryland	Bush, G. W.	2005-

Associate Justices			
Rutledge, John	South Carolina	Washington	1790-1791
Cushing, William	Massachusetts	Washington	1790-1810
Wilson, James	Pennsylvania	Washington	1789-1798
Blair, John	Virginia	Washington	1789-1796
Iredell, James	North Carolina	Washington	1790-1799
Johnson, Thomas	Maryland	Washington	1791-1793
Paterson, William	New Jersey	Washington	1793-1806
Chase, Samuel	Maryland	Washington	1796-1811
Washington, Bushrod	Virginia	Adams, John	1798-1829
Moore, Alfred	North Carolina	Adams, John	1799-1804
Johnson, William	South Carolina	Jefferson	1804-1834
Livingston, Henry Brockholst	New York	Jefferson	1806-1823
Todd, Thomas	Kentucky	Jefferson	1807-1826
Duvall, Gabriel	Maryland	Madison	1811-1836
Story, Joseph	Massachusetts	Madison	1811-1845
Thompson, Smith	New York	Monroe	1823-1843
Trimble, Robert	Kentucky	Adams, J. Q.	1826-1828

*Acting Chief Justice; Senate refused to confirm appointment.

McLean, John	Ohio	Jackson	1829-1861
Baldwin, Henry	Pennsylvania	Jackson	1830-1844
Wayne, James Moore	Georgia	Jackson	1835-1867
Barbour, Philip Pendleton	Virginia	Jackson	1836-1841
Catron, John	Tennessee	Jackson	1837-1865
McKinley, John	Alabama	Van Buren	1837-1852
Daniel, Peter Vivian	Virginia	Van Buren	1841-1860
Nelson, Samuel	New York	Tyler	1845-1872
Woodbury, Levi	New Hampshire	Polk	1845-1851
Grier, Robert Cooper	Pennsylvania	Polk	1846-1870
Curtis, Benjamin Robbins	Massachusetts	Fillmore	1851-1857
Campbell, John Archibald	Alabama	Pierce	1853-1861
Clifford, Nathan	Maine	Buchanan	1858-1881
Swayne, Noah Haynes	Ohio	Lincoln	1862-1881
Miller, Samuel Freeman	Iowa	Lincoln	1862-1890
Davis, David	Illinois	Lincoln	1862-1877
Field, Stephen Johnson	California	Lincoln	1863-1897
Strong, William	Pennsylvania	Grant	1870-1880
Bradley, Joseph P.	New Jersey	Grant	1870-1892
Hunt, Ward	New York	Grant	1873-1882
Harlan, John Marshall	Kentucky	Hayes	1877-1911
Woods, William Burnham	Georgia	Hayes	1880-1887
Matthews, Stanley	Ohio	Garfield	1881-1889
Gray, Horace	Massachusetts	Arthur	1882-1902
Blatchford, Samuel	New York	Arthur	1882-1893
Lamar, Lucius Quintus C.	Mississippi	Cleveland	1888-1893
Brewer, David Josiah	Kansas	Harrison	1889-1910
Brown, Henry Billings	Michigan	Harrison	1890-1906
Shiras, George, Jr.	Pennsylvania	Harrison	1892-1903
Jackson, Howell Edmunds	Tennessee	Harrison	1893-1895
White, Edward Douglass	Louisiana	Cleveland	1894-1910
Peckham, Rufus Wheeler	New York	Cleveland	1896-1909
McKenna, Joseph	California	McKinley	1898-1925
Holmes, Oliver Wendell	Massachusetts	Roosevelt T.	1902-1932
Day, William Rufus	Ohio	Roosevelt T.	1903-1922
Moody, William Henry	Massachusetts	Roosevelt T.	1906-1910
Lurton, Horace Harmon	Tennessee	Taft	1910-1914
Hughes, Charles Evans	New York	Taft	1910-1916
Van Devanter, Willis	Wyoming	Taft	1910-1937
Lamar, Joseph Rucker	Georgia	Taft	1911-1916
Pitney, Mahlon	New Jersey	Taft	1912-1922
McReynolds, James Clark	Tennessee	Wilson	1914-1941
Brandeis, Louis Dembitz	Massachusetts	Wilson	1916-1939
Clarke, John Hessin	Ohio	Wilson	1916-1922
Sutherland, George	Utah	Harding	1922-1938
Butler, Pierce	Minnesota	Harding	1923-1939

Sanford, Edward Terry	Tennessee	Harding	1923-1930
Stone, Harlan Fiske	New York	Coolidge	1925-1941
Roberts, Owen Josephus	Pennsylvania	Hoover	1930-1945
Cardozo, Benjamin Nathan	New York	Hoover	1932-1938
Black, Hugo Lafayette	Alabama	Roosevelt F.	1937-1971
Reed, Stanley Forman	Kentucky	Roosevelt F.	1938-1957
Frankfurter, Felix	Massachusetts	Roosevelt F.	1939-1962
Douglas, William Orville	Connecticut	Roosevelt F.	1939-1975
Murphy, Frank	Michigan	Roosevelt F.	1940-1949
Byrnes, James Francis	South Carolina	Roosevelt F.	1941-1942
Jackson, Robert Houghwout	New York	Roosevelt F.	1941-1954
Rutledge, Wiley Blount	Iowa	Roosevelt F.	1943-1949
Burton, Harold Hitz	Ohio	Truman	1945-1958
Clark, Tom Campbell	Texas	Truman	1949-1967
Minton, Sherman	Indiana	Truman	1949-1956
Harlan, John Marshall	New York	Eisenhower	1955-1971
Brennan, William J., Jr.	New Jersey	Eisenhower	1956-1990
Whittaker, Charles Evans	Missouri	Eisenhower	1957-1962
Stewart, Potter	Ohio	Eisenhower	1958-1981
White, Byron Raymond	Colorado	Kennedy	1962-1993
Goldberg, Arthur Joseph	Illinois	Kennedy	1962-1965
Fortas, Abe	Tennessee	Johnson L.	1965-1969
Marshall, Thurgood	New York	Johnson L.	1967-1991
Blackmun, Harry A.	Minnesota	Nixon	1970-1994
Powell, Lewis F., Jr.	Virginia	Nixon	1972-1988
Rehnquist, William H.	Arizona	Nixon	1972-1986
Stevens, John Paul	Illinois	Ford	1975-2010
O'Connor, Sandra Day	Arizona	Reagan	1981-2006
Scalia, Antonin	Virginia	Reagan	1986-2016
Kennedy, Anthony M.	California	Reagan	1988-2018
Souter, David H.	New Hampshire	Bush, G. H. W.	1990-2009
Thomas, Clarence	Georgia	Bush, G. H. W.	1991-
Ginsburg, Ruth Bader	New York	Clinton	1993-2020
Breyer, Stephen G.	Massachusetts	Clinton	1994-2022
Alito, Samuel A., Jr.	New Jersey	Bush, G. W.	2006-
Sonia Sotomayor	New York	Obama	2009-
Elena Kagan	New York	Obama	2010-
Neil M. Gorsuch	Colorado	Trump	2017
Brett M. Kavanaugh	Washington, D.C.	Trump	2018
Amy Coney Barrett	Louisiana	Trump	2020

GLOSSARY OF IMPORTANT PEOPLE AND CONCEPTS

Abortion laws: Abortion was generally legal in the United States until the second half of the 19th century when the American Medical Association lobbied for outlawing forms of abortion that endangered women. More restrictive laws became the norm by the early 20th century and remained in place until the *Roe v. Wade* decision.

Affirmative Action: A federal policy launched in 1970 in which all federal agencies and contractors had to meet "numerical goals and timetables" in hiring a proportionally representative number of African Americans, Mexican Americans, women and other groups that had historically experienced discrimination.

Agricultural Adjustment Act (AAA): Federal law of the New Deal era that restricted agricultural production by paying farmers subsidies and government purchases of farm commodities.

Aguinaldo, Emilio (1869-1964): Leader of the Filipino rebellion against the United States from 1898 until his capture in 1901. After his release he supported groups promoting independence of the Philippines.

AIDS (Acquired Immune Deficiency Syndrome): a potentially fatal disease caused by an infection with a specific virus (HIV) that attacks the human immune system.

Alaska purchase: Secretary of State William H. Seward negotiated the 1867 purchase of Alaska from Russia for $7.2 million. Though often ridiculed as "Seward's Folly" for its sizeable expense for a land mostly of ice and tundra, the land has proven to be invaluable to American security and a provider of immense resource wealth in the form of gold, oil, and natural gas.

Al Qaeda: Fundamentalist Muslim terrorist organization formed by Osama bin Laden that carried out a series of attacks on Western personnel and installations beginning in the early 1990s.

American Federation of Labor: Founded by Samuel Gompers in the aftermath of Haymarket Square. A new union out of the ashes of the Knights of Labor. Gompers organized the AFL by craft rather than industry, and thus the AFL became a union of mostly skilled workers.

American GI Forum: A Latino civil rights organization formed in Corpus Christi, Texas, in 1948, by Dr. Hector Garcia to help Mexican-American veterans experiencing trouble receiving Veterans Administration benefits.

American Recovery and Reinvestment Act 2009: Passed by the Obama administration in an effort to address the nation's high unemployment caused by the 2008 Great Recession.

Anthracite Coal Strike: A 1902 walkout of Pennsylvania coal miners that resulted in Theodore Roosevelt establishing the first federal arbitration commission to settle a major labor disagreement.

Anti-Saloon League (ASL): Leading national organization that campaigned for the prohibition of alcoholic beverages.

Antrim, Henry, also known as "William Bonney" or "Billy the Kid" (c. 1859-1881): A drifter and outlaw accused of the murders of more than 20 people. Antrim's misdeeds were mostly the product of legend.

***Apollo* Program**: The space program inaugurated by the Kennedy administration that resulted in manned flights to the moon with landings by the crews of *Apollo* 11 and 12, and *Apollo* 14 through 17 from 1969 until 1972.

Arab Spring: The populist uprisings that began in Egypt and Tunisia in early 2011 and spread throughout the Middle East and even into the Gulf states (Yemen and Bahrain) that overthrew long-standing dictatorships.

Baby Boom: The sharp increase in live births in the United States from the years 1946 to 1964 when approximately 77 million children were added to the population. Baby Boomers had a great impact on the American economy and their tastes deeply shaped American culture from the 1950s until the present.

Ballinger-Pinchot Affair: Chief Forester Gifford Pinchot's much-publicized disagreement with Interior Secretary Richard Ballinger over conservation matters that resulted in President Taft's firing of Pinchot.

Battle of the Atlantic: Naval fight between German submarines and Allied supply convoys to Europe during WWII.

Battle of Britain: Air battle over England in 1940 that led to Hitler calling off his planned invasion of the British Isles.

Battle of Leyte Gulf: Largest naval battle in world history fought in October 1944 off the coast of the Philippines. As a result of the U.S. Navy's ability to repel assaults by the remnants of the Japanese Navy, American forces were able to continue with their invasion of the Philippines.

Battle of Manila Bay: Naval battle early in the Spanish-American War (May 1, 1898) in which the U.S. fleet under Commodore George Dewey annihilated the Spanish Pacific fleet.

Battle of Midway: Pivotal naval battle fought in 1942 that ended Japanese offensive naval operations in the Pacific.

Battle of Stalingrad: Turning point battle fought in southern Russia from late-1942 to early 1943 resulting in a massive German defeat and the loss of Nazi momentum on the Eastern Front.

Battle of the Little Bighorn ("Custer's Last Stand"): The battle in which the Seventh Cavalry led by General George A. Custer were defeated by the Cheyennes and Sioux led by Sitting Bull and Crazy Horse in 1876.

Bay of Pigs Invasion: A failed attempt to overthrow dictator Fidel Castro in April 1961 by anti-Castro Cubans.

Beats: Non-conformist writers of the 1950s whose desire for experimentation and freedom from societal constraints influenced the more numerous "hippies" of the 1960s.

Bell, Alexander Graham (1847-1922): Scottish immigrant who invented the telephone in 1876.

Berlin Crisis of 1961: The Soviet blockade of land to U.S. access to West Berlin.

bin Laden, Osama (1957-2011): Leader of the Islamist extremist organization Al Qaeda who declared war on the West in the 1990s and was responsible for not only the 9/11 attacks on the Pentagon and the World Trade Center but the earlier bombing of the WTC in New York during the Clinton administration.

Black Codes: Laws passed denying many rights of citizenship to free blacks by the newly-elected southern white governments during presidential reconstruction.

Black Friday: A financial panic leading to a crash of the New York Stock Exchange September 24, 1869 caused by a failed attempt by railroad magnate Jay Gould and financier Jim Fisk to corner the American gold market.

"Black Lives Matter": Grass-roots movement that emerged in 2014 after a series of police killings of unarmed African-American suspects.

Black Panther Party: Established in Oakland, California, emphasizing black economic and political power.

Boland Amendment: A provision added to spending bills passed between 1982 and 1984 by the U.S. House to stop the CIA and Defense Department from funding the right-wing *Contra* rebels.

Bolsheviks: The communist revolutionary faction led by V.I. Lenin that overthrew the Provisional Government, established after the toppling of Czar Nicholas II.

Bonus Army: World War I Army veterans who demonstrated in Washington D.C., for the advance payment of their service bonuses. Hoover ordered the U.S. Army to drive the veterans and family members out of Washington.

Boxer Rebellion: A Chinese nationalist rebellion against the European imperialist powers that began in May 1900 and lasted for over two months.

Brady Bill: A law passed by Congress in response to the attempted assassination of President Ronald Reagan in which press secretary James Brady was severely wounded.

Branch Davidians: An extremist religious cult led by David Koresh, who established his church on the outskirts of Waco, Texas.

***Brown et al v. Board of Education of Topeka, et. al.* (1954):** A Supreme Court decision that ruled "separate but equal" public schools violated the Constitution.

Bryan, William Jennings (1860-1925): The three-time Democratic presidential nominee from Nebraska who served as the party's standard bearer in 1896, 1900 and 1908.

Buffalo slaughter: The mass extermination of buffalo in the West by U.S. troops and paid hunters encouraged by the U.S. government during the 1880s as an effort to force numerous Native American groups who relied on the animals for their livelihood onto reservations.

Buffalo Soldiers: African-American soldiers attached to the United States Army's Ninth and Tenth Cavalry Regiments. These units performed bravely in Indian wars in the West, explored unmapped regions, built forts and guarded railroad and telegraph lines from the New Mexico Territory to the Wyoming Territory.

Bureau of Indian Affairs (BIA): Established in 1824 as part of the War Department, the BIA was given responsibility for physically protecting Native Americans, controlling trade with indigenous peoples, and supervising their relocation to reservations.

Burke, Martha Jane, also known as "Calamity Jane" (c. 1852-1903): A former prostitute who became a trick equestrian and sharpshooter performing for William "Buffalo Bill" Cody's "Wild West" show.

Bush, George H.W. (1924-): The 41st President of the United States who presided over the end of the Cold War and led the nation during the Gulf War but failed to achieve re-election due to a major recession occurring during the latter part of his term.

Bush, George W. (1946-): Republican Governor of Texas who became the 43rd President of the United States. Bush was president on 9/11 and subsequently led the U.S. into lengthy wars in Afghanistan and Iraq.

Bush Tax Cuts: Supported by President George W. Bush, the biggest tax cut in U.S. history, which ultimately returned $1.3 trillion to taxpayers through 2010, largely benefited individuals and companies in the higher tax brackets.

Bush v. Gore: The 2000 decision of the U.S. Supreme Court stated that despite many irregularities, no recounting of any ballots in Florida would be permitted, thus allowing Florida's Secretary of State to certify the results of the election in that state. As a result, George W. Bush narrowly carried Florida and, therefore, the national presidential election by a slim margin of electoral votes.

Camp David Accords: 1978 agreements brokered by President Jimmy Carter that established a framework for peace between former enemies Egypt and Israel.

Carnegie, Andrew (1835-1919): Scottish immigrant who rose to become the leader of the American steel industry through a combination of sound business practices, exploitation of workers, and occasional ruthless destruction of competitors.

"Carpetbaggers": Name given to all northern whites who migrated south allegedly to take advantage of a prostrated southern people and economy.

Carson, Rachel (1907-1964): The author of the 1962 environmental classic *Silent Spring*, which demonstrated the dangers to the ecology of pesticides.

Carter, James Earl "Jimmy" (1924-): Democratic Governor of Georgia who became the 39th President of the United States after defeating Gerald Ford in the 1976 election. For his work in brokering the 1978 Camp David Accords and his energetic post-presidential efforts at promoting world peace, he received the Nobel Peace Prize in 2002.

Central Intelligence Agency (CIA): The major U.S. government agency responsible for gathering and analyzing foreign intelligence data. Created in 1947, the agency also undertook covert operations during the Cold War to aid anti-communist groups in numerous countries and to destabilize nations with governments unfriendly to the United States.

Chávez, César (1927-1993): Co-founder of the United Farm Workers who used non-violent tactics to improve working conditions for largely Mexican-American agricultural labor.

Chiang Kai-shek (1887-1975): The corrupt dictator of China from 1925 until 1949 who abused his own people while accepting billions in aid from the United States; an ardent anti-communist, he failed to stop Mao Zedong's communist revolution.

Chicano Movement: Inspired by Black Nationalists, the Chicano Movement promoted pride in Mexican culture, the Spanish language, and political autonomy for their community.

Child separation policy: Donald Trump's controversial immigration policy from April-June 2018 that involved separating children of illegal immigrants and parents claiming refugee status at the Mexican border.

Chinese Exclusion Act: Law passed by Congress in 1882 banning the further immigration of Chinese laborers into the United States.

Civil Rights Act of 1964: A law banning segregation at public facilities and racial discrimination in the work place.

Civil Service Reform: Changes in federal hiring practices under President Chester A. Arthur that aimed to end the "spoils system" in which federal jobs were handed out by incoming administrations as political favors. As part of the reform efforts, laws were passed to require applicants for federal positions to take competitive qualifying exams and to shield civil service employees from being fired for purely political reasons.

Civilian Conservation Corps (CCC): One of many federally-sponsored job initiatives enacted by President Franklin Roosevelt to address unemployment.

Clinton, Bill (1946-): Democratic governor of Arkansas who became the 42nd President of the United States. Despite leading the nation to a period of steady economic growth, his legacy was tarnished by his improper relationship with a White House intern.

Clinton Boom: The longest period of sustained, uninterrupted economic growth in U.S. economic history taking place during Bill Clinton's presidency in the 1990s.

Clinton, Hillary (1947--): Democrat who challenged Obama for the presidential nomination in 2008, then became his Secretary of State when he was elected.

Cody, William F. "Buffalo Bill" (1846-1917): The producer of a series of "Wild West" stage shows that starred famous Native Americans like Sitting Bull, rope twirlers and trick shooters such as Annie Oakley (Phoebe Butler). Cody's show crisscrossed America and Europe.

Cold War: Term first used by American journalist Walter Lippmann to describe the growing global rivalry between the United States and the Soviet Union.

Committee on Public Information (CPI): A government wartime propaganda agency headed by George Creel to promote the American war effort at home especially among the various immigrant communities, whose loyalty the Wilson administration wanted to ensure.

Compromise of 1877: Informal agreement made by Republican and Democratic Party leaders to resolve the impasse produced by the disputed Election of 1876, resulting in the election of Republican Rutherford B. Hayes as president in return for allowing the Democrats to gain control of the final three unredeemed states in the South and other concessions.

Comstock Lode: One of the biggest silver and gold deposits ever discovered in North America, which yielded up to $500,000,000 worth of precious metals from the Virginia Range in Western Nevada between its discovery in 1859 and 1879 when the deposits were exhausted.

Congress of Industrial Organizations (CIO): Union founded in 1935 by UMW leader John L. Lewis and Sidney Hillman of the Amalgamated Clothing Workers, for the purpose of organizing all non-union workers regardless of skill, occupation, gender, race, or religion.

Containment: The fundamental premise that the U.S. would "contain" communism (preventing its expansion), wherever and whenever it threatened democratic governments and free people in the world.

Contract With America: The 1994 "counter-revolution" led by Republican House Minority Leader Newt Gingrich against the Clinton administration.

Contras: Right wing rebels determined to overthrow the leftist *Sandinista* regime in Nicaragua. President Ronald Reagan referred to the guerrillas as "freedom fighters" and through the CIA and other agencies supported them with money and arms.

Coolidge, Calvin (1872-1933): Staunchly conservative Republican President of the United States from 1923-1929.

Court Packing: Label given to Franklin Roosevelt's failed effort during his second term to reform the Supreme Court by adding new members for every justice who did not retire upon reaching the age of 70.

Crédit Mobilier: A Grant administration scandal involving the siphoning off of millions of dollars in government funds to a "dummy company" to build the Union Pacific Railroad. The railroad company owners sold bogus stock to greedy Congressmen, who believed they could make a quick buck.

Cuban Missile Crisis: The face-off between the United States and the Soviet Union when the American military discovered on October 12, 1962, that the USSR was constructing nuclear missile launch sites in Cuba in response to the American-organized Bay of Pigs invasion the year before.

Dance Marathons: Popular craze during the 1920s involving individuals and couples engaged in organized competitions for prizes based on endurance as opposed to style.

Dawes Severalty Act: An 1887 law passed by the United States Congress that authorized the president to distribute land to individual Indians provided they broke all ties to their tribes.

de Lôme Letter: The stolen communiqué of the Spanish ambassador to the United States in which de Lôme insulted President William McKinley. The letter found its way to American newspapers, further inflaming the increasing anti-Spanish temperament of the American people, leading to the Spanish-American War of 1898.

Delgado v. Bastrop ISD: Legal case in which a federal court ruled against the segregation of Hispanic children in Texas without the existence of a state law supporting the customary practice.

Détente: French term used by Secretary of State Henry Kissinger to describe improved relations between the U.S. and the U.S.S.R. after the United States formally recognized China, the Soviet Union's main communist rival.

Diem, Ngo Dinh (1901-1963:): Anti-communist leader of South Vietnam whose repressive regime ended in 1963 when he was overthrown and murdered during a military coup undertaken by some of his generals.

Direct Primary: The popular election of nominees from a political party for a public office.

Dodd-Frank Wall Street Reform and Consumer Protection Act: A measure the Obama administration lobbied for since the Wall Street collapse, passed by Congress in July 2010. The bill overhauled the nation's financial system and re-established the government's regulatory powers over the financial system, safeguarding the system from future abuses, which had caused the 2008 collapse.

Dodge City (Western) Trail: The most traveled of the great Texas cattle trails. From 1875 to 1885, over 5 million head of cattle trekked from Texas to Dodge City, Kansas along this route.

"Dollar diplomacy": Foreign policy initiatives of Teddy Roosevelt's successor in the White House, William Howard Taft, supporting U.S. corporations that invested in Latin American countries.

Domino Theory: The belief that if South Vietnam fell to the communists, then communist regimes would be established across Asia.

"Don't Ask, Don't Tell": The government's policy toward gays in the military during the Clinton and Bush administrations. Known gay and bisexual men and women were expelled from the service but could remain in the military provided they kept their sexuality secret.

Du Bois, W.E.B. (1868-1963): African-American activist who strongly disapproved of Booker T. Washington's accommodationist approach and called for blacks to agitate for civil rights. In 1909, he helped to found the National Association for the Advancement of Colored People (NAACP).

Dulles, John Foster (1888-1959): U.S. Secretary of State under Dwight Eisenhower who adopted the hardline "New Look" foreign policy based on "massive retaliation."

Dust Bowl: The Great Plains area of the U.S. that suffered choking dust storms in the 1930s because farmers had overworked the land, stripping it of topsoil and nutrients, causing the dirt to become very thin.

Edison, Thomas (1847-1931): America's pioneer inventor in the realm of electricity, he received patents for hundreds of inventions, most notably the light bulb, the record player, DC electric power distribution, the stock ticker, and motion pictures.

Eighteenth Amendment: A provision prohibiting the sale and manufacture of alcoholic beverages in the United States until repealed in 1933.

El Salvador: Central American country whose anti-communist military dictatorship received aid from the Reagan administration during the 1980s.

Emergency Banking Act: Legislation passed at the beginning of Franklin Roosevelt's presidency authorizing extension of the bank holiday until expert teams of analysts investigated a particular bank's assets and liabilities. Those institutions found to be in sound financial shape received government approval to quickly reopen, those eligible for government aid received low-interest RFC loans or government purchase of bank stock to infuse them with cash to keep them in business, while banks determined to be on the verge of collapse were closed forever.

Energy Crisis (1973): A fuel shortage kicked off when the Organization of Petroleum Exporting Countries boycotted oil shipments to the United States in response to American support for Israel in the 1973 Yom Kippur War.

Equal Rights Amendment (ERA): A proposed amendment to the United States Constitution approved by Congress in 1972 that fell three states short of the required three-fourths of the states needed for ratification.

Espionage Act: Of 1917 made it a crime to interfere with U.S. military operations, including the promotion of insubordination in the military or interference with military recruitment.

Eugenics: The racist pseudo-science of producing superior humans through selective breeding.

Exodusters: African-American migrants to the West, primarily to Kansas, who left the South after the end of Reconstruction to escape violence and persecution.

"Fair Deal": Harry Truman's domestic agenda calling for the extension of the New Deal in the postwar years through such proposals as a national health insurance program, federal housing legislation, civil rights initiatives, increased minimum wages, and broader eligibility for Social Security and unemployment compensation.

Fascism: An extreme right-wing ideology characterized by ultra-nationalism, corporatism, militarism, rabid anticommunism, opposition to democracy, and submission to the state.

Faubus, Orval (1910-1994): The segregationist Democratic Governor of Arkansas from 1955 to 1967. Faubus ordered the Arkansas National Guard to prevent the integration of Central High School, but President Dwight Eisenhower nationalized the Guard and implemented the order.

Federal Deposit Insurance Corporation (FDIC): Government corporation operating as an independent agency that oversees the mandatory insurance fund into which banks are required to contribute funds in order to support guarantee of Americans' bank deposits. Originally set in 1933 at $5,000, the current limit is $250,000.

Federal Emergency Relief Administration (FERA): First direct welfare assistance/relief program ever enacted in U.S. history in which the federal government authorized money for the poor as well as other assistance such as food, clothing, and medicine for free to recipients.

Federal Employee Loyalty Program: Truman administration initiative to undercut the clamor of political opponents that many government bureaucrats were communists by subjecting federal employees to background checks and requiring them to take an oath of loyalty to the U.S. government.

Federal Reserve Act: Federal law passed in 1913 establishing the Federal Reserve System as the nation's central banking system under direction of the Federal Reserve Board.

Federal Trade Commission: Independent agency of the federal government created in 1914 to eliminate anti-competitive business practices by enforcing the nation's antitrust statutes.

Ferraro, Geraldine: (1935-2011): First woman ever chosen in U.S. history to be a vice-presidential running mate. Ferraro had been a several term Democratic member of the House from New York when Walter Mondale, Democratic nominee, chose her as his running mate in 1984.

Fifteenth Amendment: A Reconstruction-era amendment that bars states from interfering with the right to vote based on "race, color, or previous condition of servitude."

Fireside Chats: Radio speeches made by Franklin Roosevelt that aimed to reassure voters and to inform citizens of his New Deal programs and their purpose.

"Flappers": Popular image of a care-free party girl who adopted new styles of dress and public behavior during the 1920s.

Foraker Act 1900: The law that established Puerto Rico as a U.S. territory and gave the U.S. the right to annex Puerto Rico without any provision for making the island an American state and its people citizens.

Ford, Gerald R. (1913-2006): The 38th President of the United States who assumed office upon the resignation of Richard Nixon on August 9, 1974. He was the first person to serve in the White House without being elected either as president or vice president.

Ford, Henry (1863-1947): Founder of the Ford Motor Company who revolutionized the manufacturing of automobiles by improving assembly line techniques.

Fourteenth Amendment: A Reconstruction-era amendment passed in 1868 that officially made the freedmen U.S. citizens while prohibiting the states from denying such individuals all the rights and privileges guaranteed any citizen of the United States.

Franz Ferdinand (1863-1914): Heir to the Austrian throne whose assassination by Gavrilo Princip, a Bosnian Serb nationalist, led to the start of World War I.

Freedmen's Bureau: First federally-sponsored and funded welfare agency created during Reconstruction to help the freedmen adjust to their new status while providing education, protection, and other services.

Freedom Riders: Seven African Americans and six whites who boarded interstate buses and rode through the South in the spring of 1961 to test federal enforcement of a court order desegregating interstate transportation terminals.

Freud, Sigmund (1856-1939): Austrian psychologist who pioneered the clinical approach of treatment through dialogue with patients.

Friedan, Betty (1921-1996): A leading feminist and author of the bestselling 1963 book, *The Feminine Mystique,* that described the frustrations of educated women with few career opportunities in 1950s and 1960s America.

Fundamentalism: The Protestant movement within many denominations characterized by strict adherence to theological doctrines, especially a literal interpretation of the Bible.

Garvey, Marcus (1887-1940): Black nationalist leader who founded the United Negro Improvement Association (UNIA).

Geneva Peace Accords: The agreement signed between Ho Chi Minh and the French that established separate North and South Vietnamese governments.

Gentlemen's Agreement: An accord reached between the U.S. and Japan over the Japanese immigration issue. Japan agreed to halt further immigration of its citizens to the U.S., while President Teddy Roosevelt agreed to stop white Californian's persecution of Japanese immigrants as well as their segregation in the school system.

Geronimo (1829-1909): A Chiricahua Apache chief who led Indian resistance in northern Mexico and the American Southwest from the 1870s until his capture in modern-day Arizona in 1886.

Glasnost **and** *Perestroika*: Mikhail Gorbachev's social, economic, and political reforms for the Soviet Union. *Perestroika* ("restructuring" of the country's economic and political system) and *glasnost* ("openness," including greater freedom of speech and the press), when coupled with simultaneous massive cuts in Soviet arms production and a new policy of close cooperation with the United States and its Western allies, led directly to an end to the Cold War.

Goldwater, Barry (1909-1998): Republican nominee for president in 1964 who lost in a landslide to Lyndon Johnson.

Good Neighbor Policy: Franklin Roosevelt's foreign policy toward Latin America based upon noninterference in the domestic affairs of Latin American nations.

Gorbachev, Mikhail (1931 -): The last leader of the Soviet Union whose social and economic reforms paved the way for the USSR's collapse, the end of communism in Russia, and the end of the Cold War.

Gore, Al (1948-): Democratic senator from Tennessee who served as Vice President of the United States under Bill Clinton and narrowly lost the 2000 presidential election to George W. Bush despite receiving over 500,000 more popular votes.

Gould, Jay (1836-1892): One of the original railroad "robber barons," he made a fortune buying dilapidated rail lines, undercutting the competition, then selling them for huge profits. During the post-Civil War years, he unsuccessfully sought to corner the gold market with Jim Fisk.

Grant, Ulysses S. (1822-1885): General-in-chief of the Union Army by the end of the American Civil War (1861-1865), Grant won credit for the North's victory and was able to ride his popularity to two terms in the White House (1869-1877).

Great Railroad Strike of 1877: The first major strike in the nation's most important industry, caused by wage cuts, some as high as 35 percent. Railroad workers walked off the job at all major rail lines from St. Louis east. Violence ensued in many states, with the death toll over 100 and resulting in millions of dollars in property damage and lost railroad revenue.

Great Society: President Lyndon Johnson's social welfare programs, including Medicare, Medicaid, Head Start, the Job Corp, and VISTA. Also included in this legislative agenda were cultural initiatives such as creation of the

Public Broadcasting System, the National Endowment for the Arts and the National Endowment for the Humanities.

"Greenbacks": Paper currency printed by the federal government during the Civil War to finance the northern war effort. Their issue caused widespread, exorbitant inflation in the North while taking the dollar off the gold standard.

Grenada: A small Caribbean island on which Cuban dictator Fidel Castro helped install a supposedly communist government. President Ronald Reagan sent American troops to invade the island in 1984 on the pretext of rescuing U.S. citizens attending medical school there.

Grey, Zane (1872-1939): American author whose best-selling westerns reinforcing traditional American values made him the most widely read fiction writer of the 1920s.

Gulf of Tonkin Resolution: A congressional resolution that gave the American president authority to "take all necessary measures to repel any armed attack against the forces of the United States, and to prevent further aggression."

Harding, Warren G. (1865-1923): A conservative Republican President of the United States from 1921 to 1923 whose administration became embroiled in the "Tea Pot Dome Scandal."

"Harlem Renaissance": An African-American cultural movement expressing racial pride through the arts during the 1920s and 1930s.

Hay-Bunau-Varilla Treaty (1903): A questionable deal made between the United States and the newly formed country of Panama and its supposed ambassador, Philipe Bunau-Varilla, who actually had been director of the French company who originally contracted to build a canal. The treaty granted the U.S. the right to build the canal across the country of Panama.

Hay-Herrán Treaty (1901): Arrangement made between Secretary of State John Hay and Colombian ambassador Tomas Herran who agreed to allow the U.S. to build a canal across the Colombian province of Panama for a one-time payment of $10 million and an annual rental fee of $250,000.

Haymarket Square: Site of a bombing during a strike for the eight-hour workday in Chicago. Workers at the McCormick farm machinery plant went on strike and while demonstrating, a bomb was thrown as the police arrived, killing six cops and causing a riot in which 50 people were wounded and 10 dead, 4 others besides the police.

Hays, William H. (1879-1954): The first president of the Motion Pictures Association of America who developed the voluntary code for filmmaking designed to produce films without objectionable material that dominated the industry until replaced by the Movie Ratings System in the late 1960s.

Hepburn Act: Federal law passed in 1906 that empowered the Interstate Commerce Commission to fix reasonable maximum railroad rates (subject to court review) based on inspection of railroad company records. The legislation marked the first time that the federal government regulated rates or prices of an American business.

Hiss, Alger (1904-1996): Former State Department official accused of passing secret information to the Soviet Union who was eventually convicted only on a perjury charge related to the case.

Hitler, Adolf (1889-1945): Nazi dictator of Germany.

Ho Chi Minh (1890-1969): Vietnamese communist who led guerilla movements against the Japanese during World War II and French colonial forces after the war. Ho also served as the leader of North Vietnam after the country's partition in the mid-1950s.

Holocaust: The murder of six million Jews and "undesirables" by the Nazi regime during WW II.

Homestead Act: A law passed by the United States Congress in 1862 that allowed farmers to obtain 160 acres of public land for free, as long as they cultivated it for five years. Farmers also had the option of buying the land for $1.25 an acre if they cultivated it for six months.

Homestead Strike: Lockout of workers in 1892 at Carnegie Steel's Homestead Works that led to an outbreak of violence between laborers and guards for the Pinkerton Detective Company sent to secure control of the plant for management.

Hoover, Herbert (1874-1964): The Commerce Secretary under President Warren Harding and Calvin Coolidge who won election as President of the United States in 1928.

Horizontal Integration: A means of dominating an industry by acquiring control of the most critical aspect of production, such as John D. Rockefeller did with oil refining in the late nineteenth century.

House Un-American Activities Committee (HUAC): Right-wing Texas Congressman Martin Dies first chaired HUAC. Established in 1937, it investigated the influence of American communists and those sympathetic to fascism in the United States. HUAC would hold hearings on supposed communist subversion in Hollywood and American universities and strongly influenced the later Senate investigations of Soviet infiltration by Joseph McCarthy.

Huerta, Victoriano (1850-1916): Mexican general who overthrew Francisco Madero in 1913 only to be overthrown himself by a coalition of opponents in 1914.

Hussein, Saddam (1937-2006): Long-time dictator of Iraq whose invasion of Kuwait led to the 1991 Gulf War. A decade later he would later be removed from power following a 2002 U.S. invasion of Iraq, tried for war crimes against his own people, and executed by hanging in 2006.

Immigration Reform and Control Act of 1986: A law passed by Congress during the Reagan administration addressing the ongoing problem of illegal immigration. The law outlawed the hiring of illegal aliens, strengthened border controls, and offered legal status to aliens who had lived in the U.S. for five years.

Impeachment: The process specified in the U.S. Constitution whereby the House of Representatives can indict a federal government official in cases of "bribery, treason, or other high crimes and misdemeanors." Those impeached are to be tried by the U.S. Senate, with a two-thirds majority needed to convict and remove the officeholder from their position.

Indian Reorganization Act of 1934: This legislation gave tribal lands back to Native Americans lost under the 1887 Dawes Act, granting them all manner of autonomy and ending the "assimilationist" crusade of the 1920s in which white authorities wanted to forcibly integrate Indians into white society.

Internet: A global system of interconnected computer systems that has led to the vast digital distribution of information as impactful on the late-20th and early 21st century as the printing press was for medieval times.

Interstate Highway Act of 1956: A bill passed by the United States Congress that authorized $130 billion to construct 46,000 miles of roads connecting the eastern coast of the United States to the western coast.

Iran-Contra Affair: A scandal during the Reagan presidency that involved the illegal sale of arms to Iran, a U.S. enemy, to pay for the release of hostages held in Lebanon by terrorist groups allied with the Iranian regime. The money from the arm sales went towards arming the *Contras*, a right-wing guerilla army seeking to overthrow the leftist *Sandinista* regime in Nicaragua, in direct violation of a congressional ban on such assistance to the Central American rebels.

Iranian Hostage Crisis: 444-day ordeal in which radical Islamic students in Teheran, Iran, with help from the new revolutionary government, seized the U.S. embassy and held many of its personnel as hostages for over a year until their release at the end of the Carter presidency.

Irreconcilables: Fierce congressional opponents of both the League of Nations and Treaty of Versailles, who were determined to defeat both. Members were hardcore isolationists.

ISIS (Islamic State in Iraq and Syria): Unrecognized jihadist state located in areas of Iraq and Syria controlled by radical Sunni forces supportive of terror attacks against their enemies in the Middle East, Europe, and the United States.

Helen Hunt Jackson (1830-1885)—An American writer who drew public attention to the desperate plight of Native Americans in the 1881 book *A Century of Dishonor* and novels such as *Ramona* (1884).

James-Younger Gang: A criminal band of bank and train robbers active in Missouri and neighboring states in 1870s and 1880s led by two brothers, Jesse and Frank James.

Jazz: Musical style originating in the southern United States at the turn of the twentieth century blending African and European musical traditions.

Johnson, Andrew (1808-1875): Abraham Lincoln's successor as President of the United States. He was impeached by the House of Representatives after clashing with Congress over Reconstruction policy but the Senate failed to remove him from office by one vote.

Johnson, Lyndon Baines (1908-1973): A Democratic member of the Texas delegation in the House of Representatives from 1937 to 1949, a senator from 1949 to 1961 (including a stint as Senate Majority Leader from 1955-1961), the vice president from 1961 to 1963, and president from 1963-1969, Johnson ascended to the White House after John Kennedy's assassination. Johnson created social welfare programs such as Medicare and Medicaid, Project Head Start and what he called "The War on Poverty."

Jungle, The: Upton Sinclair's 1906 novel that attempted to draw attention to the plight of the working class and to promote socialism, but ended up generating public outrage over unsanitary meatpacking conditions and passage of the Meat Inspection Act.

Katrina (Hurricane): One of the nation's worst natural disasters that caused the destruction of much of New Orleans in the summer of 2005.

Keating-Owen Act: Federal legislation outlawing the shipment across state lines of items manufactured in whole, or in part, by labor under the age of 14. The U.S. Supreme Court ruled the law unconstitutional in 1919.

Kelley, Florence (1859-1932): Progressive reformer who campaigned for regulating the working conditions and the wages and hours of women and children.

Kennan, George (1904-2005): Considered by most Cold War historians to be the individual who had the most influence on the development of the containment policy adopted by President Harry Truman.

Kennedy, John F. (1917-1963): The 35th President of United States. Kennedy's administration has been associated with the start of the *Apollo* moon mission, troubled relations with the Soviet Union characterized by the Bay of Pigs invasion and the Cuban Missile Crisis, the start of the Vietnam War, and his administration's occasional support of the Civil Rights Movement. An assassin, Lee Harvey Oswald, murdered Kennedy in Dallas, Texas, November 22, 1963.

Kennedy-Nixon Debates: Four televised debates between John Kennedy and Richard Nixon during the 1960 campaign. These encounters were also the first presidential debates in American history among nominees of the major political parties.

Kent State Shooting: The fatal shooting of four students and injuring of nine others at the Kent State University campus on May 4, 1970, by National Guardsmen during protests over the American invasion of Cambodia.

Kerensky, Alexander (1881-1970): Leader of Russia's first attempt at parliamentary, democratic government following the overthrow of Czar Nicholas II in the Russian Revolution in February 1917.

Khrushchev, Nikita (1894-1971): Joseph Stalin's successor as the leader of the Soviet Union.

Kim Jong-un (1984 -): Dictator of North Korea since the death of his father, Kim Jong-Il, in 2011.

King, Martin Luther, Jr. (1929-1968): The primary leader of the African-American civil rights movement from the Montgomery Bus Boycott until his assassination in Memphis, Tennessee, April 4, 1968. For many, King's 1963 "I Have a Dream Speech" during the March on Washington on August 28, 1963, summarized the highest ideals of the 1960s protest movement.

Kinsey, Alfred (1894-1956): An American sex researcher whose books *Sexual Behavior in the Human Male* (1948) and *Sexual Behavior in the Human Female* (1953) documented much higher rates of premarital sex, marital infidelity, sexual experimentation among teens, and homosexuality in the American population than previously assumed.

Kissinger, Henry (1923--): President Nixon's National Security Advisor and Secretary of State under Nixon and President Gerald Ford.

Knights of Labor: One of the nation's first prominent labor organizations, formed in 1869 and reaching the peak of its strength in the 1880s. The union allowed both unskilled and skilled workers to join, as well as women and African Americans.

Kosovo: Serb province whose bid for independence led to genocidal attacks on Albanian Muslim rebels. During Bill Clinton's second term, the president ordered air strikes against Serb forces and selected targets in their capital of Belgrade, leading to an eventual cease fire and the arrival of United Nations peacekeeping troops.

Ku Klux Klan: A white supremacist group that aimed to destroy the Reconstruction-era Republican Party in the South, to force the withdrawal of Union troops from the region, and to terrify African Americans into not voting or demanding better working conditions.

Laissez-faire: A notion by 18th century English economist Adam Smith that capitalism operates for the greater benefit of all individuals if free from government interference and other artificially imposed restraints.

League of Nations: The "fourteenth point" of Wilson's grand post-World War I peace plan that called for the creation of a world organization to address global disputes before they escalated into war.

League of United Latin American Citizens (LULAC): A Latino civil rights group formed in 1929 in Corpus Christi, Texas, that sought to end discrimination against Hispanics and also sought to promote "Americanism" in the community through English language classes.

Lend-Lease Act: Legislation pushed by Roosevelt in 1941 that empowered the president "to sell, transfer title to, exchange, lease, lend, or otherwise dispose of" any American defense articles to the government of any country whose defense the president deemed vital to the protection of the United States.

Lenin, Vladimir (1870-1924): Leader of the Russian communists (Bolsheviks) who overthrew the Provisional government of Alexander Kerensky, withdrew Russian participation in World War I, and established the Soviet Union.

"Letter From a Birmingham Jail": The letter was written by Martin Luther King, Jr., in 1963 while he was held in jail after violating an Alabama state court order to stop a boycott of Birmingham's segregated department stores. Soon published, the letter condemned the inaction of so-called "moderates" who stood by while southern states denied African Americans their constitutional rights.

Lewinsky, Monica (1973-): Young White House intern whose improper relationship with Bill Clinton led to Republican efforts to impeach him and tarnished his legacy as president.

Lewis, John (1940-): Civil rights activist who led the Freedom Rides and the Selma Marches.

Liberal Republicans: Anti-Grant faction within the Republican Party that allied with Democrats in the 1872 election in an unsuccessful attempt to deny Grant a second term as president. They condemned the scandals of the Grant era, favored civil service reform, and sought an end to the Republicans' Reconstruction policies.

Liliuokalani, Queen (1838-1917): Hawaiian monarch deposed by American sugar planters in 1893 after she sought to restore complete royal rule of the islands by disbanding the national assembly dominated by the sugar producers.

Lincoln, Abraham (1809-1865). An Illinois politician who served as president from 1861 to his assassination in 1865. Before 1860, Lincoln, a successful lawyer, served a single term in the House of Representatives. In 1858, he lost a contest for the Senate to Stephen Douglas, but then defeated Douglas in the 1860 presidential election. As president, Lincoln shepherded the United States through a bitter Civil War.

Lindbergh, Charles A. (1902-1974): First pilot to fly solo across the Atlantic Ocean in 1927. He was a famous isolationist aviator who clashed with the Roosevelt Administration over foreign policy during the 1930s.

Little Rock Crisis: The battle over desegregation at Little Rock, Arkansas' Central High School in 1957. Arkansas Governor Orval Faubus dispatched the state National Guard to prevent black students from entering the school, forcing Dwight Eisenhower to nationalize the Guard and enforce a federal court's desegregation order. In response, Faubus shut down all of Little Rock's high schools in the 1958-1959 school year.

Lodge, Henry Cabot, Jr. (1902-1985): Republican Senator from MA whose opposition to the Treaty of Versailles while serving as Chairman of the Senate Foreign Relations Committee (because of the treaty's inclusion of the collective security provision for the League of Nations) ultimately led to the treaty never being ratified by the U.S. Senate.

Long, Huey (1893-1935): Popular Louisiana governor and senator who in 1934 began sharply criticizing the New Deal from the political left.

Los Angeles Riots: Outbreak of violence that occurred in April 1992 after a jury acquitted local cops who had been shown on videotape beating black motorist Rodney King after a police chase even though King was not resisting arrest.

Lusitania: A British luxury liner sunk in 1915 during World War I by a German submarine on the suspicion that U.S. arms manufacturers were smuggling weapons onboard such ships. De-classified U.S. government documents confirmed the German suspicion.

MacArthur, Douglas (1880-1964): World War II general who commanded U.S. forces at the beginning of the Korean War. Harry Truman fired him in 1951 after the general continued to publicly criticize the president's handling of the war.

McCabe, E.P. (1850-1920): African-American attorney, land agent, and public office holder who became a leading figure in encouraging black migration into Oklahoma after the Civil War. His efforts led to the creation of several black towns that exist today, including Langston, Oklahoma.

McCain, John (1936 -): U.S. senator from Arizona who received the 2008 Republican nomination for president and was defeated by Barack Obama.

McCarthy, Joseph (1908-1957): Republican senator from Wisconsin whose ceaseless hunts for communists within the United States were characterized by paranoia and baseless allegations that nevertheless cost many innocent Americans their livelihoods during the early 1950s.

McKinley, William (1843-1901): Republican senator from Ohio elected the 25th President of the United States in 1896. He served as president during the Spanish-American War and was re-elected in 1900. His assassination in 1901 led to his vice president, Theodore Roosevelt, becoming president.

McNamara, Robert (1916-2009): The Ford Motor Company executive who served for seven years as President John Kennedy's and President Lyndon Johnson's Secretary of Defense and the chief architect of American military strategy in South Vietnam from 1965 to 1968.

McPherson, Aimee Simple (1890-1944): Theatrical fundamentalist preacher who opened the first megachurch in Los Angeles in 1923.

Madero, Francisco (1873-1913): Mexican revolutionary leader who ousted longtime dictator Porfirio Diaz but was overthrown as President of Mexico and murdered by supporters of Victoriano Huerta in 1913.

Mahan, Alfred Thayer (1840-1914): American naval officer who wrote one of the most influential military history books in United States history, advocating for the United States to not only become a world power but the process by which such status was to be attained through sea power.

Malcolm X or Malcolm Little (1925-1965): A former street hustler converted by the eccentric Nation of Islam sect who as an NOI minister became a leading advocate of black self-assertion and black self-awareness before his assassination in New York on February 21, 1965.

Manhattan Project: A secret joint American and British research program that developed the atomic bomb.

Mao Zedong (1893-1976): Leader of the Chinese Communist Party who fiercely battled the Japanese invaders of his country in the 1930s and 1940s before winning in 1949 the long civil war he waged against the U.S.-supported Chiang Kai-shek dictatorship.

March on Washington: A civil rights rally held on the Mall in Washington, D.C., August 28, 1963, that galvanized congressional support for a proposed civil rights law passed the following year.

Marshall Plan: An initiative put forward by Secretary of State George C. Marshall to provide American loans and investment to the devastated economies of Europe in order not only to revitalize those economies but to prevent possible communist takeovers, especially of western Europe.

"Massive Resistance": The attempt by southern states to undermine implementation of the Supreme Court's *Brown* decision requiring desegregation of public schools through closing public schools, passing laws allowing white parents to receive vouchers for attending all-white private schools, harassment lawsuits against the NAACP, and so on.

Mattachine Society: The first American gay civil rights organization, formed in Los Angeles in 1951.

Meat Inspection Act: A federal law passed in 1906 empowering the U.S. Department of Agriculture to establish regulations for the sanitary processing of meat products and to provide for regular inspections of meat processing facilities.

Medicine Lodge Treaty of 1867: A coerced agreement that relocated Arapaho, Cheyennes, Comanches, Apaches, and Kiowas onto reservations to be shared with already resident Bannocks, Navajos, Shoshones, and Sioux. Eventually more than 100,000 people scrabbled for existence on these lands, which became infamous for malnutrition, disease, alcoholism, and depression.

Mellon, Andrew W. (1855-1937): Secretary of the Treasury under Harding, Coolidge, and Hoover who favored tax reduction for corporations and the wealthy to spur investment during the 1920s.

Milk, Harvey (1930-1978): The political leader of the San Francisco gay community who was assassinated shortly after becoming the first openly gay candidate to win a seat as supervisor on the San Francisco County Board of Supervisors.

Miranda v. Arizona: 1966 case in which the U.S. Supreme Court famously ruled that a person under arrest must be apprised of their constitutional rights to legal counsel and against self-incrimination (the "right to remain silent").

Montgomery Bus Boycott: A 381-day civil rights campaign that began on December 1, 1955, against Montgomery, Alabama's segregated public transportation that begun by Rosa Parks, an African American woman, who refused to surrender her seat to a white man.

Moral Majority: Reverend Jerry Falwell's organization founded in 1979 to mobilize Christian conservative voters behind candidates acceptable to the group's social values that became an influential group contributing to the resurgence of the Republican Party in the South and in national elections.

Mortgage-backed securities: Marketable securities based on the cash flows of mortgage loans. This device became a highly lucrative unregulated investment until a wave of mortgage defaults culminating in 2008 had devastating effects on investors and many key Wall Street financial institutions, which went bankrupt, triggering the economic downturn commonly called the "Great Recession" on the eve of the Obama presidency.

"Muckrakers": Theodore Roosevelt's label for the Progressive Era's investigative reporters.

Mueller investigation: Special counsel inquiry established within the Justice Department led by former FBI Director Robert Mueller to investigate Russian interference in the 2016 presidential election, as well as the possible involvement of members of the Trump campaign.

Munich Conference: A meeting between the leaders of Germany, Italy, Great Britain, and France that led to an agreement allowing Germany's annexation of Czechoslovakia's Sudetenland.

"Municipal housekeeping": Argument used by many urban progressive women to justify their activism in the political sphere. These women claimed that by engaging in reform efforts such as city beautification projects, library and hospital construction, and establishment of juvenile courts for youth offenders they were merely reinforcing their traditional role as protector of family and home.

Mussolini, Benito (1883-1945): The fascist dictator of Italy from 1922 to 1943 who allied his nation with Adolf Hitler's Germany during World War II.

National American Woman Suffrage Association (NAWSA): Leading national organization that campaigned beginning in the 1890s for women's right to vote.

National Origins Act: A law passed by Congress in 1924 that reduced the maximum level of legal foreign immigration to 150,000 while altering the nationality quotas to 2 percent of the number of each nationality residing in the United States in 1890.

National Recovery Administration (NRA): New Deal agency created in June 1933 by passage of the National Industrial Recovery Act (NIRA) and charged with generating economic recovery through the application of industry-created and government-approved wage and price "codes of fair practice" to be followed in hundreds of businesses across the country. After initial optimism that the codes would eliminate cutthroat competition and thereby stabilize wages and prices, the effort failed to sustain economic growth, and the NIRA was eventually ruled unconstitutional in May 1935.

National Security Act of 1947: Following the crisis over Greece and Turkey, this legislation restructured the U.S.'s military and intelligence agencies. The Department of Defense replaced the War Department, created the United States Air Force, and brought all military branches under the oversight of the Secretary of Defense. It also established the Central Intelligence Agency (CIA), and the National Security Agency to advise the president on intelligence and security issues and policies.

Nazi-Soviet Non-Aggression Pact: An agreement between Germany and the Soviet Union in 1939 in which the two powers pledged mutual neutrality and secretly authorized the partition of Poland.

Negro Leagues: African-American professional players spent their careers in several black baseball associations known as Negro Leagues.

Neutrality Acts: Legislation passed by Congress between 1935 and 1937 that outlawed the selling of arms or the issuance of loans to nations at war and only allowed the trading of non-military items to nations at war on a "cash and carry" basis.

"New Frontier": John F. Kennedy's term for his legislative program during his 1961-1963 presidency. Included were moderate support of African American civil rights, vigorous backing of the American space program, and continuation of Harry Truman and Dwight Eisenhower's policy of containing communism.

"New Immigrants": Immigrants from Eastern and Southern Europe, as well as China, Japan, and, after the 1910 Mexican Revolution, from Mexico, who formed the majority of immigrants arriving in the United States from 1880 to the start of World War I in 1914. "Old Immigrants," the majority of newcomers before 1880, came primarily from Northern and Western Europe.

"New Look": Foreign policy promoted by President Eisenhower and Secretary of State John Foster Dulles that placed primary national defense priority on the use of atomic weapons, so-called "massive retaliation," rather than conventional weapons.

"New South": Post-Civil War economic philosophy popularized by Henry Grady among others, promoting diversification of the southern economy through a concerted effort to break the region's dependence upon cotton and to espousing the benefits of industrialization.

Nhu, Ngo Dinh (1910-1963): The influential brother of Ngo Dinh Diem who headed South Vietnam's secret police and initiated the strategic hamlet program. Ngo Dinh Nhu died alongside his brother in the November 1963 military coup.

Nineteenth Amendment: Ratified in 1920, the amendment that forbade states from denying an individual from voting because of their gender.

Noriega, Manuel (1934--): Panamanian dictator who George H.W. Bush overthrew in 1989 for his involvement with the South American (primarily Colombian) drug cartels. He served time in prison in the United States and France following his capture by U.S. forces.

North American Free Trade Agreement (NAFTA): A pact ratified during the Clinton administration that went into effect in 1994 that established complete free trade between Mexico, the U.S., and Canada. NAFTA served part of President Bill Clinton's goal of expanding U.S. global markets, which he believed could only occur via free trade.

North Atlantic Treaty Organization (NATO): A collective security alliance created in 1949 between the United States, Canada and several Western European nations that aimed to counter the military threat posed by the Soviet Union and its satellite states in Eastern Europe.

North, Oliver (1943 -): Marine Lt. Colonel who became a central figure in the Iran-Contra Scandal when it was revealed that during his time as a National Security Council staff member worked out the logistics for the arms-for-hostages deals that coincided with illegally channeling the proceeds of the arms sales to the anti-communist contras in Nicaragua.

Northern Securities Company: A consolidated railroad system put together by investment banker J.P. Morgan during the 1890s in response to the economic panic of that decade. It reflected the increasing consolidation of the American economy by the wealthy in the late 19th century and was dissolved by order of the U.S. Supreme Court in 1904.

Obama, Barack (1961 -): Former Democratic Senator from Illinois elected the 44th President of the United States and the first African-American president in 2008.

Obergefell v. Hodges: Landmark 2015 Supreme Court case in which the Court held that same-sex couples had a fundamental right to marry under the Fourteenth Amendment of the U.S. Constitution.

Occupy Wall Street: A massive protest movement against the nation's present plutocracy and their hegemony over the nation's economic system. The protesters believed these individuals were responsible for the nation's financial collapse and continued economic woes, such as unemployment.

Office of Price Administration (OPA): A government agency that oversaw price restrictions and rationing programs during World War II.

O'Keefe, John (1950-): A liberal Catholic antiwar activist who adopted the sit-in tactic of civil rights protestors to agitate against abortion clinics during the 1970s.

Oklahoma City bombing, 1995: Domestic terrorist attack killing 168 people at the Murrah Federal Building in Oklahoma City in 1995. The bombers, Timothy McVeigh and Terry Nichols, carried out the attack in response to the fiery standoff between federal law enforcement and members of the Branch Davidian sect in Waco, Texas, in 1993.

On The Road: A seminal 1957 novel of the Beat generation of the 1950s written by Jack Kerouac.

Open Door Policy: Term used by Secretary of State John Hay to describe U.S. relations with China, which, by 1900, had been cut up by the European imperial powers into spheres of influence. After occupying a specific region of China, the Europeans then closed off their sphere from all outside trade. The United States was the only major world power without a sphere in China and thus locked out of the lucrative China trade.

Operation Desert Storm (the First Gulf War): The 1991 U.S.-led military invasion of Kuwait, in response to Iraq's conquest of that nation the previous year.

Operation Enduring Freedom (Afghan War): The U.S. invasion of Afghanistan launched on October 7, 2001, with the goal of capturing or killing Osama bin Laden and bringing down the Taliban government that had harbored him and his Al Qaeda organization.

Operation Iraqi Freedom (Iraq War): The long, drawn-out conflict launched in March 2003 by the U.S. invasion of Iraq resulting from the George W. Bush administration's efforts to overthrow Saddam Hussein because of the false belief that Hussein had a connection to Al Qaeda terrorists and was developing chemical and nuclear weapons of mass destruction for use against Western targets.

Operation Overlord: Code name for the 1944 Allied invasion of Normandy during World War II.

Operation Rolling Thunder: An intensive bombing campaign against North Vietnam from March 1965 to November 1968 in which more than 7 million tons of explosives were dropped.

"Operation Wetback": A federal government crackdown on undocumented Mexican workers carried out in 1950.

Palmer, A. Mitchell (1872-1936): U.S. Attorney General under Woodrow Wilson known for launching a series of raids against radicals leading to mass deportations during the "Red Scare" of 1919.

Panama Canal: After Theodore Roosevelt aided Panamanian rebels in their fight for independence against Colombia in 1903, the U.S. obtained the right to build this canal linking the Pacific and Atlantic Oceans (completed in 1914) across the Isthmus of Panama. In 1999, the U.S. transferred ownership of the canal to Panama.

Panic of 1873: A financial crisis triggered by the collapse of banks involved in railroad speculation resulting in a seven-year-long economic depression, business failures, and high unemployment.

Parks, Rosa (1913-2005): An African-American activist in the NAACP who launched the Montgomery Bus Boycott.

Patient Protection and Affordable Care Act ("Obamacare"): Major reform of the nation's health care system passed in 2010 and approved by the Supreme Court in 2012, the law eliminates medical discrimination (such as denial of coverage due to pre-existing conditions) and mandates coverage for an additional 30 million Americans (leaving only 6 percent of the total population uninsured). Controversially, it attempts to control health care costs by instituting an "individual mandate" on citizens by stipulating that all adults have health insurance coverage or be subject to tax penalties. This last provision had been demanded by insurance companies to help with the added cost of covering individuals with pre-existing conditions. Meanwhile, the legislation provides premium subsidies for low-income Americans to make their new health insurance affordable.

Patriot Act: Federal law passed by Congress after 9/11 that conferred unprecedented powers to law enforcement agencies charged with preventing the new and vaguely defined crime of "domestic terrorism." Such agencies could now wiretap, perform surveillance, open letters, read e-mail, and obtain personal records from third parties without a suspect's knowledge.

Paul, Alice (1885-1977): "Militant" woman suffragist leader and advocate for the Equal Rights Amendment (ERA), first proposed in 1923.

Pearl Harbor attack: Japanese sneak attack upon the U.S. Navy's Pacific base in Hawaii on December 7, 1941, that led to America's entry into World War II.

Pendleton Act: One of the most far-reaching reform measures of the federal government's civil service system, passed in 1883, which established the modern procedure for positions within the federal bureaucracy.

Pentagon Papers: An official, secret Pentagon history of the Vietnam war, complete with vast collections of memos produced by government officials on the conflict put together by orders of Lyndon Johnson's Defense Secretary Robert McNamara and published by *The New York Times* and the *Washington Post* in 1971. Publication of these papers would lead President Nixon to order the formation of the White House Plumbers unit.

People's or Populist Party: A minor political party formed in the 1890s that sprang from various farmers movements in the last three decades of the 19th century and elected members of Congress and state legislatures in the elections of 1892, 1894, and 1896.

Pershing, John J. (1860-1948): U.S. Army general who President Woodrow Wilson assigned to chase Pancho Villa in northern Mexico in 1916 before being recalled to command the American forces in Europe during World War I.

Perot, Ross (1930--): The founder of EDS, a Texas high-tech firm, who led one of the more popular third party movements in American history. Perot ran as an independent in the 1992 and 1996 presidential races.

Pinchot, Gifford (1865-1946): Head of the U.S. Forest Service from 1905 to 1910 and main conservation advisor to President Theodore Roosevelt.

Platt Amendment: Approved by the Congress in 1903, this measure recognized the right of the United States to annex Cuba as a "protectorate."

Plessy v. Ferguson: 1896 Supreme Court decision legalizing public segregation through the principle that the establishment of "separate but equal" accommodations were constitutional.

Political Machines: Political arrangement whereby a group that controls a state or local political organization ("machine") provides employment or other necessities to voters in exchange for their votes.

"Predatory lending": Mortgage companies that sold adjustable-rate high interest loans to unsuspecting home-buyers, many of whom did not qualify with sufficient income to own a home or once in possession could not keep up with the escalating mortgage interest and payments. Such a practice led to unprecedented foreclosures beginning a year before the Wall Street collapse.

Presley, Elvis (1935-1977): One of the bestselling recording artist of all times, Presley introduced to white audiences in the 1950s numerous songs originally performed by black artists and ushered in the era in which the youth market came to dominate the music industry.

Professional Air Traffic Controller's Organization (PATCO): A powerful union that went on strike in 1981 demanding more pay and less hours for its members. President Ronald Reagan eventually ordered the firing of over 11,000 workers. His action signaled the start of a long decline in American union influence and activism.

Progressive ("Bull Moose") Party: Theodore Roosevelt's third party organized for the 1912 election (disbanded in 1916).

Progressivism: Term given to the diverse reform efforts of the late 19th century and early 20th century responding to the social, political, and cultural changes caused by the Industrial Revolution.

Public Works Administration (PWA): Established under the auspices of the National Industrial Recovery Act, passed in 1933 during the Roosevelt administration. The program hired tens of thousands of unemployed and underemployed Americans to build the Hoover and Grand Coulee dams, thousands of new schools and public libraries, and the 100 mile causeway linking Florida to Key West.

Pure Food and Drug Act: Federal law passed in 1906 creating the Food and Drug Administration to test and approve drugs before being allowed for sale on the market.

Putin, Vladimir (1952 -): President of Russia whose seizure of the Crimean Peninsula and aid to eastern Ukrainian separatists greatly increased tensions in eastern Europe during Barack Obama's second term.

"Race Suicide": A fear promoted by white supremacist racial theorists in the late 19th and early 20th centuries that supposedly inferior African Americans, and immigrants from Eastern and Southern Europe and Mexico, were reproducing faster than supposedly superior Anglo-Saxons.

Radical Republicans: Republicans opposed to President Abraham Lincoln and Andrew Johnson's Reconstruction policies from 1863-1868. The Radicals believed the South should be punished for their "treason" and that the freedmen should become full-fledged United States citizens and their new status protected by the federal government.

Randolph, A. Phillip (1889-1979): Leader of the Brotherhood of Sleeping Car Porters, the largest African American labor union in the country, whose mobilization of blacks for a potential mass march on Washington led President Franklin Roosevelt in 1941 to issue Executive Order 8802, which forbade discrimination by defense industry employers or government agencies based on race, color, creed, or national origin.

Reagan, Ronald (1911-2004): The 40th President of the United States whose tenure during the 1980s marked the beginning of conservative resurgence in national politics and the rise of the Republican Party after decades of minority party-status.

Reaganomics: Desiring a balanced federal budget, Ronald Reagan sought to reduce social welfare programs but also wanted greatly to increase military spending while cutting taxes across the board.

Rebel Without A Cause: A 1955 movie starring James Dean as a troubled juvenile trying to find his identity in spite of his domineering mother and his emasculated father.

Reconstruction Acts of 1867: Represented the end of Presidential Reconstruction and the beginning of Congressional or Radical Reconstruction. These laws restarted the political process in the South, with the 10 unreconstructed southern states divided into five military districts administered by Army generals.

Reconstruction Finance Corporation (RFC): Government agency created by Congress in 1932, the final year of Herbert Hoover's presidency, which provided $1.5 billion in low-interest government loans to ailing banks and corporations in order to prevent their collapse. During the New Deal, the RFC under Texas banker Jesse Jones became a major investment device for government attempts to stimulate the economy.

Red Scare: The first outbreak of hysteria over communist subversion in 1919 in the aftermath of World War I.

Redeemers: The antebellum elite who sought to end "Yankee domination" and regain political power in the South after the Civil War.

Repatriation: The policy of removing of Mexican residents in the Southwest during the Great Depression, leading to the breakup of families or forced relocation of American-born Hispanics to Mexico in order to keep families together.

Reservationists: Those congressional Republicans and Democrats who, in 1919, opposed the Treaty of Versailles ending World War I, especially Article 10 of the League of Nations charter, which called for collective security among League members to deal with aggressor nations.

"Roaring Twenties": Stereotypical depiction of the 1920s as a carefree period characterized by people dressing and behaving in nontraditional ways.

Robber Barons: Super wealthy businessmen in the late nineteenth and early twentieth century such as John D. Rockefeller and Jay Gould whose lives were marked by ruthless business practices, mistreatment of their workers, and conspicuous consumption (enhancing one's social standing by living opulently).

Robinson, Jackie (1919-1972): A baseball player who in 1947 became the first African American to play in the major leagues since the late 1880s. Robinson played first and second base for the Brooklyn Dodgers until 1956.

Rock 'n' Roll: Popular music art form fusing African American rhythm and blues with country western and other genres that gained its initial popularity with the youth of the 1950s Baby Boom generation.

Rockefeller, John D. (1839-1937): American businessman who emerged from ruthless competition to gain monopoly control of oil refining in the United States by the turn of the twentieth century.

***Roe v. Wade* (1973)**: The controversial United States Supreme Court decision that legalized abortion in the first two trimesters of pregnancy.

Roosevelt Corollary: President Theodore Roosevelt's addendum to the Monroe Doctrine, in which he announced that the U.S. had the right to intervene in the internal affairs of any nation in the Western Hemisphere if the U.S. deemed it essential for "hemispheric security and stability."

Roosevelt, Eleanor (1884-1962): First Lady of the United States known for her activities on behalf of the rights of workers and minorities during the Great Depression.

Roosevelt, Franklin D. (1882-1945): Longest-serving President of the United States who led the nation through the Great Depression with his New Deal programs and to ultimate victory during World War II.

Roosevelt, Theodore (1858-1919): Progressive Republican who served as governor of New York before becoming the 26th President of the United States (1901-1909). He later became the candidate of the Progressive ("Bull Moose") Party in the 1912 presidential election.

Rosenberg, Ethel (1915-1953) and Julius (1918-1953): American couple convicted of spying for the Soviet Union and executed in 1953.

"Rough Riders": Nickname given to Theodore Roosevelt's all-volunteer military outfit of individuals ranging from cowboys, Ivy League graduates, Hispanics, and an assortment of European immigrants, who went to Cuba during the 1898 Spanish-American War.

Rural Electrification Administration (REA): A New Deal program during Franklin Roosevelt's administration that, in the 1930s, brought federally funded electrical power and other utilities to rural areas.

Russo-Japanese War: An important conflict in East Asia between two rival Asian powers, Japan and Russia, between 1904-05. The war shocked Europeans and white Americans as supposedly inferior Asians handily defeated an important European empire.

Samoa: Island group on the route between Hawaii and Australia/New Zealand. The U.S. annexed the eastern islands, including the natural harbor of Pago Pago, in 1899.

Sand Creek Massacre: A November 29, 1864, attack on Cheyenne women, children and elderly men carried out by a white militia, the "Colorado Volunteers," that left 200 dead.

Sandinistas: Marxist/leftist insurgents who had overthrown the corrupt Anastasio Somoza dictatorship in Nicaragua in 1979 and implemented land reform and

forged a close relationship with the communist governments in the Soviet Union and Cuba.

Santo Domingo Affair: The attempt by the Grant administration in 1869 to annex the present-day country of the Dominican Republic. This ended in political disaster for President Ulysses Grant who failed to consult with key Republican senators before drawing up a treaty with the Dominican leadership, and who did not lobby for ratification of the agreement.

"Scalawags": A term given during the Reconstruction Era in the 1860s and 1870s to southern whites who had supported the Union during the Civil War and the Republican Party during Reconstruction.

Schenck v. United States **(1919)**: A United States Supreme Court decision upholding the constitutionality of both Espionage Act and Sedition Act on the grounds that during times of war the need for state security supersedes the free speech rights of individual citizens.

Schlieffen Plan: A German military plan first formulated after the Franco-Prussian War in 1870-1871 that called, in the event of another war with the French, for the army to invade Belgium as a means of more quickly reaching Paris. This plan leaked out during World War I (1914-1918) and played a role in Great Britain entering the war on the side of the French.

Schlafly, Phyllis (1924--): A political conservative, opponent of abortion and gay rights, and leader, during the 1970s, of the successful opposition to the Equal Rights Amendment.

Scopes "Monkey Trial": A trial in Dayton, Tennessee, in 1925, of teacher John Scopes for teaching evolution in violation of state law.

Segregation: The mandating of racial separation by law or by social custom. Southern states implemented segregation laws creating "whites only" neighborhoods, schools, hospitals, businesses, water fountains, and even blood supplies in the late nineteenth and early twentieth centuries.

Selective Service Act: The draft instituted by the Wilson administration in 1917 to ensure the nation's armed services had adequate manpower for World War I. All men between the ages of 18 and 30 had to register with the federal government for possible conscription.

September 11 attacks: Al Qaeda terrorist attacks undertaken on September 11, 2001, by terrorists who simultaneously hijacked three jumbo jets and crashed them into the World Trade Center in New York City and the Pentagon Building outside of Washington, D.C. Hijackers of a fourth jet were challenged by some brave passengers who heard of the other attacks and forced the plane to crash into a field in Pennsylvania before reaching an undetermined target in Washington, probably the White House or the Capitol.

Settlement houses: Houses established in urban slums where college-educated social workers lived and provided the poor with vital social services.

"sick industries": Industries such as coal mining, textile manufacturing, and railroads plagued by excessive productive capacity with declining demand and labor conflict during the 1920s.

Sitting Bull (1834-1890): A Hunkpapa Sioux chief credited with prophetic visions in which he saw white soldiers falling into Native American hands. Sitting Bull was one of three Native American leaders who defeated General George Armstrong Custer's forces at the Little Big Horn River in present-day Montana on June 25, 1876.

Edward Snowden (1983-): Former contractor for the U.S. government who leaked classified National Security Agency (NSA) documents before fleeing to Russia in 2013 to avoid prosecution for sedition.

Social Darwinism: The application in the late 19th and early 20th century by social scientists such as Herbert Spencer in England and William Graham Sumner in the U.S. of Charles Darwin's theory of natural selection in nature to human society. As there were higher and lower orders of species in the animal kingdom, so there were superior and inferior individuals and races among people.

Social Security Act (1935): A social insurance program funded by payroll taxes and employer matching funds to provide retirement funds for Americans age 65 and older and financial assistance to those with disabilities, as well as survivor's benefits for dependent spouses and children.

Somalia: East African country where U.S. troops in 1993 engaged in a series of firefights, first to try and capture criminal warlords then to rescue the crews of downed helicopters in the capital city of Mogadishu.

Spanish Civil War: A civil war in Spain from 1936-1939 resulting in the overthrow of the elected republican government by fascist forces under Francisco Franco with aid from Germany and Italy. Franco established a dictatorship that lasted until his death in 1975.

Sputnik: Soviet satellite that in 1957 became the first man-made object sent into space. Fear over its launch led to the creation of NASA.

Starr, Belle [Myra Maybelle Shirley] (1848-1889): Famous female outlaw of the Old West, she associated with members of the James-Younger Gang, harbored wanted criminals, and engaged in various horse and cattle rustling operations in Texas before her murder in Oklahoma at age 41.

Stonewall Uprising: A series of violent demonstrations by members of the gay (LGBT) community against a police raid that took place on June 28, 1969, at the Stonewall Inn

Strategic bombing campaign: A high-altitude bombing campaign against Axis targets in Europe during WW II.

Strategic Defense Initiative (SDI) or "Star Wars": A theoretical weapons system advocated by President Ronald Reagan in which space satellites would use lasers to disable Soviet nuclear missiles.

Strong, Josiah (1847-1916): American clergyman whose influential sermons, lectures, and writings (most notably his book *Our Country* published in 1885) in favor of missionary work touted America's racial superiority and need to uplift the inferior peoples of the world.

Students for a Democratic Society (SDS): A student activist group that became a leading force in the anti-war movement during the Vietnam era.

Suez Crisis: Crisis resulting from the attack on Egypt by Israeli, French, and British forces after Gamel Abdel Nasser announced the nationalization of the Suez Canal in 1956 leading to Russian threats to intervene and strong pressure by Dwight Eisenhower leading to a withdrawal by the aggressors.

Sunday, Billy (1862-1935): A former major-league baseball player who emerged as the most popular fundamentalist preacher of the 1910s and 1920s.

Sweatt v. Painter (1950): A United States Supreme Court decision that ruled that the University of Texas's segregated law school violated the Constitution.

Taft, William Howard (1857-1930): The 27th President of the United States (1909-1913) and later the 10th Chief Justice of the United States. Taft was Teddy Roosevelt's chosen successor, but proved a highly conservative chief executive who disappointed his mentor, prompting Roosevelt to run against him in 1912.

Taliban: Afghani Muslim extremists who once controlled most of Afghanistan from 1996 to 2001, imposing one of the most oppressive Islamist regimes anywhere in the world. The Taliban harbored Osama bin Laden, the mastermind of the September 11, 2001, terrorist attacks against the United States, prompting George Bush's decision to invade Afghanistan in December of that year.

Tax Cuts and Jobs Act: Legislation passed by Congress in 2018 that created the first major changes to the U.S. federal tax code in 30 years.

Tea Party: A grass-roots conservative/libertarian backlash movement that emerged in 2009 protesting the government bailouts and alleged general "big-government" policies of both Republican and Democratic administrations and congressional policies as well.

Teapot Dome Scandal: The controversy surrounding the leasing of government-owned petroleum fields to two oil companies found to be authorized by Interior Secretary Albert Fall after receiving gifts valued over $300,000.

Teller Amendment: Passed by Congress before the outbreak of the Spanish-American War in 1898, which renounced all U.S. claims on Cuba and any possibility of U.S. acquisition of Cuba as an American colony.

Ten Percent Plan: Abraham Lincoln's wartime Reconstruction Plan, whereby a presidential pardon would be given to all southern whites (excluding Confederate government officials and high-ranking military officers) who took an oath of allegiance to the United States and accepted the abolition of slavery. Further, any state where the number of white males over 20 years old who took this oath exceeded 10 percent of the eligible voters in 1860 could establish a new state government that he would recognize as legitimate.

Tennessee Valley Authority (TVA): Begun in 1933, the most massive undertaking by the federal government at rural reclamation; the building of dams, hydroelectric plants, and reservoirs, all of which ended the problem of flooding and the ruining of land and businesses in a four-state area.

Tenure of Office Act of 1867: Bill passed by Radical Republican-controlled Congress designed to further strip President Andrew Johnson of his power by making it illegal for him to remove any cabinet member without Senate approval.

Tet Offensive: A massive communist assault along the length of South Vietnam, particularly targeting cities, that began on January 30, 1968, and lasted until March 28.

Texas Rangers: A law enforcement agency established in the days of the Texas Republic and frequently implicated in violence against Native Americans and Mexican Americans.

Thaddeus, Stevens (1792-1868): A member of the United States House of Representatives from Pennsylvania who supported abolition before and during the Civil War and who became a leader of the Radical Republican faction during after the War.

Thirteenth Amendment: The amendment, ratified in 1865, that abolished slavery and involuntary servitude in the United States.

Thompson, Hugh (1943-2006): American chopper crew commander who bravely intervened to try and stop the My Lai Massacre before he and his men evacuated a handful of survivors.

Three Mile Island: A nuclear power plant near Harrisburg, Pennsylvania, that overheated and nearly melted down on March 28, 1979.

Tiananmen Square: A public square in Beijing that became the scene of pro-democracy protests that were brutally crushed by Chinese troops in 1989.

Till, Emmett (1941-1955): A 14-year-old Chicago youth beaten to death by two white men in Money, Mississippi, August 28, 1955, after supposedly flirting with a white woman. His murder helped galvanize the 1950s civil rights movement.

Townsend, Francis (1867–1960): Popular California physician who made concern for the elderly a personal crusade during the Great Depression in the 1930s. In a pamphlet published in 1934, he advocated the payment of $200 monthly to every retired American over the age of 60 provided they spend all of the money within 30 days, which would then open up jobs for younger Americans.

Treaty of Paris (1898): Peace treaty formally ending the Spanish-American War that proclaimed the independence of Cuba, authorized the transfer of Guam and Puerto Rico to the United States, and included the sale of the Philippines by Spain to the United States for $20 million.

Treaty of Versailles: The treaty ending World War I and creating the League of Nations.

Troubled Assets Relief Program (TARP): U.S. government program instituted by the Bush administration in late 2008 and continued by the Obama administration to purchase troubled assets from banks and other financial institutions in order to stabilize the economy in the midst of the "Great Recession."

Trump, Donald (1946-): Billionaire Republican Party nominee elected 45th President of the United States in 2016.

Tuskegee Airmen: African-American combat pilots who distinguished themselves in Europe during WW II.

Twilight Zone, The: A popular horror and science fiction anthology series that ran on the CBS television network from 1959 to 1964 that dealt with contemporary issues like racism, McCarthyism, and the Holocaust in highly symbolic fashion.

U-2 Incident: The shooting down of an American U-2 spy plane piloted by Francis Gary Powers over the Soviet Union in 1960 leading Soviet Premier Nikita Khrushchev to cancel a planned summit meeting with Dwight Eisenhower.

U-Boat: Abbreviated term given to a German submarine, called by the Germans an *unterseeboot*.

Underwood-Simmons Tariff Act: The 1913 act that reduced tariffs and levied the first federal income tax.

Unilateralism: A foreign policy that deemphasizes the building of coalitions with allies before undertaking military operations and reserves the right to launch preemptive strikes against any potential adversaries.

USS Maine: American battleship whose destruction in Havana Harbor in February 1898 by an internal explosion (not an external blast by saboteurs as suspected at the time) led directly to war between the United States and Spain.

Vertical Integration: A means of dominating an industry and limiting production costs by acquiring control of every step of production, such as Andrew Carnegie accomplished with American steel in the late nineteenth century.

Vietnamization: Label given to the effort begun by LBJ and continued under Nixon to gradually draw down the size of U.S. forces in Vietnam and place more of the burden of fighting the Viet Cong back onto the Army of the Republican of Vietnam (ARVN).

Villa, Pancho (1878-1923): Mexican revolutionary leader whose attacks on American citizens in northern Mexico, and a cross-border raid on Columbus, New Mexico in 1916 led President Woodrow Wilson to order U.S. forces into Mexico on a futile hunt to capture him.

Voluntarism (Voluntary Cooperation): Herbert Hoover's main approach to combatting the Great Depression through the collective effort of citizens and private-sector businesses with government guidance rather than financial assistance.

Voting Rights of 1965: Landmark federal civil rights legislation that designed to prohibit racial discrimination in voting through such means as the outlawing of literacy tests and similar devices historically used to limit voting and by overseeing the administration of elections.

Wade-Davis Bill: The Radical Republicans' counter-proposal to President Abraham Lincoln's "10 percent plan," calling for all southern whites to take an "iron-clad" oath that they had never taken up arms against the United States government before they would be eligible to vote or hold office. The Radicals also proposed requiring 50 percent of a state's white population to swear their allegiance to the United States before that state would be eligible for re-admission.

Wagner Labor Relations Act: In 1935, the United States Supreme Court declared unconstitutional the National Industrial Recovery Act unconstitutional.

War Industries Board (WIB): Government agency led by Bernard Baruch charged with bringing order and efficiency to industrial production during World War I.

War on Terror: The term used by President George W. Bush (2001-09) to describe the struggle of the United States against terrorist networks like Al Qaeda, which launched the strikes against the World Trade Center and the Pentagon on September 11, 2001.

War Powers Act: Passed by Congress in 1973, the legislation requires a president to notify Congress within 48 hours of any military deployment where battle conditions prevail or where combat was likely to take place. If the Congress does not sign off on the military action, the president has to withdraw troops within 60 days.

Warren Court: The United States Supreme Court under Chief Justice Earl Warren who was appointed by President Dwight Eisenhower. The Warren Court was known for several landmark liberal rulings in the 1950s and 1960s that banned school segregation, expanded the rights of criminal defendants, narrowed the definition of pornography, and overturned laws banning contraceptives and restricting school-directed prayers at public school campuses.

Washington, Booker T. (1856-1915): African-American leader who publicly called for blacks to temporarily accept segregation and the denial on voting rights in order to focus more on economic gains that he believed would eventually lead to white acceptance and the granting of equal rights.

Washington Naval Conference: The world's first international disarmament conference, held from 1921-22, which resulted in limits placed on naval construction and tentative economic agreements among nations trading in China.

Watergate: The scandal enveloping the Nixon White House from 1972-1974 which included charges of domestic spying, tampering with witnesses, abuse of the IRS by the White House to punish political enemies, illegal wiretapping, bribery and burglary.

Watt, James (1938 -): Ronald Reagan's conservative, pro-western development Secretary of the Interior who was forced to resign in 1983 due to a series of political gaffes.

Watts Riot: A civil disturbance that started in the predominantly African-American neighborhood of Watts in Los Angeles on August 11, 1965, and did not quiet until August 15, by which time 34 people had died and $40 million in property damage had occurred.

Westmoreland, William (1914-2005): U.S. general and main military advisor in South Vietnam who later commanded American ground troops during the Vietnam War.

Weyler, Valeriano (1838-1930): Commander of Spanish forces in Cuba before the Spanish-American War who instituted the "reconcentration policy" of rounding up civilians in rural areas and holding them in armed camps and villages in order to allow more freedom of movement for his men in the countryside, leading to thousands of Cuban deaths from disease and starvation.

Wilson, Woodrow (1856-1924): Democratic governor of New Jersey who became the 28th President of the United States (1913-1921). His administration oversaw the creation of the Federal Reserve Board and the Federal Trade Commission and the American victory in World War I.

"Wise Old Men": A group of Johnson advisors who, in the spring of 1968, tried to convince Johnson to end America's involvement in the Vietnam War.

Women Airforce Service Pilots (WASPs): Female civilian pilots during World War II who aided the U.S. military by undertaking a variety of support roles.

Works Progress Administration (WPA): An offshoot of other work project programs during the New Deal in the 1930s, only this particular initiative focused on the visual and performing arts with the purpose of keeping the American creative and aesthetic tradition alive.

Wounded Knee Creek Massacre: The U.S. Army's brutal massacre in 1890 of Sioux men, women and children.

Yalta Conference: Meeting of U.S. President Franklin Roosevelt, British Prime Minister Winston Churchill and Soviet Premier Joseph Stalin in February 1945 to plan the final stages of World War II and postwar arrangements.

Yellow journalism: The sensationalistic style of newspapers beginning in the late 1890s that emphasized war, crime and scandal.

Zimmermann Telegram: A 1917 secret communiqué from the German foreign office to German ambassador to Mexico, Arthur Zimmerman, offering military aid and assistance in taking U.S. territory if Mexico came to war with the United States.

Index